BETTANE & DESSEAUVE'S
GUIDE TO THE
WINES
OF FRANCE

BETTANE & DESSEAUVE'S
GUIDE TO THE
WINES
OF FRANCE

Michel Bettane and
Thierry Desseauve

Stewart, Tabori & Chang
New York

Published in 2011 by Stewart, Tabori & Chang
An imprint of ABRAMS

First published in French by Éditions Minerva, Geneva
Copyright © 2011 BDT Médias, Paris
www.bettanedesseauve.com

Library of Congress Cataloging-in-Publication Data

Bettane, Michel.
  [Grand guide des vins de France. English]
  Bettane & Desseauve's guide to the wines of France / Michel Bettane and
Thierry Desseauve.
     p. cm.
  Includes index.
  ISBN 978-1-58479-732-6 (alk. paper)
  1. Wine and wine making—France. 2. Wine—Flavor and odor. 3. Wine
tasting. I. Desseauve, Thierry. II. Title. III. Title: Guide to the wines
of France. IV. Title: Bettane and Desseauve's guide to the wines of France.
  TP553.B4813 2011
  641.2'20944—dc22
                          2010044131

For Bettane & Desseauve:

Tasting Notes: Michel Bettane, Alain Chameyrat, Guy Charneau, Thierry Desseauve,
Hélène Durand, Denis Hervier, Amy Lillard, Thierry Meyer, Guillaume Puzo, Barbara
Schroeder

Translations: Florence Brutton with Sharon Bowman, Delia Dent, Melissa
Dowd, Raphael Knapp, Eric Lecours, Amy Lillard, Madeleine Vedel

Final Editing and Translation: Amy Lillard

Database Design: Jean-Paul Viau

Graphic Design: Francism.com and Hicham Abou Raad

Cover Photography: © Isabelle Rozenbaum

Maps: Légendes Cartographes

For STC:

Copyeditors: Anne O'Connor, Tara Q. Thomas, Janet McDonald

Production Manager: Tina Cameron

Cover Design: Galen Smith

The text of this book was composed in Grotesque MT.

Stewart, Tabori & Chang books are available at special discounts when purchased in
quantity for premiums and promotions as well as fundraising
or educational use. Special editions can also be created to specification.
For details, contact specialsales@abramsbooks.com or the address below.

Printed and bound in China
10 9 8 7 6 5 4 3 2 1

THE ART OF BOOKS SINCE 1949
115 West 18th Street
New York, NY 10011
www.abramsbooks.com

Contents

About the Authors

In 1977, while teaching as an associate professor of Classics (ancient Greek and Latin), **Michel Bettane** decided to enroll in classes at the Académie du Vin in Paris. The Académie was run by some of the most passionate and knowledgeable wine educators and tasters in the world. These classes would be the beginning of an extraordinary career in wine journalism, now spanning more than thirty years. Bettane has spent countless hours in the wine cellars of France, meeting the winemakers and tasting their wines, with a desire to truly comprehend the foundation of his country's fabled drink. Since 1996, along with his colleague Thierry Desseauve, Bettane has published *Le Grand Guide des Vins de France*, an extensive guide to French wines and wineries, which has secured his reputation as one of the most respected tasters in the world. He travels extensively in search of a better understanding of the trends in the wine industry and in public tastes, and also to share his unparalleled knowledge with wine professionals and enthusiasts alike. His desire to comprehend wines from around the world, his wonderful ability to communicate his knowledge, his exceptional palate, and his amazing ability to recall precise vintages and characteristics of wines that he has tasted have made him one of the greatest wine critics of our time.

Thierry Desseauve was introduced to wine at the age of eighteen when he raided the cellar of his father, a distinguished lung specialist and wine lover. The articles he later wrote for renowned French magazines and newspapers in the mid-eighties earned him his reputation. Desseauve understands that wine is a world of unlimited richness and complexity. The people and their stories, the intricacies of the vineyards and their regions, the varieties and techniques, the economic context and market trends, the fashions and gurus—he leaves no aspect uncharted. His encounter with Michel Bettane provided him with a new perspective to help him fine-tune his perceptions when tasting a wine. Since 1996 Desseauve and Bettane have been the co-writers of *Le Grand Guide des Vins de France*. Winemakers around the world, whether captains of the industry or more modest producers, recognize Thierry Desseauve's natural talent for translating the potential, quality, style, and consistency of a terroir.

The New Face of French Wine

All too often, new books and guides on French wine simply regurgitate information and opinions founded on the historical facts and don't truly reflect the important changes that have been going on in the past twenty years in France. The majority of our *appellations d'origine contrôlée*, or AOCs, are still anchored in their centuries-old history and traditions, but they are also changing with the times and are responding to the tastes and demands of a new generation of wine drinkers. The very best of our winemakers/winegrowers (there is no term in English that combines the two) have been able to adapt the winemaking and winegrowing techniques taught to them by their ancestors to make wines that are different from their predecessors.

The relentless pace of our current society drives us to drink younger and younger wines, often in the month or week or even on the same day they were purchased. It is no longer an option to wait many years for the initial strength or intensity of a wine to evolve peacefully: wine science, aided by the improvements in winemaking equipment, now enables us to make young wines that are fruitier, softer, and more pleasant in their youth. It is simply necessary to harvest very ripe grapes, to carefully handle the grapes during fermentation, and to control flavor and tannin extraction to avoid the excesses or imbalances commonly found in the past. If the grapes are of excellent quality, from intelligently farmed vineyards, the wines will wholly retain the personality of the terroir and age well, despite the fact that they are drinkable from the moment they are released. Mediocre, diluted, boring wines made by producers with no talent whatsoever haven't disappeared, of that we are sure; but that is precisely why we have written this guide, so we can steer you in the direction of the best wineries!

Today we can enjoy a Château Latour 2003, only eight years old, but we can also guarantee that in twenty years it will be just as glorious, deserving comparison with the legendary vintages of the twentieth century, as long as the cork doesn't betray the wine. Therefore we are required to reexamine the optimal drinking times for a wine, to adapt them to the characteristics of each vintage. The riper the vintage, the earlier we can drink the wine, even if it is super-powerful and concentrated; but in less fabulous vintages, we have to wait a bit longer, which is the opposite of what many wine lovers tend to do. They wrongly think that great vintages should be aged longer.

Many irresponsible wine critics continue the traditional hierarchy of vintages, to the detriment of the wine collector. They decree which vintages are the best and should be sought out, no matter what the cost is, and which vintages are only average and should be bought only at the best price, and they identify little vintages that they determine are not worthy of any wine lover's cellar. This is no longer reality. Just thirty years ago winemakers were unable to make good wines in rainy or sunless years, and even less so in vintages where the harvest was damaged by disease or rot. Today managed yields, the condition of the grapes, and above all meticulous grape sorting are completely changing our vision of vintages.

If only the best grapes from old vines are kept for the premium wine, it is possible in virtually every vintage to produce a good wine. The differences between vintages are a result of the characteristics of the year; the wine may be either more robust or more delicate, for example. Therefore we would choose a specific vintage for the style of wine, depending on each individual's preference: the true wine lover will have much more fun drinking good wines from the in-between years than he or she will collecting only the best wines from the "best" vintages, especially since the wines' aging potential will be similar. This was also the case in years past; the 1948s aged much better than the 1947s and the 1950s better than the 1949s. The greatest change in the wine world, though, is still largely unknown: it is the amazing shift in the hierarchy between the classic appellations and the wines of other regions. The supremacy of white Burgundy or red Bordeaux is now being challenged by the arrival of very high-quality wines from lesser-known appellations in the Loire, the Rhone, the Languedoc-Roussillon, the huge Southwest region, Provence and Corsica, Alsace, or even the Jura and Savoie regions. Numerous comparative blind tastings have shown that the best wines from each of these regions have as much personality and complexity as the greatest historical and traditional Grand Cru, and provide equal pleasure given that the difference in price is often considerable.

In many prestigious wine regions, some growers have lost the passion they once had for their craft: they sell their wines much too easily and fall into a routine that makes it impossible for them to make quality wines that are true to the prestige of their appellation. Only the snobby and quite frankly stupid wine drinker (who often has too much money) would limit himself or herself to La Romanée-Conti, Dom Pérignon, or Château Lafite. These wines and their equals remain extraordinary, especially if they are drunk at the right time, at the right temperature, and with the proper glassware and drinking conditions. But to only drink these wines would be to limit one's taste, ignoring all other aromatic characteristics, other flavors, other harmonies, and above all the excitement of discovery. The wines from each of these regional appellations hold a very important place in our guide, and we are proud to help increase the exposure of these great wines to international connoisseurs.

The Style of Wine We Defend

French vineyards, like those of our Italian, Spanish, Portuguese, Swiss, German, Austrian, and many other Central European neighbors, come from the same ancient tradition, begun by the Greeks and Romans, and then disseminated by the monks of the Middle Ages. Despite individual exceptions, this shared tradition created a common taste and style of wine. The French were simply lucky to have such a great diversity of soils and sub-climates that gave birth to a broad palette of flavors and colors. To this diversity were added better farming and vinification practices in the nineteenth century, which allowed for the production of the most sought-after wines in trade, because they were the most appreciated by the consumers. This superiority is regularly diminished with the continual advances in other viticultural regions, and with their adoption of similar winemaking practices. French wines continue, though, to serve as benchmarks and sources of competition, because at their best they possess a sureness of style that must be preserved at all costs in a time when new consumers, lacking in experience or tradition, risk simplifying the worldwide taste for wine.

How is it possible to define the style that the best French winemakers/ winegrowers keep alive and continue to perfect, and that we use as reference points in the critiques that we give each of the wines represented in this guide? We could say that it rests upon three fundamental principles: the sense of place (terroir), the balance of the wine, and its drinkability. The great enologist Jacques Puisais had a wonderful saying that summarizes this "sense of place": "a good wine should have the face of the place in which it was made and of the person who made it." Born of the soil, the wind, the rain, the sun, a wine should recall all of these things, just as it should carry the imprint of the character, the taste, the wishes and abilities of the person who made it. It's up to each consumer to do for wine what he or she does for a good film, that is choose a film he or she likes and one that relates the most to his or her ideas.

But to keep from making mistakes or from liking just about anything, it was best to decide upon one ideal quality: this quality, linked to the temperate climate of almost all French vineyards, is that of the quest for balance. The word *balance* is defined negatively to mean the rejection of excess, and positively to mean unity in a wine, combining all of its various components (alcohol, acidity, tannins, wood, the relationship between the bouquet and the flavors). Why did we choose balance over performance? Quite simply to preserve the drinkability of what we consider to be the most healthy, the most hygienic, and the most delicious of all drinks!

True to French tradition, wine is an integral part of our cuisine and therefore our eating habits, whether it be consumed every day or for celebrations. We taste wine because we drink wine, and not the opposite, as is more and more often the case. That is the only danger of globalization of the production and consumption of wine, in fact: that the wines on the market are judged by quick critiques, on their immediate impressions and in very tiny amounts. The danger is that we will then drink them less often due to the fact that high scores have made the prices skyrocket, often absurdly, to levels that are twenty, thirty, even a hundred times more than their base price! The less we drink them, the more we desire to be dazzled or shocked, as if it were a drug or a special effect at the movies. But one day this shock factor wears off and we are left with wines that all taste the same, and a wine drinker who tires of drinking them. We obviously would prefer to see a different ending, one that finishes with a better understanding and appreciation of the balanced, harmonious wines we recommend in this guide, and of all of the other similarly balanced wines of the world.

How to Understand French Wine Labels

French wines have a not very flattering reputation for being too difficult to pick out or to buy because of the large number of appellations, with labels that don't provide any information or sufficient quality assurances. Serious variations in quality certainly exist, especially in regard to international sales. This unpredictable quality is due to a lack of discipline or talent of many winemakers/growers (but not those who are in the guide!); it absolutely does not reflect, however, the philosophy and the logic behind the appellation system. On the contrary, this logic emphasizes transparency of information and makes the consumer's choice easier.

If France decided to give priority on wine labels to geographic origin, it is because the *appellation contrôlée* model was built upon the highest-quality wines, those that were expected to sell well not only in France but also in export markets. Their flavors and character being linked to the place from which they came, it seemed more honest vis-à-vis the consumer that this information appear in bold print on the label. It seems so natural and even obvious that all other European countries have little by little adopted the same labeling practices, and would that the New World might do the same!

But, you ask, why then didn't they also indicate the name or names of the grape varieties? It's not at all because the winemakers/growers considered the varieties to be of secondary importance, or that they weren't used to mentioning them; in fact, very often when they served their wines to wine lovers they referred to them by the name of the grape and not by the appellation. In the Touraine they offered tastes of sauvignon, gamay, breton, cot, pinot (not to be confused with pineau, the local name for chenin blanc). Condrieu presented their beloved viognier; in the Languedoc it was their cinsault or their carignan. But since it was a tradition to plant several different grape varieties in one vineyard, in order to lower the risk of or to be better prepared for different weather conditions in different vintages, by being overly honest, the winemaker—knowing that he never quite produced the same blend—stopped naming the grape variety altogether. In Burgundy, where both white and red wines are made from a single grape variety—chardonnay, aligoté, or pinot noir—the winemakers never mentioned the grape variety because they assumed that everyone knew the rules and it would be more interesting and informative to promote the diversity of the appellations and their individual terroirs!

No one could have ever predicted the industrial production of wine whereby the grape would be synonymous with a particular taste, always the same and easy to recognize, in short similar to the way soda or mass-produced beer is made. Since the general public has, over time, gotten used to choosing any type of wine by the name, or names, of the grapes, even for New World wines, the grape variety is appearing more and more often on French wine labels, but usually on the back label, though we'll certainly start to see them on the front labels too (some appellations like Burgundy white and red have already begun to do that). The general trend would be toward simplified labels with an easier-to-read font, with the principal region written in large type above the smaller mention of the appellation, if it were not for all of the strict labeling rules on food products, which will eventually lead to a required list of ingredients on all wine labels. But on this point the New World and the Old World agree!

9

Everything You Need to Know about Wine: Twenty Frequently Asked Questions

Is the AOC label always a mark of quality?

Far from it. The AOC designation (which stands for *appellation d'origine contrôlée* or "appellation of controlled origin") is just one shining example of the so-called "French model" that has gradually lost all credibility. Fact is, truckloads of wine without a trace of personality are approved without comment, while outstanding local wines whose misfortune it is to be "atypical" are rejected out of hand by parochially minded bureaucrats. Another joke is the assumption that all appellations are founded on "loyal and constant usages." This could be said of historic AOCs such as Champagne and the celebrated crus of Burgundy, Bordeaux, or the Rhone Valley. These are vineyards with age-old reputations whose success is built on traditional practices now enshrined in legislation (choice of vines, territorial boundaries, growing methods, and others). But younger appellations (from the 1970s onward) were simply founded on a market-driven approach that was then wrapped up in vague notions of pseudo-typicity. Examples range from vast regional entities such as Bordeaux or the Côtes du Rhône, to the new premium vineyards of the Languedoc or Southwest France. Because AOC wine sold better than ordinary wine, more than half of French wines were granted appellation status. Producers then had no alternative but to jump on the bandwagon; in particular, it stymied all hope that a large non-AOC holding might compete with the big boys outside France. What we needed was a strong industrial sector counterbalanced by a vibrant artisan sector; instead, we allowed supply to grow unfettered, leaving us with the jumble of appellations we find today. Sorting out that jumble is what we humbly propose to do in this book.

Is an organic wine better than a nonorganic wine?

There is a lot of confusion over organic wine—deliberately encouraged, of course, by a handful of professionals and journalists with vested interests in its sale and production. The terms *organic* and *biodynamic* viticulture refer to a form of agriculture based on strict working criteria and a rigorous certification process. But the term *organic wine* is a misnomer, in France, since only the grapes from which that wine is made are organically produced. In fact, all wine is by definition organic since it is made from the living micro-organisms in yeast. The quality of organically grown grapes, on the other hand, is not in question. Providing the producer gets it right, they will reflect the characteristics of the terroir and the vintage in a more natural and complex fashion than conventionally grown grapes. In theory, then, organically grown grapes make better wine—but it all depends on proper fermentation. Without that, the wine cannot possibly deliver a full and faithful expression of the fruit. This is where the problems start. Too many organic producers believe that only naturally occurring yeasts can do justice to their wine, and they reject the addition of sulfites as an abomination to be avoided at all costs. The result, all too often, is a wine that is unstable in terms of both appearance and taste: dull, cloudy color, inelegant aromas spoiled by volatile acidity, and, in particular, adulterated fruit flavors that interfere with the "local fingerprint" of the wine. The fact is that naturally occurring yeasts are a mixture of good and bad micro-organisms, and by the end of fermentation it is the bad ones that tend to prevail. The only way to render them harmless is to treat the crop with sulfites. When all goes well, of course, "natural" wines are remarkably pure and digestible, but for every good example there are countless bad ones: well-intentioned but unsuccessful efforts, cherished with an almost fatherly pride by lunatic winegrowers and foisted upon us by an irresponsible coterie of sommeliers, journalists, chefs, and wine merchants. Thank goodness therefore that France's great biodynamic growers (Humbrecht, Leroy, Leflaive, Morey, Lafon, Viret . . .) are also seasoned winemakers who fully understand the importance of control and precision in the making of a product that can certainly be described as "noble."

Is wine good for you?

It was in November 1991 that Dr. Serge Renaud first coined the expression "the French paradox," on the CBS program *Sixty Minutes*. This was the moment when millions of Americans discovered that although a diet high in saturated fat can lead to serious heart disease, this was oddly not the case in France (particularly in Southwest France), where the French routinely drink wine with their meals. Wine contains chemicals that attack LDL (bad cholesterol) and help accelerate the elimination of it from the arteries. Since then, there has been increasing evidence to show that the consumption of two to three glasses of red wine a day (not any other type of alcohol) does lower overall mortality and cancer-related mortality rates in men. Research currently under way indicates that it is only a question of time before these findings can also be extrapolated to the female population. The health benefits of wine are linked to polyphenols: compounds present in the grape skins with proven antibacterial, antiviral, and antioxidant properties. It is this antioxidant effect of polyphenols that helps to combat the cellular damage caused by the free radicals that are thought to play a role in the development of certain diseases, most notably cardiovascular disease and cancer.

Then there is the mineral composition of wine, which is rich in essential daily nutrients such as potassium, calcium, magnesium, sodium, iron, sulfates, and phosphorous. Wine is also a good source of B-group vitamins and particularly Vitamin P flavonoids, which are known to promote blood vessel health by increasing capillary resistance to hemorrhage, rupture, and edema. Yes, we can definitely say that wine is good for you—but only if drunk in moderation. As much as the wine industry might like us to think otherwise, the scientific evidence in favor of wine is plainly no excuse for drunk driving or the consumption of excessive but socially acceptable amounts of alcohol. Too much of a good thing can be bad for you and wine is no exception. For wine lovers like us, wine is an inseparable part of French civilization and the French "art of living." We have never needed any convincing of its health benefits when consumed in moderation (nice though it is to have our convictions confirmed). But we do believe that drinkers should not put others at risk, so please drink responsibly.

Is it true that French wines have become "Americanized"?

The success of the film *Mondovino* and the simplistic comments of bar flies—two key components of the so-called "French cultural exception"—have popularized the notion that French wines, particularly the most sought-after and expensive French wines, have been Americanized to please new consumers with more money than sense. The obvious culprits include specialists of dubious taste and morality, and enologists who have betrayed their own country. All of this, of course, is out-and-out nonsense. Our top wines have improved considerably over the past twenty years, in terms of both consistent quality and terroir expression, thanks to advances in viticulture and enology, and to the effects of global warming, too. These factors have also modified the aromatic profile and structure of French wine in general. Grapes, today, are harvested riper with lower acidities, making for those heady, sensual, tactile sensations that you get with higher-alcohol wines. Consumers love them because wines made from riper grapes are immediately tastier and more approachable; they also are thought to be more ethically acceptable since they no longer require chaptalization or "doctoring." The only snag is that you can't drink as much of them, so if you're really thirsty you have to find something else. This new trend in wine naturally coincides with a drop in alcohol consumption, much to the delight of the authorities but to the eternal chagrin of a few nostalgic enthusiasts who value quantity of booze more than quality. And it's not just France that is at issue here: wines are changing all over the world. Spanish and Italian growers are equally vulnerable to global warming, as are New World producers. Across the Atlantic, they have to resort to de-alcoholization to get rid of those unwanted extra degrees of alcohol—no doubt a heavy-handed process that, for the present at least, French producers have been spared. In this sense, and only in this sense, it is fair to speak of a tendency toward standardized flavors. If global warming gets any worse, of course, then we might start to see a loss of terroir character. There remains the widespread problem of over-oaking—but that's a different story to which we will return in the answer to the next question.

Can too much oak ruin a good wine?

Every self-respecting enologist knows the correct proportion of wood to wine. However, since this is something that can only be measured in esthetic and therefore ideological terms, it is also one of the most hotly debated issues in the wine arena. Bear in mind that great wine, even from the most sought-after terroirs, by no means presupposes aging in wood. Some of our finest white and rosé wines, from Champagne to Provence, are fermented entirely in cement or stainless-steel tanks. They never see a splinter of oak, and no one thinks less of them for it. The great Bordeaux châteaus of the past would do without barrels altogether when times were hard: Mr. Gasqueton himself freely admits that the sublime Calon Ségur of 1947 and 1953 saw hardly any oak. Nor have some of those fabulous Margaux wines that the idealistic Pierre Boyer (Bel-Air Marquis d'Aligre) produces in ancient cement tanks! The reason winemakers use oak—setting aside the beauty of the material itself and the advantages of aging wine in small batches—is because it allows controlled oxidation. It has long been recognized that the porous nature of wood (and especially new wood) lets in a certain amount of air, which produces a more refined wine of plainly superior "finish" in terms of aroma and texture. Traditionally, however, French producers never thought of new oak as a source of flavor. That changed with the arrival of American oak, which adds sweetness and aromas of Bourbon vanilla that appeal to consumers on both sides of the Atlantic, and especially with the introduction of "toasting": the heavy charring of barrels that produces vulgar toasty, caramelized flavors in wine. As the demand for barrels grew, coopers could no longer afford the three years it takes for staves to dry naturally—so they toasted them to disguise the fact that the barrels were not properly seasoned. For the undiscerning drinker, alas, toasty flavors chimed with preconceived ideas about luxury wines. They indicated a wine worth paying for, not just in the New World but also in France, where gullible people still equate heavy oak with great terroir. The increasing use of new oak coincided with the overcropping typical of the 1970s and 1980s that knocked the stuffing out of French wines. Some of these wines were absurdly over-oaked, which was more the fault of a lack of substance in the wine than excess oak per se. Now the pendulum seems to be swinging the other way, bringing about a welcome change: wines richer in alcohol have more of the substance required to stand up to oak; and winemakers with more exacting standards of craftsmanship expect better-quality barrels (no expense spared) and make more discerning use of new wood. New World producers have gone farther still, forsaking what they once loved in favor of "non-oaked" cuvées (especially white wines) that appeal to the snobbishness typical of the present time—and naturally fetch higher prices. All the same, we are plainly not out of the woods yet, particularly when it comes to base wines. The temptation to make them seem "classier" by adding oak shavings is almost irresistible.

"The new wine terroirs now outshine yesterday's stars." True or false?

Vested interests apart, people in democratic societies do generally cherish openness and detest rigid hierarchies, hence their desire to see wines from "new terroirs" rival or even outshine the stars of yesterday. In France, the replanting of thin, well-drained soils in the south with noble varietals has in some cases proved the salvation of former high-quality terroirs that opted for mass production following the phylloxera epidemic. Note, however, that venerable reputations have the advantage of age-old experience: in some areas every inch of cultivable land has been planted with vines for ten centuries or more, in which time the wines have been continuously tasted and compared. The terroirs that delivered the most refined and complex wines were immediately snapped up by the richest, most discerning owners, laypeople and clerics alike. It was this combination of natural and human privileges that created those great "historic" crus that sold well outside France and fetched the highest prices—wines that remain basically unchanged today. Assuming the land is properly worked, every one of these vineyards will be blessed with certain favorably exposed parcels that are universally recognized for the quality of their wines. Vineyards do go in and out of fashion, of course, usually depending on the cultural preferences of the elite at the time. Today's favorites, in France at least, are the subtle, complex wines of the Loire and the generous, fruity wines of the Languedoc. Both are now regaining a well-deserved popularity, unlike the very expensive and sometimes unreliable Bordeaux and Burgundies that, apart from the most famous crus, arouse markedly less interest. True wine enthusiasts show no such favoritism because they understand good wine wherever they find it. New World wines? Many of the newer vineyards in America and the Southern Hemisphere have the potential to produce great wines— it would be absurd to think otherwise. They encourage loyal competition with the historic European crus and foster a healthy spirit of emulation that keeps winegrowers on their toes. May the best man win!

Are very expensive wines worth the price?

The price of great wines reflects two main cost elements. First, the production costs, which include the cost of cultivation, fermentation, and bottling. Second, the amortized cost of the vineyard's value: either the purchase price, if a first-generation property; or in the case of a family property, the amortization of French inheritance tax liability—which is particularly hard on families. Wines from low-yield/high-quality vineyards usually fetch from sixty to seventy or sometimes eighty dollars a bottle. Wines that cost more than this are the exception. The most sought-after wines can fetch up to ten times this price from the date of release, and sometimes much, much more—witness the 2005 Bordeaux Premiers Crus. Star wines are naturally at the mercy of market forces, price being dictated by supply and demand and attracting speculation that benefits middlemen of every stripe. Even in periods of economic recession or stagnation, such as the one we are currently experiencing worldwide and especially in France, wine will continue to rise in price as demand develops from a new global clientele with a far greater buying power than our own. We may not like it, but a bottle of Pétrus or La Tâche is actually less expensive for the increasing numbers of unthinkably rich Chinese or Indian wine enthusiasts than a bottle of mineral water is for the common man. People in wine-growing countries find this shocking because they know that wine is no more than the product of fermented grapes. It is not caviar. They find it hard to understand those dreamy connotations that raise wine so far beyond its agricultural origins—connotations that equate wine with sought-after luxury products that people today use to display social status and wealth. Price then ceases to bear any relation to quality. No wine, however great, can be fifty times better than a very good wine that costs one fiftieth of its price! Our greatest estates did not just sit back and grow fat on the proceeds of global stardom: most of them at least did commit to making the most of their good fortune. They perfected the tools of their trade and working procedures. They set an example to winegrowers throughout France. Open-minded wine enthusiasts can, therefore, still find wines from the same or neighboring appellations that offer similar quality for half the price. Good for them!

Can you still find good wines for less than ten dollars?

Considering the current state of the French economy in general and the wine-growing sector in particular, ten dollars would seem to be the minimum price for a wine that lives up to expectations, i.e. delivers a decent expression of its vineyard—AOC wine, or a wine from another country with similar standards. Below ten dollars the producer is sure to lose money, jeopardizing his future as a winegrower. Those many producers who do under-price their wines are spiraling into disaster. Slashing production costs to keep price down inevitably compromises quality, which in turn reduces demand, and so it goes until eventually the entire vineyard has to be ripped up. The only effective cost-cutting option is mass production, with all the rationalization and mechanization that this implies. But rest assured, you can still find plenty of wines with loads of character for about five to ten dollars a bottle, especially if you know where to look. Some areas enjoy lower production costs, either because the particular microclimate reduces the need for costly vine treatments, or because a low planting density per acre brings savings in cultivation costs.

Is quality compromised by the new alternatives to cork?

Wine lovers remain very attached to the traditional cork stopper. They like the ritual pulling of the cork and the sometimes highly ingenious devices that are designed to make this task easier. There are, however, a range of efficient alternatives to cork, all of them sponsored by the increase in wine production that has reduced the available quality of traditional corks. Growing demand forced cork manufacturers to harvest immature cork that performs less well as a seal. This coincided with an alarming increase in tainted wines, as air and water pollution took their toll. It wasn't just that the wines smelled strongly and unmistakably of mold—"corked," in wine parlance. The problem ran deeper than that. White wines, for instance, would suddenly oxidize due to the practice of washing the corks in peroxide solution. A whole range of chlorinated flavors began to appear, the most dangerous being the now notorious taste of wet, musty cardboard caused by TCA (trichloroacetic acid) contamination. This can also be caused by pollution in the place where the wine is fermented, aged, or bottled. By the end of the 1990s, TCA contamination affected roughly 10 percent of all bottles produced, a rate of spoilage that was quite clearly unacceptable in any consumer product. The industry reacted with the introduction of new ways to seal wine bottles. The most effective of these is the Stelvin screw cap, first used in Switzerland and now popular in countries throughout the Southern Hemisphere. Developed by French manufacturer Pechiney (now Alcan), the Stelvin is practical and very reliable, at least for wines that should be consumed within five years of vintage—and that covers 90 percent of all the wine produced worldwide. Screw caps have actually performed better than cork in all of our comparative tastings, though like corks they do have to be fitted properly, particularly in the case of rosé and white wines. In fact, once you get used to the purer, cleaner aromas of screw-capped wines, cork-sealed wines seem quite tainted by comparison. For real cork diehards, there are now cork lookalikes made from reconstituted natural cork granules that are completely TCA-free (DIAM technology, Œneo Bouchage). There are also synthetic corks and glass corks. The cork industry, meanwhile, has taken great measures to ensure quality, entirely rethinking its approach. Quality control has been stepped up across the board and corks may now be customized, according to increasingly stringent specifications. For great wines, no one would yet dispute that good-quality cork, proven to stand the test of time, remains a most elegant material.

Will today's wines age as well as those made in the past?

This is another one of those curious effects of Judeo-Christian thinking that deeply mistrusts anything pleasurable. Just because today's wines are more approachable when young does not necessarily mean that they won't age as well as their predecessors. Many of the wines made in the past actually depended on prolonged bottle aging, not so much to reveal their true nature as to lose those nasty birth defects—excess acid, harsh tannins—brought about by rustic winemaking. Wines that were otherwise excellent could age beautifully—witness such great late developers as the 1928, 1934, or 1945. But people forget that other great wines from times past, including the milestone vintages of 1929, 1947, 1953, and 1959, could be quite quickly approachable if made from very ripe grapes that were low in acid—an objective met by all good producers today. The prophets of doom were already predicting the end of Grands Crus back in the 1960s when Émile Peynaud defined the modern style of great Bordeaux wine. Such wines, they said, would never age. Forty years on, nobody questions their unrivaled balance and faithful terroir expression. People who say the same today about wines made by fashionable winemakers like Michel Rolland will also come to discover that their fears were groundless— providing, of course, that these producers keep crop loads under control and avoid distorting the taste of the fruit through excessive manipulation. Modern, well-made wines from great French terroirs are actually superior to their predecessors in terms of chemical analysis: higher in alcohol, with more dry extract and richer tannins. What we perceive as a supple, easy-drinking style is simply the deceptive effect of qualities that are better blended from birth. Take, for example, the 1982, the first of the great modern Bordeaux vintages. By around 1994, experts were predicting that it couldn't last much longer, jeering at the American taste for what they called a perverse and "decadent" style of wine. Today, however, such hugely expressive wines are more youthful and sprightly than ever!

Are the Grand Cru wines on sale in supermarkets the same as those available at the winery?

This is a question that applies mainly to Bordeaux wines, French consumers being increasingly suspicious about the consistency of quality. Are there special bottlings for journalists, luxury wine merchants, and top restaurants and other, more ordinary bottlings for supermarkets and "lower-end" consumers? It's true that the price of Bordeaux wines can vary considerably from one distributor to another, but we think it highly unlikely that there is any genuine cause for misgiving. To start with, there are solid technical reasons for thinking that bottled wines these days are actually more consistent than before, not less. Modern bottling equipment is faster and more efficient: gone are the days when wine was drawn straight from the barrel, one bottle at a time, as and when customers required it. Blends are produced in large batches that make for much more consistent results—even if there is no such thing as absolute perfection. Also, the short-lived popularity gained from overly flattering samples is not worth the risk of giving the brand a reputation for variable quality. In the end, tasting is the only way to be sure that producers are not courting disaster in this fashion, or simply taking the public for fools. What's needed here is a huge blind tasting of samples and crus from a wide variety of outlets, the judges being professional tasters, wine enthusiasts, and the producers themselves. Leave it to us!

How can you choose a good wine shop?

The importance of getting to know your local independent wine shop is paramount. Buying wine in grocery stores or large chains may save you a dollar or two here and there, but getting good advice from an experienced wine store owner or employee will save you even more in the long run. Wine shop owners these days are committed professionals with a real love of wine. They often hold regular promotions, and tastings eschewing top wines (whether Bordeaux or Champagne) that are too easily available from other outlets in favor of real finds from often little-known vineyards all over France. The enthusiastic neighborhood wine merchant has been a great success, breathing new life into a distribution channel that remains particularly well adapted to the varied, complicated demands of the wine market. That said, there are good wine merchants and not-so-good wine merchants. At first glance, it's hard to tell one from the other—but there are a few telltale signs. The first and most obvious of these is the range of stock itself. Setting aside those who specialize in wines from one particular region, any good wine merchant should carry a truly representative selection of wines from all over the world. Of course, there should be some real finds, but the list should also include household names, wines referenced here or in other good wine books. The other real giveaway lies with the particular wine merchant: enthusiastic certainly, but always ready to be humbled by/or to acknowledge great wines that succeed purely on their own merits. The ones to watch out for are those fiercely idealistic wine merchants—fortunately rare, but not necessarily unheard of—who give their blessing to some wines but condemn others for grave offenses that they qualify as follows: "unnatural" (i.e., contains a small amount of sulfur for stabilization purposes); "short on terroir" (raised in good-quality oak or, worse still, under the watchful eye of an internationally famous enologist); "profiteering" (made by a négociant or major producer). Whether the wine is any good or not is another story... Suffice it to say that any wine merchant worth trusting actually listens to what the customer wants before giving advice.

When eating out, how can you choose a good wine that doesn't cost a fortune?

Choosing a wine when eating out is an increasingly risky business; wine prices in restaurants have skyrocketed, with bottle prices being from three to five and sometimes even ten times higher than normal retail. The simplest and most obvious solution is to seek a recommendation from the chef or sommelier. Nobody knows what's in the restaurant cellar better than they do and in principle at least they have a vested interest in keeping the customer satisfied. That said, we have lost count of the times we have had some vile dishwater fobbed off on us by unscrupulous professionals hell-bent on clearing out their stocks. Provincial restaurants in wine-growing areas carry a good choice of local wines that naturally cost less than the great classic crus. The Michelin Guide, which is committed to recommending local wines, can often make life easier in this respect. Otherwise, go for wines from regions that aren't overpriced. Any Muscadet, for instance, even a very good one, is relatively under-priced compared to a Sancerre and makes an excellent match for seafood and grilled fish. Likewise, some of the less fashionable Beaujolais crus offer better value for the money than their Rhone Valley counterparts. A good-quality riesling will be more reasonably priced than a Burgundy chardonnay. Another good tip for the discerning wine lover is to study the wine list carefully, preferably the day before so as to have plenty of time to spot any bargains: those "forgotten" wines whose prices compare favorably with younger vintages at today's prices. Sadly, such opportunities are rare in these days of increasingly price-savvy restaurateurs!

When buying direct from the producer, how can you be sure you're making the right choice?

Buying direct from the property is a national pastime for French, Belgian, and Swiss wine lovers. It combines retail therapy with an opportunity to meet the producer—and no one knows better than we do how interesting that can be. Over the past two or three decades we have always enjoyed meeting the thousands of men and women who actually produce the wines. Those ten minutes or so spent with a winegrower (not always the case when buying direct) are invariably fascinating; few professions boast such eloquent practitioners. But there is something so endearing and at times truly unique about buying direct that it can interfere with the buyer's freedom of choice. The Burgundy winegrower who takes barrel samples with a pipette then lines up his fragrant array for tasting in his dark, mossy cellar. The view you get of the glorious Provençal hinterland, or the sloping vineyards of the Rhone Valley or the terraces of Banyuls, as you make your way to the sales room. All of these things exercise a powerful hold over our capacity for objective tasting, which is why you need to have a clear idea of what you want to buy before setting off (armed with this guide, of course!). Then use the cellar tasting to put your principles to the test. The chance to get to know the winegrower personally can be very useful when it comes to allocated wines. Pricewise, direct sales rarely represent a winegrower's main distribution channel so you won't necessarily find lower prices here. Quite right, too. Winegrowers should not treat wine merchants and restaurateurs as little more than ambassadors for their wines, and give the same preferential rates (or almost) to private buyers. Such suppliers are the bane of many a good wine merchant, and may drive restaurateurs to choose other wines of lesser quality.

What are the major pitfalls to avoid when cellaring wine at home?

Ideally, of course, wine should be stored in spacious chalk cellars deep underground, far from the hustle and bustle of human life, in a place where temperature and humidity remain constant whatever the weather. Note, however, that even this acme of perfection in wine cellaring suffers from one major drawback: the labels are slowly but surely eaten away by damp, forcing you to wrap all of your bottles in cellophane. For the vast majority of our readers, in any case, this kind of facility is an unlikely option. Another solution then is to install a wine cellar in the basement (a warm, dry, unventilated space, whether under a private house or apartment block); or purchase an apartment wine cellar (designed to provide the ideal storage conditions described above). Failing that, a few basic precautions are essential to minimize the major risks. What are they? The number-one problem is light: storing bottles in full sunlight is the surest way to ruin a good wine. A few days are enough to destroy your whites, a few months for your darkest reds. We refuse to believe anyone who says they have no space for their finest crus in a cupboard somewhere in their apartment! The next, but rather more long-term, problem is warmth, especially at these latitudes in the dehumidified atmosphere of central heating. Within a few months—one to two years at most—the cork will start to shrink (usually imperceptibly but some bottles will show signs of leakage). This allows in air that oxidizes the wine and hastens the aging process. Novice collectors who think they are getting around the problem by storing their wines in an outdoor shelter—a garage, say—are in for a disappointment. Temperatures of 23°F in winter (when there was still such a thing as winter) and 104°F in summer will just as surely accelerate aging—particularly when combined with a lack of humidity. The simplest solution all round is to use an unheated room—the basement or a storage room if living in an apartment—and humidify the air with a bucket of cold water placed in a corner. The main point, however, is this: without the necessary equipment, there is no point in storing wine for more than two to three years.

What are the fatal blunders when serving wine?

Any wine, however great, can be drained of its magic by clumsy service—those unforgiveable faux pas that happen more often than we would like to think, whether eating in or dining out in plush restaurants staffed by the most solicitous and, in principle at least, most competent personnel. The first thing to remember is that when it comes to wine appreciation, temperature matters. So always use a thermometer to measure the temperature to the nearest degree. The rest is largely a question of common sense, such as not serving white wines too cold nor red wines too warm. White wines are ideally served at 50 to 55°F, red wines at 61 to 65°F. But don't underestimate the effects of the ambient temperature in the room: wine left standing for too long before serving is likely to be too warm, as is wine that sits around in a warm glass or carafe on summer days. In hot weather, wine should be drunk within moments of serving. In winter, it can be enjoyed at a more leisurely pace. Very old wines gain a lot from being placed upright in a cool place close by for at least twenty-four hours before serving. This allows any sediment to settle and decreases the effects of prolonged contact with an old cork. No one knows more about serving venerable crus than François Andouze, founder of the Académie des Vins Anciens. His advice is to open them several hours beforehand (not decant them) so as to give them time to wake up. Very young white and rosé wines, on the other hand, can benefit from decanting. Produced by reductive processes, they need plenty of air to bring out their aromas. We strongly recommend using a wide-necked decanter as this allows the wine to be poured from a good height without spilling. Another very important factor is the wine glass itself: a thick-rimmed glass will make the tactile sensations in wine feel that much heavier, while a thin-lipped glass will have the opposite effect. Tests have shown that the shape of the wine glass can even affect a taster's perception of alcohol and tannins. You can see why the quest for the perfect wine glass has become the holy grail of leading glass manufacturers. Riedel, Spiegelau, Schott, and Mikasa all offer highly specialized glasses. Professional tasting glasses are quite unsuitable for serving wine at table since they are designed to show up the flaws in wine, not optimize its enjoyment!

Is there such a thing as universal taste?

It seems that the old adage "To each his own" does really hold true. Scientists have recently discovered that the perception of flavors and their translation into thoughts then words depends on individual genetic heritage. In theory, therefore, there is no such thing as universal taste and no style guru should try to convince us otherwise! In practice, of course, it's more complicated. The fact is that it isn't all determined by Nature. Society also plays its part, dictating fashions and behavior patterns that encroach on the inner self. Gastronomy, like other "cultural" constructs, is largely dependent on history and the evolution of technologies and lifestyles. It is an area where instincts are overcome by dreams, desires, and even fantasies—to say nothing of those learned conventions that belong to the age and society we live in. Wine, then, is an acquired taste that changes with the times. When great festive meals were built around game and marinades with a high fat content, wines had to be very robust and tannic to aid the digestion. Such wines are, of course, anathema to molecular avant-garde gastronomy, which favors sparkling wines or delicately aromatic whites. Demi-sec wines are also headed for a comeback. Having gone out of fashion along with Nouvelle Cuisine and its penchant for rarefied fish and shellfish dishes, demi-sec wines are now a popular ingredient of the sweet-and-sour sauces used in Asian cuisine. These macro-trends do obviously leave room for micro-trends based on personal preference. Organic, "sulfur-free" wines may be considered more ethical though not everybody agrees on where the best organic wines come from. Some people like the easy-drinking, convivial qualities of pale rosé wines, while others find them too neutral, preferring a more vinous style of "claret" that is closer to red wine. Highly aromatic white wines may hit the spot with some consumers, but seem too heady to people with a taste for more mineral wines—which in turn will strike others as dry-tasting and even unpleasant. The sheer wealth of French wines is incredibly diverse and it is not about to get any simpler, so there is no reason whatsoever to fear a standardization of taste. The only possible exception relates to the luxury wine market where the simplicity of stereotypes may appeal to a highly conservative clientele. But it hasn't come to that yet.

Can certain wines kill the taste of certain dishes and vice versa?

Definitely. A Camembert cheese, for instance, will wreck your enjoyment of the greatest cru in a single mouthful. The creamy center may look inviting, but behind that rotund exterior lurks the insidious scourge of every great wine. Cheese and wine suffer equally, of course: all that's left of the wine is the sensation of astringency and the Camembert tastes of soap—a non-perfumed soap at that. The older the wine, the worse the detergent-like effects. And yet time and again we are forced to watch stoically as great Médoc wines commit suicide. (We have said it before and we will say it again: the cabernet grape and Camembert cheese are sworn enemies.) It happens in grand châteaus, where the oldest, most venerable wines are invariably reserved for the cheese course, and in houses throughout France where people feel just as confident about serving very old wines with creamy-centered cheeses. Other death-dealing combinations include: young red wines with game; old wines with grilled meat; Provençal rosés with spicy dishes; and chardonnays with oysters. But none of these is as heinous as the most common crime of all: serving the same wine throughout the meal, whether or not it is an obvious match. Your poor old pinot cannot be expected to hold its own against three separate courses— far better to dedicate the bottle of Burgundy to the guinea-fowl and drink plain water with the salad and Roquefort. Without going into details about ideal wine and food pairings, our advice to any amateur wine enthusiast is to set aside any preconceptions about wine and rely solely on their own senses. When preparing a dinner at home, for instance, open your chosen bottle before the meal so as to taste the wine and see how it matches up to your cooking ingredients. Half a mouthful, sometimes just a good whiff, will tell you whether the combination works—even if it does mean making some slight change to the composition of the main dish—or whether it is irretrievably wrong. In that case, simply select another wine and keep the first bottle you opened for the following day: a good wine will easily keep for forty-eight hours after opening.

How can one become a real connoisseur without wearing oneself out in the process?

Becoming a "real connoisseur" doesn't have to be an exhausting activity. It takes time, that's for sure, because what really matters to the genuine oenophile is absolute fluency in the language of wine. Every wine tells a story. It speaks to our senses, of course, but it also says a lot about the places, times, vineyards, grapes, and people that produced it. The more we know about these, the more we can bring them to mind at different points in their history, and the better our perception of a wine becomes. We can, for instance, see how the taste and texture of the raw adolescent wine compares with those of its now much older incarnation; or what effect a brand-new wine storehouse has had on a château that seemed wedded to ancient technology. It is the same for wine as it is for other forms of arts and crafts that produce esthetic pleasure: the more you know about them, the greater the pleasure. A wine that seems hugely impressive to a complete philistine will take on another dimension entirely for the person who has really got to know wine culture through the patient exploration of taste. Overzealous wine tastings and a passion for wine encyclopedias have got nothing to with it.

Can a wine critic's opinion really be trusted?

People in Latin countries tend to take a dim view of the professional wine critic. They see us as members of an old-boy network, incapable of delivering fair and impartial advice. Some even question our professional competence and the very criteria that form the basis of our opinions. Rest assured, if we had wanted to get rich, selling or producing wine would have been a far, far better bet than educating the public. We are not handsomely paid for what we do, not in France at least, and so, yes, we do rely on producers to provide us with tasting samples free of charge. Most of them accept that their wines might score badly—something that all those consumers who are suspicious about us would be unlikely to do in their place! The wines we drink socially, on the other hand, should obviously be paid for out of our own pockets—in which respect the present authors are beyond reproach! As for our views about wine, we are surely better placed to give advice than consumers themselves in wine chat rooms. To begin with, we have the advantage that comes from seeing thousands of different wines develop over a huge number of vintages. In particular, we have a much clearer idea of how wines are made, varying in style from one winemaker to another, according to local traditions and available technology. Most of all, we are more even-handed when it comes to assessing wines: in the course of our work, it would be unthinkable to judge the work of so many producers and not become friends with a few of them. This is precisely why we are less likely to show favoritism than all those wine enthusiasts who pride themselves on their particular choice of supplier. Lastly, we have nothing to do with selling wine, which is more than can be said for a good many of the professionals who sit on tasting panels (wine producers, merchants, brokers, sommeliers, etc). The fact that we are impartial, however—and the evidence does seem compelling—certainly doesn't mean that we are infallible. Let me say it loud and clear then: even wine critics can get it wrong! This is why we taste wines throughout their lives, from the cask right through to old age; why we scour the vineyards and wineries; and why we ply producers with questions.

French Grape Varieties

A world-class wine must be made from high-quality grape varieties, grown on the appropriate terroir, by a winemaker who knows how to bring out the best of the grape. Each grape variety brings a specific flavor profile and structure. The richness of a chardonnay is completely different than the immediate freshness of a muscadet, whose flavors have nothing to do with the scents of rose and litchi in a gewürztraminer. Some wines are made from a single grape variety. This is the case in Burgundy, where virtually all white wines are made from chardonnay and all red wines from pinot noir. Other regions use many different grape varieties in order to create a blend that is more interesting and complex than would have been possible simply using a single grape variety. In Bordeaux, sauvignon blanc makes a wine that is immediately drinkable, but that doesn't age very well. The semillon grape, which is typically quite closed in the first few years, has the ability to get better with time, developing very interesting flavors as it ages.

Terroir is a word that is virtually impossible to translate into other languages. It encompasses everything that could influence the quality of the grapes: climate, geology, and geography. In order to grow, grapes need a mild climate. It's very hard to grow grapes north of Champagne. In the south, grapes cannot grow in a desert climate. The geology of a good terroir is directly related to how it retains water. The soil and sub-soil must be well drained in seasons of heavy rain, but must also be able to retain enough water in order to nourish the plant in the dry season. This balance is of utmost importance in the Languedoc-Roussillon and in Provence, where the summer months can go by without a drop of rain. The geology of the soils, the altitude, the exposition and the slope of a vineyard all play an important role in the quality of the wine. Great terroirs are rare and in many cases are made up of poor soils in which it would be hard to grow anything else. One of the best places to help understand the notion of terroir is in the cellar of a Burgundian winemaker who vinifies each of his vineyards separately, some of which are located within a few hundred feet of each other. The wines, made from a single varietal by the same winemaker, will be strikingly different. Above all, though, the essential element in making a great wine is man. He must plant varieties that are appropriate to each of his terroirs and assure quality grape production without excessive yields. The winemaker will decide when to pick the grapes at the optimal time, while respecting the quality of the grapes during vinification, followed by a careful aging process. A winemaker who doesn't have the savoir-faire and proper facilities will in many cases turn over the grapes to a more qualified and better-equipped négociant in order to make the best wine possible.

The Great White Grape Varieties

There are twenty or so white grape varieties in France that are capable of producing great white wines. Riesling, gewürztraminer, pinot gris, and muscat convey the greatness of the Alsatian terroirs. Chardonnay is the base of great Champagnes and Burgundies, and has been grown successfully throughout the world. Farther south in Provence and the Languedoc-Roussillon, the most qualitative grapes are grenache blanc, clairette, and rolle, which is also known as vermentino in Corsica. In the Southwest, gros manseng and petit manseng are what make the marvelous wines of Jurançon and Pacherenc du Vic-Bihl. A little more to the north, sauvignon blanc and semillon make the great whites of Bordeaux such as Sauternes and Barsac. At the mouth of the Loire River muscadet gives its name to the fresh and lively whites from the region. Farther east in the Anjou and Touraine, chenin blanc is capable of producing amazing dry and sweet wines, while the zone around Sancerre owes its reputation to sauvignon blanc.

The Great Red Grape Varieties

Pinot noir, the grape of Burgundy, is also found in Alsace, Sancerre, and Champagne. In the south it prefers the cooler climates and does well in the area around Limoux. Gamay is at its best when grown on the granite hills of the Beaujolais and makes for fruity, pleasant wines in the Loire. In the Touraine and Anjou, cabernet franc has the ability to produce some very elegant wines. Farther south, syrah makes wines that are spicy with notes of black pepper. Syrah is at its best in the northern Rhone, but also adds structure to the blends in the south. Brought from Spain, grenache has spread throughout southern France. While it can produce just average wines when not planted in the right soils, grenache is capable of reaching the highest summits in the southern Rhone and the Languedoc-Roussillon. Châteauneuf-du-Pape is, of course, where grenache is king. Cabernet sauvignon, cabernet franc, and merlot are the great varieties of Bordeaux. In the Médoc and Graves, cabernet sauvignon is the predominant grape, while merlot is the most widely planted grape on the northern side of the Garonne River, notably in the prestigious vineyards of Saint-Émilion and Pomerol.

White Grapes Worth Discovering

Different varieties of muscat are grown in both Alsace and the Languedoc-Roussillon and are worth checking out for their dry whites. They pair surprisingly well with asparagus where all other grape varieties have given up! In the northern Rhone, roussanne is well known for its marvelous qualities in Hermitage, and it is also being planted more and more in the southern part of the Savoie where it is known as bergeron. This little-known grape can be transformed into some amazing wines when it is planted on an appropriate terroir. Near the town of Vienne, in the Condrieu appellation, viognier makes amazingly aromatic wines of the highest quality. It is also being used more and more in the south along the Mediterranean coast for its delicate aromas of violets and apricot. In the Languedoc-Roussillon, grenache gris, wrongly excluded from many AOC wines, makes wonderfully aromatic and smoky wines. It can still be found around the town of Collioure in a few Vin de Pays wines. Finally there's the savagnin grape of the Jura, one of the most distinctive white grapes in France. It has been identified as a cousin of Hungarian furmint and Alsatian traminer. This variety's balance of ripeness and acidity is responsible for the great Vins Jaunes of the Jura, which are aged in barrel under a veil of yeast that develops on the surface of the wine, creating a nutty, oxidized character. These wines have a unique flavor profile and amazing aging potential. More and more winemakers are vinifying savagnin as they would any other white, without trying for the oxidation found in Vin Jaune, and the results are stunning.

Red Grapes Worth Discovering

Mondeuse, the little-known grape from the Savoie region, is actually related to the great syrah of the northern Rhone and makes wines well worth checking out. Mourvèdre is the principal grape in Bandol and is also widely planted along the Mediterranean coast. A finicky variety, it is at its best when planted in full sun within view of the sea, which provides it with the moisture it needs. When planted in the right areas it can hold its own with some of France's best wines. In the Southwest, the regions of Madiran and Cahors produce wines made principally from the tannat grape (known as malbec in the rest of the world). As its name implies, the grapes are powerfully tannic, which means they can be transformed into terribly astringent wines when not harvested at optimal ripeness. But in the hands of the best winemakers, tannat can result in truly noble wines. Poulsard (also called ploussard), the principal red grape of the Jura, makes wines with little color that are not very tannic, though they can be wonderfully fruity and supple. Another red grape found in the region is trousseau. It makes wines with a bit more color and tannins when on its own, and is often blended with pinot noir.

How to Use This Guide

Understanding Our Scoring System

This guide lists and ranks the best wine producers in France on a scale of one to five, and the wines on a 100-point scale.

The wineries listed in this guide are rated on a scale of one to five BD ⚜. This ranking constitutes the French winemaking elite, or at least those that we have been able to get to know. Each of these producers makes at least one wine that is worthy of being part of any professional or amateur wine collection. Wineries that receive only one BD ⚜ should not in any case be considered mediocre vis-à-vis the others; the intelligent reader will understand that you must carefully read the critiques and should definitely not ignore their wines, especially if the style, price, and quality are what you are looking for. The BD ⚜ have a global value, all regions and all prices combined; this means that a producer in the Loire, Corsica, or Alsace that has 3 BDs ⚜ makes quality wine across the board, obviously taking into account differences in their climates and grape varieties.

Producer Ratings

1 (BD) ⚜ ⚜ ⚜ ⚜ ⚜
Denotes a serious winery that is recommended, meeting the expectations of the appellations in which it produces wine.

2(BD) ⚜ ⚜ ⚜ ⚜ ⚜
Denotes a serious and recommended winery that is slightly more dependable and homogenous than the previous.

3(BD) ⚜ ⚜ ⚜ ⚜ ⚜
Denotes a high-quality winery that serves as a standard in its area.

4(BD) ⚜ ⚜ ⚜ ⚜ ⚜
Denotes a very high-quality winery that represents the best of French wine production.

5(BD) ⚜ ⚜ ⚜ ⚜ ⚜
Denotes an exceptional winery that represents the absolute pinnacle of quality in France and throughout the world.

How the Scoring System Was Established

Our tasting notes include a description of each recommended wine, our suggestion for when the wine should be drunk, and the wine's score on a 100-point scale. We have only included wines that scored above 84 points.

Wine Ratings:

84-87	A solid, well-made wine that is a good example of its appellation or origin.
88-90	A very good wine, an excellent representation of its appellation or origin.
91-94	A standard for the appellation or origin in this vintage.
95-98	An exceptional wine, worthy of the most special occasions (given the appropriate aging and the proper serving conditions).
99 and 100	Our idea of perfection . . . at least on the particular day it was tasted.

Not just a guidebook, but also a full-service Web site!

Stay up to date on all of the happenings in the French wine world on our Web site:

www.bettanedesseauve.com

The wine world is ever-changing: there are great and not-so-great vintages, wineries are bought and sold, winemakers move on, and new stars are born. . . . In order to keep up with all of the latest news, subscribe to our Web site at www.bettanedesseauve.com.

On this restricted-access Web site, you'll find exclusive information and services not included in this guide.

> Complete access to our extensive tasting notes: more than 30,000 wines and 2,500 wineries profiled and rated
Around 7,500 wines are described and rated in this guide, but you'll have access to almost three times that number, all searchable, on the site. You can search by multiple criteria, allowing you to choose a wine according to price, score, drinking age, or type.

> Our complete guide to the Bordeaux Primeur tastings
One of the most exciting times of the year for wine lovers is the start of the Grand Cru Bordeaux Futures sales. The 2009 was an exceptional vintage, and on our site you'll have complete access to our tasting notes and commentaries for more than 500 of Bordeaux's greatest producers. Starting in April 2011, you'll have complete access to our full coverage of the 2010 vintage!

> Feature articles
Each month we'll provide you with articles on the important trends in the French wine industry, as well as features on French lifestyle in various formats such as videos, wine classes, and buyers' guides.

> In-depth reports
Throughout the year, the site will feature in-depth reports on the greatest wine regions of France. From Châteauneuf-du-Pape to Pomerol, from Gevrey-Chambertin to Hermitage, you'll be able to discover the different terroirs, their appellations and vineyards, a breakdown of the different vintages, and descriptions of the wines and how they've aged. In short, you'll get an in-depth look at the vineyards, the wines, and the people who make them.

The Wines

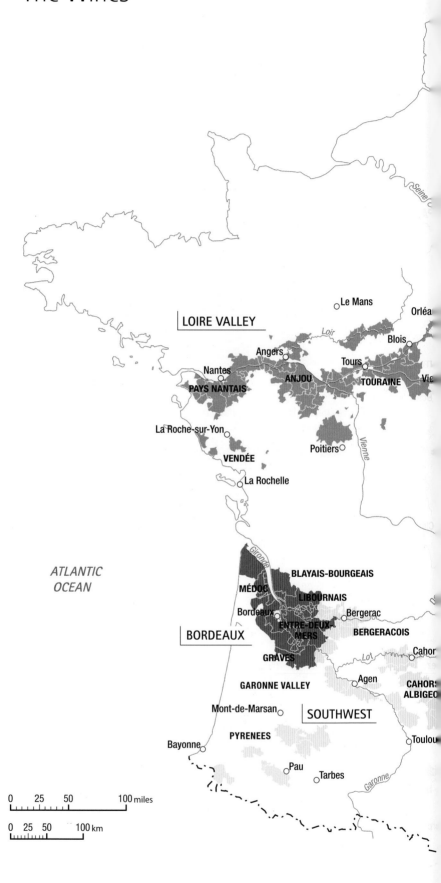

LOIRE VALLEY

Le Mans

Orléa

Blois

Loir

Angers

Tours

Vie

Nantes

ANJOU

TOURAINE

PAYS NANTAIS

La Roche-sur-Yon

Poitiers

Vienne

VENDÉE

La Rochelle

ATLANTIC
OCEAN

Gironde

BLAYAIS-BOURGEAIS

MÉDOC

LIBOURNAIS

Bordeaux

Bergerac

ENTRE-DEUX-
MERS

BERGERACOIS

BORDEAUX

Cahor

GRAVES

Lot

GARONNE VALLEY

Agen

CAHORS
ALBIGEO

Mont-de-Marsan

SOUTHWEST

PYRENEES

Toulou

Bayonne

Pau

Tarbes

Garonne

| 0 | 25 | 50 | 100 miles |

| 0 | 25 | 50 | 100 km |

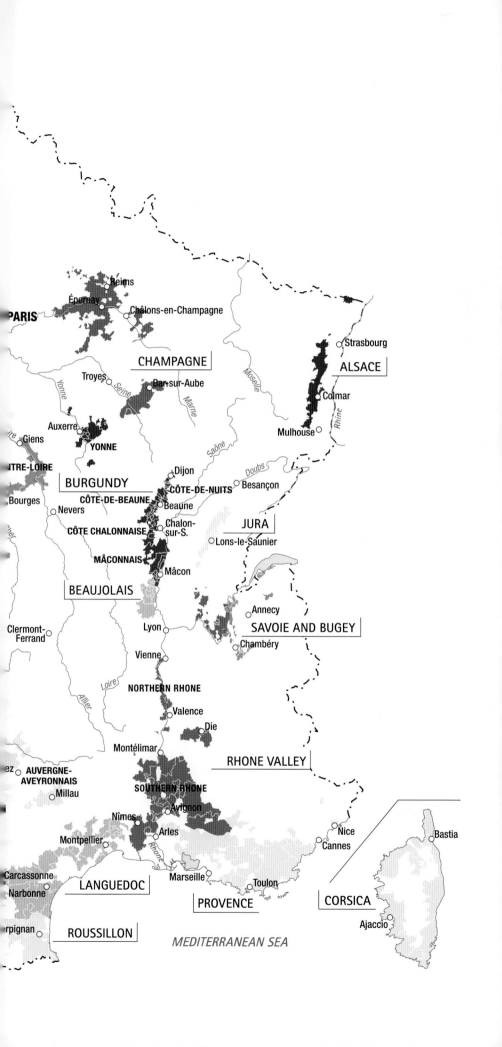

PARIS

Reims

Épernay

Châlons-en-Champagne

CHAMPAGNE

Strasbourg

ALSACE

Troyes

Bar-sur-Aube

Colmar

Mulhouse

Auxerre

Giens

YONNE

NTRE-LOIRE

Bourges

Nevers

Dijon

BURGUNDY

CÔTE-DE-NUITS

Besançon

CÔTE-DE-BEAUNE

Beaune

JURA

CÔTE CHALONNAISE

Chalon-sur-S.

Lons-le-Saunier

MÂCONNAIS

Mâcon

BEAUJOLAIS

Clermont-Ferrand

Annecy

Lyon

SAVOIE AND BUGEY

Chambéry

Vienne

NORTHERN RHONE

Valence

Die

Montélimar

RHONE VALLEY

ez

AUVERGNE-AVEYRONNAIS

Millau

SOUTHERN RHONE

Avignon

Nîmes

Nice

Arles

Cannes

Bastia

Montpellier

Carcassonne

Marseille

Narbonne

LANGUEDOC

Toulon

PROVENCE

CORSICA

rpignan

ROUSSILLON

MEDITERRANEAN SEA

Ajaccio

Bettane & Desseauve
Selections for Alsace

Alsace

This captivating region has many similarities to its German neighbor to the east, and produces some of the best white wines France has to offer. The characteristics of the grape varieties that excel here are unmistakable—the elegance of riesling, the exuberance of gewürztraminer, the depth of pinot gris, and even the easygoing character of sylvaner. Whether they are dry or late-harvest wines, the qualities of the grapes come through brilliantly in this region. Although it is easy to get lost in the labyrinth of the appellation system here, one thing is for sure: the Grand Cru wines of Alsace are among the best white wines in the world.

Two categories of Alsace AOC Wines
• **AOC Alsace:** Followed by the name of the approved varietal where wines are exclusively produced from a single grape variety.

• **AOC Alsace Grand Cru:** Followed by the name of one of the four approved noble varietals (riesling, pinot gris, muscat, gewürztraminer) and one of the fifty-one official grands crus titles, including the recently added Kaefferkopf Grand Cru.

The designations "Alsace Vendanges Tardives" and "Alsace Sélection de Grains Nobles" refer to quality wines that are made from very ripe grapes in accordance with strict growing, winemaking, and tasting procedures. Vendanges Tardives wines are produced from naturally sugar-rich fruit that gives them superior body and aging potential. They usually retain a small quantity of residual sugar, which limits their food-friendliness.

Sélections de Grains Nobles wines, as their name suggests, are based on grapes enriched by noble rot and can compete with the greatest dessert wines in the world. Chaptalization (the addition of sugar to the grape juice in order to increase alcohol levels) is not permitted for either of these wines—a feature that makes them unique among French wines.

Crémant d'Alsace is a sparkling wine that is made in a process identical to that of Champagne.

Varietal Styles
• **Sylvaner:** A fresh, delicate wine that is all too often dumbed down by excessive harvesting, it is best bought from top producers only.

• **Pinot Blanc:** The source of the best standard wines, offering consistent quality vintage after vintage.

• **Auxerrois:** A more interesting variety of pinot blanc, producing wines that are richer in alcohol, often with traces of residual sugar that make them more like pinot gris.

• **Muscat varieties (Muscat Ottonel and Muscat d'Alsace):** The source of light, fruity wines that, in principle at least, retain the taste of fresh grapes.

• **Riesling (known as the King of Grapes):** Produces a crisp, intensely fruity wine, with the potential to convey even the slightest nuances of its terroir when made from properly controlled yields and sufficiently ripe grapes. The sad truth is that the average riesling varies enormously in quality because two-thirds of the crop is harvested too early.

• **Pinot Gris:** A pink-skinned grape, originally from Burgundy. Wines made from underripe pinot gris hold little interest, but those produced from late-harvest grapes, or grapes affected by noble rot, can be rich in flavor and offer outstanding quality—they are fabulously age-worthy, too.

• **Gewürztraminer:** A very spicy, aromatic version of the traminer, producing original wines that are among the most perfumed in Alsace—though like other forms of perfume, they range from the most vulgar to the most refined. Gewürztraminer is transformed by the effects of noble rot and can produce a nectar comparable to great Sauternes.

The Terroir Factor

The varietals are the basis of Alsace wine production, but the terroir plays a key role in the top-end wines. The recognition of that role came much later than it did elsewhere in France. Today there is a policy of identifying wines by the *lieu-dit* (place-name) and commune of origin. The fifty best *lieux-dits* have even been promoted to Grand Cru status. The most fruit-forward wines come from granitic, sandy soils, such as those deposited in alluvial zones (on the Colmar plain, for instance). Sandstone soils tend to give a mineral quality to the wines, though clay-limestone soils produce an even more accentuated minerality and often need more time to develop in bottle. Schistose and volcanic soils favor the development of intensely aromatic, complex grapes that produce decidedly memorable wines.

The Lower Rhine Crus

Wines from the Lower Rhine are naturally more restrained than those from the Upper Rhine, though some of them can exhibit outstanding finesse (Andlau terroir) or power (Barr terroir). Sylvaner wines from these rather colder, more mountainous microclimates are often superbly distinguished. Riesling also performs well here, whereas the gewürztraminer tends to under-deliver.

The Upper Rhine Crus

The northern end of the department, from Bergheim to Kaysersberg, yields the most balanced and seductive of the region's wines. Since 1945, this region has been largely responsible for the success of Alsace wines thanks to the efforts of leading négociants. It is certainly home to the finest, classiest rieslings and pinots gris, and to gewürztraminers that favor elegance over power. The microclimate in Colmar suits these last two varietals particularly well, encouraging the development of botrytis and wines with opulent textures. The south is often too warm for riesling (with the exception of the sandstone terroirs around Guebwiller and the famous lava flows of the Rangen vineyard in Thann), but the area brings out all the power in gewürztraminer and pinot gris.

Alsace Vineyards

DOMAINE LUCIEN ALBRECHT

9, Grand-Rue
68500 Orschwihr
Phone 00 33 3 89 76 95 18
Fax 00 33 3 89 76 20 22
lucien.albrecht@wanadoo.fr
www.lucien-albrecht.fr

Jean Albrecht is an enterprising winemaker with the drive and determination to grow his business in line with those other great historic wine houses of Alsace that have made this region renowned throughout the world. Top of the range are two flagship rieslings from holdings in and around the Pfingstberg Grand Cru. The remaining estate-bottlings come from plots around the village of Orschwihr, including a substantial slice in the Grand Cru itself, and in the neighboring Bollenberg vineyard. Completing the range are some tastefully styled crémants made from purchased grapes, plus a range of single-varietal wines known as the Réserve Lucien Albrecht that tend to be less uniform than the estate-produced bottlings; the distinction should really be made clear on the label. The preferred wines are the remarkably refined Pfingstberg bottlings and the must-have Pinot Noir Weid from Bollenberg.

Recently tasted

ALSACE GRAND CRU PFINGSTBERG PINOT GRIS 2007
Semi-Dry White I 2011 up to 2022   **90**

ALSACE GRAND CRU PFINGSTBERG RIESLING 2006
White I 2011 up to 2016   **90**

AUXERROIS CUVÉE BALTHAZAR 2006
White I 2011 up to 2013   **87**

CLOS HIMMELREICH RIESLING 2007
White I 2011 up to 2027   **91**

CLOS SCHILD RIESLING 2005
White I 2011 up to 2020   **91**

CRÉMANT D'ALSACE
Brut Rosé sparkling I 2011 up to 2013   **88**

PINOT GRIS CUVÉE MARIE ET CÉCILE 2007
White I 2011 up to 2015   **89**

PINOT NOIR AMPLUS 2003
Red I 2011 up to 2023   **91**

PINOT NOIR WEID 2006
Red I 2011 up to 2021   **92**

RIESLING CUVÉE HENRI ALBRECHT 2006
White I 2011 up to 2016   **86**

RIESLING VENDANGES TARDIVES 2005
Sweet White I 2011 up to 2020   **89**

Older vintages

ALSACE GRAND CRU PFINGSTBERG PINOT GRIS 2005
Semi-Dry White I 2011 up to 2020   **88**
The nose is ripe with quince, honey, and smoke notes. The palate is sweet with lots of finesse, finishing on ripe fruits. A handsome Pfingstberg.

ALSACE GRAND CRU PFINGSTBERG RIESLING 2005
White I 2011 up to 2015   **87**
A very pure wine, this has the finesse of its sandstone terroir, delicate on the nose with a dry finish and good length.

CLOS HIMMELREICH RIESLING 2004
White I 2011 up to 2020   **90**
From a clos in the limestone-rich soils at the summit of Pfingstberg, overlapping the Grand Cru, this wine is still closed and compact, with a subtle nose and a dense, powerful, and very mineral palate. Definitely hold to see this great riesling reawaken.

CLOS SCHILD RIESLING 2003
White I 2011 up to 2020   **91**
Situated in the heart of the Grand Cru Pfingstberg, this wine transcends the 2003 vintage with a lightly smoky nose and a full, pure, and very mineral palate.

GEWÜRZTRAMINER VENDANGES TARDIVES 2004
Sweet White I 2011 up to 2019   **89**
The wine unveils a complex nose of exotic fruit and a sweet palate showing depth, purity, and honey on the finish.

Red: 12.4 acres. White: 74.1 acres.

DOMAINE BARMÈS-BUECHER

30, rue Sainte-Gertrude
68920 Wettolsheim
Phone 00 33 3 89 80 62 92
Fax 00 33 3 89 79 30 80
barmesbuecher@terre-net.fr
www.barmes-buecher.com

Geneviève Buecher and François Barmès merged their family estates to create this winery in 1985. Geneviève took charge of marketing and finance, while François became responsible for viticulture and winemaking. He is a careful, pragmatic winegrower who assesses the impact of everything he does in the vineyard, measuring and recording the effect on the vines. His decision to convert to biodynamics in 1998 came entirely naturally, as a way of bringing out the expression in each terroir. The result is a range of more than twenty different small-volume cuvées, sourced from a growing area that rarely exceeds more than a few acres. The hands-off approach to vinification means that the wine can vary widely in alcohol and residual sugar content from one year to another.

Recently tasted

ALSACE GRAND CRU HENGST GEWÜRZTRAMINER
SÉLECTION DE GRAINS NOBLES 2007
Sweet White | 2011 up to 2030   **97**

ALSACE GRAND CRU HENGST RIESLING 2007
White | 2012 up to 2027   **94**

ALSACE GRAND CRU LEIMENTHAL RIESLING
VENDANGES TARDIVES 2007
Sweet White | 2011 up to 2022   **91**

ALSACE GRAND CRU PFERSIGBERG
GEWÜRZTRAMINER VENDANGES TARDIVES 2007
Sweet White | 2011 up to 2027   **95**

ALSACE GRAND CRU STEINGRÜBLER
GEWÜRZTRAMINER VENDANGES TARDIVES 2007
Sweet White | 2011 up to 2027   **93**

CLOS SAND RIESLING 2007
White | 2012 up to 2027   **90**

CRÉMANT D'ALSACE BRUT 2007
Brut White sparkling | 2011 up to 2013   **89**

RIESLING TRADITION 2007
White | 2011 up to 2017   **87**

ROSENBERG GEWÜRZTRAMINER 2007
White | 2011 up to 2022   **90**

ROSENBERG RIESLING 2007
White | 2011 up to 2022   **90**

Older vintages

ALSACE GRAND CRU HENGST GEWÜRZTRAMINER 2005
White | 2011 up to 2020   **94**
An ample wine with leather and spice aromas, this has depth and power on the palate with a sensation of great richness. A wine for aging, it already possesses an almost dry character.

ALSACE GRAND CRU HENGST
GEWÜRZTRAMINER VENDANGES TARDIVES 2006
Sweet White | 2012 up to 2026   **93**
Nose still closed, honeyed and spicy; racy on the palate with depth and purity. The acidity is great. This wine requires patience; great potential.

ALSACE GRAND CRU HENGST RIESLING 2006
White | 2011 up to 2021   **88**
Closed on the nose, rich and dense on the palate with a strong minerality, this wine has powerful acidity and a dry finish. To age.

ALSACE GRAND CRU PFERSIGBERG
GEWÜRZTRAMINER VENDANGES TARDIVES 2006
Sweet White | 2011 up to 2026   **94**
A Pfersigberg bursting with fruit, this is very pure and mineral on the palate with a rare elegance. Open and easy to drink, with phenomenal length.

ALSACE GRAND CRU STEINGRÜBLER
GEWÜRZTRAMINER 2006
Sweet White | 2011 up to 2020   **93**
The terroir of this Grand Cru, less known than that of its neighbor, Hengst, often yields wines open in their youth. The 2006 does not escape the tendency, with a mineral balance of great purity and depth.

ALSACE GRAND CRU STEINGRÜBLER RIESLING 2006
White | 2011 up to 2016   **89**
With very pure, fresh citrus on the nose, this Steingrübler offers great purity, lovely minerality, and a zesty finish. Harvested before the rains.

CLOS SAND RIESLING 2006
White | 2011 up to 2016   **86**
A rich, crisp, and profound wine, already very open with very lovely fruit.

GEWÜRZTRAMINER WINTZENHEIM CUVÉE MAXIME 2006
Sweet White | 2011 up to 2016   **90**
Harvested at Vendange Tardive ripeness, this wine shows great purity and length, with an exotic nose and sweet palate.

PINOT NOIR H VIEILLES VIGNES 2005
Red | 2011 up to 2020   **90**
From the Grand Cru Hengst, matured in oak barrels, this is a rich wine, powerful and full, with fresh, fine tannins that need more time to integrate.

Annual production: 100,000 bottles

DOMAINE LAURENT BARTH

3, rue du Maréchal-de-Lattre
68630 Bennwihr
Phone 00 33 3 89 47 96 06
Fax 00 33 3 89 47 96 06
laurent.barth@wanadoo.fr

Laurent Barth returned to the family domaine in 1999 when he was still under contract to the local cooperative winery. He vinified and released his first vintage in 2004. With advice from several talented winegrowers, he practices organic viticulture and adopts a hands-off approach to vinification and aging, allowing each wine to settle slowly in the vat. His wines possess serious concentration and assertive personality, but their style is quite different depending on the vineyard source: precision and finesse from the granitic sands of the Clos Rebgarten; deep, smoky character from the Marckrain Grand Cru.

Recently tasted

ALSACE GRAND CRU MARCKRAIN GEWÜRZTRAMINER 2008
Semi-Dry White | 2011 up to 2028   **92**

MUSCAT 2008
White | 2011 up to 2013   **88**

PINOT NOIR M 2008
Red | 2011 up to 2018   **90**

RIESLING 2008
White | 2011 up to 2014   **86**

RIESLING VIEILLES VIGNES 2008
White | 2011 up to 2014   **88**

SYLVANER 2008
White | 2011 up to 2014   **87**

Older vintages

ALSACE GRAND CRU MARCKRAIN GEWÜRZTRAMINER VENDANGES TARDIVES 2005
Sweet White | 2011 up to 2025   **91**
All of this Grand Cru was harvested as Vendanges Tardives in 2005. A sweet wine with depth, this possesses much purity and finesse, enhanced by an elegant floral note on the finish. Still dominated by the fruit, it needs time for the power of the terroir to establish itself.

ALSACE GRAND CRU MARCKRAIN GEWÜRZTRAMINER 2007
Semi-Dry White | 2011 up to 2022   **94**
The only wine produced in 2007 with estate fruit, this is a magnficient success: the nose is intense with aromas of flowers, ripe fruit, spice, and a leather note; the palate is concentrated, full, and deep, with a long, spicy finish. A superb Marckrain, almost dry.

ALSACE GRAND CRU MARCKRAIN GEWÜRZTRAMINER 2006
Semi-Dry White | 2011 up to 2020   **90**
A powerful wine, sweet and pure on the palate, with aromas of pepper, smoke, and honey. It's so completely dominated by terroir that listing the variety on the label is no longer necessary.

GEWÜRZTRAMINER RÉCOLTES NOMADES EGUISHEIM 2007
Sweet White | 2011 up to 2022   **91**
From Pfersigberg and harvested superripe, this wine is full and sweet with deep, candied citrus flavors and a smoky note on the long finish.

GEWÜRZTRAMINER RÉCOLTES NOMADES HATTSTATT 2007
Sweet White | 2011 up to 2017   **89**
From the Kastelweg vineyard in Hattstatt, the wine is superripe with candied fruit notes on the nose, but retains lovely elegance on the palate, with marked acidity that counterbalances its sweetness.

PINOT NOIR 2007
Red | 2011 up to 2015   **87**
Produced from grapes from Eguisheim and from Strangenberg in Westhalten, this wine is ripe with good purity on the nose and density on the palate, with a fruity finish.

PINOT NOIR M 2005
Red | 2011 up to 2020   **90**
Of the two pinot noirs produced by the domaine, the Cuvée M comes from a parcel in the Marckrain Grand Cru. The 2005 is concentrated, very ripe and deep, displaying a smoky and full-bodied balance that is reminiscent of certain great Burgundy terroirs.

RIESLING REBGARTEN 2006
White | 2011 up to 2015   **90**
A rich and concentrated riesling with very fine acidity that gives the wine elegance. A great success.

RIESLING RÉCOLTES NOMADES EGUISHEIM 2007
White | 2011 up to 2017   **88**
Produced from grapes coming from Eguisheim's limestone soils, this wine is dry and full, with a long, citrus finish.

Red: 1.1 acres; pinot noir 13%. White: 8 acres; pinot gris 9%, auxerrois 22%, gewürztraminer 20%, muscat d'Alsace 8%, riesling 23%, sylvaner 5%.
Annual production: 15,000 bottles

DOMAINE JEAN-PHILIPPE ET JEAN-FRANÇOIS BECKER

4, route d'Ostheim, Zellenberg
BP 24
68340 Riquewihr
Phone 00 33 3 89 47 90 16
Fax 00 33 3 89 47 99 57
vinsbecker@aol.com

This property is family-owned and operated by the Jean Becker Négociant Company. It boasts a lovely portfolio of holdings around the village of Zellenberg, some in the little-publicized Froehn Grand Cru. At the helm of the estate today are the three Becker children: Jean-François in the vineyards and Jean-Philippe in the cellars while their multilingual sister Martine takes care of sales and communication. The wines are organically produced and very nicely defined, with good structure thanks to high levels of acidity, particularly those from the Froehn Grand Cru. The 2005 vintage brought a welcome move toward more ripeness and depth, with most of the cuvées taking on broad, muscular balance.

ALSACE GRAND CRU RIESLING FROEHN 2005
White | 2011 up to 2020   90
The nose is still closed but very mineral, leading to a very pure, mineral palate lifted by powerful acidity that results in a lemon-juice finish. A dry and racy riesling.

ALSACE GRAND CRU SCHOENENBOURG RIESLING 2005
White | 2011 up to 2020   89
A ripe Schoenenbourg of good purity, complex and already open on the nose, elegant and saline on the palate, with a long finish.

PINOT GRIS 2005
Sweet White | 2011 up to 2015   89
A blend of several parcels around Zellenberg, this wine is clean, full, and rich. It manages an intense sugar-acid balance and finishes on a touch of vanilla that recalls the wine's maturation in 600-liter demi-muids.

RIMELSBERG GEWÜRZTRAMINER 2006
Sweet White | 2011 up to 2016   88
A rich wine, this shows ripe fruit and spice on the nose and fullness on the palate, with well-integrated sweetness. A lovely success.

RIMELSBERG GEWÜRZTRAMINER 2005
Sweet White | 2011 up to 2013   88
A very pure sweet wine marked by aromas of rose and praline, this displays a lovely, clean character.

DOMAINE JEAN-MARC ET FRÉDÉRIC BERNHARD

21, Grand-Rue
68230 Katzenthal
Phone 00 33 3 89 27 05 34
Fax 00 33 3 89 27 58 72
vins@jeanmarcbernhard.fr
www.jeanmarcbernhard.fr

This family estate in Katzenthal is heir to an unusual variety of holdings and is becoming increasingly well known. Frédéric Bernhard is now in charge of winemaking, helped by the rest of the family, turning out exceptionally honest and elegant wines at (so far) sensible prices. The most sought-after cuvées sell out quickly, so don't delay in placing your order. Must-haves include the muscat, the gewürztraminer Vieilles Vignes, and the excellent gewürztraminer Kaefferkopf.

Recently tasted

ALSACE GRAND CRU FURSTENTUM PINOT GRIS 2007
Sweet White | 2011 up to 2022   90

ALSACE GRAND CRU MAMBOURG GEWÜRZTRAMINER 2007
Sweet White | 2011 up to 2022   91

ALSACE GRAND CRU SCHLOSSBERG RIESLING 2007
White | 2011 up to 2022   91

ALSACE GRAND CRU WINECK-SCHLOSSBERG RIESLING 2007
White | 2011 up to 2017   92

KAEFFERKOPF GEWÜRZTRAMINER 2007
Semi-Dry White | 2011 up to 2017   89

RIESLING SÉLECTION DE GRAINS NOBLES 2007
Sweet White | 2011 up to 2022   92

Older vintages

ALSACE GRAND CRU FURSTENTUM PINOT GRIS 2005
Sweet White | 2011 up to 2020   90
Harvested at a Vendange Tardive level, this wine is sweet and concentrated with superb botrytis, finishing on aromas of citrus peel. The power of the Furstentum is enveloped by ripe fruit, resulting in a fine balance of depth and purity.

ALSACE GRAND CRU WINECK-SCHLOSSBERG RIESLING 2006
White | 2011 up to 2016   92
A wine of reference: the citrus on the nose possesses strong salinity on the palate, and the minerality of the Wineck-Schlossberg's disintegrated granite is expressed without question. Superb wine.

GEWÜRZTRAMINER SÉLECTION DE GRAINS NOBLES 2005
Sweet White | 2011 up to 2025   **94**
Careful selection in the old vines of Mambourg and its neighbor Vogelgarten made it possible to produce this sweet wine, with aromas of praline and butter that unveil a molten sweetness of great depth and finesse.

HINTERBURG PINOT GRIS
SÉLECTION DE GRAINS NOBLES 2005
Sweet White | 2011 up to 2020   **92**
A luscious wine, very pure and powerful on the palate, with very fine sweetness enhanced by good acidity. The aromas of candied fruits, dried apricots, and quince are still subtle.

MUSCAT VENDANGES TARDIVES 2005
Sweet White | 2011 up to 2015   **91**
A delicate Vendange Tardive, this offers aromas of acacia and honey that lead to a clean, full, honeyed palate and a spicy finish.

Red: 1.9 acres; pinot gris 18%, pinot noir 8%. White: 21.6 acres; auxerrois/pinot blanc 17%, gewürztraminer 24%, muscat 7%, riesling 24%, sylvaner 2%. Annual production: 60,000 bottles

DOMAINE LÉON BEYER

2, rue de la Première-Armée
68420 Eguisheim
Phone 00 33 3 89 21 62 30
Fax 00 33 3 89 23 93 63
contact@leonbeyer.fr
www.leonbeyer.fr

This historic winery continues to work toward that consistency and classicism on which the reputation of the great Alsace wine producers is built. On the genealogical front, Léon Beyer is now in active retirement and Marc Beyer is at the helm, recently joined by his son Yann. The best cuvées are sourced from decent-size holdings in the Eichberg and Pfersigberg Grands Crus but make no mention of Grand Cru status anywhere. The top wines are marketed under the Comtes d'Eguisheim designation, being produced only in the best years and from the best parcels. A selection of very dependable, classical offerings made from purchased grapes rounds off this range. Most of the wines make no concessions whatsoever to residual sugar except for the Vendanges Tardives and Sélection de Grains Nobles bottlings: deliciously concentrated, very pure, and made only in great years. The wines are often austere in early youth and need a few years' cellaring; we are pleased to report that every bottle is stored on the property for several years before release.

Recently tasted
GEWÜRZTRAMINER COMTES D'EGUISHEIM 2007
White | 2012 up to 2027   **93**

PINOT GRIS 2007
White | 2011 up to 2015   **86**

PINOT GRIS COMTES D'EGUISHEIM 2007
White | 2012 up to 2027   **92**

PINOT NOIR RÉSERVE 2007
Red | 2011 up to 2015   **87**

RIESLING 2007
White | 2011 up to 2015   **86**

RIESLING COMTES D'EGUISHEIM 2007
White | 2012 up to 2027   **91**

RIESLING LES ÉCAILLERS 2007
White | 2012 up to 2022   **89**

RIESLING R DE BEYER 2007
White | 2011 up to 2027   **90**

RIESLING R DE BEYER 2005
White | 2011 up to 2025   **88**

RIESLING RÉSERVE 2007
White | 2011 up to 2017   **87**

RIESLING VENDANGES TARDIVES 1998
Sweet White | 2011 up to 2018   **92**

SYLVANER 2007
White | 2011 up to 2013   **86**

Older vintages

GEWÜRZTRAMINER COMTES D'EGUISHEIM 2005
White | 2011 up to 2025   **91**
Complex on the nose with spice, yeast, and vanilla, the wine is dry and rich on the palate. The finish is long, expressing the wine's noble origin. A full wine, possessing power on the mid-palate. For long keeping, with great potential to improve.

GEWÜRZTRAMINER COMTES D'EGUISHEIM 2003
White | 2011 up to 2023   **92**
A magnificent wine, in a vintage where the gewürztraminer found its own in the great argilo-limestone terroirs. The nose is intense with notes of violet, raisins, and sweet spices. The palate is full and completely dry, with richness and a finish of ripe fruit aromas, culminating in a magnificent balance. Already accessible and of great aging potential. There was no 2004.

GEWÜRZTRAMINER COMTES D'EGUISHEIM 2001
White | 2011 up to 2021   **90**
An unusual, limited-production wine, this is superripe, roasted, and complex on the nose. The palate is still marked by sweetness, with fine acidity and roasted notes on the long finish. A medium-dry balance that has its charm.

GEWÜRZTRAMINER COMTES D'EGUISHEIM 2000
White | 2011 up to 2020   **91**
The wine is very ripe with a nose that is already open, softly revealing a rich, full, deep palate with subtle acidity. A dry gewürztraminer perfect for the table.

GEWÜRZTRAMINER
SÉLECTION DE GRAINS NOBLES 2005
Sweet White | 2011 up to 2045   **96**
A rare wine produced with high-quality botrytis, this should qualify for the Quintessence designation the domaine uses for its greatest dessert wines. The nose is clean and toasty with a praline note; the palate is luscious and full with depth, minerality, and great purity. The complete opposite of its dry version, this wine demonstrates the extent of the house's dessert wine knowhow. Great aging potential.

GEWÜRZTRAMINER SÉLECTION DE GRAINS NOBLES QUINTESSENCE 1998
Sweet White | 2011 up to 2030   **97**
A wine that opens slowly into aromas of intense red fruits, praline, and honey. The palate is luscious and powerful with impressive concentration, depth, and fat. A wine that will follow the same path as the legendary 1983 Quintessence cuvée.

GEWÜRZTRAMINER SÉLECTION DE GRAINS NOBLES QUINTESSENCE 1983
Sweet White | 2011 up to 2023   **98**
After long aging at the domaine, this wine has been newly released, much to our great pleasure. The nose is complex and youthful in its aromas of praline and honey blossom, leather and spice. The palate is luscious, deep, and elegant, with fine acidity that adds an ethereal touch to the sweetness. One of the great dessert wines of Alsace of the twentieth century, this shows the path that the 1998 and 2005 will follow.

GEWÜRZTRAMINER
VENDANGES TARDIVES 2004
Sweet White | 2011 up to 2024   **90**
The nose is superripe with notes of exotic fruit and pineapple. The palate is clean, sweet, and full with lots of elegance. The finish is long with candied fruit. A seductive wine, already open.

PINOT GRIS COMTES D'EGUISHEIM 2005
White | 2011 up to 2025   **91**
A worthy successor to the 2000, here is a great dry pinot gris—clean, complex, and honest on the nose with aromas of hazelnuts, honey, and dried fruit and a smoky note. The palate is full, pure, and fat, unveiling good minerality. A wine to save for the best poultry.

RIESLING COMTES D'EGUISHEIM 2005
White | 2011 up to 2030   **90**
The nose is still closed with aromas of flowers and citrus. The palate is full and deep with pure minerality. The finish is long with a spicy character. A wine with great aging potential that requires time.

RIESLING COMTES D'EGUISHEIM 2003
White | 2011 up to 2023   **92**
The nose is powerful with roasted notes and dried flower aromas, leading to a palate of great purity and fullness with a long finish. Pfersigberg's old vines produced a very dense wine with aging potential.

Red: 7.4 acres; pinot noir 100%. **White:** 42 acres; gewürztraminer 46%, muscat d'Alsace 5%, pinot gris 18%, riesling 31%. **Annual production:** 700,000 bottles

DOMAINE PAUL BLANCK

32, Grand-Rue
68240 Kientzheim
Phone 00 33 3 89 78 23 56
Fax 00 33 3 89 47 16 45
info@blanck.com
www.blanck.com

This estate owns vineyards around Kientzheim and is managed today by two of Paul Blanck's grandsons, Frédéric on the winemaking side and his cousin Philippe handling marketing and sales, with particular attention to export markets. With holdings in the best Grands Crus, the winery can offer a broad range of wines, highlighting the specific character of each terroir across a range of grape varieties. The vintages for sale range from impeccably made classic cuvées that sell out quickly to cask-aged Grands Crus that are released only after several years' bottle aging. The 2004, 2005, and 2006 vintages produced very pure wines, with something to suit every taste. As an additional plus, this winery has one of the most detailed of all the Alsace Web sites.

Recently tasted

ALSACE GRAND CRU FURSTENTUM
GEWÜRZTRAMINER VIEILLES VIGNES 2004
Sweet White | 2011 up to 2024   93

ALSACE GRAND CRU FURSTENTUM PINOT GRIS 2004
Semi-Dry White | 2011 up to 2024   91

ALSACE GRAND CRU MAMBOURG
GEWÜRZTRAMINER 2006
White | 2011 up to 2026   92

ALSACE GRAND CRU SOMMERBERG RIESLING 2005
White | 2011 up to 2020   89

ALSACE GRAND CRU SYLVANER
VIEILLES VIGNES 2007
White | 2011 up to 2017   86

ALTENBOURG GEWÜRZTRAMINER 2007
Sweet White | 2011 up to 2022   89

GEWÜRZTRAMINER 2007
White | 2011 up to 2017   88

PATERGARTEN PINOT GRIS 2006
White | 2011 up to 2016   88

PINOT AUXERROIS VIEILLES VIGNES 2007
White | 2011 up to 2015   88

PINOT NOIR F 2005
Red | 2011 up to 2020   91

Older vintages

ALSACE GRAND CRU FURSTENTUM
GEWÜRZTRAMINER SÉLECTION DE GRAINS
NOBLES 2001
Sweet White | 2011 up to 2021   93
The nose is very ripe and clean with aromas of dried apricots, quince paste, and candied tropical fruit. The palate is sweet and crisp, evolving toward spice, orange peel, and smoke on the finish. Superb, mature wine that will age well.

ALSACE GRAND CRU FURSTENTUM
GEWÜRZTRAMINER VENDANGES TARDIVES 2005
Sweet White | 2011 up to 2025   95
A powerful Vendange Tardive, this offers up a delicate nose of rose, praline, and sweet spices. It is sweet and elegant on the palate, with purity and depth. The finish is long, on notes of honey and licorice. The terroir accents the variety and its superripeness, to yield a complete wine that will evolve well with aging.

ALSACE GRAND CRU FURSTENTUM
GEWÜRZTRAMINER VENDANGES TARDIVES 2004
Sweet White | 2011 up to 2025   93
A great sweet wine, this combines overripe fruit with a deep sense of terroir. It is full and generous, with a long finish.

ALSACE GRAND CRU FURSTENTUM
GEWÜRZTRAMINER VIEILLES VIGNES 2002
Sweet White | 2011 up to 2025   92
A profound and concentrated wine that opens slowly with complex aromas of orange blossom and bergamot, its pedigree evident on the palate. A wine of great aging potential.

ALSACE GRAND CRU FURSTENTUM
PINOT GRIS 2003
Semi-Dry White | 2011 up to 2020   92
An extreme pinot gris, this is very deep and mineral, scented with smoke and vanilla. It has a purity equal to the riesling. Try with roasted poultry.

ALSACE GRAND CRU FURSTENTUM
RIESLING 2004
White | 2011 up to 2024   91
Harvested very ripe, this wine offers very clean fruit and a full palate still marked by sweetness, but also depth and power, with a long finish on bitter notes.

ALSACE GRAND CRU FURSTENTUM
RIESLING 2003
White | 2011 up to 2020   90
In an exuberant vintage, the Furstentum played its cards just right, retaining remarkable elegance: this is a medium-dry, full wine with depth and crystalline purity.

ALSACE GRAND CRU SCHLOSSBERG
RIESLING 2006
White | 2011 up to 2021   **91**
The nose is elegant, floral, and smoky; the
palate is taut and elegant, with richness.
The medium-dry balance offers lovely min-
erality. A wine for aging.

ALSACE GRAND CRU SCHLOSSBERG
RIESLING 2005
White | 2011 up to 2020   **90**
The nose is racy, intense, and floral, with a
note of smoke. The palate is dense and rich
with light sweetness and very present acidity
on the finish. A mineral wine of great aging
potential.

ALSACE GRAND CRU SCHLOSSBERG
RIESLING 2004
White | 2011 up to 2020   **90**
A streamlined and taut wine, this has an elegant and mineral nose leading to a full and very
clean palate. A great vintage for Schlossberg.

ALSACE GRAND CRU WINECK-SCHLOSSBERG
RIESLING 2005
White | 2011 up to 2015   **89**
The nose is elegant and perfumed with aromas of wildflowers and almonds. The palate
is dry, full, and delicately saline and finishes
on a spicy note. A wine worthy of a terroir
that yields very fine wines. To serve with the
finest fish after several years of aging.

ALTENBOURG GEWÜRZTRAMINER 2006
Sweet White | 2011 up to 2016   **89**
A pure gewürztraminer with a clean nose
of roses, exotic fruit, and a flint note, this is
full on the palate, with well-integrated sweetness. The finish is crisp and spicy.

ALTENBOURG GEWÜRZTRAMINER 2005
Sweet White | 2011 up to 2020   **90**
Quality botrytis yielded an unctuous, sweet
Altenbourg with deep aromas of butter and
praline.

PATERGARTEN RIESLING 2005
White | 2011 up to 2015   **87**
A dry riesling, hazelnut and spice on the
nose, clean and straight on the palate, with
a finish of smoke and flint.

ROSENBOURG RIESLING 2006
White | 2011 up to 2016   **87**
The nose is pure and smoky with aromas of
citrus. The palate is full, clean, and dry, with
a floral note and very saline acidity. Altogether dry and fine.

Red: 7.4 acres; pinot 16%, pinot gris 15.5%, pinot noir
7%. White: 81.5 acres; chasselas 5%, gewürztraminer 22%, muscat 3%, riesling 31%, sylvaner 5%.
Annual production: 230,000 bottles

DOMAINE LÉON BOESCH

6, rue Saint-Blaise
68250 Westhalten
Phone 00 33 3 89 47 01 83
Fax 00 33 3 89 47 64 95
domaine-boesch@wanadoo.fr

Owner-operators Gérard Boesch and his
son Mathieu hold all the cards when it
comes to making deep, refined wines: biodynamically grown vines, controlled yields,
slow pressing, and vinification on lees in
oak vats. The 2006 vintage is just a shade
less splendid than the 2005, but still very
pure and clean with lovely acidity. The
entire range is consistent and utterly
dependable—a sure sign of a top Alsace
producer.

Recently tasted
ALSACE GRAND CRU ZINNKOEPFLÉ
GEWÜRZTRAMINER 2007
Sweet White | 2011 up to 2022   **90**

ALSACE GRAND CRU ZINNKOEPFLÉ
GEWÜRZTRAMINER VENDANGES TARDIVES 2007
Sweet White | 2011 up to 2022   **94**

BREITENBERG GEWÜRZTRAMINER 2007
Sweet White | 2011 up to 2017   **88**

BREITENBERG RIESLING 2007
Semi-Dry White | 2011 up to 2017   **88**

CLOS ZWINGEL PINOT GRIS 2007
Semi-Dry White | 2011 up to 2017   **87**

LUSS RIESLING 2007
White | 2011 up to 2017   **87**

PINOT BLANC KLEVNER 2007
White | 2011 up to 2013   **87**

SYLVANER TRADITION 2007
White | 2011 up to 2013   **86**

Older vintages
ALSACE GRAND CRU ZINNKOEPFLÉ
GEWÜRZTRAMINER 2006
Sweet White | 2011 up to 2021   **92**
A very aromatic wine, full on the palate with
depth, fat, and subtle sweetness. The finish is long, smoky, and spicy. A wine of
character.

ALSACE GRAND CRU ZINNKOEPFLÉ
GEWÜRZTRAMINER 2005
Sweet White | 2011 up to 2020   **92**
Fashioned for long aging, this wine is already
open, with a delicate, floral nose and a taut,
saline palate with fullness, depth, and citrus zest on the finish. It has all of the finesse
of Zinnkoepflé.

ALSACE GRAND CRU ZINNKOEPFLÉ
GEWÜRZTRAMINER VENDANGES TARDIVES 2006
Sweet White I 2011 up to 2026   **94**
Smoky on the nose, with a note of candied fruit, this wine is sweet and fat with strong salinity, very pure flavors, and a finish of citrus peel and honey. Already superb, the wine will improve with time.

ALSACE GRAND CRU ZINNKOEPFLÉ
GEWÜRZTRAMINER VENDANGES TARDIVES 2005
Sweet White I 2011 up to 2020   **92**
The wine is delicate, with rose and praline on the nose and sweet and mineral notes on the palate, with a lightness surprising for a wine so rich. Remarkable purity with a long finish on noble spices.

ALSACE GRAND CRU ZINNKOEPFLÉ
PINOT GRIS 2006
White I 2011 up to 2016   **89**
A very ripe pinot gris: yellow fruit on the nose and sweet on the palate, a fat and smoky finish. Aging will integrate the wine's sweetness.

ALSACE GRAND CRU ZINNKOEPFLÉ
RIESLING 2005
White I 2011 up to 2020   **92**
Fashioned for long aging, this wine is already open, with a delicate floral nose and a saline palate of depth. Full and citrusy on the finish, this has all of the finesse of the Zinnkoepflé.

BREITENBERG PINOT GRIS
SÉLECTION DE GRAINS NOBLES 2006
Sweet White I 2011 up to 2026   **93**
Very candied on the nose, with light oak scents, this is luscious on the palate with great purity. The balance is still tipped toward its strong sweetness, but the wine possesses good minerality. For keeping.

BREITENBERG PINOT GRIS
VENDANGES TARDIVES 2006
Sweet White I 2011 up to 2021   **90**
A lovely Vendange Tardive, with candied fruits on the nose and a fleshy sweetness on the palate. Fine acidity lends precision, and a finish is long on zest and candied fruit.

Red: 2.5 acres; pinot noir 15%. White: 29.7 acres; gewürztraminer 22%, muscat d'Alsace 2%, pinot blanc 15%, riesling 21%, sylvaner 6%. Annual production: 80,000 bottles

DOMAINE BOTT-GEYL

1, rue du Petit-Château
68980 Beblenheim
Phone 00 33 3 89 47 90 04
Fax 00 33 3 89 47 97 33
info@bott-geyl.com
www.bott-geyl.fr

Now entirely biodynamic, this estate boasts lovely parcels in several Grands Crus, starting with Furstentum and Schoenenbourg but also in the less-publicized crus of Mandelberg and Sonnenglanz. Jean-Christophe Bott harvests ripe fruit and keeps his wines on their lees for the sake of depth and richness. Committed to bringing out the precise expression of each terroir, he separates riesling fruit from the Grand Cru Schoenenbourg and that of the Kronenbourg lieu-dit in Zellenberg (where the plots would qualify as Grand Cru sites). Bott-Geyl rieslings are dry and sometimes austere as young wines. The pinot gris and gewürztraminer Grands Crus are more opulent but remain nicely precise, with enough acidity for good structure. The Mandelberg and Schoenenbourg rieslings are produced in small quantities, so get in quick while stocks last. The 2005 vintage produced some magnificent dry wines but also memorable dessert wines, sure to reward patient aging. The 2006 Grands Crus are also very successful, courtesy of very ripe grapes.

Recently tasted
ALSACE GRAND CRU FURSTENTUM
GEWÜRZTRAMINER 2007
Sweet White I 2011 up to 2027   **94**

ALSACE GRAND CRU SONNENGLANZ
GEWÜRZTRAMINER 2007
White I 2011 up to 2030   **97**

ALSACE GRAND CRU SONNENGLANZ GEWÜRZTRAMINER
SÉLECTION DE GRAINS NOBLES 2007
Sweet White I 2013 up to 2030   **96**

ALSACE GRAND CRU SONNENGLANZ PINOT GRIS 2007
Semi-Dry White I 2011 up to 2027   **93**

GENTIL D'ALSACE MÉTISS 2007
White I 2011 up to 2013   **86**

GEWÜRZTRAMINER LES ÉLÉMENTS 2007
Semi-Dry White I 2011 up to 2017   **89**

Older vintages
ALSACE GRAND CRU FURSTENTUM
GEWÜRZTRAMINER 2005
Sweet White I 2011 up to 2020   **97**
A superb wine, this shows intense rose, peach, and white truffle aromas that lead to a full palate of depth and great purity. Great wine, this is already approachable but should age marvelously.

ALSACE GRAND CRU FURSTENTUM GEWÜRZTRAMINER 2004
Sweet White | 2011 up to 2020   92
A very ripe and spicy wine that displays power and depth on the palate in a medium-dry balance.

ALSACE GRAND CRU FURSTENTUM PINOT GRIS 2005
Sweet White | 2011 up to 2020   90
Harvested ripe but not overripe, this wine shows a very clean nose of yellow fruits and citrus, followed by a sweet, full, mineral palate with purity. A wine to age for several years.

ALSACE GRAND CRU MANDELBERG RIESLING 2006
White | 2011 up to 2021   92
Harvested overripe, the 2006 is labeled "Cuvée Botrytis l'Exception." The nose is closed with a smoky note; the palate is full and lightly sweet with depth and richness. A wine for the cellar.

ALSACE GRAND CRU MANDELBERG RIESLING 2005
White | 2011 up to 2020   94
A very pure Mandelberg with its characteristic minerality and richness, this is ripe on the nose with depth on the palate. The lemony finish is clean and pure.

ALSACE GRAND CRU SCHOENENBOURG RIESLING 2006
White | 2011 up to 2021   92
Harvested overripe, the 2006 is labeled "Cuvée Botrytis l'Exception." The nose is still closed with a peppery note; the palate is saline and lightly sweet with lovely bitterness reminiscent of grapefruit. A racy wine of great density that will evolve well.

ALSACE GRAND CRU SCHOENENBOURG RIESLING 2004
White | 2011 up to 2020   92
Marked by botrytis on the nose, the wine shows crystalline purity on the palate with pronounced minerality and a medium-dry balance that enhances its fine, fluid character.

ALSACE GRAND CRU SONNENGLANZ GEWÜRZTRAMINER 2005
White | 2011 up to 2025   94
A powerful wine with a rich, spicy, and racy nose, full on the palate with acidity quite present. A wine for long aging.

ALSACE GRAND CRU SONNENGLANZ GEWÜRZTRAMINER 2004
White | 2011 up to 2013   92
The richness and minerality typical of Sonnenglanz brings a remarkably tender touch to the palate of this superripe wine. Brilliant and pure.

ALSACE GRAND CRU SONNENGLANZ GEWÜRZTRAMINER SÉLECTION DE GRAINS NOBLES 2005
Sweet White | 2011 up to 2025   96
A very concentrated wine, this shows honey and praline on the nose, with depth and great purity on the palate. The intensity of the liqueur and richness of sugar mask neither the wine's precision of fruit nor the aromatic finesse on the long finish. This will benefit from long aging.

ALSACE GRAND CRU SONNENGLANZ GEWÜRZTRAMINER VENDANGES TARDIVES 2006
Sweet White | 2011 up to 2026   92
The nose is ripe—even candied—with citrus and smoke notes. The palate is sweet, very fine, and crisp, with a spicy character and intense fruit very present on the finish. A powerful wine of depth that retains much finesse. Wait several years.

ALSACE GRAND CRU SONNENGLANZ GEWÜRZTRAMINER VENDANGES TARDIVES 2005
Sweet White | 2011 up to 2025   91
A rich Vendange Tardive, spicy on the nose and sweet on the palate, that possesses a lot of concentration. A powerful wine for long aging.

ALSACE GRAND CRU SONNENGLANZ PINOT GRIS 2005
Semi-Dry White | 2011 up to 2020   93
2005 yielded a great, racy wine with a pure, overripe, and lightly smoky nose leading to a palate of elegance and depth. With its powerful acidity, it strikes a lovely medium-dry balance with a sweetness of great finesse.

ALSACE GRAND CRU SONNENGLANZ PINOT GRIS SÉLECTION DE GRAINS NOBLES 2005
Sweet White | 2011 up to 2025   93
A very rich, luscious wine, this has a nose of lemon, dates, honey, and a touch of spice, and a palate of depth and great finesse with massive concentration. A great wine to age.

ALSACE GRAND CRU SONNENGLANZ PINOT GRIS VENDANGES TARDIVES 2005
Sweet White | 2011 up to 2025   96
The nose is open and very ripe with notes of apricot and smoke; the palate is rich, very fine, and crisp, with an intense minerality. The finish is long on citrus peel. A splendid Vendange Tardive from a great terroir.

SCHLOESSELREBEN DE BEBLENHEIM GEWÜRZTRAMINER 2005
Sweet White | 2011 up to 2015   88
A wine harvested very ripe that is labeled "Botrytis l'Exception," this is already open on the nose with candied rose and honey aromas. The palate is sweet, clean, and full, with purity. The finish is ethereal, with exotic fruit and light bitterness.

Red: 1.2 acres; pinot 4%. White: 30.9 acres; gewürztraminer 26%, muscat 3%, pinot blanc 17%, pinot gris 24%, riesling 24%, sylvaner 2%. Annual production: 85,000 bottles

DOMAINE ALBERT BOXLER

78, rue des Trois-Épis
68230 Niedermorschwihr
Phone 00 33 3 89 27 11 32
Fax 00 33 3 89 27 70 14
albert.boxler@9online.fr

Jean Boxler makes creative use of the granitic soils around Niedermorschwihr. Half of
his parcels are located in the Sommerberg
and Brand Grands Crus, each one providing
the raw materials for a variety of cuvées that
express all the subtle nuances at the heart of
the individual terroirs. His range of riesling
Sommerberg wines are his finest bottlings;
his Brand wines exhibit more power; his
wines from the granitic terroirs around the
village are concentrated and refined. All of
the wines are made from ultraripe fruit and
need a few years to mellow out.

Recently tasted

ALSACE GRAND CRU BRAND PINOT GRIS 2007
Semi-Dry White | 2011 up to 2027   **95**

ALSACE GRAND CRU BRAND RIESLING 2007
White | 2012 up to 2027   **96**

ALSACE GRAND CRU BRAND RIESLING K 2007
White | 2012 up to 2027   **93**

ALSACE GRAND CRU SOMMERBERG PINOT GRIS 2007
Semi-Dry White | 2011 up to 2027   **91**

ALSACE GRAND CRU SOMMERBERG RIESLING 2007
White | 2011 up to 2027   **96**

ALSACE GRAND CRU SOMMERBERG RIESLING D 2007
White | 2012 up to 2027   **95**

ALSACE GRAND CRU SOMMERBERG RIESLING
SÉLECTION DE GRAINS NOBLES 2007
Sweet White | 2012 up to 2030   **97**

BRAND GEWÜRZTRAMINER
VENDANGES TARDIVES 2007
Sweet White | 2011 up to 2027   **92**

GEWÜRZTRAMINER 2007
Semi-Dry White | 2011 up to 2022   **91**

PINOT BLANC B 2007
White | 2011 up to 2017   **92**

Older vintages

ALSACE GRAND CRU BRAND MUSCAT 2006
White | 2011 up to 2016   **90**
A blend of equal parts muscat Ottonel and
muscat d'Alsace, this wine is perfumed and
very floral on the nose and full and crisp on
the palate, with great salinity. A very dry, very
mineral terroir wine. The Grand Cru appellation is used when the vintage permits it.

ALSACE GRAND CRU BRAND PINOT GRIS 2006
Semi-Dry White | 2011 up to 2021   **91**
From Steinglitz, the wine has a very pure
nose of hazelnut and ripe fruit, and a full
and sweet palate with very pure acidity. Very
saline but still sweet, the wine will gain balance after several years of aging.

ALSACE GRAND CRU BRAND RIESLING 2006
White | 2011 up to 2021   **93**
A blend of fruit from Steinglitz and Kirchtal,
this wine is rich and super-ripe on the nose,
unctuous and profound on the palate, with
the salinity and purity typical of the vintage.

ALSACE GRAND CRU BRAND RIESLING 2005
White | 2011 up to 2020   **92**
A blend of fruit from Steinglitz and Kirchtal,
this wine is fuller than the Sommerberg, with
a very clean, floral nose and a full, mineral
palate that points to the presence of limestone under the granitic soils.

ALSACE GRAND CRU BRAND RIESLING K 2006
White | 2011 up to 2021   **95**
From the Kirchberg parcel of the Grand Cru
Brand, this wine possesses a pure nose of
white flowers and fresh grapefruit, a profound, full palate, and great length.

ALSACE GRAND CRU PINOT GRIS BRAND
SÉLECTION DE GRAINS NOBLES 2005
Sweet White | 2011 up to 2025   **95**
From Steinglitz, here is a very rich wine of
incredible youth and freshness, a pure and
mineral liqueurlike wine with lovely acidity
that integrates on the long dried-apricot and
candied-lemon finish.

ALSACE GRAND CRU SOMMERBERG
PINOT GRIS VENDANGES TARDIVES 2006
Sweet White | 2011 up to 2016   **92**
A wine with a candied nose, marked by ripe
citrus fruits and honey, this is sweet on the
palate with lovely acidity. The combination
of its sweet character and acidity yields a
very palatable balance.

ALSACE GRAND CRU SOMMERBERG RIESLING 2006
White | 2011 up to 2021   **92**
A classic Sommerberg, with a nose of sour
fruits and flowers, this is fresh and lively on
the attack with a light roundness that softens the finish. Lovely bitter notes and perfect maturity yield a great wine of profound
minerality.

ALSACE GRAND CRU SOMMERBERG RIESLING 2005
White | 2011 up to 2020   **90**
The cuvée from the base of this Grand Cru
displays a sunny profile, warm and mineral,
with all the finesse of a concentrated Grand
Cru in a dry style.

ALSACE GRAND CRU SOMMERBERG RIESLING D 2006

White | 2011 up to 2021   **95**

From a parcel within Dudenstein, the wine is perfumed with ripe citrus notes and smoke, rich and very pure on the palate, with a saline finish of great length. A full wine that possesses depth and great purity; the vineyard is close to more limestone-heavy terrains.

ALSACE GRAND CRU SOMMERBERG RIESLING E 2006

White | 2011 up to 2021   **93**

From Eckberg, this fragrant wine has a very distinct, intense structure supporting flint and fresh citrus fruit notes. It is concentrated and saline on the palate, with marked acidity that enhances the lovely bitter notes on the finish. Dry concentration, savory.

ALSACE GRAND CRU SOMMERBERG RIESLING E 2005

White | 2011 up to 2020   **91**

From the lovely Eckberg parcel, this wine was harvested very ripe but retains a fine and elegant character with remarkable purity.

GEWÜRZTRAMINER 2006

Semi-Dry White | 2011 up to 2016   **90**

Produced from Pfoeller's limestone soils, this 2006 integrates declassified Grand Cru Brand fruit. The wine is clean and intense on the nose, with pepper and exotic fruit aromas, then full and saline on the palate, with concentration and finesse. A remarkable, balanced wine from start to finish.

PINOT BLANC B 2006

White | 2011 up to 2016   **89**

Produced from Kirchberg pinot blanc, at the heart of the Grand Cru Brand, this wine is dry and floral with a smoky note on the nose, and dense on the palate with a long finish. A structured wine that will age.

RIESLING 2006

White | 2011 up to 2016   **88**

From declassified young vines in Sommerberg, the wine is ripe and fresh with citrus aromas, clean and full on the palate, with light sweetness on the finish.

Red: 1.2 acres; pinot noir 4%. **White:** 29.7 acres; chasselas 1.5%, gewürztraminer 13%, muscat 2%, pinot blanc 18%, pinot gris 19.5%, riesling 38%, sylvaner 4%. **Annual production:** 60,000 bottles

DOMAINE ERNEST BURN

⚜ ⚜ ⚜ ⚜ ⚜

8, rue Basse
68420 Gueberschwihr
Phone 00 33 3 89 49 20 68
Fax 00 33 3 89 49 28 56
contact@domaine-burn.fr
www.domaine-burn.fr

The Clos Saint Imer in the Goldert Grand Cru accounts for 50 percent of this family holding, managed by Joseph and Francis Burn. Their four noble-varietal wines come from the deep, almost exclusively limestone soils in the upper part of the Clos where each takes on its own particular expression. The remaining varietal wines come from the other parcels in the Goldert Grand Cru. Reasoned viticulture is what they practice here, combined with classical vinification and long aging in stainless-steel tanks. Virtually all of the wines are then routinely raised in old oak vats. The results are rich and concentrated, often with noticeable residual sugar, particularly when young, but with enough natural acidity to achieve superb balance after a few years' cellaring.

ALSACE GRAND CRU GOLDERT CLOS SAINT-IMER GEWÜRZTRAMINER LA CHAPELLE 2005

Sweet White | 2011 up to 2020   **92**

A rich cuvée, this offers praline and orange-blossom scents on the nose, with a butter note, and a full, clean palate with an integrated sweetness and a spicy finish. Lovely purity, rich and crisp.

ALSACE GRAND CRU GOLDERT CLOS SAINT-IMER GEWÜRZTRAMINER LA CHAPELLE 2004

Sweet White | 2011 up to 2020   **92**

The nose is exotic and floral with a spicy note; the palate is rich and tender with much depth and lots of purity. A charming gewürztraminer to drink or hold.

ALSACE GRAND CRU GOLDERT CLOS SAINT-IMER GEWÜRZTRAMINER VENDANGES TARDIVES 2005

Sweet White | 2011 up to 2025   **94**

The ideal marriage of variety and terroir, this wine is rich and opulent without losing its freshness, blending candied citrus, pralines, and rose on the nose and a clean balance and depth on the palate.

ALSACE GRAND CRU GOLDERT CLOS SAINT-IMER GEWÜRZTRAMINER VENDANGES TARDIVES 2003

Sweet White | 2011 up to 2020   **92**

A pure, rose-scented nose leads to a sweet, pure, and mineral palate that is very elegant. From passerillage (raisined fruit), this Vendange Tardive displays the potential gewürztraminer from this terroir can have in a very warm year.

ALSACE GRAND CRU GOLDERT CLOS SAINT-IMER
MUSCAT LA CHAPELLE 2005
Semi-Dry White | 2011 up to 2020 **91**
Produced from muscat d'Alsace and muscat Ottonel, this wine is ripe with aromas of grapes and elderflowers, rich and crisp on the palate with perceptible sweetness on the finish. The wine is already delicious but possesses great capacity to improve with age, Goldert being one of the terroirs of Alsace the most apt to the production of muscats for long aging.

ALSACE GRAND CRU GOLDERT CLOS SAINT-IMER
MUSCAT LA CHAPELLE 2004
Semi-Dry White | 2011 up to 2020 **90**
A very classic terroir muscat, very ripe on the nose and supple on the palate, with minerality and lots of fruit. The wine is already delicious but has great capacity to improve with age, Goldert being one of the terroirs of Alsace the most apt to produce muscat for aging.

ALSACE GRAND CRU GOLDERT CLOS SAINT-IMER
MUSCAT VENDANGES TARDIVES 2005
Sweet White | 2011 up to 2030 **96**
A rare cuvée, the most recent vintages being 1995 and 2000. Harvested at Sélection de Grains Nobles maturity but released as a Vendange Tardive, the wine follows worthily the 1989 SGN, with a perfumed nose of fresh grapes and honey that leads to a sweet, mineral palate of great depth and purity.

ALSACE GRAND CRU GOLDERT CLOS SAINT-IMER
PINOT GRIS VENDANGES TARDIVES 2005
Sweet White | 2011 up to 2025 **92**
The wine is very rich, with a nose of citrus, sour fruits, and apricots. The palate is sweet, full, and rich, with great clarity, but the sweetness still dominates, and the wine must be aged to gain integration.

ALSACE GRAND CRU GOLDERT CLOS SAINT-IMER
RIESLING LA CHAPELLE 2004
Semi-Dry White | 2011 up to 2020 **91**
This was an ideal vintage in Goldert to produce a rich, pure, and crisp riesling with lots of length and minerality on the palate. The 1996, in a very similar style, suggests the wine will profit from several years of aging.

Red: 1.2 acres; pinot gris 20%, pinot noir 5%. **White:** 23.5 acres; gewürztraminer 30%, muscat 20%, pinot blanc 10%, riesling 15%, sylvaner 5%. **Annual production:** 50,000 bottles

DOMAINE AGATHE BURSIN

11, rue de Soultzmatt
68250 Westhalten
Phone 00 33 3 89 47 04 15
Fax 00 33 3 89 47 04 15
agathe.bursin@wanadoo.fr

Young Agathe Bursin came back to Westhalten after studying enology and has been producing her own wines since 2000. Her small, family estate used to sell most of its grapes but now vinifies an increasing proportion on the property, using small fermentation tanks. The scale of production is unlikely to exceed a dozen or so cuvées, even using all of the grapes on the estate.

Recently tasted
ALSACE GRAND CRU ZINNKOEPFLÉ
GEWÜRZTRAMINER 2008
Sweet White | 2011 up to 2028 **92**

ALSACE GRAND CRU ZINNKOEPFLÉ RIESLING 2008
White | 2011 up to 2018 **90**

BOLLENBERG MUSCAT 2008
White | 2011 up to 2018 **89**

DIRSTELBERG RIESLING 2008
White | 2011 up to 2018 **88**

L'AS DE B 2008
Semi-Dry White | 2011 up to 2018 **88**

SYLVANER ÉMINENCE 2008
White | 2011 up to 2018 **88**

Older vintages
ALSACE GRAND CRU ZINNKOEPFLÉ
GEWÜRZTRAMINER 2007
Sweet White | 2011 up to 2027 **92**
A full gewürztraminer with very ripe fruit and sweet spice, sweet on the palate with depth and great purity. The finish is long on notes of exotic fruit. A superb Zinnkoepflé for long-term aging.

ALSACE GRAND CRU ZINNKOEPFLÉ
GEWÜRZTRAMINER SÉLECTION DE GRAINS
NOBLES 2006
Sweet White | 2011 up to 2026 **95**
The nose is marked by mango, lychee, and papaya with notes of honey; the palate is sweet and balanced, at once profound and ethereal, possessing great finesse. The finish is long on notes of honey and exotic fruit. A delicious wine that combines great terroir with quality botrytis.

ALSACE GRAND CRU ZINNKOEPFLÉ GEWÜRZTRAMINER
VENDANGES TARDIVES 2006
Sweet White | 2011 up to 2016   **92**
A Vendange Tardive of great freshness, with
exotic candied fruits on the nose and deep,
sweet flavors on the taut palate. The finish is
long with great purity. A great Zinnkoepflé.

ALSACE GRAND CRU ZINNKOEPFLÉ
PINOT GRIS 2007
Sweet White | 2011 up to 2017   **90**
A rich wine, ripe fruit on the nose, dense
and crisp on the palate, with salinity that
supports a long finish.

ALSACE GRAND CRU ZINNKOEPFLÉ
RIESLING 2007
White | 2011 up to 2022   **92**
A Zinnkoeplflé still marked by riesling fruit
on the nose, full and very pure on the palate, with magnificent salinity. A wine of great
potential.

BOLLENBERG MUSCAT 2007
White | 2011 up to 2017   **90**
A superb muscat with a very clean and
intense nose of fresh grapes and elderber-
ries. The palate possesses the typical depth
of fruit grown on the limestone terrain of
Bollenberg, while retaining its freshness.
An exceptional muscat.

DIRSTELBERG RIESLING 2007
White | 2011 up to 2017   **88**
From the sandy soils of Dirstelberg, the wine
is ripe on the nose, rich and saline on the
palate, with a long finish of pink grapefruit.

L'AS DE B 2007
Semi-Dry White | 2011 up to 2017   **88**
From an old vineyard coplanted with six white
varieties, the wine is ripe and fruity on the
nose, full and fat on the palate, with a long,
aromatic finish. It is drier than previous vintages, marked by very clean fruit.

PARAD'AUX 2007
White | 2011 up to 2017   **88**
A new pinot auxerrois from Bollenberg, intense
and floral on the nose, dense and pure on the
palate. A promising wine to follow.

SYLVANER ÉMINENCE 2007
White | 2011 up to 2022   **88**
From Grand Cru Zinnkoepflé vines, the wine
is still discreet on the nose, yet rich on the
palate with fine salinity. A terroir wine that
merits patience.

Red: .6 acres; pinot noir 100%. White: 8.9 acres;
gewürztraminer 28%, muscat 2%, auxerrois 13%,
riesling 20%, sylvaner 26%. Annual production:
20,000 bottles

DOMAINE MARCEL DEISS

15, route du Vin
68750 Bergheim
Phone 00 33 3 89 73 63 37
Fax 00 33 3 89 73 32 67
marceldeiss@marceldeiss.fr
www.marceldeiss.com

Jean-Michel Deiss is one of those winemakers who will never be content with simply
making great wine: he also wants to change
history, and the way we think about wine. In
a region like Alsace where the dominant
ideology is to make wines that express the
individual fruit characteristics of each
grape, Deiss believes that it's the terroir
that should speak above all, even the grape
variety. In the sector of Bergheim, he
decided to bring back the old tradition of
planting several different grape varieties
side by side in the same vineyard. After a
long battle, first to make this new kind of
wine legal, and then to convince other colleagues to do the same, he can be proud of
the result, thanks also to very demanding
farming practices and to harvesting the
grapes at perfect ripeness. His wines have
never been as rich and flavorful, and the
winemakers in Bergheim have now adopted
this idea of blended varities for their Grand
Cru Altenberg vineyard. The absence of a
single-variety character in the wines has
also made it necessary to rethink the traditional food and wine pairings of Alsatian
wines. It's taken a few years for Deiss to put
his various cuvées in place, but the 2005
vintage reveals, as never before, the incredible diversity of the mosaic of terroirs created by the Ribeauvillé fault line.

Recently tasted
ALSACE 2007
White | 2011 up to 2015   **88**

ALSACE GRAND CRU ALTENBERG DE BERGHEIM 2007
Sweet White | 2015 up to 2027   **97**

ALSACE GRAND CRU ALTENBERG DE BERGHEIM 2006
Sweet White | 2012 up to 2026   **97**

ALSACE GRAND CRU SCHOENENBOURG 2007
Sweet White | 2012 up to 2027   **98**

BURG 2007
White | 2011 up to 2027   **95**

BURLENBERG 2006
Red | 2011 up to 2021   **93**

BURLENBERG 2005
Red | 2012 up to 2025   **92**

GEWÜRZTRAMINER 2007
White | 2011 up to 2017   **90**

GEWÜRZTRAMINER QUINTESSENCE
SÉLECTION DE GRAINS NOBLES 2007
Sweet White | 2011 up to 2027   **97**

GEWÜRZTRAMINER VENDANGES TARDIVES 2007
Sweet White | 2011 up to 2027   **92**

GRASBERG 2007
White | 2012 up to 2022   **92**

GRUENSPIEL 2007
White | 2011 up to 2027   **94**

HUEBUHL 2007
Sweet White | 2012 up to 2027   **96**

LANGENBERG 2007
White | 2011 up to 2022   **91**

MUSCAT BERGHEIM 2007
White | 2011 up to 2015   **89**

PINOT GRIS 2007
White | 2011 up to 2017   **88**

RIESLING 2007
White | 2011 up to 2017   **88**

ROTENBERG 2007
White | 2011 up to 2027   **93**

ROUGE DE SAINT-HIPPOLYTE 2007
Red | 2011 up to 2017   **88**

SCHOFFWEG 2007
White | 2012 up to 2027   **95**

Older vintages
ALSACE GRAND CRU
ALTENBERG DE BERGHEIM 2005
Sweet White | 2011 up to 2030   **99**
Always a great wine, recently recognized
as a varietally coplanted Grand Cru, the 2005
Altenberg is the most accomplished terroir
wine in Alsace and the domaine's most successful from this terroir to date. Combining
a very ripe, fresh nose and a full, mineral,
rich palate of great finesse, the wine strikes
a fine balance of finesse and power. Obviously of great aging potential.

ALSACE GRAND CRU
ALTENBERG DE BERGHEIM 2004
Sweet White | 2011 up to 2024   **95**
The first Grand Cru coplanted at the
domaine, the Altenberg displays power, with
unctuous and very deep flavors. It has an
almost perfect expression of the minerality
of the terroir. A wine for the very long term.

ALSACE GRAND CRU MAMBOURG 2005
White | 2011 up to 2030   **96**
A dry wine matured in barrels, this is full
and powerful with remarkable depth and
richness and great purity. A bottle of great
aging potential, with the power of the argilo-
limestone terroir.

ALSACE GRAND CRU SCHOENENBOURG 2005
Sweet White | 2011 up to 2030   **98**
An overripe version of this historic vineyard,
this Schoenenbourg possesses a complex,
very fresh nose and a dense, taut palate that
displays the minerality of its exceptional terroir.

ALSACE GRAND CRU SCHOENENBOURG 2004
Sweet White | 2011 up to 2024   **93**
From an old coplanted parcel largely of riesling, this wine is nervier and more mineral
than the Altenberg, offering a perfect combination of quality overripeness and crystalline purity.

BEBLENHEIM PINOT GRIS 2005
Semi-Dry White | 2011 up to 2015   **90**
A dry pinot gris, full and fine on the palate,
with light sweetness on the finish.

BURG 2005
White | 2011 up to 2025   **95**
An ample wine, with dried fruit and citrus
peel on the nose and depth, great concentration, and brilliant fullness on the palate.
A wine to keep.

BURLENBERG 2004
Red | 2011 up to 2024   **91**
From a coplantation of pinot noir and pinot
beurrot, this wine is rich but still closed on
the palate, with a tight frame. A wine to keep
several years to integrate the tannins, and
a reference red in the region.

BURLENBERG 2003
Red | 2011 up to 2023   **94**
A coplantation of pinot noir and pinot beurrot, this wine is rich and powerful, with
roasted and very spicy aromas on the nose,
a full body, and thick tannin. The finish is
long on black fruits and spices. This remarkable wine remains a reference for great
Alsace red.

ENGELGARTEN 2005
White | 2011 up to 2020   **93**
From a coplantation of seven varieties in
gravel soil, this wine is fresh and ripe on the
nose, full and fat on the palate, with a strong
savory character. A rich, well-made wine;
let it age to reveal its elegance.

GRASBERG 2005
White | 2011 up to 2020   **96**
From poor limestone soils, this wine is aromatic with candied citrus notes, and pure and crisp on the palate with fine acidity that literally gushes in the mouth. A powerful wine of remarkable purity and a long finish.

GRASBERG 2004
White | 2011 up to 2015   **90**
Riesling, pinot gris, and gewürztraminer coplanted in poor limestone soil produced a profound wine of great purity, chiseled by crisp acidity that gives the wine savor.

GRUENSPIEL 2004
White | 2011 up to 2024   **94**
Produced from the marl soils of Keuper, this wine is still closed on the nose with aromas of small red fruits, yet full and fat on the palate with strong minerality. A powerful wine with depth.

HUEBUHL 2002
Sweet White | 2011 up to 2022   **97**
An overripe wine with a nose that remains very fresh, a rich palate of great purity and acidity, and length on notes of yellow fruits. Try with a crayfish gratin.

LANGENBERG 2006
White | 2011 up to 2016   **92**
From the granitic slope of Langenberg, this wine is very elegant on the nose with delicate floral notes, and very fine on the palate with great salinity. The finish is long on floral notes.

ROUGE DE SAINT-HIPPOLYTE 2006
Red | 2011 up to 2016   **88**
Harvested from the Langenberg slope, this pinot noir is ripe, rich, and spicy on the nose with delicate, concentrated fruit on the palate. A noble Saint-Hippolyte red.

SCHOFFWEG 2005
White | 2011 up to 2020   **96**
From the limestone soils of Alanéen, this wine has a fresh nose with a touch of vanilla and citrus. It feels full and silky, with fine acidity on the finish. A very suave, dry wine.

SCHOFFWEG 2004
White | 2011 up to 2020   **92**
Riesling and pinot gris coplanted in limestone soils yield a dry wine outside the norm in depth and power, marked by barrel maturation.

Red: 4.9 acres. White: 61.8 acres. Annual production: 135,000 bottles

DOMAINE DIRLER-CADÉ

13, rue d'Issenheim
68500 Bergholtz
Phone 00 33 3 89 76 91 00
Fax 00 33 3 89 76 85 97
dirler-cade@terre-net.fr
www.dirler-cade.com

Jean Dirler and Ludivine Cadé practically doubled the size of this property when they merged their two holdings through marriage. Today, the finesse and renowned lightness of the Dirler style have made way for more generous wines, sometimes with a touch of sweetness, that retain the mineral character of their terroirs. The estate will soon be fully biodynamic and already offers a very long list of wines that include many single-vineyard offerings (lieux-dits). The wines from the four Bergholtz and Guebwiller Grands Crus make a good introduction to the range as a whole, with several cuvées available including some magnificent late-harvest Vendanges Tardives.

Recently tasted
ALSACE GRAND CRU KESSLER GEWÜRZTRAMINER 2007
Sweet White | 2011 up to 2027   **92**

ALSACE GRAND CRU KESSLER GEWÜRZTRAMINER
VENDANGES TARDIVES 2007
Sweet White | 2012 up to 2027   **90**

ALSACE GRAND CRU KESSLER RIESLING 2007
White | 2011 up to 2022   **90**

ALSACE GRAND CRU KESSLER RIESLING
HEISSE WANNE 2007
White | 2011 up to 2022   **91**

ALSACE GRAND CRU KESSLER RIESLING
SÉLECTION DE GRAINS NOBLES 2007
Sweet White | 2011 up to 2022   **92**

ALSACE GRAND CRU KITTERLÉ
GEWÜRZTRAMINER 2007
Sweet White | 2011 up to 2022   **91**

ALSACE GRAND CRU SPIEGEL GEWÜRZTRAMINER
SÉLECTION DE GRAINS NOBLES 2007
Sweet White | 2011 up to 2027   **94**

ALSACE GRAND CRU SPIEGEL MUSCAT 2007
White | 2011 up to 2022   **90**

Older vintages
ALSACE GRAND CRU KESSLER GEWÜRZTRAMINER 2005
Sweet White | 2011 up to 2020   **93**
The nose is delicate and smoky with rose aromas. The palate is clean, tender, and mineral with a very delicate sweetness. The coupling of variety and terroir is remarkable here, resulting in a very well-integrated wine with remarkable texture.

ALSACE GRAND CRU KESSLER GEWÜRZTRAMINER
VENDANGES TARDIVES 2006
Sweet White | 2011 up to 2021   **94**
The nose is marked by fruit paste and smoke, the palate by its sweet, pure intensity, with praline aromas on the finish. Very well made, this wine will integrate further with age.

ALSACE GRAND CRU KESSLER PINOT GRIS 2005
Sweet White | 2011 up to 2020   **91**
Marked by high-quality botrytis, the wine is already intense on the nose. The palate is sweet, full, and very clean with a long finish marked by praline and smoke notes.

ALSACE GRAND CRU KESSLER RIESLING 2006
White | 2011 up to 2016   **92**
The wine is very clean, floral and mineral on the delicate nose, fine and mineral on the palate, marked by white-fleshed fruit. The finish is long and saline. A great success for the vintage.

ALSACE GRAND CRU KESSLER
RIESLING HEISSE WANNE 2006
White | 2011 up to 2021   **94**
More and more often, this domaine is bottling the parcels at the heart of this Grand Cru separately. This 2006 has very ripe aromas with a pure minerality and crispness on the palate; the finesse is unrivaled. A great success, superior to the 2005, which displays magnificent terroir.

ALSACE GRAND CRU KESSLER
RIESLING HEISSE WANNE 2005
White | 2011 up to 2020   **93**
When the vintage allows it, the rieslings from Heisse Wanne in the heart of Kessler are vinified separately, yielding a mineral wine with depth and finesse.

ALSACE GRAND CRU KITTERLÉ
GEWÜRZTRAMINER 2005
Sweet White | 2011 up to 2020   **91**
The nose is mineral and smoky; the palate is still round and dominated by terroir notes that give the wine much power. A rich wine, long on the finish.

ALSACE GRAND CRU SPIEGEL RIESLING 2005
White | 2011 up to 2020   **90**
The wine displays fullness and generosity, minerality and finesse, with a light sweetness enhanced by good acidity.

Red: 3.5 acres; pinot noir 9%. White: 37.4 acres; various 17%, auxerrois 9%, chasselas 1%, gewürztraminer 22%, muscat Ottonel 6%, pinot blanc 2%, riesling 27%, sylvaner 7%. Annual production: 100,000 bottles

DOMAINE PAUL GINGLINGER

8, place Charles-de-Gaulle
68420 Eguisheim
Phone 00 33 3 89 41 44 25
Fax 00 33 3 89 24 94 88
info@paul-ginglinger.fr
www.paul-ginglinger.fr

The unassuming Michel Ginglinger has gradually taken control here since 2000, following in the footsteps of his father, Paul, who made these wines the top-ranking Alsace offerings that they are today. A qualified enologist who also trained abroad, Michel looks to capture that honesty and balance that best express the special qualities of these lovely lands around Eguisheim. His limited range of about fifteen wines includes dry and dense offerings, often discreet and austere when newly made but opening up after two years in bottle and age splendidly. The gewürztraminers, like the rieslings, are rich and sometimes very slightly sweet but always balanced and never exuberant. The crémants and pinots noirs show the same attention to balance.

Recently tasted
ALSACE GRAND CRU EICHBERG GEWÜRZTRAMINER 2007
Sweet White | 2012 up to 2027   **91**

ALSACE GRAND CRU EICHBERG PINOT GRIS 2007
Semi-Dry White | 2012 up to 2027   **90**

ALSACE GRAND CRU EICHBERG RIESLING 2007
White | 2011 up to 2027   **92**

ALSACE GRAND CRU PFERSIGBERG
GEWÜRZTRAMINER 2007
Sweet White | 2011 up to 2027   **92**

ALSACE GRAND CRU PFERSIGBERG RIESLING 2007
White | 2012 up to 2027   **92**

ALSACE GRAND CRU PFERSIGBERG RIESLING
CUVÉE 42H 2007
White | 2012 up to 2027   **90**

GEWÜRZTRAMINER WAHLENBOURG 2007
White | 2011 up to 2022   **89**

RIESLING DREI EXA 2007
White | 2011 up to 2017   **88**

Older vintages
ALSACE GRAND CRU EICHBERG
GEWÜRZTRAMINER 2006
Sweet White | 2011 up to 2020   **91**
The wine is superripe, with notes of praline on the nose and a fruity, sweet palate of depth and great purity. It lasts on aromas of stone fruit.

ALSACE GRAND CRU EICHBERG
PINOT GRIS 2006
Semi-Dry White | 2011 up to 2020   **93**
Harvested without overripeness, clean and
healthy on the nose, here is a great pinot
gris, mineral, saline, elegant, and powerful.
Remarkably clean, this was partly matured
on the lees in barrel, which gives the wine
the richness necessary for its Grand Cru
volume to emerge. Magnificent terroir wine.

ALSACE GRAND CRU EICHBERG RIESLING 2006
White | 2011 up to 2021   **91**
Already open, this is smoky on the nose,
powerful and dry on the palate, with fruit
and citrus peel on the finish. The marly terroir character brings added finesse. For early
consumption.

ALSACE GRAND CRU PFERSIGBERG
GEWÜRZTRAMINER 2006
Sweet White | 2011 up to 2021   **90**
The nose of exotic fruit is very pure, leading
to a rich palate of superb volume and integrated sweetness. Long finish on flavors of
peach. A wine for aging.

ALSACE GRAND CRU PFERSIGBERG
RIESLING 2006
White | 2011 up to 2021   **90**
A ripe wine, this is fruity on the nose, clean,
streamlined, and mineral on the attack, then
grows in volume and richness. Long finish
on pineapple with lovely bitter notes. A wine
for long aging.

GEWÜRZTRAMINER
SÉLECTION DE GRAINS NOBLES 2005
Sweet White | 2011 up to 2025   **92**
The nose is very clean, with notes of praline,
honey, and candied fruits. The palate is luscious with elegance and depth, the minerality lifting the sweetness and yielding a drier
finish. An easy-drinking, luscious wine.

GEWÜRZTRAMINER VENDANGES TARDIVES 2005
Sweet White | 2011 up to 2020   **90**
From limestone soils around the village, this
wine is elegant on the nose, with dried apricot and honey scents. The palate is sweet
and rich, supported by lovely acidity. Already
open, this will keep for the long term.

Red: 2.5 acres; pinot noir. White: 27.2 acres; riesling
22.7%, pinot blanc 20.9%, pinot gris 15.7%,
gewürztraminer 19.1%, muscat 4.5%, chardonnay
12.4%, sylvaner and chasselas 4.7%. Annual
production: 80,000 bottles

DOMAINE RÉMY GRESSER

2, rue de l'École
67140 Andlau
Phone 00 33 3 88 08 95 88
Fax 00 33 3 88 08 55 99
domaine@gresser.fr
www.gresser.fr

Rémy Gresser's holdings are scattered
around the village of Andlau in a variety of
terroirs, including vines in the three Andlau Grands Crus, exclusively planted to
riesling. The estate is organic and gets
very ripe grapes producing rich and fruity
wines that are sometimes blurred by
excessive residual sugar.

Recently tasted
ALSACE GRAND CRU KASTELBERG RIESLING 2005
White | 2011 up to 2020   **89**

ALSACE GRAND CRU MOENCHBERG RIESLING 2005
Semi-Dry White | 2011 up to 2020   **91**

ALSACE GRAND CRU WIEBELSBERG RIESLING 2005
White | 2011 up to 2020   **90**

ANDLAU RIESLING 2007
White | 2011 up to 2017   **88**

Older vintages
ALSACE GRAND CRU KASTELBERG RIESLING 2006
White | 2011 up to 2021   **92**
The health of the fruit is evident in the pure,
floral nose and full, spicy palate. With depth
and lots of pedigree, this is a very lovely
Kastelberg.

ALSACE GRAND CRU MOENCHBERG RIESLING 2006
Semi-Dry White | 2011 up to 2016   **88**
This riesling is clean on the nose with floral
and mineral aromas, then straight and full
on the palate with a dry, long balance on
the finish.

ALSACE GRAND CRU WIEBELSBERG RIESLING 2006
White | 2011 up to 2016   **89**
A clean wine of great finesse, pure with fat
on the palate, with the fine salinity of Wiebelsberg.

ALSACE GRAND CRU WIEBELSBERG
RIESLING VIEILLES VIGNES 2006
Semi-Dry White | 2011 up to 2021   **90**
Produced from superripe grapes, this wine
is rich with a nose of ripe citrus and a sweet,
saline palate with good length.

Red: 1.2 acres; pinot noir 6%. White: 23.5 acres;
gewürztraminer 21%, muscat 4%, muscat d'Alsace
4%, muscat Ottonel 4%, pinot blanc 13%, pinot gris
10%, riesling 41%, sylvaner 5%. Annual production:
80,000 bottles

DOMAINE HÉRING

6, rue du Docteur-Sultzer
67140 Barr
Phone 00 33 3 88 08 90 07
Fax 00 33 3 88 08 08 54
jdhering@wanadoo.fr
www.vins-hering.com

Jean-Daniel Héring's estate boasts a large holding in the Kirchberg de Barr Grand Cru and includes a sizeable slice of the Clos Gaensbroennel at the center of the cru. The vines are cultivated in accordance with the Tyflo charter for environmentally friendly viticulture in Alsace. Héring wines are honest, pure, and nicely concentrated; be sure to check out the superb tasting room at the foot of the Grand Gru.

ALSACE GRAND CRU KIRCHBERG DE BARR GEWÜRZTRAMINER 2006
Sweet White I 2011 up to 2021   **90**
Elegant on the nose with notes of flowers and ripe fruits, this wine displays depth and salinity on the palate, with well-integrated sweetness.

ALSACE GRAND CRU KIRCHBERG DE BARR RIESLING VENDANGES TARDIVES 2006
Sweet White I 2011 up to 2021   **89**
Still dominated by sweetness, this is a rich Vendange Tardive, with candied citrus and zest accents leading to fine salinity on the finish. For keeping.

GEWÜRZTRAMINER LES COTEAUX 2007
Semi-Dry White I 2011 up to 2015   **88**
Rich and ample, with a nose of rose and spices, this wine is fat on the palate with integrated sweetness and a long, floral finish.

RIESLING CLOS DE LA FOLIE MARCO 2007
White I 2011 up to 2017   **88**
Well made in a great vintage, this wine displays dry balance and a density balanced by fine minerality. The finish is long.

ROSENEGERT 2007
Semi-Dry White I 2011 up to 2020   **87**
A coplantation of noble varieties, of which half is riesling from the western slope of Kirchberg, provides a full, spicy, and powerful wine, rich and lightly sweet on the palate. Lovely material for a wine for aging.

Red: 3.2 acres; pinot noir 100%. White: 21.5 acres; gewürztraminer 20%, muscat Ottonel 4%, pinot blanc 17%, riesling 20%, sylvaner 10%. Annual production: 75,000 bottles

HUGEL ET FILS

3, rue de la Première Armée
BP 32
68340 Riquewihr
Phone 00 33 3 89 47 92 15
Fax 00 33 3 89 49 00 10
info@hugel.com
www.hugel.fr

This venerable Alsace wine house needs no introduction: its unmistakable yellow-labeled wines have been distinguishing themselves in markets all over the world for more than half a century. Patriarch Jean Hugel passed away in 2009. At the helm of this estate today are young cousins Marc and Étienne; Marc in the cellars and vineyard, Étienne scouring the planet for new outlets and opportunities. The range of still wines covers three categories that form a coherent hierarchy of offerings: Hugel, Tradition, and Jubilée. The first two are focused dry and neat wines, sourced partly from bought-in grapes. The Jubilée range covers wines from great terroirs but makes no mention of their Grand Cru status anywhere. A separate category is reserved for the late-harvest Vendange Tardive and Sélection de Grains Nobles wines, all of which are available in good quantities across a range of varieties and vintages—proof of this estate's skill in the making of wines from nobly rotted grapes.

Recently tasted
GENTIL HUGEL 2007
White I 2011 up to 2015   **86**

GEWÜRZTRAMINER HUGEL 2007
White I 2011 up to 2015   **86**

GEWÜRZTRAMINER JUBILÉE 2007
Semi-Dry White I 2011 up to 2027   **92**

GEWÜRZTRAMINER SÉLECTION DE GRAINS NOBLES S 2007
Sweet White I 2012 up to 2040   **98**

GEWÜRZTRAMINER TRADITION 2007
Semi-Dry White I 2011 up to 2017   **88**

GEWÜRZTRAMINER VENDANGES TARDIVES 2007
Sweet White I 2012 up to 2027   **96**

MUSCAT TRADITION 2007
White I 2011 up to 2013   **87**

PINOT GRIS JUBILÉE 2007
White I 2012 up to 2027   **90**

PINOT NOIR JUBILÉE 2007
Red I 2011 up to 2022   **89**

PINOT NOIR JUBILÉE 2002
Red | 2011 up to 2017   90

RIESLING JUBILÉE 2007
White | 2012 up to 2027   93

RIESLING TRADITION 2007
White | 2011 up to 2017   89

Older vintages
GEWÜRZTRAMINER
SÉLECTION DE GRAINS NOBLES 2005
Sweet White | 2011 up to 2030   99
An almost perfect expression of a great, luscious gewürztraminer, this combines a fresh,
remarkably light nose with aromas of rose,
praline, butter, and fresh dates, with a deep,
luscious palate of great purity. It is an exceptional wine today, but patience is required
to experience nirvana.

GEWÜRZTRAMINER VENDANGES TARDIVES 2005
Sweet White | 2011 up to 2030   96
Marked by the delicacy of its pure botrytis,
this wine is already seductive, with a complex nose of praline, rose, and ripe fruit and
a clean palate of depth and elegance. Its
flesh yields tender sweetness. One must be
patient: wait ten years.

PINOT GRIS JUBILÉE 2005
White | 2011 up to 2020   91
Produced from the domaine's vines on limestone soils, here is a great dry wine with ripe
fruits on the nose, dominated by pear spirits and quince. It is full and fat on the palate, with depth and a finish of spices and
praline. Lees maturation, ideal in rich vintages, yields by all measures a great, dry
pinot gris.

PINOT GRIS VENDANGES TARDIVES 2001
Sweet White | 2011 up to 2030   95
A very ripe Vendange Tardive from a very
great vintage, this offers white truffle,
quince, and ripe fruit on the nose with a
touch of honey, and a concentrated sweetness worthy of a Sélection de Grains Nobles.
With a remarkable finish, purity, and high-
quality botrytis, this is perfectly structured
with great aging potential.

PINOT NOIR JUBILÉE 2006
Red | 2011 up to 2016   88
Matured in barrels, this wine posseses a
perfumed nose with ripe fruit and high-
quality oak. The palate is supple and well
concentrated, with good integration of its
evolved flavors. A lovely success for a flavorful wine that should be drunk before the
2005.

PINOT NOIR JUBILÉE 2005
Red | 2011 up to 2020   90
The wine is already integrated with a frame
of very ripe black fruit and cherries leading
to a full palate, rich and integrated, with ripe
tannins that accompany a long finish.

RIESLING JUBILÉE 2005
White | 2011 up to 2030   94
From the domaine's Schoenenbourg parcel,
this wine offers an open nose, complex on
aromas of ripe citrus with a touch of bal-
samic. The palate is rich and full, with fat,
power, and a fine acidity that underlines the
class of the wine. A Jubilée of great class,
this joins the magnificent 1990.

RIESLING TRADITION 2005
White | 2011 up to 2020   88
Primarily from Schoenenbourg, this wine is
elegant with aromas of white flowers on the
mineral nose and a full, clean, and mineral
palate with good length. The finish lasts with
a note of lemongrass. A very clean riesling
that will be a perfect companion at the table.

RIESLING VENDANGES TARDIVES 2001
Sweet White | 2011 up to 2030   95
Schoenenbourg grapes affected by high-
quality botrytis in the great 2001 vintage
yielded a medium-dry wine, very pure and
mineral, with great finesse. Already open
with a candied-lemon nose, it is very fine
on the palate with measured sweetness and
firm minerality. A wine of great aging potential. The wine was not produced in 2002 and
2006.

Red: 21.3 acres; pinot noir 100%. White: 292.5 acres;
gewürztraminer 27%, muscat d'Alsace 1%, pinot
blanc 16%, pinot d'Alsace 12%, riesling 30%,
sylvaner 14%. Annual production: 1,300,000 bottles

JOSMEYER

76, rue Clemenceau
68920 Wintzenheim
Phone 00 33 3 89 27 91 90
Fax 00 33 3 89 27 91 99
domaine@josmeyer.com
www.josmeyer.com

Domaine Josmeyer needs no introduction. It is managed by Jean Meyer (who has forty vintages to his credit) and is known worldwide for easily digested, refined, fat wines that avoid unnecessary residual sugar. Since Josmeyer moved toward biodynamic methods in 2000, the wines have acquired an even greater density plus a welcome consistency that brings out their noble origins. To simplify its conversion to full biodynamic production, the property has become increasingly self-sufficient in grapes, renting or purchasing vineyard plots rather than buying in from other growers.

Recently tasted

ALSACE GRAND CRU FLEUR DE LOTUS 2007
White | 2011 up to 2013   **87**

ALSACE GRAND CRU GRI-GRI 2006
White | 2011 up to 2013   **86**

GEWÜRZTRAMINER LES FOLASTRIES 2008
White | 2011 up to 2018   **88**

PINOT A NOIR 2007
White | 2011 up to 2015   **88**

PINOT BLANC MISE DU PRINTEMPS 2008
White | 2011 up to 2013   **88**

PINOT GRIS 1854 FONDATION 2007
White | 2011 up to 2022   **90**

SYLVANER PEAU ROUGE 2008
White | 2011 up to 2013   **86**

Older vintages

ALSACE GRAND CRU BRAND GEWÜRZTRAMINER 2007
White | 2011 up to 2027   **96**
A perfumed, full wine, profound and ethereal at the same time. The balance between the varietal fruit and the structured acidity is magical.

ALSACE GRAND CRU BRAND PINOT GRIS 2006
White | 2011 up to 2026   **95**
A very great, dry Brand, with splendid finesse and depth. The variety brings a touch of fat that renders the wine perfectly balanced.

ALSACE GRAND CRU BRAND RIESLING 2007
White | 2011 up to 2027   **95**
A wine of ripe citrus aromas and very fine acidity. The wine is concentrated, with fat and a long finish. Great potential for aging.

ALSACE GRAND CRU HENGST GEWÜRZTRAMINER 2007
Sweet White | 2012 up to 2030   **98**
The great depth on the palate gives this wine density and purity; it is ripe without being over the top. The finish is very long.

ALSACE GRAND CRU HENGST GEWÜRZTRAMINER VENDANGES TARDIVES 2001
Sweet White | 2011 up to 2025   **95**
A wine with an intense, complex nose, offering a mineral palate with much depth, finesse, and remarkable purity. The sweetness is already integrated. The wine finishes long on aromas of honey and sweet spices.

ALSACE GRAND CRU HENGST PINOT GRIS 2007
White | 2011 up to 2027   **95**
A rich and powerful pinot gris, this has great fullness and depth. Its minerality suggests that it will become a great food wine with several years of aging.

ALSACE GRAND CRU HENGST RIESLING 2007
White | 2011 up to 2027   **96**
Harvested ripe, this is a powerful wine, rich on the palate with a long finish. A very promising wine.

ALSACE GRAND CRU HENGST RIESLING L'EXCEPTION 2006
Semi-Dry White | 2011 up to 2026   **91**
Hengst was harvested very ripe in 2006, resulting in a wine of Vendange Tardive ripeness. Honeyed on the nose with a smoky note, the wine is full and mineral on the palate with well-integrated sweetness.

ALSACE GRAND CRU HENGST RIESLING SAMAIN 2007
White | 2011 up to 2027   **98**
Harvested superripe, this cuvée retains a dry character on the palate with much depth.

ALSACE GRAND CRU HENGST RIESLING VENDANGES TARDIVES 2001
Sweet White | 2011 up to 2030   **96**
A rare wine produced in the best years, the 2001 has nothing to envy in the splendid 1995 that it follows. Power, minerality, finesse, and great length combine to yield a medium-dry wine of taut balance that makes the palate resonate with each mouthful.

GEWÜRZTRAMINER LES ARCHENETS 2007
White | 2011 up to 2022   **90**
A well-made, ripe wine, fruity on the nose, rich and dense on the palate, with lots of volume and fat.

GEWÜRZTRAMINER VENDANGES TARDIVES 2006
Sweet White | 2011 up to 2026   **90**
The nose is complex with notes of citrus peel, caramel, and apricot. Lovely balance on the palate, both unctuous and fine. A superb Vendange Tardive.

MUSCAT LES FLEURON 2007
White | 2011 up to 2015   **89**
A dense and structured muscat made from a large proportion of old-vine fruit, this is still closed on the nose. Structured and long, this is a powerful wine that will evolve well with aging.

PINOT AUXERROIS H VIEILLES VIGNES 2007
White | 2011 up to 2027   **93**
The old vines planted in the Hengst Grand Cru yielded a wine fresh and floral on the nose and full on the palate, with great density and depth. A terroir wine of great aging potential, to cellar as one would a Grand Cru.

PINOT BLANC LES LUTINS 2007
White | 2011 up to 2017   **90**
After the 2004 vintage, the 2007 is very promising: this Rotenberg auxerrois gives a rich wine, dense and full on the palate, with fine acidity on the finish.

PINOT BLANC MISE DU PRINTEMPS 2007
White | 2011 up to 2015   **87**
An aromatic and ripe wine, dense on the palate, with pronounced, fine acidity that provides freshness on the finish. An everyday wine that transforms each day into a special occasion!

RIESLING LE KOTTABE 2007
White | 2011 up to 2017   **88**
A dry, elegant riesling, straightforward on the nose with citrus aromas, forthright on the palate with lovely fat and body in a dry balance.

RIESLING LES PIERRETS 2007
White | 2011 up to 2027   **90**
The domaine's most well-known riesling, this vintage offers fresh fruit on the nose and density on the palate, with body and very clean acidity. A very savory wine that will be perfect at the table after several years of aging.

Red: 1.2 acres; pinot gris 100%. White: 60.5 acres; gewürztraminer 19%, muscat Ottonel 3%, pinot blanc and pinot auxerrois 24%, riesling 28%, chasselas and sylvaner 5%, pinot gris 21%. Annual production: 200,000 bottles

DOMAINE ANDRÉ KIENTZLER

50, route de Bergheim
68150 Ribeauvillé
Phone 00 33 3 89 73 67 10
Fax 00 33 3 89 73 35 81
domaine@vinskientzler.com

André Kientzler has fairly clear ideas about great wine: focus and dryness but a fat style nonetheless, plus that purity and concentration that is necessary for the terroir to express itself. Holdings are located in three of the Ribeauvillé Grands Crus, including the much coveted, steeply terraced Geisberg. You see the full measure of his talents in his superb Geisberg and Osterberg riesling Grands Crus, regarded as the benchmark for great terroir-based rieslings. In years of noble rot, André gets equal results with high-quality botrytised grapes, producing sweeter wines but with no loss of balance or crystalline purity—witness his "Cuvées Exceptionnelles," Vendanges Tardives, and Sélections de Grains Nobles. The other wines in the range are taut, pure, very homogeneous, and ideal with a meal.

Recently tasted
ALSACE GRAND CRU GEISBERG RIESLING 2007
White | 2012 up to 2027   **98**

ALSACE GRAND CRU KIRCHBERG DE RIBEAUVILLÉ MUSCAT 2007
White | 2012 up to 2027   **93**

AUXERROIS K 2007
Semi-Dry White | 2012 up to 2022   **90**

GEWÜRZTRAMINER 2007
White | 2011 up to 2017   **89**

GEWRZTRAMINER RÉSERVE PARTICULIÈRE 2007
Semi-Dry White | 2011 up to 2027   **90**

MUSCAT 2007
White | 2011 up to 2013   **88**

PINOT GRIS 2007
White | 2011 up to 2017   **89**

RIESLING 2007
Semi-Dry White | 2011 up to 2015   **87**

RIESLING RÉSERVE PARTICULIÈRE 2007
White | 2011 up to 2022   **88**

Older vintages
ALSACE GRAND CRU GEISBERG PINOT GRIS 2004
Semi-Dry White | 2011 up to 2020   **94**
A very limited cuvée, this pinot gris captures the great depth and purity of the Geisberg riesling, with supplemental richness and intense minerality on the palate. Very long. A great dry wine.

ALSACE GRAND CRU GEISBERG RIESLING 2006
White | 2011 up to 2021   **92**

The only Grand Cru wine produced in 2006, this is a small production from a selection of parcels. The nose is citrusy and open; the palate shows great purity with pronounced minerality, finishing on lightly bitter notes. A great wine that will open rapidly.

ALSACE GRAND CRU GEISBERG RIESLING 2005
White | 2011 up to 2025   **97**

A magnificent wine, powerful and mineral, and a worthy successor to the 2004. With a nose of great purity and fresh citrus notes, the wine is already very open on the palate with a depth and elegance that is all too rare. Superb tension between fruit and minerality; great aging potential.

ALSACE GRAND CRU GEISBERG RIESLING CUVÉE EXCEPTIONNELLE 2004
Semi-Dry White | 2011 up to 2030   **95**

Medium-dry with great depth, this superripe wine is still sweet on the palate, with the fine bitterness of grapefruit on the finish. Great potential.

ALSACE GRAND CRU GEISBERG RIESLING SÉLECTION DE GRAINS NOBLES 2001
Sweet White | 2011 up to 2030   **97**

A rare wine, extreme in its precision and balance: the minerality on the nose blends citrus zest with a sweet palate, deep and pure and lifted by a fine acidity. The wine resonates long on the palate with a finish of fresh apricots. The perfect expression of the domaine's style applied to a great terroir, with superb botrytis.

ALSACE GRAND CRU GEISBERG RIESLING VENDANGES TARDIVES 2005
Sweet White | 2013 up to 2030   **97**

The wine possesses great concentration, already evident on the nose and in the dense and sweet palate, which opens slowly to reveal the wine's depth. From a parcel harvested late at the limit of a Sélection de Grains Nobles, this is an exceptional wine, of great aging potential.

ALSACE GRAND CRU KIRCHBERG DE RIBEAUVILLÉ MUSCAT 2005
White | 2011 up to 2020   **93**

A dry muscat, intense on the nose with white fruit and a pepper note, and a profound palate of great finesse. A reference among terroir muscats. No production in 2006.

ALSACE GRAND CRU KIRCHBERG DE RIBEAUVILLÉ PINOT GRIS VENDANGES TARDIVES 2005
Sweet White | 2011 up to 2025   **94**

Only one late-harvest pinot gris came from the Kirchberg vineyard in 2005. The nose is intense with aromas of candied fruits and a smoky note. The palate is pure, sweet, and finely crisp with the bitterness of orange zest. A tender, mineral balance with superripeness that accents the spicy character of the wine.

ALSACE GRAND CRU OSTERBERG GEWÜRZTRAMINER 2007
Semi-Dry White | 2011 up to 2022   **94**

The first gewürztraminer produced by this domaine from this Grand Cru, and a complete makeover: the delicate nose has aromas of antique roses leading to a palate of great depth and so much richness that it provides a sensation of sweetness—yet the wine is dry. Magnificent success in a great vintage.

ALSACE GRAND CRU OSTERBERG RIESLING 2007
White | 2011 up to 2022   **92**

A superb Osterberg of great purity, streamlined and long on the palate with a lemony finish. Consistent with the 2005; great potential. No production in 2006.

AUXERROIS K 2005
Semi-Dry White | 2011 up to 2015   **90**

From Ribeauvillé's Grand Cru Kirchberg, auxerrois is harvested here slightly overripe to balance its medium-dry, mineral character while preserving its purity. Don't rush to drink this wine, so that the residual sugar can integrate. No production in 2006.

GEWÜRZTRAMINER 2006
White | 2011 up to 2016   **89**

A forthright gewürztraminer with exotic fruit on the nose and a very pure palate with sweet spices. A superb success for a practically dry wine that will be perfect at the table.

GEWÜRZTRAMINER VENDANGES TARDIVES 2005
White | 2011 up to 2015   **90**

A delicate wine with great purity on the nose, lightly honeyed with a note of rose, and a pure palate with taut sweetness enhanced by a slight bitter note on the finish. Rich. Drink beginning now.

RIESLING CUVÉE FRANÇOIS ALPHONSE 2007
White | 2011 up to 2022   **90**

From declassified vines in the Grand Crus of Osterberg and Geisberg, the wine is young, full, and fat, with lovely definition of fruit and good balance.

White: 32.1 acres: chasselas 4%, gewürztraminer 25%, muscat Ottonel 6%, pinot blanc 21%, riesling 25%, sylvaner 4%, various 15%. **Annual production:** 80,000 bottles

DOMAINE MARC KREYDENWEISS

12, rue Deharbe
67140 Andlau
Phone 00 33 3 88 08 95 83
Fax 00 33 3 88 08 41 16
marc@kreydenweiss.com
www.kreydenweiss.com

Manfred and Antoine Kreydenweiss are in charge of this property today, their father having recently decided to concentrate all of his energies on his vineyard in the South of France. Manfred has been working here since 1990, committed to biodynamic viticulture, while Antoine has been in charge of vinification since 2004. Some of the cuvées produced from 1999 to 2003 were overly heavy on sugar. Since then they have shown crisper, dryer balance at no expense to that fabulous finesse and purity for which this winery is renowned. Owner of some very fine holdings in Andlau, Kreydenweiss turned out a range of offerings in 2005 that were very precise across the entire gamut of terroirs.

Recently tasted

ALSACE GRAND CRU KASTELBERG RIESLING 2007
White | 2012 up to 2027   **94**

ALSACE GRAND CRU KASTELBERG RIESLING
VENDANGES TARDIVES 2006
Sweet White | 2011 up to 2026   **92**

ALSACE GRAND CRU MOENCHBERG PINOT GRIS 2007
Semi-Dry White | 2011 up to 2022   **92**

ALSACE GRAND CRU WIEBELSBERG RIESLING 2007
White | 2011 up to 2022   **92**

ANDLAU RIESLING 2007
White | 2011 up to 2017   **88**

CLOS DU VAL D'ELÉON 2007
White | 2011 up to 2022   **89**

CLOS REBBERG PINOT GRIS 2007
Sweet White | 2011 up to 2022   **92**

CLOS REBBERG RIESLING 2007
White | 2011 up to 2022   **92**

KRITT GEWÜRZTRAMINER 2007
Sweet White | 2011 up to 2022   **91**

LERCHENBERG PINOT GRIS 2007
White | 2011 up to 2017   **88**

PINOT BLANC KRITT 2007
White | 2011 up to 2015   **88**

PINOT BLANC LA FONTAINE AUX ENFANTS 2007
White | 2011 up to 2013   **87**

Older vintages

ALSACE GRAND CRU KASTELBERG
RIESLING 2006
White | 2011 up to 2026   **92**
A Vendange Tardive that will probably assert itself with time, this is full, powerful, and very rich on the palate, with fat and a light, subtle sweetness that is already integrated (10 grams per liter of residual sugar). A wine for aging.

ALSACE GRAND CRU KASTELBERG
RIESLING 2005
White | 2011 up to 2025   **93**
The nose is balanced, spicy, and smoky; the palate is pure and linear with an intense mark of Kastelberg schist.

ALSACE GRAND CRU MOENCHBERG
PINOT GRIS 2006
Semi-Dry White | 2011 up to 2020   **88**
An elegant wine, ripe on the nose, deep on the palate, with a spicy finish. Still dominated by sweetness, the wine will gain balance with aging.

ALSACE GRAND CRU PINOT GRIS MOENCHBERG
VENDANGES TARDIVES 2005
Sweet White | 2011 up to 2025   **93**
The entire parcel was harvested as a Vendange Tardive, yielding a wine rich and delicate on the nose, marked by butter and praline. It has lovely depth, with lots of minerality and a subtle, well-integrated sweetness on the palate. A great terroir wine.

ALSACE GRAND CRU WIEBELSBERG
RIESLING 2006
White | 2011 up to 2021   **90**
With its fresh, clean citrus nose, this is ripe and lightly sweet with very pure balance. The finish is long.

ALSACE GRAND CRU WIEBELSBERG
RIESLING 2005
White | 2011 up to 2020   **90**
The wine is very ripe with an open nose and a saline palate that possesses fat and volume. The fine acidity is still subtle, resulting in a round finish.

CLOS DU VAL D'ELÉON 2006
White | 2011 up to 2016   **90**
Pinot gris and riesling from this clos resulted in a dry, clean, fine blend with ripe acidity. A saline fresh and pleasant wine, this is a magnificent success in 2006.

CLOS REBBERG PINOT GRIS 2006
Sweet White | 2011 up to 2016   **91**
Pretty hazelnut nose; full, finely crisp palate, with remarkable purity. A dry wine with delicate balance.

CLOS REBBERG PINOT GRIS 2005
Sweet White I 2011 up to 2015   **90**
Very ripe on the nose with a white rum note, this is rich and supple on the palate and lightly sweet.

CLOS REBBERG RIESLING 2006
White I 2011 up to 2016   **89**
From schist terroir in Villé, this wine is smoky and spicy on the nose, with a dry, dense palate that finishes on good acidity.

CLOS REBBERG RIESLING 2005
White I 2011 up to 2015   **90**
A full and ripe wine, this has pointed acidity that gives the wine expressive fruit. Hold so that its components integrate a bit.

KRITT GEWÜRZTRAMINER 2006
Sweet White I 2011 up to 2021   **90**
The nose is delicate and very pure, with blood-orange notes. The palate is full and saline, with light sweetness, purity, and richness, finishing on a spicy note.

PINOT GRIS CLOS REBBERG
SÉLECTION DE GRAINS NOBLES 2005
Sweet White I 2011 up to 2025   **90**
A luscious, concentrated, and powerful wine, with lovely finesse on the nose and nice depth on the palate. The citrus zest and spices give the wine an ethereal finish.

White: 29.7 acres: gewürztraminer 10%, muscat 5%, pinot blanc 15%, riesling 50%. Annual production: 65,000 bottles

DOMAINE PAUL KUBLER

103, rue de la Vallée
68570 Soultzmatt
Phone 00 33 3 89 47 00 75
Fax 00 33 3 89 47 65 45
kubler@lesvins.com

Philippe Kubler took over the family estate in 2003 and has placed his stamp on every vintage since 2004. Drawing on his Burgundy experience, he fine-tuned his management of the clayey limestone vineyards around Soultzmatt, going for long maturation and bâtonnage (stirring the lees at intervals). The Paul Kubler K range encompasses generic wines and is named after the estate, since, like some other Alsace wines, it is not entitled to call itself a Grand Cru. The Sylvaner Z Paul Kubler, on the other hand, nods to neighbor Seppi Landmann and makes no secret of its Grand Cru origins (Zinnkoepflé). Prices are reasonable so far, but stocks are running out fast.

Recently tasted

ALSACE GRAND CRU ZINNKOEPFLÉ
GEWÜRZTRAMINER 2007
White I 2011 up to 2027   **93**

ALSACE GRAND CRU ZINNKOEPFLÉ
GEWÜRZTRAMINER SÉLECTION DE GRAINS
NOBLES 2007
Sweet White I 2011 up to 2027   **94**

ALSACE GRAND CRU ZINNKOEPFLÉ
GEWÜRZTRAMINER VENDANGES TARDIVES 2007
Sweet White I 2011 up to 2027   **96**

ALSACE GRAND CRU ZINNKOEPFLÉ PINOT GRIS
SÉLECTION DE GRAINS NOBLES 2007
Sweet White I 2011 up to 2022   **92**

BREITENBERG RIESLING 2007
White I 2011 up to 2017   **86**

GEWÜRZTRAMINER K 2007
Semi-Dry White I 2011 up to 2017   **88**

RIESLING K 2007
White I 2011 up to 2017   **88**

SYLVANER Z 2007
White I 2011 up to 2022   **92**

WEINGARTEN GEWÜRZTRAMINER 2007
Semi-Dry White I 2011 up to 2017   **89**

ZINNKOEPFLÉ PINOT GRIS 2007
Sweet White I 2011 up to 2022   **90**

Older vintages

ALSACE GRAND CRU ZINNKOEPFLÉ GEWÜRZTRAMINER 2005
White | 2011 up to 2020   **92**
A very successful wine, this combines the ripe fruit and fine minerality of Zinnkoepflé with an almost dry balance, lightly bitter on the finish.

ALSACE GRAND CRU ZINNKOEPFLÉ GEWÜRZTRAMINER VENDANGES TARDIVES 2006
Sweet White | 2011 up to 2021   **90**
In 2006, the entire harvest was Vendange Tardive, resulting in a rich and crisp wine with a smoky finish and fresh balance.

ALSACE GRAND CRU ZINNKOEPFLÉ GEWÜRZTRAMINER VENDANGES TARDIVES 2005
Sweet White | 2011 up to 2020   **93**
A very pure and mineral wine with perfectly integrated sweetness, this possesses the ethereal touch common to wines from Zinnkoepflé. A fine balance, remarkably smooth.

SYLVANER Z 2006
White | 2011 up to 2021   **90**
From the Grand Cru Zinnkoepflé and matured in barrel, this wine is already open, with a nose of honeysuckle and pure, rich, ample flavor. A great dry sylvaner.

SYLVANER Z 2005
White | 2011 up to 2020   **90**
From the Grand Cru Zinnkoepflé and matured in oak barrels, this wine is marked by oak but possesses the finesse and minerality very typical of the vineyard, with strong salinity.

Annual production: 60,000 bottles

DOMAINE SEPPI LANDMANN

20, rue de la Vallée
68570 Soultzmatt
Phone 00 33 3 89 47 09 33
Fax 00 33 3 89 47 06 99
contact@seppi-landmann.fr
www.seppi-landmann.fr

Seppi Landmann is an irrepressible figure in the Alsace landscape, with that combination of wit and generosity typical of outspoken personalities. But it is not just his larger-than-life personality that gives this estate its quality. The grapes are meticulously harvested with the help of customers who come to make some small contribution to every bottle. The wines show exceptional ripeness and purity, possessing all the characteristic finesse of the sandstone and limestone terroirs around Soultzmatt. This often makes them seem closed when young, and they have a tendency to lag behind other wines in blind tastings. Fact is, it takes about three to four years for the Zinnkoepflé wines to wake up and take on an intensity and length that is worthy of their terroirs. The crémants and pinots noirs are of good quality, and the range of sylvaner offerings demonstrates the benefits of growing sylvaner on the neighboring slopes. All of the wines are flawlessly consistent, with—vintage permitting—some particularly sumptuous late-harvest bottlings (Vendanges Tardives and Sélections de Grains Nobles).

Recently tasted

ALSACE GRAND CRU ZINNKOEPFLÉ GEWÜRZTRAMINER 2007
Sweet White | 2011 up to 2021   **92**

ALSACE GRAND CRU ZINNKOEPFLÉ GEWÜRZTRAMINER VENDANGES TARDIVES 1998
Sweet White | 2011 up to 2013   **91**

ALSACE GRAND CRU ZINNKOEPFLÉ MUSCAT 2007
White | 2011 up to 2017   **89**

ALSACE GRAND CRU ZINNKOEPFLÉ PINOT GRIS 2007
Semi-Dry White | 2012 up to 2022   **89**

SYLVANER VIN DE GLACE 2007
Sweet White | 2011 up to 2022   **90**

VALLÉE NOBLE MUSCAT 2007
White | 2011 up to 2013   **88**

VALLÉE NOBLE PINOT GRIS 2007
White | 2011 up to 2017   **88**

VALLÉE NOBLE RIESLING 2007
White | 2011 up to 2017   **86**

Older vintages

ALSACE GRAND CRU GEWÜRZTRAMINER ZINNKOEPFLÉ VENDANGES TARDIVES 2004
Sweet White I 2011 up to 2015   **93**
The sweetness and finesse of Zinnkoepflé is apparent in this wine's ripe, exotic fruit nose and great purity on the palate.

ALSACE GRAND CRU ZINNKOEPFLÉ GEWÜRZTRAMINER 2006
Sweet White I 2011 up to 2016   **90**
A rich and sweet wine, very pure on the palate with depth and a finish of spice. Lovely material.

ALSACE GRAND CRU ZINNKOEPFLÉ GEWÜRZTRAMINER 1992
Sweet White I 2011 up to 2013   **88**
Elegant, spicy, lovely noble palate of medium-dry balance with a finish of dried fruits.

ALSACE GRAND CRU ZINNKOEPFLÉ GEWÜRZTRAMINER SÉLECTION DE GRAINS NOBLES VIN DE GLACE 2005
Sweet White I 2012 up to 2030   **94**
Delicate nose of praline, quince, and honey. Luscious, deep, and fine palate with a spicy finish. A wine that must be aged, joining the magnificent 2001.

ALSACE GRAND CRU ZINNKOEPFLÉ PINOT GRIS 2006
Semi-Dry White I 2011 up to 2016   **88**
A wine clean and floral on the nose, pure on the palate, with sweetness that needs to integrate. Lovely purity.

ALSACE GRAND CRU ZINNKOEPFLÉ PINOT GRIS SÉLECTION DE GRAINS NOBLES 2005
Sweet White I 2011 up to 2025   **94**
The nose is candied; the palate has exceptional purity, with salinity and great length.

ALSACE GRAND CRU ZINNKOEPFLÉ RIESLING 2006
White I 2011 up to 2020   **89**
Clean and pure, saline on the palate with lovely minerality, this is an elegant wine with fine acidity on the finish.

ALSACE GRAND CRU ZINNKOEPFLÉ RIESLING VENDANGES TARDIVES 2005
White I 2011 up to 2025   **90**
Great-quality superripeness resulted in a sweet balance that remains fresh, with a citrus finish.

BOLLENBERG PINOT GRIS VENDANGES TARDIVES 2005
White I 2011 up to 2025   **93**
An elegant wine with praline on the nose, depth and power on the palate, and a long finish. Of great purity, this is a wine of excellent aging potential.

Red: 1.5 acres; pinot noir 8%. White: 20.8 acres; gewürztraminer 22%, muscat 4%. pinot blanc 27%, pinot gris 8%, riesling 11%, sylvaner 11%. Annual production: 65,000 bottles

DOMAINE LOEW

28, rue Birris
67310 Westhoffen
Phone 00 33 3 88 50 59 19
Fax 00 33 3 88 50 59 19
domaine.loew@orange.fr
www.domaineloew.com

When Étienne Loew took over the family estate ten years ago, he introduced château bottling and radically reduced the yields. He suscribes to the Tyflo charter for sustainable viticulture in Alsace and matures his wines on their lees for as long as it takes to produce vins de terroir with exceptional concentration for the north of the region. Some of the cuvées could still do with more precision, but the overall style of the wines grows more refined every year. Sensible prices keep sales buoyant, so move quickly to grab a few bottles of the latest vintage release while you still can. The wines show that deep, fat character typical of their marly-limestone terroirs around Westhoffen and Balbronn.

Recently tasted

ALSACE GRAND CRU ALTENBERG DE BERGBIETEN GEWÜRZTRAMINER 2008
Sweet White I 2011 up to 2028   **94**

ALSACE GRAND CRU ALTENBERG DE BERGBIETEN RIESLING 2008
White I 2012 up to 2028   **91**

ALSACE GRAND CRU ENGELBERG PINOT GRIS 2008
White I 2011 up to 2028   **92**

BRUDERBACH PINOT GRIS 2008
Semi-Dry White I 2011 up to 2023   **90**

RIESLING MUSCHELKALCK 2008
White I 2011 up to 2023   **87**

Older vintages

ALSACE GRAND CRU ALTENBERG DE BERGBIETEN GEWÜRZTRAMINER 2007
Sweet White I 2011 up to 2022   **92**
A powerful Altenberg de Bergbieten, this offers notes of antique rose on the nose and a very saline deep and rich palate. The sweetness is very subtle, concealed by the mineral character of the terroir. A well-made wine that will need to be aged for several years.

ALSACE GRAND CRU ALTENBERG DE BERGBIETEN GEWÜRZTRAMINER SÉLECTION DE GRAINS NOBLES 2005
Sweet White I 2011 up to 2025   **93**
A luscious wine of great class, elegant on the nose, with a profound palate of great finesse. Already pleasant to drink, but with good potential to improve with age.

ALSACE GRAND CRU ALTENBERG
DE BERGBIETEN RIESLING 2007
White | 2011 up to 2022   **92**
A dry wine, still closed, this unveils subtle
citrus and smoke notes on the nose. Powerful and clean on the palate, it has intense
salinity and volume that is tempered by pronounced acidity. A rich wine, it will be ready
after the superb 2005.

ALSACE GRAND CRU ENGELBERG PINOT GRIS 2007
White | 2011 up to 2022   **93**
Vinified completely dry and matured on its
lees, the wine offers intense fruit aromas—
not overripe—and a palate of remarkable
depth and richness. A great white wine from
a terroir of great potential.

BRUDERBACH PINOT GRIS 2007
Semi-Dry White | 2011 up to 2017   **89**
The wine is rich, with a ripe quince nose
and a full, fruity palate with lovely purity.
The sweetness is delicate. This wine will
make a superb match to a foie gras appe-
tizer.

GEWÜRZTRAMINER CORMIER 2007
Sweet White | 2011 up to 2022   **89**
The black marl terroir of this wine always
yields a wine slow to open in its youth. The
nose is closed, with clean fruit; the palate
is full, velvety, and very saline, with a long,
spicy finish. Lovely definition for a mineral
wine that will age very well.

OSTENBERG RIESLING 2007
White | 2011 up to 2017   **89**
The latest riesling of the house's range, this
wine is elegant on the nose, with aromas of
white-fleshed fruit and citrus, then full and
pure on the palate. A dry wine, easy to drink
young, this will keep for many years.

PINOT GRIS CORMIER 2007
Semi-Dry White | 2011 up to 2017   **87**
The nose is open and clean, with aromas of
ripe pear. The palate is rich and full with a
light sweetness that is enhanced by good
acidity. A wine that will drink dry after several years of aging.

PINOT GRIS SÉLECTION DE GRAINS NOBLES 2005
Sweet White | 2011 up to 2020   **89**
A luscious and concentrated wine with
honey on the nose, this is finely crisp on the
palate with a finish of dried apricot and date
notes.

Annual production: 50,000 bottles

GUSTAVE LORENTZ

91, rue des Vignerons
68750 Bergheim
Phone 00 33 3 89 73 22 22
Fax 00 33 3 89 73 30 49
info@gustavelorentz.com
www.gustavelorentz.com

This small négociant business produces
a well-defined range of homogeneous
wines. The top offerings come from its own
vines in the Altenberg de Bergheim and
Kanzlerberg Grands Crus. The "Cuvée
Particulière" range and the wines from the
Altenberg Grand Cru combine good quality with commercial availability, a real plus
for the restaurant trade. The wines are
released soon after bottling except for the
Grands Crus and dessert wines that are
cellared for several years beforehand and
reach the shelves fully mature. All of the
wines age admirably, with clear improvements in the Grands Crus and late-harvest
offerings (Vendanges Tardives and Sélections de Grains Nobles).

Recently tasted

GEWÜRZTRAMINER CUVÉE PARTICULIÈRE 2005
Sweet White | 2011 up to 2015   **87**

PINOT GRIS LIEU-DIT SAINT-GEORGES 2007
Semi-Dry White | 2011 up to 2017   **87**

PINOT NOIR FÛT DE CHÊNE 2006
Red | 2011 up to 2021   **89**

Older vintages

ALSACE GRAND CRU ALTENBERG DE BERGHEIM
GEWÜRZTRAMINER 2004
Sweet White | 2011 up to 2024   **89**
Clean on the nose with an aromatic character of gentian and white bouillon typical
of the vintage, this wine's palate is dense
with depth. The finish is drier.

ALSACE GRAND CRU ALTENBERG DE BERGHEIM
GEWÜRZTRAMINER VENDANGES TARDIVES 2000
Sweet White | 2011 up to 2020   **92**
A sweet and delicate Vendange Tardive dominated by minerality that brings very clean
salinity. The finish is long on aromas of dried
fruit. An elegant Vendange Tardive, carried
by the terroir.

ALSACE GRAND CRU ALTENBERG DE BERGHEIM
MUSCAT 2003
White | 2011 up to 2023   **92**
Great terroir muscat, full and deep, fresh
on the nose and very pure on the palate,
with a menthol finish. A wine produced only
in the best vintages.

ALSACE GRAND CRU ALTENBERG DE BERGHEIM
MUSCAT VENDANGES TARDIVES 2003
Sweet White | 2011 up to 2023   **93**
A very aromatic wine with notes of fresh
mint and lemongrass, this is very pure and
full on the palate with imposing minerality.
The sweetness is integrated and the finish
more dry. A rare wine.

ALSACE GRAND CRU ALTENBERG DE BERGHEIM
PINOT GRIS 2004
Semi-Dry White | 2011 up to 2020   **84**
Full and fat, this is a dry wine of great depth,
with smoky notes on the finish. Perfect at
the table, with fatty fish or poultry.

ALSACE GRAND CRU ALTENBERG DE BERGHEIM
RIESLING 2002
White | 2011 up to 2020   **92**
More approachable than the serious Kanzler-
berg, Altenberg offers minerality and fat with
lots of depth, and finishes on lovely bitter notes.
A full, savory wine, of great potential.

ALSACE GRAND CRU ALTENBERG DE BERGHEIM
RIESLING 1999
White | 2011 up to 2019   **90**
Mineral, full, and fat on the palate, this is a
profound Altenberg with a long finish of
white flowers, at maturity.

ALSACE GRAND CRU GEWÜRZTRAMINER
ALTENBERG DE BERGHEIM VIEILLES VIGNES
2002
Sweet White | 2011 up to 2020   **90**
In great vintages, only the old vines are used
for this Grand Cru wine, thus the specific
name. In 2002, the Altenberg produced a
mineral gewürztraminer of great depth,
lightly sweet with lovely acidity and spicy
aromas and zest on the finish.

PINOT GRIS SÉLECTION DE GRAINS NOBLES
RÉSERVE EXCEPTIONNELLE 1989
Sweet White | 2011 up to 2015   **88**
The color is intense gold, with nuances of
age. The nose is perfumed, clean, and full,
with aromas of raisins, honey, and smoke.
The palate is fine with integrated sweetness,
evolving on smoky and roasted notes. The
ensemble is integrated, with a lovely patina.

Annual production: 1,500,000 bottles

DOMAINE ALBERT MANN

13, rue du Château
68920 Wettolsheim
Phone 00 33 3 89 80 62 00
Fax 00 33 3 89 80 34 23
vins@albertmann.com
www.albertmann.com

This family estate represents the coming
together of two winegrowing families, con-
solidated in 1989 when Jacky Barthelmé
joined forces with his brother Maurice and
sister-in-law Marie-Claire Mann (daughter
of Albert Mann). The estate today boasts a
fine legacy of vineyards in five Grands Crus
and three lieux-dits (single-block vineyards),
spread between Wettolsheim and Kientzheim. Maurice manages the vineyards while
Jacky takes care of winemaking, sparing no
effort to produce wines that offer the truest
possible expression of the vineyard. Viticulture is now entirely biodynamic, having originally been organic. This, combined with
strictly limited yields, produces very ripe
grapes that are vinified with the least intervention possible: gentle pressing, followed
by prolonged fermentation, then aged on
the lees, almost exclusively in stainless-
steel tanks. The wines are sealed using a
mixture of corks and screw caps, and the
time of bottling is always perfectly judged.
The delicate 2006 vintage was a resounding
success, particularly the rieslings (all harvested before the rains in late September);
also the early-harvest pinot noir and pinot
gris wines, whose crisp dry balance emphasizes the expression of the vineyard. All of
these wines exhibit good, clean acidity that
underlines their purity.

Recently tasted
ALSACE GRAND CRU FURSTENTUM
GEWÜRZTRAMINER SÉLECTION DE GRAINS
NOBLES 2007
Sweet White | 2011 up to 2030   **97**

ALSACE GRAND CRU FURSTENTUM
GEWÜRZTRAMINER VIEILLES VIGNES 2007
Semi-Dry White | 2011 up to 2030   **96**

ALSACE GRAND CRU FURSTENTUM PINOT GRIS 2007
Semi-Dry White | 2011 up to 2027   **92**

ALSACE GRAND CRU FURSTENTUM
PINOT GRIS LE TRI 2007
Semi-Dry White | 2012 up to 2030   **96**

ALSACE GRAND CRU FURSTENTUM RIESLING 2007
White | 2012 up to 2027   **92**

ALSACE GRAND CRU HENGST PINOT GRIS 2007
White | 2011 up to 2027   **95**

ALSACE GRAND CRU SCHLOSSBERG RIESLING 2007
White | 2011 up to 2027   96

ALSACE GRAND CRU SCHLOSSBERG RIESLING
SÉLECTION DE GRAINS NOBLES 2007
Sweet White | 2011 up to 2027   97

ALSACE GRAND CRU SCHLOSSBERG RIESLING
VENDANGES TARDIVES 2007
Sweet White | 2011 up to 2027   96

ALTENBOURG GEWÜRZTRAMINER
VENDANGES TARDIVES 2007
Sweet White | 2011 up to 2027   95

ALTENBOURG MUSCAT LE TRI 2007
Sweet White | 2011 up to 2027   96

ALTENBOURG PINOT GRIS
SÉLECTION DE GRAINS NOBLES LE TRI 2007
Sweet White | 2012 up to 2030   92

ALTENBOURG PINOT GRIS VENDANGES
TARDIVES 2007
Sweet White | 2011 up to 2027   94

AUXERROIS VIEILLES VIGNES 2007
White | 2011 up to 2015   88

GEWÜRZTRAMINER 2007
Semi-Dry White | 2011 up to 2017   89

PINOT BLANC 2007
White | 2011 up to 2015   86

PINOT GRIS CUVÉE ALBERT 2007
White | 2011 up to 2017   89

RIESLING CUVÉE ALBERT 2007
White | 2011 up to 2017   88

RIESLING ROSENBERG 2007
White | 2011 up to 2022   90

Older vintages

ALSACE GRAND CRU FURSTENTUM GEWÜRZTRAMINER
SÉLECTION DE GRAINS NOBLES 2005
Sweet White | 2011 up to 2025   94
A dessert wine with a nose of praline and
orange zest and a deep, unctuous, and very
supple palate that retains incredible elegance.

ALSACE GRAND CRU FURSTENTUM
PINOT GRIS 2006
Semi-Dry White | 2011 up to 2021   91
Vinified and aged a year in oak, this aromatic
wine shows good fruit underneath the barrel aging notes, and a clean palate, mineral
and very pure. The dry balance and long
finish make this a wine for long aging.

ALSACE GRAND CRU FURSTENTUM PINOT GRIS 2005
Semi-Dry White | 2011 up to 2020   90
A pinot gris aged in oak, rich and profound
with an already marked minerality, this needs
time to integrate the wood.

ALSACE GRAND CRU FURSTENTUM RIESLING 2005
White | 2011 up to 2020   92
A full riesling, still discreet on the nose, this
has a profound, pure palate that progressively reveals the power of the terroir. Long
finish of citrus zest.

ALSACE GRAND CRU HENGST PINOT GRIS 2006
White | 2011 up to 2021   93
A remarkable Hengst, this is clean on the
nose, powerful and rich on the palate, with
depth and strong minerality to strengthen
its great purity and light, delicate tannins
on the finish. Pinot gris can also produce
great terroir wines, not necessarily from
superripe fruit.

ALSACE GRAND CRU HENGST PINOT GRIS 2005
White | 2011 up to 2020   91
This balanced, medium-dry pinot gris displays richness, depth, and power with
marked minerality on a spicy finish.

ALSACE GRAND CRU SCHLOSSBERG RIESLING 2006
White | 2011 up to 2021   94
A remarkable wine, floral with a touch of flint
on the nose, pure and very elegant. The palate is mineral and saline, with exceptional purity
that expresses the crisp freshness of Schlossberg. Long finish with lovely bitter notes.

ALSACE GRAND CRU SCHLOSSBERG RIESLING 2005
White | 2011 up to 2020   91
A Schlossberg of very great concentration
in 2005: crystalline, mineral, and elegant,
with a dry, saline balance of great promise.

ALSACE GRAND CRU STEINGRÜBLER
GEWÜRZTRAMINER 2006
Semi-Dry White | 2011 up to 2021   92
The terroir of Steingrübler gives gewürztraminer a touch of elegance that doesn't con-
ceal the wine's depth. The nose is very clean
with flowers and ripe fruits; on the palate it
is full and mineral, with fine, pronounced
acidity and a long finish. Great potential.

PINOT NOIR GRAND P 2006
Red | 2011 up to 2021   92
From Pfersigberg, this wine possesses a
nose marked by barrel aging, with notes of
ripe fruit and smoke. The palate is rich, with
sappy concentration. One of the greatest
pinot noirs produced in 2006.

Red: 5.4 acres; pinot noir 100%. White: 44 acres;
gewürztraminer 22%, muscat 5%, pinot blanc 26%,
pinot gris 18%, riesling 27%. Annual production:
120,000 bottles

DOMAINE MEYER-FONNÉ

24, Grand-Rue
68230 Katzenthal
Phone 00 33 3 89 27 16 50
Fax 00 33 3 89 27 34 17
felix.meyer-fonne@libertysurf.fr
meyer-fonne.com

Félix Meyer makes wines that grow more refined with every passing vintage, aiming for an ideal balance of maturity and elegance. He owns holdings all around the village of Katzenthal: the granitic Wineck-Schlossberg Grand Cru (whose finesse and salinity show through beautifully in the wines); the neighboring, soon-to-be Grand Cru of Kaefferkopf; and the lieux-dits of Dorfbourg, Hinterbourg, and Pfoeller (the extension of the Sommerberg Grand Cru). His wines are concentrated, ripe, and well defined—excellent value for the money, too.

Recently tasted

ALSACE GRAND CRU KAEFFERKOPF
GEWÜRZTRAMINER 2007
Sweet White | 2011 up to 2027   **91**

ALSACE GRAND CRU KAEFFERKOPF RIESLING 2007
White | 2011 up to 2027   **92**

ALSACE GRAND CRU SCHOENENBOURG RIESLING 2007
White | 2011 up to 2022   **90**

ALSACE GRAND CRU SPOREN
GEWÜRZTRAMINER 2007
White | 2011 up to 2027   **92**

ALSACE GRAND CRU SPOREN GEWÜRZTRAMINER
SÉLECTION DE GRAINS NOBLES 2007
Sweet White | 2012 up to 2027   **96**

ALSACE GRAND CRU WINECK-SCHLOSSBERG
RIESLING 2007
White | 2011 up to 2027   **92**

DORFBOURG GEWÜRZTRAMINER
VIEILLES VIGNES 2007
Semi-Dry White | 2011 up to 2022   **90**

PFOELLER RIESLING 2007
White | 2011 up to 2022   **90**

PFOELLER RIESLING VENDANGES TARDIVES 2007
Sweet White | 2011 up to 2027   **90**

PINOT BLANC VIEILLES VIGNES 2007
White | 2011 up to 2017   **87**

VIGNOBLE DE KATZENTHAL MUSCAT 2007
White | 2011 up to 2013   **88**

VIGNOBLE DE KATZENTHAL RIESLING 2007
White | 2011 up to 2017   **88**

Older vintages

ALSACE GRAND CRU KAEFFERKOPF
GEWÜRZTRAMINER 2006
Sweet White | 2011 up to 2016   **90**
From the argilo-sandstone part of the vineyard, this wine is rich on the nose with spices and candied fruits, and sweet on the palate, finishing on notes of pepper and candied fruits. A wine close to Vendange Tardive.

ALSACE GRAND CRU KAEFFERKOPF RIESLING 2006
White | 2011 up to 2021   **90**
From the marly sandstone part of the vineyard near Wineck-Schlossberg, this wine is rich and spiced on the nose with citrus notes, full and finely crisp on the palate, with a light sweetness that will integrate with time. A wine for long aging.

ALSACE GRAND CRU WINECK-SCHLOSSBERG
GEWÜRZTRAMINER 2005
White | 2011 up to 2020   **90**
A gewürztraminer, ethereal and delicate on the nose, mineral and saline on the palate, with a delicate texture reminiscent of rose petals.

ALSACE GRAND CRU WINECK-SCHLOSSBERG
GEWÜRZTRAMINER VENDANGES TARDIVES 2006
Sweet White | 2011 up to 2016   **90**
A very pure wine, rose and praline on the nose, very sweet on the palate, with fine salinity already present.

ALSACE GRAND CRU WINECK-SCHLOSSBERG
RIESLING 2006
White | 2011 up to 2021   **91**
A very successful Wineck-Schlossberg: very ripe, fresh lemon on the nose; saline and finely crisp on the palate, with very pure, rich balance. A wine to keep several years to gain integration.

DORFBOURG GEWÜRZTRAMINER VIEILLES
VIGNES SÉLECTION DE GRAINS NOBLES 2005
Sweet White | 2011 up to 2025   **94**
Limestone soils and high-quality botrytis yield an extravagant wine, exotic and fresh on the nose, with profound, fine, and very pure sweetness on the palate. A wine of brilliant balance, with subtle notes of rose on the finish.

PFOELLER RIESLING 2006
White | 2011 up to 2021   **89**
From the limestone soils of Muschelkalk, this wine is floral on the nose and full and concentrated on the palate, with depth and great purity. A full wine that will age well.

Red: 1.5 acres: pinot noir 100%. White: 29.5 acres: gewürztraminer 19%, pinot blanc 28%, riesling 25%, muscat 7%, pinot gris 18%. Annual production: 75,000 bottles

DOMAINE MITTNACHT-KLACK

8, rue des Tuileries
68340 Riquewihr
Phone 00 33 3 89 47 92 54
Fax 00 33 3 89 47 89 50
info@mittnacht.fr
www.mittnacht.fr

Jean Mittnacht and son Franck continue to bring out the particular character of their terroirs in Riquewihr, Hunawihr, and Ribeauvillé. Thanks to sustainable viticulture and a hands-off approach in the winery, their wines are well balanced, generous, and deep. The three Grand Cru bottlings from Sporen, Schoenenbourg, and Rosacker show good depth and definition while their lieux-dits wines (from named vineyard sites) boast plenty of character plus a variety of styles to suit a variety of foods.

Recently tasted

ALSACE GRAND CRU SCHOENENBOURG
PINOT GRIS 2007
White | 2012 up to 2027   90

ALSACE GRAND CRU SCHOENENBOURG
RIESLING 2006
Sweet White | 2011 up to 2021   88

GEWÜRZTRAMINER
SÉLECTION DE GRAINS NOBLES 2003
Sweet White | 2011 up to 2023   90

RIESLING 2007
White | 2011 up to 2015   86

RIESLING SÉLECTION DE GRAINS NOBLES 2004
Sweet White | 2011 up to 2024   92

Older vintages

ALSACE GRAND CRU ROSACKER RIESLING 2005
White | 2011 up to 2020   89
A straight Rosacker, acacia on the nose, dry on the palate, with depth. A wine to age to reveal its potential.

ALSACE GRAND CRU SCHOENENBOURG
GEWÜRZTRAMINER 2005
Semi-Dry White | 2011 up to 2020   89
A lovely expression of finesse, elegance, and the minerality of Schoenenbourg with a variety that offers fat, sweetness, and spice. Superb wine to try with fusion cuisine.

ALSACE GRAND CRU SCHOENENBOURG
PINOT GRIS 2005
White | 2011 up to 2020   90
A medium-dry wine, honey and hazelnut on the nose, full and forward on the palate, with fine acidity that gives the wine length.

ALSACE GRAND CRU SCHOENENBOURG
RIESLING 2005
Sweet White | 2011 up to 2020   90
Characteristically Schoenenbourg on the nose, this is dense on the palate with fat and depth. Already accessible, it will benefit from aging.

ALSACE GRAND CRU SCHOENENBOURG
RIESLING 2004
Sweet White | 2011 up to 2019   89
A rich and elegant Schoenenbourg, this wine blends aromas of citrus and smoke and a deep palate, ending on a lovely, bitter finish.

ALSACE GRAND CRU SPOREN
GEWÜRZTRAMINER 2005
Sweet White | 2011 up to 2020   89
A rich wine with quite a bit of depth, good acidity, and good length on the finish. The wine is still marked by sweetness.

ALSACE GRAND CRU SPOREN
GEWÜRZTRAMINER 2004
Sweet White | 2011 up to 2019   88
The very perfumed nose offers notes of rose and yellow fruit; the palate is round and deep with a hazelnut note on the finish. A full wine with great aging potential.

CLOS SAINT-ULRICH RIESLING 2005
White | 2011 up to 2015   88
A forward and dry riesling, scented with white flowers on the nose, full and mineral on the palate.

MUHLFORST RIESLING 2003
White | 2011 up to 2023   88
A ripe and very aromatic riesling in the style of the 2003 vintage, this is full and deep on the palate with light sweetness and great purity.

MUSCAT KRONENBERG 2005
White | 2011 up to 2015   89
The closed and slightly musky nose is followed by a full, deep, and pure palate, lightly sweet with lovely crispness. A muscat that merits some years of patience.

ROSENBOURG PINOT GRIS 2004
Semi-Dry White | 2011 up to 2015   88
The wine is streamlined and clean with a dense, fine, and long palate. A pinot gris of dry balance, elegant and well structured.

Red: 1.5 acres; pinot noir 7%. White: 24.2 acres; gewürztraminer 21%, muscat d'Alsace 4%, pinot blanc 21%, pinot gris 14%, riesling 32%, sylvaner 1%. Annual production: 60,000 bottles

DOMAINE FRÉDÉRIC MOCHEL

56, rue Principale
67310 Traenheim
Phone 00 33 3 88 50 38 67
Fax 00 33 3 88 50 56 19
infos@mochel.net
www.mochel.net

Frédéric Mochel has developed this estate considerably and with it the Altenberg de Bergbieten Grand Cru, which accounts for roughly half of total plantings. Son Guillaume has meanwhile concentrated on building up a range of wines with a clean, characteristic expression of the terroirs around Traenheim. The riesling, gewürztraminer, and especially the muscat wines from the Altenberg de Bergbieten Grand Cru are all top-notch, driven by the mineral qualities of their terroir.

Recently tasted

ALSACE GRAND CRU ALTENBERG DE BERGBIETEN
GEWÜRZTRAMINER 2007
Sweet White I 2011 up to 2027   **91**

ALSACE GRAND CRU ALTENBERG DE BERGBIETEN
MUSCAT 2007
White I 2011 up to 2027   **94**

ALSACE GRAND CRU ALTENBERG DE BERGBIETEN
RIESLING CUVÉE HENRIETTE 2007
White I 2011 up to 2027   **92**

GEWÜRZTRAMINER 2007
Semi-Dry White I 2011 up to 2017   **88**

GEWÜRZTRAMINER VENDANGES TARDIVES 2007
Sweet White I 2011 up to 2027   **94**

MUSCAT 2007
White I 2011 up to 2015   **87**

PINOT GRIS 2007
Semi-Dry White I 2011 up to 2017   **87**

PINOT GRIS VENDANGES TARDIVES 2007
Sweet White I 2011 up to 2027   **92**

PINOT NOIR 2007
Red I 2011 up to 2017   **88**

RIESLING SÉLECTION DE GRAINS NOBLES 2007
Sweet White I 2012 up to 2030   **95**

RIESLING VENDANGES TARDIVES 2007
Sweet White I 2011 up to 2027   **93**

Older vintages

ALSACE GRAND CRU ALTENBERG DE BERGBIETEN
GEWÜRZTRAMINER 2006
Sweet White I 2011 up to 2021   **90**
2006 yielded a gewürztraminer that is sweet, pure, and honeyed, with lots of depth and a flinty note on the finish.

ALSACE GRAND CRU ALTENBERG DE BERGBIETEN
GEWÜRZTRAMINER 2005
Sweet White I 2011 up to 2020   **90**
The elegant nose of citrus peel leads to a full and mineral palate with integrated sweetness. Superb expression of Altenberg in a variety that brings out a spicy character.

ALSACE GRAND CRU ALTENBERG DE BERGBIETEN
MUSCAT 2006
White I 2011 up to 2016   **92**
Clean on the nose with delicate perfume, this is full and mineral on the palate with great purity. A great terroir muscat.

ALSACE GRAND CRU ALTENBERG DE BERGBIETEN
MUSCAT 2005
White I 2011 up to 2015   **94**
The nose already offers lovely aromatic purity, and the palate delivers intense minerality with lots of concentration. A muscat Ottonel of great aging potential that calls for seafood.

ALSACE GRAND CRU ALTENBERG DE BERGBIETEN
RIESLING CUVÉE HENRIETTE 2005
White I 2011 up to 2020   **90**
From vines fifty-plus years of age, the Henriette is perfumed and mineral on the nose with fullness and depth on the palate. A dry wine of great potential.

Red: 1.2 acres; pinot noir 7%. White: 23.5 acres; chardonnay 9%, gewürztraminer 20%, muscat Ottonel 10%, pinot blanc 9%, riesling 30%, pinot gris 14%. Annual production: 75,000 bottles

RENÉ MURÉ – CLOS SAINT LANDELIN

RN 83
68250 Rouffach
Phone 00 33 3 89 78 58 00
Fax 00 33 3 89 78 58 01
rene@mure.com
www.mure.com

The Clos Saint Landelin is located on the south-facing flank of the Vorbourg Grand Cru. It is operated by René Muré, now assisted by his children Véronique and Thomas, who have gone to great lengths to improve the quality of these wines since 1998. The pinot noir and the crémant were the first to receive attention and have improved tremendously with every passing year. Réné then gradually rethought his approach to the entire vineyard, aiming to encourage physiological ripeness, but not at the price of excess sugar. The results have been obvious for some years now: wines with all the mineral character, opulence, and depth of a rich sunny terroir, but none of its heaviness. Those made with purchased grapes, marketed under the "René Muré" label, display a ripe, generous, and very homogeneous style. The 2004 and 2005 vintages coaxed some memorable sweet wines out of the Clos Saint Landelin, but the other wines are drier than ever. Regular customers, familiar with the style of each wine, can safely buy en primeur in the year following each harvest—adding to their stock of older vintages!

Recently tasted

ALSACE GRAND CRU VORBOURG RIESLING 2007
White | 2011 up to 2022   91

CLOS SAINT LANDELIN GEWÜRZTRAMINER
VENDANGES TARDIVES 2007
Sweet White | 2011 up to 2027   94

CLOS SAINT LANDELIN GEWÜRZTRAMINER
VENDANGES TARDIVES 2002
Sweet White | 2011 up to 2022   92

CLOS SAINT LANDELIN MUSCAT VENDANGES
TARDIVES 2007
Sweet White | 2011 up to 2027   97

CLOS SAINT LANDELIN PINOT GRIS 2007
Semi-Dry White | 2011 up to 2022   92

CLOS SAINT LANDELIN PINOT NOIR 2007
Red | 2011 up to 2027   90

CLOS SAINT LANDELIN RIESLING 2007
White | 2011 up to 2022   92

CLOS SAINT LANDELIN SYLVANER
CUVÉE OSCAR 2007
Sweet White | 2012 up to 2022   90

LUTZELTAL PINOT GRIS
VENDANGES TARDIVES 2007
Sweet White | 2011 up to 2017   90

PINOT NOIR V 2006
Red | 2011 up to 2016   90

Older vintages

ALSACE GRAND CRU CLOS SAINT LANDELIN
RIESLING VENDANGES TARDIVES 2001
Sweet White | 2011 up to 2020   92
A pure and intense Vendange Tardive, this is aromatic with citrus zest, full and sweet on the palate, with acidity that provides lots of the finesse.

ALSACE GRAND CRU VORBOURG
GEWÜRZTRAMINER VENDANGES TARDIVES 2005
Sweet White | 2011 up to 2020   90
This wine is racy, with a nose of honey and smoke and a rich, sweet palate, unctuous and spicy. Still closed, this merits aging.

ALSACE GRAND CRU ZINNKOEPFLÉ
RIESLING VENDANGES TARDIVES 2005
Sweet White | 2011 up to 2020   94
This splendid Vendange Tardive shows the finesse given by the sandy limestone soils of Zinnkoepflé: acacia honey on the nose, very pure on the palate, with integrated sweetness and fine salinity that yields a savory character. An elegant wine that possesses a long finish.

CLOS SAINT LANDELIN GEWÜRZTRAMINER
SÉLECTION DE GRAINS NOBLES 2006
Sweet White | 2011 up to 2021   94
This wine is very full-bodied, with a nose of candied fruit and a sweet, saline, and pure palate. The finish is long on red fruits. A splendid cuvée that combines very pure fruit and fine acidity.

CLOS SAINT LANDELIN GEWÜRZTRAMINER
VENDANGES TARDIVES 2005
Sweet White | 2011 up to 2025   92
A superripe wine of great depth, this has a honeyed nose that leads to a full palate, unctuous and concentrated. The finish is long, with spices and a smoky note. Age it to allow the flavors to integrate.

CLOS SAINT LANDELIN GEWÜRZTRAMINER
VENDANGES TARDIVES 2001
Sweet White | 2011 up to 2025   92
With perfect balance and lovely botrytis, this wine combines a very pure, fruity nose with a sweet, fine, very elegant palate. An already delicious Vendange Tardive that finishes on notes of peach and honey.

**CLOS SAINT LANDELIN MUSCAT
VENDANGES TARDIVES 2004**
Sweet White | 2011 up to 2025   **97**
For several years, Clos Saint Landelin has produced sweet, classy muscats that are reminiscent of the great muscats of the South of France. This 2004 has a brilliant balance, with a very pure nose of exotic fruit, apricot, and mint and a sweet, pure palate of great depth and finesse.

**CLOS SAINT LANDELIN PINOT GRIS
SÉLECTION DE GRAINS NOBLES 2004**
Sweet White | 2011 up to 2013   **97**
A monumental wine produced from high-quality botrytised grapes: the nose is clean on aromas of candied fruit, quince, and a hint of vanilla; the palate is luscious, with very pure, fine sweetness balanced by pronounced acidity. The very promising 2007 follows in the same vein.

CLOS SAINT LANDELIN PINOT NOIR 2006
Red | 2011 up to 2021   **93**
The nose is still marked by a smoky note from oak maturation, but the palate offers a fleshy, full profile of great depth and beauty. A worthy successor to the great 2005 vintage.

CLOS SAINT LANDELIN RIESLING 2006
White | 2011 up to 2016   **90**
A rich wine, aromas of citrus and orange peel on the nose, full and fat on the palate, with lovely minerality, depth, and a savory character.

CRÉMANT D'ALSACE MILLÉSIMÉ 2005
Brut White sparkling | 2011 up to 2015   **92**
Chardonnay grown at the foot of Clos Saint Landelin, vinified and matured in barrel, yields a splendid crémant here, full and fine with lovely, ripe concentration and a long finish. A magnificent crémant to age several years.

Red: 8.6 acres; pinot noir 100%. White: 53.2 acres; gewürztraminer 26%, pinot blanc 28%, riesling 25%, sylvaner 8%, muscat 1%, pinot gris 12%. Annual production: 300,000 bottles

DOMAINE ANDRÉ OSTERTAG

87, rue Finkwiller
67680 Epfig
Phone 00 33 3 88 85 51 34
Fax 00 33 3 88 85 58 95
domaine.ostertag@orange.fr

André Ostertag continues to make finely chiseled wines that radiate the vibrancy of their terroir—whether traditionally matured or barrel-aged, such as his pinot gris bottlings. His "vins de fruit" are varietal-driven and sourced from the Epfig vineyard; his "vins de pierre" (stone) are soil-driven and come from other selected terroirs. Both categories are dry, with a purity and finesse that make them agreeable even when young. His climate-driven "vins de temps" (weather), made from ultramature fruit, are exceptionally pure and age harmoniously.

Recently tasted

**ALSACE GRAND CRU MUENCHBERG PINOT GRIS
CUVÉE A360P 2007**
White | 2011 up to 2027   **96**

ALSACE GRAND CRU MUENCHBERG RIESLING 2007
White | 2011 up to 2022   **97**

**ALSACE GRAND CRU MUENCHBERG RIESLING
VENDANGES TARDIVES 2007**
Sweet White | 2011 up to 2027   **95**

CLOS MATHIS RIESLING 2007
White | 2012 up to 2027   **92**

**FRONHOLZ GEWÜRZTRAMINER
SÉLECTION DE GRAINS NOBLES 2007**
Sweet White | 2011 up to 2022   **94**

**FRONHOLZ GEWÜRZTRAMINER
VENDANGES TARDIVES 2007**
Sweet White | 2011 up to 2022   **92**

FRONHOLZ RIESLING 2007
White | 2011 up to 2022   **92**

GEWÜRZTRAMINER VIGNOBLE D'E 2008
Sweet White | 2011 up to 2018   **90**

**GEWÜRZTRAMINER VIGNOBLE D'E
SÉLECTION DE GRAINS NOBLES 2007**
Sweet White | 2011 up to 2017   **92**

HEISSENBERG RIESLING 2007
White | 2011 up to 2022   **91**

LES VIEILLES VIGNES DE SYLVANER 2008
White | 2011 up to 2018   **90**

RIESLING VIGNOBLE D'E 2007
White | 2011 up to 2017   **88**

ZELLBERG PINOT GRIS 2007
White | 2011 up to 2022   **92**

Older vintages

ALSACE GRAND CRU FRONHOLZ MUSCAT 2006
White | 2011 up to 2016   **90**
An excellent muscat, intense on the nose
with aromas of elderflowers and dry on the
palate with good concentration and richness. The finesse of Fronholz brings a touch
of elegance to this wine.

ALSACE GRAND CRU MUENCHBERG
PINOT GRIS CUVÉE A360P 2006
White | 2011 up to 2021   **95**
An immense wine with depth and power,
this has a delicate nose, lightly smoky with
tea notes, and a powerful palate, very mineral and fine, with strong salinity that
emerges on the finish. The wine already possesses amazing balance, but it will benefit
from several more years of aging.

ALSACE GRAND CRU MUENCHBERG
PINOT GRIS CUVÉE A360P 2005
White | 2011 up to 2025   **94**
The nose is still marked by its élevage, but
the palate is remarkably precise, full, and
concentrated with strong minerality. The
smoke notes on the finish are the mark of
this fiery volcanic terroir.

ALSACE GRAND CRU MUENCHBERG
RIESLING 2006
White | 2011 up to 2021   **95**
Along the lines of the magnificent 2005, the
2006 offers again a terroir wine. The nose
is still discreet, complex with aromas of white
peach, flint, and smoke. The palate is concentrated, extended by very fine acidity that
brings forth strong salinity. The finish is long
with floral and smoky notes that resonate
intensely with its minerality.

ALSACE GRAND CRU MUENCHBERG RIESLING 2005
White | 2011 up to 2020   **94**
Great success for riesling, this wine is completely dominated by terroir. Smoky and
toasty on the nose and strongly mineral on
the palate, the wine already possesses a lot
of depth. If it were as open as the pinot gris,
the two wines would resemble each other.
A great Muenchberg.

CLOS MATHIS RIESLING 2006
White | 2011 up to 2021   **91**
The gneiss soil in Ribeauvillé produces a dry,
full, fleshy, and mineral wine. This great example stands out among the others of the domaine
because of the marked typicity of the Ribeauvillé terroir. A great purity, with a nose of white
flowers and a full palate, which finishes on a
smoky note.

FRONHOLZ GEWÜRZTRAMINER
SÉLECTION DE GRAINS NOBLES 2005
Sweet White | 2011 up to 2030   **94**
Superb botrytis for this cuvée, with praline
and orange blossom on the nose and a very
pure sweetness. A rich Sélection de Grains
Nobles that retains great freshness.

FRONHOLZ GEWÜRZTRAMINER VENDANGES TARDIVES 2006
Sweet White | 2011 up to 2021   **91**
A Vendange Tardive with intense fruit on
the candied nose and the very sweet, full
palate. The finish remains very fresh, with
exotic fruit aromas.

FRONHOLZ PINOT GRIS 2006
White | 2011 up to 2016   **91**
Fronholz produced a profound wine, dry and
rich with oak notes still evident on the nose
but well integrated on the palate with the
wine's pronounced minerality.

FRONHOLZ RIESLING 2006
White | 2011 up to 2016   **91**
A riesling that is fruity on the nose and long
and finely crisp on the palate, with ethereal
balance and great finesse.

GEWÜRZTRAMINER VIGNOBLE D'E 2007
Sweet White | 2011 up to 2017   **90**
Full, rich scents of ripe fruit, rose, and a touch
of pepper and clove lead into a full, sweet
palate with fine acidity and a long finish of
exotic fruit and spice.

LES VIEILLES VIGNES DE SYLVANER 2007
White | 2011 up to 2017   **88**
The most famous sylvaner of Alsace shows
magnificently well in a great year. Still young,
the nose is already aromatic, leading to a
fleshy, rich palate. Lovely fullness.

Red: 1.9 acres; pinot noir 5%. White: 32.7 acres;
gewürztraminer 19%, muscat 2.2%, pinot blanc
6.30%, pinot gris 14%, riesling 40%, sylvaner 13.50%.
Annual production: 100,000 bottles

CAVE DE RIBEAUVILLÉ

2, route de Colmar
68150 Ribeauvillé
Phone 00 33 3 89 73 61 80
Fax 00 33 3 89 73 31 21
cave@cave-ribeauville.com
www.cave-ribeauville.com

The Ribeauvillé wine cooperative enjoys an ideal location at the heart of the great, multifaceted Ribeauvillé region. This oldest wine co-op in France has taken on a new look since new director Philippe Dry joined at the turn of the millennium and committed to producing dry, fresh, and very mineral wines. A new code of practice is now in place, drawn up in consultation with enologist Évelyne Bléger-Dondelinger and the forty or so co-op members. Guidelines for quality include strictly limited yields, site-specific monitoring, and exclusively handpicked grapes. The improvements are immediately apparent: the 2005 vintage is magnificent, and average quality gets better all the time, spurred on by great wines that express all the diversity of the co-op's ten Grands Crus and many lieux-dits. A new processing facility installed before the 2006 harvests makes for even purer, more homogeneous wines. All the signs of a winery poised on the threshold of greatness— one to watch. The tasting cellar offers a selection of single-parcel, limited-run cuvées.

Recently tasted

ALSACE GRAND CRU ALTENBERG DE BERGHEIM
GEWÜRZTRAMINER 2007
Sweet White | 2011 up to 2027   **91**

ALSACE GRAND CRU ALTENBERG DE BERGHEIM
RIESLING 2007
White | 2011 up to 2027   **91**

ALSACE GRAND CRU GLOECKELBERG
GEWÜRZTRAMINER 2007
Semi-Dry White | 2011 up to 2017   **89**

ALSACE GRAND CRU KIRCHBERG DE RIBEAUVILLÉ
RIESLING 2007
White | 2011 up to 2022   **92**

ALSACE GRAND CRU MUHLFORST RIESLING 2007
White | 2011 up to 2022   **88**

ALSACE GRAND CRU OSTERBERG
GEWÜRZTRAMINER 2007
Semi-Dry White | 2011 up to 2027   **92**

ALSACE GRAND CRU OSTERBERG RIESLING 2007
White | 2011 up to 2022   **91**

ALSACE GRAND CRU ROSACKER RIESLING BIO
(ORGANIC) 2007
White | 2011 up to 2027   **90**

ALSACE GRAND CRU SCHOENENBOURG
RIESLING 2007
White | 2012 up to 2022   **92**

AUXERROIS VIEILLES VIGNES 2008
White | 2011 up to 2013   **87**

CLOS DU ZAHNACKER 2007
White | 2012 up to 2027   **94**

GEWÜRZTRAMINER VENDANGES TARDIVES 2007
Sweet White | 2011 up to 2027   **91**

HAGUENAU 2007
Semi-Dry White | 2011 up to 2017   **88**

HAGUENAU GEWÜRZTRAMINER 2007
Sweet White | 2011 up to 2017   **88**

HAGUENAU RIESLING 2007
White | 2011 up to 2022   **89**

KUGELBERG PINOT NOIR 2007
Red | 2011 up to 2017   **88**

MUSCAT 2008
White | 2011 up to 2013   **87**

PINOT NOIR RODERN 2007
Red | 2011 up to 2015   **87**

RIESLING 113 ANS 2007
White | 2011 up to 2017   **88**

RIESLING SÉLECTION DE GRAINS NOBLES 2007
Sweet White | 2011 up to 2022   **92**

SYLVANER VIEILLES VIGNES 2008
White | 2011 up to 2013   **87**

Older vintages

ALSACE GRAND CRU ALTENBERG DE BERGHEIM
GEWÜRZTRAMINER 2005
Sweet White | 2011 up to 2020   **90**
A great wine with intensely honeyed fruit and a soft palate with lots of depth and great dry extract. A full and mineral-laden wine with excellent concentration.

ALSACE GRAND CRU ALTENBERG DE BERGHEIM
RIESLING 2006
White | 2011 up to 2016   **89**
A rich wine, this has a nose of ripe fruits and a full and powerful palate with depth and fat. A lovely Altenberg, already balanced.

GEWÜRZTRAMINER 2006
Semi-Dry White | 2011 up to 2016   **90**
A magnificent success in 2006: fresh fruit and spice on the nose, elegant and sweet

on the palate, finely saline with lots of purity and a rare elegance.

ALSACE GRAND CRU OSTERBERG RIESLING 2005
White | 2011 up to 2015   **89**
A full-bodied riesling with an elegant nose of spring flowers, this has a density that gives it lots of power. Great potential.

ALSACE GRAND CRU ROSACKER
RIESLING BIO (ORGANIC) 2005
White | 2011 up to 2020   **90**
A great Rosacker with aromas of acacia flowers and smoke, this is fat and profound on the palate, with good supporting acidity providing lovely structure.

ALSACE GRAND CRU SCHLOSSBERG RIESLING 2006
White | 2011 up to 2016   **88**
2006 yielded a handsome, racy Schlossberg, floral on the nose, fine and elegant on the palate, with density and purity. Long, smoky finish.

CLOS DU ZAHNACKER 2005
White | 2011 up to 2025   **92**
A pioneering plot of varietal coplantation in Alsace, Clos du Zahnacker has been the property of the Cave de Ribeauvillé since 1935. A blend of riesling, pinot gris, and gewürztraminer from a parcel in the heart of the Grand Cru Osterberg, the 2005 has depth and minerality with a very pure, medium-dry balance. A great terroir wine.

CRÉMANT D'ALSACE GRANDE CUVÉE
Brut White sparkling | 2011 up to 2013   **86**
A blend of pinot noir and chardonnay, this crémant is perfumed with a floral nose, full and rich on the palate, with a tight mousse that releases slowly. An elegant wine with an ethereal finish, this will be perfect from aperitif to dessert.

GEWÜRZTRAMINER
SÉLECTION DE GRAINS NOBLES 2005
Sweet White | 2011 up to 2025   **94**
A very good selection in 2005, this shows a nose of honey and dates and a very pure palate with powerful sweetness. The finish is long with citrus zest, praline, and raisins.

PINOT GRIS BIO (ORGANIC) 2005
Semi-Dry White | 2011 up to 2015   **88**
A dry pinot gris, with a very fine yeasty nose of dry fruit and fine mineral flavors, with a saline finish. Perfect at the table.

Red: 44.5 acres; pinot noir 100%. White: 602.9 acres; gewürztraminer 16%, muscat 2%, pinot blanc 25%, riesling 26%, sylvaner 9%, pinot gris 13%. Annual production: 2,500,000 bottles

DOMAINE ANDRÉ RIEFFEL

11, rue Principale
67140 Mittelbergheim
Phone 00 33 3 88 08 95 48
andré.rieffel@wanadoo.fr
www.andrerieffel.com

The unassuming Lucas Rieffel took over this estate from his father about ten years ago and embarked on a major quality overhaul. Soil maintenance, the assessment of vine vigor, and long maturation on lees are all part of an ongoing program that spares no effort in pursuit of pure, richly concentrated wines. Prices have not yet caught up with quality, but people are starting to wise up. Some of the cuvées are in short supply, especially the gewürztraminer and crémant. Apply early if you want a few bottles of the rarest cuvées.

ALSACE GRAND CRU WIEBELSBERG
RIESLING 2006
White | 2011 up to 2021   **90**
The flagship wine of the domaine merits praise in this vintage: Wiebelsberg produced a concentrated and pure Vendange Tardive, sweet but well integrated with dense, mineral richness. Age it to allow it to completely reveal itself.

ALSACE GRAND CRU WIEBELSBERG
RIESLING 2005
White | 2011 up to 2020   **90**
From vines ideally situated on a fully south-facing slope of this Grand Cru, the wine displays balance, concentration, and light overripeness, with fine acidity and strong minerality. For aging.

ALSACE GRAND CRU ZOTZENBERG
RIESLING 2006
White | 2011 up to 2021   **91**
Clean, racy, and of great purity, the wine displays remarkable salinity and balance worthy of the best vintages.

PINOT NOIR RUNZ 2004
Red | 2011 up to 2020   **90**
A racy wine with deft extraction of high-quality tannins and a rich and powerful balance. Superb winemaking for this limited-production wine.

Red: 2.5 acres; pinot noir 10%. White: 21 acres; gewürztraminer 15%, muscat 5%, pinot blanc 20%, pinot gris 10%, riesling 30%, sylvaner 10%. Annual production: 60,000 bottles

DOMAINE ROLLY-GASSMANN

2, rue de l'Église
68590 Rorschwihr
Phone 00 33 3 89 73 63 28
Fax 00 33 3 89 73 33 06
rollygassmann@wanadoo.fr

Rorschwihr is located at the heart of the Ribeauvillé fault zone, in a remarkable geological patchwork that includes twelve marl-and-limestone-dominated terroirs that have been identified for centuries. Pierre Gassmann has been running this family estate in Rorschwihr since 1997. He grows and vinifies his grapes in accordance with ancient practices, picking them when superripe and giving particular emphasis to the specific differences between each terroir. The result is deep wines that sometimes show distinctive sweetness when young but age to perfection across twenty years or more. Thanks to its impressive stocks, Rolly-Gassmann can leave its cuvées to mature before release. Recent vintages show even more depth and finesse, with a marked tendency toward higher acidity—a change that will increasingly affect all the wines on the market.

Recently tasted

MOENCHREBEN MUSCAT 2007
Sweet White | 2012 up to 2027   **90**

OBERER WEINGARTEN GEWÜRZTRAMINER 2007
Sweet White | 2012 up to 2027   **94**

PINOT GRIS VENDANGES TARDIVES 2005
Sweet White | 2011 up to 2020   **92**

RIESLING VENDANGES TARDIVES 2005
Sweet White | 2011 up to 2020   **90**

ROTLEIBEL AUXERROIS 2005
Semi-Dry White | 2011 up to 2015   **88**

Older vintages

HAGUENAU GEWÜRZTRAMINER
VENDANGES TARDIVES 2002
Sweet White | 2011 up to 2022   **94**
Still marked on the nose by pretty botrytis, this shows notes of exotic fruit followed by very pure, saline flavors with integrated sweetness. It is remarkable in its expression of the clay and gypsum soils of Keuper.

KAPPELWEG GEWÜRZTRAMINER
VENDANGES TARDIVES 2001
Sweet White | 2011 up to 2021   **90**
A rich wine, this has an ethereal character, with white flowers on the nose followed by very pure sweetness on a taut palate. It finishes long with aromas of roses and spice. Gas is still perceptible, supplementing the freshness.

MOENCHREBEN MUSCAT VENDANGES TARDIVES 1997
Sweet White | 2011 up to 2017   **92**
A sweet muscat from a Grand Cru, complex on the nose with aromas of mint and smoke, this offers an elegant, mineral, deep palate with great density, and a long finish on aromas of white flowers. The youth of this wine is incredible, with good potential for aging.

OBERER WEINGARTEN GEWÜRZTRAMINER 1998
Sweet White | 2011 up to 2018   **91**
Since the release of the wines is dictated by their state of readiness here, the successor of the famous 2002 will be the 1998, perfectly integrated with a nose of spice and exotic fruit that leads to a harmonious palate of depth. The long finish lasts on notes of ginger.

PFLAENZERREBEN RIESLING 2002
White | 2011 up to 2022   **90**
From a magnificent terroir of clay over a Muschelkalk limestone base, Pflaenzerreben yields a wine redolent of flowers and sour fruit with a fresh, mineral palate of great purity. A powerful wine with great aging potential.

PINOT GRIS RÉSERVE ROLLY GASSMANN 2001
Semi-Dry White | 2011 up to 2021   **90**
A super-ripe, well-balanced pinot gris, this is pure and very clean, with density and a long finish on blood oranges. In several years, the wine will take on an almost dry character and will be perfect at the table.

PINOT GRIS RORSCHWIHR VENDANGES
TARDIVES 2000
Sweet White | 2011 up to 2025   **90**
A very fine, botrytised Vendange Tardive with sweet balance, finely crisp. Still closed on the nose, this must be decanted.

ROTLEIBEL PINOT GRIS VENDANGES TARDIVES 2006
Sweet White | 2011 up to 2026   **90**
A wine fashioned for aging, this is pefumed, with sour fruit on the nose and sweetness on the palate, with great purity and pronounced acidity that underpin the long finish. Great potential.

SILBERBERG RIESLING SÉLECTION DE GRAINS NOBLES 2006
Sweet White | 2011 up to 2026   **92**
The first Sélection de Grains Nobles produced at the domaine, and a great success: citrus fruits on the nose, dominated by grapefruit; sweetness and acidity on the palate, with density and length on the finish. To keep.

Red: 7.9 acres; pinot 9%. White: 103.3 acres; auxerrois 24%, gewürztraminer 26%, muscat 4%, pinot gris 17%, riesling 12%, sylvaner 7%. Annual production: 200,000 bottles

DOMAINE ÉRIC ROMINGER

16, rue Saint-Blaise
68250 Westhalten
Phone 00 33 3 89 47 68 60
Fax 00 33 3 89 47 68 61
vins-rominger.eric@wanadoo.fr

Eric and Claudine Rominger's estate continues to grow at a steady pace. The new cellar in 1997 marked the start of the couple's conversion to organic farming and biodynamic principles. Maturation on lees is closely monitored and the latest vintages have produced elegant wines, especially the increasingly refined late-harvest wines, Vendanges Tardives and Sélections de Grains Nobles.

Recently tasted

ALSACE GRAND CRU SAERING RIESLING 2007
White I 2011 up to 2017   **86**

ALSACE GRAND CRU ZINNKOEPFLÉ GEWÜRZTRAMINER LES SINNELLES 2007
Semi-Dry White I 2011 up to 2022   **91**

ALSACE GRAND CRU ZINNKOEPFLÉ GEWÜRZTRAMINER SÉLECTION DE GRAINS NOBLES 2006
Sweet White I 2011 up to 2026   **90**

ALSACE GRAND CRU ZINNKOEPFLÉ PINOT GRIS LES SINNELLES 2007
White I 2011 up to 2017   **86**

ALSACE GRAND CRU ZINNKOEPFLÉ RIESLING LES SINNELLES 2006
White I 2011 up to 2016   **89**

PINOT BLANC 2007
White I 2011 up to 2013   **86**

Older vintages

ALSACE GRAND CRU GEWÜRZTRAMINER ZINNKOEPFLÉ VENDANGES TARDIVES 2004
Sweet White I 2011 up to 2020   **91**
Harvested very ripe and very sweet, the wine possesses lovely freshness, lots of elegance, and fine acidity on the palate. The apricot and honey finish is long.

ALSACE GRAND CRU ZINNKOEPFLÉ GEWÜRZTRAMINER LES SINNELLES 2006
Semi-Dry White I 2011 up to 2021   **90**
A pure wine with integrated sweetness, this possesses fullness and intense salinity, bringing length on the finish.

ALSACE GRAND CRU ZINNKOEPFLÉ GEWÜRZTRAMINER LES SINNELLES 2005
Semi-Dry White I 2011 up to 2020   **90**
The wine is ripe with exotic fruits on the nose, full and fruity on the palate, marked by lovely botrytis. Very pure and fresh balance.

ALSACE GRAND CRU ZINNKOEPFLÉ GEWÜRZTRAMINER SÉLECTION DE GRAINS NOBLES 2005
Sweet White I 2011 up to 2025   **94**
This wine has great purity, intense on the nose with aromas of rose and praline, luscious on the palate with an ethereal balance that gives the wine tremendous charm.

ALSACE GRAND CRU ZINNKOEPFLÉ GEWÜRZTRAMINER SÉLECTION DE GRAINS NOBLES 2004
Sweet White I 2011 up to 2020   **93**
The honey and hazelnut aromas lead to a round, supple palate with a very clean finish of exotic fresh fruit. A concentrated and rich wine with very pure balance.

ALSACE GRAND CRU ZINNKOEPFLÉ PINOT GRIS VENDANGES TARDIVES 2005
Sweet White I 2011 up to 2025   **90**
A super-ripe, delicate wine, very saline on the palate, with well-integrated sweetness.

ALSACE GRAND CRU ZINNKOEPFLÉ PINOT GRIS LES SINNELLES 2005
White I 2011 up to 2020   **88**
A wine marked by superripeness on the nose and salinity on the palate, this is lightly sweet with a finely crisp finish.

ALSACE GRAND CRU ZINNKOEPFLÉ PINOT GRIS SÉLECTION DE GRAINS NOBLES 2005
Sweet White I 2011 up to 2025   **92**
A luscious wine of great concentration, this is candied on the nose with notes of honey, and intense on the palate with a deep sweetness that finishes on aromas of dried fruit. Hold to let all the components integrate.

ALSACE GRAND CRU ZINNKOEPFLÉ RIESLING LES SINNELLES 2005
White I 2011 up to 2020   **90**
An open and intense wine from Zinnkoepflé, with a nose of white flowers, this is lovely and streamlined, with sour fruits and minerality on the palate.

SCHWARZBERG PINOT GRIS 2005
Sweet White I 2011 up to 2015   **88**
A rich pinot gris, ripe on the nose with roasted notes, this is elegant, fine, and mineral on the palate. The sweetness is still present but will integrate going forward.

Red: 4.9 acres; pinot noir 9%. White: 24.7 acres; 21%, gewürztraminer 19%, muscat Ottonel 5%, pinot blanc 23%, riesling 16%, sylvaner 7%. Annual production: 70,000 bottles

DOMAINE MARTIN SCHAETZEL

3, rue de la Cinquième-Division-Blindée
68770 Ammerschwihr
Phone 00 33 3 89 47 11 39
Fax 00 33 3 89 78 29 77
jean.schaetzel@wanadoo.fr

Jean Schaetzel teaches at the Lycée Viticole de Rouffach (a viticultural high school) and has trained many of the new generation of Alsace winegrowers, passing on his preference for natural growing methods that respect terroir diversity. He himself separately vinifies and bottles the grapes from his holdings in the smallest, exceptionally limestone sector at the heart of the predominantly granitic and soon-to-be Grand Cru of Kaefferkopf. In addition to the Marckrain Grand Cru, he also bought holdings in the celebrated Schlossberg and Rangen Grands Crus, which today allow him to offer a range of top-notch and very distinctive rieslings. The entry-level wines made from purchased grapes are nicely crafted in the classical style but lack the purity and fullness of Schaetzel's ripe but dry, low-yield estate bottlings (which also tend to be more alcoholic).

Recently tasted

ALSACE GRAND CRU KAEFFERKOPF
GEWÜRZTRAMINER 2007
White I 2011 up to 2022   90

ALSACE GRAND CRU KAEFFERKOPF RIESLING
CUVÉE NICOLAS 2007
White I 2011 up to 2022   90

ALSACE GRAND CRU MARCKRAIN PINOT GRIS 2007
White I 2011 up to 2027   95

ALSACE GRAND CRU RANGEN RIESLING 2007
White I 2012 up to 2027   95

ALSACE GRAND CRU SCHLOSSBERG RIESLING 2007
White I 2012 up to 2022   93

GEWÜRZTRAMINER CUVÉE ISABELLE 2006
Semi-Dry White I 2011 up to 2016   88

GEWÜRZTRAMINER RÉSERVE 2007
Semi-Dry White I 2011 up to 2013   86

PINOT NOIR CUVÉE MATHIEU 2007
Red I 2011 up to 2015   87

ROSENBOURG PINOT GRIS 2007
White I 2011 up to 2015   88

Older vintages

ALSACE GRAND CRU KAEFFERKOPF
GEWÜRZTRAMINER 2006
White I 2011 up to 2016   88
A dry gewürztraminer of great purity, spicy on the nose, dense on the palate, with pronounced acidity. A dry wine that is an ideal accompaniment at the table.

ALSACE GRAND CRU KAEFFERKOPF
GEWÜRZTRAMINER CUVÉE CATHERINE 2006
Semi-Dry White I 2011 up to 2016   90
From the marly limestone part of the vineyard, this wine is sweet on the attack, then develops depth, fruit freshness, and great length on the palate.

ALSACE GRAND CRU KAEFFERKOPF PINOT GRIS 2006
White I 2011 up to 2016   88
An ethereal wine, this has fleshy white fruit and vanilla on the nose and a very pure, straight and saline palate with light bitterness on the finish. A dry, promising pinot gris.

ALSACE GRAND CRU KAEFFERKOPF RIESLING
CUVÉE NICOLAS 2006
White I 2011 up to 2016   88
From the part of the vineyard with the highest limestone content, this wine is open, with citrus notes on the nose and fullness, depth, and fat on the palate. The balance remains rich.

ALSACE GRAND CRU KAEFFERKOPF
RIESLING GRANIT 2006
White I 2011 up to 2016   87
A very dry, linear wine with fruit intensity on the nose, this is very crystalline on the palate, with bitterness on the finish.

ALSACE GRAND CRU MARCKRAIN
PINOT GRIS 2006
White I 2011 up to 2021   91
Matured in barrels, this wine has a nose marked by wood and smoky notes, then displays fullness and depth on the palate with lovely definition. A reference Marckrain.

ALSACE GRAND CRU RANGEN RIESLING 2006
White I 2011 up to 2021   92
The wine is very marked by volcanic terroir, with its smoky, open nose and dry, saline balance on the palate. It has a long finish.

ALSACE GRAND CRU SCHLOSSBERG
RIESLING 2006
White I 2011 up to 2021   92
Harvested very ripe, this riesling displays a floral nose and is full and very pure on the palate with pronounced minerality. It possesses lots of flesh and a long finish of pineapple and exotic fruit aromas. A worthy successor of the 2005.

Red: 3 acres; pinot noir 100%. White: 26.7 acres; 7%, gewürztraminer 20%, pinot blanc 18%, pinot gris 15%, riesling 22%, sylvaner 8%. Annual production: 90,000 bottles

DOMAINE SCHLUMBERGER

100, rue Théodore-Deck
BP 10
68500 Guebwiller
Phone 00 33 3 89 74 27 00
Fax 00 33 3 89 74 85 75
mail@domaines-schlumberger.com
www.domaines-schlumberger.com

With more than 340 acres of vines in production, half of them located in the four
local Grands Crus, this is by far the largest
private holding in Alsace. Some money has
been spent here since Séverine Beydon-
Schlumberger and new cellar master Alain
Freyburger arrived on the scene in 2000.
More than half of the vineyard is now biodynamic; the fermentation room and impressive barrel-storage area have both been
renovated; and the harvest is processed in
a gravity-fed system installed in 2005. The
portfolio of wines is built around Grands
Crus made from selectively harvested
grapes, plus the winery's basic range, Les
Princes Abbés, a homogeneous family of
wines often containing a high proportion of
Grand Cru grapes. The sweet (moelleux)
wines—Christine, Clarisse, Anne, and
Ernest—are now labeled Vendanges Tardives or Sélection de Grains Nobles as
appropriate. The estate owns the lion's
share of the Kitterlé Grand Cru plus some
lovely parcels at the heart of the Kessler
and Saering Grands Crus—home to exceptional wines, built for long aging. The wines
are drier than ever and produced in sufficient quantities to keep prices down; you
won't find many Alsace wines of this quality
that offer better value for the money. The
riesling Grand Cru Saering is always very
popular, so order while stocks last.

Recently tasted

ALSACE GRAND CRU KITTERLÉ RIESLING 2005
White | 2011 up to 2020　　92

ALSACE GRAND CRU PINOT GRIS VENDANGES
TARDIVES 2005
Sweet White | 2011 up to 2020　　92

ALSACE GRAND CRU SAERING RIESLING 2007
White | 2011 up to 2022　　90

GEWÜRZTRAMINER CUVÉE CHRISTINE
VENDANGES TARDIVES 2006
Sweet White | 2011 up to 2016　　91

GEWÜRZTRAMINER CUVÉE CHRISTINE
VENDANGES TARDIVES 2005
Sweet White | 2011 up to 2025　　97

GEWÜRZTRAMINER LES PRINCES ABBÉS 2007
Semi-Dry White | 2011 up to 2017　　88

MUSCAT LES PRINCES ABBÉS 2008
White | 2011 up to 2013　　87

PINOT GRIS LES PRINCES ABBÉS 2007
Semi-Dry White | 2011 up to 2017　　88

PINOT NOIR LES PRINCES ABBÉS 2008
Red | 2011 up to 2013　　86

RIESLING LES PRINCES ABBÉS 2007
White | 2011 up to 2015　　86

SYLVANER LES PRINCES ABBÉS 2007
White | 2011 up to 2017　　88

Older vintages

ALSACE GRAND CRU KESSLER
GEWÜRZTRAMINER 2004
Sweet White | 2011 up to 2019　　92
An ethereal wine, stone fruit and truffle on
the nose, concentrated on the palate, with
fine salinity and completely integrated
sweetness, showing a long, smoky, and
delicately spicy finish, perfumed with rose-
water notes.

ALSACE GRAND CRU KESSLER
GEWÜRZTRAMINER 2002
Sweet White | 2011 up to 2020　　91
A racy wine with exotic fruit and spice on
the nose, medium-dry, mineral and fresh
on the palate, with a honeyed finish.

ALSACE GRAND CRU KESSLER PINOT GRIS 2004
Sweet White | 2011 up to 2019　　90
Rich, very ripe, and fruity, this offers notes
of quince and honey on the nose and a full,
mineral palate with integrated sweetness
and very fine acidity. The finish is long and
crisp, with truffle notes.

ALSACE GRAND CRU KESSLER RIESLING 2005
White | 2011 up to 2020　　90
The wine is mineral and taut with fine acidity, expressing the purity typical of the vineyard. This is the first young-vine Kessler to
be sold as a Grand Cru, and a lovely success.

ALSACE GRAND CRU KITTERLÉ
GEWÜRZTRAMINER 2005
Sweet White | 2011 up to 2025　　95
A very powerful wine marked by the mineral
character of Kitterlé: the nose is pure, on
aromas of rose and mirabelle, with a note of
toasted almonds; the palate is rich, powerful, mineral, and deep, with a dry character
on the finish. A food wine that will age well.

ALSACE GRAND CRU KITTERLÉ
GEWÜRZTRAMINER 2003
Sweet White | 2011 up to 2020　　90
The only Grand Cru produced in 2003, the
other parcels having been declassified and
integrated into the Princes Abbés cuvées,

this offers rose and pepper on the nose and sweetness on the palate, with a beautiful, spicy finish.

ALSACE GRAND CRU KITTERLÉ PINOT GRIS 2006
Sweet White | 2011 up to 2021   **92**
Once again a wine marked by the vineyard's sandstone-volcanic soils, this has a ripe nose dominated by honey, vanilla, and dried fruit. It is rich on the palate, with integrated sweetness and pronounced salinity. The combination yields a wine with lovely flavor and purity.

ALSACE GRAND CRU KITTERLÉ PINOT GRIS 2005
Sweet White | 2011 up to 2020   **95**
From a perfect marriage of variety and site, this powerful wine is smoky and roasted on the nose with a sweet, rich, and unctuous palate rapidly dominated by its minerality. More so than the riesling, the pinot gris here displays a pure and very savory balance that shows clearly the salinity of its terroir.

ALSACE GRAND CRU KITTERLÉ RIESLING 2004
White | 2011 up to 2013   **92**
As in 2001 and 2002, the stony character of Kitterlé is very present in this dry wine, very mineral on the nose and palate, with ripe acidity.

ALSACE GRAND CRU SAERING RIESLING 2006
White | 2011 up to 2018   **92**
From the best part of this limestone-sandstone soil, this wine possesses a clean nose of fresh citrus and a pure palate with fine acidity and volume. The long finish demonstrates the success of this 2006.

ALSACE GRAND CRU SAERING RIESLING 2005
White | 2011 up to 2020   **91**
A clean and streamlined Saering, this has very precise, ripe acidity that draws a full-bodied and saline balance on the palate.

GEWÜRZTRAMINER CUVÉE CHRISTINE VENDANGES TARDIVES 2004
Sweet White | 2011 up to 2024   **95**
From old vines in the Heisse Wanne at the heart of the Kessler vineyard, this wine is already open, with an intense nose of exotic fruit, honey, and quince paste followed by a sweet palate of great purity and salinity. Still very young, this is among the great vintages of the cuvée Christine.

Red: 19.4 acres; pinot noir 100%. White: 286.4 acres; gewürztraminer 25%, riesling 31%, sylvaner 8%, muscat 2%, pinot blanc 15%, pino gris 19%. Annual production: 870,000 bottles

DOMAINE FRANÇOIS SCHMITT

19, rue de Soultzmatt
68500 Orschwihr
Phone 00 33 3 89 76 08 45
Fax 00 33 3 89 76 44 02
info@francoisschmitt.fr
www.francoisschmitt.fr

The Domaine François Schmitt is a family-run enterprise with holdings in the Bollenberg lieu-dit and the Pfingstberg Grand Cru. François and Marie-France Schmitt concentrate on viticulture and sales while son Frédéric takes care of winemaking—supervised by his brother Alain, who works as an independent enologist. Certain cuvées show especially good use of oak, making for balanced, generous wines—red and white alike. Those from the Bollenberg cru do sell out fast, so buy some while you still can. Try to get your hands on a few precious bottles of the pinot noir Coeur de Bollenberg or the riesling Pfingstberg Paradis.

Recently tasted
ALSACE GRAND CRU PFINGSTBERG RIESLING 2007
White | 2011 up to 2017   **90**

AUXERROIS BOLLENBERG 2007
White | 2011 up to 2013   **86**

BOLLENBERG PINOT GRIS 2007
White | 2011 up to 2022   **89**

MUSCAT 2008
White | 2011 up to 2013   **87**

PINOT NOIR COEUR DE BOLLENBERG 2007
Red | 2011 up to 2022   **90**

Older vintages
ALSACE GRAND CRU PFINGSTBERG GEWÜRZTRAMINER 2007
Sweet White | 2011 up to 2022   **88**
Rich and dense with great finesse, the 2007 is pure, with vanilla aromas. Great potential.

ALSACE GRAND CRU PFINGSTBERG RIESLING CUVÉE PARADIS 2005
White | 2011 up to 2020   **91**
A special cuvée from a parcel whose name was predestined to be at the heart of the Grand Cru, this wine takes on a new dimension in 2005 with a ripe floral nose and a palate of great depth, minerality, and length.

AUXERROIS FÛT DE CHÊNE 2007
White | 2011 up to 2013   **86**
From Bollenberg, this wine is still maturing in barrel. The oak is pronounced and the wine is dry, combining extract with crisp acidity. Great potential. To retaste.

BOLLENBERG GEWÜRZTRAMINER 2006
Sweet White | 2011 up to 2016   86
An honest and profound gewürztraminer, elegant and floral on the nose, with great purity on the palate. The sweetness is integrated, the finish spicy.

BOLLENBERG RIESLING 2007
White | 2011 up to 2017   88
Still in alcoholic fermentation, the wine is fizzy. To retaste.

EFFENBERG SYLVANER 2007
White | 2011 up to 2013   84
Straight and clean with notes of almonds on the nose, this is fresh and dry on the palate, with good acidity and length.

GEWÜRZTRAMINER CUVÉE MARIE-FRANCE 2007
Sweet White | 2011 up to 2017   88
A full and very ripe wine, sweet on the palate, with good acidity.

GEWÜRZTRAMINER
SÉLECTION DE GRAINS NOBLES 2005
Sweet White | 2011 up to 2025   90
A powerful, luscious wine, this offers fig and honey scents that accompany a sweet, intense, and pure palate. The good acidity and good level of alcohol guarantee long ageability.

GEWÜRZTRAMINER VENDANGES TARDIVES 2005
Sweet White | 2011 up to 2020   90
From Bollenberg, this wine shows great purity, with aromas of ripe fruit on the nose and a fleshy, round palate that retains lots of freshness.

PINOT NOIR COEUR DE BOLLENBERG 2005
Red | 2011 up to 2020   92
From ripe grapes grown on a great terroir and vinified with care in oak barrels, this is a full, powerful, and very pure wine with finely integrated tannins. The balance is close to perfect for an Alsace pinot noir.

PINOT NOIR ROUGE D'ALSACE 2007
Red | 2011 up to 2013   86
A red, light in color, that posseses body and depth with silky tannins.

Red: 6.2 acres; pinot noir 15%. White: 24.7 acres; chardonnay 1%, gewürztraminer 24%, muscat d'Alsace 2%, pinot blanc 25%, pinot gris 14%, riesling 15%, sylvaner 4%. Annual production: 100,000 bottles

DOMAINE SCHOFFIT

66-68, Nonnenholzweg
68000 Colmar
Phone 00 33 3 89 24 41 14
Fax 00 33 3 89 41 40 52
domaine.schoffit@free.fr

This winery in Colmar, far from the sloping vineyards of the Route des Vins, has its feet in two worlds. On the one hand, the alluvial plain of the Harth forest where vines pruned for tiny yields produce pure, highly concentrated and sought-after wines. And on the other, the steeply sloping Rangen de Thann vineyard, planted to the four noble varietals and home to very characteristic wines. A small riesling parcel in the Sommerberg Grand Cru completes the range. The late-harvest bottlings, Clos Saint-Théobald (Vendanges Tardives and Sélection de Grains Nobles) are as sumptuous as ever, while the dry wines are a tribute to Schoffit's hard work in the vineyards and more refined vinification since 1986: all unnecessary sweetness has been shed in favor of a fatter, more pronounced mineral character.

Recently tasted
ALSACE GRAND CRU RANGEN
CLOS SAINT-THÉOBALD GEWÜRZTRAMINER 2007
Sweet White | 2011 up to 2027   94

ALSACE GRAND CRU RANGEN
CLOS SAINT-THÉOBALD GEWÜRZTRAMINER
VENDANGES TARDIVES 2007
Sweet White | 2011 up to 2027   95

ALSACE GRAND CRU RANGEN
CLOS SAINT-THÉOBALD PINOT GRIS 2007
Sweet White | 2012 up to 2027   92

ALSACE GRAND CRU RANGEN CLOS SAINT-
THÉOBALD PINOT GRIS CUVÉE SCHISTES 2007
Semi-Dry White | 2011 up to 2027   93

ALSACE GRAND CRU RANGEN
CLOS SAINT-THÉOBALD PINOT GRIS SÉLECTION
DE GRAINS NOBLES 2007
Sweet White | 2013 up to 2030   96

ALSACE GRAND CRU RANGEN
CLOS SAINT-THÉOBALD PINOT GRIS VENDANGES
TARDIVES 2007
Sweet White | 2015 up to 2027   94

ALSACE GRAND CRU RANGEN
CLOS SAINT-THÉOBALD RIESLING 2007
Sweet White | 2012 up to 2027   92

ALSACE GRAND CRU RANGEN
CLOS SAINT-THÉOBALD RIESLING CUVÉE
SCHISTES 2007
White | 2011 up to 2027   **96**

PINOT GRIS LARMES DE LAVE 2007
Sweet White | 2015 up to 2030   **96**

RIESLING HARTH TRADITION 2007
White | 2011 up to 2017   **88**

Older vintages

ALSACE GRAND CRU RANGEN
CLOS SAINT-THÉOBALD GEWÜRZTRAMINER 2005
Sweet White | 2011 up to 2020   **94**
Extreme wine from an extreme terroir. The
nose is still closed, spicy, and smoky with
rose notes. The palate possesses the full
and sweet character of the vintage, but with
great purity and delicacy, and smoke aromas on the long finish.

ALSACE GRAND CRU RANGEN
CLOS SAINT-THÉOBALD GEWÜRZTRAMINER
SÉLECTION DE GRAINS NOBLES 2006
Sweet White | 2011 up to 2026   **95**
The wine is very candied on the nose, with
aromas of exotic fruit, then pure and luscious on the palate with great purity. A balanced wine that remains easy to drink.

ALSACE GRAND CRU RANGEN
CLOS SAINT-THÉOBALD MUSCAT 2006
White | 2011 up to 2026   **94**
A rare cuvée, only a few hundred bottles
produced in the best years, this 2006 follows
2003 with the same success: harvested at
Vendange Tardive ripeness, the wine is ripe
on the nose with a muscaty note, then full
and concentrated on the palate with lovely
acidity. A rich and racy muscat, as only
Alsace can produce.

ALSACE GRAND CRU RANGEN
CLOS SAINT-THÉOBALD PINOT GRIS
SÉLECTION DE GRAINS NOBLES 2002
Sweet White | 2011 up to 2025   **91**
A candied wine, very botrytised and lus-
cious with aromas of praline and citrus peel
that dominate the underlying notes of smoke.
Hold to see the volcanic character emerge.

ALSACE GRAND CRU RANGEN
CLOS SAINT-THÉOBALD PINOT GRIS
VENDANGES TARDIVES 2006
Sweet White | 2011 up to 2026   **96**
The color is very deep; the nose is very candied, with an intense smoked and roasted
character. The palate is luscious, very fine,
with pronounced acidity that adds extraordinary lightness to the ensemble. The finish
is long on aromas of candied fruits. A wine
of great aging potential, to be savored alone.

ALSACE GRAND CRU RANGEN
CLOS SAINT-THÉOBALD RIESLING 2006
Sweet White | 2011 up to 2021   **92**
Harvested very ripe, this wine is rich and
honeyed on the nose, pure on the palate,
and very sweet without masking the smoky,
peaty character of the wine. A rich wine,
with great acidity, for aging.

ALSACE GRAND CRU RANGEN
CLOS SAINT-THÉOBALD RIESLING 2005
Sweet White | 2011 up to 2020   **92**
A sunny and racy wine, very ripe and smoky
on the nose with a dry, fat palate with pronounced salinity. A little botrytised, the wine
is elegant and fine with good acidity.

ALSACE GRAND CRU SOMMERBERG RIESLING 2006
White | 2011 up to 2021   **90**
A sunny riesling marked by notes of citrus
peel on the nose, this is rich on the palate,
with fine salinity and light bitterness on the
finish.

CHASSELAS VIEILLES VIGNES 2007
White | 2011 up to 2015   **88**
This chasselas is fat, full, and remarkably
well structured, with a floral nose and delicate palate. This is the Alsacian reference
for the variety, 2007 a worthy successor to
the great 2005.

COLMAR PINOT GRIS TRADITION 2006
Semi-Dry White | 2011 up to 2016   **87**
A full, dry pinot gris, very clean on the nose,
with great purity on the palate. A splendid
wine in a difficult vintage that will make an
excellent companion at the table.

Red: 1.7 acres; pinot 5%. **White:** 40.3 acres;
gewürztraminer 20%, muscat 4%, pinot 16%, pinot
gris 20%, riesling 25%, sylvaner and chasselas 6%.
Annual production: 120,000 bottles

LOUIS SIPP

5, Grand-Rue
68150 Ribeauvillé
Phone 00 33 3 89 73 60 01
Fax 00 33 3 89 73 31 46
louis@sipp.com
www.sipp.com

This large property boasts a rich heritage of vines on the slopes of Ribeauvillé, plus some more recently acquired parcels. For years now, Étienne Sipp has been producing pleasingly dense and pure wines, built on an uncompromising work ethic. Soil and vineyard maintenance is in accordance with "reasoned" viticulture, pending conversion to fully organic methods. The entire harvest undergoes long and gentle pressing, and all of the wines are aged on lees in oak vats. The result is a very wide but homogeneous range of wines that offer different levels of terroir expression. The new label design features a sugar code that indicates the level of perceived sweetness, the wines being more or less sweet depending on the vintage. The traditional flagship offering is the riesling Grand Cru Kirchberg, available across at least six vintages. Vying for supremacy today is the very promising riesling Grand Cru Osterberg, first released in 2004.

Recently tasted

ALSACE GRAND CRU KIRCHBERG
DE RIBEAUVILLÉ PINOT GRIS 2007
White | 2011 up to 2027   93

ALSACE GRAND CRU KIRCHBERG
DE RIBEAUVILLÉ RIESLING 2007
White | 2012 up to 2027   92

ALSACE GRAND CRU KIRCHBERG DE RIBEAUVILLÉ
RIESLING SÉLECTION DE GRAINS NOBLES 2006
Sweet White | 2011 up to 2026   92

ALSACE GRAND CRU OSTERBERG GEWÜRZTRAMINER
VENDANGES TARDIVES 2006
Sweet White | 2011 up to 2026   90

ALSACE GRAND CRU OSTERBERG RIESLING 2007
White | 2011 up to 2027   93

GEWÜRZTRAMINER 2007
White | 2011 up to 2015   88

GEWÜRZTRAMINER SÉLECTION DE GRAINS
NOBLES 2006
Sweet White | 2011 up to 2026   94

ROTENBERG GEWÜRZTRAMINER 2007
Sweet White | 2011 up to 2022   90

Older vintages

ALSACE GRAND CRU KIRCHBERG DE RIBEAUVILLÉ
PINOT GRIS 2004
White | 2011 up to 2019   91
A great, dry pinot gris, floral on the nose without overripeness, dense and mineral on the palate, with purity and great length. It has lovely balance and will drink well young.

ALSACE GRAND CRU KIRCHBERG DE RIBEAUVILLÉ
PINOT GRIS VENDANGES TARDIVES 2005
Sweet White | 2011 up to 2025   92
The delicate, praline- and honey-scented nose leads to a taut palate, mineral and elegant. A beautiful wine with high-quality botrytis. Great aging potential.

ALSACE GRAND CRU KIRCHBERG DE RIBEAUVILLÉ
RIESLING 2006
White | 2011 up to 2021   91
The nose is marked by ripe fruit with an almond note; the palate is very mineral, full, elegant, and clean. A splendid Kirchberg.

ALSACE GRAND CRU KIRCHBERG DE RIBEAUVILLÉ
RIESLING 2005
White | 2011 up to 2021   93
Splendid Kirchberg, still closed yet floral and smoky on the nose, full and dense on the palate, with pronounced minerality and remarkable purity. Great length on the finish.

ALSACE GRAND CRU KIRCHBERG DE RIBEAUVILLÉ
RIESLING VENDANGES TARDIVES 2005
Sweet White | 2011 up to 2025   92
From a selection of botrytised grapes, this wine is still young, with a nose of exotic fruit and a sweet, mineral palate with great finesse and purity. It is remarkably fresh, with a very pure, long, tangerine-scented finish. Will gain complexity with aging.

ALSACE GRAND CRU OSTERBERG
GEWÜRZTRAMINER 2005
Semi-Dry White | 2011 up to 2025   94
This rose-scented gewürztraminer shows the density and the elegance of the terroir with rarely achieved depth and purity. A dry, high-caliber wine.

ALSACE GRAND CRU OSTERBERG
GEWÜRZTRAMINER VENDANGES TARDIVES 2005
Sweet White | 2011 up to 2025   92
A very ripe Vendange Tardive, this shows candied honey, dried fruit, and toasted hazelnuts on the nose, with sweetness and fine minerality on the palate and a long, spicy finish. This deserves age.

Red: 6.7 acres; pinot noir 100%. White: 92.2 acres; auxerrois 11%, chardonnay 1.1%, chasselas 1.9%, gewürztraminer 24.8%, muscat 1.4%, pinot blanc 11.5%, pinot gris 13.4%, riesling 28.2%, sylvaner 6.7%. Annual production: 450,000 bottles

DOMAINE SIPP-MACK

1, rue des Vosges
68150 Hunawihr
Phone 00 33 3 89 73 61 88
Fax 00 33 3 89 73 36 70
sippmack@sippmack.com
www.sippmack.com

Domaine Sipp-Mack is owned and worked by brothers Jacques and Vincent Sipp and their respective wives. Having recently expanded, it now extends to fifty acres of plantings, partly in the Osterberg de Ribeauvillé Grand Cru but mainly in Bergheim and Hunawihr, including in the Rosacker Grand Cru. The vines are cultivated using integrated pest management, and all of the grapes have been wholepressed since 1998. The product is deliciously pure, the wines from the chalkiest terroirs being notable for perfectly integrated residual sugar.

Recently tasted

ALSACE GRAND CRU OSTERBERG PINOT GRIS 2005
Semi-Dry White | 2011 up to 2020   **90**

ALSACE GRAND CRU OSTERBERG RIESLING 2005
White | 2011 up to 2020   **89**

ALSACE GRAND CRU ROSACKER RIESLING 2007
White | 2011 up to 2027   **90**

GEWÜRZTRAMINER VIEILLES VIGNES 2007
Sweet White | 2012 up to 2022   **88**

RIESLING VIEILLES VIGNES 2007
White | 2011 up to 2017   **88**

Older vintages

ALSACE GRAND CRU OSTERBERG RIESLING 2004
White | 2011 up to 2019   **90**
Delicate aromas of ripe fruit lead to a palate of depth and great purity. The light sweetness is already integrated.

ALSACE GRAND CRU ROSACKER RIESLING 2004
White | 2011 up to 2020   **89**
A ripe riesling, deep and very mineral on the palate with good purity. Still very young and dominated by the variety's fruit notes, this merits aging.

Red: 2.5 acres; pinot noir 100%. White: 34.6 acres; gewürztraminer 17%. pinot blanc 14%, riesling 40%, sylvaner 6%. Annual production: 120,000 bottles

DOMAINE STENTZ-BUECHER

21, rue Kleb
68920 Wettolsheim
Phone 00 33 3 89 80 68 09
Fax 00 33 3 89 79 60 53
stentz-buecher@wanadoo.fr
www.stentz-buecher.com

Jean-Jacques and Stéphane Stentz continue to develop their family estate. The cellars have been expanded to allow for a gravity-fed system that helps to bring out the wine's pure, natural fruit expression. The marly limestone terroirs around Wettolsheim yield high-acid wines, fermented by Stéphane to deliver plenty of power but with a crisp, dry balance and sometimes plenty of alcohol, too. The pinots noirs are just as carefully made and equally excellent. The overall range may seem to lack finesse in the first few years; but since some of the cuvées are released for sale only following several years' storage after bottling, there is some seriously food-friendly wine here.

Recently tasted

ALSACE GRAND CRU HENGST GEWÜRZTRAMINER 2007
Semi-Dry White | 2011 up to 2022   **90**

ALSACE GRAND CRU HENGST PINOT GRIS 2006
White | 2011 up to 2021   **91**

ALSACE GRAND CRU STEINGRÜBLER RIESLING 2007
White | 2011 up to 2022   **90**

PINOT NOIR OLD OAK 2007
Red | 2011 up to 2017   **89**

PINOT NOIR TRADITION 2007
White | 2011 up to 2017   **88**

STEINGRÜBLER GEWÜRZTRAMINER 2006
Semi-Dry White | 2011 up to 2021   **90**

Older vintages

ALSACE GRAND CRU HENGST PINOT GRIS 2005
White | 2011 up to 2020   **90**
The Hengst Grand Cru, vinified dry with the pinot gris, yields a full and fat wine, with depth and lovely balance on the palate.

ALSACE GRAND CRU PFERSIGBERG GEWÜRZTRAMINER 2004
White | 2011 up to 2020   **89**
A fine gewürztraminer, hazelnut and spice on the nose, full and rich on the palate, with a dry, mineral balance that enhances the long ginger finish.

ALSACE GRAND CRU STEINGRÜBLER
RIESLING 1998
White | 2011 up to 2018   **90**
While the age of the wine brings complexity to the bouquet, the palate remains young, full, and fat, with good concentration of fruit. Take advantage of the availability of this wine at maturity.

MARKEN PINOT GRIS
SÉLECTION DE GRAINS NOBLES 2003
Sweet White | 2011 up to 2025   **90**
An extreme wine from an extreme vintage: dates and dried apricots on the nose, luscious and very pure on the palate, with a long finish of great aromatic complexity.

ORTEL RIESLING 2005
White | 2011 up to 2020   **88**
Still closed on the nose, this wine shows power on the palate with fresh, ripe acidity that supports good concentration. A riesling for aging.

PFLECK GEWÜRZTRAMINER
SÉLECTION DE GRAINS NOBLES 2001
Sweet White | 2011 up to 2021   **91**
A very concentrated wine, candied fruit on the nose with a touch of smoke; very rich on the palate with a sweetness moderated by good acidity, which gives it a balance of rare freshness.

PINOT BLANC VIEILLES VIGNES
ÉLEVÉ EN BARRIQUE 2005
White | 2011 up to 2015   **89**
Very old vines of unknown age on the top of Hengst produced a concentrated pinot blanc. It is marked on the nose by barrel aging and is dense and deep on the palate, with a long finish. An atypical wine for the region but of great quality.

PINOT NOIR OLD OAK 2005
Red | 2011 up to 2020   **90**
From the Grand Cru Steingrübler and matured in neutral barrels, the wine displays perfumed aromas of small black fruits, then a full and spicy palate with a long finish.

TANNENBUEHL RIESLING
VENDANGES TARDIVES 2001
Sweet White | 2011 up to 2021   **90**
An intense and profound Vendange Tardive, already mineral on the nose, sweet on the palate, with great length. Drink now or keep.

Red: 4.9 acres; pinot noir 10%. White: 27.2 acres; gewürztraminer 18%, pinot blanc 23%, pinot gris 17%, riesling 23%, chasselas 5%, sylvaner 4%.
Annual production: 50,000 bottles

DOMAINE STOEFFLER

1, rue des Lièvres
67140 Barr
Phone 00 33 3 88 08 52 50
Fax 00 33 3 88 08 17 09
info@vins-stoeffler.com
www.vins-stoeffler.com

Vincent Stoeffler's family estate includes holdings in the Barr area and in the Upper Rhine, between Ribeauvillé and Riquewihr. The wines are made from organically grown grapes that undergo very slow pressing, followed by slow fermentation and maturation on lees in oak vats. The 2005 vintage is very homogeneous: the rieslings are delicately mineral and the pinots noirs are precisely crafted. The muscat and most of the gewürztraminers and pinots gris have already fallen victim to their own success, so buy the 2006s if you can find them.

Recently tasted
ALSACE GRAND CRU GEWÜRZTRAMINER
VENDANGES TARDIVES 2007
Sweet White | 2011 up to 2017   **90**

ALSACE GRAND CRU KIRCHBERG DE BARR
RIESLING 2007
White | 2012 up to 2022   **88**

PINOT NOIR ÉLEVÉ EN BARRIQUE 2007
Red | 2011 up to 2017   **88**

Older vintages
ALSACE GRAND CRU KIRCHBERG DE BARR
GEWÜRZTRAMINER 2007
Sweet White | 2011 up to 2022   **90**
A very powerful wine, rich and sweet with depth and good acidity. A well-made wine of great aging potential, this will evolve well.

ALSACE GRAND CRU KIRCHBERG DE BARR
GEWÜRZTRAMINER 2005
Sweet White | 2011 up to 2020   **88**
The nose is typical, spicy with some pedigree, followed by a sweet, mineral, and full palate. A great Barr Kirchberg, already open.

ALSACE GRAND CRU KIRCHBERG DE BARR
GEWÜRZTRAMINER SÉLECTION DE GRAINS
NOBLES 2001
Sweet White | 2011 up to 2025   **92**
Intense on the nose, this possesses a supple sweetness that evokes the juice of ripe fruit. A pure wine with a long finish, to keep several years to unveil its mineral side.

GEWÜRZTRAMINER 2007
Semi-Dry White | 2011 up to 2017   **87**
Ripe with an almost dry palate, this is a full wine with a spicy finish. A good companion at the table.

KRONENBOURG RIESLING 2005
White | 2011 up to 2015   87
A wine still closed, dense on the palate with good salinity.

MUHLFORST RIESLING 2007
White | 2011 up to 2017   88
Rich and very ripe with light sweetness, this wine has lovely material balanced by ripe acidity.

MUHLFORST RIESLING 2005
White | 2011 up to 2015   89
A ripe riesling that possesses lots of volume and minerality, this has a balance tipped toward richness as the acidity is still subtle at this stage.

MUHLFORST RIESLING VENDANGES TARDIVES 2004
Sweet White | 2011 up to 2024   90
This offers a superripe nose with accents of candied citrus and a luscious palate with great richness. It is finely crisp, with a long finish on aromas of citrus peel.

PINOT GRIS KIRCHBERG DE BARR 2005
Sweet White | 2011 up to 2020   88
A very ripe and rich pinot gris with intense sweetness that masks the minerality of the vineyard. Age it to let the sugar integrate.

PINOT GRIS VENDANGES TARDIVES 2005
Sweet White | 2011 up to 2015   88
Rich in aromas of praline, this wine is sweet on the palate with candied fruit notes of great purity. To drink now.

PINOT GRIS VIEILLES VIGNES 2007
Semi-Dry White | 2011 up to 2017   88
A rich pinot gris, dense and very pure, with lovely structure.

PINOT NOIR XXC 2005
Red | 2011 up to 2020   92
A splendid pinot noir from the Kirchberg Grand Cru of Barr. It expresses lovely maturation in a full, deep palate that shows fruit concentration and silky, high-quality tannins. Superb pinot noir from great terroir.

Red: 4.2 acres; pinot noir 100%. White: 32.9 acres; chardonnay 4%, gewürztraminer 20%, muscat d'Alsace 4%, pinot blanc 18%, riesling 26%, savagnin 3%, sylvaner 7%. Annual production: 110,000 bottles

DOMAINE MARC TEMPÉ

16, rue du Schlossberg
68340 Zellenberg
Phone 00 33 3 89 47 85 22
Fax 00 33 3 89 47 97 01
marctempe@wanadoo.fr
www.marctempe.fr

Marc Tempé is an exacting, impetuous winegrower who since his beginnings in 1995 has taken a lot of risks for the sake of ultra-high-quality wines: biodynamic viticulture, minimum yields, and very long, mainly hands-off vinification. His first vintages were produced with limited resources that often involved a careful balancing act. The wines were very uneven, always concentrated, and frequently exceptional; but they could also be rustic, with too much sweetness and oak. Little by little he has steadied the ship, and his efforts are starting to produce more homogeneous results. All of his offerings since 2001 have shown more finesse at no expense to ripeness.

Recently tasted

ALSACE GRAND CRU FURSTENTUM PINOT GRIS 2004
Sweet White | 2011 up to 2024   92

ALSACE GRAND CRU MAMBOURG GEWÜRZTRAMINER 2006
Sweet White | 2011 up to 2026   96

ALSACE GRAND CRU MAMBOURG GEWÜRZTRAMINER SÉLECTION DE GRAINS NOBLES 2003
Sweet White | 2011 up to 2023   97

ALSACE GRAND CRU MAMBOURG GEWÜRZTRAMINER VENDANGES TARDIVES 2002
Sweet White | 2011 up to 2022   97

ALSACE GRAND CRU MAMBOURG RIESLING 2005
Semi-Dry White | 2012 up to 2025   92

ALSACE GRAND CRU SCHOENENBOURG GEWÜRZTRAMINER 2005
Sweet White | 2011 up to 2025   92

ALSACE GRAND CRU SCHOENENBOURG PINOT GRIS 2004
Sweet White | 2011 up to 2024   93

ALSACE GRAND CRU SCHOENENBOURG PINOT GRIS SÉLECTION DE GRAINS NOBLES 2002
Sweet White | 2011 up to 2022   94

ALSACE GRAND CRU SCHOENENBOURG PINOT GRIS VENDANGES TARDIVES 2003
Sweet White | 2011 up to 2023   92

GRAFFENREBEN RIESLING 2005
White | 2011 up to 2020   89

ZELLENBERG GEWÜRZTRAMINER 2006
Semi-Dry White | 2011 up to 2016   **89**

Older vintages

ALSACE GRAND CRU FURSTENTUM PINOT GRIS 2001
Sweet White | 2011 up to 2020   **94**
A powerful and rich wine with great minerality, this has integrated its oak flavors well. The grapefruit finish is long.

ALSACE GRAND CRU MAMBOURG
GEWÜRZTRAMINER 2005
Sweet White | 2011 up to 2030   **97**
From old vines in the central part of the vineyard, this wine is already open on the nose, with candied citrus, honey, and white truffle. The palate has depth, elegance, and light sweetness on the attack, but it is rapidly curbed by superb acidity. The finish is very long, on flavors of ripe white peach, lemon, and ginger with a rose note. A superlative wine. Magical balance.

ALSACE GRAND CRU MAMBOURG GEWÜRZTRAMINER
SÉLECTION DE GRAINS NOBLES 1999
Sweet White | 2011 up to 2020   **94**
A worthy successor to the flavorful 1998, the 1999 presents a nose of candied citrus, fig, and honey, with a toasty note from maturation in oak. The palate is rich and very unctuous, with aromas of cocoa and dates on the long finish.

ALSACE GRAND CRU MAMBOURG
GEWÜRZTRAMINER VENDANGES TARDIVES 2003
Sweet White | 2011 up to 2023   **96**
Produced from very old vines in the Steinigerweg vineyard that were affected by botrytis, rare in 2003, this wine possesses an intense, toasty nose of dried apricots and a palate that is sweet, intense, pure, and deep. The finish is long and crystalline and leaves an impression of remarkable purity. Great wine with great aging potential.

ALSACE GRAND CRU MAMBOURG RIESLING 2004
Semi-Dry White | 2011 up to 2018   **90**
Very typical riesling, with a nose of flowers and almonds, this is full, saline, and very clean with a spicy, dry finish. It was vinified and matured in barrel but the oak remains subtle. A wine for aging.

ALSACE GRAND CRU SCHOENENBOURG
PINOT GRIS VENDANGES TARDIVES 2005
Sweet White | 2011 up to 2025   **94**
The nose is still marked by the oak of barrel maturation, evolving into scents of ripe fruits with a note of smoke. The palate is deep, sweet, and finely crisp, leaving an impression of great purity. A wine for long aging.

BURGREBEN RIESLING 2004
White | 2011 up to 2021   **90**
This terroir, dominated by limestone, yields a separate wine in the best vintages. The nose is ripe and mineral with citrus and a note of flint; the palate is full, powerful, lightly sweet, and fat, finishing on bitter notes supported by pronounced acidity. A very successful 2004.

GEWÜRZTRAMINER RIMELSBERG VENDANGES
TARDIVES 2003
Sweet White | 2011 up to 2015   **94**
Marked by rose and noble spice notes, the wine is fine and mineral with already integrated sweetness. Remarkable texture on a very pure palate.

RIESLING SAINT-HIPPOLYTE 2005
White | 2011 up to 2015   **89**
From sandy granitic soil with a sandstone base in Saint-Hippolyte, below the village, the wine is fresh and fruity with aromas of fleshy white fruits, pure and finely crisp on the palate with a light softness. Lovely bitter notes emerge on a long finish of pink grapefruit.

RODELSBERG 2005
Semi-Dry White | 2011 up to 2020   **89**
This comes from an iron-rich parcel co-planted to gewürztraminer and pinot gris at the top of the Mambourg hill. The maturation in 600-liter demi-muids reinforces the wine's ripe character, with its nose of praline, honey, and spice. The palate is full and dry and finishes long and crisp. Perfect for spicy cuisine.

Red: .5 acre. White: 19.3 acres. Annual production: 40,000 bottles

TRIMBACH

15, route de Bergheim
68150 Ribeauvillé
Phone 00 33 3 89 73 60 30
Fax 00 33 3 89 73 89 04
contact@maison-trimbach.fr
www.maison-trimbach.com

Trimbach stands out as one of those great wineries that helped to build market demand for Alsace wine in France and abroad thanks to a homogeneous range of wines that show consistent quality year after year. The Frédéric-Émile and Clos Sainte-Hune cuvées have become the standard-bearers for the great Alsace rieslings, but it doesn't stop there; the rest of the range is equally interesting. The estate-produced Prestige cuvées often come from the classed growths around Ribeauvillé and include the rare but always very precise moelleux wines. Trimbach's clever policy of buying grapes from holdings throughout the region, many of them located in Grands Crus, means that it can also produce Classique and Réserve bottlings—all very good whatever the varietal—in quantities sufficient to export worldwide. Pierre Trimbach heads up this side of the family business and orchestrates the blending of the wines, looking to produce cuvées with crisp, dry balance and great purity, vintage on vintage. Quality and quantity: a unique combination for an Alsace producer.

Recently tasted

CLOS SAINTE-HUNE RIESLING 2004
White | 2011 up to 2024   **97**

GEWÜRZTRAMINER 2007
White | 2011 up to 2015   **88**

GEWÜRZTRAMINER 2006
White | 2011 up to 2016   **86**

GEWÜRZTRAMINER SEIGNEURS DE RIBEAUPIERRE 2004
White | 2011 up to 2024   **92**

MUSCAT RÉSERVE 2007
White | 2011 up to 2013   **86**

PINOT BLANC 2007
White | 2011 up to 2013   **86**

PINOT GRIS RÉSERVE PERSONNELLE 2007
White | 2011 up to 2027   **90**

RIESLING 2007
White | 2011 up to 2017   **86**

RIESLING M 2004
White | 2011 up to 2024   **92**

RIESLING RÉSERVE 2007
White | 2011 up to 2022   **90**

Older vintages

CLOS SAINTE-HUNE RIESLING 2003
White | 2011 up to 2030   **93**
The Rosacker soils were spared the dehydration of the vintage, producing a full Sainte-Hune with depth, great purity, and a light sweetness that renders the wine already pleasant to drink.

CLOS SAINTE-HUNE RIESLING 2002
White | 2011 up to 2030   **96**
The order of release of each vintage is dictated by the readiness of the wine, and so the 2002 follows the 2003 and 2001. Its nose is open and smoky with a note of white flowers; its palate is full-bodied on the attack, with enormous dry extract. It is powerfully concentrated with very fine, intense acidity and a finish long on floral aromas.

GEWÜRZTRAMINER
SÉLECTION DE GRAINS NOBLES 2001
Sweet White | 2011 up to 2021   **96**
A superb wine with apricot and honey on the nose, luscious and unctuous on the palate, with great finesse. Splendid wine, already delicious, this will age very well.

PINOT GRIS SÉLECTION DE GRAINS NOBLES 2000
Sweet White | 2011 up to 2030   **93**
An incredible blend of botrytised extract and very fresh fruitiness, this cuvée combines sweetness and freshness with remarkable integration.

PINOT GRIS VENDANGES TARDIVES 2000
Sweet White | 2011 up to 2020   **91**
A ripe Vendange Tardive, this offers ripe peach and honey on the nose and sweetness on the palate, with body and a long, smoky finish.

RIESLING CUVÉE FRÉDÉRIC-EMILE 375ÈME ANNIVERSAIRE 2001
White | 2011 up to 2030   **94**
A special cuvée selected from the old vines of this parcel in celebration of the house's 375th anniversary, this wine is lightly over-ripe with very fine, ripe acidity. A wine not to be missed upon release.

RIESLING CUVÉE FRÉDÉRIC-ÉMILE 2004
White | 2011 up to 2024   **92**
From a historical, horse-plowed vineyard above the domaine in the Grands Crus of Geisberg and Osterberg, this riesling is already open, with scents of white flowers and smoke and a mineral palate with fine acidity.

RIESLING CUVÉE FRÉDÉRIC-ÉMILE
SÉLECTION DE GRAINS NOBLES 2000
Sweet White | 2011 up to 2030   **97**
A luscious wine, exceptionally upright,
offering the crystalline purity of great late-
harvest rieslings. Rare and of great aging
potential.

RIESLING RÉSERVE 2006
White | 2011 up to 2021   **90**
Blended from several great terroirs, this
Reserve riesling possesses a nose of white
flowers and citrus and a full, well-integrated
palate. This is a benchmark dry riesling for
the table, with depth that will make it magnificent for saltwater fish.

Red: 4.9 acres; pinot noir 100%. White: 84 acres;
gewürztraminer 32%, muscat d'Alsace 1%, pinot
blanc 10%, pinot gris 15%, riesling 42%. Annual
production: 1,200,000 bottles

GUY WACH – DOMAINE DES MARRONNIERS

5, rue de la Commanderie
67140 Andlau
Phone 00 33 3 88 08 93 20
Fax 00 33 3 88 08 45 59
info@guy-wach.fr
www.guy-wach .fr

Riesling enthusiast Guy Wach coaxes a very
enthusiastic performance out of his parcels
in the three Andlau Grands Crus, each one
with its own, very forceful character. Vintage
permitting, the trio of dry rieslings is rounded
off by sweeter, old-vine cuvées and some
splendid late-harvest bottlings (Vendanges
Tardives and Sélections de Grains Nobles).
The rest of the range is superbly uniform and
very consistent from vintage to vintage: as
strictly vinified as the rieslings, with plenty of
integrity and the occasional, very discreet
trace of residual sugar. Vinification in oak
vats and aging on lees are precisely calcu-
lated to produce fat but balanced wines.

Recently tasted
ALSACE GRAND CRU KASTELBERG RIESLING
VENDANGES TARDIVES 2006
Sweet White | 2011 up to 2030   **94**

ALSACE GRAND CRU KASTELBERG RIESLING
VIEILLES VIGNES 2007
White | 2012 up to 2027   **93**

ALSACE GRAND CRU MOENCHBERG RIESLING 2007
White | 2012 up to 2027   **91**

ALSACE GRAND CRU MOENCHBERG RIESLING 2006
White | 2011 up to 2021   **90**

ALSACE GRAND CRU WIEBELSBERG RIESLING 2007
White | 2011 up to 2022   **92**

ANDLAU RIESLING 2007
White | 2011 up to 2017   **88**

GEWÜRZTRAMINER SÉLECTION DE GRAINS
NOBLES 2000
Sweet White | 2011 up to 2025   **92**

GEWÜRZTRAMINER VIEILLES VIGNES 2007
Sweet White | 2011 up to 2022   **89**

PINOT NOIR CUVÉE SAINT-HUBERT 2007
Red | 2011 up to 2015   **87**

Older vintages
ALSACE GRAND CRU KASTELBERG RIESLING 2005
White | 2011 up to 2020   **91**
The flagship of the range, from the only
Grand Cru on schist soil in Alsace, this wine
has typical aromas of stones and citrus peel
and a rich palate with lovely finesse.

ALSACE GRAND CRU KASTELBERG
RIESLING VENDANGES TARDIVES 2005
Sweet White | 2011 up to 2025   94
From eighty-plus-year-old vines, this is a super-ripe wine that displays botrytis of great quality: the nose is candied with aromas of honey and citrus and a smoky note; the palate is full, sweet without being heavy, and very powerful. The finish takes on notes of dried apricots and smoke. The wine has great potential and needs several years of bottle age to reveal all its class.

ALSACE GRAND CRU KASTELBERG
RIESLING VIEILLES VIGNES 2005
White | 2011 up to 2025   93
From eighty-plus-year-old vines, this wine is produced in the best years. This vintage is very mineral on the nose with a spicy note, and concentrated on the palate with evident class. A great dry wine that will age well.

ALSACE GRAND CRU MOENCHBERG
RIESLING 2005
White | 2011 up to 2020   90
Still closed on the nose, this wine gives notes of white peach, lemon, and white flowers, leading to a palate of fullness, depth, and great purity. As is often the case, the Moenchberg needs several years of aging to completely reveal itself. The 2006 is an old-vine cuvée harvested overripe, more powerful still.

ANDLAU RIESLING 2006
White | 2011 up to 2016   88
From a sandstone parcel under the Grand Cru Wiebelsberg, this wine's terroir character is pronounced, with a smoky nose marked by a note of citrus peel and a dry palate, fine and saline, with a long finish on pink grapefruit. A great success for the vintage.

DUTTENBERG SYLVANER 2007
White | 2011 up to 2022   88
From the back slope of the Grand Cru Moenchberg, this sylvaner is very fresh with floral notes on the nose, and full and deep on the palate, with good purity. A pleasant, young sylvaner with the depth to age well.

GEWÜRZTRAMINER VENDANGES TARDIVES 2005
Sweet White | 2011 up to 2020   90
A Vendange Tardive, very pure on the nose with aromas of rose and praline, full on the palate with good richness. Drink for its pleasure from now, or hold to gain complexity.

Red: .7 acre: pinot noir 100%. White: 18.5 acres; chardonnay 4%, gewürztraminer 16%, muscat d'Alsace 5%, pinot blanc 8%, pinot gris 10%, riesling 37%, sylvaner 20%. Annual production: 50,000 bottles

DOMAINE WEINBACH – COLETTE, CATHERINE ET LAURENCE FALLER

25, route du Vin
Clos des Capucins
68240 Kaysersberg
Phone 00 33 3 89 47 13 21
Fax 00 33 3 89 47 38 18
contact@domaineweinbach.com
www.domaineweinbach.com

This domaine is surrounded by the vines of the Clos des Capucins and owns plots in all of the south-facing terroirs at the mouth of the Weiss Valley. The perfectly matched grape variety and environment here make for a homogeneous range of superbly precise wines. Laurence Faller creates flawlessly pure wines of high quality. Witness the expression of the Schlossberg Grand Cru, magnified by the riesling across a range of cuvées; or the depth of the Furstentum and Mambourg Grands Crus, magnificently emphasized by the gewürztraminer. The Altenbourg lieu-dit (unclassified but worthy of Grand Cru status) yields generous, deep wines based on pinot gris. The Clos des Capucins produces much-sought-after single-varietal wines that, thanks to biodynamic principles, achieve exceptional purity and concentration with no loss of crisp, dry balance. The sweet and liqueur wines are largely unrivaled for concentration and purity, underlining the harmony between the varietals and their terroir. This domaine continues to push forward the quality and reputation of the great Alsace wines.

Recently tasted
ALSACE GRAND CRU FURSTENTUM
GEWÜRZTRAMINER 2007
Sweet White | 2011 up to 2030   96

ALSACE GRAND CRU FURSTENTUM
GEWÜRZTRAMINER SÉLECTION DE GRAINS
NOBLES 2006
Sweet White | 2012 up to 2026   98

ALSACE GRAND CRU FURSTENTUM
GEWÜRZTRAMINER VENDANGES TARDIVES 2006
Sweet White | 2011 up to 2026   96

ALSACE GRAND CRU MAMBOURG GEWÜRZTRAMINER
QUINTESSENCE DE GRAINS NOBLES 2006
Sweet White | 2011 up to 2030   98

ALSACE GRAND CRU MAMBOURG GEWÜRZTRAMINER
SÉLECTION DE GRAINS NOBLES 2007
Sweet White | 2011 up to 2027   98

ALSACE GRAND CRU MAMBOURG GEWÜRZTRAMINER
SÉLECTION DE GRAINS NOBLES 2006
Sweet White | 2011 up to 2030   98

ALSACE GRAND CRU SCHLOSSBERG RIESLING 2007
White | 2011 up to 2022   **93**

ALSACE GRAND CRU SCHLOSSBERG RIESLING
CUVÉE SAINTE-CATHERINE 2007
White | 2011 up to 2027   **96**

ALSACE GRAND CRU SCHLOSSBERG RIESLING
CUVÉE SAINTE-CATHERINE L'INÉDIT 2007
Sweet White | 2011 up to 2027   **98**

ALSACE GRAND CRU SCHLOSSBERG RIESLING
SÉLECTION DE GRAINS NOBLES 2007
Sweet White | 2011 up to 2030   **98**

ALSACE GRAND CRU SCHLOSSBERG RIESLING
SÉLECTION DE GRAINS NOBLES 2006
Sweet White | 2011 up to 2026   **96**

ALSACE GRAND CRU SCHLOSSBERG RIESLING
VENDANGES TARDIVES 2007
Sweet White | 2011 up to 2027   **94**

ALTENBOURG GEWÜRZTRAMINER 2007
Sweet White | 2011 up to 2022   **92**

ALTENBOURG GEWÜRZTRAMINER 2006
Sweet White | 2011 up to 2026   **92**

ALTENBOURG GEWÜRZTRAMINER
QUINTESSENCE DE GRAINS NOBLES 2007
Sweet White | 2011 up to 2030   **97**

ALTENBOURG PINOT GRIS 2007
Semi-Dry White | 2011 up to 2027   **92**

ALTENBOURG PINOT GRIS 2006
Semi-Dry White | 2011 up to 2021   **91**

ALTENBOURG PINOT GRIS
SÉLECTION DE GRAINS NOBLES 2007
Sweet White | 2011 up to 2027   **95**

GEWÜRZTRAMINER CUVÉE LAURENCE 2007
Sweet White | 2011 up to 2022   **90**

GEWÜRZTRAMINER CUVÉE THÉO 2007
Semi-Dry White | 2011 up to 2017   **89**

GEWÜRZTRAMINER RÉSERVE PERSONNELLE 2007
Semi-Dry White | 2011 up to 2015   **88**

PINOT BLANC RÉSERVE 2007
White | 2011 up to 2015   **89**

PINOT GRIS CUVÉE LAURENCE 2007
Sweet White | 2011 up to 2022   **90**

PINOT GRIS CUVÉE SAINTE-CATHERINE 2007
White | 2011 up to 2017   **88**

RIESLING CUVÉE THÉO 2007
White | 2011 up to 2017   **90**

SYLVANER RÉSERVE 2007
White | 2011 up to 2017   **89**

Older vintages

ALSACE GRAND CRU FURSTENTUM
GEWÜRZTRAMINER 2004
Sweet White | 2011 up to 2024   **95**
Elegant and complex on the nose with
roasted notes; of great depth on the palate
with remarkable purity, this is a collector's
gewürztraminer.

ALSACE GRAND CRU FURSTENTUM
GEWÜRZTRAMINER VENDANGES TARDIVES 2005
Sweet White | 2011 up to 2030   **97**
Rich and profound with a honeyed character and notes of toasted hazelnuts and
smoke, this is almost dry with a spicy character on the finish. Great potential.

ALSACE GRAND CRU MAMBOURG GEWÜRZTRAMINER
SÉLECTION DE GRAINS NOBLES 2005
Sweet White | 2011 up to 2030   **95**
Very rich with notes of honey and dates, this
wine is luscious, with phenomenal power.

ALSACE GRAND CRU MARCKRAIN
GEWÜRZTRAMINER 2005
Sweet White | 2011 up to 2020   **93**
The first vintage this domaine has produced
from this vineyard, this wine is rich and full
with good tension, lovely depth, and a finish on candied fruits and smoke.

ALSACE GRAND CRU SCHLOSSBERG RIESLING 2006
White | 2011 up to 2016   **90**
A dry riesling, elegant with fat, very crystalline, with very linear acidity. A dry wine of
breeding.

ALSACE GRAND CRU SCHLOSSBERG
RIESLING CUVÉE SAINTE-CATHERINE 2006
White | 2011 up to 2026   **94**
Old vines from midslope yield again an
exceptional wine, concentrated and very
pure with a long finish.

ALSACE GRAND CRU SCHLOSSBERG RIESLING
CUVÉE SAINTE-CATHERINE L'INÉDIT 2006
Sweet White | 2011 up to 2030   **97**
Harvested slightly overripe, l'Inédit offers a
medium-dry balance and elegance, with
notes of citrus peel on the finish. A wine to
age to integrate its sweetness.

ALSACE GRAND CRU SCHLOSSBERG RIESLING
SÉLECTION DE GRAINS NOBLES 2004
Sweet White | 2011 up to 2030   **98**
With the true concentration of Schlossberg
carried by the fruit and acidity of riesling,
this wine is a tour de force, combining crystalline purity, botrytis, and great concentration. A luscious wine of great precision.

ALSACE GRAND CRU SCHLOSSBERG RIESLING
VENDANGES TARDIVES 2004
Sweet White | 2011 up to 2024   92
A fine, sweet Vendange Tardive with lovely
purity, finishing on aromas of citrus peel
and a note of exotic fruit.

ALSACE GRAND CRU SCHLOSSBERG RIESLING
VENDANGES TARDIVES "TRIE SPÉCIALE" 2004
Sweet White | 2011 up to 2020   94
A late selection of a parcel of Schlossberg
yielded a sweet wine, very crystalline, with
aromas of citrus fruits and zest. The real
essence of riesling.

ALTENBOURG GEWÜRZTRAMINER 2005
Sweet White | 2011 up to 2020   92
A very pure, intense wine with good structure supported by good ripeness. It retains
a remarkable balance that combines the
depth of the terroir with a long finish.

ALTENBOURG GEWÜRZTRAMINER
VENDANGES TARDIVES 2005
Sweet White | 2011 up to 2030   96
A wine with fresh aromas, superb volume,
and a finish remarkable in its depth and purity.

ALTENBOURG GEWÜRZTRAMINER
QUINTESSENCE DE GRAINS NOBLES 2005
Sweet White | 2011 up to 2040   97
The quintessence of balance and depth, this
is luscious and perfectly balanced by pronounced acidity that leaves the finish clean
and fresh. An extreme wine.

ALTENBOURG PINOT GRIS 2005
Semi-Dry White | 2011 up to 2020   92
A very seductive wine, spices and praline
on the nose, full and lightly sweet on the
palate, with depth. Great terroir, great vintage: superb.

GEWÜRZTRAMINER CUVÉE LAURENCE 2005
Sweet White | 2011 up to 2015   90
At the same time floral and superripe on the
nose, this wine is elegant and sweet, with a
smoky note that emerges on the finish.

PINOT GRIS CUVÉE LAURENCE 2005
Sweet White | 2011 up to 2015   90
The wine is sweet, dry, and very clean with
pronounced ripeness that brings richness
to the ensemble.

RIESLING CUVÉE SAINTE-CATHERINE 2007
White | 2011 up to 2020   92
Floral and ripe on the nose, pure and fat on
the palate, this is clean and full, a superb
success.

Red: 2.7 acres; pinot noir 18%. White: 68.9 acres;
muscat and chasselas 5%, pinot blanc and auxerrois
6%. Annual production: 135,000 bottles

DOMAINE ZIND-HUMBRECHT

4, route de Colmar
68230 Turckheim
Phone 00 33 3 89 27 02 05
Fax 00 33 3 89 27 22 58
o.humbrecht@zind-humbrecht.fr

Léonard Humbrecht revolutionized winemaking practice in Alsace back in the 1960s and
1970s by focusing on limited yields from great
terroirs. Ten years later, the Zind-Humbrecht
winery ranked among the finest in the world.
Since then, the business has gradually been
taken over by Léonard's son Olivier, now at
the peak of his talents and supported by an
enthusiastic winemaking team who share his
commitment to quality improvement in the
cellars and vineyards alike. In the 1990s, the
wines were distinguished by a well-balanced
sweetness that came from very ripe grapes.
Following conversion to biodynamic methods
at the turn of the millennium, the wines are
now drier and more acidic, sometimes more
alcoholic, too. Witness the magnificent 2005
vintage and the terrifically pure 2006 with its
well-balanced, perfectly ripe acidity. The
gewürztraminer performed particularly well,
but the terroir also shines through in every
other bottle—deliciously smoky in the Rangen and perfectly acidic in the Clos Windsbuhl. The wines show a brisk mineral edge
that is unlikely to please fans of the richly
styled pinots gris of the 1990s. But others
will love these wines for their endless food-
pairing possibilities—many of them being
driven more by terroir than by fruit.

Recently tasted
ALSACE GRAND CRU BRAND RIESLING 2007
White | 2012 up to 2027   97

ALSACE GRAND CRU BRAND RIESLING
VIEILLES VIGNES 2007
White | 2012 up to 2030   98

ALSACE GRAND CRU GOLDERT
GEWÜRZTRAMINER 2007
Sweet White | 2015 up to 2030   96

ALSACE GRAND CRU GOLDERT GEWÜRZTRAMINER
SÉLECTION DE GRAINS NOBLES 2007
Sweet White | 2015 up to 2030   96

ALSACE GRAND CRU GOLDERT MUSCAT 2007
White | 2012 up to 2027   92

ALSACE GRAND CRU HENGST
GEWÜRZTRAMINER 2007
Sweet White | 2012 up to 2030   97

ALSACE GRAND CRU HENGST GEWÜRZTRAMINER
SÉLECTION DE GRAINS NOBLES 2007
Sweet White | 2015 up to 2030   97

ALSACE GRAND CRU RANGEN
GEWÜRZTRAMINER 2007
Sweet White | 2012 up to 2030   **97**

ALSACE GRAND CRU RANGEN PINOT GRIS 2007
White | 2012 up to 2027   **96**

ALSACE GRAND CRU RANGEN RIESLING 2007
White | 2012 up to 2027   **98**

CLOS HÄUSERER RIESLING 2007
White | 2011 up to 2022   **91**

CLOS JEBSAL PINOT GRIS
SÉLECTION DE GRAINS NOBLES 2007
Sweet White | 2015 up to 2030   **96**

CLOS JEBSAL PINOT GRIS
VENDANGES TARDIVES 2007
Sweet White | 2015 up to 2030   **96**

CLOS WINDSBUHL GEWÜRZTRAMINER 2007
Sweet White | 2011 up to 2027   **97**

CLOS WINDSBUHL PINOT GRIS 2007
Semi-Dry White | 2012 up to 2022   **94**

CLOS WINDSBUHL RIESLING 2007
White | 2011 up to 2027   **99**

GUEBERSCHWIHR GEWÜRZTRAMINER 2007
Sweet White | 2011 up to 2022   **90**

GUEBERSCHWIHR RIESLING 2007
White | 2011 up to 2017   **90**

HEIMBOURG GEWÜRZTRAMINER 2007
Sweet White | 2011 up to 2022   **93**

HEIMBOURG PINOT GRIS 2007
Sweet White | 2011 up to 2022   **91**

HEIMBOURG RIESLING 2007
White | 2011 up to 2017   **91**

HERRENWEG GEWÜRZTRAMINER VIEILLES
VIGNES 2007
Semi-Dry White | 2011 up to 2022   **92**

PINOT GRIS CALCAIRE 2007
Semi-Dry White | 2011 up to 2027   **91**

PINOT GRIS VIEILLES VIGNES 2007
Sweet White | 2011 up to 2017   **92**

ROTENBERG PINOT GRIS 2007
Sweet White | 2012 up to 2027   **92**

VIN DE TABLE CLOS WINDSBUHL 2007
White | 2011 up to 2022   **92**

VIN DE TABLE ZIND 2007
White | 2011 up to 2022   **91**

Older vintages

ALSACE GRAND CRU BRAND
RIESLING SÉLECTION DE GRAINS NOBLES 2006
Sweet White | 2011 up to 2036   **97**
The first Sélection de Grains Nobles produced from the Brand vineyard and the third riesling SGN ever produced at the domaine, this wine is still closed on the nose, with light aromas of fresh citrus and truffle, and strong concentration on the palate with very intense, pure sweetness. Less accessible than the Vendange Tardive, this is a wine with enormous potential for aging.

ALSACE GRAND CRU BRAND
RIESLING VENDANGES TARDIVES 2006
Sweet White | 2011 up to 2030   **98**
Produced from the Grand Cru's old vines, this wine is delicate on the nose with ripe sour fruit, and sweet on the palate with crystalline purity. A magnificent wine that surpasses the previous vintages.

ALSACE GRAND CRU GOLDERT GEWÜRZTRAMINER
VENDANGES TARDIVES 2006
White | 2011 up to 2026   **95**
A powerful Vendange Tardive, smoky on the nose, dense and crisp on the palate, with a long finish. The terroir is very present in this wine of great aging potential.

ALSACE GRAND CRU HENGST
GEWÜRZTRAMINER 2005
Sweet White | 2011 up to 2030   **91**
The wine is still closed with a subtle nose and full palate, sweet and powerful, remaining marked by tannins that confer the terroir. The power of the wine is tempered by the brilliant balance of concentration, sweetness, and acidity. A wine that must be aged for several years.

ALSACE GRAND CRU HENGST
GEWÜRZTRAMINER VENDANGES TARDIVES 2006
Sweet White | 2011 up to 2030   **98**
Already open on the nose, this wine slowly reveals incredible power. The strong concentration largely surpasses the sweetness. A wine with enormous potential, definitely for aging.

ALSACE GRAND CRU RANGEN
GEWÜRZTRAMINER 2005
Sweet White | 2011 up to 2030   **97**
Dominated by noble rot and terroir, here is an intense wine, rich and powerful with great unctuousness that brings it lots of precision. Spices, salty caramel, and gunflint accompany a very long finish that remains pure.

ALSACE GRAND CRU RANGEN
GEWÜRZTRAMINER VENDANGES TARDIVES 2006
Sweet White | 2011 up to 2026   **94**
Strongly marked by terroir, this amber-colored wine possesses a smoky, roasted nose of good intensity, rich on the palate with a spicy character. The finish is long and spicy.

ALSACE GRAND CRU RANGEN PINOT GRIS 2006
White | 2011 up to 2026   **96**
A Rangen of very typical amber color, this wine's smoky nose is marked by dried fruit and gunflint with a peaty note. The palate is dry, of great finesse and obvious class. An exceptional wine, real Rangen concentration.

ALSACE GRAND CRU RANGEN PINOT GRIS 2005
White | 2011 up to 2025   **98**
This Rangen is a total success in 2005. It already expresses its terroir with finesse: there's a finely smoky and spicy nose as well as a pure and mineral palate with concentration and incredible elegance. The long finish makes each mouthful a great tasting moment.

ALSACE GRAND CRU RANGEN RIESLING 2006
White | 2011 up to 2026   **94**
Harvested at a ripeness close to Vendange Tardive, this is very marked by stones and smoke on the nose. The wine is still sweet on the palate, rich with fine salinity. The finish is very long with lovely bitter notes. A wine for aging.

ALSACE GRAND CRU RANGEN RIESLING 2005
White | 2011 up to 2030   **97**
The stony nose is still closed, dry and concentrated on the palate with incredible finesse, leaving a long sensation of stones on the finish. A very great terroir wine.

CLOS HÄUSERER RIESLING 2006
White | 2011 up to 2026   **92**
An open wine, ripe citrus on the fresh nose, still lightly sweet on the palate, with lots of volume. The minerality already expresses itself very well, but the wine merits patience to achieve better integration.

CLOS JEBSAL PINOT GRIS
SÉLECTION DE GRAINS NOBLES 2005
Sweet White | 2011 up to 2040   **93**
The nose is candied, very intense. The palate is luscious, rich with acidity that emerges through the notes of fruit paste and honey. An extreme dessert wine, rich in residual sugar and low in alcohol, giving the wine a great candied character. A wine that will benefit from a number of years of aging.

CLOS JEBSAL PINOT GRIS
VENDANGES TARDIVES 2006
Sweet White | 2011 up to 2026   **97**
The wine is very concentrated with a nose of yellow fruit; very rich on the palate with ripe acidity that gives freshness. The balance is very pure with a long finish on aromas of apricot and quince.

CLOS JEBSAL PINOT GRIS VENDANGES
TARDIVES 2005
Sweet White | 2011 up to 2030   **94**
A luscious wine, this is already open with overripe aromas. The palate is powerful, concentrated, and very fine with notes of cocoa on the finish, marking great-quality botrytis. A wine for long aging.

CLOS WINDSBUHL GEWÜRZTRAMINER 2006
Sweet White | 2011 up to 2026   **96**
A Clos Windsbuhl with a peppery nose, this is harmonious and of great purity on the palate, with depth and fat. Its texture is remarkable.

CLOS WINDSBUHL GEWÜRZTRAMINER
VENDANGES TARDIVES 2005
Sweet White | 2011 up to 2030   **99**
The second Vendange Tardive gewürztraminer harvested in Clos Windsbuhl since 1988; in 2005, the entire parcel was harvested late. The nose is a pure marvel, already open on aromas of zest and ripe fruit with great finish. The palate possesses exceptional purity and depth that amplify the sensation of sweetness; then the acidity takes over, rapidly yielding a dessert wine of rare elegance. The finish, pure as mineral water, reinforces the balance of this great dessert wine.

CLOS WINDSBUHL PINOT GRIS 2006
Semi-Dry White | 2011 up to 2026   **96**
A wine harvested superripe, this offers depth and remarkable purity with praline and honey notes on the palate. The still-present sweetness is perfectly integrated with balanced volume.

CLOS WINDSBUHL PINOT GRIS
VENDANGES TARDIVES 2005
Sweet White | 2011 up to 2030   **98**
The average intensity of the nose hides a palate of great precision, luscious and profound. The limestone soils bring good acidity, great depth, and lemongrass notes on the finish. A great dessert wine, close to perfection.

CLOS WINDSBUHL RIESLING 2006
White | 2011 up to 2026   **98**
The limestone soil of Clos Windsbuhl yielded a splendid wine, fruity on the nose, marked by stones, with a full palate of depth. A dry wine with perfectly balanced alcohol and acidity, lots of minerality, and great length on the finish.

CLOS WINDSBUHL RIESLING 2005
White | 2011 up to 2025   96
The nose is already strongly marked by lime-stone terroir, leading to a powerful palate, mineral and very concentrated. A dry Clos Windsbuhl with a long finish.

GUEBERSCHWIHR GEWÜRZTRAMINER 2006
Sweet White | 2011 up to 2016   90
A very ripe gewürztraminer, this is fine on the palate with sweetness and intense fruit. It feels rich, with a long finish.

GUEBERSCHWIHR RIESLING 2006
White | 2011 up to 2021   90
Harvested ripe, this wine is very aromatic, with a full palate that possesses fat. A flavorful wine.

HEIMBOURG PINOT GRIS SÉLECTION DE GRAINS NOBLES 2005
Sweet White | 2011 up to 2030   95
A pure wine affected by high-quality botrytis, this offers a fine, full-bodied sweetness that is balanced by still-subtle acidity. The terroir of Heimbourg is just beginning to express itself, bringing depth to the wine. The finish is very long without any heaviness. Needs several years of aging.

HEIMBOURG PINOT NOIR 2005
Red | 2011 up to 2020   90
An intense pinot noir marked by black fruits and maturation in new oak barrels, very powerful on the palate with pronounced tannin. The material is there but needs time to digest the wood.

HEIMBOURG RIESLING 2006
White | 2011 up to 2021   91
A riesling very ripe and fruity on the nose, full and fat on the palate, with a spicy finish.

HERRENWEG GEWÜRZTRAMINER 2006
Semi-Dry White | 2011 up to 2021   90
The wine is rich and concentrated with great purity on the palate, very full with a long finish on aromas of rose and spices. A fat wine of dry balance that will be ideal at the table in several years.

HERRENWEG GEWÜRZTRAMINER 2005
Semi-Dry White | 2011 up to 2020   92
The nose is very intense and very pure with fragrances of rose and sweet spice. The palate is ripe, very mineral, with a velvety character reminiscent of rose petals. A powerful wine that retains the finesse of Herrenweg.

HERRENWEG GEWÜRZTRAMINER VIEILLES VIGNES 2006
Semi-Dry White | 2011 up to 2013   91
From old vines at the heart of Herrenweg, the wine offers a deep gold color, a very ripe roasted nose with notes of dried flowers, and a full, fat palate with dry balance. A powerful wine that retains much elegance.

PINOT GRIS THANN 2005
Sweet White | 2011 up to 2020   90
From the higher part of the Grand Cru Rangen (although this wine is not sold as a Grand Cru), this is already open with smoky aromas typical of the volcanic terroir. The palate offers minerality and acidity that strongly balance the residual sugar, resulting in a taut, racy wine.

PINOT GRIS VIEILLES VIGNES 2006
Sweet White | 2011 up to 2021   91
From sixty-plus-year-old vines in Herrenweg, this wine was harvested very ripe, giving a nose of ripe fruits and a concentrated palate, sweet and very fat. The purity of the wine is remarkable.

ROTENBERG PINOT GRIS 2006
Sweet White | 2011 up to 2026   92
A wine harvested very ripe, this offers quince and honey on the nose with a note of under-brush, while it is deep and sweet on the palate, with a spicy finish. Concentrated with great purity, this merits patience.

ROTENBERG PINOT GRIS SÉLECTION DE GRAINS NOBLES 2005
Sweet White | 2011 up to 2025   95
Matured in new, 600-liter barrels, this wine is ripe and toasty with an intense nose of honey and dried fruit, then rich on the palate with very intense sweetness. A very concentrated wine of great aging potential.

TURCKHEIM GEWÜRZTRAMINER 2006
White | 2011 up to 2016   90
A dry gewürztraminer, roasted and smoky on the nose, aromatic on the palate, with fat and a finish on noble spices. This powerful wine will marry well with spicy cuisine.

WINTZENHEIM GEWÜRZTRAMINER 2006
Sweet White | 2011 up to 2021   92
From equal parts Herrenweg and Grand Cru Hengst, the wine is very intense on the nose with aromas of sweet spices and a smoky note and presents a full palate, dense and very fat. A wine with depth.

WINTZENHEIM GEWÜRZTRAMINER 2005
Sweet White | 2011 up to 2015   92
Half Herrenweg and half Grand Cru Hengst, this wine is fat, crystalline, and mineral with a pronounced spicy character that finishes on notes of rose and exotic fruits. A dry and dense gewürztraminer that will be a perfect companion at the table.

Red: 2.5 acres; pinot 1.6%. White: 96.4 acres; gewürztraminer 30.8%, muscat 1.5%, pinot d'Alsace 7%. pinot gris 28%, riesling 30.5%. Annual production: 160,000 bottles

DOMAINE VALENTIN ZUSSLIN

57, Grand-Rue
68500 Orschwihr
Phone 00 33 3 89 76 82 84
Fax 00 33 3 89 76 64 36
info@zusslin.com
www.zusslin.com

Jean-Marie Zusslin is part of a family team that includes son Jean-Paul in the cellar and daughter Marie in charge of sales and communication. Grape quality and the standard of vinification continue to improve since the estate converted to biodynamics in 1997. The fruit is picked in several batches and arrives at the winery in shallow bins for slow, direct-to-press processing. This is followed by natural fermentation and long maturation on lees in tanks and oak vats. The wines have the power and structure of their native terroirs but not at the expense of superb purity and a delicate, supple mouthfeel. The aim is to ferment very ripe grapes to dryness, producing alcohol levels that often add a perceived sweetness (moelleux). The pinot noir and crémant wines are made in the same way—with devastatingly charming results.

Recently tasted

ALSACE GRAND CRU PFINGSTBERG RIESLING 2007
White | 2011 up to 2022　　　　　94

BOLLENBERG MUSCAT 2007
White | 2011 up to 2015　　　　　88

BOLLENBERG RIESLING 2007
White | 2011 up to 2022　　　　　91

CLOS LIEBENBERG SYLVANER 2007
White | 2011 up to 2015　　　　　87

PINOT NOIR CUVÉE HARMONIE 2007
Red | 2011 up to 2022　　　　　91

Older vintages

ALSACE GRAND CRU PFINGSTBERG RIESLING 2005
White | 2011 up to 2020　　　　　92
A perfect expression of the terroir, with great finesse, concentration, and elegance, and with aromas of great purity.

ALSACE GRAND CRU PFINGSTBERG RIESLING 2003
White | 2011 up to 2020　　　　　90
The nose is very pure and already mineral. The palate is also mineral, full and very fine with a light sweetness supported by fine acidity. Well nourished by underground sources, Pfingstberg suffers less dehydration than other vineyards, resulting in a wine of remarkable freshness.

BOLLENBERG GEWÜRZTRAMINER 2006
White | 2011 up to 2016　　　　　90
A rich wine with dried flowers and spices on the nose, this is dry on the palate, full and mineral on the long finish. Suberb depth. An ideal companion for great spicy cuisine.

BOLLENBERG GEWÜRZTRAMINER
LA CHAPELLE 2005
White | 2011 up to 2020　　　　　91
A concentrated gewürztraminer, straight and dry, with depth and great purity on the palate. The finish is long.

BOLLENBERG GEWÜRZTRAMINER VENDANGES TARDIVES 2004
Sweet White | 2011 up to 2020　　　90
A perfectly structured Vendange Tardive, with a nose of candied citrus and spices, a sweet palate kept taut by good acidity, and an almost dry finish on aromas of citrus zest.

BOLLENBERG MUSCAT 2005
White | 2011 up to 2013　　　　　88
Very beautiful muscat, terribly seductive on the nose, supple on the palate with ripe extract of great purity. A superb aperitif muscat.

CLOS LIEBENBERG PINOT GRIS 2005
White | 2011 up to 2015　　　　　89
A dry pinot gris of great beauty, this offers hazelnut and yeast aromas that lead to a pure palate, dense, with very fine acidity.

CLOS LIEBENBERG PINOT GRIS 2003
White | 2011 up to 2013　　　　　92
Situated at the edge of Pfingstberg, Clos Liebenberg yielded a dry pinot gris, very rich and floral on the nose, with pronounced minerality and fat on the palate. A very successful pinot gris in a delicate vintage.

CLOS LIEBENBERG RIESLING 2005
White | 2011 up to 2020　　　　　90
A dry, mineral wine with remarkable acidity. Maturation on the lees in cask brings the wine fat as well as a light touch of wood. A riesling for grand tables, for aging.

PINOT NOIR CUVÉE HARMONIE 2005
Red | 2011 up to 2015　　　　　90
A cuvée produced only in the best vintages, the 2005 follows and even surpasses the 2003 with its ripe, concentrated flavor, depth, and silky tannins. Drink or keep.

Red: 4.1 acres; pinot noir 13%. White: 26.7 acres; riesling 19%, auxerrois 20%, chardonnay 3%, chasselas 2%, gewürztraminer 18%, muscat Ottonel 6%, sylvaner 2%. Annual production: 90,000 bottles

Bettane & Desseauve
Selections for Beaujolais

Beaujolais

Beaujolais, land of the Pierres Dorées (Golden Stones) and Beaujolais Nouveau, is a region that is often overlooked for high-quality wines. The worldwide phenomenon that is Beaujolais Nouveau has been both a blessing and a curse for the area. On the one hand, impressive marketing campaigns carried out by large suppliers have made the region of Beaujolais known around the planet; on the other hand, a large majority of the wines shipped on the third Thursday of November are little more than an industrial product that could come from almost anywhere. For high-quality producers, the success of Beaujolais Nouveau has hurt the region's image, making it harder for their wines to be taken seriously. Nonetheless, there are countless winemakers located throughout the region who are dedicated to making high-quality wines from great terroirs, wines that can be drunk young but also have the capacity to age quite well.

The northern end of the Beaujolais marks a brilliant start to the gamay territory, being home to the most robust of the Beaujolais crus: Saint-Amour, Juliénas, Fleurie, Moulin-à-Vent, and Chénas. Exclusively made from the gamay grape, the wines they produce are fruit-forward and rich in natural alcohol, and should be served slightly chilled. Left to age for more than five years, the best of them come close to good burgundy. Note that declassified wines from any of these crus may also be sold as generic burgundy. Cru Beaujolais wines from the villages of Brouilly, Chiroubles, and Regnié are fruitier, with a more precocious bouquet. A good Morgon, meanwhile, exhibits a power and aging potential that is reminiscent of Moulin-à-Vent. Beaujolais and Beaujolais Villages wines are altogether simpler in terms of flavor and should be drunk within one or two years of the vintage.

Beaujolais Vineyards

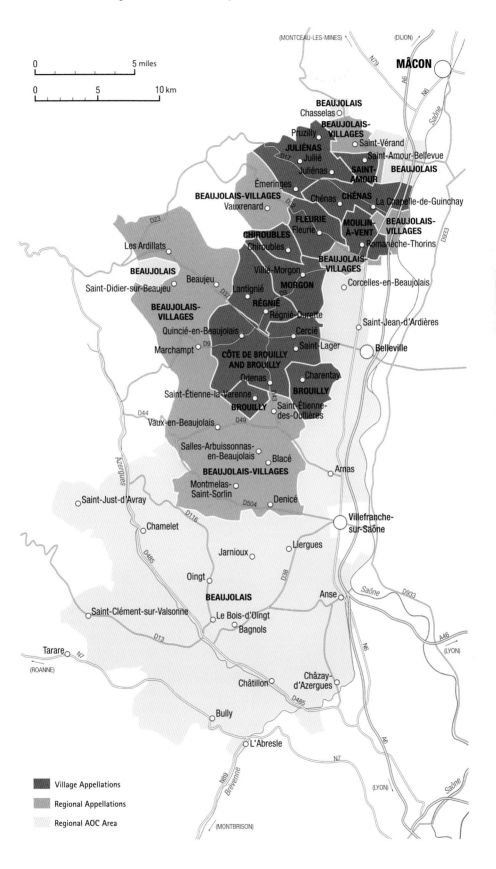

0 ——— 5 miles

0 — 5 — 10 km

(MONTCEAU-LES-MINES)   (DIJON)

MÂCON

N79
A6
N6
Saône

BEAUJOLAIS
Chasselas ○
Pruzilly ○ **BEAUJOLAIS-VILLAGES**
JULIÉNAS   ○ Saint-Vérand
○ Jullié   Saint-Amour-Bellevue ○
Juliénas ○   **SAINT-AMOUR**   **BEAUJOLAIS**
Émeringes ○   **CHÉNAS**
BEAUJOLAIS-VILLAGES   Chénas ○   La Chapelle-de-Guinchay ○
Vauxrenard ○   **FLEURIE**   **MOULIN-À-VENT**   **BEAUJOLAIS-VILLAGES**
Fleurie ○
CHIROUBLES   ○ Romanèche-Thorins
Chiroubles ○   **BEAUJOLAIS-VILLAGES**
Les Ardillats ○   Villié-Morgon ○
○ Corcelles-en-Beaujolais
BEAUJOLAIS   Beaujeu ○   **MORGON**
Saint-Didier-sur-Beaujeu ○   Lantignié ○   **RÉGNIÉ**
BEAUJOLAIS-VILLAGES   Régnié-Durette ○   ○ Saint-Jean-d'Ardières
Quincié-en-Beaujolais ○   Cercié ○
Marchampt ○   Saint-Lager ○   ○ **Belleville**
CÔTE DE BROUILLY AND BROUILLY
Odenas ○   Charentay ○
Saint-Étienne-la-Varenne ○   **BROUILLY**
BROUILLY   Saint-Étienne-des-Oullières ○
Vaux-en-Beaujolais ○
D44   D49
Salles-Arbuissonnas-en-Beaujolais ○
○ Blacé   ○ Arnas
BEAUJOLAIS-VILLAGES
Montmelas-Saint-Sorlin ○
Saint-Just-d'Avray ○   Denicé ○   **Villefranche-sur-Saône** ○
Chamelet ○   Liergues ○
Jarnioux ○   Saône
Oingt ○   Anse ○   D933
BEAUJOLAIS
Saint-Clément-sur-Valsonne ○   Le Bois-d'Oingt ○
Bagnols ○   A46
Tarare ○   N7   (LYON)
(ROANNE)   Châzay-d'Azergues ○
Châtillon ○   D485
Bully ○
○ L'Abresle   N7   Saône
N89   (LYON)
Brévenne   (MONTBRISON)

■ Village Appellations

■ Regional Appellations

■ Regional AOC Area

DOMAINE DANIEL BOULAND

Lieu-dit Corcelette
69910 Villié-Morgon
Phone 00 33 4 74 69 14 71
Fax 00 33 4 74 69 14 71
bouland.daniel@free.fr

Daniel Bouland—remember the first name, because he is one of many Boulands in Villié-Morgon—is one of the most perfectionist winegrowers in the entire Beaujolais region. The way he tends his vines is an example to all. He harvests ripe grapes and aims to make wines for cellaring that express their terroir—not that overheated fruit seen in so many wines these days! His Corcelette wines are fabulously harmonious and full-bodied; his Château Thivin–like Côte de Brouilly is cast in the same mold but sourced from an even classier terroir.

CÔTE DE BROUILLY MÉLANIE 2007
Red I 2011 up to 2015　　　　　　**90**
Superb aromatic definition, a marvelous cherry finish, velvety and fresh. Great art for this Beaujolais cru!

CÔTE DE BROUILLY MÉLANIE 2006
Red I Drink now　　　　　　**90**
A perfect expression of the vintage and the terroir, great aromas, great grapes, great mastery. A master at work, and there aren't many in Beaujolais!

MORGON CORCELETTE 2007
Red I 2011 up to 2017　　　　　　**92**
Superb presence of the terroir, full body, but less finesse on the finish than in the Côte de Brouilly.

MORGON CORCELETTE 2006
Red I Drink now　　　　　　**88**
There is a strong presence of the terroir. The flesh is less complete than in the Côte de Brouilly because of the slightly rustic tannins.

MORGON VIEILLES VIGNES 2007
Red I 2011 up to 2022　　　　　　**93**
Perfection, or almost, for this vintage and vineyard, perfectly velvety and rounded, the grapes harvested at the pinnacle of ripeness: a great example for its peers!

Red: 14.8 acres; gamay 100%. **Annual production:** 36,000 bottles

DOMAINE JEAN-MARC BURGAUD

Morgon
69910 Villié-Morgon
Phone 00 33 4 74 69 16 10
Fax 00 33 4 74 69 16 10
jeanmarcburgaud@libertysurf.fr
www.jean-marc-burgaud.com

With ambitious and competent young winemakers such as Jean-Marc Burgaud, Morgon's future is guaranteed. His vineyards are located at the heart of the historic "Côte du Py" vineyard, and also in other high-quality terroirs in Regnié and Villié-Morgon, and he makes wines that are meant to be cellared. His 2005s are the most harmonious yet, and the 2006s will also be worthy wines.

Recently tasted

MORGON CÔTE DU PY 2008
Red I 2011 up to 2018　　　　　　**89**

MORGON CÔTE DU PY JAMES 2007
Red I 2011 up to 2017　　　　　　**90**

MORGON CÔTE DU PY RÉSERVE 2007
Red I 2011 up to 2017　　　　　　**88**

MORGON LES CHARMES 2008
Red I 2011 up to 2015　　　　　　**87**

Older vintages

MORGON CÔTE DU PY 2006
Red I 2011 up to 2013　　　　　　**86**
Great color, very marked spicy notes on the nose, powerful body that is somewhat drying due to the winemaking, taut and wild character, great vinous quality for the vintage. Wait two years.

MORGON CÔTE DU PY 2005
Red I 2011 up to 2015　　　　　　**90**
The truly "historic" part of this plot's terroir, at General Sauzey's cross, gives the most refined, subtle Py, here vinified with perfect respect for the terroir.

MORGON CÔTE DU PY JAMES 2006
Red I 2011 up to 2016　　　　　　**86**
The same intensity of character and the same rigid tannins, with more marked wiriness than the two other cuvées. It would need a little more fruit to have good balance.

MORGON CÔTE DU PY RÉSERVE 2006
Red I 2011 up to 2013　　　　　　**87**
Very tannic and taut, with tannins a little more rustic than we might hope, but it does not lack for character!

Red: 46.9 acres; gamay 100%. **Annual production:** 60,000 bottles

DOMAINE CHIGNARD

69820 Fleurie
Phone 00 33 4 74 04 11 87
Fax 00 33 4 74 69 81 97
domaine.chignard@wanadoo.fr

Michel Chignard is the most skillful wine-maker in Fleurie. No one knows better than he how to capture those famous floral aromas that are typical of this cru, while retaining the characteristic expression of vines grown in granitic sands. The powerful and elegant cuvée Les Moriers comes from one of the finest parcels in this cru, while his cuvée Spéciale is a rare example of masterful cask aging.

Recently tasted
FLEURIE CUVÉE SPÉCIALE 2007
Red | 2011 up to 2017   **91**

Older vintages
FLEURIE CUVÉE SPÉCIALE 2006
Red | 2011 up to 2014   **90**
With its maturation in oak and the choice of grapes, this cuvée outdoes the Moriers in vinosity and power of expression. It will take another year for the various elements to come into balance.

FLEURIE CUVÉE SPÉCIALE 2005
Red | 2011 up to 2015   **92**
Finesse, grace, complexity, and commendable oak aging (so hard to accomplish in Fleurie). One of the pinnacles of Beaujolais and a model for all serious winemakers in the area to follow.

FLEURIE LES MORIERS 2007
Red | 2011 up to 2015   **89**
Excellent aromatic purity, and plenty of charm and freshness in the floral aromas. A nice texture. A perfect Fleurie!

FLEURIE LES MORIERS 2006
Red | 2011 up to 2013   **88**
Quite complete for the vintage. Tender and velvety but well supported by very expressive tannins. Not a bit diluted!

Red: 20.5 acres; gamay 100%. Annual production: 35,000 bottles

DOMAINE LOUIS-CLAUDE DESVIGNES

135, rue de la Voûte
69910 Villié-Morgon
Phone 00 33 4 74 04 23 35
Fax 00 33 4 74 69 14 93
louis.desvigne@wanadoo.fr
www.louis-claude-desvignes.com

We regard this winery as *the* reference point for Morgon wines—far superior to other producers who may be more fashionable in Paris or Lyon but who make superficial wines. Depth is what they deal in here: deep Morgons from outstanding terroirs that aim to express the most original aspects of the soil, even if it does make them a bit robust en primeur. Louis-Claude has now passed the baton to his children, who have adopted their father's credo and inherited his gift for winemaking. As always, the Javernières showed slightly more flesh than the Côte du Py.

Recently tasted
MORGON CÔTE DU PY 2007
Red | 2012 up to 2022   **92**

MORGON CÔTE DU PY JAVERNIÈRES 2007
Red | 2012 up to 2022   **93**

Older vintages
MORGON CÔTE DU PY 2006
Red | 2011 up to 2013   **92**
Slightly deeper in color than the Javernières, more wiry, longer, almost like a Côte Rôtie in its violet aromas, firm tannins; very great Beaujolais!

MORGON CÔTE DU PY 2005
Red | 2011 up to 2025   **90**
A well-rounded Morgon, as satisfying and faithful an expression of its robust terroir as can be. Can be cellared for twenty years!

MORGON CÔTE DU PY JAVERNIÈRES 2006
Red | 2011 up to 2013   **90**
Excellent aromas of kirsch and violet, a tender body, the perfect definition of its terroir, a generous, tender wine that is already very appealing today.

MORGON CÔTE DU PY JAVERNIÈRES 2005
Red | 2011 up to 2020   **91**
The same great tension and strong expression of the terroir as the Côte du Py, with slightly more elegance and silkiness to the texture. Very firm tannins: just what you would expect from a wine made for aging.

Red: 32.1 acres; gamay 100%. Annual production: 50,000 bottles

GEORGES DUBOEUF

Quartier de la Gare
71570 Romanèche-Thorins
Phone 00 33 3 85 35 34 20
Fax 00 33 3 85 35 34 24
gduboeuf@duboeuf.com
www.duboeuf.com

The "king of Beaujolais" knows how to make every kind of wine and plenty of it, too, whether good French table wines or niche wines and elite bottlings from the northern crus, with aromas ranging from hard candies (not our favorite) to complex nuances of granite or schistose soils. He offers a complete range of Beaujolais wines, each one made in a style to suit the whims and palates of his various customers. The white Mâcon offerings show a tendency to premature aging, and the Beaujolais can't take more than three or four years' aging either. The range is very broad but is whittled down here to include only those wines likely to appeal to devotees of grand vin—who would be making a big mistake if they disregarded them.

Recently tasted

BROUILLY 2007
Red | 2011 up to 2013   **86**

BROUILLY DOMAINE DES PIERRES SOLEIL 2007
Red | 2011 up to 2017   **89**

CHÉNAS 2007
Red | 2011 up to 2015   **88**

CHIROUBLES 2007
Red | 2011 up to 2015   **89**

CÔTE DE BROUILLY 2007
Red | 2011 up to 2014   **87**

FLEURIE 2007
Red | 2011 up to 2017   **90**

MORGON 2007
Red | 2011 up to 2013   **85**

MORGON BELLES GRIVES 2007
Red | 2011 up to 2017   **88**

MOULIN-À-VENT 2007
Red | 2011 up to 2015   **87**

SAINT-AMOUR 2007
Red | 2011 up to 2013   **86**

SAINT-AMOUR DOMAINE LOUIS DAILLY 2007
Red | 2011 up to 2013   **87**

Older vintages

BEAUJOLAIS-VILLAGES CHÂTEAU DE VARENNES 2006
Red | Drink now   **88**
One of the best Village wines of the tasting, bluish, fat, long, with good personality and stuffing and a Brouilly character that hardly comes as a surprise.

BROUILLY 2006
Red | Drink now   **88**
Round, fat, easy-drinking, with the house's obvious style and a slight acetone note, but long, ripened to perfection, and ready to drink.

CHIROUBLES 2006
Red | Drink now   **86**
Deeply colored, fleshy, given a little heat for more body, but balanced, easy-drinking. We would have liked the impression of a little more granite!

CÔTE DE BROUILLY 2006
Red | Drink now   **89**
The terroir takes over from the house style here, with delicate licorice and aniseed aromas and great purity.

FLEURIE 2006
Red | 2011 up to 2013   **88**
Great color for the vintage, a substantial nose, excellent body, finer tannins than the Morgon, very successful, and representative of the year's potential.

JULIÉNAS CHÂTEAU DES CAPITANS 2006
Red | 2011 up to 2013   **87**
Very deep in color, with a powerful nose of plums, wonderfully velvety texture, firm tannins, a wine made from very ripe grapes; carefully made, though it lacks a bit of freshness to the fruit.

MORGON 2006
Red | 2011 up to 2013   **86**
Kirsch on the nose, excellent volume on the palate, somewhat drying tannins, a serious wine that is faithful to the terroir.

MOULIN-À-VENT 2006
Red | 2011 up to 2013   **87**
More Burgundian in color than the Fleurie, with vanilla barrel notes on the nose, supple, suave, fairly long, but the terroir's tautness is a little bit smoothed out by the oak!

Annual production: 30,000,000 bottles

DOMAINE JEAN-PAUL DUBOST

Le Tracot
69430 Lantignié
Phone 00 33 4 74 04 87 51
Fax 00 33 4 74 69 27 33
j.p-dubost@wanadoo.fr
www.domaine-dubost.com

This very genial, enterprising estate continues to make progress despite the current economic crisis. Its wines come from a wide range of appellations, from Brouilly to Moulin-à-Vent, and include an absolutely stunning selection of Beaujolais-Villages from the Regnié area. Sadly, the urge to use no sulfur is producing somewhat unstable wines, although these remain in the minority.

BEAUJOLAIS-VILLAGES LES MONTHIEUX 2006
Red | 2011 up to 2013   89
Powerful, fat, thick, with enveloping fleshiness for the vintage, a fine complex taste of ripe grapes, very slippery, a great success!

FLEURIE 2007
Red | 2011 up to 2013   88
Much more finesse than the 2006, powerful, velvety, still somewhat reduced, but it has yet to be bottled. The wine might deserve a better score.

MORGON 2006
Red | 2011 up to 2014   88
Fine color, rich, complex; the oak is better integrated than in the Fleurie; fat, ample, ambitious (frank vinification and sophisticated élevage).

MOULIN-À-VENT 2007
Red | 2011 up to 2013   90
The best of the 2007s, supple, suave, natural, long, but should be decanted at least two hours before serving.

Red: 29.7 acres; gamay 100%. White: 19.8 acres; chardonnay 70%, viognier 30%. Annual production: 140,000 bottles

CHÂTEAU DES JACQUES

Les Jacques
71570 Romanèche-Thorins
Phone 00 33 3 85 35 51 64
Fax 00 33 3 85 35 59 15
château-des-jacques@wanadoo.fr
www.louisjadot.com

In just a few years Louis Jadot's estate has become a reference point for high-flying Beaujolais—and the preferred supplier of those who believe that Beaujolais wines can be as respectable as those of the Côte-d'Or. One of Jadot's claims to fame is to have persuaded wine lovers and increasing numbers of producers that cask-aged wines do not dry out if properly handled. Needless to say, Jadot's bottlings from five separate parcels are the last word in modern-style Beaujolais. That said, it is his blended Moulin-à-Vent bottling that tends to stand out in most of our tastings—remarkable for its full body and standard of "finishing."

Recently tasted
BEAUJOLAIS-VILLAGES
GRAND CLOS DE LOYSE 2007
White | 2011 up to 2013   87

BOURGOGNE CLOS DE LOYSE 2007
White | 2011 up to 2013   88

MOULIN-À-VENT CHAMP DE COUR 2007
Red | 2011 up to 2017   90

MOULIN-À-VENT CLOS DES THORINS 2007
Red | 2011 up to 2017   88

MOULIN-À-VENT CLOS DU GRAND CARQUELIN 2007
Red | 2011 up to 2022   92

MOULIN-À-VENT GRAND CLOS DE ROCHEGRÈS 2007
Red | 2011 up to 2022   93

MOULIN-À-VENT LA ROCHE 2007
Red | 2011 up to 2022   92

Older vintages
MOULIN-À-VENT 2006
Red | 2011 up to 2014   86
The color isn't too dense. The mellow gamay aromas are cleverly matured in oak. Supple, delicate, good expression of the granitic soils of the area, but only average length.

MOULIN-À-VENT CHAMP DE COUR 2006
Red | 2011 up to 2016   88
Clearly rounder and fleshier than the basic Moulin-à-Vent, with notes of flowers and plums on the nose. Very round but with a distinctly earthy finish. Excellent élevage.

MOULIN-À-VENT CLOS DES THORINS 2006
Red | 2011 up to 2016   **89**
Very full, but with a more tender, open fruit character than the Champ de Cour. Stays focused on the tactile sensations of gamay.

MOULIN-À-VENT CLOS DES THORINS 2005
Red | 2011 up to 2025   **93**
Splendid structure, a great licorice scent, noble oak influence, very long. Superlative élevage, which is rare in the Beaujolais. A Grand Cru in all its power.

MOULIN-À-VENT
CLOS DU GRAND CARQUELIN 2006
Red | 2011 up to 2018   **90**
Great color, the most dense of the series. A powerful nose, more imposing body than the La Roche, nicely coated tannins. Once again, this feels more like a Gevrey-style pinot noir than gamay. Should age well.

MOULIN-À-VENT
GRAND CLOS DE ROCHEGRÈS 2006
Red | 2011 up to 2018   **91**
The ripest grapes and best taffeta texture of all the Clos wines. Ample, luscious body, well-coated tannins, very long. The most complete wine of the vintage.

MOULIN-À-VENT
GRAND CLOS DE ROCHEGRÈS 2005
Red | 2011 up to 2020   **95**
A masterpiece, undoubtedly the best young wine of the appellation that we have ever tasted. All the power of the vintage and distinction of the terroir. Classy élevage.

MOULIN-À-VENT LA ROCHE 2006
Red | 2011 up to 2016   **90**
A spicier, tauter nose than the Thorins. A different expression of the oak, better integrated, but because of its more ethereal texture it's starting to head in the direction of pinot noir. Refined, long, very Moulin-à-Vent in the aristocratic sense.

MOULIN-À-VENT LA ROCHE 2005
Red | 2011 up to 2020   **94**
A pleasant bouquet of brambles, leather, and spices. A stunning texture that reveals the gritty, sandy soil with incredible precision. Very long, with a taffeta finish.

Red: 79.1 acres; gamay 100%. White: 24.7 acres; chardonnay 100%. Annual production: 180,000 bottles

DOMAINE PAUL ET ÉRIC JANIN

71570 Romanèche-Thorins
Phone 00 33 3 85 35 52 80
Fax 00 33 3 85 35 21 77
pauljanin.fils@club-internet.fr

The Janins' estate is one of the leading lights of Romanèche-Thorins. Its manicured vineyards are predominantly planted in manganese-rich soils that emphasize the wines' spicy, very original taste of terroir and improve their aging potential. This is wine made for cellaring and vinified accordingly, pumping juice over the cap using special plates. Under Eric's influence, more of the wines are now aged in wood—and very successful it is, too!

Recently tasted
BEAUJOLAIS-VILLAGES
DOMAINE DES VIGNES DES JUMEAUX 2007
Red | 2011 up to 2013   **89**

MOULIN-À-VENT CLOS DU TREMBLAY 2007
Red | 2012 up to 2017   **93**

MOULIN-À-VENT
DOMAINE DES VIGNES DU TREMBLAY 2007
Red | 2011 up to 2015   **88**

MOULIN-À-VENT SÉDUCTION 2007
Red | 2012 up to 2017   **90**

Older vintages
MOULIN-À-VENT CLOS DU TREMBLAY 2006
Red | 2011 up to 2014   **91**
A model of terroir expression in this very fine bottling, which is spicy and firm but without being backward, full and plush. Will age beautifully, perhaps better than the 2005.

MOULIN-À-VENT CLOS DU TREMBLAY 2005
Red | 2011 up to 2013   **90**
Well rounded, velvety, racy, truffled, silky, long: a very pretty wine much in the style of the producer's great vintages.

MOULIN-À-VENT DOMAINE DES VIGNES DU TREMBLAY 2005
Red | 2011 up to 2013   **88**
Very expressive of its terroir, subtly marked by manganese, refined texture; precise and effective work.

MOULIN-À-VENT SÉDUCTION 2005
Red | 2011 up to 2015   **92**
Great winemaking, wonderful complexity, truly what one would expect of a great vintage.

Red: 24.7 acres; gamay 100%. Annual production: 50,000 bottles

DOMAINE HUBERT LAPIERRE

Les Gandelins cedex 324
71570 La Chapelle-de-Guinchay
Phone 00 33 3 85 36 74 89
Fax 00 33 3 85 36 79 69
hubert.lapierre@wanadoo.fr
www.domaine.lapierre.com

Hubert Lapierre's Chénas and Moulin-à-Vent wines are more remarkable for their easy-drinking immediate appeal than for deep texture or aging potential. Lovely, thirst-quenching wines that we just can't get enough of! His latest vintages are first-rate.

Recently tasted
CHÉNAS FÛT DE CHÊNE 2005
Red | 2011 up to 2015   89

CHÉNAS TRADITION 2007
Red | 2011 up to 2013   88

MOULIN-À-VENT TRADITION 2007
Red | 2011 up to 2015   88

Older vintages
CHÉNAS VIEILLES VIGNES 2007
Red | 2011 up to 2017   90
Excellent overall balance, joining smoothness, firmness, aromatic charm, and seriousness in the great tradition of the cru.

CHÉNAS VIEILLES VIGNES 2006
Red | 2011 up to 2013   88
Excellent balance for the vintage, a violet note close to those of the great Moulin-à-Vent wines, the tannins firm but in no way rustic. Very commendable.

MOULIN-À-VENT VIEILLES VIGNES 2007
Red | 2011 up to 2017   91
Full, fleshy, the aromas very powerful and more assertive than in 2006, very firm tannins for this producer, an excellent compromise between fruity and serious.

MOULIN-À-VENT VIEILLES VIGNES 2006
Red | 2011 up to 2013   88
Very supple, ultraripe grapes, mellow, unctuous, very representative of this excellent producer's style.

Red: 19.2 acres; gamay 100%. **Annual production:** 35,000 bottles

CHÂTEAU DES LUMIÈRES

Château des Jacques
71570 Romanèche-Thorins
Phone 00 33 3 85 35 51 64
Fax 00 33 3 85 35 59 15
château-des-lumieres@wanadoo.fr
www.louisjadot.com

Formerly Château Bellevue, this property is to Morgon what Château des Jacques is to Moulin-à-Vent. The same brilliant technical team, headed by winemaking guru Jacques Lardière, makes complete and generous wines in the same spirit as Château des Jacques, with a particular emphasis on precision in recent years. We have a soft spot for the Terres Noires, one of the tastiest and most accomplished of all the 2005s.

Recently tasted
MORGON 2007
Red | 2011 up to 2015   87

MORGON CÔTE DU PY 2007
Red | 2011 up to 2022   91

MORGON ROCHES NOIRES 2007
Red | 2011 up to 2017   90

Older vintages
MORGON 2006
Red | 2011 up to 2016   88
This remarkable blend produced a wine more full-bodied and deeply colored than the Jacques's Moulin-à-Vent. The firm tannins and generous body demand another three or four years of cellaring.

MORGON 2005
Red | 2011 up to 2015   88
A quintessential Morgon, masculine, firm, a bit too tannic.

MORGON CÔTE DU PY 2006
Red | 2011 up to 2021   91
Exceptional substance for the vintage, and perfectly adapted to aging in oak. The candy flavors of gamay disappear here to make room for a racy complex of secondary notes (pit fruits) and the texture of a cellaring wine. One of the pinnacles of this vintage in the Beaujolais: quite the opposite of the easy-drinking style of Parisian wine bars.

MORGON CÔTE DU PY 2005
Red | 2011 up to 2025   92
Great color and substance. A meaty wine with an imposing body and very firm tannins. Needs long cellaring.

Red: 86.5 acres; gamay 100%. **Annual production:** 80,000 bottles

DOMAINE LAURENT MARTRAY

Combiaty
69460 Odenas
Phone 00 33 4 74 03 51 03
Fax 00 33 4 74 03 50 92
martray.laurent@akeonet.com

As Desvignes is to Morgon, so, you might say, this estate is to Odenas: manicured vines and well-controlled fermentation processes that aim for texture and shape rather than immediate aromatic expression. Gourmet wines, in other words, for people who care about food. And given that they get better all the time, we fully expect this producer to go up a notch in our wine hierarchy before too long.

Recently tasted

BROUILLY CORENTIN 2007
Red | 2011 up to 2017　　92

BROUILLY MAS DE BAGNOLS 2007
Red | 2012 up to 2017　　89

Older vintages

BROUILLY CORENTIN 2006
Red | 2011 up to 2013　　89
Noticeable oak, but that gives the wine greater length and precision in its definition of the terroir and vintage; a very classy Brouilly.

BROUILLY LOÏS 2007
Red | 2011 up to 2017　　88
Fine color, the most harmonious of these three 2007s, the most typical of its appellation, and the longest on the palate. This wine is destined for true gamay lovers!

BROUILLY VIEILLES VIGNES 2007
Red | 2011 up to 2013　　90
Supple, very fruity, with charming texture, but slightly lacking in body.

BROUILLY VIEILLES VIGNES 2006
Red | 2011 up to 2009　　86
A nice pruny nose, supple, fleshy; fairly noticeable tannins; a terroir that is expressed with precision. A carefully made wine that nonetheless lacks great complexity.

CÔTE DE BROUILLY LES FEUILLÉES 2007
Red | 2011 up to 2017　　88
The old vines have made for a slightly more velvety, deeper wine, which nonetheless has the same slight touch of underripe grapes, heightening the aromatic charm but simplifying the texture a little.

Red: 22.2 acres; gamay 100%. **Annual production:** 30,000 bottles

MOMMESSIN

Le Pont des Samsons
69430 Quincié-en-Beaujolais
Phone 00 33 4 74 69 09 30
Fax 00 33 4 74 69 09 28
information@mommessin.fr

This house still turns out too many nondescript wines but, like all of the estates in the huge Boisset empire, it is committed to doing better. Its best cuvées are now vinified in a newly built, high-performance winery in Monternot. Mommessin sells production from the Boisset-owned Château de Pierreux, now sumptuously restored and doing better all the time.

Recently tasted

MORGON CÔTE DU PY 2007
Red | 2011 up to 2015　　87

MORGON LES CHARMES 2007
Red | 2011 up to 2015　　87

MOULIN-À-VENT LES CAVES 2007
Red | 2011 up to 2015　　87

Older vintages

BROUILLY CHÂTEAU DES PIERREUX RÉSERVE 2006
Red | 2011 up to 2016　　90
Wonderful color, a nose of cedar; the oak is still somewhat bitter and drying, though more so on the nose than on the palate. The wine shows rare qualities on the palate for the vintage, with a particularly tight mid-palate. A Brouilly for aging, which can be quite a rare occurrence!

BROUILLY CHÂTEAU DES PIERREUX RÉSERVE 2005
Red | 2011 up to 2015　　90
With its Bordeaux-shaped bottle, this wine might create a stir in the region! But it's hard to find a better-made Brouilly: its body and tannins and the integration of its oak are exemplary.

MOULIN-À-VENT LES CAVES 2006
Red | 2011 up to 2014　　88
A typical nose, with its notes of iris and licorice; powerful, velvety, very pronounced sense of terroir, good follow-through on the palate; earthier than the Fleurie, though the two are very close, geographically speaking, which is of course a sign of the mysteries of terroir.

POUILLY-FUISSÉ DEUX TERROIRS 2006
White | 2011 up to 2014　　92
Ultraripe grapes, a taste of candied fruit that is remarkably Pouilly, long, savory, a splendid expression of the vintage.

Annual production: 25,000,000 bottles

DOMAINE DES NUGUES

Les Pasquiers
69220 Lancié
Phone 00 33 4 74 04 14 00
Fax 00 33 4 74 04 16 73
earl-gelin@wanadoo.fr
www.domainedesnugues.com

This estate remains one of our benchmark Beaujolais-Villages producers, offering densely colored, powerful, but also very agreeable wines. The top wine is the cuvée Quintessence du Gamay. Lovely 2005; pity about the seriously corked bottle of Fleurie.

Recently tasted

BEAUJOLAIS-VILLAGES 2007
Red | 2011 up to 2013   **90**
Brambly with floral notes. A chewy wine, solid and concentrated, aromatic and elegant.

BEAUJOLAIS-VILLAGES 2006
Red | 2011 up to 2013   **89**
A full-bodied and concentrated wine, with a rich and powerful core. A Beaujolais that will go well with fortifying food.

FLEURIE 2007
Red | 2011 up to 2017   **90**
At this point, the wine is fruity and full rather than minerally.

Older vintages

BEAUJOLAIS-VILLAGES QUINTESSENCE DU GAMAY 2006
Red | 2011 up to 2016   **90**
Notes of spice on the nose, a lot of volume for the appellation, long, complex, luscious, worthy of a good many crus. A reference.

Red: 59.8 acres; gamay 100%. White: 2 acres. Annual production: 130,000 bottles

DOMAINE PIRON

Morgon
69910 Villié-Morgon
Phone 00 33 4 74 69 10 20
Fax 00 33 4 74 69 16 65
dominiquepiron@domaines-piron.fr
www.domaines-piron.fr

Dominique Piron is a conscientious wine-grower and skillful winemaker whose wines convey all the power of their terroir, wisely avoiding those fake-tasting flavors that are all too common these days. His Morgons from the famous Côte du Py are deep, fleshy, and expressive; and his latest acquisition, the Chénas Quartz (a joint venture with his friend Lafont), can rival many a Moulin-à-Vent for sheer finesse and class.

Recently tasted

BEAUJOLAIS DOMAINE DE LA CHANAISE 2007
White | 2011 up to 2013   **88**

BROUILLY DOMAINE DE COMBIATY 2007
Red | 2011 up to 2013   **88**

CHÉNAS DOMAINE PIRON-LAMELOISE CUVÉE QUARTZ 2007
Red | 2012 up to 2022   **93**

MORGON DOMAINE DE LA CHANAISE 2007
Red | 2011 up to 2013   **88**

MORGON DOMAINE DE LA CHANAISE CÔTE DU PY 2007
Red | 2011 up to 2017   **92**

MOULIN-À-VENT LES VIGNES DU VIEUX BOURG 2007
Red | 2011 up to 2017   **91**

Older vintages

CHÉNAS DOMAINE PIRON-LAMELOISE CUVÉE QUARTZ 2005
Red | 2011 up to 2050   **90**
A fine chocolaty nose that is nevertheless not heavy; a rich wine, velvety, long, racy, with the powerful characteristic of the vintage.

MOULIN-À-VENT LES VIGNES DU VIEUX BOURG 2006
Red | 2011 up to 2013   **90**
An excellent nose that is broad and generous, a powerful wine with very noticeable terroir, earthy, spicy, complex, a true old-vine Moulin-à-Vent. Drink this over a meal and don't overchill it.

Red: 118.6 acres; gamay 100%. White: 4.9 acres; chardonnay 100%. Annual production: 300,000 bottles

DOMAINE DES TERRES DORÉES

Crière
69380 Charnay
Phone 00 33 4 78 47 93 45
Fax 00 33 4 78 47 93 38
terresdorees@wanadoo.fr

Those familiar with Jean-Paul Brun's style find it difficult to drink any other kind of Beaujolais: his wines retain all the natural charm of the grapes thanks to cutting-edge vinification and the avoidance of those stupid stereotypes that have destroyed the credibility of one of the most popular appellations there is! His whites are by far the best we have ever tasted. When the year and inane legislation require it, he turns out "cuvées Spéciales" that often make for some thrilling tasting.

Recently tasted

BEAUJOLAIS CHARDONNAY
VINIFICATION BOURGUIGNONNE 2007
White | 2011 up to 2014   88

MOULIN-À-VENT 2007
Red | 2011 up to 2017   92

BEAUJOLAIS L'ANCIEN 2007
Red | 2011 up to 2015   88
A fruit-filled nose, vinous, deep with subtle notes of the élevage. On the palate, it is round, with elegant tannins. A pinot-like Beaujolais!

FLEURIE 2007
Red | 2011 up to 2017   91
Very floral, beautiful expression of the terroir. The mouth is concentrated, fleshy; the tannins are rich with an expressive minerality.

MORGON 2007
Red | 2011 up to 2017   92
Cherries and plums that evolve toward fresh fruit with a bit of air. The wine is concentrated and structured, and the tannins are velvety.

Older vintages

BEAUJOLAIS CHARDONNAY 2007
White | 2011 up to 2013   86
A precise fruit character, although not yet as developed as is usually the case, clean, nervy, a bit short.

BEAUJOLAIS L'ANCIEN 2005
Red | 2011 up to 2013   90
The perfect cellaring Beaujolais from the southern part of the region, powerful, taut, with noble tannins and plenty of pith; it promises to age well. Just as good as the crus of the north!

Red: 42 acres; gamay 90%, pinot 10%. White: 7.4 acres; chardonnay 100%. Annual production: 200,000 bottles

CHÂTEAU THIVIN

La Côte de Brouilly
69460 Odenas
Phone 00 33 4 74 03 47 53
Fax 00 33 4 74 03 52 87
geoffray@château-thivin.com
www.château-thivin.com

Château Thivin was one of the first to bottle its wines on the property and looks in better shape than ever today. Every wine, from the most supple and velvety Brouilly to the more mineral Côte de Brouilly, is a model of precision and finish: luscious, with the occasional hint of youthful feistiness. Claude Geoffray should be put in charge of the entire Beaujolais industry; his 2005 is a historic success.

Recently tasted

BEAUJOLAIS-VILLAGES MARGUERITE 2007
White | 2011 up to 2013   87

CÔTE DE BROUILLY LES SEPT VIGNES 2007
Red | 2011 up to 2017   89

CÔTE DE BROUILLY ZACCHARIE 2007
Red | 2012 up to 2022   92

BROUILLY 2007
Red | 2011 up to 2015   89
Elegant with nice floral notes. A rich, ripe, and succulent wine.

CÔTE DE BROUILLY LA CHAPELLE 2007
Red | 2011 up to 2017   90
Delicate fruit, a full-bodied wine, succulent with round tannins. Delicate aromas, subtle, lots of finesse. Not to be served too cold, as is often the problem with wines from Beaujolais.

Older vintages

BROUILLY 2006
Red | 2011 up to 2013   91
Exceptional finesse and aromatic purity for the vintage. Balanced body, great precision in the vinification. The benchmark Brouilly.

CÔTE DE BROUILLY ZACCHARIE 2006
Red | 2011 up to 2013   93
It's hard to imagine better grapes and better quality wine in this vintage, with deep fruit character and well-coated tannins despite their firmness.

Red: 61 acres; gamay 100%. Annual production: 140,000 bottles

TRÉNEL

33, chemin du Buéry
71850 Charnay-lès-Mâcon
Phone 00 33 3 85 34 48 20
Fax 00 33 3 85 20 55 01
contact@trenel.com
www.trenel.com

André Trénel ran this small négociant business for many years, specializing in wines from the Mâconnais and Beaujolais areas that were much sought after by restaurants in Lyon. To judge from the wines we have tasted, the business now tends toward a more modern style of wine—darker, deeper reds and fruitier whites—but just as carefully made as before and always deliciously drinkable from the day of bottling. Just what most consumers want!

Recently tasted
MÂCON-VILLAGES 2007
White | 2011 up to 2014   **92**

MORGON CÔTE DU PY 2007
Red | 2011 up to 2017   **90**

Older vintages
JULIÉNAS 2007
Red | 2011 up to 2013   **89**
Doubtless the bottling with the strongest personality in the lineup, with even a slight leathery note that is not unpleasant and will reassure lovers of "natural" wines! Powerful, fleshy, fairly long but not aggressive.

CHIROUBLES 2007
Red | 2011 up to 2013   **89**
An excellent pleasure-drinker, if drunk chilled to 54° to 55°F; fairly deep in color with abundant ripe fruit on both the nose and palate, very plush texture, judicious tannins. An excellent, modern wine and a stylistic model for the appellation and its international distribution.

MOULIN-À-VENT 2007
Red | 2011 up to 2015   **88**
Good color, a fat, fruity wine. The terroir is more marked by the texture than the taste, and the palate is lacking a bit in iris notes, but the wine may be consumed sooner than others, and with pleasure!

Annual production: 350,000 bottles

DOMAINE DU VISSOUX

Vissoux
69620 Saint-Vérand
Phone 00 33 4 74 71 79 42
Fax 00 33 4 74 71 84 26
domaineduvissoux@chermette.fr
wwww.chermette.fr

Pierre-Marie and Martine Chermette richly deserve their international acclaim. Hardworking and born communicators, they are holding their own despite the current downturn in the wine industry, thanks to their very charming Beaujolais wines. No forced naturalness, no over-the-top expression of terroir, just all the freshness, elegance, and sleekness you could wish for. The couple's refined approach to winemaking works wonders for the offerings from their superb northern plots: the Fleurie Les Garants is one of the triumphs of modern-day Beaujolais.

Recently tasted
BEAUJOLAIS CUVÉE TRADITIONNELLE 2007
Red | 2011 up to 2013   **86**

BEAUJOLAIS LES GRIOTTES 2007
Red | 2011 up to 2013   **85**

BROUILLY PIERREUX 2007
Red | 2011 up to 2014   **88**

FLEURIE PONCIÉ 2007
Red | 2011 up to 2014   **88**

Older vintages
BEAUJOLAIS COEUR DE VENDANGES 2007
Red | 2011 up to 2014   **88**
Nice texture. Clean, well-defined aromas, less complex than the Fleurie, of course, but quite pleasant to drink.

FLEURIE LES GARANTS 2007
Red | 2011 up to 2017   **89**
A very pretty floral nose, masterful extraction, supple and pleasant but with plenty of flesh. Truly a great wine of pleasure!

MOULIN-À-VENT LES TROIS ROCHES 2007
Red | 2011 up to 2017   **90**
Nice floral aromas, fruity and supple. A good foundation, nice texture but not heavy.

Red: 71.7 acres; gamay 100%. White: 2.5 acres.
Annual production: 250,000 bottles

Bettane & Desseauve
Selections for Bordeaux

Bordeaux

The largest grape-growing region in France, the Gironde produces the most famous and the most expensive wines on the planet, but also countless bottles of great wine at very reasonable prices.

Between the Dordogne and the Gironde, Entre-Deux-Mers is a great source for everyday Bordeaux, producing wonderful wines with small price tags. In the different regions that attach "côtes" to their names (Castillon, Francs, Blaye . . .), more and more wineries are highlighting their terroirs and are making wines with lots of personality; these wines are definitely worth taking a look at. The Graves vineyards, the source of what we think of as traditional Bordeaux, begin just outside the city of Bordeaux and reach all the way to the town of Lagnon. The whites and reds share the same balance and finesse. Sauternes is an enclave in the southern part of the area that specializes in the production of sweet white wines with a worldwide reputation that are in a class of their own.

On the right bank, the wines are more welcoming and voluptuous, the silkiness of the merlot grape matching the breathtaking views and the light of the Dordogne. The wines of Fronsac and Saint-Émilion are more structured, and those of Pomerol and Lalande de Pomerol rounder and smoother, but all have the advantage of being seductive when young while also having great aging potential.

Appellation Overview
Generic Appellations
• **Bordeaux and Bordeaux Blanc Sec:** These are the basic appellations of the Gironde department. There is a mixture of good and bad, with the best of the bunch offering excellent value for the money. Generally intended for relatively early drinking: within two to five years of harvest for the reds, and one to two years for the whites.

• **Bordeaux Supérieur:** A category that in theory covers the best of the generic Bordeaux reds.

• **Bordeaux Clairet and Bordeaux Rosé:** Two different styles of rosé. The Clairet, more vinous and a darker shade of pink, definitely worth getting to know.

• **Crémant de Bordeaux:** This recent appellation denoting sparkling wines made by the Champagne method is nothing to get excited about yet.

The Entre-Deux-Mers Terroirs
• **Entre-Deux-Mers:** White wines originating from vineyards between the Dordogne and Garonne rivers. Dry, floral, and fresh, these are straightforward wines, often technically well made. Red wines from this region are labeled Bordeaux or Bordeaux Supérieur.

• **Premières Côtes de Bordeaux:** Wines from vineyards along the Garonne, from Bordeaux to Cadillac. Good-quality, straightforward, fruity reds, for drinking within two to three years of bottling.

• **Cadillac, Loupiac, Sainte-Croix-du-Mont:** Dessert wines from three appellations facing the Sauternes area, on the other side of the Garonne. Can produce some very good wines in good vintages: lighter and crisper than a Sauternes; reasonably priced, too.

• **Sainte-Foy-Bordeaux, Bordeaux-Haut-Benauge:** Wines from two recently created appellations covering the east of the department, home to ambitious winegrowers who pull out all the stops to match the great Bordeaux crus.

Fronsac, Libourne, and Côtes Sub-region

• **Fronsac and Canon-Fronsac:** Source of fleshy, dense red wines that take on Pomerol-like aromas of truffles as they age. Too little known—and it's a shame, since they are surprisingly well priced for wines of this quality.

• **Bordeaux Côtes de Francs:** A small but up-and-coming area, with a few wineries that stand out among the crowd.

• **Côtes de Castillon:** A little-known appellation in the eastward extension of Saint-Émilion. Definite signs of progress here: full-bodied, refined reds, the best of which perform better than some Saint-Émilions.

Saint-Émilion and its Satellites

• **Lussac Saint-Émilion, Montagne Saint-Émilion, Puisseguin Saint-Émilion, and Saint-Georges Saint-Émilion:** Small vineyards neighboring Saint-Émilion, producing a similar style of wine but lighter and very uneven in terms of performance.

• **Saint-Émilion and Saint-Émilion Grand Cru:** A huge appellation with a widely varied geography—a sandy plain to the south and more interesting slopes and plateaus to the north. The best of the Saint-Émilion combine well-defined structure with plump, lush flesh, but quality varies across the appellation. This is also true of the Saint-Émilion Grand Cru appellation (not to be confused with classified Saint-Émilion growths), even though these wines are made to stricter standards than generic Saint-Émilion wines.

The Pomerol Region

• **Lalande de Pomerol:** A neighboring Pomerol appellation, home to a few recently established producers who have raised these wines to a new level. The best of these offerings are in the same league as top-quality Pomerols.

• **Pomerol:** Famous for very fleshy, rounded wines with a structure that is less austere than great Bordeaux, plus those typically Pomerol tertiary aromas of truffles and earthiness. Expensive, sometimes too much so, but pretty dependable otherwise.

Côtes de Bourg and Côtes de Blaye

• **Côtes de Blaye, Premières Côtes de Blaye, Blaye:** Good-quality, sensibly priced red and white wines, with a few outstanding offerings.

• **Côtes de Bourg:** In terms of red wines, definitely one of the most interesting wine-producing areas of the "Côtes." These are solidly built, robust wines, a bit short on finesse, coming into their own after four to six years' cellaring.

Médoc

• **Médoc and Haut-Médoc:** Regional appellations covering an inevitably mixed bag of wines but home to a wide variety of good-quality Crus Bourgeois.

• **Moulis and Listrac:** Two adjoining, somewhat inland appellations, between Margaux and Saint-Julien. Good wines, but not as delicate as those of neighboring crus.

• **Margaux:** Very classy red wines, with good structure and lots of finesse. However, the quality does vary from wine to wine, and some of the classified growths have underperformed for some years now.

• **Saint-Julien:** Well structured, balanced, and harmonious. Not many producers, but all of a very high standard, especially when it comes to the classified growths.

Bordeaux Vineyards

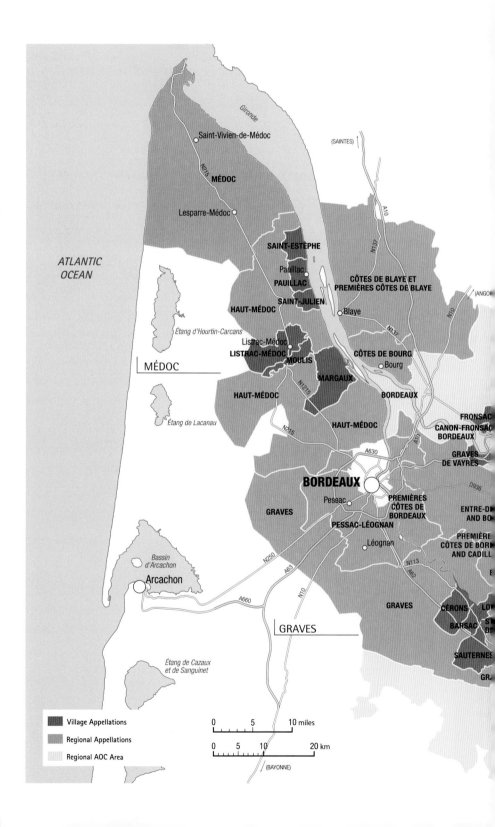

Gironde

(SAINTES)

Saint-Vivien-de-Médoc

MÉDOC

Lesparre-Médoc

ATLANTIC
OCEAN

SAINT-ESTÈPHE

Pauillac

PAUILLAC

CÔTES DE BLAYE ET
PREMIÈRES CÔTES DE BLAYE

SAINT-JULIEN

(ANGO

Blaye

HAUT-MÉDOC

Étang d'Hourtin-Carcans

Listrac-Médoc

LISTRAC-MÉDOC

MOULIS

CÔTES DE BOURG

Bourg

MÉDOC

MARGAUX

HAUT-MÉDOC

BORDEAUX

Étang de Lacanau

HAUT-MÉDOC

FRONSAC

CANON-FRONSAC
BORDEAUX

GRAVES
DE VAYRES

BORDEAUX

Pessac

PREMIÈRES
CÔTES DE
BORDEAUX

ENTRE-D
AND BO

PESSAC-LÉOGNAN

PREMIÈRE
CÔTES DE BOR
AND CADILL

GRAVES

Léognan

Bassin
d'Arcachon

Arcachon

GRAVES

CÉRONS

LO
S
B

BARSAC

Étang de Cazaux
et de Sanguinet

SAUTERNES

GR

Village Appellations

Regional Appellations

Regional AOC Area

| 0 | 5 | 10 miles |

| 0 | 5 | 10 | 20 km |

(BAYONNE)

• **Pauillac:** Great structure, class, and power, and austere in youth. Aside from rare exceptions, Pauillac wines are at least as good as you would expect of their respective classified growths.

• **Saint-Estèphe:** Robust and fleshy, the best are as sophisticated as their Pauillac neighbors. Some of the classified growths are a cut above the rest and at least ten of the many Saint-Estèphe Crus Bourgeois rank among the best in their category.

Graves

• **Pessac-Léognan:** This part of the Graves appellation encompasses the vineyards closest to Bordeaux, including all of the Bordeaux grands crus. The red wines are seriously crafted with a tight, harmonious texture; the white wines are fat, rich, and fresh and show significant improvement. High overall standard.

• **Graves (excluding Pessac-Léognan):** The vineyards start around Portets and extend south as far as Langon. The red wines are balanced and fruity but on the same level as those of Pessac-Léognan; the white wines are very good-quality and full of character. There are signs of progress, certainly, but the overall standard of wine remains very uneven.

• **Cérons:** A small Graves enclave with the potential to produce beautifully refined dessert wines in good years.

The Sauternes Region

• **Barsac, Sauternes:** Very elegant dessert wines that age magnificently. Barsac wines are particularly fresh and crisp and may be labeled Barsac, Sauternes, or Sauternes-Barsac. There was significant improvement overall in the 1980s, but given the sheer cost and labor required to make these wines, there is really no excuse for mediocrity.

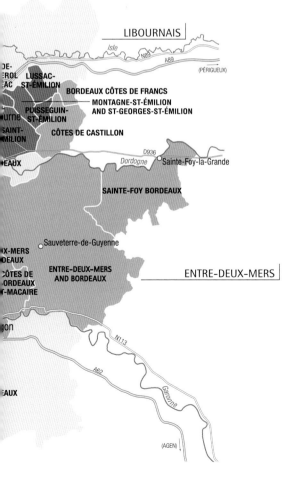

Graves and Sauternes Vineyards

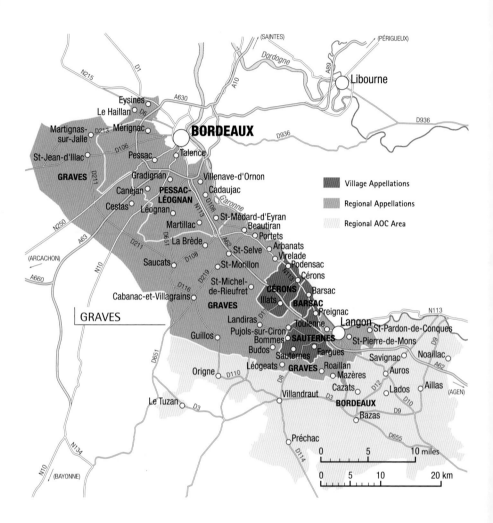

Village Appellations
Regional Appellations
Regional AOC Area

GRAVES

(SAINTES) (PÉRIGUEUX)

Dordogne

Libourne

N215

D1

A10

A89

A630

A10

D936

D936

Eysines
Le Haillan
D6
Martignas-
sur-Jalle
D213
Merignac
D106
St-Jean-d'Illac
Pessac
BORDEAUX
Talence

GRAVES
D211
Gradignan
Villenave-d'Ornon
Canéjan
PESSAC-
LÉOGNAN
Cadaujac
Cestas
Léognan
N113
D108
Garonne
Martillac
St-Médard-d'Eyran
Beautiran
La Brède
D651
A62
Portets
Saucats
D108
St-Selve
Arbanats
St-Morillon
Virelade
Podensac
Cérons
D116
St-Michel-
de-Rieufret
D219
CÉRONS
Barsac
Cabanac-et-Villagrains
GRAVES
Illats
BARSAC
Preignac
Landiras
D1
Toulenne
Langon
N113
Guillos
Pujols-sur-Ciron
SAUTERNES
St-Pardon-de-Conques
Bommes
St-Pierre-de-Mons
D651
Budos
Sauternes
Fargues
Savignac
Noaillac
Origne
D110
Léogeats
GRAVES
Roaillan
Auros
A62
Le Tuzan
D3
Villandraut
D8
Mazères
Lados
Aillas
(AGEN)
Cazats
D12
N134
D3
BORDEAUX
Bazas
D10
D9
N10
(BAYONNE)
Préchac
D655
D114

ARCACHON
A63
N250
A660
N10
D211
D108

0   5   10 miles
0   5   10   20 km

CHÂTEAU D'ARCHE

33210 Sauternes
Phone 00 33 5 56 76 66 55
Fax 00 33 5 56 76 64 38
châteaudarche@wanadoo.fr
www.château darche-sauternes.com

The vineyard here is flanked by the châteaux of Lamothe and Filhot and more recently became home to a luxury hotel, built by the owners to boost tourism in the Sauternes region. The wine is very seriously crafted—even if the owners cannot yet afford the same kind of viticultural practices as Yquem—and gets better all the time.

Recently tasted
SAUTERNES 2006
Sweet White | 2012 up to 2018   84

Older vintages
SAUTERNES 2005
Sweet White | 2013 up to 2030   91
Beautiful roasted quality, a rather rich wine, broad, unctuous, long; a nicely typical expression of the appellation.

SAUTERNES 2003
Sweet White | 2011 up to 2028   92
Golden color, broad and powerful nose of honey and citrus, imposing body, sumptuous sweetness, a very generous style of wine typical for this vintage with its phenomenal concentration and richness. Likely has a great future ahead of it—and may even compete with the greatest.

SAUTERNES 2002
Sweet White | 2011 up to 2022   90
Pale color, slightly unbalanced oak, youthful, fresh, rich; crafted with care, charm, and energy; still very young.

SAUTERNES 2001
Sweet White | 2011 up to 2021   88
Strong notes of mirabelle plum on the nose, rather full-bodied, nicely roasted, but less complex and less harmonious than the Premiers Crus.

SAUTERNES 1999
Sweet White | 2011 up to 2025   90
Bright golden color, reserved nose, no oxidation, with that slightly bitter and oceanic note reminiscent of the 2000 vintage; a food-friendly wine that should be given ten-plus years to age. Should marry well with frangipane-based desserts.

White: 108.7 acres; sauvignon 10%, sémillon 90%.
Annual production: 100,000 bottles

CRU BARRÉJATS

Clos de Gensac
Mareuil
33210 Pujols-sur-Ciron
Phone 00 33 5 57 31 02 01
Fax 00 33 5 56 27 01 15
contact@cru-barrejats.com
www.cru-barrejats.com

This perfectionist winery in Barsac produces wines that make no compromises. Vintage after vintage there is the same rigorous grape selection and the same scrupulous vinification process that eschews all chaptalization—a degree of care rarely seen in Sauternes. The wines are rich and natural but sometimes slightly heavy, a penalty often paid by producers who dare to use the least sulfur dioxide possible.

SAUTERNES 2003
Soft White | 2011 up to 2023   89
Golden, notes of camphor. Very rich in sugar, long, not pure, but very flavorful and ambitious.

SAUTERNES 2002
Soft White | 2011 up to 2020   90
Unctuous, sumptuous body, immense length, high-quality oak. For those who love wines that are truly liquorous.

SAUTERNES 2001
Soft White | 2011 up to 2021   87
The very gold color and powerful notes of beeswax indicate that the wine is evolving a bit too quickly, but the finish is very attractive, very jammy. They may have tried to make the wine too rich.

White: 12.4 acres; muscadelle 5%, sauvignon 10%, sémillon 85%. Annual production: 6,000 bottles

CHÂTEAU BASTOR-LAMONTAGNE

Domaine de Lamontagne
33210 Preignac
Phone 00 33 5 56 63 27 66
Fax 00 33 5 56 76 87 03
bastor@bastor-lamontagne.com
www.bastor-lamontagne.com

Bastor has been perfectly managed by owners Crédit Foncier for twenty years now, producing a very pleasant Sauternes that aims to deliver high-quality fruit at an affordable price. Not as sweet as the greatest in these parts, but usually excellent value for money. The 2003 is the best vintage produced by this estate in recent history.

Recently tasted
SAUTERNES 2007
Sweet White | 2011 up to 2019   **87**
Lightly colored, pretty notes of citrus and white flowers, with a delicately nuanced palate, not as spectacular as others but delicate with a pleasant bitterness on the finish. Perfect with a meal.

Older vintages
SAUTERNES 2006
Sweet White | 2011 up to 2016   **86**
Pale color, as is often the case, this wine is neither powerful nor exuberant; the nose is subtle, the sweetness balanced, not very concentrated. All in all it is an enjoyable and refreshing wine.

SAUTERNES 2005
Sweet White | 2011 up to 2020   **87**
Pale color, the nose is pure but without the complexity one would expect, less noble rot, but with nice fruit, and a very respectable fresh finish.

White: 138.4 acres; sauvignon blanc 20%, sémillon 80%. Annual production: 30,000 to 100,000 bottles

CHÂTEAU BOUSCAUT

1477, avenue Toulouse
33140 Cadaujac
Phone 00 33 5 57 83 12 20
Fax 00 33 5 57 83 12 21
cb@château-bouscaut.com
www.château-bouscaut.com

This classified estate in Cadaujac is distinguished from its neighbors by its highly calcareous soils, which tend to suit white varietals particularly well. Indeed, Sophie Cogombles and her genial husband make a very successful white wine: sappy and complex, with a lovely synergy of sauvignon and sémillon fruit. The merlot-driven red is also polished, harmonious, and velvety though not as complex as the big boys in Pessac-Léognan. Recent vintages are all good and offer excellent value for the money. The second wines could still do with a bit more character and definition.

Recently tasted
PESSAC-LÉOGNAN 2007
White | 2011 up to 2015   **92**
Musky aromas; a very rich, very complex wine, with notes of herbal infusions (linden, lemon verbena), long, flavorful, original, highly recommended!

PESSAC-LÉOGNAN 2006
Red | 2011 up to 2016   **87**
Softer and not as complex as its peers at this stage in its evolution; fleshy, supple, lacking a bit of tension. Slightly disappointing, certainly due to a recent racking.

Red: 98.8 acres; cabernet franc and malbec 5%, cabernet sauvignon 45%, merlot 50%. White: 24.7 acres; sauvignon 50%, sémillon 50%. Annual production: 250,000 bottles

CHÂTEAU CAILLOU

9, Caillou
33720 Barsac
Phone 00 33 5 56 27 16 38
Fax 00 33 5 56 27 09 60
contact@châteaucaillou.com
www.châteaucaillou.com

Château Caillou is a Second Growth Barsac, planted on the slopes in the center of the village. Its owners tend to avoid the limelight, valuing their peaceful Barsac existence and doing nothing to raise any eyebrows. Wine lovers old enough to have tasted very old Barsac vintages know the real thing when they see it; and we are delighted to say that this estate's 1997 and 2001 are the genuine article!

Recently tasted
BARSAC 2006
Sweet White | 2014 up to 2018   **82**
Medicinal nose, pale, no hit of noble rot, much too simple for this property that has made much better wines in recent vintages.

Older vintages
BARSAC 2005
Sweet White | 2017 up to 2030   **92**
Very slightly straw-colored, nicely oaked, classic notes of lemon and acacia flowers, a beautiful wine with well-defined noble rot, and a perfectly delineated terroir. Highly recommended in this exceptional vintage.

BARSAC 2003
Sweet White | 2013 up to 2028   **92**
The nose shines with complexity, distinction, and the intense expression of its Barsac origins, and exotic aromas of ginger make it a perfect wine to accompany Asian cuisine. We were very impressed with this wine; true Barsac lovers should seek it out.

BARSAC 2002
Sweet White | 2012 up to 2022   **90**
Very rich, with the standout aromas of acacia flowers typical of this winery; young, powerful, but not as polished as some of its neighbors.

Red: 4.9 acres . White: 39.5 acres; sauvignon blanc 10%, sémillon 90%. Annual production: 25,000 bottles

CHÂTEAU CARBONNIEUX

33850 Léognan
Phone 00 33 5 57 96 56 20
Fax 00 33 5 57 96 59 19
www.carbonnieux.com

A very classical Pessac-Léognan producer, both in terms of output volume (especially white wines) and consistent, characteristic style. The white wines are very pale, fresh, and nervous with superlative finesse, if a bit too linear for lovers of flesh; the reds have gained enormously in power and density and can now compete with the best. The 2006 is excellent and clearly influenced by the younger generation.

Recently tasted
PESSAC-LÉOGNAN 2007
White | 2011 up to 2017   **88**
The barrel-aging made the wine thinner, revealing underripe grapes as compared to its peers. It's lively and elegant but lacking a vinous quality.

Older vintages
PESSAC-LÉOGNAN 2006
White | 2016 up to 2026   **90**
Dense color, wonderful barrel-aging already allowing a perfect integration of the oak; elegant, with focused and distinguished notes of spice and cedar, a characteristically svelte body, and noble tannins. An exemplary Pessac-Léognan.

PESSAC-LÉOGNAN 2006
Red | 2016 up to 2026   **90**
Pretty color, very spicy nose, linear and tight, but full, very Léognan, classic texture and flavor, worthy of its appellation. The wine shows the results of strict grape selection. Experience shows that this style of wine will age wonderfully.

PESSAC-LÉOGNAN 2005
Red | 2018 up to 2028   **91**
One of the most powerful wines made in the last few years, the tannins strongly marked by the terroir, very respectable personality and structure. It's even better now than it was early on, thus we've raised the score by a few points.

PESSAC-LÉOGNAN 2005
White | 2013 up to 2020   **90**
Expressive notes of lemon and acacia, elegant, fluid, delicate, and clean. For the time being the wine is restrained, but experience shows that in five or six years, the wine will show all of its splendor.

Red: 123.6 acres; cabernet franc 10%, cabernet sauvignon 60%, merlot 30%. White: 111.2 acres; sauvignon 65%, sémillon 35%. Annual production: 500,000 bottles

CHÂTEAU LES CARMES HAUT-BRION

197, avenue Jean-Cordier
33600 Pessac
Phone 00 33 5 56 93 23 40
Fax 00 33 5 56 93 10 71
château@les-carmes-haut-brion.com
www.les-carmes-haut-brion.com

This small cru, saved from the urbanization of Pessac as was its neighbor Haut-Brion, is home to a very harmonious and subtle wine that is particularly noted for the incomparable finesse of cabernet franc. All of the latest vintages are exceptional. The 2005 is quite simply the finest wine ever to come out of this estate!

Recently tasted
PESSAC-LÉOGNAN 2007
Red | 2011 up to 2017　　　　　　　　**88**
Made in the house style, this 2007 shows a complex and elegant nose, a flavorful mouth, with a silky and tight tannic grain, well-ripened fruit, pleasant oak, and a perfectly balanced finish.

Older vintages
PESSAC-LÉOGNAN 2005
White | 2011 up to 2030　　　　　　　**92**
Wide-ranging aromas, currant and raspberry, slightly smoky notes, very harmonious, elegant, clean, and very Bordeaux-like balance in an over-the-top vintage. Bravo!

PESSAC-LÉOGNAN 2004
Red | 2011 up to 2020　　　　　　　　**90**
Pretty notes of cedar on the nose, delicate and well-integrated oak, notes of resin and smoke typical of Pessac, fresh, elegant, complex—in short, a wine with style!

PESSAC-LÉOGNAN 2001
Red | 2011 up to 2015　　　　　　　　**89**
Generous, distinguished, with rather short but noble tannins. The wine as a whole is long and dignified.

Red: 11.6 acres; cabernet franc 30%, cabernet sauvignon 15%, merlot 55%. Annual production: 25,000 bottles

CHÂTEAU DE CHANTEGRIVE

Route de Saint-Michel-de-Rieufret
33720 Podensac
Phone 00 33 5 56 27 17 38
Fax 00 33 5 56 27 29 42
courrier@château-chantegrive.com
www.chantegrive.com

This huge southern Graves property has had a few ups and downs over the past ten years, mainly due to the ill health of owner Henri Lévêque. The appointment of Hubert de Boüard (Château Angélus) as technical director was, however, a wise and brave decision that paid off with his first vintage in 2006. The red and white alike are delicately aromatic, with all the charm and taste typical of this appellation—sure to be a terrific success. The 2005, too, does much to erase the memory of certain recent vintages and restore confidence in this producer.

Recently tasted
GRAVES 2007
White | 2011 up to 2013　　　　　　　**87**
Pale yellow color. Floral nose. The mouth combines vigor and liveliness.

Older vintages
GRAVES 2006
Red | 2011 up to 2015　　　　　　　　**89**
Black color, very pretty nose, rich and complex red fruit, sweet spices, and toasty oak; ample and flattering in the mouth, with tight tannins and a lively finish.

GRAVES 2006
White | drink now　　　　　　　　　　**86**
Fruity and balanced, this is a nice white that would be perfect with a platter of oysters.

GRAVES 2005
Red | 2011 up to 2013　　　　　　　　**86**
An intense purple color, black fruit in the nose, with notes of minerals and toasty oak; a generous and fat attack, very solid, quite oaky, and a touch of bitterness on the finish. The wine has potential, but it needs time.

GRAVES CAROLINE 2006
White | 2011 up to 2016　　　　　　　**90**
Remarkable fresh fruit, perfectly ripe grapes, immediate pleasure guaranteed, impeccably vinified under the watchful eye of Hubert de Boüard.

GRAVES CAROLINE 2005
White | 2011 up to 2013　　　　　　　**88**
Exotic sauvignon blanc bouquet, fresh, more personality than the red, more elegant than but not as vigorous as the best of them.

Red: 148.3 acres; cabernet sauvignon 50%, merlot 50%. White: 89 acres; sauvignon blanc 50%, sémillon 50%. Annual production: 500,000 bottles

DOMAINE DE CHEVALIER

102, chemin de Mignoy
33850 Léognan
Phone 00 33 5 56 64 16 16
Fax 00 33 5 56 64 18 18
olivierbernard@domainedechevalier.com
www.domainedechevalier.com

Everyone agrees that this superb single-block vineyard around the château is one of the best kept in Bordeaux. Olivier Bernard is a worldwide ambassador for Bordeaux wines—and not just his own—and a pace-setter at attracting visitors. The daily tastings that he lays out for those countless visitors have made him intimately aware of the value of his products. The whites are the finest in the commune and the reds boast all the proportion and flavor of the most classical Bordeaux wines. The most recent reds are particularly noted for their added body and complexity.

Recently tasted

PESSAC-LÉOGNAN 2007
White | 2011 up to 2022   **95**

Older vintages

PESSAC-LÉOGNAN 2006
Red | 2016 up to 2026   **93**
Subtle nose with the slightly spicy nuances typical of cabernets, as well as a note that falls in between soot and smoke that is becoming more pinelike with age. With a very well-balanced core and noble tannins, this is a classic wine of the vintage in the making.

PESSAC-LÉOGNAN 2006
White | 2011 up to 2021   **95**
Very pure nose of white fruit with a touch of apricot. The elegant body hasn't yet fully taken shape, but it gives the impression of a strong personality and complexity yet to come.

PESSAC-LÉOGNAN 2005
White | 2011 up to 2025   **96**
Extremely delicate aromas. Still very young, with an ethereal body. Needs time.

PESSAC-LÉOGNAN 2004
Red | 2011 up to 2024   **94**
Aromatic, welcoming, complex, sauvignon-dominated, subtle!

PESSAC-LÉOGNAN 2003
Red | 2011 up to 2025   **96**
Beautiful color, magnificent nose of perfectly ripe grapes, notes of licorice, intense core, remarkably refined tannins: a complete wine.

PESSAC-LÉOGNAN 2002
Red | 2011 up to 2020   **96**
Pretty garnet color, dense and youthful; remarkably focused and defined nose with hints of fruit and licorice; superbly extracted tannins, elegant flavors. A very promising future.

PESSAC-LÉOGNAN 2001
Red | 2011 up to 2017   **91**
Garnet color; clean, focused nose combining cedar and licorice; nice body, but less refined texture than the 2002 and 2003. Firm tannins, slightly tight; will age well.

PESSAC-LÉOGNAN 2000
Red | 2011 up to 2020   **96**
Wonderfully complete nose, the seductive notes of ripe fruit and noble hints of oak perfectly fused. Very rich constitution for the growth, with firm but smooth tannins. A great wine.

Red: 87.7 acres; cabernet franc 2%, cabernet sauvignon 65%, merlot 30%, petit verdot 3%. **White:** 11.1 acres; sauvignon blanc 70%, sémillon 30%. **Annual production:** 118,000 bottles

CHÂTEAU CLIMENS

6, rue Plantey
33720 Barsac
Phone 00 33 5 56 27 15 33
Fax 00 33 5 56 27 21 04
contact@château-climens.fr
www.château-climens.fr

Everyone agrees that Château Climens is the leading Barsac wine. Soils overlaying a limestone bedrock give it that extra acidity required for perfectly balanced residual sugar (often high in recent vintages) and youthful, fresh qualities that withstand long aging. But there remains something mysterious about the extraordinary, some would even say transcendental, finesse of its aromas—even when you bear in mind the dedication of the present owner, Bérénice Lurton, who is responsible for running this estate. Just be sure you do justice to those aromas by enjoying them with like-minded companions! There is no such thing as a minor Climens vintage: when the year simply isn't up to it, the game passes to Climens's second wine, Les Cyprès de Climens. Recent vintages have all been good, producing blends that perfectly express the nobility of this terroir.

Recently tasted
Barsac 2006
Sweet White | 2018 up to 2036   **94**

Older vintages
Barsac 2005
Sweet White | 2011 up to 2050   **98**
This wine's pure breeding is immediately detectable on the nose, very rich and sweet, youthful, with an opulent and almost extravagant style for the cru. Will age slowly.

Barsac 2004
Sweet White | 2016 up to 2024   **94**
Pale gold color. Vanilla-oak, fat, long on the palate. Refined but less finished than the 2005. Its stability when aerated points to a great future.

Barsac 2003
Sweet White | 2021 up to 2030   **95**
With its notes of lemon and citrus and an astonishing crispness for the vintage, this wine is all about finesse and complexity, with additional nuances of rhubarb and green Chartreuse at the finish—quite original. A long cellar life ahead.

Barsac 2002
Sweet White | 2012 up to 2022   **96**
Ultra-classic on the palate, balancing alcohol, acidity, and sweetness. Immense finesse typical of the cru. A bright future ahead.

Barsac 2001
Sweet White | 2011 up to 2030   **98**
Exceptional breadth. Bouquet of transcendent smoothness, combining both tangerine and nougat. Never-ending length.

Barsac 2000
Sweet White | 2011 up to 2020   **93**
Rather gold in color for this wine at this phase, notes of mandarin on the nose. Full, not yet fully mellowed (still a little bitter), not as taut as other vintages from this millenium, but extremely tasty.

Barsac 1999
Sweet White | 2011 up to 2013   **91**
Sustained golden color, still rather closed and defensive on the nose, powerful, less supremely refined than other vintages, but accomplished—and not yet in its prime. All the same, it's still a notch below the superb 2002 and 2004.

Barsac 1998
Sweet White | 2011 up to 2028   **94**
First bottle was corked, an all-too-common problem for this vintage, regardless of the producer. However, it does seem that this château could improve on its cork quality. Second bottle was classic, more refined than 1999, with all the complexity of the terroir.

Barsac 1997
Sweet White | 2011 up to 2024   **97**
Phenomenal concentration, the nose bursting with citrus and wildflower honey aromas, perfect harmony; the citrus notes have an unforgettable finesse. The best 1997 of the whole tasting. And it's still young!

White: 74.1 acres; sémillon 100%. **Annual production:** 30,000 bottles

CHÂTEAU COUHINS

Chemin de la Gravette
BP 81
33883 Villenave-d'Ornon cedex
Phone 00 33 5 56 30 77 61
Fax 00 33 5 56 30 70 49
couhins@bordeaux.inra.fr
www.château-couhins.fr

This cru is owned by INRA (the French National Institute for Agricultural Research), which for many years never did much to promote it, despite the estate's status as a classified growth. These days, thanks to a highly competent winemaking team, Château Couhins is gradually catching up with its peers. Its delicately spicy bouquet, in the classic Léognan style, is sure to appeal to lovers of traditional Bordeaux.

Recently tasted
PESSAC-LÉOGNAN 2007
White | 2011 up to 2014   **90**
Notes of lemon and citrus, delicately built, with wonderful aromatic purity, well preserved by the aging; an excellent example of the quality of vinification currently practiced in Léognan's classified crus.

PESSAC-LÉOGNAN 2006
White | 2014 up to 2021   **90**

PESSAC-LÉOGNAN COUHINS LA GRAVETTE 2007
White | 2012 up to 2019   **88**

Older vintages
PESSAC-LÉOGNAN 2006
Red | 2011 up to 2016   **87**
Scents of cedar typical to Léognan, supple core, not as vinous as the best wines, but with focused, well-extracted tannins.

PESSAC-LÉOGNAN 2005
Red | 2013 up to 2017   **88**
Deeply colored, soft spices in the nose, the wine is edgy and delicate, clean, slightly weakened by bottling (surely temporarily); a classic.

PESSAC-LÉOGNAN 2004
Red | 2012 up to 2016   **88**
Well vinified, soft, subtle spice, with more straightforward flavors than many other wines, and with the discreet charm of reds made from this type of soil.

Red: 37.1 acres; cabernet franc 7%, cabernet sauvignon 40%, merlot 50%, petit verdot 3%. White: 17.3 acres; sauvignon blanc 80%, sauvignon gris 15%, sémillon 5%. Annual production: 90,000 bottles

CHÂTEAU COUHINS-LURTON

33420 Grézillac
Phone 00 33 5 57 25 58 58
Fax 00 33 5 57 74 98 59
andrelurton@andrelurton.com
www.andrelurton.com

This property has just been lavishly upgraded by André Lurton and now also produces a red wine from a nonclassed growth of young vines. Though very fruity and quite supple, it is simply no match for the estate's traditional offering: an exceptionally refined and quintessentially sauvignon white wine that with age evolves toward the spiciness typical of this terroir.

Recently tasted
PESSAC-LÉOGNAN 2007
White | 2011 up to 2017   **92**

Older vintages
PESSAC-LÉOGNAN 2006
Red | 2011 up to 2021   **90**
Much more balanced and elegant than it was early on, this has an unexpectedly beautiful aromatic character and substance. A wine with lots of personality.

PESSAC-LÉOGNAN 2006
White | 2011 up to 2018   **88**
Slightly reduced, vegetal nose, more nervous and tightly wound than most, nice extraction, dry tannins: a true Bordeaux-style cabernet, vinified without concession. It needs time.

PESSAC-LÉOGNAN 2005
White | 2011 up to 2025   **90**
Very typical notes of acacia and pine. This wine is richer than usual, with more body and a very noble aromatic character due to a wonderfully pure vinification. For those who appreciate pure cabernet character.

PESSAC-LÉOGNAN 2005
Red | 2011 up to 2013   **90**
Deeply colored, powerful, tight, and sappy, this is classic Graves. It is a wine with character, which requires a certain knowledge of this type of Bordeaux in order to fully appreciate it. Clearly better in terms of substance than previous vintages.

PESSAC-LÉOGNAN 2004
Red | 2011 up to 2013   **88**
Deeply colored, ripe, a touch of chocolate, an enveloping body: this does not have much acidity, but it does have a future.

Red: 43 acres; cabernet sauvignon 23%, merlot 77%. White: 14.8 acres; sauvignon 100%. Annual production: 45,000 bottles

CHÂTEAU COUTET

33720 Barsac
Phone 00 33 5 56 27 15 46
Fax 00 33 5 56 27 02 20
info@château coutet.com
www.château coutet.com

Coutet (pronounced "Coutette," Gascony-style) is forever doomed to compete with Climens in Barsac—an inevitable though not entirely unenviable destiny! That said, there are subtle differences in the soil. Coutet wines are slightly more nervous and mineral than those of its rival, but with the same lemony notes typical of a limestone bedrock. The estate is judiciously managed by the Baly family, originally from Alsace, who signed an agreement giving exclusive distribution rights to Baron Philippe de Rothschild S.A.—a reminder of just how much the baron himself loved this cru! Its peerlessly creamy finesse is immediately apparent on opening a bottle of the superbly accomplished 1989. The 2001 and 2005 promise to be every bit as good. Coutet today is in great shape thanks to state-of-the-art harvesting practices and winemaking techniques that preserve the extraordinary variety of perfumes in botrytised grapes. The 2002, though not as sought-after as some, is one of the triumphs of the vintage!

Recently tasted
BARSAC 2006
Sweet White | 2014 up to 2030   **95**

Older vintages
BARSAC 2005
Sweet White | 2015 up to 2030   **97**
This has aromatic splendor and great force of character: it will go even farther than this château's great 1989 or 1997 bottlings. A must-have for the vintage.

BARSAC 2004
Sweet White | 2012 up to 2019   **89**
More golden than most, a well-developed nose of citrus fruit, slight oxidation, lacking in richness. Has a deceptive tendency toward musk a little at the beginning, but evolves favorably toward guava and finishes with magnificent distinction.

BARSAC 2003
Sweet White | 2011 up to 2030   **92**
Pale hue, an elegant and subtle wine of remarkable purity, despite a finish that is slightly less spectacular than that of others. It deftly hides its powerful richness under a citrus-fruit freshness. Thanks to skillful vinification, it is sure to age long and slowly.

BARSAC 2002
Sweet White | 2012 up to 2022   **96**
Delicate, fresh, smooth, with marvelous purity of sweetness—an almost ideal Barsac, splendid right now.

BARSAC 2001
Sweet White | 2011 up to 2026   **93**
Remarkable nose of acacia honey, ample but delicate in its sweetness; evolving more discreetly than others for the moment.

BARSAC 2000
Sweet White | 2011 up to 2013   **86**
Clumsy iodized hints on the nose, obviously a difficult harvest, which gave the fruit a bitter, white-peach-pit quality, too pharmaceutical.

BARSAC 1999
Sweet White | 2011 up to 2019   **95**
Superbly expresses the vintage, with notes of acacia and toast and a richly honeyed finish. Young, made for lobster Thermidor.

BARSAC 1998
Sweet White | 2011 up to 2018   **95**
Young, pale; great aromatic finesse, sweet but not at all heavy. Still a little too simple at present and too centered on acacia on the palate, but it has a great future ahead.

White: 95.1 acres: muscadelle 2%, sauvignon 23%, sémillon 75%. Annual production: 50,000 bottles

CHÂTEAU CRABITEY

63, route du Courneau
33640 Portets
Phone 00 33 5 56 67 18 64
Fax 00 33 5 56 67 14 73
vignobles@debutler.fr

This is one of the best-groomed crus in the Portets area and definitely the first stop for well-balanced wines—the quintessence of classic Bordeaux taste.

GRAVES 2007
Red | 2011 up to 2015   **87**
Very dark color. Deep nose of ripe fruit. Full-bodied, with a touch of oak. Delicate tannins.

GRAVES 2006
Red | 2011 up to 2016   **87**
Typified by the Graves terroir, the Château Crabitey made a pleasant red in 2006. Its elegant tannins and the bright black fruit will make for a great wine in the coming years.

Red: 24.7 acres; cabernet sauvignon 45%, merlot 55%. White: 4.9 acres; sauvignon blanc 50%, sémillon 50%. Annual production: 60,000 bottles

CLOS DADY

Les Remparts
33210 Preignac
Phone 00 33 5 56 62 20 01
Fax 00 33 5 56 62 33 11
clos.dady@wanadoo.fr
www.clos-dady.com

This beautifully manicured cru in Preignac has gone from strength to strength in recent years thanks to the devoted attentions of its charming owner, Catherine Gachet. The wine is now up to the standard of a Premier Cru and is quite as lavishly oaked. A tiny output of a splendid red Graves—the best in its appellation—is offered exclusively to the estate's most loyal (and very privileged) customers.

Recently tasted
SAUTERNES 2007
Sweet White | 2011 up to 2016   ·**87**
Deep gold color; expressive nose, unctuous and complex with notes of noble rot, long and rich finish, and notes of candied figs. Harvested and vinified on the edge.

Older vintages
SAUTERNES 2005
Sweet White | 2011 up to 2025   **91**
Superb aromas of acacia honey; perfect sweetness. This is richly built and luxuriously oaked, on the level of a Cru Classé.

SAUTERNES 2004
Sweet White | 2011 up to 2020   **88**
Pale, straw-colored, clean and elegant, smooth, pure, nicely balanced, well made.

SAUTERNES CHÂTEAU DE BASTARD 2001
Sweet White | 2011 up to 2016   **86**
This second wine shows finesse and precision on the nose, though it is not as rich as it has been in other years. The winery has continued to improve with every year since this vintage.

Red: 4.1 acres. White: 16.1 acres; muscadelle 2%, sauvignon 10%, sémillon 88%. Annual production: 5,000 bottles

CHÂTEAU DOISY-DAËNE

10, Gravas
33720 Barsac
Phone 00 33 5 56 62 96 51
Fax 00 33 5 56 62 14 89
reynon@wanadoo.fr
www.denisdubourdieudomaines.com

Denis Dubourdieu and his sons run their Grand Cru vineyard in masterful style, making effective use of cutting-edge technology (agronomic and enological) to curb the whims of nature. The result is a wine with elegant aromas and ideal levels of alcohol (14°) and sugar (80–90 grams)—testament to the Dubourdieus's innately Barsac sense of balance. When the vintage allows, production includes a tiny quantity of very sweet wine (3,000 bottles) that is marketed under the L'Extravagant de Doisy-Daëne label. The wine is flamboyantly rich but with an almost crystalline purity that is a real tour de force, considering that the newly picked grapes contain 25° potential alcohol. The same winemaking team also vinifies two remarkable nonclassed crus, the Château Cantegril and Château de Carles: both make terrific aperitifs.

BARSAC 2006

Sweet White | 2014 up to 2024   **94**
One of the most aromatic, pure, and balanced wines of the vintage, magnified by its remarkable acidity—which is typical of Barsac—and the judicious balance between alcohol and sugar. It is slightly less rich than other wines, but rich enough.

BARSAC 2005

Sweet White | 2015 up to 2025   **95**
Very complex and fresh on the nose, with notes of citrus (grapefruit). Well made, rich without being heavy. The wine has evolved perfectly over the past year.

BARSAC 2004

Sweet White | 2012 up to 2019   **94**
Light color, a marvelously fresh nose, harmonious and complex, perfect balance between body and barrel aging. A monumental success, quite nearly the model for Barsac.

BARSAC 2003

Sweet White | 2013 up to 2023   **93**
With a very light color and well-defined notes of raisined grapes (citrus and raisins), this is a rich and powerful wine with a good balance of alcohol and sweetness, which will make it shine with food.

BARSAC 2001

Sweet White | 2011 up to 2026   **94**
Light, delicate, a touch of reduction in the nose, which is a good sign of long aging potential, more linear than broad on the palate. Huge potential.

BARSAC 2000

Sweet White | 2011 up to 2020   **90**
Straw-colored with a botrytised nose, this is less focused and subtle than the 2004. It is clean, pleasant, and very flavorful, but it doesn't truly assert the characteristics of its terroir. Maybe it needs more time.

BARSAC L'EXTRAVAGANT DE DOISY-DAËNE 2006

Sweet White | 2011 up to 2030   **96**
There were only a few barrels produced, but this is a small gem of aromatic purity and refinement in the richness of the liqueur.

BARSAC L'EXTRAVAGANT DE DOISY-DAËNE 2005

Sweet White | 2011 up to 2050   **99**
Sublime finesse and brilliance, in which the extremely rich sweetness is perfectly balanced by noble acidity and extraordinary aromatic purity. Genius in the bottle!

White: 38.8 acres; muscadelle 1%, sauvignon blanc 12%, sémillon 87%. **Annual production:** 60,000 bottles

CHÂTEAU DOISY-VÉDRINES

33720 Barsac
Phone 00 33 5 56 27 15 13
Fax 00 33 5 56 27 26 76
doisy-vedrines@orange.fr

Château Doisy-Védrines is a classic Barsac estate in terms of vineyard location and style of wine and is as pampered as it deserves to be by the Castéja family, who like their wine sweet and richly fragrant. Price is a steal—particularly since anyone prepared to wait twenty years can look forward to opening a wine that rivals Climens for quality. We have a weakness for the estate's 2000 and 2002 bottlings, bearing in mind that great Barsac vintages don't always tally with those of Sauternes!

Recently tasted
Barsac 2006
Sweet White | 2012 up to 2018   **86**

Older vintages
Barsac 2005
Sweet White | 2015 up to 2025   **93**
Very diverse aromatics, a classic foundation of apricot and yellow fruit, beautiful acidity, A long, fresh, very well made wine.

Barsac 2004
Sweet White | 2011 up to 2025   **94**
Pale gold. Distinguished aromas (wildflower honey, pear), no oxidation, great finesse. Splendid length and purity of botrytis. Erudite, complex; a remarkable success.

Barsac 2003
Sweet White | 2011 up to 2020   **86**
Yet again, this doesn't reach the recent level of the winery's elevated reputation: the wine is powerful but heavy, monolithic, with rather banal apple notes. To reexamine.

Barsac 2002
Sweet White | 2011 up to 2022   **95**
Pale, honeyed, roasted, very young, very elegant, very Barsac. A classic from this vintage and representative of the property in the density and elegance of its structure and sweetness.

Barsac 2001
Sweet White | 2011 up to 2050   **91**
Discreet but finely aromatic, seems less botrytised than others or even other vintages of the same wine, but everything feels fresh. In short: very Barsac.

Barsac 2000
Sweet White | 2011 up to 2020   **90**
Bright gold color, powerful, sweet, tasty citrus fruit notes, yet somehow the wine lacks transparency and purity.

Barsac 1999
Sweet White | 2011 up to 2013   **82**
Premature amber color, acidic, unbalanced, even violent aromas and taste. It does not live up to the true ability of this château.

Barsac 1998
Sweet White | 2011 up to 2028   **93**
Pale, completely the opposite (fortunately) of the 1999, with grand finesse and freshness; a broad wine, youthful and vivacious, with a promising future!

Barsac 1997
Sweet White | 2011 up to 2017   **95**
Golden color, reminiscent of great Champagne and apricot nectar, sensual, almost muscat-like, with beautiful sweetness. This is unconventional but extremely delicious! A second bottle offered a much more traditional balance with the splendid, rich sweetness characteristic of this vintage.

White: 66.7 acres; muscadelle 5%, sauvignon 15%, sémillon 80%. Annual production: 80.000 bottles

CHÂTEAU DE FARGUES

33210 Fargues-de-Langon
Phone 00 33 5 57 98 04 20
Fax 00 33 5 57 98 04 21
fargues@château-de-fargues.com
www.château-de-fargues.com

Owner Alexandre de Lur Saluces grows and picks his grapes here exactly as he did in Yquem, which he ran for more than a quarter of a century! The result is a wine that can rival the Premier Crus Classés: complete, generously aromatic, and always loaded with roasted character. The sumptuous 2003 and 2005 can compete with the big boys!

SAUTERNES 2006
Sweet White | 2011 up to 2030   **95**
A remarkable success for the cru: the wine is rich in sweetness with perfect noble rot, long, classical, up there with the greats of previous years.

SAUTERNES 2005
Sweet White | 2011 up to 2030   **95**
Outstanding noble rot, ample flavor, great length on the palate, classically made.

SAUTERNES 2001
Sweet White | 2011 up to 2030   **96**
Fat, powerful, roasted, and long, this is a classical wine from a great vintage. Wait ten more years.

White: 37.1 acres; sauvignon 20%, sémillon 80%.
Annual production: 15,000 bottles

CHÂTEAU DE FIEUZAL

124, avenue de Mont-de-Marsan
33850 Léognan
Phone 00 33 5 56 64 77 86
Fax 00 33 5 56 64 18 88
infochato@fieuzal.com
www.fieuzal.com

This cru used to be famous for its white wine, one of the most complete of all the Pessac-Léognans, even if it isn't as subtly crafted as some of the wines available today. The very robust red, on the other hand, was rarely a match for an Haut-Bailly or Chevalier. We hope new owner Lochlann Quinn will give this estate that extra push required to perform as well as it did in the 1980s. The latest reds are a long way from that precise expression achieved by neighboring Pomerols, but the whites can once again compete with the best.

PESSAC-LÉOGNAN 2006
Red | 2014 up to 2021   **91**
Bluish hue, charming, rather delicate and precise in its terroir definition, with refined tannins.

PESSAC-LÉOGNAN 2005
Red | 2011 up to 2015   **86**
The wine continues to develop flavors less frank than expected.

PESSAC-LÉOGNAN 2004
Red | 2011 up to 2014   **86**
This wine is complete and classic, with fullness but also a slight tannic rigidity at the finish.

PESSAC-LÉOGNAN 2003
Red | 2011 up to 2015   **88**
A lovely success, smooth and velvety, full but still tender, softened, and ready to drink.

PESSAC-LÉOGNAN 2002
Red | 2011 up to 2013   **82**
Straightforward, rather thin vegetative aromatic character.

PESSAC-LÉOGNAN 2000
Red | 2011 up to 2020   **91**
Firm, almost mineral on the palate, this wine matches the noble austerity of the terroir with the beautiful plushness given by very ripe grapes.

Red: 98.8 acres. White: 19.8 acres. Annual production: 250,000 bottles

CLOS FLORIDÈNE

Château Reynon
21, route de Cardan
33410 Beguey
Phone 00 33 5 56 62 96 51
Fax 00 33 5 56 62 14 89
reynon@wanadoo.fr
www.denisdubourdieu.com

This estate is a testament to the skills and experience of foremost Bordeaux enologist Professor Denis Dubourdieu (the name "Floridène" is a combination of his and his wife Florence's given names). The white wines in particular are now much improved, playing up their stunning limestone mineral expression rather than the (local) varietal aromas. Recent vintages are fabulously pure and crystalline. The red wine, produced in much smaller quantities, is carefully made but lacks the individuality of the whites.

GRAVES 2006
White | 2011 up to 2016   **93**
Quite pale in color. Complex nose with mineral notes. The palate is pure elegance, rich and fruity, with wonderful aromatic length and hints of citrus.

GRAVES 2006
Red | 2011 up to 2013   **90**
Deep ruby-red color. Deep and complex nose with spicy, slightly gamey notes. Wonderfully smooth and supple on the palate, with peppery, spicy notes. Nice length, elegant tannins.

GRAVES 2005
Red | 2011 up to 2013   **93**
Dark, concentrated color; deep, complex, powerful, and refined on the nose; structured in the mouth with a very fine texture and harmonious and wonderfully long tannins. Classic and elegant.

GRAVES 2004
Red | 2011 up to 2013   **92**
Dense purple color; intense and smoky on the nose with notes of leather; flavorful and soft on the palate. This is very a classy Graves with wonderfully long flavors.

GRAVES 2003
Red | 2011 up to 2015   **92**
Remarkable aromas of red and black fruit without any hint of heavy prune or chocolate notes; velvety texture, elegant tannins, wonderful length: a perfect red Graves in a vintage that saw very few successful wines.

Red: 40.3 acres; cabernet sauvignon 71%, merlot 29%. White: 46.9 acres; muscadelle 1%, sauvignon blanc 39%, sémillon 60%. Annual production: 135,000 bottles

CHÂTEAU GILETTE

4, rue du Port
33210 Preignac
Phone 00 33 5 56 76 28 44
Fax 00 33 5 56 76 28 43
contact@gonet-medeville.com
www.gonet-medeville.com

Gilette is a specialty of the Médeville family and the only Sauternes to undergo at least fifteen years' aging in small tanks, then five years' aging in the bottle before release for sale. This unique technique uses a lengthy reduction process to concentrate the wine's natural fruitiness and bring out its citrus notes. The result is a wine that is practically immortal. Fabulously complex nose, stupendous length, and a naturally high alcohol content make this Preignac Sauternes a gourmet's delight.

SAUTERNES CRÈME DE TÊTE 1986
Sweet White | 2011 up to 2030   **93**
Completely golden in color with a subtle nose marked by citrus notes and marvelous finesse. The complexity is there, but for the time being the wine is still quite reserved.

SAUTERNES CRÈME DE TÊTE 1983
Sweet White | 2011 up to 2028   **97**
Hints of amber are beginning to show at the edge of the glass. Wonderfully complex nose of crème brûlée and mandarin orange, tremendous concentration on the palate with a slight hint of bitterness balancing out the sugar. A monumental wine.

SAUTERNES CRÈME DE TÊTE 1982
Sweet White | 2011 up to 2022   **95**
Golden color, rich nose that is not as complex as the 1983, botrytised, suave, not grandiose but surprising for such a difficult vintage in Sauternes. After ten hours of air, it develops prodigious finesse.

SAUTERNES CRÈME DE TÊTE 1981
Sweet White | 2011 up to 2016   **93**
Fully golden color, less amber than the 1983. The nose is less complex but quite savory, evoking acacia, honey cake, and violets all at the same time. The sweetness is not excessive. Almost ready to drink.

SAUTERNES CRÈME DE TÊTE 1979
Sweet White | 2011 up to 2019   **94**
Light amber nuances and more noticeable "rancio" flavors than in previous vintages, with notes of caramel, bitter orange, and cocoa, and a lingering texture. A delicate, very elegant wine.

SAUTERNES CRÈME DE TÊTE 1978
Sweet White | 2011 up to 2028 **95**
One of the most amazing wines of a vintage with very little noble rot. The raisined grapes made the wine, and what a wine it made. Admirable nose of acacia honey, wonderfully bright, still very young.

SAUTERNES CRÈME DE TÊTE 1976
Sweet White | 2011 up to 2016 **92**
The color is quite golden; the nose is slightly lacking in purity and elegance, with notes of iodine and caramel. The generous body tends to mask the lack of finesse.

SAUTERNES CRÈME DE TÊTE 1975
Sweet White | 2011 up to 2025 **99**
A sumptuous wine, elegant and distinguished, with an amazingly generous bouquet and a refined fruit quality unique in this vintage. Perfection, or near perfection, made by Château Gilette.

SAUTERNES CRÈME DE TÊTE 1971
Sweet White | 2011 up to 2021 **96**
Marvelous finesse and aromatic complexity, wonderful noble rot, sumptuous followthrough on the palate: a truly grandiose Sauternes in all its glory.

SAUTERNES CRÈME DE TÊTE 1967
Sweet White | 2011 up to 2015 **97**
Admirable aromatic complexity, impossible to describe in only a few words; wonderful essence, bright fruit finesse, and marvelously expressive sweetness. At its peak.

SAUTERNES CRÈME DE TÊTE 1961
Sweet White | 2011 up to 2016 **99**
A masterpiece in the nose, with notes of bitter orange marmalade and spices (nutmeg and cloves). Amazingly botrytised, with impressive sweetness.

SAUTERNES CRÈME DE TÊTE 1953
Sweet White | 2011 up to 2013 **94**
This wine, which remained closed for a long time, has slowly gained in finesse and character, yet still does not equal the best vintages of the château. It leans toward the style of a Barsac.

SAUTERNES CRÈME DE TÊTE 1937
Sweet White | 2011 up to 2017 **99**
An amazing vintage, and this bottle lives up to all expectations. It has an incredibly powerful and expressive nectar quality and marvelously elegant fruit carried by a transcendent sweetness.

White: 11.1 acres; muscadelle 2%, sauvignon blanc 8%, sémillon 90%. Annual production: 5,000 bottles

CHÂTEAU GUIRAUD

33210 Sauternes
Phone 00 33 5 56 76 61 01
Fax 00 33 5 56 76 67 52
dgalhaud@châteauguiraud.com
www.châteauguiraud.com

This Premier Cru estate was acquired by the Peugeot consortium in 2006, in association with whiz-kid winemaking trio Xavier Planty, Stephan de Neipperg, and Olivier Bernard. Château Guiraud was always an able producer of wines grown and made in accordance with the classical standards of sweet-wine production. But the improvement since its acquisition is undeniable, particularly in terms of refined aging—witness the very promising 2006. Some of the recent vintages started off very pure but now show signs of premature aging.

SAUTERNES 2006
Sweet White | 2016 up to 2026 **95**
Golden color, savory aromas, precise structure, with excellent noble rot and more complexity than most. A remarkable diversity and freshness of aromas for such a rich body.

SAUTERNES 2005
Sweet White | 2011 up to 2030 **96**
Superb aromas of perfectly ripe grapes, striking a magnificent balance of power and finesse. This wine is the most complete of this château, to our knowledge.

SAUTERNES 2004
Sweet White | 2011 up to 2020 **89**
Weighty color, oak a bit insistent, spicy, with a slight lack of freshness.

SAUTERNES 2003
Sweet White | 2011 up to 2020 **87**
Lovely bouquet but undefined body, the finish slightly bitter and too short for a wine of such pedigree.

SAUTERNES 2002
Sweet White | 2011 up to 2022 **94**
Pale yellow with great aromatic elegance, freshness, smoothness, and complexity. A splendid bottle, undoubtedly the most accomplished in its category in the last ten years.

SAUTERNES 2001
Sweet White | 2011 up to 2026 **94**
Seductive and full, very richly aromatic, lengthy and persistent, superb noble rot.

SAUTERNES 2000

Sweet White | 2011 up to 2020   **93**
Pale color, complex nose, classical notes of apricot and citrus fruits, no premature oxidation, charming, long, slightly less pure than the 2002.

SAUTERNES 1999

Sweet White | 2011 up to 2017   **92**
A little too bitter and heavy with crème brûlée flavors, this is full-bodied for the vintage, tasty and ripe, but less refined than the vintages that immediately follow it.

SAUTERNES 1998

Sweet White | 2011 up to 2013   **89**
Light golden color, with notes of bitterness and iodine (but without heaviness) that render the wine less captivating than those from the vintages that followed. It is clean, but the sweetness is a little dried out by the oak.

SAUTERNES 1997

Sweet White | 2011 up to 2013   **90**
Evolved color, curious aromas recalling great Champagnes and apricot nectar. The acidity comes up with air, but the wine lacks purity for the vintage and the flavors are rapidly evolving. To drink with pleasure, but not recommended for Sauternes purists.

Annual production: 100,000 bottles

CHÂTEAU HAUT-BAILLY

103, avenue de Cadaujac
33850 Léognan
Phone 00 33 5 56 64 75 11
Fax 00 33 5 56 64 53 60
mail@château-haut-bailly.com
www.château-haut-bailly.com

This famous cru is the quintessence of that balance and refinement possessed by the finest red Bordeaux. The age of its vines is an advantage, of course, but so too is the first-class team in charge, managed by Gabriel Vialard and headed by Véronique Sanders, granddaughter of former proprietor Daniel Sanders. Haut-Bailly's new owner is American banker Robert Wilmers, a man of enormous culture and finesse who is committed to giving his estate what it needs to go even farther. The rest depends on the combined talents of enological consultants Jean Delmas and Denis Dubourdieu. Château Haut-Bailly has always possessed great class, but recent vintages show more distinction and precision than ever before. The 2005 is sure to be a worthy successor to the 1928.

PESSAC-LÉOGNAN 2006

Red | 2016 up to 2026   **93**
Discreetly spicy aromas, very harmonious, less "roasted" than the 2005, long-limbed, elegant, yet not fully developed. Noble tannins.

PESSAC-LÉOGNAN 2005

Red | 2011 up to 2025   **96**
Great color, generous nose, almost smoky in the Pessac style, evolving toward Havana tobacco. Full, velvety, with firm, authoritative tannins.

PESSAC-LÉOGNAN 2004

Red | 2012 up to 2024   **93**
Black, great nose, civilized, powerful, taut, crafted, refined, and vinous, this deserves an award of excellence for the vintage. One of the great successes of Bordeaux.

PESSAC-LÉOGNAN 2003

Red | 2011 up to 2023   **94**
Crimson color, great spice, and subtle aromas, rather tender and attenuated body for the vintage. Its remarkable smoothness compensates for the slight lack of energy. Wine lovers looking for refinement will appreciate this wine.

PESSAC-LÉOGNAN 2002
Red | 2011 up to 2017   **89**
With hints of musk and leather on the nose, this starts out viscous and creamy, but the tannins tighten at the finish and limit its ambitions, despite the wine's excellent craftsmanship.

PESSAC-LÉOGNAN 2001
Red | 2011 up to 2026   **95**
With grand, complex aromas and a harmonious, very full body, this possesses the velvet texture celebrated in this cru, but supported by upright, firm tannins. A complex wine, distinguished, very promising, and much greater than 2002.

PESSAC-LÉOGNAN 2000
Red | 2011 up to 2030   **97**
Ultra-distinguished, deep, supremely balanced, and endowed with firm tannins, cut out for the long haul.

PESSAC-LÉOGNAN 1999
Red | 2011 up to 2017   **93**
The nose is very subtle and infinitely typical of the designation, with notes of cherry pit, spice, and fresh leather presented with exemplary precision. The tannins are a little tight but let up on the finish, charming as they melt into the wine. Very elegant wine of exemplary, classic craftsmanship.

PESSAC-LÉOGNAN LA PARDE DE HAUT-BAILLY 2006
Red | 2011 up to 2018   **89**
An exemplary second wine, with charming fruit and refined tannins, this is precise, velvety, and especially very faithful to the style of the Premiers Crus, just more supple and immediate.

Red: 74.1 acres; cabernet franc 6%, cabernet sauvignon 64%, merlot 30%. Annual production: 150,000 bottles

CHÂTEAU HAUT-BERGEY
🍷 🍷 🍷 🍷 🍷

69, cours Gambetta
33850 Léognan
Phone 00 33 5 56 64 05 22
Fax 00 33 5 56 64 06 98
info@vignoblesgarcin.com
www.vignoblesgarcin.com

Haut-Bergey is one of those nonclassed Léognan growths that can now compete with the classed crus on equal terms. The Garcin family enlisted the help of Michel Rolland, Jean-Luc Thunevin, and Alain Raynaud to help transform this estate into one of the stars of Pessac-Léognan. The white wines today show just a touch more personality than the reds, displaying a rare degree of aromatic finesse and a superbly rich constitution. A small quantity of red wine, bottled as Château Branon, is sourced from the best terroirs and vinified in a separate tank. Famous American wine critics love it, but, though robust and distinctly woodier than Haut-Bergey, it isn't necessarily any better in terms of originality and sheer finesse.

Recently tasted
PESSAC-LÉOGNAN 2006
Red | 2011 up to 2015   **92**
With its powerful and radiant bouquet, ripe fruit, and minerals; its pleasant, full, fruity mouth; and its savory and balanced tannins, this vintage fits perfectly into the profile of the property.

PESSAC-LÉOGNAN 2004
Red | 2011 up to 2013   **87**
A nice wine with character, an intense and complex nose, black fruit, mineral, and smoke; dense, emblematic, tight; and very long on the palate.

Older vintages
PESSAC-LÉOGNAN 2006
White | 2011 up to 2014   **93**
Very remarkable in the complexity of the aromas and body: the grapes were harvested at peak maturity and the terroir is beginning to show its true potential, notably in the length and tension of its flavors.

PESSAC-LÉOGNAN 2005
Red | 2011 up to 2015   **87**
Deeply colored, serious, clean, straightforward, supple, fine tannins, will age. Good in the style of the vintage.

Red: 64.2 acres; cabernet sauvignon 60%, merlot 40%. White: 4.9 acres; sauvignon 80%, sémillon 20%. Annual production: 80,000 bottles

CHÂTEAU HAUT-BRION

33608 Pessac cedex
Phone 00 33 5 56 00 29 30
Fax 00 33 5 56 98 75 14
info@haut-brion.com
www.haut-brion.com

Being inside the town of Bordeaux itself, this majestic cru enjoys a very warm, urban microclimate and ripens earlier than any of its peers. Every Haut-Brion is a model of consistency and every vintage has been massive. Even in less favorable years, it remains hugely aromatic, with that famous "smoky" taste typical of wines from the Pessac-Léognan appellation, and with an astonishing capacity to grow even stronger with long aging. Its beautifully civilized tannins are universally admired, though alcohol content has tended to increase over the past five years due to global warming, making the tannic support more powerful. The tiny quantity of exceptionally forceful white wine shows more marked sauvignon aromas than Laville, and it rivals Montrachet itself for sheer power. The château's second wine, the Bahans, is similar in style to the first wine, with a finesse, class, and precision that is unique by Bordeaux standards. The most recent reds are more robust than any other wines this century, while the whites are the most richly aromatic.

Recently tasted
PESSAC-LÉOGNAN 2006
Red | 2021 up to 2034   95
Wonderful color, high in alcohol, a rich, complex wine, closed for the time being. This vintage is in the wines that had a tendency to be very merlot focused; this phase ends with the 2007 and 2008, which bring back the cabernet character.

Older vintages
PESSAC-LÉOGNAN 2006
White | 2011 up to 2018   97
Immense promise with the usual differences in character from Laville Haut-Brion, the sauvignon and its mentholated thiols being more obvious. Finish is very pure. Everything was done to ensure a wine of certain aging potential.

PESSAC-LÉOGNAN 2005
Red | 2020 up to 2035   95
Monumental wine, of a natural alcoholic richness very rare in this cru, with super-powerful tannins but also remarkable depth. This wine completely sets itself apart in its appellation, in the grandeur of very great merlots.

PESSAC-LÉOGNAN 2005
White | 2011 up to 2020   98
A brush with perfection! An aroma of divine finesse, where floral and lemony notes irresistibly harmonize; and, above all, a vivacity and expression of breed on the finish of this young wine that is greater than that of all the preceding vintages.

PESSAC-LÉOGNAN 2004
Red | 2011 up to 2024   95
The initial scents are the cedar aromas of the cabernets. The wine is full, very classic in its proportions and form compared to the overpowering 2005, with noble tannins. It offers a better rapport between quality and price than that of the speculative vintages.

PESSAC-LÉOGNAN 2004
White | 2011 up to 2014   97
In its current state, a splendor. Distinctive scent of linden, oak completely integrated, unforgettable flavor. Ready.

PESSAC-LÉOGNAN 2003
Red | 2011 up to 2020   95
Deep color but less intense than many from the Médoc; harmonious aromas of ripe fruit, a beautiful creaminess, and the velvet tannins that are a signature of the house. Beautiful length.

PESSAC-LÉOGNAN 2003
White | 2011 up to 2013   96
In our opinion, this is more successful than the red from this château: the terroir and style expression is exceptional in its viscosity and ample body, as well as in the generosity of the bouquet, which has none of the reductive aspects that spoil the pleasure of white Graves of a certain age. À point.

PESSAC-LÉOGNAN 2002
Red | 2011 up to 2025   96
A great success for this cru in an irregular vintage that remains unappreciated. The wine possesses formidable brilliance and distinction, expressed in flavors that are very structured and fresh without heaviness, with remarkably defined tannins. Perhaps the most accomplished wine of the vintage.

PESSAC-LÉOGNAN 2002
White | 2011 up to 2013   98
The finest, most harmonious wine of all, with a purity and a complexity worthy of the grandest Montrachet. This type of wine is absolutely exceptional in Bordeaux, enough to make you cry due to its scarcity. Unfortunately, previous vintages aged rather badly, but this had the happy effect of inspiring the proprietors to find the key to making a wine of this formal perfection. Avoid 2000, 1999.

PESSAC-LÉOGNAN 2001
Red | 2011 up to 2025   95
The body is ample and round, with an impressive texture free of any heaviness or overextraction. The tannins possess the inimitable silkiness of the cru.

PESSAC-LÉOGNAN 2001
White | 2011 up to 2020   90
The gives an immediate impression of generous flesh and character, but it has a little less freshness and persistence than Laville in this vintage.

PESSAC-LÉOGNAN 2000
Red | 2011 up to 2030   98
With its unmatched fine tannin texture splendidly integrated into its body, this is a chef d'oeuvre of harmony. For very long aging.

PESSAC-LÉOGNAN 1999
Red | 2011 up to 2024   94
Very classic style from this property, taut and spicy with a hint of smoke, with elegant, noble tannins and great personality despite its rather reserved character.

PESSAC-LÉOGNAN 1998
Red | 2011 up to 2029   98
One of the most accomplished wines of the decade, this shows admirable aromatic purity, an extraordinary noblesse of tannins, and an ultra-precise, complete expression of this great terroir.

PESSAC-LÉOGNAN 1997
Red | 2011 up to 2013   86
The only "weak" vintage we know of from this property: the grapes lacked maturity, even if the wine is more balanced than Mission.

PESSAC-LÉOGNAN 1996
Red | 2011 up to 2021   94
A powerful and tannic wine, rich in personality but certainly less harmonious and refined than the 2002 and 2004, and less noble than the impressive 1998.

Red: 118.7 acres; cabernet franc 12.8%, cabernet sauvignon 44.2%, merlot 42.1%. White: 7.1 acres; sauvignon 47.4%, sémillon 52.6%. Annual production: 144,000 (red) bottles

CLOS HAUT-PEYRAGUEY

ⵣ ⵣ ⵣ ⵣ

33210 Bommes
Phone 00 33 5 56 76 61 53
Fax 00 33 5 56 76 69 65
clos.haut.peyraguey@orange.fr
www.closhautpeyraguey.com

This cru is located on the "Haut Bommes," not really a peak but the highest point of the Bommes plateau. The view from here looks slightly downward on all the neighboring Premier Crus. Clay-rich soil gives the wine considerable body and smoothness and explains in particular why it is usually slow to age. The most recent vintages are impeccably made from meticulously harvested fruit and deserve rave reviews, particularly since price remains reasonable for what is one of the finest sweet wines on the planet. The 2002 is palpable evidence of the strides taken to produce a sumptuous Sauternes in years without "obvious" vintage appeal. That said, the great 2001 and 2003 vintages are certainly nothing to sniff at.

Recently tasted
SAUTERNES 2006
Sweet White | 2014 up to 2026   93

Older vintages
SAUTERNES 2005
Sweet White | 2013 up to 2030   99
Full, fresh nose, somehow managing to be both roasted and deliciously lemony all at the same time, syrupy, with a rich sweetness that has already marvelously mellowed and an incredibly long-lasting finish: a glorious Sauternes.

SAUTERNES 2004
Sweet White | 2014 up to 2024   93
Pale gold color, slightly reduced on the nose, grapefruit aromas, refined, more fluid than La Tour Blanche, less plush, easy, pleasant.

SAUTERNES 2003
Sweet White | 2013 up to 2023   97
Golden color, intense aromatic richness, complete, and full-bodied; this wine is radiant and fully developed, far beyond its promising beginnings. Right up at the level of Yquem!

SAUTERNES 1998
Sweet White | 2011 up to 2028   93
Golden color, toast and spice aromas on the nose, powerful, lively, almost explosive. Much more vivacious on the palate than the 1999. Bright future.

White: 42 acres; sauvignon 10%, sémillon 90%.
Annual production: 25,000 bottles

CHÂTEAU LES JUSTICES

33210 Preignac
Phone 00 33 5 56 76 28 44
Fax 00 33 5 56 76 28 43
gonet.medeville@wanadoo.fr

One of the best and most reliable of the nonclassed Sauternes growths: very fruity, like many of the Preignac Sauternes, and growing increasingly complex with age, but especially notable for an ideal grape sugar/alcohol ratio (often more than 14°) that makes it a great companion to gourmet cuisine. The latest vintages are even richer than the 1970 offerings—just one stunningly well-made Sauternes after another!

Recently tasted
SAUTERNES 2006
Sweet White | 2011 up to 2022   **90**

Older vintages
SAUTERNES 2005
Sweet White | 2011 up to 2020   **92**
Excellent, classic Sauternes, with all the nobility of the botrytis of the vintage and a richness of constitution superior to all recent celebrated vintages.

SAUTERNES 2004
Sweet White | 2011 up to 2019   **88**
Golden with straw effects. Powerful, roasted, still a little simple but delicious with classic flavors of pineapple and grapefruit. Correctly made. Beautiful foreseeable bottle aging.

SAUTERNES 2003
Sweet White | 2011 up to 2028   **95**
Splendid power and complexity of fruit, which was well protected from oxidation from the beginning. Great volume of body and a vigor not seen for the last thirty vintages. This has the timeless style of excellent vintages in Sauternes, with its incredible length in the mouth.

SAUTERNES 2002
Sweet White | 2011 up to 2024   **90**
Very fruity and "Justices" on the nose, with luscious citrus notes. It is refined and complex, but less monumental than the 2003.

SAUTERNES 2001
Sweet White | 2011 up to 2030   **92**
Lemony but discreet on the nose, complete in the mouth, this is tight and long with noble aromatics and huge potential.

White: 21 acres; various 8%, muscadelle 2%, sémillon 90%. Annual production: 20,000 bottles

CHÂTEAU LAFAURIE-PEYRAGUEY

33210 Bommes
Phone 00 33 5 56 76 60 54
Fax 00 33 5 56 76 61 89
info@lafaurie-peyraguey.com
www.lafaurie-peyraguey.com

This attractive vineyard with its grandiose, Moorish-style walled château makes a monumental, equally eye-catching wine that is a perfect ambassador for wines from the top of Sauternes: a boatload of syrupy fruit, admirable consistency, and all the potential and style to be expected at this level. The 1988s and 1990s are now drinking magnificently, with a body and sumptuous palate to rival Yquem. The wines of 2002 to 2005 are very reasonably priced for the quality. Given the price, more people should be buying them!

Recently tasted
SAUTERNES 2006
Sweet White | 2014 up to 2026   **94**

Older vintages
SAUTERNES 2005
Sweet White | 2015 up to 2030   **96**
This cru has come into its own perfectly since the first samples: a wine of masterly amplitude and exemplarily classic aromas!

SAUTERNES 2004
Sweet White | 2011 up to 2024   **93**
Pale golden color, aromatically less open than others, with a little more pineapple. It may be more pointed, less harmonious, and a little less formally perfect than La Tour Blanche, but it has freshness, very great length, lots of character, and a great future ahead.

SAUTERNES 2003
Sweet White | 2013 up to 2025   **94**
With a golden color and honey aromas bursting with acacia, this is rich, fat, and as perfectly botrytised as one can imagine, with a sweetness made sumptuous by its persistence and richness. A monumental wine, even if in the absolute one can dream of a little more aromatic purity.

SAUTERNES 1997
Sweet White | 2011 up to 2017   **96**
With still-youthful color and intense notes of acacia on the nose, this has less acidity than in a great traditional vintage (like all the 1997s), but it is more youthful, better preserved, and slimmer in its sweetness than its peers. Great achievement!

White: 89 acres; muscadelle 2%, sauvignon blanc 8%, sémillon 90%. Annual production: 75,000 bottles

CHÂTEAU LARRIVET HAUT-BRION

84, route de Cadaujac
33850 Léognan
Phone 00 33 5 56 64 75 51
Fax 00 33 5 56 64 53 47
larrivethautbrion@wanadoo.fr

This winery lies between Haut-Bailly and Smith Haut-Laffite, at the heart of the Pessac-Léognan appellation. It has been nicely taken in hand by Philippe Gervoson (of Société Andros, France's largest jam manufacturer) and his wife, and produces wines in consultation with Michel Rolland. The reds in particular are modern-style, fat, vinous, and warm by Pessac-Léognan standards. The white wines are much more substantial and precise than they were but could still do with more finesse.

Recently tasted
PESSAC-LÉOGNAN 2006
Red | 2011 up to 2015   86

Older vintages
PESSAC-LÉOGNAN 2006
White | 2011 up to 2050   85
Aromas of mirabelle plum, round ample wine, very perfumed, but a little heavy in its musky notes.

PESSAC-LÉOGNAN 2005
Red | 2011 up to 2025   90
A brilliant achievement, this is complete, generous, and elegant, with especially finely spicy tannins. In principle made for long aging.

PESSAC-LÉOGNAN 2004
Red | 2011 up to 2014   86
Lovely nose of prune and a touch of leather; smooth, appealing, commercial. No freshness.

PESSAC-LÉOGNAN 2001
Red | 2011 up to 2015   90
This wine does not lack vitality and seduces with its fleshy, deep body, structured by ripe and dense tannins.

Red: 111.2 acres; cabernet sauvignon 50%, merlot 50%. White: 22.2 acres; sauvignon 50%, sémillon 50%. Annual production: 240,000 bottles

CHÂTEAU LATOUR-MARTILLAC

33650 Martillac
Phone 00 33 5 57 97 71 11
Fax 00 33 5 57 97 71 17
latourmartillac@latourmartillac.com
www.latourmartillac.com

Somewhat isolated from the rest of Martillac, this Graves Cru Classé is the archetypal family estate. The Kressman children, brothers Loïc and Tristan, display an almost filial attachment to their heritage, showing themselves to be wise and careful managers. The white wines rely on a complex mix of vines, many of them old, and have always been renowned for their generous flavors and good aging potential. They remain very popular in Bordeaux, where they continue to sell well. The red wines display classic Graves style: robust and austere en primeur, without that seductive fruit that wannabe wine buffs like so much. They age slowly, concentrating the spicy, slightly smoky, meaty notes typical of Pessac-Léognan—it takes fifteen to twenty years for a good vintage to become truly expressive of this mighty terroir. The tannins and texture could still do with a bit more finesse—an improvement that the owners have been working toward for some years now.

PESSAC-LÉOGNAN 2007
White | 2012 up to 2019   93
Pale color, amazing aromatic expression, quite characteristic of the vintage, fresh, elegant, tight on the finish, gives the impression that it's holding itself back for aging; a wine of wonderful character.

PESSAC-LÉOGNAN 2006
White | 2011 up to 2016   93
Pale, quite complex and stylish on the nose, the essence of mandarin and citron fruit, fat, ripe, and long. Truly remarkable.

PESSAC-LÉOGNAN 2006
Red | 2015 up to 2021   93
This wine has evolved exceptionally since we last tasted it, developing distinguished notes of graphite that we didn't perceive in the "primeurs" tastings, and an authentic elegance in the tannins, not at all overdone. A stylish wine for the experienced and demanding Bordeaux lover.

Red: 84 acres; cabernet franc and petit verdot 5%, cabernet sauvignon 60%, merlot 35%. White: 24.7 acres; muscadelle 5%, sauvignon 35%, sémillon 60%. Annual production: 290,000 bottles

CHÂTEAU LAVILLE HAUT-BRION

Domaine Clarence Dillon
33608 Pessac cedex
Phone 00 33 5 56 00 29 30
Fax 00 33 5 56 98 75 14
info@haut-brion.com
www.haut-brion.com

As of the 2009 vintage the wine is no longer called Laville Haut-Brion but rather Mission Haut-Brion Blanc. Produced from a very small vineyard, this just might be the greatest dry white wine in Bordeaux: richly sappy, with a supremely aristocratic nose and tactile sensations as sumptuous as those of the greatest Burgundy crus. The sémillon overtakes the sauvignon with age, adding considerable length to the finish. Magnificent in 2005, sublime in 2006, but in the 1990s there were several vintages that evolved much too quickly.

Pessac-Léognan 2006
White | 2011 up to 2021   **97**
With extraordinary purity and finesse, the acidity magnificently in balance with texture and savor, this has unparalleled nobility of character. The makers of this masterpiece would be disappointed if aging were to betray the promises of youth!

Pessac-Léognan 2005
White | 2011 up to 2020   **95**
The wine begins on scents of pine and acacia, leading into generous and noble flavors.

Pessac-Léognan 2004
White | 2011 up to 2020   **96**
Peacefully, royally, without excess, Laville brings out the big guns of an impressive Bordeaux white wine, at the level of the best Montrachets. The magical nose shows delicate finesse. The marvelously fine and full mouth is long, round, intense, fresh, and distinguished, developing notes of acacia honey of great persistence and without any heaviness.

Pessac-Léognan 2003
White | 2011 up to 2013   **90**
Powerful and spicy, this shows noticeable notes of stress in the vineyard. It seems that the terroir of Haut-Brion coped better with the difficulties of this vintage.

Pessac-Léognan 2002
White | 2011 up to 2013   **95**
A wine of spectacular purity and substantial aromatic finesse, very long and noble, perfectly aged. Its salinity will mingle perfectly with the best ocean fish.

Pessac-Léognan 2001
White | 2011 up to 2013   **94**
More triumphant than Haut-Brion, and particularly better preserved, with all the character intensity specific to this terroir. At its peak. Older vintages like 1999, 1998, 1997, and 1996 unfortunately aged suddenly and should be avoided.

White: 6.3 acres; sauvignon blanc 12%, sémillon 88%.
Annual production: 9,000 bottles

CHÂTEAU LA LOUVIÈRE

🍷🍷🍷🍷

149, route de Caudajac
33850 Léognan
Phone 00 33 5 56 64 75 87
Fax 00 33 5 56 64 71 76
lalouviere@andrelurton.com
www.andrelurton.com

The majestic Château La Louvière is flanked on either side by Carbonnieux and Haut-Bailly, and is one of the world's most effective ambassadors for the Pessac-Léognan appellation. These are powerful wines—slightly austere but flawlessly consistent and built to age. André Lurton, who even in his eighties remains as indefatigable as ever, gives this estate that all-important technical edge. Screw-cap closures for the white wines are a good example. All he has to do now is successfully pass the baton to the younger generation!

Recently tasted
PESSAC-LÉOGNAN 2006
Red | 2011 up to 2018   89

PESSAC-LÉOGNAN 2006
White | 2011 up to 2015   90

Older vintages
PESSAC-LÉOGNAN 2005
Red | 2011 up to 2015   88
Pretty floral nose. Spicy, distinguished, lengthy, fresh, elegant, bilberry notes, good tannins but dimensionally limited, a little too dry.

PESSAC-LÉOGNAN 2005
White | 2011 up to 2013   88
Pineapple, grapefruit, finesse, and subtlety, more aromatic than flavorful. There is vivacity but not real length.

Red: 118.6 acres; cabernet sauvignon 64%, merlot 36%. White: 33.4 acres; sauvignon 85%, sémillon 15%. Annual production: 250,000 bottles

CHÂTEAU MALARTIC-LAGRAVIÈRE

🍷🍷🍷🍷🍷

43, avenue de Mont-de-Marsan
33850 Léognan
Phone 00 33 5 56 64 75 08
Fax 00 33 5 56 64 99 66
malartic-lagraviere@malartic-lagraviere.com
www.malartic-lagraviere.com

The perfectionist owners of this estate, the Bonnie family, have dramatically revamped the technical facilities, restored and expanded the vineyard, and, most notably, transformed the wines. The reds in particular are among the most robust but also the most harmonious in this appellation. The most recent whites show a smoother, more voluminous palate but do tend to close up after two years in bottle. What you need then is patience, because in time they will be just as charming but more complex. The most recent vintages are all exceptionally well crafted and rank among the best of the Pessac-Léognans.

Recently tasted
PESSAC-LÉOGNAN 2007
White | 2011 up to 2015   93

Older vintages
PESSAC-LÉOGNAN 2006
White | 2011 up to 2018   93
For the moment, it is the technical excellence of winemaking that dominates, in particular the great freshness and impeccable purity of the classic aromas of Bordeaux sauvignon blanc, spicier than Loire sauvignon. Impressive density of texture.

PESSAC-LÉOGNAN 2006
Red | 2016 up to 2026   95
Beautiful color, assertive nose of very ripe grapes, full and delightful flavors, and a very confident finish. One of the most complete samples in our comparative tasting.

PESSAC-LÉOGNAN 2005
White | 2011 up to 2027   94
Powerful musky nose, very sappy and tense in mouth, great future. The wine, previously a touch closed, is finding all the force of expression it had while in the barrel.

PESSAC-LÉOGNAN 2005
Red | 2011 up to 2025   95
With ample but fine body, racy aromas of cedar and noble tannins, this feels very nuanced. Superb winemaking.

PESSAC-LÉOGNAN 2004
White | 2011 up to 2019 **90**
Pale color, very fine and fresh nose with notes of acacia honey free of heaviness. With a full body, lively acidity, and great length, this has incontestably great potential. A new success that demonstrates that this cru can produce white wines of grand personality.

PESSAC-LÉOGNAN 2004
Red | 2011 up to 2025 **95**
Impressive color and a superb expression of a revered terroir, with pure and complex aromas of violet and red fruit. It has an especially exemplary structure on the palate: a complete body and an exquisite velvety texture that will surprise those who associate Léognan wines with austerity, as well as especially magnificent, complex, purebred tannins, infinitely more civilized early on than those of most Right Bank crus.

PESSAC-LÉOGNAN 2002
Red | 2011 up to 2017 **92**
With a delicate spicy nose, very elegant texture, and exceptional grape maturity for this vintage, this is purebred, complex, and very classic, made for true aficionados of this type of great red Bordeaux.

PESSAC-LÉOGNAN 2000
Red | 2011 up to 2025 **95**
A monumental wine and a major success of the vintage, combining freshness and power with obvious authority.

PESSAC-LÉOGNAN 1999
Red | 2011 up to 2019 **92**
With saturated color and an evolved and complex nose with notes of cedar and fresh leather, this is elegant, full-bodied, and purebred. Firm but fresh tannins without heaviness, and with splendid substance for the vintage. A perfect example of the tension and harmony of a beautiful Graves wine.

PESSAC-LÉOGNAN 1998
Red | 2011 up to 2023 **94**
Superb freshness and complexity on the nose, body as elegant as usual but with more distinguished and complex flavors than the 1999, great raciness on the finish. It confirms the success of the appellation in 1998.

Red: 113.7 acres; cabernet franc 10%, cabernet sauvignon 40%, merlot 50%. White: 17.3 acres; sauvignon 85%, sémillon 15%. Annual production: 130,000 bottles

CHÂTEAU DE MALLE

Château de Malle
33210 Preignac
Phone 00 33 5 56 62 36 86
Fax 00 33 5 56 76 82 40
accueil@château-de-malle.fr
www.château-de-malle.fr

Surrounded by its magnificent Italianesque garden, Château de Malle is as historic as the wine it produces. This is your archetypal Preignac sweet wine, somewhere between the very forward fruit of a Barsac and the opulence of a Sauternes. Textbook harvesting and vinification produce a wine that is an excellent value for the money. The 2001 promises to rank alongside the benchmark Sauternes of 1990 and 1997, a marriage of opulence and aromatic intensity. Malle also turns out some classy red and white Graves— such as the deliciously delicate dry white Graves M. de Malle. It is sourced from a small seven-acre parcel with an annual production capacity of just 7,000 bottles. The red Graves is bottled under the Château de Cardaillan label and comes from a fifty-acre vineyard, evenly planted to the sauvignon and merlot (part of Château de Malle).

Recently tasted
SAUTERNES 2006
Sweet White | 2014 up to 2021 **86**

Older vintages
GRAVES CHÂTEAU DE CARDAILLAN 2005
Red | 2011 up to 2013 **87**
Dense crimson color, rich and beautifully complex nose of pure and mature fruit. Dense and smooth on the palate, with plenty of fruit and a beautiful, tightly tannic weave. Long and balanced finish.

GRAVES M. DE MALLE 2006
White | 2011 up to 2013 **89**
Dark golden yellow color. Complex and rich nose. Full mouthfeel, with a beautifully rich texture and much freshness. Lovely oak.

GRAVES M. DE MALLE 2005
White | 2011 up to 2015 **88**
Colors of green, gold, and yellow, the nose delicate, fine, and purebred, with lovely ripe fruit. Fleshy palate, fruity, with lovely oak and a beautiful freshness on the finish. Great length for this very pleasant white wine.

SAUTERNES 2005
Sweet White | 2015 up to 2030 **92**
Splendid, complex aroma, great viscosity, noble and immediately seductive fruitiness, great continuity on the palate; perhaps the most beautiful wine from Malle in more than fifty years.

SAUTERNES 2004
Sweet White | 2012 up to 2019   **90**
Golden green hue. Vanilla, honest, creamy, long, very citrusy. Very pleasant and balanced, good compromise of the strengths and weaknesses of the vintage. Well done.

SAUTERNES 2002
Sweet White | 2011 up to 2022   **88**
Light color, charming but fairly complex, round, smooth, almost ready to drink. To serve with appetizers.

SAUTERNES 2001
Sweet White | 2011 up to 2021   **90**
Fairly open on the nose, showing finesse and aromatic vivacity. Fat, sweet, and tender, this has evolved much faster than expected—than the best of the Barsacs, for example.

SAUTERNES 2000
Sweet White | 2011 up to 2015   **89**
Evolved color, powerful bitter orange aroma, but less refined than the 2002. There's a beautiful density to the texture, but the lack of purity compared to that of an ideal Sauternes suggests the harvest was not entirely pleasurable!

SAUTERNES 1999
Sweet White | 2011 up to 2014   **90**
Golden color, very unctuous and graceful, more balanced than the 2000, fruitier, very pleasant.

SAUTERNES 1998
Sweet White | 2011 up to 2018   **90**
Beautiful golden color, strong note of acacia or bitter peach pit, with the style, the behavior and, as usual, the velvety and very pleasant finish that seems to be a hallmark of the château, even if it is missing the complexity of the greatest wines from Preignac.

SAUTERNES 1997
Sweet White | 2011 up to 2017   **92**
Light color, powerful aroma, original, more lactic than usual, enormous noble rot on the palate, rich sweetness, velvety, better preserved than others, but it lacks the expected classicism of the great year dreamed of when we tasted it en primeur. Perhaps we must admit to have overestimated it.

Red: 56.8 acres; cabernet sauvignon 50%, merlot 50%. **White:** 74.1 acres; muscadelle 3%, sauvignon blanc 25%, sémillon 72%. **Annual production:** 170,000 bottles

CHÂTEAU LA MISSION HAUT-BRION

Domaine Clarence Dillon
33608 Pessac cedex
Phone 00 33 5 56 00 29 30
Fax 00 33 5 56 98 75 14
info@haut-brion.com
www.mission-haut-brion.com

This holding had to be largely replanted in the 1980s, which explains some of its past inconsistencies. Today it once again boasts all the style that has made it famous throughout the world: that rare combination of a very voluptuous texture and a very powerful, very original bouquet that develops rapidly in the glass, plus tannins of superlative finesse.

Recently tasted
PESSAC-LÉOGNAN 2006
Red | 2018 up to 2031   **95**

Older vintages
PESSAC-LÉOGNAN 2005
Red | 2020 up to 2030   **96**
One finds the high class and the natural sensuality of this terroir, with more immediate charm than in the Haut-Brion. Not to open for another fifteen or twenty years.

PESSAC-LÉOGNAN 2004
Red | 2011 up to 2026   **95**
Already open on the nose, with notes of leather, fur, spices; opulent, enrobing tannins, and much sensuality for a Bordeaux.

PESSAC-LÉOGNAN 2003
Red | 2011 up to 2023   **94**
More successful and harmonious than Haut-Brion, this has a very developed nose—almost Burgundian—and a velvety texture that is slightly exotic. But it is difficult to imagine its future.

PESSAC-LÉOGNAN 2002
Red | 2011 up to 2024   **95**
Classic character, very lovely cedar and spice aromas, completely fitting body, aristocratic texture, great honesty, excellent price-quality ratio. A wine made for true aficionados.

PESSAC-LÉOGNAN 2001
Red | 2011 up to 2019   **94**
More tender, less firm, and precise in aromas and texture than the 2002, but a little more voluptuous, urban, and certainly very well positioned to accompany modern culinary genius.

Pessac-Léognan 2000
Red | 2011 up to 2030   **97**
Very high-class wine, full in form and texture, with very noble tannins, perfectly balanced in spite of its monumentality. Immense future.

Pessac-Léognan 1999
Red | 2011 up to 2019   **93**
A very open nose, with notes of spice and menthol; tender and full, easy and generous, a little less refined in texture than the 2002.

Pessac-Léognan 1998
Red | 2011 up to 2018   **97**
A grand vintage chez Dillon, with elegance in form, flavor, and texture, and undoubtedly more aromatic freshness than found in the great, recent sunny vintages. It can already be opened and enjoyed.

Pessac-Léognan 1997
Red | 2011 up to 2013   **84**
Evolved color, vegetative aroma, and insufficient body and complexity for this level of prestige.

Pessac-Léognan 1996
Red | 2011 up to 2016   **88**
Delicate and nervy but lacking lift and tension for a cru of this reputation, this class of terroir, and the price. Since 1998, the owners have rectified their aim.

Red: 51.1 acres; cabernet franc 7.9%, cabernet sauvignon 47.6%, merlot 44.5%. Annual production: 84,000 bottles

CHÂTEAU MYRAT
33720 Barsac
Phone 00 33 5 56 27 09 06
Fax 00 33 5 56 27 11 75
myrat@châteaudemyrat.fr

Jacques de Pontac is one of the most genial Barsac producers we know, committed to making great dessert wines despite his lack of resources. He is not helped by plantings that, as we saw in 1998, do not always favor the noblest development of botrytis. All of his fruit, however, comes from a very strict grape selection. We were a bit optimistic about the 2000, which now shows signs of premature aging, but the 2002 is drinking well, and every vintage since then offers super value for the money.

Sauternes 2006
Sweet White | 2011 up to 2025   **90**
The oak is a bit overpowering; they should reprimand their supplier. For the rest, though, the wine is rich, perfect noble rot, with the additional acidity found in Barsac, which is useful in this type of vintage. The long finish is that of a perfectly executed harvest.

Barsac 2005
Sweet White | 2013 up to 2030   **92**
Beautiful Barsac, richly sweet, meticulously made, a price-quality ratio that is certainly hard to beat.

Barsac 2003
Sweet White | 2011 up to 2021   **90**
A luminous gold color, very complex nose from a rich harvest, perfectly combining raisined grapes and noble rot (notes of citrus and acacia, and also apricot). Fruit-filled, long, elegant, candied.

Barsac 2002
Sweet White | 2012 up to 2022   **90**
Lighter color, straightforward, citrus nose, nice noble rot, good length, a well-made wine, highly recommended.

White: 54.4 acres; muscadelle 4%, sauvignon blanc 8%, sémillon 88%. Annual production: 30,000 bottles

CHÂTEAU NAIRAC

33720 Barsac
Phone 00 33 5 56 27 16 16
Fax 00 33 5 56 27 26 50
contact@château-nairac.com
www.château-nairac.com

Nicole Tari and her children are passionate about this estate, pouring their energies into making a rich and authentic wine that really does justice to the excellent Nairac soils. They focus solely on Grand Vin, keep their winery squeaky-clean, and never cheat and never chaptalize. Some of the vintages produced in the 1990s seemed a bit heavy and tired, but steps were taken to put that right and all the latest vintages are superb.

Barsac 2006
Sweet White | 2016 up to 2028   **93**
With a golden color, beautiful pineapple aromas, and an overall balance that feels very natural and satisfying, this is a very precise expression of the vintage. A meticulous, elegant Barsac that can be enjoyed rather young.

Barsac 2005
Sweet White | 2013 up to 2025   **97**
Very great richness in botrytis, but without heaviness and, most remarkably, without any oxidative notes. High-class wine, infinitely better than the 2001.

Barsac 2004
Sweet White | 2014 up to 2019   **94**
Advanced gold color. On the nose, powerful, with good oak. On the palate, expressive, complex, great sweetness, frankness, and length. Very pleasant and well harvested.

Barsac 2003
Sweet White | 2011 up to 2018   **93**
A beautiful golden color and an extremely expressive nose of citrus make this wine immediately appealing. Rich and roasted, this is ideal with Asian food.

Barsac 2002
Sweet White | 2011 up to 2014   **88**
Delicate, floral, oak a little dominant, very relaxed on the palate but balanced by a charming acidity. It will make an excellent aperitif, but wait three to five years, when the oak will be better integrated.

Barsac 2001
Sweet White | 2011 up to 2021   **88**
With much opulence and aromatic charm, this is rich in orange marmalade flavors, long and complex. Oak a little forward.

White: 42 acres; muscadelle 4%, sauvignon 6%, sémillon 90%. Annual production: 15,000 bottles

CHÂTEAU OLIVIER

175, avenue de Bordeaux
33850 Léognan
Phone 00 33 5 56 64 73 31
Fax 00 33 5 56 64 54 23
mail@château-olivier.com
www.château-olivier.com

Château Olivier is owned by the de Bethmann family, who have very successfully protected their magnificent property from the rampant urbanization of the Pessac-Léognan area. After many years of fairly lackluster performance, the winery recently underwent a change of heart and completely rethought its day-to-day workings—with immediate results. The white wine is sappy and complex, and the reds are much better vinified and truer to their excellent terroir—a performance finally worthy of a Cru Classé! The château continues to make rapid and consistent progress: the 2006 reds and whites are without doubt the most accomplished of the estate's recent offerings.

Pessac-Léognan 2006
Red | 2014 up to 2018   **89**
Beautiful color, fine and precise nose of fennel, velvety texture of perfectly ripe grapes, spicy, complex.

Pessac-Léognan 2006
White | 2011 up to 2014   **91**
Rich aromatic nose with notes of green tea and a touch of sea breeze (useful for gastronomy); round, salty, complete.

Pessac-Léognan 2005
Red | 2011 up to 2023   **90**
Discreet cherry aromas, generously fleshy and smooth body with tannins that are less spicy than others. The velvety texture renders it more directly approachable than other more complex wines. Good winemaking. We slightly overestimated it during barrel tasting.

Pessac-Léognan Le Dauphin d'Olivier 2005
Red | 2011 up to 2015   **86**
Supple and grounded wine, with very frank fruity aromas and no tannic unevenness. Not really complex but easy to drink.

Red: 116.1 acres; cabernet franc 4%, cabernet sauvignon 35%, merlot 45%. White: 19.8 acres; sémillon 8%. Annual production: 300,000 bottles

CHÂTEAU PAPE CLÉMENT

216, avenue du Docteur-Nancel-Pénard
33600 Pessac
Phone 00 33 5 57 26 38 38
Fax 00 33 5 57 26 38 39
château@pape-clement.com
www.pape-clement.com

Pape Clément makes one of the most deservedly popular choices in Bordeaux wine, omitting no detail that might compromise its commitment to quality. It is now famous for destemming its grapes by hand: dozens of busy fingers remove the grapes one by one. The reds are in many ways reminiscent of La Mission Haut-Brion, with a voluptuous texture not seen in any other Pessac-Léognan wine and a finesse and elegance that is shared by the whites.

Recently tasted
PESSAC-LÉOGNAN 2007
White | 2011 up to 2017   90

Older vintages
PESSAC-LÉOGNAN 2006
White | 2011 up to 2020   90
Rich, plump, alcohol quite obvious, citrus flavor slightly masked at this stage by its persistent oak, more creamy than nervy.

PESSAC-LÉOGNAN 2006
Red | 2016 up to 2024   95
This has a charming texture, with a full and balanced fruity character and skillfully extracted tannins from ripe grapes. It is a very pleasant wine, smooth and scented by powerful leather notes on the finish, capable of seducing the masses.

PESSAC-LÉOGNAN 2005
Red | 2011 up to 2030   97
The most complex of these Pape Clément wines on the nose and palate. It is splendidly built, long, generous, in Olympic shape.

PESSAC-LÉOGNAN 2005
White | 2011 up to 2018   89
Paler than its peers, this is in a severe phase of reduction, with struck flint notes, undefined but tight. To retaste on a more forgiving day.

PESSAC-LÉOGNAN 2004
White | Drink now   91
Aromatic, reduced, toasty, amusing, alive, tempting!

PESSAC-LÉOGNAN 2004
Red | 2011 up to 2013   93
Very beautiful color, powerful oak, notes of bramble. A well-made, well-aged modern wine, long and multilayered.

PESSAC-LÉOGNAN 2003
Red | 2011 up to 2023   95
With a deep color and ample nose of prune, this is rich and warm but without excess. The tannins are particularly voluptuous, which was not easy in this vintage. A great accomplishment, this will age well and for a long time.

PESSAC-LÉOGNAN 2002
Red | 2011 up to 2017   89
Spicy notes stronger than usual. Vivacious, frank, but with a certain simplicity in the tannins, which makes it not quite up to the level of the 2001.

PESSAC-LÉOGNAN 2001
Red | 2011 up to 2025   95
From an over-publicized harvest, in which all the grapes were manually destemmed, this 2001 impresses with its extraordinary texture, silky and very racy. A new stage for the château.

PESSAC-LÉOGNAN 2000
Red | 2011 up to 2025   94
This is charming and rich with plump tannins and beautiful persistence, but has less depth than the great vintages that followed at this château.

PESSAC-LÉOGNAN 1998
Red | 2011 up to 2023   96
Very elegant nose, very typical of Pessac, with smoky notes already quite perceptible. Distinguished and velvety body, excellent tannic base. A great vintage of a classic style. Great future.

Red: 74.1 acres; cabernet sauvignon 60%, merlot 40%. White: 6.2 acres; muscadelle 5%, sauvignon blanc 45%, sauvignon gris 5%, sémillon 45%. Annual production: 99,000 bottles

CHÂTEAU RABAUD-PROMIS

33210 Bommes
Phone 00 33 5 56 76 67 38
Fax 00 33 5 56 76 63 10
rabaud-promis@wanadoo.fr

This estate was formed when Château Rabaud divided into two, part of the vineyard going to the Sigalas family (Château Rabaud-Sigalas), the other to the Dejeans, who own this property today. The vines occupy a kind of transitional zone, in between the Haut-Sauternes and the crus some thirty feet lower down. The Dejeans are experts when it comes to noble rot, but their hyper-cautious approach and unwillingness to take risks means that some of their vintages lack that famous roasted note. In good years, though, the wine is richly fragrant and ages admirably. Prices remain very reasonable.

Recently tasted
SAUTERNES 2006
Sweet White | 2014 up to 2021   **88**

Older vintages
SAUTERNES 2005
Sweet White | 2015 up to 2025   **96**
Splendidly floral nose. The noble rot is magnificently transparent. With elegance, power, and an amazing sincerity in the mouth, this is a great vintage for the château, with a price-quality ratio that is surely exceptional.

SAUTERNES 2004
Sweet White | 2014 up to 2024   **93**
Pale color, well protected from oxidation; wonderful aromatic finesse, invigorating acidity, less raisiny than the 2005, but well balanced, pure, an irreproachable style that will age well.

SAUTERNES 2003
Sweet White | 2011 up to 2025   **93**
More golden in color than the 2004 or 2005, with concentrated flavors of apricots in the mouth, this shows the wonderful quality of the grapes and excellent vinification. Good progress.

SAUTERNES 2001
Sweet White | 2011 up to 2020   **92**
Powerful and rich wine, nice late-harvest character, with a very long finish. Very well made.

White: 81.5 acres; muscadelle 2%, sauvignon 18%, sémillon 80%. Annual production: 50,000 bottles

CHÂTEAU RAHOUL

4, route du Courneau
33640 Portets
Phone 00 33 5 57 97 73 33
Fax 00 33 5 57 97 73 36
château-rahoul@thienot.com

Major Champagne Group Thiénot recently took a major stake in leading Bordeaux négociant CVBG Dourthe-Kressmann. Increasingly active in Bordeaux, Thiénot started with a few little-known properties, managed then as now on a quality-based policy. This one in Portets has the potential to produce typically sémillon white wines for fans of delicately honeyed aromas. The estate does need to try harder, though—especially with its red wines.

GRAVES 2006
White | 2011 up to 2013   **88**
Supple and graceful, more delicately made than the previous vintages.

GRAVES 2006
Red | 2011 up to 2013   **88**
Linear and elegant, nice depth, and noticeable freshness in the finish. Delightful.

GRAVES 2005
White | 2011 up to 2015   **88**
Pale hay color, very intense nose of flowery honey, showing the predominance of sémillon. Original, fine, slightly bitter flavors of peach pit and fennel. The opposite of the usual style in this region, and very well made. It is not the flavor of the moment, but we bet that it will come back in fashion.

GRAVES 2005
Red | 2011 up to 2013   **87**
Ruby color. Spicy, peppery nose. Palate is fresh and elegant with beautiful length. Tannins quite firm in the finish.

GRAVES 2004
Red | 2011 up to 2014   **86**
Medium intense in color. Spicy nose, fairly developed. Supple, easy to drink, with fine tannins, not very expansive but in keeping with the character of this terroir. Meticulous winemaking. It is starting to acquire more length on the palate, in a register somewhat feral and smoky.

Red: 91.4 acres; cabernet 20%, merlot 80%. White: 7.4 acres; sauvignon 20%, sémillon 80%. Annual production: 260,000 bottles

CHÂTEAU RAYMOND-LAFON

🍷🍷🍷🍷🍷

4, Au Puits
33210 Sauternes
Phone 00 33 5 56 63 21 02
Fax 00 33 5 56 63 19 58
famille.meslier@château-raymond-lafon.fr
www.château-raymond-lafon.fr

Raymond-Lafon boasts a magnificent location in the upper Sauternes region, alongside some of the finest Premiers Crus Classés. For years now, its wines have rivaled the best of them, meticulously crafted by Pierre Meslier and his children. Originally from the Médoc, Pierre Meslier was the brilliant director of Château d'Yquem from the 1970s to the 1980s, and he knows all about making great sweet wines. These easily live up to their worldwide reputation: richly honeyed, with an impeccable roasted character and guaranteed aging potential.

Recently tasted
SAUTERNES 2006
Sweet White | 2013 up to 2024   **91**

Older vintages
SAUTERNES 2005
Sweet White | 2011 up to 2035   **95**
A wonderfully complete wine, bringing to mind the 1962, which was made under similar climatic conditions. It sports an imposing sweetness, perfectly adapted to its extended time in oak.

SAUTERNES 2004
Sweet White | 2011 up to 2029   **92**
Very powerful floral notes in the nose; wonderfully pure flavors despite the difficult vintage; very small production.

SAUTERNES 2003
Sweet White | 2011 up to 2028   **93**
With a pronounced raisiny quality, light notes of caramel and exotic fruit linked to noble rot, this has great body and sweetness, but its apogee is several years away.

SAUTERNES 2001
Sweet White | 2011 up to 2021   **95**
Amazing wine, with classic aromas of apricot and citrus, expertly integrated oak, a remarkable balance of alcohol and body, and wonderful length.

White: 42 acres; sauvignon blanc 20%, sémillon 80%.
Annual production: 20,000 bottles

CHÂTEAU DE RAYNE-VIGNEAU

🍷🍷🍷🍷🍷

109, rue Achard - BP 154
33210 Bommes
Phone 00 33 5 56 59 00 40
Fax 00 33 5 56 59 36 47
contact@cagrandscrus.fr
www.cagrandscrus.com

With the possible exception of Yquem, Rayne-Vigneau is unrivaled for ideal vineyard exposure and natural drainage. The wine itself, on the other hand, has rarely been a match for Yquem over the past fifty years. But it seems that the estate's new owners, the all-powerful French bank Crédit Agricole, have finally understood that such a great cru deserves to shine. The 2006 should easily outrank the wines from those intrinsically superior vintages produced at the start of the century.

SAUTERNES 2006
Sweet White | 2014 up to 2021   **90**
Very pure nose, beautiful aromatic hints of lemon and pineapple, well-balanced liqueur in the body and texture, a neat and ambitious vinification; among the most, if not the most, successful of the latest vintages, in spite of the difficulties of 2006!

SAUTERNES 2005
Sweet White | 2013 up to 2017   **90**
Exuberant aromas of passion fruit, a sign of excellent technical mastery; pure, tasty, long, complex.

SAUTERNES 2004
Sweet White | 2012 up to 2016   **86**
Rich, not very complex or finessed, but tasty. Not stringent enough standards in grape selection, or at least less than other Premiers Crus.

SAUTERNES 2003
Sweet White | 2013 up to 2021   **86**
Reserved in aroma, with jammy flavors that are powerful but marked by the burning sensation of alcohol and that lack aromatic detail. A monolithic wine to follow as it develops in the bottle.

SAUTERNES 2002
Sweet White | Now to 2017   **93**
Delicate, complex, lovely botrytis flavors, one of the most elegant wines of late from this château.

SAUTERNES 2001
Sweet White | 2011 up to 2016   **86**
Rich enough, but not as refined or complex as its peer Premiers Crus, and absolutely less pure. This terroir deserves better.

SAUTERNES 2000
Sweet White | 2011 up to 2015　　86
Golden in color, this lacks the definition and texture expected for its classification and terroir, but overall, it remains enjoyable to taste.

SAUTERNES 1999
Sweet White | 2011 up to 2014　　87
The viscosity and bouquet are too simple for a Premier Cru, but good general balance and good tension suggest it will age favorably.

SAUTERNES 1998
Sweet White | 2011 up to 2018　　89
Honey and soft spice aromas, good body, fatter and more complete than the 1999, with a slight lack of finesse.

SAUTERNES 1997
Sweet White | 2011 up to 2017　　92
The color is beginning to show hints of amber. Powerful, concentrated, richly sweet, hints of citrus fruits and crème brûlée rather typical of the vintage. Consistent, long, yet lacks a little purity and freshness as it develops in the glass.

White: 182.9 acres. Annual production: 100,000 bottles

CHÂTEAU RESPIDE-MÉDEVILLE
🜹 🜹 🜹 🜹 🜹

4, rue du Port
33210 Preignac
Phone 00 33 5 56 76 28 44
Fax 00 33 5 56 76 28 43
contact@gonet-medeville.com
www.gonet-medeville.com

Vines were planted in the Graves region earlier than anywhere else in Bordeaux, predating even the Romans. By medieval times, Bordeaux wine had come to mean Graves wine, white varietals having gradually been overtaken by red varietals. We see this illustrated in Château Respide-Médeville where twenty acres of plantings are devoted to the production of a fine red Graves. This compares with just ten acres for the white wine, an elegant white Graves, renowned for its consistent quality. Owned by the Médeville family (of Sauternes Château Gilette fame), the estate has been nicely taken in hand by the new generation and the wines are now back in top form.

Recently tasted
GRAVES 2006
Red | 2011 up to 2014　　90

GRAVES LA DAME DE RESPIDE 2006
Red | 2011 up to 2013　　86

Older vintages
GRAVES 2006
White | 2011 up to 2013　　88
Pale color. Notes of acacia flowers and white fruit. Nervy but without searing acidity; hints of iodine, typical of the two great local grape varieties. Truly perfect with seafood.

GRAVES 2005
White | 2011 up to 2013　　88
Golden yellow to green in color, this is rich, complex, and perfectly ripe on the nose, with honeyed notes. On the palate, it is full, generous, and filled with fruit, with freshness and a long, well-balanced finish.

GRAVES 2005
Red | 2011 up to 2013　　92
Black color, expressive, ripe and complex nose, powerful and rich palate, with nice, tight tannins and a long, fresh, well-balanced finish. Superbly elegant.

Red: 19.8 acres; cabernet sauvignon 60%, merlot 40%. White: 9.8 acres; muscadelle 5%, sauvignon blanc 45%, sémillon 50%. Annual production: 70,000 bottles

CHÂTEAU RIEUSSEC

33210 Fargues-de-Langon
Phone 00 33 5 57 98 14 14
Fax 00 33 5 57 98 14 10
rieussec@lafite.com
www.lafite.com

This Premier Cru Classé is currently the most lionized in its category, thanks partly to the undeniable quality of its very sweet and remarkably consistent wine, and partly to the power and marketing acumen of the Rothschild holdings. Head of Lafite, Charles Chevallier has built his career here and continues to watch lovingly over the style of the sweet wine, which is vinified using state-of-the-art technology. Some of the poetry may have been lost but definitely none of the quality. Even the so-called "intermediary" vintages remain very sweet, and all of the wines now show more refined balance—even those from a year as climatically flamboyant as 2003!

Recently tasted

SAUTERNES 2006
Sweet White | 2014 up to 2026   **92**
Pretty golden color, almost coppery, lovely botrytis on the nose, with amazingly concentrated notes of candied fruit, almost over the top. Sumptuous, for those who like this style of Sauternes.

Older vintages

SAUTERNES 2005
Sweet White | 2013 up to 2030   **97**
A wine of magnificent strength, this has huge potential for the future. A classic for this exceptional vintage.

SAUTERNES 2004
Sweet White | 2012 up to 2024   **94**
A stunning success. Great sweetness; generous; meticulously sorted by multiple passes; majestic class. A model of its type.

SAUTERNES 2003
Sweet White | 2011 up to 2030   **95**
This holds to a marvelous balance on the palate despite a rich sweetness superior to all vintages we've known, with the light touch of caramel common to this vintage. Sumptuous wine, with no doubt about its ability to age.

SAUTERNES 2002
Sweet White | 2011 up to 2022   **94**
Pale color, honey and mead on the nose, nice acidity, freshness, finesse, roundness, complexity, and charm. Confirms the general success of this vintage, which had been underestimated at first.

SAUTERNES 2001
Sweet White | 2011 up to 2030   **95**
This has a monumental body matched in rich sweetness. Enormous length, considerable promise.

SAUTERNES 2000
Sweet White | 2011 up to 2018   **90**
Golden color, lush but with a certain heaviness on the nose and palate, and an overwhelming aroma of concentrated bitter orange. Much less attractive than the 2002 at this stage.

SAUTERNES 1999
Sweet White | 2011 up to 2027   **93**
With its pale color and notes of acacia with a slight touch of iodine—very "oceanic"—this will pair well with Maine and Caribbean lobster. Vivid, younger, and more complex than the 2000.

SAUTERNES 1998
Sweet White | 2011 up to 2028   **93**
Pale gold color, rich aromas of citrus, saffron, and iodine (but not pharmaceutical). Powerful, tonic, still much too young, with a slight lack of noble rot character.

SAUTERNES 1997
Sweet White | 2011 up to 2027   **95**
Youthful color, complex nose, refined noble rot character. This offers the concentrated flavors typical of this terroir but with purity that we expect from a First Growth and a longevity worthy of the vintage. Very well vinified and aged.

White: 185.3 acres; muscadelle 1.5%, sauvignon 6.5%, sémillon 92%. Annual production: 90,000 bottles

CHÂTEAU ROÛMIEU-LACOSTE

Le Plantey
33720 Barsac
Phone 00 33 5 56 27 16 29
Fax 00 33 5 56 27 02 65
hervedubourdieu@aol.com

What owner Hervé Dubourdieu mainly produces here are dry Graves wines from his vineyards in the neighboring Graves appellation (they get around, these Dubourdieus). This small, little-known Barsac cru consists of a few acres of plantings near Climens, perfectly managed by Hervé, who vinifies one of today's most powerful and uncompromising Barsac wines.

SAUTERNES CHÂTEAU ROÛMIEU-LACOSTE 2005
Sweet White | 2011 up to 2025   **93**
Sumptuously rich sweetness, a nose of wonderfully botrytised grapes. A bottle for true lovers of sweet wines.

SAUTERNES CHÂTEAU ROÛMIEU-LACOSTE 2001
Sweet White | 2011 up to 2026   **92**
A wonderfully complete wine with a rich nose, perfectly botrytised, sweet but not heavy. Great future ahead.

Annual production: 20,000 bottles

CHÂTEAU SIGALAS-RABAUD

33210 Bommes
Phone 00 33 5 57 31 07 45

This domaine owns a small (thirty-five-acre) but perfectly exposed, single-block vineyard next door to Lafaurie-Peyraguey, with the potential to produce a very sweet but fabulously delicate dessert wine. The development of noble rot is particularly splendid on these early-ripening varietals—witness the sublime 1988, 1990, 1996, and 1997 Sigalas Rabaud. Recent vintages seem to us to fall somewhat short of the mark, but bottle aging may prove us wrong. The Lambert des Granges family is devoted to this property, and we earnestly hope that they take full charge of viticulture and winemaking.

Recently tasted
SAUTERNES 2006
Sweet White | 2014 up to 2021   **93**

SAUTERNES LIEUTENANT DE SIGALAS 2006
Sweet White | 2012 up to 2016   **90**

Older vintages
SAUTERNES 2005
Sweet White | 2013 up to 2027   **95**
A wine of great richness in extract and of unbelievable aromatic distinction. Cellar for another ten years.

SAUTERNES 2004
Sweet White | 2012 up to 2019   **90**
Fine, very enjoyable, supple. Lovely style, not too syrupy, and structured by a pleasant acidity, with good length. Not for long aging.

SAUTERNES 2003
Sweet White | 2011 up to 2023   **93**
This is fairly pure, but with a little touch of heaviness (caramel) from the 2003 vintage. Bottle age will help to improve the balance by bringing refinement and the development of more complex aromas.

SAUTERNES 2002
Sweet White | 2011 up to 2027   **94**
Pale color but powerful wine, complex and refined. There is a touch of bitterness that needs to meld in, and slightly too much oak character for a supreme balance, but it has considerable body and will age well.

SAUTERNES 2001
Sweet White | 2011 up to 2030   **96**
With extremely elegant aromas and a great purity of expression, this splendidly hides its force. An archetype of wine made from truly noble rot!

SAUTERNES 2000

Sweet White | 2011 up to 2020   **93**

Pale color and strong notes of iodine (more like the ocean than the pharmacy), as is common in 2000. Close to the 2001 for its oak component. Well preserved, still young but without the expected purity and extreme finesse.

SAUTERNES 1998

Sweet White | 2011 up to 2018   **94**

Very generous notes of honey. Ample, long, delicious, this one also has a little iodine note recalling ocean mist. Oak more integrated than in the vintage that followed. A great achievement for the vintage.

SAUTERNES 1997

Sweet White | 2011 up to 2017   **95**

Golden color, notes of mead in the nose and palate, long, noble rot character, a touch evolved but infinitely flavorful.

White: 34.6 acres; muscadelle 1%, sauvignon 14%, sémillon 85%. Annual production: 30,000 bottles

CHÂTEAU SMITH HAUT-LAFITTE

33650 Martillac
Phone 00 33 5 57 83 11 22
Fax 00 33 5 57 83 11 21
smith-haut-lafitte@smith-haut-lafitte.com
www.smith-haut-lafitte.com

Smith Haut-Lafitte is the most "go-to" property in Martillac, with a well-equipped winery and tourist facilities that earned it the "Best of Wine Tourism" award in 2003. It is also a pioneer in its category, with a viticultural philosophy largely inspired by the principles of Rudolph Steiner and biodynamic thinking. Its white wines always were irresistible; today they are magnificent for their sappiness and aromatic class. The reds grow more corpulent and precise with every passing vintage and age delightfully; we have occasionally underestimated them when newly born. The Cathiards's other property, Cantelys, makes altogether more commonplace wines.

Recently tasted
PESSAC-LÉOGNAN 2007
White | 2011 up to 2017   **94**

PESSAC-LÉOGNAN LES HAUTS DE SMITH 2007
White | 2011 up to 2013   **91**

PESSAC-LÉOGNAN LES HAUTS DE SMITH 2006
Red | 2011 up to 2014   **87**

Older vintages
PESSAC-LÉOGNAN 2006
Red | 2014 up to 2021   **93**
Good color, quite supple, less complex in aromas, and less dense than Domaine de Chevalier, but more voluptuous in texture. This wine has not yet said its last word.

PESSAC-LÉOGNAN 2006
White | 2011 up to 2016   **95**
Slightly musky, round, long, and very richly aromatic, with an oak note that is strong but perfectly harmonious with the intensity of the wine body. Terrific length. Remarkable and inimitable.

PESSAC-LÉOGNAN 2005
Red | 2011 up to 2025   **93**
This has a refined texture for the vintage, well-defined fruit, harmonious tannins, and great balance between strength and finesse. The end of barrel aging brought out some notes of chocolate from this extremely sunny vintage.

PESSAC-LÉOGNAN 2005
White | 2011 up to 2020   **95**
With a complex nose, distinguished, deep, great, and sophisticated, this is pure, complex, and magnificently crafted, a wine that did not change an iota in a year. Marvelously expressive notes of vine blossom and white peach developing on the nose.

PESSAC-LÉOGNAN 2004
Red | 2011 up to 2025   **93**
Big nose, spicy, feral, a little bit too open, but the texture is very voluptuous, caressing, long and sensual, with delicate tannins. High-quality wine.

PESSAC-LÉOGNAN 2004
White | 2011 up to 2020   **88**
Flavorful, oaky, long, approachable, tidy, just about ready to drink.

PESSAC-LÉOGNAN 2001
White | 2011 up to 2015   **95**
A great achievement: wonderful aromatic finesse and superb length.

PESSAC-LÉOGNAN 2001
Red | 2011 up to 2020   **93**
Spicy with assertive but smooth tannins, this wine is an achievement, with a deep, elegant, lingering finish.

PESSAC-LÉOGNAN 2000
Red | 2011 up to 2020   **90**
Fine, harmonious, and aromatic, with a powerful and vivid body.

Red: 138.4 acres; cabernet franc 10%, cabernet sauvignon 59%, merlot 30%, petit verdot 1%. **White:** 27.2 acres; sauvignon blanc 90%, sauvignon gris 5%, sémillon 5%. **Annual production:** 200,000 bottles

CHÂTEAU SUDUIRAUT

33210 Preignac
Phone 00 33 5 56 63 61 92
Fax 00 33 5 56 63 61 93
acceuil@suduiraut.com
www.suduiraut.com

This immense holding is certainly not the easiest of the Sauternes crus in terms of viticulture, but today's management is the best in fifty years. Like Yquem, Suduiraut plays on the diversity of its terroirs and is an unfailing favorite with all lovers of great sweet wines: complete character, tremendous aromatic development, and impressively opulent sweetness.

Recently tasted
SAUTERNES 2006
Sweet White | 2016 up to 2030   **96**

Older vintages
SAUTERNES 2005
Sweet White | 2015 up to 2050   **96**
A wine of amazing concentration and sumptuous sweetness. Huge cellar-aging potential.

SAUTERNES 2004
Sweet White | 2012 up to 2022   **92**
Pale; nose of honey, hay, and classic notes of citrus. Supple and very delicate.

SAUTERNES 2003
Sweet White | 2011 up to 2030   **95**
With a golden color, this has a little splash of iodine on the nose, which will reduce its score by one-half to one point, because some of its peers do not have this character. Huge richness and sweetness. Great future.

SAUTERNES 2002
Sweet White | 2011 up to 2022   **94**
This offers a lot of finesse and harmony and pure, generous fruit. This vintage is decidedly surprising and tasting very well right now.

SAUTERNES 2001
Sweet White | 2011 up to 2029   **96**
With great aromatic finesse and remarkably opulent sweetness, this is noble and full-bodied with huge potential.

SAUTERNES 2000
Sweet White | 2011 up to 2030   **94**
Eye-catching bright golden-yellow color. Well constructed, with exceptional balance between richness and freshness and a noble and complex finish. A very beautiful 2000.

SAUTERNES 1999

Sweet White | 2011 up to 2017   **93**

A beautiful success for the vintage: a rich, fleshy wine, full, spicy on the palate but finishing on bitter orange notes very specific to this region. The best of its terroir.

SAUTERNES 1998

Sweet White | 2011 up to 2013   **93**

Color still youthful with a hay hue; nose scented with dry fruit and a lovely noble rot character. This is less vibrant than the 1999 but more delicate, and, most importantly, has not a trace of oxidation.

SAUTERNES 1997

Sweet White | 2011 up to 2017   **93**

Amber color, good development of fruit aromas toward mead, as well as some notes that are less attractive than we might wish. It has a velvety texture and great sweetness, but one might prefer the style of the 1998.

White: 227.3 acres; sauvignon blanc 7%, sauvignon gris 1%, sémillon 92%. Annual production: 130,000 bottles

CHÂTEAU LA TOUR BLANCHE

1 Ter Tour Blanche
33210 Bommes
Phone 00 33 5 57 98 02 73
Fax 00 33 5 57 98 02 78
tour-blanche@tour-blanche.com
www.tour-blanche.com

The château here is owned by the French state and houses an official research center for winemakers. Mostly, though, Château La Tour Blanche is renowned throughout the world for its magnificent sweet wine: very rich, with a foundation of aromatic finesse and subtly nuanced flavors. There is a tendency to premature aging in some of its latest releases, which suggests it might be even better if fermentation were kicked up a notch. An extra half or one degree of alcohol would help to prevent oxidation. The current winemakers look to achieve a very high degree of residual sugar (often more than 100 grams), which explains the exquisite smoothness of all the recent vintages.

Recently tasted

SAUTERNES 2006

Sweet White | 2014 up to 2026   **92**

Older vintages

SAUTERNES 2005

Sweet White | 2013 up to 2030   **94**

The richness in liqueur is incredible, yet the wine retains an admirable aromatic purity. The texture and the persistence of sweetness are lavish.

SAUTERNES 2004

Sweet White | 2012 up to 2022   **92**

Pale golden color, very developed nose (pear, citrus fruit), well defined, ultrarich, refined, smooth. Very long, youthful, distinguished. Great future.

SAUTERNES 2003

Sweet White | 2011 up to 2025   **96**

Grand aromas of noble rot, marvelously preserved without alteration by vinification; immense sweetness, great length. Lavish but without heaviness, this is masterfully vinified, and resembles Yquem more than any of the others.

SAUTERNES 2002

Sweet White | 2011 up to 2022   **94**

Practically ideal balance, transcendent finesse; the most harmonious vintage of the last decade.

SAUTERNES 2001

Sweet White | 2011 up to 2026   **94**

Complex aromas, more mirabelle plum than citrus; grand finesse, perfect botrytis. Great future.

SAUTERNES 1999

Sweet White | 2011 up to 2024   **92**

With a golden color, spicy aromas, sharper acidity than 1998, and much more balanced sweetness than the 1997, this has volume, nobility, and length. There is a slight bitterness that has yet to blend in.

SAUTERNES 1998

Sweet White | 2011 up to 2020   **94**

Clearer and more youthful color than the 1997, very refined, floral and honey aromas, grand finesse, and tenderness, well within the style of the château.

SAUTERNES 1997

Sweet White | 2011 up to 2013   **88**

Nose a little too evolved, just like the color, with a loss of freshness and aromatics; good suavity but finish too simple.

Red: 7.4 acres; malbec 10%, merlot 90%. White: 91.4 acres; muscadelle 5%, sauvignon blanc 12%, sémillon 83%. Annual production: 60,000 bottles

VIEUX CHÂTEAU GAUBERT

35, avenue du 8-mai-1945
33640 Portets
Phone 00 33 5 56 67 18 63
Fax 00 33 5 56 67 52 76
dominique.haverlan@libertysurf.fr

Dominique Haverlan comes from a long line of vignerons and for the past two decades has ranked as a benchmark producer of Graves wines. His merlot-driven red is made from stringently selected fruit and barrel-matured for twelve months. The estate's second wine is the Benjamin de Vieux Château Gaubert. The white wine also sees wood, and is fermented and raised on lees for nine months. Château Gaubert may have some catching up to do in terms of aromatic precision and elegant composition, but it remains a top Graves nonetheless.

Recently tasted

GRAVES 2007

White | 2011 up to 2013   **86**

GRAVES 2006

Red | 2011 up to 2014   **87**

GRAVES BENJAMIN DE VIEUX CHÂTEAU GAUBERT 2006

Red | 2011 up to 2013   **87**

Older vintages

GRAVES 2005

White | 2011 up to 2013   **86**

A yellow-gold color with hints of green, and a powerful and complex nose of ripe fruit and spicy oak. Broad on the palate and very ripe, with a finish that could have used a bit more acidity.

GRAVES 2005

Red | 2011 up to 2013   **87**

Purple-black color. Expressive nose of super-ripe black fruit, with hints of spice. Solid, full, and voluminous in the mouth with good length. A Graves that is more powerful than elegant.

Red: 49.4 acres; cabernet sauvignon 50%, merlot 50%. White: 12.4 acres; sauvignon blanc 50%, sémillon 50%. Annual production: 120,000 bottles

CHÂTEAU D'YQUEM

🏅 🏅 🏅 🏅

33210 Sauternes
Phone 00 33 5 57 98 07 07
Fax 00 33 5 57 98 07 08
info@yquem.fr
www.yquem.fr

One could almost say that Château d'Yquem is to Bordeaux what the Mona Lisa is to art: so unique as to be beyond criticism. There is no such thing as a minor or even average Yquem vintage, because there is no compromise. Either the year is good enough for a vintage or it isn't. Nature decides whether or not there will be that ideal spread of *Botrytis cinerea* together with that smaller proportion of shriveled grapes that is sometimes required for perfect balance. The final shape of the wine may simply reflect the preferences of the person in charge at the time: sparkle, finesse, and creaminess under the long reign of Alexandre de Lur-Saluces; purity, freshness, and a subtle flexibility characteristic of each vintage under the present incumbent, Pierre Lurton, wisely guided by Denis Dubourdieu. Château d'Yquem's big advantage is the sheer variety of terroirs at its disposal—some earlier-ripening than others; some clayey, others sandy—which allows it to capture great grapes in their prime, wherever they may be found. The wine has continued to grow in freshness, crispness, and aromatic finesse, with no loss of that sumptuous character seen in its three masterpieces: the resoundingly successful 2004, 2005, and 2006.

SAUTERNES 2006
Sweet White | 2016 up to 2030   **97**
Superlative balance of alcohol and sugar for the vintage. Optimal aromatic purity. The grace, precision, and individuality of this wine places it above the rest!

SAUTERNES 2005
Sweet White | 2011 up to 2030   **100**
The wine blends the most beautifully rich constitution imaginable with an immediate freshness and elegance previously unheard of, which places this wine in a category of its own.

SAUTERNES 2004
Sweet White | 2011 up to 2030   **97**
An admirable success, and the beginning of a stylistic evolution toward more immediate freshness and aromatic purity, without losing any of its splendid substance. Not only the best, but also without a doubt the most well-made wine of 2004.

SAUTERNES 2003
Sweet White | 2011 up to 2030   **97**
The nose is already developing with confidence; the wine has a precision and purity that would have been unthinkable just ten years ago. This is a complete wine with slightly more body than in previous vintages, all of the elements in perfect balance.

SAUTERNES 2002
Sweet White | 2011 up to 2030   **96**
An exquisite nose of splendid fruit, with the grace of true noble rot. This offers richness and elegance of the highest echelon, accessible and open at this early stage thanks to modern vinification techniques.

SAUTERNES 2001
Sweet White | 2011 up to 2050   **100**
Perfection, if it exists on Earth! Sublime nose of yellow and white fruit melded with notes of supremely elegant vanilla; perfect balance between alcohol and sweetness; amazing length and, above all, a feeling of harmony and restraint that surpasses all other vintages of this growth.

SAUTERNES 2000
Sweet White | 2011 up to 2030   **95**
Wonderfully botrytised nose, very elegant and integrated, with slightly fewer nuances and less freshness than the 2001. Rich and balanced on the palate with sumptuous sweetness. Wonderful future. The rigorous selection of grapes that is unique to Yquem has yet again put it at the top of the appellation.

SAUTERNES 1999
Sweet White | 2011 up to 2020   **93**
Pretty nose of apricot, mango, and honey, typical of Sauternes, but lacking the extra botrytis expected of Yquem. It is rich and elegant, not very tight in texture, with a less forceful personality than other vintages. Wonderful élevage.

SAUTERNES 1998
Sweet White | 2011 up to 2025   **96**
Classic Yquem, generous, deep, with magnificently focused richness. It will age beautifully.

SAUTERNES 1997
Sweet White | 2011 up to 2030   **98**
The classic power and concentration of Yquem are there, but in addition there is also an amazing freshness that erases any heaviness in the wine. The length makes it impeccably distinguished. A work of art!

White: 254.5 acres; sauvignon 20%, sémillon 80%.
Annual production: 95,000 bottles

Médoc Vineyards

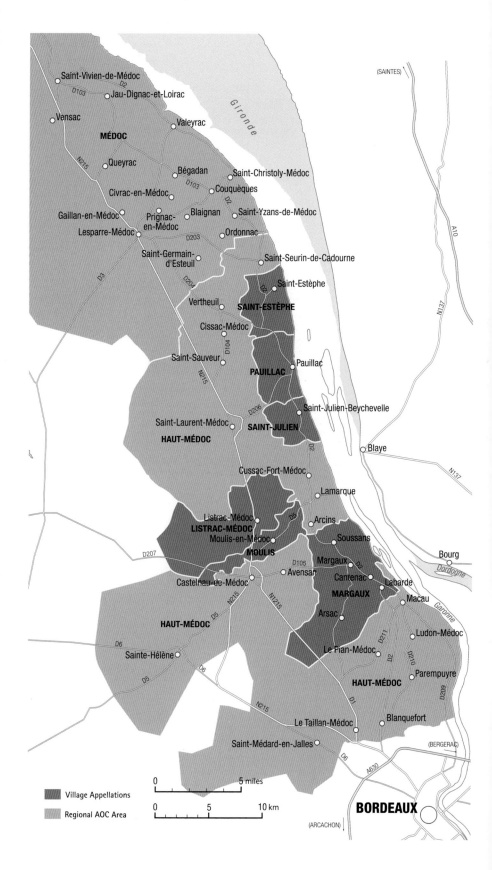

(SAINTES)

Saint-Vivien-de-Médoc
D103
Jau-Dignac-et-Loirac
Vensac
Valeyrac
MÉDOC
Gironde
N215
Queyrac
Bégadan
Saint-Christoly-Médoc
D103
Couquèques
Civrac-en-Médoc
D2
Gaillan-en-Médoc
Blaignan
Saint-Yzans-de-Médoc
Prignac-
en-Médoc
Lesparre-Médoc
Ordonnac
D203
Saint-Germain-
d'Esteuil
Saint-Seurin-de-Cadourne
D3
D204
Vertheuil
Saint-Estèphe
D2
SAINT-ESTÈPHE
Cissac-Médoc
Saint-Sauveur
D104
Pauillac
PAUILLAC
N215
Saint-Julien-Beychevelle
D206
Saint-Laurent-Médoc
SAINT-JULIEN
HAUT-MÉDOC
Blaye
D2
Cussac-Fort-Médoc
N137
Lamarque
Listrac-Médoc
Arcins
LISTRAC-MÉDOC
D6
Moulis-en-Médoc
Soussans
D207
MOULIS
D105
Margaux
Castelnau-de-Médoc
Avensan
Cantenac
Bourg
Dordogne
Labarde
MARGAUX
N215
Macau
N215
Arsac
Garonne
HAUT-MÉDOC
Ludon-Médoc
D211
D6
Le Pian-Médoc
D2
Sainte-Hélène
D210
Parempuyre
D5
D6
D209
HAUT-MÉDOC
N215
Le Taillan-Médoc
Blanquefort
D1
Saint-Médard-en-Jalles
(BERGERAC)
D6
A630

A10
N137

0   5 miles
0   5   10 km

■ Village Appellations
■ Regional AOC Area

BORDEAUX

(ARCACHON)

CHÂTEAU D'ARMAILHAC

33250 Pauillac
Phone 00 33 5 56 59 22 22
Fax 00 33 5 56 73 20 44
webmaster@bpdr.com
www.bpdr.com

The vineyards adjoin those of Mouton-Rothschild but are planted in lighter, less perfectly drained gravel. The not inconsiderable proportion of cabernet franc here leads to wines with refined aromas but a characteristically slender structure that has sometimes bordered on thinness. Since 2000, greater attention has been paid to viticulture and harvesting, resulting in more muscular expression at no expense to finesse. Philippine de Rothschild holds this château dear and makes sure it produces the most complete wine possible. Since Philippe Dalhuin arrived on the scene, the results speak for themselves: witness the remarkable 2005.

PAUILLAC 2006
Red | 2014 up to 2021   90
Fat, fruity, subtle, but a little less energetic than some of its peers.

PAUILLAC 2005
Red | 2011 up to 2020   93
Impressive finesse on both the nose and palate, particularly fine, clean texture, harmonious tannins; a high-class wine that is now reaching its peak.

PAUILLAC 2004
Red | 2011 up to 2017   89
Beautiful color, delicious notes of raspberry on the nose, less spice in both tannins and flavor than other bottlings; delicate tannins and greater emphasis on the wine's floral and fruity notes.

PAUILLAC 2001
Red | 2011 up to 2020   90
A remarkable wine: the body, the aromatic finesse, the texture, and the tannins are all perfectly balanced, making it the most accomplished of all the Pauillac Fifth Growths of this vintage.

PAUILLAC 2000
Red | 2011 up to 2020   90
This wine is powerful and harmonious, with impeccably extracted tannins.

Red: 123.6 acres; cabernet franc 20%, cabernet sauvignon 56%, merlot 22%, petit verdot 2%. Annual production: 220,000 bottles

CHÂTEAU BATAILLEY

86, cours Balguerie-Stuttenberg
33250 Pauillac
Phone 00 33 5 56 00 00 70
Fax 00 33 5 56 52 29 54
domaines@borie-manoux.fr

This cru has developed enormously in just five years: as vinous and powerfully expressive as some of the vintages seen in the past, particularly in the 1940s and 1950s, but with infinitely purer, more refined aromas. Philippe Castéja, with advice from foremost enologist Denis Dubourdieu, has made all the changes required and the results speak for themselves. Batailley has become one of the most highly recommended crus in this appellation and at a very attractive price. The 2005 and 2006 represent its best-ever performance, showing classical cedar and spice on the nose and gorgeous vinosity. Sure to reward the patient oenophile!

PAUILLAC 2006
Red | 2016 up to 2026   93
Dense on the palate but softened by a remarkably velvety texture and racy tannins. Classy wine, undoubtedly the best in the last fifty years.

PAUILLAC 2005
Red | 2011 up to 2020   90
Truffle and spice aromas, remarkably balanced, full, deep body, with pure tannins and a bit mineral for this area of Pauillac.

PAUILLAC 2004
Red | 2011 up to 2020   92
Well made and well vinified, a complete wine, with refined tannins. A clear expression of its terroir and appellation.

PAUILLAC 2002
Red | 2011 up to 2017   90
Very elegant and complete for its vintage, with classic notes of cigar box and graphite and pure tannins. Warmly recommended.

PAUILLAC 2000
Red | 2011 up to 2020   88
Generous body, tannins less refined than in recent vintages. Will gain balance with time.

Red: 135.9 acres; cabernet 30%, merlot 70%. Annual production: 320,000 bottles

CHÂTEAU BELGRAVE

33112 Saint-Laurent-du-Médoc
Phone 00 33 5 56 35 53 00
Fax 00 33 5 56 35 53 29
contact@cvbg.com
www.dourthe.com

This cru has been fully up to speed for only the past three years. Before that, it produced a solid, carefully vinified but rather over-extracted wine. For enological consultant Michel Rolland, this was a necessary step toward the harmonious, aromatically seductive style we see displayed in the most recent vintages. Thanks to cutting-edge technology, this cru now delivers all the style and precise expression to be expected of its excellent terroir.

HAUT-MÉDOC 2006
Red | 2011 up to 2020   **90**
Powerful, fleshy wine, with tannins of a complexity never before seen at this château. Good for long cellaring.

HAUT-MÉDOC 2005
Red | 2011 up to 2025   **89**
Rich in color, alcohol, and tannins. Powerful wine, straightforward, well made, if a tiny bit rigid.

HAUT-MÉDOC 2004
Red | 2011 up to 2019   **87**
Slightly feral, tender for this cru, long-lasting on the palate, refined tannins, well extracted, but overall lacks some personality.

HAUT-MÉDOC 2003
Red | 2011 up to 2015   **87**
Saturated crimson color, spicy aroma, noticeable oak, lovely velvet texture, viscous, with a dry, tannic finish.

HAUT-MÉDOC 2002
Red | 2011 up to 2014   **86**
Generous body for the vintage but tannins a little coarse and tight.

HAUT-MÉDOC 2001
Red | 2011 up to 2013   **87**
Cozy body, tannins firm but velvety and harmonious. Drinkable now.

HAUT-MÉDOC 2000
Red | 2011 up to 2013   **86**
Solid wine. Generous. Lively, but not especially refined.

Red: 148.3 acres; cabernet franc 4%, cabernet sauvignon 44%, merlot 48%, petit verdot 4%. Annual production: 280,000 bottles

CHÂTEAU BELLE-VUE

69, route de Louens
33460 Macau
Phone 00 33 5 57 88 19 79
Fax 00 33 5 57 88 41 79
vincent.mulliez@château-belle-vue.fr
www.château-belle-vue.fr

Vincent Mulliez acquired this southern Médoc property in 2004, together with the neighboring Château de Gironville. Château Belle-Vue is often impressive as a young wine but can tend to close up for a while as it gets older. The 2005 vintage seems to have marked a turning point, characterized by a much silkier tannic structure. The same could be said of the Gironville, which has displayed exceptional elegance in recent vintages.

BORDEAUX SUPÉRIEUR CHÂTEAU BOLAIRE 2006
Red | Drink now   **86**
Round and pleasant wine, with notes of jammy red fruit, well built, for immediate drinking.

HAUT-MÉDOC 2006
Red | 2011 up to 2018   **88**
Black color, powerful nose, complex and soft; on the palate it's full, fleshy, vigorous, with ripe tannins and nice aromatic length. Well balanced.

HAUT-MÉDOC 2005
Red | 2011 up to 2020   **90**
Fuller and more structured than the 2006 and 2004, this is a hearty wine with ripe tannins and great aromatic length. Great potential.

HAUT-MÉDOC CHÂTEAU DE GIRONVILLE 2006
Red | 2011 up to 2018   **90**
A nice wine, in the style of the best wines of the southern Médoc, with an elegance that approaches that of a good Margaux. A focused nose of small red berries, luxurious body, svelte and elegant; splendid balance, length, and freshness.

HAUT-MÉDOC CHÂTEAU DE GIRONVILLE 2005
Red | 2011 up to 2017   **90**
Slightly less complex than the 2006, but on the same scale, fruity, supple, and substantial.

HAUT-MÉDOC CHÂTEAU DE GIRONVILLE 2004
Red | 2011 up to 2014   **89**
Fruit-filled wine, fleshy, elegantly assembled, with body and freshness. Good length with structured tannins.

Red: 257 acres; cabernet sauvignon 53%, merlot 27%, petit verdot 20%. Annual production: 55,000 bottles

CHÂTEAU BEYCHEVELLE

🦆 🦆 🦆 🦆 🦆

33250 Saint-Julien-Beychevelle
Phone 00 33 5 56 73 20 70
Fax 00 33 5 56 73 20 71
beychevelle@beychevelle.com
www.beychevelle.com

This magnificent property boasts some of the finest, most elegant buildings in Saint-Julien and produces a grand vin to match: enough finesse to compete with any wine, even a Margaux, and a texture so delicate that you need the sensibilities of an aesthete to appreciate it properly. True, it can seem thin and green in difficult years, but, that said, performance is much more consistent than it used to be. Note also that this cru reveals its true colors only with time (the sublime 1996 is a good example), and present winemaker Philippe Blanc refuses to do anything that might compromise the dignity of this terroir for the sake of precocious charm! Recent vintages are sure to go down well with those mainly in search of finesse and that subtly spicy nose typical of cabernet. The barrels they use here today are much better than in the past.

Saint-Julien 2006
Red | 2014 up to 2021   **90**
Elegant, straightforward, and refined: the vintage will be a fine classic from the château.

Saint-Julien 2005
Red | 2011 up to 2030   **94**
Marvelous finesse and remarkably subtle aromas and tannins, which largely compensate for this wine's slight lack in body. A wine for connoisseurs—comparable to the château's phenomenal 1928!

Saint-Julien 2004
Red | 2011 up to 2016   **88**
Feral and reductive on the nose, less refined than expected. Rather dry tannins but racy, with good vinosity. Could be a pleasant surprise with age.

Saint-Julien 2003
Red | 2011 up to 2025   **91**
An admirably faultless body but, above all, tannins of a rare quality. Smooth, refined, subtle, true to the Saint-Julien tradition. A stunning wine from a vintage that itself broke all the records. For the connoisseur.

Saint-Julien 2002
Red | 2011 up to 2017   **89**
Lovely cedar nose, more slender than vinous, tannins still tight, stylish, and full of character, less fleshy than its peers, but not diluted.

Saint-Julien 2001
Red | 2011 up to 2019   **92**
A classic wine, combining suppleness and vinosity and at the same time playing on finesse and freshness.

Saint-Julien 2000
Red | 2011 up to 2025   **94**
A racy wine of rare power for this cru and a very tight texture; a good example of the classicism of Saint-Julien.

Red: 222.4 acres; cabernet franc 5%, cabernet sauvignon 62%, merlot 31%, petit verdot 2%. Annual production: 480,000 bottles

CHÂTEAU BOYD-CANTENAC

11, route de Jean Faure
33460 Cantenac
Phone 00 33 5 57 88 90 82
guillemet.lucien@wanadoo.fr
www.boyd-cantenac.fr

Boyd-Cantenac often escapes the hallowed "en primeur" tastings—which is not a bad thing, because this wine really takes shape only in the bottle, acquiring the firm body and complex nose that its rank commands. Pierre Guillemet is one of a kind in the Médoc: an independent owner-winemaker who cherishes his freedom and handles himself like the true professional that he is. Recent vintages reflect their terroir and year, and are complete in every way. Built to age and very reasonably priced, too.

Recently tasted
Margaux 2006
Red | 2014 up to 2021   **89**

Older vintages
Margaux 2005
Red | 2011 up to 2030   **95**
This wine was the most impressive of all the Margaux Crus Classés presented at the blind tasting. Splendid cedar aromas, dedicated to true lovers of cabernet sauvignon. Remarkable body, racy tannins, a tension and vitality unmatched among its peers.

Margaux 2004
Red | 2011 up to 2020   **90**
Deeply colored, powerful, vinous, ripe, with quality oak and good breadth: the style of this appellation keeps changing. This is an attention-getter.

Margaux 2003
Red | 2011 up to 2018   **88**
A somewhat underdeveloped wine, clean, solid. Only age will give it the harmony it presently lacks—but the wine has a very solid structure from the start.

Margaux 2002
Red | 2011 up to 2017   **89**
Beautifully balanced and straightforward, yet also refined and full of life: a product of quality viticulture and serious vinification.

Margaux 2000
Red | 2011 up to 2020   **91**
Quality depth in its makeup and great integrity in its expression of terroir. A monumental wine—the epitome of cabernet sauvignon.

Red: 44.5 acres; cabernet sauvignon 66%, merlot 30%, petit verdot 4%. Annual production: 70,000 bottles

CHÂTEAU BRANAIRE-DUCRU

Lieu-dit Le Bourdieu
33250 Saint-Julien-Beychevelle
Phone 00 33 5 56 59 25 86
Fax 00 33 5 56 59 16 26
branaire@branaire.com
www.branaire.com

Rigorous viticulture and quality winemaking have earned this winery a place among the top Saint-Julien producers. Vineyard management has to be particularly strict here because the parcels are scattered throughout the appellation. Winemaking is equally disciplined (Branaire was the first in Saint-Julien to reintroduce gravity-fed vinification processes). Branaire-Ducru wines are known for their consistency, finesse, and full-bodied constitution—even the second wine—but don't expect them to match the vinosity of crus from the Pauillac area.

Saint-Julien 2006
Red | 2014 up to 2021   **91**
Long, full-bodied, and subtle. Barrel aging has nicely helped this wine come into its prime.

Saint-Julien 2005
Red | 2011 up to 2025   **93**
Very fleshy wine, more supple than many of its peers, with an enveloping mouthfeel and quality tannins. Vinified for balance and elegance rather than to achieve the ultimate expression of the vintage.

Saint-Julien 2003
Red | 2011 up to 2021   **90**
A generous wine with a delicate texture but a tendency to thin out with aeration. Fine, intelligently extracted tannins, good palate length.

Saint-Julien 2002
Red | 2011 up to 2017   **93**
Superb aromatic precision, with seductive notes of violet and licorice, particularly refined tannins. Bright future ahead.

Saint-Julien 2001
Red | 2011 up to 2021   **90**
Classic form and texture with an excellent tannic structure, undisputedly built for long aging.

Saint-Julien 2000
Red | 2011 up to 2020   **95**
Particularly powerful for this cru, plump, mouth-coating tannins and good length. Brilliantly precise, with outstanding balance and authenticity.

Red: 123.6 acres; cabernet franc 5%, cabernet sauvignon 70%, merlot 22%, petit verdot 3%. Annual production: 250,000 bottles

CHÂTEAU BRANE-CANTENAC

33460 Cantenac
Phone 00 33 5 57 88 83 33
Fax 00 33 5 57 88 72 51
contact@brane-cantenac.com
www.brane-cantenac.com

This historic winery is centered on a nicely homogeneous terroir, source of a typical, very dependable, and carefully made Margaux. Until recent vintages at least, the wine was more attractive for its refined nose than its mouthfeel. The grand vin these days reflects the work put in by Henri Lurton: a brawnier, more dynamic expression of terroir but still relatively restrained on first impression; you might say this is the innate politeness of the Brane-Cantenac soils. All of the recent vintages are excellent: built on finesse but with that tautness typical of great terroirs that just needs a bit of time to come into its own.

Recently tasted
MARGAUX 2006
Red | 2014 up to 2021   90

Older vintages
MARGAUX 2005
Red | 2011 up to 2030   90
The years of barrel aging have brought strength to this wine, with tannins that now almost overpower the palate, to the detriment of texture and taste. The quality of the vineyard is almost lost to the vintage. But give it about ten years, and the terroir will prevail.

MARGAUX 2004
Red | 2011 up to 2020   94
Very balanced wine with a perfectly elegant texture. Strict but racy flavor, true to the Médoc.

MARGAUX 2003
Red | 2011 up to 2025   95
Great color, fantastic finesse on the nose; grapes of ideal ripeness, rich with notes of licorice and prunes, admirably silken texture, racy tannins. Full of the inimitable charm of Margaux's grand terroir.

MARGAUX 2000
Red | 2011 up to 2020   90
A harmonious wine that practically oozes with flavor, held together by its tight texture.

Red: 210 acres; cabernet franc 4%, cabernet sauvignon 52%, merlot 43%. Annual production: 180,000 bottles

CHÂTEAU CALON-SÉGUR

33180 Saint-Estèphe
Phone 00 33 5 56 59 30 08
Fax 00 33 5 56 59 71 51
calon-segur@calon-segur.fr

With its sumptuous walled vineyard on the northern borders of the appellation, the magnificent Château Calon-Ségur seems magically suspended in time. Now as stylish as ever thanks to current owner Madame Gasqueton, the domaine is home to one of the classiest and most consistent of all the Médoc wines. Its aromatic finesse and generous texture come close to the great Pauillacs, and its natural expression is out of this world—as is its longevity. Given another fifty years or so, the 2000, 2003, and 2005 are sure to be as stunning as the 1947 or the 1953.

SAINT-ESTÈPHE 2006
Red | 2016 up to 2026   94
A beautiful wine, though no particular sophistication has been brought to its maturation. Effortlessly expresses the beautiful fruit of this vintage and the nobility of the terroir. Almost ideal balance of alcohol and tannins, judiciously extracted.

SAINT-ESTÈPHE 2005
Red | 2011 up to 2030   96
Sublime cedar and red-fruit aromas, full body, noble tannins: this wine flirts with the Premiers Crus and commands respect for its authenticity, sincerity, and magnificent expression of terroir.

SAINT-ESTÈPHE 2004
Red | 2011 up to 2024   95
Great harmony of flavor and tannins, nobly spicy, with a truly aristocratic mouthfeel. Splendid success.

SAINT-ESTÈPHE 2003
Red | 2011 up to 2025   95
Very elegant shape and structure, with a dreamily velvety texture. The flavor has more pronounced notes of cabernet sauvignon than most of the other Second Growths from this appellation. Great follow-through on the palate.

SAINT-ESTÈPHE 2002
Red | 2011 up to 2020   93
Very beautiful wine, precise and racy, with an elegant aroma of cedar and the mouthfeel of a Lafite; dry, but charming and refined. The most successful wine of its appellation for this vintage.

SAINT-ESTÈPHE 2001
Red | 2011 up to 2020   **87**
A harmoniously built wine, but much simpler on the nose and palate than the best of its peers from this vintage.

SAINT-ESTÈPHE 2000
Red | 2011 up to 2020   **92**
Expansive and almost exotic on the nose, with notes of eucalyptus and ripe bell peppers, held in check by a tight texture.

SAINT-ESTÈPHE 1999
Red | 2011 up to 2014   **96**
Impressively refined and distinguished aromas of cedar, great follow-through on the palate. What elegance!

SAINT-ESTÈPHE 1998
Red | 2011 up to 2013   **93**
Complex and racy notes of cedar and spice on the nose, tannins slightly stiffer than in the 1998, tight and classy nevertheless.

SAINT-ESTÈPHE 1996
Red | 2011 up to 2016   **93**
Racy cedar aromas, long, fresh, and distinguished, but a slight lack of vinosity.

Red: 135.9 acres; 60%, merlot 35%, petit verdot 5%.

CHÂTEAU CANTEMERLE

33460 Macau
Phone 00 33 5 57 97 02 82
Fax 00 33 5 57 97 02 84
cantemerle@cantemerle.com
www.cantemerle.com

This estate boasts magnificent grounds and buildings in the southern Médoc. The vineyards are meticulously tended and planted in a fine gravel soil. The wines are packed with charm and immediately aromatic, becoming enormously full-bodied and complex after about ten years' aging. Recent vintages show a delightful absence of those less-than-necessary animal notes seen in previous years. The 2004 and 2005 are both superb: supple, fleshy, and velvety, with a particularly interesting mouthfeel. Excellent value for the money.

HAUT-MÉDOC 2006
Red | 2014 up to 2026   **92**
A rich and creamy wine, a complex nose of prunes and spice; the wine is more tannic than usual, but not at all aggressive. On the whole the wine seems harmonious and leads us to believe it will age wonderfully.

HAUT-MÉDOC 2005
Red | 2011 up to 2025   **89**
Very ripe grapes have left the nose slightly overpowered by notes of cooked fruit; the wine has body and personality, but it lacks in finesse and purity when tasted blind. On the other hand, the tannins are refined and silky.

HAUT-MÉDOC 2004
Red | 2011 up to 2014   **88**
Nice volume in the mouth, velvety tannins, clean, balanced, just waiting for its peak.

Red: 222.4 acres; cabernet franc 3%, cabernet sauvignon 58%, merlot 33%, petit verdot 6%. **Annual production:** 560,000 bottles

CHÂTEAU CANTENAC-BROWN

🍷🍷🍷🍷🍷

33460 Cantenac
Phone 00 33 5 57 88 81 81
Fax 00 33 5 57 88 81 90
contact@cantenacbrown.com
www.cantenacbrown.com

We can expect some great things from this estate following its recent acquisition by Syrian-born property magnate Simon Halabi. An admirer of great Médoc wines, Halabi is counting on his highly motivated technical team to produce wines with even more personality and truer expression of terroir than ever. Cantenac-Brown wines were always richly colored and tannic, but the aromas never really hit the mark. The 2005 bottling boasts a remarkable finish, with an overall harmony to rival a good many of its peers, and the 2006 follows suit. The 2005 vintage of the château's second wine, Brio, was notable for its clean character and assertive style—in the manner of Palmer's Alter Ego, which is a compliment indeed.

Recently tasted
MARGAUX 2006
Red | 2014 up to 2018   86
This wine didn't taste well in early 2009, with bitter tannins, and with a texture that lacked filling. We have a feeling (which we hope will be proved wrong in the years to come) that the wine is too concentrated for the ripeness of the grapes.

Older vintages
MARGAUX 2005
Red | 2011 up to 2015   92
A powerful wine, with very generous, almost truffled notes, a powerful core, and an almost candied texture; the tannins have really rounded out since our last tasting. A very distinguished wine.

MARGAUX 2004
Red | 2011 up to 2015   86
Deeply colored, the merlot really comes out in the nose; the wine has silky tannins, though it lacks some finesse. A well-made wine, easygoing, just as it was early on.

Red: 103.8 acres; cabernet franc 5%, cabernet sauvignon 65%, merlot 30%. Annual production: 244,000 bottles

CHÂTEAU CHASSE-SPLEEN

🍷🍷🍷🍷🍷

33480 Moulis-en-Médoc
Phone 00 33 5 56 58 02 37
Fax 00 33 5 57 88 84 40
info@chasse-spleen.com
www.chasse-spleen.com

Château Chasse-Spleen now encompasses the splendid vineyards of Château Gressier, added to its original plantings in the excellent Gunzian gravel of the celebrated plateau of Grand Poujeaux. This gives it the capacity to produce large quantities of richly colored, fleshy wines, packed with charm but vinous and as ageworthy as you would expect of wines of this pedigree—even if they can be a bit showy at times. The Chasse-Spleen label has become famous worldwide, proving that the Merlaut family is as good at selling wines as they are at producing them. The latest vintages are unusually warm and velvety (courtesy of global warming), though some of them could do with a touch more finesse.

MOULIS 2006
Red | 2011 up to 2020   89
Much more convincing in our tastings at the end of its maturation than en primeur: upright and rather strict, but unquestionably deep and purebred.

MOULIS 2005
Red | 2011 up to 2025   87
Ripe grapes, velvety and charming texture, vinous but not very complex, at least for the moment.

MOULIS 2004
Red | 2011 up to 2015   88
Beautiful color, full fruit, firm tannins, lots of volume on the palate, smooth, less refined than others but certainly built for the long haul.

MOULIS 2002
Red | 2011 up to 2017   88
Beautiful color, great richness of fruit for the vintage, cozy oak, rather voluptuous wine— a perfect expression of the style that has made this cru so popular with the public.

MOULIS 2000
Red | 2011 up to 2015   90
Palate full of flavor, with a luscious texture and terrifically ripe fruit. A beautiful wine with fantastic length.

Red: 205.1 acres; cabernet sauvignon 65%, merlot 30%, petit verdot 5%. White: 4.4 acres; sauvignon 50%, sémillon 50%. Annual production: 600,000 bottles

CHÂTEAU CLARKE

33480 Listrac
Phone 00 33 5 56 58 38 00
Fax 00 33 5 56 58 26 46
contact@cver.fr
www.cver.fr

Famous proprietor Benjamin de Rothschild keeps a close eye on this state-of-the-art winery in Listrac—and so does his mother, Nadine. The vineyard is operated like a Premier Cru: it is harvested parcel by parcel (séléction parcellaire), and the yields are reduced for the sake of the ultimate in harmonious, distinctive taste. The wine is made using modern techniques, in line with the teachings of enologist Michel Rolland, and it combines very ripe grapes with a tasty expression of terroir. You won't find a better Listrac anywhere.

Recently tasted
LISTRAC-MÉDOC 2006
Red | 2011 up to 2025   90

Older vintages
LISTRAC-MÉDOC 2005
Red | 2011 up to 2025   92
A remarkable success, full-bodied, refined tannins, a wine in the modern style, perfectly vinified.

LISTRAC-MÉDOC 2002
Red | 2011 up to 2017   88
Extremely generous, spicy oak, full, tasty, with harmonious tannins, the most finely crafted of its appellation, but also the most accomplished.

LISTRAC-MÉDOC 2001
Red | 2011 up to 2013   88
Concentrated wine, well crafted, with a full and powerful structure that supports the terrific length.

LISTRAC-MÉDOC 2000
Red | 2011 up to 2013   88
Full-bodied, good volume, with nice length. Modern and seductive style, vinified with care.

Red: 133.4 acres; cabernet sauvignon 30%, merlot 70%. White: 4.9 acres; muscadelle 10%, sauvignon blanc 70%, sémillon 20%. Annual production: 250,000 bottles

CHÂTEAU CLÉMENT-PICHON

33290 Parempuyre
Phone 00 33 5 56 35 23 79
Fax 00 33 5 56 35 85 23
info@vignobles.fayat.com
www.vignobles.fayat.com

This cru is luxuriously maintained by Clément Fayat, who recently appointed Jean-Luc Thunevin to manage the estate and make it more stylish. We can therefore expect to see rapid progress in what already ranks as a very nicely balanced, beautifully consistent Cru Bourgeois—in the real sense of that term.

HAUT-MÉDOC 2006
Red | 2011 up to 2020   89
With superripe fruit on the nose and palate, this smooth wine distinguishes itself from the others with its wonderful freshness.

Red: 61.8 acres; cabernet franc 10%, cabernet sauvignon 40%, merlot 50%. Annual production: 110,000 bottles

CHÂTEAU CLERC-MILON

33250 Pauillac
Phone 00 33 5 56 59 22 22
Fax 00 33 5 56 73 20 44
webmaster@bpdr.com
www.bpdr.com

Clerc-Milon is planted in the deep gravel beds typical of this appellation and has always produced a very well-defined Pauillac: vinous, smooth, and complex, skillfully matured by the Mouton wine-making teams. Today it is more precisely crafted than ever thanks to a newly reno-vated vinification cellar. The domain's rich merlots have a smoothness that sets them apart from those of Château d'Armailhac, which are slender and finer but less sappy. All of the recent vintages are excellent and are sure to seduce every Pauillac lover.

Pauillac 2006
Red | 2016 up to 2021   **92**
Beautifully defined aromatics, velvety tex-ture, full of the deep, earthy notes that are so characteristic of this terroir.

Pauillac 2005
Red | 2011 up to 2030   **94**
Very rich cedar aroma, great vinosity and tannic complexity. A perfectly matured wine that is at its best now.

Pauillac 2004
Red | 2011 up to 2019   **90**
A little more vigorous and full than Armailhac, slightly less refined in its tactile sensations but with remarkable individuality.

Pauillac 2003
Red | 2011 up to 2025   **88**
Intense color, powerful, warm, but lacking finesse, overshadowed in this respect by the grand Mouton, and even by its Petit. Excel-lent vinosity on the other hand, which has us hoping for the best with some age.

Pauillac 2002
Red | 2011 up to 2017   **88**
Fleshy, spicy, vinous, and full-bodied, with remarkably well-integrated oak. This is a tra-ditional Pauillac that should be ready to drink soon.

Red: 74.1 acres; cabernet franc 15%, cabernet sauvignon 46%, merlot 35%, petit verdot 4%. **Annual production:** 170,000 bottles

CHÂTEAU COS D'ESTOURNEL

33180 Saint-Estèphe
Phone 00 33 5 56 73 15 50
Fax 00 33 5 56 59 72 59
estournel@estournel.com
www.estournel.com

Cos has always been more solid than its immediate neighbor, Lafite, with a fleshi-ness that comes from the greater proportion of merlot and from slightly more rigid but less refined tannins. Quality was remarkably consistent from 1971 to 1996 under the direc-tion of Bruno Prats but then wavered a bit until Jean Guillaume, Bruno's son, took over. Cos today is fully back on form: sappier than ever with an unprecedented harmony of tex-ture and tannins and generous qualities to rival the most accomplished of all the north-ern Médoc offerings. The technical improve-ments currently under way should add even greater finesse and purity. The second wine, Les Pagodes, is not yet up to the standard of the best in this category.

Recently tasted
BORDEAUX LES PAGODES DE COS 2006
White | 2011 up to 2013   **86**

Older vintages
SAINT-ESTÈPHE 2006
Red | 2018 up to 2024   **96**
The most nobly aromatic and most accom-plished wine in its category for the recent vintages from this château. Admirable aro-matic freshness (thanks to a high percent-age of cabernet sauvignon), a fat and velvety texture, immense follow-through on the palate.

SAINT-ESTÈPHE 2005
Red | 2011 up to 2050   **94**
Very structured, domineering tannins; long cellaring is a necessity. A monument; but those who love pure finesse should look else-where.

SAINT-ESTÈPHE 2004
Red | 2011 up to 2024   **95**
Great color, voluptuous but precise texture, noble palate of cedar, tremendous length. We deem it a worthy match for the 2005: it has the same smoothness, but pulls it off with a certain flair.

SAINT-ESTÈPHE 2003
Red | 2011 up to 2025   **97**
Magnificent color, powerful aromas domi-nated by spice, oak well integrated on both the nose and palate. A wine with all the body and structure of a great vintage. Tannins are neither aggressive nor tight; tremendous length. A superb wine, very generous.

SAINT-ESTÈPHE 2002
Red | 2011 up to 2020   90
Rich, fleshy, and full, but without the extreme precision of the previous or following vintages. A sensuous wine nevertheless, generously aromatic.

SAINT-ESTÈPHE 2001
Red | 2011 up to 2025   92
With its powerful and racy bouquet of tobacco and spice, this is a voluptuous, very precise wine that perfectly expresses its terroir and varietal composition.

SAINT-ESTÈPHE 2000
Red | 2011 up to 2025   97
A Casanova of a wine! Fabulously dense on the palate, with an unctuous mouthfeel and mellow tannins. The truffle and spice notes just go on and on.

Red: 224.9 acres; cabernet franc 2%, cabernet sauvignon 70%, merlot 28%. Annual production: 300,000 bottles

CHÂTEAU COS LABORY

33180 Saint-Estèphe
Phone 00 33 5 56 59 30 22
Fax 00 33 5 56 59 73 52
cos-labory@wanadoo.fr

Much of the vineyard here lies on a perfect ridge of gravel that is also home to the illustrious Cos d'Estournel. Unlike its more lavishly maintained neighbor, however, Cos Labory paid the price of mechanical harvesting and machine-friendly vine-training systems—rather like Pichon-Longueville Baron back in the 1980s. Having now gone back to manual picking (and other such salutary practices), its latest vintages range from good to excellent, with a spicy, very savory character. Exceptional value for the money.

Recently tasted
SAINT-ESTÈPHE 2006
Red | 2011 up to 2016   89

Older vintages
SAINT-ESTÈPHE 2005
Red | 2011 up to 2023   91
Without losing any of the classic spicy notes of its terroir, this wine has continued to gain in suppleness, in tannic finesse, and in the freshness of its fruit. Good overall balance. Tasting blind, we have a hard time telling it apart from its prestigious neighbors!

SAINT-ESTÈPHE 2004
Red | 2011 up to 2019   87
Vinous, nicely colored, with appealing plum fruit; very well made, even if lacking in individualized character.

SAINT-ESTÈPHE 2003
Red | 2011 up to 2023   91
Rich bouquet, abundant and noble tannins, the product of particularly ripe grapes: this wine perfectly embodies the classicism of great Médoc in a year that was anything but traditional.

SAINT-ESTÈPHE 2002
Red | 2011 up to 2017   90
Good body and a masculine vinosity typical of this appellation. The tannins are still lacking a little finese and precision in the texture; they are just a touch too coarse. Age will soften this minor flaw.

Red: 44.5 acres; cabernet franc 10%, cabernet sauvignon 55%, merlot 35%. Annual production: 100,000 bottles

CHÂTEAU LE CROCK

Marbuzet
33180 Saint-Estèphe
Phone 00 33 5 56 59 73 05
Fax 00 33 5 56 59 30 33
lp@leoville-poyferre.fr

This eighty-acre estate backs onto Château Cos d'Estournel and Château Montrose. It has been owned by the Cuvelier family since 1903 (also the owners of Château Léoville Poyferré, which was acquired twenty years later). The winemaking facilities were entirely rebuilt in 1998. Cabernet sauvignon represents the bulk (60 percent) of the plantings, and the wines are made in consultation with Michel Rolland, focusing on aging potential. Time softens their youthful austerity, making way for refinement and complexity.

SAINT-ESTÈPHE 2006
Red | 2011 up to 2017   **89**
Dark color. Nice, rich nose. On the palate it is elegant, fresh, and solidly supported by a serious tannic streak.

SAINT-ESTÈPHE 2001
Red | 2011 up to 2013   **88**
A full wine with good ripeness and a seductive bouquet. A nice style that is long and generous.

SAINT-ESTÈPHE 2000
Red | 2011 up to 2013   **90**
In the same vein as the 2001, with more concentration and potential, rich and smooth with great substance and length.

Red: 79.1 acres; cabernet franc 10%, cabernet sauvignon 60%, merlot 25%, petit verdot 5%. Annual production: 140,000 bottles

CHÂTEAU DAUZAC

33460 Labarde
Phone 00 33 5 57 88 32 10
Fax 00 33 5 57 88 96 00
châteaudauzac@châteaudauzac.com
www.châteaudauzac.com

Château Dauzac is the twin of Château Siran (the Cru Bourgeois from Margaux) and is owned by the insurance company MAIF. It is planted on excellent gravel soils in the commune of Dauzac and produces densely colored wines with a robust character, made even more emphatic over the past several years by André Lurton's winemaking teams. What we see today is a welcome move toward more finesse. The wines offer excellent value for the money.

MARGAUX 2006
Red | 2011 up to 2020   **90**
Impeccable on the technical level, firm but without heaviness, with very elegant tannins, the wine reconciles freshness with the vivacity typical of the vintage and the advanced ripeness of the fruit.

MARGAUX 2005
Red | 2011 up to 2030   **92**
The ambitious craftsmanship has left the wine quite oaky, which masks the generous fruit of the vintage. A wine of great dimensions with racy tannins, it is still youthfully rough, but should age magnificently.

MARGAUX 2004
Red | 2011 up to 2017   **89**
A little less body than the norm, tight, taut texture, beautiful freshness, clean tannins; these characteristics combined, it is certain to age well.

MARGAUX 2003
Red | 2011 up to 2018   **90**
With a very pure cedar aroma, the wine is delicate despite its power, with an enveloping texture and tannins judiciously integrated into the body.

MARGAUX 2000
Red | 2011 up to 2015   **88**
Very powerful Margaux, vigorously extracted, with rather dry tannins.

Red: 111.2 acres; cabernet franc 5%, cabernet sauvignon 65%, merlot 30%. Annual production: 280,000 bottles

CHÂTEAU DUCRU-BEAUCAILLOU

𝕴 𝕴 𝕴 𝕴

33250 Saint-Julien-Beychevelle
Phone 00 33 5 56 73 16 73
Fax 00 33 5 56 59 27 37
je-borie@je-borie-sa.com
www.château-ducru-beaucaillou.com

This celebrated cru will sometimes rank among the finest, most elegant Médocs—as it did in 1961, 1970, and 1982—but it can also suffer from a serious lack of substance or sometimes purity, most notably in the difficult decade of 1983 to 1992. Production of the 2001 and 2002 vintages then faltered following the demise of Jean-Eugène Borie, but quality soon returned to normal under the direction of his son Bruno, whose highly personal style has done much to modernize the visitor facilities and overall atmosphere of the château. Since 2003 this estate has been as high-achieving as ever, crafting wines of formal, almost ethereal perfection that make no concessions whatsoever to the universe of "international taste." This is great cabernet sauvignon at its most magical: terrific cedar nose, distinguished tannins. The splendid 2004s, 2005s, and 2006s have a lovely vinosity and structure but with a very refined texture, and deserve to be regarded as the very epitome of Saint-Julien. All we ask now is for the La Croix de Beaucaillou, this estate's second wine, to develop a bit more character—particularly now that it has the advantage of the vines recently acquired from Terrey Gros Cailloux.

Recently tasted
SAINT-JULIEN LA CROIX DE BEAUCAILLOU 2006
Red | 2012 up to 2018   **86**

Older vintages
SAINT-JULIEN 2006
Red | 2016 up to 2026   **95**
A wonder of delicacy and power, with a rare, marvelously creamy feeling on the palate and already considerable length.

SAINT-JULIEN 2005
Red | 2011 up to 2050   **98**
Profoundly deep and extraordinarily charming in the textural realm, this is a brilliant example of this superb vintage. Immense future.

SAINT-JULIEN 2004
Red | 2011 up to 2024   **95**
A great success, with a nearly perfect definition of the aromatic nobility of cabernet grown on the soils that accommodate it best. In addition to the refined cedar aromas, it finishes with great viscous density.

SAINT-JULIEN 2003
Red | 2011 up to 2023   **96**
One finds with pleasure, in all its fullness of constitution, a character ever so particular and yet classic of this celebrated cru, with notes of cedar in the Lafite tradition (more aromatically refined than usual in this vintage), a perfectly balanced body, and noble, perfectly integrated tannins. A great wine with a great future.

SAINT-JULIEN 2002
Red | 2011 up to 2017   **88**
Fine and precise, a little thin for the vintage, this wine does not live up to the best of the cru, but the class of the terroir comes through nevertheless.

SAINT-JULIEN 2001
Red | 2011 up to 2016   **88**
Harmonious and supple, with broad tannins and excellent ripeness, yet its tannic structure lacks some density.

SAINT-JULIEN 2000
Red | 2011 up to 2020   **91**
A refined wine, but more linear and less subtle than the château's 1995s and 1996s, and far behind the 2005s.

Red: 271.8 acres; cabernet franc 5%, cabernet sauvignon 70%, merlot 25%.

CHÂTEAU DUHART-MILON

🍷🍷🍷🍷🍷

33250 Pauillac
Phone 00 33 5 56 73 18 18
Fax 00 33 5 56 59 26 83
visites@lafite.com
www.lafite.com

Duhart-Milon stands on the impressive Carruades plateau, near Lafite but without the latter's famous deep gravel soils over limestone bedrock. The latest vintages show even greater harmony of constitution than before, with more thoroughbred, better-integrated tannins. A healthy dollop of merlot gives the wine a characteristically cushiony texture, with whiffs of cedar and spice typical of the Rothschild style.

PAUILLAC 2006
Red | 2016 up to 2021   90
Very accomplished: the cru shows in its smoothness, purity, and complexity, without losing the body given by superb merlot.

PAUILLAC 2005
Red | 2011 up to 2030   92
Powerful yet refined tannins, very long flavors, with impressive clarity in its terroir expression.

PAUILLAC 2004
Red | 2011 up to 2020   88
Rich in color and rather intense in its cedar aromas, but the tannins are a little dry.

PAUILLAC 2003
Red | 2011 up to 2021   88
Beautiful color, almost roasted aromas, good vinosity, fruit leaning a little to prune (from the merlot), a powerful wine sturdily supported by firm tannins. Not particularly refined or distinguished, but well suited to winter drinking and small game-bird dishes.

PAUILLAC 2002
Red | 2011 up to 2014   87
With its bouquet of cedar and leather, this offers typical Pauillac character. It is sufficiently vinous for aging, but it lacks a little purity and subtlety in its terroir expression.

PAUILLAC 2001
Red | 2011 up to 2019   88
The wine is balanced and has refined tannins, with fresh fruit and a strong finish, but it lacks smoothness and purity.

PAUILLAC 2000
Red | 2011 up to 2020   90
Vigorous and precise in its defined texture and tannins.

Red: 173 acres; cabernet franc 5%, cabernet sauvignon 65%, merlot 30%. Annual production: 240,000 bottles

CHÂTEAU DURFORT-VIVENS

🍷🍷🍷🍷🍷

33460 Margaux
Phone 00 33 5 57 88 31 02
Fax 00 33 5 57 88 60 60
infos@durfort-vivens.com
www.durfort-vivens.com

This wine used to be a bit on the thin side, but it gets bigger all the time in the hands of Gonzague Lurton, a man as passionate about terroir as his father, Lucien, but stricter about the routine side of the job. The wine is distinctly cabernet sauvignon and starts out straighter, more linear, and slightly more rigid than most, but is nonetheless refined, distinguished, and complex and—for the past three years at least—always made from perfectly ripe grapes. Good value for the money. The 2005s and 2006s are the most complete wines made by this château in recent years: very pure, direct, and subtle. Just a touch more vinosity and they would compete with the finest Second Growths.

MARGAUX 2006
Red | 2014 up to 2021   91
Very full body with firm and complex tannins and a very distinct cabernet character. Perfectly ripe, very Médoc in style, certain to age superbly in the bottle.

MARGAUX 2005
Red | 2011 up to 2030   89
Firm wine, precise, purebred, and racy, but, as is common in this vintage, the tannins are overpowering, which is a shock given the usual style of this appellation. The wine will age well, but aficionados will prefer the 2006.

MARGAUX 2004
Red | 2011 up to 2020   88
With its lovely bramble aroma, this is an elegant wine, taut and longer in flavor than Dauzac, with firm tannins, style, and structure. Tannins a little more drying than those in Brane, less balanced.

MARGAUX 2002
Red | 2011 up to 2017   88
Classic Margaux, elegant but reserved, linear, very cabernet. Good aging potential.

MARGAUX 2000
Red | 2011 up to 2020   90
Very classic in aroma, body, and texture, with firm tannins.

Red: 123.6 acres; cabernet franc 7%, cabernet sauvignon 70%, merlot 23%. Annual production: 200,000 bottles

CHÂTEAU DES EYRINS

27, cours Pey-Berland
33460 Margaux
Phone 00 33 5 57 88 95 03
Fax 00 33 5 57 88 37 75
eric.grangerou@free.fr

Eric Grangeroux's small but impeccably maintained Margaux cru delivers a wine that is tight, dense, and deep—intense, but not at the expense of that distinguished expression typical of its Margaux origins. The second offering from this quality producer is an honestly crafted, pretty, and thirst-slaking wine that does justice to its name: Cru Monplaisir (my pleasure). The property has recently been bought by the Gonet-Médeville family, owner of the famous Château Gilette Sauternes.

Recently tasted
MARGAUX SÉLECTION GRANGEROU 2006
Red | 2011 up to 2014   **90**

Older vintages
MARGAUX 2006
Red | 2011 up to 2020   **90**
Delightfully floral, this wine combines concentration, elegance, and freshness.

MARGAUX 2005
Red | 2011 up to 2015   **92**
Most certainly the best vintage from this winery: showing fresh fruit, the wine reveals depth, length, intense personality, and a wonderful essence.

BORDEAUX CRU MONPLAISIR 2005
Red | 2011 up to 2013   **89**
Seductive notes of ripe black cherries lead to a savory palate underscored by ripe tannins. Absolutely delicious!

Red: 22.2 acres; cabernet sauvignon 60%, merlot 35%, petit verdot 5%. **Annual production:** 50,000 bottles

CHÂTEAU FERRIÈRE

33 bis, rue de la Trémoille
33460 Margaux
Phone 00 33 5 57 88 76 65
Fax 00 33 5 57 88 98 33
château@ferriere.com
www.ferriere.com

This small cru never really shines in barrel tastings, but its wines firm up well in the bottle, developing good structure and a distinguished nose and palate. Quite masculine for a Margaux, though, but still not as refined as the best of them. Prices remain reasonable for the time being.

Recently tasted
MARGAUX 2006
Red | 2014 up to 2021   **88**

Older vintages
MARGAUX 2005
Red | 2011 up to 2030   **91**
One finds on the nose the "roast" nuances common to most Margaux in this vintage, and the same breadth and constitutional power. The tannins are of excellent makeup and should make this a very beautiful "vin de garde."

MARGAUX 2004
Red | 2011 up to 2020   **89**
Fleshy wine with a frank nose, ripe and fragrant, savory tannins, and beautiful persistence. Complete Margaux, well vinified and probably of great aging potential.

MARGAUX 2003
Red | 2011 up to 2020   **88**
Fleshy wine, firmly built, rather rich in alcohol.

MARGAUX 2002
Red | 2011 up to 2014   **88**
Firm and balanced with smoky notes in the Pauillac style, due to the high percentage of cabernet sauvignon in the blend. It should age well but lacks a little of the generosity of the vintage.

MARGAUX 2001
Red | 2011 up to 2013   **90**
A beautiful wine with generous aromas, its savory flavors blended with an immediate charm, finesse, and voluptuousness.

MARGAUX 2000
Red | 2011 up to 2020   **88**
A sturdily built wine, firm and seriously structured.

Red: 19.8 acres; cabernet sauvignon 80%, merlot 15%, petit verdot 5%. **Annual production:** 50,000 bottles

CHÂTEAU GISCOURS

10, route de Giscours
33460 Margaux
Phone 00 33 5 57 97 09 09
Fax 00 33 5 57 97 09 00
giscours@château-giscours.fr
www.château-giscours.fr

The vineyard here still belongs to the Tari family, but the wine is made by talented winemakers Alexander Van Beek and Jacques Pellissié, with guidance from Albada Jelgersma despite his serious accident. The wine itself is now fully back on form: very robust for a Margaux, with a sumptuous bouquet and the quality to rival Château Palmer as the second Margaux.

MARGAUX 2005
Red | 2011 up to 2030   **93**
Deeply colored and very powerful on the nose, with the dark chocolate aroma typical of very hot years. Firm tannins, high alcohol. A very vigorous wine that will slowly find its balance over the course of bottle aging.

MARGAUX 2004
Red | 2011 up to 2020   **93**
Frank and precise, this wine impresses with its upright tannins and its aromatic personality, subtler and more elegant in certain respects than that of the 2005.

MARGAUX 2003
Red | 2011 up to 2023   **95**
Great color, a nose radiating aromas of plum, remarkable volume, great fruit maturity, with a texture largely superior to the average. A great success in this very particular vintage.

MARGAUX 2002
Red | 2011 up to 2024   **92**
Great color, very vinous and complex, seductive in the complexity of its aromas and the abundance of tactile sensations it delivers. Remarkably well done for the vintage.

MARGAUX 2001
Red | 2011 up to 2021   **93**
A great success for the cru: the richness and the harmony of body, the nobility of texture, and the refinement of the tannins are splendid.

MARGAUX 2000
Red | 2011 up to 2025   **93**
Aromatically racy, this wine stands apart for its fullness, creaminess, and the exceptional quality of its tannins.

Red: 197.7 acres; cabernet franc 5%, cabernet sauvignon 60%, merlot 32%, petit verdot 3%. **Annual production:** 280,000 bottles

CHÂTEAU GLORIA

33250 Saint-Julien-Beychevelle
Phone 00 33 5 56 59 08 18
Fax 00 33 5 56 59 16 18
domainemartin@wanadoo.fr
www.domaines-henri-martin.com

Proud possession of late owner Henri Martin, Château Gloria nestles at the heart of Saint-Julien, alongside some of the finest crus classés. For ten years or so, it seems there was some debate as to how to style and position this wine in relation to Château Saint Pierre, the Martins' other property. Today, however, Château Gloria can once again rival its neighbors: supple, fleshy, and deliciously fruity, less closed on the nose but also built to age. Just our kind of archetypal Saint-Julien.

SAINT-JULIEN 2006
Red | 2011 up to 2025   **90**
Round, harmonious, precise in its fruit expression and supple tannins, with classic structure. It should rather quickly become elegant, perhaps even more so than the 2005.

SAINT-JULIEN 2005
Red | 2011 up to 2025   **92**
Beautiful, complex flavors of red fruits and cedar, smooth texture, grand finesse. It will be ready earlier than the crus classés.

SAINT-JULIEN 2004
Red | 2011 up to 2015   **91**
Brilliantly constructed, this classic from Saint-Julien excels in 2004. This vintage unquestionably marks a new level for the cru, with a silkiness of tannins worthy of a classification.

Red: 108.7 acres; cabernet franc 5%, cabernet sauvignon 65%, merlot 25%, petit verdot 5%. **Annual production:** 300,000 bottles

GOULÉE

33180 Saint-Estèphe
Phone 00 33 5 56 73 15 50
Fax 00 33 5 56 59 72 59
estournel@estournel.com
www.estournel.com

Goulée is a brilliant undertaking, conceived and executed by Jean-Guillaume Prats. His idea was that the strict growing practices used in the greatest Grands Crus could work just as well in the little-known vineyards of the northern Médoc. Today his well-placed confidence in his terroir has paid off. Goulée is a vigorous, sappy wine with a refined, complex bouquet. Pity so few of Prats's neighbors share his uncompromising standards.

MÉDOC 2006
Red | 2011 up to 2016   **89**
A solid, serious wine, less expressive than previous vintages, but with depth, a velvety texture, and elegant, silky tannins.

MÉDOC 2005
Red | 2011 up to 2015   **91**
This has all of the generous flavors of Médoc wines, and it is not dry or rustic in any way: it is deep and succulent, in the same aromatic vein as the 2004, but with more density on the palate.

MÉDOC 2004
Red | 2011 up to 2013   **88**
Beautifully deep color, an unusual and seductive bouquet of red fruit combined with notes of nougat, full-bodied, rich, tender, ready to drink.

Red: 173 acres; cabernet 60%, merlot 40%.

CHÂTEAU GRAND-PUY-DUCASSE

4, quai Antoine-Ferchaud
33250 Pauillac
Phone 00 33 5 56 59 00 40
Fax 00 33 5 56 59 36 47
contact@cagrandscrus.com
www.cagrandscrus.com

This wine is a combination of parcels that should by rights represent the spirit of Pauillac. But despite all the efforts made since the 1990s—starting with the building of a new fermentation facility—the performance from this cru is still not up to the standard of the best Pauillac Fifth Growths. Which is not to say things haven't improved: the 2005 and 2006 vintages show more precise expression of terroir than ever before. What would really make the difference is more of those great cabernet sauvignons.

Recently tasted
PAUILLAC 2006
Red | 2014 up to 2018   **86**

Older vintages
PAUILLAC 2005
Red | 2011 up to 2023   **92**
Excellent body, filled with the savor of red fruits but no cedar; very pure fruit, lovely vinosity; without doubt the best wine recently released from this winery.

PAUILLAC 2004
Red | 2011 up to 2015   **87**
Solid wine, rather intense, but without very nuanced aromas.

PAUILLAC 2003
Red | 2011 up to 2015   **85**
Completely adequate body, but our sample had heavy and questionable aromas of cooked fruit and fox. Tannins a little bitter. The wine has neither the purity nor the distinction expected.

PAUILLAC 2002
Red | 2011 up to 2014   **86**
Fairly forward, carefully crafted, rather fine tannins, but this vintage does not reach the level of vinosity expected from a classified cru of Pauillac.

PAUILLAC 2000
Red | 2011 up to 2020   **86**
Generous texture but a bit taut with dry tannins. Good vinosity, frank finish.

Red: 98.8 acres; cabernet sauvignon 60%, merlot 40%. **Annual production:** 140,000 bottles

CHÂTEAU GRAND-PUY-LACOSTE

Château Grand-Puy-Lacoste
33250 Pauillac
Phone 00 33 5 56 59 06 66
Fax 00 33 5 56 59 22 27
dfxb@domainesfxborie.com

Grand-Puy-Lacoste—GPL to aficionados—is a textbook example of the Pauillac terroir and one of the most consistently reliable Crus Classés. François-Xavier Borie runs a tight ship and has completely renovated the winemaking facilities. Ancient cabernet sauvignon vines give this wine a remarkable vinosity with classy aromas of spice; great vintages benefit enormously from long aging in the bottle (fifteen years plus). Recent vintages show greater precision than ever—refined tannins, focused aromas—and include the truly exceptional 2005.

Pauillac 2006
Red | 2016 up to 2026   **93**
Completely classic in its body, its cigar box aromas, its texture, and its overall balance. It does not share the aromatic genius of the 2005, but it does resemble the 1996.

Pauillac 2005
Red | 2011 up to 2030   **95**
Complex aromas, clean, very defined and above all less "roasted" than other crus of the same vintage. Its power and breed are outstanding. A wine of great aging potential and ultra-classic craftsmanship.

Pauillac 2004
Red | 2011 up to 2016   **89**
Reduced on the nose; very long, smooth, and complex on the palate, this is still very young and austere, but has good juice and lovely tannins.

Pauillac 2003
Red | 2011 up to 2018   **90**
The wine is marked more by its strength and the sensation of heat from the alcohol than by its tension and the tightness of its texture.

Pauillac 2002
Red | 2011 up to 2017   **88**
Solid and harmonious, with very classic notes of cedar, but the texture lacks a little refinement.

Pauillac 2000
Red | 2011 up to 2020   **92**
A balanced wine, rather supple and delicate for the cru and the vintage.

Red: 135.9 acres; cabernet franc 5%, cabernet sauvignon 70%, merlot 25%. Annual production: 200,000 bottles

CHÂTEAU GREYSAC

18, route de By
33340 Bégadan
Phone 00 33 5 56 73 26 56
Fax 00 33 5 56 73 26 58
info@greysac.com
www.greysac.com

This enormous property in the commune of Bégadan produces a refined and refreshingly spicy wine—something increasingly rare these days—and plenty of it, too. Its astonishing notes of red peppers are definitely not to be mistaken for greenness and reveal their thoroughbred character with prolonged aging. Sure to appeal to lovers of authentic Médoc!

Médoc 2005
Red | 2011 up to 2020   **88**
A very balanced wine, one of the cleanest and most refined of its vintage, particularly in regard to the tannins. It's long, complex, and in a style we like and defend for the northern Médoc.

Médoc 2004
Red | 2011 up to 2013   **86**
Beautiful color, fresh red pepper aromas, lovely fruit, distinguished tannins, good length; a wine of character.

Médoc 2002
Red | 2011 up to 2013   **86**
A pepper note lends this wine charm and freshness. The tannins are finely textured.

Red: 227.3 acres; cabernet franc 2%, cabernet sauvignon 38%, merlot 58%, petit verdot 2%. Annual production: 550,000 bottles

CHÂTEAU GRUAUD-LAROSE

🐎 🐎 🐎 🐎

33250 Saint-Julien-Beychevelle
Phone 00 33 5 56 73 15 20
Fax 00 33 5 56 59 64 72
gl@gruaud-larose.com
www.gruaud-larose.com

The soils here are some of the most magnificent in the Médoc: a deep, homogeneous gravel bed that yields consistently flawless wines, quality combined with quantity. Château Gruaud-Larose is a perfect alliance of strength and finesse, though the fullness of its structure may not be obvious en primeur, appearing only after twenty to thirty years' aging. Those animal notes mingled with classical cedar and tobacco aromas seen in the 1970s and 1980s (attributed to the terroir; people either loved or hated them) are increasingly rare these days, which is not a bad thing. The direction taken by this cru today says a lot about Jean Merlaut's wise governance: the wine is cleaner and more precise than in the past but with the same generous bouquet and charming texture.

SAINT-JULIEN 2006
Red | 2016 up to 2026   93
The wine has the power and the energy of the vintage and has opened up during its élevage, gaining in subtlety and precision of definition.

SAINT-JULIEN 2005
Red | 2011 up to 2030   95
Just before bottling, the great Saint-Juliens are often similar. Gruaud's terroir and vintage character have become more apparent than they were at the offset: remarkably elegant and fresh, and thankfully not a hint of barnyard!

SAINT-JULIEN 2004
Red | 2011 up to 2020   93
A festival of fruit and flowers on the nose, extremely fine and delicate texture; completely open, smooth, and long.

SAINT-JULIEN 2003
Red | 2011 up to 2025   92
At first the wine seems thin, but the return of the tannins in the aftertaste assures that it has a great wealth of dry extract and thus a beautiful potential for cellaring.

SAINT-JULIEN 2002
Red | 2011 up to 2022   92
Lots of flesh and harmony for the vintage, with surprising notes of citrus fruit. This vintage definitely makes a mark, but it needs time.

SAINT-JULIEN 2001
Red | 2011 up to 2020   88
Simpler in body and bouquet than the 2002, this is clean and pleasant but a little impersonal.

SAINT-JULIEN 2000
Red | 2011 up to 2020   96
Exceptional in size and complexity, with profound body and impressive length. A great success.

SAINT-JULIEN 1999
Red | 2011 up to 2014   92
Charming cedar aroma, a lot of body for the vintage, a little leather and musk on the nose; very classic for the terroir and this château.

SAINT-JULIEN 1998
Red | 2011 up to 2025   94
Good viscosity, developed aromas of cedar, spice, and leather, with considerable finesse. An excellent success for this vintage.

Red: 326.2 acres; cabernet franc 8%, cabernet sauvignon 57%, malbec 2%, merlot 31%, petit verdot 2%. **Annual production:** 450,000 bottles

CHÂTEAU HAUT-BAGES LIBÉRAL

Saint-Lambert
33250 Pauillac
Phone 00 33 5 57 88 76 65
Fax 00 33 5 57 88 98 33
château@ferriere.com
www.hautbagesliberal.com

Part of this vineyard lies next to Château Latour, a terroir that heightens the expression in this robust and generous Pauillac that is always a sleeper of the vintage: the bottled wine ends up much more complex and accomplished than the barrel sample. It continues to offer very good value for the money, debunking preconceived notions about overpriced Bordeaux. All the latest vintages are in line with expectations: densely colored, robust, and generously aromatic. This is distinctly Pauillac in style, though the texture is not quite as refined as the best of them.

Pauillac 2006
Red | 2014 up to 2021   87
A true Pauillac, with a spicy nose and a touch of graphite, corpulent, virile, licorice on the finale. It can certainly be aged for many years.

Pauillac 2004
Red | 2011 up to 2016   88
Beautiful viscosity, generous, tannic, and complete, with a beautiful terroir expression. This didn't show as well when tasted en primeur. All the better!

Pauillac 2003
Red | 2011 up to 2018   87
Crimson color, open and giving aromas of very ripe plum, marked by the class of its merlot, rich, supple, velvety, and easy to drink. Could have been a little denser in this vintage.

Pauillac 2002
Red | 2011 up to 2014   87
Full and robust with firm tannins, even a bit overbearing. This is serious wine, though less refined than some of its peers.

Pauillac 2000
Red | 2011 up to 2020   89
Generous wine, with a particularly smooth texture despite the firm tannins.

Red: 69.2 acres; cabernet sauvignon 80%, merlot 17%, petit verdot 3%. Annual production: 170,000 bottles

CHÂTEAU HAUT-BATAILLEY

33250 Pauillac
Phone 00 33 5 56 59 06 66
Fax 00 33 5 56 59 27 37
je-borie@je-borie-sa.com

Château Haut-Batailley is the product of an inheritance that was divided between two families from the Corrèze region (of France), the Bories and the Castéjas. The terroirs are quite similar, but the wines are as different as their owners. François-Xavier Borie aims to give Haut-Batailley a finesse and degree of suppleness that will distinguish it from Grand-Puy-Lacoste—and with very few exceptions, he pulls it off perfectly. Haut-Batailley seems to have grown more forceful since 2005, making it better value for the money than ever.

Pauillac 2006
Red | 2014 up to 2021   89
Precise in its cedar aromas, supple, fine; tannins carefully extracted, without aggressiveness; a little short on the palate.

Pauillac 2005
Red | 2011 up to 2025   92
With a beautiful nose of ripe fruit, this is powerful, long, and complex, with perfectly controlled tannin extraction. One of the best quality-price ratios for the vintage.

Pauillac 2004
Red | 2011 up to 2020   84
Relatively easy, reduced, with simple and astringent tannins and a soft body.

Pauillac 2003
Red | 2011 up to 2020   88
Supple, pleasant wine with refined tannins, this is very mainstream, ideal for fine dining, where it can be served immediately.

Pauillac 2002
Red | 2011 up to 2017   86
Average body and rather dry tannins, classic style: not very hedonistic although it gets better with air. It could gain much in character with time in the bottle.

Pauillac 2000
Red | 2011 up to 2020   90
A very beautiful wine made with classic craftsmanship, developing lovely spicy nuances without heaviness or the sensation of sweetness. It will please European palates.

Red: 54.4 acres; cabernet franc 10%, cabernet sauvignon 65%, merlot 25%. Annual production: 110,000 bottles

CHÂTEAU HAUT-CONDISSAS AND CHÂTEAU ROLLAN DE BY

3, route du Haut-Condissas
33340 Bégadan
Phone 00 33 5 56 41 58 59
Fax 00 33 5 56 41 37 82
infos@rollandeby.com
www.rollandeby.com

This vineyard in Bégadan yields two quite distinct brands of wine. The first is Haut-Condissas, drawn from premium parcels of vines that are governed by particularly stringent growing standards. Owner Jean Guyon, one of Bordeaux's most notorious entrepreneurs, gambled that he could create an outstanding representation of a great Médoc red—and for some years now, he has been winning his bet. Haut-Condissas exhibits that spicy, sappy nose typical of a great, quintessentially classical Médoc cru. Rollan de By, the second brand, is sleek but more straightforward, with a skillful blend of muscle and flexibility.

Recently tasted
BORDEAUX ROSÉ ROLLAN DE BY 2008
Rosé | 2011 up to 2013   **90**

MÉDOC HAUT-CONDISSAS 2006
Red | 2011 up to 2014   **90**

Older vintages
MÉDOC CHÂTEAU TOUR SÉRAN 2005
Red | 2011 up to 2014   **87**
Purple color. Fine nose of concentrated red fruit. Palate is smooth and full-bodied with nice length, finishing on lovely, smooth tannins.

MÉDOC HAUT-CONDISSAS 2005
Red | 2011 up to 2015   **93**
Inky dark color. The nose is extremely intense and mature, developing aromas of red and black fruits, sweet spices, and toasty oak. Delightful, ample, and dense on the palate, richly aromatic, with tight and silky tannins and a long finish. Voluptuous and distinguished.

MÉDOC ROLLAN DE BY 2006
Red | 2012 up to 2018   **90**
This is full-bodied with a powerful structure, tight, complex tannins, and an exceptionally assertive Médoc character. Huge aging potential.

Red: 207.6 acres; cabernet franc 3%, cabernet sauvignon 28%, merlot 63%, petit verdot 6%. **Annual production:** 450,000 bottles

CHÂTEAU HAUT-MARBUZET

Vignobles H. Duboscq & Fils
33180 Saint-Estèphe
Phone 00 33 5 56 59 30 54
Fax 00 33 5 56 59 70 87
infos@haut-marbuzet.net

This cru has achieved worldwide fame thanks to the commitment of its owner, Henri Duboscq, one of the most remarkable of all the Médoc producers. In his hands, the often rustic Saint Estèphe style becomes rounded and immediately voluptuous thanks to just the right proportion of merlot and skillful use of new oak. What Duboscq created was a modern, attractive style of wine that he perfected to the highest degree. His sons continue their father's work—which has been copied by neighboring producers who now strive to make very similar wines. All the recent vintages are successful although their unprecedented subtlety may tend to detract from their immediate impact. Fact is, Haut-Marbuzet is becoming more classical!

SAINT-ESTÈPHE 2006
Red | 2011 up to 2025   **92**
Beautiful, velvety texture, abundant fruit, body a little less imposing than those of the Crus Classés in this appellation: very pleasant.

SAINT-ESTÈPHE 2005
Red | 2011 up to 2025   **93**
Classic Saint-Estèphe on the nose, this is full-out creamy, long, and complex, with flavorful tannins—a rather immediate and convincing expression of a very beautiful vintage!

SAINT-ESTÈPHE 2004
Red | 2011 up to 2018   **94**
The freshness and succulence of fruit and velvety texture makes one forget the shortcomings of many wines of the vintage in this area!

SAINT-ESTÈPHE 2001
Red | 2011 up to 2018   **93**
Dense wine, spicy, chewy, and lengthy. Beautiful intensity on the finish. Lovely, long wine, a very fine success.

SAINT-ESTÈPHE 2000
Red | 2011 up to 2015   **92**
In this vintage, Haut-Marbuzet is a wine of good harmony, but without the usual richness and intensity. It is a supple wine, with a velvety and balanced weave.

Red: 173 acres; cabernet franc 10%, cabernet sauvignon 50%, merlot 40%. **Annual production:** 400,000 bottles

CHÂTEAU D'ISSAN

BP 5
33460 Cantenac
Phone 00 33 5 57 88 35 91
Fax 00 33 5 57 88 74 24
issan@château-issan.com
www.château-issan.com

A very typically Margaux cru, from excellent gravel soils on the borders of the Gironde River; the château here is one of the finest in the southern Médoc region. The wine can seem rather too straightforward when young, but aging brings out that refined bouquet and texture to be expected of a Third Growth. Emmanuel Cruse is plainly the most ambitious owner this winery has ever known: the remarkable vinosity of recent vintages says a lot about his stringent selection. If what you want is that characteristic Margaux elegance and freshness, then this one is for you.

MARGAUX 2005
Red I 2011 up to 2030   **92**
Very powerful and tannic, a noble wine with the firm tannins so characteristic of cabernet; "wild" leather notes bring a slight stiffness to the usual finesse of this terroir.

MARGAUX 2004
Red I 2011 up to 2020   **89**
A straightforward and complete Margaux, with a solid tannic structure; made for long keeping.

MARGAUX 2003
Red I 2011 up to 2020   **91**
Strong color, nose marked by nuances of plum and chocolate (typical for this vintage, which endured a heat wave), virile tannins, generous and expressive style; the wine is just beginning to mellow, with the tannins nicely integrating into the texture.

MARGAUX 2002
Red I 2011 up to 2015   **91**
Full of aromatic elegance and freshness, a genuine Margaux texture, unbelievably satiny. One of the most underestimated wines of the vintage.

MARGAUX 2001
Red I 2011 up to 2016   **88**
This wine is more striking for the density of its body and the tightness of its texture than for its aromatic generosity.

Red: 131 acres; cabernet sauvignon 60%, merlot 40%. Annual production: 300,000 bottles

CHÂTEAU KIRWAN

33460 Cantenac
Phone 00 33 5 57 88 71 00
Fax 00 33 5 57 88 77 62
mail@château-kirwan.com
www.château-kirwan.com

This estate underwent a cultural revolution in the 1990s under the inspired guidance of Michel Rolland. Riper fruit and luxurious use of new wood made for some surprisingly irresistible wines, though they tended to lose their character with age. We are pleased to report that recent vintages seem as pure as they are seductive.

MARGAUX 2005
Red I 2011 up to 2025   **93**
Very ripe grapes, yet the intense sun of the vintage did not mask the finesse of the terroir in this wine. The wine has a remarkable balance between high alcohol and elegance in body and texture. A future classic of the vintage.

MARGAUX 2004
Red I 2011 up to 2020   **90**
Lovely floral aroma, very tender, velvety, seductive, refined. Very Margaux. Music to the ears.

MARGAUX 2003
Red I 2011 up to 2020   **92**
Beautiful color, complex and sensual leather and plum aromas, lots of body, cozy tannins, persistent flavor, opulent, already very open, made to give pleasure and to be enjoyed.

MARGAUX 2001
Red I 2011 up to 2015   **91**
A powerful and tempting wine with grand aromas opening into notes of spice, cedar, and nuts; a broad body, a silky texture, refined tannins, and much length.

MARGAUX 2000
Red I 2011 up to 2020   **90**
Very rich wine, with an exuberance that borders on Margaux classicism. Very beautiful length. It seems immovable.

Red: 91.4 acres; cabernet franc 15%, cabernet sauvignon 45%, merlot 30%, petit verdot 10%.
Annual production: 180,000 bottles

CHÂTEAU LAFITE-ROTHSCHILD

33250 Pauillac
Phone 00 33 5 56 73 18 18
Fax 00 33 5 56 59 26 83
clesure@lafite.com
www.lafite.com

This supremely aristocratic Pauillac owes its unrivaled finesse to a gravel terroir over limestone bedrock north of Pauillac. It is this type of soil that will forever distinguish it from Latour. The nose is pungently cabernet sauvignon (often accounting for more than ninety percent of the blend), revealing incredible aromas of cedar and graphite that are the complete antithesis of conventional fruit. The texture would be impossible to reproduce anywhere else in the world, especially those dry but caressing tannins that make Lafite an aesthete's delight. The unforgivable inconsistencies of the 1960s and 1970s are now no more than a bad memory thanks to stringent selection (often rejecting more than half of the crop) and exceptional aging in some of the best new wood we have ever seen. Our warmest congratulations to Charles Chevallier and his team! Lafite's second wine, Les Carruades, is more remarkable for its finesse than its body and lacks the consistency of a Forts de Latour. Lafite's most recent vintages are noted for their perfect balance, with a near-ideal combination of grace and power. The most inimitable wines, however, are probably the intermediary vintages, particularly the 2001 and 2004 that offer (by far) the best value for the money.

Pauillac 2006
Red | 2016 up to 2026   97
Delightful, very supple, silky, subtle wine, among the most accomplished of the last vintages.

Pauillac 2005
Red | 2011 up to 2050   99
Very powerful and masculine with an ultra-tight texture, dense tannins, and great volume on the palate. Monumental Lafite, requiring a long, patient wait.

Pauillac 2004
Red | 2011 up to 2024   94
With great color and a very distinguished aroma of cedar, this is a tight, subtle, very elegant wine but with a relatively unadorned core, which will please those who seek refinement rather than sensuality in their wines.

Pauillac 2003
Red | 2011 up to 2028   97
A wine of great proportions, with a very sharp cedar aroma, sumptuous flavors, and tannins of extreme nobility.

Pauillac 2002
Red | 2011 up to 2027   95
Outstanding aroma of cedar; creamy, magical texture but without heaviness; marvelously noble and pure tannins from great cabernet sauvignon.

Pauillac 2001
Red | 2011 up to 2023   97
The pure, precise, magnificently spicy nose is in perfect balance with the wine's vigorous body. The texture has sublime substance.

Pauillac 2000
Red | 2011 up to 2030   97
Intense, magnificently spicy wine. The texture is as refined as one would wish, yet this is still a style that requires patience.

Pauillac Les Carruades de Lafite 2006
Red | 2014 up to 2018   90
One of the best in recent years, with a very "Lafite" nose of cedar, excellent volume on the palate, and noble notes of almond. One can sense that it contains ultra-premium merlot.

Pauillac Les Carruades de Lafite 2005
Red | 2011 up to 2023   91
This has impressive body, aromas strongly dominated by black chocolate, and tannins that are better harmonized than those of wines from a few vintages back. Yet, instinctively, we prefer the style of the 2006 vintage, which is more faithful to the character of this château.

Pauillac Les Carruades de Lafite 2004
Red | 2011 up to 2015   88
Slender and distinguished, Lafite's second wine has the nobility of the cru, with a lesser dimension.

Red: 271.8 acres; cabernet franc 4%, cabernet sauvignon 75%, merlot 20%, petit verdot 1%. **Annual production:** 250,000 bottles

CHÂTEAU LAFON-ROCHET

Lieu-dit Blanquet
33180 Saint-Estèphe
Phone 00 33 5 56 59 32 06
Fax 00 33 5 56 59 72 43
lafon@lafon-rochet.com
www.lafon-rochet.com

Michel Tesseron, with his son now working alongside him, has fully updated the technical facilities here and restored the vineyard to the appearance befitting a great Cru Classé. All of these lands around Lafite provide ideal ripening conditions for Médoc varietals. Tesseron relies heavily on the merlot, which certainly makes for a very plump and charming texture. But in great vintages a higher proportion of cabernet sauvignon would add just a shade more weight and precision to the body of the wine.

Recently tasted
SAINT-ESTÈPHE 2006
Red | 2014 up to 2021   90

Older vintages
SAINT-ESTÈPHE 2005
Red | 2011 up to 2030   92
This has a complete body, firm tannins, and great aging possibilities, but not as much finesse as Calon-Ségur. The sunny vintage strongly shaped this bottling.

SAINT-ESTÈPHE 2004
Red | 2011 up to 2015   90
With ripe fruit flavors, straight and distinguished, this is a beautiful, velvety Saint-Estèphe.

SAINT-ESTÈPHE 2003
Red | 2011 up to 2013   92
Round, generous wine with velvety tannins and pleasing length, this is much less rigid in its youth than one might expect from this appellation. Beautiful future.

SAINT-ESTÈPHE 2001
Red | 2011 up to 2019   91
One of the best Lafon-Rochet vintages in history: good color, vigor, and depth with generous persistence.

SAINT-ESTÈPHE 2000
Red | 2011 up to 2020   89
Supple, creamy, and forward, this wine does not hide its terroir. Beautifully spicy, firm and earthy tannins.

Red: 111.2 acres; cabernet franc 3%, cabernet sauvignon 55%, merlot 40%, petit verdot 2%. Annual production: 240,000 bottles

CHÂTEAU LAGRANGE

33250 Saint-Julien-Beychevelle
Phone 00 33 5 56 73 38 38
Fax 00 33 5 56 59 26 09
château-lagrange@château-lagrange.com
www.château-lagrange.com

This lovely property in the heart of prime vine-growing country serves as a link between Château Gruaud-Larose, the rear-line Léoville crus, and the Saint-Laurent-du-Médoc Crus Classés. Marcel Ducasse has been the winemaker here since 1983 when the estate was acquired by Japanese multinational Suntory. He crafts a classically Médoc wine, somewhat strict when young but sappy, distinguished, and very consistent. The second wine, Fiefs de Lagrange, deserves all the credit it gets: supple, precise, refined, and digestible. Remarkably good value for the money, too. Recent vintages have added extra finesse and refinement to the texture of the wines, making them more like a Léoville in terms of class and value.

SAINT-JULIEN 2006
Red | 2014 up to 2021   91
Rich in color, tannins, and alcohol. Firm, full, promising.

SAINT-JULIEN 2005
Red | 2011 up to 2030   94
Great power, very meticulous definition of the terroir, impeccable finish. This is the work of a talented professional working with the gravels of Saint-Julien.

SAINT-JULIEN 2004
Red | 2011 up to 2019   91
Very complex nose with licorice, anise, mint, spices, and more. With superb substance and integrated oak, this is appealing, creamy.

SAINT-JULIEN 2001
Red | 2011 up to 2019   92
The wine displays very fine tannins and a great purity on the retro-nasal aromas, with the body of a marvelous vintage.

SAINT-JULIEN 2000
Red | 2011 up to 2020   91
Spicy and candied aromas, imposing body, powerful and harmonious tannins, and some finesse, more integrated and robust than refined.

Red: 279.2 acres; cabernet sauvignon 66%, merlot 27%, petit verdot 7%. Annual production: 700,000 bottles

CHÂTEAU LA LAGUNE

🍷🍷🍷🍷🍷

33290 Ludon-Médoc
Phone 00 33 5 57 88 82 77
Fax 00 33 5 57 88 82 70
contact@château-lalagune.com
www.château-lalagune.com

Now produced with cutting-edge technology, Château La Lagune has improved significantly in terms of aromatic purity and overall definition, but with no loss of that distinctive character owed to the sandy-siliceous soils unique in the Médoc. The wine plays increasingly on a harmonious, refined style that suits it well, and looks set to rival the best Third Growths. Witness the highly successful 2005 and 2006: supple and creamy, with refined tannins. We look forward to more body and vinosity as viticulture progresses.

Haut-Médoc 2006
Red | 2012 up to 2020   **92**
Full-bodied but elegant, nice tannins, but with good acidity on the finish, well vinified and very typical of the vintage.

Haut-Médoc 2005
Red | 2015 up to 2025   **91**
Ripe grapes and elegant notes of cedar and leather, with hints of the chocolaty notes typical of 2005; a very nice texture even if it's not the height of vinosity.

Haut-Médoc 2004
Red | 2012 up to 2016   **89**
Deeply colored, a touch of leather in the nose, which seems to be characteristic of the property; nice body, straightforward, classic tannins, a bit of menthol on the finish, excellent style.

Haut-Médoc 2003
Red | 2011 up to 2015   **86**
Dark color, particularly unctuous texture, but follows through with dry, hard tannins.

Haut-Médoc 2002
Red | 2011 up to 2017   **87**
Elegant, pleasing, a bit too chocolaty to attain the heights of purity, but possesses noble tannins.

Haut-Médoc 2001
Red | 2011 up to 2013   **88**
A powerful wine, but with an elegant texture and refined tannins. If it were just a bit more vinous, it would be up there with the best.

Red: 197.7 acres. Annual production: 150,000 bottles

CHÂTEAU LANGOA-BARTON

🍷🍷🍷🍷🍷

33250 Saint-Julien-Beychevelle
Phone 00 33 5 56 59 06 05
Fax 00 33 5 56 59 14 29
château@leoville-barton.com
www.leoville-barton.com

This exquisite Chartreuse-style château is the seat of the Barton family and the place where both Langoa-Barton and Léoville-Barton wines are vinified. Sourced from the very heart of the Saint-Julien appellation, the wines can be hard to tell apart when tasted "en primeur," although Léoville wines do tend to be fuller bodied with a denser texture. Langoa is very classically crafted—dense, tannic, and very spicy—but not always quite as pure as it should be on the nose and finish. Great vintages age superbly; all the recent vintages seem splendid!

Recently tasted
Saint-Julien 2006
Red | 2014 up to 2021   **91**

Older vintages
Saint-Julien 2005
Red | 2011 up to 2030   **93**
Very similar to Léoville, this is complete, ample, and full-bodied, with refined, long tannins. A great future.

Saint-Julien 2004
Red | 2011 up to 2022   **91**
With a beautiful nose of red fruit, this is clean, very elegant, and long with smooth tannins. Extraordinary in its almost Margaux style.

Saint-Julien 2003
Red | 2011 up to 2023   **93**
A classic grand vin of Saint-Julien, this is very similar in style to Léoville-Barton, which should not surprise. It is absolutely as majestic but slightly more rustic in its tannins.

Saint-Julien 2002
Red | 2011 up to 2017   **90**
A beautiful wine, generous and complete for the vintage. Nobly tannic and blessed with a very vivid and ripe acidity.

Saint-Julien 2000
Red | 2011 up to 2020   **92**
Full-bodied wine, this is slightly more supple than Léoville-Barton, with spicy tannins and a long, complex, and harmonious finish. A classic representation of its kind.

Red: 42 acres. Annual production: 85,000 bottles

CHÂTEAU LASCOMBES

1, cours de Verdun
BP 4
33460 Margaux
Phone 00 33 5 57 88 70 66
Fax 00 33 5 57 88 72 17
châteaulascombe@château-lascombes.fr
www.château-lascombes.com

The current owners are intent on restoring Château Lascombes to its past glory, and their efforts are paying off. The aromas and texture of the newly made wine can seem a bit over-flattering on occasion, but time adds a very pleasing balance between perfect form and, especially, fine-textured tannins.

Margaux 2006
Red | 2014 up to 2021   **92**
Complex nose, incredibly velvety texture, creamy tannins: here is an accomplished wine in a modern style but in keeping with (at least in our eyes) great Médoc tradition.

Margaux 2005
Red | 2011 up to 2025   **94**
In the bottle, this wine is distinguished by its texture and tannins, which are more delicate and molten than most others (perhaps due to a skillful oxygenation during the barrel aging), but it should cellar very well. Gorgeous complexity of flavors.

Margaux 2004
Red | 2011 up to 2020   **88**
Deeply colored, sappy, long, with more substance than the others; ripe grape flavors, spice, and very firm tannins.

Margaux 2003
Red | 2011 up to 2023   **93**
Beautiful texture, generous and ideally ripe fruit flavors, velvety tannins, long and seductive.

Margaux 2002
Red | 2011 up to 2017   **89**
Profusely aromatic, this has a well-balanced body and refined texture. A modern wine but not over-the-top, with very meticulous oak integration.

Red: 207.6 acres; cabernet sauvignon 45%, merlot 50%, petit verdot 5%. Annual production: 250,000 bottles

CHÂTEAU LATOUR

Saint-Lambert
33250 Pauillac
Phone 00 33 5 56 73 19 80
Fax 00 33 5 56 73 19 81
s.favreau@château-latour.com
www.château-latour.com

This cru was already a model of consistency but has clearly not rested on its laurels. François Pinault gave Frédéric Engerer a free hand to raise the bar even higher, and since then the great Château Latour—with a newly renovated vinification cellar that permits more precise single-batch fermentations—has been pushing the boundaries of wine perfection. Global warming has brought slightly riper grapes that produce plumper, fleshier, more supple wines despite their high tannin content. The inimitable integrity of this terroir nevertheless remains intact and brings a superb gravitas to the finish. The second wine, the Forts de Latour, combines fruit from the young vines in the Grand Vin vineyard Enclos with grapes from other top-quality Pauillac terroirs. The product is a wine with a vinosity and brilliance not seen in any other Médoc in this category. Recent vintages offer a supreme expression of a magical terroir and are all grandiose. The mouthfeel of the 2003, made in a year of extreme weather, simply defies description. The choice is yours: the genially baroque qualities of the latter or the absolute classicism of the 2005, a modern-day reprise of the 1949 or the 1929.

Pauillac 2006
Red | 2018 up to 2030   **97**
Very powerful and noble, with the return of mineral and iron notes common to the ultra-traditional vintages of the château, this has splendid tightness of the tannins and a very balanced body.

Pauillac 2005
Red | 2011 up to 2050   **99**
Very impressive tannin extraction makes this possibly the most harmonious wine in this vintage. It is majestic, long, and more traditional than the brilliant 2003. Alas, it is out of reach for most people because of the speculative value of the vintage.

Pauillac 2004
Red | 2011 up to 2029   **95**
A great achievement for the vintage, combining full body, elegance, and plenty of sap, with a more "friendly" character than Lafite, a more enveloping texture, and tannins that are a touch more harmonious.

PAUILLAC 2003
Red | 2011 up to 2030   **99**
A wine of a transcendent harmony at birth, it has managed to preserve all its charms and the original character of its structure and flavor. The nose is admirably pure and natural with fully integrated oak, but what remains most striking is the tender, silky texture, which effortlessly carries the noblest flavors of cabernet sauvignon at peak ripeness. Everything is big and smooth in this wine, which has a dazzling finish.

PAUILLAC 2002
Red | 2011 up to 2027   **94**
The oak expression is finely sappy, perfectly supporting the mineral and iron notes supplied by the terroir. It is complete, precise, and refined, with an inimitable feeling of nobility and a great future.

PAUILLAC 2001
Red | 2011 up to 2023   **94**
Very classic and rigorous definition of the cru, with a great integrity of structure and a uniquely velvety texture and sophistication.

PAUILLAC 2000
Red | 2011 up to 2030   **96**
With its aromas of cedar and its formal perfection, this wine is a model of classicism from Médoc.

PAUILLAC FORTS DE LATOUR 2006
Red | 2011 up to 2020   **90**
Very powerful and noble, with the return of mineral and iron notes common to the ultra-traditional vintages of the château, this has splendid tightness in its tannins and a very balanced body.

PAUILLAC FORTS DE LATOUR 2005
Red | 2011 up to 2013   **92**
Sumptuous substance extremely rare in a second wine, noble and spicy flavor, and a finish worthy of the reputation of the vintage. Great future.

Red: 197.7 acres; cabernet franc 1%, cabernet sauvignon 75%, merlot 23%, petit verdot 1%. **Annual production:** 320,000 bottles

CHÂTEAU LÉOVILLE-BARTON
🎖 🎖 🎖 🎖 🎖

33250 Saint-Julien-Beychevelle
Phone 00 33 5 56 59 06 05
Fax 00 33 5 56 59 14 29
château@leoville-barton.com
www.leoville-barton.com

Anthony Barton's restrained, honest, and thoughtful winemaking philosophy has placed this cru among the ranks of the Médoc elite, without sending prices through the roof. Its success is due to a significant proportion of ideally located old vines that combine quantity with quality, plus a collective determination to improve performance while maintaining a supremely classical Médoc style. Where these wines get their personality from is less easy to explain. It seems to be innate, characterized by an unmistakable, almost creamy consistency that makes this wine immediately likable. The key factor in the end is a respect for traditional methods—such as wood fermenting vats, for instance—that should offer food for thought to other Médoc wineries. The most recent vintages are all true to their lineage: complete in every way and instantly recognizable as wines of great class and great expectations.

SAINT-JULIEN 2006
Red | 2016 up to 2026   **94**
Very powerful nose of cedar; very masculine character, with full body, firm tannins, spicy notes, and lots of extract. A great wine with excellent aging potential.

SAINT-JULIEN 2005
Red | 2011 up to 2030   **96**
With power, generosity, and body, this has enormous aging potential and great elegance. A wine true to itself.

SAINT-JULIEN 2004
Red | 2011 up to 2024   **93**
Ultraripe, silky, long, and more full in body than Gruaud-Larose, this has impressive length and profoundly deep character.

SAINT-JULIEN 2003
Red | 2011 up to 2030   **96**
Without a doubt, the most complete of the three Léovilles in this vintage. The great nose is delicately oaky and spicy; the body is deep, harmonious, less abrupt than Las Cases in tannins and texture and more complex than Poyferré. Outstanding retro-nasal aromas, which raises this wine to the level of the First Growths.

SAINT-JULIEN 2002
Red | 2011 up to 2022   **94**
Marvelous in its balance and aromatic charm, this offers notes of cedar and tobacco and all the nuances specific to cabernet sauvignon, with the creamy texture that is a mark of the château.

SAINT-JULIEN 2001
Red | 2011 up to 2025   **90**
Beautiful cedar aromas but a little less body and definition than usual. Perhaps the wine is in a less expressive period of its bottle development.

SAINT-JULIEN 2000
Red | 2011 up to 2020   **96**
Great extract, rounded and vigorous tannins, noble texture. Certainly a classic of the vintage.

Red: 123.6 acres; cabernet franc 8%, cabernet sauvignon 70%, merlot 22%. Annual production: 210,000 bottles

CHÂTEAU LÉOVILLE-LAS CASES

33250 Saint-Julien-Beychevelle
Phone 00 33 5 56 73 25 26
Fax 00 33 5 56 59 18 33
leoville-las-cases@wanadoo.fr

This leading Médoc property owes everything to the pristine vines at its heart: the Grand Clos, a walled vineyard alongside Latour's Grand Enclos, where a perfect combination of soil, aspect, and microclimate ripens the cabernet sauvignon to perfection. This estate is also fortunate to have been managed by some remarkable personalities: Michel Delon and now his son Jean-Hubert, still striving for perfection on a daily basis in vineyards and winery. Always the first to taste and judge their wines, these men know what makes a great wine, since they often taste their wines against some of the greatest crus in the world (their private cellar is the best in Bordeaux). The future is plainly safe in their hands. The second wine, the Clos du Marquis, is made from younger plantings, even if now thirty years old, "outside" the Clos. It is the best in its category alongside the Forts de Latour and as good as at least half the Crus Classés.

SAINT-JULIEN 2006
Red | 2016 up to 2026   **95**
Astonishing tightness of body and tannins, admirable aromatic richness leaning toward Pauillac, nearly ideal balance between the magnitude of texture and the alcohol, and refreshing acidity on the finish.

SAINT-JULIEN 2005
Red | 2011 up to 2050   **96**
True Léoville, very generous in body, this has a tight texture, with ultra-firm but complex tannins. Grand nobility, immense future.

SAINT-JULIEN 2004
Red | 2011 up to 2026   **95**
Intense color, cedar, opulently rich texture, complex tannins, spice, and tobacco; great nobility. One of the best in this vintage.

SAINT-JULIEN 2003
Red | 2011 up to 2030   **93**
With intense color and a still-closed nose, this is very powerful wine, tight, with a density of substance rare for the vintage, which will ensure certainly a very slow aging in the bottle, but it falls a little short in flavor and in the pure finesse expected from this level of concentration in the grapes.

SAINT-JULIEN 2002
Red | 2011 up to 2027   **94**
Ideal for the vintage, this offers considerable classic aromas, with perfectly articulated notes of cedar and an outstanding density of texture—although for once its overall character is more Saint-Julien than Pauillac.

SAINT-JULIEN 2001
Red | 2011 up to 2025   **94**
The nose of cedar and licorice possesses all the expected flair, and the stunning palate displays plenitude and brightness.

SAINT-JULIEN 2000
Red | 2011 up to 2025   **98**
Everything we like in a great Saint-Julien: the finesse and subtlety of the aromas, texture, and tannins, with a vinosity superior to all the others.

SAINT-JULIEN 1998
Red | 2011 up to 2023   **95**
Absolutely complete and emblematic of this terroir, with noble aromas of cedar and incomparably classy tannins. Few wines surpass it in the vintage.

SAINT-JULIEN 1996
Red | 2011 up to 2026   **98**
One of the best Léovilles in history, majestic in form and character, with rigorous tannins and a distinction that approaches Lafite.

SAINT-JULIEN CLOS DU MARQUIS 2006
Red | 2011 up to 2030   **91**
A remarkable achievement, deep and intense, loaded with terrific cabernet franc and merlot.

SAINT-JULIEN CLOS DU MARQUIS 2005
Red | 2011 up to 2025   **93**
With a powerful nose, strong notes of overripe berries, opulent substance, and complex tannins, this is a wine to cellar, at the level of the appellation's best Premiers Crus.

SAINT-JULIEN CLOS DU MARQUIS 2004
Red | 2011 up to 2019   **91**
Delicately spicy and with a fine structure regardless of the solidity of its extract; noble notes of cedar. In line with the château's usual wines, made without compromise.

Red: 239.7 acres; cabernet franc 13%, cabernet sauvignon 65%, merlot 19%, petit verdot 3%. **Annual production:** 180,000 bottles

CHÂTEAU LÉOVILLE-POYFERRÉ

33250 Saint-Julien-Beychevelle
Phone 00 33 5 56 59 08 30
Fax 00 33 5 56 59 60 09
lp@leoville-poyferre.fr
www.leoville-poyferre.fr

A large part of this holding faces Léoville–Las Cases and adjoins Latour and Pichon-Longueville; we are therefore in prime Médoc country. This family estate has been very intelligently managed for the last quarter-century by Didier Cuvelier. The vineyard has been totally replanted several times, and the technical installations have been modernized so as to bring out all the magic in Léoville-Poyferré. The picking and processing of the grapes too has had the benefit of advice from foremost enologist Michel Rolland—apparently as much in his element in the Médoc as in his native Libourne! The cru today fulfills all expectations: vinous, classy, and very complex—not quite enough immediate charm, perhaps, but a match for the best of them after five years' aging. The wines show remarkable consistency from year to year, cleaner on the nose thanks to better-quality wood and a more powerful constitution. With another five or six years' aging, the best of the cabernets will rival their illustrious neighbors!

SAINT-JULIEN 2006
Red | 2016 up to 2026   **93**
Feminine tannins, smooth texture, elegant volume, a little less multilayered than 2005.

SAINT-JULIEN 2005
Red | 2011 up to 2030   **95**
With great elegance of aroma and texture and an imposing body, as is fitting for the vintage, this is a grand vin de garde. One of the future masterpieces of this vintage.

SAINT-JULIEN 2004
Red | 2011 up to 2020   **92**
Marked by the oak, this wine is tight, firm, spicy, racy, and linear.

SAINT-JULIEN 2003
Red | 2011 up to 2025   **93**
Very deep color with a bluish hue, nose typical of very ripe merlot bordering on notes of currants. Powerful, generous, tannic, even a little astringent.

SAINT-JULIEN 2002

Red | 2011 up to 2022   **92**

A well-made wine with the classic tobacco and graphite notes specific to northern Saint-Juliens. Slightly less immediately appealing than Barton and less monumental than Las Cases, but balanced well for bottle aging.

SAINT-JULIEN 2001

Red | 2011 up to 2020   **92**

Magnificent Saint-Julien of an aristocratic and irreproachable balance, with rich body and character.

SAINT-JULIEN 2000

Red | 2011 up to 2020   **94**

The nose, the palate, and the tannins are in complete harmony, relying more on finesse and elegance than body. A lovely and aristocratic wine.

SAINT-JULIEN 1999

Red | 2011 up to 2015   **90**

Beautiful color, oak a little insistent but very beautiful texture.

SAINT-JULIEN 1998

Red | 2011 up to 2020   **94**

Classic cedar aroma, tight texture, oak less noble than the extract, but this wine should have a beautiful future.

SAINT-JULIEN 1997

Red | 2011 up to 2015   **89**

Almost merlot-like, this offers finesse and momentum but without the true breeding of the terroir. Nevertheless, it is enjoyable and ready to drink.

SAINT-JULIEN 1996

Red | 2011 up to 2014   **93**

A precise and elegant wine with a stylish nose of cedar, this is not as dense as the best but demonstrates very good winemaking and better oak integration than 1998 or 1999.

SAINT-JULIEN 1995

Red | 2011 up to 2015   **90**

This has a round body, velvety texture, and complexity but lacks a little purity and transparency in the flavors compared to the very best Second Growths. One senses that their barrel inventory was not as impeccable as others.

Red: 197.7 acres; cabernet franc 2%, cabernet sauvignon 65%, merlot 25%, petit verdot 8%. **Annual production:** 450,000 bottles

CHÂTEAU LYNCH-BAGES

BP 120
33250 Pauillac
Phone 00 33 5 56 73 24 00
Fax 00 33 5 56 59 26 42
infochato@lynchbages.com
www.lynchbages.com

A worldwide reputation for opulence and consistency places this Pauillac Fifth Growth at the same level as a First Growth. Rich soil and a high proportion of cabernet sauvignon grapes that are picked at the peak of ripeness give this wine exceptional body and lovely, mouth-filling texture. Vinification is skillfully conducted under the expert eyes of Daniel Llose. Jean-Michel Cazes has now handed the reins to the next generation, who should be truly grateful to him for watching lovingly over this château's destiny for more than thirty years. The wine did seem to lose its oomph for a bit, but it was back with a vengeance in 2006—as stunning and forceful as ever!

PAUILLAC 2006

Red | 2018 up to 2026   **94**

Splendid velvety texture, very powerful but enrobing tannins; great personality! Very beautiful wine.

PAUILLAC 2005

Red | 2011 up to 2030   **91**

The velvety texture and smoothness emblematic of this château is admirable. Nevertheless, on the nose as well as on the palate, the new oak component is not in balance with the texture, and the wine's positive aspects may seem less elegant than one would like.

PAUILLAC 2004

Red | 2011 up to 2013   **91**

This round and refined wine is seductive with its graceful, subtle finish and its elegance. An accomplishment for this vintage.

PAUILLAC 2003

Red | 2011 up to 2025   **92**

Intense nose with leather, spice, and Havana tobacco notes. Body more broad than deep. It is voluptuous, easy, and smooth, but not as structured or defined as we ideally would expect. Beautiful future.

PAUILLAC 2002

Red | 2011 up to 2017   **91**

Relaxed and creamy, in the great tradition of the château, this 2002 will always have more nose than palate, but with a sufficient body to surprise during aging.

PAUILLAC 2001
Red | 2011 up to 2020   **91**
Rich, voluptuous wine but a touch heavy, with particularly concentrated notes of Havana cigars.

PAUILLAC 2000
Red | 2011 up to 2020   **95**
Evolved aromas of very ripe grapes with the roasted notes of hot vintages; abundant volume in mouth and appreciable persistence.

PAUILLAC 1998
Red | 2011 up to 2016   **92**
The powerful nose recalls the exotic clove notes in other Pauillacs. The tannins are less refined than the 1999. Well built but with a certain rusticity.

PAUILLAC 1997
Red | 2011 up to 2013   **88**
Light, refined, supple, harmonious. Slightly unripe grapes; will this evolve?

PAUILLAC 1996
Red | 2011 up to 2016   **95**
With a very pure and racy nose, complete body, and very discernible terroir, this round wine is archetypical of this great vintage for the Médoc.

Red: 222.4 acres; cabernet franc 10%, cabernet sauvignon 73%, merlot 15%, petit verdot 2%. **White:** 11.1 acres; muscadelle 20%, sauvignon 40%, sémillon 40%. **Annual production:** 420,000 bottles

CHÂTEAU LYNCH-MOUSSAS

33250 Pauillac
Phone 00 33 5 56 59 57 14
Fax 00 33 5 57 87 60 30
contact@moueix.com
www.moueix.com

This cru in the Pauillac hinterland under-performed for many years, but the vines now average a respectable age and—most important—this estate like all the Castéja vineyards has been properly taken in hand. The wine's fleshy, very rounded texture and forward nose make it a worthy second choice while you wait for the Castejas' other classed growth: Château Batailley, a denser, more classically styled Pauillac. Excellent value for the money. The two most recent vintages are very successful. This is a cru that continues to improve in terms of character and attractive style.

PAUILLAC 2006
Red | 2012 up to 2018   **90**
With beautiful color, this is a dense wine, with the truffle and spicy flavors typical of Pauillac wines from the "back" area. Lovely personality.

PAUILLAC 2005
Red | 2011 up to 2025   **91**
A sun-drenched wine with a very toasty nose. It is broad, voluptuous, and very "modern." Denis Dubourdieu directed the winemaking. More voluptuous than refined.

PAUILLAC 2004
Red | 2011 up to 2014   **88**
More elegant on the nose than many Médoc wines, with tannins that are refined yet a bit astringent, it finishes on notes of tobacco and truffle, which is classic for this sector of Pauillac.

PAUILLAC 2003
Red | 2011 up to 2013   **84**
Supple and fluid wine, lacking definition on both mid-palate and finish, with slightly bitter tannins and the sensation of vine stress.

PAUILLAC 2002
Red | 2011 up to 2014   **87**
Vigorous wine from a rather light vintage, but with roundness due to good merlot components. Evolving rather quickly for a Pauillac.

Red: 86.5 acres; cabernet 70%, merlot 30%. **Annual production:** 220,000 bottles

CHÂTEAU MALESCOT SAINT-EXUPÉRY

33460 Margaux
Phone 00 33 5 57 88 97 20
Fax 00 33 5 57 88 97 21
malescotsaintexupery@malescot.com
www.malescot.com

Owner Luc Zuger and superstar winemaker Michel Rolland combine their complementary talents here to produce wines that perform better than ever: complete, with a creamy warmth in the modern style but a very classical expression of terroir nonetheless, and a high proportion of cabernet sauvignon that keeps them beautifully in line! Flawlessly consistent since 1990.

MARGAUX 2006
Red I 2015 up to 2022   **90**
Freshness, finesse, elegance, with very markedly Margaux character (a menthol freshness at the end of the finish). A beautiful success, this should reach its apogee in ten to twelve years!

MARGAUX 2005
Red I 2011 up to 2030   **93**
A wine of huge dimensions with very powerful tannins. It has become even a little stiffer than it was before bottling, so it is necessary to wait.

MARGAUX 2004
Red I 2011 up to 2025   **91**
Full, sincere, tight, and tannic but with balance and unity. A true Médoc wine, for aficionados who can appreciate its solemnity.

MARGAUX 2003
Red I 2011 up to 2025   **93**
Precise floral nose likely to develop with time; perfectly balanced body with a broad texture but without heaviness; noble tannins. Bright future.

MARGAUX 2000
Red I 2011 up to 2020   **93**
Great Médoc classicism, with typical Margaux aromas. It has a generous body and plump texture without heaviness and impeccably extracted tannins.

Red: 58.1 acres; cabernet franc 10%, cabernet sauvignon 50%, merlot 35%, petit verdot 5%. Annual production: 220,000 bottles

CHÂTEAU MARGAUX

33460 Margaux
Phone 00 33 5 57 88 83 83
Fax 00 33 5 57 88 31 32
château-margaux@château-margaux.com
www.château-margaux.com

This cru has not disappointed since its acquisition by the Mentzelopoulos family in 1977 and now easily outclasses all the other wines in this appellation. There are two reasons for Château Margaux's superiority. The first is its terroir, ideally spread throughout the appellation on well-drained gravel soils that bring out the best in the cabernet sauvignon, the flagship grape of Château Margaux and the Médoc as a whole. The second is Paul Pontallier's brilliant winemaking team, always ready to take risks but never departing from the most classical Bordeaux style. The "grand vin" remains an exemplary expression of Château Margaux, showing density but finesse, opulence but freshness, while never relying on overripe grapes. Pavillon Rouge, the second wine, owes a lot to the hotter temperatures in recent years and exploits the Château's finest merlot, which is now increasingly excluded from the top wine. Pavillon Blanc, produced from thirty acres planted to white grapes, boasts a rich constitution and aristocratic aromas of ideally ripe sauvignon that place it among the three or four greatest dry white wines in Bordeaux.

Recently tasted
BORDEAUX PAVILLON BLANC 2007
White I 2011 up to 2017   **94**

Older vintages
BORDEAUX PAVILLON BLANC 2006
White I 2011 up to 2016   **95**
With exceptional grape maturity, this is undoubtedly more monumental in proportion than the red wine.

BORDEAUX PAVILLON BLANC 2005
White I 2011 up to 2015   **96**
At the top of an opulent vintage (also) for white wines: this has great depth but a light constitution, with freshness and purity that shows the perfect maturity of the sauvignon blanc, and refreshing persistence.

BORDEAUX PAVILLON BLANC 2004
White I 2011 up to 2016   **94**
Great smoothness and length, delicate and extremely classy aromas, remarkable density, and, especially on the finish, exceptional freshness and brightness.

Margaux 2006
Red | 2016 up to 2026   **95**
Very noble and fresh aromas of red berries and fruits, cedar and rose petal. Marvelous body with generosity and elegance, ultra-purebred tannins, and remarkable persistence. Inimitably Margaux. In short, an impressive achievement.

Margaux 2005
Red | 2011 up to 2040   **100**
An absolute masterpiece, the most accomplished wine that we have seen in thirty vintages! The structure is monumental but the texture is silky, with tannins of transcendent freshness and nobility.

Margaux 2004
Red | 2011 up to 2024   **95**
Admirably pure in aromas and very elegant and clean in texture, this wine has a pure expression of this unsurpassed terroir within its tannic frame. It will bring comfort to those who will not be able to afford the 2005 vintage.

Margaux 2003
Red | 2011 up to 2023   **98**
A wonder of finesse and delicacy within density, with tannins that are at the same time sublime in texture but certainly still far away from their apogee. Amazing length. An artistic wine.

Margaux 2002
Red | 2011 up to 2017   **94**
Very pure and classic on the nose; body perhaps a little thin in mid-palate, but with remarkably highly civilized tannins. The 2004 will undoubtedly have a little more body, but some may prefer the smoothness of this delicious 2002.

Margaux 2001
Red | 2011 up to 2013   **93**
Despite obvious qualities of finesse and complexity, this is not our favorite vintage for this château; its textural definition is a bit blurry.

Margaux 2000
Red | 2011 up to 2030   **98**
The nose shows an impressive aromatic intensity for its age, still showing toasty new oak notes and a "roasted" character from intense sun. It is a splendid wine with considerable and hedonistic charm. Its ample body should make for a rather slow evolution, and so it should not be opened until much later.

Margaux 1999
Red | 2011 up to 2019   **94**
This has more intensity and precision in its aromatic definition than the 2001. It is very much a "grand Médoc," delicately spiced, viscous, and, for the moment, without any corky notes, one of the defects of this vintage.

Margaux 1998
Red | 2011 up to 2023   **95**
A very beautiful vintage, expressing the incomparable personality of this terroir with strength, nobility, and precision. If you like notes of cedar, even ripe red bell pepper and pencil lead, you might just prefer it to the 2000.

Margaux 1997
Red | 2011 up to 2013   **88**
Bell peppery, simple, and sincere, but compared to the latest vintages this is clearly below what we can expect from a château of this value and price point.

Margaux Pavillon Rouge 2006
Red | 2011 up to 2021   **90**
Beautifully opulent and refined substance. Spicy, firm and noble tannins, very classic substance. This will comfort those who missed the 2005 vintage, but they will have to wait on it.

Margaux Pavillon Rouge 2005
Red | 2011 up to 2016   **94**
One of the greatest Pavillons in history, thanks to the beautiful merlot not selected for the grand wine. It has a remarkable richness, full and velvety, with noble aromas.

Red: 197.7 acres; cabernet franc 2%, cabernet sauvignon 75%, merlot 20%, petit verdot 3%. **White:** 29.7 acres; sauvignon blanc 100%. **Annual production:** 383,000 bottles

CHÂTEAU MARQUIS DE TERME

3, route de Rauzan
BP 11
33460 Margaux
Phone 00 33 5 57 88 30 01
Fax 00 33 5 57 88 32 51
mdt@château-marquis-de-terme.com
www.château-marquis-de-terme.com

Veteran Médoc winemaker Jean-Pierre Hugon has personally vinified more than thirty-five vintages. Today, thanks to a well-thought-out program of modernization, he can at last produce a wine worthy of its terroir: richly colored, vigorous but refined, and capable of rivaling the best in good vintages such as 1985 and 1989. That said, some of the younger vintages could do with purer, better-integrated wood. A new winemaker has been in charge since 2009. A revolution in the style is more than probable.

Margaux 2006
Red | 2011 up to 2016　　　　　**90**
The élevage was good for this wine: distinguished, slender, and energetic, a remarkable wine made for the long run.

Margaux 2005
Red | 2011 up to 2025　　　　　**91**
A powerful wine with very firm tannins, still-noticeable oak, and an unusually masculine feel for the appellation. Very frank but far from ready.

Margaux 2004
Red | 2011 up to 2020　　　　　**86**
The nose is spicy with oak notes but not very pure, with a slight foxy note. Good extract, but the fruit character is masked.

Margaux 2003
Red | 2011 up to 2027　　　　　**89**
Solid wine, this is guaranteed to age well and become more harmonious with time, as it was produced from ripe grapes.

Margaux 2002
Red | 2011 up to 2017　　　　　**88**
Good integration of merlot and cabernet sauvignon gives this wine a solid body and a full texture that will benefit from aging.

Margaux 2000
Red | 2011 up to 2020　　　　　**91**
Generous in body and flavors, bright finish.

Red: 93.9 acres; cabernet franc 3%, cabernet sauvignon 55%, merlot 35%, petit verdot 7%. Annual production: 150,000 bottles

CHÂTEAU MEYNEY

La Croix-Baccalan
109, rue Achard - BP 154
33042 Bordeaux cedex
Phone 00 33 5 56 59 00 40
Fax 00 33 5 56 59 36 47
contact@cagrandscrus.fr
www.cagrandscrus.com

Château Meyney, in the Saint-Estèphe appellation, lies next door to Château Montrose on one of the finest gravel ridges overlooking the Gironde River. The estate was in its heyday in the 1960s as part of the Cordier portfolio, ranking alongside Château Talbot. Today, after too many imprecise and overly thin vintages, it is fully back on form and a match for the best in its appellation. The bouquet sometimes gives off just the faintest whiff of truffles—doubtless a legacy of the blue marls in the subsoil (as in Pétrus). Great value for the money. All the latest vintages were among the top five nonclassed Médoc growths, each one highly recommended.

Saint-Estèphe 2006
Red | 2011 up to 2025　　　　　**91**
Great, racy aromas, powerful and clean body, complex tannins, splendid purity of expression.

Saint-Estèphe 2005
Red | 2011 up to 2030　　　　　**95**
More complete and racy than many in this vintage, this has a full, round body, noble texture, and quite an assertive finish. The best wine from this property for the past fifty vintages and undoubtedly the best value of this vintage, if you like archetypal Médoc wines.

Saint-Estèphe 2004
Red | 2011 up to 2020　　　　　**89**
A multilayered and distinguished wine in a very distinct Médoc style, with a solid frame, aromas of cedar and cigar, and an energetic finish.

Saint-Estèphe 2002
Red | 2011 up to 2022　　　　　**92**
Complete for the vintage and splendid return to the spotlight for this major Saint-Estèphe château: a flavor of cedar, a texture like velvet, with noble tannins.

Saint-Estèphe 2001
Red | 2011 up to 2013　　　　　**88**
Beautiful, deep, dense color, massive and expressive palate with powerful tannins, slightly dry.

Red: 126 acres; cabernet franc 8%, cabernet sauvignon 56%, merlot 26%, petit verdot 10%. Annual production: 320,000 bottles

CHÂTEAU MONBRISON

1, allée Monbrison
33460 Arsac
Phone 00 33 5 56 58 80 04
Fax 00 33 5 56 58 85 33
lvdh33@wanadoo.fr
www.châteaumonbrison.com

Home to the finest gravel soils in Arsac, Monbrison produces one of the most elegant and expressive of all the Margaux wines—seeming a bit thin when young, but fleshing out nicely with time in oak. The latest vintages show slightly more vinosity as young wines and look in great shape. The exceptional 2005s and 2006s are possibly the most refined of all the nonclassed growths in this appellation!

Margaux 2006
Red | 2011 up to 2025   **92**
The wine is equal to many classed growths in the finesse and purity of its cedar aromas and precision. It shows the flawlessness and refinement typical of great vintages from this château!

Margaux 2005
Red | 2011 up to 2025   **94**
This offers a great deal of personality and style, with an extremely elegant nose of red fruit aromas and fine tannins. Classy Margaux, worthy of the grand wines from the late 1980s.

Margaux 2004
Red | 2011 up to 2020   **90**
Beautiful, graceful aromas, tannins under control and almost at ease, a medium body emphasizing the wine's textural refinement: a feminine Margaux, extremely well made.

Margaux 2002
Red | 2011 up to 2022   **89**
With superior aromatic finesse and complex tannins perfectly integrated with its body, this is worthy of a good classified growth.

Margaux 2001
Red | 2011 up to 2018   **88**
A wine of good intensity, with a concentrated substance. Beautiful style, long and linear.

Margaux 2000
Red | 2011 up to 2015   **90**
A beautiful, complete wine, spicy, creamy, harmonious, full, and long.

Red: 32.6 acres; cabernet franc 15%, cabernet sauvignon 50%, merlot 30%, petit verdot 5%. **Annual production:** 80,000 bottles

CHÂTEAU MONTROSE

33180 Saint-Estèphe
Phone 00 33 5 56 59 30 12
Fax 00 33 5 56 59 71 86
château@château-montrose.com
www.château-montrose.com

The sale of this cru came as a surprise to its admirers, since the Charmolüe family seemed forever attached to their property and had no obvious financial difficulties. The lucky buyer is French construction giant Bouygues, which has shelled out a small fortune for one of the finest, most homogeneous vineyards in the entire Médoc. Ideally located on the Gironde River like Château Latour, this cru has always been much sought after by lovers of classical Bordeaux, who appreciate its clean but voluminous palate, supported by very classy if sometimes slightly rigid tannins—a tendency that veteran winemaker Jean Delmas plans to put right. The 2005 will not equal the sumptuous Château Montrose 1996, 2000, or 2003—models to be followed by the present winemaking team if they add just a shade more finesse.

Saint-Estèphe 2006
Red | 2016 up to 2026   **93**
Very beautiful wine, richly made, lifted, with diverse aromas and a remarkable mineral dimension.

Saint-Estèphe 2005
Red | 2011 up to 2025   **93**
Beautifully balanced wine, easy enough for the château, with supple and appealing tannins, but we cannot find the monumentality of its peers nor the body of great vintages like 2000 or 2003.

Saint-Estèphe 2004
Red | 2011 up to 2024   **93**
This has the deep color, harmonious and full body, magically precise and purebred tannins, and persistence worthy of a First Growth. It is perhaps relatively more accomplished than the 2005.

Saint-Estèphe 2003
Red | 2011 up to 2028   **95**
Good color, nose powerful, but not fully developed, majestic body; this is obviously one of the big players of the vintage. The tannins are slightly tight at the moment, as is typical for Montrose.

Saint-Estèphe 2002
Red | 2011 up to 2022   **91**
This is rich in color and tannins, round and creamy, but not as refined as the best Margaux or Pauillac wines of the vintage.

Saint-Estèphe 2001
Red | 2011 up to 2026   **94**
Splendid, classic Saint-Estèphe, with fleshy and ripe tannins, energy, and great distinction.

Saint-Estèphe 2000
Red | 2011 up to 2025   **96**
A crimson color with admirable luminosity, noble and spicy aromas, and a superlative body with a small dab of austerity: this is high-class wine, living up to its stardom in this vintage.

Saint-Estèphe 1996
Red | 2011 up to 2026   **96**
Powerful, nervy, and refreshing, framed with drier tannins than the 2000 and 2003. This 1996 is aligned with beautiful oceanic vintages, which please the experts but require from the beginners an education that they do not always wish to (or cannot) acquire. Tannins of great class.

Saint-Estèphe 1990
Red | 2011 up to 2020   **94**
Entering its apogee. The nose, for a long time showing notes of "barnyard," is evolving to rose-petal, musk, and black truffle. Its body and texture are also out of the ordinary with an accentuated plumpness that evokes Rhone wines, but with an indubitable opulence as well as a very long aromatic persistence.

Saint-Estèphe 1989
Red | 2011 up to 2015   **95**
With sumptuous aromas, this is high-class wine, appealing, complex, posing on spicy tannins admirably representing the northern Médoc terroir. It tastes magnificent right now but will slowly continue to become finer—if the cork, of course, does not fail.

Red: 173 acres; cabernet franc 4%, cabernet sauvignon 65%, merlot 30%, petit verdot 1%. Annual production: 340,000 bottles

CHÂTEAU MOUTON-ROTHSCHILD

33250 Pauillac
Phone 00 33 5 56 59 22 22
Fax 00 33 5 56 73 20 44
webmaster@bpdr.com
www.bpdr.com

Mouton is beyond question the most distinctly Pauillac of all the Pauillacs in terms of opulence, velvety texture, and longevity. But it hasn't been the most dependable of the First Growths these past thirty years, which makes its present performance all the more commendable. Back on form with a vengeance, Mouton wines place emphasis on fruit selection over quantity, but the main distinction is a truly extraordinary level of technical perfection—testament to an impeccable harvesting process and effective, ultraprecise aging. The refined tannins and perfectly integrated wood are beyond reproach, a credit to Philippe Dalhuin, who joined Mouton in 2004. The second wine, Le Petit Mouton de Mouton Rothschild, is "petit" in name alone, displaying a character and vinosity that now rank it with the Forts de Latour wines. The 2004, 2005, and 2006 show a precision of texture and purity of flavor that surpass even the remarkable 2000. The 2005 is sure to prove a modern reincarnation of the sensational 1949 vintage.

Recently tasted
Bordeaux Ailes d'Argent 2007
White | 2012 up to 2017   **93**

Older vintages
Pauillac 2006
Red | 2011 up to 2020   **99**
A splendid silky texture, thanks to an élevage of admirable precision, great power, and great refinement, all in magical balance.

Pauillac 2005
Red | 2011 up to 2050   **99**
This wine has not stopped growing in power and refinement of texture, and seems like the most formally achieved of the last half-century; it may even be the most nobly aromatic of the Pauillac First Growths. Time will confirm or it won't.

Pauillac 2004
Red | 2011 up to 2026   **95**
Frank and rich flavors, aristocratic texture, infinitely more refined oak than in the past, and great length. Undeniably one of the pinnacles of the vintage.

Pauillac 2003
Red | 2011 up to 2030 **96**

Great color, very developed nose, warm but refined with an already complete integration of new oak. It has a splendid velvety texture, with tannins that feel very smooth, even molten, typical of the current phenolic extractions at the château. Gigantic length.

Pauillac 2002
Red | 2011 up to 2027 **93**

A grand wine, intensely aromatic with classic Pauillac aromas of cedar and tobacco, very powerful on the palate, with refined tannins. We slightly prefer the 2004, and the 2006 even more.

Pauillac 2001
Red | 2011 up to 2026 **94**

Fat and rich, very deep, with the opulent style of Mouton, but with a little less vigor and amplitude than the 2000.

Pauillac 2000
Red | 2011 up to 2013 **98**

This is incredibly fleshy, with a velvety texture that delivers seductive tactile sensations and phenomenal persistence.

Pauillac Petit Mouton 2006
Red | 2016 up to 2026 **93**

This strikes an impressive balance despite the undeniable power of all its components. It has very refined tannins, a character that we like in Mouton wines, without reduction in structure or complexity, in a style that will age more quickly.

Pauillac Petit Mouton 2005
Red | 2011 up to 2025 **93**

This offers much character, complexity, and nobility in its oak integration and in the class of its tannins. A remarkable wine in its vintage and category.

Red: 192.7 acres; cabernet franc 10%, cabernet sauvignon 77%, merlot 11%, petit verdot 2%. White: 9.8 acres; muscadelle 2%. sauvignon blanc 51%, sémillon 47%. Annual production: 300,000 bottles

CHÂTEAU LES ORMES DE PEZ

33180 Saint-Estèphe
Phone 00 33 5 56 73 24 00
Fax 00 33 5 56 59 26 42
infochato@ormesdepez.com
www.ormesdepez.com

A typical Saint-Estèphe cru, home to fleshy, spicy, smooth-tasting wines of dependable quality. Praised by some for its mouth-filling volume; criticized by others for its slight lack of finesse and complexity compared with other Crus Bourgeois of similar standing. Think of it more as an excellent wine from clay-limestone rather than from gravel soils.

Recently tasted
Saint-Estèphe 2007
Red | 2011 up to 2015 **89**

Older vintages
Saint-Estèphe 2006
Red | 2011 up to 2014 **91**

Purple crimson color. Fine and spicy nose. Palate does not have much intensity, but it is fine and elegant, showing an attractive freshness. Fine tannins.

Saint-Estèphe 2004
Red | 2011 up to 2020 **86**

In this particular bottle, the tannins appeared much drier than in the other Saint-Estèphe wines. It will have to be reexamined with another bottle.

Saint-Estèphe 2001
Red | 2011 up to 2018 **89**

Good stature on the palate with harmonious and dense tannins. Lovely, long, and pleasant wine.

Saint-Estèphe 2000
Red | 2011 up to 2015 **89**

Complete wine, of beautiful maturity and accomplished traditional Médoc style.

Red: 86.5 acres; cabernet franc 11%. cabernet sauvignon 57%, merlot 32%. Annual production: 23,000 bottles

CHÂTEAU PALMER

Cantenac
33460 Margaux
Phone 00 33 5 57 88 72 72
Fax 00 33 5 57 88 37 16
château-palmer@château-palmer.com
www.château-palmer.com

This cru is rightly famous for its consistent quality and compelling aromas and texture. Crafted by the Chardon family for two generations, it always retained a genuine expression of terroir that was a source of admiration throughout the world. Thomas Duroux merges that traditional style with modern enological expertise to achieve even more textbook perfection. The "grand vin" does contain slightly more cabernet sauvignon these days, but its body and texture is distinguished by the opulence of the estate-grown merlot and petit verdot. This gives it an immediate sensuality that goes down well with newcomers and seasoned connoisseurs alike. Alter Ego, the aptly named second wine, exhibits very neat balance and texture.

MARGAUX 2006
Red | 2014 up to 2021   **94**
A rich wine, harmonious, very diversified in aromas, precise and noble in texture, very velvety and long.

MARGAUX 2005
Red | 2011 up to 2030   **97**
Splendid, complex, and refined nose with a minty note that gives it a rare freshness for the vintage. Superb and balanced body, marvelously velvety, with subtle tannins. A grand wine, worthy of the vintage and the château.

MARGAUX 2004
Red | 2011 up to 2020   **93**
The aromas have distinct class and the texture is refined, with great length due to the exemplary quality of tannins. Wine of great style in a vintage less preferred than others.

MARGAUX 2003
Red | 2011 up to 2020   **92**
Beautiful floral and light nose, full but soft texture, caressing tannins. Wine of great charm but less complete than the 2005.

MARGAUX 2002
Red | 2011 up to 2020   **91**
This is tasty, smooth, and fresh in aroma and texture, with the creamy characteristic of excellent merlot harvested at perfect maturity.

MARGAUX 2001
Red | 2011 up to 2021   **90**
The wine is generous, even opulent, for the vintage, with a remarkable velvety texture but a slight lack of complexity.

MARGAUX 2000
Red | 2011 up to 2020   **92**
Spiced, truffled, and roasted, this wine has remarkable volume on the palate, framed with firm tannins, a touch astringent. Nice length.

MARGAUX ALTER EGO 2006
Red | 2011 up to 2018   **90**
With beautiful fruit character, elegant texture, and fresh and pure tannins, this is a wine of class and style that will probably develop rather quickly.

MARGAUX ALTER EGO 2005
Red | 2011 up to 2020   **93**
This has a superb aromatic expression with violet notes that are rare in this vintage, a velvety texture and charming tannins despite its intensity and alcohol level. A remarkable second wine.

Red: 135.9 acres; cabernet sauvignon 47%, merlot 47%, petit verdot 6%. Annual production: 200,000 bottles

CHÂTEAU PETIT-BOCQ

3, rue de la Croix-de-Pez
33180 Saint-Estèphe
Phone 00 33 5 56 59 35 69
Fax 00 33 5 56 59 32 11
châteaupetitbocq@hotmail.com

From just five acres in 1993, this estate has grown to thirty-five acres today: a patchwork collection of some eighty subsequently acquired parcels that reflect the variety of terroirs and soils in Saint-Estèphe, and unfailingly deliver all the character and aromatic complexity typical of this appellation. The estate's happy owner, Dr. Lagneaux, cares for his vines as lovingly as he does his patients, planting mainly merlot for the sake of his charming and beguiling Saint-Estèphe.

SAINT-ESTÈPHE 2006
Red | 2011 up to 2013   **88**
Brilliant black color. Rich and complex nose with hints of chocolate. In the mouth it is broad, massive, charming, and silky in its extract, finishing with elegant, refined tannins. A very sophisticated wine.

SAINT-ESTÈPHE 2005
Red | 2011 up to 2020   **87**
Black in color, rich and expansive on the nose, with ripe fruit and floral notes. Charming in the mouth, silky with round tannins, great aromatic persistence and elegance. Very stylish.

SAINT-ESTÈPHE 2004
Red | 2011 up to 2020   **87**
Dense purple color. Intense nose with good complexity, aromas of dark fruit, minerals, and light oak; broad on the palate, dense and powerful with very solid tannins, good length, and great balance. Flavorful and rich.

Red: 33.9 acres; cabernet franc 2%, cabernet sauvignon 43%, merlot 55%. **Annual production:** 80,000 bottles

CHÂTEAU DE PEZ

33180 Saint-Estèphe
Phone 00 33 5 56 59 30 26
Fax 00 33 5 56 59 39 25
pmoureau@châteaudepez.com
www.champagne-roederer.com

Pez rightly ranks as one of the most respectable nonclassed growths, renowned for its neat vineyards, careful winemaking, and spicy, ultra-classical wines. Owned by Louis Roederer Champagne, Pez was the spearhead of the company's presence in the Médoc prior to the acquisition of Pichon-Lalande. This is a wine that always needs a few years in the bottle to show its true colors. Roederer's second Saint-Estèphe property, Haut-Beauséjour, produces a simpler but tidy wine with a decently spicy bouquet.

Recently tasted
SAINT-ESTÈPHE 2006
Red | 2011 up to 2016   **92**

Older vintages
SAINT-ESTÈPHE 2005
Red | 2011 up to 2030   **92**
Full-bodied, with massive tannins. A very bright future.

SAINT-ESTÈPHE 2004
Red | 2011 up to 2016   **88**
Intense ruby-red color, notes of cedar on the nose, serious and linear on the palate, with firm tannins. A serious style with a great future ahead.

SAINT-ESTÈPHE 2001
Red | 2011 up to 2013   **91**
A wine with elegant substance and nice density. One of the successes of the vintage, without a doubt.

SAINT-ESTÈPHE 2000
Red | 2011 up to 2013   **91**
Nice intensity with finesse and personality. Generous, with great length on the finish.

Red: 93.9 acres; cabernet franc 5%, cabernet sauvignon 45%, merlot 45%, petit verdot 5%. **Annual production:** 150,000 bottles

CHÂTEAU PHÉLAN-SÉGUR

33180 Saint-Estèphe
Phone 00 33 5 56 59 74 00
Fax 00 33 5 56 59 74 10
phelan@phelansegur.com
www.phelansegur.com

This walled property, magnificently located on the banks of the Gironde River, is in a sense the first cousin of Calon-Ségur, but the two wines have always been very different in character. The notes of cedar and sandalwood are more pronounced in Phélan-Ségur, which is more lithely structured, especially on the mid-palate. And it has never been more consistent and precise than it is today, crafted under the judicious direction of the Gardinier family. In fact, the character is so like a Lafite or Ducru-Beaucaillou that Phélan-Ségur often surprises in blind tastings!

Recently tasted
SAINT-ESTÈPHE 2006
Red | 2011 up to 2025   **93**

Older vintages
SAINT-ESTÈPHE 2005
Red | 2011 up to 2025   **93**
Very elegant and fresh notes of cedar for cabernet sauvignon in this vintage. It is full in body but long-limbed, with racy tannins. Great future.

SAINT-ESTÈPHE 2004
Red | 2011 up to 2020   **92**
Very complex aromas, remarkably built and balanced body; a major achievement for the château.

SAINT-ESTÈPHE 2002
Red | 2011 up to 2017   **90**
Very balanced wine, framed with supple, racy tannins, this is long, particularly subtle and elegant, thanks to the cabernet sauvignon from parcels near Montrose.

SAINT-ESTÈPHE 2001
Red | 2011 up to 2015   **90**
This is a beautiful wine with fine aromas and perfect balance. A beautiful achievement in this vintage.

SAINT-ESTÈPHE 2000
Red | 2011 up to 2015   **93**
Beautiful, powerful wine, with lovely substance improved by beautiful aging. Very balanced with a fruit maturity that lives up to the stature of this great vintage.

Red: 222.4 acres; cabernet franc 2%, cabernet sauvignon 51%, merlot 47%. **Annual production:** 500,000 bottles

CHÂTEAU PIBRAN

33250 Pauillac
Phone 00 33 5 56 73 17 17
Fax 00 33 5 56 73 17 28
contact@pichonlongueville.com
www.château pichonlongueville.com

A good, nonclassified Pauillac Growth that draws on the skills and experience of the Pichon-Baron technical team. This is a fleshy, very classical Pauillac, rather more supple and fruity than the classified growths and made in an earlier-drinking style. You can judge this wine only once it is bottled; the best of the bunch so far is the 2000.

Recently tasted
PAUILLAC 2006
Red | 2011 up to 2018   **89**

Older vintages
PAUILLAC 2005
Red | 2011 up to 2025   **88**
A beautiful body, fleshy and spicy, rather traditional and comfortable. Good tannins, perhaps a touch too astringent.

PAUILLAC 2004
Red | 2011 up to 2018   **88**
Full with expressive extract, this looks to be the most beautiful achievement of the Cru Bourgeois in Pauillac. It is certainly one of the most classic expressions of this appellation in this vintage.

PAUILLAC 2002
Red | 2011 up to 2017   **86**
Good volume on the palate, strict tannins, a little rustic.

PAUILLAC 2001
Red | 2011 up to 2015   **88**
The wine displays a beautiful substance in a full and masculine style, typical of its appellation.

PAUILLAC 2000
Red | 2011 up to 2018   **91**
Similar to the 2001, with even more powerful substance. A traditional Pauillac, strong, with assuredly great aging potential.

Red: 42 acres; cabernet sauvignon 45%, merlot 54%, petit verdot 1%. **Annual production:** 90,000 bottles

CHÂTEAU PICHON-LONGUEVILLE BARON

🦎 🦎 🦎 🦎

33250 Pauillac
Phone 00 33 5 56 73 17 17
Fax 00 33 5 56 73 17 28
contact@pichonlongueville.com
www.château pichonlongueville.com

This estate's first wine comes from the deep gravel beds underpinned by clay opposite Latour, with the benefit of the microclimate particular to the banks of the Gironde River. The wine has all the vigor and power of the greatest Médocs, but made in a very pure style, lovingly watched over by the estate's excellent director, Jean-Louis Matignon. The second wine has yet to equal the best in its category, but the winery's long-awaited expansion will allow longer, more ambitious aging. All recent vintages are exceptional, with that honest character that comes partly from the cabernet sauvignon and partly from that hint of minerals contributed by the best Saint-Lambert soils—a perfect transition between Pauillac and Saint-Julien.

Recently tasted
PAUILLAC LES TOURELLES
DE PICHON-LONGUEVILLE 2006
Red | 2014 up to 2018   89

Older vintages
PAUILLAC 2006
Red | 2016 up to 2026   95
Powerful and muscular, this offers an intense expression of the vintage, with splendidly present Pauillac character (cigar box and spice). Very great future.

PAUILLAC 2005
Red | 2011 up to 2030   96
Great, racy nose of tobacco; ample body with very noble and frank texture, firm tannins. A very big Pauillac, a touch less voluptuous than Pontet-Canet.

PAUILLAC 2004
Red | 2011 up to 2022   93
Multilayered, powerful, warm, full, delightful, noble wine. A beautiful success with bright aging potential.

PAUILLAC 2003
Red | 2011 up to 2025   95
The wine justifies its classification with the extra body and generosity of texture it offers compared to its peers. Moreover, it will be much more classic than one might think in its aromas and texture. Great wine.

PAUILLAC 2002
Red | 2011 up to 2022   93
With its deep color, racy, severe, and smoky nose, dense and tight body, and ample, firm tannins, this is a wine of great character without concessions, destined for real aficionados.

PAUILLAC 2001
Red | 2011 up to 2016   92
An ample wine of great stature with round tannins, this will fully reveal itself in the next decade.

PAUILLAC 2000
Red | 2011 up to 2025   96
Remarkable plenitude of constitution and evident nobility: a grand Pauillac, strong and complex, with very racy tannins. A must.

PAUILLAC 1998
Red | 2011 up to 2016   92
This has a velvety texture and complex aromas but less concentration than the vintages that followed. We sense that the grapes were less ripe than those for the best wines.

PAUILLAC 1996
Red | 2011 up to 2016   92
The color is still deep, the nose very spicy: this is a tight wine, outstanding but without the supplement of finesse and complexity of Pichon-Comtesse, which wins when we taste them side by side.

PAUILLAC LES TOURELLES
DE PICHON-LONGUEVILLE 2005
Red | 2011 up to 2013   91
Excellent substance on the nose, very Pauillac, with notes of cedar and cigar box that make it more classic than most wines in this vintage. Lovely body, noble tannins. A true, highly recommended success.

Red: 180.4 acres; cabernet franc 3%, cabernet sauvignon 61%, merlot 35%, petit verdot 1%. Annual production: 400,000 bottles

CHÂTEAU PICHON-LONGUEVILLE COMTESSE DE LALANDE

BP 72
33250 Pauillac
Phone 00 33 5 56 59 19 40
Fax 00 33 5 56 59 26 56
pichon@pichon-lalande.com
www.pichon-lalande.com

When Louis Roederer Champagne acquired this cru from then-owner May-Eliane de Lencquesaing, the emphasis was firmly on continuity. The vineyards are located right next door to Latour but have always produced wines with a very different expression due to a complex mix of vines—mainly merlot, but also subsidiary plantings of the petit verdot, which contribute natural sweetness and mellowness. Velvety and quick to open up, the wine also ages superbly, retaining all of its charm and hugely classy tannins. A greater proportion of cabernet sauvignon in the most recent vintages gives them a Pauillac-like classicism but with no loss of their fabulous finesse. The second wine, La Réserve de la Comtesse, is one of the most consistent in its category. The 2005s and 2006s are spicier than usual due to that greater proportion of cabernet sauvignon, displaying a barely perceptible hint of ripe peppers that gives them a particular freshness and charm.

Recently tasted

PAUILLAC 2006
Red | 2016 up to 2026 **92**

PAUILLAC RÉSERVE DE LA COMTESSE 2006
Red | 2014 up to 2018 **90**

Older vintages

PAUILLAC 2005
Red | 2011 up to 2050 **95**
With great opulence and refined flavors of cedar, this is long, sappy, and charming, with very rare body for the appellation!

PAUILLAC 2004
Red | 2011 up to 2019 **90**
Good grapes made for a generous and ripe wine, slightly rustic in its aromas of green pepper, which will evolve in the bottle.

PAUILLAC 2003
Red | 2011 up to 2025 **94**
Noble cedar aroma with a dab of red pepper. Generous, open, and very sappy with very fine-grained tannins, this wine already has a great, persistent presence.

PAUILLAC 2002
Red | 2011 up to 2022 **94**
With very noble aromas and a velvety texture, this is marvelous for this vintage, with good length. A flavorful wine, long, complex, and typical of the current evolution of the appellation.

PAUILLAC 2001
Red | 2011 up to 2021 **91**
Spicy and flavorful on the palate, this is rather angular for this château, solidly built, very Pauillac.

PAUILLAC 2000
Red | 2011 up to 2030 **95**
Powerful, complex, and noble, this is a wine of great aromatic freshness, with a smooth, deep texture. Its evolution will be very long but sure.

PAUILLAC 1999
Red | 2011 up to 2017 **92**
Finely aromatic with notes of cedar and red pepper and smooth in texture, this has a slight lack of body but not of elegance.

PAUILLAC 1998
Red | 2011 up to 2018 **93**
This is intensely expressive and defined on the nose, with notes of cedar, spices, green pepper, leather, and a touch of clove. Very Pauillac, almost too exuberant, but this characteristic will please many.

PAUILLAC 1996
Red | 2011 up to 2021 **96**
The nose is exceptional in its nobility, precision, and élan, a mark of great cabernet sauvignon vintages. Full body, remarkable finesse, and great length. A wine that approaches the status of a First Growth. Our favorite of the last twenty vintages from this château.

Red: 210 acres; cabernet franc 12%, cabernet sauvignon 45%, merlot 35%, petit verdot 8%. **Annual production:** 400,000 bottles

CHÂTEAU PONTET-CANET

33250 Pauillac
Phone 00 33 5 56 59 04 04
Fax 00 33 5 56 59 26 63
info@pontet-canet.com
www.pontet-canet.com

These magnificent vineyards alongside Mouton-Rothschild have very quickly rewarded all the hard work put into this holding under Alfred Tesseron's passionate, perfectionist leadership. No other estate in this sector takes so many risks for the sake of eco-friendly vineyard management. The picked grapes are placed in small baskets then gravity-fed into the fermentation tanks. We were extremely impressed by the gorgeous texture and palate of the most recent vintages.

Recently tasted
PAUILLAC 2006
Red | 2016 up to 2026   93

Older vintages
PAUILLAC 2005
Red | 2011 up to 2030   97
Sumptuous body and texture. Truly a special achievement in a terrific vintage for Pauillac, showing the usual intelligent viticulture at this estate.

PAUILLAC 2004
Red | 2011 up to 2019   93
A remarkable success: a very rich wine, harmonious, long, with a dense and silky texture, which seems unique among its peers in this vintage.

PAUILLAC 2003
Red | 2011 up to 2025   95
Significant body and tannins delivering ultra-refined tactile sensations. Strong aromas of cigar box and plum. Persistent, very close to a First Growth in the quality of its nose and body. Spectacular success in a vintage that was not easy for Pauillac.

PAUILLAC 2002
Red | 2011 up to 2017   91
Polished in its aromas and texture, this is one of the most balanced wines of this vintage. It will probably evolve faster in the bottle than the vintages that followed it.

PAUILLAC 2001
Red | 2011 up to 2019   90
This shows the true attributes of Pauillac, which can be defined as a forthrightness and fullness of the body and a solid tannic foundation; but it lacks the "genius" of a great vintage.

PAUILLAC 2000
Red | 2011 up to 2025   94
An incredible success on several levels: generous, harmonious, hedonistic, and rigorous all at the same time.

PAUILLAC 1999
Red | 2011 up to 2014   92
With a nose of cedar, refined texture, charm, and complexity, this shows grand precision in winemaking. Equal to the best Second Growths.

PAUILLAC 1998
Red | 2011 up to 2018   94
Very subtle and spicy nose, without the clove note from other crus. Classic body, significant harmony among aromas, alcohol, and tannins. A wine of great character.

PAUILLAC 1997
Red | 2011 up to 2013   92
With a very expressive and remarkable, complex nose of cedar, this has more youth and precision in its structure and subtlety in the texture of its tannins than almost any other Pauillac in this vintage. An immense achievement. À point.

PAUILLAC 1996
Red | 2011 up to 2016   91
In the context of this vintage and the amazing success of all the others that followed, we are a little disappointed. It has the finesse and the class of cabernet sauvignon in this vintage, but with less richness than the 1998, for example.

Red: 200.2 acres; cabernet franc 5%, cabernet sauvignon 61%, merlot 32%, petit verdot 2%. **Annual production:** 280,000 bottles

CHÂTEAU POTENSAC

33340 Ordonnac
Phone 00 33 5 56 73 25 26
Fax 00 33 5 56 59 18 33
leoville-las-cases@wanadoo.fr
www.potensac.com

Potensac is probably the most respected of all the Médoc crus. It owes its success to some first-rate winemaking teams, carefully selected by the Delon family, who also own Léoville-Las-Cases. The same exacting production standards apply to this cru that also has the advantage of some seriously old vines—which remain as productive as ever despite their age. This is classical wine of the highest degree: notes of cedar on the nose, spicy tannins, and plenty of firmness. Today's offerings show a tendency toward more immediate finesse and suppleness.

MÉDOC 2006
Red | 2011 up to 2018   89
Wonderful color. This is a very good wine for its appellation, vinous and full, powerful yet without being aggressive. It will certainly age a long time.

MÉDOC 2005
Red | 2011 up to 2018   91
Dark purple color with hints of violet. Superb nose, rich, full, appealing, all while remaining elegant. The palate is full with a tight tannic grain, a velvety texture, complex and persistent flavors, and an excellent acidity on the finish. Huge aging potential.

MÉDOC 2004
Red | 2011 up to 2015   91
Deep purple color, expressive nose with subtle notes of spice and rich fruit. Full, soft, and harmonious in the mouth, with fruity notes, pretty vanilla oak, velvety tannins, and a good finish. A picture of elegance.

MÉDOC 2001
Red | 2011 up to 2013   88
Pretty, saturated color, nose strongly marked by the oak but of nice intensity, full and powerful in the mouth with intense extract.

Red: 173 acres; cabernet franc 16%, cabernet sauvignon 46%, carménère 2%, merlot 36%. Annual production: 240,000 bottles

CHÂTEAU POUGET

33460 Cantenac
Phone 00 33 5 57 88 90 82
guillemet.lucien@wanadoo.fr
www.boyd-cantenac.fr

We rarely get to taste this wine because it is all spoken for by a local négociant. Under the same ownership as Boyd-Cantenac, next door, this small cru produces quite a different style of wine: less complex in terms of aroma though with much the same vinosity. Once plagued by poor-quality barrels it has improved greatly over the past years and now delivers the performance expected of a Grand Cru Classé: decently rustic but with handsome body and that tight-knit texture of fruit from old vines.

MARGAUX 2005
Red | 2011 up to 2025   87
With a lovely nose of cedar, this is a muscular and complex wine with classy tannins. A complete wine and positively the best value of the vintage in Margaux.

MARGAUX 2004
Red | 2011 up to 2013   87
Good color and full-bodied, but less pure on the nose than Boyd. More structure than finesse.

MARGAUX 2003
Red | 2011 up to 2015   87
Powerful wine, actually a bit rough, this is long, but not aged in the same quality of oak barrels as its peers.

MARGAUX 2002
Red | 2011 up to 2014   87
This is more impressive in its frankness and streamlined body than in its aromatic appeal. A strong wine, it will age nicely.

MARGAUX 2001
Red | 2011 up to 2013   90
A charming achievement, with tannins that stand out in their finesse, class, and tenderness.

Red: 24.7 acres; cabernet franc 10%, cabernet sauvignon 60%, merlot 30%. Annual production: 55,000 bottles

CHÂTEAU POUJEAUX

33480 Moulis-en-Médoc
Phone 00 33 5 56 58 02 96
Fax 00 33 5 56 58 01 25
contact@château-poujeaux.com
www.château-poujeaux.com

This classic Moulis estate boasts a well-stocked vineyard planted in the finest Gunzian gravel surrounding Grand Poujeaux. It dependably produces one of the fleshiest and most thoroughbred of the Médoc Crus Bourgeois, known for its plump tannins and rich texture. The 1990s brought a slight loss of character that is gradually being put right although we're not quite there yet!

Recently tasted
MOULIS 2006
Red | 2011 up to 2014   91

Older vintages
MOULIS 2005
Red | 2011 up to 2020   88
Powerful, full-bodied, and complete, but without the sophisticated texture that others achieve these days. The elegance of the terroir will compensate.

MOULIS 2004
Red | 2011 up to 2018   88
Round, ample, and complete, this possesses tannins of remarkable finesse. Racy and voluptuous.

Red: 168 acres; cabernet franc 5%, cabernet sauvignon 50%, merlot 40%, petit verdot 5%. Annual production: 350,000 bottles

CHÂTEAU PRIEURÉ-LICHINE

34, avenue de la Cinquième-République
33460 Cantenac
Phone 00 33 5 57 88 36 28
Fax 00 33 5 57 88 78 93
contact@prieure-lichine.fr
www.prieure-lichine.fr

The vineyard here is typical of the Margaux appellation, consisting of a huge collection of parcels in varied but complementary terroirs. Scattered plots do of course mean harder work and more stringent selection, but the result is a wine with the refined aromas and pure, textured mouthfeel that are characteristic of Margaux. The estate's well-heeled owners, the Ballande family, spare no expense to provide the technical team with the best and have brought in Stéphane Derenoncourt to advise on winemaking. The latest vintages are greatly improved: deliciously delicate but complete with all the suppleness and charm you could wish for. Good value for the money, too.

MARGAUX 2006
Red | 2014 up to 2018   89
Attractive color, extremely balanced body, flavors of perfectly ripe grapes. Fleshy wine, sinuous, smooth, detailed, very Margaux.

MARGAUX 2005
Red | 2011 up to 2030   91
With a grand richness of body for this terroir, this is a generous wine, powerfully built, with high alcohol and muscular tannins. It has a grand stature, but finesse is not its primary trait, at least for now.

MARGAUX 2004
Red | 2011 up to 2020   91
Fine, elegant, fresh, light green pepper, mint, delicate, tannins not harsh, long: devilishly Margaux.

MARGAUX 2003
Red | 2011 up to 2020   91
Spicy nose, lean body but full, aromas of cedar, fine and detailed tannins, slight lack of vinosity compared to wines at the highest level, but charming and stylish.

MARGAUX 2000
Red | 2011 up to 2015   91
A classic Margaux in this vintage, elegant and racy.

Red: 168 acres. Annual production: 450,000 bottles

CHÂTEAU RAUZAN-GASSIES

Rue Alexis-Millardet
33460 Margaux
Phone 00 33 5 57 88 71 88
Fax 00 33 5 57 88 37 49
rauzangassies@domaines-quie.com
www.domaines-quie.com

Margaux lovers have often been disappointed by the lack of ripeness and the rough, strict appearance of these wines. Things have plainly improved over the past ten years, though consistency leaves room for improvement. The wines today are sappy and neat but somewhat oversimple for such a blue-blooded terroir. The new generation of the Quié family now runs the show, fully aware of just how much work is required to get this winery back up to speed. Could and should do better.

Margaux 2006
Red | 2014 up to 2018   **87**
Good richness, although the tannins and acidity are still a little bit aggressive. A masculine and energetic Margaux, this is a noticeable step forward, even if it does not yet show the spark and subtlety of the very best.

Margaux 2005
Red | 2011 up to 2020   **88**
The wine has softened and it seems more evolved than its peers. A clear effort in winemaking gave this wine the finesse that past vintages have too often lacked, as well as defined tannins. However, it does not create excitement.

Margaux 2003
Red | 2011 up to 2021   **86**
Intense color, powerful nose of ripe grapes, a tad heavy with notes of leather and musk. The tannins lack great refinement and there is a slight bitterness in the finish, but this has a solid structure and will age well.

Margaux 2002
Red | 2011 up to 2017   **87**
Seriously built but discreet in the aromas, this still lacks a bit of purity and immediate seduction to completely live up to its class.

Margaux 2001
Red | 2011 up to 2015   **91**
A remarkable wine, classically built, with a generous and giving body and sophisticated tannins.

Red: 74.1 acres; cabernet franc 5%, cabernet sauvignon 65%, merlot 25%, petit verdot 5%. Annual production: 120,000 bottles

CHÂTEAU RAUZAN-SÉGLA

Rue Alexis-Millardet - BP 56
33460 Margaux
Phone 00 33 5 57 88 82 10
Fax 00 33 5 57 88 34 54
contact@rauzan-segla.com
www.châteaurauzansegla.com

The cabernet sauvignon vines here are not quite old enough yet to rival the power of Château Margaux, but on every other front this wine is a model of Margaux finesse, tender textures, and pure expression of terroir. Kudos to John Kolasa and his associates for the new spirit and style that they breathe into this property.

Recently tasted
Margaux 2006
Red | 2014 up to 2021   **91**

Older vintages
Margaux 2005
Red | 2011 up to 2030   **93**
Quite distinct oak on the sample bottle, masking the noble aroma of strong black licorice a little too much. Very ripe grapes gave this a "roasted" texture and very smooth tannins. Nice wine from a hot vintage.

Margaux 2004
Red | 2011 up to 2020   **91**
Dense, full-bodied, with firm but slightly drying tannins, this is serious but lacks charm and pure grace.

Margaux 2003
Red | 2011 up to 2025   **93**
With a beautiful color, generous and spicy nose, well-balanced body, and silky texture, this is a distinguished and very polished wine.

Margaux 2002
Red | 2011 up to 2020   **93**
Ideally refined and subtle in the finish, here is a wine of flawless style, an example of what a true Margaux should be. Its evolution in the mouth confirms its perfect elegance but also a slight lack of body, which will bother only those who prefer heavyweight wines.

Margaux 2000
Red | 2011 up to 2025   **95**
This has immaculate balance between acidity and alcohol, great finesse of aromas, subtle and elegant tannins, great clarity, and admirable precision in the terroir definition.

Red: 128.5 acres; cabernet franc 1%, cabernet sauvignon 54%, merlot 40%, petit verdot 5%. Annual production: 220,000 bottles

CHÂTEAU SAINT-PIERRE

33250 Saint-Julien-Beychevelle
Phone 00 33 5 56 59 08 18
Fax 00 33 5 56 59 16 18
domainemartin@wanadoo.fr
www.domaines-henri-martin.com

This cru may not have the worldwide renown of the other Saint-Julien Fourth Growths, but it does have plenty of seriously old vines in prime locations at the heart of the village. Thanks to them, recent vintages from this estate have been as good as if not better than its more illustrious peers: stylistically impeccable, with a combination of power, class, and complexity rarely seen outside Léoville—but much more reasonably priced and sure to appeal to bona fide oenophiles because of it! A proud achievement for Jean-Louis Triaud, current president of the Girondins de Bordeaux soccer club and son-in-law of Henri Martin (founder of the Commanderie du Bontemps): all the recent vintages seem splendid!

Saint-Julien 2006
Red | 2016 up to 2021   **92**
The character of this wine is brightly defined, with a remarkable aroma of cedar and firm tannins. Comparable to the very best.

Saint-Julien 2005
Red | 2011 up to 2030   **94**
Very noble nose with Médoc's classic cedar note; spectacular vinosity and considerable length. This may be the best value of the vintage in Médoc, and the most complete vintage of the cru.

Saint-Julien 2004
Red | 2011 up to 2019   **91**
Very Saint-Julien on the nose (cedar, spices), this is tight and distinguished with rather dry tannins and excellent style.

Saint-Julien 2003
Red | 2011 up to 2025   **94**
Very distinguished and vibrant nose of cedar, plum, and spices. Magnificent texture in both its dimension and creaminess. Opulent flavors, typical of a sunny vintage, with a little touch of the roasted character specific to the southern part of Saint-Julien.

Saint-Julien 2001
Red | 2011 up to 2016   **91**
A rich wine, enveloping and fairly long, this is a wine of style and character, built to age.

Red: 42 acres; cabernet franc 10%, cabernet sauvignon 70%, merlot 20%. **Annual production:** 60,000 bottles

CHÂTEAU SÉNÉJAC

Allé Saint-Seurin
33290 Le Pian-Médoc
Phone 00 33 5 56 70 20 11
Fax 00 33 5 56 70 23 91
château.senejac@wanadoo.fr

This southern Médoc property owes a lot to the late Jean-Luc Vonderheyden, who, with the help of New Zealand cellar-master extraordinaire Jenny Robson, revived a very interesting Margaux-style Graves vineyard back in the 1980s. This particular cru was acquired by the owners of Château Talbot in 1999 and looks in better shape than ever, producing very balanced, well-groomed wines that offer attractive value for the money.

Haut-Médoc 2006
Red | 2011 up to 2020   **89**
There is good substance in this wine: it has remained supple and conveys pretty notes of violets.

Haut-Médoc 2005
Red | 2011 up to 2013   **90**
Purple color. Delicate nose of concentrated red fruit. The palate is fresh and smooth, full-bodied with nice length, finishing with well-integrated tannins.

Haut-Médoc 2004
Red | 2011 up to 2013   **87**
Pretty tannins; the ripeness of an imperfect vintage. The wine is elegant and well made.

Haut-Médoc 2003
Red | 2011 up to 2016   **89**
Delicate and balanced with the elegance of the vintage.

Haut-Médoc 2002
Red | 2011 up to 2013   **86**
This wine is simpler than the following vintages, but reasonably balanced for the vintage and ready to drink.

Haut-Médoc 2001
Red | 2011 up to 2013   **86**
A wine for aficionados, one that seduces with its round tannins and its fresh finish.

Haut-Médoc 2000
Red | 2011 up to 2013   **87**
The tannins are still bitter, but the wine is ripe and deep.

Red: 98.8 acres; cabernet franc 11%, cabernet sauvignon 48%, merlot 37%, petit verdot 4%. **Annual production:** 180,000 bottles

CHÂTEAU SIRAN

BP 10
33460 Labarde-Margaux
Phone 00 33 5 57 88 34 04
Fax 00 33 5 57 88 70 05
info@châteausiran.com
www.châteausiran.com

Château Siran makes an excellent Margaux Cru Bourgeois: robust, generous, and hugely complex with age, developing notes of antique rose and spice that are unmatched by any of its neighbors. The vineyard in Labarde boasts fine gravel soils identical to those of Château Dauzac. The estate also produces an excellent Bordeaux Supérieur from its plantings in the Palus (alluvial land). The wine is now very dependable, with tannins that since 2005 seem just that bit more refined.

Recently tasted
MARGAUX 2006
Red | 2011 up to 2016   **92**

Older vintages
MARGAUX 2005
Red | 2011 up to 2025   **91**
This has a lot of flesh but impeccable balance between alcohol and tannins, which are well integrated into the extract. Skillful barrel aging. Bright future.

MARGAUX 2004
Red | 2011 up to 2018   **91**
The most robust of the Bourgeois growths from Margaux, this has firm tannins but a magnificent vinosity and excellent length.

MARGAUX 2001
Red | 2011 up to 2015   **89**
An expressive wine, full-bodied with round tannins and generous length, with perfect fruit maturity on the finish.

MARGAUX 2000
Red | 2011 up to 2015   **90**
A beautiful bottle, this offers elegant oak notes and nice structure, with lavish, generous flavors backed up by very nice tannins.

Red: 98.8 acres; cabernet franc 2%, cabernet sauvignon 41%, merlot 46%, petit verdot 11%.
Annual production: 170,000 bottles

CHÂTEAU SOCIANDO-MALLET

33180 Saint-Seurin-de-Cadourne
Phone 00 33 5 56 73 38 80
Fax 00 33 5 56 73 38 88
scea-jean-gautreau@wanadoo.fr
www.sociandomallet.com

Sociando-Mallet is beyond question the best nonclassed Médoc cru in twenty-five years. Production is unfailingly consistent, thanks first to Sociando-Mallet's Montrose-like terroir on the banks of the Gironde River, where it never freezes and the grapes ripen to perfection practically every year. Jean Gautreau is one of the few owners who personally supervise winemaking, aiming for a style of wine that maintains the grand tradition of the Médoc: generously spicy aromas of noble cabernet sauvignon, and the velvety texture of stunning merlot grapes from somewhat heavier soils. Sure to please every wine lover. Recent vintages have shown an added refinement and subtlety that some devotees might find surprising—the benefit of vines planted in the early 1980s that have now reached maturity.

Recently tasted
HAUT-MÉDOC LA DEMOISELLE
DE SOCIANDO-MALLET 2006
Red | 2011 up to 2013   **88**

Older vintages
HAUT-MÉDOC 2006
Red | 2011 up to 2020   **92**
Beautiful color, very developed nose of cedar, excellent oak integration, firm and full-bodied texture. Powerful, balanced wine.

HAUT-MÉDOC 2005
Red | 2011 up to 2025   **94**
Very well designed, with high-quality oak, a tight texture, elegant flavors of cedar and spices, especially refined tannins, and excellent length. Very classy, as usual the most accomplished Cru Bourgeois.

HAUT-MÉDOC 2004
Red | 2011 up to 2019   **92**
Great color, classic nose of cedar, excellent structure, powerful and complex tannins. Altogether absolutely classic.

HAUT-MÉDOC 2003
Red | 2011 up to 2028   **93**
Dark color, aromas of almost jammy red fruit, still strongly reduced. It has an imposing body with a lot of heat from its elevated alcohol level, and it still feels very young. A giant just coming out of early childhood!

HAUT-MÉDOC 2002
Red | 2011 up to 2022   93
Nearly black, this has a nose that is very pure in its cedar note but still very youthful. The body is very impressive for the vintage, with the velvety texture typical of a vineyard in its middle age. This is a wine made without concession to fashion, and should become a fantastic bottle in five to ten years.

HAUT-MÉDOC 2000
Red | 2011 up to 2013   93
Curiously enough for this very ripe vintage, this wine's nose shows floral notes and even a touch of green pepper, a caprice of cabernet's expected nature. The wine possesses balanced tannins but they are less dense and energetic than we might have imagined. The oak expression is not up to the expected standard. Aeration dramatically improves this wine.

HAUT-MÉDOC 1998
Red | 2011 up to 2016   91
Powerful but tending toward drying tannins. A very austere and masculine style!

Red: 210 acres; cabernet franc 5%, cabernet sauvignon 55%, merlot 40%. Annual production: 450,000 bottles

CHÂTEAU TALBOT
🍇 🍇 🍇 🍇 🍇

33250 Saint-Julien-Beychevelle
Phone 00 33 5 56 73 21 50
Fax 00 33 5 56 73 21 51
château-talbot@château-talbot.com
www.château-talbot.com

This property is still run by the late Jean Cordier's daughters and rightly ranks among the most popular of all the Médoc producers. Production levels are high, but consistency is hard to fault. For many, Château Talbot is the archetypal Saint-Julien: generously aromatic, with stable, solid aging potential. It has seemed even more vinous over the past three or four years, back up to the standard of those quintessential Cordier Talbots of the 1940s and 1950s. Caillou Blanc is Talbot's prettily aromatic, nervous, and dry white wine.

Recently tasted
BORDEAUX CAILLOU BLANC 2007
White | 2011 up to 2014   89

SAINT-JULIEN 2006
Red | 2014 up to 2026   88

Older vintages
BORDEAUX CAILLOU BLANC 2006
White | 2011 up to 2014   90
A wonderful wine, velvety and fresh, with an elegant constitution that is already delicious.

BORDEAUX CAILLOU BLANC 2005
White | 2011 up to 2013   90
Talbot's white, devoid of pretension or heavy oak, is one of the most pleasant white Bordeaux wines made. This 2005 is rich but with nice acidity and delicate hints of lemon. It can be enjoyed now, but it will also age gracefully for a few more years.

SAINT-JULIEN 2005
Red | 2011 up to 2025   93
Remarkable nose of cabernet, slightly less dense and concentrated than the Saint-Pierre. Wonderfully vinous, with classic tannins. Excellent balance.

SAINT-JULIEN 2004
Red | 2011 up to 2020   89
Wonderful nose of leather and game but not overpowering; rich color, ripe grapes, really nice length. Flavorful, but with a slight lack of acidity.

SAINT-JULIEN 2003
Red | 2011 up to 2021   90
With nuances of very ripe fruit, this is a very powerful wine. The heat of the alcohol is palpable and tends to overpower the aromas in the glass.

SAINT-JULIEN 2002
Red | 2011 up to 2017   89
Quite open aromatically and cleaner on the
nose than past vintages, free of gamey qualities. Soft, full, and very pleasant on the palate, as always.

SAINT-JULIEN 2001
Red | 2011 up to 2019   92
Nice, very traditional Saint-Julien, with notes
of licorice and cigars, an elegant tannic
grain, and wonderful length on the finish.

SAINT-JULIEN 2000
Red | 2011 up to 2020   93
Powerful and expressive, this is rich and
silky without any hint of austerity.

SAINT-JULIEN CONNÉTABLE DE TALBOT 2006
Red | 2011 up to 2014   86
Supple but long and svelte, this is a very
classic and pure Bordeaux with well-defined
tannins and clean length. Distinguished,
ready to drink now.

SAINT-JULIEN CONNÉTABLE DE TALBOT 2005
Red | 2011 up to 2015   86
A softly structured Saint-Julien, pretty, with
focused tannins and good length; it is ready
to drink now.

Red: 252 acres; cabernet franc 3%, cabernet
sauvignon 66%, merlot 26%, petit verdot 5%. White:
14.8 acres. Annual production: 550,000 bottles

CHÂTEAU DU TERTRE

Chemin de Ligondras
33460 Arsac
Phone 00 33 5 57 88 52 52
Fax 00 33 5 57 88 52 51
receptif@château du tertre.fr
www.château du tertre.fr

The Château du Tertre vineyards form a
single, somewhat isolated block on a magnificent gravel and silica hillock. Quality
has really taken off here since the property
was acquired by Dutch proprietor Albada
Jelgersma. The wine's deliciously fresh
and elegant aromatic character owes a lot
to the cabernet franc and to the winemaking talents of Jacques Pelissié. The latest
vintages are highly individual and a great
success: seemingly light but full-bodied
with plenty of aromatic finesse. Excellent
value for the money, too.

MARGAUX 2006
Red | 2011 up to 2025   89
Lively, elegant, lifted, very original and honest, a priority for aficionados seeking finesse!

MARGAUX 2005
Red | 2011 up to 2025   91
Beautiful flavor of licorice, less marked by
the sun than other wines from other crus,
tight body and creamy texture, good length.
A wine of high class that displays a freshness on the finish rare for this vintage.

MARGAUX 2004
Red | 2011 up to 2020   90
Cedar aromas, very pure, very elegant, floral, delicate tannins. Very feminine and
smooth, a pretty style.

MARGAUX 2003
Red | 2011 up to 2021   93
An aromatic explosion of antique rose, in
the manner of a great pinot noir, remarkably
fleshy, with impressive length.

MARGAUX 2002
Red | 2011 up to 2014   90
Very aromatic wine, subtle, fresh, complex,
with the classic texture of Margaux, ready
to drink young.

MARGAUX 2000
Red | 2011 up to 2015   90
Pleasant texture, tannins barely dry, beautiful follow-through: a wine of character.

Red: 128.5 acres; cabernet franc 30%, cabernet
sauvignon 32%, merlot 33%, petit verdot 5%. Annual
production: 200,000 bottles

CHÂTEAU LA TOUR CARNET

Route de Saint-Julien-Beychevelle
33112 Saint-Laurent-du-Médoc
Phone 00 33 5 56 73 30 90
Fax 00 33 5 56 59 48 54
latour@latour-carnet.com
www.bernard-magrez.com

This cru has been brought right up to date in the past ten years under Bernard Magrez's shrewd and ambitious management, along with some help from Michel Rolland. The wine is increasingly true to its unique vineyard, on an impressive limestone hillock that yields first-class merlot grapes. Rich and voluptuous, sometimes too much so, La Tour Carnet epitomizes the modern Médoc and does it in style—still a bit lacking in finesse, though. Bernard Magrez has also created a single-parcel bottling from this cru, Servitude Volontaire, which shows amazingly rich constitution and gets more refined with every passing day.

HAUT-MÉDOC 2006
Red | 2011 up to 2020   **92**
This has a remarkable texture, fat with firm and complex tannins and much class. The once overpowering oak has now been fully integrated into the wine, leaving it superbly refined.

HAUT-MÉDOC 2005
Red | 2011 up to 2025   **92**
Deeply colored, strongly oaked yet well integrated, full, long, complex. An extremely seductive expression of a great vintage.

HAUT-MÉDOC 2004
Red | 2011 up to 2016   **88**
Clean oak, rich, rather ample but not hollow, taffeta texture but firm and astringent tannins, spicy.

HAUT-MÉDOC 2003
Red | 2011 up to 2021   **91**
Intense crimson color. The nose is very vanilla but beginning to successfully integrate the oak. Pulpy texture, round, generous, with perfectly ripe tannins (which wasn't easy in this vintage) and an open finish. Very well-made wine.

HAUT-MÉDOC 2002
Red | 2011 up to 2016   **88**
This has a very dense color, flattering oak that does not simplify or betray the lovely blueberry aromas, a round and flattering body, and a lovely finish with finely worked, enveloping tannins.

HAUT-MÉDOC 2001
Red | 2011 up to 2013   **88**
The palate is all richness and sweetness, but without any softness; on the contrary, this is a taut and vigorous style.

HAUT-MÉDOC 2000
Red | 2011 up to 2020   **90**
Velvety wine, this is supple, with judiciously extracted tannins. Classy, worthy of the cru's rank in the Haut-Médoc hierarchy.

HAUT-MÉDOC LA SERVITUDE VOLONTAIRE 2005
Red | 2011 up to 2025   **92**
In the same intense and viscous style as in 2004, but with incontestably smoother tannins: this wine will impress just as much in ten years.

HAUT-MÉDOC LA SERVITUDE VOLONTAIRE 2004
Red | 2011 up to 2019   **89**
The color is very deep and the nose is still dominated by oak, but this wine incontestably has a great sappiness, deep and consistent, which will open up over the long haul. The tannins are, however, less ideally ripe than in 2005.

Red: 170.5 acres; cabernet franc 3%, cabernet sauvignon 45%, merlot 50%, petit verdot 2%. White: 29.7 acres; sauvignon blanc 40%, sauvignon gris 20%, sémillon 40%. Annual production: 350,000 bottles

CHÂTEAU TOUR HAUT-CAUSSAN

27 bis, rue de Verdun
33340 Blaignan-Médoc
Phone 00 33 5 56 09 00 77
Fax 00 33 5 56 09 06 24
courriel@tourhautcaussan.com

This cru has long been at the forefront of quality in Médoc wines thanks to the efforts of charismatic proprietor Philippe Courrian: merlot driven, with a lovely velvet texture and youthful appeal from élevage in new oak—and none the worse for that! The latest vintages are just a shade routine, as may so often happen when a producer has been at it for so long.

MÉDOC 2006
Red | 2011 up to 2013   **87**
Deep purple color. Delicate nose of red fruit. Fresh, suave, and round on the palate with slight hints of licorice. Pretty tannins on the finish.

MÉDOC 2002
Red | 2011 up to 2013   **86**
A serious, discreet, and reserved wine, very classic in this sector, fairly supple, and ready to drink.

MÉDOC 2001
Red | 2011 up to 2013   **86**
Classic color, soft nose and mouthfeel, but with a wonderfully balanced core and perfectly ripe fruit. This wine is always pleasant, made in a very traditional Bordeaux style.

Red: 42 acres; cabernet sauvignon 50%, merlot 50%.
Annual production: 110,000 bottles

Right Bank Vineyards

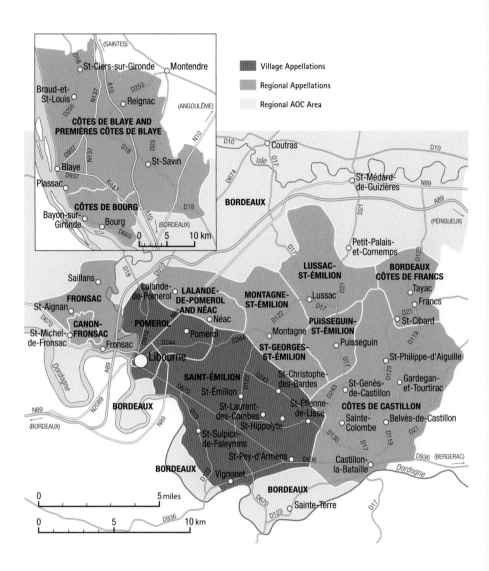

Village Appellations
Regional Appellations
Regional AOC Area

(SAINTES)

St-Ciers-sur-Gironde   Montendre

Braud-et-
St-Louis
Reignac   (ANGOULÊME)

**CÔTES DE BLAYE AND
PREMIÈRES CÔTES DE BLAYE**

D23

Blaye   St-Savin

Plassac

CÔTES DE BOURG

Bayon-sur-
Gironde   Bourg   (BORDEAUX)

0   5   10 km

Coutras

Isle

St-Médard-
de-Guizières

BORDEAUX

(PÉRIGUEUX)

Petit-Palais-
et-Cornemps

Saillans

Lalande-
de-Pomerol   **LALANDE-
DE-POMEROL
AND NÉAC**

**LUSSAC-
ST-ÉMILION**

**BORDEAUX
CÔTES DE FRANCS**

Tayac

Lussac

St-Aignan   **FRONSAC**

**MONTAGNE-
ST-ÉMILION**

Francs

Néac

**CANON-
FRONSAC**   **POMEROL**

**PUISSEGUIN-
ST-ÉMILION**

St-Cibard

St-Michel-
de-Fronsac

Pomerol

Montagne

Puisseguin

Fronsac

**ST-GEORGES-
ST-ÉMILION**

St-Philippe-d'Aiguille

Libourne

Gardegan-
et-Tourtirac

SAINT-ÉMILION

St-Christophe-
des-Bardes

St-Genès-
de-Castillon

St-Émilion

St-Étienne-
de-Lisse

CÔTES DE CASTILLON

BORDEAUX

St-Laurent-
des-Combes

(BORDEAUX)

St-Hippolyte

Sainte-
Colombe

Belvès-de-Castillon

St-Sulpice-
de-Faleyrens

St-Pey-d'Armens

Castillon-
la-Bataille

Dordogne   (BERGERAC)

BORDEAUX   Vignonet

BORDEAUX

Sainte-Terre

0   5 miles

0   5   10 km

DOMAINE DE L'A

Lieu-dit Fillol
33350 Sainte-Colombe
Phone 00 33 5 57 24 60 29
Fax 00 33 5 57 24 75 95
contact@vigneronsconsultants.com

Stéphane Derenoncourt is now one of the most sought-after enological consultants in Bordeaux. He has put his experience to work for wineries great and small, from those in the more modest appellations to the most celebrated properties in Saint-Émilion, Pomerol, and also the Médoc. It's fascinating to watch him at work in this property in Castillon, which he bought with his wife and christened the Domaine de l'A. Less than five years later, it had already become known for its characteristically elegant, deep, and creamy wines.

Recently tasted
Côtes de Castillon 2007
Red | 2011 up to 2015   90

Older vintages
Côtes de Castillon 2006
Red | 2011 up to 2013   89
A magnificent Castillon, this stands out among the wines of this appellation in this vintage: excellent nose with subtle fruit, remarkable balance in the mouth, refined texture with ripe tannins, and great acidity.

Côtes de Castillon 2005
Red | 2011 up to 2013   89
Wonderfully defined, unctuous and deep, with a soft nose of black and red fruit and impeccably fine-grained tannins. Brilliant!

Côtes de Castillon 2004
Red | 2011 up to 2013   87
With its deep color, expressive fruit, velvety palate, and good depth, this is one of the best wines of the vintage in this appellation.

Côtes de Castillon 2001
Red | 2011 up to 2013   89
This is a wine with great style: it is delicate and penetrating, with a full-bodied balance, very silky tannins, and a refreshing acidity. The finish is crisp, rich, and long.

Red: 19.8 acres; cabernet franc 20%, cabernet sauvignon 10%, merlot 70%. Annual production: 15,000 bottles

CHÂTEAU D'AIGUILHE

33350 Saint-Philippe-d'Aiguilhe
Phone 00 33 5 57 40 60 10
Fax 00 33 5 57 40 63 56
info@neipperg.com
www.neipperg.com

The ancient Château d'Aiguilhe is named after the Saint-Philippe-d'Aiguilhe plateau on which it is located. Its immense vineyards extend along the slopes bordering the Dordogne River, planted in soils that are typical of this sector and derived from the same foundation as the hill of Saint-Émilion: a thin layer of clayey limestone over deep limestone substrate that protects the vines from drought and extremes of heat. The cru was always a standard-bearer for this appellation, but since it was acquired by Stephan von Neipperg (Château Canon-la-Gaffelière) it has transcended its pedigree and grown to be one of the Right Bank's most valuable assets. The wines are creamy, deep, and silky—a lovely combination of strength, suppleness, and power.

Côtes de Castillon 2006
Red | 2011 up to 2017   88
A powerful, very rich, and full-bodied wine with structured tannins and depth. Can be cellared for a few more years.

Côtes de Castillon 2005
Red | 2011 up to 2013   91
A powerful yet very refined wine, with fine, elegant tannins and generous length, accented by a profusion of spice and black fruit.

Côtes de Castillon 2004
Red | 2011 up to 2013   90
Virile, energetic, and immediately seductive for its nose of black fruit and plums, its delicate structure, silky core, and velvety length. A work of art.

Côtes de Castillon 2001
Red | 2011 up to 2013   90
A wonderful, generous style, with a delicately spicy character that blends perfectly with its notes of ripe fruit. The wine opens up splendidly on the finish.

Côtes de Castillon 2000
Red | 2011 up to 2015   90
Wonderful, intense fruit, unctuous and deep on the palate: a great 2000!

Red: 123.6 acres; cabernet franc 20%, merlot 80%. Annual production: 115,000 bottles

CHÂTEAU ANGÉLUS

33330 Saint-Émilion
Phone 00 33 5 57 24 71 39
Fax 00 33 5 57 24 68 56
château-angelus@château-angelus.com
www.angelus.com

Château Angélus enjoys a fabulous location at the heart of the hill of Saint-Émilion, west of the village—a top-quality terroir in the classical style of this appellation, where the generous merlot is partnered by significant plantings of cabernet franc for an added touch of freshness and brilliance. As always, it takes human expertise to draw the full value from natural assets. Angélus has taken on a new dimension since 1987, when Hubert de Boüard took command and the wine rose quickly to the rank of Bordeaux "Super Second." The vintages of the 1990s are remarkably full-bodied. Those of the new century add a certain tannic finesse and aromatic sparkle that take this wine to yet another level. The consistency of production is incomparable: we have not seen one disappointing vintage in the past twenty years.

Recently tasted
SAINT-ÉMILION GRAND CRU 2007
Red | 2012 up to 2020   **91**

Older vintages
SAINT-ÉMILION GRAND CRU 2006
Red | 2012 up to 2018   **93**
An intense and complete wine: deep color, very expressive fruit, unctuous attack, ultra-fine-grained tannins, wonderful length.

SAINT-ÉMILION GRAND CRU 2005
Red | 2011 up to 2025   **98**
The best Angélus of recent history: deep color; distinguished nose; wonderful, harmonious volume; ultra-silky, magnificently refined texture; amazing length.

SAINT-ÉMILION GRAND CRU 2004
Red | 2011 up to 2020   **92**
Intense, opaque color; a wonderful nose that is ripe and full; unctuous, profound, rich, and generous on the palate; a beautifully deep, big, and dense wine.

SAINT-ÉMILION GRAND CRU 2003
Red | 2011 up to 2020   **96**
Deep color, black fruit, generously built, silky with profound, tightly wound tannins and a fruit-filled finish. Quite reserved, with impeccable style: at the top of its game.

SAINT-ÉMILION GRAND CRU 2002
Red | 2011 up to 2014   **88**
Deep color, intense nose, floral and black fruits, full in the mouth, tight volume and depth, robust and intense. A wonderful and generous wine.

SAINT-ÉMILION GRAND CRU 2001
Red | 2012 up to 2022   **94**
This is Angélus at its best, combining a deep body and magnificent fruit with grace.

SAINT-ÉMILION GRAND CRU 2000
Red | 2011 up to 2020   **94**
Deeply colored, bright, rich, supple, and deep, this is wonderfully elegant without having extraordinary depth.

SAINT-ÉMILION GRAND CRU 1999
Red | 2011 up to 2017   **90**
Notes of black truffle, deep color, fat and generous, nice length but only average freshness and vitality for the growth.

SAINT-ÉMILION GRAND CRU 1998
Red | 2011 up to 2018   **93**
A full and generous wine, ample and savory, definitely hedonistic.

Red: 57.8 acres; cabernet franc 47%, cabernet sauvignon 3%, merlot 50%. Annual production: 110,000 bottles

CHÂTEAU L'ARROSÉE

🦎🦎🦎🦎🦎

1, Larosé
33330 Saint-Émilion
Phone 00 33 5 57 24 69 44
Fax 00 33 5 57 24 66 46
château.larrosee@wanadoo.fr
www.châteaularrosee.com

Château L'Arrosée enjoys a splendid location on the slopes west of Saint-Émilion, hidden from the Libourne-Périgueux highway by the imposing building of the Saint-Émilion cooperative winery. Years of underperformance at the hands of the previous owner ended in 2003, when L'Arrosée was acquired by Lyon entrepreneur Roger Caille, who wasted no time developing its potential. Trusted, experienced enologist Gilles Pauquet was retained as winemaker. Stricter attention to viticulture and new, ultramodern, tailor-made winemaking facilities soon brought the wine up to par. Caille's first vintage, the 2003, was an outstanding success, but, sadly, he passed away in 2008 before seeing the full impact of the improvements he initiated. The wines have since acquired a finesse and tannic clout that place it among the great Saint-Émilion crus.

Recently tasted

SAINT-ÉMILION GRAND CRU 2007
Red | 2012 up to 2020   92

SAINT-ÉMILION GRAND CRU 2006
Red | 2012 up to 2017   92

Older vintages

SAINT-ÉMILION GRAND CRU 2005
Red | 2012 up to 2025   95
The body has amazing dimension and depth and an ultrafine texture, unquestionably distinguished, with splendid length: this vintage is a benediction.

SAINT-ÉMILION GRAND CRU 2004
Red | 2011 up to 2015   93
This wine shines for its freshness and, above all, for its genuinely distinguished tannins, which give it an ethereal elegance and a perfect succulence. Excellent fruit, wonderful finish.

SAINT-ÉMILION GRAND CRU 2003
Red | 2011 up to 2017   90
A full and profound wine, with tannins that are less elegant than in the following vintages, but perfectly constructed, distinguished, and refined.

Red: 24.7 acres; cabernet franc 20%, cabernet sauvignon 20%, merlot 60%. Annual production: 35,000 bottles

CHÂTEAU AUSONE

🦎🦎🦎🦎🦎

33330 Saint-Émilion
Phone 00 33 5 57 24 24 57
Fax 00 33 5 57 24 24 58
château.ausone@wanadoo.fr
www.château-ausone.com

The Château Ausone vineyards enjoy an ideal exposure at the entrance to the village of Saint-Émilion, planted in a limestone mound with a thin layer of gravel topsoil. Present owner Alain Vauthier has taken advantage of this unique location to drive up the quality at Ausone, placing the cru among the best Right Bank Bordeauxs in each of the past ten years. Every vintage since 1997 has been a winner—supremely velvety tannins, stunningly fresh fruit—with the 2000s and 2005s coming close to perfection. If you can can't get your hands on the grand vin (very highly allocated), remember that the second wine, La Chapelle d'Ausone, puts in a performance entirely worthy of its mighty relative, especially in terms of finesse.

Recently tasted

SAINT-ÉMILION GRAND CRU 2007
Red | 2012 up to 2030   94
Elegant length, soft and persistent volume, with a beautifully focused and refined finish.

SAINT-ÉMILION GRAND CRU 2006
Red | 2012 up to 2030   96
Amazingly smooth, ethereal, and delicately framed, with intense fruit, the wine is absolutely stunning with wonderfully elegant length.

SAINT-ÉMILION GRAND CRU 2005
Red | 2011 up to 2035   100
This wine shows a bouquet of unparalleled elegance, an unctuous and profound palate, and taffeta-like tannins with extraordinary length and freshness. The wine of the vintage!

SAINT-ÉMILION GRAND CRU
CHAPELLE D'AUSONE 2007
Red | 2012 up to 2018   89
Bursting with fruit, delicate and smooth, not as long as the 2006 at this point.

SAINT-ÉMILION GRAND CRU
CHAPELLE D'AUSONE 2006
Red | 2012 up to 2020   91
Ethereal, distinguished, suave, and long, the wine shows magnificently focused red fruit and is very well balanced. Brilliant.

SAINT-ÉMILION GRAND CRU 2004
Red | 2012 up to 2025   **95**
Remarkable for its subtle elegance and the finesse of the tannins, especially in a year where these qualities are not often found in Saint-Émilion.

SAINT-ÉMILION GRAND CRU 2003
Red | 2015 up to 2030   **98**
Magnificent wine, with unprecedented richness and tannic elegance, refined length, and subtle, complex aromas. Not a hint of the drying tannins so often found in the wines of this vintage.

SAINT-ÉMILION GRAND CRU 2002
Red | 2011 up to 2025   **94**
Nice, soft balance, slightly less depth.

SAINT-ÉMILION GRAND CRU 2001
Red | 2011 up to 2030   **97**
Wonderfully smooth tannins and perfect balance for a year that is, in reality, much better than its reputation.

SAINT-ÉMILION GRAND CRU 2000
Red | 2011 up to 2030   **99**
Stunning balance and grace for this legendary wine; can be aged practically for eternity!

SAINT-ÉMILION GRAND CRU 1999
Red | 2011 up to 2019   **93**
Here as in other places in Saint-Émilion, 1999 isn't the greatest vintage of the past ten years: deep, linear, but the freshness and energy aren't quite as stunning as in other vintages.

SAINT-ÉMILION GRAND CRU 1998
Red | 2011 up to 2028   **99**
An ultra-refined wine, surprisingly elegant, linear, fresh, and voluptuous!

SAINT-ÉMILION GRAND CRU
LA CHAPELLE D'AUSONE 2004
Red | 2011 up to 2017   **89**
Long, fine, not at all severe or harsh, with a more subtle volume on the palate than in the "grand vin," but charmingly aromatic and smooth.

SAINT-ÉMILION GRAND CRU
LA CHAPELLE D'AUSONE 2000
Red | 2011 up to 2018   **92**
Elegant and distinguished nose, wonderfully focused fruit, ripe, deep, delicate, long.

SAINT-ÉMILION GRAND CRU
LA CHAPELLE D'AUSONE 1999
Red | 2011 up to 2016   **90**
Close in style to the "grand vin," with less focused tannins but more freshness.

Red: 17.3 acres; cabernet franc 55%, merlot 45%.
Annual production: 18,000 bottles

CLOS BADON–THUVENIN

Établissements Thunevin
6, rue Guadet
33330 Saint-Émilion
Phone 00 33 5 57 55 09 13
Fax 00 33 5 57 55 09 12
thunevin@thunevin.com
www.thunevin.com

The Clos Badon is well located at the foot of the Pavie hillside, alongside Château Pavie and Château Larcis-Ducasse. Since it was acquired by Jean-Luc Thunevin in 1998, this cru has been as carefully cultivated as Valandraud, and the wine today is much improved: not as intense as Château Valandraud but elegant and supple with that velvety character and refined tannic profile that Jean-Luc and Murielle Thunevin like so much. Drinks well young.

Recently tasted
SAINT-ÉMILION GRAND CRU 2007
Red | 2012 up to 2017   **89**

Older vintages
SAINT-ÉMILION GRAND CRU 2006
Red | 2012 up to 2017   **90**
The oak is currently slightly drying on the palate, but the tannins are elegant and the ensemble is long and complete.

SAINT-ÉMILION GRAND CRU 2005
Red | 2011 up to 2017   **90**
Since bottling, this wine has filled out and is now more convincing than it was en primeur: it is deeply colored with toasty oak that is present but not drying, elegant tannins, and a long and silky palate.

SAINT-ÉMILION GRAND CRU 2004
Red | 2011 up to 2013   **86**
Dark color, aromas of black fruit, dense in the mouth, generous and powerful with a touch of bitterness on the finish.

SAINT-ÉMILION GRAND CRU 2003
Red | 2011 up to 2014   **91**
Suave, elegant, and tender, with fine tannins that have no tendency toward drying, this is a lovely and charming success.

Red: 16.1 acres; cabernet franc 30%, merlot 70%.
Annual production: 12,000 bottles

CHÂTEAU BARDE-HAUT

33330 Saint-Christophe-des-Bardes
Phone 00 33 5 56 64 05 22
Fax 00 33 5 56 64 06 98
info@vignoblesgarcin.com
www.vignoblesgarcin.com

The Garcin family bought this property in Saint-Christophe-des-Bardes in the late 1990s and soon turned it into one of the region's most dependable producers. The wines are always solidly built, sometimes slightly austere in average vintages but very successful in good years, made in a generous, intense, and honest style.

Recently tasted
SAINT-ÉMILION GRAND CRU 2007
Red | 2012 up to 2017   **86**

Older vintages
SAINT-ÉMILION GRAND CRU 2006
Red | 2012 up to 2017   **86**
Deep and intense, this wine's tannins are a bit rigid, but it has solid potential.

SAINT-ÉMILION GRAND CRU 2005
Red | 2011 up to 2015   **89**
A succulent wine, rich with fresh and luminous fruit, this is full of vitality and allure.

SAINT-ÉMILION GRAND CRU 2004
Red | 2011 up to 2013   **84**
Bright garnet color; nose of plums with a slightly vegetal note; full-bodied but limited by the rigid tannins.

SAINT-ÉMILION GRAND CRU 2003
Red | 2011 up to 2013   **86**
A powerful wine but with vegetal tannins, this is full but without finesse, characteristic of the difficult vintage.

SAINT-ÉMILION GRAND CRU 2002
Red | 2011 up to 2013   **87**
This wine is powerful and richly composed, with volume, color, pretty substantial oak, substance, and fairly ripe tannins.

SAINT-ÉMILION GRAND CRU 2001
Red | 2011 up to 2015   **91**
An imposing but supple wine, the balance achieved by a refreshing acidity. Great length.

Red: 42 acres; cabernet franc 10%, merlot 90%.
Annual production: 50,000 bottles

CHÂTEAU BEAUREGARD

33500 Pomerol
Phone 00 33 5 57 51 13 36
Fax 00 33 5 57 25 09 55
pomerol@château-beauregard.com
www.château-beauregard.com

This large estate (large by Pomerol standards) has been owned by a finance company since the early 1990s. State-of-the-art viticulture and vinification make Beauregard one of the most dependable producers in this appellation, turning out well-built wines with a roundness and velvetiness supported by sturdy, refreshing structure. The wines are made in an accessible style but also age quite well.

Recently tasted
POMEROL 2007
Red | 2011 up to 2017   **88**

Older vintages
POMEROL 2006
Red | 2012 up to 2017   **88**
A classic Pomerol with notes of black truffles, this is supple and round, pleasing and plentiful.

POMEROL 2005
Red | 2011 up to 2020   **89**
Bright color, finesse, fresh fruit, elegant length, nice style.

POMEROL 2004
Red | 2011 up to 2015   **87**
With good color, the wine shows wonderful fruit finesse and a soft palate, long and quite well built.

POMEROL 2001
Red | 2011 up to 2015   **89**
Rich, refined, elegant, and long, this is a modern Pomerol, but expertly vinified and aged.

POMEROL BENJAMIN DE BEAUREGARD 2005
Red | 2011 up to 2013   **84**
A solid second wine, fat and well structured.

Red: 43.2 acres; cabernet franc 30%, merlot 70%.
Annual production: 90,000 bottles

CHÂTEAU BEAUSÉJOUR-BÉCOT

33330 Saint-Émilion
Phone 00 33 5 57 74 46 87
Fax 00 33 5 57 24 66 88
contact@beausejour-becot.com
www.beausejour-becot.com

This cru lies to the west of the village of Saint-Émilion on a clay and limestone plateau overlooking the hillside. Since 1985, it has been run by brothers Dominique and Gérard Bécot, now assisted by Gérard's daughter, Juliette, sparing no effort to restore this vineyard to its past glory. The wines are immediately savory, rich, and robust, with ripe fruit forward, thanks to careful aging. La Gomerie, first released in 1995, is a very ambitious single-parcel bottling: sappy and intense but in our opinion not always as harmoniously seductive as the Bécot. Beauséjour-Bécot wines are certainly refined, but they retain a joyous and instant deliciousness that makes them immediately appealing to the newcomer— particularly since the quality of production has been stunningly consistent for more than a decade.

Recently tasted
SAINT-ÉMILION GRAND CRU 2007
Red | 2012 up to 2020   90

Older vintages
SAINT-ÉMILION GRAND CRU 2006
Red | 2011 up to 2020   91
Beautifully deep color, ripe black fruit on the nose. It is marked by oak, but it is delicate and fine, not at all harsh, and long and distinguished.

SAINT-ÉMILION GRAND CRU 2005
Red | 2011 up to 2022   95
A dazzling wine, full of freshness, long and very stylish. Wonderfully elegant fruit. The wine is coming around splendidly in the bottle.

SAINT-ÉMILION GRAND CRU 2004
Red | 2011 up to 2016   90
With bright fruit, this is elegant in the mouth, with very fine tannins, a velvety texture, and clean length.

SAINT-ÉMILION GRAND CRU 2003
Red | 2011 up to 2020   92
A great success, combining richness, roundness, freshness, and distinction.

SAINT-ÉMILION GRAND CRU 2002
Red | 2011 up to 2015   90
A rich and generous style, with round tannins and a nice silkiness on the palate.

SAINT-ÉMILION GRAND CRU 2001
Red | 2011 up to 2014   92
Full-flavored, rich, and hot, this is succulent, powerful, and unctuous.

SAINT-ÉMILION GRAND CRU 2000
Red | 2011 up to 2018   98
Magnificent color, distinguished elegance, superb tannins, intensity, length, and finesse. The wine is now entering its apogee.

SAINT-ÉMILION GRAND CRU 1998
Red | 2011 up to 2018   94
Lovely, fully alluring, with a richness that is less vibrant than the 2000 but splendid in volume.

Red: 40.8 acres; cabernet franc 24%, cabernet sauvignon 6%, merlot 70%. Annual production: 60,000 bottles

CHÂTEAU BEAUSÉJOUR DUFFAU-LAGAROSSE

33330 Saint-Émilion
Phone 00 33 5 57 24 71 61
Fax 00 33 5 57 74 48 40
beausejourhdl@beausejourhdl.com
www.beausejourhdl.com

Château Beauséjour (full name Beauséjour Duffau-Lagarosse) is admirably located on the western flank of the hill of Saint-Émilion and represents one of the soundest producers in this appellation. Every vintage bears witness to its noble origins, but that said, overall performance is always less than stellar. The style relies on elegance, not power, but it could still do with more precise tannins and brighter aromas. In 2009 Nicolas Thienpont and Stéphane Derenoncourt were brought in as consulting enologists.

Recently tasted
SAINT-ÉMILION GRAND CRU 2007
Red | 2012 up to 2020   88

Older vintages
SAINT-ÉMILION GRAND CRU 2006
Red | 2012 up to 2018   88
Expressive aromas of black fruit and chocolate introduce a rich, smooth wine with soft tannins. A flavorful style, lacking in great finesse.

SAINT-ÉMILION GRAND CRU 2005
Red | 2011 up to 2020   90
Youthful color, lots of freshness. With still-intense oak, notes of red fruit, and relatively firm tannins, this is clean but lacking a bit of complexity.

SAINT-ÉMILION GRAND CRU 2004
Red | 2011 up to 2015   88
Deep color, nice nose, notes of ripe fruit, toast, and black fruit jam. Full on the palate, though the tannins lack perfect finesse.

SAINT-ÉMILION GRAND CRU 2003
Red | 2011 up to 2015   89
Nice color, vanilla oak, floral, soft, not super-concentrated, very delicate tannins, long and fresh, elegant in a reserved and well-mannered style.

SAINT-ÉMILION GRAND CRU 2002
Red | 2011 up to 2014   89
Not particularly dense in color, this has rich black fruit, generous but somewhat simple tannins, and a finish of average length and freshness.

Red: 17.3 acres; cabernet franc 20%, cabernet sauvignon 10%, merlot 70%. **Annual production:** 30,000 bottles

CHÂTEAU BELAIR-MONANGE

6, Madeleine
33330 Saint-Émilion
Phone 00 33 5 57 51 78 96
belair@châteaubelair.com
www.châteaubelair.com

Château Belair is the immediate neighbor of Château Ausone and Château Magdelaine, located on a magnificent limestone plateau at the southernmost entrance to Saint-Émilion. Pascal Delbeck has been in charge of the property for more than two decades and now co-owns it with the Moueix family. Despite its obvious advantages, Belair has not always lived up to our expectations: many of the wines produced in the 1990s and even the early 2000s seemed to lack intensity on the nose and palate. The most recent vintages, by contrast, show a welcome change in personality, still as elegantly refined and alluring as ever but with more immediate charm and tannic precision.

Recently tasted
SAINT-ÉMILION GRAND CRU 2006
Red | 2012 up to 2022   90

Older vintages
SAINT-ÉMILION GRAND CRU 2005
Red | 2012 up to 2025   92
Very elegant, delicately built, with fine-grained, silky tannins that are ideal. Without being exceptionally concentrated, this is a wonderfully distinguished wine, and certainly the best Belair of the past twenty years.

SAINT-ÉMILION GRAND CRU 2004
Red | 2011 up to 2015   84
Light in color, the fruit leaning toward raspberry, very soft, with good acidity. A very subtle wine.

SAINT-ÉMILION GRAND CRU 2002
Red | 2011 up to 2015   87
Pale in color. Dried flowers and underbrush on the nose, with hints of wild strawberries. Soft attack, with elegant tannins that are a bit drying. Lacks a bit of intensity on the palate. Supple finish.

SAINT-ÉMILION GRAND CRU 2001
Red | 2011 up to 2020   88
A very distinctive wine with well-defined tannins, but we'd like to see more depth.

SAINT-ÉMILION GRAND CRU 2000
Red | 2011 up to 2020   88
The not-so-concentrated color still has a touch of youth. It is softly vegetal on the nose and supple on the palate, with a tender, lively finish.

SAINT-ÉMILION GRAND CRU 1999
Red | 2011 up to 2013   86
There is still some fruit, but there are also some vegetal notes. Delicate, with rather rigid tannins.

SAINT-ÉMILION GRAND CRU 1998
Red | 2011 up to 2020   92
A wonderfully distinguished success: this is an elegant and pretty wine, very smooth, with freshness and everlasting distinction, even down to the slightly vegetal notes.

Red: 30.9 acres; cabernet franc 20%, merlot 80%.
Annual production: 60,000 bottles

CHÂTEAU BELLEFONT-BELCIER

33330 Saint-Laurent-des-Combes
Phone 00 33 5 57 24 72 16
Fax 00 33 5 57 74 45 06
château.bellefont-belcier@wanadoo.fr
www.bellefont-belcier.fr

This cru boasts a superb terroir right next door to Larcis-Ducasse but has really reached its potential only in recent times. The wines are made in one of Bordeaux's most innovative "traditional" gravity-fed cellars, with recent vintages showing a tempting combination of generous body, velvety texture, and a classical nose characteristic of great merlot. Add to that a potential for bottle aging that rivals that of its neighbor and you have a wine that more than justifies its recent promotion to a Premier Cru Classé.

Recently tasted
SAINT-ÉMILION GRAND CRU 2007
Red | 2012 up to 2017   90

Older vintages
SAINT-ÉMILION GRAND CRU 2006
Red | 2012 up to 2017   90
The 2006 confirms the spectacular progress of this property, which was suggested by the 2005: a full wine, very elegant, refined, and silky, displaying a wonderful bouquet of red fruit.

SAINT-ÉMILION GRAND CRU 2005
Red | 2011 up to 2015   91
After bottling, the wine is starting to reveal its true potential: elegantly oaked, unctuous body, velvety, and delicate length. Easily the best wine this château has made.

SAINT-ÉMILION GRAND CRU 2004
Red | 2011 up to 2013   87
Full, deep color, toasty and fat: this is a beautifully seductive and well-structured wine.

SAINT-ÉMILION GRAND CRU 2003
Red | 2011 up to 2015   89
An elegant wine with a subtle smokiness, this is long and delicate on the palate, unquestionably distinguished. Lovely, fresh finish.

SAINT-ÉMILION GRAND CRU 2002
Red | 2011 up to 2013   89
An elegant and aromatically fresh wine, full-bodied and svelte, with fine tannins and length. This wine is not lacking in grace.

Red: 32.1 acres; cabernet franc 20%, cabernet sauvignon 10%, merlot 70%. **Annual production:** 60,000 bottles

CHÂTEAU BELLEVUE

Route du Milieu
33330 Saint-Émilion
Phone 00 33 5 57 51 06 07
Fax 00 33 5 57 51 59 61
contact@horeau-beylot.fr
www.horeau-beylot.fr

This cru enjoys magnificent exposure on the hill of Saint-Émilion, but it attracted attention only when the owners commissioned Nicolas Thienpont and Stéphane Derenoncourt to justify a classification that no one had questioned for twenty years. They were the impetus behind Bellevue's tremendous leap forward at the start of the millennium, turning out wines with a tempting fullness and savory elegance that offer immediate appeal. The cru is now owned and managed by the talented Hubert de Boüard (Château Angélus).

Recently tasted

SAINT-ÉMILION GRAND CRU 2007
Red | 2012 up to 2017   **90**

Older vintages

SAINT-ÉMILION GRAND CRU 2006
Red | 2012 up to 2017   **87**
Full-bodied and deep with a very dark color, this is dense and stylish with long and rich fruit, and a slight hint of bitterness that is certain to disappear after bottling.

SAINT-ÉMILION GRAND CRU 2005
Red | 2011 up to 2015   **91**
A much better wine than the previous vintage, with an intense color, a ripe and expressive nose of red fruit, and a full-bodied, intense, long, and flavorful palate.

SAINT-ÉMILION GRAND CRU 2004
Red | 2011 up to 2013   **84**
Aromatically subdued at this point, this wine lacks neither color nor substance, but it does not possess great liveliness.

SAINT-ÉMILION GRAND CRU 2003
Red | 2011 up to 2015   **92**
The wine is developing an ambitious style, very rich and unctuous, but in addition to this wonderfully smooth and silky density, the wine also shines in its balance and freshness, demonstrated by its clean and peppery finish.

SAINT-ÉMILION GRAND CRU 2001
Red | 2011 up to 2015   **90**
The aromatic palette is delicately spiced and floral; the palate is very elegant. Perfectly balanced, with a silky and stylish texture.

Red: 15.3 acres; cabernet franc 20%, merlot 80%.
Annual production: 22,000 bottles

CHÂTEAU BELLEVUE-MONDOTTE

Château Pavie
33330 Saint-Émilion
Phone 00 33 5 57 55 43 43
Fax 00 33 5 57 24 63 99
contact@vignoblesperse.com
www.vignoblesperse.com

Gérard Perse is the brilliant owner of the Châteaux Pavie, Pavie-Decesse, and Monbousquet. He created this microcuvée in 2001 from a tiny parcel of vines planted on a limestone plateau above Pavie-Decesse, at the top of Mondot. Born to impress, this is an ultra-powerful, luxuriously matured wine that always delivers. That said, we have never found it to be as harmonious as the Pavie or the Pavie-Decesse—which some might prefer for their more balanced style.

SAINT-ÉMILION GRAND CRU 2007
Red | 2012 up to 2025   **91**
Dark, distinguished, rich, and voluminous, not quite as linear and long as it could be, but full-bodied just the same.

SAINT-ÉMILION GRAND CRU 2006
Red | 2012 up to 2025   **92**
Deep and dark, unctuous, intense, less of a caricature than in the past, still a touch bitter on the finish, but this is a nice, deep wine.

SAINT-ÉMILION GRAND CRU 2005
Red | 2014 up to 2024   **92**
Powerful, dense, and imposing, the wine is more imposing than it is expressive right now . . . it needs time.

SAINT-ÉMILION GRAND CRU 2004
Red | 2011 up to 2020   **90**
Beautifully deep color, rich, intense, and long, this concentrated wine is developing expressive notes of red fruit.

Red: 6.2 acres; cabernet franc 5%, cabernet sauvignon 5%, merlot 90%. **Annual production:** 4,800 bottles

CHÂTEAU BERLIQUET

33330 Saint-Émilion
Phone 00 33 5 57 24 70 48
Fax 00 33 5 57 34 70 24
château.berliquet@wanadoo.fr

This small, classified estate is a solo opera-
tor once again after years of working as a
cooperative producer. It now delivers all
the quality to be expected of a Grand Cru
Classé, relying mainly on expansive merlot
fruit from a sloping vineyard with clay and
limestone soils. Berliquet makes wine in
classic Saint-Émilion style: generously proportioned but with no trace of heaviness
and well matured in barrels (if occasionally
just a touch too showy). It grows increasingly elegant after a few years' cellaring,
displaying all the strong personality of its
terroir.

Recently tasted
SAINT-ÉMILION GRAND CRU 2007
Red | 2012 up to 2017   86

Older vintages
SAINT-ÉMILION GRAND CRU 2006
Red | 2012 up to 2017   87
A rich and full-bodied wine with generous
and very ripe fruit and enrobed tannins, voluminous and straightforward.

SAINT-ÉMILION GRAND CRU 2005
Red | 2011 up to 2018   90
Now that the wine has incorporated the oak,
it admirably demonstrates the elegance of
its terroir: the length is delicately fruity with
subtle depth.

SAINT-ÉMILION GRAND CRU 2004
Red | 2011 up to 2014   87
Classically built wine, with a long and clean
body.

SAINT-ÉMILION GRAND CRU 2003
Red | 2011 up to 2013   88
Fruity, aromatically elegant, this wine is
developing a dense, fat, ripe, and very rich
body.

SAINT-ÉMILION GRAND CRU 2002
Red | 2011 up to 2013   86
A powerful and dark wine with pronounced
notes of chocolate, indulgent but slightly
heavy.

Red: 22.2 acres; cabernet franc 25%, cabernet
sauvignon 5%, merlot 70%. **Annual production:**
40,000 bottles

CHÂTEAU LE BON PASTEUR

Maillet
33500 Pomerol
Phone 00 33 5 57 51 52 43
Fax 00 33 5 57 51 52 93
contact@rollandcollection.com
www.rollandcollection.com

This property belongs to famous wine consultant Michel Rolland. The laboratory that
he runs with his wife, Dany, is in fact just a
few hundred yards away from the winery. It
is located in the area known as Maillet,
near the Barbanne River, which marks the
border of the appellation. Obviously Le
Bon Pasteur is emblematic of the Michel
Rolland style: the wines are always ripe
and seductive right from the start, full-
bodied, with velvety but well-defined tannins. Though the wines don't have the
extreme finesse that comes with the best
terroirs of the appellation, the wines are
very well made and impressively consistent.

POMEROL 2007
Red | 2012 up to 2020   90
Blackberry jam, fat and smooth, with soft
tannins, the wine is generous and shows
the style of the vintage with hedonistic
appeal.

POMEROL 2006
Red | 2013 up to 2022   90
Dark, truffly oak, solid and firm, nice length,
with fruit that is less exuberant than in 2005.
Deep, but currently quite severe.

POMEROL 2005
Red | 2011 up to 2020   95
Wonderfully young color, notes of black fruit
and chocolate, rich, full, a refined tannic
structure with a bright and fresh finish.

POMEROL 2004
Red | 2011 up to 2015   86
A young, not very deep color, a pleasantly
peppery nose, soft and appealing but limited.

POMEROL 2003
Red | 2012 up to 2022   93
Deep, young color. Though the wine isn't
super-expressive aromatically, the tautness
(quite rare in Bon Pasteur), the depth, the
tight and velvety tannins, and the length
make for a surprisingly lively wine with great
potential for cellaring.

Red: 17.3 acres. **Annual production:** 25,000 bottles

CHÂTEAU BONALGUE

🍷🍷🍷 🍷🍷

62, quai du Priourat
BP 79
33500 Libourne cedex
Phone 00 33 5 57 51 62 17
Fax 00 33 5 57 51 28 28
contact@jbaudy.fr
www.vignoblesbourotte.com

Château Bonalgue, like its sister estate Clos du Clocher, is a very dependable producer on the outskirts of Libourne, expertly managed by longstanding owner Pierre Bourotte, one of the friendliest, most conscientious winegrowers in Pomerol. The wine is generous, supple, and fleshy— fairly early-drinking, but with the capacity to age splendidly for ten to twenty years, depending on the vintage.

Recently tasted
POMEROL 2007
Red | 2012 up to 2017   **91**
Nice, deep color, toasty nose, full-bodied without being austere, silky texture, round, very pleasant.

POMEROL 2006
Red | 2012 up to 2017   **90**
Pretty color, elegant oak, delicate, but structured on the palate, refined with a silky texture.

POMEROL 2005
Red | 2011 up to 2020   **89**
Fairly exotic nose, black fruit with a touch of coconut, this deeply colored wine is rich, smooth, and full.

Red: 16.1 acres; cabernet franc 10%, merlot 90%.
Annual production: 28,000 bottles

CHÂTEAU BONNET

🍷🍷 🍷🍷🍷

33420 Grézillac
Phone 00 33 5 57 25 58 58
Fax 00 33 5 57 74 98 59
andrelurton@andrelurton.com
www.andrelurton.com

Now over eighty years old, André Lurton is still as surprisingly full of energy and innovative as ever, especially now that his son Jacques is working alongside him. As at ease in the small appellations as he is in the great ones, he's always had a soft spot for Château Bonnet, a magnificent 670-acre property in the Entre-Deux-Mers appellation. His latest creation, in 2005: low-trained vines, in narrow rows and planted with ground cover, so that he can harvest super-ripe grapes that are then fermented and aged in barrel for just a short time in order to produce a fruit-forward wine.

Recently tasted
BORDEAUX DIVINUS 2006
Red | 2011 up to 2013   **88**
A very nice Bordeaux, dense with ripe, complex fruit, and a solid tannic streak, which will benefit from a bit of time in the cellar.

BORDEAUX RÉSERVE 2007
Red | 2011 up to 2013   **86**
A very pleasant wine, showing a rich, complex nose of black fruit with hints of spice, honey, and minerals on the palate. The wine finishes with a tender, fresh, and delicately tannic mouthfeel.

BORDEAUX RÉSERVE 2006
Red | 2011 up to 2013   **86**
A wine with lots of character, pure and expressive fruit, with a nice minerality in the mouth, it is straightforward with good acidity on the finish.

BORDEAUX RÉSERVE 2005
Red | Drink now   **87**
Tasting this wine for a second time, we are happy to confirm that it hasn't lost its fruit, its smooth texture, and its freshness.

Red: 370.7 acres; cabernet sauvignon 50%, merlot 50%. White: 370.7 acres; muscadelle 10%, sauvignon 45%, sémillon 45%. Annual production: 1,600,000 bottles

CHÂTEAU BOURGNEUF–VAYRON

1, le Bourg Neuf
33500 Pomerol
Phone 00 33 5 57 51 42 03
Fax 00 33 5 57 25 01 40
châteaubourgneufvayron@wanadoo.fr

This beautifully located cru, next to Trotanoy, is very carefully managed by the Vayron family, with a record of consistent performance. Its wines are harmonious, typically Pomerol, and at their peak after five to ten years' aging. Every wine since the turn of the century has delivered, but price remains reasonable compared with most of this winery's increasingly expensive neighbors. Warmly recommended.

Recently tasted
POMEROL 2007
Red | 2011 up to 2017   86
A fresh wine with good structure, elegant tannins, and pure aromatic definition, it is pleasant, with only average concentration.

POMEROL 2006
Red | 2012 up to 2017   89
Ruby red, with a soft nose, the wine is a mixture of indulgence and elegance on the palate, with interesting notes of black truffle.

POMEROL 2005
Red | 2011 up to 2023   88
A seductive wine with pretty notes of chocolate, full-bodied and smooth.

POMEROL 2004
Red | 2011 up to 2020   86
A fruity bouquet and a rich body, this is a round, smooth, and pleasant Pomerol.

Red: 22.2 acres; cabernet franc 10%, merlot 90%.
Annual production: 40,000 bottles

CHÂTEAU CANON

BP 22
33330 Saint-Émilion
Phone 00 33 5 57 55 23 48
Fax 00 33 5 57 24 68 00
contact@château-canon.com
www.château-canon.com

All the work put into this estate by Médoc winemaker John Kolasa and his team since it was bought up by the Wertheimer family in 1996 is gradually paying off. Witness a wine that fulfills all expectations, characterized not by power but by a finesse and linear style that will handsomely repay several years' cellaring. The new millennium clearly marked a turning point, and this estate has not looked back since.

Recently tasted
SAINT-ÉMILION GRAND CRU 2007
Red | 2012 up to 2020   91

Older vintages
SAINT-ÉMILION GRAND CRU 2006
Red | 2011 up to 2021   93
In the same wonderful line as the 2005: bright color, a subtle and fruity nose, a svelte and delicate body, and not a hint of rigidity in the tannins. Undeniably profound.

SAINT-ÉMILION GRAND CRU 2005
Red | 2011 up to 2020   93
Deep but not opaque in color, this has very pure fruit, wonderfully distinctive flavors, and elegant length. Bright, suave, and profound.

SAINT-ÉMILION GRAND CRU 2004
Red | 2011 up to 2017   91
Deep color, focused, delicately toasted. Magnificent wine, harmonious and elegant, with silky and precise texture, superb length, and persistence.

SAINT-ÉMILION GRAND CRU 2003
Red | 2011 up to 2017   87
The wine has fine tannins, vigor, and persistent aromas but disappoints in its lack of substance and richness.

SAINT-ÉMILION GRAND CRU 2002
Red | 2011 up to 2014   90
Moderately concentrated color. The nose of red fruit and white pepper is discreet but elegant. Svelte, delicate, and persistent on the palate.

SAINT-ÉMILION GRAND CRU 2001
Red | 2011 up to 2014   87
Quite linear and multilayered, not at all heavy, this boasts tannins that are spicy and refined, with wonderful length on the palate.

SAINT-ÉMILION GRAND CRU 2000
Red | 2011 up to 2020   **93**
Remarkably refined texture and flavors, with very noble, fine-grained tannins.

Red: 54.4 acres; cabernet franc 25%, merlot 75%.
Annual production: 70,000 bottles

CHÂTEAU CANON-LA-GAFFELIÈRE

BP 34
33330 Saint-Émilion
Phone 00 33 5 57 24 71 33
Fax 00 33 5 57 24 67 95
info@neipperg.com
www.neipperg.com

Canon-la-Gaffelière, flagship domaine of Stephan Von Neipperg, is located on the hill of Saint-Émilion, almost at the southern entrance to the village. Since his arrival on the scene in the early 1980s, Von Neipperg has shown himself to be one of the most talented winegrowers on Bordeaux's Right Bank. He understood immediately that perfectly ripe grapes in pristine condition are the sine qua non of great wine production. The results speak for themselves. Canon-la-Gaffelière shows a quality and maturity of substance that never fails to impress: beautifully balanced, bursting with fruit, and superbly aged. Von Neipperg plays as much on powerful constitution as on refined tannins, putting in a nearly flawless performance that started in the 1990s and continues today. This cru is one of the commune's most valuable assets, even without Premier Cru status.

Recently tasted
SAINT-ÉMILION GRAND CRU 2007
Red | 2012 up to 2020   **94**

Older vintages
SAINT-ÉMILION GRAND CRU 2006
Red | 2012 up to 2020   **94**
Wonderfully rich and succulent, this has intense fruit, everything in beautiful balance.

SAINT-ÉMILION GRAND CRU 2005
Red | 2013 up to 2030   **97**
Hugely powerful, tight tannins, similar texture, very young, but with a fresh finish that is immediately recognizable as cabernet franc. Much more masculine than usual, this wine has a great future.

SAINT-ÉMILION GRAND CRU 2004
Red | 2011 up to 2015   **89**
More supple and clearly more limited than the 2005, this was made in a focused and elegant style that can be appreciated already.

SAINT-ÉMILION GRAND CRU 2003
Red | 2011 up to 2020   **93**
One of the great wines of the complicated 2003 vintage, this has ripe, almost hot notes on the nose, but it is also deep on the palate, unctuous, and silky, with wonderful acidity and freshness.

SAINT-ÉMILION GRAND CRU 2002
Red | 2011 up to 2015   **92**
A wonderful wine in a modern style, this has intense color, expressive fruit combined with ambitious oak, a smooth body, and perfectly silky tannins.

SAINT-ÉMILION GRAND CRU 2001
Red | 2011 up to 2020   **90**
Very round and powerful, richly unctuous, almost sweet, underscored by a nice tannic structure that is fresh and elegant.

SAINT-ÉMILION GRAND CRU 2000
Red | 2011 up to 2020   **92**
Full, very flavorful, this has a rich but nervy body without the slightest hint of flabbiness.

SAINT-ÉMILION GRAND CRU 1999
Red | 2011 up to 2015   **88**
Warm and rich, this is generous but lacking in freshness.

SAINT-ÉMILION GRAND CRU 1998
Red | 2011 up to 2013   **98**
This has a wonderfully deep personality, distinguished and intense, refined and luminous in substance. This is the finest vintage of the decade.

SAINT-ÉMILION GRAND CRU 1996
Red | 2011 up to 2015   **90**
A pretty, fresh, and firm wine, made in an almost Médoc-like style, with fresh acidity, red fruit flavors, and serious tannins.

Annual production: 65,000 bottles

CHÂTEAU CERTAN DE MAY

33500 Pomerol
Phone 00 33 5 57 51 41 53
Fax 00 33 5 57 51 88 51
château.certan-de-may@wanadoo.fr

Château Certan de May enjoys a splendid setting opposite Vieux Château Certan, planted in a clay soil with patches of gravel and sand. The vineyard is some fifty years old, owner-operator Jean-Luc Bareau preferring to replace vines on a regular basis. The wines have neither the precision nor the finesse of the greatest (despite all the potential of this terroir), but they are made in a generous, very classical style, with plenty of tasty truffle character.

POMEROL 2006
Red | 2011 up to 2020   **91**
This wine, now in bottle, lives up to its promises from the "primeur" tastings: suave and full-bodied, generously round, with refined and elegant length.

POMEROL 2005
Red | 2012 up to 2020   **90**
This wine is generous and well oaked: the terroir shows through, but with firmly extracted tannins.

POMEROL 2004
Red | 2011 up to 2018   **87**
Fleshy and full-bodied, with solid tannins, but it lacks a bit of finesse.

POMEROL 2001
Red | 2011 up to 2015   **90**
Powerful yet elegant, with solid tannins, though not quite as refined as the very best.

Red: 12.4 acres; cabernet franc 25%, cabernet sauvignon 5%, merlot 70%. Annual production: 24,000 bottles

CHÂTEAU CHEVAL BLANC

🍷 🍷 🍷 🍷 🍷

33330 Saint-Émilion
Phone 00 33 5 57 55 55 55
Fax 00 33 5 57 55 55 50
contact@château-chevalblanc.com
www.château-cheval-blanc.com

Cheval Blanc's performance throughout the latter half of the twentieth century was by far the most consistent of all the top-ranking Right Bank Bordeaux estates. What makes it distinctive is an unusual encépagement (mix of vine varieties) dominated by the cabernet franc; plus a sandy-gravelly terroir on the Pomerol plateau, right next door to the eponymous appellation. In the mid-1990s, Cheval Blanc was sold to Bernard Arnault and investor Albert Frère. But the guiding philosophy remains in line with Pierre Lurton's genial but precise vision of a civilized cru that bucks fashionable trends in favor of increasingly sharp definition. What strikes you first about Cheval Blanc is its classy, fruity balance—fresh, elegant, and pure but with plenty of liveliness. The 2005 is a prodigious Cheval Blanc that challenges the 1998 as one of the most memorable vintages since the legendary 1947. Some of the intermediary vintages, on the other hand, such as the 2002 and the 2004, are not quite the all-around performers that they should be for such a great cru.

Recently tasted
SAINT-ÉMILION GRAND CRU 2006
Red | 2012 up to 2025   93

Older vintages
SAINT-ÉMILION GRAND CRU 2005
Red | 2015 up to 2030   98
Combining tannic finesse, fullness, and energy, this is one of the greatest Cheval Blanc wines of the past fifty years. The pedigree of the bouquet and its explosive freshness give it a magnificent impact.

SAINT-ÉMILION GRAND CRU 2004
Red | 2011 up to 2020   93
With its notes of wild strawberries, blueberries, and musk and its full, long flavors, this wine is very elegant, though it lacks a dimension that leaves it a notch below the wines in the highest echelon.

SAINT-ÉMILION GRAND CRU 2003
Red | 2011 up to 2025   96
This wine associates the charm, freshness, and crispness of the cru with a full and ripe aromatic palette typical of the vintage. This is a bright wine, ample and long, without any heaviness and with wonderful complexity.

SAINT-ÉMILION GRAND CRU 2002
Red | 2011 up to 2020   92
The tannins are quite lively; the wine has personality and depth.

SAINT-ÉMILION GRAND CRU 2001
Red | 2012 up to 2022   90
Similar in style to the 2000, with a bit less depth.

SAINT-ÉMILION GRAND CRU 2000
Red | 2011 up to 2030   95
An elegant achievement: deeply colored, wonderfully succulent, fresh in fruit, rich, dense, and profound. Very distinguished.

SAINT-ÉMILION GRAND CRU 1999
Red | 2011 up to 2013   91
An indisputably distinguished wine with nice length, this isn't the most complex wine ever, but it is charming for its bright style and its harmony.

SAINT-ÉMILION GRAND CRU 1998
Red | 2011 up to 2013   99
For us, this is the most amazing Cheval in the past fifteen years, and our most recent tastings brilliantly confirm the superiority of this wine, especially in comparison with the charming and racy 2000: splendid color, extraordinary aromatic freshness, silky texture, and an extra-fine tannic grain, grandeur, and pedigree. Unforgettable!

Red: 91.4 acres; cabernet franc 57%, merlot 43%.
Annual production: 150,000 bottles

CHÂTEAU LA CLÉMENCE

33500 Pomerol
Phone 00 33 5 57 24 77 44
Fax 00 33 5 57 40 37 42
contact@vignoblesdauriac.com
www.vignoblesdauriac.com

Château La Clémence was acquired in 1996 by Christian Dauriac, the owner of Saint-Émilion's fine Château Destieux. Both properties have made spectacular progress in the past decade, the product of Dauriac's meticulous genius. The wine plays on all the nuances of Pomerol geology, made in an elegant, circular winemaking facility that is specifically designed for careful vinification. Made in a creamy style with a very delicate bouquet, La Clémence has quickly become one of the rising stars of this appellation.

Recently tasted
Pomerol 2007
Red | 2012 up to 2020   90

Older vintages
Pomerol 2006
Red | 2012 up to 2020   92
A deeply colored, rich, and truffle-laced wine with a beautiful texture, silky and dense. Excellent.

Pomerol 2005
Red | 2011 up to 2020   92
A powerful and very rich wine, this is full-bodied and ample, with expressive notes of black cherry and tannins that are both elegant and distinguished.

Pomerol 2004
Red | 2011 up to 2020   93
One of the best wines of the vintage for its refined aromas and the surprisingly perfect tannins, infinitely smoother and silkier than most Pomerols, including the most famous.

Pomerol 2003
Red | 2011 up to 2013   88
This displays wonderfully refined aromas and an amazingly delicate mouthfeel for the vintage, but there's a slight lack of substance on the mid-palate.

Pomerol 2001
Red | 2011 up to 2015   88
Remarkably concentrated and unctuous texture, abundantly aromatic.

Pomerol 2000
Red | 2011 up to 2015   90
Rich, unctuous, and deep, with a full body that is underscored by smooth tannins.

Red: 7.4 acres Annual production: 6,000 bottles

CHÂTEAU CLINET

16, chemin de Feytit
33500 Pomerol
Phone 00 33 5 57 25 50 00
Fax 00 33 5 57 25 70 00
contact@châteauclinet.com
www.châteauclinet.com

Château Clinet, magnificently located at the heart of the appellation, was one of the spearheads of the winemaking revolution that took hold of the Bordeaux region throughout the 1980s. Then crafted under the direction of the talented Jean-Michel Arcaute, the cru stood out for a modern, irresistible, generous, and mature style that won approval with leading restaurateurs worldwide. That personality has gained in refinement since Jean-Marie Laborde's arrival in the 1990s, but at the cost of consistency: superb one year, nothing special the next.

Recently tasted
Pomerol 2007
Red | 2012 up to 2017   89

Pomerol 2006
Red | 2012 up to 2017   92

Older vintages
Pomerol 2005
Red | 2011 up to 2020   92
As much as the 2004 disappoints, this vintage delights: beautiful style, elegant and intense, graceful volume, lovely length.

Pomerol 2004
Red | 2011 up to 2015   85
The wine is classically built but lacking in finesse and aromatic precision: spicy oak, robust tannins, a touch astringent.

Pomerol 2001
Red | 2011 up to 2020   92
The wine shows a remarkably silky texture with a warm mouthfeel that is long and harmonious.

Pomerol 2000
Red | 2011 up to 2020   90
A very powerful wine, generous, complex, and openly hedonistic.

Pomerol Fleur de Clinet 2006
Red | 2011 up to 2014   88
A supple, elegant, and quite refined Pomerol, this opens with notes of violets and black fruit, expanding into a velvety fruit-filled finish.

Red: 21.3 acres; cabernet franc 5%, cabernet sauvignon 10%, merlot 85%. **Annual production:** 35,000 bottles

CHÂTEAU LA CLOTTE

33330 Saint-Émilion
Phone 00 33 5 57 24 66 85
Fax 00 33 5 57 24 79 67
château-la-clotte@wanadoo.fr
www.châteaulaclotte.com

Château La Clotte is a small estate splendidly located in the sector of Bergat, in the heart of the limestone hillside. This property, long a part of the Moueix portfolio, regained its independence in the 1990s and is now making some charming wines, round and generous, that are drinkable early on. Located near the center of the village, the winery is open for visits, and their tasting room is in a troglodyte cave.

SAINT-ÉMILION GRAND CRU 2007
Red | 2012 up to 2019   92
Deeply colored, this very distinguished wine is elegant and its limestone terroir shows through, smooth but with a nice grip and wonderful length.

SAINT-ÉMILION GRAND CRU 2006
Red | 2012 up to 2019   90
This wine is evolving nicely in the bottle: pretty, dark color, toasty red fruit in the nose, ample and well built on the palate, with distinguished length.

SAINT-ÉMILION GRAND CRU 2005
Red | 2011 up to 2019   90
Really beautiful wine, the nose is quite elegant and focused; deliciously silky texture. Very 2005, with the grace and acidity that balances out the massive structure of the wine.

SAINT-ÉMILION GRAND CRU 2003
Red | 2011 up to 2013   88
A pretty Saint-Émilion, round and smooth, with a nice, full balance. This is an elegant and stylish wine that isn't flashy but has a lasting finish.

Red: 9.8 acres; cabernet franc 15%, cabernet sauvignon 5%, merlot 80%. Annual production: 15,000 bottles

CHÂTEAU LA CONSEILLANTE

33500 Pomerol
Phone 00 33 5 57 51 15 32
Fax 00 33 5 57 51 42 39
contact@la-conseillante.com
www.la-conseillante.com

Only Château La Conseillante can boast such an exceptional constellation of neighbors: Cheval Blanc and Figeac to the south, L'Évangile to the east, Vieux Château Certan to the north, and Petit-Village to the west. More important still, it is the only Pomerol that can draw on the quintessence of these different terroirs, combining like no other the smoothness and mellowness of a Pomerol with the refined texture of the sandy-gravelly soils of Saint-Émilion. Its destiny has been lovingly presided over by successive generations of the Nicolas family, the current one by far the most dynamic. Viticulture in the past few years has grown more precise thanks to closer attention to press loads and stricter selection in the blending of the "grand" wine. The most recent vintages remain as voluptuous as ever, with more precision in the texture, more sparkle in the aromas, without compromising the delicious notes of violets and truffles.

Recently tasted
POMEROL DUO DE CONSEILLANTE 2007
Red | 2012 up to 2017   87

Older vintages
POMEROL 2007
Red | 2012 up to 2022   92
A beautiful wine, deep, with a finely sculpted texture and a long and very distinguished mouthfeel. A wine with conviction.

POMEROL 2006
Red | 2012 up to 2022   92
A beautifully sculpted wine, very fresh, lively, and lean, with a wonderfully refined texture and nice length.

POMEROL 2005
Red | 2012 up to 2025   96
Definitely one of the great Pomerols in this vintage, this is a finely perfumed wine, fat, rich, expansive, on a grand scale, but also with very refined tannins.

POMEROL 2004
Red | 2011 up to 2020   91
Built with finesse and grace, this wine appears delicate without any hint of rigidity: it has round and luscious fruit and wonderfully elegant length.

POMEROL 2001
Red | 2011 up to 2020   **94**
One of the stars of the vintage: very racy bouquet, silky, amazing balance, perfect velvety texture in the mouth.

POMEROL 1998
Red | 2011 up to 2020   **90**
Quite delicate and fine, the wine is at its aromatic peak right now, and is developing a long and subtle body. It has elegant tannins but is lacking the density and precision of the best vintages of the last decade.

Red: 29.7 acres; cabernet franc 20%, merlot 80%.
Annual production: 50,000 bottles

CHÂTEAU LA COUSPAUDE

BP 40
33330 Saint-Émilion
Phone 00 33 5 57 40 15 76
Fax 00 33 5 57 40 10 14
vignobles.aubert@wanadoo.fr
www.aubert-vignobles.com

La Couspaude is owned by Jean-Claude Aubert, who also owns two interesting crus in the Libourne satellites (Jean de Gué in Lalande and Messine-Aubert in Montagne). This particular winery improved significantly in the early 1990s and has since produced one of the most consistently dependable Saint-Émilion crus. Its style bears the unmistakable mark of La Couspaude's wine consultant, Michel Rolland. The wine is generous, rounded, luscious, and very well matured—perfect with the hearty cuisine of Southwest France. All of the wines are approachable when young but will also reward after ten years' aging or longer—longer still in good vintages.

Recently tasted
SAINT-ÉMILION GRAND CRU 2007
Red | 2012 up to 2019   **91**

Older vintages
SAINT-ÉMILION GRAND CRU 2006
Red | 2011 up to 2019   **90**
Round, smooth, and refined, this is a nice wine with a very distinguished character that isn't trying to be overpowering.

SAINT-ÉMILION GRAND CRU 2005
Red | 2011 up to 2020   **92**
This has a fine structure, elegant, with a hedonistic silkiness. The rich style and perfectly ripe fruit make for a wine that is a huge success in this vintage.

SAINT-ÉMILION GRAND CRU 2004
Red | 2011 up to 2015   **89**
The wine has a beautifully deep color. Generously endowed, the fat, robust, truffle-laced character is truly seductive. The finish, however, doesn't have the same silky quality as the most impressive vintages from this property.

SAINT-ÉMILION GRAND CRU 2002
Red | 2011 up to 2015   **88**
With its appealing nose combining elegant fruit and toasty oak, this is an immediately seductive and full-bodied wine.

SAINT-ÉMILION GRAND CRU 2001
Red | 2011 up to 2015   **89**
Pretty strongly oaked, this wine has good length and isn't lacking balance.

SAINT-ÉMILION GRAND CRU 2000
Red | 2011 up to 2015   92
Very well made: full, soft texture, generous, rich, a natural bouquet with sober yet powerful tannins.

SAINT-ÉMILION GRAND CRU CHÂTEAU
SAINT-HUBERT 2006
Red | 2011 up to 2015   86
The second label of Jean-Claude Aubert in Saint-Émilion, this is a concentrated and deeply colored wine structured with good fruit and a soft finish. It can be enjoyed in its youth, especially with wild game.

Red: 17.3 acres; cabernet franc 20%, cabernet sauvignon 5%, merlot 75%. Annual production: 36,000 bottles

CHÂTEAU LA CROIX

37, rue Pline-Parmentier
33506 Libourne Cedex
Phone 00 33 5 57 51 41 86
Fax 00 33 5 57 51 53 16
info@j-janoueix-bordeaux.com
www.j-janoueix-bordeaux.com

La Croix is a twenty-five-acre vineyard in Catusseau, opposite La Croix Saint-Georges and Petit-Village. It belongs to the Janoueix family, also the owners of La Croix Saint-Georges and some ten other Pomerol, Saint-Émilion, and Castillon properties. Originally from Corrèze, the Janoueixes, like the Moueix family, have been big players in Libourne since the early twentieth century. Their wines have come a long way over the past decade and now rank as very good Pomerols indeed.

POMEROL 2006
Red | 2011 up to 2018   89
A quite complete wine with nice balance, floral and fruity, deep with lots of freshness, smooth and full.

POMEROL 2005
Red | 2011 up to 2018   88
Well made and not at all rustic, this supple 2005 is fat, succulent, generous, and clean.

Annual production: 54,000 bottles

CHÂTEAU LA CROIX DE GAY

33500 Pomerol
Phone 00 33 5 57 51 19 05
Fax 00 33 5 57 51 81 81
contact@château-lacroixdegay.com
www.château-lacroixdegay.com

This winery, which is located at the northern edge of the appellation, belongs to the Raynaud family and is now run by Chantal Lebreton, the sister of Alain Raynaud of Château Quinault l'Enclos in Saint-Émilion. The wine is elegantly made with those shapely curves and truffle notes typical of a classic Pomerol, but there's still room for improvement when it comes to consistency—ordinary vintages lack intensity. Since the 1980s the château has also been making an ambitious reserve bottling from specially selected vineyards.

Recently tasted
Pomerol 2007
Red | 2012 up to 2017   89

Older vintages
Pomerol 2006
Red | 2012 up to 2017   89
This wine is very promising: intense and fat, nice, racy volume, precise tannins, lots of concentration.

Pomerol 2005
Red | 2012 up to 2020   88
The wine possesses much more intensity and flavor than the previous vintage. For the time being, the aromas are muted; it needs time.

Pomerol La Fleur de Gay 2006
Red | 2011 up to 2022   92
A true success with a superb élevage: delicately oaked, elegant, dense, and structured, with great length that is full of freshness.

Pomerol La Fleur de Gay 2005
Red | 2011 up to 2022   91
The wine is powerful and rich, with a very oaky character and a spicy palate. The élevage has amplified the wine's intensity.

Pomerol La Fleur de Gay 2001
Red | 2011 up to 2020   91
Expressive and very delicate, with an unctuous and supple body, integrated tannins, and a beautifully persistent finish.

Pomerol La Fleur de Gay 2000
Red | 2011 up to 2020   92
A robust wine, intensely aromatic, with a wonderfully deep texture.

Red: 24.7 acres; cabernet franc 5%, cabernet sauvignon 5%, merlot 90%. Annual production: 40,000 bottles

CHÂTEAU DASSAULT

1, Couprie
33330 Saint-Émilion
Phone 00 33 5 57 55 10 00
Fax 00 33 5 57 55 10 01
lbv@châteaudassault.com
www.châteaudassault.com

This estate, as the name suggests, is owned by the French industrialist family Dassault, who acquired it in 1956. It is run today by Laurent Dassault, who also has interests in vineyards in Argentina and Chile, assisted by Laurence Brun. In the 1990s, Château Dassault showed supple body but no real intensity; since then it has steadily gained in depth, recent vintages often showing brilliant character.

Recently tasted
Saint-Émilion 2007
Red | 2012 up to 2017   90

Saint-Émilion 2006
Red | 2012 up to 2017   89

Older vintages
Saint-Émilion 2005
Red | 2011 up to 2015   90
With a beautiful, bright color and notes of red fruit and roasted coffee, this has length, freshness, and good flavor. Well done.

Saint-Émilion 2004
Red | 2011 up to 2015   88
An elegant and harmonious wine: it has a nice intensity of color, and it is full-bodied and generous on the palate, with supple tannins and reasonable length.

Saint-Émilion 2003
Red | 2011 up to 2015   90
A rich and full wine, this has tannins that aren't drying and a fresh finish, with notes of red fruit. Well made.

Saint-Émilion 2002
Red | 2011 up to 2015   89
A success in the classic style of Saint-Émilion, perfectly made, this intensely colored, concentrated wine is deep, delicate, fine, and linear, elegantly combining intensity and verve.

Red: 66.7 acres; cabernet franc 30%, cabernet sauvignon 5%, merlot 65%. Annual production: 75,000 bottles

CHÂTEAU DESTIEUX

1, lieu-dit Destieux
33330 Saint-Hippolyte
Phone 00 33 5 57 24 77 44
Fax 00 33 5 57 40 37 42
contact@vignoblesdauriac.com
www.vignoblesdauriac.com

Château Destieux stands on a steep hillock in the eastern part of Saint-Émilion. Acquired by the Dauriac family in the 1970s, it has made steady progress over the past ten years and is now warmly recommended for wines that are remarkably consistent vintage after vintage and increasingly well aged. In the 1990s, the wines always appeared powerful but they could also seem rustic. Since the turn of the millennium, however, they have taken on a very elegant and harmonious tannic structure.

Recently tasted
SAINT-ÉMILION GRAND CRU 2007
Red | 2012 up to 2017   88

Older vintages
SAINT-ÉMILION GRAND CRU 2006
Red | 2012 up to 2017   91
Velvety, flavorful, rich, and elegant, this wine is perfectly built and offers wonderful freshness on the finish. A major success for the growth, and one of the best Saint-Émilions of the vintage.

SAINT-ÉMILION GRAND CRU 2005
Red | 2011 up to 2015   91
Deep color, ambitiously oaked, intense and long volume without any hint of heaviness, lots of backbone and pedigree. Combining power and generosity, with enrobed tannins and virtually no severity, this is a great achievement.

SAINT-ÉMILION GRAND CRU 2004
Red | 2011 up to 2015   90
With a deep and elegant bouquet, perfectly aged, this is a linear and long wine, underscored by fine, drawn-out tannins. A fine, noble wine.

SAINT-ÉMILION GRAND CRU 2003
Red | 2011 up to 2017   90
A nice, racy wine, very rich, dense, and ripe, with savory fruit.

SAINT-ÉMILION GRAND CRU 2002
Red | 2011 up to 2013   88
A solid Saint-Émilion for the vintage, dense and truffle-laced.

SAINT-ÉMILION GRAND CRU 2001
Red | 2011 up to 2015   90
In the dense and tightly wound style of the growth, this wine has lots of intensity and energy, and shows noble notes of black truffles.

Red: 19.8 acres; cabernet 34%, merlot 66%. Annual production: 30,000 bottles

CHÂTEAU DU DOMAINE DE L'ÉGLISE

86, cours Balguerie-Stuttenberg
33082 Bordeaux
Phone 00 33 5 56 00 00 70
Fax 00 33 5 57 24 71 34
domaines@borie-manoux.fr

Quality has soared here since the turn of the millennium, as in all of the Castéja crus (Trottevieille, Batailley, and Lynch-Moussas). Vineyards close to the heart of the Pomerol appellation (holdings in Clinet and Clos l'Église) produce a wine that is known for its generously sappy character with not a trace of heaviness or flabbiness. This is a high-volume Pomerol, perfectly balanced, every vintage since 2000 impeccably made.

Recently tasted
POMEROL 2007
Red I 2012 up to 2017   **88**

Older vintages
POMEROL 2006
Red I 2012 up to 2017   **90**
Deeply colored, dense, and deep, this has lots of substance, pronounced notes of chocolate, and a finish that is rich and quite massive. A wine to be aged.

POMEROL 2005
Red I 2011 up to 2025   **92**
This wine has huge potential: pretty texture, pedigree and depth, delicate spice. Brilliant length.

POMEROL 2004
Red I 2011 up to 2022   **90**
Excellent and very characteristic of Pomerol. Bright color, svelte body, elegant tannins, deep and sappy length.

POMEROL 2001
Red I 2011 up to 2020   **90**
Tender but deep, this wine exhibits a subtle texture, never-ending velvetiness, and particularly delicate tannins.

POMEROL 2000
Red I 2011 up to 2020   **92**
This is the first real success in the winery's recent history: generous body, elegant texture, firm but not hard tannins, amazingly natural in its tone and majestically balanced.

Red: 17.3 acres; cabernet franc 5%, merlot 95%.
Annual production: 36,000 bottles

DOURTHE

35, rue de Bordeaux
33290 Parempuyre
Phone 00 33 5 56 35 53 00
Fax 00 33 5 56 35 53 29
contact@cvbg.com
www.dourthe.com

Négociants like Dourthe are the backbone of the Bordeaux region, constantly inventing ever more precise cuvées and steering châteaux toward the top of their appellations. You know where you are with a house like this. It was recently taken over by Champagne producer Alain Thiénot, who picked the current winemaking team. It will be interesting to see how it develops.

Recently tasted
BORDEAUX DOURTHE LA GRANDE CUVÉE 2008
White I 2011 up to 2013   **87**

BORDEAUX DOURTHE LA GRANDE CUVÉE 2006
Red I 2011 up to 2013   **88**

GRAVES DOURTHE TERROIRS D'EXCEPTION HAUTES GRAVIÈRES 2006
Red I 2011 up to 2013   **87**

Older vintages
BORDEAUX DOURTHE LA GRANDE CUVÉE 2005
Red I 2011 up to 2013   **88**
This wine, with its dark purple color, offers generous and rich flavor punctuated by elegant and fine tannins.

BORDEAUX DOURTHE NO. 1 2007
White I 2011 up to 2013   **89**
Very traditional and typical, with remarkable fruit, a pretty core, and a wonderfully fresh and aromatic finish. A great accomplishment.

BORDEAUX DOURTHE NO. 1 2006
Red I 2011 up to 2013   **89**
Always perfectly vinified, this cuvée has a very expressive and open nose and a full, round palate. A rich, velvety, fruity, and fresh Bordeaux; a true pleasure!

BORDEAUX DOURTHE NO. 1 2005
Red I 2011 up to 2013   **88**
Black color, powerful and expressive nose with nice complexity; good presence in the mouth, balanced and full with excellent freshness. A perfect example of a truly classic Bordeaux.

BORDEAUX SUPÉRIEUR CHÂTEAU PEY LA TOUR RÉSERVE DU CHÂTEAU 2006

Red | 2011 up to 2013   **89**

The nose is delicately fruity with pretty floral notes; the mouth is full and robust, with nice acidity and fruit. A pleasant Bordeaux, ready to drink.

BORDEAUX SUPÉRIEUR CHÂTEAU PEY LA TOUR RÉSERVE DU CHÂTEAU 2005

Red | 2011 up to 2013   **90**

Dense, dark color, powerful nose, nice attack in the mouth with richness, pretty tannins, good acidity, and very persistent aromas. Wonderfully elegant. The wine belongs in a rare category: it is a kind of mini-great Bordeaux, full of personality, with all the qualities of a classic Grand Cru Bordeaux, just a notch below!

Red: 24.7 acres **Annual production:** 6,000 bottles

CLOS L'ÉGLISE

33500 Pomerol
Phone 00 33 5 56 64 05 22
Fax 00 33 5 56 64 06 98
info@vignoblesgarcin.com
www.vignoblesgarcin.com

There have been some huge improvements here since 1997 when Château Clos l'Église—a tiny estate right next to Château l'Église-Clinet—was purchased by the Garcins (also the owners of Haut-Bergey in Pessac Léognan). Indeed, its superb 1998 and 2000 offerings placed it among the rising stars of the Right Bank Bordeaux. The wines are made in a very modern, forward style: dense, deep color; ripe fruit nose with notes of toast, mocha, and cocoa; and a generous, ample body with no hard edges whatsoever! Immediately seductive but with all the pedigree required for long aging.

POMEROL 2007

Red | 2012 up to 2017   **88**

Dark, rich, solid, truffle-laced, the tannic structure lacks a bit of finesse, but there's nice, full volume.

POMEROL 2006

Red | 2012 up to 2017   **91**

The wine is currently quite hard, with tannins that are not as immediately velvety as in 2005, but the wine has great density and great cellaring potential.

POMEROL 2005

Red | 2011 up to 2020   **92**

An unctuous and silken triumph: a deeply colored wine with delicate fruit, full-bodied and dense, not harsh or bitter. Generous volume, full-flavored, and luscious.

POMEROL 2004

Red | 2011 up to 2018   **88**

A generous and seductive Pomerol: beautiful fruit aromas, smooth length, limited depth, but harmonious.

POMEROL 2001

Red | 2011 up to 2017   **92**

Powerful and spectacularly built, this ultra-rich and velvety 2001 is seductive in its unctuous texture and intense structure.

POMEROL 2000

Red | 2011 up to 2020   **95**

A great success that represents the key to the cru: a powerful but elegant Pomerol, delicately built, with silky length.

Red: 14.8 acres; cabernet franc 20%, merlot 80%.
Annual production: 15,000 bottles

CHÂTEAU L'ÉGLISE-CLINET

33500 Pomerol
Phone 00 33 5 57 25 96 59
Fax 00 33 5 57 25 21 96
denis@durantou.com
www.eglise-clinet.com

Denis Durantou is one of those rare Pomerol "artistes"—a winemaker of terrific talent and intuition who has a very clear idea of the style that best suits his small but remarkable Clinet terroir: clay-gravel soils planted with ancient merlot and even more venerable bouchet vines that take on fabulous violet aromas. The fragrance is quite unlike the truffle notes found in wines from the more clay-rich soils on the Certan plateau. Everything else about Durantou's wines—refined fabric and texture, expertly balanced ripeness and freshness, masterful aging—can be credited to Durantou himself. This property has a unique elegance that invariably places it among the five top-ranking estates in the Pomerol appellation.

Recently tasted
POMEROL 2007
Red | 2011 up to 2013   **94**

Older vintages
POMEROL 2006
Red | 2012 up to 2025   **92**
Though it doesn't possess the impressive volume of the best vintages of the growth, it has an unctuous body, and the refined tannins of this 2006 will make this a classic from the property.

POMEROL 2005
Red | 2012 up to 2035   **98**
This has an incredible nose of violets and marvelous focus. It is sumptuous on the palate and explodes on the finish, a wonderful wine that reveals its terroir, and was clearly vinified by an artist!

POMEROL 2004
Red | 2011 up to 2019   **92**
Great color, fresh and complex aromas, a surprising and magnificent vinosity worthy of a great vintage. A pure wine, made without compromise. Exemplary.

POMEROL 2003
Red | 2011 up to 2030   **94**
Very powerful, truffled and intense, with massive tannins and a firm mouthfeel that is uncommon for the growth: this musn't be drunk too early.

POMEROL 2001
Red | 2011 up to 2020   **93**
Wonderfully rich constitution, exuding ripe and complex fruit, with a rich and tightly wound tannic structure.

POMEROL 2000
Red | 2011 up to 2028   **97**
A creamy, very deep wine with an unctuous core, still quite youthful but at the same time remarkably vigorous, tight, and very refined—as if it had been refined by its élevage.

POMEROL 1999
Red | 2011 up to 2020   **92**
Less incredibly energetic than the 1998 or 2000. That said, this 1999 is a splendid Pomerol, suave and long with a wonderfully velvety texture.

POMEROL 1998
Red | 2011 up to 2024   **99**
Now hitting its peak, but still capable of evolving over the next twenty years (at least!), this suave and amazingly profound wine is certainly one of the greatest Bordeaux wines of the vintage. Completely unforgettable.

Red: 14.8 acres; cabernet franc 10%, merlot 90%.
Annual production: 26,500 bottles

CHÂTEAU L'ÉVANGILE

2, chemin Vieux Maillet
33500 Pomerol
Phone 00 33 5 57 55 45 55
Fax 00 33 5 57 55 45 56
levangile@lafite.com
www.lafite.com

Baron Eric de Rothschild was co-owner of this cru until the start of the twenty-first century, when he acquired it outright. Since then he has equipped l'Évangile with the technical expertise to be expected of a property of this potential and reputation, magnificently located on the Pomerol Plateau. Vinification in small vats is a particular feature and helps to focus more closely on the vintage and refine the blending. Naturally, all of these improvements are reflected in the early 2000 vintages, which are made in a smooth, gourmand style.

POMEROL 2006
Red | 2015 up to 2025   93
Richly constituted, this is an unctuous and immediately seductive wine with bright and expressive fruit.

POMEROL 2005
Red | 2012 up to 2020   95
Exquisitely succulent, this has a generous and truffle-laden nose, an incomparably velvety texture, and a more pure and transparent expression of the terroir than previous vintages. This is the most distinctively accomplished wine that we have seen come to life in the last twenty years.

POMEROL 2004
Red | 2011 up to 2017   92
The result of rigorous sorting of the grapes, this wine is profound and unctuous. It expands generously on the palate, with an expressive bouquet of black fruits.

POMEROL 2001
Red | 2011 up to 2020   89
A fine, elegant, and classic wine, not lacking in finesse or smoothness, but with only average complexity.

Red: 34.6 acres; cabernet franc 22%, merlot 78%.
Annual production: 60,000 bottles

CHÂTEAU FAUGÈRES

33330 Saint-Étienne de Lisse (Saint-Émilion)
Phone 00 33 5 57 40 34 99
Fax 00 33 5 57 40 36 14
info@château-faugeres.com
www.château-faugeres.com

Château Faugères stands on the hill of Saint-Émilion itself, within striking distance of the Côtes de Castillon appellation (production includes the excellent Cap de Faugères Côtes de Castillon). The estate is one of Saint-Émilion's biggest success stories from the 1990s, when it rocketed to fame thanks to owner Corinne Guisez's deliciously powerful and intense range of wines—wines for hedonists, created under the guidance of Michel Rolland. In 2005, Corinne sold the estate to Swiss businessman Silvio Denz, who has raised the bar even higher. The grapes are more rigorously selected than ever, not only for the single-parcel Péby-Faugères but also for the Saint-Émilion Grand Cru. Both are definitely wines to watch: very powerful and intense, with the potential to take their place in the pantheon of great Saint-Émilion wines in years to come. Spectacular new buildings designed by the famous architect Botha are perhaps the most striking of all in the Bordeaux area.

Recently tasted
SAINT-ÉMILION GRAND CRU 2007
Red | 2012 up to 2017   89

SAINT-ÉMILION GRAND CRU PÉBY-FAUGÈRES 2007
Red | 2012 up to 2017   90

Older vintages
CÔTES DE CASTILLON CAP DE FAUGÈRES 2006
Red | 2011 up to 2013   86
Fat, dense, and suave like other wines of Faugères, but accessible earlier.

SAINT-ÉMILION GRAND CRU 2006
Red | 2011 up to 2013   89
Tasted in the middle of its élevage, this deeply colored wine shows notes of prunes and is developing a full-bodied and silky texture and a wonderful generosity. Very promising.

SAINT-ÉMILION GRAND CRU 2005
Red | 2011 up to 2015   90
Deep color, jammy red-fruit nose: this is a generous and intense wine, full and silky.

SAINT-ÉMILION GRAND CRU 2004
Red | 2011 up to 2013   90
A fat, round, harmonious wine, with perfectly ripe and elegant tannins, which is far from the norm in this vintage. Long and pleasing.

SAINT-ÉMILION GRAND CRU 2003
Red | 2011 up to 2015   **91**
This is very deeply colored, with notes of roasted coffee, a rich and fat body, generous tannins, and a full, fruit-filled palate. Wonderful acidity on the finish. Well done.

SAINT-ÉMILION GRAND CRU 2002
Red | 2011 up to 2013   **88**
A lovely, rich, and generous wine, with a chocolaty bouquet and elegant tannins, this feels broad and full.

SAINT-ÉMILION GRAND CRU 2001
Red | 2011 up to 2015   **89**
A round, supple, and deep wine, with a soft tannic structure.

SAINT-ÉMILION GRAND CRU 2000
Red | 2011 up to 2013   **88**
An ample and generous character, blackberry jam on the nose, a rich body, average acidity: a modern and savory wine, but without a true terroir identity.

SAINT-ÉMILION GRAND CRU 1999
Red | 2011 up to 2013   **86**
Rich, generous, and quite straightforward with notes of cooked fruit.

SAINT-ÉMILION GRAND CRU 1998
Red | 2011 up to 2013   **90**
The best vintage by far in this transitional period around the millennium: ample, spicy, and very full-bodied, but with balance and acidity.

SAINT-ÉMILION GRAND CRU
PÉBY-FAUGÈRES 2006
Red | 2012 up to 2017   **88**
Ultrarich, overpowering, creamy, unquestionably heavy, but intense.

SAINT-ÉMILION GRAND CRU
PÉBY-FAUGÈRES 2005
Red | 2011 up to 2020   **91**
Much better balanced than the previous vintage, this cuvée always has an impressively rich constitution and intensity. The lack of freshness noted in the prebottling tastings has now disappeared.

SAINT-ÉMILION GRAND CRU
PÉBY-FAUGÈRES 2004
Red | 2011 up to 2015   **86**
The wine is very powerful, intensely colored, dense and extracted, but here also the classic cuvée seems to be more balanced and harmonious.

SAINT-ÉMILION GRAND CRU
PÉBY-FAUGÈRES 2003
Red | 2011 up to 2015   **90**
An ample and generous wine, very rich and broad with black fruit flavors. It is so intense it gives the impression of sweetness, but also offers a nice richness and concentration in the mouth, though slightly lacking in finesse.

SAINT-ÉMILION GRAND CRU
PÉBY-FAUGÈRES 2002
Red | 2011 up to 2013   **92**
Deep color, noble oak, very elegant, fine tannins: this is well made in a grand style that is unctuous and profound.

SAINT-ÉMILION GRAND CRU
PÉBY-FAUGÈRES 2001
Red | 2011 up to 2020   **90**
The wine exudes a powerful constitution, a richness of fruit, and imposing oak that is just now beginning to mellow.

SAINT-ÉMILION GRAND CRU
PÉBY-FAUGÈRES 2000
Red | 2011 up to 2016   **88**
Gutsy wine, spicy and rich, lacking, unfortunately, acidity on the finish.

SAINT-ÉMILION GRAND CRU
PÉBY-FAUGÈRES 1999
Red | 2011 up to 2014   **88**
Structured, dense and tight, lacking in aromatic vibrancy, like many 1999s.

SAINT-ÉMILION GRAND CRU
PÉBY-FAUGÈRES 1998
Red | 2011 up to 2016   **91**
Without a hint of fatigue, this elegant and profound wine has both vitality and character. A wonderful wine.

Red: 197.7 acres; cabernet franc 10%, cabernet sauvignon 5%, merlot 85%. **Annual production:** 200,000 bottles

CHÂTEAU FEYTIT-CLINET

33500 Pomerol
Phone 00 33 5 57 25 51 27
Fax 00 33 5 57 25 93 97
jeremy.chasseuil@orange.fr

This admirably located estate, a neighbor to Trotanoy, emerged from almost total obscurity in the late 1990s when the Chasseuil family severed their rental agreement with a Libourne négociant and regained control of their magnificent terroir. Jérémy Chasseuil was free to refine the growing practices, since then producing sleek, slender Pomerols that contrast sharply with the invariably boring offerings of the past. The wines are deep and very distinguished, with none of that heaviness on the nose or body that we see in too many Pomerols. Good aging potential, too.

Recently tasted
POMEROL 2006
Red | 2012 up to 2017   91

Older vintages
POMEROL 2005
Red | 2012 up to 2025   93
Deep, elegant, distinguished, and graceful: the wine is intensely built, with tightly wound and delicate tannins, nice length, and intense flavors. This is the most successful vintage from the winery.

POMEROL 2004
Red | 2011 up to 2014   91
A beautiful wine in this vintage, which is often just average in the region: richly flavored, fat, refined and complete, pretty, with racy length on the palate.

POMEROL 2001
Red | 2011 up to 2015   88
A full-bodied, robust wine, solid and smooth, more straightforward than complex, but sincere and with depth.

POMEROL 2000
Red | 2011 up to 2020   92
This wine, quite harmonious in the nose, is on par with the best wines of the area in its generosity and harmony.

Red: 15.7 acres; cabernet franc 10%, merlot 90%.
Annual production: 30,000 bottles

CHÂTEAU FIGEAC

33330 Saint-Émilion
Phone 00 33 5 57 24 72 26
Fax 00 33 5 57 74 45 74
château-figeac@château-figeac.com
www.château-figeac.com

Château Figeac comes from the gravelly plateau bordering Pomerol and is often referred to as the most Médoc-like of all the Saint-Émilions because cabernet franc and cabernet sauvignon make up two-thirds of the blend. It's true that the wine is honest, direct, slender, and fresh—a rather unfashionable profile these days and in sharp contrast with the rounded power of so many of the Right Bank wines. In the 1980s, Figeac's character was on the thin side, but since 1995 it has showed renewed vigor, with that particular freshness and balance that are surely the first qualities one looks for in a great Bordeaux. Thierry Manoncourt, the dedicated owner of the property, whose first vintage was 1949, died in 2010.

Recently tasted
SAINT-ÉMILION GRAND CRU 2007
Red | 2012 up to 2022   91

Older vintages
SAINT-ÉMILION GRAND CRU 2006
Red | 2015 up to 2025   91
A full, rich wine with a refined and ample texture, this is seductive in its freshness and velvety finish.

SAINT-ÉMILION GRAND CRU 2005
Red | 2011 up to 2022   93
This wine tastes better now that it is in bottle than it was in barrel: it is fat and elegant with nice volume, aristocratically forthright.

SAINT-ÉMILION GRAND CRU 2004
Red | 2011 up to 2015   88
Endowed with more harmonious fruit, this is a tender Figeac, with nice length.

SAINT-ÉMILION GRAND CRU 2003
Red | 2011 up to 2020   91
Quite firm, with notes of ripe peppers on the nose, the wine is developing unquestionable distinction, great length, finesse, and aristocratic tannins. It needs time.

SAINT-ÉMILION GRAND CRU 2002
Red 2011 up to 2015   90
Loaded with class and wonderfully bright aromatics, this is a wine with elegant tannins, confirming its superiority with excellent balance and acidity.

SAINT-ÉMILION GRAND CRU 2001
Red | 2011 up to 2025   **94**

The wine is impressive for its finesse and texture, its wonderfully elegant palate, its noble, truffle-laced tannins, and its harmonious length.

SAINT-ÉMILION GRAND CRU 2000
Red | 2011 up to 2025   **92**

This wine has currently entered into an austere phase, though it has a balance and distinction that should allow it to age well.

SAINT-ÉMILION GRAND CRU 1999
Red | 2011 up to 2016   **91**

An elegant and fresh wine, meaty and earthy without being common, this has distinguished length, a full body, and freshness on the palate.

SAINT-ÉMILION GRAND CRU 1998
Red | 2011 up to 2025   **98**

The best Figeac in recent memory, and one of the greatest wines of the vintage: this is an amazingly complete wine, elegant and muscular, distinguished, classy, and vigorous, with superb style and energy.

Red: 98.8 acres; cabernet franc 35%, cabernet sauvignon 35%, merlot 30%. **Annual production:** 120,000 bottles

CHÂTEAU FLEUR CARDINALE

Le Thibaud
33330 Saint-Étienne-de-Lisse
Phone 00 33 5 57 40 14 05
Fax 00 33 5 57 40 28 62
fleurcardinale@wanadoo.fr
www.château-fleurcardinale.com

The Asseo family did a lot to refine the style of wine from this lovely hillside cru close to Castillon—then found some buyers as committed, hardworking, and passionate about quality as they were themselves. New owners the Decoster family are even more strict about viticulture and work closely with Jean-Luc Thunevin (Fleur Cardinale and Valandraud are close neighbors). The wine today expresses all the potential of these exceptionally rich soils where the vines ripen later than in the heart of the appellation. It's high time this region was known for more than simply producing the blending wines used by Libourne négociants to flesh out those that are more famous but too lightweight.

Recently tasted
SAINT-ÉMILION GRAND CRU 2007
Red | 2012 up to 2017   **90**

SAINT-ÉMILION GRAND CRU 2006
Red | 2012 up to 2017   **90**

Older vintages
SAINT-ÉMILION GRAND CRU 2005
Red | 2011 up to 2019   **91**

The natural qualities of this vintage serve this growth well. Showing very pretty fruit, this is a rich, generous, and long wine. Certainly one of the best of Saint-Émilion.

SAINT-ÉMILION GRAND CRU 2004
Red | 2011 up to 2013   **86**

Very deep and bright in color, this has very apparent oak and a rich, ample palate, but the ripeness of both the fruit and the tannins isn't optimal for a wine made in such an ambitious style.

SAINT-ÉMILION GRAND CRU 2003
Red | 2011 up to 2015   **92**

Delicate, long, and complex with superbly elegant tannins and long fruit flavors in the mouth, this has marvelous style. Marvelous wine!

SAINT-ÉMILION GRAND CRU 2002
Red | 2011 up to 2013   **87**

Gracefully fruited with elegant tannins, this is a delicate, easygoing wine to drink now.

Red: 45.7 acres; cabernet franc 15%, cabernet sauvignon 15%, merlot 70%. **Annual production:** 70,000 bottles

CHÂTEAU LA FLEUR D'ARTHUS

La Grave
33330 Vignonet
Phone 00 33 6 08 49 18 11
Fax 00 33 5 57 84 61 76
fleurdarthus@orange.fr
www.fleurdarthus.fr

Who would have thought that the village of Vignonet, tucked away at the back of the Saint-Émilion plain on the banks of the Dordogne, would one day produce such great wines? Kudos to Grand Cru fanatic and tasting supremo Jean-Denis Salvert for his excellent choice of parcels, all with perfect exposure and drainage, and a top-notch vineyard management worthy of the cult vineyards on the hillsides. Congratulations in particular for getting the most out of the aging process by delaying bottling until the wine is in its prime.

Recently tasted
SAINT-ÉMILION GRAND CRU 2007
Red | 2012 up to 2017   86

Older vintages
SAINT-ÉMILION GRAND CRU 2006
Red | 2012 up to 2017   88
Deeply colored, fat, supple, and silky, definitely promising.

SAINT-ÉMILION GRAND CRU 2005
Red | 2011 up to 2017   91
Wonderfully deep color, pure and clean fruit, silky tannins from the oak aging, magnificent length. Another smashing success.

SAINT-ÉMILION GRAND CRU 2004
Red | 2011 up to 2019   93
One of the great wines of the vintage, with a richness and tension that many Premiers Grands Crus Classés of the appellation were not able to obtain. Noble tannins, great potential; a wine to be decanted two hours in advance.

SAINT-ÉMILION GRAND CRU 2002
Red | 2011 up to 2013   89
The deep color and profound nose reveal a concentrated palate, dense, generous, and tightly wound, with elegant tannins and nice length.

Red: 9.8 acres; merlot 100%. **Annual production:** 16,000 bottles

CHÂTEAU LA FLEUR DE BOÜARD

33500 Pomerol
Phone 00 33 5 57 25 25 13
Fax 00 33 5 57 51 65 14
contact@lafleurdebouard.com
www.lafleurdebouard.com

Acquired by Hubert de Boüard in 1998, this Lalande de Pomerol estate relies on fruit from two mainstay plots, one planted in gravel soils, the other in sand and clay. Since the very first vintage, these have yielded generous, very deep wines with exceptionally refined tannins and concentration unmatched by any other Lalande. All the recent vintages of La Fleur de Boüard rank as very good Pomerols indeed. Le Plus, sourced from gravel soils, is Hubert de Boüard's very ambitious offering—what he calls an OVNI (French for UFO, altered here to mean "unidentified vinified object"), which is matured for thirty-three months in new oak.

Recently tasted
LALANDE DE POMEROL 2007
Red | 2011 up to 2015   90

Older vintages
LALANDE DE POMEROL 2006
Red | 2011 up to 2016   90
Tasted the day it was bottled, the wine didn't suffer at all: it showed a delicate and tender nose, and a palate that was fruity, floral, spicy, and wonderfully harmonious, with fine tannins, pure fruit, and a long, fresh finish.

LALANDE DE POMEROL 2005
Red | 2011 up to 2015   91
Elegant, long, and refined. With this vintage, La Fleur de Boüard has achieved more noble clarity.

LALANDE DE POMEROL 2004
Red | 2011 up to 2015   90
A suprisingly velvety texture, ultra-precise aromatic definition, ultra-harmonious tannins, nice length. Expertly made.

LALANDE DE POMEROL 2003
Red | 2011 up to 2015   91
Deep color, elegant fruit and tannins, length and freshness, elegant and distinguished. In line with the other great wines of the growth.

LALANDE DE POMEROL 2002
Red | 2011 up to 2013   91
An impressive success: this has the sort of balance and intensity found only in the best wines, especially in a difficult vintage. The wine is generous and graceful.

LALANDE DE POMEROL 2001
Red | 2011 up to 2015   91
Very deep, this is a wine with wonderfully
flavorful fruit, nicely balanced on the palate.

LALANDE DE POMEROL
LE PLUS DE LA FLEUR DE BOÜARD 2005
Red | 2011 up to 2018   93
Quite naturally, considering its name, this
cuvée has even more power and depth than
La Fleur.

LALANDE DE POMEROL
LE PLUS DE LA FLEUR DE BOÜARD 2004
Red | 2011 up to 2017   91
Remaining faithful to its name, this is more
intense than the "regular" cuvée from the
property. It is suave and long, with wonderful body and splendidly fine-grained tannins.

Red: 49.8 acres; cabernet franc 15%, cabernet
sauvignon 5%, merlot 80%. Annual production:
70,000 bottles

CHÂTEAU LA FLEUR-PÉTRUS
🍷 🍷 🍷 🍷 🍷

33500 Pomerol
Phone 00 33 5 57 51 78 96
Fax 00 33 5 57 51 79 79
info@jpmoueix.com
www.moueix.com

La Fleur-Pétrus enjoys a very favorable
location in the clayey belt of the Pomerol
plateau. Like Pétrus itself (but not Château
Lafleur!), this estate is part of the Moueix
holdings and is managed by Jean-Claude
Berrouet. The wine is less immediately
expansive than most of the Pomerols bottled under the Moueix label and needs
time to reveal its classy, truffle character
and elegant but taut length.

Recently tasted
POMEROL 2006
Red | 2012 up to 2018   91

Older vintages
POMEROL 2005
Red | 2011 up to 2018   91
Without being overpowering, the 2005
seduces with its distinguished elegance and
length, elevated by a bouquet of fresh and
delicate fruit. The ensemble is long and persistent.

POMEROL 2004
Red | 2011 up to 2013   88
The fruit is tender and the body elegant, but
the tannins, with a slight vegetal note, don't
have the same suppleness of the following
vintage.

POMEROL 2001
Red | 2011 up to 2015   91
With its silky body and restrained tannins,
this is a perfectly vinified wine.

POMEROL 2000
Red | 2011 up to 2018   92
A magnificently structured wine, powerful
and harmonious at the same time, with perfectly integrated tannins.

Red: 33.2 acres; cabernet franc 15%, merlot 85%.
Annual production: 40,000 bottles

CHÂTEAU FOMBRAUGE

33330 Saint-Christophe-des-Bardes
Phone 00 33 5 57 24 77 12
Fax 00 33 5 57 24 66 95
château@fombrauge.com
www.fombrauge.com

This large estate to the northeast of Saint-Émilion has improved enormously since it was acquired by Bernard Magrez at the turn of the millennium. After years of generous but rustic performance, no one could have guessed that Château Fombrauge had such potential for class and balance. The wine is full, delicious, and impeccably matured, impressively built, and exceptionally harmonious. The estate takes even greater care (in vineyard and winery alike) with its single-parcel Magrez-Fombrauge: a richer, more powerful wine than the "ordinary" Fombrauge, with those same superbly refined tannins but not, we think, the same delicious balance.

Recently tasted

SAINT-ÉMILION GRAND CRU 2007
Red | 2012 up to 2017   89

SAINT-ÉMILION GRAND CRU
MAGREZ-FOMBRAUGE 2007
Red | 2013 up to 2020   90

Older vintages

BORDEAUX 2005
White | 2011 up to 2015   90
This white wine is more than a curiosity: it is ample and perfumed, perfectly aged, with substance and breadth that develop perfectly on the palate, thanks to the bright acidity throughout.

SAINT-ÉMILION GRAND CRU 2006
Red | 2012 up to 2017   90
Deeply colored, supple with nice ripe tannins, substance, and black fruit, this has a pleasant balance and immediately seductive flavors.

SAINT-ÉMILION GRAND CRU 2005
Red | 2011 up to 2015   88
The wine is very dark in color, fruity, and richly oaked, with nice volume that melts in your mouth, a fat and silky body, and a harmonious finish.

SAINT-ÉMILION GRAND CRU 2004
Red | 2011 up to 2013   88
This wine is more basic than Magrez-Fombrage, but is also better balanced and fresh: dark color, dense, suave, and silky, made in a modern and flavorful style.

SAINT-ÉMILION GRAND CRU 2003
Red | 2011 up to 2013   90
Dark color, roasted coffee and truffle scents, succulent, long and indulgent, very generous, pleasurable length. Immediately enjoyable.

SAINT-ÉMILION GRAND CRU 2002
Red | 2011 up to 2013   90
Impressive style: the wine is opaque and deep, with high-quality oak, concentrated fruit, and a rich, ample body with fantastic volume.

SAINT-ÉMILION GRAND CRU 2001
Red | 2011 up to 2020   89
A wine with an unctuous and ripe body, highlighted by a smooth, tannic structure.

SAINT-ÉMILION GRAND CRU
MAGREZ-FOMBRAUGE 2005
Red | 2011 up to 2018   86
The same observations as for the 2004, with still quite obvious oak and a finish that is, at this point, overpowering.

SAINT-ÉMILION GRAND CRU
MAGREZ-FOMBRAUGE 2004
Red | 2011 up to 2015   87
Rich and intensely colored, this combines ripe fruit and toasty oak. On the palate, the wine is amazingly rich and made in a resolutely hedonistic style, with an imposing structure, an oaky character, and very exotic notes on the finish, but it lacks acidity.

Red: 133.4 acres; cabernet franc 14%, cabernet sauvignon 9%, merlot 77%. White: 4.9 acres. Annual production: 160,000 bottles

CHÂTEAU FONPLÉGADE

33330 Saint-Émilion
Phone 00 33 5 57 74 43 11
Fax 00 33 5 57 74 44 67
karine.queron@fonplegade.fr
adamsfrenchvineyards.fr

Fonplégade, just above Canon-la-Gaffelière, belonged to Armand Moueix from 1953 until his death in 1999. Since then, the estate has been acquired by American banker Steve Adams, who has reportedly spent a small fortune on restoring this château's reputation. His efforts are sure to be rewarded, given Fonplégade's prime location right on the hill of Saint-Émilion. The year 2004 marked a distinct change in style that has been confirmed by every vintage since. If properly worked, this terroir could plainly win Fonplégade a place in that elite club of great Saint-Émilions.

Recently tasted
SAINT-ÉMILION GRAND CRU 2007
Red | 2012 up to 2019　　　　　　　91

Older vintages
SAINT-ÉMILION GRAND CRU 2006
Red | 2011 up to 2018　　　　　　　91
A rich and fat wine with a very fruity, modern nose, this is endowed with tannins that are imminently more elegant than in previous vintages, which bring both a silky texture and a long finish to the wine, more fresh than heavy.

SAINT-ÉMILION GRAND CRU 2005
Red | 2011 up to 2019　　　　　　　89
The wine is powerful and richly structured, with enrobed tannins and an aromatic palette that combines toasty oak and black fruit. The finish is complex, even if the finesse of the terroir is not yet apparent.

SAINT-ÉMILION GRAND CRU 2004
Red | 2011 up to 2015　　　　　　　88
A seductive and well-made wine with good volume, this was nicely vinified. Delicate tannins make for a soft, elegant wine.

Red: 44.5 acres; cabernet franc 7%, cabernet sauvignon 2%, merlot 91%. **Annual production:** 40,000 bottles

CHÂTEAU FONTENIL

33141 Saillans
Phone 00 33 5 57 51 23 05
Fax 00 33 5 57 51 66 08
rolland.vignobles@wanadoo.fr
www.rollandcollection.com

Dany and Michel Rolland bought this property in 1986 and made it their primary residence. Merlot thrives on these clayey slopes, allowing the Rollands to refine that generous, luscious style that has become their trademark throughout the world. Their performance here is as professional and rigorous as ever. The wines are well structured, concentrated, and fleshy, with an expressive array of pretty red-fruit flavors and toasty aromas; drink within two to three years of the vintage date. Recent bottlings, like so many of the regional wines, are more refined than in the past.

FRONSAC 2006
Red | 2011 up to 2016　　　　　　　91
Rich and simultaneously full of vitality, this is a deep and flavorful wine, suberbly made. Perfect balance.

FRONSAC 2005
Red | 2011 up to 2016　　　　　　　91
This is one of the best vintages at Fontenil, with hints of black truffle, rich and generous. It is entering into a closed phase, but be patient and don't worry: this is an indisputable success.

FRONSAC 2004
Red | 2011 up to 2013　　　　　　　90
Ready to drink now: creamy, harmonious, and truffly, a nice, flavorful, and complete wine.

FRONSAC 2003
Red | 2011 up to 2015　　　　　　　90
Nice substance: full and velvety volume, great aromatic presence, subtle notes of black truffle and spice, long and persistent.

Red: 22.2 acres; cabernet sauvignon 10%, merlot 90%. **Annual production:** 45,000 bottles

CLOS FOURTET

🏅 🏅 🏅 🏅 🏅

33330 Saint-Émilion
Phone 00 33 5 57 24 70 90
Fax 00 33 5 57 74 46 52
closfourtet@closfourtet.com
www.closfourtet.com

This small but attractive winery is easy to spot when you visit Saint-Émilion: it faces the church on the spectacular limestone plateau that extends beyond the hill. Having belonged to the Lurton family for generations, the Clos Fourtet was acquired in 2001 by Parisian businessman Philippe Cuvelier, who undertook to restore this cru to greatness, a process that continues today. Recent vintages show more precise tannins and longer length, while remaining immediately seductive and complete as young wines and as ineffably classy as ever.

Recently tasted
SAINT-ÉMILION GRAND CRU 2007
Red | 2012 up to 2020   **88**

Older vintages
SAINT-ÉMILION GRAND CRU 2006
Red | 2012 up to 2018   **90**
Tasted a few months before bottling, the wine seems very promising: deep color, full, linear, very refined, brilliant length, pure fruit.

SAINT-ÉMILION GRAND CRU 2005
Red | 2011 up to 2020   **92**
Intense color; bright, lively fruit; long, nice silky volume, with lots of character.

SAINT-ÉMILION GRAND CRU 2004
Red | 2011 up to 2015   **87**
With a toasty nose, rich attack, nice tannins, and ripe fruit, the structure is a bit soft, but there's generous volume.

SAINT-ÉMILION GRAND CRU 2003
Red | 2011 up to 2015   **90**
The tannins aren't the most elegant of the First Growths, and the alcohol is more present, but the wine is generous, succulent, and devilishly seductive.

SAINT-ÉMILION GRAND CRU 2002
Red | 2011 up to 2014   **86**
Very full-bodied and perfectly vinified in a modern style, though lacking that touch of acidity that would place it among the great wines of the appellation.

SAINT-ÉMILION GRAND CRU 2001
Red | 2011 up to 2014   **87**
This vintage, the first under the direction of the new owners, is quite a success, showing perfectly ripe fruit and finishing with restrained definition.

SAINT-ÉMILION GRAND CRU 2000
Red | 2011 up to 2020   **91**
A rich, unctuous and seductive wine, this is missing the precision and the structure of previous vintages, but it is quite tasty.

SAINT-ÉMILION GRAND CRU 1999
Red | 2011 up to 2015   **90**
Round, rich, medium body, but with lots of length, this is savory and fruity, with fine tannins.

SAINT-ÉMILION GRAND CRU 1998
Red | 2011 up to 2015   **89**
Fresh, floral, refined, not super-dense for the vintage.

Red: 49.4 acres; cabernet franc 5%, cabernet sauvignon 10%, merlot 85%. Annual production: 80,000 bottles

CHÂTEAU LA GAFFELIÈRE

BP 65
33330 Saint-Émilion
Phone 00 33 5 57 24 72 15
Fax 00 33 5 57 24 69 06
contact@château-la-gaffeliere.com
www.château-la-gaffeliere.com

Château La Gaffelière is a very pretty estate at the southern entrance to the village of Saint-Émilion. Owned by the Malet Roquefort family, La Gaffelière boasts ideally exposed vineyards that are the western equivalent of those of Château Pavie. Unlike its neighbor, however, La Gaffelière has never gone in for overly powerful, forward fruit. It looks instead to produce palpably generous, luscious wines with thoroughbred character and a balance that is unfailingly classical—freshness and harmony to the fore. The vintages from the past decade are better than ever: faithfully styled but showing much more intensity and promise.

SAINT-ÉMILION GRAND CRU 2007
Red | 2012 up to 2020   **89**
Deep garnet color, bright nose of black cherry; the palate is round and ample, but the wine hasn't yet revealed its full potential.

SAINT-ÉMILION GRAND CRU 2006
Red | 2012 up to 2018   **88**
Suave and supple, elegant and long, this is minerally but less concentrated than other Premier Crus of the vintage.

SAINT-ÉMILION GRAND CRU 2005
Red | 2011 up to 2020   **92**
Intensely colored, wonderful texture, a wonderfully intense and expressive wine, with lots of character, black fruit, tropical fruit, and roasted coffee, deep and soulful.

SAINT-ÉMILION GRAND CRU 2002
Red | 2011 up to 2014   **88**
Light, fruity nose, soft on the palate, delicate and fresh, round on the finish.

SAINT-ÉMILION LÉO DE LA GAFFELIÈRE 2006
Red | 2011 up to 2017   **86**
Soft and enjoyable, immediately drinkable.

Red: 54.4 acres; cabernet franc 15%, cabernet sauvignon 5%, merlot 80%. **Annual production:** 55,000 bottles

CHÂTEAU LE GAY

33500 Pomerol
Phone 00 33 5 57 25 34 34
Fax 00 33 5 57 25 56 45

This estate boasts one of the finest terroirs on the northern part of the Pomerol plateau and was for many years owned by the same family as Lafleur but never enjoyed the same level of care and expertise. It is now starting to realize its potential under new owner Catherine Péré-Vergé and consultant winemaker Michel Rolland. Innovations include a very handsome, purpose-built cellar and a policy of detailed attention to vineyard management. Since buying Le Gay in 2003, Catherine Péré-Vergé has poured all her energies into producing statuesque wines with a lot of class and impeccable definition. She is also currently resurrecting another legendary Pomerol estate, La Violette (whose first vintage, the 2006, is said to be a stunning success). A brilliant first effort from a lady who gambled and won!

Recently tasted
POMEROL 2007
Red | 2012 up to 2022   **93**

Older vintages
POMEROL 2006
Red | 2012 up to 2020   **92**
Very round and seductive with hints of rose and a velvety quality, this is a linear wine, long and intense.

POMEROL 2005
Red | 2012 up to 2020   **93**
A truly great wine, deep, silky, and rich, brightly structured with great intensity in the mouth.

POMEROL 2004
Red | 2011 up to 2014   **90**
Beautifully deep color, noble, integrated oak, suave, and elegant, an indisputable triumph.

POMEROL MANOIR DE GAY 2006
Red | 2011 up to 2018   **86**
Supple and elegant body, currently a bit overshadowed by the oak.

POMEROL MANOIR DE GAY 2005
Red | 2011 up to 2018   **88**
This has very fresh fruit and a supple constitution not lacking in depth, truly characteristic of this second wine. A very well-made cuvée.

Red: 79.1 acres; cabernet franc 7%, cabernet sauvignon 3%, merlot 90%. **Annual production:** 10,000 bottles

CHÂTEAU GAZIN

Le Gazin
33500 Pomerol
Phone 00 33 5 57 51 07 05
Fax 00 33 5 57 51 69 96
contact@gazin.com
www.gazin.com

Château Gazin boasts a large and lovely vineyard in prime Pomerol country—so large, in fact, that it ranks as something of a giant compared with most of the other famous Pomerol crus. This estate has improved considerably over the past twenty years, rising to become one of the great names in Pomerol thanks to stringent grape selection and vineyard practice. Gazin is not an opulent style of Pomerol but is supple and fresh with very elegant aromas and no trace of heaviness whatsoever.

Recently tasted
POMEROL 2007
Red | 2012 up to 2017   89

POMEROL 2006
Red | 2012 up to 2017   92

Older vintages
POMEROL 2005
Red | 2012 up to 2022   93
A wine with splendid color, distinguished and elegant length, and true freshness. Ultra-refined wine, with an artistic touch.

POMEROL 2004
Red | 2011 up to 2018   88
In a supple and elegant tone, this 2004 opens up with softness, if not intensity.

POMEROL 2001
Red | 2011 up to 2018   90
A wonderfully complex and expressive bouquet; a robust and full body, with generous notes of black truffle. A beautiful wine, full of personality.

POMEROL L'HOSPITALET DE GAZIN 2006
Red | 2011 up to 2016   87
Beautiful composition, succulent and complete, with nice freshness, precise fruit, elegant tannins. A true success; the winery should be proud.

Red: 56.8 acres; cabernet franc 3%, cabernet sauvignon 7%, merlot 90%. Annual production: 100,000 bottles

GIROLATE

Le Touyre
33420 Naujan-et-Postiac
Phone 00 33 5 57 84 55 08
Fax 00 33 5 57 84 57 31
contact@despagne.fr
www.despagne.fr

The Despagnes are not the sort of people to rest on their laurels—a dynasty wholly committed to wine for nearly 250 years. The present generation includes no less than four enologists and one agronomical engineer! The estate certainly offers plenty of scope for creativity: 750 acres planted to traditional Bordeaux varietals. The latest discovery is the Girolate cuvée: no tanks, no pumps, just one single container (the barrel) all the way to the point of bottling. The result is an extraordinary, ultra-sweet, and perfumed wine that definitely smacks of tomorrow's grand vin. The other wines are a more traditional take on good Bordeaux, but very tasty nonetheless.

BORDEAUX GIROLATE 2006
Red | 2011 up to 2013   88
For those who love dense wines. This is in a true Girolate style, with a delicately jammy and spicy nose, a warm and voluptuous mouthfeel, ripe tannins, and perfectly integrated oak. Great aging potential.

BORDEAUX GIROLATE 2005
Red | 2011 up to 2013   88
Black color. Strong notes of ripe fruit and intense oak introduce the nose. Wonderfully rich on the palate with extremely ripe and velvety tannins, nice fruit, and good follow-through. A pleasingly seductive wine, although one glass is enough.

BORDEAUX GIROLATE 2003
Red | 2011 up to 2013   87
Dark, dense, purple color; strong notes of black fruit, spice, and toasty oak on the nose; rich in the mouth, warm with lots of fruit and still-firm tannins, but with nice length. Good aging potential.

Red: 24.7 acres; merlot 100%. Annual production: 22,000 bottles

CHÂTEAU LA GOMERIE

Château Beauséjour-Bécot
33330 Saint-Émilion
Phone 00 33 5 57 74 46 87
Fax 00 33 5 57 24 66 88
contact@beausejour-becot.com
www.beausejour-becot.com

This tiny cru of just over six acres was purchased in the 1990s by the Bécot family, who are making wine in an ambitious style, using 100 percent merlot. The vineyards are divided into two plots, one at the foot of the hillside in very old sandy soils, the other contiguous to Beauséjour-Bécot, on a limestone plateau. Their vinification style, hedonistic and elegant at the same time, is the same that the Bécot brothers employ at Beauséjour, but the wines here are round, succulent, and focused.

Recently tasted

SAINT-ÉMILION GRAND CRU 2007
Red | 2012 up to 2017   90
Opaque color, powerful; the tannins are a bit harder than in 2006, but the wine is full and deep, with good definition.

SAINT-ÉMILION GRAND CRU 2006
Red | 2012 up to 2017   92
Beautifully deep color, focused fruit, and elegant toast, expansive on the palate, good structure, but with rounded tannins, nice harmony, deep and persistent.

Older vintages

SAINT-ÉMILION GRAND CRU 2005
Red | 2011 up to 2020   91
Deep color, smooth and refined, elegant tannins, nice velvety length, and pretty notes of red and black fruit.

SAINT-ÉMILION GRAND CRU 2004
Red | 2011 up to 2015   88
This wine is powerful, extracted, with good substance, but a bit overdone when compared to Beauséjour-Bécot.

Red: 6.22 acres; merlot 100%. **Annual production:** 12,000 bottles

CHÂTEAU GRAND CORBIN-DESPAGNE

33330 Saint-Émilion
Phone 00 33 5 57 51 08 38
Fax 00 33 5 57 51 29 18
f-despagne@grand-corbin-despagne.com
www.grand-corbin-despagne.com

This cru has belonged to the Despagne family for years and ranks as one of the most dependable Saint-Émilion producers on the Pomerol plateau. In the 1980s and early 1990s, there was something thin and anodyne about many of these wines, which brought about the estate's demotion in 1996 followed by a much-needed restructuring. It has shaped up nicely since, now producing very full and harmonious wines: well balanced, often quite austere when young, though they mellow out after four to five years' cellaring.

Recently tasted

SAINT-ÉMILION GRAND CRU 2007
Red | 2012 up to 2018   89

Older vintages

SAINT-ÉMILION GRAND CRU 2006
Red | 2012 up to 2018   89
Remarkable wine of elegant dimensions, good élevage. Profound, with pure fruit expression.

SAINT-ÉMILION GRAND CRU 2005
Red | 2011 up to 2015   88
Beautifully svelte volume, streamlined and balanced. The tannins are a bit rigid, but the wine has potential as well as density.

SAINT-ÉMILION GRAND CRU 2004
Red | 2011 up to 2013   87
Intensely colored, the wine seems serious and well made, quite long, fairly acidic, but with body.

SAINT-ÉMILION GRAND CRU 2003
Red | 2011 up to 2013   86
Powerful but quite simple, this is rich in ripe fruit and fat tannins.

SAINT-ÉMILION GRAND CRU 2002
Red | 2011 up to 2013   87
A good Saint-Émilion made in a classic style: pleasantly balanced and fleshy, with nice acidity and clean fruit.

Red: 66.2 acres; cabernet franc 24%, cabernet sauvignon 1%, merlot 75%. **Annual production:** 85,000 bottles

CHÂTEAU GRAND-MAYNE

33330 Saint-Émilion
Phone 00 33 5 57 74 42 50
Fax 00 33 5 57 74 41 89
grand-mayne@grand-mayne.com
www.grand-mayne.com

Château Grand-Mayne is the heart of an ancient winegrowing estate that had already made a name for itself by the six-teenth century. Since the turn of the millennium, Grand-Mayne has been run by Marie-Françoise Nony and her sons. Their wines recapture a style that made this estate successful back in the early 1990s: intense and deep, with a solid tannic structure but no roughness, and lush, fleshy fruit. The latest vintages also benefit from more carefully extracted tannins.

Recently tasted
SAINT-ÉMILION GRAND CRU 2007
Red | 2012 up to 2017   **90**

SAINT-ÉMILION GRAND CRU 2006
Red | 2012 up to 2017   **90**

Older vintages
SAINT-ÉMILION GRAND CRU 2005
Red | 2011 up to 2017   **92**
A deeply colored wine, immediately seduc-tive on both the nose and the palate, savory, hedonistic, and ripe. This is undeniably the best wine produced by this property in the last ten years.

SAINT-ÉMILION GRAND CRU 2004
Red | 2011 up to 2015   **90**
One of the great wines of this difficult vin-tage. Deeply colored, fruity, elegant, refined tannins, distinguished, and long. Wonder-fully fresh on the finish.

SAINT-ÉMILION GRAND CRU 2003
Red | 2011 up to 2015   **89**
A solid and powerful wine, this has tannins that are brusquer than in other vintages from the château, but it is full-bodied and sus-tained by alluring aromas of dried plums.

SAINT-ÉMILION GRAND CRU 2002
Red | 2011 up to 2015   **89**
A fresh-fruit character is apparent on the palate of this full, dense, and vibrant wine.

SAINT-ÉMILION GRAND CRU 2000
Red | 2011 up to 2015   **90**
An ample, rich and well-built wine, with still-perceptible fruit and no drying tannins. A beautiful Saint-Émilion that will age well.

Red: 42 acres; cabernet franc 20%, cabernet sauvignon 5%, merlot 75%. Annual production: 55,000 bottles

CHÂTEAU GRAND-PONTET

33330 Saint-Émilion
Phone 00 33 5 57 74 46 88
Fax 00 33 5 57 74 45 31
château.grand-pontet@wanadoo.fr

Château Grand-Pontet lies on the lime-stone plateau to the west of Saint-Émilion, next to Château Beauséjour-Bécot. Well managed by the Bécot brothers, the estate is a dependable producer of lush, fruity, generous wines—though many still display slightly rustic tannins. In average vintages, this estate never disappoints, producing early-developing wines of consistent qual-ity. In great vintages, on the other hand, it invariably misses the mark.

Recently tasted
SAINT-ÉMILION GRAND CRU 2007
Red | 2011 up to 2013   **89**

Older vintages
SAINT-ÉMILION GRAND CRU 2006
Red | 2012 up to 2017   **88**
A rich and powerful wine, generously oaked, this one must be aged. The tannins are unc-tuous.

SAINT-ÉMILION GRAND CRU 2005
Red | 2012 up to 2019   **89**
Deeply colored, elegant fruit, velvety tan-nins, wonderful length, powerful and in-tense. Patience is necessary.

SAINT-ÉMILION GRAND CRU 2004
Red | 2011 up to 2013   **88**
An honorable wine with a pretty color, noble and refined aromas, and freshness on the palate. It is distinguished, with tannins that are elegant but not perfectly smooth, and with serious length.

SAINT-ÉMILION GRAND CRU 2003
Red | 2011 up to 2015   **89**
An ultrarich wine, black in color, expressive with ripe fruit, rich and generous in volume, but lacking a bit of brightness.

SAINT-ÉMILION GRAND CRU 2002
Red | 2011 up to 2013   **87**
Vinous and fat, in a very concentrated aro-matic style, this is a generous wine, but it lacks finesse.

Red: 34.6 acres; cabernet franc 15%, cabernet sauvignon 10%, merlot 75%. Annual production: 50,000 bottles

CHÂTEAU GRAND-VILLAGE

33240 Mouillac
Phone 00 33 5 57 84 44 03
Fax 00 33 5 57 84 83 31

Château Lafleur owners Jacques and Sylvie Guinaudeau also own this estate on the far side of Fronsac. What they produce here is a straightforward Bordeaux, made with the same careful attention to viticulture and winemaking as they apply in their legendary Pomerol property. For some vintages now, Château Grand-Village has been one of the most harmonious of all Bordeaux thanks to its immediately accessible fruit, refined texture, and refreshing balance. The estate also makes a very good white—straightforward, but very honest.

BORDEAUX SUPÉRIEUR 2006
Red | 2011 up to 2013   87
With elegant fruit, intense substance, and a finish that is still a bit angular, this pure, seductive, and lively Bordeaux needs another year in the bottle.

BORDEAUX SUPÉRIEUR 2005
Red | 2011 up to 2013   88
A distinguished, first-class Bordeaux, with unctuous and drawn-out length, splendid aromatic purity, and perfect balance.

BORDEAUX SUPÉRIEUR 2004
Red | 2011 up to 2013   87
The tannins are a bit more austere here than in the vintages immediately preceding and following, but this focused wine is seductive with its elegant fruit and freshness.

BORDEAUX SUPÉRIEUR 2003
Red | 2011 up to 2013   88
Showing a fruity and pure nose, this straightforward, fresh, and pleasing Bordeaux reveals a remarkably precise texture and balance without being heavy or harsh.

CHÂTEAU LES GRANDES MURAILLES

33330 Saint-Émilion
Phone 00 33 5 57 24 71 09
Fax 00 33 5 57 24 69 72
lesgrandesmurailles@wanadoo.fr
www.lesgrandesmurailles.fr

This small vineyard stands at the foot of a famous wall (muraille) now in ruins, on the edge of the village of Saint-Émilion. The wine is as solidly built as its name suggests: impressive in good vintages, with a firm presence on the palate and a powerful but never coarse structure. The estate is owned, like Château Côte de Baleau and the Clos Saint-Martin, by the Reifers family, who for more than a decade now have worked hard to turn this property and the Clos Saint-Martin into real little gems.

Recently tasted
SAINT-ÉMILION GRAND CRU 2007
Red | 2012 up to 2019   89

Older vintages
SAINT-ÉMILION GRAND CRU 2006
Red | 2012 up to 2020   90
This vintage reaffirms the progress that we noted with the previous year: a pure bouquet of small red fruits, a silky and intense body, and wonderfully balanced depth.

SAINT-ÉMILION GRAND CRU 2005
Red | 2011 up to 2018   91
The élevage lives up to its promises with this ample and refined wine, very deep with notes of red fruit. The silkiness of the tannins is brilliant. This is one of the major successes of the growth.

SAINT-ÉMILION GRAND CRU 2003
Red | 2011 up to 2015   88
Powerful wine with expressive aromas of black cherry, this has a ripe and appealing style and a long and generous body that doesn't dry out on the finish.

SAINT-ÉMILION GRAND CRU 2001
Red | 2011 up to 2015   89
This is a wonderful vintage, a powerful wine with a seductive nose and an unctuous body that combines freshness with velvety tannins.

SAINT-ÉMILION GRAND CRU 2000
Red | 2011 up to 2015   90
This has a very rich body with a decidedly truffly finish. The terroir as well as the vintage are expressed with authority.

Red: 4.8 acres. Annual production: 8,000 bottles

CHÂTEAU LA GRAVE-À-POMEROL

33500 Pomerol
Phone 00 33 5 57 51 78 96
Fax 00 33 5 57 51 79 79
info@jpmoueix.com
www.moueix.com

This estate is located at the eastern tip of the Pomerol appellation, planted in the excellent gravel and sand soils typical of this sector. The wines are supple and increasingly deep and, unlike those from the more clayey parts of the appellation, never play on opulence. Formerly known as La Grave–Trigant de Boisset, the estate is owned by the Jean-Pierre Moueix company and has made significant progress over the past ten years.

POMEROL 2006
Red | 2012 up to 2018   86
There's a certain amount of fruit here, but the wine is austere; it needs time.

POMEROL 2005
Red | 2011 up to 2020   88
Subtle notes of black truffle on the nose, lush fruit, fine tannins, a slightly vegetal note, with a deep finish.

POMEROL 2004
Red | 2011 up to 2014   87
A good 2004, soft tannins, and delicate fruit expression, not super-intense, but quite pleasing.

Red: 21.5 acres; cabernet franc 15%, merlot 85%.
Annual production: 36,000 bottles

CHÂTEAU HAUT-CARLES

1, Château de Carles
33141 Saillans
Phone 00 33 5 57 84 32 03
Fax 00 33 5 57 84 31 91
châteaudecarles@free.fr
www.haut-carles.com

This magnificent and historic property has made a dazzling comeback under the direction of its present owners, Constance and Stéphane Droulers, who have established perfectly laid-out vineyards, impeccable viticulture, and brand-new custom-designed, gravity-fed winemaking facilities. The wines have never been so complete and harmonious. The Haut-Carles cuvée accounts for just under half of all the wines produced and is especially praiseworthy: silky tannins make this a wine you can cellar with confidence.

Recently tasted
FRONSAC 2007
Red | 2011 up to 2013   91

Older vintages
FRONSAC 2006
Red | 2011 up to 2016   90
Deep color, luxurious oak, spicy, rich flavor, and a wonderfully silky, deep volume. Great style.

FRONSAC 2005
Red | 2011 up to 2013   90
Wonderfully made, with a silky body and an underlying tannic structure that is intense but focused. Fruity and well made, this is a great wine and a clear success.

FRONSAC 2004
Red | 2011 up to 2013   88
Not heavy or obvious, this wine shows perfectly mastered hedonistic ambition. It is long, structured, and undeniably elegant.

FRONSAC 2003
Red | 2011 up to 2013   89
The wine is still as full and distinguished as it was at the outset, but the tannins are losing their suppleness. It has now entered into a secondary phase, less flattering but still showing depth.

FRONSAC 2001
Red | 2011 up to 2013   91
This wine is quite an achievement; it perfectly blends its elegant texture and silky core with a superbly rich essence that is quite rare.

Red: 49.4 acres; cabernet franc 5%, merlot 95%.
Annual production: 80,000 bottles

CHÂTEAU HOSANNA

33330 Saint-Émilion
Phone 00 33 5 57 74 48 94
Fax 00 33 5 57 74 47 18
info@jpmoueix.com
www.moueix.com

The evocatively named Château Hosanna, formerly part of Certan-Giraud, was rechristened Château Hosanna by the Moueix family in the late 1990s. The wine since then has been sourced from grapes that are grown and vinified in the same spirit as the other Moueix crus. Based on a decade of tasting Château Hosanna, we would describe its character as suave, velvety, and generous—often immediately appealing, more sharply defined than Trotanoy but not as complex as Pétrus.

POMEROL 2006
Red | 2012 up to 2018 **91**
Fruity, floral, slightly vegetal, delicate length, elegant definition, nice persistence on the finish.

POMEROL 2005
Red | 2014 up to 2025 **91**
This wine has shut down and seems tighter than it did during the primeur tastings, but it is undeniably rich and dense, with a very tight and fine tannic structure. It is imperative to age it for at least four years.

POMEROL 2004
Red | 2011 up to 2018 **90**
Developing a slightly chocolaty nose, this Pomerol is unctuous, fat, and round without being at all heavy. Its personality is more seductive than profound.

POMEROL 2001
Red | 2011 up to 2015 **94**
A wonderfully accomplished wine, combining aromatic finesse with an ample body, supple and very precise.

POMEROL 2000
Red | 2011 up to 2020 **92**
This wine plays on elegance and subtlety, with an elegant and ethereal body.

Red: 11.1 acres; cabernet franc 30%, merlot 70%.
Annual production: 18,000 bottles

CHÂTEAU HOSTENS-PICANT

33220 Les Leves et Thoumeyrague
Phone 00 33 5.57.46.54.54
châteauHP@aol.com
www.châteauhostens-picant.fr

Located in the outlying sector of Sainte-Foy-la-Grande, this worthy property has achieved its high level of quality thanks to the hard work of Nadine and Yves Picant, who purchased the winery in 1986. The well-tended vineyards have the classic blend of grape varieties, mostly merlot for the reds, but with equal proportions of sémillon and sauvignon blanc for the whites. The reds have always been intense and robust, but now there is an added softness, and the tannic structure is much more velvety.

Recently tasted
SAINTE-FOY-BORDEAUX 2007
Red | Drink now **88**
Enticing, lots of personality, and very well balanced, the powerful nose reveals notes of blueberry, blackberry, juniper, and spice, a warm, super-aromatic, lively, and fresh mouthfeel.

SAINTE-FOY-BORDEAUX CUVÉE DES DEMOISELLES 2008
White | 2011 up to 2013 **88**
Made in an identical style to that of 2007, this wine has a subtle and complex nose, with nice fruit and minerals, full on the palate with a great minerality, fresh acidity, and length; very well made.

SAINTE-FOY-BORDEAUX CUVÉE DES DEMOISELLES 2007
White | 2011 up to 2013 **88**
Beautiful white wine, quite refined with a powerful nose of honey, minerals, and ripe white fruit. Similar on the palate, it is rich and mouth-filling with concentrated flavors and a long, lively finish.

SAINTE-FOY-BORDEAUX LUCULLUS 2006
Red | 2011 up to 2014 **88**
A complete, harmonious wine, full and elegantly structured. Expressive and flavorful fruit character.

CLOS DES JACOBINS

4 Gomerie
33330 Saint-Émilion
Phone 00 33 5 57 24 70 14
Fax 00 33 5 57 24 68 08
contact@closdesjacobins.com
www.closdesjacobins.com

The Clos des Jacobins enjoys a superb location, overlooking the road from Libourne to
Saint-Émilion. It has changed hands twice
in the past decade, having previously been
a long-standing flagship estate of French
négociant Cordier. At the start of the millennium, it was acquired by French industrialist
Gérard Frydmann, who appointed the very
talented Hubert de Boüard (Château Angélus) as manager. The wine improved tremendously under his guidance; even the
2004 was magnificent. Present owner Bernard Decoster has maintained that lead
since he took over in 2005, making classy
wines without a trace of heaviness.

Recently tasted

SAINT-ÉMILION GRAND CRU 2007
Red | 2012 up to 2019   **90**

SAINT-ÉMILION GRAND CRU
CHÂTEAU LA COMMANDERIE 2007
Red | 2012 up to 2018   **88**

Older vintages

SAINT-ÉMILION GRAND CRU 2006
Red | 2012 up to 2019   **90**
Velvety, generous, and concentrated with
beautifully elegant tannins, this is a modern
and very successful style.

SAINT-ÉMILION GRAND CRU 2005
Red | 2011 up to 2020   **91**
A bright and intense color, nose of raspberries and black fruit with hints of coffee, generous, well-built volume, tannins that are racy
and smooth, a finish of wonderful length.

SAINT-ÉMILION GRAND CRU 2004
Red | 2011 up to 2015   **90**
Wonderful, lively color, notes of coffee and
black truffle, pretty and deep on the palate,
supple but elegant tannins, intense.

SAINT-ÉMILION GRAND CRU 2003
Red | 2011 up to 2015   **89**
Made in a rich and impressive style, this is
black as ink, dense and thick in the mouth,
with a super-ripe aromatic character that
lasts. It develops a wonderfully deep amplitude with a truly silky texture.

Red: 21 acres; cabernet franc 23%, cabernet
sauvignon 2%, merlot 75%. **Annual production:**
40,000 bottles

CHÂTEAU JEAN-FAURE

33330 Saint-Émilion
Phone 00 33 5 57 51 34 86
Fax 00 33 5 57 51 94 59
châteaujeanfaure@wanadoo.fr
www.châteaujeanfaure.com

Château Jean-Faure is admirably situated
on the Pomerol plateau but, due to years of
mismanagement, never really lived up to
its location. Taken over by Olivier Decelle
in 2003, the estate now boasts a fully renovated cellar and uses viticultural methods
as rigorous as those that have made
Decelle famous in the Roussillon (he also
owns the Mas Amiel in Maury).

Recently tasted

SAINT-ÉMILION GRAND CRU 2007
Red | 2012 up to 2017   **90**

Older vintages

SAINT-ÉMILION GRAND CRU 2006
Red | 2011 up to 2017   **89**
Nice color, excellent fruit, supple and fleshy,
round and long.

SAINT-ÉMILION GRAND CRU 2005
Red | 2011 up to 2015   **91**
Unctuous, suave, and fresh, without
aggressiveness, this is very nice to drink,
with very delicate tannins and a generous
personality.

SAINT-ÉMILION GRAND CRU 2004
Red | 2011 up to 2013   **88**
A classy wine. On the finish the tannins simply lack a bit of age.

Red: 44.5 acres; cabernet franc 54%, malbec 6%,
merlot 40%. **Annual production:** 70,000 bottles

CHÂTEAU LAFLEUR

Grand-Village
33240 Mouillac
Phone 00 33 5 57 84 44 03
Fax 00 33 5 57 84 83 31
scea.guinaudeau@orange.fr

Jacques and Sylvie Guinaudeau consider Château Lafleur their garden. They became the outright owners of this micro-vineyard in 2001 after running it for twenty-five years. In this meticulously tended vineyard, every parcel, even those no bigger than half a row, represents a negotiation between specific growing practices and the nature of the soil. Château Lafleur, previously owned by the same family for more than a century, faces Pétrus on a gently undulating hill that is fabulously gravelly at the top but also unusually varied, with some clay and deeper soils in places. The Guinaudeaus have always been passionately interested in these tiny variations and took them into account in 1986 when they created a second wine, Les Pensées de Lafleur, that in practice often rivals the top-ranking Pomerols. Simple vinification showcases the quality of the harvest, producing wines with an impressive, Ausone-like balance and naturalness. Witness the magisterial wines produced in the late 1980s. Production in the early 1990s may have suffered while the vineyards got a much-needed renovation; but all of the wines in the past ten years have measured up to the highest Bordeaux standards.

POMEROL 2006
Red | 2011 up to 2045   97
Exquisitely refined, with a taffeta-like texture, a lavishly fresh bouquet of red fruit, and an incomparable velvety character. This wine meets all expectations, and demonstrates the greatness of the vintage.

POMEROL 2005
Red | 2015 up to 2045   100
Currently, the nose of this wine is much more muted in comparison to its youthful body, which is to be expected. But the depth on the palate, the complexity of flavors, the silky texture, the fullness, the freshness and overall harmony are extraordinary.

POMEROL 2004
Red | 2012 up to 2030   92
This wine is clearly more reserved and austere than any other recent vintage from this domaine, but the tight tannins have a lot of finesse and the length is there. We need to be patient.

POMEROL 2003
Red | 2011 up to 2023   98
With an enchantingly floral nose with hints of raspberry, this is rich and delectable, with good acidity, harmony, and a wonderful balance. It's far from showing the heat of the vintage.

POMEROL 2001
Red | 2011 up to 2030   96
The nose explodes after a little aeration; the texture is supremely elegant and fine. A wine that is ethereal and succulent at the same time.

POMEROL 2000
Red | 2011 up to 2025   95
Deep and serious, this is a wine to age, but it is not as perfect as in previous vintages.

POMEROL LES PENSÉES DE LAFLEUR 2006
Red | 2011 up to 2022   90
More precise in the nose and on the palate than Lafleur, this is a pretty wine with refined texture, velvety length, and focused fruit.

POMEROL LES PENSÉES DE LAFLEUR 2005
Red | 2011 up to 2022   92
A great Pomerol, unctuous, velvety, and intense, with a wonderfully refined texture and remarkable flavors.

POMEROL LES PENSÉES DE LAFLEUR 2004
Red | 2011 up to 2018   86
Surprisingly spicy, the wine is solid but also quite rigid, without the usual velvety character of the growth.

POMEROL LES PENSÉES DE LAFLEUR 2003
Red | 2011 up to 2013   88
A rich wine, currently very seductive with notes of raspberry and strawberry and a fresh attack. The finish is a bit drier. It can be enjoyed right away.

Red: 11.1 acres; cabernet franc 50%, merlot 50%.
Annual production: 20,000 bottles

CHÂTEAU LARCIS-DUCASSE

1, Grottes d'Arsis
Saint-Laurent-des-Combes
33330 Saint-Émilion
Phone 00 33 5 57 24 70 84
Fax 00 33 5 57 24 64 00
larcis-ducasse@nicolas-thienpont.com
www.nicolas-thienpont.com

In the 2005 Bordeaux En Primeur campaign this estate recorded the highest-ever price increase for any wine in any category (up by more than 300 percent on the year). Rocketing prices, however, are just part of the story. Despite its often austere nose, Larcis-Ducasse could always be relied upon to reveal a classy, delicately balanced palate, with a harmony founded on freshness and finesse that made it one of the most attractive Saint-Émilion crus; few wines age so well, that's for sure. Since wunderkind duo Nicolas Thienpont and Stéphane Derenoncourt took over in 2005 they have done nothing to disturb that balance, but they have made the wine more immediately appealing. The velvety texture is even more refined and the aromas now show magisterial precision.

Recently tasted
SAINT-ÉMILION GRAND CRU 2007
Red | 2012 up to 2022   **93**

Older vintages
SAINT-ÉMILION GRAND CRU 2006
Red | 2012 up to 2017   **92**
The purity of the fruit shines; the wine is developing an ample body, elegant and quite distinguished, similar to the style of 2005, with a more immediate softness.

SAINT-ÉMILION GRAND CRU 2005
Red | 2012 up to 2025   **95**
An ultra-refined, superb wine, with an intense and deep body, a velvety texture, and sophisticated richness: unquestionably one of the great Saint-Émilions of the vintage.

SAINT-ÉMILION GRAND CRU 2004
Red | 2011 up to 2020   **89**
Aromatically austere, the wine reveals an unctuous volume, well balanced and underscored by elegant tannins.

SAINT-ÉMILION GRAND CRU 1998
Red | 2011 up to 2018   **92**
A great wine, profound and distinguished, with an earthy, truffled nose, opening up with linear elegance on the palate.

Red: 27.2 acres; cabernet franc 22%, merlot 78%.
Annual production: 35,000 bottles

CHÂTEAU LARMANDE

33330 Saint-Émilion
Phone 00 33 5 57 24 71 41
Fax 00 33 5 57 74 42 80
contact@soutard-larmande.com
www.château-larmande.com

Following more than eighty years' successful ownership, the Méneret family sold Château Larmande to the La Mondiale insurance group in the mid-1990s. Its performance since then seems very consistent, producing solid, well-built wines that tend to be at their best early on. A dependable producer but plainly not in the same league as the best in this appellation. La Mondiale recently acquired Château Soutard, another very promising Saint-Émilion estate.

Recently tasted
SAINT-ÉMILION GRAND CRU 2006
Red | 2012 up to 2017   **88**

SAINT-ÉMILION GRAND CRU
LE CADET DE LARMANDE 2006
Red | 2012 up to 2015   **84**

Older vintages
SAINT-ÉMILION GRAND CRU 2005
Red | 2011 up to 2016   **90**
An ambitiously made wine, this offers a bouquet of red fruit, notes of roasting coffee, and a full-bodied palate, firmly built but long, generous, and already seductive.

SAINT-ÉMILION GRAND CRU 2004
Red | 2011 up to 2015   **85**
A very structured wine, this is developing notes of red fruit and green peppers in the nose and on the palate; on the whole it is svelte, although the tannins are a bit abrupt.

SAINT-ÉMILION GRAND CRU 2003
Red | 2011 up to 2014   **89**
Full, fat, not drying, this wine appears to be hitting its peak now.

SAINT-ÉMILION GRAND CRU 2001
Red | 2011 up to 2015   **89**
A full, ripe wine with a very substantial texture, a touch drying on the finish.

SAINT-ÉMILION GRAND CRU 2000
Red | 2011 up to 2013   **86**
With a beautifully deep color, notes of prune, and generous, if not delicate, tannins, this is a powerfully built wine. It is flavorful and ready to drink all the same.

Red: 61.8 acres; cabernet franc 30%, cabernet sauvignon 5%, merlot 65%. Annual production: 80,000 bottles

CHÂTEAU LATOUR-À-POMEROL

33500 Pomerol
Phone 00 33 5 57 69 60 03
Fax 00 33 5 57 51 79 79
info@jpmoueix.com
www.moueix.com

The gravel and clay soils here are characteristic of the best Pomerol vineyards, located on the plateau that borders the left side of the Libourne–to–Saint-Émilion highway. Jean-Pierre Moueix now owns this small and distinguished Pomerol winery that has hardly missed a step in twenty-five years. Its wines are well structured, luscious, and deep, developing truffly undertones with age.

Recently tasted
POMEROL 2006
Red | 2012 up to 2018   90

Older vintages
POMEROL 2005
Red | 2012 up to 2020   92
Deep color, expressive nose combining hints of red fruit and black truffle with a delicate touch of chocolate, ample and deep texture, round and robust. A great future lies ahead.

POMEROL 2004
Red | 2011 up to 2016   90
Aromas of black truffle and red fruit. Very elegant texture, silky and refined, and beautiful, aromatic, and velvety length. Undoubtedly one of the great successes of the vintage.

POMEROL 2001
Red | 2011 up to 2015   88
Precise, silky, and elegant, not lacking in complexity.

POMEROL 2000
Red | 2011 up to 2020   90
A harmonious wine with a particularly velvety texture, noble licorice flavors, and medium length.

Red: 19.8 acres; cabernet franc 10%, merlot 90%.
Annual production: 30,000 bottles

CHÂTEAU LOUBENS

Château Loubens
33410 Sainte-Croix-du-Mont
Phone 00 33 5 56 62 01 25
Fax 00 33 9 55 62 01 25
contact@loubens.com

Loubens owns the most celebrated terroir in Sainte-Croix-du-Mont, famous for its fossilized oyster beds overlooking the Garonne River. Its prudent owner, Arnaud de Sèze, has never had the means to make spectacular wines and so decided years ago to focus on very balanced dessert wines that were true to their origins. More honeyed and a tad simpler en primeur than the great Sauternes, they become truly sumptuous with age, developing those rich flavors of candied apricot and citrus that distinguish great sémillon wines.

SAINTE-CROIX-DU-MONT
CHÂTEAU LOUBENS 2001
Sweet White | 2011 up to 2020   88
Golden color, powerful and distinguished wine, wonderful length on the palate. Patience is required, as is often the case with this growth!

SAINTE-CROIX-DU-MONT
CHÂTEAU LOUBENS 1998
Sweet White | 2011 up to 2014   87
Perfectly ripe, with a yellowy-gold hue and a brilliant nose, rich with preserved fruit, resin, tobacco, and minerals, this Sainte-Croix is distinguished, offering an elegant, fresh mouthfeel leaning toward minerality.

Red: 17.3 acres. White: 34.6 acres. Annual production: 40,000 bottles

CHÂTEAU MAGDELAINE

33330 Saint-Émilion
Phone 00 33 5 57 55 05 80
Fax 00 33 5 57 25 13 30
info@jpmoueix.com
www.moueix.com

Château Magdelaine, which belongs to the Moueix family, neighbors some of the most celebrated names in Saint-Émilion. It boasts a truly outstanding location, on a limestone slope at the gateway to the medieval village itself. You can see why it has enjoyed Premier Cru status since the first official Saint-Émilion classification of 1955. The wines display a delicate, very refined style but do seem to lack substance and depth compared with their peers—including some that achieve the same effect but without added heaviness.

Saint-Émilion grand cru 2007
Red | 2011 up to 2013   **87**
The texture of this wine always seems too flabby given its potential and its terroir. The wine is delicate and fresh, but lacks substance for a Premier Cru.

Saint-Émilion grand cru 2005
Red | 2011 up to 2020   **89**
Fruity and aromatically distinguished, this is soft and delicate with silky tannins and standard depth.

Saint-Émilion grand cru 2004
Red | 2011 up to 2015   **86**
Subtle nose. This is a linear and supple wine, not very intense, with decent length but limited.

Saint-Émilion grand cru 2003
Red | 2011 up to 2015   **88**
This has tender volume, combining the elegance, fruit, and alcohol of the vintage. The tannins are elegant, but the wine again lacks intensity and length.

Saint-Émilion grand cru 2002
Red | 2011 up to 2015   **87**
The color is not very intense. With delicate fruit on the nose, a smooth body, and light tannins, the wine lacks length, even if the style is elegant.

Saint-Émilion grand cru 2001
Red | 2011 up to 2020   **90**
Supple in the mouth, this is a wine of great finesse, with a crisp character that is quite delicious.

Saint-Émilion grand cru 2000
Red | 2011 up to 2015   **87**
The wine seems quite thin, tender, and pretty at this time. The tannins are delicate and tightly wound, but on the whole it lacks density.

Saint-Émilion grand cru 1999
Red | 2011 up to 2013   **84**
Very soft wine, with limited character and personality.

Saint-Émilion grand cru 1998
Red | 2011 up to 2016   **86**
With notes of plum and cooked fruit and a round body, this is appealing but lacking in vitality.

Red: 27.2 acres; cabernet franc 10%, merlot 90%.
Annual production: 30,000 bottles

BERNARD MAGREZ

Château Pape Clément
216, avenue du Docteur Nancel Pénard
33600 Pessac
Phone 00 33 5 57 26 38 38
Fax 00 33 5 57 26 38 39
contact@luxurywinetourism.fr
boutique-pessac@bernard-magret.com
www.pape-clément.com

Having spent the first half of his life building up his luxury wine and spirits empire, French wine magnate Bernard Magrez then poured his energies into the high-end wine market. His first move was to acquire Grands Crus such as Pape Clément, Fombrauge, and La Tour Carnet, later creating his own wines and buying up unknown properties. With advice from enologist Michel Rolland, Magrez went mainly for small vineyards in leading terroirs in Bordeaux (such as Saint-Seurin de Cadourne for the Magrez-Tivoli) as well as the Languedoc- Roussillon and abroad (especially in Spain). The wines are made in a very powerful style and lavishly barrel-aged—a bit short on freshness at times, but often with unbelievably refined tannins and real character. The best of the bunch just need one to three years' bottle aging to show their stuff.

Recently tasted

MÉDOC CHÂTEAU TOUR BLANCHE 2006
Red | 2011 up to 2014   86

PREMIÈRES CÔTES DE BLAYE
LA CROIX DE PÉRENNE 2006
Red | 2014 up to 2017   87

PREMIÈRES CÔTES DE BLAYE
LA CROIX DE PÉRENNE 2005
Red | 2012 up to 2017   88

Older vintages

BERGERAC LE DOMAINE DES SONGES 2005
Red | 2011 up to 2009   84
A supple, fat wine with ripe tannins, quite simple.

BERGERAC LE DOMAINE DES SONGES CUVÉE
ANNE 2005
Red | 2011 up to 2013   87
A powerful and intense wine, with aromas of roasted coffee and fruit and unctuous length.

BORDEAUX EGREGORE 2006
Red | 2011 up to 2013   88
Less exuberant than the same cuvée in 2007, but full-bodied with good structure, this is a truly luxurious Bordeaux, generous, with wonderfully rich flavors.

CÔTES DE BOURG CHÂTEAU GUERRY 2005
Red | 2011 up to 2013   89
Unctuous, fresh, full, and spicy, the wine lacks neither subtlety nor freshness despite its power.

MÉDOC CHÂTEAU LA TEMPÉRANCE 2006
Red | 2011 up to 2016   88
Nice, deep length; dense but free of harsh tannins: a full and well-structured wine.

MÉDOC CHÂTEAU LA TEMPÉRANCE 2005
Red | 2011 up to 2013   88
Generously oaked, the wine is becoming deep, full-bodied, and intense; nicely balanced, it finishes with freshness.

MÉDOC CHÂTEAU LES GRANDS CHÊNES 2006
Red | 2012 up to 2017   88
A Médoc that is generous and full, loaded with fresh tannins, not at all harsh. On the whole it has volume and potential.

MÉDOC MAGREZ TIVOLI 2005
Red | 2011 up to 2016   92
A beautifully rich wine, intense and complete, with integrated and ripe tannins, generous length, and magnificent potential.

MÉDOC MAGREZ TIVOLI 2004
Red | 2011 up to 2015   90
A powerful and intense wine, currently closed, but with great potential.

PESSAC-LÉOGNAN LA SÉRÉNITÉ 2006
Red | 2011 up to 2018   90
Wonderfully complex wine, long and harmonious, very rich and powerful, but with elegance and silky tannins. Now we must simply wait for the wine to fully integrate the oak.

PESSAC-LÉOGNAN LA SÉRÉNITÉ 2005
Red | 2011 up to 2013   91
A very rich wine with silky, unctuous tannins, long and savory with notes of black fruit and cloves, and an intense body.

PREMIÈRES CÔTES DE BLAYE
CHÂTEAU PÉRENNE 2006
Red | 2011 up to 2015   88
Gracefully built, nice, silky tannins, elegant length, pleasantly smooth.

PREMIERES CÔTES DE BLAYE
CHÂTEAU PÉRENNE 2005
Red | 2011 up to 2014   88
A suave and velvety wine, very deep, still showing a touch of bitterness due to the ambitious oak aging, but on the whole brilliantly made.

CHÂTEAU LA MAURIANE

Rigaud
33570 Puisseguin
Phone 00 33 5 57 74 68 06
Fax 00 33 5 57 74 50 97
lamauriane@vignobles-taix.com

For about a decade now, this small cru in Puisseguin has plainly been one of the best ambassadors for the so-called Saint-Émilion satellite appellations—if not the best. Fact is, Mauriane wines can easily hold their own against many of the most distinguished Saint-Émilions, in terms of both rich constitution and careful wine-making. They also age extremely well and can be enjoyed at their best after three to five years' bottle aging.

PUISSEGUIN-SAINT-ÉMILION 2006
Red | 2011 up to 2017   88
The nose is superb, offering wonderfully pure fruit and delicate oak. It is harmonious in the mouth, with a tight tannic vein, fruit, and good balance.

PUISSEGUIN-SAINT-ÉMILION 2005
Red | 2011 up to 2017   90
A modern wine, powerful, heavily oaked, with notes of black fruit and nougat, smooth acidity, and tannins that are still a bit bitter.

PUISSEGUIN-SAINT-ÉMILION 2004
Red | 2011 up to 2015   88
Once again the subtle and elegant texture and bouquet are admirable, unique among these so-called "satellite appellations." Thanks to a nice acidity, this wine has at least five years ahead of it!

PUISSEGUIN-SAINT-ÉMILION 2003
Red | 2011 up to 2013   90
Very powerful, generous, rich, unctuous, and charming, with wonderfully intense fruit.

Red: 10.7 acres; cabernet franc 25%, merlot 75%.
Annual production: 12,000 bottles

CHÂTEAU MONBOUSQUET

42, route de Saint-Émilion
33330 Saint-Sulpice-de-Faleyrens
Phone 00 33 5 57 55 43 43
Fax 00 33 5 57 24 63 99
contact@vignoblesperse.com
www.vignoblesperse.com

In 2006 Château Monbousquet became the first-ever vineyard at the foot of the Saint-Émilion hill to be elevated to Grand Cru status. Before that, these ancient deposits of sand, gravel, and clay had always been looked down upon by Bordeaux specialists. Monbousquet certainly deserves its promotion, which is of course testament to the extraordinary efforts of owner Gérard Perse, who bought Monbousquet in 1993, five years before buying Pavie. His sole ambition, then as now, was to make the greatest wine possible. Château Monbousquet is a real stunner when young—dark ruby tones, aromas of cocoa, black-skinned fruit, and roasted coffee beans; full, smooth body and lovely freshness—but it also ages very gracefully, thanks to some particularly refined tannins. All of which goes to show just how good these soils can be when they are properly drained and worked.

Recently tasted
SAINT-ÉMILION GRAND CRU 2007
Red | 2012 up to 2017   91

Older vintages
SAINT-ÉMILION GRAND CRU 2006
Red | 2011 up to 2020   90
Focused and fresh fruit, deep, without rigidity, a superfine tannic grain and silky length.

SAINT-ÉMILION GRAND CRU 2005
Red | 2012 up to 2020   93
A splendid Saint-Émilion with wonderfully unctuous volume, this combines rich flavors and a voluptuous texture, with straightforward fruit that has not the slightest hint of bitterness.

SAINT-ÉMILION GRAND CRU 2004
Red | 2011 up to 2015   88
A rich and supple wine, with completely non-aggressive tannins. It's lacking the vibrancy of a great Montbousquet, but it has nice length.

SAINT-ÉMILION GRAND CRU 2003
Red | 2011 up to 2020   92
The nose is still closed, but this wine is wonderfully smooth thanks to its unctuous, languid body and tannins that are almost sweet. An excellent wine made in a style that is archetypal for the growth.

SAINT-ÉMILION GRAND CRU 2002
Red | 2011 up to 2013   **90**
Wonderfully deep color, toasty oak, smooth and fresh fruit; full-bodied, silky, and long; nicely balanced without being hard or green.

SAINT-ÉMILION GRAND CRU 2001
Red | 2011 up to 2020   **91**
The harmonious balance of this vintage is a huge success. The wine is elegant, round, and silky, long and perfectly structured.

SAINT-ÉMILION GRAND CRU 2000
Red | 2011 up to 2018   **92**
The tannins are suave and much more elegant than many typical Saint-Émilions, which have a tendency to be hardening up in this vintage. It is focused, with flavorful length.

SAINT-ÉMILION GRAND CRU 1999
Red | 2011 up to 2016   **90**
Very youthful color. The fruit is still very apparent, rich, and meaty. Very seductive on the whole.

SAINT-ÉMILION GRAND CRU 1998
Red | 2011 up to 2016   **90**
Suave and round, lacking a bit of intensity in comparison with the best wines of Saint-Émilion.

Red: 79.1 acres; cabernet franc 30%, cabernet sauvignon 10%, merlot 60%. White: 2.5 acres; sauvignon blanc 66%, sauvignon gris 34%. Annual production: 90,000 bottles

LA MONDOTTE

BP 34
33330 Saint-Émilion
Phone 00 33 5 57 24 71 33
Fax 00 33 5 57 24 67 95
info@neipperg.com
www.neipperg.com

Planted in very clayey soils on the limestone plateau east of Saint-Émilion, this small vineyard features merlot vines lovingly tended by Stephan Von Neipperg with the help of Stéphane Derenoncourt. In 1996 their efforts produced what was rapidly to become a cult wine—proving Von Neipperg's claim that this cru is indeed "a laboratory for excellence." It has allowed him to develop an assertive style that combines great depth and power with huge finesse. All of the vintages since 1996 are top-notch.

Recently tasted
SAINT-ÉMILION 2007
Red | 2012 up to 2025   **93**

Older vintages
SAINT-ÉMILION 2006
Red | 2012 up to 2025   **95**
Still very young, this wine feels less massive than the 2005, but it has an unctuous body, refined, tight tannins, and intense length.

SAINT-ÉMILION 2005
Red | 2011 up to 2020   **97**
A smooth and velvety wine with wonderful density and volume, beautifully built.

SAINT-ÉMILION 2004
Red | 2011 up to 2015   **91**
With a deep color, the wine is immediately seductive on the nose and palate, with intense fruit and a succulent generosity that isn't lacking in acidity.

SAINT-ÉMILION 2003
Red | 2011 up to 2025   **93**
As with all great vintages from La Mondotte, it is imperative to age this wine. Still quite young and massive, it has impressive depth.

SAINT-ÉMILION 2001
Red | 2011 up to 2022   **93**
This is an impressive wine thanks to its charming and savory texture. The finish is long, with good acidity.

SAINT-ÉMILION 2000
Red | 2011 up to 2025   **96**
The perception of sweet silkiness is as intense as the perception of depth and vigor. The refined tannins show that this restrained wine can age for a good while longer.

SAINT-ÉMILION 1999
Red | 2011 up to 2017   92
Less intense than the 1998 and 2000, this is
an opulent, suave, and silky wine, very tasty
right now.

SAINT-ÉMILION 1998
Red | 2011 up to 2030   98
This has an impressively youthful personality for a thirteen-year-old wine: it is still tight
but velvety and deep, with firm but elegant
tannins, wonderful length, and amazingly
persistent aromas. Let's revisit it in a few
years!

SAINT-ÉMILION 1997
Red | 2011 up to 2017   94
Very silky and delicately perfumed, the wine
is currently softer than the following vintages, but it has a very nice persistence on
the finish.

SAINT-ÉMILION 1996
Red | 2011 up to 2017   90
The vintage that started it all: an ambitious
wine with a coffee character, rich and super-
tannic. The finish is less explosive than the
attack would have led us to believe.

CHÂTEAU MONTVIEL

1, rue du Grand-Moulinet
33500 Pomerol
Phone 00 33 5 57 51 87 92
Fax 00 33 3 21 93 21 03
pvp.montviel@skynet.be

Catherine Péré-Vergé, whose family owns
Cristalleries d'Arques, has become one of
Pomerol's big players since buying Châteaux Le Gay and La Violette. Her success
story started in the mid-1980s when she
created this small cru, produced from two
quite separate vineyard plots. It has made
steady progress ever since—no bells and
whistles, just a perfect balance of strength
and fluidity, with graceful length. Definitely one of the best wines in this appellation.

Recently tasted
POMEROL 2007
Red | 2011 up to 2018   90
Full, linear, not heavy, developing a very pure
fruit quality. Remarkable.

POMEROL 2006
Red | 2011 up to 2018   90
A rich and refined wine, with a very elegant
and deep structure. Proof of the clear progress this winery has made.

POMEROL 2005
Red | 2011 up to 2020   90
This wine is certainly a notch above all of
the wines ever made here. Still tightly wound,
but distinguished and elegant, it's a wine
that must be cellared.

CHÂTEAU LE MOULIN

Moulin de Lavaud
33500 Pomerol
Phone 00 33 5 57 55 19 60
Fax 00 33 5 57 55 19 61
m.querre@orange.fr

Michel Querre has transformed this small vineyard in the northwest of the appellation. Since 1997 it has been turning out a couture wine that is testament to rigorous standards of viticulture, winemaking, and maturation. The style is very modern, of course—deeply colored and richly oaked, with emphatic, very ripe fruit that mixes with more exotic nuances—developing generous, velvety body but with no loss of honesty and freshness.

POMEROL 2005
Red | 2011 up to 2021   **92**
Generously oaked, this is an inspired and seductive wine, ample and round as is usual with this growth, but also with magnificent depth and tannic definition.

POMEROL 2004
Red | 2011 up to 2017   **89**
Marked by oak, loaded with personality, with subdued tannins: here is a Pomerol that was very well made within the context of the vintage.

POMEROL 2003
Red | 2011 up to 2015   **90**
Of remarkable balance, this full-bodied, warm wine has savory tannins that show that it was expertly vinified.

POMEROL 2001
Red | 2011 up to 2013   **90**
Long and rich, with nice tannins, this wine is impressive for its density and spicy aromatic character.

Red: 5.9 acres; cabernet franc 20%, merlot 80%. Annual production: 10,000 bottles

CHÂTEAU MOULIN PEY-LABRIE

33126 Fronsac
Phone 00 33 5 57 51 14 37
Fax 00 33 5 57 51 53 45
moulinpeylabrie@wanadoo.fr
www.moulinpeylabrie.com

This small winery in Fronsac is now one of the most dependable in its area. It sits at the top of a slope ("pey" in the regional patois, hence the name Pey-Labrie) on clay-limestone soils typical of this region, known as Molasse du Fronsadais. Careful attention to viticulture and winemaking produce very sincere wines, as robust and straightforward as any Fronsac but also showing exquisitely graceful definition.

CANON-FRONSAC 2006
Red | 2011 up to 2016   **89**
An earthy, full, and solid wine, made in a restrained style that needs a few years of aging in order for it to fully express its character.

CANON-FRONSAC 2005
Red | 2011 up to 2013   **89**
This wine is exemplary in terms of its terroir expression, aromatic complexity, and the quality of its tannins. It is on the same level as a good Cru Classé from Saint-Émilion.

CANON-FRONSAC 2004
Red | 2011 up to 2013   **86**
This wine is now more pleasurable than it was early on. Straightforward, long, and not lacking class.

CANON-FRONSAC 2003
Red | 2011 up to 2013   **84**
Solid, but with drying tannins, notably affected by the heat wave.

Red: 32 acres; malbec 5%, merlot 95%. Annual production: 30,000 bottles

CHÂTEAU MOULIN SAINT-GEORGES

33330 Saint-Émilion
Phone 00 33 5 57 24 24 57
Fax 00 33 5 57 24 24 58
château-ausone@wanadoo.fr
www.château-ausone.fr

Alain Vauthier of Château Ausone fame vinifies this small cru according to the same principles. The terroir here isn't the same, and the wine doesn't share the same superb finesse as Vauthier's Premier Grand Cru Classé, but its overall harmony, velvety palate, and aromatic freshness are instantly recognizable. All of the vintages released since 2009 have shown Moulin Saint-Georges to be one of the top-performing Saint-Émilion producers.

Recently tasted
SAINT-ÉMILION GRAND CRU 2006
Red | 2012 up to 2017   91

Older vintages
SAINT-ÉMILION GRAND CRU 2005
Red | 2011 up to 2020   91
Broad and harmonious, showing intense fruit carried by superbly defined tannins, this wine is deeply flavorful and has great potential.

SAINT-ÉMILION GRAND CRU 2004
Red | 2011 up to 2014   89
Svelte and well made for the vintage, with a very nice tannic grain.

SAINT-ÉMILION GRAND CRU 2003
Red | 2011 up to 2013   91
The velvety texture immediately indicates the influence of Alain Vauthier. The wine is richly structured and amazingly vigorous, one of the best wines of the cru.

SAINT-ÉMILION GRAND CRU 2002
Red | 2011 up to 2015   90
A wonderfully charming wine with very elegant and refined fruit. The tannins have a finesse that can be outdone only by its big brother, Ausone.

SAINT-ÉMILION GRAND CRU 2000
Red | 2011 up to 2013   88
Nice volume, with ripe tannins and a full, fresh finish.

Red: 17.3 acres; cabernet franc 20%, cabernet sauvignon 10%, merlot 70%. Annual production: 30,000 bottles

CHÂTEAU NÉNIN

44, route de Montagne
33500 Pomerol
Phone 00 33 5 56 73 25 26
Fax 00 33 5 56 59 18 33
leoville-las-cases@wanadoo.fr

Things looked pretty bleak for this huge property in the period 1970–1990 until it was bought up by Domaines Delon, the owners of Château Léoville–Las Cases in Saint-Julien. Considerable money has been spent since then, reviving and expanding the vineyard through the purchase of new parcels with excellent soils in Certan-Giraud and building modern, high-performance fermentation facilities. The style of vinification is largely Médoc-inspired and aims to produce wines for long cellaring: somewhat austere "en primeur" compared to many of Nénin's boldly hedonistic neighbors, but with very distinguished tannins. Only since 2005, however, have we seen this cru take on that extra level of complexity that places it alongside the very great Pomerols. The second wine, Fugue de Nénin, is one of the most dependable in its category.

POMEROL 2006
Red | 2011 up to 2020   89
Delicately articulated tannins and harmonious length, but it is not as deep as the 2005.

POMEROL 2005
Red | 2012 up to 2025   91
Powerful and harmonious, this is the best wine since the new owners took over the property, with remarkably defined terroir character and great length.

POMEROL 2004
Red | 2011 up to 2019   88
An adequate structure, tight texture, tannins a bit austere. The truffle notes are stronger than usual, which softens the tannins.

POMEROL 2003
Red | 2011 up to 2020   88
Firm and straightforward in the mouth, this has a velvety texture but feels limited by the hearty tannins of a wine made to age. You can definitely tell that the vines suffered.

POMEROL 2001
Red | 2011 up to 2020   90
With a wonderfully fine texture and harmony, this wine has a light, ethereal quality and elegant length.

Red: 79.1 acres. Annual production: 50,000 bottles

CLOS DE L'ORATOIRE

BP 34
33330 Saint-Émilion
Phone 00 33 5 57 24 71 33
Fax 00 33 5 57 24 67 95
info@neipperg.com
www.neipperg.com

Clos de l'Oratoire is the third of Stephan Von Neipperg's Saint-Émilion properties. The vineyard lies to the northeast of the town itself, planted in exceptionally clayey limestone soils that suit merlot to a T. The wine is less famous than Neipperg's other two Saint-Émilion crus, La Mondotte and Canon-la-Gaffelière, but no less typical of his distinctive style: lush and intense but still with delicate structure and obvious class. This is a wine that can be enjoyed very young for its charming, superbly expressive fruit. Cellaring potential, on the other hand, is definitely not up to the standard of Canon-la-Gaffelière.

Recently tasted
SAINT-ÉMILION GRAND CRU 2007
Red | 2012 up to 2017   **90**

Older vintages
SAINT-ÉMILION GRAND CRU 2006
Red | 2011 up to 2017   **92**
A magnificent wine. The color is bright and opaque, the nose fresh and focused. The palate reveals an unctuous body of superbly elegant tannins, long and distinguished.

SAINT-ÉMILION GRAND CRU 2005
Red | 2011 up to 2020   **92**
The wine asserts itself with power and charm: it is deeply colored with full and lively tannins, wonderfully harmonious length, and superbly balanced acidity.

SAINT-ÉMILION GRAND CRU 2004
Red | 2011 up to 2015   **90**
A beautifully deep wine with dark color, expressive fruit, a supple and dense character, and an undeniably long finish.

SAINT-ÉMILION GRAND CRU 2003
Red | 2011 up to 2017   **91**
If the structure is taut and more severe than usual, it is perfectly blended with a silky body and an amazing richness, giving this wine remarkable distinction.

SAINT-ÉMILION GRAND CRU 2001
Red | 2011 up to 2015   **91**
Extremely rich with a tight, tannic streak, this is an impressive wine that has wonderfully flavorful density without compromising its balance.

SAINT-ÉMILION GRAND CRU 2000
Red | 2011 up to 2015   **89**
The color is still lively and the nose very aromatic, dominated by blackberry jam. Fat, ambitious, and powerful, this is in a style that is a bit heavier than usual.

SAINT-ÉMILION GRAND CRU 1999
Red | 2011 up to 2013   **87**
Nice, rich body, aromatically diverse, with a finish that is a bit heavy.

SAINT-ÉMILION GRAND CRU 1998
Red | 2011 up to 2015   **88**
The wine is powerful and long, with tannins that are undeniably less refined than in more recent vintages.

SAINT-ÉMILION GRAND CRU 1996
Red | 2011 up to 2013   **84**
Powerful, but the aromas are slightly vegetal, and the tannins are much drier than they are in the wines of the following decade.

Red: 25.5 acres: cabernet franc 5%, cabernet sauvignon 5%, merlot 90%. Annual production: 45,000 bottles

CHÂTEAU PAVIE

33330 Saint-Émilion
Phone 00 33 5 57 55 43 43
Fax 00 33 5 57 24 63 99
contact@vignoblesperse.com
www.vignoblesperse.com

Château Pavie enjoys one of the best locations and aspects in the entire appellation, on the eastern flank of the impressive hill bordering Saint-Émilion. Despite its long-standing and flattering reputation, this cru did not participate in the cultural and enological revolution that took hold of the best Bordeaux estates in the 1980s. Its spectacular transformation dates from 1997 when Gérard Perse took over. Every vintage since then has been remarkable for its power, with a sunny, generous fullness plus the ultrarefined tannins that are required of truly great wines. There's no denying the ambitious, demonstrative personality of Perse's wines—nor that it has led some critics to make hasty judgments based on that first, overriding impression of power. But given time to come into their own, his wines display a silky texture and natural freshness that place the great Pavies in the same category as the most classically expressive great Bordeaux. All you need is patience.

Recently tasted
SAINT-ÉMILION GRAND CRU 2007
Red | 2012 up to 2020   92

Older vintages
SAINT-ÉMILION GRAND CRU 2006
Red | 2012 up to 2018   93
Dense and multifaceted, with silky and noble tannins and wonderful pedigree. A wine to age, with a timeless future.

SAINT-ÉMILION GRAND CRU 2005
Red | 2011 up to 2030   98
Fat and intense, corpulent, solid but well built. Pavie is amazingly full-bodied and impressively reserved at the same time. Aging is imperative.

SAINT-ÉMILION GRAND CRU 2004
Red | 2011 up to 2025   92
Immediately impressive in color alone, this wine combines a wonderful succulence with elegant tannins, which is not very common in this vintage. A magnificently generous wine.

SAINT-ÉMILION GRAND CRU 2003
Red | 2011 up to 2030   97
With age, this wine is showing its expansive dimensions and demonstrating its nobility and class. The bouquet is still lively with notes of black fruit and figs; the rich, deep, and unctuous body is becoming supremely elegant.

SAINT-ÉMILION GRAND CRU 2002
Red | 2011 up to 2014   92
With velvety, silky volume and good acidity, this is a very stylish and profound wine, a great achievement in a complicated vintage.

SAINT-ÉMILION GRAND CRU 2001
Red | 2012 up to 2022   92
This is brilliant wine, with a perfectly harmonious body, superb tannins, complex aromas, and a fresh and unctuous finish.

SAINT-ÉMILION GRAND CRU 2000
Red | 2011 up to 2025   98
A beautifully sculpted wine, this has magnificent vigor and elegance. The tannins are superbly silky.

SAINT-ÉMILION GRAND CRU 1999
Red | 2011 up to 2019   91
Massive and linear, with fewer nuances than the vintages from the Perse era.

SAINT-ÉMILION GRAND CRU 1998
Red | 2011 up to 2022   97
A wine with amazing intensity and an impressively powerful constitution, elegant and mineral.

Red: 91.4 acres: cabernet franc 20%, cabernet sauvignon 10%, merlot 70%. Annual production: 90,000 bottles

CHÂTEAU PAVIE-DECESSE

33330 Saint-Émilion
Phone 00 33 5 57 55 43 43
Fax 00 33 5 57 24 63 99
contact@vignoblesperse.com
www.vignoblesperse.com

Gérard Perse acquired this property on the hill of Saint-Émilion in 1997, at the same time as neighboring Château Pavie. He chose to keep their two identities separate, though both have undergone the same careful transformation. The fermentation and aging cellars have been rebuilt, and the vineyard has been restructured. Château Pavie-Decesse today impresses with every new vintage. Its wines are powerful and full-bodied with sultry, brooding tannins and overall class—spectacular wines that can be safely stashed away in the cellar for a few years to make the most of all that class and refined structure.

Recently tasted
SAINT-ÉMILION GRAND CRU 2007
Red | 2012 up to 2025　　　　90

Older vintages
SAINT-ÉMILION GRAND CRU 2006
Red | 2012 up to 2025　　　　91
Pure notes of both red and black fruit, rich and multifaceted in body, with an unctuous finish.

SAINT-ÉMILION GRAND CRU 2005
Red | 2012 up to 2025　　　　95
An inky color and amazing richness suggest perfectly ripe grapes; the volume is impressive without the slightest hint of bitterness; the omnipresent tannins have remarkable finesse, with a superb, almost creamy finish. A great wine with great potential.

SAINT-ÉMILION GRAND CRU 2004
Red | 2011 up to 2016　　　　91
A great wine with a deep and vivid color and hints of roasted coffee and truffles on the nose, full-bodied, intense, succulent, and vigorous.

SAINT-ÉMILION GRAND CRU 2003
Red | 2011 up to 2023　　　　95
Very rich, unctuous, and dense, this wine has, like Pavie, an unequaled volume and is evolving superbly thanks to ultrapure fruit and an amazing freshness.

SAINT-ÉMILION GRAND CRU 2002
Red | 2011 up to 2015　　　　90
Brilliantly profound wine, deeply colored, dense and suave on the palate, splendidly highlighted by velvety tannins.

SAINT-ÉMILION GRAND CRU 2001
Red | 2011 up to 2020　　　　92
An elegant and multilayered wine, with a texture that is intense but not heavy. The finish has sophistication and length.

SAINT-ÉMILION GRAND CRU 2000
Red | 2011 up to 2025　　　　95
A monumental and unctuous wine, with a nice minerality emerging on the nose.

SAINT-ÉMILION GRAND CRU 1999
Red | 2011 up to 2019　　　　90
Not as well-rounded this vintage as Monbousquet, this is elegant and fine, with a touch of acidity on the finish.

SAINT-ÉMILION GRAND CRU 1998
Red | 2011 up to 2018　　　　92
Good acidity, broad and fruit-filled palate, long finish.

Red: 9 acres; cabernet franc 10%, merlot 90%.
Annual production: 10,000 bottles

CHÂTEAU PAVIE-MACQUIN

33330 Saint-Émilion
Phone 00 33 5 57 24 74 23
Fax 00 33 5 57 24 63 78
pavie-macquin@nicolas-thienpont.com
www.pavie-macquin.com

Pavie-Macquin, right next door to Troplong-Mondot, is another estate that was recently promoted to a Premier Cru Classé—a logical move given its valuable terroir. The property did not perform well in the 1980s but then made a spectacular comeback thanks to the determined and largely unfunded efforts of manager Maryse Barre, assisted by her very young deputy, Stéphane Derenoncourt. He and winemaking consultant Nicolas Thienpont now form a winning team, capturing the best in the terroir but expressing it in that modern style that suits the popular taste. Very robust and fleshy, Pavie-Macquin grows more refined and harmonious with every new vintage—always with that distinctively Pavie whiff of truffles and taut mineral character. The success of this cru is a tribute to the achievements of two men who together and separately are now seminal figures of the Bordeaux Right Bank. Pavie-Macquin marked the start of their collaboration and individual rise to fame, and it has since become the ultimate expression of their creative effort.

Recently tasted
SAINT-ÉMILION GRAND CRU 2007
Red | 2012 up to 2020   **92**

Older vintages
SAINT-ÉMILION GRAND CRU 2006
Red | 2012 up to 2018   **91**
A great wine, ultrarefined, with brilliant oak aging, aristocratic tannins, a svelte body, and great length. A complete wine.

SAINT-ÉMILION GRAND CRU 2005
Red | 2011 up to 2025   **97**
Very powerfully built and richly structured, this wine shines for its intensity and aromatic vitality. It is made for long-term aging, with delicate but tightly wound tannins and notes of truffles on the velvety finish.

SAINT-ÉMILION GRAND CRU 2004
Red | 2011 up to 2015   **89**
Deeply colored, notes of black fruit on the nose, full in the mouth, generous, a bit hard on the finish, but with volume and breadth. Nice tannins.

SAINT-ÉMILION GRAND CRU 2003
Red | 2011 up to 2020   **92**
Nice, well-rounded wine, dense and harmonious, with superbly elegant tannins.

SAINT-ÉMILION GRAND CRU 2002
Red | 2011 up to 2014   **90**
A great success, bright and deep: garnet color, intensely built, round, suave, velvety, long and refined, with wonderful balance.

SAINT-ÉMILION GRAND CRU 2001
Red | 2011 up to 2014   **90**
An absolute success, this shows perfect harmony on the palate and a magnificently precise texture. One of the five best Saint-Émilions of the year.

SAINT-ÉMILION GRAND CRU 2000
Red | 2011 up to 2015   **92**
Pretty color, good acidity and distinction, nice persistence, remarkable freshness.

SAINT-ÉMILION GRAND CRU 1999
Red | 2011 up to 2013   **89**
This wine seems a bit tired, with an aromatic palette of cooked fruit and soft tannins, though it is not lacking in length.

SAINT-ÉMILION GRAND CRU 1998
Red | 2011 up to 2018   **97**
This wine is tasting wonderfully now, deep, unctuous, generous, with amazingly rich aromas and a full and flavorful structure.

Red: 37.1 acres: cabernet franc 14%, cabernet sauvignon 2%, merlot 84%. **Annual production:** 55,000 bottles

CHÂTEAU PETIT-GRAVET AÎNÉ AND CLOS SAINT-JULIEN

33330 Saint-Émilion
Phone 00 33 5 57 24 72 44
Fax 00 33 5 57 24 74 84
château.gaillard@wanadoo.fr

The winemaker here is Catherine Papon-Nouvel, now widely recognized as one of the most sensitive, capable performers on the Bordeaux Right Bank. Her wines show plenty of power and generosity, but what you mainly notice is a superb freshness and balance that make them genuinely fit for their purpose, that is, to be drunk! Her two (small) principal crus, Clos Saint-Julien and Petit-Gravet Aîné, rely on a significant proportion of the cabernet franc.

Recently tasted
SAINT-ÉMILION GRAND CRU
CHÂTEAU PETIT-GRAVET AÎNÉ 2007
Red | 2011 up to 2015   **90**

SAINT-ÉMILION GRAND CRU
CLOS SAINT-JULIEN 2007
Red | 2011 up to 2014   **90**

Older vintages
SAINT-ÉMILION GRAND CRU
CHÂTEAU PETIT-GRAVET AÎNÉ 2005
Red | 2011 up to 2015   **92**
Striking a richer balance than the 2004, this is an ample and enveloping wine, but also deep and quite refined. The silkiness of the texture and body are magnificent.

SAINT-ÉMILION GRAND CRU
CHÂTEAU PETIT-GRAVET AÎNÉ 2004
Red | 2011 up to 2013   **90**
Beautiful, intense color, elegant oak, not heavy, focused fruit, deep and long in the mouth, with velvety tannins, firm length, and a very harmonious balance.

SAINT-ÉMILION GRAND CRU
CHÂTEAU PETIT-GRAVET AÎNÉ 2001
Red | 2011 up to 2015   **89**
The third vintage from Catherine Papon-Nouvel is a huge success, with lots of class and surprising finesse.

SAINT-ÉMILION GRAND CRU
CLOS SAINT-JULIEN 2005
Red | 2011 up to 2015   **90**
An intense wine, more focused than the previous vintage, with a true internal energy and wonderful aromatic palette of red and black fruit. A beautiful wine, refined and pure.

SAINT-ÉMILION GRAND CRU
CLOS SAINT-JULIEN 2004
Red | 2011 up to 2013   **87**
A soft and full-bodied wine with notes of plum and raspberry, this is harmonious but not overpowering, with a suave and supple composition.

Red: 6.2 acres: cabernet franc 80%, merlot 20%.
Annual production: 8,000 bottles

CHÂTEAU PETIT-VILLAGE

Catusseau
33500 Pomerol
Phone 00 33 5 57 51 21 08
Fax 00 33 5 57 51 87 31
contact@petit-village.com
www.petit-village.com

Petit-Village has been much slower to show its stuff than the other major Pomerol players. Production in the 1970s and 1980s was no better than average by local standards and, though its performance definitely improved under new owners AXA Millésimes (of Pichon-Longueville fame), it remained less than stellar. Recent vintages do finally show signs of change: the 2005 has depth and the 2006, the first vintage made under the watchful eye of Stéphane Derenoncourt, sure looks promising.

Recently tasted
POMEROL 2007
Red | 2012 up to 2020   90

Older vintages
POMEROL 2006
Red | 2011 up to 2022   90
The body and structure of this wine have never been so velvety and elegant. It expands on the palate without becoming too heavy, all the while displaying wonderful depth and fruity length.

POMEROL 2005
Red | 2011 up to 2022   88
A wine that is rich, fruit-driven, and fat, unquestionably more concentrated than before, but lacking refinement in its tannic structure.

POMEROL 2004
Red | 2011 up to 2015   84
The wine is smooth, sun-soaked, and pleasant but seriously lacking in depth.

POMEROL 2001
Red | 2011 up to 2015   88
A modern and savory wine, but it doesn't possess the extremely fine texture that one would expect from a great Pomerol.

POMEROL 2000
Red | 2011 up to 2020   92
A full wine, quite suave and long on the palate, very sensual without being heavy.

Annual production: 40,000 bottles

PÉTRUS

1, rue Pétrus-Arnaud
33500 Pomerol
Phone 00 33 5 57 51 17 96
info@jpmoueix.com
www.moueix.com

Pétrus, the fabled Pomerol estate, makes one of the best-known wines in the world, including several now legendary prewar (1921, 1929) and postwar vintages (1945, 1947, 1949, 1961, 1964). Its original rise to success was driven by wine merchant extraordinaire Jean-Pierre Moueix, Château Pétrus having for many years been no more than an anonymous building at the heart of the Pomerol appellation. It has now been entirely renovated and includes a new cellar; but what really makes Pétrus is not bricks but terroir: that precious pocket of clay that sets it apart from its otherwise illustrious neighbors. The nature of the soil protects the vines and retains moisture, which is perfect for the merlot, by far the predominant planting here. Vinified since the 1980s by Jean-Claude Berrouet, the winemaking genius of Domaine Moueix, Pétrus has acquired a refined character that is sometimes at the expense of intensity (witness the offerings from the 1980s and 1990s). What it has also gained, however, is a taffeta-like texture, brightened by a particularly seductive, often almost exotic, bouquet.

Recently tasted
POMEROL 2006
Red | 2015 up to 2030   94

Older vintages
POMEROL 2005
Red | 2015 up to 2040   99
Understated aromas blend notes of black truffles, red fruit, tropical fruit, and green tea; the body is smooth and velvety, round and enveloping, with a delicate texture worthy of the vintage and the growth. Enchanting.

POMEROL 2004
Red | 2011 up to 2020   93
Very refined, this does not have exceptional depth, but it was built with great tannic precision. The wine seduces with its complex aromatic nuances, combining exotic fruit and delicate notes of oak.

POMEROL 2001
Red | 2011 up to 2020   93
Generous and exuberant, this is a Pétrus that will age well although it doesn't possess the depth or polished texture of the 2000 or the 2005.

POMEROL 2000
Red | 2011 up to 2030   **98**

Complex, refined, and velvety, the 2000 is one of the greatest Pétrus wines in recent history. Its intensity and focus reveal much more power than previous vintages, except for the remarkable 1998.

POMEROL 1998
Red | 2011 up to 2030   **99**

A grandiose vintage, one of the most intense and powerful in recent history, but also built with a refined and delicate sophistication. This wine has amazing length and will age for years. Definitely the best wine of the 1990s.

Red: 28.4 acres; cabernet franc 5%, merlot 95%.
Annual production: 32,000 bottles

LE PIN

Les Grands-Champs
33500 Pomerol
Phone 00 33 5 57 51 33 99
Fax 00 33 0 32 55 31 09
wine@thienpontwine.com

This estate founded in the early 1980s by Jacques Thienpont was the first of the micro-wineries that toppled the traditional hierarchy of the Right Bank Bordeaux wines, predating the "garage wines" by a decade. The vineyard enjoys a (very discreet) location on the edge of the village of Catusseau. It produces a remarkably smooth, merlot-driven wine with an often exuberant and exotic bouquet, but much more assertive balance and freshness than in the past. Its rarity and aura of mystery make it the archetypal speculator's wine, while the quality it achieves today is simply out of this world.

Recently tasted
POMEROL 2007
Red | 2012 up to 2020   **92**

Older vintages
POMEROL 2006
Red | 2012 up to 2025   **93**

At the end of its barrel aging, the exuberant character of the growth is for the moment suppressed. On the other hand, the palate offers a glimpse of sophistication that belongs only to Pomerol.

POMEROL 2005
Red | 2011 up to 2020   **93**

Incredibly soft and velvety texture, silky tannins, incredible finesse: a wonderfully natural style.

POMEROL 2002
Red | 2011 up to 2015   **91**

A velvety, smooth wine with extraordinary aromatic charm.

POMEROL 2001
Red | 2011 up to 2015   **93**

Exotic and smooth, the wine has immense density, with exceptionally suave tannins, surprising and wonderful.

Red: 4.9 acres; merlot 92%, other 8%. Annual production: 8,000 bottles

CHÂTEAU LA POINTE

33500 Pomerol
Phone 00 33 5 57 51 02 11
Fax 00 33 5 57 51 42 33
contact@châteaulapointe.com
www.châteaulapointe.com

This estate, huge by Pomerol standards, really is a landmark on the road out of Libourne, as you enter the Pomerol AOC. The sandy and sandy-clay soils here produce fairly early-drinking wines, whose suppleness used to verge on wateriness until about twelve years ago, when the owners introduced much stricter selection processes. La Pointe today is known as a producer of Pomerol wines that are accessible in every sense: affordable, enjoyable, and age-worthy.

Recently tasted
POMEROL 2007
Red | 2012 up to 2017   **88**

POMEROL 2006
Red | 2012 up to 2017   **86**

Older vintages
POMEROL 2005
Red | 2011 up to 2015   **88**
The wine's aromas are very focused, the result of high-quality grapes, and it is just as pleasing in the mouth. Very well made.

POMEROL 2004
Red | 2011 up to 2013   **84**
This has good color and a spicy, open, and precise nose, but the tannins are hard, angular.

POMEROL 2003
Red | 2011 up to 2013   **84**
The wine is supple, almost to the point of being flabby, then finishes with rigid tannins.

POMEROL 2001
Red | 2011 up to 2013   **88**
A well-made Pomerol with an elegant core, not lacking in distinction. The finish seems a bit short.

Red: 53 acres; cabernet franc 10%, cabernet sauvignon 15%, merlot 75%. Annual production: 97,000 bottles

CHÂTEAU POMEAUX

Lieu-dit Toulifaut
33500 Pomerol
Phone 00 33 5 57 51 98 88
Fax 00 33 5 57 51 88 99
j.palous@wine-and-vineyards.com
www.pomeaux.com

Château Pomeaux was sold at the turn of the millennium to enterprising new owners who have since produced a series of superbly constructed vintages with immediately irresistible character, turning this once entirely anonymous example of its appellation into a wine built on velvetiness and generosity. Can be enjoyed relatively young.

Recently tasted
POMEROL 2006
Red | 2012 up to 2017   **88**

Older vintages
POMEROL 2005
Red | 2011 up to 2020   **90**
This wine is seductive for its beautiful color and robust, generous, and long texture.

POMEROL 2004
Red | 2011 up to 2020   **90**
Beautiful color, elegantly oaked, rich and velvety, with lots of charm, suavity, and persistence on the finish.

Red: 5.4 acres; merlot 100%. Annual production: 6,000 bottles

CLOS PUY ARNAUD

7, Puy Arnaud
33350 Belvès-de-Castillon
Phone 00 33 5 57 47 90 33
Fax 00 33 5 57 47 90 53
clospuyarnaud@wanadoo.fr

Thierry Valette settled in Puy Arnaud in 2000. An exacting, ultratalented wine-grower, he soon became known for a particular style of wine that combines plenty of sap with fine-grained texture. In a region where producers tend to play on roundness and overripe fruit to the point of heaviness, Valette's wines are refreshingly honest, elegant, and crisp, with a clean mineral edge. Today they rank among the most elegant and thoroughbred of the Côtes de Castillon.

Recently tasted
CÔTES DE CASTILLON 2007
Red | 2011 up to 2015   **90**

Older vintages
CÔTES DE CASTILLON 2006
Red | 2011 up to 2013   **88**
Wonderful elegance, with pure fruit and pleasant notes of eucalyptus. The fine-grained, savory tannins make for a wine with wonderful length and perfect balance.

CÔTES DE CASTILLON 2005
Red | 2011 up to 2018   **91**
A sublime wine of amazingly expressive fruit, with a dense and harmonious mouthfeel. Huge aging potential. One of the best of the appellation.

CÔTES DE CASTILLON 2004
Red | 2011 up to 2013   **89**
This wine has great length and acidity underlined by tannins that aren't aggressive in the least. Expressive, long, and complete.

CÔTES DE CASTILLON 2001
Red | 2011 up to 2013   **90**
A brilliant accomplishment. This wine offers an immaculate pedigree, elegant tannins, and a magnificently full body.

Red: 29.7 acres; cabernet franc 30%, merlot 70%.
Annual production: 25,000 bottles

CHÂTEAU PUYGUERAUD

33570 Saint-Cibard
Phone 00 33 5 57 56 07 47
Fax 00 33 5 57 56 07 48
puygueraud@nicolas-thienpont.com
www.nicolas-thienpont.com

When purchased in 1946 by George Thienpont, father of Nicolas Thienpont, Château Puygueraud was in bad shape. Over the years Thienpont improved the soils, notably by planting grains and raising livestock here, not planting any vines until the 1970s. The location, at the upper part of the appellation on very clayey soils, provides these wines with power and structure. In 2000, Nicolas Thienpont purchased the eleven acres of Château La Prade. Half of the vineyards are located on a limestone plateau with nice clay, the other half on southern-facing hillsides.

Recently tasted
CÔTES DE FRANCS 2007
Red | 2011 up to 2013   **88**

CÔTES DE FRANCS CUVÉE GEORGES 2006
Red | 2011 up to 2016   **89**

Older vintages
CÔTES DE FRANCS 2006
Red | 2011 up to 2013   **86**
An elegant nose, with delicate fruit and pretty floral notes that also appear on the soft, fresh, and pleasant palate. Already very enjoyable to drink.

CÔTES DE FRANCS 2005
Red | 2011 up to 2013   **88**
This wine is impressive for its density and structure. The vintage brings out all of the classic characteristics of the growth, with a remarkably refined texture.

CÔTES DE FRANCS CHÂTEAU LA PRADE 2006
Red | 2011 up to 2013   **87**
The nose is superb, intense, ripe, and rich. The palate is along the same lines. It's a pleasing, well-balanced wine.

CÔTES DE FRANCS CHÂTEAU LA PRADE 2005
Red | 2011 up to 2013   **87**
Generous and intense with a nice, velvety mouth, this is a pleasant Côtes de Francs, with wonderful depth.

Red: 86.5 acres; cabernet franc 15%, malbec 5%, merlot 80%. Annual production: 120,000 bottles

CHÂTEAU QUINAULT L'ENCLOS

30, chemin Videlot
33500 Libourne
Phone 00 33 5 57 74 19 52
Fax 00 33 5 57 25 91 20
www.château-quinault.com

Quinault-l'Enclos is an oasis of greenery in the heart of the bustling little city of Libourne. For more than ten years now, it has been lovingly tended by Alain Raynaud, who turns out one of the most harmonious, seductive expressions of modern-style Saint-Émilion. The wine is very lush, fat, and rich, immediately exhibiting quite irresistible fruit, highlighted by careful, ambitious aging. Characteristics like these make this wine enjoyable when young and positively delightful in super-ripe vintages—particularly now that Alain Raynaud has found a way of making his generous wine fresher still.

SAINT-ÉMILION GRAND CRU 2006
Red I 2011 up to 2016   89
Soft, seductive nose of stone fruit; broad and well built, with a delicate and pleasant body.

SAINT-ÉMILION GRAND CRU 2005
Red I 2011 up to 2015   89
A wine without aggressiveness, this has nice finesse, being naturally soft, delicate, and round. It is developing a rich, fruity, and clean finish.

SAINT-ÉMILION GRAND CRU 2003
Red I 2011 up to 2015   92
Tasty, silky, deep, and refined with elegant tannins, this is a pretty and distinguished wine.

SAINT-ÉMILION GRAND CRU 2002
Red I 2011 up to 2013   88
Dark color. The nose is rich but not heavy, the body muscular with solid tannins; balanced.

SAINT-ÉMILION GRAND CRU 2001
Red I 2011 up to 2013   90
A very well-balanced wine, dense and profound, but also smooth on the finish.

SAINT-ÉMILION GRAND CRU 2000
Red I 2011 up to 2013   90
A succulent and rich wine that should be drunk now, made in a pretty style, with freshness and a truly lavish elegance.

Red: 44.5 acres; cabernet franc 15%, malbec 5%, merlot 70%, sauvignon 10%. **Annual production:** 75,000 bottles

ROC DE CAMBES

33710 Bourg
contact@roc-de-cambes.com
www.roc-de-cambes.com

François Mitjaville was the founding genius of Tertre-Roteboeuf in Saint-Émilion. About ten years ago, he embarked on an even more amazing venture: the creation of a grand vin from the Côtes de Bourg, one of the least-known Bordeaux appellations. The product is Roc de Cambes, made to the same exacting standards as all Mitjaville's offerings. Like Tertre-Roteboeuf, Roc de Cambes has turned out to be a brilliant success. The wine is highly sought after but still only produced in painfully small quantities.

CÔTES DE BOURG 2006
Red I 2011 up to 2016   90
The nose, with hints of little red fruits, is of absolute precision and freshness; in the mouth, the wine is evolving with much intensity and focus, with very elegant and fine-grained tannins.

CÔTES DE BOURG 2005
Red I 2011 up to 2018   92
The magnificent nose strikes a perfect balance between wood and fruit. It has an unctuously deep body, subtle and ethereal, and rises easily above the leaders of the appellation. A majestic wine.

CÔTES DE BOURG 2001
Red I 2011 up to 2013   91
This wine gracefully combines ripe fruit, fine texture, and backbone with a full body; the tannins are present but not at all aggressive.

CÔTES DE BOURG 2000
Red I 2011 up to 2018   88
Amazingly youthful wine, linear and cheerful, still showing notes of bright red fruit.

CÔTES DE BOURG 1999
Red I 2011 up to 2016   88
Lots of personality, linear, firm, with distinctive flavors and a remarkable freshness in the mouth.

Red: 24.7 acres; cabernet sauvignon 20%, malbec 5%, merlot 75%. **Annual production:** 45,000 bottles

CHÂTEAU ROL VALENTIN

5, Cabanes Sud
33330 Saint-Émilion
Phone 00 33 5 57 74 43 51
Fax 00 33 5 57 74 45 13
e.prissette@rolvalentin.com
www.rolvalentin.com

Éric Prissette, who sold this cru in 2009, began his career as a professional soccer player from the north of France. A love of competition and the drive for excellence were plainly what led him to acquire this estate in 1994. Since then, Rol Valentin has repeatedly been acclaimed for the intensity and quality of its great Saint-Émilion vintages. Sourced from a small vineyard, planted in a mixture of clay, limestone, and sandy soils, his wine delivers all the vigor but also charm of modern, merlot-driven Saint-Émilions: generous aromas, intense structure, all the power and depth you could wish for, and perfect balance. Rol Valentin is instantly seductive when young but also ages gracefully—now one of today's top wines.

Recently tasted
SAINT-ÉMILION GRAND CRU 2007
Red | 2011 up to 2017   **90**

Older vintages
SAINT-ÉMILION GRAND CRU 2006
Red | 2011 up to 2017   **90**
Powerful and dense, surprisingly austere at this tasting, this is a wine that is very well constructed but requires patience.

SAINT-ÉMILION GRAND CRU 2005
Red | 2011 up to 2018   **90**
Deep and intense, with the richness, flavor, and generosity that are the signature of this growth.

SAINT-ÉMILION GRAND CRU 2004
Red | 2011 up to 2015   **89**
Toasted, rich, broad, and powerful, this is an immediately flavorful wine with ripe and long volume on the palate.

SAINT-ÉMILION GRAND CRU 2001
Red | 2011 up to 2015   **89**
A super-concentrated wine, very ample and rich, with ultratight and enrobed tannins.

Red: 18.5 acres; cabernet sauvignon 3%, merlot 97%.
Annual production: 20,000 bottles

CHÂTEAU ROUGET

Route de Saint-Jacques-de-Compostelle
33500 Pomerol
Phone 00 33 5 57 51 05 85
Fax 00 33 5 57 55 22 45
château.rouget@wanadoo.fr
www.château-rouget.com

Mâcon businessman Jean-Pierre Labruyère (now also the owner of holdings on the Côte d'Or) has restored this lovely vineyard on the northern edge of the Pomerol plateau to the reputation it enjoyed some sixty years ago. The wines are intensely built and solidly structured, though the tannins still lack the silkiness and precision to equal the best.

Recently tasted
POMEROL 2007
Red | 2012 up to 2020   **90**

Older vintages
POMEROL 2006
Red | 2012 up to 2020   **92**
A refined and distinguished red, developing a bouquet of red fruit and a svelte body. Not as expansive as in 2005 but fresh and long.

POMEROL 2005
Red | 2011 up to 2025   **90**
Deeply colored, fruity, toasty and spicy, unctuous in texture, well rounded, richer but less elegant than the 2006.

POMEROL 2004
Red | 2011 up to 2018   **87**
A spicy and fat wine with tannins that lack a bit of finesse.

POMEROL 2001
Red | 2011 up to 2020   **93**
One of the great wines of the vintage in Pomerol. Great power, but also a fleshy texture that is particularly seductive.

POMEROL 2000
Red | 2011 up to 2020   **93**
An aromatic wine with superb substance and a sumptuous finish. A clear success.

Red: 43.2 acres; cabernet franc 15%, merlot 85%.
Annual production: 60,000 bottles

CAVE COOPÉRATIVE DE SAINT-ÉMILION

Haut-Gravet
BP 27
33330 Saint-Émilion
Phone 00 33 5 57 24 70 71
Fax 00 33 5 57 24 65 18
contact@udpse.com
www.udpse.com

This co-op can now hold its own against the best from Saint-Émilion, turning out some remarkable wines that position it among the leading cooperative wineries in France and among the top producers in its appellation. The range is huge but includes three very approachable and affordable bottlings that have never disappointed to date: Côte Rocheuse, Galius, and Aurélius. The emphasis remains firmly on disciplined viticulture, now supported by the co-op's own state-of-the-art winemaking facility. The results speak for themselves.

Recently tasted
SAINT-ÉMILION GRAND CRU AURÉLIUS 2007
Red | 2012 up to 2017   88

SAINT-ÉMILION GRAND CRU CÔTE ROCHEUSE 2007
Red | 2012 up to 2017   86

SAINT-ÉMILION GRAND CRU GALIUS 2007
Red | 2012 up to 2017   87

Older vintages
SAINT-ÉMILION GRAND CRU 2006
Red | 2011 up to 2013   83
The entry-level cuvée from the co-op is a very respectable offering of a half-million bottles. It is supple and well built, with clean fruit free of vegetal notes.

SAINT-ÉMILION GRAND CRU AURÉLIUS 2006
Red | 2011 up to 2013   89
Softer in personality than the 2005, but with pretty tannins and a nice élevage. A refined wine.

SAINT-ÉMILION GRAND CRU AURÉLIUS 2005
Red | 2011 up to 2015   89
A dense and solid wine, wonderful in its virility and its firm, long tannins.

SAINT-ÉMILION GRAND CRU AURÉLIUS 2004
Red | 2011 up to 2013   88
With nicely melded tannins, this wine is harmonious and deep, with a lovely and modern texture and a long finish.

SAINT-ÉMILION GRAND CRU
CHÂTEAU FLEUR-LARTIGUE 2006
Red | 2011 up to 2013   85
A supple and fresh wine with straightforward notes of red fruit, round on the palate.

SAINT-ÉMILION GRAND CRU
CHÂTEAU LAMARTRE 2006
Red | 2011 up to 2015   86
With softer tannins than the 2005, this is a rich wine with nice density.

SAINT-ÉMILION GRAND CRU
CÔTE ROCHEUSE 2006
Red | 2011 up to 2014   86
A dense and generous wine, slightly more firm than the 2005.

SAINT-ÉMILION GRAND CRU
CÔTE ROCHEUSE 2005
Red | 2011 up to 2014   87
Fat and rich, this very classic and full-bodied Saint-Émilion is immediately drinkable.

SAINT-ÉMILION GRAND CRU
CÔTE ROCHEUSE 2004
Red | 2011 up to 2013   86
Fruity, round, and harmonious, this is a nice Saint-Émilion, quite pleasant to drink now.

SAINT-ÉMILION GRAND CRU GALIUS 2006
Red | 2011 up to 2013   88
A nice, silky expression of a ripe merlot. Smooth and complete.

SAINT-ÉMILION GRAND CRU GALIUS 2005
Red | 2011 up to 2013   88
Beautiful color, pure fruit, balanced freshness, body, and length. The tannins have softened.

SAINT-ÉMILION GRAND CRU GALIUS 2004
Red | 2011 up to 2013   86
The hints of chocolate are a bit heavy, but this robust wine is at its peak now.

SAINT-ÉMILION GRAND CRU GALIUS 2003
Red | 2011 up to 2013   87
Ample, appetizing, no drying tannins, ready to drink.

Red: 1,977 acres. Annual production: 5,000,000 bottles

CLOS SAINT-MARTIN

GFA Les Grandes Murailles
Château Côte de Baleau
33330 Saint-Émilion
Phone 00 33 5 57 24 71 09
Fax 00 33 5 57 24 71 09
lesgrandesmurailles@wanadoo.fr
www.lesgrandesmurailles.fr

The tiny Clos Saint-Martin boasts a magnificent location on the Côte de Beauséjour, between two eponymously named vineyards. Since the late 1990s, this fabulous cru has been painstakingly cultivated and vinified by owners determined to take it to the forefront of quality. Its wines are rich but velvety and concentrated, with perfectly judged use of new oak.

Recently tasted
SAINT-ÉMILION GRAND CRU 2007
Red | 2012 up to 2017   89

Older vintages
SAINT-ÉMILION GRAND CRU 2006
Red | 2012 up to 2017   89
More softly built than the 2005, this is an elegant and distinguished wine, gracefully conveying pure and delicate fruit.

SAINT-ÉMILION GRAND CRU 2005
Red | 2011 up to 2020   92
Magnificent wine, encouragingly so. Now that it is in the bottle, it has wonderfully noble aromas and a texture that combines density and finesse. Superbly mouth-filling, easily at the level of a Premier Cru.

SAINT-ÉMILION GRAND CRU 2004
Red | 2011 up to 2015   89
Good intensity of color. The fruit is combined with notes of torrefaction and toast. Ample and succulent body, nice length.

SAINT-ÉMILION GRAND CRU 2002
Red | 2011 up to 2015   91
Delicious and complete: deep color, wonderfully fresh notes of red and black fruit, velvety, silky, elegant, and full body.

SAINT-ÉMILION GRAND CRU 2001
Red | 2011 up to 2015   90
Deep and elegant, with lovely, fine-grained tannins and a rich, smooth finish.

SAINT-ÉMILION GRAND CRU 2000
Red | 2011 up to 2020   92
Rich tannins, nice length: a modern wine, seductive, remarkably revealing of its terroir.

Red: 3.3 acres; cabernet franc 20%, cabernet sauvignon 10%, merlot 70%. **Annual production:** 5,000 bottles

CHÂTEAU SOUTARD

BP 4
33330 Saint-Émilion
Phone 00 33 5 57 24 71 41
Fax 00 33 5 57 74 42 80
contact@soutard-larmande.com
www.soutard-larmande.com

Château Soutard belonged to the same family from 1811 to 2006 when it was purchased by the French insurance group La Mondiale. Under previous owner François des Ligneris, Soutard was very much an estate apart, committed to organic production but otherwise strictly traditional. Given that Ligneris never submitted his wines for tasting by the press, we have little by which to judge the latest vintages. It will be interesting to see how this property develops under new ownership, bearing in mind that it boasts one of the largest vineyards of any of the Crus Classés.

Recently tasted
SAINT-ÉMILION LES JARDINS DE SOUTARD 2006
Red | 2011 up to 2015   85

Older vintages
SAINT-ÉMILION GRAND CRU 2007
Red | 2012 up to 2017   91
Much more convincing than Larmande, the other property owned by the insurance group La Mondiale, Soutard has an ample and silky body, with a supple, tannic grain.

SAINT-ÉMILION GRAND CRU 2005
Red | 2011 up to 2020   86
This is similar to this property's second wine in this vintage, but the tannins are more elegant. It has nice length, but the wine is austere. Needs time.

SAINT-ÉMILION GRAND CRU 2003
Red | 2011 up to 2020   90
With the absence of oak, this wine doesn't attract attention. Aromatically very discreet at first, it needs time to open up and reveal its wonderfully profound length and charming aromas that seem to come from an earlier era.

SAINT-ÉMILION GRAND CRU
CADET DE SOUTARD 2005
Red | 2011 up to 2015   84
Linear, quite restrained, but with nice notes of red fruit and good depth. The finish is still a bit hard.

Red: 66.7 acres; cabernet franc 30%, merlot 70%.
Annual production: 65,000 bottles

CHÂTEAU TAILLEFER

BP 9
33501 Libourne cedex
Phone 00 33 5 57 25 50 45
Fax 00 33 5 57 25 50 45
contact@moueixbernard.com
www.châteautaillefer.fr

This classic cru was the first to be acquired by the Moueix family and is owned today by Bernard Moueix's children, with Catherine Moueix at the helm. The vineyard is planted in sand and gravel soils on the southern half of the Pomerol plateau. Thanks to Catherine's astute management, the estate has come a long way over the past ten years. The vineyards are meticulously maintained, and the wines are carefully vinified and matured, with help from enologist Denis Dubourdieu. The result is a very precise Pomerol, deliciously clean with not a showy aroma in sight.

Recently tasted
POMEROL 2007
Red | 2011 up to 2017   88

POMEROL 2006
Red | 2012 up to 2018   89

Older vintages
POMEROL 2005
Red | 2011 up to 2015   88
Pretty with classic aromas of red fruit and spice and a slight touch of minerality, this is a very pleasurable wine, fleshy and endowed with firm but elegant tannins. A very traditional style in this region, with a density worthy of the vintage.

POMEROL 2004
Red | 2011 up to 2020   90
Generously but delicately oaked, this wine seems rich, with an elegant texture, but it also has a streak of rich juiciness, unctuous and torrefied. A great success.

POMEROL 2001
Red | 2011 up to 2013   88
Fat and well balanced, the wine has tannins that are neither aggressive nor heavy.

Red: 32.1 acres; cabernet franc 25%, merlot 75%.
Annual production: 60,000 bottles

CHÂTEAU LE TERTRE-ROTEBOEUF

33330 Saint-Laurent-des-Combes
Fax 00 33 5 57 74 42 11
tertre.roteboeuf-roc.de.cambes@wanadoo.fr
www.tertre-roteboeuf.com

François Mitjaville has more artistic sensibility than any other great Bordeaux winegrower. His passion for philosophy and art history has carried his natural, and obvious, talent for wine tasting to a new level, using it as a tool to fashion the personality of the wine. The magnificent arching hill of the Tertre effectively marks the end of the Côte Pavie. The cooler microclimate here prolongs ripening times and vegetative growth in general, encouraging the development of fantastic aromas that are unique in Saint-Émilion. The winemaking process strives to capture and stabilize those aromas, and the only way to do that (as the intuitive, empirically minded François Mitjaville was sharp enough to realize) is to apply enological science. He works hand-in-hand with one of today's foremost authorities on wine microbiology, aiming to strike that happy balance between oxidation and reduction that distinguishes a masterfully aged wine. Lavish in body and nose, with voluptuous texture, Tertre-Roteboeuf attracts a devoted following of esthetes who rank it among their all-time favorite wines.

Recently tasted
SAINT-ÉMILION GRAND CRU 2007
Red | 2015 up to 2025   94
Refined and delicate, this wine is a jewel, showing delicacy and depth: a palette of ripe red fruit, silky length, almost fragile but also extremely long, focused, distinguished, and balanced.

SAINT-ÉMILION GRAND CRU 2006
Red | 2014 up to 2030   95
The wine opens up in the mouth, with a quite extraordinary velvety smooth depth. The tannic grain is out of this world, with mind-blowing finesse.

SAINT-ÉMILION GRAND CRU 2005
Red | 2015 up to 2030   96
The wine shows impressive aromas of perfectly ripened grapes; notes of plum, blackberry, young leather, sweet spices; and an absolutely unique texture and constitution. Everything is perfectly integrated, despite the concentration and power of the fruit, thanks to a perfectly executed oxidation process. A marvelous wine.

Saint-Émilion grand cru 2004
Red | 2012 up to 2019   **93**
One of the richest, most balanced, and most complex of the vintage, despite the huge risks taken during vinification. A mouthfeel that is unique to the property.

Saint-Émilion grand cru 2003
Red | 2013 up to 2018   **96**
In an exceptionally hot year, Tertre's cooler and later-ripening terroir allowed them to produce a giant, but a civilized giant, with aristocratic composure and majestic texture.

Saint-Émilion grand cru 2001
Red | 2011 up to 2020   **96**
Svelte and dense, not at all heavy or hot, this is an elegant wine, full of depth.

Saint-Émilion grand cru 2000
Red | 2011 up to 2020   **98**
Delicately fruity and floral, showing subtlety thanks to an expertly handled élevage, this is a wine that is smooth, but devilishly artistic and extraordinarily refined.

Saint-Émilion grand cru 1999
Red | 2011 up to 2019   **96**
A delicate bouquet of moss and flowers that transcends the limitations of the vintage, combining a freshness and an energy that many wines have already lost.

Saint-Émilion grand cru 1998
Red | 2011 up to 2018   **98**
A monumental wine, with stunning youth, fruit, and sparkle. Unforgettable!

Red: 14 acres; cabernet franc 15%, merlot 85%.
Annual production: 27,000 bottles

ÉTABLISSEMENTS THUNEVIN

🍷🍷 🍷🍷

6, rue Guadet
33330 Saint-Émilion
Phone 00 33 5 57 55 09 13
Fax 00 33 5 57 55 09 12
www.thunevin.com

Château Valandraud owner Jean-Luc Thunevin also works as négociant and consultant for numerous châteaux. His specialty is top-end wines, but a few years ago he branched out into inexpensive Bordeaux, creating Présidial, a unique cuvée offered in bottles or as box wine. On a more ambitious front, he is building up a range of tasty estate-bottled wines—such as Compassant, vinified by Guillaume Quéron.

Recently tasted
Bordeaux Bad Boy 2007
Red | 2011 up to 2013   **89**

Lalande de Pomerol Domaine des Sabines 2007
Red | 2011 up to 2013   **88**

Margaux Bellevue de Tayac 2007
Red | 2011 up to 2014   **87**

Older vintages
Bordeaux Bad Boy 2006
Red | 2011 up to 2013   **88**
A pretty Bordeaux, charming but well built. Very appealing attack, with a beautifully fruity nose and good aging potential.

Bordeaux Bad Boy 2005
Red | 2011 up to 2013   **92**
Super-dark color. Almost overripe on the nose with lots of fruit and opulence; rich, flavorful, and velvety on the palate with a really nice tannic weave. The finish is tight and long. With wonderful character, this wine is ambitious yet restrained, not trying to imitate a Grand Cru.

Bordeaux Présidial 2006
Red | 2011 up to 2013   **86**
An easy and pleasant Bordeaux, well made with an elegant nose of spicy, ripe fruit and a straightfoward, minerally, and full mouthfeel.

Bordeaux Présidial 2005
Red | 2011 up to 2013   **88**
In the same style as the 2004, with an intense nose of black fruit and smoke; full, tight, and fresh on the palate. Yet another very drinkable wine.

Annual production: 230,000 bottles

CHÂTEAU LA TOUR FIGEAC

BP 007
33330 Saint-Émilion
Phone 00 33 5 57 51 77 62
Fax 00 33 5 57 25 36 92
latourfigeac@wanadoo.fr
www.latourfigeac.com

As its name suggests, this cru originally formed part of Château Figeac until the plot was sold off in the late nineteenth century. It shares the gravel terroir that is specific to the Graves area and relies, indeed, on a high proportion of cabernet franc, which thrives in these soils. The estate was purchased by a German family in 1973 and is owned and managed today by son and heir Otto Rettenmaier. Things have progressed splendidly since he took over in 1994, ably supported by technical director Christine Dernoncourt. Viticulture, for instance, has been entirely biodynamic for a decade.

Recently tasted

SAINT-ÉMILION GRAND CRU 2007
Red | 2012 up to 2017　　　　　　86

SAINT-ÉMILION GRAND CRU 2006
Red | 2012 up to 2017　　　　　　87

Older vintages

SAINT-ÉMILION GRAND CRU 2005
Red | 2011 up to 2015　　　　　　90
A well-made wine that is rich and full: nice color, flawlessly built, ripe tannins, long and svelte.

SAINT-ÉMILION GRAND CRU 2004
Red | 2011 up to 2013　　　　　　86
Rich and full with a more supple constitution than the previous and following vintages.

SAINT-ÉMILION GRAND CRU 2003
Red | 2011 up to 2015　　　　　　89
A solid and powerful wine, generous in body, intense in heady aromas, but also with a seductive liveliness on the finish.

SAINT-ÉMILION GRAND CRU 2001
Red | 2011 up to 2015　　　　　　90
This wine has a wonderful succulence, which is expressed with richness and elegance thanks to well-integrated and polished tannins.

SAINT-ÉMILION GRAND CRU 2000
Red | 2011 up to 2020　　　　　　91
Nice style, openly hedonistic. Aromatic and suave.

Red: 35.8 acres; cabernet franc 35%, merlot 65%. Annual production: 45,000 bottles

CHÂTEAU TRIANON

33330 Saint-Émilion
Phone 00 33 5 57 25 34 46
Fax 00 33 5 57 25 28 61
contact@château-trianon.com

Château Trianon is located on the outskirts of Libourne, on interesting sandy soils that require proper drainage to give of their best. This they now have thanks to new owner Dominique Hébrard, who took over in 2001 and set about achieving great things. Quality has really taken off in recent years, especially the 2001, 2003, and 2005 vintages. These are lush, fat, sappy wines, made for early drinking.

Recently tasted

SAINT-ÉMILION GRAND CRU 2007
Red | 2012 up to 2017　　　　　　90

Older vintages

SAINT-ÉMILION GRAND CRU 2006
Red | 2012 up to 2017　　　　　　88
Good color, expressive aromas of black fruit, full and silky mouth, long and quite elegant.

SAINT-ÉMILION GRAND CRU 2005
Red | 2011 up to 2017　　　　　　90
Long and profound, fruity nose, rounded out by a touch of elegant oak. Succulent, more tannic than usual, long. We will happily wait two to three more years in order to fully appreciate its charm.

SAINT-ÉMILION GRAND CRU 2004
Red | 2011 up to 2014　　　　　　84
The wine is powerful, but the aromas and tannins have vegetal notes.

SAINT-ÉMILION GRAND CRU 2003
Red | 2011 up to 2015　　　　　　90
Deep color, pure and subtle fruit, round and soft in the mouth, elegant, fine, and rich, lacking the depth of the wines grown on the hillsides, but soft and charming.

SAINT-ÉMILION GRAND CRU 2002
Red | 2011 up to 2013　　　　　　87
This wine is solid and robust with nice body and round tannins, but the finish lacks the desired freshness.

SAINT-ÉMILION GRAND CRU 2001
Red | 2011 up to 2015　　　　　　89
Softly built, but with substance, and a delicate and elegant tannic structure.

Red: 24.7 acres; cabernet franc 10%, cabernet sauvignon 5%, carmenère 5%, merlot 80%. Annual production: 50,000 bottles

CHÂTEAU LES TROIS CROIX

Lieu-dit Les-Trois-Croix
33126 Fronsac
Phone 00 33 5 57 84 32 09
Fax 00 33 5 57 84 34 03
lestroiscroix@aol.com
www.châteaulestroiscroix.com

This very old Fronsac property dates from the early eighteenth century and is named after the three church spires visible in the distance, each one located in a different Fronsac commune. The property was purchased in 1995 by well-known enologist and winemaker Patrick Léon (Mouton-Rothschild), who now runs it with his son and daughter. The wines reflect his winemaking philosophy, focusing on balance and finesse for the sake of length and slenderness rather than power and heaviness. All of which now makes this estate a benchmark producer of Fronsac wines.

FRONSAC 2006
Red | 2012 up to 2016   90
Dark color. This is deep and full-bodied, rich and flavorful, with clear potential.

FRONSAC 2005
Red | 2011 up to 2015   90
Built to age, this vintage is intense with lots of vitality and volume. With an additional year in the bottle the tannins have, fortunately, softened a bit.

FRONSAC 2004
Red | 2011 up to 2013   88
This wine, focused and harmoniously built, reveals expressive fruit and a structure that has not the slightest hint of weight or rusticity. Nice length.

FRONSAC 2003
Red | 2011 up to 2013   89
With notes of sweet pepper and ripe fruit, the voluminous body is long and radiant. This is a wine with lots of character and length.

Red: 37.6 acres; cabernet franc 15%, merlot 85%.
Annual production: 60,000 bottles

CHÂTEAU TROPLONG-MONDOT

33330 Saint-Émilion
Phone 00 33 5 57 55 32 05
Fax 00 33 5 57 55 32 07
contact@château-troplong-mondot.com
www.château-troplong-mondot.com

The vineyards of Troplong-Mondot run from the top of the Côte Pavie all along the escarpment—a magnificent site where time and fashion seem to have no importance. And yet some remarkable work has gone into this cru, which for several years now has been one of the foremost Saint-Émilion producers. Its recent promotion to Premier Cru Classé is a just reward for owner Christine Valette's committed efforts over the past twenty years, using state-of-the-art viticultural techniques to bring out the best in her remarkable terroir. The soils and microclimate are very similar to those around Pavie, yielding deep, robust, but harmonious wines that slowly develop an elegant bouquet of spice and truffles. The "grand vin" is made from a rigorous selection of the best wines, which guarantees consistently high quality, with truly outstanding results in great vintages such as 1990, 1995, 1998, 2000, 2003, and 2005.

Recently tasted
SAINT-ÉMILION GRAND CRU 2007
Red | 2012 up to 2020   92

Older vintages
SAINT-ÉMILION GRAND CRU 2006
Red | 2012 up to 2018   93
Fat, succulent, ample, truffle-laced, rich, and long, this is an intensely concentrated wine that needs time.

SAINT-ÉMILION GRAND CRU 2005
Red | 2012 up to 2025   96
A wine of great stature, with a truffly, rich nose and a full and luscious body, wonderfully deep and generous.

SAINT-ÉMILION GRAND CRU 2004
Red | 2011 up to 2017   90
A pleasant but not very powerful vintage, with notes of jammy fruit, a silky palate, persistence, and a fresh finish.

SAINT-ÉMILION GRAND CRU 2003
Red | 2011 up to 2020   94
Powerful, solid, magnificently flavorful and robust, this is a Troplong for aging, with a characteristic nose of ripe fruit and roasted coffee.

Saint-Émilion grand cru 2002
Red | 2011 up to 2014   **90**
Similar in style to the 1988, this is a beautifully dense and profound wine, slightly austere, but exhibiting wonderfully ripe volume.

Saint-Émilion grand cru 2001
Red | 2011 up to 2020   **92**
The wine is ample and tannic with impressive volume. The balance is a bit heavier than the 2000, but it can be aged without hesitation.

Saint-Émilion grand cru 2000
Red | 2011 up to 2020   **95**
Lively, dense, and tight, this is a wine to be forgotten in the cellar. Right now it is austere, but the body is exceptionally distinguished.

Saint-Émilion grand cru 1999
Red | 2011 up to 2019   **93**
A nicely made wine in this vintage: delicate and well-delineated fruit, lovely acidity, fine tannins, wonderful length.

Saint-Émilion grand cru 1998
Red | 2011 up to 2020   **94**
This shows a wonderfully deep color, ripe fruit, and richness with notes of licorice and wonderful volume, but with less precision than the 2005.

Red: 56.8 acres; cabernet franc 5%, cabernet sauvignon 5%, merlot 90%. **Annual production:** 100,000 bottles

CHÂTEAU TROTANOY

33500 Pomerol
Phone 00 33 5 57 51 78 96
Fax 00 33 5 57 51 79 79
info@jpmoueix.com
www.moueix.com

Trotanoy, like neighboring Pétrus, is planted on very clayey soils that favor a mix of vines heavily dominated by merlot. Its wines—also like Pétrus and indeed all the "Moueix group" offerings—are vinified and aged by Jean-Claude Berrouet. Trotanoy and Pétrus are both wines to be reckoned with, but in terms of personality they are actually quite different. Trotanoy always seems more structured, straighter, less exuberant, and smoother than Pétrus. Its fairly lively fruit withstands aging and adds extra freshness to that truffly range of aromas seen in the mature wine. All of the recent vintages are deep and intense.

Recently tasted
Pomerol 2006
Red | 2012 up to 2025   **95**

Older vintages
Pomerol 2005
Red | 2011 up to 2025   **96**
The bouquet, which is just starting to develop, is subtle and diverse, with notes of violet and wild strawberries; in the mouth it reveals itself to be quite profound, with freshness and a long, intense, and velvety finish. Huge potential.

Pomerol 2004
Red | 2011 up to 2020   **92**
The color is not very intense, but the wine shows notes of pure red fruit and wonderful freshness in the mouth. The structure is linear and refined with nice length.

Pomerol 2001
Red | 2011 up to 2020   **92**
With very firm tannins, this is a tightly wound, powerful Pomerol, made for long-term aging.

Pomerol 2000
Red | 2011 up to 2025   **95**
Remarkable body, rich and ample but tightly wound with noble notes of black truffles: an earthy wine but very harmonious and long.

Red: 17.8 acres; cabernet franc 10%, merlot 90%.
Annual production: 25,000 bottles

CHÂTEAU TROTTEVIEILLE

33330 Saint-Émilion
Phone 00 33 5 56 00 00 70
Fax 00 33 5 57 87 60 30
bordeaux@borie-manoux.fr

Although very well located at the northeast edge of Saint-Émilion, this cru's performance in the 1980s and 1990s never justified its Premier Cru Classé classification. Not until Philippe Castéja took over, supported by brilliant enologist Denis Dubourdieu, did this cru take on that extra dimension also seen in Lynch-Moussas and Batailley, Castéja's other properties. The dawn of the millennium definitely marked a turning point for Trottevieille, now showing a charming, very bold intensity, balanced by finesse and freshness and all the thoroughbred character of a long, slender Saint-Émilion that is irresistible even when very young.

Recently tasted

SAINT-ÉMILION GRAND CRU 2007
Red | 2012 up to 2020   90

Older vintages

SAINT-ÉMILION GRAND CRU 2006
Red | 2012 up to 2018   90
The wine seems pretty tight at this point and is cautiously coming to life: it should be tasted again in another year.

SAINT-ÉMILION GRAND CRU 2005
Red | 2011 up to 2020   94
Filled with sparkle and distinction, this is wonderfully fresh and bright, and magnificently restrained.

SAINT-ÉMILION GRAND CRU 2004
Red | 2011 up to 2015   88
Nice color, pretty oak on the nose, soft and round, quite agreeable, a friendly wine, medium body, but straightforward and very well balanced.

SAINT-ÉMILION GRAND CRU 2003
Red | 2011 up to 2020   92
The first truly great wine from this property in a long time: deep color, super-toasty oak, fat, rich, generous, a well-defined and direct personality. What a pleasure!

SAINT-ÉMILION GRAND CRU 2002
Red | 2011 up to 2014   85
Garnet color, not super-deep, red fruit, soft attack with tannins that are soft but dry; pleasant but limited.

SAINT-ÉMILION GRAND CRU 2001
Red | 2011 up to 2014   88
The wine is harmonious and complete, finishing with originality and class.

SAINT-ÉMILION GRAND CRU 2000
Red | 2011 up to 2015   90
The tannins are slightly green at this point, but the wine is elegant and refined, alluring.

SAINT-ÉMILION GRAND CRU 1999
Red | 2011 up to 2015   90
Not super-concentrated but pretty and refined, this has retained its fruit.

SAINT-ÉMILION GRAND CRU 1998
Red | 2011 up to 2015   89
Delicate, evolved, but with very subtle fruit, this is elegant up until the finish, which is a bit drying.

Red: 24.7 acres; cabernet franc 45%, cabernet sauvignon 5%, merlot 50%. **Annual production:** 40,000 bottles

CHÂTEAU VALANDRAUD

6, rue Guadet
33330 Saint-Émilion
Phone 00 33 5 57 55 09 13
Fax 00 33 5 57 55 09 12
thunevin@thunevin.com
www.thunevin.com

Jean-Luc Thunevin started this estate from scratch in the early 1990s. Since then it has grown exponentially, from one and a half acres to twenty-four acres today. The Cru Valandraud, which began the craze for so-called "garage wines," has in that time turned into one of the most harmonious and distinguished of all the Saint-Émilions: ultraripe and perfumed with a solid backbone of smooth, rich, velvety wood. Valandraud is an accomplished wine, broad-minded and broad-shouldered but with delicate, refined tannins—a modern and original take on a certain idea of the perfect wine.

Recently tasted

SAINT-ÉMILION GRAND CRU 2007
Red | 2012 up to 2017   92

SAINT-ÉMILION GRAND CRU VIRGINIE DE VALANDRAUD 2007
Red | 2012 up to 2017   90

Older vintages

SAINT-ÉMILION GRAND CRU 2006
Red | 2012 up to 2017   93
Still tightly wrapped, this is deeply colored, meaty, and extracted, with notes of black fruit, but also elegant in its tannins and length. The alcohol is still evident.

SAINT-ÉMILION GRAND CRU 2005
Red | 2011 up to 2020   96
The wine is quite seductive, with well-integrated oak, a velvety, rich body, and nice length. There is also a deep and powerful structure that guarantees a terrifically long evolution in the bottle.

SAINT-ÉMILION GRAND CRU 2004
Red | 2011 up to 2015   92
Pretty color, deep and brilliant; an imposing nose of black fruit and ample toast; vinous, powerful, and long. One of the great successes of the vintage.

SAINT-ÉMILION GRAND CRU 2001
Red | 2011 up to 2020   96
This magnificent wine has a wonderfully fine texture and pedigree, a deep body, and great length, all fresh and delicately flavored.

SAINT-ÉMILION GRAND CRU 2000
Red | 2011 up to 2020   96
A 2000 that is keeping its promises with regal elegance: deep, unctuous, silky, very rich, and showing pure fruit on the palate. Still a youngster.

SAINT-ÉMILION GRAND CRU 1999
Red | 2011 up to 2016   88
Supple and elegant but lacking the intensity and vivacity of the 1998, 2000, or 2001.

SAINT-ÉMILION GRAND CRU 1998
Red | 2011 up to 2020   98
Magnificent wine with brilliantly silky tannins and unctuous depth. The finish, with notes of prunes and mocha, is at its peak.

SAINT-ÉMILION GRAND CRU
VIRGINIE DE VALANDRAUD 2006
Red | 2012 up to 2017   91
Quite deeply colored, offering red fruit and oak notes, this is straightfoward and linear, only average in complexity, but very clean.

SAINT-ÉMILION GRAND CRU
VIRGINIE DE VALANDRAUD 2005
Red | 2011 up to 2015   88
Unctuous and supple, a harmonious wine with elegant tannins.

SAINT-ÉMILION GRAND CRU
VIRGINIE DE VALANDRAUD 2004
Red | 2011 up to 2013   89
A full-bodied, harmonious wine with lots of body and substance.

Red: 24 acres; cabernet franc 25%, cabernet sauvignon 2.5%, malbec 2.5%, merlot 70%. Annual production: 12,000 bottles

Bettane & Desseauve
Selections for Burgundy

Burgundy

This historical region is a veritable work of art with its multifaceted diversity of soils and microclimates, each of which merits its own individual AOC. Burgundy has never before been so faithfully studied and followed by lovers of pinot noir and chardonnay, which grow here in their native soils.

The white soils of Chablis are the perfect growing place for minerally, elegant white wines. Though sometimes austere in cold years, they have the amazing ability to come alive once they are served with food. Global warming has given some of the lesser-known Chablis appellations a second chance, and the wines often closely resemble their more famous neighbors. In the small appellation of Saint-Bris, the whites made from sauvignon blanc and the reds made from pinot noir are actually starting to resemble wine!

The Côtes de Nuits, a tiny strip of vineyards, produces some of the most famous wines on the planet, but you must choose carefully, as the quality can vary widely from one producer to the next. Near the wonderfully tourist-friendly city of Beaune, whites and reds of the Côte de Beaune can reach the greatest heights of finesse, complexity, and personality.

In the Côte Chalonnaise, we find ourselves in the heart of "old France" with its wonderfully charming, tranquil villages, where they produce very pleasant early-drinking wines.

Le Mâconnais region is stunningly beautiful and in the midst of a true revolution in terms of quality. Chardonnay is king here, and the wines are more opulent thanks to warmer temperatures and more sun. When this opulence is reined in by the limestone soils, the resulting wine has a solid backbone, and it can be pure pleasure! The prices have thankfully remained reasonable.

Beaujolais, a little farther south, is one of the most beautiful wine regions in France. The wines made here are justifiably popular, but the worldwide success of Beaujolais Nouveau has unfairly tarnished the reputation of the most expressive wines of the region. Some of the wines achieve unexpected greatness. It's time to rediscover Beaujolais!

Appellation Overview
Winegrowing Burgundy, with its myriad communes and traditions, represents a geological and human puzzle like no other—and French legislation makes sure it stays that way. When trying to make sense of it all, however, you will find there is a clearly defined hierarchy of appellations.

Regional Appellations
Burgundy at its most basic level is a simple, straightforward wine from vineyards throughout the Burgundy terroir (departments of the Yonne, Côte d'Or, Saône-et-Loire, and Rhone). The label may specify the name of the varietal (Bourgogne Aligoté) or the particular sub-region where the wine is produced (Bourgogne Côte Chalonnaise, Bourgogne Côte d'Auxerre, Bourgogne Hautes-Côtes de Nuits). The appellations Bourgogne Passe-Tout-Grain (a blend of pinot noir and gamay grapes) and Bourgogne Grand Ordinaire (from terroirs that are in principle inferior) are relics of former times and are hardly ever used today.

Communal Appellations
The best villages may be appellations in their own right or part of an appellation shared with neighboring communes. They may be associated with a particular (precisely defined) vineyard, which in some cases may rank as a classified growth: for instance, Pommard, Pommard La Vache, Pommard Rugiens (part of this *lieu-dit* falls under village appellation; the other half is classified as premier cru).

Grands Crus

The top Burgundy vineyards are classified growths and rank as appellations in their own right, but the name of the village is no longer anywhere to be seen (e.g., Chambertin, Bonnes-Mares, and Richebourg). Just to complicate matters, some villages won the right to attach their own names to those of their most famous grand cru vineyard—for instance, Chambolle-Musigny or Gevrey-Chambertin. The wines from these villages are not to be confused with those from the grands crus in question, and are always less expensive.

Yonne Wines

This is as far north as red grapes will ripen in France and, except for a few cuvées from the Irancy area, the reds lack color and body. The whites, on the other hand, are famous for their crispness and finesse, the top performers coming from the premier Chablis terroirs. In theory there are four quality levels of Chablis, but the varying fortunes of the region as a whole have led to considerable overlap. Village wines made from old vines can outclass washed-up, badly made grands crus.

Whatever the case, a good Chablis really shows its stuff only after five years' cellaring; some are stunning after twenty years.

Côte d'Or Wines

The Côte d'Or is the historic heart of Burgundy. The road from Dijon to Chagny passes a procession of villages that are unrivaled in France for their incomparably aromatic red and white wines—even though the discipline required to produce them is still not as widespread as it should be. Red Côte de Nuits wines, particularly those from Gevrey-Chambertin and Nuits-Saint-Georges, tend to be more robust than their Côte de Beaune counterparts, even slightly aggressive as young wines. Wines from Chambolle-Musigny and Vosne-Romanée are more delicate but also fleshier and creamier. Of the Côte de Beaune wines, the most robust (in principle at least) come from the Corton Grand Cru and the best Pommard vineyards. The softest and most delicate come from Savigny, Beaune, and Volnay. At both ends of the Côte d'Or, you find little-known villages (just moments away from their over-hyped neighbors) that turn out little gems at very reasonable prices—a real treat for the curious connoisseur. At the same time you also find wines that are nothing special.

Prices vary widely but, because the grands crus are so expensive, people tend to overlook all those other, much more affordable wines that are already well appreciated by people who know a good producer when they see one. So be guided by our ratings.

One thing we can never hope to change however is the inconsistency of vintages. Once or twice every decade we get a year that sees no sun at all, and there is nothing that can make up for that.

Saône-et-Loire Wines

This huge and diverse region extends from the Côte Chalonnaise to the Mâconnais (on the northern border of Beaujolais). The Côte Chalonnaise produces very agreeable red and white wines—slightly less complex than those from the Côte d'Or, but very reasonably priced. The Mâconnais specializes in white wines that deserve to be better known.

Chablis Vineyards

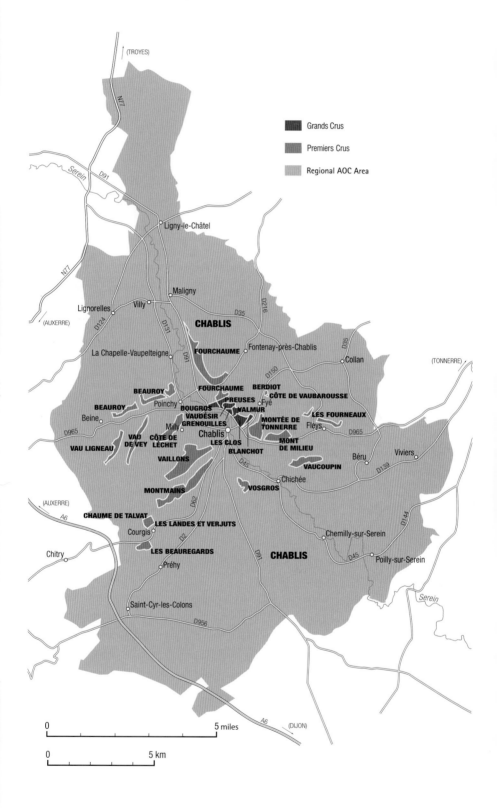

Grands Crus
Premiers Crus
Regional AOC Area

(TROYES)

N77

Serein

D91

Ligny-le-Châtel

N77

Maligny

Lignorelles

Villy

D124

D131

D91

D35

D216

(AUXERRE)

CHABLIS

La Chapelle-Vaupelteigne

FOURCHAUME

Fontenay-près-Chablis

D35

Collan

(TONNERRE)

D150

BEAUROY

FOURCHAUME

BERDIOT

CÔTE DE VAUBAROUSSE

BEAUROY

Poinchy

PREUSES

Fyé

LES FOURNEAUX

Beine

BOUGROS

VAUDÉSIR

MALMUR

Fleys

D965

GRENOUILLES

Milly

MONTÉE DE TONNERRE

D965

VAU DE VEY

CÔTE DE LÉCHET

Chablis

MONT DE MILIEU

VAU LIGNEAU

LES CLOS

BLANCHOT

Béru

Viviers

VAILLONS

D45

VAUCOUPIN

D139

Chichée

MONTMAINS

VOSGROS

(AUXERRE)

D62

CHAUME DE TALVAT

A6

LES LANDES ET VERJUTS

Courgis

Chemilly-sur-Serein

D144

Chitry

D2

LES BEAUREGARDS

CHABLIS

D45

Poilly-sur-Serein

Préhy

D91

Saint-Cyr-les-Colons

Serein

D956

A6

(DIJON)

0 ———————— 5 miles

0 ———————— 5 km

Yonne Vineyards

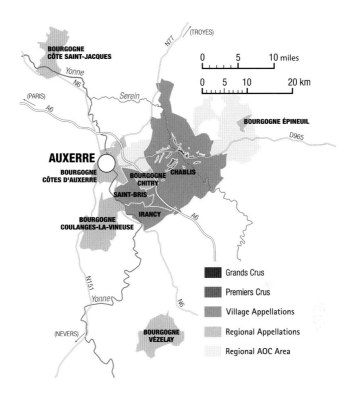

DOMAINE JEAN-CLAUDE BESSIN

18, rue de Chitry
89800 Chablis
Phone 00 33 3 86 42 46 77
Fax 00 33 3 86 42 85 30
dnejcbessin@wanadoo.fr

Jean-Claude Bessin has run this thirty-acre property for the past eighteen years. Being the reserved but gifted winemaker that he is, he lets his wines do the talking. Thanks to tiny yields, his Chablis are concentrated and pure, with incisive mineral edge. His vintage 2005, in particular, received top marks! The entire Bessin range is worth a look, as they are exceptionally well priced.

Recently tasted

CHABLIS GRAND CRU VALMUR 2007
White | 2012 up to 2022   91

CHABLIS PREMIER CRU FOURCHAUME 2007
White | 2012 up to 2017   88

CHABLIS PREMIER CRU FOURCHAUME LA PIÈCE AU COMTE 2007
White | 2012 up to 2022   90

CHABLIS PREMIER CRU LA FORÊT 2007
White | 2012 up to 2022   90

CHABLIS PREMIER CRU MONTMAINS 2007
White | 2012 up to 2017   86

CHABLIS VIEILLES VIGNES 2007
White | 2011 up to 2014   86

Older vintages

CHABLIS GRAND CRU VALMUR 2006
White | 2011 up to 2018   92
A concentrated, taut wine. The grapes' juice is superbly mature, and the fairly high alcohol is perfectly balanced by good acidity. Peppery finish.

CHABLIS PREMIER CRU LA FORÊT 2006
White | 2011 up to 2016   89
This is the first vintage of this cuvée sold. Mineral, marked by notes of underbrush. The palate offers mature, lip-smacking, juicy fruit. The character of Montmains comes through clearly.

CHABLIS PREMIER CRU MONTMAINS 2006
White | 2011 up to 2016   89
Fruity and opulent, this is a rich, generous wine. Its juicy tastiness makes you want to bite into it. It ends on a fresher note than the Fourchaume. It is a notch above—and, not surprisingly, it is already sold out at the domaine.

White: 29.7 acres; chardonnay 100%. **Annual production:** 55,000 bottles

DOMAINE BILLAUD-SIMON

1, quai de Reugny
BP 46
89800 Chablis
Phone 00 33 3 86 42 10 33
Fax 00 33 3 86 42 48 77
bernard.billaud@online.fr
www.billaud-simon.com

Samuel Billaud's lovely fifty-acre property turns out an excellent range of Chablis from some handsome terroirs. His wines are pure but fat and made in a style quite unlike a Droin, say. The only catch is that some of the cuvées are bottled in batches, and length of maturation varies accordingly. So too, of course, does the taste, a point that should be made clear to the consumer!

Recently tasted

CHABLIS GRAND CRU LES BLANCHOTS 2006
White | 2011 up to 2021   94

CHABLIS GRAND CRU LES CLOS 2006
White | 2011 up to 2021   93

CHABLIS GRAND CRU VAUDÉSIR 2006
White | 2011 up to 2017   93

CHABLIS PREMIER CRU LES FOURCHAUMES 2007
White | 2011 up to 2017   90

CHABLIS TÊTE D'OR 2007
White | 2011 up to 2017   88

Older vintages

CHABLIS GRAND CRU LES BLANCHOTS 2005
White | 2011 up to 2020   91
On the palate, this is a fat, rich wine, but it lacks length and freshness compared to the Clos or the Preuses. It clearly has not yet found its final balance but shows great potential.

CHABLIS GRAND CRU LES CLOS 2005
White | 2011 up to 2025   94
An intense, concentrated, straightforward nose. Rich and taut on the palate, with a superb minerality, a bit closed right now, but it will slowly develop. The finish is tight but long.

CHABLIS GRAND CRU LES PREUSES 2005
White | 2011 up to 2020   93
Very elegant, delicate, and sharply defined, this is a pure, straightforward Grand Cru. The clean attack is drawn out by a pleasant crystalline sensation. A highly seasoned, racy finish.

CHABLIS GRAND CRU VAUDÉSIR 2005
White | 2011 up to 2020   92
A powerful, dense, expressive nose showing intense floral notes and blackberries;
almost spicy. Fat and taut on the palate, with
good concentration. Definitely needs to age.
A nicely balanced, saline finish.

CHABLIS PREMIER CRU
LES FOURCHAUMES 2005
White | 2011 up to 2013   90
A very floral nose, dominated by honey and
flower aromas. The palate is elegant, tending toward sunny floral notes. Good freshness and a concentrated mineral tension
on the finish.

CHABLIS PREMIER CRU MONT DE MILIEU 2006
White | 2011 up to 2016   90
The nose is marked by ripe, slightly exotic
fruit. The palate is fat and rich, with a minerality that will dominate for several years,
even though there is heat on the finish.

CHABLIS PREMIER CRU
MONT DE MILIEU VIEILLES VIGNES 2005
White | 2011 up to 2020   90
A very rich wine with good concentration.
Rich and fat, with good tension on the pal-
ate. A nice freshness.

CHABLIS PREMIER CRU
MONTÉE DE TONNERRE 2006
White | 2011 up to 2016   90
A powerful, expressive nose with floral notes
already blending with the minerality. But this
one will require patience. The palate is fat,
rich, and well concentrated. The finish is
taut and tight.

CHABLIS PREMIER CRU VAILLONS 2006
White | 2011 up to 2016   90
The floral nose is a bit wild. The palate is
pure and well defined, long and fat, but also
balanced and fresh. The finish of juicy white
fruit and flowers is quite succulent. To be
drunk young.

White: 46.9 acres; chardonnay 100%.

LA CHABLISIENNE

8, boulevard Pasteur
BP 14
89800 Chablis
Phone 00 33 3 86 42 89 89
Fax 00 33 3 86 42 89 90
chab@chablisienne.fr
www.chablisienne.com

The Chablis wine co-op is one of the most
famous in France and probably one of the
best managed. Cuvée after cuvée and
year after year, all of the wines presented
here are impeccably crafted, with honest,
sincere expression of terroir—even if one
does occasionally come across deeper,
more articulate wines made by independent producers. Our particular favorite
was the Cuvée de Vieilles Vignes—it's a
real treat finding that on a restaurant
menu—and the Château Grenouilles, a
very long-lived wine from the Grand Cru
Grenouilles "monopole" (owned by a single winery).

Recently tasted
CHABLIS GRAND CRU CHÂTEAU
GRENOUILLES 2006
White | 2011 up to 2021   92

CHABLIS GRAND CRU LE FIEF DE
GRENOUILLES 2006
White | 2011 up to 2016   89

CHABLIS GRAND CRU LES PREUSES 2006
White | 2011 up to 2021   91

CHABLIS PREMIER CRU CÔTE DE LECHET 2006
White | 2011 up to 2016   86

CHABLIS PREMIER CRU L'HOMME MORT 2006
White | 2011 up to 2021   89

CHABLIS PREMIER CRU MONTÉE DE TONNERRE 2006
White | 2011 up to 2021   89

CHABLIS PREMIER CRU MONTMAINS 2006
White | 2011 up to 2016   88

Older vintages
CHABLIS GRAND CRU BLANCHOT 2005
White | 2011 up to 2017   89
A refined, elegant nose. Nice depth, with
white and yellow fruit. Very ample on the
palate, but the finish is clean and precise.

CHABLIS GRAND CRU CHÂTEAU
GRENOUILLES 2005
White | 2011 up to 2022   **94**
A racy, refined, concentrated nose that is
already becoming mineral. Great energy in
this wine, which will evolve over a long period
of time. Pure; a great Chablis.

CHABLIS GRAND CRU LE FIEF DE
GRENOUILLES 2005
White | 2011 up to 2022   **91**
A succulent and rich wine with a fine expression of white and citrus fruit. Pure, with a
nice cleanness to it. A rich, mineral finish
that remains long and balanced.

CHABLIS GRAND CRU LES CLOS 2005
White | 2011 up to 2017   **88**
A closed, crystalline wine. Very disappointing for a Clos, because its volume on the
palate does not hold up. Clearly the fault
lies in excessive yields.

CHABLIS GRAND CRU LES PREUSES 2005
White | 2011 up to 2022   **93**
Dense, deep. A well-rounded, open wine.
The tension on the finish is wonderful, underscored by a fine backbone of acidity. Enormous potential.

CHABLIS LA SEREINE 2005
White | 2011 up to 2014   **87**
A new name for the former L.C. bottling.
Marked by citrus fruit and minerality. Good
balance on the palate, with its fattiness
stretching into good, fresh, savory length.
A very good quality-price ratio.

CHABLIS LES VÉNÉRABLES VIEILLES VIGNES 2005
White | 2011 up to 2017   **88**
A great classic from this cellar, always at
the top of its game. It is taut on the palate
and very long. Nice density; it will come
together slowly.

CHABLIS PREMIER CRU FOURCHAUME 2005
White | 2011 up to 2017   **88**
A very floral wine that suffers from a slight
lack of concentration on the mid-palate, but
it is pure and classy.

Red: 49.4 acres; gamay 25%, pinot 75%. White: 2965.2
acres; aligoté 1%, chardonnay 98%, sauvignon 1%.
Annual production: 8,500,000 bottles

DOMAINE ANITA, JEAN-PIERRE ET STÉPHANIE COLINOT

Jean-Pierre et Stéphanie Colinot
1, rue des Chariats
89290 Irancy
Phone 00 33 3 86 42 33 25
Fax 00 33 3 86 42 33 25

At the helm of this estate today is Jean-
Pierre Colinot's charming and talented
daughter Stéphanie. The wines are still the
benchmark for the appellation, but their
style has shifted toward purer fruit and
silkier tannins. The great estate bottlings
are as always the refined and perfumed
Palotte (finesse and fragrance), the Côte
du Moutier (more richness), and the
Mazelots Cuvée César, the most concentrated of the three with nice smoky notes.
Stéphanie is now experimenting with oak
aging, and while the first vintage did seem
slightly heavy, she can be counted on to
fine-tune her work as the years go by. A
lady with a brilliant future ahead!

Recently tasted
IRANCY LES CAILLES 2007
Red | 2011 up to 2015   **89**

IRANCY LES MAZELOTS 2007
Red | 2011 up to 2014   **88**

IRANCY PALOTTE 2007
Red | 2011 up to 2017   **90**

IRANCY VIEILLES VIGNES CUVÉE CÉSAR 2007
Red | 2011 up to 2015   **89**

Older vintages
IRANCY CÔTE DU MOUTIER
ÉLEVÉ EN FÛT DE CHÊNE 2006
Red | 2011 up to 2016   **86**
After the Mazelots in 2005, it's the Côte du
Moutier that had the honor of the barrels in
2006. Powerful, spicy, rich. The palate is taut,
with lots of tannin. Better than the 2005: with
the age of the barrels advancing, the oak
influence is more mellow.

IRANCY LES CAILLES 2006
Red | 2011 up to 2016   **88**
Concentrated fruit, black and red. The palate is more mineral than on the Vieilles
Vignes. Rich, dense, and quite taut. Needs
time. A great wine, maybe one of the best
of the estate this year!

IRANCY LES MAZELOTS 2006
Red | 2011 up to 2016   **87**
The nose is delicate, deep, and elegant;
rather floral and mineral. The palate is taut,
long, with firm tannins on the finish. Straightforward.

IRANCY PALOTTE 2006
Red | 2011 up to 2016   87
The César varietal offers a note of intense
black fruits, a bit wild. The palate is slightly
smoky, with nice density. An elegant wine
with good structure.

IRANCY VEAUPESSIOT 2006
Red | 2011 up to 2014   86
A nice wine with flesh and substance. Meaty,
with an elegant fruity finish. The Palotte is
softer.

Red: 30.9 acres; césar 5%, pinot 95%. Annual
production: 70,000 bottles

DOMAINE RENÉ ET VINCENT DAUVISSAT

🍷🍷🍷🍷

8, rue Émile-Zola
89800 Chablis
Phone 00 33 3 86 42 11 58
Fax 00 33 3 86 42 85 32

Vincent Dauvissat is a gifted, passionate
winegrower who heads up one of the best
sources of Chablis wines. His approach to
viticulture is not officially organic but
close, and all those hours spent tending
his vines no doubt explain how he manages to craft wines with such focused palate expression—particularly his La Forest,
Les Preuses, and Les Clos. All of his wines
spend time in (fairly old) casks and share a
common elegance and crystalline purity.
They age to perfection.

Recently tasted
CHABLIS 2007
White | 2011 up to 2017   88

CHABLIS GRAND CRU LES CLOS 2007
White | 2017 up to 2027   96

CHABLIS GRAND CRU LES PREUSES 2007
White | 2017 up to 2027   93

CHABLIS PREMIER CRU LA FOREST 2007
White | 2012 up to 2022   92

CHABLIS PREMIER CRU SÉCHET 2007
White | 2012 up to 2022   89

CHABLIS PREMIER CRU VAILLONS 2007
White | 2012 up to 2022   90

PETIT CHABLIS 2007
White | 2011 up to 2015   87

Older vintages
CHABLIS 2006
White | 2011 up to 2014   89
Fine fat, with nice notes of underbrush and
wild mushrooms. Expressive.

CHABLIS GRAND CRU LES CLOS 2006
White | 2011 up to 2026   94
Refined, elegant, with pretty mineral notes.
On the palate, the attack is pure and crys-
talline. A chiseled, very linear wine.

CHABLIS GRAND CRU LES CLOS 2005
White | 2011 up to 2020   96
Very mineral. Great crystalline purity on the
palate. A great wine: concentrated, refined,
and linear. Very pure. It will age very well.

CHABLIS GRAND CRU LES PREUSES 2006
White | 2011 up to 2026   93
A powerful, compact, fairly massive nose.
On the palate, the wine is dense, rich, but
pure and subtly balanced. A wine that finishes tight, with nice pepper notes (white
pepper). Tasty, rich length. A wine with a
future.

CHABLIS PREMIER CRU LA FOREST 2006
White | 2011 up to 2021   92
A taut, concentrated wine. On the palate it
is ripe, very taut, with a finish that ends up
compact, with noble bitter notes, as well as
underbrush and pepper.

CHABLIS PREMIER CRU LA FOREST 2005
White | 2011 up to 2020   94
Pure and linear, this is a rich Chablis with
good fat to it. The raw materials have been
well crafted through careful work with oak.
The minerality on the finish should gain in
intensity, because this is a bottle made for
cellaring. Well-rounded, rich, and harmonious. Long and savory.

CHABLIS PREMIER CRU SÉCHET 2006
White | 2011 up to 2021   91
More powerful than the Chablis, a little more
expressive, very ripe. On the palate, it finishes off compact and taut. A massive, concentrated wine with a great future.

CHABLIS PREMIER CRU SÉCHET 2005
White | 2011 up to 2020   91
A straight, mineral wine that is pure and
concentrated. Very linear, with great cleanness to its aromas. On the palate, it has crystalline purity. Its great freshness on the
finish will allow it to evolve very well. The
élevage is hardly noticeable.

CHABLIS PREMIER CRU VAILLONS 2006
White | 2011 up to 2021   91
More powerful and a little more expressive
than the Séchet. Very ripe. On the palate,
it finishes off compact and taut. A massive,
concentrated wine with a great future.

CHABLIS PREMIER CRU VAILLONS 2005
White | 2011 up to 2020   93
More slender than the Séchet, this wine is
more linear and more mineral. It is an elegant, very pure wine with good minerality
that crystallizes on the finish. The balance
and vivacity on the finish are remarkable.
Great artistry. Amazing style and charm!

White: 28.4 acres; chardonnay 100%.

DOMAINE JEAN-PAUL ET BENOÎT DROIN

🏵 🏵 🏵 🏵 🏵

14 bis, rue Jean-Jaurès
89800 Chablis
Phone 00 33 3 86 42 16 78
Fax 00 33 3 86 42 42 09
benoit@jeanpaulbenoit-droin.fr
www.jeanpaulbenoit-droin.fr

Benoît Droin took over the family domaine
in 1999 and has focused exclusively on
making estate-produced wines. The style
is progressively less oaked (80 percent of
the wines are fermented in stainless-steel
tanks), though the casks themselves are
quite young (five years max). What the
wines have in common is a solid backbone
of acidity that gives them good aging
potential; they always take a few years to
develop that stunning purity that makes
them so tasty with food.

Recently tasted

CHABLIS GRAND CRU GRENOUILLES 2007
White | 2012 up to 2022   93

CHABLIS GRAND CRU LES CLOS 2007
White | 2012 up to 2027   93

CHABLIS GRAND CRU VALMUR 2007
White | 2012 up to 2022   91

CHABLIS GRAND CRU VAUDÉSIR 2007
White | 2012 up to 2022   91

CHABLIS PREMIER CRU MONT DE MILIEU 2007
White | 2011 up to 2017   88

CHABLIS PREMIER CRU MONTÉE DE TONNERRE 2007
White | 2011 up to 2017   87

PETIT CHABLIS 2007
White | 2011 up to 2013   85

Older vintages

CHABLIS GRAND CRU BLANCHOT 2006
White | 2011 up to 2021   90
Dominated by its fresh white fruitiness, this
wine is rich, savory, and balanced on the
palate. A lush, juicy finish that is nonetheless a little hot.

CHABLIS GRAND CRU GRENOUILLES 2006
White | 2011 up to 2021   91
Fairly discreet, even austere nose at this
point. But on the palate, the wine is straightforward, pure, and chiseled. A long, fresh
style with subtle winemaking. It will age
slowly. Taut finish, straight as an arrow.

CHABLIS GRAND CRU LES CLOS 2006
White | 2011 up to 2021   93
A fine Clos, taut and mineral. The elegant use of oak dominates for now, but the minerality and tension gradually become present on the palate, a sign of the terroir's great quality.

CHABLIS GRAND CRU LES CLOS 2005
White | 2011 up to 2020   93
Very fine oak texture on the nose. The palate is immediately mineral, with some perceptible oak. It's a wine with great potential. Superb finish, taut and pure. This is really a very great wine.

CHABLIS GRAND CRU VAUDÉSIR 2006
White | 2011 up to 2021   91
A wine that is very much Côte d'Or in style, thanks to its élevage. Subtle, elegant, grilled oakiness. Noble, very tasty at this point. The body is ripe, rich, and the barrel treatment is ambitious but mastered. A refined, elegant, stylish wine.

CHABLIS PREMIER CRU FOURCHAUME 2006
White | 2011 up to 2016   90
A powerful, rich nose marked by nice, elegant oak. On the palate, it is cutting, incisive in style, with minerality on the finish.

CHABLIS PREMIER CRU MONT DE MILIEU 2006
White | 2011 up to 2016   91
Nose slightly less open than the Fourchaume. Very ripe, on the palate it is taut, sunny, with ripe fruit and citrus aromas and minerality. Very nice.

CHABLIS PREMIER CRU MONTÉE DE TONNERRE 2006
White | 2011 up to 2021   92
Quintessential Chablis, a wine with notes of woodsy mushroom and underbrush. The wine is cutting, sharpened like flint. The finish is taut, linear, yet fresh. A wine worth patiently waiting for.

CHABLIS PREMIER CRU MONTMAINS 2006
White | 2011 up to 2016   89
A fine Montmains, a rich wine from a rather heavy plot. The barrel aging gives it elegance and length.

CHABLIS PREMIER CRU VAILLONS 2006
White | 2011 up to 2014   87
Slightly caramel, more marked by the fruit. A sense of warmth and sunlight! On the palate, it's expressive, fairly open. Good balance. It's starting to open up more. More tasty than refined.

White: 61.8 acres; chardonnay 100%. Annual production: 165,000 bottles

DOMAINE JEAN DURUP ET FILS

4, Grande-Rue
89800 Maligny
Phone 00 33 3 86 47 44 49
Fax 00 33 3 86 47 55 49
contact@domainesdurup.com
www.durup-chablis.com

This domaine is the largest private owner of Chablis vineyards, with 480 acres of land, of which 335 acres are Chablis, 57 acres are Petit Chablis, and 86 acres are Premier Cru Chablis. Surprisingly, the family doesn't own any Grand Cru vineyards. All of the wines made from proprietary vineyards are sold under two brand names, L'Églantière and Château de Maligny, both are made with the same philosophy—"never in oak"—as Jean-Paul Durup (who is now working alongside his father) likes to emphasize. The wines are linear, with a good acidic backbone, as they are entirely aged in stainless-steel tanks. Rigorous technical practices in the winery make for excellent consistency, despite the fact that the sheer volume of wine produced requires that the same lot be bottled at different times. The most representative and unique wines come from the Vigne de la Reine, La Marche du Roi, and Carré de César bottlings, three single vineyards in the Chablis appellation. There is also, of course, La Reine Mathilde, a Premier Cru blended from several different Premier Cru vineyard holdings. Recent vintages are all good.

CHABLIS L'ÉGLANTIÈRE LA MARCHE DU ROI 2007
White | 2011 up to 2014   85
More mineral and complete than La Vigne de la Reine. A complete, well-balanced wine with a pleasant bitterness on the finish, and with nice notes of wild mushrooms.

CHABLIS L'ÉGLANTIÈRE LA VIGNE DE LA REINE 2007
White | 2011 up to 2014   84
More complete than the simple Chablis, ripe and well balanced, with great aromatic generosity on the palate. Open and radiant.

CHABLIS L'ÉGLANTIÈRE LE CARRÉ DE CÉSAR 2007
White | 2011 up to 2015   87
More taut, more mineral, a bit more closed, and maybe a bit less balanced than the Marche du Roi.

CHABLIS L'ÉGLANTIÈRE VIEILLES VIGNES 2007
White | 2011 up to 2015   86
Fat, concentrated, well-balanced. A harmonious, elegant wine. Already appealing.

CHABLIS PREMIER CRU L'HOMME MORT L'ÉGLANTIÈRE 2007

White | 2011 up to 2017　　　**87**

More delicate and accomplished than the Fourchaume, which is nevertheless where it came from. The aromatic expression is more delicate; it is more sharply defined and yet also more tender. The comparison to the Fourchaume is fascinating!

CHABLIS PREMIER CRU MONTÉE DE TONNERRE L'ÉGLANTIÈRE 2007

White | 2011 up to 2017　　　**85**

A very nice wine, dense and mineral, all about tension and expression. Racy, appetizing, but not yet recovered from the bottling.

CHABLIS PREMIER CRU MONTMAINS L'ÉGLANTIÈRE 2007

White | 2011 up to 2017　　　**88**

Racy, elegant, this is a wine that is tasting particularly well. Ripe and resplendent. Generous and rich. The finish is long and fresh.

CHABLIS PREMIER CRU MONTMAINS L'ÉGLANTIÈRE 2005

White | 2011 up to 2013　　　**89**

Delicate and elegant. The aromas are candid and pure, with citrus and white fruits. A few iodized notes on the finish. Pure and stylized. Well-balanced, with richness but also finesse.

CHABLIS PREMIER CRU REINE MATHILDE-JEAN DURUP 2007

White | 2011 up to 2017　　　**87**

Fat, complete, rich, and complex. A very nice "brand" wine that finishes fresh and well balanced.

CHABLIS PREMIER CRU REINE MATHILDE-JEAN DURUP 2005

White | 2011 up to 2013　　　**88**

A true "brand" wine that blends several Premiers Crus. A complex, refined nose (you would swear it spent time in oak, but it didn't!). Rich and fat on the palate, with good length. A bit atypical compared to the rest of the range.

CHABLIS PREMIER CRU VAU DE VEY L'ÉGLANTIÈRE 2007

White | 2011 up to 2017　　　**86**

Fat, well-balanced, quite accomplished. This cru is already accessible but will keep for several more years.

White: 479.4 acres; chardonnay 100%. **Annual production:** 1,500,000 bottles

DOMAINE WILLIAM FÈVRE

21, avenue d'Oberwesel
89800 Chablis
Phone 00 33 3 86 98 98 98
Fax 00 33 3 86 98 98 99
contact@williamfevre.com
www.williamfevre.com

William Fèvre's estate-bottled and négociant wines share a common identity: rich, concentrated, refined, and mineral, with that subtle, elegantly matured character that makes them unmistakable in blind tastings. Testament to a quality-driven policy—hard labor in the vineyards, handpicked and meticulously sorted grapes—that leaves nothing to chance!

CHABLIS 2007

White | 2011 up to 2014　　　**89**

Ripe, with delicate, elegant aromatic finesse. A delicious Chablis, with good presence on the palate, long and fresh.

CHABLIS 2006

White | 2011 up to 2013　　　**88**

Floral, elegant, ripe and fat. This is a good Chablis: supple, open, balanced, with a fresh, subtle finish.

CHABLIS GRAND CRU BOUGROS 2007

White | 2014 up to 2027　　　**90**

This wine boasts an extra richness with respect to the other Premiers Crus. A ripe, elegant wine that is well balanced. Great aromatic purity and a saline, lemony finish.

CHABLIS GRAND CRU BOUGROS 2006

White | 2011 up to 2021　　　**92**

A powerful, rich nose that is a mix of fruit and spices. Great purity. On the palate, it is concentrated, with a good fruity expression that is extended by a taut, mineral finish.

CHABLIS GRAND CRU BOUGROS CÔTE DE BOUGUEROTS 2007

White | 2014 up to 2027　　　**95**

Made from a parcel at the heart of the Bougros vineyard, it has a sunnier, more concentrated nose that is more marked by floral notes than the Bougros. On the palate, it is more elegant, more chiseled, even more delicate.

CHABLIS GRAND CRU BOUGROS CÔTE DE BOUGUEROTS 2006

White | 2011 up to 2021　　　**93**

Even sharper and deeper than the Bougros. This is a wine of exquisite juice, aromatic and concentrated.

CHABLIS GRAND CRU LES CLOS 2007
White | 2017 up to 2027   96
A very taut nose that is almost austere, with a bit of citrus fruit. On the palate, it is remarkably linear and mineral. A long, straightforward, tight finish, with lemon notes. Harder at this point than the Preuses or Valmur, but it, too, will go far.

CHABLIS GRAND CRU LES CLOS 2006
White | 2016 up to 2026   95
Taut, linear, deep, this wine is in a difficult phase but promises to have a very fine future. Its score will certainly improve with time.

CHABLIS GRAND CRU LES PREUSES 2007
White | 2014 up to 2027   95
A superb Grand Cru, ripe and unctuous. Well-rounded, harmonious, elegant. Great ripeness, very good presence on the palate: this is a wine of great class. In terms of style, it's the polar opposite of Valmur.

CHABLIS GRAND CRU LES PREUSES 2006
White | 2011 up to 2026   95
Still somewhat closed and discreet on the nose at this stage. But on the palate, it is chiseled, taut, very linear. This is an elegant, well-rounded wine. Very slow to evolve.

CHABLIS GRAND CRU VALMUR 2007
White | 2014 up to 2027   94
Tight, mineral nose. On the palate, it is taut. A dense, very linear wine. Great precision.

CHABLIS GRAND CRU VALMUR 2006
White | 2015 up to 2026   94
Very racy nose. A wine of deep, intense fruitiness that is taut on the palate with good energy. Fat, balanced, and fresh. A very great bottling. Needs time.

CHABLIS GRAND CRU VAUDÉSIR 2007
White | 2014 up to 2027   92
Very nice, very ripe fruit, rich with candied citrus. Powerful and generous. On the palate, it is thick, almost creamy, unctuous. More citrus fruit on the finish.

CHABLIS GRAND CRU VAUDÉSIR 2006
White | 2012 up to 2021   93
This Grand Cru is all about floral and fruit notes. Balanced and tasty. Without being heavy, it is powerful and rich.

CHABLIS PREMIER CRU BEAUROY 2007
White | 2011 up to 2015   87
Pure, with a ripe, round nose and very expansive on the palate. A fat, well-balanced wine.

CHABLIS PREMIER CRU FOURCHAUME 2006
White | 2011 up to 2016   89
Ripe, open, very appetizing, with an expressive flavor profile of flowers and yellow fruit.

CHABLIS PREMIER CRU LES LYS 2006
White | 2011 up to 2016   90
Very floral, with an elegant nose. On the palate, it is tasty, linear, and pure. A finish of fine, juicy white fruit. Very appealing.

CHABLIS PREMIER CRU MONT DE MILIEU 2006
White | 2011 up to 2016   90
A pure, subtle nose that combines white fruit and pepper. On the palate, it is linear, racy, elegant, with remarkable purity.

CHABLIS PREMIER CRU MONTÉE DE TONNERRE 2007
White | 2012 up to 2022   91
Pure, very elegant nose. On the palate, it is linear, taut, pure, and precise. A wine that will evolve well.

CHABLIS PREMIER CRU MONTÉE DE TONNERRE 2006
White | 2011 up to 2021   92
Taut, a linear wine that already shows pleasant wild mushroom notes. Great purity to its definition on the palate. A magnificent, chiseled wine. Rich but structured.

CHABLIS PREMIER CRU MONTMAINS 2007
White | 2011 up to 2017   89
Mineral nose, very much marked by the chalk soil. Good body on the palate, great purity, nice work with the barrel treatment, which is almost imperceptible. A rich finish. Let this one age.

CHABLIS PREMIER CRU VAILLONS 2007
White | 2011 up to 2017   88
Very ripe, very yellow fruit. On the palate, it is rich, in a fairly powerful style.

CHABLIS PREMIER CRU VAILLONS 2006
White | 2011 up to 2016   90
More fruity than the Montmains, but purer, too, and more chiseled. A refined, elegant bottling, very light and long. Cellar this one patiently.

CHABLIS PREMIER CRU VAULORENT 2007
White | 2012 up to 2022   92
A concentrated wine with great balance. On the palate, it is rich but taut, with length and breadth but also finesse and freshness. There is a superior dimension here compared to the other Premiers Crus.

CHABLIS PREMIER CRU VAULORENT 2006
White | 2011 up to 2021   91
Very taut, chiseled, elegant. Very linear. Here is the linear quality we did not find in the "simple" Fourchaume, and yet the vines are very close to each other.

White: 116.1 acres; chardonnay 100%.
Annual production: 312,500 bottles

DOMAINE GHISLAINE ET JEAN-HUGUES GOISOT

30, rue Bienvenu-Martin
89530 Saint-Bris-le-Vineux
Phone 00 33 3 86 53 35 15
Fax 00 33 3 86 53 62 03
jhetg.goisot@cerb.cernet.fr

This is certainly one of the greatest Yonne estates. No holdings in Chablis (sadly) but a record of outstanding performance in the small commune of Saint-Bris. The estate is totally biodynamic and makes wines of remarkable purity and concentration. There's a lot of thinking behind these Saint-Bris terroirs: witness the new cuvées sourced from parcels in Gueule de Loup, Biaumont, and Gondonne. Simply stunning.

Recently tasted

BOURGOGNE ALIGOTÉ 2007
White | 2011 up to 2014   90

BOURGOGNE CÔTES D'AUXERRE
CORPS DE GARDE 2007
Red | 2011 up to 2015   90

BOURGOGNE CÔTES D'AUXERRE GONDONNE 2007
White | 2011 up to 2017   90

IRANCY LES MAZELOTS 2007
Red | 2011 up to 2017   90

SAINT-BRIS CORPS DE GARDE 2007
White | 2011 up to 2017   91

SAINT-BRIS EXOGYRA VIRGULA 2007
White | 2011 up to 2014   90

Older vintages

BOURGOGNE ALIGOTÉ 2006
White | 2011 up to 2013   88
Delicate, pure, elegant. Pleasantly fat on the palate. A rich, appealing wine with a tender but clearly defined palate.

BOURGOGNE CÔTES D'AUXERRE 2006
White | 2011 up to 2013   87
Nice aromatic variety (delicate fruit and elegant floral notes). Fat on the palate, the attack clean and direct. A very pure wine with a nice fatness and a fresh, appealing finish.

BOURGOGNE CÔTES D'AUXERRE
BIAUMONT 2006
White | 2011 up to 2016   89
More clayey soils than in the Gueule de Loup. A more opulent, broad bouquet with notes of yellow fruits. Powerful. Fat, generous, but well-balanced on the palate, without the mineral tension of the Gueule de Loup.

BOURGOGNE CÔTES D'AUXERRE
CORPS DE GARDE 2006
Red | 2011 up to 2013   86
A fruity, delicate, profound nose. Very pure, straightforward, elegant. Taut and direct on the palate, with delicate tannins and a gourmand fruit character.

BOURGOGNE CÔTES D'AUXERRE
CORPS DE GARDE 2006
White | 2011 up to 2016   88
Racy on the palate, pure, fresh, the maturation gives good length. Nice tension on the finish. A slender, delicate wine, long and fresh. Very pure. Superb.

BOURGOGNE CÔTES D'AUXERRE
GONDONNE 2006
White | 2011 up to 2016   91
The attack has a crystalline purity. Svelte, long and fresh on the palate. The purity and elegance surpass the two other single-vineyard wines.

BOURGOGNE CÔTES D'AUXERRE
GUEULES DE LOUP 2006
White | 2011 up to 2016   89
Very pure, marked by a few anise notes and a bit of white pepper. Fat on the palate, with a nice mineral tension. Long and direct.

IRANCY LES MAZELOTS 2006
Red | 2011 up to 2016   89
Very strong notes of roots, compost, and tobacco. The tannins are ripe and fat. Subtle balance. A luscious wine, fleshy and fresh, with a velvety finish.

SAINT-BRIS CORPS DE GARDE 2006
White | 2011 up to 2014   89
Less exuberant than the two other Saint-Bris, but nicely direct, elegant, and long. The finish finds more volume, with ripe fruit notes.

SAINT-BRIS EXOGYRA VIRGULA 2006
White | 2011 up to 2014   88
A delicate nose, more mineral than the Moury (slightly iodized). Fatter on the palate, but just as sharp and pure. A nice aromatic range on the finish.

SAINT-BRIS MOURY 2006
White | 2011 up to 2013   87
Pure, straightforward. A nice aromatic range: flowers, herbal teas, ferns. Just as highly perfumed on the palate, with a nice vivacity on the finish.

Red: pinot noir 28%. White: 51.9 acres; aligoté 22%, chardonnay 23%, fié Gris (sauvignon gris) 7%, sauvignon blanc 20%. Annual production: 150,000 bottles

DOMAINE CORINNE ET JEAN-PIERRE GROSSOT

4, route de Mont-de-Milieu
89800 Fleys
Phone 00 33 3 86 42 44 64
Fax 00 33 3 86 42 13 31

This lovely domaine is located in the village of Fleys, just east of Chablis. Beautifully managed by owners Jean-Pierre Grossot and his wife, Corinne, the estate boasts a modern, generously equipped winery and flawless hygiene conditions. This excellence is reflected in wines that deliver the very purest expression of the grape. A very homogeneous range, whatever the appellation.

CHABLIS 2007
White | 2011 up to 2017   **88**
Concentrated and rich. A full Chablis with good tension on the palate. Very full but with good acidity that also gives length. Greater potential than the 2006.

CHABLIS PREMIER CRU CÔTE DE TROÈMES 2007
White | 2012 up to 2017   **86**
Sharper, but also more concentrated, than the generic Chablis. A pure, straightforward wine, currently showing frank fruit aromas, but it will become more complex with age. A svelte mineral finish.

CHABLIS PREMIER CRU FOURCHAUMES 2007
White | 2012 up to 2017   **89**
A very floral nose, powerful, open, very direct. Fat on the palate, rich, and luscious. Long, intense, rich. A nicely vivacious finish.

CHABLIS PREMIER CRU FOURCHAUMES 2006
White | 2011 up to 2021   **91**
Very open, sunny, and floral. A powerful wine, almost opulent on the attack. It finishes on a very pure, crystalline note.

CHABLIS PREMIER CRU LES FOURNEAUX 2007
White | 2012 up to 2017   **87**
Richer and more powerful than the Troëmes and very full. Ample and generous, this well-balanced wine is very lively on the palate. Long and intense.

CHABLIS PREMIER CRU MONT DE MILIEU 2006
White | 2011 up to 2016   **90**
Taut, very straightforward, it glides like water from a rock into the mouth. And yet, it also has plenty of substance. Ripe, luscious, but long and above all slow-aging.

White: 44.5 acres; chardonnay 100%. Annual production: 100,000 bottles

DOMAINE LAROCHE

22, rue Louis-Bro
89800 Chablis
Phone 00 33 3 86 42 89 00
Fax 00 33 3 86 42 89 29
info@michellaroche.com

Michel Laroche is one of those media-friendly Chablis personalities, famous as a talented businessman, ace communicator, but also (and mostly?) as a great wine-grower. Chablis was the starting point of his now worldwide wine business (with holdings in the Languedoc, South Africa, and Chile) and it remains a good showcase for Laroche's very particular style of wines: fat but pure, with rich but subtle palate expressions that always finish fresh and balanced. Vintage on vintage, all of his wines are impeccable, whether estate-bottled (labeled Domaine Laroche) or négociant wines. The top-of-the-range offering is of course the Grand Cru Réserve de l'Obédience: magnificently matured at no expense to precision and mineral character. As a complement to his winegrowing activities, Laroche recently opened a restaurant in Chablis specializing in world cuisine, plus a delightful hotel on the banks of the River Bief.

Recently tasted

CHABLIS GRAND CRU BLANCHOT RÉSERVE DE L'OBÉDIENCE 2007
White | 2012 up to 2022   **93**

CHABLIS GRAND CRU LES BLANCHOTS 2007
White | 2014 up to 2022   **90**

CHABLIS GRAND CRU LES BOUGUEROTS 2007
White | 2014 up to 2022   **89**

CHABLIS GRAND CRU LES CLOS 2007
White | 2015 up to 2022   **92**

CHABLIS PREMIER CRU LES FOURCHAUMES VIEILLES VIGNES DOMAINE LAROCHE 2007
White | 2011 up to 2017   **88**

CHABLIS PREMIER CRU LES VAILLONS VIEILLES VIGNES 2007
White | 2011 up to 2017   **90**

CHABLIS PREMIER CRU LES VAUDEVEY DOMAINE LAROCHE 2007
White | 2011 up to 2017   **87**

CHABLIS SAINT-MARTIN 2007
White | 2011 up to 2015   **87**

PETIT CHABLIS LAROCHE 2008
White | 2011 up to 2013   **84**

Older vintages

CHABLIS GRAND CRU BLANCHOT
RÉSERVE DE L'OBÉDIENCE 2006
White | 2011 up to 2026   **95**
Fat, rich, powerful, but with good wiriness and perfect balance between power and freshness. This is a rich, savory wine with a subtle, aromatic palate, nicely balanced by the oak. Magnificent length. Very fine vinification work. Great style.

CHABLIS GRAND CRU BLANCHOT
RÉSERVE DE L'OBÉDIENCE 2005
White | 2011 up to 2025   **96**
The nose is delicate. On the palate, it is more expressive, with nice notes of roasted coffee beans and, especially, a broad aromatic palette: wild mushrooms, caramel, underbrush, dried fruits, spices. Lush and generous, but with remarkable balance on the palate. Its balance and depth are greater than in the 2006s.

CHABLIS GRAND CRU LES BLANCHOTS 2006
White | 2011 up to 2021   **92**
The wine is concentrated and dense. This is a linear wine with good acidity that gives it structure on the palate. Very pure juice. A wine that presents a great deal of elegance and harmony. Great potential.

CHABLIS GRAND CRU LES CLOS 2006
White | 2011 up to 2026   **94**
More taut, more mineral, and tighter than the Blanchots. Some tension on the palate, but quite promising. The minerality is now gaining the upper hand over the élevage. A wine of great style.

CHABLIS LAROCHE 2007
White | 2011 up to 2013   **85**
Nice floral notes on the nose. On the palate, it is taut and precise, and the aromatics are nicely straightforward. Pure and elegant, but with a slight lack of concentration on the mid-palate.

CHABLIS PREMIER CRU LES FOURCHAUMES
VIEILLES VIGNES DOMAINE LAROCHE 2006
White | 2011 up to 2021   **91**
A concentrated, refined nose with ripe, generous fruitiness. On the palate, it is superb, unctuous, rich, and dense, with a depth that comes from old vines. Juicy and mouthwatering. An open finish with good length. Very generous.

CHABLIS PREMIER CRU LES VAILLONS
VIEILLES VIGNES 2006
White | 2011 up to 2021   **89**
Ripe, generous fruit. Powerful on the palate, with nice fattiness. A nice, ripe wine with acidity that is already well integrated, round, and generous. Balanced, despite its brawniness.

CHABLIS PREMIER CRU LES VAUDEVEY
DOMAINE LAROCHE 2006
White | 2011 up to 2016   **88**
A pretty wine, rich and ripe. The attack is fatty, rich, with very ripe yellow fruit notes. Concentrated and pure, it ends with a bit of slightly bitter minerality.

CHABLIS SAINT-MARTIN 2006
White | 2011 up to 2013   **88**
More refined than the Laroche Chablis, it offers fattiness on the palate, with nice, ripe aromas of fruit and underbrush. Complex and savory.

White: 247.1 acres; chardonnay 100%.

DOMAINE LONG-DEPAQUIT

45, rue Auxerroise
89800 Chablis
Phone 00 33 3 86 42 11 13
Fax 00 33 3 86 42 81 89
château-long-depaquit@wanadoo.fr

This lovely estate in the heart of Chablis actually belongs to the Maison Albert Bichot in Beaune. The healthy growing environment here produces wines with very natural, pure, and honest aromas: plenty of powerful floral expression, chorused by floral and citrus notes; not much mineral expression in their youth. The 2005 offerings are sumptuous, with a range of breathtakingly pure Grands Crus that are stunningly expressive of their terroir (the Moutonne in particular deserves to be anthologized).

Recently tasted
CHABLIS PREMIER CRU LES BEUGNONS 2007
White | 2012 up to 2017   88

Older vintages
CHABLIS 2007
White | 2011 up to 2015   86
Ripe, chiseled; a pure and elegant wine. Linear, long, with a fresh finish.

CHABLIS 2006
White | 2011 up to 2016   88
A fine, complex expression, with fruit and floral notes. On the palate, it is linear and pure. An excellent Village wine.

CHABLIS GRAND CRU LA MOUTONNE 2007
White | 2012 up to 2022   93
Pure and elegant, this is a refined, delicate wine with great natural aromatics. It is incredibly classy.

CHABLIS GRAND CRU LA MOUTONNE 2006
White | 2011 up to 2026   95
Very fine, superbly fat on the palate. An elegant Grand Cru that shows potential slightly above the other Grands Grus in this vintage.

CHABLIS GRAND CRU LA MOUTONNE 2005
White | 2011 up to 2025   96
A very pure, very elegant nose that is finely concentrated on floral and citrus notes (ripe lemon). On the palate, it is also pure and delicate, but with a voluminous side that takes over as it blossoms. The finish is long and ample, balanced and fresh. This is great art! A wine that is deeply moving in its purity and the splendor of its aromas. There is real genius in this bottle.

CHABLIS GRAND CRU LES BLANCHOTS 2007
White | 2012 up to 2022   91
Very floral, elegant. Concentrated on the palate, with good volume. Lusciously rich.

CHABLIS GRAND CRU LES BLANCHOTS 2006
White | 2011 up to 2026   92
Ripe, with nice tastes of white fruit. On the palate, it is rich, concentrated, lush.

CHABLIS GRAND CRU LES BLANCHOTS 2005
White | 2011 up to 2025   94
A delicate, very floral nose with fine, ripe citrus notes (grapefruit). On the palate, it is chiseled, taut, linear, with great purity to its expression. Here is another refined, elegant wine. More tension and depth than Vaudésirs, though the latter was more charming.

CHABLIS GRAND CRU LES CLOS 2007
White | 2014 up to 2022   93
Taut, very mineral. Great aromatic purity, very elegant. On the palate, it is particularly chiseled. It should be cellared patiently.

CHABLIS GRAND CRU LES CLOS 2006
White | 2011 up to 2026   94
Superb mineral tension in this wine, which is as crystalline as mountain spring water. Elegant and chiseled, its vinification is very skillful and respects the terroir.

CHABLIS GRAND CRU LES CLOS 2005
White | 2011 up to 2025   96
A fine, elegant nose, with oak that remains discreet. On the palate, the wine is linear, with a nice expression of pepper notes. A taut wine, it is now opening up and will last for a long time. Even if it is still subdued, it is more racy than La Moutonne.

CHABLIS GRAND CRU LES VAUDÉSIRS 2007
White | 2012 up to 2022   92
A rich, very ripe, sun-drenched wine. A good mineral expression on the palate, with a rich, generous finish.

CHABLIS GRAND CRU LES VAUDÉSIRS 2006
White | 2011 up to 2026   94
Still expressive, but it will close down; this is a powerful, generous, opulent wine, which nonetheless has a very pure finish, despite so much body.

CHABLIS GRAND CRU LES VAUDÉSIRS 2005
White | 2011 up to 2020   93
A refined, delicate nose, with white fruit, citrus, and flowers. On the palate are similar notes, with greater persistence of the citrus ones (very ripe grapefruit), as well as some licorice. This wine is elegant and open, already very tempting, but its presence on the palate assures it will age well. Very refined.

CHABLIS PREMIER CRU LES LYS 2007
White | 2012 up to 2017   88
Pure, linear, with nice fattiness on the palate. A nice floral expression on the finish.

CHABLIS PREMIER CRU LES VAILLONS 2006
White | 2011 up to 2016   87
Ripe, elegant, with great purity on the palate, this is refined and fresh.

CHABLIS PREMIER CRU LES VAUCOPINS 2007
White | 2012 up to 2022   90
Fat, with good body, a ripe, long, fresh, and lively Chablis. A fine expression, concentrated and taut. A long, fatty finish.

CHABLIS PREMIER CRU LES VAUCOPINS 2006
White | 2011 up to 2016   88
Nice richness on the palate; it finishes with a pure sensation of very ripe fruit.

White: 160.6 acres; chardonnay 100%.

DOMAINE CHRISTIAN MOREAU PÈRE ET FILS

26, avenue d'Oberwesel
89800 Chablis
Phone 00 33 3 86 42 86 34
Fax 00 33 3 86 42 84 62
contact@domainechristianmoreau.com
www.domainechristianmoreau.com

Domaine Christian Moreau is one of four wineries to contain the name Moreau in the town of Chablis, so it's very important to know their first name! This particular Moreau is located on the outskirts of the village at the foot of the Grand Cru vineyards, which make up the majority of the 60,000 bottles they produce annually, an amazing family vineyard inheritance! All in all the family makes eight wines: one Chablis, two Chablis Premier Cru, and five Chablis Grand Cru, including the wonderful Clos des Hospices, a parcel located at the bottom of Les Clos. The winery was created in 2002, a result of the sale of the family négociant business, J. Moreau, being sold to the Boisset group. Their philosophy is to focus on meticulous vineyard work: canopy management, plowing. The grapes are harvested by hand: "Since we are a small winery, we can," says Fabien Moreau, who is the sixth generation to carry on the family tradition of winemaking. The grapes are partially fermented in vat, partially in barrel, depending on the terroir of the vineyard. Both the 2005s and 2006s are impeccable; the flavors are always honest and pure.

Recently tasted
CHABLIS GRAND CRU BLANCHOT 2007
White | 2012 up to 2022   92

CHABLIS GRAND CRU LES CLOS 2007
White | 2013 up to 2027   93

CHABLIS GRAND CRU LES CLOS LE CLOS DES HOSPICES 2007
White | 2013 up to 2027   94

CHABLIS GRAND CRU VALMUR 2007
White | 2013 up to 2022   93

CHABLIS GRAND CRU VAUDÉSIR 2007
White | 2012 up to 2022   90

CHABLIS PREMIER CRU VAILLON GUY MOREAU 2007
White | 2011 up to 2017   90

PETIT CHABLIS 2007
White | 2011 up to 2013   86

Older vintages

CHABLIS GRAND CRU BLANCHOT 2006
White | 2011 up to 2021   **91**
More taut, floral, and unctuous on the palate than the Vaudésir. The oak aging aggrandizes it but still dominates. Needs time. At this point, the Vaudésir is more natural and spontaneous.

CHABLIS GRAND CRU LES CLOS 2006
White | 2011 up to 2021   **93**
A taut cru that will open up slowly. But it's concentrated, mineral, with a good showing of white fruit, and the minerality reemerges on the finish.

CHABLIS GRAND CRU LES CLOS LE CLOS DES HOSPICES 2006
White | 2011 up to 2021   **94**
Concentrated, dense, and taut. A wine of great character, even if the finish reveals the limited freshness of the vintage. A notch above the Clos.

CHABLIS GRAND CRU VALMUR 2006
White | 2011 up to 2021   **92**
Taut, closed, this is a Grand Cru in the making. On the palate, it settles on citrus notes (lemon) but promises much more. The oak influence still needs to mellow out. The structure and backbone show a greater potential than the Vaudésir and Blanchot.

CHABLIS GRAND CRU VAUDÉSIR 2006
White | 2011 up to 2021   **91**
This wine is still marked by the barrels at this stage. Aromas of yellow and white fruits. A mouthwatering, seductive wine. Fresh on the palate. A powerful modern style, but controlled.

White: 29.7 acres. Annual production: 60,000 bottles

DOMAINE GILBERT PICQ ET FILS

3, route de Chablis
89800 Chichée
Phone 00 33 3 86 42 18 30
Fax 00 33 3 86 42 17 70
domaine.picq-gilbert@wanadoo.fr

This estate produces only four wines, each one spoken for well in advance—sad, but hardly surprising considering the care that goes into them. From the vine to the finished product, everything about this winery is meticulous. The wines are sourced from sustainable vineyards and vinified in stainless-steel tanks. With 32 acres under production, there are no plans to expand—though it would be nice to see such a great estate operate one or two parcels in a Grand Cru vineyard!

CHABLIS 2007
White | 2011 up to 2013   **85**
Pure, straightforward, and quite rich. Fruity and fresh. Well-balanced. Nice vivacity.

CHABLIS PREMIER CRU VAUCOUPIN 2007
White | 2011 up to 2015   **88**
Candid floral aromas. Rather sunny on the nose. Pure and elegant on the palate, with a mineral finish.

CHABLIS PREMIER CRU VAUCOUPIN 2006
White | 2011 up to 2016   **90**
A very pure nose, more delicate, less mineral. Notes of yellow fruits (peaches, dried apricots). Fat, rich, and very pure. Only the age of the vines prevents (for the moment) this cuvée from going further! Very elegant.

CHABLIS PREMIER CRU VOSGROS 2007
White | 2011 up to 2014   **87**
Elegant, with delicate fruity and floral aromas. Very pure. A pretty and pleasantly sapid wine with a saline minerality on the finish.

CHABLIS PREMIER CRU VOSGROS 2006
White | 2011 up to 2016   **91**
A concentrated, taut wine. All about mineral tension. It will evolve slowly but well. Rich, with nice lemony aromas, and the freshness of the finish nicely balances the rich core.

CHABLIS VIEILLES VIGNES 2007
White | 2011 up to 2013   **86**
More concentrated, more marked by notes of ripe (yellow) fruits. Dense on the palate. Concentrated and delicate, with integrity.

White: 32.1 acres; chardonnay 100%. Annual production: 90,000 bottles

DOMAINE RAVENEAU

9, rue de Chichée
89800 Chablis
Phone 00 33 3 86 42 17 46
Fax 00 33 3 86 42 45 55

The Domaine Raveneau is the ultimate expression of Chablis, and has been so for some decades. Yesterday it was François, today it is Jean-Marie and Bernard. What they have in common are supremely expressive cuvées of a quality that is consistent in any year. So how do they do it? They pay meticulous attention to cultivation and pruning. They vinify all their cuvées with the same care and then age them for twelve months in casks, with a careful eye on the lees. They do all of this and more. Whatever the case, this domaine is home to a wine that is unmatched for sheer complexity of flavor and finesse. The wine will delight every Chablis lover.

Recently tasted

CHABLIS 2007
White I 2011 up to 2017   88

CHABLIS GRAND CRU BLANCHOT 2007
White I 2012 up to 2027   91

CHABLIS GRAND CRU LES CLOS 2007
White I 2012 up to 2027   95

CHABLIS GRAND CRU VALMUR 2007
White I 2012 up to 2027   93

CHABLIS PREMIER CRU BUTTEAUX 2007
White I 2012 up to 2022   91

CHABLIS PREMIER CRU MONTÉE DE TONNERRE 2007
White I 2012 up to 2017   89

CHABLIS PREMIER CRU VAILLONS 2007
White I 2012 up to 2022   91

Older vintages

CHABLIS GRAND CRU BLANCHOT 2006
White I 2014 up to 2021   93
Powerful, rich, with some spicy notes. On the palate, it is fat and expressive, with a tasty fruity register. Marked by forcefulness.

CHABLIS GRAND CRU BLANCHOT 2005
White I 2011 up to 2035   94
An aniseed note on the nose. Concentrated and taut, with great richness to it. This is a very great wine that will last a long time.

CHABLIS GRAND CRU LES CLOS 2006
White I 2014 up to 2026   95
Ethereal, subtle, mineral nose. On the palate, it is taut, concentrated. The finish is almost saline. It will go far.

CHABLIS GRAND CRU LES CLOS 2005
White I 2011 up to 2035   99
This is perfection. Taut, pure, crystalline. The quintessence of a great Chablis: a great terroir in a great vintage! The mineral tension on the palate is prodigious. This wine will be expressive in ten years minimum, and even more so after that. This is simply a knockout. Its length is phenomenal.

CHABLIS GRAND CRU VALMUR 2006
White I 2014 up to 2021   94
More taut than Blanchot, though less powerful. A precise, pure, elegant wine. Its minerality is concentrated on the finish, which is vivid and fresh. This has the same minerality we found in the Montée de Tonnerre.

CHABLIS GRAND CRU VALMUR 2005
White I 2011 up to 2025   96
More refined, more subtle and elegant than the Blanchot. More lemony aromas. On the palate, it is chiseled, linear, with a very fresh finish. Crystalline and mineral, but rich and concentrated.

CHABLIS PREMIER CRU BUTTEAUX 2006
White I 2014 up to 2021   91
Rich, generous. The oak is perceptible in this sample, but this is a ripe, well-rounded wine. A tasty finish.

CHABLIS PREMIER CRU BUTTEAUX 2005
White I 2011 up to 2025   93
Rich, with good concentration on the palate. This is a powerful, generous wine with great density in the mouthfeel. The age of the vines adds depth, but it also requires more time! This is rich, well-rounded, elegant.

CHABLIS PREMIER CRU FOREST 2006
White I 2014 up to 2021   92
More mineral, purer, more chiseled than Montmain. Very elegant, very linear. A thing of purity and great length.

CHABLIS PREMIER CRU FOREST 2005
White I 2011 up to 2025   92
Very pure, very fine, linear. Disarming aromatic depth. A slight aniseed, licorice note on the palate. Even in its youth, it crushes all other sources. The vines are young; it will be ready to drink more quickly.

CHABLIS PREMIER CRU
MONTÉE DE TONNERRE 2006
White | 2014 up to 2021   93
Elegant, linear, very pure. This is a wiry, pure wine. Its minerality is concentrated on the mid-palate through to the finish. The terroir has modified the impact of the oak treatment. Great depth.

CHABLIS PREMIER CRU
MONTÉE DE TONNERRE 2005
White | 2011 up to 2025   94
A somewhat austere wine with a touch of minerality that crystallizes on the finish. Powerful, taut, and concentrated. Pure, and very long and linear. Great raciness: it will age very well.

CHABLIS PREMIER CRU MONTMAIN 2006
White | 2014 up to 2021   90
Powerful, subtle, with fine root notes. On the palate, spicy and delicately robust juices. Succulent, with dense juice.

CHABLIS PREMIER CRU MONTMAIN 2005
White | 2011 up to 2015   93
This wine offers more richness, fat, and concentration than Forest. Very pure. The complexity of its taste is perfect. Its balance is magnificent. Pure, linear, well-rounded.

CHABLIS PREMIER CRU VAILLONS 2006
White | 2014 up to 2021   92
Fatter, more opulent, more generous than Forest. Great volume on the palate. This is tasty, smooth, balanced, dense, racy.

CHABLIS PREMIER CRU VAILLONS 2005
White | 2011 up to 2025   92
Rich, elegant, with great power and rich material. A wine with more stuffing than the Montmain, but less minerality.

White: 18.5 acres; chardonnay 100%.

DOMAINE SERVIN

20, avenue d'Oberwesel
89800 Chablis
Phone 00 33 3 86 18 90 00
Fax 00 33 3 86 18 90 01
contact@servin.fr
www.servin.fr

François Servin makes a wide variety of Chablis, including newly released wines from past vintages. His old-vines Chablis is a triumph of massal selection, entirely sourced from the beautifully exposed site of Les Pargues, a Premier Cru until World War Two. It was destroyed in the war and has not been reclassified since. The Premiers Crus nicely capture the differences between terroirs while sharing a clean, pure palate with a crystalline finish. The Grands Crus are impressively voluminous, powerful, and balanced.

Recently tasted
CHABLIS 2007
White | 2011 up to 2014   86

CHABLIS GRAND CRU BOUGROS 2007
White | 2011 up to 2017   92

CHABLIS GRAND CRU LES CLOS 2007
White | 2012 up to 2022   93

CHABLIS GRAND CRU LES PREUSES 2007
White | 2011 up to 2017   90

CHABLIS PREMIER CRU BUTTEAUX 2007
White | 2011 up to 2017   89

PETIT CHABLIS 2007
White | 2011 up to 2013   87

Older vintages
CHABLIS 2006
White | 2011 up to 2013   87
A nose of floral aromas. The palate is fat, expressive, with good stuffing. Already round, it can be appreciated now.

CHABLIS GRAND CRU BLANCHOT 2006
White | 2011 up to 2016   90
Powerful, rich, lots going on. The noble Chablis notes are starting to appear (wild mushrooms). On the palate, it is fat, long, balanced. It has, however, less density on the palate than the other Grands Crus in the lineup.

CHABLIS GRAND CRU BLANCHOT 2005
White | 2011 up to 2020   92
A powerful, ripe nose. Aromas of grapes and raisins. A nice example of a Chablis that is more fruity than mineral. On the palate, it is subtle, with fine, savory juice and a harmonious and very well-balanced finish.

CHABLIS GRAND CRU BOUGROS 2006
White | 2011 up to 2021   92
Rich, powerful, with marked oak at this point. But it is noble and pure, and the aromas are very frank. Concentrated but balanced and very precise in its aromatic definition. Very nice quality-price ratio for a Grand Cru!

CHABLIS GRAND CRU LES CLOS 2006
White | 2012 up to 2021   93
Taut, precise, very linear; here is a Clos that should be patiently waited for. It is powerfully constructed, but its density and tension will gradually come to the fore.

CHABLIS GRAND CRU LES CLOS 2005
White | 2011 up to 2020   94
On the nose, the oak is a little bit more noticeable, but it is still refined and elegant. Notes of grapes and ripe yellow fruit. On the palate, it is linear, concentrated, with superb juice that is fine and elegant. The finish is taut and mineral, with slight (but noble) bitterness. It will be truly great in four or five years. Rich and taut, but pure and precise.

CHABLIS GRAND CRU LES PREUSES 2006
White | 2011 up to 2021   91
Fine, savory aromas. On the palate, it is taut, chiseled, pure, and linear.

CHABLIS GRAND CRU LES PREUSES 2005
White | 2011 up to 2013   90
This is a rich, fat wine with lots going on. On the palate, it is powerful, rich. This is a very colorful Chablis! Its only pitfall might be a slight lack of freshness compared to the Blanchot. Doubtless due to its barrel aging!

CHABLIS PREMIER CRU BUTTEAUX 2006
White | 2011 up to 2016   89
A subtle, refined nose. Very pure, very fine—between flowers and white fruit. On the palate, it is suave, with a rich, piquant finish. Very good balance.

CHABLIS PREMIER CRU LES FORÊTS 2006
White | 2011 up to 2016   88
Still young, it is dense on the palate, and not very open at this point. But a nice mineral, taut expression on the finish. Have patience.

CHABLIS PREMIER CRU LES FORÊTS 2005
White | 2011 up to 2020   91
Very much marked by the floral register, with underbrush. Very refined. On the palate, it is suave, subtle, and very elegant. Its purity on the palate is sublime. A Chablis from a very fine terroir in which the vinification has shown off the terroir's potential to the best effect.

CHABLIS PREMIER CRU MONTÉE DE TONNERRE 2006
White | 2011 up to 2016   90
A taut, linear nose with a bit of minerality mixed with some citrus notes. On the palate, it is fat, and is starting to open up.

CHABLIS PREMIER CRU VAILLONS 2006
White | 2011 up to 2016   88
More earthy, more grounded than the other Premiers Crus. A massive, fairly powerful wine that is even a little heavy in its aromas. But good balance on the palate. Nice depth of taste.

CHABLIS VIEILLES VIGNES 2006
White | 2011 up to 2016   89
Opulent, generous. On the palate, notes of yellow fruit. Powerful and ripe, with good purity.

CHABLIS VIEILLES VIGNES 2005
White | 2011 up to 2015   91
A superb nose with floral intensity, very powerful and concentrated. A terrifically balanced juice on the palate, velvety, refined, tasty, with a tautness to the finish. Wonderful! Rush to get this one, because there is little left!

White: 81.5 acres; chardonnay 100%. Annual production: 250,000 bottles

DOMAINE GÉRARD TREMBLAY

12, rue de Poinchy
89800 Chablis
Phone 00 33 3 86 42 40 98
Fax 00 33 3 86 42 40 41
gerard.tremblay@wanadoo.fr

The Tremblay family is heir to one of the great names in Chablis, and this estate is definitely the region's flagship winery. Although the grapes are entirely machine harvested (except for Grand Cru parcels) and then matured in tanks (with one exception), the estate has stopped using chaptalization since the 2005 and 2006 vintages. Low-temperature fermentation accounts for dominant notes of white flowers, all of the wines being very pure and delicate—more fruity than mineral, with superb aging potential. The Montmain 1985, for instance, which we tasted at the domaine itself, was a fabulously complex mouthful of flavor.

Recently tasted
CHABLIS CUVÉE HÉLÈNE 2007
White | 2011 up to 2017   **86**

CHABLIS PREMIER CRU FOURCHAUME VIEILLES VIGNES 2007
White | 2012 up to 2022   **90**

Older vintages
CHABLIS 2007
White | 2011 up to 2013   **85**
Ripe, lively, straightforward, a nicely expressive Chablis, moderately concentrated. It will evolve quickly.

CHABLIS CUVÉE HÉLÈNE 2005
White | 2011 up to 2015   **89**
A powerful, clearly oaky nose. But the depth of the wine immediately reappears on the palate, with notes of roots, nice underbrush, and a mineral, lively finish. A great wine, a bit atypical for the estate, but in a direct, pure style. Quite stylish. Great technical mastery.

CHABLIS GRAND CRU VAUDÉSIR 2007
White | 2012 up to 2022   **91**
A powerful, floral, spicy nose, with yellow flowers marked by the sun. Fat on the palate. Though its final balance hasn't been reached yet, it already has good density. Wait patiently for this one.

CHABLIS GRAND CRU VAUDÉSIR 2006
White | 2011 up to 2021   **91**
Hints of oak aging are still perceptible on the nose, but there are also elegant notes of flowers and underbrush. Fat, with a rather chalky finish. Very nice expression. Well balanced and long, with a nicely spicy finish.

CHABLIS PREMIER CRU BEAUROY 2007
White | 2011 up to 2017   **86**
Frank, lively, with lemony aromas, quite fruity. Ripe on the palate, a bit short.

CHABLIS PREMIER CRU CÔTE DE LÉCHET 2007
White | 2011 up to 2017   **87**
More floral than the Beauroy, with nice structure. Elegant, open.

CHABLIS PREMIER CRU CÔTE DE LÉCHET 2006
White | 2011 up to 2014   **87**
More tension and concentration than the Beauroy. A balanced cru, rather tender, but with good length.

CHABLIS PREMIER CRU FOURCHAUME 2007
White | 2011 up to 2017   **87**
Fatter, richer, more elegant and delicate than the Montmain. A fleshy wine with nice, juicy fruit on the palate. Good acidity on the finish. Well balanced, long, and fresh.

CHABLIS PREMIER CRU FOURCHAUME 2006
White | 2011 up to 2016   **88**
Good ripe, floral expression on the nose. Fat, pure, with a nice, luscious fruit character. Nice structure and length.

CHABLIS PREMIER CRU FOURCHAUME VIEILLES VIGNES 2006
White | 2011 up to 2021   **90**
These old vines planted in 1951 offer a deeper, more distinguished nose than on the classic cuvée. Luscious, with mushroom notes that are already elegant and food-friendly. The finish is delicately smoky, long, and luscious. A very nice energy thanks to the old vines. The difference in price from the classic Fourchaume is justified!

CHABLIS PREMIER CRU MONTMAIN 2007
White | 2011 up to 2017   **88**
More concentrated than the Côte de Léchet, with a nice, taut bitterness on the finish. A concentrated wine that will evolve nicely. Well balanced.

CHABLIS PREMIER CRU MONTMAIN 2006
White | 2011 up to 2016   **88**
A more elegant, racy nose than the Côte de Léchet. Nice notes of ripe white fruit. On the palate, more concentrated, more balanced, quintessentially Chablis.

CHABLIS VIEILLES VIGNES 2007
White | 2011 up to 2014   **86**
A wine with a nice tension on the palate. Mineral, with a nice, noble bitterness on the finish. Well above the generic Chablis.

Côte-d'Or Vineyards

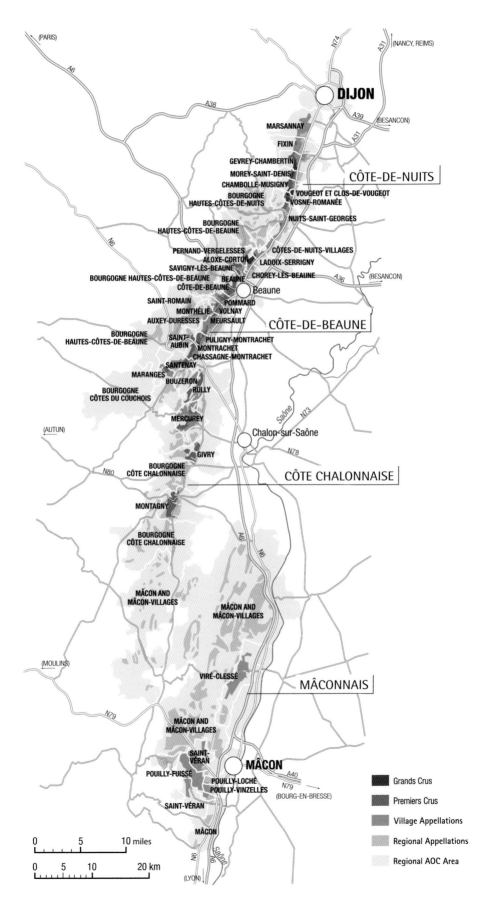

(PARIS)

A6

A38

A39 (BESANCON)

N74

A31

(NANCY, REIMS)

DIJON

A31

MARSANNAY

FIXIN

GEVREY-CHAMBERTIN

MOREY-SAINT-DENIS

CHAMBOLLE-MUSIGNY

CÔTE-DE-NUITS

VOUGEOT ET CLOS-DE-VOUGEOT

VOSNE-ROMANÉE

BOURGOGNE
HAUTES-CÔTES-DE-NUITS

NUITS-SAINT-GEORGES

N6

BOURGOGNE
HAUTES-CÔTES-DE-BEAUNE

CÔTES-DE-NUITS-VILLAGES

PERNAND-VERGELESSES

ALOXE-CORTON

LADOIX-SERRIGNY

SAVIGNY-LÈS-BEAUNE

CHOREY-LÈS-BEAUNE

A36

(BESANCON)

BOURGOGNE HAUTES-CÔTES-DE-BEAUNE

BEAUNE

CÔTE-DE-BEAUNE

Beaune

SAINT-ROMAIN

POMMARD

MONTHÉLIE

VOLNAY

CÔTE-DE-BEAUNE

AUXEY-DURESSES

MEURSAULT

BOURGOGNE
HAUTES-CÔTES-DE-BEAUNE

SAINT-
AUBIN

PULIGNY-MONTRACHET

MONTRACHET

CHASSAGNE-MONTRACHET

SANTENAY

MARANGES

BUUZERON

BOURGOGNE
CÔTES DU COUCHOIS

RULLY

Saône

N73

MERCUREY

(AUTUN)

Chalon-sur-Saône

N78

GIVRY

BOURGOGNE
CÔTE CHALONNAISE

N80

CÔTE CHALONNAISE

MONTAGNY

BOURGOGNE
CÔTE CHALONNAISE

A6

N6

MÂCON AND
MÂCON-VILLAGES

MÂCON AND
MÂCON-VILLAGES

(MOULINS)

VIRÉ-CLESSÉ

MÂCONNAIS

N79

MÂCON AND
MÂCON-VILLAGES

SAINT-
VÉRAN

MÂCON

POUILLY-FUISSÉ

A40

POUILLY-LOCHÉ

N79

POUILLY-VINZELLES

(BOURG-EN-BRESSE)

SAINT-VÉRAN

MÂCON

N6

Saône

A6

(LYON)

0	5	10 miles
0	5	10	20 km

Grands Crus

Premiers Crus

Village Appellations

Regional Appellations

Regional AOC Area

Côte de Nuits Vineyards

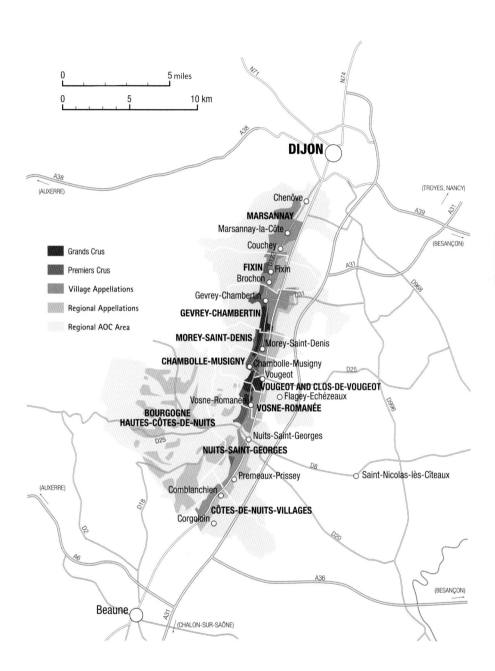

0   5 miles

0   5   10 km

DIJON

(TROYES, NANCY)

(BESANÇON)

A38
(AUXERRE)

Chenôve

MARSANNAY
Marsannay-la-Côte
Couchey

FIXIN   Fixin
Brochon
Gevrey-Chambertin
GEVREY-CHAMBERTIN

MOREY-SAINT-DENIS
Morey-Saint-Denis

CHAMBOLLE-MUSIGNY
Chambolle-Musigny
Vougeot
VOUGEOT AND CLOS-DE-VOUGEOT
Flagey-Echézeaux
Vosne-Romanée
VOSNE-ROMANÉE

**BOURGOGNE
HAUTES-CÔTES-DE-NUITS**

Nuits-Saint-Georges
NUITS-SAINT-GEORGES

Saint-Nicolas-lès-Cîteaux

(AUXERRE)

Premeaux-Prissey

Comblanchien

CÔTES-DE-NUITS-VILLAGES
Corgoloin

Beaune

(CHALON-SUR-SAÔNE)

(BESANÇON)

- Grands Crus
- Premiers Crus
- Village Appellations
- Regional Appellations
- Regional AOC Area

JEAN-LUC & PAUL AEGERTER

🜍 🜍 🜍 🜍 🜍

49, rue Henri-Challand
21700 Nuits-Saint-Georges
Phone 00 33 3 80 61 02 88
Fax 00 33 3 80 62 37 99
infos@aegerter.fr
www.aegerter.fr

Jean-Luc Aegerter is an astute négociant who knows that good wines are good business. He works with his son Paul and owns a small winery in Nuits-Saint-Georges, now complemented by holdings in some exceptional plots close by. Father and son have a particular expertise in maturation. They also own a very chic wine boutique in Beaune, specializing in fine, rare, and hard-to-find Burgundies.

Recently tasted

BEAUNE PREMIER CRU REVERSÉES 2007
White | 2013 up to 2019   90

BONNES-MARES GRAND CRU 2007
Red | 2017 up to 2027   94

BOURGOGNE 2007
White | 2011 up to 2015   86

BOURGOGNE PINOT NOIR 2007
Red | 2011 up to 2019   88

CORTON-CHARLEMAGNE GRAND CRU 2007
White | 2015 up to 2022   94

GRANDS-ECHÉZEAUX GRAND CRU 2007
Red | 2015 up to 2019   92

MERCUREY 2007
Red | 2013 up to 2019   90

MEURSAULT 2007
White | 2013 up to 2019   90

NUITS-SAINT-GEORGES
RÉCOLTE DU DOMAINE 2007
Red | 2015 up to 2022   89

POMMARD PREMIER CRU BERTINS 2007
Red | 2017 up to 2022   93

SAINT-ROMAIN SOUS LE CHÂTEAU 2007
White | 2011 up to 2015   87

SAVIGNY-LÈS-BEAUNE RÉSERVE PERSONNELLE 2007
White | 2011 up to 2015   87

Older vintages

BONNES-MARES GRAND CRU 2006
Red | 2011 up to 2013   93
A specialty of the house, very noble, complex aromas of dark fruit, refined texture, racy tannins, great length. Slightly drying tannins.

BONNES-MARES GRAND CRU 2004
Red | 2011 up to 2019   93
Fairly well rounded for the vintage, racy but somewhat sharp spicy tastes; remarkably well-calculated use of oak.

BONNES-MARES GRAND CRU 2003
Red | 2011 up to 2025   95
A magnificent wine, well rounded, with great unctuousness and balance.

CORTON-LES VERGENNES GRAND CRU 2006
Red | 2011 up to 2021   86
Acceptable color, a nose of red fruit and licorice, too fluid in texture for a Grand Cru, somewhat forced, drying tannins; this has finesse, but the winemaking choices in the élevage are too demonstrative.

CORTON-LES VERGENNES GRAND CRU 2005
Red | 2011 up to 2025   93
Power, full body, length, class—a true Corton!

GEVREY-CHAMBERTIN 2006
Red | 2011 up to 2018   90
Excellent cherry fruit, a more elegant, typical expression of the vintage and village than the Vosne; an elegant, well-rounded wine that is very successful for a Village wine!

GRANDS-ECHÉZEAUX GRAND CRU 2006
Red | 2011 up to 2026   94
Racy on the nose and on the palate, with greater length and brightness than the Bonnes-Mares; slightly forced tannins, though they are justified by the wine's body and the need to allow it to age well and over a long period of time. Superb class.

MEURSAULT 2006
White | 2011 up to 2016   88
Very typical, with fine hazelnut notes, fluid without being hollow, well-integrated oak, nice acidity, a good expression of the terroir.

NUITS-SAINT-GEORGES
RÉCOLTE DU DOMAINE 2004
Red | 2011 up to 2015   90
Rich with black currant and a remarkable expression of this wine's character. No earthy flaws, long, with subtle tannins and silky texture. Bravo!

Red: 13.6 acres; pinot noir 100%. **White:** 1.2 acres; chardonnay 100%. **Annual production:** 480,000 bottles

DOMAINE AMIOT-SERVELLE

🍇 🍇 🍇 🍇 🍇

34, Caroline Aigle
21220 Chambolle-Musigny
Phone 00 33 3 80 62 80 39
domaine@amiot-servelle.com
www.amiot-servelle.com

Christian Amiot has the good fortune to own parcels in the best Chambolle-Musigny vineyards, such as Amoureuses, Charmes, Derrière la Grange (Gruenchers), and he generally makes very good Village wines. His vinification style often results in somewhat austere wines when young, but they are clean and complex, capable of aging well. Recent vintages seem to better highlight the inherent finesse of these prestigious terroirs right from the start.

Recently tasted
CHAMBOLLE-MUSIGNY 2007
Red | 2014 up to 2019   87

CHAMBOLLE-MUSIGNY PREMIER CRU
AMOUREUSES 2007
Red | 2015 up to 2025   88

CHAMBOLLE-MUSIGNY PREMIER CRU
LES CHARMES 2007
Red | 2017 up to 2027   90

Older vintages
CHAMBOLLE-MUSIGNY PREMIER CRU
AMOUREUSES 2006
Red | 2011 up to 2024   93
Firm body, typical of this estate's vinification, tight texture, dense tannins but very nice aromatic distinction and remarkable tension in a vintage where that is not the dominant character.

CHAMBOLLE-MUSIGNY PREMIER CRU
DERRIÈRE LA GRANGE 2006
Red | 2011 up to 2021   93
An intense color. Great aromatic nobility and finesse, firm tannins. Perfectly marries power and delicacy.

CHAMBOLLE-MUSIGNY PREMIER CRU
LES CHARMES 2006
Red | 2011 up to 2021   93
Great color, imposing body. A complete wine, very solidly anchored on unaggressive tannins.

CHAMBOLLE-MUSIGNY PREMIER CRU
LES CHARMES 2004
Red | 2011 up to 2050   86
More accomplished and precise than the first wines tasted, but not really complex or elegant. The year didn't help, but other producers did better.

Red: 16.1 acres; pinot 100%. White: 1.2 acres; chardonnay 100%. Annual production: 30,000 bottles

DOMAINE DE L'ARLOT

🍇 🍇 🍇 🍇 🍇

Route Nationale 74
21700 Prémeaux-Prissey
Phone 00 33 3 80 61 01 92
Fax 00 33 3 80 61 04 22
dom.arlot@freesbee.fr

These wines have always played on finesse but never more successfully than today, with a refinement that avoids any trace of dilution—very soothing in this too-often brutal universe of Nuits-Saint-Georges. A white Arlot remains the most original and accomplished of all the Côte de Nuits offerings.

Recently tasted
NUITS-SAINT-GEORGES PREMIER CRU
CLOS DE L'ARLOT 2006
Red | 2011 up to 2013   90

NUITS-SAINT-GEORGES PREMIER CRU
CLOS DES FORÊTS SAINT-GEORGES 2006
Red | 2014 up to 2021   93

Older vintages
NUITS-SAINT-GEORGES LA GERBOTTE 2004
White | 2011 up to 2013   88
Pure, clean, elegant, with citrus notes, and once again that suaveness that makes chardonnay and viognier more of a pair, at least on these terroirs!

NUITS-SAINT-GEORGES PREMIER CRU
CLOS DE L'ARLOT 2004
White | 2011 up to 2014   92
Ultraripe for the vintage, luscious, suave, rich in natural glycerol, always the most original and accomplished white of the Côte de Nuits.

NUITS-SAINT-GEORGES PREMIER CRU
CLOS DES FORÊTS SAINT-GEORGES 2004
Red | 2011 up to 2019   93
Plain color, a marvelous and highly varied floral nose. This wine shows a rare elegance and freshness, contrary to all the current trends! Great length.

NUITS-SAINT-GEORGES PREMIER CRU
LES PETITS PLETS 2004
Red | 2011 up to 2019   86
Transparent. The floral aromas border on vegetal, and the finish is still too bitter. The wine hasn't found its balance yet, but you can still appreciate its natural quality.

Red: 29.7 acres; pinot noir 100%. White: 4.9 acres; chardonnay 100%. Annual production: 60,000 bottles

ROBERT ARNOUX

3, Route Nationale 74
21700 Vosne-Romanée
Phone 00 33 3 80 61 08 41
Fax 00 33 3 80 61 36 02
arnoux.lachaux@wanadoo.fr

A well-known Vosne-Romanée domaine with impeccable vineyards. The wines are fleshy and rich, perhaps not as refined and pure as some others but easy to understand and love. They age very well, especially the excellent Clos Vougeot (from the high part of the slope) and the superb Suchots. The Village range is less memorable.

Recently tasted

ECHÉZEAUX GRAND CRU 2007
Red | 2015 up to 2022   **89**

VOSNE-ROMANÉE PREMIER CRU SUCHOTS 2007
Red | 2015 up to 2022   **89**

Older vintages

ECHÉZEAUX GRAND CRU 2005
Red | 2011 up to 2050   **89**
Very rich in color with cocoa notes on the nose, voluptuous, with a tendency toward sugariness and richness, which some will love, and others will find a little insistent.

NUITS-SAINT-GEORGES 2006
Red | 2011 up to 2018   **89**
Licorice tastes, very linear, ample body for a Village wine; a clean wine with perfectly limpid terroir.

NUITS-SAINT-GEORGES LES POISETS 2006
Red | 2011 up to 2021   **89**
Dark in color, a very rich wine that is almost excessive in its "cooked" aromas, but with obvious, seductive voluptuousness.

NUITS-SAINT-GEORGES PREMIER CRU CORVÉES PAGETS 2006
Red | 2011 up to 2021   **93**
Dark in color, a great nose of reductive black currants that will please many (and that enchants us!); the smoothest and perhaps the most noble of the Nuits from this domaine.

VOSNE-ROMANÉE 2005
Red | 2011 up to 2050   **87**
Fine color and an open, spicy, tender, easy-going nose, sufficient body, a slight leathery note that weighs down the finish.

Red: 33.4 acres; pinot noir 100%. **White:** 1.2 acres.
Annual production: 70,000 bottles

DOMAINE BART

23, rue Moreau
21160 Marsannay-la-Côte
Phone 00 33 3 80 51 49 76
Fax 00 33 3 80 51 23 43
domaine.bart@wanadoo.fr

With each new vintage, Martin Bart seems to perfect his style. Bruno Clair's cousin, he shares not only some of the same appellations but also the same serious, classic, and timeless vision of Burgundy, preferring a strict and exact expression of the terroir to that of aromatic explosion or purely hedonistic textures. His 2007s, and notably his large range of Marsannay wines, are excellent.

Recently tasted

BONNES-MARES GRAND CRU 2007
Red | 2017 up to 2027   **95**

CHAMBERTIN-CLOS DE BÈZE GRAND CRU 2007
Red | 2017 up to 2027   **94**

CHAMBOLLE-MUSIGNY VÉROILLES 2007
Red | 2013 up to 2019   **88**

FIXIN 2007
Red | 2011 up to 2015   **86**

FIXIN PREMIER CRU LES HERVELETS 2007
Red | 2014 up to 2019   **89**

MARSANNAY LES CHAMPS SALOMON 2007
Red | 2011 up to 2013   **87**

Older vintages

CHAMBERTIN-CLOS DE BÈZE GRAND CRU 2006
Red | 2011 up to 2026   **94**
The best Clos de Bèze of our tasting, with generous aromas, body, and texture. Very noble tannins. A Chambertin with a great future ahead.

FIXIN PREMIER CRU LES HERVELETS 2005
Red | 2011 up to 2030   **90**
A nice color, a rich wine, taut, the tannins just a tad too marked, but with a sure and sincere expression of a good terroir. A good future ahead.

MARSANNAY ECHÉZEAUX 2006
Red | 2011 up to 2018   **88**
Nice bramble aromas. A pure wine, more taut and mineral than Les Longerois. Great finesse and a bright future. A exemplary, classy Marsannay.

MARSANNAY GRANDES VIGNES 2006
Red | 2011 up to 2016   **88**
The most openly fruity of the estate's red Marsannays. Creamy, sensual, open, and very nicely vinified.

MARSANNAY LES CHAMPS SALOMON 2005

Red | 2011 up to 2025   92

Riper and more unctuous than Les Longeroies. Distinguished, connected to the quality of the vegetal material. A great future ahead.

MARSANNAY LES LONGEROIES 2006

Red | 2011 up to 2018   87

Great color, ripe grapes, well-coated tannins. A wine with character and obvious loyalty to the terroir. The archetype of classic Marsannay.

MARSANNAY LES LONGEROIES 2005

Red | 2011 up to 2025   90

Rich, balanced, tannic, with great style.

Red: 44.5 acres; pinot noir 100%. White: 7.4 acres; aligoté 55%, chardonnay 45%. Annual production: 70,000 bottles

BERTRAND AMBROISE

Rue de l'Église
21700 Prémeaux-Prissey
Phone 00 33 3 80 62 30 19
Fax 00 33 3 80 62 38 69
bertrand.ambroise@wanadoo.fr
www.ambroise.com

In the 1990s, this estate turned out highly colored, very tannic red wines that appealed to lovers of the modern style but seemed excessive to enthusiasts of classic Burgundy. The latest offerings show a welcome return to more traditional winemaking, with no loss of pristine technique. The whites age superbly in the bottle, whether the Corton-Charlemagne or the outstanding Saint-Romain—the most complete Saint-Romain we have ever tasted.

Recently tasted

HAUTES CÔTES DE NUITS 2008

White | 2011 up to 2017   88

LADOIX PREMIER CRU LES GRECHONS 2007

White | 2011 up to 2015   86

MEURSAULT PREMIER CRU PORUSOT 2007

White | 2013 up to 2019   90

SAINT-ROMAIN 2007

White | 2011 up to 2015   90

SAINT-ROMAIN 2006

White | 2011 up to 2013   90

Older vintages

CLOS DE VOUGEOT GRAND CRU 2006

Red | 2011 up to 2021   88

A nice wine, very aromatic, fleshy, velvety, supple even for this vineyard, relatively sensual and to be drunk earlier than others.

CORTON-CHARLEMAGNE GRAND CRU 2006

White | 2011 up to 2021   92

Nicely ripe grapes, a supple, tender wine but meaty, substantial length, more charming than structured.

NUITS-SAINT-GEORGES PREMIER CRU VAUCRAINS 2006

Red | 2011 up to 2024   92

A complete, great wine. Rich, mellow, monumental in body but nicely coated in its tannins; worthy of this great terroir.

SAINT-ROMAIN 2005

White | 2011 up to 2013   93

A remarkable vinosity for the appellation; complex, racy, long, nobly mineral, resembling a little Charlemagne!

Red: 32.1 acres; pinot 100%. White: 17.3 acres; aligoté 5%, chardonnay 95%. Annual production: 150,000 bottles

DOMAINES ALBERT BICHOT

6 bis, boulevard Jacques-Copeau
21200 Beaune
Phone 00 33 3 80 24 37 37
Fax 00 33 3 80 24 37 38
bourgogne@albert-bichot.com
www.albert-bichot.com

One of the oldest and largest of all the Burgundy wineries, Albert Bichot remains bravely determined to revise its philosophy and the quality of its wines. The négociant wines are now kept entirely separate from the domaine-sourced bottles. See under Chablis for our review of the Domaine Long-Depaquit and its celebrated Chablis wines. Albert Bichot owns two wineries on the Côte d'Or, the Domaine du Clos Frantin in Nuits-Saint-Georges and the Domaine du Pavillon in Beaune. Its Clos Frantin and Château Gris properties are slightly ahead of the rest in terms of quality improvements and are starting to make very stylish wines indeed. The négociant side of the business, on the other hand, could still do better.

Recently tasted

CLOS DE VOUGEOT GRAND CRU
DOMAINE DU CLOS FRANTIN 2007
Red | 2017 up to 2022   88

CORTON-CHARLEMAGNE GRAND CRU 2007
White | 2014 up to 2019   90

MEURSAULT PREMIER CRU
CHARMES DOMAINE DU PAVILLON 2007
White | 2013 up to 2017   90

POMMARD PREMIER CRU RUGIENS
DOMAINE DU PAVILLON 2007
Red | 2015 up to 2022   88

Older vintages

BEAUNE PREMIER CRU BRESSANDES 2006
Red | 2011 up to 2021   90
Produced under the Lupé-Chollet label. A very well-balanced wine, spicy, complex, led by very civilized tannins. Notes of soot and spices that are typical of this remarkable Beaune terroir.

CLOS DE VOUGEOT GRAND CRU
DOMAINE DU CLOS FRANTIN 2006
Red | 2011 up to 2021   93
Very fleshy, elegant wine with comfortable mocha aromas, a refined texture, racy tannins, great length, and excellent vinification.

CLOS DE VOUGEOT GRAND CRU
DOMAINE DU CLOS FRANTIN 2005
Red | 2011 up to 2025   90
Solid, very straightforward as far as its aromas go, with a slight cocoa note, but it lacks genius.

CORTON-CHARLEMAGNE GRAND CRU 2005
White | 2011 up to 2017   95
Remarkably racy with a powerful body and great sensuality for a Corton, with very great persistence. One of the pinnacles of this appellation in 2005.

CORTON GRAND CRU CLOS DES MARÉCHAUDES
DOMAINE DU PAVILLON 2005
Red | 2011 up to 2023   90
Deeply colored, ample and fleshy, with firm but well-integrated tannins and obviously racy terroir, complex fruit, though the whole is a little too heavy.

ECHÉZEAUX GRAND CRU
DOMAINE DU CLOS FRANTIN 2005
Red | 2011 up to 2025   91
A little more refined than the Malconsorts, more floral on the nose, with a slightly silkier texture, a fine style with a nice future ahead of it.

MEURSAULT PREMIER CRU
CHARMES DOMAINE DU PAVILLON 2005
White | 2011 up to 2015   88
Satisfactory balance, a clean expression of the terroir, but there are not yet all of the nuances and flavor tones of the great bottlings.

VOSNE-ROMANÉE PREMIER CRU MALCONSORTS
DOMAINE DU CLOS FRANTIN 2005
Red | 2011 up to 2025   90
Fine color, a firm, generous wine with promising floral and spicy aromas, a rich texture that is nonetheless a little impersonal for a cru of its kind; great persistence. A classy wine, even if it's not yet perfect!

Red: 76.6 acres; pinot 100%. White: 170.5 acres; chardonnay 100%. Annual production: 500,000 bottles

BOISSET

5, quai Dumorey
21703 Nuits-Saint-Georges
Phone 00 33 3 80 62 61 61
Fax 00 33 3 80 62 61 59
mallinger@boisset.fr
www.boisset.com

Over the past five years, this large house has completely revolutionized its Burgundian universe and changed the style of its wines. The Boisset family, certainly concerned by the usual critiques, and proud of the redevelopment of their Domaine de Vougeraie, had the wonderful idea to hire the talented Grégory Patriat, young, brilliant, and above all a nonconformist. He was trained in the school of Lalou Bize-Leroy to make wines worthy of the best producers. The Boisset brand focuses on wines that are 100 percent vinified by the company. The grapes are purchased from growers that follow a strict set of guidelines and the wines, as a result, gain in finesse, purity, and distinctiveness with each new vintage. The 2006s tasted were splendid, receiving some of our best scores, village after village! We can't encourage enough the courageous initiative taken by Grégory Patriat, who has decided to bottle a large part of the production under screw cap. So far the results are impeccable; all of the bottles have been identical.

Recently tasted

CHAMBOLLE-MUSIGNY PREMIER CRU LES CHARMES 2007
Red | 2014 up to 2019   89

FIXIN 2007
White | 2011 up to 2013   86

GEVREY-CHAMBERTIN CRÉOT 2007
Red | 2011 up to 2013   87

MARSANNAY 2007
White | 2011 up to 2015   86

MOREY-SAINT-DENIS MONTS LUISANTS 2007
White | 2012 up to 2015   87

NUITS-SAINT-GEORGES LAVIÈRES 2007
Red | 2014 up to 2019   91

NUITS-SAINT-GEORGES LAVIÈRES 2007
Red | 2013 up to 2019   89

SAINT-AUBIN 2007
White | 2011 up to 2015   87

SANTENAY PREMIER CRU BEAUREPAIRE 2007
White | 2011 up to 2015   88

SANTENAY PREMIER CRU LA COMME 2007
Red | 2013 up to 2017   87

SAVIGNY-LÈS-BEAUNE 2007
White | 2011 up to 2013   86

SAVIGNY-LÈS-BEAUNE PREMIER CRU LA DOMINODE 2007
Red | 2012 up to 2017   89

VOSNE-ROMANÉE 2007
Red | 2013 up to 2017   89

Older vintages

BEAUNE PREMIER CRU GRÈVES 2006
Red | 2011 up to 2021   89
Clean aromas of small fruits, suitable body, supple tannins, velvety. A subtle, racy finish. Another impeccably vinified wine from this estate.

MEURSAULT PREMIER CRU CHARMES 2006
White | 2011 up to 2018   92
One of the best Charmes of the tasting: strong expression of terroir, great stability of aromas, charming in its power. A wine of consensus!

MOREY-SAINT-DENIS PREMIER CRU MONTS LUISANTS 2006
Red | 2011 up to 2016   91
A powerful nose, very 2006, with notes of plums and chocolate, rich, unctuous, even creamy, complete because it also flaunts a beautiful finesse on the mouthfeel.

POMMARD VAUMURIENS 2006
Red | 2011 up to 2018   91
A superb cuvée with a magnificent nose of roses. Fleshy, long, complex, truly at the level of a Premier Cru.

SAVIGNY-LÈS-BEAUNE PREMIER CRU VERGELESSES 2006
Red | 2011 up to 2018   91
A pretty, spicy nose, a deliciously velvety texture, round, delicate, subtle, long—all the charm of Savigny!

VOSNE-ROMANÉE 2006
Red | 2011 up to 2018   91
Deeply colored, rich, with generous but elegant tannins. A complete wine from this Village-level appellation, with all the fruity personality expected. Bravo!

VOSNE-ROMANÉE QUARTIERS DE NUITS 2006
Red | 2011 up to 2018   91
A lot of style for a very floral wine. Tender, delicate, subtle. Vinified in the very spirit of the appellation.

DOMAINE RENÉ BOUVIER

Chemin de Saule Brochon
21220 Gevrey-Chambertin
Phone 00 33 3 80 52 21 37
Fax 00 33 3 80 59 95 96
rene-bouvier@wanadoo.fr

This domaine is a good source of local Burgundies for people who like healthy, robust wines that perform best at table. The range is broad and the winemaking is increasingly regular. The 2006s are worthy successors to the 2005s.

Recently tasted

CHARMES-CHAMBERTIN GRAND CRU 2007
Red | 2015 up to 2022   90

FIXIN CRAIS DE CHÊNE 2007
Red | 2013 up to 2017   86

MARSANNAY CLOS DU ROI 2007
Red | 2012 up to 2019   90

MARSANNAY LONGEROIES 2007
Red | 2011 up to 2017   87

Older vintages

CHARMES-CHAMBERTIN GRAND CRU 2006
Red | 2011 up to 2021   93
Dark in color with great black currant flavors and a wonderfully suave texture: very successful winemaking. A great pleasure-giving wine.

FIXIN CRAIS DE CHÊNE 2005
Red | 2011 up to 2020   89
Dark in color, slightly reductive, straightforward flavors, more refined tannins than in the past, a fine style and a fine future ahead of it.

GEVREY-CHAMBERTIN PREMIER CRU
PETITE CHAPELLE 2005
Red | 2011 up to 2020   90
Not yet bottled, which explains the slightly blowsy note, great color, great texture, great promise: all the finesse of this tiny terroir!

GEVREY-CHAMBERTIN RACINES DU TEMPS 2005
Red | 2011 up to 2020   92
A remarkably complex aroma of brambles, velvety texture, great raciness, a magnificent Village wine in this exceptional vintage.

MARSANNAY CLOS DU ROI 2006
Red | 2011 up to 2018   90
Exceptional density to its body, perfect balance on the palate, a well-rounded wine.

Red: 32.1 acres; pinot 100%. **White:** 9.8 acres; aligoté 10%, chardonnay 90%. **Annual production:** 100,000 bottles

SYLVAIN CATHIARD

20, rue de la Goillotte
21700 Vosne-Romanée
Phone 00 33 3 80 62 36 01
Fax 00 33 3 80 61 18 21
sylvain.cathiard@orange.fr

We have included this winery in the guide, despite the fact that they never present samples for tasting, because time and again we find that we enjoy the style of the wines, and also because Sylvain Cathiard owns some of the best-situated vineyards in the village of Vosne-Romanée. We tasted the 2006s at the Grands Jours de Bourgogne tastings: they most certainly won't equal the legendary 1999 and 2005s, but they are undeniably among the elite of the village. The wines seem to have become more precise and focused since the owner spent some time in Bordeaux. At its best, his Romanée-Saint-Vivant, which wasn't presented for tasting, is one of the most impressive ever.

Recently tasted

VOSNE-ROMANÉE PREMIER CRU
MALCONSORTS 2007
Red | 2015 up to 2022   91

VOSNE-ROMANÉE PREMIER CRU ORVEAUX 2007
Red | 2014 up to 2019   89

Older vintages

VOSNE-ROMANÉE PREMIER CRU
MALCONSORTS 2006
Red | 2011 up to 2013   88
Excellent general balance, a sincere, classic style, but with far fewer aromatic nuances and less nobility to its tannins than in the bottling from the Domaine Dujac. A fine wine for aging, but inferior to the magnificent 1999.

VOSNE-ROMANÉE PREMIER CRU ORVEAUX 2006
Red | 2011 up to 2013   89
More supple, more open than Malconsorts, with the same frankness, the same natural feel, and also the same slight lack of complexity.

VOSNE-ROMANÉE PREMIER CRU REIGNOTS 2006
Red | 2011 up to 2024   88
A nice wine that is spicy, long, and subtle, with barrel treatment that is slightly less accomplished than the vinification.

Annual production: 22,000 bottles

DOMAINE PHILIPPE CHARLOPIN-PARIZOT

🐟🐟🐟🐟

18, route de Dijon
21220 Gevrey-Chambertin
Phone 00 33 3 80 58 50 46
Fax 00 33 3 80 58 55 98
charlopin.philippe21@orange.fr

In less than twenty years, Philippe Charlopin has considerably expanded his family vineyard and is now heir to one of the most formidable holdings on the entire Côte de Nuits. A tour around the domaine cellars is a privileged journey through a world of great wines, all of them brilliantly made in accordance with state-of-the-art vinification practices: grapes harvested at peak maturity; meticulous grape sorting; long prefermentation maceration; aging almost exclusively in new casks. "Toutoune," as he is known here, focuses on bringing out the best in the terroir and the vintage—and he rarely gets it wrong. His wines have improved enormously since 1996, gaining in purity and finesse and achieving a textbook balance that only the meanest of spirits would deny. They are irresistible when young but also have everything it takes to age well—the mark of a classic Burgundy made in a modern style. With each new vintage the empire expands: this time with his son, Charlopin purchased vineyards in Chablis and has added several whites to his line, but their obvious oak won't please everyone.

Recently tasted

ALOXE-CORTON 2007
Red | 2014 up to 2019   90

CHARMES-CHAMBERTIN GRAND CRU 2007
Red | 2016 up to 2022   95

GEVREY-CHAMBERTIN VIEILLES VIGNES 2007
Red | 2014 up to 2019   89

MARSANNAY 2007
Red | 2015 up to 2022   93

MARSANNAY ECHEZOTS 2007
Red | 2013 up to 2019   90

Older vintages

CHAMBERTIN GRAND CRU 2006
Red | 2011 up to 2026   93
Rich in color, spectacular in texture and aromas, but also full of complexity. A baroque wine with classical foundations.

CHARMES-CHAMBERTIN GRAND CRU 2006
Red | 2011 up to 2024   90
A creamy texture that contrasts with its firm tannins; powerful tastes that are on par with the vigorousness of this wine's constitution.

CLOS DE VOUGEOT GRAND CRU 2006
Red | 2011 up to 2024   92
Superb mouthfeel, a wine that is generous in its proportions and texture, marked by its long stay on the lees, much more sensual than the style many winemakers seek out.

CLOS SAINT-DENIS GRAND CRU 2006
Red | 2011 up to 2021   95
With wonderful finesse and aromatic suavity and silky tannins, this Clos Saint-Denis comes close, as is often the case, to an ideal Musigny, which is a great compliment. The most refined Grand Cru in our tasting.

CLOS SAINT-DENIS GRAND CRU 2004
Red | 2011 up to 2050   93
Powerful, chocolaty, full-bodied, with remarkable texture, great length, very suave tannins for the vintage. Lots of character!

ECHÉZEAUX GRAND CRU 2005
Red | 2011 up to 2025   94
Very spicy, reductive, smoky, long, complex; splendid style.

GEVREY-CHAMBERTIN LA JUSTICE 2005
Red | 2011 up to 2025   92
Powerful, severe, almost rough for a bottling from this source!

GEVREY-CHAMBERTIN PREMIER CRU BEL AIR 2006
Red | 2011 up to 2018   88
A classic nose of leather and spice, nice generous fruit, firm tannins, accomplished winemaking; a stricter style of wine than the domaine's other bottlings, made to age.

GEVREY-CHAMBERTIN VIEILLES VIGNES 2005
Red | 2011 up to 2020   93
Noble bramble aromas, well-rounded, racy, exciting.

MAZIS-CHAMBERTIN GRAND CRU 2006
Red | 2011 up to 2026   93
Slight reduction on its lees, but a splendid suave texture. A sensual, complex wine that fits right in with this legendary domaine.

MOREY-SAINT-DENIS 2006
Red | 2011 up to 2018   92
Very skillfully vinified and aged, this Village wine is brilliant in its great finesse and the stunning suavity of its texture and tannins; and once again, this wine is the domaine's best quality-price ratio.

Red: 44.5 acres: pinot noir 100%. White: 17.3 acres; chardonnay 100%. Annual production: 200,000 bottles

DOMAINE GEORGES CHICOTOT

15, rue du Général-de-Gaulle
BP 118
21703 Nuits-Saint-Georges
Phone 00 33 3 80 61 19 33
Fax 00 33 3 80 61 38 94
chicotot@aol.com
www.domaine-chicotot.com

This small artisan winery shows plenty of consistency once again, producing stunningly authentic and sincere Nuits-Saint-Georges that are very respectably priced for wines of this standing.

Recently tasted

NUITS-SAINT-GEORGES LES PLANTES AU BARON 2007
Red | 2015 up to 2022   92

NUITS-SAINT-GEORGES PREMIER CRU
LA RUE DE CHAUX 2007
Red | 2015 up to 2025   93

NUITS-SAINT-GEORGES PREMIER CRU
LES SAINT-GEORGES 2007
Red | 2017 up to 2027   95

NUITS-SAINT-GEORGES PREMIER CRU
VAUCRAINS 2007
Red | 2019 up to 2027   94

Older vintages

NUITS-SAINT-GEORGES
LES PLANTES AU BARON 2006
Red | 2011 up to 2021   92
Great color, magnificent pith, delicate black currant flavors, soft tannins. Remarkable for a Village-level wine.

NUITS-SAINT-GEORGES PREMIER CRU
LA RUE DE CHAUX 2003
Red | 2011 up to 2013   93
Excellent finesse and a remarkable balance for the vintage. Highly recommended.

NUITS-SAINT-GEORGES PREMIER CRU
LES SAINT-GEORGES 2006
Red | 2011 up to 2028   96
One of the top two ratings in the grand blind tasting hosted by the wine union, this Nuits is perfect in its body, tension, aromatic nobility, and aging potential.

NUITS-SAINT-GEORGES PREMIER CRU
VAUCRAINS 2006
Red | 2011 up to 2028   95
The admirable nose of a great wine of the Côte de Nuits, joining brambles, black currants, spices, and leather. Full and sumptuous, with noble tannins, great length, a vinification that in our opinion is perfect.

Red: 16.1 acres; pinot noir 100%. **Annual production:** 30,000 bottles

DOMAINE BRUNO CLAIR

5, rue du Vieux-Collège
BP 22
21160 Marsannay-la-Côte
Phone 00 33 3 80 52 28 95
Fax 00 33 3 80 52 18 14
brunoclair@wanadoo.fr
www.bruno-clair.com

This quintessentially classical Burgundian domaine produces unbelievably pure and elegant wines, although maybe a bit short on immediate generosity of fruit. The most recent vintages put that right, thanks to a combination of stricter vineyard management and global warming. The heritage of vines is one of the noblest anywhere, boasting such Gevrey gems as the Clos Saint-Jacques, Les Cazetiers, and the Clos de Bèze, which since 2006 includes part of the Bonnes-Mares vineyard inherited by Bernard Clair. Among the many other jewels adorning this magnificent crown are the ancient La Dominode vineyard; exceptional Marsannays that offer excellent value for money; and of course, the impeccable Corton-Charlemagne. The 2007s deserve a standing ovation.

Recently tasted

BONNES-MARES GRAND CRU 2007
Red | 2017 up to 2025   92

GEVREY-CHAMBERTIN PREMIER CRU
CLOS SAINT-JACQUES 2007
Red | 2017 up to 2027   94

GEVREY-CHAMBERTIN PREMIER CRU
LES CAZETIERS 2007
Red | 2015 up to 2027   92

MARSANNAY LES LONGEROIES 2007
Red | 2012 up to 2019   89

MARSANNAY VAUDENELLES 2007
Red | 2014 up to 2019   90

PERNAND-VERGELESSES 2007
White | 2011 up to 2017   90

Older vintages

CHAMBERTIN-CLOS DE BÈZE GRAND CRU 2006
Red | 2011 up to 2026   92
A complete, vigorous wine, generous in alcohol and tannins, with no drying on the finish. All it needs is time!

CHAMBERTIN-CLOS DE BÈZE GRAND CRU 2005
Red | 2011 up to 2030   97
One of the prizes of this unforgettable vintage: a refined wine with a fullness and precision of expression that cannot be beaten. From one of the four greatest terroirs of Burgundy!

CHAMBERTIN-CLOS DE BÈZE GRAND CRU 2004
Red | 2011 up to 2024   **96**
Admirable overall balance. Very ripe grape pulp, distinguished tannins, very long. Will continue to age beautifully.

CHAMBOLLE-MUSIGNY LES VÉROILLES 2006
Red | 2011 up to 2016   **90**
Excellently ripe grapes. A full wine, fleshy, voluminous, but endowed with well-controlled tannins. A perfectly defined Village-level wine, with obvious class!

GEVREY-CHAMBERTIN PREMIER CRU
CLOS DU FONTENY 2006
Red | 2011 up to 2018   **89**
Precise, spicy aromas but still serious. Generous body, taut tannins. A rich wine, certainly well balanced. Consume it slowly at maturity in seven or eight years.

GEVREY-CHAMBERTIN PREMIER CRU
CLOS DU FONTENY 2005
Red | 2011 up to 2025   **90**
A very dense color. Powerful, noble aromas of brambles. A complete wine, refined and natural compared to all the cuvées with tannins stupidly added!

GEVREY-CHAMBERTIN PREMIER CRU
CLOS DU FONTENY 2004
Red | 2011 up to 2019   **94**
The award goes to this great signature wine of Burgundy, triumphant in its color worthy of a Roman emperor's cape. Rich and firm, with precise tannins. The magnificently concentrated palate has a lot of style. The aromatics—spices, licorice, and black fruit—hold up nicely on the palate.

GEVREY-CHAMBERTIN PREMIER CRU
CLOS SAINT-JACQUES 2006
Red | 2011 up to 2024   **92**
Great vinosity, a serious wine in its aromas and tannins. Clearly classic workmanship. It will slowly but surely evolve.

GEVREY-CHAMBERTIN PREMIER CRU
CLOS SAINT-JACQUES 2005
Red | 2011 up to 2050   **96**
An intense color, just a hint less deeply colored than the Cazetiers. The bouquet has a refinement and fullness superior to all recent vintages; the tannins are perfectly integrated. Another admirable wine from an estate that is master of its style!

GEVREY-CHAMBERTIN PREMIER CRU
CLOS SAINT-JACQUES 2004
Red | 2011 up to 2024   **95**
This complete wine, with a remarkably velvety texture for the vintage, expresses its incredible terroir with precision and charm. A pinnacle of Burgundian classicism.

GEVREY-CHAMBERTIN PREMIER CRU
LES CAZETIERS 2005
Red | 2011 up to 2050   **96**
Black. Sumptuous and substantive, with all the generosity and the "wild" character of this vineyard, brought into harmony by an exceptional vintage. Admirable!

GEVREY-CHAMBERTIN PREMIER CRU
LES CAZETIERS 2004
Red | 2011 up to 2019   **90**
Aromas of blackberry and spices. A supple texture, quite welcoming for the cru, a bit alcoholic. Not as long as its neighbor, the Saint-Jacques.

MARSANNAY LES LONGEROIES 2006
Red | 2011 up to 2018   **87**
Close in style to the wine of the Bart estate. Nice red-berry aromas, firm tannins, a serious finish, complex and likely to soften with age. The tannins are just a touch rustic.

MARSANNAY LES LONGEROIES 2005
Red | 2011 up to 2025   **93**
Almost black. Taffeta mouthfeel, a marvelous fruit character from perfectly ripe grapes. Exemplary.

MOREY-SAINT-DENIS EN LA RUE DE VERGY 2005
Red | 2011 up to 2025   **93**
Fleshy, suave, very seductive. Lightly smoky, like a Lambrays. A great vintage!

SAVIGNY-LÈS-BEAUNE PREMIER CRU
LA DOMINODE 2006
Red | 2011 up to 2018   **90**
Generous fruit character, precise, with even the dark chocolate note of ultraripe grapes. An excellent tannic backbone; only excellent, whereas the 2005 was brilliant.

SAVIGNY-LÈS-BEAUNE PREMIER CRU
LA DOMINODE 2005
Red | 2011 up to 2030   **95**
The extraordinary density is the result of old vines. The fruit character has a nobility that is not surprising from this terroir. Firm, complex tannins. An immense success.

VOSNE-ROMANÉE CHAMPS PERDRIX 2005
Red | 2011 up to 2020   **94**
Deeply colored, spicy, velvety, suave. Vosne to perfection. This vintage clearly expresses the wine's relation to the greatest terroirs of the area. It will not soon be forgotten!

Red: 46.4 acres; pinot 100%. White: 11.3 acres; chardonnay 100%. **Annual production:** 100,000 bottles

DOMAINE CHRISTIAN CLERGET

10, ancienne RN
Gilly-les-Cîteaux
21640 Vougeot
Phone 00 33 3 80 62 87 37
Fax 00 33 3 80 62 84 37
domainechristianclerget@wanadoo.fr

We decided to include this winery in the guide after tasting his 2006s: wonderfully generous wines, true to the classic style, but with barrel aging infinitely superior to the wines of ten years ago. There is a bright future here.

Recently tasted
CHAMBOLLE-MUSIGNY 2007   88
Red | 2013 up to 2017

CHAMBOLLE-MUSIGNY PREMIER CRU
CHARMES 2007
Red | 2015 up to 2022   90

Older vintages
CHAMBOLLE-MUSIGNY PREMIER CRU
CHARMES 2006
Red | 2011 up to 2024   93
Great color, imposing body for a Chambolle, even in this vintage, with racy, complex tannins. The most complete of the stars of our tasting.

VOUGEOT PREMIER CRU LES CRAS 2006
Red | 2011 up to 2018   87
This wine has a similar character to that of the Clos. With plenty of substance, energy, and a finesse that makes the transition with Vosne, this classically made wine is well vinified.

Annual production: 20,000 bottles

DOMAINE JACK CONFURON-COTETIDOT

10, rue de la Fontaine
21700 Vosne-Romanée
Phone 00 33 3 80 61 03 39
Fax 00 33 3 80 61 17 85
domaine-confuron-cotetidot@wanadoo.fr

This exemplary artisanal estate boasts a heritage of vines ideally distributed across the main communes of the Côte de Nuits. It also now has a foothold in Pommard, where Yves Confuron does wonderful things as manager of the Domaine de Courcel. Back home, he works in partnership with his brother Jean-Pierre (director of Chanson and consultant to the Domaine Labet), a double act that preserves the noble but robust style perfected by their father. Remember that all of the cuvées are vinified from whole bunches, producing wines with extraordinary staying power once bottled, plus a unique freshness in very sunny years but a tendency to ruggedness at the outset! The strong point of this domaine is the exceptionally full-bodied personality of its Villages wines.

Recently tasted
CLOS DE VOUGEOT GRAND CRU 2007
Red | 2017 up to 2027   94

ECHÉZEAUX GRAND CRU 2007
Red | 2017 up to 2027   95

GEVREY-CHAMBERTIN 2007
Red | 2014 up to 2019   89

GEVREY-CHAMBERTIN PREMIER CRU
CRAIPILLOTS 2007
Red | 2015 up to 2019   90

GEVREY-CHAMBERTIN PREMIER CRU
LAVAUT SAINT-JACQUES 2007
Red | 2017 up to 2027   90

GEVREY-CHAMBERTIN PREMIER CRU
PETITE CHAPELLE 2007
Red | 2017 up to 2022   92

NUITS-SAINT-GEORGES 2007
Red | 2015 up to 2022   93

NUITS-SAINT-GEORGES PREMIER CRU
VIGNES RONDES 2007
Red | 2015 up to 2022   93

POMMARD PREMIER CRU ARVELETS 2007
Red | 2015 up to 2022   93

VOSNE-ROMANÉE 2007
Red | 2015 up to 2019   90

Vosne-Romanée premier cru Les Suchots 2007
Red | 2017 up to 2027 **95**

Older vintages

Chambolle-Musigny 2004
Red | 2011 up to 2019 **93**
Great color, enveloping blackberry aromas, powerful but with very firm tannins! Exceptional vinosity for a Village-level wine, without the earthy notes you so often find!

Charmes-Chambertin grand cru 2006
Red | 2011 up to 2026 **94**
A great nose of peonies evokes the great vintages of five decades ago. Generous body, with firm, suave tannins. A very distinguished wine, harmonious despite the presence of stems during vinification. But the grapes were so ripe!

Charmes-Chambertin grand cru 2005
Red | 2011 up to 2030 **96**
Very noble flavors, very long, great style, an exquisite wine, more velvety and delicate right now than its neighbors in the cellar.

Clos de Vougeot grand cru 2006
Red | 2011 up to 2026 **96**
A considerably delicate, refined texture for a lower vineyard, but the quality of the whole-grape vinification and the nature of the vintage reinforced the usual qualities of this micro-cuvée.

Clos de Vougeot grand cru 2005
Red | 2011 up to 2050 **96**
The definition, body, and aromatic complexity are ideal for long aging. A very stylish wine.

Clos de Vougeot grand cru 2004
Red | 2011 up to 2016 **90**
More fluid than the Echézeaux; the tannins are too raw; but the terroir is quite present and will show itself with time.

Echézeaux grand cru 2005
Red | 2011 up to 2030 **90**
Great color, cherry aromas, full-bodied but the tannins are very astringent. We'll have to come back to this one in five years.

Gevrey-Chambertin Lavaux Saint-Jacques 2006
Red | 2011 up to 2024 **92**
Great aromatic nobility. A serious wine, firm yet ripe tannins. A great future ahead.

Gevrey-Chambertin premier cru Lavaut Saint-Jacques 2005
Red | 2011 up to 2030 **90**
Not as complete as the Suchots, but very taut, racy, with the firm tannins of whole-bunch vinification; it won't find its true form for another ten to twelve years.

Gevrey-Chambertin premier cru Craipillots 2005
Red | 2011 up to 2025 **94**
Very tender, very subtle, immense elegance, very long.

Gevrey-Chambertin premier cru Petite Chapelle 2006
Red | 2011 up to 2026 **90**
Noble floral aromas, generous yet tender, the tannins a bit rustic for the moment, but whole-grape vinification typically gives a slower development of the tannins, and ultimately greater longevity.

Mazis-Chambertin grand cru 2005
Red | 2011 up to 2050 **95**
Very firm, very concentrated, tremendous substance, the tannins still just a hint rustic. Unfortunately, a tiny production.

Nuits-Saint-Georges 2005
Red | 2011 up to 2020 **89**
Good color, anise and menthol on the nose, fresh, elegant, tannic, very honest.

Nuits-Saint-Georges premier cru Vignes Rondes 2006
Red | 2011 up to 2021 **90**
A more evolved color than some others, refined aromas of roses and candied almonds, very delicate for a Nuits-Saint-Georges, but the firm tannins on the finish suggest that it will gain body toward the end of its time in barrel.

Nuits-Saint-Georges premier cru Vignes Rondes 2005
Red | 2011 up to 2025 **93**
A great nose, very powerful, considerable body, firm tannins.

Pommard 2005
Red | 2011 up to 2020 **90**
A nose of brambles, very fresh, firm tannins, a true Pommard.

Vosne-Romanée 2006
Red | 2011 up to 2021 **90**
Distinguished, complex aromas of flowers, ideal body for a Village-level wine, with firm, fresh tannins and good aging potential.

Vosne-Romanée premier cru Les Suchots 2006
Red | 2011 up to 2025 **93**
A noble style, very precise floral aromas harmonized by notes of cocoa. Remarkably well balanced, very natural tannins: a wine of great expression and with perfect transparency in the expression of the terroir.

Red: 28.4 acres; gamay 5%, pinot noir 95%. **White:** 1.2 acres; aligoté 2%, chardonnay 98%. **Annual production:** 35,000 bottles

DOMAINE PIERRE DAMOY

11, rue du Maréchal-de-Lattre-de-Tassigny
21220 Gevrey-Chambertin
Phone 00 33 3 80 34 30 47
Fax 00 33 3 80 58 54 79
info@domaine-pierre-damoy.com

Pierre Damoy's magnificent estate accounts for the lion's share of the Chambertin–Clos de Bèze Grand Cru and often delighted us in the late 1990s with powerful, thoroughbred wines that culminated in the 2002, a wine that deserves to be anthologized. The wines since then have seemed less consistent, flawed by earthy, vegetal notes that spoil the nose and tannins. This will not have gone unnoticed by Pierre Damoy. Being an experienced and committed winemaker, he is sure to do everything he can to put this bad patch behind him. Some wines of the 2004 and 2006 vintage exhibit a slight bitter aftertaste. But the 2007 are back to the 2002 excellence.

Recently tasted

CHAMBERTIN-CLOS DE BÈZE GRAND CRU 2007
Red | 2017 up to 2027   96

GEVREY-CHAMBERTIN LE TAMISOT 2007
Red | 2015 up to 2025   92

Older vintages

CHAMBERTIN GRAND CRU 2004
Red | 2011 up to 2050   93
The only 2004 from the domaine in this great tradition, full-bodied, tannic but fleshy, obviously racy terroir, more powerful than refined.

CHAMBERTIN-CLOS DE BÈZE GRAND CRU 2006
Red | 2011 up to 2026   89
The aromatic raciness that is distinctive of this parcel is present, as is its rich constitution. This sample showed no aromatic trouble, but spicy, dry tannins that recalled the problems with the grapes in the Clos de Bèze near Chambertin.

CHAPELLE-CHAMBERTIN GRAND CRU 2006
Red | 2011 up to 2024   90
A dense, generous, even monumental wine built on a considerable tannic base, very straightforward and clean tasting.

GEVREY-CHAMBERTIN 2004
Red | 2011 up to 2014   90
A fine, complex nose with vanilla and licorice notes, racy texture, great aging potential, very much in halftones.

Red: 25.9 acres; pinot 100%. **Annual production:** 20,000 bottles

DOMINIQUE LAURENT

Rue Principale
21220 L'Étang-Vergy
Phone 00 33 3 80 61 49 94
Fax 00 33 3 80 61 49 95
dominiquelaurent@club-internet.fr

In the latter part of the 1980s Dominique Laurent invented the concept of a "haute couture" négociant, specializing in the highest-quality barrel aging of tiny quantities of wines that were selected for their exceptional grapes (old-vine pinot noir). His unique process of keeping wines on their lees for extended periods of time, without racking and with a minimum of sulfur (or none at all), make the wines very difficult to judge before their final racking and bottling. But it's worth the wait, for the wines acquire a fullness of texture and an aromatic complexity that really set them apart. Especially since the quality of the oak aging has been refined. They now use less new wood, and employ only barrels made by their own cooperage from Tronçais oak, which is incomparably dried and toasted. The house range starts with the "Tradition" (aimed at restaurants and wide distribution), which is similar to a second wine from a Bordeaux château, and continues with the "Villages n°1" and the old-vines cuvées made from the best lots and the best barrels, bottled the old-fashioned way, by hand, one by one, which may explain certain micro-variations from one bottle to another. The 2006 vintage is certainly one of the most successful ever, and will become collector's items, especially the Côte de Nuits Grand Crus.

Recently tasted

BEAUNE PREMIER CRU 2007
Red | 2012 up to 2019   90

CHAMBERTIN-CLOS DE BÈZE GRAND CRU 2007
Red | 2017 up to 2022   95

CHAMBOLLE-MUSIGNY PREMIER CRU CHARMES 2007
Red | 2017 up to 2022   93

CLOS SAINT-DENIS GRAND CRU
VIEILLES VIGNES 2007
Red | 2015 up to 2019   93

ECHÉZEAUX GRAND CRU 2007
Red | 2015 up to 2022   93

GEVREY-CHAMBERTIN PREMIER CRU
CLOS SAINT-JACQUES 2007
Red | 2017 up to 2027   96

MAZIS-CHAMBERTIN GRAND CRU
VIEILLES VIGNES 2007
Red | 2017 up to 2022   93

MEURSAULT PREMIER CRU PORUZOTS 2007
White | 2012 up to 2017   90

POMMARD 2007
Red | 2015 up to 2019   90

POMMARD PREMIER CRU CHARMOTS 2007
Red | 2015 up to 2022   92

POMMARD PREMIER CRU ÉPENOTS 2007
Red | 2011 up to 2013   94

POMMARD PREMIER CRU RUGIENS VIEILLES
VIGNES 2007
Red | 2017 up to 2025   92

VOLNAY PREMIER CRU CLOS DES CHÊNES
VIEILLES VIGNES 2007
Red | 2017 up to 2027   92

VOSNE-ROMANÉE PREMIER CRU BEAUMONTS
VIEILLES VIGNES 2007
Red | 2011 up to 2013   90

Older vintages

BONNES-MARES GRAND CRU 2006
Red | 2011 up to 2026   95
Admirable aromas of small red fruit, an ideally velvety texture; tends toward the Chambolle style, but with all the body, stuffing,
length, and harmony one expects from this
great terroir.

CHAMBERTIN GRAND CRU 2006
Red | 2011 up to 2026   96
Wonderfully racy on the nose, even if the
aromas are more discreet than in other
Grands Crus; impressive body and intensity
for the vintage, and an ideal presentation
of the terroir (a blend of two sources situated at very different spots).

CHAMBERTIN-CLOS DE BÈZE GRAND CRU 2006
Red | 2011 up to 2028   97
One of the absolute pinnacles of the vintage
in Burgundy, a wine made from a single parcel that was much less affected by hail than
others, with miraculous intensity to its color
and aromas, a creamy texture and soft tannins that contrast with the harder tannins
of most of the wines from this appellation.

CHAMBOLLE-MUSIGNY VIEILLES VIGNES 2006
Red | 2011 up to 2021   90
Very pronounced color, with a more licorice
taste than the Morey; the tannins are still
somewhat harsh, but there is a very pretty
texture on the mid-palate. A wine for aging.

CHARMES-CHAMBERTIN GRAND CRU
VIEILLES VIGNES 2006
Red | 2011 up to 2021   93
Tender and long; suave in texture; plays the
card of finesse and delicacy in its aromas

and tannins, typical of its cru and very
appealing, with better aromatic purity than
in other vintages.

CLOS SAINT-DENIS GRAND CRU
VIEILLES VIGNES 2006
Red | 2011 up to 2028   97
One of the best wines imaginable from this
terroir, with divine aromas of spicy roses
worthy of a great Musigny, a body so harmonious it brings tears to your eyes, immense
length and distinguished character. One of
our favorites.

GEVREY-CHAMBERTIN PREMIER CRU ESTOURNELLES
SAINT-JACQUES VIEILLES VIGNES 2006
Red | 2011 up to 2013   96
Ultra-racy aromas of bramble and rose, practically identical to those of a Clos Saint-
Jacques, dense texture, very racy tannins,
a wine of great subtlety made for aesthetes,
though the production volume is minuscule.

GEVREY-CHAMBERTIN PREMIER CRU
LAVAUT SAINT-JACQUES VIEILLES VIGNES 2006
Red | 2011 up to 2028   95
These vines are almost a hundred years old.
The bramble aromas are wonderfully faithful to what made the great bottlings of the
1920s and 1930s so glorious, and the texture
is truly fabulous—all of which should be food
for thought for many agronomists on the
quality of old pinot noir vines.

GRANDS-ECHÉZEAUX GRAND CRU 2006
Red | 2011 up to 2028   96
Two sources, one of which is a little more
reliable and reasonable in the volatility of
its acidity, perfectly balancing out the other,
which is more fragile but incredibly racy.
The blend produces a prodigious Grands-
Echézeaux that is more mouth-filling than
any other we have ever encountered.

LATRICIÈRES-CHAMBERTIN GRAND CRU 2006
Red | 2011 up to 2013   97
A wine of transcendent elegance, a little
offbeat as compared to the other Grands
Crus from this house, but only insofar as it
is a little less opulent and baroque on an
aromatic level; nonetheless, its finesse and
definition of terroir will be hard to surpass,
with an élevage of uniquely high quality.

MAZIS-CHAMBERTIN GRAND CRU
VIEILLES VIGNES 2006
Red | 2011 up to 2028   95
Completely different in form and aroma from
the Latricières; firmer, earthier, but with rare
elegance to its oak and a textural quality
that sets it apart. One can immediately
sense, upon tasting such a wine, the crucial
importance of the winemaking choices taken
during the élevage.

MOREY-SAINT-DENIS VIEILLES VIGNES 2006
Red | 2011 up to 2018   90
Aromas of small dark fruit, mocha, soot; firm, slightly untamed tannins, a quintessential Village wine, taut for the vintage and fleshy—a style that has become rare. Something indefinable about it feels similar to the Latricières.

NUITS-SAINT-GEORGES PREMIER CRU
LES SAINT-GEORGES VIEILLES VIGNES 2006
Red | 2011 up to 2026   94
Once again, a well-rounded Nuits, with great bramble aromas and a richer, more harmonious texture than that of many other producers.

POMMARD PREMIER CRU RUGIENS
VIEILLES VIGNES 2006
Red | 2011 up to 2026   94
In the house's habitual match between this and the Épenots, whose vines are even older, it is the Rugiens that takes the crown in 2006 (the same as for most other producers). It has more tension to its body and tannins and a plush feel from the naturally rich levels of glycerol in the grapes, which removes their habitual youthful austerity.

VOLNAY PREMIER CRU CLOS DES CHÊNES
VIEILLES VIGNES 2006
Red | 2011 up to 2024   92
Powerful, spicy, long on the palate, lots of character and subtlety, and great intensity to it.

VOSNE-ROMANÉE PREMIER CRU
BEAUMONTS VIEILLES VIGNES 2006
Red | 2011 up to 2026   95
A superb and inimitable expression of the finesse of the Vosne terroirs, with a slightly more ideal suavity than the Suchots; a well-rounded, refined wine made for true connoisseurs.

VOSNE-ROMANÉE PREMIER CRU
SUCHOTS VIEILLES VIGNES 2006
Red | 2011 up to 2024   93
A fine, complex aroma of hawthorn flower, with a slight touch of chocolate that we find in certain Clos de Vougeots; broad, distinguished, a very fine quality to the raw materials.

Red: 12.4 acres; pinot 100%. White: 2.5 acres; chardonnay 100%. Annual production: 300,000 bottles

DOMAINE DROUHIN-LAROZE

20, rue du Gaizot
21220 Gevrey-Chambertin
Phone 00 33 3 80 34 31 49
Fax 00 33 3 80 51 83 70
drouhinlaroze@wanadoo.fr
www.drouhin-laroze.com

This famous estate boasts an impressive heritage of vines and for five or six years now has had its sights set on achieving the ultimate in quality—a reasonable enough ambition, given its standing!

Recently tasted
CHAPELLE-CHAMBERTIN GRAND CRU 2007
Red | 2015 up to 2025   90

Older vintages
BONNES-MARES GRAND CRU 2006
Red | 2011 up to 2024   92
Great color, imposing body, nicely present tannins, slightly hardened by the oak influence, clean, ample, generous, but without the purity necessary to attain supreme excellence.

CHAMBERTIN-CLOS DE BÈZE GRAND CRU 2005
Red | 2011 up to 2030   90
Powerful, wild, but the tannins are abrupt.

CHAMBERTIN-CLOS DE BÈZE GRAND CRU 2004
Red | 2011 up to 2017   89
Elegant, pure, fresh, but on some level lacking in depth and in complexity in the tannins.

CLOS DE VOUGEOT GRAND CRU 2006
Red | 2011 up to 2030   92
Rich in color and tannins, vinous, ample, built like a long-distance runner. The tannins could be more delicate.

GEVREY-CHAMBERTIN 2005
Red | 2011 up to 2020   88
Deeply colored, powerful, rich, ripe, with notes of mint and tannins with no finesse.

GEVREY-CHAMBERTIN 2004
Red | 2011 up to 2016   88
Lactic, but with generous body and texture, a bit green on the finish. Plenty of energy!

GEVREY-CHAMBERTIN PREMIER CRU
AU CLOSEAU 2005
Red | 2011 up to 2030   90
Very deeply colored, powerful, ripe, rich, but the tannins are excessive.

GEVREY-CHAMBERTIN PREMIER CRU
AU CLOSEAU 2004
Red | 2011 up to 2017   88
Black currants. Elegant, tannic, fresh, well vinified.

Red: 29.7 acres; pinot noir 100%. Annual production: 40,000 bottles

DOMAINE DAVID DUBAND

36, rue de la Fontaine
21220 Chevannes
Phone 00 33 3 80 61 41 16
Fax 00 33 3 80 61 49 20
domaine.duband@wanadoo.fr

David Duband is the right-hand man of François Feuillet, who appointed him director of the superb Domaine Truchot holding in Morey-Saint-Denis. But brilliant winemaker though he is, we never seem to have any luck with his wines: the 2005 entries suffered from astringent wood—or at least they did when we tasted them. But we will of course taste his new range, which includes a lovely bunch of Nuits-Saint-Georges Premiers Crus. The style of the latest vintages places them squarely in the modern camp: highly colored, with very assertive but somewhat trite flavors compared to the greatest contemporary offerings.

Recently tasted

HAUTES CÔTES DE NUITS LOUIS AUGUSTE 2007
Red | 2011 up to 2016   88

NUITS-SAINT-GEORGES PREMIER CRU
CHABOEUFS FRANÇOIS FEUILLET 2007
Red | 2015 up to 2022   90

NUITS-SAINT-GEORGES PREMIER CRU LES PROCÈS 2007
Red | 2015 up to 2022   91

NUITS-SAINT-GEORGES PREMIER CRU
LES PRULIERS 2007
Red | 2013 up to 2022   94

Older vintages

NUITS-SAINT-GEORGES PREMIER CRU
LES CHABOEUFS 2005
Red | 2011 up to 2050   87
Fleshy and clean, great progress compared to the Village wines, but more powerful than delicate and still with rather dry oak tannins.

NUITS-SAINT-GEORGES PREMIER CRU
LES PROCÈS 2005
Red | 2011 up to 2015   86
Deeply colored, a nose of spices and brambles, fair body but dried out by barrel aging.

NUITS-SAINT-GEORGES PREMIER CRU
LES PRULIERS 2005
Red | 2011 up to 2017   89
A very dense color, by far the most noble of the estate's Premier Crus, complex, racy, a bit dried out by barrel aging.

Red: 40.8 acres; pinot 100%. White: 1.2 acres; chardonnay 100%. Annual production: 40,000 bottles

DOMAINE BERNARD DUGAT-PY

Rue de Planteligone
BP 31
21220 Gevrey-Chambertin
Phone 00 33 3 80 51 82 46
Fax 00 33 3 80 51 86 41
dugat-py@wanadoo.fr
www.dugat-py.com

Bernard Dugat, like his cousin Claude, has inherited family holdings of incomparable pinot noir vines, patiently selected over time. Winegrower extraordinaire Bernard makes wines that are a testament to the advantages of meticulous vineyard practices based on limiting the number of clusters per vine. His plots are essentially located in the Villages and Premier Cru Côte de Nuits appellations, although output from Charmes-Chambertin has increased and is not as exclusive as it used to be. In just a few years, Bernard Dugat has risen to become one of the top Côte de Nuits producers, crafting wines of admirable power and noble expression—but they really develop a recognizable form only after many years of aging. He is now joined by his equally talented son, perhaps even more of a perfectionist than his father.

CHARMES-CHAMBERTIN GRAND CRU 2005
Red | 2011 up to 2030   96
Great, complex nose where the noble notes of magnificent oak harmonize with the licorice notes of very ripe grapes. Offers the power of a Perrot-Minot but with extra fresh-fruit character and depth.

GEVREY-CHAMBERTIN COEUR DU ROY
VIEILLES VIGNES 2005
Red | 2011 up to 2025   94
Great color and aromatic power, very firm texture, magnificent tannic grain, but a rather uncontrolled character that needs time to soften.

GEVREY-CHAMBERTIN LES ÉVOCELLES 2005
Red | 2011 up to 2030   97
A stunning Village-level wine, with an intense, firm texture and astonishing flavor. For those who love monumental wines. But when it starts to open up . . .

GEVREY-CHAMBERTIN PREMIER CRU 2005
Red | 2011 up to 2025   94
Powerful flavor, racy, with tannins that are still firm. Less unctuous than the best Village wines but perhaps with a more solid foundation. A great wine for the cellar.

GEVREY-CHAMBERTIN PREMIER CRU
CHAMPEAUX 2005
Red | 2011 up to 2030   **95**
A great, complete wine with a pure, spicy
nose, a splendid texture with very firm, distinguished tannins. A long future lies ahead.

GEVREY-CHAMBERTIN PREMIER CRU
LAVAUT SAINT-JACQUES 2005
Red | 2011 up to 2030   **97**
Marvelously unctuous body and texture,
monumental but very distinguished. The
grand style of Gevrey, for those who know
what a great wine is!

GEVREY-CHAMBERTIN PREMIER CRU
PETITE CHAPELLE 2005
Red | 2011 up to 2025   **95**
Very deep color, a strong presence of high-
quality new oak. Sumptuous, but the terroir
brings suppleness and finesse. It will open
before some of the Village wines!

MAZIS-CHAMBERTIN GRAND CRU 2005
Red | 2011 up to 2030   **98**
This wine is admirable for its body, texture,
refinement of flavor, and depth and exact-
ness of terroir expression. This is the absolute pinnacle of the vintage and of Burgundy
(but unfortunately with just 1,200 bottles).

VOSNE-ROMANÉE VIEILLES VIGNES 2005
Red | 2011 up to 2025   **93**
Great substance, but in this vintage and on
the day of the tasting the tannins were abrupt
compared to those of Gevrey.

Red: 23.5 acres; pinot noir 100%. White: 1.2 acres;
chardonnay 100%. Annual production: 35,000 bottles

DOMAINE DUJAC

🍷🍷🍷🍷🍷

7, rue de la Bussière
21220 Morey-Saint-Denis
Phone 00 33 3 80 34 01 00
Fax 00 33 3 80 34 01 09
dujac@dujac.com
www.dujac.com

This estate already boasted more than its
fair share of Grands and Premiers Crus and
has expanded by purchasing the prestigious Domaine Thomas holdings, which
includes pristine parcels in Chambertin,
Romanée-Saint-Vivant, and Les Malconsorts! The 2002, 2003, 2005, and 2006s are
all exceptional and more masterfully styled
than ever before: all the aromatic purity
you could wish for but still instantly appealing and very long-lived, with magnificently
distinguished, ultra-classy tannins! A small
proportion of négociant wines sold under
the Dujac Fils et Père label make a very
worthy addition to this winery's offerings.

Recently tasted
BONNES-MARES GRAND CRU 2007
Red | 2015 up to 2019   **93**

CHAMBOLLE-MUSIGNY 2007
Red | 2017 up to 2027   **94**

CHARMES-CHAMBERTIN GRAND CRU 2007
Red | 2019 up to 2027   **95**

CLOS DE LA ROCHE GRAND CRU 2007
Red | 2017 up to 2027   **94**

CLOS SAINT-DENIS GRAND CRU 2007
Red | 2017 up to 2023   **98**

ECHÉZEAUX GRAND CRU 2007
Red | 2017 up to 2022   **93**

GEVREY-CHAMBERTIN PREMIER CRU
AUX COMBOTTES 2007
Red | 2017 up to 2025   **94**

MOREY-SAINT-DENIS 2007
Red | 2019 up to 2027   **95**

VOSNE-ROMANÉE PREMIER CRU
LES BEAUX MONTS 2007
Red | 2015 up to 2019   **90**

Older vintages
CHAMBOLLE-MUSIGNY 2005
Red | 2011 up to 2025   **94**
Nice aromatic opening, distinguished body
and tannins, great follow-up on the palate.

CHAMBOLLE-MUSIGNY DUJAC FILS & PÈRE 2006
Red | 2011 up to 2021 **90**
An exceptional Village-level wine for its fullness, aromatic complexity, texture, and potential.

CHAMBOLLE-MUSIGNY PREMIER CRU
LES GRUENCHERS 2005
Red | 2011 up to 2023 **92**
Plenty of charm and finesse, distinguished tannins, great style, without the density of the more complete wines of this vintage.

CHARMES-CHAMBERTIN GRAND CRU 2005
Red | 2011 up to 2025 **94**
Very generous, with plenty of style in its aromas and velvety texture, and more graceful than the Grands Crus of Morey.

CLOS DE LA ROCHE GRAND CRU 2006
Red | 2011 up to 2024 **92**
Great color, a nobly spicy, oaky nose, powerful, a taut texture, tight, the tannins still austere but, as is often the case in this vintage, the Clos Saint-Denis surpasses it in refinement of texture and even in vinosity.

CLOS DE LA ROCHE GRAND CRU 2005
Red | 2011 up to 2025 **93**
Remarkable body, rather firm tannins, less charm and aromatic finesse than in 2004.

CLOS SAINT-DENIS GRAND CRU 2006
Red | 2011 up to 2026 **95**
A very great wine, marrying power and noble aromatics at the highest level, which will surprise those who consider this vineyard inferior to the other Grands Crus of the village. Magnificent integration of the oak.

CLOS SAINT-DENIS GRAND CRU 2005
Red | 2011 up to 2025 **94**
Nice intense color, a clean, racy nose of small black fruits, elegant but lacking agility in the tannic structure.

MOREY-SAINT-DENIS PREMIER CRU 2005
Red | 2011 up to 2023 **94**
Almost as distinguished as the Grands Crus of this vintage, and more marked finesse. Magnificent!

VOSNE-ROMANÉE PREMIER CRU LES
MALCONSORTS 2006
Red | 2011 up to 2026 **95**
Admirable aromas of flowers and spices, a sensationally dense texture with noble tactile sensations, great length. We're not far, in all senses of the word, from La Tâche.

Red: 34.1 acres. White: 3.6 acres. Annual production: 90,000 bottles

DUPONT-TISSERANDOT

2, place des Marronniers
21220 Gevrey-Chambertin
Phone 00 33 3 80 34 10 50
Fax 00 33 3 80 58 50 71
dupont.tisserandot@orange.fr
www.duponttisserandot.com

This winery was the surprise discovery of our blind tastings. We have long known of its remarkable vineyard heritage, especially the large and impressive plot of Cazetiers. We've noted, over the past five years, several welcome changes in the way the vineyards are farmed that have transformed the style of the wines. Since then they combine fullness, sensuality, and remarkably precise expression of the terroirs, like few others in the village. We highly recommend all of the 2006s!

Recently tasted
CHARMES-CHAMBERTIN GRAND CRU 2007
Red | 2015 up to 2022 **92**

GEVREY-CHAMBERTIN PREMIER CRU
CAZETIERS 2007
Red | 2015 up to 2022 **93**

GEVREY-CHAMBERTIN PREMIER CRU LAVAUX
SAINT-JACQUES 2007
Red | 2015 up to 2025 **87**

MAZIS-CHAMBERTIN GRAND CRU 2007
Red | 2015 up to 2022 **89**

Older vintages
CHARMES-CHAMBERTIN GRAND CRU 2006
Red | 2011 up to 2021 **94**
Great color, a powerful yet wiry wine with considerably velvety texture; long and wonderfully confectionary, because it is not heavy in the least!

GEVREY-CHAMBERTIN PREMIER CRU CAZETIERS 2006
Red | 2011 up to 2026 **95**
The crème de la crème of great pinot noir, practically perfect on the whole, at once for the level of its form, its tastiness, and its respect for a magnificent terroir. One imagines that Henri Leroy, who was so proud of his legendary 1955s, would have bought the whole harvest!

GEVREY-CHAMBERTIN PREMIER CRU
LAVAUX SAINT-JACQUES 2006
Red | 2011 up to 2024 **93**
Superbly dense color, great racy nose of perfectly ripe grapes, majestic body, completely dominated by wonderful floral nuances in its tastes. Stunningly silky tactile sensations.

GEVREY-CHAMBERTIN PREMIER CRU
PETITE CHAPELLE 2006
Red | 2011 up to 2018   **89**
Elegance and subtlety in a less flamboyant
style than the Combe de Lavaux bottlings.
Excellent vinification.

MAZIS-CHAMBERTIN GRAND CRU 2006
Red | 2011 up to 2026   **94**
A remarkable nose of blackberries, great
breadth to its constitution, and a velvety texture comparable to all of the other bottlings
from this domaine; great length.

Red: 48.5 acres; pinot noir 100%. White: 1.5 acres;
chardonnay, aligoté. Annual production: 100,000
bottles

DOMAINE SYLVIE ESMONIN

1, rue Neuve
Clos Saint-Jacques
21220 Gevrey-Chambertin
Phone 00 33 3 80 34 36 44
Fax 00 33 3 80 34 17 31

This small winery is the darling of authentic Gevrey enthusiasts, and it's easy to
understand why: the wines here have
nobility and classicism in both craftsmanship and flavor. Sylvie Esmonin has progressively moved toward whole-cluster
fermentation, from grapes that are even
more rigorously farmed than in the past.
This has led to legendary 2002, 2003, 2004,
and 2005s, recalling the consistency and
perfume of the mythic wines of the nineteenth century. The 2006 Clos Saint
Jacques will be worthy of them too once
the oak is better integrated, and the 2007
promises to be one of the best reds of the
vintage. One shouldn't underestimate the
remarkable Côte de Nuits Villages and in
minuscule quantities, a delicious Volnay
Santenots.

Recently tasted
GEVREY-CHAMBERTIN PREMIER CRU
LE CLOS SAINT-JACQUES 2007
Red | 2017 up to 2027   **98**

GEVREY-CHAMBERTIN VIEILLES VIGNES 2007
Red | 2015 up to 2022   **90**

Older vintages
GEVREY-CHAMBERTIN PREMIER CRU
LE CLOS SAINT-JACQUES 2006
Red | 2011 up to 2026   **93**
Great tension and noble constitution, still
very marked by its oak, firm tannins, a highly
expressive wine, to be cellared for many
years before opening.

GEVREY-CHAMBERTIN PREMIER CRU
LE CLOS SAINT-JACQUES 2005
Red | 2011 up to 2050   **98**
Dark in color, with black currants, bramble,
and flowers on the nose; even more magical than the 2004! To our tastes, this is the
greatest vinification possible for the parcel
and the vintage, in the tradition of the unforgettable wines of the nineteenth century.

GEVREY-CHAMBERTIN PREMIER CRU
LE CLOS SAINT-JACQUES 2004
Red | 2011 up to 2024   **94**
Admirably dense in color for the year, a very
open nose with wonderful smoky notes, as
well as vanilla, bramble, and hawthorn; fresh
taste, and the tannic backbone of whole-
cluster grapes that accentuates the overall
freshness. Great length. Wonderful!

GEVREY-CHAMBERTIN VIEILLES VIGNES 2006
Red | 2011 up to 2021   89

Very marked by the oak treatment, but with a well-rounded body for the vintage, firm tannins. The richness in natural sugar from the grapes explains its generous texture. This wine will offer a very authentic style, once the oak has been absorbed.

GEVREY-CHAMBERTIN VIEILLES VIGNES 2005
Red | 2011 up to 2025   95

Dark in color, with a well-rounded nose of licorice, candied fruit, and spices, a wonderfully velvety, full texture; an exceptional Village wine from an exceptional year!

Red: 17.3 acres; pinot noir 100%. Annual production: 35,000 bottles

DOMAINE FAIVELEY

8, rue du Tribourg
21700 Nuits-Saint-Georges
Phone 00 33 3 80 61 04 55
Fax 00 33 3 80 62 33 37
accueil@bourgognes-faiveley.com
www.bourgognes-faiveley.com

We can expect some big changes here now that Erwan Faiveley is working with Bernard Hervet to drive up the quality of production. The Domaine Faiveley is one of the great traditional Burgundy estates, with impressive holdings in the loftiest Gevrey-Chambertin crus. Its wines were very deftly made in the early 1990s, but recent vintages have been marred by an astringent finish. The winery has been completely reorganized since then, and we will be keeping a close eye on the 2007s to see whether they deliver the change in style that the 2006s merely suggested. The white wines seem more even than the reds. All the 2008s will be brilliant.

Recently tasted

CHAMBERTIN-CLOS DE BÈZE GRAND CRU 2007
Red | 2017 up to 2027   94

CHAMBOLLE-MUSIGNY PREMIER CRU
COMBE D'ORVEAU 2007
Red | 2015 up to 2019   93

CHAMBOLLE-MUSIGNY PREMIER CRU
FUÉES 2007
Red | 2015 up to 2022   89

CLOS DE VOUGEOT GRAND CRU 2007
Red | 2017 up to 2025   92

CORTON-CHARLEMAGNE GRAND CRU 2007
White | 2016 up to 2022   95

GEVREY-CHAMBERTIN PREMIER CRU
CAZETIERS 2007
Red | 2017 up to 2027   92

LATRICIÈRES-CHAMBERTIN GRAND CRU 2007
Red | 2017 up to 2025   93

MAZIS-CHAMBERTIN GRAND CRU 2007
Red | 2015 up to 2025   90

MEURSAULT 2007
White | 2013 up to 2017   89

MEURSAULT PREMIER CRU CHARMES 2007
White | 2015 up to 2022   95

NUITS-SAINT-GEORGES PREMIER CRU
LES CHAIGNOTS 2007
Red | 2015 up to 2019   88

NUITS-SAINT-GEORGES PREMIER CRU
SAINT-GEORGES 2007
Red | 2017 up to 2022   92

Older vintages

CORTON-CHARLEMAGNE GRAND CRU 2005
White | 2011 up to 2025   95
Very rich, complete, broad, long-aging. The
oak is a bit simple for such a noble wine.

GEVREY-CHAMBERTIN PREMIER CRU
CAZETIERS 2005
Red | 2011 up to 2030   88
Powerful, dense, refined on the mid-palate.
The tannins are too astringent.

MEURSAULT PREMIER CRU
LES BOUCHÈRES 2005
White | 2011 up to 2015   86
Broad, generous, rather complex, but
weighted down by inelegant oakiness.

MONTAGNY LES JONCS 2005
White | 2011 up to 2015   90
One of the consistent successes of the
estate, nervy, mineral, with splendid substance. The best of Montagny.

NUITS-SAINT-GEORGES PREMIER CRU
LES CHAIGNOTS 2006
Red | 2011 up to 2026   93
Complete, deeply colored, noble aromas of
brambles, magnificently vigorous, finishing
on tannins infinitely more civilized than in
the past, yet still firm. A great future ahead.

Red: 222.4 acres. White: 74.1 acres. Annual
production: 1,000,000 bottles

RÉGIS FOREY

2, rue Derrière-le-Four
21700 Vosne-Romanée
Phone 00 33 3 80 61 09 68
Fax 00 33 3 80 61 12 63
domaineforey@orange.fr

This serious producer likes his wines very
solidly built, and he does a great job with
his Nuits-Saint-Georges wines, where he
has excellent vineyard holdings. In general, the wines here are more natural and
balanced than his Vosne-Romanée offerings, save the confidential bottling of Gau-
dichots (800 bottles). The 2007s shown
were excellent.

Recently tasted

NUITS-SAINT-GEORGES 2007
Red | 2014 up to 2019   90

NUITS-SAINT-GEORGES PREMIER CRU
LES SAINT-GEORGES 2007
Red | 2017 up to 2025   93

NUITS-SAINT-GEORGES PREMIER CRU
PERRIÈRES 2007
Red | 2017 up to 2027   93

Older vintages

NUITS-SAINT-GEORGES 2006
Red | 2011 up to 2021   87
Blue-black in color, with a powerful nose.
Both tannic and spicy, this is a wine pow-
ered by ripe grapes and strong tannins, with
perfectly expressed terroir. A Village wine
for aging.

NUITS-SAINT-GEORGES PREMIER CRU
LES SAINT-GEORGES 2006
Red | 2011 up to 2026   93
One of the pinnacles of the vintage for this
Village and cru, with great aromatic nobility owing to the quality of the grapes and
the impeccable quality of the new oak used.
Racy and complex on the palate, on the level
of the best Grands Crus, which will come
as no surprise!

NUITS-SAINT-GEORGES PREMIER CRU
PERRIÈRES 2006
Red | 2011 up to 2024   88
Deeply colored, very tannic, with tannins
that are even slightly astringent. A dark,
untamed character in the very spirit of Nuits
wines from this sector.

Red: 19.8 acres; pinot noir 100%. White: 1.2 acres;
chardonnay 100%. Annual production: 30,000 bottles

DOMAINE JEAN FOURNIER

34, rue du Château
21160 Marsannay-la-Côte
Phone 00 33 380522438
Fax 00 33 380527740
domaine.jean.fournier@orange.fr

Laurent Fournier, who is little by little taking the reins at this traditional family winery, is one of the brightest talents of the new generation in Burgundy. He truly pleased us in searching out and finding the secrets of the great wines of old, vinified with whole clusters but with the help of modern materials, which allow for better hygiene and much more precision. His "cuvée spéciale de vin à l'ancienne" is simply the greatest and the most beautiful Marsannay that we've tasted, and little by little the excellent Echezots and Clos du Roy are catching up to it.

Recently tasted

MARSANNAY CLOS DU ROY 2007
Red | 2013 up to 2019   89

MARSANNAY CUVÉE SAINT-URBAIN 2007
Red | 2013 up to 2019   90

MARSANNAY LONGEROIES 2007
Red | 2013 up to 2019   89

Older vintages

MARSANNAY CLOS DU ROY 2006
Red | 2011 up to 2014   90
Refined oak influence, remarkably ripe grapes, a very vibrant fruit character, generous, luscious, long, truly stunning. A wine that shows off this winemaker's quick mastery of his craft. A model for the appellation.

MARSANNAY ECHEZOTS 2006
Red | 2011 up to 2016   88
Great aromatic finesse, a very pure style of wine. It was promising when tasted during the Great Days of Burgundy.

MARSANNAY TROIS TERRES
VIEILLES VIGNES 2005
Red | 2011 up to 2017   95
We don't know if there is any more available, but this 2005 Marsannay, apparently from whole-grape vinification, offers a distinguished nose rivaling those of the Grands Crus of the Côte and the same level of refinement in the tactile sensation, showing the ultimate potential of this commune's vineyards. A revelation.

Annual production: 70,000 bottles

DOMAINE GEANTET-PANSIOT

3, route de Beaune
21220 Gevrey-Chambertin
Phone 00 33 3 80 34 32 37
Fax 00 33 3 80 34 16 23
domaine.geantet@wanadoo.fr
www.geantet-pansiot.com

Vincent Geantet is one of the most competent winegrowers in Gevrey-Chambertin, with a particular admiration for wines in the Chambolle-Musigny style. The latest addition to his portfolio is the very excellent Les Baudes Premier Cru, a wine sourced from parcels just below Bonnes-Mares that increase his holdings in Chambolle-Musigny. His daughter Emilie is also showing increasing initiative and looks, in her own personal way, to take the wines toward more finesse and a silkier texture. All of the estate wines are fairly quick to open in the bottle but built for aging; they usually need to sit in the decanter for a while.

Recently tasted

CHARMES-CHAMBERTIN GRAND CRU 2007
Red | 2017 up to 2025   94

FIXIN ÉMILIE GEANTET 2007
Red | 2013 up to 2017   88

GEVREY-CHAMBERTIN 2007
Red | 2014 up to 2019   89

GEVREY-CHAMBERTIN EN CHAMPS 2007
Red | 2014 up to 2019   88

GEVREY-CHAMBERTIN PREMIER CRU
POISSENOT 2007
Red | 2015 up to 2022   90

MAZIS-CHAMBERTIN GRAND CRU ÉMILIE
GEANTET 2007
Red | 2017 up to 2025   90

Older vintages

CHAMBOLLE-MUSIGNY PREMIER CRU
LES BAUDES 2005
Red | 2011 up to 2025   90
Great color, a bit reduced on the nose, great vinosity and complexity. A very long future ahead.

CHAMBOLLE-MUSIGNY VIEILLES VIGNES 2005
Red | 2011 up to 2017   90
Good color, a clean, pure fruit character, firm tannins, good substance, stylish in a modern way.

CHARMES-CHAMBERTIN GRAND CRU 2006
Red | 2011 up to 2026   95
The greatest Charmes of our immense tasting, in which the selection was overall top-

notch, and one of the pinnacles of the vintage in the Côte de Nuits. Admirable finesse of texture and flavor, great length; it will outshine many Chambertins and Clos de Bèze in this vintage.

CHARMES-CHAMBERTIN GRAND CRU 2005
Red | 2011 up to 2025   **93**
Rich, complete, with very Bordeaux-like tannins, good length, ready for long aging, but we would like a bit more finesse.

GEVREY-CHAMBERTIN 2005
Red | 2011 up to 2017   **89**
Clean, fruity, elegant, nice oak influence, generous and appetizing, a nice technical execution.

GEVREY-CHAMBERTIN ÉMILIE GEANTET VIEILLES VIGNES 2006
Red | 2011 up to 2018   **88**
A nice rich, fleshy wine, ripe grapes, firm tannins; a long future is guaranteed. A more classic style, in a way, than that of the father.

GEVREY-CHAMBERTIN EN CHAMPS 2006
Red | 2011 up to 2016   **87**
The oak influence is pronounced but seductive. Fleshy, very clean, harmonious tannins, good length, but not very nuanced.

GEVREY-CHAMBERTIN JEUNES ROIS 2006
Red | 2011 up to 2018   **87**
Great color, a generous nose, powerful, fleshy, very ripe, with a slight lack of finesse.

GEVREY-CHAMBERTIN PREMIER CRU CHAMPEAUX ÉMILIE GEANTET 2006
Red | 2011 up to 2021   **89**
Strong color, a powerful nose that marries cocoa and licorice, very structured, classic tannins. Will age very well.

GEVREY-CHAMBERTIN PREMIER CRU POISSENOT 2006
Red | 2011 up to 2026   **88**
Powerful, the tannins robust but not aggressive, great unity, the noble yet rustic terroir clearly shows through.

GEVREY-CHAMBERTIN PREMIER CRU POISSENOT 2005
Red | 2011 up to 2017   **92**
Subtle licorice notes, long, silky, perfectly ripe grapes, excellent!

MAZIS-CHAMBERTIN GRAND CRU ÉMILIE GEANTET 2006
Red | 2011 up to 2026   **90**
Power worthy of the cru, great strawberry flavor, the tannins a bit rustic but quite abundant. A very long future ahead.

Red: 32.1 acres; pinot 100%. **White:** 2.5 acres; chardonnay 100%. **Annual production:** 100,000 bottles

DOMAINE FRANÇOIS GERBET
2, route nationale
21700 Vosne-Romanée
Phone 00 33 3 80 61 07 85
Fax 00 33 3 80 61 01 65
vins.gerbet@wanadoo.fr

The Gerbet sisters continue to move their domaine forward, not changing their vinification style, favoring finesse over power, but with infinitely more rigor and precision. The wines have gained in definition, terroir, and body. The 2006s were ravishing, for they are the ambassadors of incomparable elegance in the village.

Recently tasted
VOSNE-ROMANÉE PREMIER CRU SUCHOTS 2007
Red | 2011 up to 2019   **90**

Older vintages
ECHÉZEAUX GRAND CRU 2006
Red | 2011 up to 2021   **93**
The same superbly floral nose as the other bottlings from the domaine, with just a few subtle differences. Long, elegant texture, no excess alcoholic heat, a general impression of great finesse.

VOSNE-ROMANÉE AUX RÉAS 2006
Red | 2011 up to 2018   **88**
A pretty, floral nose and very fine tastes of wild strawberries—a feature shared by all the best Vosnes of the vintage. Delicate and long, with a skillful smoky nuance that spices up the floral notes. Vinification respectful of the terroir.

VOSNE-ROMANÉE PREMIER CRU PETITS MONTS 2006
Red | 2011 up to 2018   **93**
Superb nose of floral essence, a long, subtle wine that is very caressing in texture, very aristocratic. Decidedly, Vosne produces inimitable wines when given the means.

VOSNE-ROMANÉE PREMIER CRU SUCHOTS 2006
Red | 2011 up to 2013   **93**
Once again, a bouquet of flowers on the nose, the same finesse and tender feel as the Petits Monts, with slightly more body. Exemplary vinification and élevage.

Annual production: 60,000 bottles

DOMAINE HENRI GOUGES

7, rue du Moulin
21700 Nuits-Saint-Georges
Phone 00 33 3 80 61 04 40
Fax 00 33 3 80 61 32 84
domaine@gouges.com
www.gouges.com

The difficult 2004 vintage seems to have been a particular problem for this classical Nuits-Saint-Georges estate. It's possible that routinely planting grass in the vineyards leads to a degree of water stress in dry years that prevents the grapes from ripening properly. Generally speaking, this estate makes powerful wines that are slightly austere en primeur but very classy when aged—though it would be nice if they could become more like the recent offerings from Bruno Clair, an old friend of the Gouges cousins.

Recently tasted

NUITS-SAINT-GEORGES PREMIER CRU
CLOS DES PORRETS SAINT-GEORGES 2007
Red | 2011 up to 2013   91

NUITS-SAINT-GEORGES PREMIER CRU
LES SAINT-GEORGES 2007
Red | 2017 up to 2027   94

NUITS-SAINT-GEORGES PREMIER CRU
PRULIERS 2007
Red | 2017 up to 2025   93

NUITS-SAINT-GEORGES PREMIER CRU
VAUCRAINS 2007
Red | 2017 up to 2027   93

Older vintages

BOURGOGNE PINOT BLANC 2007
White | 2011 up to 2013   88
Very pale, lemony, no noticeable oak influence, fruity, simple, mineral.

NUITS-SAINT-GEORGES PREMIER CRU
LA PERRIÈRE 2005
White | 2011 up to 2017   88
Very clean, full, straightforward, rich, but with the simplicity of pinot blanc.

NUITS-SAINT-GEORGES PREMIER CRU
LES SAINT-GEORGES 2006
Red | 2011 up to 2030   93
Black color, a very powerful nose, majestic body, very forward tannins. The fruit character is less precise than on the Chicotot. Great aging potential.

Red: 32.6 acres; pinot noir 100%. White: 3.2 acres; chardonnay 100%. Annual production: 60,000 bottles

DOMAINE JEAN GRIVOT

6, rue de la Croix-Rameau
21700 Vosne-Romanée
Phone 00 33 3 80 61 05 95
Fax 00 33 3 80 61 32 99
www.domainegrivot.fr

This famous Vosne-Romanée winery revolutionized its style in the late 1980s, and since then has remained faithful to the idea of making wines that are rich in color and tannins, quite firm before bottling, almost Bordeaux-like in their linearity and tactile sensations, and very slow to evolve in bottle. The 2006s are along the same lines, powerful, austere, but superbly built for aging.

Recently tasted

ECHÉZEAUX GRAND CRU 2007
Red | 2015 up to 2027   93

NUITS-SAINT-GEORGES PREMIER CRU
BOUDOTS 2007
Red | 2015 up to 2022   90

NUITS-SAINT-GEORGES PREMIER CRU
PRULIERS 2007
Red | 2017 up to 2027   93

NUITS-SAINT-GEORGES PREMIER CRU
RONCIÈRES 2007
Red | 2015 up to 2022   90

RICHEBOURG GRAND CRU 2007
Red | 2019 up to 2027   94

VOSNE-ROMANÉE PREMIER CRU
BEAUMONTS 2007
Red | 2017 up to 2022   93

Older vintages

ECHÉZEAUX GRAND CRU 2006
Red | 2011 up to 2024   89
A fine nose of wild strawberries, imposing body, firm tannins; not the most elegant Echézeaux, but one of the healthiest and most expressive from its year: in the end, the grapes in this vintage offered a concentration that was good, but extreme!

NUITS-SAINT-GEORGES PREMIER CRU
BOUDOTS 2006
Red | 2011 up to 2024   90
A deep, almost opaque color, with a great nose of dark fruit, ample body, more sensual in texture than most of the domaine's wines, great ripe tannins; excellent!

NUITS-SAINT-GEORGES PREMIER CRU RONCIÈRES 2006
Red | 2011 up to 2024   **92**
Notes of blackberry, wild strawberry, and black currant, in the spirit of the vintage's grapes, which are even more typical of Nuits than Boudots is; a wine of great character for informed connoisseurs.

VOSNE-ROMANÉE BOSSIÈRES 2006
Red | 2011 up to 2024   **89**
A well-rounded Village wine with powerful rose and peony aromas; tannic, complex, very assured in its style, and made for aging.

VOSNE-ROMANÉE PREMIER CRU SUCHOTS 2006
Red | 2011 up to 2021   **92**
Complex, delicate, refined, more subtle in its tannins and more diversified than Beaumonts; very successful and highly recommended—but there is sadly little of it, due to the tiny size of the domaine's parcel.

Red: 36.3 acres; pinot noir 100%. Annual production: 65,000 bottles

DOMAINE GROS FRÈRE ET SOEUR
🍷 🍷 🍷 🍷 🍷

6, rue des Grands-Crus
21700 Vosne-Romanée
Phone 00 33 3 80 61 12 43
Fax 00 33 3 80 61 34 05
bernard.gros2@wanadoo.fr

This winery is now managed by Bernard Gros, who took over the prestigious vineyards from his aunt and uncle, leaving his parents' vineyards to his brother Michel. His style is different from any other winery bearing the name Gros, with immediately forward aromatics and a voluptuous texture that is surprising at each tasting, for you ask yourself the question: can this charm last? While waiting to find out, these wines can be thoroughly enjoyed, especially since the prices have remained relatively reasonable for such rare and sought-after vineyard designations. Enthusiasts who are in a hurry to drink sensual and complex wines will be thrilled with the 2007s.

Recently tasted
GRANDS-ECHÉZEAUX GRAND CRU 2007
Red | 2012 up to 2019   **92**

HAUTES CÔTES DE NUITS 2007
White | 2011 up to 2016   **90**

HAUTES CÔTES DE NUITS 2007
Red | 2011 up to 2017   **89**

RICHEBOURG GRAND CRU 2007
Red | 2013 up to 2027   **94**

VOSNE-ROMANÉE 2007
Red | 2012 up to 2017   **90**

Older vintages
CLOS DE VOUGEOT GRAND CRU LE MUSIGNI 2006
Red | 2011 up to 2016   **94**
As its name suggests, this wine is from a parcel from the upper part of the vineyard, immediately below Musigny, and tradition holds that this is the part of the parcel that gives wines with the greatest finesse. This cuvée confirms this idea and shines with a truly unctuous texture, creamy and melty. But those who love Clos de Vougeot might find this wine too snobby.

RICHEBOURG GRAND CRU 2006
Red | 2011 up to 2021   **93**
A great, complex, chocolaty nose. A velvety wine with an immediate sensuality, certainly not orthodox but boundlessly pleasing right away.

Red: 42 acres; pinot noir 100%. White: 7.4 acres; chardonnay 100%. Annual production: 100,000 bottles

DOMAINE JEAN-MICHEL GUILLON & FILS

33, route de Beaune
21220 Gevrey-Chambertin
Phone 00 33 3.80.51.83.98
Fax 00 33 3.80.51.85.59
contact@domaineguillon.com
www.domaineguillon.com

Jean-Michel Guillon leads the dynamic Gevrey growers' union with authority and his own unique sense of humor, and maintains the spirit of competition that has so helped the appellation advance. His wines are perfect ambassadors of their terroir in 2006, powerful and elegant. And we tasted only part of his production.

Recently tasted

GEVREY-CHAMBERTIN PREMIER CRU
CHAMPONNETS 2007
Red | 2015 up to 2022   93

GEVREY-CHAMBERTIN PREMIER CRU
PETITE CHAPELLE 2007
Red | 2014 up to 2019   86

GEVREY-CHAMBERTIN VIEILLES VIGNES 2007
Red | 2015 up to 2022   88

MAZIS-CHAMBERTIN GRAND CRU 2007
Red | 2012 up to 2017   89

Older vintages

GEVREY-CHAMBERTIN PREMIER CRU
PETITE CHAPELLE 2006
Red | 2011 up to 2018   89
Notes of raspberry and bramble on the nose; precise, racy body; somewhat abrupt tannins; a confirmed style that is very faithful to the terroir.

GEVREY-CHAMBERTIN VIEILLES VIGNES 2006
Red | 2011 up to 2018   88
An elaborate, subtle nose in the spirit of the terroir, combining floral, spicy (bramble, peony) notes with the "roasted" overtone of the very ripe grapes of that year; very pleasant on the palate, both vinous and quaffable.

Red: 27.2 acres; pinot noir 100%. White: 2.5 acres; chardonnay 100%. Annual production: 70,000 bottles

DOMAINE OLIVIER GUYOT

4, rue des Carrières
21160 Marsannay-la-Côte
Phone 00 33 3 80 52 39 71
Fax 00 33 3 80 51 17 58
domaine.guyot@wanadoo.fr
www.domaineguyot.fr

This very conscientious artisan winery still uses horse-drawn plows, and vinifies and raises its wines in accordance with time-honored practice. Its Marsannays are just about the most complete wines to come out of this village, particularly the Cuvée Montagne. Its Gevreys meanwhile can rival those of the Domaine Mortet—clearly a source of inspiration for Olivier Guyot. Less stunning are the two Morey Grand Crus, sourced from holdings acquired from a large Morey Saint-Denis estate.

Recently tasted

CLOS DE LA ROCHE GRAND CRU 2007
Red | 2015 up to 2019   89

CLOS SAINT-DENIS GRAND CRU 2007
Red | 2015 up to 2019   89

GEVREY-CHAMBERTIN EN CHAMPS 2007
Red | 2014 up to 2019   87

GEVREY-CHAMBERTIN PREMIER CRU LES
CHAMPEAUX 2007
Red | 2017 up to 2022   89

MARSANNAY LA MONTAGNE 2007
Red | 2013 up to 2019   84

MARSANNAY LES FAVIÈRES 2007
Red | 2011 up to 2015   85

Older vintages

CHAMBOLLE-MUSIGNY PREMIER CRU
LES CHARMES 2005
Red | 2011 up to 2020   93
Fine dark color, very ripe grapes, irreproachable balance, a superb expression of the parcel and vintage.

CLOS DE LA ROCHE GRAND CRU 2006
Red | 2011 up to 2021   87
Clearly distinguished, aromatically speaking, but markedly less well rounded and complex than the Clos Saint-Denis. Slight dilution seems to be the explanation for this.

CLOS DE LA ROCHE GRAND CRU 2005
Red | 2011 up to 2050   88
Deep color, bramble on the nose, fairly supple texture for the year, a little more vinous than the Clos Saint-Denis, but not really more interesting as a wine than the Marsannay La Montagne!

CLOS DE LA ROCHE GRAND CRU 2004
Red | 2011 up to 2019   **89**
A lactic nose, a very tender wine for the parcel, though it is elegant, without any excess extraction; supple, fresh, harmonious: it is drinking very well!

CLOS SAINT-DENIS GRAND CRU 2006
Red | 2011 up to 2021   **93**
Floral and subtle, very tender despite its power, refined tannins, an aristocratic wine, clearly superior to the Clos de La Roche of the same vintage.

CLOS SAINT-DENIS GRAND CRU 2005
Red | 2011 up to 2020   **88**
Deeply colored, robust, harmonious but less full and less expressive in its aromas and texture than the Chambolle Les Charmes.

GEVREY-CHAMBERTIN EN CHAMPS 2005
Red | 2011 up to 2020   **90**
Excellent color, a very balanced wine, straightforward, finely tannic, fresh, very carefully vinified.

**GEVREY-CHAMBERTIN PREMIER CRU
LES CHAMPEAUX 2005**
Red | 2011 up to 2020   **89**
Fine dense color, a fresh, elegant wine with well-integrated tannins, with finesse and minerality, even if it does not go all the way in its expression of these undeniably great grapes.

MARSANNAY 2006
White | 2011 up to 2014   **87**
Perceptible yet well-integrated oak, classic notes of fern and floral honey, a clean wine that is fairly wiry for the vintage, simple but very straightforward.

MARSANNAY LA MONTAGNE 2006
Red | 2011 up to 2021   **88**
A creamy texture, a fleshy wine, complex tastes, authentic pinot noir tannins produced by healthy viticultural practices; a fine future. Already a remarkable wine, but one that should improve even more with time.

MARSANNAY LA MONTAGNE 2005
Red | 2011 up to 2020   **90**
Great color, a beautiful nose of red fruit, perfectly ripe grapes, firm but well-integrated tannins, one of the most harmonious current expressions of the village.

Red: 29.7 acres; pinot noir 100%. White: 7.4 acres; aligoté 65%, chardonnay 35%. Annual production: 50,000 bottles

DOMAINE HARMAND-GEOFFROY

1, place des Lois
21220 Gevrey-Chambertin
Phone 00 33 3 80 34 10 65
Fax 00 33 3 80 34 13 72
harmand-geoffroy@wanadoo.fr
www.harmand-geoffroy.com

This estate is always a good sport about its entries—which represent the entire gamut of offerings. We were delighted with the average standard of the 2005s, those foxy notes having largely disappeared. The best cuvées are powerful and energetic with sincere expression of terroir, but they still need a bit more finesse.

Recently tasted
GEVREY-CHAMBERTIN EN JOUISE 2007
Red | 2013 up to 2017   **86**

**GEVREY-CHAMBERTIN PREMIER CRU
LAVAUX SAINT-JACQUES 2007**
Red | 2013 up to 2022   **87**

Older vintages
GEVREY-CHAMBERTIN PREMIER CRU CHAMPEAUX 2006
Red | 2011 up to 2021   **93**
The most harmonious and distinguished of all of this estate's wines presented at our grand tasting. An ultra-elegant flavor of spicy flowers, and almost perfect tannins for their stability and integration into the wine. Highly recommended.

**GEVREY-CHAMBERTIN PREMIER CRU
LA PERRIÈRE 2005**
Red | 2011 up to 2025   **89**
A mocha nose, strong licorice notes, very evolved, an unctuous texture but with drying underlying tannins.

**GEVREY-CHAMBERTIN PREMIER CRU
LAVAUX SAINT-JACQUES 2006**
Red | 2011 up to 2021   **88**
A nice nose of wild strawberries, a generous wine, suave, supple, but other Lavaux showed more complexity and allure, just like the estate's Champeaux.

GEVREY-CHAMBERTIN VIEILLES VIGNES 2005
Red | 2011 up to 2017   **89**
Black. An enormous bouquet of black fruits, very powerful, rich flavors, wild. Made for pairing with game.

MAZIS-CHAMBERTIN GRAND CRU 2006
Red | 2011 up to 2021   **92**
Here, in all its integrity, is the powerful build of this vineyard, with noble, complex aromas of smoke, spices, black fruits, and brambles. The texture is creamy but not as refined as one might like.

Red: 22.2 acres; pinot noir 100%. Annual production: 47,000 bottles

DOMAINE HERESZTYN

27, rue Richebourg
21220 Gevrey-Chambertin
Phone 00 33 3 80 34 13 99
Fax 00 33 3 80 34 13 99
domaine.heresztyn@wanadoo.fr

A serious producer of lovely Village and Premier Cru wines from the northern part of the Côte de Nuits. The wines are solid, well balanced, and true to their terroir but without that extra dimension of finesse and purity that is always such a thrill. The Grand Cru Clos Saint-Denis—usually the estate's top offering—was not entered for our recent tastings.

Recently tasted

GEVREY-CHAMBERTIN PREMIER CRU 2007
Red | 2013 up to 2019　　　　　　　86

GEVREY-CHAMBERTIN VIEILLES VIGNES 2007
Red | 2013 up to 2019　　　　　　　88

Older vintages

GEVREY-CHAMBERTIN PREMIER CRU
LES CORBEAUX 2005
Red | 2011 up to 2020　　　　　　　88
A nice, deep color, spicy nose, not overextracted, but with this wine, we prefer spicy aromas to very elegant floral and fruity notes.

GEVREY-CHAMBERTIN VIEILLES VIGNES 2005
Red | 2011 up to 2020　　　　　　　87
Good color, a serious wine, made with care, still a bit limited in its aromatic variety.

GEVREY-CHAMBERTIN VIEILLES VIGNES 2004
Red | 2011 up to 2016　　　　　　　86
Limpid color, a bit evolved, and a spicy nose. A simple, well-balanced, direct wine, a bit short.

MOREY-SAINT-DENIS PREMIER CRU
LES MILLANDES 2005
Red | 2011 up to 2020　　　　　　　88
Nice color, the oak influence still quite marked, a bit of tannic bitterness but the body is very satisfying and the flavors frank and expressive. There could be more finesse.

Red: 26.7 acres; pinot noir 100%. Annual production: 60,000 bottles

DOMAINE HUMBERT FRÈRES

Rue de Planteligone
21220 Gevrey-Chambertin
Phone 00 33 3 80 51 80 14
Fax 00 33 3 80 51 80 14

The owners of this estate represent the little-known, third branch of the Dugat family (related on the mother's side). The label no longer says Dugat but the wines work the usual Dugat magic—although the mouthfeel may be just a touch more delicate here and the texture less monumental. The 2005s are worthy successors to the delightful 2002s. The estate's strong point once again is its remarkable range of Premiers Crus: elegant, authentic, and highly recommended. As always with Dugat, all of these offerings are extremely limited.

Recently tasted

CHARMES-CHAMBERTIN GRAND CRU 2007
Red | 2015 up to 2025　　　　　　　92

GEVREY-CHAMBERTIN PREMIER CRU
ESTOURNELLES SAINT-JACQUES 2007
Red | 2015 up to 2025　　　　　　　87

Older vintages

CHARMES-CHAMBERTIN GRAND CRU 2004
Red | 2011 up to 2019　　　　　　　91
More tannic than the Petite Chapelle but less natural in its form, tauter, with nicely ripe grapes.

GEVREY-CHAMBERTIN PREMIER CRU
ESTOURNELLES SAINT-JACQUES 2004
Red | 2011 up to 2019　　　　　　　93
Powerful, with licorice notes, dense. Great promise of long aging.

GEVREY-CHAMBERTIN PREMIER CRU
LAVAUX SAINT-JACQUES 2006
Red | 2011 up to 2013　　　　　　　89
The oak influence is a bit too strong, long, and lean in body, a bit less vinosity than the Poissenot, finer-grained texture, adept vinification, but the maturation a bit less so!

GEVREY-CHAMBERTIN PREMIER CRU
PETITE CHAPELLE 2004
Red | 2011 up to 2016　　　　　　　92
Plenty of nuances on the nose, less full than the Estournelles but more suave, very soft tannins.

GEVREY-CHAMBERTIN PREMIER CRU
POISSENOT 2005
Red | 2011 up to 2020　　　　　　　92
Deeply colored, wild, with strong toasty notes on the palate, generous, very characteristic, the flavors still wild but not the tannins, perfectly velvety.

Red: 17.3 acres; pinot noir 100%. Annual production: 25,000 bottles

DOMAINE JAYER-GILLES

21700 Magny-les-Villers
Phone 00 33 3 80 62 91 79
Fax 00 33 3 80 62 99 77

The talented Gilles Jayer is a favorite with leading restaurateurs for his lush, immediately appealing Hautes-Côtes de Beaune, especially the whites. His sumptuous Echézeaux offering comes from the heart of the eponymous Grand Cru (which is rather too broadly delimited in our opinion) and boasts an incomparable black-currant nose. All of the wines are made in a powerfully reduced style and are best decanted two to three hours before serving.

CÔTE DE NUITS-VILLAGES 2004
Red | 2011 up to 2014   **87**
A wine showing this estate's black-currant style in a vintage when it was difficult to get well-ripened grapes. Not very complex beyond the black currant!

ECHÉZEAUX GRAND CRU 2004
Red | 2011 up to 2019   **90**
Good color, good volume on the palate, noble flavors of licorice, the tannins a bit too insistent.

NUITS-SAINT-GEORGES
LES HAUTS POIRETS 2004
Red | 2011 up to 2014   **86**
Moderately steady color, a slightly earthy nose, fresh but not very complex.

NUITS-SAINT-GEORGES PREMIER CRU
LES DAMODES 2004
Red | 2011 up to 2016   **89**
More suave, fresher, a pleasant wine, delicate and very perfumed.

Red: 13.6 acres; pinot 100%. White: 13.6 acres; chardonnay 50%, pinot 50%. Annual production: 65,000 bottles

DOMAINE FRANÇOIS LAMARCHE

9 rue des Communes
21700 Vosne-Romanée
Phone 00 33 3 80 61 07 94
Fax 00 33 3 80 61 24 31
vins.lamarche@wanadoo.fr
www.domaine-lamarche.com

What we have here is a domaine with a heritage of vines that makes it a candidate for top-ranking Burgundy status. After years of under-performance, the wines have now recovered a good deal of their character and focused terroir expression, but they remain held back by notes of new barrels that are not as elegant as the wine itself—in which respect, they are not alone in the very imperfect universe of present-day Burgundy cooperage.

CLOS DE VOUGEOT GRAND CRU 2005
Red | 2011 up to 2030   **93**
Powerful, racy, but still dominated by a slightly drying oak influence. Great pedigree; a long future ahead.

LA GRANDE RUE GRAND CRU 2005
Red | 2011 up to 2030   **94**
The oak influence is a bit too pronounced and not quite well integrated, but the wine is splendid for its body, its aromatic nobility, its intensity. Sumptuous!

VOSNE-ROMANÉE PREMIER CRU
LES SUCHOTS 2005
Red | 2011 up to 2025   **90**
Great color, a bit too oaky, racy, full—but it hasn't found its balance yet. A long future ahead. A different kind of oak should be used.

Red: 27 acres; pinot noir 97%. Annual production: 60,000 bottles

DOMAINE DES LAMBRAYS

31, rue Basse
21220 Morey-Saint-Denis
Phone 00 33 3 80 51 84 33
Fax 00 33 3 80 51 81 97
clos.lambrays@wanadoo.fr
www.lambrays.com

For some vintages now, this estate's wealthy German proprietor has left manager Thierry Brouin to apply the selective picking employed in Bordeaux, culling overly young and less-than-perfectly exposed vines so as to get the best possible performance out of the top wine. The result has been a succession of great wines in an ultrapure style with that inimitable charm that comes from whole-bunch fermented grapes. The 2005 vintage is even better: a top-notch Burgundy to rival its neighbor Clos de Tart but made in a tauter, more mineral style; the 2006 and 2007 follow close behind. The 2005 and the 2003 are definitely the greatest recent vintages from this estate, more robust and complete than the otherwise excellent 1999 and 2002—sure to become the stuff of legend.

Recently tasted
CLOS DES LAMBRAYS GRAND CRU 2007
Red | 2017 up to 2027   **94**

Older vintages
CLOS DES LAMBRAYS GRAND CRU 2006
Red | 2011 up to 2026   **94**
Very complex aromas of peonies and roses, mellow, suave, the grapes so ripe that the tannins are concentrated and almost melty, great length. A magnificent wine.

CLOS DES LAMBRAYS GRAND CRU 2005
Red | 2011 up to 2030   **97**
A great, perfectly balanced wine with exemplary finesse and sincerity! It always starts off a bit less flamboyant than the Clos de Tart, its immediate neighbor, and takes its time!

CLOS DES LAMBRAYS GRAND CRU 2004
Red | 2011 up to 2022   **93**
A very precise nose of brambles, blackberries, and sweet spices, full but tight body, very delicate, the tannins still tight, not much sensuality but plenty of complexity.

CLOS DES LAMBRAYS GRAND CRU 2003
Red | 2011 up to 2030   **97**
Magnificent body, a great, complex nose, at once floral and earthy; noble tannins, great follow-up on the palate. Up to this point, the estate's most complete wine since being classed a Grand Cru in 1985.

MOREY-SAINT-DENIS PREMIER CRU LES LOUPS 2005
Red | 2011 up to 2020   **92**
A light smoky note on the nose, full body but clearly less full than the Grand Cru, great finesse in the tannins, complex, very taut.

PULIGNY-MONTRACHET PREMIER CRU CAILLERETS 2006
White | 2011 up to 2014   **90**
Very ripe grapes, a full body, round, tender, lots of charm and refinement. Can be drunk young!

Red: 24.8 acres; pinot noir 100%. White: 1.6 acres; chardonnay 100%. Annual production: 38,000 bottles

DOMAINE PHILIPPE ET VINCENT LECHENEAUT

🜋 🜋 🜋 🜋 🜋

14, rue des Seuillets
21700 Nuits-Saint-Georges
Phone 00 33 3 80 61 05 96
Fax 00 33 3 80 61 28 31
lecheneaut@wanadoo.fr

This small, artisan winery is just the sort we like: meticulously tended vines and wines made in a very assertive style but with that essentially classical balance that comes from a combination of strength and finesse. The wines are less reduced and more "mature" than a few years ago and no longer need such a long resting time.

Recently tasted

CHAMBOLLE-MUSIGNY PREMIER CRU 2007
Red | 2015 up to 2022   92

CLOS DE LA ROCHE GRAND CRU 2007
Red | 2017 up to 2025   92

MOREY-SAINT-DENIS 2007
Red | 2015 up to 2022   90

MOREY-SAINT-DENIS CLOS DES ORMES 2007
Red | 2013 up to 2019   86

Older vintages

CHAMBOLLE-MUSIGNY 2005
Red | 2011 up to 2017   89
Crimson in color, fine floral nose, a very precise wine of exemplary classicism.

CHAMBOLLE-MUSIGNY PREMIER CRU 2006
Red | 2011 up to 2018   90
A very classic wine in shape and construction, superb tastes of licorice, nice length, always a reliable choice for this appellation.

CHAMBOLLE-MUSIGNY PREMIER CRU 2005
Red | 2011 up to 2025   90
Very pretty crimson, remarkable body for a Chambolle, deep, dark flavors that do not feel forced; very nice balance at the start.

CLOS DE LA ROCHE GRAND CRU 2006
Red | 2011 up to 2024   95
A tiny production, but the wine is remarkable for its well-mastered force and the harmony of its body, texture, and tannins. Its persistence is greater than that of most of its peers!

CLOS DE LA ROCHE GRAND CRU 2005
Red | 2011 up to 2025   93
Once more, a very exactingly defined expression of the terroir, classic vinification, not moody but rather precise and dedicated; truly a remarkable wine.

MOREY-SAINT-DENIS CLOS DES ORMES 2005
Red | 2011 up to 2020   88
Intense crimson in color, fresh nose, the natural texture of a fine vintage, precise, sincere, very satisfying!

MOREY-SAINT-DENIS PREMIER CRU
CLOS DES ORMES 2006
Red | 2011 up to 2018   90
A fine nose, complex and racy, wafting with a delicate truffle note that will certainly show up again in the Grands Crus; nice balance on the palate, a powerful yet refined wine.

NUITS-SAINT-GEORGES LES DAMODES 2006
Red | 2011 up to 2016   92
Deeply colored, very precise in its aromas, magnificent extraction to its tannins, limpid terroir; in short, everything we like in fine wine and intelligently modern vinification! This wine is made not from the vines in this parcel that are classified Premier Cru but from those immediately above.

NUITS-SAINT-GEORGES LES DAMODES 2005
Red | 2011 up to 2017   90
Very typical with its bramble and blackcurrant notes, tender, elegant, long, and delicious!

NUITS-SAINT-GEORGES PREMIER CRU
LES PRULIERS 2006
Red | 2011 up to 2021   90
Generous and fleshy, with good fat and unctuousness to its texture.

NUITS-SAINT-GEORGES PREMIER CRU
LES PRULIERS 2005
Red | 2011 up to 2030   94
Sumptuous stuffing, the most precise definition of this terroir, with a very slight metallic note; delicate, complex, remarkable!

Red: 22.2 acres; gamay 5%, pinot 95%. White: 2.5 acres; aligoté 60%, chardonnay 40%. Annual production: 55,000 bottles

DOMAINE PHILIPPE LECLERC

Rue des Halles
21220 Gevrey-Chambertin
Phone 00 33 3 80 34 30 72
Fax 00 33 3 80 34 17 39
philippe.leclerc60@wanadoo.fr
www.philippe-leclerc.com

Philippe Leclerc is one of the most eccentric but also the most engaging personalities in the village of Gevrey. He made himself known in the 1980s with intensely built wines that were far from the widespread banality of the time, but they soon became excessive, strange, or flawed. We had lost track of his wines, but are very happy to rediscover them with a remarkable lineup of 2006s, that are once again at the level of what we would expect from him.

Recently tasted

GEVREY-CHAMBERTIN PREMIER CRU CAZETIERS 2007
Red | 2017 up to 2025   **93**

GEVREY-CHAMBERTIN PREMIER CRU
CHAMPEAUX 2007
Red | 2017 up to 2025   **89**

Older vintages

GEVREY-CHAMBERTIN EN CHAMPS 2006
Red | 2011 up to 2018   **88**
A reductive nose, but not excessively so, very black-currant on the palate, a fleshy wine that is long and complex.

GEVREY-CHAMBERTIN PREMIER CRU
CAZETIERS 2006
Red | 2011 up to 2026   **94**
Sensational texture, ultimate, almost absolute ripeness of the grapes, plush tannins, with a tiny bit more complexity than the Combe aux Moines. A great future, and a very original style, marked yet well mastered.

GEVREY-CHAMBERTIN PREMIER CRU
CHAMPEAUX 2006
Red | 2011 up to 2021   **92**
Noble, complex aromas with a striking truffle scent, powerful, fleshy, dense, but with tannins that are balanced out by the great ripeness of the grapes.

GEVREY-CHAMBERTIN PREMIER CRU
COMBE AUX MOINES 2006
Red | 2011 up to 2026   **93**
Great bramble aromas, ample texture, firm yet harmonious tannins, great length, a remarkable expression of the terroir and vintage; a wine that hews to the straight and narrow, despite a clearly very late harvest date!

Red: 19.8 acres; pinot noir 100%.

DOMAINE LEROY

15, rue de la Fontaine
21700 Vosne-Romanée
Phone 00 33 3 80 21 21 10
Fax 00 33 3 80 21 63 81
domaine.leroy@wanadoo.fr
www.domaineleroy.com

This magnificent domaine was built by Lalou Bize-Leroy on the vineyards she purchased from Charles Noëllat and Philippe Rémy: nine Grands Crus and seven Premiers Crus that extend along the finest slopes of the Côte d'Or, from Savigny to Corton to Chambertin. The vines are biodynamically cultivated, producing incredibly small yields but to a level of quality unrivaled by any other pinot noir grapes in the world. The resulting crus have beautiful aromas, matched only by their supremely elegant texture and pure expression of terroir. Wines like these set an absolute benchmark for quality, universally acclaimed and therefore widely sought after. Price is unlike anything else available in Burgundy, partly because the real production costs are significant and partly because tiny quantities of such magical wines do inevitably fuel speculation! After the disappointments of 2004, when many of these wines were declassified, Domaine Leroy is now fully back on form. Witness the perfectly classical 2005 and the movingly perfumed 2006 (perhaps even more so than its predecessor). Admirable from the first to the last drop.

Recently tasted

CHAMBERTIN GRAND CRU 2007
Red | 2019 up to 2027   **98**

CHAMBOLLE-MUSIGNY PREMIER CRU LES
CHARMES 2007
Red | 2017 up to 2027   **95**

CLOS DE LA ROCHE GRAND CRU 2007
Red | 2017 up to 2027   **94**

CLOS DE VOUGEOT GRAND CRU 2007
Red | 2019 up to 2037   **96**

GEVREY-CHAMBERTIN PREMIER CRU
COMBOTTES 2007
Red | 2015 up to 2025   **93**

LATRICIÈRES-CHAMBERTIN GRAND CRU 2007
Red | 2019 up to 2027   **99**

MUSIGNY GRAND CRU 2007
Red | 2017 up to 2027   **98**

NUITS-SAINT-GEORGES LAVIÈRES 2007
Red | 2015 up to 2022   **93**

NUITS-SAINT-GEORGES PREMIER CRU
AUX BOUDOTS 2007
Red | 2015 up to 2027   94

NUITS-SAINT-GEORGES PREMIER CRU
VIGNES RONDES 2007
Red | 2015 up to 2022   94

POMMARD LES VIGNOTS 2007
Red | 2015 up to 2022   93

RICHEBOURG GRAND CRU 2007
Red | 2019 up to 2037   95

ROMANÉE-SAINT-VIVANT GRAND CRU 2007
Red | 2017 up to 2027   98

SAVIGNY-LÈS-BEAUNE PREMIER CRU
LES NARBANTONS 2007
Red | 2015 up to 2027   93

VOSNE-ROMANÉE PREMIER CRU
LES BEAUX MONTS 2007
Red | 2017 up to 2027   97

Older vintages
CHAMBERTIN GRAND CRU 2006
Red | 2011 up to 2030   99
Grandiose, slightly more robust than the
Latricières, perfect in its balance, though it
does not offer more emotion than its little
brother, which is slightly more refined and
"artistic." Still, a true wonder! Great age
should make the difference.

CHAMBERTIN GRAND CRU 2005
Red | 2011 up to 2050   97
Still bears the mark of strong reduction in
the barrel: monumental, grandiose in its
potential, but slightly less pure than the
Latricières.

CHAMBOLLE-MUSIGNY PREMIER CRU
LES CHARMES 2006
Red | 2011 up to 2026   97
Once again, the most noble of the domaine's
Premiers Crus, for the intensity and rigor-
ousness of its construction, giving an overall impression of inimitable elegance! The
quality of the winemaking helped avoid all
of the aromatic pollution noticed in other
producers' wines.

CHAMBOLLE-MUSIGNY PREMIER CRU
LES CHARMES 2005
Red | 2011 up to 2050   97
The most elegant and sublime, on an aromatic level, of the domaine's Premiers Crus,
with infinitely suave and racy texture and
immense length!

CLOS DE LA ROCHE GRAND CRU 2006
Red | 2011 up to 2013   95
Powerful, sensual, but rigorous, with balance only this producer, to our knowledge,
attains with this terroir. A note of burnt rock
is uncommon and gives a sensation many
would call mineral.

CLOS DE VOUGEOT GRAND CRU 2006
Red | 2011 up to 2026   95
Noble aromas of spicy rose, supple, long,
refined, with great raciness perceptible in
the tannins and tactile sensations, great
length, obviously marked by the incomparable charm of whole-cluster vinification.

CLOS DE VOUGEOT GRAND CRU 2005
Red | 2011 up to 2050   98
A masterpiece of density and seriousness
in its body and texture, less openly opulent
than the Richebourg and, to our tastes, more
satisfying. A glorious Clos de Vougeot.

CORTON-CHARLEMAGNE GRAND CRU 2006
White | 2014 up to 2018   93
Taut, powerful, austere, but racy, with the
slight bitterness of a white wine grown on
red wine soil; wait before opening.

CORTON-CHARLEMAGNE GRAND CRU 2005
White | 2011 up to 2030   95
Immense material, a very powerful, tight,
almost tannic wine that is opulent, long on
the palate, but less sensual than the wines
from the Domaine d'Auvenay.

CORTON-RENARDES GRAND CRU
AUX RENARDES 2006
Red | 2011 up to 2013   97
The most noble of the 2006 Cortons, with
distinguished texture and astonishing tannins and absolutely nothing "animal" or
musky on the nose or the palate. Very small
yields are to thank for this.

CORTON-RENARDES GRAND CRU
AUX RENARDES 2005
Red | 2011 up to 2050   95
Great raciness, an imposing body, firm yet
complex tannins, taut yet fleshy; an immense
future.

GEVREY-CHAMBERTIN PREMIER CRU
COMBOTTES 2006
Red | 2011 up to 2021   92
If we had to feel slight disappointment about
something in order to appear more "objective," it would be about this bottling, despite
its high quality. On the whole, compared to
Les Boudots, Les Beaumonts, and Les
Charmes, it seems a little more simple. In
another context, the wine would obviously
have seemed brilliant!

LATRICIÈRES-CHAMBERTIN GRAND CRU 2006
Red | 2011 up to 2026 **98**
Extreme purity and finesse, all in a well-rounded body rooted in the perfectly noble, well-integrated tannins of whole-cluster grapes. A masterpiece that shows the lofty peaks Latricières can attain!

LATRICIÈRES-CHAMBERTIN GRAND CRU 2005
Red | 2011 up to 2050 **98**
Wonderful finesse, racy, complex, and subtle: an absolute model of a grand Burgundian style from a great vintage.

MUSIGNY GRAND CRU 2006
Red | 2011 up to 2013 **99**
A dream! Sublime floral scents, a silky texture, length, class, refinement in all of its components, a wine that should give pause to the appellation's largest producer, Comte Georges de Vogüé.

MUSIGNY GRAND CRU 2005
Red | 2011 up to 2050 **97**
Very powerful and tight, noble but with a more masculine texture than usual. The 2006 will be more aromatic.

NUITS-SAINT-GEORGES 2006
Red | 2011 up to 2013 **92**
A blend of Allots, Bas de Combe, and Lavière, a Village wine that is remarkable for its harmony, the cleanness of its expression and its tannins—firm yet not aggressive and, above all, natural, which helps avoid the charade of tannified wines.

NUITS-SAINT-GEORGES PREMIER CRU AUX BOUDOTS 2006
Red | 2011 up to 2026 **95**
Inimitably pulpy character, with a very pure nose and, this year, nothing reductive, a velvety texture; an incomparable introduction to the grandeur of this domaine!

NUITS-SAINT-GEORGES PREMIER CRU AUX BOUDOTS 2005
Red | 2011 up to 2050 **95**
A Nuits-Saint-Georges twin hailing from Vosne's Beaumont, overflowing with charm and energy, very high-quality tannins, great length, ideally ripe grapes, with the inimitable style of whole-cluster harvests.

NUITS-SAINT-GEORGES PREMIER CRU VIGNES RONDES 2006
Red | 2011 up to 2021 **93**
A great harmony of scents and textures, refined tannins, great length, a charming Nuits.

POMMARD LES VIGNOTS 2006
Red | 2011 up to 2018 **93**
An exceptionally full, round, velvety, and balanced Village wine, more refined to our tastes than the monumental 2005.

POMMARD LES VIGNOTS 2005
Red | 2011 up to 2030 **90**
Deeply colored, powerful, earthy, fleshy, good balance, and important openness compared to other bottlings. Wait ten to twelve years for the wine's bite to soften.

RICHEBOURG GRAND CRU 2006
Red | 2011 up to 2024 **98**
This year, this wine surpasses the Romanée Saint-Vivant in its formal perfection: the body is imposing, as it should be, but the harmony of the tannins and tastes and the precision of all the sensations it conjures have no equal among the 2006 Richebourgs tasted, even Domaine de la Romanée-Conti's, which is nonetheless of great nobility.

RICHEBOURG GRAND CRU 2005
Red | 2011 up to 2050 **97**
Great opulence and monumental body. The Romanée Saint-Vivant perhaps surpasses it in finesse and harmony.

ROMANÉE-SAINT-VIVANT GRAND CRU 2006
Red | 2011 up to 2013 **97**
Magnificently velvety texture, remarkable length, the inimitable presence of whole-cluster grapes, a finish in line with the body's sweep; but if we were to split hairs, this wine is less perfect on a formal level than the Richebourg or the Musigny.

ROMANÉE-SAINT-VIVANT GRAND CRU 2005
Red | 2011 up to 2050 **98**
Wonderful for its satiny density and ethereal freshness, despite the high alcohol and tannins. One of the best wines of the vintage.

SAVIGNY-LÈS-BEAUNE PREMIER CRU LES NARBANTONS 2006
Red | 2011 up to 2013 **93**
Great color, tremendously vinous, with tannins that are still somewhat tight and taut, remarkably racy, exceptionally expansive on the palate for the appellation!

SAVIGNY-LÈS-BEAUNE PREMIER CRU LES NARBANTONS 2005
Red | 2011 up to 2023 **94**
Very dense, magnificent flesh, firm tannins, a wine that can be cellared for a long time, with exceptional class for the appellation.

VOLNAY PREMIER CRU SANTENOTS 2006
Red | 2011 up to 2026   **93**
Very powerful, concentrated, and noble, but
here the tannins from the stems take on a
(temporarily) severe dimension that they
don't in the other bottlings. Wait for this one!

VOSNE-ROMANÉE PREMIER CRU
LES BEAUX MONTS 2006
Red | 2011 up to 2013   **94**
A twin of the Boudots, with tiny differences:
floral notes that are less spicy on the nose,
a texture as velvety but a little more distinguished, and a more neutral finish, if such
terms can apply to this extremely high level
of quality.

VOSNE-ROMANÉE PREMIER CRU
LES BEAUX MONTS 2005
Red | 2011 up to 2030   **95**
Wonderfully satiny texture, great classy tan-
nins, great length, the ideal Vosne, or nearly.

Red: 44.8 acres; gamay 2%, pinot noir 81%. White:
9.5 acres; aligoté 11%, chardonnay 6%. Annual
production: 40,000 bottles

DOMAINE CHANTAL LESCURE

34A, rue Thurot
21700 Nuits-Saint-Georges
Phone 00 33 3 80 61 16 79
Fax 00 33 3 80 61 36 64
contact@domaine-lescure.com
www.domaine-lescure.com

Now here is a serious domaine, which
owns vineyards in several quality appellations in the southern part of the Côte de
Nuits, where the precise vinifications have
found a successful balance between tradition and modernity. The wines have body,
vigor, and fairly powerful tannins but lack
aggressiveness. But above all, it's the naturalness and clarity of the terroir that
speaks. A trustworthy source.

Recently tasted
CHAMBOLLE-MUSIGNY LES MOMBIES 2007
Red | 2013 up to 2019   **86**

CLOS DE VOUGEOT GRAND CRU 2007
Red | 2017 up to 2027   **93**

NUITS-SAINT-GEORGES 2007
Red | 2013 up to 2019   **89**

NUITS-SAINT-GEORGES LES DAMODES 2007
Red | 2014 up to 2019   **90**

NUITS-SAINT-GEORGES PREMIER CRU
VALLEROTS 2007
Red | 2015 up to 2019   **92**

Older vintages
BEAUNE PREMIER CRU CHOUACHEUX 2006
Red | 2011 up to 2021   **87**
Modern vinification, with very ripe grapes.
A strong color. Very full and energetic. The
terroir is still influenced by technology.

CLOS DE VOUGEOT GRAND CRU 2006
Red | 2011 up to 2026   **93**
A great, complete cellaring wine, endowed
with complex but firm tannins. In the great—
and best—tradition of this vineyard site.

NUITS-SAINT-GEORGES LES DAMODES 2006
Red | 2011 up to 2018   **88**
Excellent vinification: a quintessential nose
of currants, licorice, and anise. The body of
a good vintage, with delicate tannins. The
terroir clearly shows through; a classy Village wine.

NUITS-SAINT-GEORGES PREMIER CRU
VALLEROTS 2006
Red | 2011 up to 2024   **93**
One of the best Nuits wines of our blind tast-
ing. Splendid aromas of ripe grapes, generous full body, much more harmonious

tannins than you find on average, great length. A classy, complex wine at a Grand Cru level.

POMMARD PREMIER CRU BERTINS 2006
Red | 2011 up to 2018   **87**
A very suave wine, with evident oak influence, a silky texture, very mellow tannins. Just a tad decadent.

VOLNAY 2006
Red | 2011 up to 2018   **88**
A nice nose with notes of cocoa beans. A refined texture and an unctuousness appropriate to the vintage but perfectly respected. Delicate tannins.

VOLNAY JEUNES FAMINES 2006
Red | 2011 up to 2018   **90**
One of the best Village wines in our tasting. Very refined in its aromas and texture, long, complex. Marvelously Volnay.

VOSNE-ROMANÉE PREMIER CRU SUCHOTS 2006
Red | 2011 up to 2021   **88**
A classic, elegant nose of spicy flowers (rose, peony). Nice overall balance, even if we would have liked some more flesh. A clean, noble finish.

Red: 43.6 acres. Annual production: 70,000 bottles

DOMAINE THIBAULT LIGER-BELAIR

32, rue Thurot
21700 Nuits-Saint-Georges
Phone 00 33 3 80 61 51 16
Fax 00 33 3 80 61 51 16
tligerbelair@wanadoo.fr
www.thibaultligerbelair.com

The Liger-Belair family is one of the last of the great, historic families of Burgundy that still owns its own vines. It's a sign of the times when two of its members, in the same decade, have gone back to operating their vineyards themselves: winegrowing has recovered its respectability! This estate has recently been taken in hand by one of the most passionate winegrowers of his generation and the most blessed with great terroirs. Sure to rise to stardom as one of the top-flight Burgundies!

Recently tasted

ALOXE-CORTON PREMIER CRU LA TOPPE AU VERT 2007
Red | 2012 up to 2017   **90**

CLOS DE VOUGEOT GRAND CRU 2007
Red | 2017 up to 2027   **93**

CORTON-LE CORTON GRAND CRU ROGNET 2007
Red | 2017 up to 2025   **93**

CORTON-RENARDES GRAND CRU 2007
Red | 2017 up to 2025   **93**

NUITS-SAINT-GEORGES LA CHARMOTTE 2007
Red | 2013 up to 2017   **90**

NUITS-SAINT-GEORGES PREMIER CRU LES SAINT-GEORGES 2007
Red | 2017 up to 2027   **94**

Older vintages

ALOXE-CORTON PREMIER CRU LA TOPPE AU VERT 2006
Red | 2011 up to 2018   **89**
Fine color, an appealing nose of cherry candy, ripe grapes, harmonious body.

ALOXE-CORTON PREMIER CRU LA TOPPE AU VERT 2005
Red | 2011 up to 2016   **88**
A fine bluish color, splendid fruit, a simple but very aromatic wine, straightforward.

CHAMBOLLE-MUSIGNY LES GRUENCHERS 2006
Red | 2011 up to 2018   **89**
A somewhat reductive nose with licorice aromas, very acceptable body, fine texture, appreciable length on the palate, very well vinified.

CHAMBOLLE-MUSIGNY LES GRUENCHERS 2005
Red | 2011 up to 2025   **95**
A remarkable nose of peonies and roses, a splendid bouquet, ideally ripe grapes.

CLOS DE VOUGEOT GRAND CRU 2006
Red | 2011 up to 2021   **91**
A domaine harvest. A very fresh nose of red fruit, slightly insolent in its flashiness; complex, fairly long, very original.

CLOS DE VOUGEOT GRAND CRU 2005
Red | 2011 up to 2015   **90**
Very blue-tinged, licorice-y, long, refined, ripe; vinified with style.

CORTON-RENARDES GRAND CRU 2006
Red | 2011 up to 2026   **94**
Remarkable aromatic finesse, well-rounded body, very engaging texture, a terroir of the first order and successful vinification. A classic!

CORTON-RENARDES GRAND CRU 2005
Red | 2011 up to 2030   **95**
Great unctuousness, a remarkably soft texture, great length, a powerful, racy wine; remarkable.

NUITS-SAINT-GEORGES LA CHARMOTTE 2005
Red | 2011 up to 2022   **95**
Sumptuously ripe grapes, a wine of grand style—a perfect Village wine from the Côte de Nuits.

NUITS-SAINT-GEORGES PREMIER CRU
LES SAINT-GEORGES 2006
Red | 2011 up to 2024   **90**
A noble bramble aroma, generous body, velvety tannins, less precision at this point than we might hope, but certainly highly promising!

NUITS-SAINT-GEORGES PREMIER CRU
LES SAINT-GEORGES 2005
Red | 2011 up to 2025   **93**
Great intensity to its tastes, powerful, tight, tannins a little too firm.

RICHEBOURG GRAND CRU 2006
Red | 2011 up to 2026   **92**
A complex nose of peonies, spices, and leather, great body, ample texture; not as precise and refined in its tannins as other great bottlings from the commune, but very present and earthy on the palate. A slight tweak seems necessary in order to transform this fine wine into a great wine.

Red: 17.3 acres; pinot noir 100%. **Annual production:** 40,000 bottles

DOMAINE DU COMTE LIGER-BELAIR

Château de Vosne-Romanée
21700 Vosne-Romanée
Phone 00 33 3 80 62 13 70
Fax 00 33 3 80 62 13 70
contact@liger-belair.fr
www.liger-belair.fr

This domaine owns some of the best land in Vosne-Romanée, and its winemaking level has never been as great as now. All the red wines are truly noble, with the exact expression of each vintage. Of course the Romanée Grand Cru is the most elegant and complex and not very different from its neighbor Conti. The 2001 wines are now ready to drink, the 2004 is as refined as possible, and the 2007 will rival the DRC range. Louis-Michel Liger-Belair has progressively brought his domaine to the top ranks of Burgundy producers, with wines that have refined textures and aromas that concede only to those of La Romanée-Conti. The jewel in their crown, La Romanée, is more and more like La Romanée-Conti, which does justice to their common roots.

Recently tasted

ECHÉZEAUX GRAND CRU 2007
Red | 2015 up to 2022   **95**

LA ROMANÉE GRAND CRU 2007
Red | 2017 up to 2027   **98**

NUITS-SAINT-GEORGES LAVIÈRES 2007
Red | 2014 up to 2019   **92**

NUITS-SAINT-GEORGES PREMIER CRU
CRAS 2007
Red | 2014 up to 2022   **92**

VOSNE-ROMANÉE CLOS DU CHÂTEAU 2007
Red | 2014 up to 2019   **90**

VOSNE-ROMANÉE PREMIER CRU REIGNOTS 2007
Red | 2017 up to 2025   **97**

VOSNE-ROMANÉE PREMIER CRU SUCHOTS 2007
Red | 2015 up to 2022   **95**

Older vintages

ECHÉZEAUX GRAND CRU 2006
Red | 2011 up to 2021   **94**
Complex, refined aromas that are both fruity (wild strawberries) and floral (roses and peonies), a very delicate texture in contrast to the massiveness of quite a few other Grands Crus; very elegant tannins. A model of stylishness for the cru.

LANGUEDOC-ROUSSILLON – LOIRE VALLEY – PROVENCE & CORSICA – RHONE VALLEY – SOUTHWEST

536   588   642   668   770

La Romanée grand cru 2006
Red | 2011 up to 2026   **96**
An admirable floral nose with just a tiny hint of reduction that clears off after fifteen minutes of aeration. A pinnacle of tenderness and refinement in a vintage that generally gave hot, sensual wines.

Vosne-Romanée Clos du Château 2006
Red | 2011 up to 2021   **93**
A light color, but with transcendent finesse for a simple Village wine. Great length, noble tannins, incredibly extracted. Bravo!

Vosne-Romanée La Colombière 2006
Red | 2011 up to 2018   **92**
A nose with great style, subtly floral, a remarkably elegant texture. A welcome adherence to the traditions of the village.

Vosne-Romanée premier cru Chaumes 2006
Red | 2011 up to 2018   **92**
Fine oaky note, delicate but more fluid than in the Suchots or Reignots, fine tannins, very long. Unfortunately, the terroir just isn't the most brilliant of the village.

Vosne-Romanée premier cru Reignots 2006
Red | 2011 up to 2026   **95**
Perfection for a Premier Cru in this vintage: a complete wine, combining an utterly refined texture with slightly firmer tannins than in the estate's other vineyards. Totally integrated and noble oak influence.

Vosne-Romanée premier cru Suchots 2006
Red | 2011 up to 2021   **94**
Very complex, inimitable aromas of wildflowers such as wild rose, very elegant body showing no weakness at all, refined tannins, a model of style, especially in the integration of the oak. It almost achieves the supreme refinement of the Domaine de la Romanée-Conti.

Red: 21 acres; pinot noir 100%. Annual production: 30,000 bottles

DOMAINE LUCIE ET AUGUSTE LIGNIER

Hameau de Corboin
21700 Nuits-Saint-Georges
Phone 00 33 3 80 61 33 84
Fax 00 33 3 80 61 33 84
la.lignier@yahoo.fr

This property is a result of the division of the Domaine Huber Lignier. Upon the premature death of Romain Lignier, one of the most brilliant winemakers of his generation, his wife bravely took over a big part of the vineyards, and she is doing her best to maintain the high quality of the wines, while waiting for her son to take over. The 2006s, super powerful and generous, are headed in the right direction.

Recently tasted
Clos de La Roche grand cru 2007
Red | 2017 up to 2027   **94**

Morey-Saint-Denis premier cru cuvée Romain Lignier 2007
Red | 2015 up to 2019   **86**

Older vintages
Clos de La Roche grand cru 2006
Red | 2011 up to 2026   **94**
A wine of incredible density for a pinot noir, recalling a majestic hillside Saint-Émilion with its body, tannins, and mineral tension (the wine comes from the high part of the parcel) and its truffle notes. The quality of the new barrels could improve it even more.

Morey-Saint-Denis premier cru Chaffots 2006
Red | 2011 up to 2021   **88**
Dark in color, a stunningly powerful wine in its expressiveness, monumental in its tannins, very healthy, doubtless more muscular than refined, especially as the barrels have given it very marked empyreumatic notes (think "burnt").

Annual production: 25,000 bottles

DOMAINE VIRGILE LIGNIER-MICHELOT

🌿 🌿 🌿 🌿 🌿

11, rue Haute
21220 Morey-Saint-Denis
Phone 00 33 3 80 34 31 13
Fax 00 33 3 80 58 52 16
virgile.lignier@wanadoo.fr

The 2006 vintage confirms the progress of this young producer, combining meticulous work in the vineyards with modern and well-managed vinifications. The current wines have style and personality, all while remaining faithful to their excellent origins.

Recently tasted

CHAMBOLLE-MUSIGNY PREMIER CRU
CUVÉE JULES 2007
Red | 2017 up to 2022   87

CLOS DE LA ROCHE GRAND CRU 2007
Red | 2017 up to 2027   93

CLOS SAINT-DENIS GRAND CRU 2007
Red | 2011 up to 2013   93

MOREY-SAINT-DENIS EN LA RUE DE VERGY 2007
Red | 2014 up to 2019   90

MOREY-SAINT-DENIS PREMIER CRU
FAÇONNIÈRES 2007
Red | 2014 up to 2019   88

MOREY-SAINT-DENIS VIEILLES VIGNES 2007
Red | 2014 up to 2019   87

Older vintages

CHAMBOLLE-MUSIGNY VIEILLES VIGNES 2006
Red | 2011 up to 2018   90
A wine vinified with precision and expertise, great aromatic finesse, delicate tannins, nice length; an excellent definition of Burgundian classicism, with all the benefits of modern vinification.

CLOS DE LA ROCHE GRAND CRU 2005
Red | 2011 up to 2020   88
Deeply colored, fleshy, fine fruit, but impersonal for this terroir.

CLOS DE LA ROCHE GRAND CRU 2004
Red | 2011 up to 2050   88
Powerful, but with a finish of bitter cherries as far as aromatics go. Long but not elegant.

GEVREY-CHAMBERTIN CUVÉE BERTIN 2005
Red | 2011 up to 2030   92
Great color, a lot of character, breadth, and class; a splendid Village wine.

MOREY-SAINT-DENIS PREMIER CRU
FAÇONNIÈRES 2006
Red | 2011 up to 2021   93
A powerful, expressive nose of blueberries and blackberries, ample curves, generous texture, racy tannins; a very noble wine, worthy of a Grand Cru.

MOREY-SAINT-DENIS PREMIER CRU
FAÇONNIÈRES 2005
Red | 2011 up to 2020   90
Finer, more diversified fruitiness than the Chenevery, pretty texture, nice classiness.

MOREY-SAINT-DENIS PREMIER CRU
FAÇONNIÈRES 2004
Red | 2011 up to 2050   88
Fine color, skillful texture, fine tannins, with something somewhat cooked on the nose.

MOREY-SAINT-DENIS PREMIER CRU
LES CHENEVERY 2005
Red | 2011 up to 2015   88
Deeply colored, powerful, tannic, fresh, well vinified, not very subtle!

MOREY-SAINT-DENIS VIEILLES VIGNES 2006
Red | 2011 up to 2018   90
A fine, complex nose with smoky notes, powerful and very fleshy for a Village wine, but the tannins are very well handled, firm and without any astringency. A second Village bottling presents the same qualities, but with a little less body.

MOREY-SAINT-DENIS VIEILLES VIGNES 2005
Red | 2011 up to 2030   90
Almost black in color, very rich and very complex for a Village wine, quite superior to the Chambolle.

Red: 20.3 acres; pinot noir 100%. Annual production: 60,000 bottles

DOMAINE BERTRAND MACHARD DE GRAMONT

13, rue de Vergy
21700 Nuits-Saint-Georges
Phone 00 33 3 80 61 16 96
Fax 00 33 3 80 61 16 96
bertrandmacharddegramont@aliceadsl.fr

This small, quality estate has become famous in recent years for its heroic replanting of the terraced Vallerots Premier Cru, on some of the most favorably exposed but also steepest slopes in Nuits-Saint-Georges. Its first vintages since then are a well-earned reward for all that careful and exceptionally eco-friendly labor.

Recently tasted

NUITS-SAINT-GEORGES HAUTS-PRULIERS 2007
Red | 2015 up to 2019   92

NUITS-SAINT-GEORGES LES VALLEROTS 2007
Red | 2015 up to 2022   90

Older vintages

BOURGOGNE PINOT NOIR 2005
Red | 2011 up to 2013   87
Rather dense and complete, with a distinctively "Nuits" character.

NUITS-SAINT-GEORGES AUX ALLOTS 2007
Red | 2013 up to 2019   89
Well made, clean, fruity, very pleasant. A night-and-day difference from the 2004!

NUITS-SAINT-GEORGES HAUTS-PRULIERS 2005
Red | 2011 up to 2020   90
Black, deep, very expressive of its terroir!

NUITS-SAINT-GEORGES LES VALLEROTS 2005
Red | 2011 up to 2025   93
A splendid terroir, a great, noble wine. Complex and stunning.

VOSNE-ROMANÉE 2006
Red | 2011 up to 2016   85
Not as full-bodied as some others. More about softness and elegance of texture, but a bit limited in its aromatics.

VOSNE-ROMANÉE 2005
Red | 2011 up to 2020   92
Precise, spicy, excellent oak influence, complete for the appellation and vintage.

Red: 14.3 acres; pinot 100%. White: 1.7 acres; aligoté 100%. Annual production: 22,000 bottles

FRÉDÉRIC MAGNIEN ET DOMAINE MICHEL MAGNIEN

26, route Nationale
21220 Morey-Saint-Denis
Phone 00 33 3 80 58 54 20
Fax 00 33 3 80 51 84 34
frederic@fred-magnien.com
www.frederic-magnien.com

We have to distinguish here between the négociant wines and the estate-produced bottlings. Both are vinified by talented, energetic winemaker Frédéric Magnien, but his own sourced wines show more precision and finesse simply because his vineyards are better managed. Being the young and passionate winegrower that he is, though, he does have a tendency to overdo extraction. Tread carefully, on the other hand, when buying the négociant wines.

Recently tasted

CHAMBERTIN-CLOS DE BÈZE GRAND CRU 2007
Red | 2017 up to 2027   95

CHAMBOLLE-MUSIGNY PREMIER CRU BORNIQUES 2007
Red | 2014 up to 2019   90

CHAMBOLLE-MUSIGNY PREMIER CRU LES SENTIERS 2007
Red | 2015 up to 2019   92

CHARMES-CHAMBERTIN GRAND CRU 2007
Red | 2017 up to 2025   95

CLOS DE LA ROCHE GRAND CRU MICHEL MAGNIEN 2007
Red | 2017 up to 2025   92

CLOS SAINT-DENIS GRAND CRU 2007
Red | 2017 up to 2025   90

GEVREY-CHAMBERTIN PREMIER CRU CAZETIERS 2007
Red | 2015 up to 2025   92

GEVREY-CHAMBERTIN PREMIER CRU CAZETIERS DOMAINE MICHEL MAGNIEN 2007
Red | 2015 up to 2025   93

GEVREY-CHAMBERTIN PREMIER CRU GOULOT 2007
Red | 2015 up to 2022   90

MOREY-SAINT-DENIS PREMIER CRU CHAFFOTS 2007
Red | 2011 up to 2019   89

MOREY-SAINT-DENIS PREMIER CRU CLOS BAULET 2007
Red | 2011 up to 2017   88

Older vintages

CHAMBERTIN-CLOS DE BÈZE GRAND CRU 2005
Red | 2011 up to 2030   90
A certain finesse and at last, softer tannins, but not very racy on the finish. This is good, but a little disappointing for the parcel and the vintage.

**CHAMBOLLE-MUSIGNY PREMIER CRU
LES SENTIERS 2006**
Red | 2011 up to 2021   93
A remarkable bottling, very elegant body, complex tastes, very fresh, and superbly typical of its origins; nice follow-through on the palate.

CHARMES-CHAMBERTIN GRAND CRU 2006
Red | 2011 up to 2026   90
Deeply colored, fleshy, powerful, firm, licorice-y, a serious, assured wine made for aging. Here, once again, there were two cuvées, the négociant (Frédéric) and the domaine (Michel). The domaine wine is a little more reductive on the nose than the négociant, but the two are very similar!

CHARMES-CHAMBERTIN GRAND CRU 2005
Red | 2011 up to 2018   88
Supple, suave, but imprecise in its aromas and texture.

**CLOS DE LA ROCHE GRAND CRU
MICHEL MAGNIEN 2005**
Red | 2011 up to 2030   93
Deeply colored, rich, tannic, tight, fairly monumental, very spicy tastes; a great future before it.

CLOS DE VOUGEOT GRAND CRU 2005
Red | 2011 up to 2025   86
Very severe, tannic, heavy. Doubtlessly over-extracted.

CLOS SAINT-DENIS GRAND CRU 2006
Red | 2011 up to 2013   93
A classic of this bottling, powerful, very linear in its tannins, very virile, more Chambertin than Bonnes-Mares.

CLOS SAINT-DENIS GRAND CRU 2005
Red | 2011 up to 2050   96
Great raciness, subtle tannins, very plush texture, great length; a wonderful future in view!

GEVREY-CHAMBERTIN AUX ECHÉZEAUX 2005
Red | 2011 up to 2017   90
Complex, with red and black fruit, good tannins, an elegant finish.

GEVREY-CHAMBERTIN ECHÉZEAUX 2006
Red | 2011 up to 2018   86
A fine nose of bramble and spice, a clean wine that is classic in its expression; slightly austere.

GEVREY-CHAMBERTIN JEUNES ROIS 2006
Red | 2011 up to 2018   87
More supple and fruity than the Echézeaux, a charming wine, pleasant to drink now.

GEVREY-CHAMBERTIN PREMIER CRU CAZETIERS 2006
Red | 2011 up to 2021   90
Good fullness to this one, with noble spice tastes and harmonious tannins; a wine of character, faithful to its type, though a little less complex than Domaine Dupond's bottling. This wine comes in two different cuvées: the négociant cuvée seems slightly more supple than the domaine.

GEVREY-CHAMBERTIN PREMIER CRU CAZETIERS 2005
Red | 2011 up to 2030   93
Well rounded, rich, tannic, unctuous, with a great future.

**GEVREY-CHAMBERTIN PREMIER CRU
PERRIÈRES 2006**
Red | 2011 up to 2018   88
Smoky notes that are classic for the vintage, a tender, elegant wine with unaggressive tannins and more relaxed vinification than in the past, which works perfectly with the nature of the vintage!

GEVREY-CHAMBERTIN SEVRÉES 2006
Red | 2011 up to 2026   93
Limpid terroir, ample body, great aromatic cleanness, though it has a little less pure finesse than others.

GEVREY-CHAMBERTIN SEVRÉES 2005
Red | 2011 up to 2020   90
Rich, complex, but with a drying finish. There is not enough oak here.

MOREY-SAINT-DENIS 2005
Red | 2011 up to 2019   90
Rich, tannic, but fresh, with nice rich sap to it.

**MOREY-SAINT-DENIS PREMIER CRU
CLOS DES SORBES 2006**
Red | 2011 up to 2026   90
A grand, smoky nose recalling certain old Clos des Lambrays; great power to its form and tastes, majestic fleshiness, and strong aging potential.

MOREY-SAINT-DENIS PREMIER CRU RUCHOTS 2006
Red | 2011 up to 2021   92
A well-rounded, generous Premier Cru with unusually ample texture underpinned by perfectly ripe tannins; virile but not aggressive.

Annual production: 150,000 bottles

DOMAINE MÉO-CAMUZET

11, rue des Grands-Crus
21700 Vosne-Romanée
Phone 00 33 3 80 61 11 05
Fax 00 33 3 80 61 11 05
meo-camuzet@wanadoo.fr
www.meo-camuzet.com

Jean-Nicolas Méo continues to turn out immensely classy wines. The jewel in the crown of this illustrious estate is the pristine vineyard in the most privileged part of the Clos de Vougeot. Méo's style, compared with that of his mentor Henri Jayer, is toward more depth of constitution and riper grape aromas, which is certainly no bad thing. It would be nice all the same to taste the Richebourg and Vosne-Romanée Cros Parantoux, even if they are produced in only tiny quantities. Production is being boosted these days by a range of négociant wines that help to meet the ever-growing demand.

Recently tasted

CHAMBOLLE-MUSIGNY PREMIER CRU
FEUSSELOTTES 2007
Red | 2013 up to 2019   **89**

NUITS-SAINT-GEORGES 2007
Red | 2013 up to 2019   **92**

NUITS-SAINT-GEORGES PREMIER CRU
MURGERS 2007
Red | 2015 up to 2022   **94**

VOSNE-ROMANÉE PREMIER CRU BRÛLÉES 2007
Red | 2017 up to 2027   **93**

VOSNE-ROMANÉE PREMIER CRU CHAUMES 2007
Red | 2014 up to 2019   **89**

Older vintages

CLOS DE VOUGEOT GRAND CRU 2006
Red | 2011 up to 2030   **94**
Great color, a generous wine with great aromatic power and a base of imposing tannins. Very long aging in sight.

CLOS DE VOUGEOT GRAND CRU 2005
Red | 2011 up to 2025   **92**
Firm, racy tannins, but it lacks something as far as textural magic goes!

HAUTES CÔTES DE NUITS
CLOS SAINT-PHILIBERT 2005
White | 2011 up to 2013   **84**
Clear, clean, supple, common, easy to drink.

MARSANNAY MÉO-CAMUZET FRÈRE ET SOEUR 2005
Red | 2011 up to 2020   **92**
Superb color and striking fruitiness, pure and modern in the best sense of the word.

NUITS-SAINT-GEORGES PREMIER CRU
AUX BOUDOTS 2005
Red | 2011 up to 2025   **96**
Nice bergamot fruit, ample and velvety, great length, excellent.

VOSNE-ROMANÉE 2005
Red | 2011 up to 2020   **90**
Somewhat richly oaked, powerful, striking, warm; alcohol slightly present.

Red: 35.6 acres; pinot noir 100%. **White:** 8.9 acres; chardonnay 90%, pinot blanc 10%. **Annual production:** 120,000 bottles

DOMAINE ALAIN MICHELOT

6, rue Camille Rodier
21700 Nuits-Saint-Georges
Phone 00 33 3 80 61 14 46
Fax 00 33 3 80 61 35 08
domalainmichelot@aol.com

We were happy to rediscover this traditional domaine, which has quite a large palette of vineyards in the village of Nuits-Saint-Georges. The farming practices had relaxed a bit in the 1990s with the over-use of weed killers, but now the grapes are better harvested and sorted, and Alain Michelot, a very experienced viticulturalist, is overseeing the operation, while waiting for the next generation to take over. The wines from the property can be characterized by their deep colors, their well-developed black fruit and brambly aromas, and their fine structure.

NUITS-SAINT-GEORGES PREMIER CRU
CAILLES 2006
Red | 2011 up to 2021   **90**
Plenty of nerve and energy, full body, the tannins powerful but more balanced than in other cuvées from this domaine. There is a great future ahead of this high-level, characteristic Nuits.

NUITS-SAINT-GEORGES PREMIER CRU
CHAIGNOTS 2006
Red | 2011 up to 2024   **89**
Almost black, with powerful aromas of brambles. A firm wine, ripe, masterfully made from a technical point of view. For fans of game birds.

NUITS-SAINT-GEORGES PREMIER CRU
RICHEMONE 2006
Red | 2011 up to 2024   **88**
Great generosity of structure. A dense wine, fleshy, ripe, tannins just a touch thick.

NUITS-SAINT-GEORGES VIEILLES VIGNES 2006
Red | 2011 up to 2018   **87**
Dark, with a powerful nose of brambles and spice. Excellent substance, firm tannins. A quintessential Nuits in the classic style.

Red: 19.8 acres. Annual production: 30,000 bottles

LUCIEN LE MOINE

1 ruelle Morlot
21200 Beaune
Phone 00 33 3 80 24 99 98
Fax 00 33 3 80 24 99 98
l.m.sas@lucienlemoine.com
www.lucienlemoine.com

The brainchild of two enologists (he's Lebanese, she's Israeli), this small wine business now has a select but worldwide following of devotees. Mounir Saouma takes his lead from Dominique Laurent, selecting wines from some of the finest crus available to the market, then maturing them with the utmost care in his small but impeccably neat and tidy cellar in Beaune. The whites (bought as juice) take on plenty of fat and become much more stable; the reds (bought vinified) combine voluptuous texture with refined vineyard expression.

BONNES-MARES 2005
Red | 2011 up to 2025   **93**
Very ample, nicely fleshy in texture; the oak is remarkably well integrated into the body of the wine, with great length, firmness, and finesse, as befits this cru.

BOURGOGNE 2005
White | 2011 up to 2050   **88**
Very clean, mineral and firm yet fat, an excellent quality-price ratio.

CHAMBOLLE-MUSIGNY PREMIER CRU
AMOUREUSES 2005
Red | 2011 up to 2025   **92**
Very evolved aromas, considerable finesse; at the same time, an ever-so-slight lack of purity and naturalness.

CHAMBOLLE-MUSIGNY PREMIER CRU
CHARMES 2005
Red | 2011 up to 2025   **92**
A little more firmness, texture, and tannins than the Amoureuses; irreproachable balance, a wine with character, it should have even more by the end of the élevage.

CLOS SAINT-DENIS GRAND CRU 2005
Red | 2011 up to 2025   **90**
Great aromatic finesse, but here the oak interferes a little with the delicate nature of the terroir.

CORTON-CHARLEMAGNE GRAND CRU 2005
White | 2011 up to 2025   **95**
Great unctuousness, absolutely stunning fat, worthy of a Montrachet, very fine balance overall; a great future ahead of it.

MEURSAULT PREMIER CRU PERRIÈRES 2005
White | 2011 up to 2020   **93**
Wonderful notes of honey, flowering vine, and hazelnut on the nose, well-integrated oak, great body.

RICHEBOURG GRAND CRU 2005
Red | 2011 up to 2030   **95**
The pinnacle of this cellar, as it should be, but the quantities are tiny! Monumental in its form, but very sophisticated in its texture and tannins; a model of good winemaking.

Red: 7.4 acres; pinot noir 100%. White: 4.9 acres; chardonnay 100%. Annual production: 30,000 bottles

DOMAINE DENIS MORTET

22, rue de l'Église
21220 Gevrey-Chambertin
Phone 00 33 3 80 34 10 05
Fax 00 33 3 80 34 16 26
denis-mortet@wanadoo.fr
www.domaine-denis-mortet.com

Denis Mortet died in 2006, leaving his wife, Laurence, and son, Arnaud, to take stock of their heritage in order to get the very best out of the delicate 2006 vintage. Standards of viticulture remain as high as ever and the methods of vinification are unchanged. The estate had acquired a name for an uncommonly expressive style of wine that had come to symbolize Burgundy wine today: exceptionally ripe grapes; immediately appealing floral and fruity nose highlighted by selective use of wood; and a texture of exemplary precision and fullness. The most recent vintages showed considerably more refined tannins than those slightly insistent tannins seen in the early 1990s. Arnaud Mortet is determined to keep up the good work. For best results, all of the estate wines should be decanted two hours before serving if drunk young, and served at 60 to 62°F (slightly below room temperature).

Recently tasted
CHAMBERTIN GRAND CRU 2007
Red | 2017 up to 2027   **97**

FIXIN CHAMP PENNEBAUT 2007
Red | 2014 up to 2022   **94**

GEVREY-CHAMBERTIN PREMIER CRU
LAVAUT SAINT-JACQUES 2007
Red | 2017 up to 2025   **94**

GEVREY-CHAMBERTIN PREMIER CRU
LES CHAMPEAUX 2007
Red | 2015 up to 2025   **94**

MARSANNAY LES LONGEROIES 2007
Red | 2014 up to 2019   **90**

Older vintages
BOURGOGNE 2006
Red | 2011 up to 2013   **85**
Oaky, structured, a well-made pinot noir. Rather powerful.

BOURGOGNE 2006
White | 2011 up to 2013   **84**
Elegant, rather delicate. Even if it is only moderately concentrated, it finishes on a good, chalky minerality.

BOURGOGNE CUVÉE DE NOBLE SOUCHE 2005

Red | 2011 up to 2015   **88**

Nice color and impeccable style: a nose of red berries, just the right extraction of ripe tannins, finesse, and plenty of character, even if it is far from having the vinosity of the Gevreys!

CHAMBERTIN GRAND CRU 2005

Red | 2011 up to 2030   **97**

A very different nose from the Clos de Vougeot, with more licorice, full body, noble texture, grandeur, and style in the tactile impressions. A great wine and a perfect homage to the talent of a great winemaker who left us too soon.

CLOS DE VOUGEOT GRAND CRU 2006

Red | 2011 up to 2026   **97**

A blue-black color, aromas of a rare purity and perfection in their expression of the most perfectly ripe grapes possible, a sublimely suave texture that melts on the tongue, noble tannins. An immense accomplishment for a young winemaker, in the same spirit as what his father would have done!

CLOS DE VOUGEOT GRAND CRU 2005

Red | 2015 up to 2030   **95**

Very vigorous, a copious bouquet, noble tannins, magnificent follow-up on the palate. A wide-reaching wine with incomparable character. Wait ten to twelve years before drinking!

FIXIN 2006

Red | 2011 up to 2018   **90**

The absolute standard for red Fixin, and unfortunately the only truly distinguished Village appellation wine of our tasting. The texture is creamy, but it is not overly fruity, oaky, or tannic. Made from near-perfect grapes and a precise vinification.

FIXIN 2005

Red | 2011 up to 2025   **90**

This wine is very representative of the Mortet style and at an accessible price: very clean aromatics, powerful, slender, tannins with no harshness, great length. Exceptional for the appellation!

GEVREY-CHAMBERTIN 2006

Red | 2011 up to 2018   **89**

A blend of various terroirs, this 2006 is complete and remarkable for its harmony and length, worthy of the fame of the estate. (But beware: one bottle was badly corked!)

GEVREY-CHAMBERTIN 2005

Red | 2011 up to 2025   **93**

A blend of the best terroirs of the village, this cuvée is quite complete for the vintage, marrying finesse and power in a modern yet luscious whole. This one is destined for great success.

GEVREY-CHAMBERTIN PREMIER CRU 2006

Red | 2011 up to 2018   **90**

A wine of pleasure, guaranteed to have luscious flavor, but with a noble finish contributed by the small Bel Air parcel above Chambertin.

GEVREY-CHAMBERTIN PREMIER CRU LAVAUT SAINT-JACQUES 2006

Red | 2011 up to 2026   **94**

One of the pinnacles of the vintage in Gevrey, with marvelously fresh aromatics for the vintage and subtlety in the expression of the terroir. Very noble tannins, and guaranteed for long cellaring.

GEVREY-CHAMBERTIN PREMIER CRU LES CHAMPEAUX 2006

Red | 2011 up to 2026   **89**

Powerful, endowed with tannins a bit rougher than in the Village wine, but with more vinosity and intensity in the tannin. A long future is certain.

GEVREY-CHAMBERTIN PREMIER CRU LES CHAMPEAUX 2005

Red | 2011 up to 2025   **94**

Very precise aromas of red berries with an undeniable mineral element (for once!), very elegant texture, good length.

MARSANNAY LES LONGEROIES 2006

Red | 2011 up to 2018   **90**

Powerful aromas of black cherries, very extracted, well-worked but not excessive tannins, great length. An extroverted but noble wine.

MARSANNAY LES LONGEROIES 2005

Red | 2011 up to 2025   **90**

Great color, a very clear nose of red berries, very vinous, firm tannins. A Marsannay of great class and great aging potential.

Red: 24.7 acres; pinot noir 100%. White: 2.5 acres; aligoté 30%, chardonnay 70%. Annual production: 65,000 bottles

DOMAINE GEORGES MUGNERET ET MUGNERET-GIBOURG

5, rue des Communes
21700 Vosne-Romanée
Phone 00 33 3 80 61 01 57
Fax 00 33 3 80 61 33 08
dgm@mugneret-gibourg.com
www.mugneret-gibourg.com

The two denominations of this domaine designate wines that are in fact made by the same producers, Dr. Georges Mugneret's two daughters. This is one of the most reliable, regular, and most respected sources of Vosne-Romanée and Nuits-Saint-Georges. The wines are vinified with rare precision, a bit less spectacular in their youth than others, but they age happily for decades. The 2006s were impeccably successful.

Recently tasted

ECHÉZEAUX GRAND CRU 2007
Red | 2015 up to 2025   92

VOSNE-ROMANÉE 2007
Red | 2014 up to 2019   90

Older vintages

CLOS DE VOUGEOT GRAND CRU 2006
Red | 2011 up to 2026   94
A superb parcel that combines power with elegance, with the typical texture of higher-altitude vines and the domaine's habitually rigorous, precise tannins. Great aging potential.

ECHÉZEAUX GRAND CRU 2006
Red | 2011 up to 2018   88
Very sharp, tight, dense, and taut; it is still somewhat short right now but very promising.

NUITS-SAINT-GEORGES PREMIER CRU
CHAIGNOTS 2006
Red | 2011 up to 2026   88
A delicious, precise nose of licorice, full-bodied, with more subtle, elegant texture than in the other bottlings from the sector; refined tannins, but the terroir is perfectly expressed and possesses a greater firmness than in Vosne. Excellent for cellaring.

VOSNE-ROMANÉE 2006
Red | 2011 up to 2018   88
Sold under the Mugneret-Gibourg label. A very fine aroma of slightly smoky wild strawberries, a tender, elegant wine that is refined in its tannins and texture and very well balanced.

Red: 14.8 acres; pinot noir 100%. Annual production: 30,000 bottles

DOMAINE JACQUES-FRÉDÉRIC MUGNIER

Château de Chambolle-Musigny
21220 Chambolle-Musigny
Phone 00 33 3 80 62 85 39
Fax 00 33 0 80 62 87 36
info@mugnier.fr
www.mugnier.fr

This estate has been perfecting its farming and vinification practices since the 1990s—but never more so than now following the return to the fold of the celebrated Clos de la Maréchale. This doubled the planting capacity and led to the reshaping of the production area and a much-needed modernization of the vinification cellar. The style of the wines today is the purest and most authentic ever, though the 1996, 1999, 2001, and 2002 vintages had already forced many other universally acclaimed producers to rethink their art. The Musigny 2004 ranks with the La Tâche, the Clos de Tart, and the Chambertin of Rousseau! The magnificent 2004 and 2005 fulfill all the promise of their vintage. The Musigny from this estate is the greatest available, excepting only the six hundred bottles produced by the Domaine Leroy.

Recently tasted

BONNES-MARES GRAND CRU 2007
Red | 2017 up to 2027   94

CHAMBOLLE-MUSIGNY 2007
Red | 2013 up to 2019   90

CHAMBOLLE-MUSIGNY PREMIER CRU
LES FUÉES 2007
Red | 2015 up to 2022   92

MUSIGNY GRAND CRU 2007
Red | 2017 up to 2027   97

NUITS-SAINT-GEORGES PREMIER CRU
CLOS DE LA MARÉCHALE 2007
White | 2011 up to 2015   89

Older vintages

BONNES-MARES GRAND CRU 2006
Red | 2011 up to 2026   95
One of the two most impressive wines of our comparative blind tasting in this cru, rich, aromatic, nobly anchored on very judiciously extracted tannins. Superb elegance.

BONNES-MARES GRAND CRU 2004
Red | 2011 up to 2016   88
Doesn't achieve the greatest level of depth and velvetiness.

CHAMBOLLE-MUSIGNY 2004
Red | 2011 up to 2017   92
Marvelous finesse and definition of terroir,
delicate, pure, subtle.

CHAMBOLLE-MUSIGNY PREMIER CRU
LES AMOUREUSES 2006
Red | 2011 up to 2024   97
Remarkable finesse and aromatic purity,
exemplary precision in the expression of the
marvelous terroir, great length, one of the
pinnacles of the vintage in the Côte de Nuits.

CHAMBOLLE-MUSIGNY PREMIER CRU
LES AMOUREUSES 2004
Red | 2011 up to 2019   95
Magnificent fullness, definition of terroir,
length, and style.

CHAMBOLLE-MUSIGNY PREMIER CRU
LES FUÉES 2004
Red | 2011 up to 2017   92
Beautifully floral on the nose, very fresh.
The texture is a bit aggressive.

MUSIGNY GRAND CRU 2006
Red | 2011 up to 2026   99
Incomparably distinguished aromas and texture, extreme precision and adroitness in
the tannic extraction, an absolute model of
style, loyal to the best of tradition.

MUSIGNY GRAND CRU 2004
Red | 2011 up to 2024   98
A perfect expression of a great terroir, inimitable. Bravo!

NUITS-SAINT-GEORGES
CLOS DE LA FOURCHE 2004
Red | 2011 up to 2013   88
A rather light color but very nice aromatic
purity. Ready to drink.

NUITS-SAINT-GEORGES PREMIER CRU
CLOS DE LA MARÉCHALE 2006
Red | 2016 up to 2026   94
The first tie of our grand tasting (134 Nuits
wines!) and a wine of great allure, with a
classic bouquet and supreme flavor! You
will especially admire the purity of the finish and the nobility of the tannins. Bravo!

NUITS-SAINT-GEORGES PREMIER CRU
CLOS DE LA MARÉCHALE 2004
Red | 2011 up to 2016   93
Rather dense color, very floral, subtle, long,
with marvelous aromatic purity.

Red: 32.1 acres; pinot noir 100%. **White:** 1.5 acres;
chardonnay 100%. **Annual production:** 60,000 bottles

DOMAINE PIERRE NAIGEON

4, rue du Chambertin
Vieil Hôtel Jobert de Chambertin
21220 Gevrey-Chambertin
Phone 00 33 3 80 34 14 87
Fax 00 33 3 80 58 51 18
pierre.naigeon@wanadoo.fr
www.DomainePierreNaigeon.com

A stunning first-ever entry from this old
and venerable wine house, which we had
lost sight of for a while: its submissions
from the 2005 vintage showed all the
finesse, complexity, and confident style of
the very best! If the price suits, buy as
much as you can. One to watch!

Recently tasted
BONNES-MARES GRAND CRU 2007
Red | 2017 up to 2027   93

CHAMBOLLE-MUSIGNY 2007
Red | 2012 up to 2019   88

GEVREY-CHAMBERTIN EN VOSNE 2007
Red | 2015 up to 2019   88

Older vintages
BONNES-MARES GRAND CRU 2006
Red | 2011 up to 2026   96
Great, complex nose that superbly expresses
the terroir, vinification that is very respectful of the vintage character, really very recommendable, especially since the vines are
situated on the raciest part of the terroir—
the chalky, high-elevation terres blanches.

FIXIN PREMIER CRU HERVELETS 2006
Red | 2011 up to 2018   89
A fine nose of raspberries and smoky black
currants in a style that is common for the vintage; fine, complex tannins, a very carefully
made wine, like everything from this producer.

GEVREY-CHAMBERTIN EN VOSNE 2006
Red | 2011 up to 2016   86
A nose of cocoa, very virile, austere, with
spicy tannins and enough body to ensure
good aging.

GEVREY-CHAMBERTIN PREMIER CRU
PERRIÈRES 2006
Red | 2011 up to 2018   89
A fine nose of raspberries, with tastes that—
in keeping with the best tradition—are closer
to brambles than red fruit. Consistent tannins help make this a wine of excellent style.

GEVREY-CHAMBERTIN VIEILLES VIGNES 2005
Red | 2011 up to 2020   89
Dark in color, remarkable material, a magnificent expression of the vintage; a stylish wine
that is authentic and very recommendable.

HAUTES CÔTES DE NUITS VIEILLES VIGNES 2005
Red | 2011 up to 2017   **89**
Dark in color, remarkable character, with rare finesse and complexity for the appellation; very pure vinification.

MOREY-SAINT-DENIS 2006
Red | 2011 up to 2013   **88**
Fine color, a very refined, precise nose of cherries, a rich wine for a Village bottling, savory, with firm tannins.

MOREY-SAINT-DENIS PREMIER CRU LA RIOTTE 2006
Red | 2011 up to 2021   **89**
Great volume on the palate, impressive flesh, a very robust wine that is certainly made for aging; all it lacks is a little finesse in the fruit and tannins.

MOREY-SAINT-DENIS PREMIER CRU LA RIOTTE 2005
Red | 2011 up to 2020   **90**
Great finesse and raciness, very natural, the true, timeless Morey, with a joyous expression of its origins. A source to watch for and encourage!

VOSNE-ROMANÉE 2006
Red | 2011 up to 2018   **88**
A fine nose, full of floral elegance, with a touch of well-calibrated oak; a charming, seductive wine, for those who like finesse.

Red: 25.9 acres; pinot noir 100%. White: 2.5 acres; aligoté 37%, chardonnay 63%. Annual production: 40,000 bottles

DOMAINE HENRI NAUDIN-FERRAND

Rue du Meix-Grenot
21700 Magny-les-Villers
Phone 00 33 3 80 62 91 50
Fax 00 33 3 80 62 91 77
info@naudin-ferrand.com
www.naudin-ferrand.com

A surefire producer of Hautes Côtes de Beaune and Bourgogne-Aligotés that really do articulate their terroir. Price remains reasonable. Claire Naudin had her work cut out for her with the top cuvée, Echézeaux, which is designed to capture the most intense, original expression possible. She pulled it off brilliantly in 2005, producing not only a superb Echézeaux but also some very good white Hautes Côtes de Beaune. Though quite different in terms of reputation and price, both wines are equally recommended and provide a brilliant demonstration of Burgundy's rich and varied heritage.

Recently tasted

BOURGOGNE ALIGOTÉ 2007
White | 2011 up to 2013   **86**

CÔTE DE NUITS-VILLAGES VIOLA ODORATA VIEILLES VIGNES 2007
Red | 2011 up to 2017   **94**

HAUTES CÔTES DE BEAUNE 2007
White | 2011 up to 2015   **88**

HAUTES CÔTES DE BEAUNE BELLIS PERENIS 2007
White | 2011 up to 2017   **88**

HAUTES CÔTES DE BEAUNE FÛT 2007
Red | 2011 up to 2017   **90**

HAUTES CÔTES DE BEAUNE ORCHIS MASCULATA 2007
Red | 2011 up to 2017   **90**

HAUTES CÔTES DE NUITS 2007
White | 2011 up to 2015   **90**

HAUTES CÔTES DE NUITS 2007
Red | 2011 up to 2017   **90**

Older vintages

ECHÉZEAUX GRAND CRU 2006
Red | 2011 up to 2021   **90**
A dense color, powerful nose, less nobly floral than on the 2005, curiously more marked by its tannins; but there is integrity, power, and a sincerity in its great stylishness on the palate. Needs time!

ECHÉZEAUX GRAND CRU 2005
Red I 2011 up to 2025   **94**
Black color, very noble violet aromas, the
inimitable style of whole grapes, not unwor-
thy of a comparison to a Romanée-Conti:
very classy, with a great future ahead.

HAUTES CÔTES DE BEAUNE 2006
White I 2011 up to 2014   **88**
Very frank flavors, a tension that is perfectly
in the spirit of this part of the Hautes Côtes.
A natural, pleasant finish, without any hint
of oxidation.

HAUTES CÔTES DE BEAUNE 2005
White I 2011 up to 2013   **88**
Clean, fresh, well defined, with much more
nerve than the Aligoté! A sincere wine,
straightforward, to be drunk by the end of
2013.

HAUTES CÔTES DE BEAUNE FÛT 2005
Red I 2011 up to 2013   **88**
A delicious nose of red berries, supple, very
elegant, ripe, natural, delicate, with a lot of
personality.

HAUTES CÔTES DE BEAUNE
ORCHIS MASCULATA 2006
Red I 2011 up to 2014   **92**
The benchmark wine for the Hautes Côtes,
at least from what we've learned in thirty
years of intensive Burgundy tastings. A delicate color (not unlike a hillside Champagne),
but the nose has a dazzling finesse in its
old rose notes that are the signature of noble
pinot noir. As a whole it is staggeringly natural. The future decision-makers of the
appellation urgently need to understand this
sort of wine!

HAUTES CÔTES DE NUITS 2005
White I 2011 up to 2013   **89**
A slightly reduced nose of hazelnuts, fresh,
distinguished, with good acidity, the finish
a bit more complex than on the Hautes Côtes
de Beaune. A wine with character!

LADOIX LA CORVÉE 2006
Red I 2011 up to 2016   **90**
Magnificent purity of style. Well balanced,
respectful of the grapes, delicate tannins,
well-integrated oak—and we would drink it
to our hearts' content if it weren't a crime
these days even to say so.

Red: 35.8 acres; gamay 8%, pinot noir 92%. White:
18.5 acres; aligoté 60%, chardonnay 34%, pinot blanc
6%. Annual production: 130,000 bottles

DOMAINE SYLVAIN PATAILLE

6, rue Roger Salengro
21300 Chenôve
Phone 00 33 3 80 51 17 35
Fax 00 33 3 80 52 49 49
domaine.sylvain.pataille@wanadoo.fr

Sylvain Pataille is a young enologist who is
prepared to set aside everything he has
been taught for the sake of pure and natural expression of fruit and vintage. The
quality of the wines remains a bit uneven
but you can tell they were made by a talented winegrower with a great future
ahead of him! The wine to buy from 2005 is
the Ancestrale.

Recently tasted
MARSANNAY CLOS DU ROY 2007
Red I 2013 up to 2019   **88**

MARSANNAY L'ANCESTRALE 2007
Red I 2013 up to 2019   **90**

Older vintages
MARSANNAY L'ANCESTRALE 2005
Red I 2011 up to 2013   **90**
Nice sap to it, with a fat texture, suave tan-
nins, and great sincerity and skill.

MARSANNAY L'ANCESTRALE 2004
Red I 2011 up to 2013   **88**
Very prettily made, despite the difficulties
of the vintage; suave, somewhat earthy but
able to age.

MARSANNAY LA CHARME AUX PRÊTRES 2006
White I 2011 up to 2014   **92**
A wine of truly surprising class and length,
one of the pinnacles of white wine production from the Côte de Nuits.

Red: 22.9 acres; gamay 10%, pinot noir 90%. White:
9.3 acres; aligoté 75%, chardonnay 25%. Annual
production: 50,000 bottles

DOMAINE DES PERDRIX

Rue des Écoles
21700 Prémeaux-Prissey
Phone 00 33 3 80 61 26 53
Fax 00 33 3 85 98 06 62
contact@domainedesperdrix.com
www.domainedesperdrix.com

This domaine owns lovely holdings in the southern part of the Côte de Nuits and vinifies its wines in a modern spirit, aiming for very ripe fruit and deep, voluptuous textures. The result has been a resounding success for some years now: very solid Village wines; a warm and subtle Côte de Nuits Premier Cru; and especially, a splendidly aristocratic Echézeaux from the best part of the cru.

Recently tasted

ECHÉZEAUX GRAND CRU 2007
Red | 2017 up to 2027   **93**

NUITS-SAINT-GEORGES 2007
Red | 2015 up to 2022   **90**

NUITS-SAINT-GEORGES PREMIER CRU
AUX PERDRIX 2007
Red | 2017 up to 2027   **94**

Older vintages

ECHÉZEAUX GRAND CRU 2006
Red | 2011 up to 2021   **89**
Strong color, powerful, fleshy, velvety, very sensual, but a bit of the inimitable refinement of the vineyard, especially in its most classic parcels, disappears (part of the wine is from the upper area of Echézeaux).

ECHÉZEAUX GRAND CRU 2005
Red | 2011 up to 2025   **94**
Great color, very powerful, marvelously unctuous, a long, caressing finish, great pedigree. A very nice Echézeaux; complete.

ECHÉZEAUX GRAND CRU 2004
Red | 2011 up to 2025   **90**
A nice color, less dense than the 2005, a spicy nose, taut texture, rather precise and pure; tends to be closed, which is a sign of good aging. The tannins are a bit drying.

NUITS-SAINT-GEORGES 2006
Red | 2011 up to 2018   **90**
Notes of black currant, typical of the way the wines of the Côte de Nuits become reduced during barrel aging; generous body; perfectly ripe, succulent grapes. Excellent.

NUITS-SAINT-GEORGES 2005
Red | 2011 up to 2015   **89**
A profound, opaque color, a very fat and complete wine. Ripe grapes, nicely unctuous, deep, displaying a well-mastered modern style but lacking finesse.

NUITS-SAINT-GEORGES PREMIER CRU
AUX PERDRIX 2006
Red | 2011 up to 2024   **94**
Black. Magnificent blackberry aromas, a concentrated, almost melty texture from the perfectly ripe grapes, more subtle and complex on the aftertaste than Les Terres Blanches; a great future ahead. Modern and proud of it.

NUITS-SAINT-GEORGES PREMIER CRU
AUX PERDRIX 2005
Red | 2011 up to 2025   **90**
Great color, unctuous; there is a bit too much cocoa in the flavor to qualify for supreme excellence.

NUITS-SAINT-GEORGES PREMIER CRU
LES TERRES BLANCHES 2006
Red | 2011 up to 2026   **93**
A complete wine, powerful, vigorous, rich, with remarkable length, just a little less complex than the great terroirs.

NUITS-SAINT-GEORGES PREMIER CRU
LES TERRES BLANCHES 2005
Red | 2011 up to 2025   **89**
Delicate, less flesh and fat than the Village wines but with more finesse and length. From young vines that did very well in this vintage!

VOSNE-ROMANÉE 2006
Red | 2011 up to 2016   **85**
Strong color, the tannins too extracted to preserve the expected finesse, typical of a wine from a hot year; possibly harvested too late.

Red: 28.4 acres; pinot 100%. White: 1.2 acres; chardonnay 100%. Annual production: 50,000 bottles

DOMAINE HENRI PERROT-MINOT ET DOMAINE CHRISTOPHE PERROT-MINOT

🍇🍇🍇🍇

Route des Grands-Crus
21220 Morey-Saint-Denis
Phone 00 33 3 80 34 32 51
Fax 00 33 3 80 34 13 57
gfa.perrot-minot@wanadoo.fr
www.perrot-minot.com

Every successive vintage shows this winery to be one of the most ambitious of the younger-generation Burgundy producers. It markets a broad range of wines, made from its own grapes and those of carefully selected suppliers, all crafted in a very assertive style that aims for powerful, taut body and texture. In truth they can be a touch over-saturating and are unlikely to satisfy seasoned connoisseurs in search of rather more natural qualities and greater transparency of fruit and texture. But they will appeal to a larger international audience and, in any case, Christophe Perrot-Minot is far too skilled and intelligent a winemaker to push his wines in anything but the right direction. The 2005s are overly powerful, but all of the Gevrey-Chambertins are exceptional, as is the Vosne Champs Perdrix—sumptuous and very Vosne-Romanée.

Recently tasted

CHAMBERTIN-CLOS DE BÈZE GRAND CRU 2007
Red | 2017 up to 2027   **97**

CHAMBOLLE-MUSIGNY PREMIER CRU
LES FUÉES 2007
Red | 2017 up to 2022   **93**

MAZOYÈRES-CHAMBERTIN GRAND CRU 2007
Red | 2017 up to 2025   **94**

VOSNE-ROMANÉE PREMIER CRU
LES BEAUX MONTS 2007
Red | 2017 up to 2022   **95**

Older vintages

CHAMBERTIN GRAND CRU
VIEILLES VIGNES 2005
Red | 2011 up to 2030   **95**
Very powerful, massive, very complex in its smoky and spicy notes, an ultra-tight texture. Immense aging potential.

CHAMBOLLE-MUSIGNY 2006
Red | 2011 up to 2018   **88**
The nose is typical of the estate, though a bit reduced (black currant, red berries); a clean and elegant wine, still reserved.

CHAMBOLLE-MUSIGNY COMBE D'ORVEAUX CUVÉE ULTRA 2006
Red | 2011 up to 2016   **90**
A super garagiste wine made from just a few rows of vines that abut Musigny. Very taut and racy but not inherently superior, at least for the moment, to the "regular" cuvée.

CHAMBOLLE-MUSIGNY PREMIER CRU
LA COMBE D'ORVEAU 2006
Red | 2011 up to 2018   **92**
Great elegance of flavor and texture, more open than the Cuvée Ultra, the terroir and vintage more apparent, undoubtedly because of better balance with the oak.

CHAMBOLLE-MUSIGNY PREMIER CRU
LA COMBE D'ORVEAU 2005
Red | 2011 up to 2020   **93**
Strong color, a great nose, the wine is very extracted but adeptly so, magnificent flesh; a great future ahead.

CHAMBOLLE-MUSIGNY PREMIER CRU
LES CHARMES 2006
Red | 2011 up to 2021   **93**
A magnificent cuvée with exceptionally ripe grapes, a taffeta texture, more open and complex than the two Combe d'Orveaus of the estate. A great future ahead.

CHAMBOLLE-MUSIGNY PREMIER CRU
LES FUÉES 2004
Red | 2011 up to 2016   **90**
Great aromatic finesse and complexity, fat and full for the vintage, no excess of tannins.

CHAPELLE-CHAMBERTIN GRAND CRU 2005
Red | 2011 up to 2030   **92**
A floral nose and rather suave texture, less monumental and affirmatory than the Mazoyères, long, velvety, appealing.

CLOS DE TART GRAND CRU 2005
Red | 2011 up to 2030   **90**
Deeply colored, straightforward, with a serious tannic foundation, a slight lack of finesse and complexity. Sure to age very well.

MAZOYÈRES-CHAMBERTIN GRAND CRU 2005
Red | 2011 up to 2030   **94**
Great color, a powerful nose, spicy, considerable body, the tannins firm but not rough, rather monumental.

MOREY-SAINT-DENIS PREMIER CRU
LA RIOTTE 2006
Red | 2011 up to 2021   **93**
Magnificent, high-quality élevage has perfectly refined this wine: it combines power and aromatic finesse in a balance that was very hard to obtain in this vintage.

Nuits-Saint-Georges premier cru
La Richemone 2006
Red | 2011 up to 2026   **93**
Great aromas driven by powerful mercaptan notes in the reduction, evoking a bit of smoke, toast, and black currants. Remarkable body, a velvety texture, great length, and a great future ahead.

Nuits-Saint-Georges premier cru
La Richemone 2005
Red | 2011 up to 2017   **93**
Very rich in color and tannin, full, fleshy, deep, still not very evolved. A great future ahead.

Nuits-Saint-Georges premier cru
La Richemone 2004
Red | 2011 up to 2019   **90**
Strong notes of black currant on the nose and palate, great pith for the vintage, very long. A wine of character!

Nuits-Saint-Georges premier cru
La Richemone cuvée ultra 2005
Red | 2011 up to 2020   **90**
Ultraripe grapes, reminiscent of a fortified wine, notes of chocolate on the nose, a concentrated, "roasted" texture; it goes all the way with something, but is it worth it? Only time will tell.

Vosne-Romanée 2006
Red | 2011 up to 2018   **88**
A precise, characteristic nose of spicy flowers, an exquisite fruit character of peonies, suave tannins, great length. A wine with charm and character.

Vosne-Romanée Champ Perdrix 2006
Red | 2011 up to 2021   **90**
A nice ruby color. An elegant texture and noble tannins rare in a Village-level wine but, when you know that the vineyard is immediately above the Reignots, you understand why.

Vosne-Romanée Champ Perdrix 2005
Red | 2011 up to 2025   **94**
Stunningly dense color, a great velvety, noble texture, expressive tannins. A truly exceptional Village-level wine, in the same vein as a Vosne-Romanée Les Reignots.

Vosne-Romanée premier cru
Les Beaux Monts 2006
Red | 2011 up to 2021   **95**
Sensational finesse and complexity, with an aromatic charm that only the commune of Vosne managed to retain in 2006. Distinguished tannins. The ideal, or almost, of a modern wine.

Red: 31.1 acres; gamay 2%, pinot 98%. White: 1 acre; aligoté 50%, chardonnay 50%. Annual production: 65,000 bottles

NICOLAS POTEL

44, rue des Blés
21700 Nuits-Saint-Georges
Phone 00 33 3 80 62 15 45
Fax 00 33 3 80 62 15 46
prevost@vfb.fr, marcocashera@vfb.fr
www.nicolas-potel.fr

Nicolas Potel continues to make a large range of wines covering the entire Côte d'Or, obviously with some offerings being better than others, like the wines from the Volnay area, for example. Remember that his father was long the director of Domaine de la Pousse d'Or, which enabled him to create excellent relationships with some of the best growers of Meursault. His wines are always honest, and sometimes even brilliant, expressions of their origins.

Recently tasted
Beaune premier cru Aigrots 2007
Red | 2015 up to 2022   **89**

Meursault premier cru Genevrières 2007
White | 2011 up to 2017   **92**

Santenay premier cru Gravières 2007
Red | 2011 up to 2015   **85**

Savigny-lès-Beaune Vieilles Vignes 2007
Red | 2012 up to 2017   **86**

Volnay premier cru Champans 2007
Red | 2015 up to 2022   **90**

Volnay premier cru Les Mitans 2007
Red | 2014 up to 2019   **90**

Volnay Vieilles Vignes 2007
Red | 2014 up to 2019   **88**

Vosne-Romanée 2007
Red | 2013 up to 2017   **90**

Older vintages
Chassagne-Montrachet premier cru
Morgeot 2006
White | 2011 up to 2016   **88**
Excellent finesse and purity, with good elegance for a Morgeot, good follow-through on the palate; a very pleasant wine.

Meursault Blagny premier cru 2006
White | 2011 up to 2018   **93**
A remarkable bottling, with the sumptuous aromatics of a Grand Cru; possesses an internal tension due to the high altitude of the parcel. That altitude was particularly useful in 2006 to give the rich body of this wine some additional yet very welcome acidity. Long, racy, highly recommended.

MEURSAULT PREMIER CRU GENEVRIÈRES 2006
White | 2011 up to 2016   **90**
Very upper-crust oakiness, lots of finesse, very delicate and long, with an obvious pedigree; for luxury restaurants.

MEURSAULT VIEILLES VIGNES 2006
White | 2011 up to 2014   **86**
Generous on the nose and on the palate; notes of honey and toast, which are classic and to be expected here; slightly soft on the palate, but with long persistence. A true 2006.

NUITS-SAINT-GEORGES 2006
Red | 2013 up to 2019   **88**
A bit of mercaptans on the nose; a fluid wine that is fairly elegant in its tannins, without being heavy-handed, aromatically speaking, even ending on a refreshing acidic note; easy-drinking.

SAVIGNY-LÈS-BEAUNE PREMIER CRU HAUTS-JARRONS 2006
Red | 2011 up to 2016   **88**
A fine harvest, with the chocolate notes of ripe grapes, nice follow-through on the palate, easy to understand and like.

VOLNAY PREMIER CRU CLOS DES CHÊNES 2006
Red | 2011 up to 2024   **90**
Deeply colored, powerful, tannic, with a structure that just manages to gain the upper hand over the fruit for the moment, but all built on a framework of racy tannins that are typical of the parcel.

VOSNE-ROMANÉE PREMIER CRU CHAUMES 2006
Red | 2011 up to 2021   **94**
A fine Côte de Nuits from the house for this vintage, and one of the most impressive Chaumes we have ever tasted. A wonderfully floral nose, a racy texture like that of the Domaine de la Romanée-Conti, subtle tannins, wonderful aromatic purity.

Red: 205.1 acres; pinot noir 100%. White: 29.7 acres; chardonnay 100%. Annual production: 450,000 bottles

DOMAINE LOUIS REMY

1, place du Monument
21220 Morey-Saint-Denis
Phone 00 33 3 80 34 32 59
Fax 00 33 3 80 34 32 23
domaine.louis.remy@wanadoo.fr
www.domaine-louis-remy.com

This small domaine with its magnificent heritage of vines produces increasingly dependable wines thanks to its dynamic and delightful proprietor, Chantal Rémy. The aim is to make very classical wines that express these great terroirs and ancient pinot noir vines with finesse, precision, and unfailing taste.

Recently tasted
CHAMBERTIN GRAND CRU 2007
Red | 2017 up to 2027   **95**

CHAMBOLLE-MUSIGNY PREMIER CRU DERRIÈRE LA GRANGE 2007
Red | 2014 up to 2019   **90**

CLOS DE LA ROCHE GRAND CRU 2007
Red | 2017 up to 2025   **92**

LATRICIÈRES-CHAMBERTIN GRAND CRU 2007
Red | 2017 up to 2027   **93**

Older vintages
CHAMBERTIN GRAND CRU 2006
Red | 2018 up to 2026   **93**
Here we can sense the influence of the high part of this parcel: very wiry and racy, with elegant, timeless discretion that is the stamp of the greatest bottlings. Wait at least until 2018.

CHAMBERTIN GRAND CRU 2004
Red | 2011 up to 2019   **90**
Very pretty black-currant aromas, fruity, delicate, long, fresh, a little simple in its tannins, but straightforward.

CHAMBOLLE-MUSIGNY PREMIER CRU DERRIÈRE LA GRANGE 2006
Red | 2011 up to 2018   **89**
A fine licorice nose, balanced body, racy and complex tannins, but a little dry, which should smooth out with age.

CHAMBOLLE-MUSIGNY PREMIER CRU DERRIÈRE LA GRANGE 2004
Red | 2011 up to 2016   **93**
Finesse, purity, discretion; great artistry that hides its art and a model of classicism in the expression of its terroir.

CLOS DE LA ROCHE GRAND CRU 2006
Red | 2011 up to 2026   **92**

Great aromatic cleanness, a rather slender body compared to most of its peers, but without any sense of being hollow. The tannins are racy but still resolving, and the wine could develop considerably with time.

CLOS DE LA ROCHE GRAND CRU 2004
Red | 2011 up to 2019   **94**

Deeper color than the domaine's other bottlings, great class.

LATRICIÈRES-CHAMBERTIN GRAND CRU 2006
Red | 2011 up to 2021   **93**

A particularly exacting and elegant expression of a bottling that is very secretive in its youth but infinitely racy with time. Noble spicy aromas, harmonious texture, complex but light-handed tannins. Great freshness and finesse from a vintage where the grapes were sometimes too ripe.

LATRICIÈRES-CHAMBERTIN GRAND CRU 2004
Red | 2011 up to 2020   **94**

Superlative finesse, distinction, class, length, and obviously racy terroir.

Red: 7.4 acres; pinot noir 100%. Annual production: 15,000 bottles

DOMAINE BERNARD ET ARMELLE RION

8, route Nationale
21700 Vosne-Romanée
Phone 00 33 3 80 61 05 31
Fax 00 33 3 80 61 34 60
rion@domainerion.fr
www.domainerion.fr

Under the influence of the new generation, a new phase is beginning for this respected and conscientious domaine in Vosne-Romanée. Armelle Rion is now in charge, and this was immediately perceptible in the 2006s presented for tasting: the wines have gained in purity and finesse, even attaining an elegance that will place them among the top ranks of the sector. This is a great thing when considering the pedigree of their vineyards; enthusiasts should still be able to buy these rare and prestigious wines at reasonable prices.

Recently tasted
NUITS-SAINT-GEORGES PREMIER CRU
DAMODES 2007
Red | 2011 up to 2013   **89**

NUITS-SAINT-GEORGES PREMIER CRU
MURGERS 2007
Red | 2014 up to 2022   **89**

Older vintages
CLOS DE VOUGEOT GRAND CRU 2006
Red | 2011 up to 2026   **91**

A nice, classic wine with the ample proportions of the vintage. Vinous, racy, built for long aging. Highly commendable.

NUITS-SAINT-GEORGES PREMIER CRU
MURGERS 2006
Red | 2011 up to 2021   **89**

A fleshy, complete wine with a texture that is firm but not aggressive. Good length and a steady future ahead of it.

VOSNE-ROMANÉE PREMIER CRU CHAUMES 2006
Red | 2011 up to 2018   **87**

Light cocoa notes on the nose like the ones you often find in certain Premier Crus, such as Les Chaumes, Les Suchots, and Les Echézeaux. A firm wine. The tannins are a bit dry, but the finish is complex. The oak might not have measured up to the wine.

VOSNE-ROMANÉE VIEILLES VIGNES 2006
Red | 2011 up to 2018   **87**

A classic nose for this village, floral and spicy. Tender texture, firm but refined tannins, excellent style.

Red: 17.8 acres; pinot noir 100%. White: 2 acres; chardonnay 100%. Annual production: 40,000 bottles

DOMAINE DANIEL RION ET FILS

17, route Nationale 74
21700 Prémeaux-Prissey
Phone 00 33 3 80 62 31 28
Fax 00 33 3 80 61 13 41
contact@domaine-daniel-rion.com
www.domaine-daniel-rion.com

A good, classical estate in the southern Côte de Nuits. Style tends to vary with the vintage and the cuvée, but the most refined wines are usually the Vignes Rondes Nuits-Saint-George Premier Cru and the Vosne-Romanée Les Chaumes Premier Cru, from the borders of Vosne-Romanée and Nuits-Saint-George. We didn't taste all of the 2005s, but overall quality seemed good to excellent, with some particularly elegant Vosnes.

Recently tasted

NUITS-SAINT-GEORGES LAVIÈRES 2007
Red | 2011 up to 2019   92

NUITS-SAINT-GEORGES PREMIER CRU
AUX VIGNES RONDES 2007
Red | 2015 up to 2022   92

NUITS-SAINT-GEORGES PREMIER CRU
HAUTS PRULIERS 2007
Red | 2013 up to 2019   89

VOSNE-ROMANÉE 2007
Red | 2014 up to 2019   90

VOSNE-ROMANÉE PREMIER CRU
LES BEAUX MONTS 2007
Red | 2015 up to 2019   93

Older vintages

NUITS-SAINT-GEORGES LES GRANDES VIGNES 2006
Red | 2011 up to 2018   90
Very aromatically seductive, well-built, elegant texture, nobly reduced and visibly from an excellent harvest.

NUITS-SAINT-GEORGES LES GRANDES VIGNES 2005
Red | 2011 up to 2020   87
Marked astringence, but contrastingly suave on the mid-palate! A lack of precision in the general definition of the flavors.

NUITS-SAINT-GEORGES PREMIER CRU
AUX VIGNES RONDES 2006
Red | 2011 up to 2021   92
Generous body, an ample wine, harmonious, preserving its freshness and finesse despite its alcohol. Precise vinification, just as we like it.

NUITS-SAINT-GEORGES PREMIER CRU
AUX VIGNES RONDES 2005
Red | 2011 up to 2020   88
A menthol nose and fittingly full body. A supple wine, sincere, but without much personality.

VOSNE-ROMANÉE PREMIER CRU
LES BEAUX MONTS 2005
Red | 2011 up to 2025   92
Plenty of finesse in the balanced body. A well-made wine, just a bit fuller than Les Chaumes.

VOSNE-ROMANÉE PREMIER CRU
LES CHAUMES 2005
Red | 2011 up to 2025   93
A nice, precise nose of black currants, very suave, with noble tannins. The pedigree of the terroir is evident! By far the best of the range.

Red: 37.1 acres; pinot 100%. White: 7.4 acres; chardonnay 90%, pinot blanc 10%. Annual production: 80,000 bottles

DOMAINE DE LA ROMANÉE-CONTI

🜚 🜚 🜚 🜚 🜚

1, rue Derrière-le-Four
21700 Vosne-Romanée
Phone 00 33 3 80 62 48 80
Fax 00 33 3 80 61 05 72

The most famous of all flagship Burgundy estates offers its usual flawless performance, with sublime 2003s and 2004s followed by no less excellent 2005s and 2006s. Exceptional terroirs and (for Burgundy) large vineyard plots have something to do with it, of course. Also the fact that those in charge have a clear and uncompromising vision of a quintessentially pure style of wine, vinified so as to remain as faithful as possible to the grapes and their aristocratic varietal aromas. This combination of impeccable ethics, pristine terroir, and competent staff is what produces the great Vosne-Romanée crus: wines of a finesse that nothing else can touch. Aubert de Villaine and his team set a fine example for other winegrowers worldwide. When you taste the admirably refined 2004 with its perfectly pure nose and structure, it's hard to believe that this was such a difficult vintage and produced so many flawed wines!

Recently tasted

ECHÉZEAUX GRAND CRU 2007
Red | 2015 up to 2022   **92**

GRANDS-ECHÉZEAUX GRAND CRU 2007
Red | 2017 up to 2022   **93**

LA TÂCHE GRAND CRU 2007
Red | 2017 up to 2027   **95**

MONTRACHET GRAND CRU 2006
White | 2016 up to 2026   **100**

RICHEBOURG GRAND CRU 2007
Red | 2015 up to 2022   **94**

ROMANÉE-CONTI GRAND CRU 2007
Red | 2019 up to 2027   **98**

Older vintages

ECHÉZEAUX GRAND CRU 2006
Red | 2011 up to 2024   **94**
A very elegant floral nose, a bit less complete proportionally than in 2004, but the texture carries all the nobility of the estate.

ECHÉZEAUX GRAND CRU 2004
Red | 2011 up to 2024   **97**
Elegantly transparent, noble floral aromas, superb body for the vintage, great precision in the expression of terroir, well-integrated tannins (which is becoming so rare!)—an admirable accomplishment for the year as with all the other crus!

GRANDS-ECHÉZEAUX GRAND CRU 2006
Red | 2011 up to 2013   **95**
We clearly move up a notch here compared to the Echézeaux in this vintage, with a deeper color, a tighter texture. Incredibly noble and distinguished, with a more meaty but less "pure" style than in 2004 because of naturally higher alcohol.

GRANDS-ECHÉZEAUX GRAND CRU 2004
Red | 2011 up to 2024   **95**
Pure in color, a floral nose of supreme elegance, the body a bit weaker than in the Echézeaux, silky, elegant tannins, with great style, but in this vintage all the other crus did even better!

LA TÂCHE GRAND CRU 2006
Red | 2011 up to 2030   **98**
An immense wine, majestic, complete—as you would expect—but the day of the tasting it didn't dominate the Saint-Vivant or the Richebourg: it was simply, and to the same extent, a marvelous expression of the originality of these great terroirs and a confirmation of the quality of this vintage.

MONTRACHET GRAND CRU 2004
White | 2014 up to 2019   **98**
Exemplary body, irresistible integrity, unparalleled aromatic distinction. Once again, the greatest white wine of Burgundy! Needs five to seven years.

RICHEBOURG GRAND CRU 2006
Red | 2011 up to 2028   **98**
Absolutely sumptuous, incredibly noble aromatics, as with all the wines of the estate in 2006, an unusual velvety texture, and confirmation that the estate's famous Grand Cru is back at the highest level imaginable.

ROMANÉE-CONTI GRAND CRU 2006
Red | 2011 up to 2030   **100**
From its first year in barrel, it was easy to understand that this cru in 2006 has something transcendent that puts it above, or rather beyond, all the other cuvées of the estate: purity, a supreme elegance of aromas and texture, incredibly fine tannins. In short, a legendary wine is born—and highborn.

ROMANÉE-CONTI GRAND CRU 2004
Red | 2011 up to 2050   **99**
On the nose you will find the strange nuance of peppers that is typical of this cru. The bouquet promises to be transcendent and inimitable in thirty years. Divinely ethereal on the palate, but you have to love great wine to understand!

ROMANÉE-SAINT-VIVANT GRAND CRU 2006
Red | 2011 up to 2026   **94**
Extraordinarily refined aromas and texture. The tannins have a nobility that would be difficult to surpass (but the Conti will do so with ease!). A marvelous success.

ROMANÉE-SAINT-VIVANT GRAND CRU 2004
Red | 2011 up to 2029   **98**
A sublime nose of old roses, silken texture, stunningly precise and pure, magically integrated tannins. What an accomplishment!

Red: 59.3 acres; pinot 100%. **White:** 2.5 acres; chardonnay 100%. **Annual production:** 80,000 bottles

DOMAINE ROSSIGNOL-TRAPET

Rue de la Petite-Issue
21220 Gevrey-Chambertin
Phone 00 33 3 80 51 87 26
Fax 00 33 3 80 34 31 63
info@rossignol-trapet.com
www.rossignol-trapet.com

Despite its rich heritage of vines, this estate rarely produces wines that fulfill expectations. The enthusiastic reviews it occasionally receives are due entirely to the personal charisma of brothers Nicolas and David Rossignol. Vineyard performance has obviously come a long way, inspired by organic principles and the example of cousin Jean-Louis Trapet. But only time will tell whether the improvements noticed in the 2002s were just a flash in the pan.

BEAUNE MARIAGES 2004
Red | 2011 up to 2014   **84**
Spicy, with a verbena note; imprecise, a slightly stewed impression.

BEAUNE PREMIER CRU TEURONS 2004
Red | 2011 up to 2016   **86**
More vegetal but purer fruit than Mariages. A certain amount of finesse. No taste of hail.

CHAMBERTIN GRAND CRU 2004
Red | 2014 up to 2016   **86**
Despite the terroir's obvious finesse, this wine is thin, with aggressive tannins. Little class, even if the terroir is perceptible.

CHAPELLE-CHAMBERTIN GRAND CRU 2004
Red | 2014 up to 2016   **89**
A more refined, precise nose than the others; acceptable body; an elegant wine, with slightly dry tannins.

GEVREY-CHAMBERTIN 2004
Red | 2011 up to 2014   **84**
Little purity or finesse, with fairly dry tannins. A straightforward wine that lacks grace.

GEVREY-CHAMBERTIN PREMIER CRU CLOS PRIEUR 2004
Red | 2011 up to 2050   **85**
Very spicy and oaky, a velvety texture that is superior to the Village wine, a cooked finish.

GEVREY-CHAMBERTIN PREMIER CRU PETITE CHAPELLE 2004
Red | 2011 up to 2014   **86**
Robust, bitter, powerful, but with dry tannins.

LATRICIÈRES-CHAMBERTIN GRAND CRU 2004
Red | 2014 up to 2019   **89**
Deep color, a firm wine with clearly racy terroir, but its extraction lacks refinement. Hold.

Red: 33.2 acres; pinot 100%. **White:** 1.5 acres; chardonnay 100%. **Annual production:** 65,000 bottles

DOMAINE GEORGES ROUMIER

🍷 🍷 🍷 🍷 🍷

4, rue de Vergy
21220 Chambolle-Musigny
Phone 00 33 3 80 62 86 37
Fax 00 33 3 80 62 83 55
domaine@roumier.com
www.roumier.com

This world-famous winery specializes in Chambolle-Musigny from vineyard parcels ideally spread throughout the commune. Christophe Roumier was the first to introduce more power and body to Chambolle-Musigny wines, at no expense to their incomparable finesse. He can be rightly proud of his efforts, paving the way for a new style of Burgundian classicism that he continues to perfect, even in difficult years. Among the estate-produced offerings, the really must-have wines are his bastions of Chambolle-Musigny classicism, the Les Cras Premier Cru and the Bonnes-Mares Grand Cru. The large Clos de La Bussière parcel produces wines of comparable quality in only very great vintages, such as 2005.

Recently tasted

BONNES-MARES GRAND CRU 2007
Red | 2017 up to 2027   **94**

CHAMBOLLE-MUSIGNY 2007
Red | 2013 up to 2019   **90**

CHAMBOLLE-MUSIGNY PREMIER CRU
LES CRAS 2007
Red | 2017 up to 2022   **91**

MOREY-SAINT-DENIS PREMIER CRU
CLOS DE LA BUSSIÈRE 2007
Red | 2015 up to 2019   **89**

Older vintages

BONNES-MARES GRAND CRU 2006
Red | 2011 up to 2026   **93**
A slightly more evolved color than on the Drouhin-Laroze, nicely full, more delicate tannins, a slight lack of finesse, at least at the moment.

BONNES-MARES GRAND CRU 2004
Red | 2011 up to 2022   **93**
Deeply colored, ample, very spicy and floral on the nose (almost a caricature of peony), intense, firm, a fresh finish, great classicism of form and flavor. Relaxing!

CHAMBOLLE-MUSIGNY 2006
Red | 2011 up to 2016   **90**
Delicate, tender, supple, with fine-grained tannins, very clear expression of the terroir, exemplary vinification.

CHAMBOLLE-MUSIGNY COMBOTTES 2006
Red | 2011 up to 2018   **93**
More expressive than Les Cras, gracious, subtle, very tender and perfumed, a classic of its type.

CHAMBOLLE-MUSIGNY PREMIER CRU LES CRAS 2006
Red | 2011 up to 2018   **90**
Full, well balanced, a refined texture, good length. A classic Chambolle.

CHAMBOLLE-MUSIGNY PREMIER CRU LES CRAS 2004
Red | 2011 up to 2019   **90**
Nice dense color, not very evolved, a floral, mineral nose much more elegant than on the Bussière. Fleshy, a steady finish, well balanced, carefully produced, distinguished.

Red: 28.9 acres; pinot noir 100%. Annual production: 40,000 bottles

DOMAINE ARMAND ROUSSEAU

❦ ❦ ❦ ❦

1, rue de l'Aumônerie
21220 Gevrey-Chambertin
Phone 00 33 3 80 34 30 55
Fax 00 33 3 80 58 50 25
contact@domaine-rousseau.com
www.domaine-rousseau.com

It was relatively easy for Eric Rousseau to restore his family estate to its rightful place at the top of the Gevrey-Chambertin appellation. His heritage was a vineyard with impeccable aristocratic credentials and consistently high standards of viticulture and vinification. But the yields were just a bit on the high side, and not all of the cuvées were made with the same care. Not anymore. The past five vintages from this estate have combined unbelievably refined aromas with an ideal density and purity of texture. The Chambertin now rivals the Romanée-Conti as the most perfect expression of contemporary Burgundy.

Recently tasted
CHAMBERTIN GRAND CRU 2007
Red | 2019 up to 2025   95

CHAMBERTIN-CLOS DE BÈZE GRAND CRU 2007
Red | 2017 up to 2027   95

GEVREY-CHAMBERTIN 2007
Red | 2013 up to 2019   88

GEVREY-CHAMBERTIN PREMIER CRU
CLOS SAINT-JACQUES 2007
Red | 2015 up to 2027   93

Older vintages
CHAMBERTIN GRAND CRU 2006
Red | 2011 up to 2026   98
Once again, the greatest Chambertin and the greatest wine of the whole tasting, getting a unanimous vote from all winemakers present (who are not always kind with each other). The finesse of the texture and the aromatic distinction of this cuvée are absolutely unmatched, and the internal tension of the tannins evokes the character of the parcels in the upper part of the cru.

CHAMBERTIN GRAND CRU 2003
Red | 2011 up to 2030   98
One of the absolute pinnacles of this exceptional vintage. The body has a goldsmith's precision, the flavor an indescribable richness and complexity, and noble tannins.

CHAMBERTIN-CLOS DE BÈZE GRAND CRU 2005
Red | 2011 up to 2021   92
Great aroma and body, worthy of this cru, but less perfection in the texture and especially the tannin than in the Chambertin, despite the grapes being ruthlessly sorted. From that point of view, the Ruchottes would be a bit better.

CHAMBERTIN-CLOS DE BÈZE GRAND CRU 2001
Red | 2011 up to 2021   97
A violet and licorice bouquet of rare class, remarkably balanced, peerless distinction of terroir. An accomplished and certainly underestimated vintage that will delight the true connoisseur!

CHARMES-CHAMBERTIN GRAND CRU 2006
Red | 2011 up to 2026   93
A refined wine with a subtly racy texture that was perfectly conserved by the élevage. Supple and delicate, but rich in alcohol and tannic backbone. This should be a beautiful wine, and more accessible than the Chambertin.

CLOS DE LA ROCHE GRAND CRU 2006
Red | 2011 up to 2026   93
A nice blackberry nose, generous body, stunning interior tension, firm tannins. A noble wine, just a hint more linear and less sensual than some other expressions of this Grand Cru.

GEVREY-CHAMBERTIN PREMIER CRU
CLOS SAINT-JACQUES 2006
Red | 2011 up to 2026   93
Nice red-berry aromas and an aristocratic mouthfeel that is immediatly appealing for its unparalleled texture, rich and harmonious flavor, in short everything we expect from this superb cru but with less panache than in 2005.

GEVREY-CHAMBERTIN PREMIER CRU
CLOS SAINT-JACQUES 2005
Red | 2011 up to 2030   97
Noble blackberry aromas; a very generous texture, gloriously delicate tannins. The Rousseau style in all its glory!

GEVREY-CHAMBERTIN PREMIER CRU
CLOS SAINT-JACQUES 2003
Red | 2011 up to 2028   97
A very precise bouquet of licorice and dark chocolate. The body has a transcendent elegance in a vintage with all of the pitfalls. A practically perfect vinification. It has already surpassed the remarkable 2002!

GEVREY-CHAMBERTIN PREMIER CRU
CLOS SAINT-JACQUES 2002
Red | 2011 up to 2022   95
Superlative finesse of aromas and texture, aristocratic tannins. A great wine!

RUCHOTTES-CHAMBERTIN GRAND CRU
CLOS DES RUCHOTTES 2006
Red | 2011 up to 2013   93
Great spicy flavor. A taut wine, nobly aromatic, with firm but clear tannins, which was not easy given the damage done here by hail. The grapes were impeccably sorted and the vinification adept.

Red: 34.6 acres; pinot 100%. **Annual production:** 65,000 bottles

DOMAINE MARC ROY

8, avenue de la Gare
21220 Gevrey-Chambertin
Phone 00 33 3 80 51 81 13
Fax 00 33 3 80 34 16 74
domainemarcroy@orange.fr
www.domainemarcroy.vinimarket.com

This modest family estate has extended its reach into domestic and overseas markets alike under the influence of Marc's daughter Alexandrine. The range of wines is small but increasingly well crafted, with the 2006 edition of the Alexandrine and Clos Prieur both achieving precision on the palate—the most consistent vintage to date.

Recently tasted
GEVREY-CHAMBERTIN ALEXANDRINE 2007
Red | 2013 up to 2019   89

GEVREY-CHAMBERTIN CLOS PRIEUR 2007
Red | 2013 up to 2017   87

GEVREY-CHAMBERTIN VIEILLES VIGNES 2007
Red | 2013 up to 2019   88

Older vintages
GEVREY-CHAMBERTIN ALEXANDRINE 2006
Red | 2011 up to 2018   88
A refined, elegant nose of peonies, generous body, suave texture, noble tannins, a very successful, immediately appealing Village wine, despite its sturdy constitution, which assures it will age well.

GEVREY-CHAMBERTIN ALEXANDRINE 2005
Red | 2011 up to 2017   89
Fine color, complex nose, fresh, elegant, pretty texture, a very precise wine that is faithful to the terroir and worthy of the vintage.

GEVREY-CHAMBERTIN CLOS PRIEUR 2006
Red | 2011 up to 2016   88
The same stylistic qualities as the Alexandrine bottling, with remarkably fine tannins for the vintage, precise fruit; very good work.

GEVREY-CHAMBERTIN CLOS PRIEUR 2005
Red | 2011 up to 2050   88
Fine color, pretty texture, a refined wine that is clean, elegant, though slightly less well rounded than Alexandrine.

Red: 9.8 acres; pinot noir 100%. Annual production: 23,000 bottles

CLOS DE TART

7, route des Grands-Crus
21220 Morey-Saint-Denis
Phone 00 33 3 80 34 30 91
Fax 00 33 3 80 51 86 70
contact@clos-de-tart.com

This eponymous estate has the good fortune to be sole owner of the Clos de Tart, one of the most illustrious Grands Crus on the Côte de Nuits. Plantings follow the contours of the hill with a perfect exposure that brings the grapes to ideal ripeness in sunny years without risk of scorching—and that's even allowing for global warming! The vineyard also owes a lot to its manager, Sylvain Pitiot, whose standards of perfection have raised this cru to its highest level ever. The nature of the soil here and its location produces a wine with the vigor of a Clos de la Roche, plus the aromatic charm of a Bonnes-Mares, and even more fullness and breeding than either of its two neighbors. Sure to please hedonists in search of immediate pleasure, and aesthetes, too, who will instantly spot its refined texture and tannins. The youngest vines are bottled as Morey Saint-Denis Clos de la Forge, one of the most distinguished Côte de Nuits Villages.

Recently tasted
CLOS DE TART GRAND CRU 2007
Red | 2019 up to 2027   95

Older vintages
CLOS DE TART GRAND CRU 2006
Red | 2016 up to 2028   94
A big, virile wine, endowed with colossal body and richness, supported by more refined tannins than one would imagine in such a full wine.

CLOS DE TART GRAND CRU 2005
Red | 2011 up to 2030   98
Close to perfection! A sublime floral nose, perfectly balanced body, very noble tannins!

CLOS DE TART GRAND CRU 2004
Red | 2011 up to 2024   98
A delicate color, a floral nose with exquisitely refined nuances, the suave texture of ultraripe grapes, silken tannins. A ridiculously charming wine, but only those enamored of pinot noir will understand its true merit! Approaches a Conti!

CLOS DE TART GRAND CRU 2003
Red | 2011 up to 2025   98
Great vigor, immense aromas of ripe grapes, with violets, licorice, and cocoa. A sumptuous texture, noble tannins, and truly exceptional substance!

CLOS DE TART GRAND CRU 2002
Red | 2011 up to 2020   97

A great, classic wine, with a perfectly full and balanced body, but without the genius or the incredible personality of the previous vintages. Conservatives will love it!

CLOS DE TART GRAND CRU 2001
Red | 2013 up to 2021   95

A great complex nose, starting to show gently spicy notes of age. Generous body, great follow-up on the palate, but it hasn't quite mellowed yet; it would be crazy to drink it at this stage.

Red: 18.5 acres: pinot 100%. **Annual production:** 25,000 bottles

DOMAINE TAUPENOT-MERME

33, route des Grands-Crus
21220 Morey-Saint-Denis
Phone 00 33 3 80 34 35 24
Fax 00 33 3 80 51 83 41
domaine.taupenot-merme@orange.fr

This family property, related to the domaine Perrot-Minnot by way of grandparents, is notable for holdings in two different areas: on the Côtes de Nuits, with remarkable vineyards from Gevrey to Nuits, and vineyards that originated with the Taupenot family in Saint-Romain and Auxey-Duresses. A new, spirited generation is at the helm, and the wines are getting better from year to year; there are still more irregularities in the Côte de Beaune than the Côte de Nuits, even though the 2005 white Saint-Romain was exemplary. The 2006s tasted were of good quality, detailed, in a classic style, recommendable for the most part.

Recently tasted
CHAMBOLLE-MUSIGNY 2007
Red | 2013 up to 2019   90

CHAMBOLLE-MUSIGNY PREMIER CRU COMBE D'ORVEAU 2007
Red | 2014 up to 2022   92

MOREY-SAINT-DENIS 2007
Red | 2013 up to 2019   89

MOREY-SAINT-DENIS PREMIER CRU RIOTTE 2007
Red | 2014 up to 2019   89

Older vintages
CHARMES-CHAMBERTIN GRAND CRU 2006
Red | 2011 up to 2021   89

The clean fruitiness of red berries, well built but without excessive extraction, precise but a little less complex on the finish than others.

CORTON GRAND CRU LE ROGNET 2006
White | 2011 up to 2018   92

Aromatic, generous, with tastes of blackberry, supple tannins. It will be ready to drink more quickly than the others but is nonetheless very well made.

MAZOYÈRES-CHAMBERTIN GRAND CRU 2006
Red | 2011 up to 2021   90

A fairly typical 2006 nose of wild strawberries and smoke; the wine seems more robust and fleshy than the Charmes and, in any case, more masculine in character, with firm yet noble tannins. Overall, a very satisfactory cru but lacking in genius.

MOREY-SAINT-DENIS 2006

Red | 2011 up to 2018   **88**

Excellent general balance, with somewhat dark fruit that is typical of the vintage, with its notes of plum; fresher and more marked by cherries on the palate, with well-integrated tannins.

MOREY-SAINT-DENIS PREMIER CRU RIOTTE 2006

White | 2011 up to 2021   **92**

Excellent styling for a Premier Cru that is more delicate than many of its peers, with a fruitiness that is generous but not too "hot" and a refined texture. A very elegant rasp-berried finish.

NUITS-SAINT-GEORGES PREMIER CRU LES PRULIERS 2006

White | 2011 up to 2021   **93**

A splendid, complex nose, ample but very likeable texture, fine tannins, excellent style, faithful to this noble terroir, to which the vintage has given even more precocious charm than usual.

SAINT-ROMAIN 2005

White | 2011 up to 2013   **88**

Clean, clear, delicately lemony, made with care, and especially well balanced for the year, thanks to the altitude of the vineyard!

Red: 26.4 acres; gamay 5%, pinot noir 95%. White: 6.2 acres; aligoté 42%, chardonnay 58%. Annual production: 80,000 bottles

CHÂTEAU DE LA TOUR

Clos de Vougeot
21640 Vougeot
Phone 00 33 3 80 62 86 13
Fax 00 33 3 80 62 82 72
contact@châteaudelatour.com
www.châteaudelatour.com

This domaine owns, by far, the largest parcel of the Grand Cru Clos de Vougeot, and has the singular privilege to be the only winery that vinifies and ages its wines within the walls of this famous vineyard. The quality of the grapes that go into the old-vines bottling is exceptional, and the whole-cluster fermentation creates a wine that has prodigious pedigree, worthy of the best Richebourg. The regular bottling (also made from fairly old vines), though excellent, doesn't reach the same heights. Once it does, this domaine will deserve a place at the top of the podium. The old-vines 2005 will join the 1999 and 2003 in the Burgundy hall of fame. The 2007s seem to be more elegant and complex than the pretty 2006s.

Recently tasted

CLOS DE VOUGEOT GRAND CRU 2007
Red | 2017 up to 2025   **92**

CLOS DE VOUGEOT GRAND CRU VIEILLES VIGNES 2007
Red | 2017 up to 2027   **94**

Older vintages

CLOS DE VOUGEOT GRAND CRU VIEILLES VIGNES 2006
Red | 2011 up to 2026   **94**

Classic body and texture in the expression of the terroir. A complete wine with no surprises. To be aged slowly.

CLOS DE VOUGEOT GRAND CRU VIEILLES VIGNES 2005
Red | 2011 up to 2050   **98**

Black, great nose and texture, monumental flavor, very pure tannins. The ultimate expression of the terroir and vintage.

CLOS DE VOUGEOT GRAND CRU VIEILLES VIGNES 2004
Red | 2011 up to 2019   **94**

Beautiful color. Brambles and very ripe peppers on the nose. A noble texture, flavors of black fruit and cocoa, very long. A wine of great distinction but reserved for true connoisseurs.

Red: 13.6 acres; pinot noir 100%. Annual production: 22,000 bottles

DOMAINE JEAN TRAPET PÈRE ET FILS

🍇 🍇 🍇 🍇 🍇

53, route de Beaune
21220 Gevrey-Chambertin
Phone 00 33 3 80 34 30 40
Fax 00 33 3 80 51 86 34
message@domaine-trapet.com
www.domaine-trapet.com

Another family domaine that is headed for greatness, thanks to the committed efforts of proprietors Jean-Louis Trapet and his wife, Andrée, an Alsace winegrower as dedicated as her husband. Holdings include parcels in some of the finest Gevrey Grands Crus, farmed under a stringently biodynamic regime that has restored the soil's vitality. The wine is as alive as the soils: eloquently expressive but at no expense to purity and aromatic neatness, since vinification here is as precise as the viticulture. The three Grands Crus are incomparable; the Gevrey Village wine is increasingly classy and definitely worth a look; and the incredible Marsannay is very attractively priced.

CHAMBERTIN GRAND CRU 2006
Red | 2016 up to 2026   94
A great, ethereal wine, sober tannins, great length, an aristocratic wine that unveils only part of its force and potential, but already remarkable for its silkiness and texture.

CHAMBERTIN GRAND CRU 2005
Red | 2011 up to 2030   99
Extraordinary finesse and frankness, fabulous length, sublime expression of the vineyard and vintage.

CHAMBERTIN GRAND CRU 2004
Red | 2011 up to 2024   97
A wonderful harmony of roses, quite charming, suave, subtle; a very moving wine!

CHAPELLE-CHAMBERTIN GRAND CRU 2006
Red | 2014 up to 2024   88
A powerful nose with smoky, spicy notes; a straightforward wine with more austere tannins than the domaine's other wines, which points to stress on the vines in this hail-hit vintage.

GEVREY-CHAMBERTIN PREMIER CRU CLOS PRIEUR 2006
Red | 2014 up to 2021   89
Smoky, brambly notes, in the spirit of the vintage; a noble, natural taste of well-respected pinot, subtle tannins, a charming wine that will help during the long wait for the Grands Crus.

GEVREY-CHAMBERTIN PREMIER CRU CLOS PRIEUR 2004
Red | 2011 up to 2019   93
Fine aromatics of strawberry and flowers, tender, aristocratic, subtle, a striking frankness to its expression.

LATRICIÈRES-CHAMBERTIN GRAND CRU 2006
Red | 2016 up to 2026   92
Great elegance and frankness, supple tannins, a tender yet complex wine that hides its power beneath the looseness of youth.

LATRICIÈRES-CHAMBERTIN GRAND CRU 2005
Red | 2011 up to 2030   95
Deep color, rich, tannic, tight, mineral, incredibly racy; expect amazing age-worthiness!

LATRICIÈRES-CHAMBERTIN GRAND CRU 2004
Red | 2011 up to 2024   93
Very precise, natural, more mineral than Chapelle; long, somewhat dry tannins.

Red: 30.9 acres; pinot 100%. White: 6.2 acres; chardonnay 100%. Annual production: 60,000 bottles

DOMAINE COMTE GEORGES DE VOGÜÉ

Rue Sainte-Barbe
21220 Chambolle-Musigny
Phone 00 33 3 80 62 86 25
Fax 00 33 3 80 62 82 38

This impressive estate owns three-quarters of the incomparable Musigny Grand Cru but declined to submit any wines for inclusion after we voiced a few very polite criticisms regarding some of its vintages from the mid-1990s. Our opinion has not changed since then. We tasted all of its 1996 offerings—which had ten years to show their stuff—and could find no fault with the body of the wines. The tannins, however, seemed rigid, and the taste had neither the naturalness nor the charm of the same crus from the Domaine Mugnier. The 1997s are slightly better balanced without being entirely convincing. Since the 2005 vintage the wines are showing better equilibrium.

BONNES-MARES 1996
Red | 2011 up to 2016 **88**
Body and nerve, but the tannins are too dry and the aromatics not subtle enough for this cru.

CHAMBOLLE-MUSIGNY PREMIER CRU 2003
Red | 2011 up to 2021 **87**
A very deep color, typical of this vintage, and a very generous body, but the aromas lack definition and purity. The finish is astringent, which is contrary to this terroir (this wine is mainly from young vines in Musigny). We tasted bottle #1614.

MUSIGNY GRAND CRU VIEILLES VIGNES 1998
Red | 2011 up to 2015 **86**
The color is still young, but the wine has a singular lack of aromatic finesse, silkiness, and length for a Musigny and for a Vieilles Vignes. There is the same note of green wood tannins that marked the 1996s. Bottle #01265.

MUSIGNY GRAND CRU VIEILLES VIGNES 1996
Red | 2011 up to 2016 **88**
This wine is unquestionably vinous, but the aromas lack precision and finesse, with over-assertive tannins and an oaky note that is more rustic than we would hope.

MUSIGNY GRAND CRU VIEILLES VIGNES 1995
Red | 2011 up to 2015 **87**
More delicate and supple than the 1996, with a floral bouquet that is more typical of the cru, but the body is a bit lean and the texture lacks refinement. A very rigorous critique, of course, but the cru demands it!

Red: 29.2 acres; pinot 100%. White: 1.6 acres; chardonnay 100%. Annual production: 36,000 bottles

DOMAINE DE LA VOUGERAIE

Rue de l'Église
21700 Prémeaux-Prissey
Phone 00 33 3 80 62 48 25
Fax 00 33 3 80 61 25 44
vougeraie@domainedelavougeraie.com
www.domainedelavougeraie.com

This domaine has the makings of a future Burgundy star. Former winemaker Pascal Marchand introduced biodynamic techniques and started to steer the wines toward an ever more authentic expression of terroir, albeit at the expense of slightly too much robustness. The new incumbent, Pierre Vincent, is a worthy successor: entirely aware of how much remains to be done and very much in tune with the thinking of owners Nathalie and Jean-Charles Boisset.

Recently tasted
CHAMBOLLE-MUSIGNY 2007
Red | 2013 up to 2019 **93**

CORTON-CLOS DU ROI GRAND CRU 2007
Red | 2015 up to 2022 **93**

GEVREY-CHAMBERTIN PREMIER CRU BEL AIR 2007
Red | 2013 up to 2019 **90**

MAZOYÈRES-CHAMBERTIN GRAND CRU 2007
Red | 2017 up to 2025 **93**

NUITS-SAINT-GEORGES PREMIER CRU DAMODES 2007
Red | 2015 up to 2022 **92**

VOUGEOT CLOS DU PRIEURÉ 2007
White | 2012 up to 2019 **90**

VOUGEOT PREMIER CRU CLOS BLANC 2007
White | 2013 up to 2019 **93**

Older vintages
BEAUNE 2005
White | 2011 up to 2013 **90**
Slightly reduced, a candid style, straightforward, rather pure, with obvious finesse. To be drunk soon.

BEAUNE PREMIER CRU GRÈVES 2005
Red | 2011 up to 2017 **89**
A spicy nose, supple, not much flesh or complexity, but it has charm and style. One ought to be able to do better with this terroir.

BONNES-MARES GRAND CRU 2006
Red | 2011 up to 2026 **97**
A sumptuous success, full body, very natural in its aromatic development and perception of texture. Obviously a wine of great pedigree. Bravo!

Charmes-Chambertin grand cru 2005
Red | 2011 up to 2020   **92**
A nice wine, very meaty and complex, well-marked terroir, luscious tannins. Excellent!

Clos de Vougeot grand cru 2005
Red | 2011 up to 2030   **90**
Nice color, suave texture, perhaps a bit empty on the mid-palate, delicate tannins; an evolution of style is expected of this estate. A nice wine, but with no thrill.

Corton-Charlemagne grand cru 2005
White | 2011 up to 2020   **94**
Vinous, rich in alcohol, the terroir is quite marked, an imposing finish. A first-class terroir and a great future ahead.

Corton-Clos du Roi grand cru 2006
Red | 2011 up to 2024   **93**
Sumptuous, very rich aromatics, a fat wine, sensual, a touch less pure than some others.

Côte de Beaune Pierres Blanches 2005
White | 2011 up to 2015   **90**
A pale color, nice fullness and richness, a harmonious finish, very nice style. A great future ahead.

Gevrey-Chambertin 2006
Red | 2011 up to 2014   **87**
This tender, refined, immediately pleasing Village wine shows more charm and delicacy than the Évocelles.

Gevrey-Chambertin Évocelles 2006
Red | 2011 up to 2016   **86**
Nice blueberry character, a delicate wine, smooth texture, slightly lacking in body for such a well-situated terroir.

Mazoyères-Chambertin grand cru 2006
Red | 2011 up to 2026   **90**
Strong color, a powerful nose, enormous tannic concentration as is often the case from this vineyard and this vintage; a vigorous wine built to go the distance.

Musigny grand cru 2005
Red | 2011 up to 2025   **93**
Noble red-berry aromas, very balanced, an elegant wine, but here again, one ought to be able to get even more transparency and purity of expression from such a magical terroir.

Nuits-Saint-Georges premier cru Damodes 2006
Red | 2011 up to 2021   **93**
Dark-colored, fleshy, deep, splendid substance. The tannins are much more delicate and pure than in past vintages. A model of the Vosne section of the Côte de Nuits.

Nuits-Saint-Georges premier cru Les Damodes 2005
Red | 2011 up to 2025   **93**
Great color, nice oak influence, luscious and melty, very long, excellent pedigree, a high-level wine that will please true connoisseurs.

Pommard Petits Noizons 2006
Red | 2011 up to 2018   **88**
A black currant nose, slightly reduced, full body, the tannins firm and fat but not astringent. True to type and to expectations.

Puligny-Montrachet Corvée des Vignes 2005
White | 2011 up to 2013   **93**
A refined nose with grape blossoms and cinnamon, great finesse, a harmonious finish. The last wine produced by the estate from this vineyard, which it has sold.

Savigny-lès-Beaune premier cru Marconnets 2006
Red | 2011 up to 2021   **92**
An exemplary Savigny for the quality of its fruit character, its velvety texture but also its body, the discretion of its tannins and its aging potential.

Vougeot Clos du Prieuré 2006
White | 2011 up to 2014   **88**
More nerve but less fullness and length than the Le Clos Blanc, and undoubtedly less refined than the great white wines of the Côte de Beaune.

Vougeot Clos du Prieuré 2005
White | 2011 up to 2015   **89**
A nose of ferns, rather nervy, clean, direct, somewhat long, not very refined but with no concession to trends.

Vougeot premier cru Le Clos Blanc 2006
White | 2011 up to 2014   **89**
Sugared almonds on the nose, well balanced, a clean wine, rather full, less nerve on the finish than in the Côte de Beaune wines.

Vougeot premier cru Le Clos Blanc 2005
White | 2011 up to 2013   **90**
Ripe grapes, a suave texture, vanilla notes that need to mellow out, nice length, just a bit too much alcohol.

Red: 71.7 acres; pinot noir 100%. White: 12.4 acres; chardonnay 100%. Annual production: 140,000 bottles

Côte de Beaune Vineyards

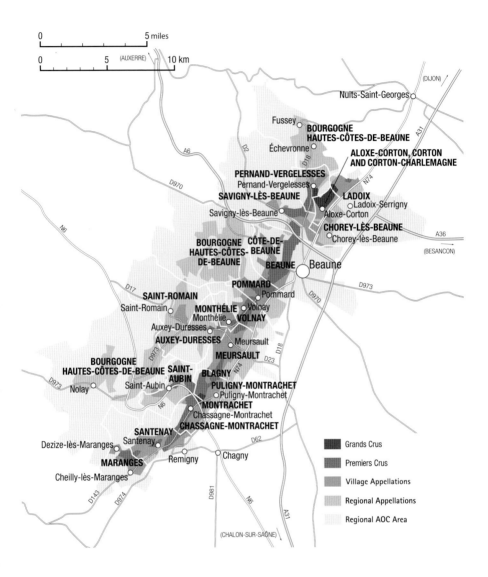

0 ___ 5 miles
0 ___ 5 (AUXERRE) 10 km

(DIJON)

Nuits-Saint-Georges

Fussey
BOURGOGNE HAUTES-CÔTES-DE-BEAUNE
Échevronne
ALOXE-CORTON, CORTON AND CORTON-CHARLEMAGNE
PERNAND-VERGELESSES
Pernand-Vergelesses
SAVIGNY-LÈS-BEAUNE
LADOIX
Ladoix-Serrigny
Savigny-lès-Beaune
Aloxe-Corton
CHOREY-LÈS-BEAUNE
Chorey-lès-Beaune
(BESANCON)
BOURGOGNE HAUTES-CÔTES-DE-BEAUNE
CÔTE-DE-BEAUNE
BEAUNE
Beaune
POMMARD
Pommard
SAINT-ROMAIN
Saint-Romain
MONTHÉLIE
Monthélie
VOLNAY
Volnay
Auxey-Duresses
AUXEY-DURESSES
Meursault
MEURSAULT
BOURGOGNE HAUTES-CÔTES-DE-BEAUNE
SAINT-AUBIN
BLAGNY
Saint-Aubin
Nolay
PULIGNY-MONTRACHET
Puligny-Montrachet
MONTRACHET
Chassagne-Montrachet
CHASSAGNE-MONTRACHET
SANTENAY
Santenay
Dezize-lès-Maranges
Chagny
MARANGES
Remigny
Cheilly-lès-Maranges
(CHALON-SUR-SAÔNE)

Grands Crus
Premiers Crus
Village Appellations
Regional Appellations
Regional AOC Area

DOMAINE D'ARDHUY

Clos des Langres
21700 Corgoloin
Phone 00 33 3 80 62 98 73
Fax 00 33 3 80 62 95 15
domaine@ardhuy.com
www.ardhuy.com

This huge domaine has progressed enormously since it became independent from the négociant side of the business. Its current offerings come from a wide variety of appellations and are noted for their tastefully classical form and texture. We have a particular weakness for the Nuits-Saint-Georges and the red Cortons that seem more accomplished than the whites.

Recently tasted
CORTON-CHARLEMAGNE GRAND CRU 2006
White | 2014 up to 2018   **92**

Older vintages
BEAUNE PREMIER CRU CHAMPIMONTS 2005
Red | 2011 up to 2020   **87**
Ripe, luscious grapes, with classic, delicately spicy nuances. The texture could be silkier.

BEAUNE PREMIER CRU
PETIT CLOS BLANC DES THEURONS 2006
White | 2011 up to 2021   **93**
For this cru, the 2006 surpasses the 2005, with more precision and elegance in the aromas and texture, and a very long finish with flavors of ripe plums.

BEAUNE PREMIER CRU
PETIT CLOS BLANC DES THEURONS 2005
White | 2011 up to 2013   **90**
This wine is all about finesse and delicacy. Judiciously applied oak, long, with balanced alcohol, but not vinous enough.

CLOS DE VOUGEOT GRAND CRU 2006
Red | 2011 up to 2026   **93**
Until now, this cuvée disappointed despite its remarkable placement above the Clos vineyard, but the 2006 is a success: powerful, meaty, racy, and long, with velvety tannins. Really very distinguished!

CLOS DE VOUGEOT GRAND CRU 2005
Red | 2011 up to 2020   **88**
Powerful and tannic, but the terroir is not as successfully defined as in the Cortons!

CORTON-CHARLEMAGNE GRAND CRU 2005
White | 2013 up to 2017   **88**
Precise, but flabby and lacking in energy: it will take a few years to see if the power of the terroir will bring it into balance.

CORTON-CLOS DU ROI GRAND CRU 2005
Red | 2011 up to 2030   **92**
Very ripe, deep, luscious but not better than the Renardes, which does not happen very often!

CORTON-RENARDES GRAND CRU 2005
Red | 2011 up to 2030   **93**
A splendid nose of plums, magnificent body, the texture of a truly great Corton: an immense future ahead.

CORTON GRAND CRU HAUTES MOUROTTES 2005
Red | 2011 up to 2030   **91**
A strong oak influence, but very full, firm, and tannic, almost a Bordeaux-like tension. A great future lies ahead.

GEVREY-CHAMBERTIN 2005
Red | 2011 up to 2017   **89**
Deeply colored, round, ripe, very mellow since its inception but not particularly refined in its taste or texture. This vintage's excellent grapes show through, but the terroir is not very present.

MEURSAULT LES PELLANS 2005
White | 2011 up to 2013   **89**
Very open and typical, with clear notes of toasted hazelnuts. To drink soon, while it is still young and charming.

NUITS-SAINT-GEORGES 2006
Red | 2011 up to 2018   **88**
Good, ripe grapes, a strong color and generous body. Not particularly delicate, but luscious and clean. In short, rather classic for this village!

NUITS-SAINT-GEORGES 2005
Red | 2011 up to 2020   **91**
A great bouquet of black currant, a nice smoky touch, substantial body, infinitely more complex than the Gevrey. Impressive for a Village-level wine!

SAVIGNY-LÈS-BEAUNE CLOS DES GODOTS 2006
Red | 2011 up to 2018   **86**
A classic nose of red berries and spices. A clean wine, well balanced, but the tannins still need to soften.

SAVIGNY-LÈS-BEAUNE PREMIER CRU PEUILLETS 2006
Red | 2011 up to 2021   **87**
Ripe grapes, good vinosity. A straightforward wine, rather rich in alcohol. Needs at least five years of aging.

VOLNAY PREMIER CRU CHANLIN 2005
Red | 2011 up to 2020   **89**
Good color, a superb floral nose, balanced body. A precise wine, the texture perhaps too simple in its tactile sensations.

Red: 79.1 acres; pinots noir and meunier 100%.
White: 19.8 acres; chardonnay 90%, pinot blanc, auxerrois 10%. Annual production: 180,000 bottles

DOMAINE D'AUVENAY

♆ ♆ ♆ ♆

21190 Saint-Romain Meursault
Phone 00 33 3 80 21 23 27
Fax 00 33 3 80 21 23 27

This micro-winery wholly owned by Lalou Bize-Leroy produces tiny quantities of sublimely intense and complex white wines even from vineyards overlooking Saint-Romain and more modest aligotés terroirs near Auxey-Duresses. It also owns two magnificent Côte de Nuits Grands Crus: a Bonnes-Mares and a Mazis-Chambertin. There is simply nothing in Burgundy to equal the splendor of this estate's Meursault, Puligny, and Auxey-Duresses white 2004 and 2005 vintages. Wines like these defy conventional scoring systems and make you realize just how far their competitors, including the most famous Burgundian white wines, lag behind.

Recently tasted

AUXEY-DURESSES 2007
White | 2012 up to 2017   92

BONNES-MARES GRAND CRU 2007
Red | 2017 up to 2022   95

CHEVALIER-MONTRACHET GRAND CRU 2007
White | 2011 up to 2019   97

MAZIS-CHAMBERTIN GRAND CRU 2007
Red | 2019 up to 2027   96

MEURSAULT NARVAUX 2007
White | 2015 up to 2019   95

MEURSAULT PREMIER CRU GOUTTES D'OR 2007
White | 2011 up to 2019   97

PULIGNY-MONTRACHET PREMIER CRU
EN LA RICHARDE 2007
White | 2011 up to 2017   95

Older vintages

AUXEY-DURESSES BOUTONNIÈRES 2006
White | 2011 up to 2013   92
The most delicate of the estate's Auxeys and the closest to the great Meursaults, with graceful notes of toast and hazelnut, remarkable body, and a remarkably natural, easy finish.

BONNES-MARES GRAND CRU 2006
Red | 2011 up to 2021   94
A floral nose, a tender, suave texture, marvelously mellow tannins despite the stems of the whole grape bunches. Long, complex, very much Chambolle in its perfect form!

BONNES-MARES GRAND CRU 2005
Red | 2011 up to 2050   96
Marvelously satiny, great aromatic complexity. A supremely balanced wine.

BOURGOGNE ALIGOTÉ 2006
White | 2011 up to 2014   91
Aligoté to perfection: supreme balance of alcohol and acidity, a pure and precise expression of the varietal. But the varietal character is nothing compared to the expression of the soil. A masterful wine and a lesson.

CHEVALIER-MONTRACHET 2006
White | 2011 up to 2018   98
A masterpiece and, in our opinion, the pinnacle in this vintage of white wines vinified by Lalou Bize-Leroy. A nose of grape blossoms, admirable purity, infinitely long, not a hint of heaviness due to the vintage; unfortunately the secrecy of how it was produced will limit its educational effect. It's impossible to come back down to earth after seeing this kind of quality.

CHEVALIER-MONTRACHET 2005
White | 2011 up to 2030   99
A sublimely delicate, velvety texture, but there is unfortunately very little volume. But whoever has tasted it knows what a Burgundy chardonnay is at its greatest.

CRIOTS-BÂTARD-MONTRACHET GRAND CRU 2006
White | 2011 up to 2013   96
A parenthesis (only 200 bottles were produced!) but unforgettable as the ultimate expression of the potential of the vintage, and essential for us to establish standards for Grands Crus. Monumental, complex, natural, a dream become wine!

MAZIS-CHAMBERTIN GRAND CRU 2006
Red | 2011 up to 2013   94
More deeply colored than the Bonnes-Mares, more taut and ample on the palate, more immediately impressive, but less refined and complex on the finish, with the firmness of the earthy tannins of this vineyard. Immense but slightly rustic. This is what you expect from a true Mazis!

MAZIS-CHAMBERTIN GRAND CRU 2005
Red | 2011 up to 2050   97
Intense color and body, an exceptional majesty of substance and flavor—the magic of a terroir when the viticulture respects it and the vinification magnifies it! Sadly so rare.

MEURSAULT NARVAUX 2006
White | 2011 up to 2016   93
Remarkable tension that nevertheless does not exclude unctuousness. A powerful wine, meaty, with naturally high alcohol; perhaps a bit less elegant than the 2004.

MEURSAULT NARVAUX 2005
White | 2011 up to 2025   **97**
Sublime finesse, an incredibly rich texture:
Meursault to perfection (or almost).

MEURSAULT PREMIER CRU GOUTTES D'OR 2006
White | 2011 up to 2016   **95**
A light note of bread on the nose, still marked
by yeast but with a truly splendid mid-palate
and finish, if you like roundness and sensuality.

MEURSAULT PREMIER CRU GOUTTES D'OR 2005
White | 2011 up to 2025   **98**
A blend of honey and hazelnuts, divinely
smooth, immensely long, an exemplary
cuvée. No Gouttes d'Or could measure up
to this one or even come near!

PULIGNY-MONTRACHET PREMIER CRU
EN LA RICHARDE 2006
White | 2011 up to 2016   **93**
Plenty of power and richness, with grape
blossom notes more delicate than in Meursault. Great purity, but proportionally less
refined than in 2005.

PULIGNY-MONTRACHET PREMIER CRU
EN LA RICHARDE 2005
White | 2011 up to 2020   **97**
Perhaps even more noble and complete than
Les Folatières. An irrestistible texture and
never-ending finish.

Red: 1.2 acres; pinot noir 100%. **White:** 8.4 acres;
aligoté 12%, chardonnay 88%. **Annual production:**
11,000 bottles

JEAN-CLAUDE BACHELET

1, rue de la Fontaine
21190 Saint-Aubin
Phone 00 33 3 80 21 31 01
Fax 00 33 3 80 21 91 71
info@domainebachelet.fr
www.jcbachelet.com

Judging by the 2006s we tasted, this is an
excellent source for whites, vinified with a
precise notion of their origins. The reds,
which we have been familiar with for some
time now, especially the Maranges,
weren't offered for tasting.

BIENVENUES-BÂTARD-MONTRACHET
GRAND CRU 2006
White | 2011 up to 2014   **92**
Exceedingly sumptuous on the nose and on
the palate, with great expression of this terroir, which is too quickly judged by some to
be inferior to the neighboring Bâtard. It
seems, on the contrary, to have a more slender, refined body to it than the latter, and in
any case, this example is a wonder of elegance.

CHASSAGNE-MONTRACHET
ENSEIGNIÈRES 2006
White | 2011 up to 2014   **87**
A fat, unctuous wine with a finish that is
voluptuous and easy to understand, both
dry and soft, more elegant on retro-olfaction
than on the attack. Stylish!

CHASSAGNE-MONTRACHET
VIEILLES VIGNES 2006
Red | 2011 up to 2014   **88**
A great deal of fruit on the nose: a pleasurable wine that is a perfect success, with
tannins that have already softened; the epitome of Chassagne.

PULIGNY-MONTRACHET PREMIER CRU
FOLATIÈRES 2006
White | 2011 up to 2016   **91**
These young winemakers have managed to
produce one of the best Folatières possible,
with deep, nuanced tastes that are pure and
fresh enough to age well.

Red: 9.9 acres; pinot noir 100%. **White:** 14.8 acres;
chardonnay 100%. **Annual production:** 60,000 bottles

DOMAINE BACHELET-RAMONET

11, rue du Parterre
21190 Chassagne-Montrachet
Phone 00 33 3 80 21 32 97
Fax 00 33 3 80 21 91 41
bachelet.ramonet@wanadoo.fr
www.bachelet-ramonet.com

This domaine has holdings in the very best sites in Chassagne, and it is unfortunate that in the past the family wasn't particularly interested in vinification, because they could have rivaled the best producers. From time to time one of their wines stood out, especially the whites, but the 2006 vintage seems to have marked a clear evolution toward higher quality, with rich, focused, and well-defined wines that are in some cases even outstanding.

Recently tasted

CHASSAGNE-MONTRACHET PREMIER CRU
CAILLERETS 2007
White | 2012 up to 2017   87

CHASSAGNE-MONTRACHET PREMIER CRU
LA GRANDE MONTAGNE VIEILLES VIGNES 2007
White | 2012 up to 2017   91

Older vintages

BÂTARD-MONTRACHET GRAND CRU 2006
White | 2011 up to 2018   94
A noble, racy wine with grape blossom aromas, impeccably defined, straightforward. An immense step forward from the previous vintages. A future classic of the vintage!

CHASSAGNE-MONTRACHET 2006
White | 2011 up to 2016   89
A revolution! A nose of rare frankness, a straightforward wine, taut, elegant, with integrated oak, harvested much riper than in the recent past but not heavy, and with a freshness that will last a long time.

CHASSAGNE-MONTRACHET PREMIER CRU
CAILLERETS 2006
White | 2011 up to 2013   90
Excellent volume on the palate, a subtle nose, still not very open, great finesse in the tannins. Subtle aromatic nuances that should make for a great wine.

CHASSAGNE-MONTRACHET PREMIER CRU
GRANDES RUCHOTTES 2006
White | 2011 up to 2014   90
Very classy on the nose and palate, with notes of white fruit, lemon, vanilla, and grape blossoms. A great future ahead.

Red: 16.1 acres; pinot 100%. White: 17.3 acres; aligoté 14%, chardonnay 86%. Annual production: 50,000 bottles

DOMAINE ROGER BELLAND

3, rue de la Chapelle
BP 13
21590 Santenay
Phone 00 33 3 80 20 60 95
Fax 00 33 3 80 20 63 93
belland.roger@wanadoo.fr
www.domaine-belland-roger.com

This large property—the largest on the southern Côte de Beaune—has a long-standing reputation as a supplier of red and white wines at every price point. All of its offerings are very seriously crafted and usually quite fresh and eloquent. They testify to a constant drive for improvement that may become more dynamic still under the new generation, much to the satisfaction of devotees. The most consistently dependable of all the estate's offerings (red and white wines alike) is the Chassagne-Montrachet Clos Pitois, from a particularly well-exposed parcel in the celebrated Morgeot vineyard. Like all of the Morgeot offerings, the Clos Pitois strikes a happy balance between power and finesse.

Recently tasted

CRIOTS-BÂTARD-MONTRACHET GRAND CRU 2007
White | 2015 up to 2019   88

MARANGES PREMIER CRU LA FUSSIÈRE 2007
Red | 2012 up to 2018   90

POMMARD LES CRAS 2007
Red | 2013 up to 2017   88

SANTENAY PREMIER CRU BEAUREGARD 2007
Red | 2013 up to 2017   89

SANTENAY PREMIER CRU LES GRAVIÈRES 2007
Red | 2013 up to 2017   89

VOLNAY PREMIER CRU LES SANTENOTS 2007
Red | 2014 up to 2019   90

Older vintages

CHASSAGNE-MONTRACHET PREMIER CRU
CLOS PITOIS 2005
Red | 2011 up to 2017   89
Deeper in color, more body, softer and more complex than the Santenays.

CHASSAGNE-MONTRACHET PREMIER CRU
MORGEOT CLOS PITOIS 2006
White | 2011 up to 2016   89
Still closed down but very typically Morgeot, solidly built but refined, complex, racy, very well made.

CHASSAGNE-MONTRACHET PREMIER CRU
MORGEOT CLOS PITOIS 2005
White | 2011 up to 2013 **88**
Straightforward, fresh, but not very complex.

CRIOTS-BÂTARD-MONTRACHET
GRAND CRU 2005
White | 2011 up to 2013 **91**
Ample, lemony, with clearly racy terroir but not enough work on the yeast autolysis. More straightforward than refined.

POMMARD LES CRAS 2005
Red | 2011 up to 2013 **85**
Truffles on the nose, with acceptable body and a slight lack of personality.

PULIGNY-MONTRACHET PREMIER CRU
LES CHAMPS GAINS 2005
White | 2011 up to 2013 **90**
More floral and ethereal than the Clos Pitois. Nice acidity, a clean wine that is perhaps too one-note.

SANTENAY CHARMES 2005
Red | 2011 up to 2015 **86**
Middling in color, with a spicy nose. A simple, straightforward wine that gives a suitable definition of the terroir, but with too much rigidity on the finish.

SANTENAY PREMIER CRU BEAUREGARD 2005
Red | 2011 up to 2015 **87**
A fairly precise floral nose, but still a somewhat severe texture.

SANTENAY PREMIER CRU LA COMME 2006
Red | 2011 up to 2016 **87**
Deeply colored, well-rounded wine made from ripe grapes, with a particularly pleasant texture.

SANTENAY PREMIER CRU LA COMME 2005
Red | 2011 up to 2015 **88**
A fairly fine floral nose, supple body, slight lack of fleshiness, with tannins that are less rustic than the Charmes.

SANTENAY PREMIER CRU LES GRAVIÈRES 2005
Red | 2011 up to 2013 **88**
Better defined on the nose than all the Santenays, with a bit more flesh and raciness on the palate.

Red: 45.7 acres; pinot noir 100%. White: 10.4 acres; chardonnay 100%. Annual production: 100,000 bottles

DOMAINE SIMON BIZE ET FILS

12, rue du Chanoine-Donin
21420 Savigny-lès-Beaune
Phone 00 33 3 80 21 50 57
Fax 00 33 3 80 21 58 17
domaine.bize@wanadoo.fr
www.domainebize.fr

The Savignys from this estate are definitely the most elegant produced today, for those who seek a red Burgundy with red-fruit aromas and that silky texture that comes mainly from whole-bunch fermentation. The tannins can be rather taut sometimes and the grapes picked rather too early—but then they do ripen early in this village, which is a problem given the very warm vintages of late. The whites are largely inspired by Jean-Marie Raveneau's Chablis wines and show outstanding finesse and mineral character.

Recently tasted
SAVIGNY-LÈS-BEAUNE 2007
White | 2011 up to 2015 **90**

SAVIGNY-LÈS-BEAUNE PREMIER CRU
AUX GUETTES 2007
Red | 2015 up to 2019 **93**

SAVIGNY-LÈS-BEAUNE PREMIER CRU
FOURNAUX 2007
Red | 2011 up to 2015 **86**

SAVIGNY-LÈS-BEAUNE PREMIER CRU
LES VERGELESSES 2007
Red | 2012 up to 2017 **93**

Older vintages
SAVIGNY-LÈS-BEAUNE PREMIER CRU
AUX VERGELESSES 2005
White | 2011 up to 2013 **88**
Heavier and more caramelized than the whites. Ends on a less pure note than Perrières.

SAVIGNY-LÈS-BEAUNE PREMIER CRU
LES MARCONNETS 2006
Red | 2011 up to 2021 **94**
As often with young wines at blind tastings, this bottling stands out above the others for its extra body and its wonderful satiny texture, the essence of great pinot ripened to perfection.

SAVIGNY-LÈS-BEAUNE PREMIER CRU
LES MARCONNETS 2005
Red | 2011 up to 2015 **93**
Great color, exceptional body, great nobility of texture and taste: a well-rounded Savigny made for aging!

SAVIGNY-LÈS-BEAUNE PREMIER CRU
LES VERGELESSES 2006
Red | 2011 up to 2016   **92**
Extreme aromatic purity and skill in the barrel treatment, a very elegant, even sophisticated wine in its aromas, and one that has retained stunning freshness!

SAVIGNY-LÈS-BEAUNE PREMIER CRU
LES VERGELESSES 2005
Red | 2011 up to 2013   **92**
A fine, vanilla nose, generous body, and magnificent freshness. Bravo!

SAVIGNY-LÈS-BEAUNE PREMIER CRU
LES VERGELESSES 2006
Red | 2011 up to 2018   **90**
Wonderfully aromatic, with notes of subtly spicy peony, acceptable body, racy tannins—but it lacks something at a higher level.

Red: 37.1 acres; pinot 100%. White: 17.3 acres; chardonnay 100%. Annual production: 100,000 bottles

DOMAINE HENRI BOILLOT

1, rue des Angles
21190 Volnay
Phone 00 33 3 80 21 61 90
Fax 00 33 3 80 21 69 84

This estate with its superb heritage of red and white vines alike is now run by "Kiki" Boillot, Jean-Marc's brother. We have been impressed for some years now with the astonishing purity and mineral edge of its white wines and the aromatic charm of its reds. The success of these exemplary wines is a testament to unwavering perfectionism. The estate-produced 2005s raise the bar even higher and rank among the loftiest Burgundies currently in production.

Recently tasted

BEAUNE PREMIER CRU CLOS DU ROI 2007
Red | 2013 up to 2017   **89**

VOLNAY PREMIER CRU LES CHEVRETS 2007
Red | 2017 up to 2025   **94**

VOLNAY PREMIER CRU LES FRÉMIETS 2007
Red | 2011 up to 2019   **91**

Older vintages

MEURSAULT PREMIER CRU
LES GENEVRIÈRES 2006
White | 2011 up to 2016   **92**
Rare acidity for a Meursault, great aromatic finesse, a little more nuanced and complex than La Mouchère.

MEURSAULT PREMIER CRU
LES GENEVRIÈRES 2005
White | 2011 up to 2020   **95**
Wonderful harmony. Everything we like in a great Meursault is here, though it requires more age!

PULIGNY-MONTRACHET PREMIER CRU
CLOS DE LA MOUCHÈRE 2006
White | 2011 up to 2016   **91**
Nicely wiry, with exemplary integration of its oak, very typical lemongrass notes that nonetheless blend seamlessly into saline, taut notes on the palate, due to the rocky terroir of this parcel, the largest one in the village held by a single winemaker.

PULIGNY-MONTRACHET PREMIER CRU
CLOS DE LA MOUCHÈRE 2005
White | 2011 up to 2017   **95**
This has exemplary finesse, purity, and transparency in the expression of its terroir. A great wine.

PULIGNY-MONTRACHET PREMIER CRU
LES PUCELLES 2006
White | 2011 up to 2018   **93**
The most refined and subtle of the domaine's white Premiers Crus, with a tautness that is truly rare for the vintage!

PULIGNY-MONTRACHET PREMIER CRU
LES PUCELLES 2005
White | 2011 up to 2017   **94**
A noble aroma of flowering vines, elegant, not heavy at all, great persistence, a very pure finish that expresses its origins well.

VOLNAY PREMIER CRU EN CAILLERET 2006
Red | 2011 up to 2021   **94**
Immense finesse and velvety texture; a dream Volnay—and confirmation that the vinification has subtly evolved toward a timelessly classical style in form and taste.

VOLNAY PREMIER CRU EN CAILLERET 2005
Red | 2011 up to 2025   **95**
Remarkable refinement to its texture and fruit, an aristocratic wine that has been superbly crafted to conserve all of its natural beauty.

VOLNAY PREMIER CRU EN CHEVRET 2006
Red | 2011 up to 2018   **94**
Certainly the bottling to follow at the domaine, with the same raciness and refinement to its texture as the Cailleret, which just happens to be next door! One of the most seductive wines from the Côte de Beaune.

VOLNAY PREMIER CRU EN CHEVRET 2005
Red | 2011 up to 2025   **93**
A fine aroma of hawthorn, impeccable body, refined tannins, an elegant, well-rounded Volnay.

VOLNAY PREMIER CRU LES FRÉMIETS 2006
Red | 2011 up to 2018   **93**
Intense ruby color, very precise nose, an irresistible taste of violets, suave texture, great finesse to its tannins, exemplary vinification.

VOLNAY PREMIER CRU LES FRÉMIETS 2005
Red | 2011 up to 2020   **93**
The domaine's great specialty for reds: more supple, tender, and quickly open than the two other Premiers Crus; just as much charm, but more accessible.

Red: 17.3 acres; pinot noir 100%. White: 17.3 acres; chardonnay 100%. Annual production: 70,000 bottles

DOMAINE BONNEAU DU MARTRAY
21420 Pernand-Vergelesses
Phone 00 33 3 80 21 50 64
Fax 00 33 3 80 21 57 19
courrier@bonneaudumartray.com
www.bonneaudumartray.com

Some of the mid-1990 offerings, like a good many other Burgundies, show signs of premature aging, probably due to defective corks. But mostly this magnificent estate produces timeless Corton-Charlemagnes of crystalline purity, and a red Corton that grows classier and more precise with every passing vintage. Thanks to its immense size (for a Burgundy), this holding can market several vintages, and its wines are not too highly allocated. Recent vintages have delivered a flawless performance; only time will tell whether the cork will let them down.

CORTON-CHARLEMAGNE GRAND CRU 2006
White | 2016 up to 2021   **95**
The character of this vintage disturbed the habitual style of the estate and gave a fatter, rounder wine, a bit less precise in its youth than the 2005 at the same age, but it hasn't had its final say yet!

CORTON GRAND CRU 2005
Red | 2011 up to 2021   **92**
Great finesse and terroir definition, more marked than the white version at the same age! Very distinguished, almost charming tannins, which is rare in this rather austere cuvée.

CORTON GRAND CRU 2004
Red | 2011 up to 2030   **95**
Very racy aromas of black fruit, magnificent body, and very noble tannins. With a great future ahead, this is one of the greatest reds of the Côte de Beaune today.

CORTON-CHARLEMAGNE GRAND CRU 2003
White | 2011 up to 2018   **94**
This wine is starting to find itself and has become significantly more refined since its birth: it shows the slight caramel scent of this vintage's heat wave, but it is young and full.

Red: 3.7 acres; pinot noir 100%. White: 23.5 acres; chardonnay 100%. Annual production: 53,000 bottles

BOUCHARD PÈRE ET FILS

15, rue du Château
BP 70
21202 Beaune
Phone 00 33 3 80 24 80 24
Fax 00 33 3 80 24 80 52
contact@bouchard-pereetfils.com
www.bouchard-pereetfils.com

This great estate is now fully back on form, with a record of ten successive vintages that meet the highest standards of vinification and aging potential. The connoisseur will of course prefer the domaine wines, produced from the greatest lieux-dits on both the Côte de Nuits and the Côte de Beaune—a really unique choice of red and white wines. The 2003 and 2005 reds have everything it takes to age admirably in keeping with the terroir and the vintage. The 2004 white wine, though relatively unknown, will deliver some of the most exciting bottles ever, four to five years from now.

Recently tasted

BONNES-MARES GRAND CRU 2007
Red | 2017 up to 2027   96

CHAPELLE-CHAMBERTIN GRAND CRU 2007
Red | 2017 up to 2022   94

CHEVALIER-MONTRACHET GRAND CRU 2007
White | 2015 up to 2022   94

CLOS DE VOUGEOT GRAND CRU 2007
Red | 2022 up to 2029   96

CORTON-CHARLEMAGNE GRAND CRU 2007
White | 2015 up to 2019   94

CORTON GRAND CRU LE CORTON 2007
Red | 2011 up to 2013   95

ECHÉZEAUX GRAND CRU 2007
Red | 2015 up to 2027   94

MEURSAULT LES CLOUS 2007
White | 2011 up to 2017   89

MEURSAULT PREMIER CRU GENEVRIÈRES 2007
White | 2012 up to 2017   93

MONTHÉLIE CHAMPS FULLIOTS 2007
Red | 2015 up to 2019   89

MONTRACHET GRAND CRU 2007
White | 2017 up to 2022   95

NUITS-SAINT-GEORGES PREMIER CRU
LES CAILLES 2007
Red | 2017 up to 2027   95

NUITS-SAINT-GEORGES PREMIER CRU
PORRETS SAINT-GEORGES 2007
Red | 2017 up to 2022   93

VOLNAY PREMIER CRU CLOS DES CHÊNES 2007
Red | 2017 up to 2022   93

VOLNAY PREMIER CRU TAILLEPIEDS 2007
Red | 2015 up to 2019   92

Older vintages

BEAUNE CLOS SAINT-LANDRY 2006
White | 2011 up to 2016   93
Little by little this prestigious Beaune cuvée finds its features: the pear nose has a brilliant purity, and the texture of the wine marks a clear progression in volume and nobility compared to the Beaune du Château.

BEAUNE DU CHÂTEAU 2006
White | 2011 up to 2014   89
The estate made about 70,000 bottles of this harmonious, clean wine, ideal for restaurants.

BEAUNE DU CHÂTEAU 2005
White | 2011 up to 2015   87
Pale, very tender, supple, subtle, no oak domination. A very agreeable wine even if the personality of the terroir is not very pronounced.

BEAUNE DU CHÂTEAU PREMIER CRU 2006
Red | 2011 up to 2018   90
To our taste, this wine is a greater success than the Blanc and is truly stunning for its aromatic delicacy and its very agreeable texture. More than 100,000 bottles produced, which makes it perfect for high-end restaurants.

BEAUNE DU CHÂTEAU PREMIER CRU 2005
Red | 2011 up to 2017   88
A pretty color, fruity, generous, spicy, very stable. Good aging potential.

BEAUNE PREMIER CRU CLOS DE LA MOUSSE 2006
Red | 2011 up to 2021   92
A melty texture, and a pretty nose that nears perfection with red berries and a few spicy notes: delectable, very "Beaune." Hidden under its pleasant exterior is a good structure that will allow for very graceful aging.

BEAUNE PREMIER CRU LES MARCONNETS 2005
Red | 2011 up to 2025   93
Bluish color, great vigor. Rich and complex.

BEAUNE PREMIER CRU LES TEURONS 2005
Red | 2011 up to 2030   92
Notes of sugared almonds. A firm wine, straightforward, long, with good aging potential.

BONNES-MARES GRAND CRU 2005
Red | 2011 up to 2030   **95**
Full-bodied, powerful, suave, complex; still immensely young!

BOURGOGNE CUVÉE DES MOINES 2007
Red | 2011 up to 2013   **86**
A magnificent suaveness, great length, and complexity.

CHAMBERTIN-CLOS DE BÈZE GRAND CRU 2006
Red | 2011 up to 2030   **97**
Great aromatic distinction, a sumptuous body for this vintage. The majesty of the terroir is very clear. This wine gained a lot from being harvested a little earlier than others, before the grapes started to shrivel.

CHAMBERTIN-CLOS DE BÈZE GRAND CRU 2005
Red | 2011 up to 2030   **96**
Very complex, racy, ample, with refined tannins and the inimitable pedigree of the terroir.

CHAMBOLLE-MUSIGNY 2005
Red | 2011 up to 2030   **91**
Estate harvested fruit. Strong color, remarkable intensity in body and aromas for a Village-level wine. An intelligently reductive vinification for a long life in bottle.

CHEVALIER-MONTRACHET GRAND CRU LA CABOTTE 2006
White | 2011 up to 2026   **97**
A special selection from a vineyard site touching Montrachet. A wine sublime in its purity, finesse, and precision. One of the indisputable pinnacles of Burgundy today, but unfortunately produced in tiny quantities.

CHEVALIER-MONTRACHET GRAND CRU LA CABOTTE 2005
White | 2013 up to 2025   **94**
Ultrapure, almost fluid in appearance, but the finish is very long and well coated. Above all the already integrated oak gives hope for great things to come in another five to seven years.

CLOS DE VOUGEOT GRAND CRU 2006
Red | 2011 up to 2030   **96**
There are two cuvées of this wine. That of the domaine is far better, so look closely at the label. It's difficult to imagine a more successful 2006 red. Outstanding in all ways ever since its birth.

CLOS DE VOUGEOT GRAND CRU 2005
Red | 2011 up to 2030   **93**
Closed on the nose, a lot of substance, good harmony for cellaring; classic chocolate notes on the palate.

CORTON-CHARLEMAGNE GRAND CRU 2006
White | 2011 up to 2026   **97**
The greatest of the 2006 whites on the day of our tasting. Tremendously powerful in its elegance, with an immediate, noble aroma of verbena, which does not show up every year in this wine. The monumental body might be the most complete ever produced since the Henriot family bought the estate.

CORTON-CHARLEMAGNE GRAND CRU 2005
White | 2013 up to 2030   **95**
A complete wine, pale and discreet yet marvelously subtle and refined in its aromas and texture; more freshness than the classic Burgundian style but also more purity.

CORTON GRAND CRU LE CORTON 2006
Red | 2016 up to 2030   **94**
Very pure, straightforward, not much charm for the moment but quite racy on the finish. Not ready yet.

CORTON GRAND CRU LE CORTON 2005
Red | 2011 up to 2030   **94**
Power, rigor, precision, and noble tannins. This wine has a great future.

ECHÉZEAUX GRAND CRU 2006
Red | 2011 up to 2028   **96**
Marvelously refined aromas, a delicate texture, and tannins of a rare elegance. This is Echézeaux as we dream of it.

ECHÉZEAUX GRAND CRU 2005
Red | 2011 up to 2025   **95**
Very rich, complete, suave. Complex, long, subtle, very classy.

GEVREY-CHAMBERTIN PREMIER CRU CAZETIERS 2006
Red | 2011 up to 2026   **95**
A magnificent success for a cuvée produced in very small quantities. One of the loveliest textures of all the Côte de Nuits wines, with all the integrity of flavor of a whole-cluster vinification.

MEURSAULT 2005
White | 2011 up to 2015   **86**
The estate wine, pale, very clean and straightforward. Not very complex but not heavy, rather tender, which makes it ready to drink now.

MEURSAULT LES CLOUS 2006
White | 2011 up to 2016   **92**
This wine seems long and linear, but it hides a superb concentration, and its delicate, highly precise fruit is exceptional. An airy Meursault, pure, truly exemplary!

Meursault Premier Cru Genevrières 2006
White | 2011 up to 2018   **95**
More body than the Goutte d'Or, but paradoxically also more purity, more delicate aromatics, and a greater length. A marvelous example of the potential of the vintage, produced in large quantities for this bottling!

Meursault Premier Cru Goutte d'Or 2006
White | 2011 up to 2016   **93**
Wonderfully delicate aromatics. This wine is all about finesse and charm, the grapes ripened to perfection. Very graceful.

Meursault Premier Cru Perrières 2006
White | 2011 up to 2021   **96**
Admirably noble aromatics, exemplary purity and transparence in the expression of terroir. A wine of great pedigree, it is bound to be the most complete of the stunning line of Meursaults from this domaine!

Meursault Premier Cru Perrières 2005
White | 2011 up to 2025   **94**
A great success: a very pure wine with subtle aromas of honey and grape blossom, superlative finesse on the palate, and just as racy as the Chevalier-Montrachet!

Monthélie Champs Fulliots 2006
Red | 2011 up to 2018   **89**
Excellently integrated oak. An elegant and racy wine, subtly spicy, very similar to the best Volnays and with just as much flesh.

Montrachet Grand Cru 2006
White | 2018 up to 2030   **97**
Typical of this area of Puligny, without the almost exotic honey notes of a Chassagne-Montrachet. Taut, full, complete, ultra-noble but with a reserve that makes it perfect for connoisseurs who know to wait at least ten years!

Montrachet Grand Cru 2005
White | 2011 up to 2030   **96**
Very pale compared to the others, an immense aromatic nobility despite a distinguished reserve that is normal for a wine this old. It has a marvelous purity that is the signature of this estate.

Nuits-Saint-Georges Premier Cru Les Cailles 2006
Red | 2011 up to 2021   **93**
A superbly velvety texture, not very full-bodied but long, suave, subtle. Very feminine for a Nuits.

Nuits-Saint-Georges Premier Cru Les Cailles 2005
Red | 2011 up to 2020   **91**
A strong color. The wine is a little reduced, with cassis on the nose, spicier on the palate, full body, straightforward, complex, but without the same flair as in 2003.

Nuits-Saint-Georges Premier Cru Porrets Saint-Georges 2006
Red | 2011 up to 2021   **93**
Ripe grapes, a nice, spicy nose and feminine texture. A racier finish than the nose would suggest.

Pommard Premier Cru Pezerolles 2006
Red | 2011 up to 2021   **95**
A remarkable cuvée with great color and a firmer body than the Volnays (which is normal); delicately aromatic, joining licorice and violet, which suggests that the flavor and the tannins are perfectly in place!

Volnay Premier Cru Clos des Chênes 2006
Red | 2011 up to 2026   **95**
A rich color, and on the day of our tasting even more nuanced and complex than the Caillerets. A perfect union of charm, finesse, and density, given that the grapes of this vintage were naturally rich in sugar.

Volnay Premier Cru Clos des Chênes 2005
Red | 2011 up to 2030   **93**
An excellently rich energy. Deep, tannic, complete.

Volnay Premier Cru Les Caillerets 2006
Red | 2011 up to 2021   **94**
A beautiful color, nose of violets, a fleshy wine, velvety, complex, seductive—but a bit overshadowed by the unusual success of the Taillepieds.

Volnay Premier Cru Les Caillerets 2005
Red | 2011 up to 2030   **95**
Violet dominates the nose; a wine of great distinction: complete, elegant, very long and subtle.

Volnay Premier Cru Taillepieds 2006
Red | 2011 up to 2030   **94**
The color is barely denser than that of the Beaunes. A magnificent nose of cherry and violet; ripe grapes, the texture of a good or even great vintage. Undoubtedly the estate's most elegant cuvée of this cru in decades!

Volnay Premier Cru Taillepieds 2005
Red | 2011 up to 2050   **90**
Deeply colored, rich, tannic, long, powerful, clean.

Vosne-Romanée 2006
Red | 2011 up to 2021   **93**
The best Villages-level cuvée vinified by the winery in 2006, aromatically the most noble and complex, the most faithful to the style that connoisseurs are used to. Exceptionally complex and undoubtedly superior to the 2005.

Red: 212.5 acres; pinot 100%. White: 108.7 acres; chardonnay 100%. Annual production: 600,000 bottles

DOMAINE J.M. BOULEY

🝒 🝒 🝒 🝒 🝒

12, chemin de la Cave
21190 Volnay
Phone 00 33 3 80 21 62 33
Fax 00 33 3 80 21 64 78
jeanmarc.bouley@wanadoo.fr
www.jean-marc-bouley.com

This artisanal winery, endowed with wonderful terroirs in Volnay and Pommard, enchanted us with the elegance and precision of the 2006 vinifications, receiving some of our highest marks. It seems that the young Thomas Bouley is one of the most talented rising stars of the village. He belongs to a group of passionate young winemakers that get together and taste wines from all over the world, broadening their horizons in order to make better wines. He will be one to rely on in the future.

Recently tasted

BEAUNE PREMIER CRU REVERSÉES 2007
Red | 2011 up to 2013   85

POMMARD 2007
Red | 2014 up to 2017   84

POMMARD PREMIER CRU FREMIERS 2007
Red | 2014 up to 2019   89

VOLNAY 2007
Red | 2011 up to 2017   86

VOLNAY CLOS DE LA CAVE 2007
Red | 2012 up to 2017   87

VOLNAY PREMIER CRU CLOS DES CHÊNES 2007
Red | 2011 up to 2017   89

VOLNAY PREMIER CRU EN CARELLE 2007
Red | 2012 up to 2017   88

Older vintages

POMMARD PREMIER CRU FREMIERS 2006
Red | 2011 up to 2016   88
Slightly reductive but very pleasant aromas of raspberries, spices, and mocha. Supple, delicate tannins, good persistence for a linear wine, but suave and very "feminine" for the appellation.

POMMARD PREMIER CRU RUGIENS 2006
Red | 2011 up to 2016   89
Spicy notes on the nose, supple, but the tannins are firmer than on the Fremiers; long and lean, serpentine, a slight lack of density on the mid-palate.

VOLNAY 2006
Red | 2011 up to 2018   93
Glints of blue, a complex and refined nose, very characteristic, with aristocratic floral notes; excellent oak influence, very high-quality tannic extraction, masterful vinification.

VOLNAY CLOS DE LA CAVE 2006
Red | 2011 up to 2016   92
Magnificent notes of roses and dark chocolate on the nose, very generous, coating tannins. A distinguished and splendidly built Village wine.

VOLNAY PREMIER CRU CLOS DES CHÊNES 2006
Red | 2011 up to 2021   94
Another complete wine from this producer, combining grace, elegance, and a full build, magnificently distinguished tannins; a great future ahead.

VOLNAY PREMIER CRU EN CARELLE 2006
Red | 2011 up to 2021   93
Very unctuous and powerful, a suave texture, very accomplished modern vinification: we are pleased to see that the natural class of the terroir is perfectly respected.

Red: 18 acres; pinot noir 100%. **Annual production:** 35,000 bottles

DOMAINE MICHEL BOUZEREAU ET FILS

3, rue de la Planche-Meunière
21190 Meursault
Phone 00 33 3 80 21 20 74
Fax 00 33 3 80 21 66 41
michel-bouzereau-et-fils@wanadoo.fr

This is a very good producer, who makes better-quality whites than reds. At their best they have finesse and purity, and in general, flavors that evolve rather quickly, but the wines have good longevity. At the end of the 1990s too many bottles were maderized before their time, but recent vintages have regained their traditional balance. Of the 2005 reds, only the Pommard can truly be recommended; the whites have more class and length. The 2006s are similar.

Beaune premier cru Vignes Franches 2005
Red | 2011 up to 2013   88
Spicy nose, somewhat reductive and animal, a soft attack, rather dry tannins; pleasant but lacks fleshiness.

Meursault Le Limozin 2006
White | 2011 up to 2014   89
Fresh, with a complex aroma of white and yellow fruit and vanilla. Great finesse for a wine that is easy, long, and ideal for restaurant wine lists.

Meursault Le Limozin 2005
White | 2011 up to 2015   90
Fat, a slight hazelnut nose, not too ripe grapes, nice persistence; solid and tasty.

Meursault Les Grands Charrons 2005
White | 2011 up to 2015   88
A bit of mercaptan on the nose, fat, ample, tannic; will age better than several earlier vintages.

Meursault Les Tessons 2005
White | 2011 up to 2015   93
Very racy, with much more finesse than the other Village wines from the domaine, with length, precision, and great style. Excellent.

Meursault premier cru Charmes 2006
White | 2011 up to 2016   92
An unusual nose with a fleeting note of clove; fine and pure texture, which is habitual for the domaine; long, hides its dry extract well. A classy wine.

Meursault premier cru Charmes 2005
White | 2011 up to 2013   90
Supple, easy, a little more commonplace than the Tessons. You can feel the vintage's lack of acidity.

Meursault premier cru Genevrières 2005
White | 2011 up to 2017   92
Great finesse, excellent overall balance, very clean, very subtle; a return to the excellence of yore.

Meursault premier cru Perrières 2005
White | 2011 up to 2016   90
Pure but less vinous and well-defined than the Genevrières. A tiny production!

Pommard Cras 2005
Red | 2011 up to 2017   89
Deeper in body and texture than the Beaune, with a nice truffled nose that is typical of the sector. A Village wine that is very representative of the village.

Puligny-Montrachet premier cru Champ Gain 2005
White | 2011 up to 2013   89
Very pleasant and balanced, with a slight touch of citrus, but not very complex. More pleasant than the 2005 Cailleret.

Puligny-Montrachet premier cru Le Cailleret 2006
White | 2011 up to 2018   92
An intense, racy nose, with considerable complexity, fine length; a wine full of elegance, just as we like them from this exceptional terroir.

Puligny-Montrachet premier cru Le Cailleret 2005
White | 2011 up to 2013   88
Too fluid and common for this terroir; curiously less successful than the Meursaults!

Red: 6.7 acres; pinot 100%. White: 23 acres; aligoté 22%, chardonnay 78%. Annual production: 70,000 bottles

DOMAINE BOUZEREAU GRUÈRE ET FILLES

🐝 🐝 🐝 🐝 🐝

22 A, rue de la Velle
21190 Meursault
Phone 00 33 3 80 21 20 05
Fax 00 33 3 80 21 68 16
hubert.bouzereau.gruere@libertysur.fr

Here is a bold family winery: Hubert Bouzereau and his two daughters farm almost thirty acres in Meursault and Chassagne. After a timid start at the beginning of the millennium, the wines became much more focused and personal, and are wonderful expressions of great terroirs. The wines are modern in their freshness and immediate purity, classic in their never-ending nuances. A winery to watch, especially since the family is so charming.

Recently tasted

CHASSAGNE-MONTRACHET 2007
White | 2011 up to 2015   89

CHASSAGNE-MONTRACHET BLANCHOT DESSOUS 2007
White | 2011 up to 2017   91

MEURSAULT PREMIER CRU CHARMES 2007
White | 2013 up to 2019   85

MEURSAULT PREMIER CRU GENEVRIÈRES 2007
White | 2012 up to 2017   91

Older vintages

CHASSAGNE-MONTRACHET 2006
White | 2011 up to 2016   90
Elegant notes of white flowers. A nice wine with great finesse and pedigree, and above all very well balanced.

CHASSAGNE-MONTRACHET BLANCHOT DESSOUS 2006
White | 2011 up to 2016   91
An absolutely remarkable pedigree and complexity for a Village-level wine, which makes sense when you know the vineyard is next door to Montrachet! This wine does honor to the talent of the young winemakers, who are hardworking and precise in their vinification.

CHASSAGNE-MONTRACHET PREMIER CRU CHAUMÉES 2006
White | 2011 up to 2016   91
Power and intensity, but also luminosity in the color and flavor. A long, complex wine, remarkable given that the grapes were extremely ripe.

MEURSAULT LES TILLETS 2006
White | 2011 up to 2014   87
A great deal of generosity in shape and flavor. The finish is a welcome change after a slightly heavy mid-palate, which is typical of the vintage.

MEURSAULT PREMIER CRU GENEVRIÈRES 2006
White | 2011 up to 2018   93
A very distinguished nose and palate. Harmonious and long, with the classic notes of this cru, more floral than toasted or buttery. A great wine of pleasure.

PULIGNY-MONTRACHET 2006
White | 2011 up to 2014   87
A very open fruit character. A clean, fat wine, quite pleasant. An almost Muscat note evokes certain wines of Alsace!

Red: 9.8 acres; pinot noir 100%. **White:** 19.8 acres; chardonnay 100%. **Annual production:** 45,000 bottles

DOMAINE BOYER-MARTENOT

17, place de l'Europe
21190 Meursault
Phone 00 33 3 80 21 26 25
Fax 00 33 3 80 21 65 62
vincent.boyer@boyer-martenot.com
www.boyer-martenot.com

This small domaine has top-notch vine-yards, and over the past few years we have watched the style evolve toward more purity and definition of terroir. The excellence of the 2006s that were offered for tasting (with an amazing energy that should be mentioned) allows this winery to be included in the guide as one of the best sources in the village. We hope for the wine enthusiast's sake that they will have a few bottles left to sell! If we had to define the personality of the wines, we'd say that they are a good mix of the opulent style of Jacques Prieur and the more strict style of Roulot, certainly closer to the latter rather than the former. Vincent Boyer should continue in this direction; it's what most wine lovers are looking for.

MEURSAULT L'ORMEAU 2006
White | 2011 up to 2016 **87**
The nice nose of honey and hazelnuts shows that the grapes were quite ripe. No heaviness; just a long, steady finish.

MEURSAULT NARVAUX 2006
White | 2011 up to 2016 **92**
This is a Village wine, and not surprisingly, it steps up the pace. A great nose of fresh hazelnuts, direct, pure, distinguished. Full-bodied but taut, with elegant tactile sensations. This might be a great wine in the making.

MEURSAULT PREMIER CRU GENEVRIÈRES 2006
White | 2011 up to 2018 **92**
Adept use of new barrels, but the distinguished character of the vineyard is absolutely preserved. A powerful wine, long, though less subtle than the Narvaux, which is truly exceptional.

MEURSAULT PREMIER CRU PERRIÈRES 2006
White | 2011 up to 2018 **94**
A perfect expression of the vineyard, nobly aromatic, more taut and saline than the Genevrières. Long, racy, and highly recommended.

Red: 4.9 acres; pinot noir 100%. White: 19.8 acres; chardonnay 100%. Annual production: 40,000 bottles

CAMILLE GIROUD

3, rue Pierre-Joigneaux
21200 Beaune
Phone 00 33 3 80 22 12 65
Fax 00 33 3 80 22 42 8
contact@camillegiroud.com
www.camillegiroud.com

The tiny Maison Camille Giroud in Beaune now belongs to an American consortium, headed by acclaimed Napa Valley vintner Ann Colgin. Her 2003s, 2004s, and 2005s were so sensational that they are now out of stock. All is not lost, however, because you can still buy some of the venerable "old-style" Giroud vintages—including one or two really top-notch offerings. The house places special emphasis on wines sourced from terroirs in Corton and Beaune: the 2005s, like the 2004s and 2003s, are remarkable for elegant, classical crafting—testament to the talents of David Croix, a young winemaker with a great future ahead of him.

Recently tasted
CHASSAGNE-MONTRACHET PREMIER CRU
VERGERS 2007
White | 2013 up to 2019 **88**

MARANGES PREMIER CRU
LE CROIX MOINES 2007
Red | 2014 up to 2022 **90**

SANTENAY 2007
Red | 2014 up to 2017 **86**

VOLNAY 2007
Red | 2015 up to 2019 **86**

VOSNE-ROMANÉE 2007
Red | 2014 up to 2019 **91**

Older vintages
BEAUNE PREMIER CRU CENT VIGNES 2006
Red | 2011 up to 2018 **87**
Tender and supple, with fine tannins. Should probably be drunk soon.

BOURGOGNE 2005
Red | 2011 up to 2017 **89**
Complete for the appellation, rich, tannic, generous. Good aging potential.

CORTON-CHARLEMAGNE GRAND CRU 2005
White | 2011 up to 2017 **91**
Golden, powerful, a little heavy but with sufficient acidity to hope for more elegance in five or six years.

CORTON-CHAUMES GRAND CRU 2006
Red | 2011 up to 2021   **94**
Once again, the most accomplished Corton of the house, with great purity of fruit, a generous yet supple body. Terrifically natural. We think we see a vinification with a bit of crushing!

CORTON-CHAUMES GRAND CRU 2005
Red | 2011 up to 2020   **93**
Very pretty color, lots of character, and vinified with great respect for the grape's intrinsic nobility.

CORTON-CLOS DU ROI GRAND CRU 2006
Red | 2011 up to 2024   **93**
Beautiful color. A very different type of wine from the Chaumes but excellent, more deeply colored, more powerful, more modern in a way but less mysterious and subtle. Highly recommended anyway!

CORTON GRAND CRU LE ROGNET 2006
Red | 2011 up to 2021   **92**
A more marked oak influence than in the other two Cortons, but behind that the wine is generous, clean, with elegant tannins and a long future.

SAVIGNY-LÈS-BEAUNE PREMIER CRU PEUILLETS 2006
Red | 2011 up to 2018   **91**
Very aromatic, with a nice oaky quality to it. Supple, fleshy, with a complex finish. Very well made.

Red: 2.8 acres; pinot 100%. **Annual production:** 60,000 bottles

DOMAINE LOUIS CARILLON ET FILS

21190 Puligny-Montrachet
Phone 00 33 3 80 21 30 34
Fax 00 33 3 80 21 90 02
contact@francois-carillon.com
contact@jacques-carillon.com
www.louis-carillon.com

The Carillons are a close-knit Burgundy family with very strong convictions! Their wines offer terrific purity and edge, for a price that is reasonable by the standards of such famous appellations—making them popular with leading French restaurants. Harvesting happens early here so as to capture all the liveliness in the grapes, which is no bad thing given how warm vintages can be these days! The young vines in Combette still have some catching up to do but in the meantime the most dependable choices are the Champ Canet and the Perrières.

PULIGNY-MONTRACHET 2006
White | 2011 up to 2018   **86**
Vinified in a reductive style to preserve its longevity, still marked by the lees, with slight mercaptan notes, refined, wiry, made for aging!

PULIGNY-MONTRACHET 2005
White | 2011 up to 2015   **88**
Still some bitter reduction in this Village bottling (perhaps due to the vinification in larger barrels), but with the finesse and wiriness that characterize the producer.

PULIGNY-MONTRACHET 2004
White | 2011 up to 2014   **88**
Pale in color, marked by some bitterness from the lees; lacking purity, with a long body and lots of wiry energy.

PULIGNY-MONTRACHET PREMIER CRU CHAMP CANET 2006
White | 2011 up to 2016   **86**
Still closed and austere, with a short finish due most likely to its recent bottling, a linear wine; wait before drinking!

PULIGNY-MONTRACHET PREMIER CRU CHAMP CANET 2004
White | 2011 up to 2014   **91**
A nice, classic nose of fern, taut, mineral, fairly pure, with a straightforward, healthy, rustic quality to it!

PULIGNY-MONTRACHET PREMIER CRU
PERRIÈRES 2006
White | 2011 up to 2018   89
A wine that is full of vitality, with intelligent reduction on its lees, longer and more complex than the Village bottling; fresh and subtle, without the heavy-handedness of the vintage.

PULIGNY-MONTRACHET PREMIER CRU
PERRIÈRES 2004
White | 2011 up to 2016   94
Nice green touches, luminous, with great aromatic finesse; the most elegant, by far, of the 2004s presented, and no worries as to its aging potential!

Red: 8.6 acres; pinot 100%. White: 21 acres; chardonnay 100%. Annual production: 60,000 bottles

CHAMPY

3, rue du Grenier-à-Sel
21200 Beaune
Phone 00 33 3 80 25 09 99
Fax 00 33 3 80 25 09 95
contact@champy.com
www.champy.com

The Champy Wine House is intelligently run by Pierre Merugey and consultant enologist Dimitri Bazas, a pupil of Kiriakos Kinigopoulos. Both are well connected with the elite of local viticulture, giving them access to good-quality grapes that they vinify in the same spirit as their wine-grower friends, focusing on terroir expression and the elegance of the raw material. Champy's minor appellations are as soigné and warmly recommended as its great ones!

Recently tasted
BEAUNE PREMIER CRU AUX CRAS 2007
Red | 2015 up to 2019   88

BOURGOGNE PINOT NOIR SIGNATURE 2007
Red | 2011 up to 2015   86

CHASSAGNE-MONTRACHET 2007
White | 2012 up to 2017   90

CORTON-CHARLEMAGNE GRAND CRU 2007
White | 2014 up to 2019   94

POMMARD PREMIER CRU GRANDS ÉPENOTS 2007
Red | 2017 up to 2022   90

Older vintages
ALOXE-CORTON 2006
Red | 2011 up to 2018   89
A pretty nose of licorice, very soft, with lots of finesse for a Village wine that often gives more rustic tannins. Deftly and expertly made.

BEAUNE PREMIER CRU CHAMPIMONTS 2005
Red | 2011 up to 2020   93
Harmonious, elegant, with refined tannins. Long and perfectly ripe.

BOURGOGNE PINOT NOIR SIGNATURE 2005
Red | 2011 up to 2013   88
An excellent generic appellation wine, combining pleasant, clean fruit with a good tannic backbone. To drink in the next three years.

CHASSAGNE-MONTRACHET 2005
White | 2011 up to 2020   92
A denser color than the Villages, an excellent nose of very ripe fruit, luscious, long. Masterfully vinified.

CORTON-CHARLEMAGNE GRAND CRU 2006
White | 2011 up to 2018   **93**
Excellently integrated oak. A rich wine, generous, complex. Perfectly ripe grapes, perhaps a tiny bit showy, but that's the character of this vintage!

CORTON-CHARLEMAGNE GRAND CRU 2005
White | 2011 up to 2013   **90**
Pure, with balanced alcohol, just a tad too lactic to show off the terroir in all its precision and originality.

PERNAND-VERGELESSES 2005
White | 2011 up to 2013   **90**
Remarkably harmonious, a very clear expression of terroir. Vinosity, elegance, clarity.

PULIGNY-MONTRACHET
LES ENSEIGNÈRES 2006
White | 2011 up to 2014   **88**
A good wine, rather fluid for the vintage but with a clean, elegant nose. A touch of citronella (as well as its purity) identifies it as a Puligny. A nicely made white wine.

PULIGNY-MONTRACHET
LES ENSEIGNÈRES 2005
White | 2011 up to 2015   **93**
A pure nose of grape blossoms, excellent vinosity. Racy and respectful expression of terroir. Very long. Highly recommended.

SAVIGNY-LÈS-BEAUNE 2006
Red | 2011 up to 2013   **88**
All the charm of a Burgundian pinot noir. Supple without being lean; fresh, delicate. An immediate pleasure.

SAVIGNY-LÈS-BEAUNE AUX FOURCHES 2005
Red | 2011 up to 2013   **88**
A slightly spicy nose, supple body, not much more character than the Bourgogne, but with the same satisfying harmony.

VOLNAY 2006
Red | 2011 up to 2018   **92**
It's hard to imagine a more accomplished Village-level wine, beautifully marrying vinosity and finesse, with perfectly polymerized tannins, the sign of an exemplary mastery of vinification.

VOSNE-ROMANÉE PREMIER CRU SUCHOTS 2006
Red | 2011 up to 2018   **89**
A pretty nose of vanilla and a classic texture tending toward elegance and discretion but without any weakness. Long, precise, carefully made.

Red: 35.8 acres; pinot noir 100%. White: 6.2 acres; aligoté 33%, chardonnay 67%. Annual production: 425,000 bottles

DOMAINE CHANDON DE BRIAILLES

1, rue Soeur-Goby
21420 Savigny-lès-Beaune
Phone 00 33 3 80 21 50 97
Fax 00 33 3 80 21 59 02
contact@chandondebriailles.com
www.chandondebriailles.com

This famous winery has holdings in the best vineyard sites in the northern part of the Côte de Beaune, practices traditional whole-bunch fermentation, and uses little new oak during the aging process. The wines sometimes lack color and seem thin when young, but they age admirably, showing an elegance once they have reached their peak. The 2006s were made along these lines. Unfortunately we weren't able to taste the entire production.

Recently tasted
SAVIGNY-LÈS-BEAUNE 2007
Red | 2013 up to 2019   **86**

SAVIGNY-LÈS-BEAUNE PREMIER CRU LAVIÈRES 2007
Red | 2015 up to 2022   **89**

Older vintages
CORTON-BRESSANDES GRAND CRU 2006
Red | 2011 up to 2021   **91**
A delicate floral nose, discreet, racy. Typical with its light color, but with the estate's firm vinification style. Seemingly light-bodied but with no emptiness on the mid-palate. A precise, noble finish.

PERNAND-VERGELESSES PREMIER CRU
ÎLE DES VERGELESSES 2006
Red | 2011 up to 2021   **88**
Not very deeply colored, but complex and refined on the nose, with delicate floral notes. Nicely balanced acidity, no excess alcohol. The tannins are well integrated but not very firm. An authentic style, no pretention in the oaky notes, and plenty of reserves for aging. A bit more flesh would make it brilliant.

SAVIGNY-LÈS-BEAUNE PREMIER CRU
LAVIÈRES 2006
Red | 2011 up to 2021   **89**
Cocoa beans on the nose. A supple attack, then more supple in its tannins, with a noble texture. The antithesis of the current fashion, but it carries the great flair of the terroir.

Red: 24.7 acres; pinot noir 100%. White: 9.8 acres; chardonnay 100%. Annual production: 60,000 bottles

CHANSON PÈRE ET FILS

10, rue Paul-Chanson
21200 Beaune
Phone 00 33 3 80 25 97 97
Fax 00 33 3 80 24 17 42
chanson@domaine-chanson.com
www.domaine-chanson.com

In the past three years this venerable Beaune wine house has completely revamped its working approach under the brilliant tutelage of Gilles de Courcel and winemaking partner Jean-Pierre Confuron. Their offerings today rank with the cream of Burgundy: the 2005 estate-produced Beaunes, Savignys, and red Pernands are the most accomplished we have ever tasted, rivaled only by those of Albert Morot. Since the 2006 vintage the whites have greatly improved and are now equal in quality to the reds. It's no mystery why this house is doing so well. Very disciplined viticulture and precise, whole-bunch vinification favor a very pure expression of terroir. Added to that is a stringent selection process that systematically downgrades any would-be Premiers Crus that are less than perfect.

Recently tasted

BEAUNE PREMIER CRU CLOS DES MARCONNETS 2007
Red | 2011 up to 2013   94

BEAUNE PREMIER CRU CLOS DES MOUCHES 2007
Red | 2017 up to 2022   94

BEAUNE PREMIER CRU LAS FÈVES 2007
Red | 2017 up to 2027   96

BOURGOGNE PINOT NOIR 2007
Red | 2012 up to 2017   88

CHARMES-CHAMBERTIN GRAND CRU 2007
Red | 2015 up to 2022   94

CHASSAGNE-MONTRACHET PREMIER CRU
CHENEVOTTES 2007
White | 2013 up to 2019   95

CLOS DE VOUGEOT GRAND CRU 2007
Red | 2017 up to 2027   95

MEURSAULT PREMIER CRU BLAGNY 2007
White | 2012 up to 2017   90

MOULIN-À-VENT 2007
Red | 2011 up to 2015   87

POMMARD 2007
Red | 2014 up to 2019   90

PULIGNY-MONTRACHET PREMIER CRU
FOLATIÈRES 2007
White | 2013 up to 2019   94

SAINT-VÉRAN 2007
White | 2011 up to 2015   88

SAVIGNY-LÈS-BEAUNE PREMIER CRU
VERGELESSES 2007
Red | 2015 up to 2022   91

Older vintages

BEAUNE PREMIER CRU BRESSANDES 2006
Red | 2011 up to 2021   93
Deeply colored, powerfully built but with great precision in the expression of terroir—particularly in the notes of spice and burning vine branches that are typical of the cru. Vigorous, fresh, scrupulously made.

BEAUNE PREMIER CRU BRESSANDES 2005
Red | 2011 up to 2021   96
Spicy and taut, but the tension is magnified by the splendor of the texture and noble tannins: another immense Beaune and, to our taste, even more satisfying than the Hospices wine!

BEAUNE PREMIER CRU CHAMPIMONTS 2006
Red | 2011 up to 2018   91
A bit more densely colored than the Teurons, a firmer wine, more slender and taut, with more complex tannins. A racy wine with a good future ahead of it.

BEAUNE PREMIER CRU CLOS DES MARCONNETS 2005
Red | 2011 up to 2050   94
A pretty, deep purple. A wine with a lot of style, typical of whole-cluster vinification but with controlled tannins. Spicier and wilder, and just a touch less delicate than the Bressandes.

BEAUNE PREMIER CRU CLOS DES MOUCHES 2006
White | 2011 up to 2014   91
A great deal of upfront charm: delicate, round, elegant, comfortable. Ideal for a restaurant.

BEAUNE PREMIER CRU CLOS DES MOUCHES 2005
Red | 2011 up to 2015   93
Absolutely no trace of the terrible hail of 2004. An ample body, velvety, with immediately delicate aromas. A very pretty Beaune!

BEAUNE PREMIER CRU GRÈVES 2006
Red | 2011 up to 2018   91
A complex floral nose with a more noticeable oaky note than the Champimonts. Very elegant, well-integrated tannins. Great delicacy and freshness. The terroir shines through.

BEAUNE PREMIER CRU LES FÈVES 2006
Red | 2011 up to 2021   94
Beautiful color with tints of blue and a very noble, authentic floral nose with a refined oak influence. An esthete's wine—one of the most delicate but also among the most well built of this village and vintage.

BEAUNE PREMIER CRU LES FÈVES 2005

Red | 2011 up to 2030   **98**

A sublime expression of the terroir of the Côte de Beaune, with an admirable fruity quality. Worthy of the greatest crus of the Côte de Nuits and carried by a velvety texture. A collector's wine.

BEAUNE PREMIER CRU TEURONS 2006

Red | 2011 up to 2018   **89**

Relatively light color, a refined nose of violets, elegant texture. The tannins are a bit rough, but the overall ensemble is very natural. With a little aeration, the wine shows pretty nuances.

CHARMES-CHAMBERTIN GRAND CRU 2006

Red | 2011 up to 2021   **94**

A wine of great style, ripe grapes, noble tannins, not a hint of hail; admirably selected and impeccably vinified.

CHASSAGNE-MONTRACHET CLOS SAINT-JEAN 2006

White | 2011 up to 2014   **90**

Notes of grape blossoms on the nose. Elegant, immediately expressive; the fruit is very ripe but not heavy. A delicate oakiness. Well made and complex.

CORTON-CHARLEMAGNE GRAND CRU 2005

White | 2011 up to 2013   **88**

Sinewy, carefully delineated, but lacking vinosity for a cru of this level.

CORTON-LES VERGENNES GRAND CRU 2005

White | 2011 up to 2015   **93**

Rich, unctuous, pure, with better-integrated oak than in the past. Unfortunately made in tiny quantities!

GEVREY-CHAMBERTIN 2006

Red | 2011 up to 2021   **89**

An exemplary Village-level wine. A subtle nose of red berries, full texture, fresh, elegant, with impeccably formed tannins. Quality grapes and highly authentic vinification.

MEURSAULT 2006

White | 2011 up to 2014   **90**

A full wine, elegant, with well-integrated oak, faithful to the best of tradition. The terroir clearly shows through. Very commendable.

SAVIGNY-LÈS-BEAUNE PREMIER CRU VERGELESSES 2006

Red | 2011 up to 2021   **91**

A deeply colored, dense wine, very full, made from an unusually ripe harvest and with a remarkable quality-price ratio. This is really a Corton-type wine, and there's enough to go around (15,000 bottles!). One of our favorites.

Red: 173 acres; pinot noir 100%. White: 74.1 acres; chardonnay 100%. Annual production: 200,000 bottles

DOMAINE DU CHÂTEAU DE CHOREY

Rue des Moutots
21200 Chorey-lès-Beaune
Phone 00 33 3 80 24 06 39
Fax 00 33 3 80 24 77 72
domaine-château-de-chorey@wanadoo.fr
www.domaine-chorey.fr

Benoît Germain is now fully in charge of these family vineyards and, like so many of his counterparts these days, has recently opened a small négociant business. The red 2004s and 2006s do not do justice to his serious winemaking talents, particularly when you consider the huge potential for depth and character in this part of Beaune. But if you come across his Teurons or Cras cuvées from the 1990s, grab them fast, as they are among the finest possible expressions of the Beaune terroir.

Recently tasted

BEAUNE PREMIER CRU
LES CRAS VIEILLES VIGNES 2007

Red | 2015 up to 2019   **87**

BEAUNE PREMIER CRU
LES VIGNES FRANCHES VIEILLES VIGNES 2007

Red | 2015 up to 2019   **87**

MEURSAULT 2007

White | 2012 up to 2017   **87**

Older vintages

BEAUNE PREMIER CRU
LES CRAS VIEILLES VIGNES 2004

Red | 2011 up to 2014   **86**

Earthy and spicy, with dry tannins but a certain substance to it.

BEAUNE PREMIER CRU
LES VIGNES FRANCHES VIEILLES VIGNES 2004

Red | 2011 up to 2016   **88**

Very spicy nose, taut, clean, tending toward a Pommard style. Straightforward but not very pure.

MEURSAULT LES PELLANS
VIEILLES VIGNES 2005

White | 2011 up to 2013   **88**

Full, with a nice citrus nose, wide, generous, a nice style, but it won't age too long.

PERNAND-VERGELESSES PREMIER CRU
LES COMBOTTES 2005

White | 2011 up to 2013   **89**

Easy, wide, generous, sufficiently mineral. An excellent quality-price ratio.

Red: 32.1 acres; pinot noir 100%. White: 9.8 acres; chardonnay 100%. Annual production: 80,000 bottles

DOMAINE CHEVALIER PÈRE ET FILS

Hameau de Buisson - cedex 18
21550 Ladoix-Serrigny
Phone 00 33 3 80 26 46 30
Fax 00 33 3 80 26 41 47
contact@domaine-chevalier.fr
www.domaine-chevalier.fr

Claude Chevalier's favorable public image and genuine love of his terroir make him an ace ambassador for the village of Ladoix. This family domaine has improved a lot in recent vintages thanks to Claude's policy of picking riper grapes, then vinifying them much more carefully so as to maintain the integrity and special character of the fruit.

Recently tasted

ALOXE-CORTON 2007
Red | 2013 up to 2017   89

ALOXE-CORTON PREMIER CRU 2007
Red | 2013 up to 2017   88

CORTON-CHARLEMAGNE GRAND CRU 2007
White | 2014 up to 2019   88

LADOIX PREMIER CRU LES GRÉCHONS 2007
White | 2011 up to 2015   90

Older vintages

ALOXE-CORTON 2005
Red | 2011 up to 2016   89
Dark color, a black-currant nose, the texture of ripe grapes, finesse, a full body. A style that's rather unusual today. Should age very well.

ALOXE-CORTON PREMIER CRU 2005
Red | 2011 up to 2013   88
A black-currant nose, oddly enough more velvety and supple than the Village wine. Nice fruit character. A wine of almost immediate enjoyment.

CORTON-CHARLEMAGNE GRAND CRU 2006
White | 2011 up to 2018   94
Lightly Muscat-like on the nose, powerful. Above all, this wine finds an unusually happy marriage between a good level of alcohol and sufficient acidity.

CORTON-CHARLEMAGNE GRAND CRU 2005
White | 2011 up to 2013   91
Great power and highly ripe grapes. A very promising wine.

GEVREY-CHAMBERTIN 2005
Red | 2011 up to 2020   89
A deep, evolved nose of licorice and black currant. Fleshy, elegant. The tannins are just a bit dry.

LADOIX BOIS DE GRÉCHONS 2005
White | 2011 up to 2013   89
A lemony note. Nice acidity for the vintage, full and clean.

LADOIX PREMIER CRU LE CLOU D'ORGE 2005
Red | 2011 up to 2020   88
Dense color, closed tannins, a tight texture, spicy, tender flavors. This wine has style and a good future. The tannins are just a bit drying.

LADOIX PREMIER CRU LES CORVÉES 2005
Red | 2011 up to 2020   90
Purple-black color, very ripe fruit flavors, an unctuous texture, good length, and a great future ahead of it. An exemplary Ladoix.

LADOIX PREMIER CRU LES GRÉCHONS 2006
White | 2011 up to 2015   90
Pleasantly frank flavors, very full, with tense, mineral finish like that of a Charlemagne. Precise vinification. An excellent quality-price ratio.

LADOIX PREMIER CRU LES GRÉCHONS 2005
White | 2011 up to 2013   89
Clean, lively, with nice acidity and freshness.

Red: 27.7 acres; pinot noir 100%. White: 7.9 acres; aligoté 48%, chardonnay 43%, pinot blanc 9%. Annual production: 60,000 bottles

DOMAINE FRANÇOISE ET DENIS CLAIR

🌿 🌿 🌿 🌿 🌿

14, rue de la Chapelle
21590 Santenay
Phone 00 33 3 80 20 61 96
Fax 00 33 3 80 20 65 19
fdclair@orange.fr

This estate is owned by a very united, warm-hearted family with an unerring instinct for precise flavor. That, and some lovely vineyard parcels in the best parts of Saint-Aubin and Santenay, have made this domaine consistently successful for nearly two decades. They were the first to grasp the advantages of cold maceration before fermentation as a means of eliminating those rustic tannins that spoiled so many of their neighbors' Santenays—and their Santenay remains ahead by a whisker today, striving for ever more harmonious structure and flavor. The white wines in particular took longer to improve but now show very sure-footed style. Despite the nasty hailstorm of 2005, this estate excelled and didn't make a wrong move all year.

Recently tasted

BÂTARD-MONTRACHET GRAND CRU 2007
White | 2013 up to 2019   **93**

SAINT-AUBIN PREMIER CRU EN REMILLY 2007
White | 2012 up to 2017   **93**

SAINT-AUBIN PREMIER CRU
LES MURGERS DES DENTS DE CHIEN 2007
White | 2011 up to 2015   **93**

SANTENAY CLOS GENET 2007
Red | 2012 up to 2017   **89**

SANTENAY PREMIER CRU CLOS DE LA COMME 2007
Red | 2012 up to 2019   **90**

SANTENAY PREMIER CRU CLOS DE TAVANNES 2007
Red | 2012 up to 2017   **88**

Older vintages

PULIGNY-MONTRACHET PREMIER CRU
LA GARENNE 2005
White | 2011 up to 2015   **89**
More nervy but less subtle and fruity than the Saint-Aubins, fresh and frank for the vintage, very agreeable and possibly destined to show more vinosity with age.

SAINT-AUBIN PREMIER CRU EN REMILLY 2006
White | 2011 up to 2014   **90**
Gold with green glints, a delicious nose of white flowers, remarkable finesse of expression, and stunning vivacity for the vintage, which offers lemony notes on the finish that make it the perfect aperitif!

SAINT-AUBIN PREMIER CRU
LES CHAMPLOTS 2006
White | 2011 up to 2014   **90**
Splendidly radiant, pure aromatics, the grapes ripe but not soft, well-integrated oak tannins, very delicate interpretation of the terroir. The maturation and bottling are improving. A reference.

SAINT-AUBIN PREMIER CRU
LES CHAMPLOTS 2005
White | 2011 up to 2013   **90**
A tender nose of vanilla, nicely fat, delicate, well-balanced, with the charm of the village and vintage. Good follow-up on the palate, but rather close to peaking.

SAINT-AUBIN PREMIER CRU
LES MURGERS DES DENTS DE CHIEN 2006
White | 2011 up to 2016   **93**
The pedigree of this terroir is no longer subject to question, and the wine reaches the level of the best Premiers Crus of Chassagne or Puligny. A crystalline purity that is unique in this hot vintage and a long, refined finish. A great wine.

SAINT-AUBIN PREMIER CRU
LES MURGERS DES DENTS DE CHIEN 2005
White | 2011 up to 2013   **91**
Pale color, lightly lemony nose, very elegant and pure, showing all the progress made by the estate in its white-wine vinification.

SANTENAY PREMIER CRU
CLOS DE TAVANNES 2006
Red | 2011 up to 2018   **90**
Great aromatic elegance, a rich wine, the tannins already well integrated (a regular mark of the estate), long. Quite a success.

SANTENAY PREMIER CRU
CLOS DE TAVANNES 2005
Red | 2011 up to 2017   **90**
Racy, taut, tight, the tannins a bit raspy. An extremely high-quality terroir, but you can tell that the grapes suffered from the hail!

SANTENAY PREMIER CRU
CLOS DES MOUCHES 2005
Red | 2011 up to 2015   **90**
Deeply colored, powerful, tannic, with very direct flavors, sincere. Santenay as we like it!

Red: 24.7 acres; pinot 100%. **White:** 12.4 acres; chardonnay 100%. **Annual production:** 75,000 bottles

DOMAINE JEAN-FRANÇOIS COCHE-DURY

9, rue Charles-Giraud
21190 Meursault
Phone 00 33 3 80 21 24 12
Fax 00 33 3 80 21 67 65

Jean-François Coche-Dury is admired to the point of adoration by wine enthusiasts worldwide—and rightly so. The cost of such idolatry, however, is rampant speculation, which prices his wines beyond the reach of the people who are really capable of appreciating their inimitably chic and refined style. Jean-François Coche-Dury is the most modest and profoundly honest of all the world's great winemakers, with a real concern that his wines should attract the consumers they deserve. Much as he regrets all this hyperbole, there is not a thing he can do about it. The reds have been too much eclipsed by the whites, despite their equally admirable finesse, inner balance, and purity of expression. What this domaine really needs are plots of vines in the great Meursault or Puligny Premiers Crus—where it would do a much better job than any other winery.

AUXEY-DURESSES 2005
Red | 2011 up to 2017   91
An irresistible aromatic delicateness, silky texture, refined tannins; that is the true and pure character of pinot noir in a great year when treated with respect.

CORTON-CHARLEMAGNE GRAND CRU 2005
White | 2011 up to 2030   98
A monument, which owing to its rarity will be highly sought after and, alas, squandered in useless high-end tastings, but the happy wine lover who manages to get his hands on a bottle or two will see the full extent of this cru's class.

CORTON-CHARLEMAGNE GRAND CRU 2004
White | 2011 up to 2016   89
More robust than the Genevrières; pure, lithe, still a little simple, aromatically speaking, but perfectly capable of finding that dimension with age.

MEURSAULT CHEVALIÈRES 2005
White | 2011 up to 2017   94
Wonderful finesse, a remarkable purity in its expression of the terroir, admirably ripe fruit, and great length.

MEURSAULT PREMIER CRU GENEVRIÈRES 2005
White | 2011 up to 2020   97
A wine that is sublime in its transparency, heft, its delicate yet powerful nature—an archetype of the Coche-Dury style.

MEURSAULT PREMIER CRU PERRIÈRES 2005
White | 2011 up to 2020   95
Fat, but without being heavy-handed; taut, pure, complex, a remarkable wine with perhaps less aromatic poetry than the Genevrières.

MEURSAULT ROUGEOTS 2005
White | 2011 up to 2020   95
The same purity as the Chevalières, but with more body and a bit more energy. A splendid success, worthy of the vintage.

MONTHÉLIE 2005
Red | 2011 up to 2017   92
Delicate floral aromas, great elegance to the texture, tannins magically integrated into the body of the wine—all in the spirit of the best Volnays, a rare thing these days!

Red: 6.2 acres; gamay 10%, pinot 90%. White: 21 acres; aligoté 5%, chardonnay 95%. Annual production: 45,000 bottles

DOMAINE BRUNO COLIN

3, impasse des Crets
21190 Chassagne-Montrachet
Phone 00 33 3 80 21 93 79
Fax 00 33 3 80 21 93 79
domainebrunocolin@wanadoo.fr

Bruno Colin's brand new estate is in fact his share of the Domaine Colin-Deleger. Its wines proved a revelation in our Chassagne-Montrachet tastings: Bruno Colin clearly has a brilliant career ahead of him. Such an acute instinct for pressing and aging is not something you can be taught. A great stylist is born!

Recently tasted

CHASSAGNE-MONTRACHET PREMIER CRU
LA BAUDRIOTTE 2007
White | 2012 up to 2017   **91**

CHASSAGNE-MONTRACHET PREMIER CRU
MORGEOT 2007
White | 2012 up to 2017   **91**

Older vintages

CHASSAGNE-MONTRACHET 2006
White | 2011 up to 2014   **86**
A well-made wine: elegant, full, harmonious, a touch less complex than all the best Village wines, but easy to drink and enjoy!

CHASSAGNE-MONTRACHET PREMIER CRU
LA BAUDRIOTTE 2005
White | 2011 up to 2013   **94**
Perfect balance for the vintage. Full, long, luscious, a very nice style.

CHASSAGNE-MONTRACHET PREMIER CRU
LA MALTROIE 2005
White | 2011 up to 2015   **93**
Deliciously fruity, complex, with no heaviness. Bright, long, nicely appetizing at the table.

CHASSAGNE-MONTRACHET PREMIER CRU
LES VERGERS 2004
White | 2011 up to 2017   **94**
A delicious balance of honey, hazelnut, and bread. Charming, long, fresh, lovingly made. Marvelously ripe for the vintage.

PULIGNY-MONTRACHET PREMIER CRU
TRUFFIÈRES 2006
White | 2011 up to 2016   **88**
Pale color and a discreet nose with a light lemon note. Good raw materials, nice dry extract. A quality wine.

Red: 10.1 acres; pinot noir 100%. White: 10.4 acres; aligoté 6%, chardonnay 94%. Annual production: 55,000 bottles

DOMAINE MARC COLIN ET FILS

1, rue de la Chatenière
21190 Saint-Aubin
Phone 00 33 3 80 21 30 43
Fax 00 33 3 80 21 90 04
domaine-colinmarc@club-internet.fr

Despite its significant growth in the past ten years, this very busy winery can still be relied upon to produce deliciously pure and elegant white wines and is especially noted for its comprehensive range of Saint-Aubin Premiers Crus. The reds are somewhat underwhelming these days except for the top wine, Cuvée de Santenay, which is stunning. We are sure that Pierre-Yves Colin (who took over from his father) can do even more to bring out the quintessential expression and character of his terroirs.

Recently tasted

CHASSAGNE-MONTRACHET
LES ENSEIGNIÈRES 2007
White | 2012 up to 2017   **91**
Wonderful aromatic purity, with notes of grapes, flowers, and lemon, tightly wound, nice length and style.

CHASSAGNE-MONTRACHET PREMIER CRU
EN CAILLERET 2007
White | 2012 up to 2017   **91**
Pretty hazelnut in the nose, with amazing balance; smooth, elegant, long, and harmonious.

Older vintages

BOURGOGNE LES COMBES 2005
White | 2011 up to 2013   **90**
Fairly broad and comfortable, with obvious cleanness in its expression of the terroir. Pure.

CHASSAGNE-MONTRACHET
LES ENSEIGNIÈRES 2005
White | 2011 up to 2013   **93**
Racy, balanced, long, very pure, very faithful to the habitual style.

CHASSAGNE-MONTRACHET PREMIER CRU
EN CAILLERET 2005
White | 2011 up to 2013   **93**
Racy, full, pure, a fitting expression of the terroir and vintage. Do not let this one age too much.

Red: 14.8 acres; pinot 100%. White: 28.4 acres; aligoté 14%, chardonnay 86%. Annual production: 115,000 bottles

DOMAINE DU COMTE ARMAND

7, rue de la Mairie
21630 Pommard
Phone 00 33 3 80 24 70 50
Fax 00 33 3 80 22 72 37
epeneaux@domaine-comte-armand.com
www.domaine-comte-armand.com

Benjamin Leroux has modified the style of these wines, going for greater elegance of aroma and texture but with no loss of that astonishing vinosity and powerful character that are the mark of the superb Clos des Épeneaux. His most recent vintages are classical Burgundies in the modern style and set an example for most if not all other Pommard producers. Witness the stunning 2004s: wines that show none of the inadequacies of the vintage and deserve a place of honor in any self-respecting Burgundy cellar.

Recently tasted
VOLNAY 2006
Red | 2013 up to 2016   **84**

Older vintages
POMMARD PREMIER CRU
CLOS DES ÉPENEAUX 2006
Red | 2016 up to 2024   **93**
Very firm for the vintage and for a wine in barrel, truffles on the nose, lots of flesh, good length. A wine with style, which will age well, but not a charmer.

POMMARD PREMIER CRU
CLOS DES ÉPENEAUX 2004
Red | 2011 up to 2024   **90**
Splendid flesh, but the oak is a bit insistent, immensely long. A very great accomplishment.

VOLNAY PREMIER CRU LES FRÉMIETS 2006
Red | 2011 up to 2024   **93**
Perfectly macerated, powerful, tannic, long; full of class, but in a masculine style.

VOLNAY PREMIER CRU LES FRÉMIETS 2004
Red | 2011 up to 2015   **93**
A magnificent success, fleshy, mouthwatering, racy, with no trace of hail. Sumptuous!

Red: 18 acres; pinot noir 100%. **Annual production:** 35,000 bottles

DOMAINE DES COMTES LAFON

Clos de la Barre
21190 Meursault
Phone 00 33 3 80 21 22 17
Fax 00 33 3 80 21 61 64
comtes.lafon@wanadoo.fr

This domaine is the most universally admired of all the Volnay and Meursault estates and boasts a unique heritage of vines. Each lieu-dit is ideally located, and the main parcel of red plantings, the Les Santenots du Milieu, has a large enough area to allow rigorous grape selection and the fermentation of a sufficient quantity of grapes for optimal extraction. As so often seen elsewhere, some of the whites produced in the 1990s show signs of premature aging, mainly due to faulty corks, but everything now seems back on track and in any case the quality of vinification has never faltered. The whites show sumptuous body and unique flavor, while the reds are perfectly poised between strength and finesse. All things considered, Dominique Lafon can be justly proud of his work.

Recently tasted
MEURSAULT 2007
White | 2012 up to 2015   **88**

MEURSAULT PREMIER CRU CHARMES 2007
White | 2015 up to 2022   **93**

MEURSAULT PREMIER CRU GENEVRIÈRES 2007
White | 2011 up to 2013   **96**

MONTRACHET GRAND CRU 2007
White | 2017 up to 2027   **98**

VOLNAY PREMIER CRU SANTENOTS DU MILIEU 2007
Red | 2017 up to 2025   **93**

Older vintages
MEURSAULT 2004
White | 2011 up to 2013   **93**
Excellent overall definition, a good balance of alcohol and acidity.

MEURSAULT CLOS DE LA BARRE 2004
White | 2011 up to 2016   **94**
Nice full body, great purity, extremely well balanced, long. Impressive for the vintage.

MEURSAULT PREMIER CRU CHARMES 2004
White | 2011 up to 2016   **93**
More supple and round than the Genevrières, perfect definition of the terroir. A bit lacking in vinosity.

MEURSAULT PREMIER CRU GENEVRIÈRES 2004
White | 2011 up to 2016   **94**
Pure, complete, but closed on the nose.

MEURSAULT PREMIER CRU PERRIÈRES 2007
White | 2017 up to 2022   **94**
Supreme finesse and delicacy in a difficult vintage, perfect grapes, ideal vinification. Exemplary integration of the oak. Possibly the greatest white of the year!

Red: 14.3 acres; pinot 100%. White: 19.8 acres; chardonnay 100%. Annual production: 60,000 bottles

DOMAINE EDMOND CORNU & FILS

Rue du Meix-Grenot
21700 Magny-les-Villers
Phone 00 33 3 80 26 40 79
Fax 00 33 3 80 26 48 34
cornu.pierre@voila.fr

Edmond Cornu is one of the most respected growers in Ladoix, a reputation that is well deserved where his vines are concerned. A few vintages have been affected by off flavors that we have often mentioned, but we are thrilled to see that the 2006 vintage seems unscathed, and better than that, they are among the top wines produced in the area for their finesse, expression of terroir, and their certain aging potential. We heartily recommend these wines.

Recently tasted
HAUTES CÔTES DE BEAUNE 2005
Red | 2011 up to 2013   **88**

HAUTES CÔTES DE NUITS 2005
Red | 2011 up to 2015   **90**

LADOIX PREMIER CRU BOIS ROUSSOT 2007
Red | 2012 up to 2017   **87**

MEURSAULT 2007
White | 2011 up to 2015   **88**

Older vintages
ALOXE-CORTON PREMIER CRU
MOUTOTTES 2006
Red | 2011 up to 2021   **90**
Deeply colored, complex aromatics with spicy notes typical of the appellation, full body, a very steady finish. A great character that will delight enthusiasts of wines from this area.

ALOXE-CORTON PREMIER CRU
VALOZIÈRES 2006
Red | 2011 up to 2021   **91**
Even more delicate and distinguished than the Moutottes, with classic floral aromas, fat and ample texture, and a pure finish.

CORTON-BRESSANDES GRAND CRU 2006
Red | 2011 up to 2021   **92**
A complete wine, superior, with complex, racy tannins and a long future ahead.

LADOIX VIEILLES VIGNES 2006
Red | 2011 up to 2016   **89**
Strong color, black fruit aromas, lots of body and length for a Village-level wine, a rediscovered mastery of style: a new and talented generation expressing itself. Another cuvée from the Carrières vineyard strongly resembles this one.

DOMAINE DE COURCEL

Place de l'Église
21630 Pommard
Phone 00 33 3 80 22 10 64
Fax 00 33 3 80 24 98 73
courcel@domaine-de-courcel.com

This estate already owned the most homogeneous vineyard in the Pommard appellation: a regal twelve-acre parcel of ancient vines in the Grand Clos des Épenots, virtually all of them classified as Premier Cru. But its wines really entered the realm of magic only when gifted, exacting winemaker Yves Confuron arrived on the scene and made them what they are today: the Côte de Beaune equivalents of Romanée-Conti on the Côte de Nuits. They have that same breadth and purity of style that comes from whole-berry fermentation, and the same legitimate expression of terroir. Judging from its impressive performance over the past five years, this estate deserves to be promoted to the very top of the Burgundy rankings.

Recently tasted

POMMARD PREMIER CRU CROIX NOIRES 2007
Red | 2017 up to 2025   91

POMMARD PREMIER CRU
GRAND CLOS DES ÉPENOTS 2007
Red | 2019 up to 2027   95

POMMARD PREMIER CRU LES FRÉMIERS 2007
Red | 2011 up to 2013   91

POMMARD PREMIER CRU RUGIENS 2007
Red | 2017 up to 2027   96

Older vintages

BOURGOGNE PINOT NOIR 2005
Red | 2011 up to 2015   90
A magnificent bouquet of black currants, noble, deep for a simple Burgundy.

POMMARD PREMIER CRU CROIX NOIRES 2005
Red | 2011 up to 2020   93
A nose of brambles, very supple, but richly constructed. It will be ready before the other Premiers Crus.

POMMARD PREMIER CRU
GRAND CLOS DES ÉPENOTS 2006
Red | 2011 up to 2021   93
A very nice nose of red berries, astonishingly meaty for the vintage. This one dominated by far—with the authority of a Grand Cru—all of the estate's other Pommard Premiers Crus except the Rugiens!

POMMARD PREMIER CRU
GRAND CLOS DES ÉPENOTS 2005
Red | 2011 up to 2030   98
Absolutely sumptuous in its body, color, and nobility of texture and tannins. We'll have to come back to it in another twenty years! For us, perhaps the greatest red wine of this vintage from the Côte de Beaune.

POMMARD PREMIER CRU
GRAND CLOS DES ÉPENOTS 2003
Red | 2011 up to 2030   97
Ultraripe grapes, a miracle in this vintage! A sumptuously rich wine with an aristocratic texture, maybe even the most distinguished of Pommard!

POMMARD PREMIER CRU
GRAND CLOS DES ÉPENOTS 2001
Red | 2011 up to 2016   93
Voluptuous despite virile tannins. Fruit oils on the nose, great power. One of the pinnacles of the vintage in the Côte de Beaune, where there aren't many.

POMMARD PREMIER CRU
GRAND CLOS DES ÉPENOTS 2000
Red | 2011 up to 2020   95
The color is starting to get brick-red glints. Marvelous overall balance. A powerful wine, but it finishes fresh thanks to the whole-grape vinification.

POMMARD PREMIER CRU RUGIENS 2006
Red | 2011 up to 2026   94
A tad more elegant and open than the Épenots at the same stage, which is rare. This wine shows supreme distinction—a well-vinified example from a whole-grape harvest.

POMMARD PREMIER CRU RUGIENS 2005
Red | 2011 up to 2030   96
A very great wine, exhilarating, with the aftertaste of a superb Grand Cru. Perfectly ripe grapes.

POMMARD VAUMURIENS 2006
Red | 2011 up to 2021   89
A very balanced Village wine with distinguished truffle notes. The tannins are a bit firm. Obviously less full than the 2005, but plenty of harmony. This terroir at the top of the slope is excellent.

POMMARD VAUMURIENS 2005
Red | 2011 up to 2025   95
An imposing definition of terroir! An exceptional vintage, and an unusual Village wine for its complexity, aromatic distinction, and potential.

Red: 19.8 acres; pinot 100%. White: 2.5 acres; chardonnay 100%. Annual production: 27,000 bottles

CHÂTEAU DE LA CRÉE

11, rue Gaudin
21590 Santenay
Phone 00 33 3 80 20 63 36
Fax 00 33 3 80 20 65 27
la.cree@orange.fr
www.la-cree.com

This new producer, located in one of the most beautiful properties in the upper part of Santenay at the heart of a particularly magnificent setting, completely seduced us with their offerings. Each wine shows a presence and a confidence that is impressive: generosity, elegant aromas, and, the most difficult of all, perfectly integrated oak. A sure bet, undoubtedly destined for the international market, bearing witness to the current revitalization happening in Burgundy.

Recently tasted

CHASSAGNE-MONTRACHET PREMIER CRU MORGEOT 2007
White | 2013 up to 2017   91

MEURSAULT TILLETS 2007
White | 2011 up to 2015   87

POMMARD PETITS NOIZONS 2007
Red | 2015 up to 2019   88

SANTENAY CLOS DE LA CONFRÉRIE 2007
Red | 2012 up to 2017   86

SANTENAY PREMIER CRU BEAUREPAIRE 2007
White | 2011 up to 2015   87

SANTENAY PREMIER CRU GRAVIÈRES 2007
White | 2011 up to 2015   90

VOLNAY PREMIER CRU CLOS DES ANGLES 2007
Red | 2012 up to 2019   87

Older vintages

MEURSAULT TILLETS 2006
White | 2011 up to 2016   90
A very nice Village-level wine, showing delicacy and purity but with a notable tension that makes it very harmonious on the palate. Remarkable style.

POMMARD PETITS NOIZONS 2006
Red | 2011 up to 2018   87
The oak is just a touch "bling" but doesn't hide the clean fruit character or the quality extraction of the tannins. A charming wine, in step with today's fashions but carefully made and potentially capable of coming around to the classic style with time.

SANTENAY PREMIER CRU GRAVIÈRES 2006
White | 2011 up to 2016   89
Exemplary vinification and élevage, its central harmony showing great skill. Length and a lot of class. The best you can find in a white from this village!

VOLNAY ECHARDS 2006
Red | 2011 up to 2016   88
Very appealing blackberry aromas, pleasantly velvety, fine tannins, excellent élevage. Remarkable for a Village-level wine.

VOLNAY PREMIER CRU CLOS DES ANGLES 2006
Red | 2011 up to 2021   90
Spicy, very powerful, with distinguished tannins and oaky notes. Long and hearty. A splendidly pleasing wine.

Annual production: 40,000 bottles

DOMAINE VINCENT DANCER

♒♒♒♒♒

23, route de Santenay
21190 Chassagne-Montrachet
Phone 00 33 3 80 21 94 48
Fax 00 33 3 80 21 39 48
vincentdancer@free.fr
www.vincentdancer.com

Like those of so many of his competitors, some bottles of Vincent Dancer's more recent vintages from the late 1990s show signs of premature aging. But since 2004, this estate has used corks that do justice to the purity and precision of Dancer's exceptional white wines. We still regard him as the most talented and meticulous of all the winemakers of his generation, producing wines that uphold but also update the canons of Burgundian classicism. The 2005 white wines, starting with Les Perrières, possess an elegance and freshness that set them apart, in a vintage that was otherwise rather heavier than expected. The red Chassagne suffered from a nasty localized hailstorm in July. It's a shame that this estate is so small: production is tiny and Dancer has to be very strict about his allocations.

Recently tasted

CHASSAGNE-MONTRACHET PREMIER CRU
LA ROMANÉE 2007
White | 2012 up to 2019   93

CHASSAGNE-MONTRACHET PREMIER CRU
MORGEOT TÊTE DU CLOS 2007
White | 2014 up to 2019   93

MEURSAULT PREMIER CRU PERRIÈRES 2007
White | 2015 up to 2019   93

Older vintages

BOURGOGNE 2005
White | 2011 up to 2009   90
Wonderful finesse and transparent texture. A somewhat over-the-hill taste to it, so expect it to evolve rapidly.

CHASSAGNE-MONTRACHET PREMIER CRU
LA ROMANÉE 2006
White | 2011 up to 2018   90
Great intensity on the nose and on the palate, marked by its terroir, with great class on the finish; a wine made for aging, with a superior constitution.

CHASSAGNE-MONTRACHET PREMIER CRU
LA ROMANÉE 2005
White | 2011 up to 2015   93
Very ripe, round, unctuous, fatty, but with less refinement than the Perrières.

CHASSAGNE-MONTRACHET PREMIER CRU
MORGEOT GRANDE BORNE 2004
Red | 2011 up to 2013   88
Clean, balanced, somewhat drying tannins.

CHASSAGNE-MONTRACHET PREMIER CRU
MORGEOT TÊTE DU CLOS 2006
White | 2011 up to 2021   93
Remarkable intensity, fullness, elegance; an almost perfect Morgeot, made to age!

CHASSAGNE-MONTRACHET PREMIER CRU
MORGEOT TÊTE DU CLOS 2005
White | 2011 up to 2013   95
More vinous than La Romanée, with considerable finesse despite its power, and wonderful overall balance. A master winemaker confirms his mastery.

CHEVALIER-MONTRACHET GRAND CRU 2006
White | 2011 up to 2016   91
A noble, delicate apricot aroma; the wine is complex and subtle, and just starting down the path to opening up, worthy of its terroir and the domaine.

CHEVALIER-MONTRACHET GRAND CRU 2005
White | 2011 up to 2020   96
A monument of finesse and intensity; like all of the other wines from the domaine, it shows a formal perfection that is extremely rare in Burgundy today.

MEURSAULT LES GRANDS CHARRONS 2005
White | 2011 up to 2015   94
Pale, very pure, very fat, marvelously ripe and aromatic grapes, almost ideally transparent vinification.

MEURSAULT PREMIER CRU PERRIÈRES 2006
White | 2011 up to 2013   91
A great aroma of very ripe grapes, with citrus notes; powerful, generous, taut—as it should be—but this bottle was showing a little more evolved than it should. Keep an eye on this wine's evolution in the bottle. Good, but not as astonishing as Gaunoux's wine.

MEURSAULT PREMIER CRU PERRIÈRES 2005
White | 2011 up to 2017   97
Transcendent purity, extraordinarily balanced ripeness for the vintage; perfection!

POMMARD PREMIER CRU PÉZEROLLES 2005
Red | 2011 up to 2020   94
Powerful, truffled, limpid terroir, a wine of great character.

Red: 5.4 acres; pinot noir 100%. White: 6.2 acres; chardonnay 100%. Annual production: 21,000 bottles

DOMAINE DOUDET

5, rue Henri-Cyrot
21420 Savigny-lès-Beaune
Phone 00 33 3 80 21 51 74
Fax 00 33 3 80 21 50 69
doudet-naudin@wanadoo.fr
www.doudet-naudin.com

Domaine Doudet sometimes produces truly grandiose wines from its plantings of old vines in the Corton Maréchaudes Grand Cru and in Savigny and Pernand Vergelesses. The whites started to improve only in 2005.

Recently tasted

CORTON-CHARLEMAGNE GRAND CRU 2007
White | 2014 up to 2019   **93**

PERNAND-VERGELESSES 2007
White | 2011 up to 2014   **88**

SAVIGNY-LÈS-BEAUNE PREMIER CRU
EN REDRESCUL 2007
White | 2011 up to 2015   **86**

SAVIGNY-LÈS-BEAUNE PREMIER CRU
LES GUETTES 2007
Red | 2011 up to 2017   **86**

SAVIGNY-LÈS-BEAUNE VERMOTS 2007
White | 2011 up to 2013   **84**

Older vintages

ALOXE-CORTON PREMIER CRU GUERETS 2006
Red | 2011 up to 2018   **90**
A nice nose of red berries, full body, elegant yet firm tannins, excellent vinification. Confirms the quality of grapes from the north of Beaune.

ALOXE-CORTON PREMIER CRU
LES MARÉCHAUDES VIEILLES VIGNES 2006
Red | 2011 up to 2021   **90**
An excellent cuvée with a perfectly velvety texture, deftly hiding powerful tannins. Lots of character!

ALOXE-CORTON PREMIER CRU
LES MARÉCHAUDES VIEILLES VIGNES 2005
Red | 2011 up to 2017   **88**
Ripe grapes, but the fruit character lacks precision. Full, supple, luscious, but not very distinguished.

BEAUNE PREMIER CRU CENT VIGNES 2006
Red | 2011 up to 2018   **88**
A very delicate texture, suitable tannins, a delicate wine, with aromatics that will surely evolve.

BEAUNE PREMIER CRU CLOS DU ROI 2006
Red | 2011 up to 2018   **90**
Great generosity, an early-opening bouquet, velvety, elegant tannins. A superb Beaune!

BEAUNE PREMIER CRU CLOS DU ROI 2005
Red | 2011 up to 2020   **90**
Insistently oaky, but a velvety texture and more finesse than in the Savigny.

CORTON-CHARLEMAGNE GRAND CRU 2006
White | 2011 up to 2025   **96**
Here we are truly at the highest level of the cru, with a very distinguished nose of hazelnuts, a rich core, and an energetic, sumptuous finish. The terroir is clearly first-rate!

CORTON-CHARLEMAGNE GRAND CRU 2005
White | 2011 up to 2025   **96**
Honey and mineral in a great vintage, and in the very elegant style of Aloxe! Marvelously long.

CORTON-MARÉCHAUDES GRAND CRU
VIEILLES VIGNES 2006
Red | 2011 up to 2026   **94**
Very ripe grapes are apparent on the nose, the color is splendid, the body generous, the tannins elegant, and the overall expression of the terroir quite natural. A superb Corton that marries power and finesse, just as it should.

CORTON-MARÉCHAUDES GRAND CRU
VIEILLES VIGNES 2005
Red | 2011 up to 2025   **93**
Nice volume, great texture, balanced tannins, the attack is a bit animal, but the wine purifies itself with aeration. A great future ahead.

PERNAND-VERGELESSES LES PINS 2005
White | 2011 up to 2013   **88**
Pale, clear, supple, mineral, tender but with pedigree.

PERNAND-VERGELESSES PREMIER CRU
SOUS FRÉTILLE 2005
White | 2011 up to 2015   **91**
Very pure, precise, transparent, refined; excellent!

Red: 23.5 acres; pinot noir 100%. **White:** 8.6 acres; aligoté 13%, chardonnay 87%. **Annual production:** 50,000 bottles

JOSEPH DROUHIN

7, rue d'Enfer
21200 Beaune
Phone 00 33 3 80 24 68 88
Fax 00 33 3 80 22 43 14
maisondrouhin@drouhin.com
www.drouhin.com

This large, historic wine house in Beaune is now expertly run by the new generation of Jousset-Drouhins, who are committed to maintaining its reputation for elegantly styled red and white wines. Their offerings meet all expectations, showing a sharper mineral profile than before. Since 2006 some welcome adjustments have been made, allowing the négociant wines to gain in balance, quality, and especially in the expression of their individual terroirs.

Recently tasted

BÂTARD-MONTRACHET GRAND CRU 2007
White | 2014 up to 2019   93

BEAUNE 2007
White | 2011 up to 2017   93

BEAUNE PREMIER CRU CLOS DES MOUCHES 2007
Red | 2013 up to 2019   89

BOURGOGNE LA FORÊT 2007
White | 2011 up to 2013   86

BOURGOGNE LA FORÊT 2007
Red | 2011 up to 2013   88

CHABLIS GRAND CRU BOUGROS 2007
White | 2011 up to 2017   89

CHABLIS VAUDON 2007
White | 2011 up to 2013   88

CHAMBOLLE-MUSIGNY PREMIER CRU 2007
Red | 2013 up to 2019   91

CHAMBOLLE-MUSIGNY PREMIER CRU
AMOUREUSES 2007
Red | 2017 up to 2022   94

CHASSAGNE-MONTRACHET
MARQUIS DE LAGUICHE 2007
White | 2012 up to 2019   95

CLOS DE VOUGEOT GRAND CRU 2007
Red | 2017 up to 2027   93

CORTON-CHARLEMAGNE GRAND CRU 2007
White | 2014 up to 2019   96

CÔTE DE BEAUNE LA CHÂTELAINE 2007
White | 2011 up to 2017   90

GEVREY-CHAMBERTIN 2007
Red | 2014 up to 2019   91

GRANDS-ECHÉZEAUX GRAND CRU 2007
Red | 2017 up to 2025   94

GRIOTTE-CHAMBERTIN GRAND CRU 2007
Red | 2017 up to 2022   94

MONTRACHET GRAND CRU MARQUIS DE LAGUICHE 2007
White | 2014 up to 2019   94

MUSIGNY GRAND CRU 2007
Red | 2017 up to 2027   97

PULIGNY-MONTRACHET 2007
White | 2012 up to 2017   91

Older vintages

BEAUNE PREMIER CRU CLOS DES MOUCHES 2006
Red | 2011 up to 2018   89
A dark-colored body for the vintage, a clean wine with affirmed tannins, doubtless less elegant in its red version than in its white for this vintage.

BEAUNE PREMIER CRU CLOS DES MOUCHES 2005
Red | 2011 up to 2015   89
Pretty ruby color, a tender, ripe, elegant wine that is a little too supple to match the greatest successes of the year in the sector, but full of charm!

BONNES-MARES GRAND CRU 2006
Red | 2011 up to 2026   95
Sure to develop into another great classic of the vintage, this Bonnes-Mares will appeal to wine lovers for the precision of its aromas and the adept extraction of its tannins.

CHAMBOLLE-MUSIGNY PREMIER CRU
AMOUREUSES 2006
Red | 2011 up to 2021   94
A pure, delicate wine that is very refined in texture, a little less vinous and well-defined than those of the Domaine Mugnier, but utterly worthy of one's expectations!

CHASSAGNE-MONTRACHET 2006
White | 2011 up to 2014   90
Excellent style, very distinct from the Puligny, with more fat and aromas, showing more white fruit than white flowers; very pleasant even in its youth.

CHASSAGNE-MONTRACHET
MARQUIS DE LAGUICHE 2006
White | 2011 up to 2016   93
One of the classics of the house, perfectly typical in 2006, fleshy but very elegant, with impeccable balance between the alcohol and the acidity, with more body than the Premier Cru Pulignys and Meursaults!

CLOS DE VOUGEOT GRAND CRU 2006
Red | 2011 up to 2026   **95**
A grand, well-rounded wine that combines
fleshiness with a noble texture, powerful yet
not harsh tannins, and great aromatic depth:
a sure sign of smooth aging on the horizon!

CLOS DE VOUGEOT GRAND CRU 2005
Red | 2011 up to 2025   **93**
Rich, fleshy, with terrifically elegant tannins,
great length and class, but the terroir could
be better sculpted in the details. This wine
will go far, though!

CORTON-BRESSANDES GRAND CRU 2006
Red | 2011 up to 2026   **93**
A wine of very fine elegance and subtlety;
delicate sap despite the high level of alcohol; precise, refined tannins that hark back
to the true values of racy pinot noir.

CORTON-CHARLEMAGNE GRAND CRU 2006
White | 2011 up to 2018   **94**
Tastes at least as good as the Montrachet,
with curious floral, racy notes and greater
tautness on the palate.

GRANDS-ECHÉZEAUX GRAND CRU 2006
Red | 2011 up to 2021   **93**
Superb volume on the palate, clear aromatic
and textural elegance, slightly less well-
rounded than the Clos de Vougeot!

MONTRACHET GRAND CRU
MARQUIS DE LAGUICHE 2006
White | 2011 up to 2018   **93**
The most widely distributed of the Montrachets presents its habitual aromatic finesse
and purity, but honestly, it lacks something
as far as the body and texture go, falling
short of the level of the greatest bottles.

MONTRACHET GRAND CRU
MARQUIS DE LAGUICHE 2005
White | 2011 up to 2020   **95**
Remarkable purity and finesse, well-balanced
body, but somewhere in the details, the power
and raciness of the terroir get lost and do not
appear with the same force we find in other
producers.

PULIGNY-MONTRACHET 2006
White | 2011 up to 2014   **90**
A very fine négociant bottling, with precise
aromas of lemongrass and white flowers, a
supple, refined body, elegant oak, and a wiry,
straightforward finish.

Red: 59.3 acres; pinot noir 100%. White: 121.1 acres;
chardonnay 100%. Annual production: 3,600,000
bottles

DOMAINE DUBREUIL-FONTAINE PÈRE ET FILS

Rue Rameau Lamarosse
21420 Pernand-Vergelesses
Phone 00 33 3 80 21 55 43
Fax 00 33 3 80 21 51 69
domaine@dubreuil-fontaine.com
www.dubreuil-fontaine.com

This was for many years the most famous
estate in the picturesque village of Pernand and one of the pioneers of estate-
bottled wines. Its own bottlings suffered
from a disappointing lack of elegance for
some twenty years or so, but, thanks to
Christine Dubreuil's more precise, fruit-
driven approach, the 2002s—and all of the
wines since—can be counted on to seduce
even the most demanding connoisseur:
robust, classically tasty reds and tauter-
than-average whites that need several
years' cellaring.

Recently tasted
CORTON-CHARLEMAGNE GRAND CRU 2007
White | 2015 up to 2019   **90**

PERNAND-VERGELESSES PREMIER CRU
ÎLE DES VERGELESSES 2007
Red | 2015 up to 2019   **87**

Older vintages
ALOXE-CORTON PREMIER CRU
LES VERCOTS 2005
Red | 2011 up to 2017   **90**
Nice ripe fruit, rich, fat; generous, with the
terroir clearly coming through.

CORTON-BRESSANDES GRAND CRU 2005
Red | 2011 up to 2025   **93**
Excellently suave, the classic character of
the terroir shows through; long, full, generous, promises to age very well.

CORTON-CHARLEMAGNE GRAND CRU 2004
White | 2011 up to 2014   **88**
Clean, but packed with carbon dioxide, and
it lacks finesse and purity. Luscious, with
plenty of nerve, not fully formed yet.

PERNAND-VERGELESSES CLOS BERTHET 2006
White | 2011 up to 2014   **89**
Delicate notes of ferns on the nose, very
clean in the expression of terroir, lots of
finesse and class, a magnificent quality-
price ratio.

PERNAND-VERGELESSES CLOS BERTHET 2006
Red | 2011 up to 2016   **86**
Not very deeply colored, but quite a subtle
bouquet of pleasant floral notes. Immediate
in its expression of the natural fruit character of the grape; tender.

PERNAND-VERGELESSES PREMIER CRU ÎLE DES VERGELESSES 2006
Red | 2011 up to 2018   **89**

Excellent character of red berries, a long wine, luscious, in a very accomplished classic style, its immediate elegance veiling its good aging potential.

POMMARD PREMIER CRU LES ÉPENOTS 2006
Red | 2011 up to 2018   **89**

Great complexity in the aromas, a candid texture, classic vinification. A clean, racy wine that will win over many connoisseurs to the appellation.

POMMARD PREMIER CRU LES ÉPENOTS 2005
Red | 2011 up to 2020   **90**

Deeply colored, rich, generous body, precise cherry character, excellent style. Will probably age well.

Red: 34.6 acres; pinot noir 100%. **White:** 14.8 acres; chardonnay 100%. **Annual production:** 90,000 bottles

DOMAINE FOLLIN–ARBELET
🏵 🏵 🏵 🏵 🏵

Les Vercots
21420 Aloxe-Corton
Phone 00 33 3 80 26 46 73
Fax 00 33 3 80 26 43 32
franck.follin-arbelet@wanadoo.fr

Follin-Arbelet is an honest winery with a total commitment to excellence. Slowly but surely, it is making its mark with wines that have that elegant bouquet and texture to be expected from such a remarkable heritage of vines. Franck Follin's style grows more refined with every vinification, never compromising the integrity of terroir expression—his greatest strength.

Recently tasted

CORTON-BRESSANDES GRAND CRU 2007
Red | 2015 up to 2022   **88**

CORTON-LE CORTON GRAND CRU 2007
Red | 2012 up to 2019   **87**

ROMANÉE-SAINT-VIVANT GRAND CRU 2007
Red | 2015 up to 2022   **91**

Older vintages

ALOXE-CORTON APPELLATION VILLAGE 2005
Red | 2011 up to 2015   **88**

Supple, full, natural, a bit hollow on the mid-palate.

ALOXE-CORTON PREMIER CRU CLOS DU CHAPÎTRE 2006
Red | 2011 up to 2026   **92**

The nose is protected by reduction, with its notes of black currants. Magnificent body, possibly even more harmonious than on the Vercots, firm tannins, with very long aging ahead. A classic of the vintage in the making.

ALOXE-CORTON PREMIER CRU CLOS DU CHAPÎTRE 2005
Red | 2011 up to 2017   **90**

Fleshy, well-balanced, natural, maybe a bit too supple.

ALOXE-CORTON PREMIER CRU CLOS DU CHAPÎTRE 2004
Red | 2011 up to 2016   **90**

Nice finesse, very clear expression of terroir, good overall balance; sincere and precise.

ALOXE-CORTON PREMIER CRU LES VERCOTS 2006
Red | 2011 up to 2021   **93**

Firm color, generous body and aromas; it captures perfectly the character of the terroir. Complete, and just as good as many Cortons.

ALOXE-CORTON PREMIER CRU
LES VERCOTS 2005
Red | 2011 up to 2020 **90**
More force and vinosity than the Clos du Chapître. Clean. Great aging potential.

CORTON-BRESSANDES GRAND CRU 2006
Red | 2011 up to 2026 **95**
A model of the Bressandes vineyard, very pure, vigorous, refined in its tannins, marrying generosity and discretion as is desirable for long aging. Another model of authenticity and classicism.

CORTON-BRESSANDES GRAND CRU 2005
Red | 2011 up to 2020 **94**
Noble black-currant notes without any vegetal character, a noble finish with notes of wild rose; marvelously fresh for the vintage.

CORTON-BRESSANDES GRAND CRU 2004
Red | 2011 up to 2016 **90**
A nice cherry note, intense, subtle, frank, strong expression of terroir, but a slight lack of refinement.

CORTON-CHARLEMAGNE GRAND CRU 2005
White | 2011 up to 2020 **93**
Very rich and fat, good substance. A wine with plenty of character, built for aging, in the great tradition of Burgundy.

CORTON-LE CORTON GRAND CRU 2006
Red | 2011 up to 2013 **94**
Great aromatic elegance, with precise, luscious notes of red berries. Noble texture, distinguished tannins, very authentic!

PERNAND-VERGELESSES PREMIER CRU
EN CARADEUX 2004
Red | 2011 up to 2016 **90**
A typical note of bell peppers, yet not vegetal. Fresh, elegant, natural, with excellent tannins.

PERNAND-VERGELESSES PREMIER CRU
LES FICHOTS 2005
Red | 2011 up to 2020 **90**
Rich, complete, tannic, long, precise. A real wine.

ROMANÉE-SAINT-VIVANT GRAND CRU 2006
Red | 2011 up to 2026 **94**
A great wine, complex, dense, taut, in a classic, steady style, undoubtedly the most complete wine vinified up to now by this estate. A very long future ahead.

Red: 12.4 acres; pinot noir 100%. White: 2.5 acres; chardonnay 100%. Annual production: 25,000 bottles

ALEX GAMBAL

14, boulevard Jules Ferry
21200 Beaune
Phone 00 33 3 80 22 75 81
Fax 00 33 3 80 22 21 66
info@alexgambal.com
www.alexgambal.com

Boston-born Alex Gambal loved Burgundy so much that he settled in Beaune and started a small wine business that soon earned the respect of locals. He purchases red grapes that he vinifies himself. His Premier and Grand Cru wines show good breeding and plenty of elegance but just a touch too much oak. His lovely red 2005 cuvées display all the class of their vintage, while his 2006s are uniformly high in quality, making him one of the most reliable sources currently to be found in Beaune.

Recently tasted
BOURGOGNE PINOT NOIR CUVÉE LES 2 PAPIS 2007
Red | 2011 up to 2015 **88**

CHAMBOLLE-MUSIGNY 2007
Red | 2014 up to 2019 **90**

CHASSAGNE-MONTRACHET 2007
White | 2012 up to 2017 **90**

CORTON-CHARLEMAGNE GRAND CRU 2007
White | 2015 up to 2019 **94**

MEURSAULT CLOS DU CROMIN 2007
White | 2012 up to 2017 **91**

SAVIGNY-LÈS-BEAUNE VIEILLES VIGNES 2007
Red | 2013 up to 2017 **87**

Older vintages
BOURGOGNE CHARDONNAY
CUVÉE PRESTIGE 2005
White | 2011 up to 2013 **89**
Fine, balanced, with noble aromas of fresh hazelnut; a great success! Here, we can see the advantage of using a blend for a generic appellation.

BOURGOGNE PINOT NOIR CUVÉE LES 2 PAPIS 2006
Red | 2011 up to 2016 **89**
A sample that is still young, saturated with carbon dioxide, but with a delicious fruitiness and delicate tannins. The style is impeccable, and many will appreciate the delicate texture of this fine Village wine.

CHAMBOLLE-MUSIGNY PREMIER CRU
LES CHARMES 2005
Red | 2011 up to 2013 **91**
Elegant, insistent yet not excessive oak, obvious finesse, fairly long, racy.

CHASSAGNE-MONTRACHET PREMIER CRU
LA MALTROIE 2006
White | 2011 up to 2016   **90**
Fine hazelnut aromas and, above all, remarkable saline, mineral tension for this vintage, which had a heat wave at the end; long, refined barrel treatment, a fine future.

CHASSAGNE-MONTRACHET PREMIER CRU
LA MALTROIE 2005
White | 2011 up to 2013   **90**
Very pure, elegant, subtle, fine in style; it's hard to imagine so much difference between two Chassagnes.

CLOS DE VOUGEOT GRAND CRU 2006
Red | 2011 up to 2018   **93**
Fine aromas of ripe grapes, a fleshy, elegant, carefully vinified wine that comes highly recommended.

CLOS DE VOUGEOT GRAND CRU 2005
Red | 2011 up to 2025   **94**
A lot of wine here; good typicity of terroir, long, an excellent expression of the vintage, as opposed to the Chambolle.

CORTON-CHARLEMAGNE GRAND CRU 2006
White | 2011 up to 2021   **95**
A great classic of the terroir on the nose, with notes of flowering vine and fresh hazelnut, well-integrated oak, a strong finish that deserves to be qualified as mineral; splendid vinification!

CORTON-CHARLEMAGNE GRAND CRU 2005
White | 2011 up to 2017   **95**
A great wine, energetic, refined, with exemplary length and freshness.

ECHÉZEAUX GRAND CRU 2005
Red | 2011 up to 2020   **93**
A very pretty body, noble fruit, length, classiness, balance.

MEURSAULT CLOS DU CROMIN 2006
White | 2011 up to 2016   **90**
A fine aromatic expression that is lactic yet pure and precise; a fat, long, complex wine with good seamlessness and excellent, racy terroir; a very classy Meursault Village wine.

SAINT-AUBIN PREMIER CRU
LES MURGERS DES DENTS DE CHIEN 2005
White | 2011 up to 2013   **91**
Excellent, rich, balanced, long, classy and completely different from the Fixin, which is to be expected as far as minerality goes, but here, the oak is integrated!

Red: 3.6 acres; pinot noir 100%. White: 2.6 acres; chardonnay 100%. Annual production: 50,000 bottles

JEAN-MICHEL GAUNOUX

1, rue de Leignon
21190 Meursault
Phone 00 33 3 80 21 22 02
Fax 00 33 3 80 21 68 45
jean-michel.gaunoux@wanadoo.fr

Jean-Michel Gaunoux split this winery from that of his father several years ago. It is worthy most of all for its whites, vinified without bowing to recent trends, and all coming from great terroirs. Their tension and lack of oxidation place them among the ranks of the best wines for aging, and the 2006s are no exception!

Recently tasted
MEURSAULT PREMIER CRU PERRIÈRES 2007
White | 2012 up to 2019   **88**

Older vintages
MEURSAULT 2006
White | 2011 up to 2014   . **88**
A great deal of aromatic nuance and delicacy to its tastes, a pure, assured finish with terrific youthfulness of character.

MEURSAULT PREMIER CRU GOUTTE D'OR 2006
White | 2011 up to 2018   **93**
A fine lemon aroma, an energetic, elegant wine with great follow-through on the palate, and the same mastery in a grand, classic style as the Perrières. Highly recommended.

MEURSAULT PREMIER CRU PERRIÈRES 2006
White | 2011 up to 2021   **95**
A very great wine, with nobility and complexity worthy of the great producers who were absent from our tasting (Roulot, Lafon, Coche Dury, etc.); great level of dry extract, perfect expression of the terroir on the mid-palate, with no decadent or overripe qualities on the finish. A pinnacle!

Red: 7.4 acres; pinot noir 100%. White: 7.4 acres; chardonnay 100%.

DOMAINE HENRI GERMAIN ET FILS

🜄 🜄 🜄 🜄 🜄

4, rue des Forges
21190 Meursault
Phone 00 33 3 80 21 22 04
Fax 00 33 3 80 21 67 82

This excellent artisan winery makes white wines that often achieve the ultimate in intense, rigorous expression of terroir—particularly the superb Meursault Charmes. A small quantity of red wine is also produced, the best by far being an Old Vines Beaune Bressandes. All of the white wines age to perfection. The Meursault Chevalières gives you an idea of what to expect from the Meursault Charmes and Perrières in another few years! Buy with confidence.

MEURSAULT 2005
White | 2013 up to 2017 **90**
Fat, clean, candid, with excellent substance and—finally—dry extract! Good aging potential.

MEURSAULT 2004
White | 2011 up to 2014 **90**
Citrus notes on the nose, ample, pure, well balanced, not at all lactic. It will age well.

MEURSAULT CHEVALIÈRES 2005
White | 2013 up to 2017 **91**
Nice oak influence, well balanced, good tension, very well defined terroir. Needs three or four years.

MEURSAULT CHEVALIÈRES 2004
White | 2011 up to 2014 **93**
Nice oak influence, elegant, very tender yet full. A remarkable accomplishment.

MEURSAULT PREMIER CRU PERRIÈRES 2005
White | 2011 up to 2018 **93**
Quite distinguished, generous, straightforward, long, uncompromising.

Red: 4.9 acres; pinot 100%. White: 7.4 acres; chardonnay 100%. Annual production: 16,000 bottles

DOMAINE VINCENT GIRARDIN

🜄 🜄 🜄 🜄 🜄

Les Champs Lins
21190 Meursault
Phone 00 33 3 80 20 81 00
Fax 00 33 3 80 20 81 10
vincent.girardin@vincentgirardin.com
www.vincentgirardin.com

This ambitious grower now runs an impressive array of great chardonnay land, and helped by a young member of the Germain family from Meursault produced impressive 2006s and 2007s after some disappointing 2005s. The red wines are very fleshy and oaky but ripe and designed for hedonists.

Recently tasted

CHASSAGNE-MONTRACHET PREMIER CRU CAILLERETS 2007
White | 2014 up to 2019 **93**

CHASSAGNE-MONTRACHET PREMIER CRU CHAUMÉES 2007
White | 2012 up to 2019 **93**

CHASSAGNE-MONTRACHET PREMIER CRU MORGEOT 2007
White | 2013 up to 2019 **93**

CORTON-CHARLEMAGNE GRAND CRU 2007
White | 2013 up to 2019 **93**

MEURSAULT PREMIER CRU CHARMES 2007
White | 2013 up to 2019 **91**

Older vintages

BIENVENUES-BÂTARD-MONTRACHET GRAND CRU 2004
White | 2011 up to 2014 **90**
Rich, balanced, with well-integrated oak, but lacks transparency on a higher level.

CHASSAGNE-MONTRACHET PREMIER CRU ABBAYE DE MORGEOT 2004
White | 2011 up to 2013 **90**
Purer than the 2005, with good balance, cleanness, and straightforwardness, but fairly simple.

PULIGNY-MONTRACHET PREMIER CRU LES FOLATIÈRES 2005
White | 2011 up to 2013 **88**
More refined and ethereal than the Chassagne, with obviously high-quality terroir but a lack of energy on the palate: this vintage was not as easy as people say for whites.

Red: 7.4 acres; pinot noir 100%. White: 42 acres; chardonnay 100%. Annual production: 150,000 bottles

DOMAINE ALBERT GRIVAULT

🐓 🐓 🐓 🐓 🐓

7, place Murger
21190 Meursault
Phone 00 33 3 80 21 23 12
Fax 00 33 3 80 21 24 70
albert.grivault@wanadoo.fr

This estate is a must for lovers of Meursault Perrières, the tautest, classiest, slowest aging and most capable of aging of all the wines from this village. The main Les Perrières vineyard boasts the most favorable aspect in the entire "climat" (a Burgundian term for a cadastral lieu-dit) and adjoins the sub-plot of Clos des Perrières, a monopoly of Albert Grivault. You might think there was no difference between the two—think again. Burgundy being as mysterious as ever, the Clos wines actually transcend those of its neighbor, possessing all the strength of a Montrachet and maybe even more finesse.

MEURSAULT 2005
White | 2011 up to 2017   **91**
Luscious, rich, long. A magnificent, classic style. A slight lack of finesse.

MEURSAULT PREMIER CRU
CLOS DES PERRIÈRES 2006
White | 2014 up to 2024   **95**
Of all the Perrières, the most marked by the citronella notes typical of soils rich in magnesium. The volume on the palate, the tension, the distinction of flavor are that of a great vintage of the Clos.

MEURSAULT PREMIER CRU
CLOS DES PERRIÈRES 2005
White | 2013 up to 2020   **95**
Very powerful and rich in alcohol, unctuous, dense, with marvelously distinguished terroir. Needs another three years.

MEURSAULT PREMIER CRU
CLOS DES PERRIÈRES 2004
White | 2011 up to 2013   **91**
Notes of caramel on the nose, clean, subtle, rather long, but without the radiance of a great vintage.

MEURSAULT PREMIER CRU PERRIÈRES 2006
White | 2014 up to 2021   **93**
Nice citrus notes, a touch of overripeness that is not found in the Clos. Long, complex, luscious, but a step down.

MEURSAULT PREMIER CRU PERRIÈRES 2005
White | 2011 up to 2017   **94**
A lot of substance, great flavor, and a very satisfying balance for the vintage.

POMMARD PREMIER CRU CLOS BLANC 2005
Red | 2011 up to 2025   **91**
Very classic vinification. A rich, harmonious wine, long, with a smoky note typical of the terroir and tannins that are firm but not hard.

Red: 2.5 acres; pinot 100%. White: 12.4 acres; chardonnay 100%. Annual production: 38,000 bottles

DOMAINE ANTONIN GUYON

2, rue de Chorey
21420 Savigny-lès-Beaune
Phone 00 33 3 80 67 13 24
Fax 00 33 3 80 66 85 87
domaine@guyon-bourgogne.com
www.guyon-bourgogne.com

The strength of this well-respected Savigny estate is its exceptional parcels in Corton and Corton-Charlemagne; but it also offers some exemplary Meursaults, Volnays, and Chambolle-Musignys. The red wines are more consistently successful than the whites, which show a disappointing tendency to premature aging. The reds, on the other hand, usually age very well and get better with every vintage.

Recently tasted

CHAMBOLLE-MUSIGNY CLOS DU VILLAGE 2007
Red | 2012 up to 2017   86

CORTON-BRESSANDES GRAND CRU 2007
Red | 2015 up to 2022   88

CORTON-CHARLEMAGNE GRAND CRU 2007
White | 2015 up to 2019   93

MEURSAULT PREMIER CRU CHARMES DESSUS 2007
White | 2014 up to 2019   93

PERNAND-VERGELESSES PREMIER CRU
SOUS FRÉTILLE 2007
White | 2011 up to 2015   88

Older vintages

ALOXE-CORTON PREMIER CRU FOURNIÈRES 2006
Red | 2011 up to 2018   90
A lot more delicate and elegant in its texture and aromas than the Vercots, and we prefer it a bit, but some others will be more drawn to the full body of its neighbor in the cellar.

ALOXE-CORTON PREMIER CRU VERCOTS 2006
Red | 2011 up to 2024   89
A spicy nose with notes of nutmeg and coriander, possibly from the oak. Vinous, tannic, very clean on the finish. A serious wine with good cellaring potential!

CORTON-BRESSANDES GRAND CRU 2006
Red | 2011 up to 2020   91
Great integrity in the expression of terroir, a bit less complete than the Clos du Roi.

CORTON-BRESSANDES GRAND CRU 2004
Red | 2011 up to 2016   90
Delicate, suave, very subtle and quite characteristic of the terroir. In a way, more appealing than the 2005. Don't hurry to drink it.

CORTON-CHARLEMAGNE GRAND CRU 2005
White | 2011 up to 2017   93
Clearly noble body and bouquet. We would have liked a bit more substance.

CORTON-CLOS DU ROI GRAND CRU
CLOS DU ROY 2006
Red | 2011 up to 2026   93
Ripe grapes, refined body, great length. A very accomplished wine right from its birth.

CORTON-CLOS DU ROI GRAND CRU
CLOS DU ROY 2005
Red | 2011 up to 2020   92
By far the most noble bouquet of the series and the most balanced body. Distinguished and without any roughness, but not as complete as some others.

CORTON-RENARDES GRAND CRU 2005
Red | 2011 up to 2020   90
The first of the series to have a bit of substance. A full wine, balanced, the terroir quite apparent (a small, gently animal note), better-coated tannins.

GEVREY-CHAMBERTIN LA JUSTICE 2005
Red | 2011 up to 2015   91
Very ripe grapes. An ultra-supple wine, charming, suave, immediate.

MEURSAULT PREMIER CRU
CHARMES DESSUS 2006
White | 2011 up to 2014   91
An elegant flavor of ripe grapes, perfectly matured in oak. It has conserved a great freshness, but for how long?

MEURSAULT PREMIER CRU
CHARMES DESSUS 2005
White | 2011 up to 2015   90
Finesse, elegance, purity, maybe a bit too fluid. Holds promise.

Red: 106.3 acres; pinot 100%. White: 9.1 acres; chardonnay 100%. Annual production: 220,000 bottles

LOUIS JADOT

21, rue Eugène-Spuller
21200 Beaune
Phone 00 33 3 80 22 10 57
Fax 00 33 3 80 22 56 03
maisonlouisjadot@louisjadot.com
www.louisjadot.com

In just a few years this winery has grown to become the largest producer in Beaune, noted for a splendid range of Mâcon and Beaujolais wines made from superbly located vineyards in both appellations. Charismatic director Jacques Lardière has made significant improvements to the style of his wines. The reds undergo very long tank fermentation and, though not always readily accessible when young, do often age superbly. They include a range of fabulously expressive domaine wines that mirror all the minute differences in the terroir, and an outstanding collection of Gevrey-Chambertins. The best of the whites are possibly even better, showing unrivaled fullness and sappiness as in, for instance, the Chevalier-Montrachet Les Demoiselles. Among the wines from the lesser-known appellations, we warmly recommend the white and red Les Santenays Clos de Malte; also, the beautifully consistent Pernand-Vergelesses and the ample Fixins.

Recently tasted

BEAUNE PREMIER CRU GRÈVES 2007
White | 2012 up to 2019   **90**

CHAMBERTIN-CLOS DE BÈZE GRAND CRU 2008
Red | 2017 up to 2027   **95**

CHAPELLE-CHAMBERTIN GRAND CRU 2007
Red | 2017 up to 2027   **94**

CHASSAGNE-MONTRACHET PREMIER CRU
MORGEOT DUC DE MAGENTA 2007
White | 2015 up to 2022   **93**

CHEVALIER-MONTRACHET GRAND CRU
DEMOISELLES 2007
White | 2017 up to 2027   **96**

CORTON-CHARLEMAGNE GRAND CRU 2007
White | 2017 up to 2022   **95**

FIXIN 2007
White | 2011 up to 2015   **87**

GEVREY-CHAMBERTIN CLOS SAINT-JACQUES 2007
Red | 2015 up to 2027   **93**

MEURSAULT 2007
White | 2014 up to 2019   **91**

PERNAND-VERGELESSES PREMIER CRU
CROIX DE PIERRE 2007
White | 2014 up to 2019   **90**

POMMARD PREMIER CRU RUGIENS 2007
Red | 2017 up to 2025   **91**

PULIGNY-MONTRACHET 2007
White | 2011 up to 2016   **90**

PULIGNY-MONTRACHET CLOS DE LA GARENNE
DUC DE MAGENTA 2007
White | 2015 up to 2022   **93**

SAVIGNY-LÈS-BEAUNE PREMIER CRU
DOMINODE 2007
Red | 2012 up to 2017   **86**

VOSNE-ROMANÉE PREMIER CRU
BEAUMONTS 2007
Red | 2015 up to 2022   **91**

VOSNE-ROMANÉE PREMIER CRU SUCHOTS 2007
Red | 2017 up to 2027   **93**

Older vintages

BEAUNE BRESSANDES 2006
Red | 2011 up to 2021   **91**
The day of the tasting, this was the most racy and well rounded of the house's Premier Cru Beaunes. Very aristocratic in its tautness and tannins; well rounded.

BEAUNE PREMIER CRU CLOS DES URSULES 2004
Red | 2011 up to 2019   **90**
A little tighter in texture than the Theurons, spicy, fleshy, complex, very accomplished, with a slight change of body for a Beaune that already looks ahead to Pommard.

BEAUNE THEURONS 2004
Red | 2011 up to 2016   **90**
Combines elegance and freshness without the slightest trace of underripeness to the grapes; gracious and ideal for those who are disturbed by the habitual tautness of this house's wines!

CHAPELLE-CHAMBERTIN GRAND CRU 2004
Red | 2011 up to 2024   **94**
Great unctuousness, a wonderful nose of cherries, stunning length. Should give food for thought to those who "massacred" this vintage by bringing out rough tannins.

CHASSAGNE-MONTRACHET PREMIER CRU
MORGEOT 2004
White | 2011 up to 2019   **93**
Produced by the Domaine de Magenta; rich in dry extract for the year, ample, complex, very taut but without being hard, with an ideal proportion of malic acid. Great aging potential.

Chevalier-Montrachet grand cru Demoiselles 2006
White | 2011 up to 2024   **97**
Sublimely refined scents, an opulent but not heavy texture, an inimitable mix of grace, power, and complexity due to inspired vinification that let the wine incorporate all the power of a unique terroir!

Chevalier-Montrachet grand cru Demoiselles 2005
White | 2011 up to 2025   **97**
Sublimely unctuous grapes, great aromatic nobility and complexity, an inimitable style!

Clos de la Roche grand cru 2006
Red | 2011 up to 2026   **94**
Once again, a well-rounded wine with a clear expression of terroir; fleshy, ample, admirably balanced and, in our opinion, richer than most of the house's Grands Crus from the Côte de Nuits, aside from the Chambertin and the Clos de Vougeot.

Clos de Vougeot grand cru 2006
Red | 2016 up to 2026   **94**
Great color, a well-rounded wine that combines power and refinement, with tannins that are almost as noble as in 2005 and with perhaps more hedonism to its texture. Remarkable!

Clos de Vougeot grand cru 2004
Red | 2011 up to 2024   **95**
Vigorous, tannic, with the noble bouquet and straightforward body so characteristic of this small parcel within the domaine's large plots. Once again surprisingly ripe grapes and surprisingly ample!

Corton-Charlemagne grand cru 2005
White | 2011 up to 2025   **97**
Grandiose purity and finesse, wonderfully balanced for cellaring.

Corton-Charlemagne grand cru 2004
White | 2011 up to 2019   **94**
Unctuous, long, with an admirable bouquet of white peaches and a texture that is anything but fluid! Stunning for the year!

Corton-Pougets grand cru 2006
Red | 2011 up to 2021   **93**
A wine of great unctuousness, rich, generous but not heavy or rigid, with the inimitable satiny texture of the house's successful vinifications, which bring forth from the grapes all they have to give, and then capture all their best qualities for eternity, or nearly!

Corton-Pougets grand cru 2004
Red | 2011 up to 2019   **90**
Raspberry notes, vinous, tannic, deep for the vintage; could still gain in refinement.

Gevrey-Chambertin premier cru Estournelles Saint-Jacques 2004
Red | 2011 up to 2019   **94**
A wonderfully suave texture for the year, remarkable refinement to its bouquet, great length; bravo!

Marsannay 2005
White | 2011 up to 2015   **93**
Broad, straightforward, fat, very long. This wine has great style and a great future.

Meursault 2005
White | 2011 up to 2025   **96**
Great sap, rich, generous, great length; a stunning wine that will mark its era!

Meursault premier cru Genevrières 2006
White | 2011 up to 2016   **95**
A wine of great aromatic refinement, suave, delicate, very fat, in which Jacques Lardière has been able to retain a bit of wonderful vivacity; a model for stylish winemaking that will please the most demanding connoisseurs.

Musigny grand cru 2004
Red | 2011 up to 2024   **97**
A wine that is sublime in its scents and texture, alas produced in tiny quantities. Sad to say, it is even more marked by its terroir than those currently being turned out by the largest producer of the appellation.

Nuits-Saint-Georges premier cru aux Boudots 2004
Red | 2011 up to 2019   **90**
Very affirmed style, fresh, long, with spicy tannins, great persistence.

Pommard 2006
Red | 2011 up to 2021   **90**
One of the house's most complete and appetizing Village wines, round, suave, and full, with particularly loose tannins, more subtle than certain Premiers Crus.

Pommard premier cru Grands Épenots 2006
Red | 2011 up to 2021   **93**
A superb bottling, with elegant scents and texture, finishing on fresh, racy tannins that are perfectly integrated into the body of the wine.

Puligny-Montrachet 2006
White | 2011 up to 2016   **89**
A large production, worthy of the size of this house (600hl/60,000l), which means it can be found in many restaurants. Rich in alcohol (14°) but not heavy, it has finesse and precision superior to the Chassagnes and Meursaults from the same source.

PULIGNY-MONTRACHET 2004
White | 2011 up to 2013   **89**
A pure, precise nose of fern; a particularly elegant, clean wine, with a finish that preserves all the freshness of the vintage.

PULIGNY-MONTRACHET LES FOLATIÈRES 2006
White | 2011 up to 2016   **95**
Ethereal, plush on the palate, ideally complex and refined, the polar opposite of the bare-boned or too linear wines of some of the larger concerns. This manages to square the circle by combining generosity, transparency, and elegance.

PULIGNY-MONTRACHET PREMIER CRU CHAMPS GAINS 2005
White | 2011 up to 2017   **94**
More floral than the Folatières, lively, elegant, with great character.

PULIGNY-MONTRACHET PREMIER CRU CLOS DE LA GARENNE, DOMAINE DUC DE MAGENTA 2005
White | 2011 up to 2020   **93**
Very full, great breadth, still somewhat harsh in its definition on the finish.

PULIGNY-MONTRACHET PREMIER CRU FOLATIÈRES 2005
White | 2011 up to 2020   **94**
Aromas of baking bread, broad, powerful, tannic, and stable; lively acidity, very long aging potential.

SANTENAY CLOS DE MALTE 2005
White | 2011 up to 2015   **93**
With a nose of wheat, fatty, very subtle and pure, this wine has a great future.

VOLNAY PREMIER CRU CLOS DE LA BARRE 2004
Red | 2011 up to 2024   **93**
A very great success: firm color, ample, soft texture, long persistence, complex tannins—one of the pinnacles of the vintage in this village.

Red: 212.5 acres; gamay 45%, pinot 55%. White: 143.3 acres; aligoté 2%, chardonnay 98%. Annual production: 8,000,000 bottles

DOMAINE PATRICK JAVILLIER

7, impasse des Acacias
21190 Meursault
Phone 00 33 3 80 21 27 87
Fax 00 33 3 80 21 29 39
contact@patrickjavillier.com
www.patrickjavillier.com

The white wines from this estate start out with plenty of body but hardly anything on the nose at all. They often improve with age, gradually developing all the characteristics of these terroirs that, though not as famous as some, do produce very fine examples of generic Burgundy. The reds show light color, tannins, and fruit, and the style is less sure-footed. The 2005 whites are made in the classical Javillier style, with a touch more complexity in the newest Cuvée Oligocène, thus making it relatively more successful than some of its smarter counterparts.

Recently tasted
PERNAND-VERGELESSES 2007
Red | 2011 up to 2014   **87**

Older vintages
BOURGOGNE OLIGOCÈNE 2005
White | 2011 up to 2015   **91**
Exceptional richness for a Bourgogne AOC: a wiry, powerful, elegant, complex, and stunning wine.

CORTON-CHARLEMAGNE GRAND CRU 2005
White | 2013 up to 2017   **90**
Broad and pure but not very complex or mineral. Wait three years for this wine's character to gain better definition.

MEURSAULT CLOS DU CROMIN 2006
White | 2011 up to 2014   **87**
A fresh nose with notes of fermentation and a fruitiness evocative of pineapple; generous, amusing, less strict than Tête de Murgers, and almost ready to drink.

MEURSAULT LES CLOUS 2005
White | 2011 up to 2015   **88**
Lemon notes on the nose; a precise wine that is fairly mineral, linear, but not very complex.

MEURSAULT PREMIER CRU CHARMES 2006
White | 2011 up to 2016   **89**
Powerful, rich, very ripe grapes that make the wine almost heavy, but very long, savory, and sensual, which largely compensates for the powerful nose.

MEURSAULT TÊTE DE MURGERS 2006
White | 2011 up to 2016   **90**
Nicely vinous, a wine that is a touch stricter on the palate than the Tillets, but with the same seductive quality and the same length; remarkably vinified.

MEURSAULT TILLETS 2006

White | 2011 up to 2016 — **90**

A classic of the style, with fine notes of toasted hazelnut and very opulent, with follow-through on the palate and nice presence of the terroir. Good balance in its acidity.

MEURSAULT TILLETS 2005

White | 2011 up to 2013 — **88**

Citrus notes on the nose, supple, fat, but not very racy.

SAVIGNY-LÈS-BEAUNE
LES GRANDS LIARDS 2006

Red | 2011 up to 2016 — **86**

A delicate nose of black currants, not very pronounced in color, vinification voluntarily angled more toward the purity of the fruit than toward extraction, elegant but a bit short.

SAVIGNY-LÈS-BEAUNE MONCHENEVOY 2006

White | 2011 up to 2014 — **87**

Very well vinified, fat, balanced, not reductive, not oxidative; easy to understand and enjoy.

Red: 4.9 acres; pinot noir 100%. White: 19.8 acres; chardonnay 100%. Annual production: 70,000 bottles

DOMAINE FRANÇOIS JOBARD

2, rue de Leignon
21190 Meursault
Phone 00 33 3 80 21 21 26
Fax 00 33 3 80 21 26 44
dom.francois.antoine.jobard@wanadoo.fr

Craftsman winemaker François Jobard is admired all over the world for his somewhat austere wines—fairly impenetrable when young, but they age superbly, developing all the strength and complex character of their handsome Meursault terroirs. The style seems to be changing now that François has his son alongside him—and a welcome change it is, too.

Recently tasted

MEURSAULT EN LA BARRE 2007

White | 2013 up to 2019 — **88**

A more pronounced golden color than average 2007s, oak and reduced lees that are slightly bitter, but hugely powerful and dense substance; great aging potential.

MEURSAULT PREMIER CRU GENEVRIÈRES 2007

White | 2015 up to 2022 — **91**

Golden with strong notes of toasted hazelnuts in the nose; toasty, very rich, long, concentrated, and complex.

Older vintages

MEURSAULT PREMIER CRU GENEVRIÈRES 2005

White | 2011 up to 2017 — **93**

Very ripe, ample, and luscious, less marked by the lees than in the past.

MEURSAULT PREMIER CRU PORUZOTS 2005

White | 2011 up to 2017 — **94**

Remarkable fullness, tight texture, and a long, explosive finish with hazelnut notes.

White: 14.8 acres; aligoté 5%, chardonnay 95%.
Annual production: 30,000 bottles

DOMAINE RÉMI JOBARD

12, rue Sudot
21190 Meursault
Phone 00 33 3 80 21 20 23
Fax 00 33 3 80 21 67 69
remi.jobard@libertysurf.fr

This estate really impressed us in the late 1990s for its consistency in general and, in particular, the introduction of a modern-style white wine based on crispness, freshness, clean aromas, and a purity of texture not unlike that of the Domaine Roulot.

MEURSAULT PREMIER CRU CHARMES 2004
White | 2011 up to 2017   86
Does not have a very strong personality. Pure on the nose and on the palate, nonetheless; let's hope it will come into its own in a few years!

MEURSAULT PREMIER CRU GENEVRIÈRES 2004
White | 2011 up to 2015   88
Very clean, without much personality, but a more rich and harmonious body than the other terroirs.

MEURSAULT SOUS LA VELLE 2004
White | 2011 up to 2013   86
A little more material than the two other Village wines; linear; the grapes lack ripeness.

Red: 6.2 acres; pinot 100%. White: 13.6 acres; aligoté 25%, chardonnay 75%. Annual production: 45,000 bottles

DOMAINE PIERRE LABET

Clos de Vougeot
21640 Vougeot
Phone 00 33 3 80 62 86 13
Fax 00 33 3 80 62 82 72
contact@châteaudelatour.com

The vineyard here belongs to François Labet's father, but the wines are vinified at the Clos de Vougeot, family seat of François's mother and aunt, by the same winemaking team and according to the same principles. That said, the level of quality is not the same, though satisfactory nonetheless, suggesting that this estate is now taking a stricter approach to viticulture! It's easier to recommend the 2005 red wines than the whites.

Recently tasted

BEAUNE CLOS DU DESSUS DES MARCONNETS 2007
White | 2011 up to 2015   86

BEAUNE CLOS DU DESSUS DES MARCONNETS 2007
Red | 2012 up to 2017   85

BEAUNE PREMIER CRU COUCHERIAS 2007
Red | 2015 up to 2022   88

BOURGOGNE VIEILLES VIGNES 2007
White | 2011 up to 2013   86

BOURGOGNE VIEILLES VIGNES 2007
Red | 2011 up to 2017   90

Older vintages

BEAUNE CLOS DES MONSNIÈRES 2006
White | 2011 up to 2014   87
Personality, with rare tautness for white Beaunes and superior oak quality to earlier vintages. A pretty white to drink now.

BEAUNE CLOS DES MONSNIÈRES 2005
White | 2011 up to 2013   89
Lactic but ample and straightforward, natural, with vitality on the finish.

BEAUNE CLOS DES MONSNIÈRES 2005
Red | 2011 up to 2017   85
A serious, somewhat severe wine, not very rich but spicy, tannic, and certainly able to age!

BEAUNE CLOS DU DESSUS DES MARCONNETS 2006
White | 2011 up to 2016   86
Broadly lactic aromas; a clean, very technical wine with a finish that lacks generosity.

BEAUNE CLOS DU DESSUS DES MARCONNETS 2005
White | 2011 up to 2017   88
A fine cherry nose, a wine that is linear, balanced, serious, very precise in the expression of its origins.

BEAUNE CLOS DU DESSUS DES MARCONNETS 2004
White | 2011 up to 2014 **87**
Delicate color, piquant nose of black currant that is nonetheless not at all vegetal, supple, charming, stylish for the vintage and no hail-afflicted tannins.

BEAUNE PREMIER CRU COUCHERIAS 2006
Red | 2011 up to 2016 **84**
Appropriate body and constitution, but the tannins lack suppleness and are not very smooth with regard to the body. We shall see how the wine integrates them.

BEAUNE PREMIER CRU COUCHERIAS 2005
Red | 2011 up to 2017 **88**
Fine color, suave on the nose, tender texture, ripe grapes, tasty but not very complex.

MEURSAULT TILLETS 2006
White | 2011 up to 2014 **87**
Pale, pure, clean, very well made, technically speaking, but lacking in a bit of immediate personality. The slightly reductive, bitter finish with its hazelnut notes gives us hope that it will develop more character as it evolves.

SAVIGNY-LÈS-BEAUNE PREMIER CRU
VERGELESSES 2006
White | 2011 up to 2014 **88**
The best white from the domaine, as often happens, with fine honey and lemon aromas but without the punch of the very best Savignys.

Red: 9.8 acres; pinot noir 100%. White: 9.8 acres; chardonnay 100%. Annual production: 40,000 bottles

DOMAINE MICHEL LAFARGE

15, rue de la Combe
21190 Volnay
Phone 00 33 3 80 21 61 61
Fax 00 33 3 80 21 67 83
contact@domainelafarge.com
www.domainelafare.com

At the turn of the millennium some of the wines from this estate were flawlessly authentic but just a shade too austere for their own good. Today, thanks to an ongoing biodynamic program and Frédéric Lafarge's personality, they show more finesse and a subtler texture.

Recently tasted
VOLNAY PREMIER CRU LES MITANS 2006
Red | 2014 up to 2018 **86**

VOLNAY VENDANGES SÉLECTIONNÉES 2006
Red | 2013 up to 2016 **84**

Older vintages
VOLNAY PREMIER CRU CAILLERETS 2004
Red | 2011 up to 2016 **94**
Flower essence on the nose, very close to the Volnay Village wine, very pure, refined, fresh, subtle.

VOLNAY PREMIER CRU CLOS DES CHÊNES 2006
Red | 2014 up to 2018 **88**
Spicy, supple, generous, charming, very pure and natural, without the hard edges that bottlings of this parcel sometimes show.

VOLNAY PREMIER CRU CLOS DES CHÊNES 2004
Red | 2011 up to 2014 **88**
More vegetal and tannic than the Caillerets, with less finesse and, especially, less affected by the character of the vintage.

VOLNAY VENDANGES SÉLECTIONNÉES 2004
Red | 2011 up to 2019 **95**
Wonderfully elegant, suave, floral, great style.

Red: 23.5 acres; gamay 2%, pinot 98%. White: 6.2 acres; aligoté 50%, chardonnay 50%. Annual production: 50,000 bottles

DOMAINE HUBERT LAMY

20, rue des Lavières
21190 Saint-Aubin
Phone 00 33 3 80 21 32 55
Fax 00 33 3 80 21 38 32
domainehubertlamy@wanadoo.fr
www.domainehubertlamy.com

This traditional estate is now run by Hubert's son Olivier Lamy, a young and very talented winegrower who certainly impressed us with the way he handled his white wines in the difficult 2005 vintage. Their finesse, charm, and freshness should give a good many more famous producers something to think about. The reds are fruity and made in that pleasing style that this estate does so well.

Recently tasted

CHASSAGNE-MONTRACHET 2007
White | 2011 up to 2015   87

CHASSAGNE-MONTRACHET PREMIER CRU MACHERELLES 2007
White | 2013 up to 2019   93

SAINT-AUBIN PREMIER CRU DERRIÈRE CHEZ ÉDOUARD VIEILLES VIGNES 2007
Red | 2012 up to 2017   86

SAINT-AUBIN PREMIER CRU EN REMILLY 2007
White | 2011 up to 2013   91

SAINT-AUBIN PREMIER CRU LES MURGERS DES DENTS DE CHIEN 2007
White | 2011 up to 2013   89

SANTENAY CLOS DES HÂTES 2007
White | 2011 up to 2015   84

Older vintages

CHASSAGNE-MONTRACHET LA GOUJONNE VIEILLES VIGNES 2005
Red | 2011 up to 2020   93
A complete wine, aromatic and refreshing but with a superb chewiness; it promises to age a long time.

CHASSAGNE-MONTRACHET PREMIER CRU MACHERELLES 2006
White | 2011 up to 2016   90
Slightly reduced, but a superbly well-made wine, mouthwatering, with noble hazelnut aromas, long, complex, racy.

PULIGNY-MONTRACHET LES TREMBLOTS 2005
White | 2011 up to 2015   93
A remarkable purity of style, transparent, very subtle and refined. As a whole, brilliant.

SAINT-AUBIN PREMIER CRU CLOS DE LA CHATENIÈRE 2006
White | 2011 up to 2016   90
Great balance, great purity, this is Saint-Aubin at its best, in a vintage when the altitude of the vineyard significantly helped preserve the finesse of the grapes.

SAINT-AUBIN PREMIER CRU CLOS DE LA CHATENIÈRE 2005
White | 2011 up to 2015   94
Exquisite citronella aromas, transparent, pure, a magic expression of the terroir, very long. A stylish wine!

SAINT-AUBIN PREMIER CRU CLOS DU MEIX 2005
White | 2011 up to 2015   90
Delicate, pure aromas of grape blossoms. A very elegant wine, transparent, typical of the terroir!

SAINT-AUBIN PREMIER CRU DERRIÈRE CHEZ ÉDOUARD VIEILLES VIGNES 2005
Red | 2011 up to 2020   93
A delicious cherry-fruit character, very subtle texture, quite precise and clean, very long. Exceptional for the commune!

SAINT-AUBIN PREMIER CRU LES MURGERS DES DENTS DE CHIEN 2006
White | 2011 up to 2018   94
Sumptuously rich, great aromatic nobility, marvelous purity. A very great wine, possibly one of the pinnacles of the vintage!

SAINT-AUBIN PREMIER CRU LES MURGERS DES DENTS DE CHIEN 2005
White | 2011 up to 2015   93
More lactic and racy than the other Premiers Crus, but a bit less complex than the Clos des Frionnes. The distinction of this terroir is evident!

Red: 11.1 acres; pinot 100%. White: 29.7 acres; chardonnay 100%. Annual production: 100,000 bottles

DOMAINE LAMY-PILLOT

31, route de Santenay
21190 Chassagne-Montrachet
Phone 00 33 3 80 21 30 52
Fax 00 33 3 80 21 30 02
contact@lamypillot.fr
www.lamypillot.fr

Domaine Lamy-Pillot often turns out white Chassagnes that offer strong character at prices that remain reasonable for such pristine terroirs (it also houses a corkscrew collection that is well worth the visit). The estate made a better job of the 2005s than many of its neighbors: the Les Caillerets and Chassagne Premier Cru are as warmly recommended as the 2004 editions. The estate's small Blagny bottling (red like almost all Blagnys, and not submitted for tasting) can sometimes rival its whites!

BLAGNY 2006
Red | 2011 up to 2016   **86**
Excellent quality, well-balanced, refined, classic for the undeservedly little-known hamlet of Blagny, which can make very tasty reds.

CHASSAGNE-MONTRACHET premier cru 2006
White | 2011 up to 2016   **88**
Elegant honey notes, great finesse and subtlety, great length; a wine with character.

CHASSAGNE-MONTRACHET premier cru 2005
White | 2011 up to 2015   **90**
Fine, clean, vinous, pure, with a fine future ahead of it; a particularly successful wine.

CHASSAGNE-MONTRACHET premier cru 2004
White | 2011 up to 2015   **90**
Fine note of floral honey, long, harmonious, very open; superb for the vintage.

CHASSAGNE-MONTRACHET premier cru
CLOS SAINT-JEAN 2005
White | 2011 up to 2015   **88**
Citrus notes on the nose, supple, ripe, but less vinous than the Morgeot.

CHASSAGNE-MONTRACHET premier cru
EN CAILLERETS 2006
White | 2014 up to 2018   **85**
Still closed on the palate, slightly disjointed, but the stamp of the terroir is present! This is one to wait for!

CHASSAGNE-MONTRACHET premier cru
EN CAILLERETS 2005
White | 2014 up to 2020   **93**
A well-rounded wine for the vintage, straightforward, vinous; most likely it will age very well.

CHASSAGNE-MONTRACHET premier cru
LA GRANDE MONTAGNE 2005
White | 2011 up to 2013   **90**
A good wine, broad-shouldered, generous, unusual.

CHASSAGNE-MONTRACHET premier cru
MORGEOT 2005
Red | 2011 up to 2015   **89**
Powerful but lacking in finesse, very straightforward on the finish—which must not have been easy to achieve, given the hail!

Red: 27.2 acres; pinot noir 100%. **White:** 19.8 acres; aligoté 5%, chardonnay 95%. **Annual production:** 100,000 bottles

DOMAINE DANIEL LARGEOT

5, rue des Brenots
21200 Chorey-lès-Beaune
Phone 00 33 3 80 22 15 10
Fax 00 33 3 80 22 60 62
domainedaniellargeot@orange.fr

A good artisan winery making carefully crafted, elegant wines at reasonable prices. Even the 2004s hit the spot. The Chorey Les Beaumonts 2004 is a good wine for everyday drinking—served cold, of course—while you wait for the 2005 and 2006 editions. But it does need to be served cold.

Recently tasted

BEAUNE PREMIER CRU GRÈVES 2007
Red | 2011 up to 2013   86

CHOREY-LÈS-BEAUNE LES BEAUMONTS 2007
Red | 2012 up to 2017   87

SAVIGNY-LÈS-BEAUNE 2007
Red | 2015 up to 2019   88

Older vintages

ALOXE-CORTON 2006
Red | 2011 up to 2018   89
Very nice style for a Village-level wine. A clean, elegant nose of red berries, excellently balanced acidity, very candid tannins, rather complex, and sold at an entirely reasonable price.

ALOXE-CORTON 2004
Red | 2011 up to 2014   88
A light color, a more complex nose than on the Savigny, a delicately smoky bouquet.

BEAUNE PREMIER CRU GRÈVES 2004
Red | 2011 up to 2016   88
Rather deep and tannic, the pedigree of the terroir is evident, but you can tell that the vines suffered!

CHOREY-LÈS-BEAUNE LES BEAUMONTS 2004
Red | 2011 up to 2014   88
Delicious notes of black currant and wild roses. A clean wine, delicate, refreshing, with plenty of style.

SAVIGNY-LÈS-BEAUNE 2006
Red | 2011 up to 2014   90
An almost perfect Savigny with rare aromatic purity and tannins that are diabolically charming but not vulgar. Long, already ready but capable of aging. A treasure of artisanal Burgundy.

Red: 24.7 acres; gamay 3%, pinot 97%. White: 2.5 acres; aligoté 100%. Annual production: 25,000 bottles

LOUIS LATOUR

18, rue des Tonneliers
BP 127
21204 Beaune
Phone 00 33 3 80 24 81 00
Fax 00 33 3 80 22 36 21
louislatour@louislatour.com
www.louislatour.com

This great house boasts a wealth of knowledge (though not always the wits to use it) and first-class vineyards that include some of the finest holdings in Corton. The most troubling thing about Latour is the lack of uniformity vintage-on-vintage. White wines are its particular specialty and range from the superlative (the sumptuous Corton-Charlemagne) to the commonplace (the Mâcon offerings are insipid and some of its Côte d'Or Village wines are nothing special). The red Latours have often shown a disappointing lack of color and body in the past but improved tremendously in 2003 and 2005, both stunningly successful. The 2001s and 2004s, on the other hand, were conspicuous failures.

Recently tasted

AUXEY-DURESSES 2007
White | 2012 up to 2017   86

BEAUNE PREMIER CRU AUX CRAS 2007
White | 2011 up to 2015   88

BEAUNE PREMIER CRU PERRIÈRES 2006
Red | 2012 up to 2016   87

BEAUNE VIGNES FRANCHES 2006
Red | 2014 up to 2018   88

CHASSAGNE-MONTRACHET PREMIER CRU MORGEOT 2007
White | 2012 up to 2017   88

CHEVALIER-MONTRACHET GRAND CRU LES DEMOISELLES 2007
White | 2015 up to 2022   96

CORTON-CHARLEMAGNE GRAND CRU 2007
White | 2015 up to 2019   93

MEURSAULT GOUTTE D'OR 2007
White | 2014 up to 2022   93

MEURSAULT PREMIER CRU BLAGNY 2007
White | 2015 up to 2022   90

MONTRACHET GRAND CRU 2007
White | 2015 up to 2022   93

NUITS-SAINT-GEORGES PREMIER CRU DAMODES 2006
Red | 2012 up to 2018   89

POUILLY-VINZELLES EN PARADIS 2006
White | 2011 up to 2015   90

SANTENAY PREMIER CRU LA COMME 2007
Red | 2012 up to 2017   87

Older vintages

BEAUNE PREMIER CRU LES CRAS 2006
White | 2011 up to 2014   87
Unusual in its citrus notes, a tender, easy, well-balanced wine without any bitter reduction.

BEAUNE VIGNES FRANCHES 2005
Red | 2011 up to 2017   89
Delicate in color, with very good general balance, supple; lacks a bit of complexity, but the wine is natural and elegant.

CHASSAGNE-MONTRACHET PREMIER CRU MORGEOT 2005
White | 2011 up to 2015   90
Rich, fat, ample; the terroir expression is not very pronounced.

CHEVALIER-MONTRACHET GRAND CRU LES DEMOISELLES 2006
White | 2011 up to 2024   94
Discreet on the nose, with the reductive note and incisive oak that characterize the wines from this house in their youth; a great deal of fat and dry extract; long, racy, but made for aging!

CORTON-CHARLEMAGNE GRAND CRU 2006
White | 2014 up to 2021   90
Greater power on the palate, with a nose that is still marked by a reductive style typical of the house (toasted hazelnuts or almonds) and that hides its considerable body. A wine that is evolving, not easy to understand right now, but with fine promise.

CORTON-CHARLEMAGNE GRAND CRU 2004
White | 2011 up to 2019   95
A very well-bred wine, with wonderful hazelnut aromas; long, racy, and pure!

CORTON GRAND CRU CHÂTEAU CORTON GRANCEY 2006
Red | 2011 up to 2024   91
Racy on the nose in its floral aromas, more immediately Corton than in the past, full of charm and promise, yet without any harsh tannins, just the way this house likes its wines to be.

CORTON GRAND CRU CHÂTEAU CORTON GRANCEY 2005
Red | 2011 up to 2027   93
Very refined on the nose and on the palate, with elegant texture to the tannins; it hides its body and potential, though; perfectly ripe grapes.

MEURSAULT PREMIER CRU PORUZOTS 2006
White | 2011 up to 2018   90
A great deal of fat and power, very clear, uncommon aromatic character, remarkable dry extract. This is a wine made for aging: wait six to eight years.

MONTRACHET GRAND CRU 2006
White | 2011 up to 2026   95
A great expression of the terroir, very generous, long, racy, and dense. This is a wine made for aging; its style might seem outmoded, but it's the only way to make a bottle guaranteed to be great fifteen years down the line!

POMMARD 2006
Red | 2011 up to 2018   87
A successful bottling for the vintage; a tender, velvety, and harmonious wine that is less earthy than others but more elegant and looser in its tannins.

ROMANÉE-SAINT-VIVANT GRAND CRU LES QUATRE JOURNAUX 2006
Red | 2011 up to 2026   96
Nothing more to say here, except that this wine's aromatic purity and refined texture stand in contradiction to some clichés about the house's reds, which no longer have any reason to be repeated. This wine is at the highest level of Burgundian craftsmanship, and twenty-five years from now, it will be a legend!

VOSNE-ROMANÉE 2006
Red | 2011 up to 2018   88
A fine Village wine with refined fruitiness; round, harmonious, fairly long and truly typical of the appellation.

Red: 98.8 acres; pinot 100%. White: 24.7 acres; chardonnay 100%. Annual production: 5,500,000 bottles

DOMAINE LATOUR-GIRAUD

6, RN 74
21190 Meursault
Phone 00 33 3 80 21 21 43
Fax 00 33 3 80 21 64 26
domaine-latour-giraud@wanadoo.fr
www.domaine-latour-giraud.com

Home to some of the finest Meursault crus, Latour-Giraud turns out wines that in good years capture all the finesse of their origins, albeit with a disappointing lack of vinosity. It's a bit of a mixed bag, but the best of the bunch is usually the Genevrières, sourced from one very large single parcel.

MEURSAULT CHARLES-MAXIME 2004
White | 2011 up to 2013   **88**
Generous bouquet, fairly long, ready to drink.

MEURSAULT PREMIER CRU CHARMES 2004
White | 2011 up to 2013   **89**
Wiry, with flowering vine notes, fairly fat; pure, but lacks finesse.

MEURSAULT PREMIER CRU GENEVRIÈRES 2006
White | 2011 up to 2016   **88**
Great ripeness to the grapes, with pronounced citrus notes. A generous, fat wine that is rich in alcohol and fairly unusual.

MEURSAULT PREMIER CRU GENEVRIÈRES 2004
White | 2011 up to 2016   **90**
Fairly well-rounded, pure, wiry. Obviously from high-quality terroir.

PULIGNY-MONTRACHET PREMIER CRU
CHAMP CANET 2006
White | 2011 up to 2014   **89**
Racy on the nose and on the palate, with the expected lemony nuances, refined, and long. Quite intense!

Red: 4.9 acres; pinot 100%. White: 19.8 acres; chardonnay 100%. Annual production: 50,000 bottles

DOMAINE LEFLAIVE

Place des Marronniers
21190 Puligny-Montrachet
Phone 00 33 3 80 21 30 13
Fax 00 33 3 80 21 39 57
sce-domaine-leflaive@wanadoo.fr
www.leflaive.fr

In terms of choice of cru, large vineyard plots, and distinctive style, Domaine Leflaive is to white wine what Romanée-Conti is to red: the absolute benchmark in quality winemaking. Anne-Claude Leflaive's conversion to biodynamics has produced purer, more abundantly structured wines with no loss of that remarkable finesse and freshness that made them famous—qualities that are the complete antithesis of the doughy, oxidized style adopted by a good many local producers. Her determination and Pierre Morey's gifted management set an example for idealistic winegrowers the world over. That whiff of reduction in the 2004 was bound to raise a few eyebrows but it's nothing that bottle aging cannot put right. The 2005, on the other hand, seems beyond reproach, showing far more elegance and purity than any other Puligny wine.

Recently tasted
BÂTARD-MONTRACHET GRAND CRU 2006
White | 2014 up to 2021   **95**

BIENVENUES-BÂTARD-MONTRACHET GRAND CRU 2006
White | 2014 up to 2021   **95**

CHEVALIER-MONTRACHET GRAND CRU 2006
White | 2016 up to 2021   **96**

MEURSAULT PREMIER CRU
SOUS LE DOS D'ÂNE 2006
White | 2011 up to 2014   **90**

PULIGNY-MONTRACHET 2006
White | 2012 up to 2016   **90**

PULIGNY-MONTRACHET PREMIER CRU
CLAVOILLON 2006
White | 2013 up to 2018   **91**

PULIGNY-MONTRACHET PREMIER CRU
COMBETTES 2006
White | 2012 up to 2016   **90**

PULIGNY-MONTRACHET PREMIER CRU
PUCELLES 2006
White | 2011 up to 2013   **94**

Older vintages
BÂTARD-MONTRACHET GRAND CRU 2005
White | 2011 up to 2020   **97**
Filled with power and nobility, it keeps its promises but is still in its infancy.

Bâtard-Montrachet grand cru 2004
White | 2011 up to 2018 **97**
To date, one of the five greatest whites of the vintage, with a vigor and aromatic nobility that put to shame other producers who misfired with this vintage.

Bienvenues-Bâtard-Montrachet grand cru 2005
White | 2011 up to 2020 **97**
Pure aromas of flowering vines, wonderfully balanced body, inimitable style. Perfection, or nearly, in a white wine.

Bienvenues-Bâtard-Montrachet grand cru 2004
White | 2011 up to 2019 **96**
Great aromatic nobility, a long, dense body; an apotheosis of the vintage!

Chevalier-Montrachet grand cru 2005
White | 2011 up to 2020 **98**
Transcendently savory, with idyllic texture, incredibly natural in its expression: the triumph of biodynamic grapes from a great terroir when vinified with precision and love.

Montrachet grand cru 2005
White | 2011 up to 2025 **98**
A body that surpasses, if such a thing is possible, the Chevalier, with the same perfect expression of the terroir and vintage, with slightly more integrated oak!

Puligny-Montrachet 2004
White | 2011 up to 2014 **95**
Wonderful aromas of hazelnut flower whose nobility has no equivalent other than the finest Manzanilla; stunning finesse, eloquently showing how this vintage—so absurdly derided—is evolving at the domaine. Perfection for a Village wine.

Puligny-Montrachet premier cru Clavoillon 2005
White | 2011 up to 2017 **95**
Remarkable body, ideally ripe grapes, a diversity of aromatic nuances that is particular to the domaine; an ideal of its type!

Puligny-Montrachet premier cru Clavoillon 2004
White | 2011 up to 2016 **90**
Full, remarkably balanced and dense for the vintage, with striking freshness on the finish.

Puligny-Montrachet premier cru Combettes 2006
White | 2011 up to 2016 **92**
More extreme than the Folatières, insofar as the grapes were even riper and the caramelized taste more pronounced, recalling the 2003. But Combettes is practically a Meursault, from the domaine's sun-drenched parcel.

Puligny-Montrachet premier cru Folatières 2006
White | 2011 up to 2016 **95**
Wondrously tender, velvety, with slightly caramelized grapes, a caress, but with perfect softness that transfigures it. Mouthfeel like this is unsurpassably rare.

Puligny-Montrachet premier cru Folatières 2005
White | 2011 up to 2020 **96**
Admirable refinement and purity to its expression. Transcendent elegance!

Puligny-Montrachet premier cru Pucelles 2005
White | 2013 up to 2017 **96**
Bottling has closed it down a little, but it still has its wonderfully full constitution. Wait three years before opening one again.

Puligny-Montrachet premier cru Pucelles 2004
White | 2011 up to 2016 **95**
Very slight reduction but incredible body for the year, and very noble aromatic persistence. Great connoisseurs will adore this wine!

White: 61.2 acres; chardonnay 100%. **Annual production:** 136,000 bottles

OLIVIER LEFLAIVE

Place du Monument
21190 Puligny-Montrachet
Phone 00 33 3 80 21 37 65
Fax 00 33 3 80 21 33 94
contact@olivier-leflaive.com
www.olivier-leflaive.com

Olivier Leflaive is never short of ideas and he knows how to pull them off. Having been the first to start a négociant business specializing in white wines, he then opened a restaurant (La Table d'Olivier) where guests can taste a wide range of his wines in situ. His latest coup is a magnificent hotel in the heart of Puligny that is sure to attract Puligny devotees from all over the world! The house wines are very adroitly crafted by Franck Grux and usually show plenty of finesse and clean, immediate fruit on the nose—sometimes at the expense of strong expression of terroir.

Recently tasted

AUXEY-DURESSES 2007
White | 2012 up to 2015 **90**

BOURGOGNE LES SÉTILLES 2007
White | 2011 up to 2015 **90**

MEURSAULT PREMIER CRU PERRIÈRES 2007
White | 2015 up to 2019 **95**

MEURSAULT TILLETS 2007
White | 2011 up to 2017 **91**

MONTAGNY PREMIER CRU 2007
White | 2011 up to 2015 **88**

PULIGNY-MONTRACHET 2007
White | 2013 up to 2019 **93**

SAINT-AUBIN DENTS DE CHIEN 2007
White | 2012 up to 2017 **93**

SAINT-AUBIN PREMIER CRU CHATENIÈRE 2007
White | 2011 up to 2017 **90**

SAINT-ROMAIN SOUS LE CHÂTEAU 2007
White | 2011 up to 2015 **90**

VOLNAY PREMIER CRU CLOS DES ANGLES 2007
Red | 2013 up to 2019 **93**

Older vintages

BÂTARD-MONTRACHET GRAND CRU 2006
White | 2011 up to 2018 **95**
Here, once again, two bottles were needed. The second was magnificent: the Grand Cru was fully expressive, with a powerful, delicately saffron-nuanced aspect on the palate and a slight note of flower honey that should open up in six or seven years.

BÂTARD-MONTRACHET GRAND CRU 2005
White | 2011 up to 2017 **88**
Too supple and upfront for a Bâtard, not vinous or brilliant enough. On the other hand, clear finesse.

BIENVENUES-BÂTARD-MONTRACHET GRAND CRU 2006
White | 2011 up to 2016 **94**
A splendid nose of flowering vine with the supreme finesse of this magic sector; more elegant and upfront, as it should be, than the Bâtard, but in five or six years, the latter will surpass it.

CHASSAGNE-MONTRACHET 2005
White | 2011 up to 2015 **90**
Well-vinified, ample; integrated oak, fine floral aromas, an assured finish; an excellent Village wine.

CHASSAGNE-MONTRACHET PREMIER CRU ABBAYE DE MORGEOT 2007
White | 2011 up to 2021 **94**
Another domaine vine, with a more vinous character, a little heavier than the Saint-Marc, broad and savory, even in need of more aging: the prototypical white from red-wine soil.

CHASSAGNE-MONTRACHET PREMIER CRU CLOS SAINT-MARC 2006
White | 2011 up to 2018 **94**
One of the house's domaine vines, at the heart of the Vergers parcel, with a precise nose of white flowers, lemon nuances, and fine honey; very pretty oak, vinified with the greatest skill. Superb.

CORTON-CHARLEMAGNE GRAND CRU 2006
White | 2011 up to 2021 **93**
A well-rounded wine that is aromatically much younger than all the others and not yet completely settled.

CORTON-CHARLEMAGNE GRAND CRU 2005
White | 2011 up to 2017 **93**
Ample, generous, large; delicate oak, satisfactorily vinous, great aging potential but a slight lack of transparency.

MEURSAULT NARVAUX 2006
White | 2011 up to 2016 **93**
This wine raises the bar, with much racier notes on the nose than the Tillets: pure on the palate, long, with rich, complex tastes; a great Meursault.

MEURSAULT PREMIER CRU PERRIÈRES 2006
White | 2011 up to 2018 **91**
More reductive than the other Meursaults on the nose, with typical toasty notes, long, racy, very young, but without all the opulence this supreme terroir is capable of.

Meursault premier cru Poruzots 2006
White | 2011 up to 2016   90
Broad-bodied, subtly fruity with the elegant lemon notes that characterize the house's vinifications in this vintage; savory and lively but, all things considered, the Narvaux seems even racier.

Meursault premier cru Poruzots 2005
White | 2011 up to 2013   89
Notes of orange and mint on the nose, fresh, elegant, middlingly vinous for the vintage. Drink this fairly young.

Meursault Tillets 2006
White | 2011 up to 2014   89
Ripe grapes, smooth oak, an unctuous body that is nonetheless not heavy-handed, excellent style; a perfect pleasure-drinking wine.

Meursault Tillets 2005
White | 2011 up to 2015   90
Nice work in the cellar, rich, unctuous, fairly long, nice potential; very well defined terroir.

Meursault Vireuils 2006
White | 2011 up to 2013   91
Fine classic aromas of hazelnut, a fat yet energetic wine that hides its rich body well. Seductive. Once again, a wine of impeccable style.

Montrachet grand cru 2006
White | 2014 up to 2024   95
The richest wine of all in dry extract, which heralds great longevity. Taut, powerful, racy, perhaps slightly too oaky in this sample, but we will have to wait a bit longer for it.

Pommard 2007
Red | 2014 up to 2019   90
The best red Village wine from this house, and a very fine example of successful Pommard: deeply colored, velvety, spicy, with the expectedly chewy mouthfeel but no rusticity.

Puligny-Montrachet 2006
White | 2011 up to 2016   93
A specialty of the house, which produces 200 barrels of it (over 50,000 bottles!), resulting from a blend of thirty-two parcels. The result is impeccable, pure, linear, and refined, but the corks need to respect this absolute aromatic precision.

Puligny-Montrachet premier cru Champs Gains 2006
White | 2011 up to 2016   91
We had to open two of these, as the first had fallen victim to a flawed cork. Very irritating, because the audience did not notice and thought that the wine was simply imprecise. A blend of eight parcels, an elegant, deliciously lemony wine that, however, does not represent much progress over the Village wine.

Puligny-Montrachet premier cru La Garenne 2006
White | 2011 up to 2016   93
Taut, racy, like a great Saint-Aubin, but a little more austere and mineral; this will be perfect with freshwater fish (perch, pike, etc.).

Puligny-Montrachet premier cru Les Folatières 2005
White | 2011 up to 2015   90
Refined, distinguished, fairly taut, fine oak, but not as vinous as it could be.

Puligny-Montrachet premier cru Referts 2006
White | 2011 up to 2016   94
The most well-rounded of the Premiers Crus, with a ravishing nose of lemongrass and infinite subtlety on the finish. The dominant feeling is one of perfect elegance.

Saint-Aubin Dents de Chien 2006
White | 2011 up to 2016   93
Supreme elegance, worthy of the best Pulignys, slightly more rich, taut, and complex than the remarkable Remilly. This terroir is decidedly exceptional.

Saint-Aubin premier cru Remilly 2006
White | 2011 up to 2014   91
Perfect typicity, pure, tender, with racy notes of flowering vines, and with a wonderful crystalline impression.

Saint-Romain 2006
White | 2011 up to 2014   91
A magnificent wine that has ideal purity to its expression, with skill and a quality of winemaking that are still too rare among the winemakers of this commune. Its subtlety on the finish makes one think that it will be drunk too young, before it completely flowers.

Volnay premier cru Clos des Angles 2006
Red | 2011 up to 2021   91
Precise, elegant, soft, even suave, a Volnay of rare elegance, and certainly as successful in style as the 2005.

Red: 5.9 acres; pinot 100%. **White:** 23.8 acres; aligoté 34%, chardonnay 66%. **Annual production:** 750,000 bottles

DOMAINE LEJEUNE

La Confrérie
1, place de l'Église
21630 Pommard
Phone 00 33 3 80 22 90 88
Fax 00 33 3 80 22 90 88
domaine-lejeune@wanadoo.fr
www.domaine-lejeune.fr

This old, traditional winery uses whole-bunch fermentation (the sort we like) and in good years turns out very pure and elegant wines. Less-than-perfect fruit, of course, presents more of a problem. François Julien de Pommerol is gradually handing over the reins to his nephew, who seems highly motivated and fully in accord with his uncle's strategy. The 2006s will not disappoint their fans.

Recently tasted

POMMARD PREMIER CRU ARGILLIÈRES 2007
Red | 2017 up to 2027   **95**

POMMARD PREMIER CRU LES POUTURES 2007
Red | 2017 up to 2022   **91**

POMMARD PREMIER CRU RUGIENS 2007
Red | 2017 up to 2027   **95**

POMMARD TROIS FOLLOTS 2007
Red | 2015 up to 2022   **90**

Older vintages

POMMARD PREMIER CRU ARGILLIÈRES 2006
Red | 2011 up to 2021   **89**
Fine color, an elegant, floral nose, refined texture, complex tannins, and the tactile sensations of whole-cluster grapes, combining a certain astringency of the stems with inimitable freshness and length.

POMMARD PREMIER CRU LES POUTURES 2006
Red | 2011 up to 2026   **90**
A great, noble, uncommon nose with notes of black olive owing to the grapes' ripeness; very enveloping terroir, truffled, spicy in its tannins—a Pommard for connoisseurs!

POMMARD PREMIER CRU LES POUTURES 2004
Red | 2011 up to 2015   **88**
Floral, supple, elegant, ripe, with vanilla from the barrel still too noticeable, but with the inimitable freshness of whole-cluster grapes.

POMMARD PREMIER CRU RUGIENS 2006
Red | 2011 up to 2026   **93**
A great nose with the same black-olive notes as Les Poutures, but with a more energetic, taut body and more intensity in its tannins, ending with great length on an incredibly racy cocoa bean note. An apex of the vintage in Pommard.

POMMARD PREMIER CRU RUGIENS 2004
Red | 2011 up to 2016   **89**
Complicated, with a slight note pointing to hail, but complex, aristocratic texture and taste.

POMMARD TROIS FOLLOTS 2006
Red | 2011 up to 2018   **89**
A fine floral nose, a delicious Village bottling, very delicate in its texture, harmonious in its tannins, loose, refined; truly remarkable for its category.

Red: 14.8 acres; gamay 5%, pinot 95%. **White:** 2.5 acres; aligoté 40%, chardonnay 60%. **Annual production:** 45,000 bottles

CHÂTEAU DE LA MALTROYE

16, rue de la Murée
21190 Chassagne-Montrachet
Phone 00 33 3 80 21 32 45
Fax 00 33 3 80 21 34 54
château.maltroye@wanadoo.fr

A classic Chassagne estate with a full palette of remarkably situated vineyards in both red and white, and they are equally talented in vinifying both. The whites are harvested very ripe and may have suffered a bit in 2005. The reds are vinous, intense, and certainly among the best wines currently produced in the village. The 2005s are to be savored, even if we have judged them to be slightly inferior to the marvelous 2003s.

Recently tasted

CHASSAGNE-MONTRACHET MORGEOT
VIGNE BLANCHE 2007
White | 2011 up to 2017   89

Older vintages

BÂTARD-MONTRACHET GRAND CRU 2005
White | 2011 up to 2020   93
Rich, fleshy, complex, just a touch heavy but very long on the palate. In short, a true mongrel!

CHASSAGNE-MONTRACHET CLOS DU CHÂTEAU
DE LA MALTROYE (MONOPOLE) 2005
White | 2011 up to 2015   90
Powerful, vinous, dense, the terroir distinct. Rigorously made. Very sensible alcohol level.

CHASSAGNE-MONTRACHET
LA DENT DE CHIEN 2006
White | 2011 up to 2016   86
A bit closed, the oak currently dominating the floral notes, but with good body, density, and style. To try again next year.

CHASSAGNE-MONTRACHET
LA DENT DE CHIEN 2005
White | 2011 up to 2018   93
The most noble of this estate's Premiers Crus. An aroma of grape blossom, very long. A good future ahead of it.

CHASSAGNE-MONTRACHET LA ROMANÉE 2005
White | 2011 up to 2016   88
Too much alcohol, imposing substance. A lack of finesse and purity.

CHASSAGNE-MONTRACHET
LES GRANDES RUCHOTTES 2005
White | 2011 up to 2015   90
Good volume on the palate, vinous, hearty. A slight lack of finesse.

Red: 16.1 acres; pinot noir 100%. White: 21 acres; chardonnay 100%. Annual production: 80,000 bottles

MARATRAY-DUBREUIL

5, place du Souvenir
21550 Ladoix-Serrigny
Phone 00 33 3 80 26 41 09
Fax 00 33 3 80 26 49 07
contact@domaine-maratray-dubreuil.com
www.domaine-maratray-dubreuil.com

This family property, historically linked to the Dubreuil family in Pernand-Vergelesses, is making better and better wines, a result of the influence of the younger generation coming of age. The vineyard legacy is superb, centered around the best terroirs north of Beaune, and the wines we've tasted over the past two years have enchanted us with the integrity of expression of their origin and their classic, timeless style.

Recently tasted

CORTON-CHARLEMAGNE GRAND CRU 2007
White | 2013 up to 2017   88

LADOIX NAGETS 2007
Red | 2012 up to 2017   88

Older vintages

CORTON-BRESSANDES GRAND CRU 2006
Red | 2011 up to 2018   88
Serious constitution, limpid terroir, firm but without drying or artificial tannins; a well-made wine that lacks only a supplementary dose of finesse.

CORTON-CHARLEMAGNE GRAND CRU 2006
White | 2012 up to 2016   88
Very developed floral aromas that are almost amylic, but without being a caricature. A full, clean, precise wine with good technical mastery; cellar it three or four years so that its terroir comes to the fore.

LADOIX PREMIER CRU LES GRÊCHONS 2006
White | 2011 up to 2014   88
An excellent expression of this fine terroir, a fluid wine that is not at all hollow; elegant, with well-integrated oak and a complex finish. This vintage was particularly good for this wine.

PERNAND-VERGELESSES
VIGNES BLANCHES 2006
White | 2011 up to 2014   89
Greenish gold in color, very luminous, a fat wine, well rounded for the appellation, very limpid terroir, well-calibrated oak, very recommendable and even finer and more saline than the Ladoix!

Red: 29.7 acres; pinot noir 100%. White: 9.8 acres; chardonnay 100%. Annual production: 80,000 bottles

DOMAINE CATHERINE ET CLAUDE MARÉCHAL

6, route de Chalon
21200 Bligny-lès-Beaune
Phone 00 33 3 80 21 44 37
Fax 00 33 3 80 26 85 01
marechalcc@orange.fr

An honest producer of red wines with fabulously natural and forward fruit that makes for some delicious drinking! Outstandingly luscious pinot noir at very reasonable prices. The 2005s are in line with the rest, if a bit richer and more firmly tannic. All things being equal, though, the 2003s were more to our taste. For the time being the excellent 2007s have very pure fruit, with particularly classic Savignys.

Recently tasted
AUXEY-DURESSES 2007
Red | 2014 up to 2019   89

CHOREY-LÈS-BEAUNE 2007
Red | 2011 up to 2017   89

SAVIGNY-LÈS-BEAUNE 2007
White | 2011 up to 2014   90

SAVIGNY-LÈS-BEAUNE PREMIER CRU
LES LAVIÈRES 2007
Red | 2011 up to 2017   89

SAVIGNY-LÈS-BEAUNE VIEILLES VIGNES 2007
Red | 2011 up to 2015   86

VOLNAY 2007
Red | 2012 up to 2017   87

Older vintages
AUXEY-DURESSES 2005
Red | 2011 up to 2015   90
A rich color. Black cherry on the nose. Tannic, full, vigorous, natural.

BOURGOGNE 2005
White | 2011 up to 2013   93
Exceptionally ripe grapes. A fat wine, long and pure, in the tradition of this marvelous estate!

BOURGOGNE GRAVEL 2005
Red | 2011 up to 2014   88
An appealing pinot noir, rich, easy to drink, delicious.

LADOIX CHAILLOTS 2005
Red | 2011 up to 2014   86
A bit lean for the year and the producer.

POMMARD LA CHANIÈRE 2005
Red | 2011 up to 2020   93
An intense fruit character and very ripe grapes. Powerful, wild, natural, but precise. A wine of great character.

POMMARD LA CHANIÈRE 2004
Red | 2011 up to 2014   87
Spicy, velvety, pleasant to drink thanks to highly extracted tannins.

SAVIGNY-LÈS-BEAUNE 2006
White | 2011 up to 2013   88
Slightly reduced, with a toasted hazelnut character, in the Meursault style. Nice energy, quite appealing.

SAVIGNY-LÈS-BEAUNE 2005
White | 2011 up to 2013   91
Full, long, harmonious, natural. Yet another benchmark!

SAVIGNY-LÈS-BEAUNE PREMIER CRU
LES LAVIÈRES 2006
Red | 2011 up to 2016   89
An ultra-tender texture. Supple, currently with incredible charm, and with an ease that makes it disappear quickly.

SAVIGNY-LÈS-BEAUNE PREMIER CRU
LES LAVIÈRES 2005
Red | 2011 up to 2015   90
A nice nose, a generous wine, full, luscious, natural.

SAVIGNY-LÈS-BEAUNE VIEILLES VIGNES 2005
Red | 2011 up to 2050   90
A rich color, ripe. An expressive fruit character. Natural, frank, really a very nice wine.

VOLNAY 2005
Red | 2011 up to 2050   91
A nice style, pure, elegant, and fresher than the other cuvées.

Red: 25.2 acres; pinot 100%. White: 4.4 acres; aligoté 28%, chardonnay 72%. Annual production: 65,000 bottles

DOMAINE MARQUIS D'ANGERVILLE

21190 Meursault
Phone 00 33 3 80 21 61 75
Fax 00 33 3 80 21 65 07
info@domainedangerville.fr

Along with Domaine de la Pousse d'Or, this long-established winery possesses the most impressive legacy of exceptional pinot noir vineyards in Volnay, which they are rightfully proud of. Over the past fifty years, they have shown impressive continuity of quality in the sector. Guillaume d'Angerville left a career in banking, where his reputation for integrity and precision was unquestioned, in order to take over from his father, Jacques. The 2006s we tasted show an exceptional continuity in the grand tradition of the domaine. But be aware, these Volnays, made for the long haul, have firm, slightly outdated tannins that in twenty years will still have the original attributes of this excellent vintage.

Recently tasted

MEURSAULT PREMIER CRU SANTENOTS 2007
White | 2013 up to 2019   90

VOLNAY PREMIER CRU CAILLERETS 2007
Red | 2014 up to 2019   90

VOLNAY PREMIER CRU CHAMPANS 2007
Red | 2017 up to 2027   90

VOLNAY PREMIER CRU CLOS DES DUCS 2007
Red | 2017 up to 2027   91

VOLNAY PREMIER CRU TAILLEPIEDS 2007
Red | 2015 up to 2019   88

Older vintages

MEURSAULT PREMIER CRU SANTENOTS 2006
White | 2011 up to 2013   93
Very pale in color, superb citrus aromas, great finesse, and very fine persistence. The domaine has greatly improved the precision of its vinification for whites.

MEURSAULT PREMIER CRU SANTENOTS 2005
White | 2011 up to 2015   95
Very noble aromas of flowering vine, great sap, magnificent raciness, ideal vinification.

MEURSAULT PREMIER CRU SANTENOTS 2004
White | 2011 up to 2050   93
Lemony and complex on the nose, fairly refined, nice follow-up on the palate; the terroir is expressed well.

VOLNAY PREMIER CRU CAILLERETS 2006
Red | 2011 up to 2030   93
Very spicy and wiry on the nose and on the palate, tannins less plush than in the Cham-

pans or Taillepieds, energetic and racy, but it will need more time in the bottle.

VOLNAY PREMIER CRU CHAMPANS 2006
Red | 2011 up to 2021   93
A discreet nose, slightly spicy, pretty texture, firm yet fine tannins, good aging potential, a classic wine. Sure to be a long-term ager.

VOLNAY PREMIER CRU CLOS DES DUCS 2006
Red | 2011 up to 2024   91
Tighter texture than the Champans, slender form, firm tannins, slightly austere but with a great deal of complexity in the relationship between the fruit and the tannins.

VOLNAY PREMIER CRU FRÉMIET 2006
Red | 2011 up to 2018   89
Aroma of small red fruit, with a serious or even strict construction in the spirit of the domaine; more bare-faced tannins than in the other Premiers Crus. Frémiet, with its delicate nature, might do better with slightly more extraction.

VOLNAY PREMIER CRU TAILLEPIEDS 2006
Red | 2011 up to 2013   94
Perfectly defined fruit and texture, with absolutely classic craftsmanship of all of its components and especially, under the current leadership of Guillaume d'Angerville, a wonderful continuity in style from the domaine's past.

Red: 29.7 acres; pinot 100%. White: 2.5 acres; chardonnay 100%. Annual production: 55,000 bottles

DOMAINE MICHELOT

31, rue de la Velle
21190 Meursault
Phone 00 33 3 80 21 23 17
Fax 00 33 3 80 21 63 62
mestremichelot@aol.com

We welcome this classic Meursault domaine back to the guide, since the time it was divided between the new generations of the Michelot family. The original entity still exists, and judging from the 2006s presented for tasting they are making wines that are warm, aromatic, easy to understand, and an excellent introduction to the subtleties of Meursault terroirs.

Recently tasted

MEURSAULT PREMIER CRU CHARMES 2007
White | 2011 up to 2015   90

MEURSAULT PREMIER CRU PERRIÈRES 2007
White | 2014 up to 2019   92

Older vintages

MEURSAULT GRANDS CHARRONS 2006
White | 2011 up to 2014   87
Nice use of barrels, a delicately toasty, grilled nose, with straightforward, complex tastes, very limpid terroir; a beginner's wine, sure, but it gives a good idea of a classic Meursault.

MEURSAULT PREMIER CRU CHARMES 2006
White | 2011 up to 2016   90
Fairly developed on an aromatic level, with even some reductive notes that recall a nice sauvignon on chalky soil, along with citrus nuances. Fairly taut on the palate for its corpulence; a typical Meursault, full of generosity.

DOMAINE FRANÇOIS MIKULSKI

7 RD 974
21190 Meursault
Phone 00 33 3 80 21 25 11
Fax 00 33 3 80 21 63 38

François Mikulski's estate is particularly famous abroad and boasts a handsome slice of the Meursault Premier Cru, plus a sizeable parcel of Santenots du Milieu—a mecca for lovers of Côte de Beaune reds. Mikulski's version, indeed, often comes across as his top offering: exceptionally powerful, balanced, and true to type. The white wines sometimes seem a trifle oxidized, as do a good many of their rivals, and lack the precision of other, more stylish efforts.

BOURGOGNE 2005
White | 2011 up to 2015   89
Good Meursault character, with toasty notes, well-vinified, long, complex.

MEURSAULT PREMIER CRU LES CHARMES 2005
White | 2011 up to 2013   90
Pleasant reductive note on the nose, very different from the 2004s that are already dead. Good mouthfeel and finesse.

VOLNAY SANTENOTS DU MILIEU 2005
Red | 2011 up to 2030   95
A great, luscious wine, deep, with perfect expression of the terroir, masterfully vinified. Just as good as the one from Comtes Lafon.

Red: 6.2 acres; pinot noir 100%. White: 14.8 acres; chardonnay 100%. Annual production: 45,000 bottles

JEAN-LOUIS MOISSENET BONNARD

Rue des Jardins
21630 Pommard
Phone 00 33 3 80 24 62 34
Fax 00 33 3 80 22 30 04
jean-louis.domaine-moissenet
-bonnard@wanadoo.fr
www.moissenet-bonnard.com

This artisan winery has become a reliable source for quality if you like your Pommard full and velvety, rustic, but in the way of a gentleman farmer, the kind of wines you drink in the fall and that go well with game birds. Recent vintages show clear progress in terms of elegance and focus, notably in the wonderful old vines bottling the Épenots.

Recently tasted

AUXEY-DURESSES PREMIER CRU
LES GRANDS CHAMPS 2007
Red | 2015 up to 2019   87

POMMARD CRAS 2007
Red | 2014 up to 2022   88

POMMARD PETITS NOIZONS 2007
Red | 2015 up to 2019   89

POMMARD PREMIER CRU ÉPENOTS 2007
Red | 2017 up to 2022   94

POMMARD PREMIER CRU PEZEROLLES 2007
Red | 2017 up to 2022   93

Older vintages

POMMARD CRAS 2006
Red | 2011 up to 2021   88
A fine, truffled nose and a full-bodied, fleshy, firm wine that shows good typicity of the rich soil in the lower part of the village; true Pommard.

POMMARD PREMIER CRU CHARMOTS 2006
Red | 2011 up to 2021   88
A classic, spicy nose; the wine is firm, fleshy, vinous, complex—exactly as one would expect it to be.

POMMARD PREMIER CRU ÉPENOTS 2006
Red | 2011 up to 2024   90
Very powerful, with a slightly wild quality made to pair with game; more truffled, in a Pezerolles spirit, than floral, eloquently illustrating one of the two personalities of this fine parcel.

Red: 10 acres; pinot noir 100%. White: 3 acres; chardonnay 100%. Annual production: 30,000 bottles

DOMAINE RENÉ MONNIER

6, rue du Docteur-Rolland
21190 Meursault
Phone 00 33 3 80 21 29 32
Fax 00 33 3 80 21 61 79
domaine-rene-monnier@wanadoo.fr

This domaine has excellent plots, from Beaune to Puligny-Montrachet, and they have come a long way in recent vintages, with wines that are more and more representative of the value of their terroirs. You can certainly count on the Meursault Charmes, which comes from old vines in the lower part of the vineyard, and also on the Puligny Folatières. The reds, especially the Clos des Chênes, are along the lines of current trends with deeply colored wines made from very ripe grapes, but with truly elegant tannins.

Recently tasted

BEAUNE PREMIER CRU TOUSSAINTS 2007
Red | 2012 up to 2019   91

BOURGOGNE 2007
White | 2011 up to 2013   86

MARANGES PREMIER CRU
CLOS DE LA FUSSIÈRE 2007
Red | 2011 up to 2015   87

VOLNAY PREMIER CRU CLOS DES CHÊNES 2007
Red | 2015 up to 2019   87

Older vintages

MEURSAULT PREMIER CRU CHARMES 2006
White | 2011 up to 2015   88
Very typical of the cru, complex, tasty, long, and both delicate and sensual. Recommended.

PULIGNY-MONTRACHET PREMIER CRU
FOLATIÈRES 2006
White | 2011 up to 2016   88
Complexity worthy of the terroir, a very elegant lemony finish; a clean, well-vinified wine that is highly recommendable, even if the vintage gives it certain limitations.

VOLNAY PREMIER CRU CLOS DES CHÊNES 2006
Red | 2011 up to 2018   89
A refined, complex nose, well crafted in its balance between the oak and the cherry and licorice notes of a very ripe harvest; luscious texture, appreciable length, fine, straightforward tannins. A very fine Volnay. From the same producer, a Pommard Vignots also appealed to us for its cleanness and balance.

Red: 19.8 acres; pinot noir 100%. White: 24.7 acres; chardonnay 100%. Annual production: 120,000 bottles

DOMAINE EDMOND MONNOT ET FILS

Rue de Borgy
71150 Dezize-les-Maranges
Phone 00 33 3 85 91 16 12
Fax 00 33 3 85 91 15 99
domaine.monnotetfils@free.fr

Monnot et Fils is plainly one of the most dependable producers in the little-known Maranges area, at the southern tip of the Côte de Beaune: quality wines, faithful to their terroir, at very attractive prices. This includes a few lovely 2005s that survived the heat and hail, at a price that won't break the bank.

HAUTES CÔTES DE BEAUNE 2005
White | 2011 up to 2013   **88**
Fat, pure, simple, and sincere! The kind of wine we like!

MARANGES PREMIER CRU LA FUSSIÈRE 2005
White | 2011 up to 2013   **90**
Well-integrated oak influence, fat, well balanced, very natural! The most delicate of the range from this producer.

Red: 16.3 acres; pinot 100%. White: 5.9 acres; aligoté 40%, chardonnay 60%. Annual production: 25,000 bottles

DOMAINE DE MONTILLE

Rue de Pied-de-la-Vallée
21190 Volnay
Phone 00 33 3 80 21 62 67
Fax 00 33 3 80 21 67 14
sales@domainedemontille.com

This family estate in Volnay has recently undergone considerable expansion following the purchase of prime holdings throughout the Côte d'Or from the Domaine Thomas (Moillard). All of the estate wines are now aged in the ancient Ropiteau and Bouchard cellars in Meursault, made in that masterfully classic style that we have come to expect from Étienne de Montille over the past decade. He works closely with his sister Alix, who shares her brother's commitment to a very particular style of wine. The first vintage from the expanded winery is the 2005—which luckily was a very good year indeed!

BEAUNE PREMIER CRU GRÈVES 2006
Red | 2011 up to 2018   **90**
Delicate on the nose, with gentle smoky nuances, tender but with good volume, a suave texture. The inimitable pedigree of the terroir is very apparent on the finish. A nice example of the potential for refinement in the best Beaune wines.

CLOS DE VOUGEOT GRAND CRU 2006
Red | 2011 up to 2024   **94**
Full, supple, but very racy and nuanced. Undoubtedly the most accomplished of the estate's red wines, but made in minuscule quantities.

CLOS DE VOUGEOT GRAND CRU 2005
Red | 2011 up to 2025   **91**
The first vinification of a new acquisition for the estate. A very precise wine, racy but the tannins a bit rigid.

CORTON-CLOS DU ROI GRAND CRU 2006
Red | 2011 up to 2021   **93**
Rich in natural alcohol, with a plumper yet also more delicate texture than the Pommards. A very distinguished wine, subtle, unquestionably the estate's best wine of the Côte de Beaune in 2006.

CORTON-POUGETS GRAND CRU 2005
Red | 2011 up to 2030   **95**
A very elegant, refined wine, impeccably balanced, from one of the best parcels in all of Corton, but which has since been entirely replanted to Chardonnay to make Corton-Charlemagne. The Corton Rouge 2006 came from a parcel in the Clos du Roi.

Nuits-Saint-Georges premier cru Les Thoreys 2006
Red | 2011 up to 2018   **90**
A very nice texture. The nose combines red berries, leather, and spices. Open, delicate, with very pleasant tannins. Can be drunk rather young.

Pommard premier cru Les Pézerolles 2006
Red | 2011 up to 2021   **93**
Excellent balance, a combination of power and finesse. A bit less energy than in the estate's Volnays.

Pommard premier cru Les Pézerolles 2005
Red | 2011 up to 2025   **94**
Pure, ample, spicy, with fine-grained tannins. All about elegance, but without the radiance of the Domaine de Courcel. Nevertheless, a splendid wine.

Pommard premier cru Rugiens 2006
Red | 2011 up to 2021   **91**
A bit tauter than the Pézerolles, a bit less immediate generosity of texture. A powerful, racy wine, but not at the same level as the very best Rugiens of the vintage.

Pommard premier cru Rugiens 2005
Red | 2011 up to 2030   **94**
A touch fuller, tauter, and more mineral than the Pézerolles but with less immediately elegant tannins. It might outstrip it in fifteen years!

Puligny-Montrachet premier cru Cailleret 2006
White | 2011 up to 2018   **94**
Those who like pure, direct chardonnays will love the finesse of this cuvée, especially since it doesn't skimp on body or vigor in a vintage that could have given flabby wines. One might wish for a bit more aromatic complexity, with a slightly more aggressive yeast autolysis.

Puligny-Montrachet premier cru Cailleret 2005
White | 2011 up to 2020   **95**
A lot of nerve for the vintage, remarkable aromatic purity and even more remarkable subtlety of the oak influence. A very distinguished wine, but only for cultivated connoisseurs!

Volnay premier cru Champans 2005
Red | 2011 up to 2025   **93**
The nose is a bit wilder and spicier than on the other Premiers Crus, the body firm, a very nice balance. All that's missing is the fullness of the very old vines.

Volnay premier cru Les Mitans 2006
Red | 2011 up to 2018   **91**
Very delicate body and graceful aromatics, a generous finish with no harshness from the tannins, typical of its appellation and perfect to drink while waiting for the 2005 and 2007.

Volnay premier cru Les Mitans 2005
Red | 2011 up to 2025   **93**
This cru is constantly reaffirming its worth: it is in the family of fine-grained Volnays, not very spicy, and the vintage gives it a fullness never seen here before.

Volnay premier cru Taillepieds 2006
Red | 2011 up to 2018   **91**
Very delicate aromas, an aristocratic texture, full and supple, but a slight lack of flesh.

Volnay premier cru Taillepieds 2005
Red | 2011 up to 2025   **94**
Irreproachable balance, clean, pure aromatics, refined, long, complex in the integration of the tannins into the body of the wine; distinguished.

Vosne-Romanée premier cru Malconsorts 2006
Red | 2011 up to 2021   **93**
A noble and varied nose, supple and suave body, clearly less intensity than there was in the 2005 and will be in the 2007.

Vosne-Romanée premier cru Malconsorts 2005
Red | 2011 up to 2025   **95**
A great deal of nobility and aromatic purity, and astounding precision for a first vinification in the expression of this great terroir.

Vosne-Romanée premier cru Malconsorts cuvée Christiane 2005
Red | 2011 up to 2025   **96**
Under this name, the estate vinifies a stunning parcel of Malconsorts, right up against La Tâche! The wine has just a hint more definition than the basic Malconsorts, and the blind tasting substantiated the estate's decision to separate them.

Red: 17.3 acres; pinot 100%. White: 2.1 acres; chardonnay 100%. Annual production: 35,000 bottles

DEUX MONTILLE

Rue Pied de La Vallée
21190 Volnay
Phone 00 33 3 80 21 62 67
Fax 00 33 3 80 21 67 14

This young négociant business was
started by Alix and Étienne de Montille,
both devoted to white Burgundy but owners of an estate that mainly specializes in
reds. Alix derives her taste from the wines
of Jean-Marc Roulot, putting honesty, ner-
vousness, and freshness before opulence:
she loves what she calls "chiseled wines"
and vinifies her own accordingly. She specializes in wines from lesser-known and
therefore less pricey appellations (roughly
50,000 bottles).

MEURSAULT PREMIER CRU BOUCHÈRES 2004
White | 2011 up to 2014   91
Lots of purity and complexity on the nose,
with a light lactic note. Fleshy without being
heavy, very elegant and long on the finish.

MEURSAULT PREMIER CRU
PORUSOT DESSUS 2005
White | 2011 up to 2017   90
Rich, unctuous without being heavy, well-
integrated oak influence. A very pure style
with a good future.

MONTAGNY LES COÈRES 2005
White | 2011 up to 2013   87
Very pure mineral aromas, finesse; subtlety
but lacking in vinosity, smooth. A good aperitif.

RULLY 2005
White | 2011 up to 2013   86
Clean and lively, the opposite of the current
trends in Rully. Finishes on an almost saline,
aperitif note. Missing a strong expression
of terroir.

SAINT-ROMAIN 2005
White | 2011 up to 2013   88
Well-integrated oak, lots of finesse and har-
mony, quite long. More vinosity than the
Rully.

DOMAINE BERNARD MOREAU ET FILS

3, route de Chagny
21190 Chassagne-Montrachet
Phone 00 33 3 80 21 33 70
Fax 00 33 3 80 21 30 05
domaine.moreau-bernard@wanadoo.fr

A first-class Chassagne estate with an
even distribution of plantings of red and
white wines that are now very deftly made.
We love their vinosity, coupled with just
enough finesse for good balance. The old-
vines offering from the magnificent
Grandes Ruchottes Premier Cru is the
best there is from this "climat" (a small
plot or single block of vineyard)—as good
as any Grand Cru.

Recently tasted
CHASSAGNE-MONTRACHET MORGEOT 2007
White | 2015 up to 2022   92

CHASSAGNE-MONTRACHET PREMIER CRU
GRANDES RUCHOTTES 2007
White | 2013 up to 2017   90

CHASSAGNE-MONTRACHET PREMIER CRU
LA MALTROIE 2007
White | 2013 up to 2019   90

Older vintages
CHASSAGNE-MONTRACHET 2006
White | 2011 up to 2014   89
A complete Village-level wine, joining power
and finesse with remarkable length. This
confirms the success both of the village and
of the estate in this vintage that is undeservedly praised for whites.

CHASSAGNE-MONTRACHET 2005
White | 2011 up to 2013   90
Excellent overall balance, nice fluidity without being too lean, no heaviness, great
finesse.

CHASSAGNE-MONTRACHET PREMIER CRU
CHENEVOTTES 2006
White | 2011 up to 2018   91
A great deal of tension and noble aromat-
ics. This wine is already quite pleasant, full
of vitality, concentrated but juicy, and long.
A true accomplishment!

CHASSAGNE-MONTRACHET PREMIER CRU
CHENEVOTTES 2005
White | 2011 up to 2013   91
Vanilla notes. Tender, harmonious, balanced,
with nice style. To drink soon.

CHASSAGNE-MONTRACHET PREMIER CRU
GRANDES RUCHOTTES 2006
White | 2011 up to 2018   **94**
Admirable floral aromas, great substance, and a long, racy finish. This is one of the great wines of the vintage and a superb expression of this top-notch parcel! A great winemaker is reaffirmed.

CHASSAGNE-MONTRACHET PREMIER CRU
GRANDES RUCHOTTES 2004
White | 2011 up to 2014   **93**
Great substance, bright acidity, an evident nobility of expression that shows in the persistence of the flavor and tactile sensations.

CHASSAGNE-MONTRACHET PREMIER CRU
MORGEOT LA CARDEUSE 2006
White | 2011 up to 2016   **90**
Powerful, remarkably characteristic of the cru, very deep but not heavy, long; complete for the vintage.

CHASSAGNE-MONTRACHET PREMIER CRU
MORGEOT LA CARDEUSE 2005
Red | 2011 up to 2013   **88**
Round, hearty, almost too marked by licorice but skillfully vinified nevertheless. To drink soon.

CHASSAGNE-MONTRACHET PREMIER CRU
MORGEOT LA CARDEUSE 2005
White | 2011 up to 2023   **90**
Black, rich, ultra-powerful. The terroir is very strongly emphasized. A great future ahead.

CHASSAGNE-MONTRACHET
VIEILLES VIGNES 2005
Red | 2011 up to 2017   **89**
Black, powerful, wild. The tannins are a bit rough but clean. A good future ahead.

SAINT-AUBIN PREMIER CRU EN REMILLY 2005
White | 2011 up to 2013   **88**
Light, pure, the racy terroir pronounced. Not quite enough vinosity.

Red: 16.8 acres; pinot 100%. White: 17.8 acres; aligoté 13%, chardonnay 87%. Annual production: 85,000 bottles

MORET-NOMINÉ

🍷 🍷 🍷 🍷 🍷

1-3, rue Goussery
21200 Beaune
Phone 00 33 3 80 24 00 70
Fax 00 33 3 80 24 79 65
moret.nomine@wanadoo.fr

This young négociant ages his wines, essentially whites, in the cellars of the Hameau de Barboron, in Savigny-lès-Beaune, one of the most pleasant hotels on the Côte d'Or. He knows how to select wines with the best provenance and to find the perfect barrels that are best adapted to the type of wine he wants to make. His wines shine for their harmonious constitution and their precise definition of each terroir. A more and more reliable source for high-end restaurants.

Recently tasted
CHASSAGNE-MONTRACHET PREMIER CRU
BAUDINES 2007
White | 2013 up to 2017   **91**

MEURSAULT PREMIER CRU CHARMES 2007
White | 2012 up to 2017   **88**

MEURSAULT PREMIER CRU GENEVRIÈRES 2007
White | 2013 up to 2017   **88**

MEURSAULT PREMIER CRU GOUTTE D'OR 2007
White | 2013 up to 2017   **91**

MEURSAULT PREMIER CRU PERRIÈRES 2007
White | 2014 up to 2019   **90**

Older vintages
MEURSAULT PREMIER CRU CHARMES 2006
White | 2011 up to 2018   **94**
A superb expression of the terroir and village on the nose; a fat yet elegant wine that is long, wonderfully crafted, and bottled with skill, without losing any of its fat or breadth!

MEURSAULT PREMIER CRU GENEVRIÈRES 2006
White | 2011 up to 2018   **94**
A racy, fat, powerful wine, but one that is currently very hard to distinguish from the Charmes. It has the same skillful balance between oxidation and reduction (honey and slightly bitter hazelnut) and the same quality of oak, which seems perfectly appropriate to Meursault.

MEURSAULT PREMIER CRU GOUTTE D'OR 2006
White | 2011 up to 2016   **91**
This shows the same reduction that we found in La Velle, but more complexity in its hazelnut notes, very intelligently integrated oak, and, especially, more finesse due to its acidity, which helps balance out the alcohol. A very fine Premier Cru.

MEURSAULT PREMIER CRU PERRIÈRES 2006
White | 2011 up to 2013   **94**
Very supple, elegant, refined, persistent; showing its distinction from the Charmes through greater transparency or a more crystalline texture and taste; very balanced. Do not drink this too cold (59° to 60°F seems ideal in order to respect its purity).

MEURSAULT SOUS LA VELLE 2006
White | 2011 up to 2016   **90**
A bit of bitter reduction on the nose, doubtless necessary for appropriate aging in the bottle, with lots of fat and purity to the tactile sensations; an excellent expression of the terroir and vintage—a very well-made wine.

PULIGNY-MONTRACHET PREMIER CRU FOLATIÈRES 2006
White | 2011 up to 2014   **90**
Very pleasant honey notes, though they do have us suspecting that the wine will evolve quickly in the bottle; very suave on the palate, long, but without the complexity of the best Meursaults. On the other hand, the purity of its tastes is as clear as day.

RULLY 2006
White | 2011 up to 2013   **90**
An absolutely delicious wine with a very rare fattiness to it and an equally astonishing harmony to the fruit despite the tendency of this vintage to be a bit "heavy." This négociant has managed to find the producer(s) who can harvest ideally ripe grapes!

Annual production: 25,000 bottles

DOMAINE MARC MOREY ET FILS

3, rue Charles-Paquelin
21190 Chassagne-Montrachet
Phone 00 33 3 80 21 30 11
Fax 00 33 3 80 21 90 20
domaine.marc-morey@wanadoo.fr

This is one of Chassagne-Montrachet's most dependable performers, thanks to vineyards in prime Chardonnay terrain, located midslope above the village itself. The wines are generally very pure—quite mineral and with good aging potential—but unlikely to age as gracefully as the vintages of the 1980s.

CHASSAGNE-MONTRACHET 2006
White | 2011 up to 2016   **89**
Straightforward, clean, ample, and complex, a well-rounded, remarkably vinified Village wine.

CHASSAGNE-MONTRACHET PREMIER CRU LES CHENEVOTTES 2005
White | 2011 up to 2015   **88**
Clean, elegant, not very complex but pure, balanced. Will be at its peak in three years.

CHASSAGNE-MONTRACHET PREMIER CRU LES VERGERS 2006
White | 2011 up to 2016   **87**
Wiry, very closed—as is, moreover, the Virondot from the same vintage—still too young and hardened by the sulfur dioxide needed for its conservation. But there is good wine here! It should get a better score with time.

CHASSAGNE-MONTRACHET PREMIER CRU LES VERGERS 2005
White | 2011 up to 2015   **89**
Refined, fresh, clean, more finesse than the Chenevottes.

CHASSAGNE-MONTRACHET PREMIER CRU VIRONDOT 2005
White | 2011 up to 2015   **91**
Fresh, mineral, fairly long on the palate, very well vinified, though we might perhaps have hoped it was a little more vinous. Virondot is part of the La Grande Montagne parcel next to La Romanée.

CHEVALIER-MONTRACHET GRAND CRU 2006
White | 2011 up to 2021   **95**
A very elegant nose with well-integrated oak, very pure, long, complex, very well protected against oxidation. Has the potential to be one of the highlights of its kind!

PULIGNY-MONTRACHET 2006
White | 2011 up to 2016   **93**
Remarkable flowering vine aromas, a great success; long, complex, absolutely at the level of the Premiers Crus, with a balance to its acidity and potential that are truly rare for the vintage!

PULIGNY-MONTRACHET PREMIER CRU
LES PUCELLES 2006
White | 2011 up to 2016   **90**
Rich, fat, unctuous, long, good body, terroir character that is worthy of its roots, excellent stuffing, should age well!

PULIGNY-MONTRACHET PREMIER CRU
LES PUCELLES 2005
White | 2011 up to 2016   **91**
Great finesse and subtlety, flowering vine aromas, middling body but very pure texture, transparent. For refined connoisseurs.

Red: 5.2 acres; pinot 100%. White: 17.9 acres; aligoté 12%, chardonnay 88%. Annual production: 55,000 bottles

DOMAINE PIERRE MOREY ET MOREY BLANC

13, rue Pierre-Mouchoux
21190 Meursault
Phone 00 33 3 80 21 21 03
Fax 00 33 3 80 21 66 38
morey-blanc@wanadoo.fr
www.morey-meursault.fr

Pierre Morey, the celebrated winemaker for Domaine Leflaive, shows the same respect for soil and environment in his own holding. The great white wines he makes here testify to the same masterful style. Their slightly reduced nose when young needs five to fifteen years' bottle aging to express the full force of the terroir. The reds exhibit more polished tannins and aromatic finesse than before, with a particularly excellent Grands Épenots. Production these days is boosted by a small range of négociant wines, sold under the Morey Blanc label, that, from the simplest to the most stunning, are similar in style to the domaine wines.

Recently tasted
BÂTARD-MONTRACHET GRAND CRU 2006
White | 2016 up to 2026   **96**

MEURSAULT LES TESSONS 2007
White | 2017 up to 2022   **93**

MEURSAULT PREMIER CRU CHARMES 2007
White | 2017 up to 2022   **94**

MEURSAULT PREMIER CRU PERRIÈRES 2006
White | 2014 up to 2021   **95**

Older vintages
BÂTARD-MONTRACHET GRAND CRU 2005
White | 2011 up to 2025   **95**
A well-rounded wine with slight reduction on the nose but extreme aromatic finesse and complexity, with the expected body and longevity.

CORTON-CHARLEMAGNE GRAND CRU 2005
White | 2011 up to 2020   **90**
Still too young and closed, with a fine, complex yet discreet nose, a very well balanced body, integrated oak; a noble wine that should be cellared for eight or ten years more.

MEURSAULT LES TESSONS 2005
White | 2011 up to 2020   **90**
A very balanced wine that combines finesse and robustness with the producer's taut, discreet style, with a vinous side that too often lacks in his production.

MEURSAULT PREMIER CRU BOUCHÈRES 2006

White | 2011 up to 2021   **90**

The only bottling presented by this producer, as the others were perhaps tired from having been bottled so recently. A fine, sober, powerful, complex wine made for aging.

MEURSAULT PREMIER CRU PERRIÈRES 2005

White | 2011 up to 2020   **95**

A great wine that is very pure, racy, subtle, with rare tension for the vintage; a great future before it.

MONTHÉLIE 2005

Red | 2011 up to 2020   **88**

Fine aniseed nose, a wine with character; very complex for a Village wine, with almost mineral tension on the palate, doubtless due to the altitude and sunlight on the vines.

POMMARD PREMIER CRU LES GRANDS ÉPENOTS 2005

Red | 2011 up to 2025   **90**

Fine color, an open, precise nose of dark fruit, balanced body, dense yet racy texture, nice length; a very carefully made wine that nevertheless lacks the personality of the neighboring parcels.

SAINT-AUBIN PREMIER CRU LES COMBES 2005

White | 2011 up to 2015   **87**

Well-produced, a pure wine that is very balanced, even if the details don't have all the purity and elegance of other terroirs, such as Les Murgers des Dents de Chien or Remilly.

VOLNAY PREMIER CRU SANTENOTS 2005

Red | 2011 up to 2025   **89**

A new acquisition by the domaine: a deeply colored, dense, taut, very tannic yet fleshy wine that is very earthy, with good aging potential ahead.

Red: 8.3 acres; pinot noir 100%. White: 16.7 acres; aligoté 36%, chardonnay 64%. Annual production: 70,000 bottles

DOMAINE ALBERT MOROT

Château de la Creusotte
20, avenue Charles Jaffelin
21200 Beaune
Phone 00 33 380223539
Fax 00 33 380224750
albertmorot@aol.com

Geoffroy Choppin de Janvry now makes some of the classiest and most exciting wines in the whole of Burgundy, and not just in Beaune and Savigny. This is the ultimate expression of the local style at its most classical and its most mysterious. The 2005s are extraordinary: buy as much as you can!

Recently tasted

BEAUNE PREMIER CRU LES MARCONNETS 2007

Red | 2015 up to 2022   **90**

BEAUNE PREMIER CRU LES TEURONS 2007

Red | 2013 up to 2019   **88**

SAVIGNY-LÈS-BEAUNE PREMIER CRU LA BATAILLÈRE AUX VERGELESSES 2007

Red | 2015 up to 2019   **90**

Older vintages

BEAUNE PREMIER CRU LES BRESSANDES 2005

Red | 2011 up to 2025   **97**

A great wine, complete, refined, with an immense future ahead of it. A masterpiece in the works, showing the potential of the great Beaunes!

BEAUNE PREMIER CRU LES CENT VIGNES 2005

Red | 2011 up to 2013   **94**

Delicate, taut, with tight tannins despite the tenderness on the middle palate. Racy.

BEAUNE PREMIER CRU LES MARCONNETS 2005

Red | 2011 up to 2025   **95**

Great grapes. Good substance, noble, with very good cellaring potential.

BEAUNE PREMIER CRU LES TEURONS 2005

Red | 2011 up to 2025   **95**

Magnificent body. A wine with great allure. Complete!

BEAUNE PREMIER CRU LES TOUSSAINTS 2005

Red | 2011 up to 2017   **90**

The tannins are a bit dry. Less fruity than the Cent Vignes. Too stiff, but what character!

SAVIGNY-LÈS-BEAUNE PREMIER CRU LA BATAILLÈRE AUX VERGELESSES 2005

Red | 2011 up to 2025   **94**

Magnificent substance, thickness, length. The tannins are a bit firm. Great cellaring potential.

Red: 19.3 acres; pinot noir 100%. White: .6 acre; chardonnay 100%. Annual production: 34,000 bottles

DOMAINE LUCIEN MUZARD ET FILS

11 bis, rue de la Cour-Verreuil
21590 Santenay
Phone 00 33 3 80 20 61 85
Fax 00 33 3 80 20 66 02
lucienmuzard@orange.fr
www.domainemuzard.com

The Muzard brothers bring a wealth of experience to their Santenays, producing a comprehensive range of exceptionally well-structured wines with stunning expression of terroir. Their small négociant business, on the other hand, seems rather less convincing.

Recently tasted

MARANGES 2007
Red | 2013 up to 2019   88

SANTENAY CHAMPS CLAUDE VIEILLES VIGNES 2007
Red | 2015 up to 2019   88

SANTENAY PREMIER CRU CLOS DE TAVANNES 2007
Red | 2015 up to 2022   91

SANTENAY PREMIER CRU CLOS DES MOUCHES 2007
Red | 2015 up to 2022   90

SANTENAY PREMIER CRU LA MALADIÈRE 2007
Red | 2013 up to 2019   87

Older vintages

CHASSAGNE-MONTRACHET
VIEILLES VIGNES 2006
Red | 2011 up to 2016   87
Fruity and suave, good presence of its terroir, a little less immediate charm than Jean-Claude Bachelet's wine, but perhaps better aging potential.

CHASSAGNE-MONTRACHET
VIEILLES VIGNES 2005
Red | 2011 up to 2015   88
The most well-rounded of the domaine's reds in this vintage, which was locally affected by hail! Volume and follow-through on the palate, but without the absolute purity of fruit unharmed vines would have given.

MARANGES 2005
Red | 2011 up to 2015   86
A fine nose of red fruit, corpulent, very tannic and astringent.

PULIGNY-MONTRACHET 2006
White | 2011 up to 2014   88
Not very fleshy, but with remarkable elegance, with fine oak and lemon notes, a supermodel.

SANTENAY CHAMPS CLAUDE
VIEILLES VIGNES 2006
Red | 2011 up to 2014   87
Skillfully vinified and aged, fine use of oak, very pleasant body, nice follow-through on the palate; demonstrates that Santenay Village wines can be immediately tasty.

SANTENAY PREMIER CRU
CLOS DE TAVANNES 2006
Red | 2011 up to 2018   91
Our best score from the union's large blind tasting, a wine with superior typicity, refined in its aromas, complex, subtle; the equal of many Chambolles for its finesse, but obviously with different character and mouthfeel. The Muzard brothers should be proud of their results with this wine.

SANTENAY PREMIER CRU
CLOS DE TAVANNES 2005
Red | 2011 up to 2017   90
Striking purity of fruit in this vintage! A racy nose of cherry and spice, a full body, good tannins.

SANTENAY PREMIER CRU
CLOS DES MOUCHES 2006
Red | 2011 up to 2018   88
Superior elegance, supple but racy tannins, precise aromas, the true, fine modern pinot noir, much better crafted than the same producer's Maladière.

SANTENAY PREMIER CRU CLOS FAUBARD 2005
Red | 2011 up to 2017   87
Powerful, but without real depth, with some rusticity to the tannins.

SANTENAY PREMIER CRU LES GRAVIÈRES 2005
Red | 2011 up to 2015   88
Fleshy and generous, with very straightforward fruit.

Red: 51.1 acres; pinot noir 100%. **White:** .9 acre; aligoté 20%, chardonnay 80%. **Annual production:** 80,000 bottles

DOMAINE ANTOINE OLIVIER

5, rue Gaudin
21590 Santenay
Phone 00 33 3 80 20 61 35
Fax 00 33 3 80 20 64 82
domaineolivier@orange.fr

This young and dynamic producer in Santenay is lucky to own a beautiful Nuits-Saint-Georges vineyard, near Vosne-Romanée, and he seems to know just how to coax the best out of it, adapting his vinification style to better suit the Côtes de Nuits. The Santenays that he produces are just as good, though, both red and white; he knows just how to make them aromatic and appealing without losing structure. The 2006s are excellent.

Recently tasted

NUITS-SAINT-GEORGES PREMIER CRU
DAMODES 2007
Red | 2015 up to 2022   95

SANTENAY LES BIÉVAUX 2007
White | 2011 up to 2015   93

SANTENAY LES CHARMES 2007
Red | 2011 up to 2017   86

SANTENAY LES COTEAUX SOUS LA ROCHE 2007
White | 2013 up to 2017   93

SANTENAY PREMIER CRU BEAUREPAIRE 2007
Red | 2014 up to 2019   87

SAVIGNY-LÈS-BEAUNE LES PETITS LIARDS 2007
Red | 2011 up to 2017   86

Older vintages

NUITS-SAINT-GEORGES PREMIER CRU
DAMODES 2006
Red | 2011 up to 2024   90
A rich, dense wine, firm in its tannins, very racy on the finish. Vinified in the grand tradition, undoubtedly with a good part of the raisins whole. Highly recommended.

SANTENAY PREMIER CRU BEAUREPAIRE 2006
Red | 2011 up to 2016   88
A pretty, appetizing wine, delicately oaky, a testament to this producer's current mastery of vinification.

SAVIGNY-LÈS-BEAUNE PREMIER CRU PEUILLETS 2006
Red | 2011 up to 2018   86
A nice, spicy nose, good body, lots of integrity and definition in the expression of the terroir, and sufficient finesse.

Annual production: 50,000 bottles

DOMAINE JEAN-MARC ET HUGUES PAVELOT

1, chemin des Guettottes
21420 Savigny-lès-Beaune
Phone 00 33 3 80 21 55 21
Fax 00 33 3 80 21 59 73
hugues.pavelot@wanadoo.fr
www.domainepavelot.com

Jean-Marc Pavelot's son Hugues now runs this Savigny estate, known for its generally full-bodied wines with a pretty, velvety texture and good aging potential. Recent vintages have been rather heavy tasting, giving off a whiff of cooked or stewed fruit that is somewhat out of character for Savigny wines. The 2005 entries, for instance, from a hot, dry vintage, were solid almost to the point of heaviness.

Recently tasted

BEAUNE PREMIER CRU BRESSANDES 2006
Red | 2014 up to 2021   90

SAVIGNY-LÈS-BEAUNE 2007
Red | 2012 up to 2017   87

SAVIGNY-LÈS-BEAUNE PREMIER CRU
AUX GRAVAINS 2007
Red | 2012 up to 2017   88

SAVIGNY-LÈS-BEAUNE PREMIER CRU
LES NARBANTONS 2007
Red | 2014 up to 2019   90

SAVIGNY-LÈS-BEAUNE PREMIER CRU PEUILLETS 2007
Red | 2014 up to 2017   88

Older vintages

SAVIGNY-LÈS-BEAUNE 2005
Red | 2011 up to 2015   86
Nice color, but a little too much extraction for the grapes' potential.

SAVIGNY-LÈS-BEAUNE PREMIER CRU
AUX GUETTES 2005
Red | 2011 up to 2017   88
Stereotyped nose (jam and spice notes). Hefty but lacking in finesse.

SAVIGNY-LÈS-BEAUNE PREMIER CRU
LES NARBANTONS 2005
Red | 2011 up to 2017   89
Dense color, powerful wine; closed, drying tannins.

Red: 28.4 acres; pinot noir 100%. White: 2.5 acres; chardonnay 100%. Annual production: 65,000 bottles

PIERRE ANDRÉ

🍷 🍷 🍷 🍷 🍷

Rue des Cortons
21420 Aloxe-Corton
Phone 00 33 3 80 26 44 25
Fax 00 33 3 80 26 43 57
info@corton-andre.com
www.pierre-andre.com

Since this house was bought out (linked to that of Reine Pédauque) by the Ballande Group, the team of Goujon and Griveau, one a Burgundian at heart and the other a passionately committed enologist, are turning out great wines. The 2006 offering is a comprehensive line of high-quality wines, true to their terroirs and often with heightened elegance.

Recently tasted

ALOXE-CORTON PREMIER CRU LES PAULANDS 2007
Red | 2014 up to 2019   87

BEAUNE PREMIER CRU LES PERRIÈRES 2007
Red | 2017 up to 2022   92

SAVIGNY-LÈS-BEAUNE CLOS DES GUETTOTES 2007
Red | 2011 up to 2017   87

VOLNAY PREMIER CRU SANTENOTS 2007
Red | 2017 up to 2027   88

VOSNE-ROMANÉE PREMIER CRU SUCHOTS 2007
Red | 2013 up to 2019   90

Older vintages

ALOXE-CORTON PREMIER CRU
LES PAULANDS 2006
Red | 2011 up to 2018   88
Great aromatic freshness in its red-fruit notes, which is rare for the vintage; judiciously extracted tannins, and confirmed terroir character.

CORTON-BRESSANDES GRAND CRU 2006
Red | 2011 up to 2021   91
Generously structured, very pleasant and pure on the nose, complex tannins that indicate it needs quite some time in the bottle before its texture softens; a wine with real character.

CORTON-CHARLEMAGNE GRAND CRU 2006
White | 2011 up to 2016   90
Fine integration of its oak, ample, rich body, the straightforward, long savoriness of ripe grapes, a slight lack of tension on the mid-palate, but a self-assured finish.

MEURSAULT PREMIER CRU CHARMES 2006
White | 2011 up to 2016   90
A fine, classic wine with the frank taste of fresh hazelnut; lively, nuanced, long. A little less exotic on the palate than Michelot's wine, but close in its components.

POMMARD 2006
Red | 2011 up to 2016   86
A Village wine that is light in color but very aromatic, supple, fleshy, harmonious, made for those who find the appellation rustic. Drink this when it is six or seven years old.

PULIGNY-MONTRACHET 2006
White | 2011 up to 2014   87
An appealing wine that tends toward floral honey tastes—a charming, nonoxidative honey, that is. Suave; very 2006.

SAVIGNY-LÈS-BEAUNE
CLOS DES GUETTOTES 2006
Red | 2011 up to 2018   90
A very refined Village wine with exemplary classicism to its aromas (red and black fruit, a slight spicy note), well-rounded body, refined texture; charming without being common.

VOLNAY PREMIER CRU CHEVRET 2006
Red | 2011 up to 2018   90
Great elegance on the nose, well-rounded body, slightly taut tannins; a wine of very fine style that truly meets our expectations.

VOLNAY PREMIER CRU SANTENOTS 2006
Red | 2011 up to 2018   88
A carnal, spicy nose, powerful body, plush tannins—very 2006 in its supple nature, its flesh, and the slightly "decadent" side to the grapes.

Red: 123.6 acres; pinot noir 100%. White: 148.3 acres; chardonnay 100%. Annual production: 3,500,000 bottles

DOMAINE FERNAND ET LAURENT PILLOT

2, place des Noyers
21190 Chassagne-Montrachet
Phone 00 33 3 80 21 99 83
Fax 00 33 3 80 21 92 60
contact@vinpillot.com
www.vinpillot.com

Laurent Pillot comes from a very serious-minded family of winegrowers who divide their attentions among several good-quality local estates. This one recently expanded to include a superb collection of Pommard crus, inherited by Laurent's wife (a Pothier). These vineyards allow the estate to offer a comprehensive portfolio of carefully made wines, the whites being especially competent and the reds showing clear signs of improvement.

Recently tasted

CHASSAGNE-MONTRACHET PREMIER CRU
LES GRANDES RUCHOTTES 2007
White | 2012 up to 2017   89

CHASSAGNE-MONTRACHET PREMIER CRU
LES VERGERS 2007
White | 2012 up to 2017   90

CHASSAGNE-MONTRACHET PREMIER CRU
VIDE BOURSE 2007
White | 2012 up to 2017   88

MEURSAULT PREMIER CRU LES CAILLERETS 2007
White | 2013 up to 2017   90

Older vintages

CHASSAGNE-MONTRACHET PREMIER CRU
LES GRANDES RUCHOTTES 2005
White | 2011 up to 2017   90
More finesse than the Morgeot, and more transparency despite the heaviness of the vintage.

CHASSAGNE-MONTRACHET PREMIER CRU
LES VERGERS 2006
White | 2011 up to 2016   87
Very full and fat, great tension due to the strong presence of dry extract; clearly in the style of the vintage, but without the superlative finesse that distinguishes the best examples.

CHASSAGNE-MONTRACHET PREMIER CRU
LES VERGERS 2005
White | 2011 up to 2013   90
Good substance and balance, dry, taut, very clear terroir, good follow-up on the palate.

CHASSAGNE-MONTRACHET PREMIER CRU
MORGEOT 2005
White | 2011 up to 2017   88
Powerful, alcoholic, good mid-palate. The bouquet still needs time to develop more complexity.

CHASSAGNE-MONTRACHET PREMIER CRU
VIDE BOURSE 2006
White | 2011 up to 2016   87
Powerful, ripe grapes, just a touch heavy but the noble terroir (close to the Criots-Bâtard-Montrachet) shows through, and as a whole it will age well.

MEURSAULT PREMIER CRU
LES CAILLERETS 2006
White | 2011 up to 2018   88
Huge bouquet, now slightly reduced (slight mercaptan odor), powerful, with great dry extract; taut, tight; good aging potential.

POMMARD LES TAVANNES 2005
Red | 2011 up to 2019   88
Powerful, spicy, straightforward, good aging potential, without any fuss.

POMMARD PREMIER CRU LES CHARMOTS 2006
Red | 2011 up to 2021   89
Complete, with truffles and spice, clearly marked terroir; long, luscious, built for aging.

POMMARD PREMIER CRU LES CHARMOTS 2004
Red | 2011 up to 2016   89
Delicate, subtle, very elegant, all about freshness; noble tannins; a nice style.

POMMARD PREMIER CRU LES RUGIENS 2004
Red | 2011 up to 2016   86
Dry tannins and great power. It just might become more elegant with age!

PULIGNY-MONTRACHET NOYER BRET 2006
White | 2011 up to 2014   86
Very ripe grapes, generous alcohol; a fat wine, broad, even opulent for a Village-level wine, but without very marked typicity.

Red: 21.9 acres; gamay 5%, pinot 95%. White: 15.2 acres: aligoté 15%, chardonnay 85%. Annual production: 65,000 bottles

PAUL PILLOT

3, rue Clos Saint-Jean
21190 Chassagne-Montrachet
Phone 00 33 3 80 21 31 91
Fax 00 33 3 80 21 90 92
contact@domainepaulpillot.com
wwww.domainepaulpillot.com

Yet another well-known winery named Pillot, with a long-standing reputation for his excellent Romanée cuvée. As chance would have it, we only recently had the opportunity to taste his entire production, and we can confirm his local reputation for pure, expressive wines, with splendidly made 2006s!

Recently tasted

CHASSAGNE-MONTRACHET PREMIER CRU
CAILLERETS 2007
White | 2012 up to 2017   89

CHASSAGNE-MONTRACHET PREMIER CRU
GRANDE MONTAGNE 2007
White | 2014 up to 2019   90

CHASSAGNE-MONTRACHET PREMIER CRU
GRANDES RUCHOTTES 2007
White | 2011 up to 2015   90

CHASSAGNE-MONTRACHET PREMIER CRU
ROMANÉE 2007
White | 2015 up to 2022   94

Older vintages

CHASSAGNE-MONTRACHET PREMIER CRU
CAILLERETS 2006
White | 2011 up to 2016   91
One of the most successful wines from this parcel in 2006: a racy nose of flowering vine, nice depth to the texture, a great deal of nuance on the finish; very expressive already.

CHASSAGNE-MONTRACHET PREMIER CRU
CLOS SAINT-JEAN 2006
White | 2011 up to 2016   90
Power and brightness, with a strong personality and precise expression of a terroir that perfectly lightens the powerful nature of classical Morgeots.

CHASSAGNE-MONTRACHET PREMIER CRU
GRANDE MONTAGNE 2006
White | 2011 up to 2018   89
A classic expression of the Chassagne slope with the best exposition and the most mineral terroir, precise in its aromas, taut and clean on the finish. This wine has excellent aging potential.

CHASSAGNE-MONTRACHET PREMIER CRU
GRANDES RUCHOTTES 2006
White | 2011 up to 2021   94
The whole is absolutely remarkable for its aromatic finesse, voluptuous texture, the precision in its persistence; subtle and powerful; truly memorable!

CHASSAGNE-MONTRACHET PREMIER CRU
ROMANÉE 2006
White | 2011 up to 2018   88
Uncommon on the nose, with notes of green coffee and a bit of bitterness, still marked by the barrel, full, long, but needs time!

Red: 12.4 acres; pinot noir 100%. White: 19.8 acres; chardonnay 100%. Annual production: 70,000 bottles

CHÂTEAU DE POMMARD

15, rue Marey-Mouge
21630 Pommard
Phone 00 33 3 80 22 12 59
Fax 00 33 3 80 24 65 88
contact@châteaudepommard.com
www.châteaudepommard.com

This large estate boasts a single-block vineyard, planted around the château in the Bordeaux style. The wines are now back to their former excellence thanks to a dynamic new owner and a ruthless selection process that eliminates every grape except the best. The superb 2004 is a testament to the expert reputation of winemaker Philippe Charlopin—who sadly has left the property. This is one of the best five wines we tasted from this village, in a very difficult year!

Pommard 2006
Red | 2011 up to 2014 — 86
A dense color and lightly reductive nose. A velvety wine with plenty of oak. The finish is steady, but we wished for a more delicate Pommard, just a touch more austere, vinified in a stricter style.

Pommard 2004
Red | 2011 up to 2019 — 91
Excellent overall harmony. Finesse, freshness, elegance, length. It's lost some of its luster in the last year.

Red: 49.4 acres; pinot 100%. **Annual production:** 40,000 bottles

DOMAINE DE LA POUSSE D'OR

Rue de la Chapelle
21190 Volnay
Phone 00 33 3 80 21 61 33
Fax 00 33 3 80 21 29 97
patrick@lapoussedor.fr
www.lapoussedor.fr

This winery boasts more great terroirs than any other Volnay estate, and its fabulous reputation is now restored. After a few years of finding his way, owner Patrick Landanger has reestablished that surefire style to be expected of a flagship estate. The red wines are produced in an ultramodern cellar, expressing their terroir and vintage with formidable precision. All of the recent vintages are stunningly successful, and the first estate-grown white wines are just as sure-footed.

Recently tasted
Pommard premier cru Jarollières 2007
Red | 2017 up to 2022 — 90

Volnay premier cru Caillerets Clos des Soixante Ouvrées 2007
Red | 2017 up to 2022 — 94

Volnay premier cru Clos d'Audignac 2007
Red | 2015 up to 2019 — 90

Volnay premier cru Clos de La Bousse d'Or 2007
Red | 2014 up to 2019 — 89

Volnay premier cru en Cailleret 2007
Red | 2015 up to 2019 — 93

Older vintages
Corton-Bressandes grand cru 2005
Red | 2011 up to 2013 — 93
Clean, ample, ripe, but without the refined texture of the great Volnays.

Corton-Clos du Roi grand cru 2006
Red | 2011 up to 2026 — 94
A complex, racy nose, generous body, a light, very clean reduction for long aging, noble tannins: a great future ahead.

Corton-Clos du Roi grand cru 2005
Red | 2020 up to 2030 — 94
Great color, noble aromas of cherries, a very tight texture, probably ready for long cellaring.

Pommard premier cru Jarollières 2004
Red | 2011 up to 2016 — 91
Rich, tannic, less noble than the Volnay Premiers Crus.

PULIGNY-MONTRACHET PREMIER CRU
LE CAILLERET 2006
White | 2011 up to 2018   93
One of the pinnacles of the vintage in
Puligny. Very delicate, toasty reductive notes
on the nose, a remarkable citronella flavor,
very fresh, magnificent texture, exemplary
purity on the finish. A recent acquisition by
the estate on a great terroir, and a success
that should make some producers in the area
think!

PULIGNY-MONTRACHET PREMIER CRU
LE CAILLERET 2005
White | 2011 up to 2015   93
Powerful, racy, full, uncompromising. A good
future ahead.

SANTENAY 2006
Red | 2011 up to 2018   90
As always, one of the best wines of Santenay, firm, subtle anise notes on the nose,
as dense as the Muzard but with a touch
more immediate charm!

SANTENAY PREMIER CRU
CLOS DE TAVANNES 2005
Red | 2011 up to 2025   94
A rich color, nobly aromatic, velvety texture;
a great future lies ahead.

SANTENAY PREMIER CRU LES GRAVIÈRES 2005
White | 2011 up to 2013   90
Powerful citrus aromas, fat, full, long, very
original and luscious.

SANTENAY PREMIER CRU LES GRAVIÈRES 2005
Red | 2011 up to 2020   90
Rich, complex, ripe grapes, firm tannins. A
wine with great style.

VOLNAY PREMIER CRU CAILLERETS
CLOS DES SOIXANTE OUVRÉES 2006
Red | 2011 up to 2024   96
Our top rating at the grand tasting of the village wine union, a perfect wine with a marvelously satiny texture, showing incomparable
pedigree on the palate and magical tannins.
It has all the elements of a Grand Cru.

VOLNAY PREMIER CRU CAILLERETS
CLOS DES SOIXANTE OUVRÉES 2005
Red | 2011 up to 2030   95
Long, suave, ultraripe, and refined; a great
wine.

VOLNAY PREMIER CRU CLOS D'AUDIGNAC 2006
Red | 2011 up to 2018   90
Supple, charming, racy, just a bit more lean
than the other prestigious Premiers Crus of
the estate.

VOLNAY PREMIER CRU CLOS D'AUDIGNAC 2005
Red | 2011 up to 2025   93
Very deeply colored, ample, vinous, ripe.
Clearly ready for long aging.

VOLNAY PREMIER CRU CLOS D'AUDIGNAC 2004
Red | 2011 up to 2014   86
A nice fruit character, generous and ripe,
but in the flavor is a hint of hail. But the work
to clean it up is quite admirable!

VOLNAY PREMIER CRU
CLOS DE LA BOUSSE D'OR 2006
Red | 2011 up to 2021   93
Supple, fleshy, perfectly velvety. An ultra-
classic build and flavor, with a satiny texture
and notes of violets.

VOLNAY PREMIER CRU
CLOS DE LA BOUSSE D'OR 2005
Red | 2011 up to 2025   90
Tender but a bit too suave.

VOLNAY PREMIER CRU
CLOS DE LA BOUSSE D'OR 2004
Red | 2011 up to 2014   86
Tender, spicy, supple, but empty on the mid-
palate.

VOLNAY PREMIER CRU
CLOS DES SOIXANTE OUVRÉES 2004
Red | 2011 up to 2016   93
A wine of great distinction, fleshy, complete
for the vintage. Everything here is well integrated.

VOLNAY PREMIER CRU EN CAILLERET 2006
Red | 2011 up to 2024   90
Elegant, supple, and clean, but several
notches below the incomparable Clos des
Soixante Ouvrées.

VOLNAY PREMIER CRU EN CAILLERET 2005
Red | 2011 up to 2030   95
Ultraripe, hearty, ample, suave; a great vintage.

VOLNAY PREMIER CRU EN CAILLERET 2004
Red | 2011 up to 2014   89
Fleshy, ripe, elegant, more vinous than its
neighbor from La Pousse d'Or, rather long.

Red: 35.8 acres; pinot 100%. White: 3 acres;
chardonnay 100%. Annual production: 65,000 bottles

DOMAINE JACQUES PRIEUR

6, rue des Santenots
21190 Meursault
Phone 00 33 3 80 21 23 85
Fax 00 33 3 80 21 29 19
info@prieur.com
www.prieur.com

This is one of the most celebrated of all the Burgundy wineries, offering a comprehensive range of Grands and Premiers Crus made in a very confident and consistent style. Martin Prieur and his enological consultant Nadine Gublin show what can be achieved when the best concepts in modern vinification are used in the service of the terroir and the vintage. Very ripe grapes, plus long, slow vinification and equally lengthy aging produce red and white wines with all the flesh and flavor possible. Flawlessly consistent output for the past fifteen years.

Recently tasted
CHAMBERTIN GRAND CRU 2007
Red | 2011 up to 2013   93

CLOS DE VOUGEOT GRAND CRU 2007
Red | 2017 up to 2027   93

ECHÉZEAUX GRAND CRU 2007
Red | 2017 up to 2025   94

MONTRACHET GRAND CRU 2007
White | 2017 up to 2022   95

MUSIGNY GRAND CRU 2007
Red | 2017 up to 2027   96

Older vintages
BEAUNE CHAMPS-PIMONT 2006
Red | 2011 up to 2018   91
One of the greatest successes in Beaune in this vintage; deeply colored, charming, velvety, long, complex, delicately smoky!

BEAUNE CHAMPS-PIMONT 2005
White | 2011 up to 2015   88
Lactic, a strong yeasty flavor, a nice fatness thanks to the "bâtonnage" (stirring of the lees), broad. Terroir less pronounced than in the red from the same vineyard.

BEAUNE CHAMPS-PIMONT 2005
Red | 2011 up to 2020   90
Very ripe grapes, deep color, fleshy, powerful; a nice cellaring wine.

BEAUNE CLOS DE LA FEGUINE MONOPOLE 2006
Red | 2011 up to 2021   90
A hint of smoking vine branches, typical of a Beaune. Finesse, tender flesh and tannins, a long satiny finish. An excellent Premier Cru.

CHAMBERTIN GRAND CRU 2006
Red | 2011 up to 2013   93
The bottle we tasted in Gevrey was not perfect. At the estate the wine awes you with its perfume and the extraction of its tannins, even if it doesn't yet have the fullness of the old-vines cuvées!

CHAMBERTIN GRAND CRU 2005
Red | 2011 up to 2030   95
Sumptuous body and texture, even fresher than the Musigny; racy; very long aging potential.

CHEVALIER-MONTRACHET GRAND CRU 2004
White | 2011 up to 2016   93
Very ripe, broad, a bit flabby, enormously full for the vintage, lactic notes that are almost heavy.

CLOS DE VOUGEOT GRAND CRU 2006
Red | 2011 up to 2026   94
Black, a great nose of ripe grapes, superbly full; the very archetype of Clos de Vougeot, vigorous and distinguished.

CLOS DE VOUGEOT GRAND CRU 2005
Red | 2011 up to 2025   94
Very powerful, ultraripe, a dark-chocolate note that could be considered fantastic or a bit heavy. A very vigorous wine that will certainly evolve well with time.

CORTON-BRESSANDES GRAND CRU 2006
Red | 2011 up to 2024   93
Complete, harmonious, subtle, a very satiny texture, nice length, no faults.

CORTON-BRESSANDES GRAND CRU 2005
Red | 2011 up to 2025   93
Powerful, well-balanced, very homogenous from the beginning of the tasting to the end, as always from this vineyard.

ECHÉZEAUX GRAND CRU 2006
Red | 2011 up to 2026   88
Very rich, powerful; the tannins are clearly too much and mask the perfume, but very heady, voluptuous texture, tending toward the style of a great Côtes du Rhone. It will be instructive to see how it evolves.

ECHÉZEAUX GRAND CRU 2005
Red | 2011 up to 2025   95
A very refined texture, long, complete, remarkable vinification!

MEURSAULT CLOS DE MAZERAY MONOPOLE 2006
White | 2011 up to 2016   89
Very rich structure, a powerful nose joining hazelnuts and citrus, voluptuous texture, very 2006. This one is for those who love round, rich Meursaults.

MEURSAULT CLOS DE MAZERAY MONOPOLE 2005
White | 2011 up to 2015   **90**
Broad, complete, pure. Proportionally more
balanced than the most elite crus!

MEURSAULT PERRIÈRES 2006
White | 2011 up to 2018   **93**
Ultrarich, almost overripe, unctuous, long,
needs some time for the vanilla and butter
from the oak to mellow out. This one is
approaching Montrachet!

MONTRACHET GRAND CRU 2006
White | 2011 up to 2018   **93**
Ultraripe and generous, with all the pedigree of its origins, but a hint of heaviness.

MONTRACHET GRAND CRU 2005
White | 2011 up to 2017   **93**
More frank and energetic than the Chevalier, with citrus notes. But there is a slight
lack of purity.

MONTRACHET GRAND CRU 2004
White | 2011 up to 2019   **95**
Young, ample, complete for the vintage and
above all more well balanced for aging than
the Chevalier or the 2005!

MUSIGNY GRAND CRU 2006
Red | 2011 up to 2026   **96**
Sumptuous, great aromatic complexity,
noble tannins, impeccable as always, with
possibly just a bit more pure finesse than
the wine of the Mugnier estate.

MUSIGNY GRAND CRU 2005
Red | 2011 up to 2030   **96**
Magnificent expression of the terroir, a sumptuously full texture, very long.

PULIGNY-MONTRACHET LES COMBETTES 2005
White | 2011 up to 2017   **89**
Less heavy than the Perrières, a bit fluid,
easy, slender, with a pure finish.

VOLNAY CHAMPANS 2006
Red | 2011 up to 2026   **95**
A remarkable success, ultra-complex nose,
satiny texture, great length, marvelously ripe
and well-vinified grapes.

VOLNAY CLOS DES SANTENOTS MONOPOLE 2005
Red | 2011 up to 2030   **93**
Complete, rich, racy, with notes of brambles
and peonies. A great future ahead!

Red: 32.1 acres; pinot noir 100%. White: 19.8 acres;
chardonnay 100%. Annual production: 90,000 bottles

DOMAINE PRIEUR-BRUNET

Rue de Narosse
21590 Santenay
Phone 00 33 3 80 20 60 56
Fax 00 33 3 80 20 64 31
uny-prieur@prieur-santenay.com
www.prieur-santenay.com

The vineyard here is in two parts, extending
from some lovely parcels of white varietals
around Meursault (the Brunet half) to plantings in Santenay (the Prieur half). The
wines are always carefully made and grew
increasingly refined throughout the 1990s.
We saw no particular change in the 2004
and 2005 entries—serious wines, with no
immediate charm and built for aging. Hail
interrupted ripening of the red grapes in
Santenay and Chassagne in 2005, which
doubtless explains the tendency to stiffness.

BÂTARD-MONTRACHET GRAND CRU 2004
White | 2012 up to 2016   **89**
Pronounced citrus notes and a fairly unclear
sense of terroir, but clearly a wine for aging,
as is always true of this domaine.

BEAUNE PREMIER CRU CLOS DU ROI 2006
Red | 2011 up to 2018   **89**
Clearly this terroir was a success in 2006:
the wine has great color, is powerfully vinous
for such light soil, and has firm yet likeable
tannins.

BEAUNE PREMIER CRU CLOS DU ROI 2005
Red | 2011 up to 2020   **89**
In 2005, this wine is much more southern,
very powerful and full of velvety force, with
a sense that the alcohol dominates the finish, but there is remarkably intense material
behind it!

CHASSAGNE-MONTRACHET PREMIER CRU
LES EMBAZÉES 2005
White | 2011 up to 2015   **87**
Great breadth, but an almost heavy wine in
a very Morgeot style, doubtless due to the
nature of the terroir. For those who love powerful whites.

MEURSAULT PREMIER CRU CHARMES 2005
White | 2012 up to 2017   **89**
A reductive nose, bitter but not excessively
so, a very fat, rich, even opulent wine, which
is for now still closed. This is a wine with
great power, at the cost perhaps of pure
finesse!

POMMARD PREMIER CRU LA PLATIÈRE 2006
Red | 2011 up to 2018   **89**
A nose of violets and roses, with a thin body for the appellation, an almost ethereal wine that is very pleasant, with impeccable aromatic maturity.

POMMARD PREMIER CRU LA PLATIÈRE 2004
Red | 2011 up to 2016   **88**
The domaine's best 2004, fairly ripe, round, truffled, with length and style.

SANTENAY PREMIER CRU
CLOS FAUBARD HOMMAGE À GUY PRIEUR 2005
White | 2011 up to 2014   **91**
Currently one of the top white Santenays, with sumptuous citrus aromas; a broad, ample wine that is comparable to a remarkable Morgeot, demonstrating this tiny parcel's vocation for producing whites. Let's hope the domaine's other luxury cuvées follow the same path.

SANTENAY PREMIER CRU
LA MALADIÈRE CUVÉE CLAUDE 2006
Red | 2014 up to 2018   **90**
A purposefully well-crafted bottling made from the best grapes in the parcel, very deeply colored, with imposing oak that is nevertheless perfectly integrated and will certainly smooth out in four to six years; great length, great sensuality, spectacular but not without finesse. But purists will see it as somewhat excessive.

SANTENAY PREMIER CRU
LA MALADIÈRE CUVÉE CLAUDE 2004
Red | 2011 up to 2016   **90**
A special cuvée, with more color than the regular bottling, marked oak, fine tannins, good complexity and a refined style seen so infrequently with Santenays. Points to the right direction.

VOLNAY PREMIER CRU SANTENOTS 2006
Red | 2011 up to 2021   **88**
Bluish in color with fine raspberry and stewed notes, body and texture that are classic for this appellation; a straightforward terroir wine with good aging potential.

VOLNAY PREMIER CRU SANTENOTS 2005
Red | 2011 up to 2020   **92**
Remarkable aromatic personality, more immediately perceptible complexity and raciness than the Clos du Roy; a superb wine that, it would seem, is still available for purchase. Don't miss this.

Red: 19.8 acres; pinot 100%. White: 19.8 acres; chardonnay 100%. Annual production: 100,000 bottles

CHÂTEAU DE PULIGNY-MONTRACHET

21190 Puligny-Montrachet
Phone 00 33 3 80 21 39 14
Fax 00 33 3 80 21 39 07
châteaudepuligny@wanadoo.fr
www.châteaudepuligny.com

This pilot estate in Puligny is owned by the Caisse d'Épargne and run by Étienne de Montille, who is steadily taking its wines to the forefront of quality: exceptional aromatic finesse and terrifically pure expression of terroir. Not quite enough depth yet for perfect style, but the now-stricter standards of viticulture here should put that right.

MEURSAULT PREMIER CRU LES PERRIÈRES 2006
White | 2011 up to 2018   **90**
Refined notes of fresh hazelnuts on the nose. A taut wine, powerful, determined but subtle. Masterful élevage. Tasted at the estate.

MEURSAULT PREMIER CRU LES PERRIÈRES 2005
White | 2011 up to 2017   **93**
The nose is a bit discreet yet pure with a very well integrated oak influence. An elegant structure, precise and pure on the finish. The style shows great mastery.

PULIGNY-MONTRACHET 2006
White | 2011 up to 2017   **89**
This wine has retained a great deal of freshness and finesse, in an ethereal style in keeping with the purest this village has to offer.

PULIGNY-MONTRACHET PREMIER CRU
LES FOLATIÈRES 2006
White | 2011 up to 2016   **90**
Delicate, pure notes of citronella on the nose. The same volume on the palate as the Perrières. This wine has style and promises to age well.

PULIGNY-MONTRACHET PREMIER CRU
LES FOLATIÈRES 2005
White | 2011 up to 2015   **93**
Noble aromas of grape blossoms, generous body but very pure and fresh on the palate, unlike many wines of this vintage. Complete.

SAINT-AUBIN PREMIER CRU EN REMILLY 2006
White | 2011 up to 2014   **93**
Remarkable finesse and complexity, ethereal style, precise and long. This success affirms the worth of the terroir in this vintage.

SAINT-AUBIN PREMIER CRU EN REMILLY 2005
White | 2011 up to 2015   **91**
Remarkable aromatic finesse, crystalline body, very pretty style. A racy wine with a good quality-price ratio.

Red: 16.8 acres; pinot 100%. White: 30.4 acres; chardonnay 100%. Annual production: 100,000 bottles

DOMAINE RAPET PÈRE ET FILS

Place de la Mairie
21420 Pernand-Vergelesses
Phone 00 33 3 80 21 59 94
Fax 00 33 3 80 21 54 01
vincent@domaine-rapet.com
www.domaine-rapet.com

No question, Vincent Rapet is one of the top white-wine makers of his generation. From his Pernand-Vergelesses Village wines to his terrific Corton-Charlemagne, this is simply the ultimate in freshness, finesse, and transparent terroir. The reds are not quite as stunning but get better all the time!

Recently tasted

BEAUNE PREMIER CRU CLOS DU ROI 2007
Red | 2012 up to 2017   **88**

CORTON-CHARLEMAGNE GRAND CRU 2007
White | 2012 up to 2017   **90**

CORTON GRAND CRU 2007
Red | 2015 up to 2022   **89**

PERNAND-VERGELESSES PREMIER CRU
EN CARADEUX 2007
White | 2011 up to 2015   **88**

PERNAND-VERGELESSES PREMIER CRU
ÎLE DE VERGELESSES 2007
Red | 2013 up to 2017   **89**

PERNAND-VERGELESSES PREMIER CRU SOUS
FRÉTILLE 2007
White | 2012 up to 2017   **90**

Older vintages

ALOXE-CORTON 2006
Red | 2011 up to 2018   **88**
A spicy bouquet that is classic for the terroir, excellent body, very extracted tannins; a wine that conforms to the best tradition.

BEAUNE PREMIER CRU CLOS DU ROI 2006
Red | 2011 up to 2018   **88**
Vanilla and spice on the nose, supple, suave, long, heady in its delicate tactile sensations, already open, very appealing.

BEAUNE PREMIER CRU GRÈVES 2005
Red | 2011 up to 2017   **88**
Supple, fleshy, and ripe, but with a lack of refinement to its texture.

CORTON-CHARLEMAGNE GRAND CRU 2006
White | 2011 up to 2018   **93**
Great cleanness to its aromas, an ample body, a savory note of basil on the nose, but not completely formed on the palate. A fine future ahead of it.

CORTON-CHARLEMAGNE GRAND CRU 2005
White | 2011 up to 2017   **96**
Broad, generous, fine hazelnut aromas, very great breadth and precision.

CORTON-POUGETS GRAND CRU 2006
Red | 2011 up to 2021   **90**
Firm in color with a fine floral nose, a tender yet fleshy wine that is subtle in the definition of its spicy tannins; elegant, in the style of the vintage.

CORTON GRAND CRU 2005
Red | 2011 up to 2025   **90**
More body and more vinous than all of the domaine's other reds, but once again with slightly drying tannins. A fine future before it.

PERNAND-VERGELESSES PREMIER CRU
CLOS DU VILLAGE 2006
White | 2011 up to 2014   **89**
Great promise, ample, precise, a very appealing finish.

PERNAND-VERGELESSES PREMIER CRU
EN CARADEUX 2005
White | 2011 up to 2015   **95**
More vinous than the Frétille, ample, fat, great aging potential, mineral, perfectly limpid terroir.

PERNAND-VERGELESSES PREMIER CRU
ÎLE DE VERGELESSES 2005
Red | 2011 up to 2017   **89**
Black-currant notes on the nose, abundant fruit, purity of texture, and precision. Slight lack of body.

PERNAND-VERGELESSES PREMIER CRU
SOUS FRÉTILLE 2006
White | 2011 up to 2018   **93**
Great purity and finesse, with mineral, lemony notes of great stylishness, and even more defined at this point than the Charlemagne. Remarkable.

PERNAND-VERGELESSES PREMIER CRU
SOUS FRÉTILLE 2005
White | 2011 up to 2013   **95**
Wonderful transparency and purity, lively, long, stunning vitality; an almost perfect style.

PERNAND-VERGELESSES PREMIER CRU
VERGELESSES 2005
Red | 2011 up to 2015   **86**
The tannins are slightly too astringent, leaving the wine's flesh somewhat stripped as a result: less successful than the same producer's whites.

Red: 29.7 acres; pinot noir 100%. White: 19.8 acres; chardonnay 100%. Annual production: 90,000 bottles

DOMAINE REBOURGEON-MURE

Grande Rue
21630 Pommard
Phone 00 33 3 80 22 75 39
Fax 00 33 3 80 22 71 00

This artisanal domaine in Pommard has very nice vineyards in some prestigious terroirs, but their approach is simple and honest, not always enabling the wines to show their full character. But when they do, there are some great deals to be found; 2006 is no exception.

POMMARD PREMIER CRU
CLOS DES ARVELETS 2005
Red | 2011 up to 2017   **87**
Nice color, tannins that are not excessive, discreet yet straightforward fruitiness, not very vinous for the year.

POMMARD PREMIER CRU CLOS MICOT 2006
Red | 2011 up to 2018   **87**
Classically made wine, very clean, precise, fairly supple, but with enough flesh to age well.

VOLNAY 2006
Red | 2011 up to 2014   **87**
A generous, straightforward wine that is classically made and presents the village character very well.

VOLNAY PREMIER CRU CAILLERETS 2006
Red | 2011 up to 2021   **93**
Perfect violet aromas, tender, unctuous, very precise in the expression of this noble parcel: it should be a priority to seek this out, even if production is limited.

Red: 17.3 acres; pinot 100%. Annual production: 30,000 bottles

DOMAINE NICOLAS ROSSIGNOL

27, rue de Mont
21190 Volnay
Phone 00 33 3 80 21 62 43
Fax 00 33 3 80 21 27 61
nicolas-rossignol@wanadoo.fr
www.nicolas-rossignol.com

We are delighted to see that, after giving his style a serious rethink, this highly gifted and enterprising young winegrower has gone back to making those timelessly classical wines for which Volnay is renowned. In no time at all, Nicolas Rossignol has learned how to give his wines an elegance that makes them unique.

Recently tasted
BEAUNE PREMIER CRU CLOS DES MOUCHES 2007
Red | 2015 up to 2022   **89**

BEAUNE PREMIER CRU CLOS DU ROY 2007
Red | 2011 up to 2013   **90**

POMMARD PREMIER CRU CHANLINS 2007
Red | 2015 up to 2022   **93**

POMMARD PREMIER CRU JAROLIÈRES 2007
Red | 2015 up to 2027   **93**

VOLNAY PREMIER CRU CAILLERETS 2007
Red | 2011 up to 2013   **93**

VOLNAY PREMIER CRU CHEVRET 2007
Red | 2011 up to 2013   **91**

VOLNAY PREMIER CRU RONCERET 2007
Red | 2015 up to 2022   **90**

Older vintages
BEAUNE 2006
Red | 2011 up to 2018   **91**
Excellent color, very ripe grapes, very pretty velvety texture, elegant fruit, a superb example of the value of this so-often underestimated village, as far as these wines are concerned.

BEAUNE PREMIER CRU CLOS DES MOUCHES 2006
Red | 2011 up to 2018   **88**
Fine color that is slightly less dense than that of the Beaune, with spicy yet refined notes on the nose; but the texture of the Village wine is far superior to that of the Premier Cru this year.

BEAUNE PREMIER CRU CLOS DU ROY 2006
Red | 2011 up to 2018   **94**
A wine with greater elegance than the Clos des Mouches, both for the delicate nature of its bouquet and for its silky texture. A wonderful example of a Beaune Premier Cru.

PERNAND-VERGELESSES 2006
Red | 2011 up to 2014   **90**
Dense color, very well defined nose of red
fruit and spice, exceptional body and texture for a generic wine, very good tannins.

SAVIGNY-LÈS-BEAUNE PREMIER CRU
LES FOURNEAUX 2006
Red | 2011 up to 2013   **91**
Dense color, a fine nose of dark fruit, excellent
silky texture, very finely extracted tannins; a
fine example of a wine that is modern yet faithful to the classic local style. Very fine grapes.

VOLNAY PREMIER CRU CAILLERETS 2006
Red | 2011 up to 2013   **96**
An absolutely well-rounded Volnay, refined
on the nose and on the palate, with an uncommonly perfect body for the vintage on the
Côte de Beaune. This wine will amaze all those
who love the great village of Volnay!

VOLNAY PREMIER CRU CAILLERETS 2005
Red | 2011 up to 2013   **91**
A floral nose, great precision and finesse in
its texture and expression of the terroir, ripe
grapes, though the finish is somewhat short.

VOLNAY PREMIER CRU CHEVRET 2006
Red | 2011 up to 2021   **95**
Very dark color, with noble aromas of violet
and licorice, sumptuous stuffing, refined
tannins; a very great Volnay and true confirmation of this producer's talent.

VOLNAY PREMIER CRU CHEVRET 2005
Red | 2011 up to 2020   **90**
Greater finesse than the Frémiets, a pretty
wine with a refined texture and an elegant
floral nose that is classic for the village.

VOLNAY PREMIER CRU LES FRÉMIETS 2005
Red | 2011 up to 2017   **89**
Deeply colored, with floral notes, but a little
too heavy in texture.

VOLNAY PREMIER CRU RONCERET 2006
Red | 2011 up to 2013   **93**
Perhaps we are a little influenced by the name
of the parcel, but we find in the bouquet of
this wine a slight wild rose and bramble note
that sets it apart from the Chevret. It does
not have the supreme elegance and the silkiness of that wine, but its natural charm and
delicate persistence are almost as admirable!

Red: 17.3 acres; pinot 100%. **Annual production:**
80,000 bottles

DOMAINE ROULOT
🍷 🍷 🍷 🍷 🍷

1, rue Charles-Giraud
21190 Meursault
Phone 00 33 3 80 21 21 65
Fax 00 33 3 80 21 64 36
roulot@domaineroulot.fr

This top-performing winery is run by professional actor Jean-Marc Roulot, who
puts the same precision into making wines
as he does into acting. His wines show
exceptional neatness, purity, and verve—
much appreciated by leading wine enthusiasts and sommeliers.

Recently tasted
BOURGOGNE 2007
White | 2011 up to 2015   **90**

MEURSAULT PREMIER CRU CHARMES 2007
White | 2015 up to 2022   **94**

MEURSAULT PREMIER CRU PERRIÈRES 2007
White | 2015 up to 2022   **95**

MEURSAULT PREMIER CRU PORUSOT 2007
White | 2015 up to 2022   **93**

MEURSAULT TESSONS CLOS DE MON PLAISIR 2007
White | 2013 up to 2019   **94**

Older vintages
MEURSAULT LUCHETS 2004
White | 2011 up to 2013   **95**
Wonderful aromatic finesse and cleanness,
a balanced body, exemplary purity of texture.

MEURSAULT PREMIER CRU BOUCHÈRES 2005
White | 2011 up to 2015   **93**
Refined, distinguished, very pure, very del-
icate texture; we might like to see more body
to it.

MEURSAULT PREMIER CRU PERRIÈRES 2005
White | 2011 up to 2020   **94**
A racy, powerful, deep, generous wine, with
an added dose of tension—the signature of
this parcel and domaine!

MEURSAULT TESSONS CLOS DE MON PLAISIR 2005
White | 2011 up to 2050   **93**
A fine, complex nose that is more generous
and sensual than it is delicate and fresh, as
the domaine is skilled at producing in vintages that are less hot than this one.

MEURSAULT TILLETS 2005
White | 2011 up to 2013   **90**
A pretty style, with confirmed ripe grape
notes but a very slight lack of intensity!

Red: 4.4 acres; pinot 100%. **White:** 20.8 acres; aligoté
10%, chardonnay 90%. **Annual production:** 57,000
bottles

ROUX PÈRE & FILS

42, rue des Lavières
21190 Saint-Aubin
Phone 00 33 3 80 21 32 92
Fax 00 33 3 80 21 35 00
roux.pere.et.fils@wanadoo.fr
www.domaines-roux.com

A new entry for this year's edition of the guide, Roux is an experienced producer, négociant, and grower. The business originated in Saint-Aubin, where the family has a wonderful, small vineyard holding. Little by little, many hardworking generations of the Roux family built a small empire, producing wines from both "Côtes." Judging by the 2006s, the reds are more expertly vinified than the whites.

Recently tasted
SAINT-AUBIN PREMIER CRU LA CHATENIÈRE 2007
White | 2011 up to 2013   86

SAINT-AUBIN PREMIER CRU LES CORTONS 2007
White | 2011 up to 2017   91

SAINT-AUBIN PREMIER CRU MURGERS DES DENTS DE CHIEN 2007
White | 2011 up to 2015   90

SANTENAY PREMIER CRU GRAND CLOS ROUSSEAU 2007
Red | 2011 up to 2015   86

Older vintages
CHAMBOLLE-MUSIGNY 2006
Red | 2011 up to 2016   86
Good use of oak, a supple, charming, even quaffable wine, the archetypal commercial Chambolle (without intending anything pejorative by the expression). It can be drunk now.

POMMARD 2006
Red | 2011 up to 2018   86
Insistent oak, but fine fruit behind it; a texture of ripe grapes, firm tannins, clear terroir.

POMMARD PREMIER CRU GRANDS ÉPENOTS 2006
Red | 2011 up to 2021   90
Marked use of oak, but an ample, fat, long wine with racy tannins, quintessentially Épenots; seductive.

Red: 74.1 acres, pinot noir 100%. White: 86.5 acres; chardonnay 100%. Annual production: 1,000,000 bottles

ÉTIENNE SAUZET

11, rue de Poiseul
21190 Puligny-Montrachet
Phone 00 33 3 80 21 32 10
Fax 00 33 3 80 21 90 89
Étienne.sauzet@wanadoo.fr
www.Étiennesauzet.com

A very respected source for Puligny wines, back again to form. Some wines from the nineties aged too quickly, but the last vintages are clean, pure, and refined.

Recently tasted
CHEVALIER-MONTRACHET GRAND CRU 2007
White | 2012 up to 2019   93

Older vintages
BÂTARD-MONTRACHET GRAND CRU 2005
White | 2011 up to 2017   93
More robust than the Bienvenues, a clean transcription of the terroir, somewhat overwhelming alcohol; the vintage really comes to the fore.

BIENVENUES-BÂTARD-MONTRACHET GRAND CRU 2005
White | 2011 up to 2017   90
Round, with fine citrus notes, but rich in alcohol and not as refined as usual.

PULIGNY-MONTRACHET 2006
White | 2011 up to 2014   88
Pale, very clean on the nose, with classic aromas of lemongrass; fat, balanced, elegant, and above all, quintessentially Puligny.

PULIGNY-MONTRACHET 2005
White | 2011 up to 2015   86
Fairly tannic and dense, but lacking in finesse and openness to its bouquet. It should age well.

PULIGNY-MONTRACHET PREMIER CRU CHAMP CANET 2005
White | 2011 up to 2017   93
An excellent nose, open, refined, with great finesse, great length: a precise, elegant wine.

PULIGNY-MONTRACHET PREMIER CRU LES COMBETTES 2006
White | 2011 up to 2014   86
Great wiriness, very fresh, austere.

PULIGNY-MONTRACHET PREMIER CRU LES COMBETTES 2005
White | 2011 up to 2013   94
Great purity, great cleanness, complex, refined in its texture and its back-palate.

White: 19.8 acres; chardonnay 100%. Annual production: 120,000 bottles

DOMAINE DU COMTE SENARD

7, rempart Saint-Jean
21200 Beaune
Phone 00 33 3 80 24 21 65
Fax 00 33 3 80 24 21 44
phsenard@club-internet.fr

A classical estate with holdings in some of the best vineyards on the hill of Corton. It occasionally excels, but consistency overall still leaves much to be desired. A broad range of wines is offered for tasting in the winery's recently opened restaurant, which pays homage to Olivier Leflaive's establishment in Puligny-Montrachet.

ALOXE-CORTON PREMIER CRU
LES VALOZIÈRES 2004
Red | 2011 up to 2013   87
Not much color, supple body, floral perfume, easy to drink for its current fruit character.

CORTON-BRESSANDES GRAND CRU 2004
Red | 2011 up to 2014   88
Delicate color, the nose is a bit vegetal (bell peppers), supple, but lacking in precision.

CORTON-PAULAND GRAND CRU 2004
Red | 2011 up to 2013   87
Light color, rather astringent tannins, suitable volume. Still a bit wild.

CORTON GRAND CRU 2005
White | 2011 up to 2015   88
Clean but impersonal! It will develop a bit more character over the next few years.

Red: 19.8 acres; pinot 100%. White: 2.5 acres; chardonnay 100%. Annual production: 35,000 bottles

DOMAINE TOLLOT-BEAUT ET FILS

Rue Alexandre-Tollot
21200 Chorey-lès-Beaune
Phone 00 33 3 80 22 16 54
Fax 00 33 3 80 22 12 61
tollot.beaut@wanadoo.fr

This property is impeccably run by a particularly united family with a tradition of making neat, precise, easily likeable wines, with well-judged oak and forward fruit. But despite their obvious elegance, they were never quite complex enough to rival the best. The 2005 vintage put that right, with some of the finest Côte de Beaune reds available anywhere in France: classically styled, accomplished, complete, and truly memorable.

Recently tasted
BEAUNE PREMIER CRU GRÈVES 2007
Red | 2013 up to 2017   87

BOURGOGNE 2007
Red | 2011 up to 2013   84

CORTON-BRESSANDES GRAND CRU 2007
Red | 2015 up to 2022   88

SAVIGNY-LÈS-BEAUNE PREMIER CRU
CHAMP CHEVREY 2007
Red | 2012 up to 2017   86

SAVIGNY-LÈS-BEAUNE PREMIER CRU LAVIÈRES 2007
Red | 2013 up to 2017   88

Older vintages
ALOXE-CORTON 2006
Red | 2011 up to 2014   87
Elegant rose aromas and oak that is more discreet than usual, a tender, easy-drinking wine that is nonetheless far from the 2005.

BEAUNE PREMIER CRU GRÈVES 2006
Red | 2011 up to 2018   87
Very pure and natural aromas of flowers and vanilla, supple body, fine tannins, nice length, a wine that is already well formed and drinkable, though slightly short on the finish.

BEAUNE PREMIER CRU GRÈVES 2005
Red | 2011 up to 2025   93
A remarkable floral nose, very balanced body, long and racy, with the oaky note that is particular to the domaine and which in this vintage perfectly underscores the wine's body.

CORTON-BRESSANDES GRAND CRU 2005
Red | 2011 up to 2025   95
A great, well-rounded wine that is racy, ample, refined in its texture and aromas, with exceptionally ripe grapes—very unlike the domaine's usual style. Wonderful.

SAVIGNY-LÈS-BEAUNE PREMIER CRU
CHAMP CHEVREY 2006
Red | 2011 up to 2018   **91**
Remarkable constitution, almost more comfortable in body than any of the Cortons. A racy, deep wine of great style.

SAVIGNY-LÈS-BEAUNE PREMIER CRU
CHAMP CHEVREY 2005
Red | 2011 up to 2020   **90**
Deeply colored, powerful, tannic, very linear and precise, with all the fantastic grape ripeness characteristic of this vintage. Good for long-term cellaring.

SAVIGNY-LÈS-BEAUNE PREMIER CRU
LAVIÈRES 2006
Red | 2011 up to 2018   **89**
A fine, complex, and racy nose with notes of licorice and very ripe grapes; suave, long on the palate, but still slightly reductive compared to the true expansiveness of this vintage in Savigny.

Red: 55.8 acres; pinot 100%. White: 3.5 acres; chardonnay 100%. Annual production: 130,000 bottles

HENRI DE VILLAMONT

Rue du Docteur Guyot
21420 Savigny-lès-Beaune
Phone 00 33 3 80 21 50 59
Fax 00 33 3 80 21 36 36
regis.abadie@hdv.fr
www.hdv.fr

This historic Savigny producer, owned by a large Swiss-German wine conglomerate, long produced wines with no clearly defined style. A radical change appeared with the 2006 vintage: each of the wines presented from several different appellations, in both white and red, stood out for their precision and their elegance, and can compete with the best of them. Especially impressive are the Chambolle-Musignys in red and the Chassagne-Montrachets in white. If this progress continues the company will quickly become a reference for many professionals, especially since they own vineyards in prestigious terroirs such as Grands Echézeaux.

Recently tasted
AUXEY-DURESSES LES HAUTES 2007
White | 2011 up to 2017   **88**

CHAMBOLLE-MUSIGNY 2007
Red | 2013 up to 2017   **88**

CHAMBOLLE-MUSIGNY PREMIER CRU BAUDES 2007
Red | 2012 up to 2019   **88**

MEURSAULT PREMIER CRU CAILLERETS 2007
White | 2013 up to 2017   **89**

SAVIGNY-LÈS-BEAUNE PREMIER CRU
VERGELESSES 2006
White | 2011 up to 2016   **90**

Older vintages
CHAMBOLLE-MUSIGNY PREMIER CRU
CHÂTELOTS 2006
Red | 2011 up to 2018   **92**
Great aromatic finesse, very clean tastes of red fruit, delicate tannins, and ideal typicity.

CHAMBOLLE-MUSIGNY PREMIER CRU
FEUSSELOTTES 2006
Red | 2011 up to 2018   **92**
A fine licorice-y nose, supple body, delicate texture, very fine tannins, impeccable style.

CHASSAGNE-MONTRACHET 2006
White | 2011 up to 2014   **91**
A wonderfully successful Village wine, ample, fat, well-rounded, tasty, like all the other wines from this source in this appellation.

CHASSAGNE-MONTRACHET 2006

Red | 2011 up to 2016   **89**
A pure delight; a licorice-y wine with generous body, well-extracted tannins, mouthwatering; very clearly a cut above most of the other Village wines; a confirmation of the winemaker's talent.

CHASSAGNE-MONTRACHET PREMIER CRU MORGEOT 2006

White | 2011 up to 2018   **91**
Decidedly, a winning streak for the Chassagnes of this domaine! The Morgeot has the structure and the purity of a great wine, with superb nuances from an exemplary élevage. The vintage was understood and respected.

CHASSAGNE-MONTRACHET PREMIER CRU VERGERS 2006

White | 2011 up to 2014   **91**
A magnificent nose of flowering vines, a superb sample of the vintage, ample, pure, natural, long: bravo!

CLOS DE VOUGEOT GRAND CRU 2006

Red | 2011 up to 2026   **95**
One of the best scores at our blind tasting, a parcel that is imperial in its breadth, generosity, and extreme length.

GRANDS-ECHÉZEAUX GRAND CRU 2006

Red | 2011 up to 2024   **91**
One of the best parcels of this incomparable terroir, and at last, a wine worthy of it; very delicate in its floral aromas, with tender body and texture; long; vinification more meticulous than inspired.

Annual production: 70,000 bottles

DOMAINE ANNE-MARIE ET JEAN-MARC VINCENT

3, rue Sainte-Agathe
21590 Santenay
Phone 00 33 3 80 20 67 37
Fax 00 33 3 80 20 67 37
VINCENT.J-M@wanadoo.fr

This tiny domaine is the most idealistic of the village and certainly the one that has the ability to make the most elegant and successful Santenays. The hail in 2005 was catastrophic for them, and their small production sold out quickly. The 2006s have wonderful substance and are evolving slowly. The 2007s are excellent.

Recently tasted

AUXEY-DURESSES LES HAUTES 2007
White | 2011 up to 2013   **93**

SANTENAY PREMIER CRU BEAUREPAIRE 2007
White | 2015 up to 2019   **93**

SANTENAY PREMIER CRU PASSE TEMPS 2007
Red | 2012 up to 2019   **88**

Older vintages

AUXEY-DURESSES LES HAUTES 2006
White | 2011 up to 2016   **90**
An exceptional success, and the best rating we gave to any Auxey. An ample wine, refined, long, very like a great Meursault and worthy of comparison to what Lalou Bize-Leroy does in this area.

AUXEY-DURESSES LES HAUTES 2005
White | 2011 up to 2013   **93**
Very distinguished. A marvelously elegant, successful wine for the appellation. Heartily recommended.

AUXEY-DURESSES PREMIER CRU LES BRETTERINS 2005
Red | 2011 up to 2017   **86**
Ripe grapes, the tannins a bit firm. A wine with character.

BOURGOGNE 2005
White | 2011 up to 2013   **88**
Full, fruity, pure, with a lot of style.

SANTENAY PREMIER CRU BEAUREPAIRE 2006
White | 2011 up to 2014   **86**
It's clear that the grapes were quite ripe. The palate-coating texture is already apparent and should make for a wine that is rich and voluptuous but not very taut or "mineral," as we say these days.

SANTENAY PREMIER CRU BEAUREPAIRE 2004
White | 2011 up to 2013   **93**
Very suave, the grapes exceptionally ripe, very long, marvelous texture.

SANTENAY PREMIER CRU GRAVIÈRES 2006
White | 2011 up to 2016   **89**
A touch reductive but with admirable power, energy, and refinement. More nuanced than the Beaurepaire. A very nice wine in the works.

SANTENAY PREMIER CRU GRAVIÈRES 2006
Red | 2011 up to 2013   **90**
The distinction of this terroir shines through on the nose with aromas of exceptional finesse. Nobler tannins and more complexity, delivering more refined tactile sensations. Exemplary vinification and maturation.

SANTENAY PREMIER CRU PASSE TEMPS 2006
Red | 2011 up to 2016   **87**
Good general harmony, supple, fleshy, with a steady finish. Made with care and highly praiseworthy.

Red: 7.2 acres; pinot noir 100%. White: 4.9 acres; chardonnay 100%. Annual production: 21,000 bottles

DOMAINE JOSEPH VOILLOT

4, place de l'Église
21190 Volnay
Phone 00 33 3 80 21 62 27
Fax 00 33 3 80 21 66 63
joseph.voillot@wanadoo.fr
joseph-voillot.com

Here we find ourselves at the heart of classic Volnay winemaking, with wines of rare delicacy and exemplary aging potential. A few of the 2004s are a bit thin, which is normal, but the 2005s are back to the usual style of the winery: wines that are discreet, elegant, that will thrill the experienced Burgundy lover. The 2007s have the elegance we would expect.

Recently tasted
POMMARD PREMIER CRU PEZEROLLES 2007
Red | 2015 up to 2019   **86**

POMMARD PREMIER CRU RUGIENS 2007
Red | 2017 up to 2027   **91**

POMMARD VIEILLES VIGNES 2007
Red | 2017 up to 2022   **90**

VOLNAY PREMIER CRU LES CHAMPANS 2007
Red | 2011 up to 2013   **91**

VOLNAY PREMIER CRU LES FRÉMIETS 2007
Red | 2015 up to 2019   **88**

Older vintages
POMMARD VIEILLES VIGNES 2005
Red | 2011 up to 2017   **86**
Full, suave, but nose marked too much by animal notes.

VOLNAY PREMIER CRU LES CHAMPANS 2005
Red | 2011 up to 2020   **91**
Rich, suave, spicy; the terroir is eminently legible; a stylish wine.

VOLNAY PREMIER CRU LES FRÉMIETS 2005
Red | 2011 up to 2020   **90**
Floral, subtle, without the animal notes of the Volnay village wine; long, refined.

VOLNAY PREMIER CRU LES FRÉMIETS 2004
Red | 2011 up to 2020   **89**
Light, mature color, but supple, subtle, delicately vinified wine; very pleasant.

Red: 23.7 acres; pinot noir 100%. Annual production: 45,000 bottles

Mâcon Vineyards

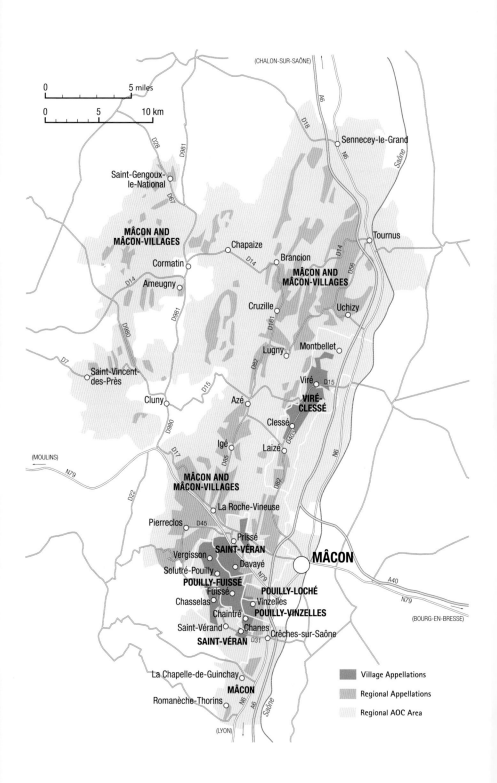

0	5 miles
0	5	10 km

(CHALON-SUR-SAÔNE)

Sennecey-le-Grand

Saint-Gengoux-le-National

MÂCON AND MÂCON-VILLAGES

Chapaize

Brancion

Tournus

Cormatin

MÂCON AND MÂCON-VILLAGES

Ameugny

Cruzille

Uchizy

Lugny

Montbellet

Saint-Vincent-des-Près

Viré

Cluny

Azé

VIRÉ-CLESSÉ

Clessé

(MOULINS)

Igé

Laizé

MÂCON AND MÂCON-VILLAGES

La Roche-Vineuse

Pierreclos

MÂCON

Prissé

SAINT-VÉRAN

Vergisson

Davayé

Solutré-Pouilly

POUILLY-FUISSÉ

Fuissé

POUILLY-LOCHÉ

Chasselas

Vinzelles

Chaintré

POUILLY-VINZELLES

Saint-Vérand

Chanes

Crêches-sur-Saône

SAINT-VÉRAN

(BOURG-EN-BRESSE)

La Chapelle-de-Guinchay

MÂCON

Romanèche-Thorins

(LYON)

Saône

■	Village Appellations
▨	Regional Appellations
░	Regional AOC Area

Côte Chalonnaise Vineyards

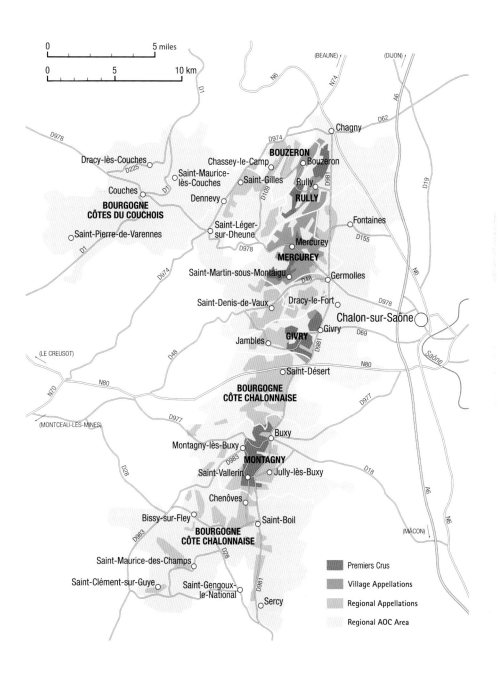

ANTONIN RODET

71640 Mercurey
Phone 00 33 3 85 98 12 12
Fax 00 33 3 85 45 25 49
rodet@rodet.com
www.rodet.com

The Maison Antonin Rodet may be in Mercurey but its wines come from all over Burgundy. Enologist Nadine Gublin supervises vinification from start to finish, aiming for that smooth, charming juiciness that all of these wines have in common.

Recently tasted

MERCUREY CHÂTEAU DE MERCEY 2007
Red | 2011 up to 2014   **84**

MERCUREY PREMIER CRU EN SAZENAY CHÂTEAU DE MERCEY 2007
Red | 2011 up to 2014   **86**

RULLY CHÂTEAU DE RULLY 2007
White | 2011 up to 2014   **84**

RULLY PREMIER CRU LA BRESSANDE CHÂTEAU DE RULLY 2007
White | 2011 up to 2014   **86**

Older vintages

MERCUREY CHÂTEAU DE MERCEY 2006
White | 2011 up to 2013   **85**
A ripe nose, fine and elegant. High-quality oak influence. Fat and rich on the palate. Harmonious yet rich. Nicely fruity, ripe finish.

MERCUREY CHÂTEAU DE MERCEY 2006
Red | 2011 up to 2013   **86**
Clean, radiant fruit. The palate is rich and well balanced. A very good Village-level wine, fruity, with pulpy flesh. Moderately concentrated, but very pleasant.

MERCUREY CHÂTEAU DE MERCEY 2005
Red | 2011 up to 2013   **88**
A concentrated nose with agreeable smoky notes. This wine has an unctuous mouthfeel with the suave lightness of a Mercurey. Pleasant and with a lovely balance, it is very precise, delicate, and elegant.

MERCUREY PREMIER CRU EN SAZENAY CHÂTEAU DE MERCEY 2006
Red | 2011 up to 2016   **87**
An expressive, open nose. Deep fruit, with good freshness. The palate is succulent and rich, with round tannins. Velvety and luscious. A long, fresh finish.

MERCUREY PREMIER CRU EN SAZENAY CHÂTEAU DE MERCEY 2005
Red | 2011 up to 2013   **89**
Very pure; beautifully ripe grapes. The juice is superb! Deep, suave, very velvety. A superb Village-appellation wine.

RULLY CHÂTEAU DE RULLY 2006
White | 2011 up to 2013   **86**
Luscious, appetizing fruitiness, tending toward yellow and white fruits (peach). Good maturity, but freshness and lightness reappear on the palate. A wine for gourmands.

RULLY CHÂTEAU DE RULLY 2005
Red | 2011 up to 2013   **87**
A good wine with straightforward tannins. A pretty, perfumed juice on the palate, tending toward black and red fruit, rather rich, with a touch of licorice at the finish.

RULLY PREMIER CRU CHÂTEAU DE RULLY 2006
White | 2011 up to 2021   **90**
Fine and elegant, with a nice aromatic complexity. A fat wine that still finds an almost crystalline freshness on the finish, as well as tautness. Racy. The very old vines give more tautness and fat than Les Pucelles.

RULLY PREMIER CRU LA BRESSANDE CHÂTEAU DE RULLY 2006
White | 2011 up to 2021   **90**
Very fine, very elegant. The palate is pure and straightforward. Concentrated, long, but fine and luscious. The finish is nicely taut. Very harmonious.

RULLY PREMIER CRU LA BRESSANDE CHÂTEAU DE RULLY 2005
White | 2011 up to 2013   **87**
This delicate, elegant wine has a very pretty palate, suave and juicy. It shows a nice maturity. This wine has a brilliant future ahead of it!

RULLY PREMIER CRU LES MOLESMES CHÂTEAU DE RULLY 2006
Red | 2011 up to 2016   **88**
More mineral, spicier, more straightforward than the Préaux. But the palate has the same luscious, appetizing quality, with fat, round tannins. Crispy fruit; a good tautness on the finish.

Red: 187.8 acres; pinot noir 100%. White: 118.6 acres; chardonnay 100%.

DOMAINE DANIEL, JULIEN ET MARTINE BARRAUD

Le Nambret
71960 Vergisson
Phone 00 33 3 85 35 84 25
Fax 00 33 3 85 35 86 98
contact@domainebarraud.com
www.domainebarraud.com

This pristine winery in Vergisson is one of many estates that was taken up by Belgian winemaker Jean-Marie Guffens. Now a model of integrity, it boasts modern and immaculate facilities where Daniel Barraud turns out refined, subtle wines. This style can suffer though, especially in hot years, which seem to be more and more frequent.

Recently tasted
POUILLY-FUISSÉ CLOS DE LA COMBE PONCET 2007
White | 2011 up to 2016   88

POUILLY-FUISSÉ LES CHÂTAIGNIERS 2007
White | 2011 up to 2015   86

Older vintages
POUILLY-FUISSÉ ALLIANCE PAR JULIEN
BARRAUD 2006
White | 2011 up to 2013   85
A wine with noticeable technique. Honest.

POUILLY-FUISSÉ EN BULAND 2006
White | 2011 up to 2014   87
Yeasty notes on the nose, but a very nice terroir character. Very promising.

POUILLY-FUISSÉ LA VERCHÈRE 2007
White | 2011 up to 2013   89
A wine built entirely on its fruit character. Mouthwatering and fat. Very well made. Luscious and counterbalanced by a nice vivacity.

POUILLY-FUISSÉ LA VERCHÈRE 2006
White | 2011 up to 2014   88
More open than the En Buland, very delicate, full, long, subtle, lemony, distinguished. Long and classy.

SAINT-VÉRAN LES POMMARDS 2007
White | 2011 up to 2015   87
An unusual but deep style. Nice balance on the palate. Well built.

SAINT-VÉRAN LES POMMARDS 2006
White | 2011 up to 2013   87
A good effort in the vinification, a bit yeasty, more substance than the other 2006s. Plenty of style!

White: 21 acres; chardonnay 100%. Annual production: 50,000 bottles

CHÂTEAU DE BEAUREGARD

71960 Fuissé
Phone 00 33 3 85 35 60 76
Fax 00 33 3 85 35 66 04
joseph.burrier@wanadoo.fr
www.joseph-burrier.com

Frédéric Burrier runs this large family estate as intelligently as he does the entire Pouilly-Fuissé appellation—which can rightly aspire to elite AOC status. Part of the vineyard is still worked by sharecroppers (according to the French system of "vigneronnage"), but the bulk of holdings are farmed directly by the property, with a level of care that is reflected in the wines. The estate also boasts some excellent parcels in Fleurie and Moulin-à-Vent.

Recently tasted
FLEURIE LES COLONIES DE ROCHEGRÈS 2007
Red | 2011 up to 2013   89

MORGON GRAND GRAS 2007
Red | 2011 up to 2015   88

MOULIN-À-VENT CLOS DES PÉRELLES 2007
Red | 2011 up to 2017   90

MOULIN-À-VENT LA SALOMINE 2007
Red | 2011 up to 2015   88

POUILLY-FUISSÉ VERS POUILLY 2007
White | 2011 up to 2017   91

SAINT-AMOUR CÔTE DE BESSET 2007
Red | 2011 up to 2014   89

Older vintages
FLEURIE LES COLONIES DE ROCHEGRÈS 2006
Red | 2011 up to 2014   90
A nice floral nose. Intelligent modern winemaking, which sets the tone for what should be done today with cru Beaujolais.

POUILLY-FUISSÉ GRAND BEAUREGARD
HOMMAGE À JOSEPH BURRIER 2005
White | 2011 up to 2014   88
An elegant nose. Well made yet with a certain simplicity. Oaky notes on the finish.

POUILLY-FUISSÉ VERS CRAS 2006
White | 2011 up to 2013   86
A pleasant wine with good structure. Once again the terroir shows through. A fleshy finish.

POUILLY-FUISSÉ VERS CRAS 2005
White | 2011 up to 2014   90
Fleshy, complex, long, powerful; a classic example of a great Pouilly-Fuissé, from a site worthy of being a Grand Cru.

Red: 29.7 acres; gamay 96%, pinot noir 4%. White: 74.1 acres; chardonnay 100%. Annual production: 300,000 bottles

DOMAINE DE LA BONGRAN – JEAN ET GAUTIER THÉVENET

Quintaine Cedex 654
71260 Clessé
Phone 00 33 3 85 36 94 03
Fax 00 33 3 85 36 99 25
contact@bongran.com
www.bongran.com

Over the years, this famous winemaker has proven the intelligence of his work ethic, despite his lofty ideas. The wines, made from ultraripe grapes, have the slightest hint of residual sugar, with a very distinctive personality. But that doesn't mean that they aren't balanced, thanks to his meticulous vineyard practices. The challenging weather in 2007 made it a winemaker's year, and this winemaker made some truly superb wines.

Recently tasted

VIRÉ-CLESSÉ DOMAINE DE LA BONGRAN 2007
White | 2011 up to 2016   **88**

VIRÉ-CLESSÉ DOMAINE DE LA BONGRAN 2005
White | 2011 up to 2014   **90**

VIRÉ-CLESSÉ DOMAINE EMILIAN GILLET-CUVÉE QUINTAINE 2005
White | 2011 up to 2015   **90**

Older vintages

VIRÉ-CLESSÉ DOMAINE DE LA BONGRAN 2004
White | 2013 up to 2016   **88**
An explosive nose of mind-boggling mineral scents. Good overall harmony, at once refined and powerful.

VIRÉ-CLESSÉ DOMAINE DE ROALLY-CUVÉE TRADITION 2005
White | 2011 up to 2013   **90**
Exceptional texture. A complex, refined wine. Infinitely long.

VIRÉ-CLESSÉ DOMAINE EMILIAN GILLET-CUVÉE QUINTAINE 2004
White | 2011 up to 2013   **88**
Golden. Very nice complexity. A magnificent wine that breathes floral scents. Elegant structure.

White: 29.7 acres; chardonnay 100%. Annual production: 40,000 bottles

DOMAINE BRINTET

105, Grande-Rue
71640 Mercurey
Phone 00 33 3 85 45 14 50
Fax 00 33 3 85 45 28 23
domaine.brintet@wanadoo.fr
www.domaine-brintet.com

Established in 1354, the Brintet family winery is located on the edge of the village of Mercurey in a splendid eighteenth-century estate. Luc Brintet took over the management of the property in 1984 and began making wines that reflect his personality, reserved and elegant, with lots of finesse. All of the wines here, red as well as white, are made in a pure and refined style, aged in oak, but with a very light touch. The single vineyard holdings of the Premier Cru La Levrière and the Premier Cru Les Champs Martin in the Mercurey appellation are often the most distinctive reds. Prices are more than reasonable.

Recently tasted

MERCUREY 2007
White | 2011 up to 2013   **87**

MERCUREY PREMIER CRU LA LEVRIÈRE 2007
Red | 2011 up to 2015   **87**

MERCUREY PREMIER CRU LES CHAMPS MARTIN 2007
Red | 2011 up to 2015   **88**

MERCUREY PREMIER CRU LES VASÉES 2007
Red | 2011 up to 2015   **87**

MERCUREY VIEILLES VIGNES 2007
White | 2011 up to 2015   **88**

RULLY 2007
White | 2011 up to 2013   **87**

RULLY 2007
Red | 2011 up to 2013   **86**

Older vintages

MERCUREY LA PERRIÈRE 2006
Red | 2011 up to 2014   **86**
Good, straightforward, fresh fruit character. The tannins are ripe and soft. Good substance. A dense wine, balanced, that finishes pleasantly fresh.

MERCUREY LA PERRIÈRE 2005
Red | 2011 up to 2013   **86**
A wine with a good, solid core and firm tannins. A rather strict Mercurey that should develop nicely over the next few years.

Mercurey premier cru La Levrière 2006

Red | 2011 up to 2016   **88**

A three-acre single vineyard under exclusive ownership of the domaine. Good fruit character, frank and deep. The palate is ripe, the tannins luscious. Good length. A balanced wine with good concentration.

Mercurey premier cru La Levrière 2005

Red | 2011 up to 2013   **89**

The nose is powerful and concentrated, mostly fruity, with a few gamey, animal notes already showing. Firm tannins, but still fleshy. A ripe wine, promising a good future. Very nice juiciness on the finish.

Mercurey premier cru Les Champs Martin 2006

Red | 2011 up to 2016   **89**

An expressive, rich nose, joining flowers and fruit. The palate is straightforward, with good body. A long, luscious, deep wine.

Mercurey premier cru Les Vasées 2006

Red | 2011 up to 2016   **87**

A fruity, floral nose, elegant and complex. The wine has a velvety texture and finishes harmoniously and quite fruity. Less full-bodied than La Levrière.

Mercurey Vieilles Vignes 2006

White | 2011 up to 2014   **86**

Fresher and more balanced than the Mercurey-Village: the old vines from 1953 give extra freshness and fullness. A fleshy wine, expansive, direct, and balanced.

Mercurey Vieilles Vignes 2006

Red | 2011 up to 2016   **87**

An appealing fruit character, deeper than La Perrière. Dense and concentrated. The tannins are direct and elegant. Good length, with a lightly spicy finish.

Rully 2006

White | 2011 up to 2013   **86**

A delicate, pure nose. The palate is direct and concentrated. A very good Village-level wine that finishes fresh and fruity.

Red: 18.5 acres; pinot 100%. White: 6.2 acres; chardonnay 100%. Annual production: 50,000 bottles

CHÂTEAU DE CHAMIREY

BP 5
71640 Mercurey
Phone 00 33 3 85 45 21 61
Fax 00 33 3 85 98 06 62
contact@châteaudechamirey.com
www.chamirey.com

The Devillard family owns vineyards in different parts of Burgundy: Nuits-Saint-Georges (Domaine des Perdrix), Mercurey (Château de Chamirey), and Givry. The wines share a common richness and depth of aroma, and they age to perfection, burying any youthful awkwardness in a very natural-seeming, mellow maturity.

Recently tasted

Givry Domaine de La Ferté 2007

Red | 2011 up to 2015   **89**

Givry premier cru Servoisine Domaine de La Ferté 2007

Red | 2011 up to 2017   **90**

Mercurey 2007

White | 2011 up to 2014   **89**

Mercurey 2007

Red | 2011 up to 2015   **90**

Mercurey premier cru Clos du Roi 2007

Red | 2011 up to 2022   **92**

Mercurey premier cru La Mission 2007

White | 2011 up to 2017   **90**

Mercurey premier cru Les Ruelles 2007

Red | 2011 up to 2022   **92**

Older vintages

Bourgogne Le Renard 2006

White | 2011 up to 2013   **87**

Fat, elegant, aromatic, tasty and fresh.

Bourgogne Le Renard 2006

Red | 2011 up to 2013   **84**

A fine pinot that is refined and straightforward. The aromas are delicate, on the palate it is linear, and the tannins are supple.

Bourgogne Le Renard 2005

White | 2011 up to 2013   **85**

Ripe, floral, open, straightforward. A pleasant aromatic palette, with a pineapple finish.

Givry premier cru Servoisine Domaine de La Ferté 2006

Red | 2011 up to 2016   **89**

More taut, more mineral (red clay soil) than the Village wine. On the palate, it is concentrated, with nice fruit. Needs time. The finish brings together fruit and mineral notes.

MERCUREY 2006
Red | 2011 up to 2013   **87**
Deep red fruitiness, refined, very pure, very linear. Mouthwatering. On the palate is the same supple, tasty register; very round.

MERCUREY 2005
White | 2011 up to 2013   **86**
Concentrated, with very expressive floral notes. But without the purity of the 2006s. Nonetheless, it's ripe, elegant, and always very fresh.

MERCUREY 2005
Red | 2011 up to 2015   **87**
Very ripe nose: dark fruit, olives, spice, tobacco. Rich and opulent. On the palate, it is fat, with savory, fine juice. Already appealing, it will hold up well.

MERCUREY PREMIER CRU CLOS DU ROI 2006
Red | 2011 up to 2016   **88**
Refined, fruity, deep. On the palate, it is suave, with an unctuous, caressing mouthfeel. Very tasty.

MERCUREY PREMIER CRU CLOS DU ROI 2005
Red | 2011 up to 2020   **89**
More taut than the Village wine of the same vintage, with a greater tannic backbone. This is a concentrated yet elegant, fresh wine.

MERCUREY PREMIER CRU LA MISSION 2006
White | 2011 up to 2021   **87**
Fine, elegant oak, but great freshness on the nose. A fat, luscious body to it that is very pure. Elegant and refined. A fresh, savory finish.

MERCUREY PREMIER CRU LES RUELLES 2006
Red | 2011 up to 2021   **89**
More concentrated than the Clos du Roi. A refined, elegant wine with great purity on the palate, a linear and slightly tight finish that requires some time.

Red: 64.2 acres; pinot noir 100%. White: 27.2 acres; chardonnay 100%. Annual production: 200,000 bottles

LES CHAMPS DE L'ABBAYE

9, rue des Roches-Pendantes
71510 Aluze
Phone 00 33 3 85 45 59 32
Fax 00 33 3 85 45 59 32
alainhasard@wanadoo.fr

Alain Hasard is considered a "young wine-maker" given that he started making wine only in 1997. Since he didn't start out with a lot of money, he set up in the unknown appellation "Côtes du Couchois," but since 2006 he has been focusing on the better known "Côtes Chalonnaises." Starting in 1999, Hasard began farming his vineyards biodynamically, and he 100 percent destems his reds. Each wine we tasted from this property was off the charts, blending purity, brilliance, and concentration. His recent offerings from the wonderful terroirs of Mercurey and Rully should shake up some preconceived ideas about the wines from this region.

Recently tasted
BOURGOGNE 2007
Red | 2011 up to 2013   **89**

BOURGOGNE ALIGOTÉ 2007
White | 2011 up to 2013   **90**

BOURGOGNE CÔTE CHALONNAISE
LE CLOS DES ROCHES 2006
Red | 2011 up to 2017   **89**

BOURGOGNE CÔTES DU COUCHOIS
LE CLOS 2007
Red | 2011 up to 2017   **91**

BOURGOGNE CÔTES DU COUCHOIS
LES ROMPEYS 2007
Red | 2011 up to 2017   **90**

MERCUREY LA BRIGADIÈRE 2007
Red | 2011 up to 2017   **90**

MERCUREY LES MARCOEURS 2007
Red | 2011 up to 2017   **91**

RULLY LES CAILLOUX 2007
White | 2011 up to 2015   **90**

Older vintages
BOURGOGNE CÔTE CHALONNAISE
LE CLOS DES ROCHES 2006
Red | 2011 up to 2016   **88**
Mineral, concentrated, taut, with remarkable purity to its fruit. On the palate, it is linear, taut with minerality, and its tannins are elegant. A firm, long, very balanced wine.

BOURGOGNE CÔTES DU COUCHOIS LE CLOS 2006
Red | 2011 up to 2016   **91**
What purity, what elegance, what depth! Taut, concentrated juice with a magnificent mineral expression. A charming, well-balanced vintage.

BOURGOGNE CÔTES DU COUCHOIS LES ROMPEYS 2003
Red | 2011 up to 2013   **92**
The nose is superb, typical of the vintage: licorice, black fruit and fruit jelly, but refined, fresh. No overripe notes. On the palate, it is full of good, savory tannins. They are firm—owing to the vintage—but not drying. The finish is spicy and licorice-y. Delicious.

MERCUREY LA BRIGADIÈRE 2006
Red | 2011 up to 2016   **90**
A fine, fruity nose. On the palate, pure, delicious fruit! What softness to the texture! What aromatic refinement! A real treat.

MERCUREY LES MARCOEURS 2006
Red | 2011 up to 2016   **90**
Tauter and more linear on the palate than La Brigadière. But still the same ripe, well-rounded juice and plush tannins. Superb balance, very fresh on the finish, which gives it its tension and length (more so than the Brigadière). Cellar this one a bit more.

RULLY LES CAILLOUX 2006
White | 2011 up to 2016   **89**
Very concentrated (flowers, aniseed, lime), very elegant. On the palate it is pure and taut, with nice mineral tension playing out good fattiness. Very natural. Excellent acidity on the finish, and doubtless more balance and freshness than the 2005s.

Red: 12.4 acres; pinor noir 100%. White: 2.5 acres; chardonnay 75%, aligoté 25%. Annual production: 18,000 bottles

DOMAINE DES DEUX ROCHES

Route de Mâcon
71960 Davayé
Phone 00 33 3 85 35 86 51
Fax 00 33 3 85 35 86 12
info@collovrayterrier.com
www.collovrayterrier.com

This large estate is a dependable source of high-volume, well-crafted Saint-Véran wines that offer excellent value for the money—from an appellation too often discredited by indifferent, mediocre wines aimed at undemanding customers. The finest bottlings, Terres Noires and Cras, show a satisfying balance and have enough finesse and honest fruit to compete with the cream of the Mâcon offerings. You can forget about the others. The partners' expertise now extends into the Limoux region with the same success.

SAINT-VÉRAN LES CRAS 2006
White | 2011 up to 2013   **88**
A very nice wine, all about finesse and intensity. Superb balance of flavors. A sumptuous finish.

SAINT-VÉRAN LES CRAS 2005
White | 2011 up to 2013   **88**
A perfectly refined, pure nose. Long, complex, lemony, with an escalating finish. Excellent!

SAINT-VÉRAN LES TERRES NOIRES 2006
White | 2011 up to 2014   **86**
The terroir already shows through on the nose. A very nice wine with good acidity this year that brings it all together. Very good length.

SAINT-VÉRAN VIEILLES VIGNES 2005
White | 2011 up to 2013   **86**
More ambitious, the oak isn't integrated yet, but with more marked finesse and no heaviness. A good 2005.

SAINT-VÉRAN VIGNES DERRIÈRE LA MAISON 2006
White | 2011 up to 2015   **88**
A magnificently intense nose. Exceptionally fresh. A velvety texture and masterful balance.

Red: 2.5 acres; gamay 100%. White: 101.3 acres; chardonnay 100%. Annual production: 300,000 bottles

DOMAINE VINCENT DUREUIL-JANTHIAL

🍷🍷🍷🍷🍷

10, rue de la Buisserolle
71150 Rully
Phone 00 33 3 85 87 26 32
Fax 00 33 3 85 87 15 01
vincent.dureuil@wanadoo.fr

Vincent Dureuil vinified his first wine in 1994. He has been a rising star of the Rully appellation for quite some years now, and his wines get better with every new vintage, proof that meticulous vineyard maintenance and precision vinification are the keys to bringing out the precise, individual character of each "climat" (single vineyard). This producer is one step away from the podium.

Recently tasted

NUITS-SAINT-GEORGES 2007
Red | 2011 up to 2015   **89**

PULIGNY-MONTRACHET PREMIER CRU
CHAMP GAINS 2007
White | 2011 up to 2022   **91**

Older vintages

BOURGOGNE 2007
White | 2011 up to 2013   **89**
Ripe, with a slightly mentholated freshness. A fat, pure wine. Nice personality on the palate. Its finish is tasty and fresh.

BOURGOGNE 2007
Red | 2011 up to 2013   **88**
Ripe fruitiness; a rich wine with natural, pure aromas. Appealing, round, and generous on the palate.

BOURGOGNE ALIGOTÉ 2007
White | 2011 up to 2013   **89**
Great aromatic expressiveness, with a very diverse floral palette. A very ripe, rich wine with astonishing purity for an aligoté.

MERCUREY 2007
Red | 2011 up to 2015   **88**
Good, straightforward fruitiness and chewy mouthfeel. More body than the Rullys, but also balanced and straightforward.

NUITS-SAINT-GEORGES PREMIER CRU
CLOS DES ARGILLIÈRES 2007
Red | 2011 up to 2022   **91**
Fine juice, racy and pure. The finish brings out the nice, slightly robust tannins. The style here has become more refined in the past few years!

RULLY 2007
White | 2011 up to 2013   **87**
Elegant, fat, with good balance between the fruitiness and the minerality. A good Village wine.

RULLY 2007
Red | 2011 up to 2013   **87**
Pure, straightforward aromas. Round on the palate, with supple tannins. Nice fruit; a tasty, linear wine.

RULLY EN GUESNES 2007
Red | 2011 up to 2013   **87**
Ripe fruit, but less strikingly pure than the old-vines bottling. Solidly built, with good, ripe tannins.

RULLY MAIZIÈRES 2007
White | 2011 up to 2015   **88**
Pure, refined juice that is quite aromatic. Pleasant minerality, an elegant, straightforward wine. Slightly lemony finish.

RULLY MAIZIÈRES 2007
Red | 2011 up to 2015   **89**
A wine with ripe fruitiness and good fat, very appetizing.

RULLY PREMIER CRU CHAPITRE 2007
White | 2011 up to 2013   **88**
Very ripe fruit, but less finesse, less precision, less minerality than the Meix Cadot. Expressive fruit notes (white, yellow fruit). On the palate, a good fattiness to it, an easy-drinking wine that is fairly supple.

RULLY PREMIER CRU LES MARGOTÉS 2007
White | 2011 up to 2022   **90**
An elegant wine with nice purity on the palate. Chiseled, linear, very long; a refined, mineral wine.

RULLY PREMIER CRU MEIX CADOT
VIEILLES VIGNES 2007
White | 2012 up to 2022   **92**
More tension, more purity, more elegance, and more minerality than the Meix Cadot bottling. The finish is crystalline, extremely linear.

RULLY VIEILLES VIGNES 2007
Red | 2011 up to 2017   **88**
Concentrated, velvety juice, with good tension on the finish. Refined and taut.

RULLY VIEILLES VIGNES 2007
White | 2011 up to 2017   **87**
More concentrated than the Village wine, with more depth on the palate.

Red: 19.8 acres; gamay 4%, pinot 96%. White: 21 acres; aligoté 3%, chardonnay 97%. Annual production: 100,000 bottles

DOMAINE J.-A. FERRET-LORTON

Le Plan
71960 Fuissé
Phone 00 33 3 85 35 61 56
Fax 00 33 3 85 35 62 74
ferretlorton@orange.fr

Colette Ferret recently passed away, but her estate continues to produce some of today's most exciting Pouilly-Fuissés—a credit to perfectly exposed vineyards in the hamlet of Pouilly itself. Leading French restaurateurs love these wines—so, too, do top négociants who buy part of production. The Le Clos is one of the rare successes of 2005, with a density and class that make it the archetypal Pouilly-Fuissé. As good as many Montrachets!

Recently tasted
POUILLY-FUISSÉ HORS CLASSE
LES MÉNÉTRIÈRES 2007
White | 2011 up to 2017   90

POUILLY-FUISSÉ TÊTE DE CRU LE CLOS 2007
White | 2011 up to 2017   90

POUILLY-FUISSÉ TÊTE DE CRU-LES PERRIÈRES 2007
White | 2011 up to 2017   95

Older vintages
POUILLY-FUISSÉ HORS CLASSE
LES MÉNÉTRIÈRES 2006
White | 2011 up to 2016   90
A splendid wine, well-balanced, deep. The minerality shines thanks to a luscious texture.

POUILLY-FUISSÉ TÊTE DE CRU LE CLOS 2006
White | 2011 up to 2016   90
Both powerful and refined. Magnificent notes of almonds and apricots. Exceptionally long and quite fresh.

POUILLY-FUISSÉ TÊTE DE CRU LE CLOS 2005
White | 2011 up to 2013   94
An admirable nose of honey, almonds, and apricots, the sign of a perfectly ripe harvest. Magnificent body, the very definition of a great Pouilly-Fuissé, which is so rare in 2005!

POUILLY-FUISSÉ TÊTE DE CRU-LES
PERRIÈRES 2006
White | 2011 up to 2015   97
A delicate texture, but perfectly balanced. Lemony flavors; a luscious, brilliant wine.

White: 45.7 acres; chardonnay 100%. Annual production: 40,000 bottles

DOMAINE GUFFENS-HEYNEN

En France
71960 Vergisson
Phone 00 33 3 85 51 66 00
Fax 00 33 3 85 51 66 09
info.verget@orange.fr
www.guffensheynen.com

This tiny domaine is home to some of the world's greatest chardonnays. Jean-Marie Guffens is the only winemaker we know who can produce a wine of such consistent eloquence, combining immaculate grape expression with the mineral character of a limestone terroir. The key to his success without a doubt are those pristine grapes, from vines that have been lovingly tended by his wife, Maine, for twenty-five years. Even at peak ripeness they retain an acidity simply unknown elsewhere. Without fiendishly precise pressing—tailored to the requirements of every vintage—Guffens could never achieve such a degree of crystalline purity. His great Pierreclos and Vergisson cuvées, like the greatest rieslings, are as limpid and pure as spring water. The masterpieces of finesse produced by this domaine in 2005 were a sharp contrast to the heavy wines seen elsewhere, and are sure to rival and even surpass the 1989s and 1997s.

Recently tasted
POUILLY-FUISSÉ TRIS DES HAUTS DE VIGNES 2007
White | 2011 up to 2017   92

Older vintages
MÂCON-VILLAGES PIERRECLOS
TRI DE CHAVIGNE 2005
White | 2011 up to 2020   95
Fantastic aromatic purity, an unthinkable level of delicate acidity for the vintage; all the components are absolutely immaculate. This is great art!

POUILLY-FUISSÉ 2005
White | 2011 up to 2020   98
A blend of the best small parcels, and the absolute paradigm of great Burgundian chardonnay: intense, pure, complex, inimitable!

POUILLY-FUISSÉ PREMIER JUS DE CHAVIGNE 2006
White | 2011 up to 2016   92
A highly stylish, elegant wine. Very long intensity, amazingly harmonious. This is one you won't forget!

POUILLY-FUISSÉ PREMIER JUS DES HAUTS
DE VIGNES 2006
White | 2011 up to 2016   86
A nice wine, well made, with a delicate simplicity. Medium finish. But overall very intense.

POUILLY-FUISSÉ SAUVÉ DES EAUX 2006
White | 2011 up to 2016   **91**
An elegant nose despite the oak influence. Silky attack. Well balanced, refined, and luscious on the palate. A gastronomic wine, all about delicacy and richness.

White: 13.2 acres; chardonnay 100%. Annual production: 25,000 bottles

DOMAINE DES HÉRITIERS DU COMTE LAFON

Cartelées
71960 Milly-Lamartine
Phone 00 33 3 85 37 78 90
Fax 00 33 3 85 37 65 21
comtes.lafon@wanadoo.fr

A very young estate on a fast track to success. It was started by Côte d'Or superstar Dominique Lafon as a way of expanding the family holdings without paying the exorbitant prices charged for vineyards around Meursault. He quite rightly went for the Mâcon, an area of untapped potential exploited (in the pejorative sense) mainly by mediocre wine co-ops. As he grows more familiar with each individual cru, he looks to bring out the maximum expression of terroir. Prices remain reasonable for the time being. Clos de la Crochette, from this estate's latest acquisition in the village of Chardonnay, is sure to become a cult-wine chardonnay. Buy while you still can!

MÂCON-VILLAGES MÂCON CHARDONNNAY
CLOS DE LA CROCHETTE 2005
White | 2011 up to 2017   **90**
The new acquisition of the estate and its best cru, with the lightly milky character of Mâcon wine. Very noble aromas of grape blossom, and it shines above all for its fuller, fatter texture. Excellent!

MÂCON-VILLAGES MÂCON MILLY-LAMARTINE
CLOS DU FOUR 2005
White | 2011 up to 2015   **89**
A nice vanilla nose, very full body for the appellation and the vintage. A very pure, complex, refined wine with a slight lack of acidity.

MÂCON-VILLAGES MÂCON-BUSSIÈRES
LE MONSARD 2005
White | 2011 up to 2013   **86**
A pale color and pure bouquet. Tender, easy, a light caramel note, less complex than some of the estate's other cuvées.

MÂCON-VILLAGES MÂCON-UCHIZY
LES MARANCHES 2005
White | 2011 up to 2015   **88**
Mineral, taut, complex, very good vinification and maturation. Here is a prototype of the potential quality when as-yet-little-known areas are well worked.

DOMAINE HENRI ET PAUL JACQUESON

5 et 7, rue de Chèvremont
71150 Rully
Phone 00 33 3 85 91 25 91
Fax 00 33 3 85 87 14 92
sceajacqueson@lesvinsfrançais.com

Paul Jacqueson has been a cutting-edge Rully producer for many years. He specializes in white wines, but the guiding principles remain the same whatever the color of the wine: carefully controlled yields and 100 percent barrel aging with no more than 20 percent new wood. The young wines are remarkable for their finesse and purity and they age superbly—testament to Paul Jacqueson's patient and painstaking labors.

Recently tasted

BOURGOGNE PASSE-TOUT-GRAINS 2008
Red | 2011 up to 2013   88

BOUZERON 2008
White | 2011 up to 2013   88

RULLY 2008
White | 2011 up to 2016   88

RULLY LES CHAPONNIÈRES 2008
Red | 2011 up to 2018   88

RULLY PREMIER CRU GRÉSIGNY 2008
White | 2011 up to 2018   92

RULLY PREMIER CRU LA PUCELLE 2008
White | 2011 up to 2017   89

RULLY PREMIER CRU LES CLOUX 2008
Red | 2012 up to 2018   90

RULLY PREMIER CRU MARGOTÉS 2008
White | 2011 up to 2023   93

Older vintages

BOURGOGNE PASSE-TOUT-GRAINS 2006
Red | 2011 up to 2013   90
An excellent wine with an explosive fruit character, deliciously lush and enticing. A gourmandise that calls for a picnic or barbecue.

RULLY PREMIER CRU GRÉSIGNY 2007
White | 2011 up to 2022   90
More pronounced minerality than in La Pucelle. A supple, luscious wine, perfumed and already quite pleasant. The finish is pure and straightforward, with plenty of elegance.

RULLY PREMIER CRU GRÉSIGNY 2006
White | 2011 up to 2013   89
This is great art: pure and crystalline, with good aromatic depth and a suave texture. Refined and subtle.

RULLY PREMIER CRU LA PUCELLE 2007
White | 2011 up to 2022   88
Radiant, with nice mellow aromatics. Ripe and balanced on the palate, with a long, direct finish.

RULLY PREMIER CRU LA PUCELLE 2006
White | 2011 up to 2013   88
More subtle, delicate, and elegant than the Villages. Very suave. An unctuous wine, mineral on the palate.

RULLY PREMIER CRU LES CLOUX 2007
Red | 2011 up to 2015   87
The fruit character is denser, the palate a bit richer than on the Chaponnières, and with more substance. A straightforward wine, clean, endowed with a nice elegance. This one can be drunk young, too!

RULLY PREMIER CRU LES CLOUX 2006
Red | 2011 up to 2015   89
Structured, with nice firm tannins. This wine is dense and well built. It will age very well! The oak aging gives it roundness and an appealing lushness.

RULLY PREMIER CRU LES CLOUX 2005
Red | 2011 up to 2025   89
A nice fruit character that is concentrated and ripe, but still elegant and fresh. There are already hints of leather. Rich on the palate, with firm but fat tannins. This is the beginning of a great career!

RULLY PREMIER CRU MARGOTÉS 2007
White | 2011 up to 2022   90
Tauter than the Grésigny, and purer, too, with very strong backbone. This wine finishes long and fresh.

RULLY PREMIER CRU MARGOTÉS 2006
White | 2011 up to 2013   89
A powerful nose with pronounced, almost violent, minerality. Fat on the palate, but with a highly seasoned flavor.

Red: 11.1 acres; pinot 100%. White: 16.1 acres; aligoté 20%, chardonnay 80%.

DOMAINE JOBLOT

4, rue Pasteur
71640 Givry
Phone 00 33 3 85 44 30 77
Fax 00 33 3 85 44 36 72
domaine.joblot@wanadoo.fr

The Domaine Joblot and the Domaine François Lumpp are the two flagship Givry estates, but they make quite different styles of wine. Like the passionate, committed winegrower that he is, Jean-Marc Joblot loves to explain what he does: how he works his vineyards so as to capture that pure fruit expression typical of this terroir; how vinification and aging are but the culmination of the year's labors.

Recently tasted

GIVRY EN VAUX 2008
White | 2011 up to 2015   **89**

GIVRY PIED DE CHAUME 2008
White | 2011 up to 2015   **89**

GIVRY PIED DE CHAUME 2008
Red | 2011 up to 2015   **89**

GIVRY PREMIER CRU CLOS DES BOIS CHEVAUX 2008
Red | 2011 up to 2018   **89**

GIVRY PREMIER CRU CLOS DU CELLIER AUX MOINES 2008
Red | 2011 up to 2018   **90**

GIVRY PREMIER CRU CLOS MAROLE 2008
Red | 2012 up to 2023   **91**

GIVRY PREMIER CRU SERVOISINE 2008
Red | 2012 up to 2023   **92**

Older vintages

GIVRY EN VAUX 2007
White | 2011 up to 2017   **88**
More taut and longer on the palate than Pied de Chaume. Pure and fresh.

GIVRY PIED DE CHAUME 2007
White | 2011 up to 2015   **87**
Good fruity juice, very ripe. An elegant, tasty, round wine.

GIVRY PIED DE CHAUME 2006
Red | 2011 up to 2013   **87**
Ripe, straightforward fruitiness. A full, expressive wine with soft tannins. Fat, rich, tasty.

GIVRY PREMIER CRU CLOS DES BOIS CHEVAUX 2007
Red | 2011 up to 2022   **89**
Floral, elegant, delicate. Less taut than Cellier aux Moines, but balanced, ripe, and linear.

GIVRY PREMIER CRU CLOS DES BOIS CHEVAUX 2006
Red | 2011 up to 2013   **89**
A refined, intense, concentrated nose. Very fine purity to the fruit. On the palate, it is pure and delicate. Very soft and silky. Nice fullness on the palate.

GIVRY PREMIER CRU CLOS DU CELLIER AUX MOINES 2006
Red | 2011 up to 2016   **90**
The aromas of this wine are more floral and intense than some pinots, but the fruity purity of the grape in all its ripeness is present on the palate, with concentrated, fresh juice. Superb balance will lead it to age well. Nice minerality on the finish.

GIVRY PREMIER CRU CLOS MAROLE 2007
Red | 2011 up to 2022   **90**
Mineral, with good tension and full bodied. Racy and well rounded. It seems to be a notch above the others, even if the techniques used are the same for all the wines!

GIVRY PREMIER CRU CLOS MAROLE 2006
Red | 2011 up to 2013   **89**
A very rocky terroir. The wine is mineral on the nose, with pretty fruit and floral notes. On the palate, it is linear and long. Very subtle!

GIVRY PREMIER CRU CLOS MAROLE 2005
Red | 2011 up to 2015   **91**
An explosive, concentrated wine: black and red fruit, flowers, honey (!). It's full of fruit; the juice is refined, concentrated. Extraordinary and suave: a great vintage. A very pure, refined wine that will age well!

GIVRY PREMIER CRU SERVOISINE 2007
White | 2011 up to 2017   **89**
Ripe and rich, a wine with good concentration, well balanced by good, mineral tension. Lively, direct finish.

GIVRY PREMIER CRU SERVOISINE 2007
Red | 2011 up to 2022   **90**
Balanced, well rounded, with good heft, fine tannins, and a velvety finish. Linear and refined.

GIVRY PREMIER CRU SERVOISINE 2006
Red | 2011 up to 2016   **91**
A wine with fine, fruity flesh on the palate. Broader and better structured than the previous wines. But still, a sense of purity, a clear, pure style and a great sense of freshness on the finish. A deep, linear wine. Superb!

Red: 27.2 acres; pinot 100%. White: 6.2 acres; chardonnay 100%. Annual production: 65,000 bottles

DOMAINE BRUNO LORENZON

71640 Mercurey
Phone 00 33 3 85 45 13 51
Fax 00 33 3 85 45 15 52
domaine.lorenzon@wanadoo.fr

Bruno Lorenzon's Mercurey estate is plainly the best there is. An overachiever among winegrowers, he is always looking to improve his performance, aiming for wines that mirror their vintage as closely as possible. There have been a few (youthful!) mistakes in the past due to overzealous extraction and use of wood. But his wines these days are pure and fresh, with not a whiff of animal or gamey notes, no overripe or crystallized fruit. The whites are as impeccable as the reds.

MERCUREY 2006
Red | 2011 up to 2016   **87**
Very berry (jam, wild strawberry). Appetizing. Round and supple on the palate. Moderately tannic, but balanced and supple. The finish is fruity and very appealing.

MERCUREY PREMIER CRU COMBINS 2006
White | 2011 up to 2016   **89**
An elegant nose with a delicate anise and almond note. The palate is more mineral, a bit tauter than the Croichots. A lightly saline finish.

MERCUREY PREMIER CRU CROICHOTS 2006
White | 2011 up to 2014   **86**
Very ripe fruit, white and even yellow. The palate is pure and direct, with an anise note on the finish. Elegant and pure. Very smooth on the palate. Appealing.

MERCUREY PREMIER CRU LES CHAMPS MARTIN 2006
White | 2011 up to 2016   **90**
The raciest of the three whites. Delicate and elegant, with a nice aromatic range and great freshness (pineapple, fennel, anise). The palate is refined, the oak fully integrated. Luscious, long, and fresh. The finish will make you salivate.

MERCUREY PREMIER CRU LES CHAMPS MARTIN 2006
Red | 2011 up to 2016   **89**
A more concentrated fruit character than in the Mercurey-Village, but still the same ripe, seductive style. The attack is tender, the tannins supple, but the long finish is very pleasant.

MERCUREY PREMIER CRU LES CHAMPS MARTIN CARLINE 2006
Red | 2011 up to 2016   **91**
A very concentrated nose. The palate is rich and pure, with good tannic presence that is ripe and soft. Superb mouthfeel. An elegant wine, very classy (even more so than the 2005!). A precise finish with a mineral touch.

VOLNAY 2006
Red | 2011 up to 2016   **89**
This wine was made from purchased grapes. The deep, elegant nose shows blackberries and red fruit (strawberries). More tension on the palate, and quite tight. Delicate and elegant, with good, long tannins and a juicy, licorice-y finish.

Red: 10.6 acres; pinot 100%. **White:** 1.7 acres; chardonnay 100%.

DOMAINE FRANÇOIS LUMPP

Le Pied du Clou
36, avenue de Mortières
71640 Givry
Phone 00 33 3 85 44 45 57
Fax 00 33 3 85 44 46 66
françois.lumpp@wanadoo.fr

It's a token of François Lumpp's emblematic status among Givry producers that he is now no longer accepting new clients—that's the penalty he pays for being so successful—but his wines are available from all good wine merchants and restaurants. His wines are oaky—that's for sure (more so than Joblot)—but with rich, ripe substance and good expression of terroir that comes with age. Mostly, though, we love their pure fruit aromas, unspoiled by gamey notes or hints of stewed fruit. Seductive and simply luscious!

GIVRY PIED DU CLOU 2007
Red | 2011 up to 2017   **87**
Nice red-berry character. Straightforward, delicate tannins. Mellow.

GIVRY PIED DU CLOU 2006
Red | 2011 up to 2013   **88**
Fleshy, rich, with a nice fruit character. The tannins are delicate and velvety. A very nice mouthfeel.

GIVRY PREMIER CRU A VIGNE ROUGE 2006
Red | 2011 up to 2016   **90**
Rich and powerful. A wine with plenty of substance, ripe, rich, velvety. The tannins are fat, and the oak influence gives even more roundness. Slick, with a saline note on the finish.

GIVRY PREMIER CRU CLOS DU CRAS LONG 2007
Red | 2011 up to 2017   **89**
Pure, elegant nose. Concentrated on the palate, with soft, delicate tannins. Fleshy, long and delicate.

GIVRY PREMIER CRU CLOS DU CRAS LONG 2006
Red | 2011 up to 2016   **88**
Deep fruit character, luscious. Perfumed on the palate, with very agreeable floral notes, delicately peppery. Mouthwatering. The tannins are fat and mellow.

GIVRY PREMIER CRU CLOS JUS 2007
Red | 2011 up to 2017   **89**
A nice, floral wine, elegant. Fleshy, concentrated, and luscious.

GIVRY PREMIER CRU CLOS JUS 2006
Red | 2011 up to 2016   **90**
Deep, luscious fruit character, infused with wild red berries. Rich and ripe. The finish is quite taut and concentrated.

GIVRY PREMIER CRU CRAUSOT 2007
White | 2011 up to 2017   **88**
More perfumed and rich than the Petit Marole. An appealing wine with juicy white fruit and a chalky mineral note on the finish.

GIVRY PREMIER CRU CRAUSOT 2007
Red | 2011 up to 2017   **88**
Nice fruit character. More substance than the Pied du Clou. A fleshy wine with a fresh, velvety finish.

GIVRY PREMIER CRU CRAUSOT 2006
White | 2011 up to 2016   **88**
Fine, fresh, lemony. Pure and elegant. Delicate, subtle mouthfeel. A luscious finish, good aromatic range, mineral and fruity (citrus). Very chalky.

GIVRY PREMIER CRU CRAUSOT 2006
Red | 2011 up to 2016   **90**
Rich and velvety, with a ripe, rich core. The tannins are fat, and the oak aging is well integrated.

GIVRY PREMIER CRU PETIT MAROLE 2006
Red | 2011 up to 2016   **90**
Delicate and racy, this Givry is quite juicy and fleshy. Velvety and elegant. Suave and refined.

Red: 16.1 acres; pinot 100%. White: 3.7 acres; chardonnay 100%. Annual production: 40,000 bottles

MERLIN

Domaine du Vieux Saint-Sorlin
71960 La-Roche-Vineuse
Phone 00 33 3 85 36 62 09
Fax 00 33 3 85 36 66 45
merlin.vins@wanadoo.fr
www.merlin-vins.com

Olivier Merlin was the right-hand man of Jean-Marie Guffens before purchasing excellent holdings centered on the village of La Roche Vineuse. He then expanded into the négociant business, making wines that displayed the full measure of his talents and rank as some of the most accomplished of all the Mâcon offerings. His latest acquisition is an exceptionally well-located parcel of red vines in Moulin-à-Vent, where he personally supervises the quality of the grapes. His recent vintages exhibit exemplary style.

Recently tasted
MÂCON-VILLAGES LA ROCHE VINEUSE
LES CRAS 2007
White | 2011 up to 2017   **95**

POUILLY-FUISSÉ CLOS DES QUARTS 2007
White | 2011 up to 2017   **88**

Older vintages
MÂCON-VILLAGES LA ROCHE VINEUSE
DOMAINE DU VIEUX SAINT-SORLIN 2006
White | 2011 up to 2013   **88**
Notes of fine, intense, small white flowers. The whole is elegant and refined. Drinking well already.

MÂCON-VILLAGES LA ROCHE VINEUSE
DOMAINE DU VIEUX SAINT-SORLIN 2005
White | 2011 up to 2013   **88**
An ample, well-balanced body, with well-integrated oak, vigorousness and style.

MÂCON-VILLAGES LA ROCHE VINEUSE
LES CRAS 2006
White | 2011 up to 2014   **90**
A well-made wine with an added dose of minerality that is the charm of the exceptional terroir of La Roche Vineuse.

MOULIN-À-VENT 2005
Red | 2011 up to 2020   **92**
One of the pinnacles of the appellation in a great year; harmonious body, racy tannins, exceptionally precise and exemplary vinification.

MOULIN-À-VENT LA ROCHELLE 2006
Red | 2011 up to 2016   **88**
This new Moulin-à-Vent bottling presents a nose of red fruit (wild blueberry) that is extremely refined. A wine with balanced structure. Very fine body.

POUILLY-FUISSÉ CLOS DES QUARTS 2006
White | 2011 up to 2013   **84**
Lacks a bit of acidity, but a fine, balanced wine all the same. Vanilla finish.

POUILLY-FUISSÉ TERROIR DE VERGISSON 2006
White | 2011 up to 2016   **89**
Mineral, vigorous, very linear on an aromatic level, even a little austere, with a fine future before it.

SAINT-VÉRAN LE GRAND BUSSIÈRE 2006
White | 2011 up to 2015   **88**
A potent nose of roses. Harmonious on the palate with a permanent intense note. Fine, powerful structure.

SAINT-VÉRAN LE GRAND BUSSIÈRE 2005
White | 2011 up to 2013   **89**
Fat, very mineral, with a slightly caramelized taste; a straightforward and exacting finish; remarkable typicity to the terroir.

Red: 8.6 acres; gamay 67%, pinot noir 33%. White: 234.7 acres; chardonnay 100%. Annual production: 150,000 bottles

CHÂTEAU DES RONTETS

Les Rontés
71960 Fuissé
Phone 00 33 3 85 32 90 18
Fax 00 33 3 85 35 66 80
châteaurontets@wanadoo.fr

Claire and Fabio Montrasi have made the transition from architecture to viticulture with all their artistic sensibilities and savvy intact. Having done an excellent job of restoring an old, Bourgeois-style property in Fuissé, they now produce a wine with outstandingly authentic expression of vineyard and vintage. Lately they have also started to vinify a small amount of Saint-Amour red wine—and very good it is, too. For once, we prefer the Pierre Folle to the Les Birbettes.

Recently tasted

POUILLY-FUISSÉ LES BIRBETTES 2007
White | 2011 up to 2017   **88**

POUILLY-FUISSÉ PIERREFOLLE 2007
White | 2011 up to 2017   **88**

Older vintages

POUILLY-FUISSÉ CLOS VARAMBON 2006
White | 2011 up to 2013   **88**
A silky, elegant wine. Good structure, but also generous. A clean substance that lingers on the finish with a nice freshness.

POUILLY-FUISSÉ LES BIRBETTES 2006
White | 2011 up to 2014   **86**
A wine with good intensity. Supple and well made. Good length.

POUILLY-FUISSÉ PIERREFOLLE 2006
White | 2011 up to 2015   **87**
Defined by subtlety and finesse. A complexity that comes out with aeration. A certain elegance.

SAINT-AMOUR 2007
Red | 2011 up to 2014   **88**
Pure, fresh fruit. Light structure but very unctuous and generous. A well-made wine. For bon vivants.

Red: 1.2 acres; gamay 100%. White: 14.8 acres; chardonnay 100%. Annual production: 3,035,000 bottles

DOMAINE RAPHAËL SALLET

Domaine de l'Arfentière
71700 Uchizy
Phone 00 33 3 85 40 50 45
Fax 00 33 3 85 40 59 86
mrsallet@orange.fr

We have included this estate because it demonstrates all the potential of the Mâcon Villages vineyards to the north of Mâcon, traditionally stifled by local winemaking routines. The Clos des Ravières comes from a superbly exposed vineyard and richly deserves the ambitious maturation it gets from Raphaël Sallet.

MÂCON-VILLAGES MÂCON UCHIZY
CLOS DES RAVIÈRES 2006
White | 2011 up to 2013   **86**
A wine that remains in the tradition of the previous vintage. A white made like a red, in which the deep raw material dominates. A wine for meat rather than fish.

MÂCON-VILLAGES MÂCON UCHIZY
CLOS DES RAVIÈRES 2005
White | 2011 up to 2013   **87**
Conscientious élevage; fairly buttery, full, long, oaky, intelligent, a little bit heavy, made for chicken more than fish.

Red: .5 acre; gamay 100%. White: 61.3 acres; chardonnay 100%. Annual production: 120,000 bottles

DOMAINE SAUMAIZE-MICHELIN

Le Martelet
71960 Vergisson
Phone 00 33 3 85 35 84 05
Fax 00 33 3 85 35 86 77
saumaize-michelin@wanadoo.fr

This is Roger Saumaize's share of the estate that he and his brother inherited from their father, a man who blazed a trail for Vergisson winemakers. Both men now work with their wives, forming committed husband-and-wife teams who make wines of very similar quality. Roger and Christine's are perhaps a bit more complex in terms of immediate aromas. Their Saint-Vérans offer exceptionally good value for the money.

Recently tasted
POUILLY-FUISSÉ AMPELOPSIS 2006
Red I 2011 up to 2016   88

POUILLY-FUISSÉ CLOS SUR LA ROCHE 2007
White I 2011 up to 2017   88

SAINT-VÉRAN LES CRÈCHES 2007
White I 2011 up to 2014   86

Older vintages
POUILLY-FUISSÉ CLOS SUR LA ROCHE 2006
White I 2011 up to 2013   87
Expressive hazelnut aromas. A lively attack. The whole is tasty, ample, rich. But this is also a terroir wine: one can feel its depth.

POUILLY-FUISSÉ LE HAUT DES CRAYS 2006
White I 2011 up to 2013   86
The whole is very lemony, but balanced. Let it age to see it become more integrated. Nice freshness.

POUILLY-FUISSÉ LES RONCHEVATS 2006
White I 2011 up to 2013   86
Very close to its terroir, with tasty, fresh body to it. Nice hold through the finish.

SAINT-VÉRAN LES CRÈCHES 2006
White I 2011 up to 2013   87
Intense mineral notes on the nose. Fine structure and balance to the wine. Nice length. A freshness that was not there in the other wines from this cellar.

SAINT-VÉRAN VIEILLES VIGNES 2006
White I 2011 up to 2013   85
Very luscious and deep. The fruit is pretty, well crafted. Not much acidity.

White: 23 acres; chardonnay 100%. **Annual production:** 70,000 bottles

DOMAINE LA SOUFRANDIÈRE-BRET BROTHERS

Aux Bourgeois
71680 Vinzelles
Phone 00 33 3 85 35 67 72
Fax 00 33 3 85 35 67 72
contact@bretbrothers.com
www.bretbrothers.com

There seems to be no stopping the Bret brothers! Witness the amazingly uniform yet flamboyant style of their 2005s. Disciplined viticulture and ambitiously precise vinification put these two young men leagues ahead of the competition and promise to keep them there.

Recently tasted
MÂCON-VILLAGES MÂCON-VINZELLES
LE CLOS DE GRAND-PÈRE 2008
White I 2011 up to 2015   86

POUILLY-VINZELLES LES LONGEAYS 2007
White I 2011 up to 2015   88

POUILLY-VINZELLES LES QUARTS
CUVÉE MILLERANDÉE 2007
White I 2011 up to 2017   90

Older vintages
MÂCON-CRUZILLE 2006
White I 2011 up to 2016   88
Perfect balance. Almost exotic fruity notes. Elegant texture and stunning length. Pure chardonnay.

MÂCON-CRUZILLE 2005
White I 2011 up to 2013   88
Broad, generous, long, lemony, fine oak aging: at last, this is the real thing from a professional winemaker who is attentive to his terroir.

MÂCON-VILLAGES MÂCON-VINZELLES
LE CLOS DE GRAND-PÈRE 2006
White I 2011 up to 2014   86
A very beautiful wine, complex and fresh. Good intensity. Healthy material with full mouthfeel.

POUILLY-FUISSÉ EN CAREMENTRANT 2006
White I 2011 up to 2015   88
Expressive nose. Subtle, intense floral notes. On the palate, very fine tastes of hazelnut.

POUILLY-FUISSÉ EN CAREMENTRANT 2005
White I 2011 up to 2013   88
Fairly nice, hazelnuts on the nose, subtle, pure, somewhat long, good balance!

POUILLY-LOCHÉ LES MÛRES 2006
White | 2011 up to 2016   **88**
Very pretty wine, elegant, long, refined. A fine success, especially for 2006. It is not unlike the magnificent 2005.

POUILLY-LOCHÉ LES MÛRES 2005
White | 2011 up to 2013   **88**
Very elegant, vinified as a dry wine, pure, long, complex, stylish. Just what one expects but so rarely finds!

POUILLY-VINZELLES LES LONGEAYS 2006
White | 2011 up to 2016   **88**
A fine wine with elegant vanilla notes, rich and tasty. And designed intelligently with respect to the raw materials.

POUILLY-VINZELLES LES LONGEAYS 2005
White | 2011 up to 2013   **90**
Great Charlemagne-style nose dominated by hazelnut, wonderful refinement and complexity, long, with lots of expressiveness. Bravo!

POUILLY-VINZELLES LES QUARTS 2006
White | 2011 up to 2016   **88**
The domaine has done a good job with the raw materials, creating a wine of magnificent elegance and purity. Beautiful!

POUILLY-VINZELLES LES QUARTS CUVÉE MILLERANDÉE 2005
White | 2011 up to 2013   **85**
Less expressive than the Longeays, but good balance in general; slower evolution in the bottle is perhaps to be expected.

POUILLY-VINZELLES X-TASTE 2006
White | 2011 up to 2016   **87**
Golden color. The bottling, which was harvested on November 18, 2006, contains 20 percent grapes with noble rot. Despite the 150 grams of residual sugar, there is good vivacity. Interesting . . . and tasty (quince notes)!

SAINT-VÉRAN CLIMAT LA CÔTE RÔTIE 2006
White | 2011 up to 2015   **87**
Very fine minerality, straightforward and pure. A supple structure. Crunchy, refined finish.

VIRÉ-CLESSÉ LA VERCHÈRE 2006
White | 2011 up to 2013   **86**
Very nice finesse and elegance. Floral, lemony notes, but with a rich backbone.

Red: 1.9 acres; gamay 100%. White: 14.9 acres; chardonnay 100%. Annual production: 80,000 bottles

VERGET

Le Bourg
71960 Sologny
Phone 00 33 3 85 51 66 00
Fax 00 33 3 85 51 66 09
contact@verget-sa.com
www.verget-sa.com

Jean-Marie Guffens's small négociant business in Sologny now concentrates on Mâcon production, while continuing to buy grapes from the finest Chablis and Côte d'Or growers. Some of his vintages, like those of his competitors, show signs of atypical aging, but he has now cut the barrel-aging time and tightened up hygiene measures. Since 2003, Guffens has once again been stacking up the winners, leading the way in great Mâcon wine. His Mâcon-Villages is unbeatable value for the money if bought en primeur. In fact, practically all of his bottlings are warmly recommended, including his Chablis and Côte d'Or offerings.

Recently tasted
MÂCON-VILLAGES TERRES DE PIERRES 2007
White | 2011 up to 2014   **88**

POUILLY-FUISSÉ LA ROCHE 2007
White | 2011 up to 2014   **86**

Older vintages
BOURGOGNE GRAND ÉLEVAGE 2005
White | 2011 up to 2013   **86**
A blend bottling that, in another context, would deserve a better score but, as it is surrounded by more precise, more personalized wines, suffers somewhat.

CHABLIS CUVÉE DE LA BUTTE 2006
White | 2011 up to 2013   **86**
Fat, round, ripe, with fine white fruit. Supple, ready to drink.

CHABLIS GRAND CRU BOUGROS 2006
White | 2011 up to 2021   **90**
An opulent nose. A racy, concentrated wine that is ripe and rich. Nice vivacity that balances out the richness on the palate.

CHABLIS GRAND CRU BOUGROS 2005
White | 2011 up to 2018   **89**
Slightly closed and impersonal if compared to the Vaulorent or Mont de Milieu, but very refined and taut, as it should be.

CHABLIS GRAND CRU LES CLOS 2006
White | 2011 up to 2021   **92**
A closed yet elegant nose. A fine parcel, linear, a little austere, but it will come together slowly with time.

CHABLIS PREMIER CRU FOURCHAUME CÔTE DE VAULORENT 2005

White | 2011 up to 2018   92

One of the best terroirs in Chablis and an exceptionally balanced wine for the vintage, with the inimitable charm of the subtle iodine and honey notes that are its hallmark.

CHABLIS PREMIER CRU LES FORÊTS 2006

White | 2011 up to 2016   88

Elegance and good concentration on the nose. A savory, balanced wine whose minerality will come to the fore with time.

CHABLIS PREMIER CRU LES VAILLONS 2005

White | 2011 up to 2015   89

Fairly open, balanced, tender in its mineral expression and ready to drink sooner than others.

CHABLIS PREMIER CRU LES VAILLONS VIEILLES VIGNES LES MINODES 2005

White | 2011 up to 2017   92

Very noble texture, magnificently brilliant finesse, great length; a model of great style!

CHABLIS PREMIER CRU MONT DE MILIEU 2006

White | 2011 up to 2013   85

The nose is closed here: a wine that is made in a heavy style and lacking finesse.

CHABLIS TERROIR DE CHABLIS 2006

White | 2011 up to 2014   87

In comparison to the Butte bottling, it presents more minerality, with greater concentration and length.

CORTON-CHARLEMAGNE GRAND CRU 2005

White | 2011 up to 2025   94

Splendid constitution, a precise expression of the terroir, a great future; exemplary Charlemagne!

MÂCON-CHARNAY LE CLOS SAINT-PIERRE 2006

White | 2011 up to 2013   88

A wine that absolutely does not smell of alcohol. Amazingly digestible. The whole is harmonious and deep.

MÂCON-VILLAGES MÂCON-BURGY EN CHÂTELAINE 2005

White | 2011 up to 2013   89

Terroir with great typicity, a full wine with very expressive character, exactly what one expects from this house!

MÂCON-VILLAGES MÂCON-BUSSIÈRES LE CLOS 2005

White | 2011 up to 2013   89

Very round, with a slight milky caramel note found in many terroirs of the Mâconnais; savory; the grapes were harvested at just the right time.

MÂCON-VILLAGES MÂCON-CHARNAY VIEILLE VIGNE DE MONBRISON 2005

White | 2011 up to 2013   90

One of the finest of all the Village wines, it even has notes of flowering vine that recall the greatest Pouilly terroirs.

MEURSAULT TÊTE DE CUVÉE 2005

White | 2011 up to 2017   89

Full and tasty, but others are making wine as good as this in the Mâconnais now, and for a more reasonable price!

POUILLY-FUISSÉ TERROIR DE FUISSÉ VERS ASNIÈRES 2006

White | 2011 up to 2013   88

A wine with good tension and deep minerality. Long, with elegant oak notes.

POUILLY-FUISSÉ TERROIR DE POUILLY LES COMBES VIEILLES VIGNES 2006

White | 2011 up to 2015   88

Fat and rich, but with good depth. A food-friendly wine that will pair as well with white meat as with fish.

POUILLY-FUISSÉ TERROIR DE VERGISSON 2005

White | 2011 up to 2015   90

The mountain vines have allowed the grapes not to ripen to too high an alcohol level and to conserve the minerality of the soil.

PULIGNY-MONTRACHET PREMIER CRU SOUS LE PUITS 2005

White | 2011 up to 2018   90

Pure, very taut but sufficiently fat that it does not seem too straight and narrow, a racy finish; a well-made wine that has benefited from its somewhat cold exposure.

SAINT-VÉRAN 2006

White | 2011 up to 2016   88

An interesting terroir wine, intense and fat. Nice balance overall.

SAINT-VÉRAN LES CHÂTAIGNIERS 2006

White | 2011 up to 2013   88

Nose of almonds; silky texture. A balanced, healthy, fresh wine.

SAINT-VÉRAN TERRES NOIRES 2006

White | 2011 up to 2013   90

Good intensity, savory on the palate: a very fine wine with nice balance between fattiness and vivacity.

VIRÉ-CLESSÉ VIEILLES VIGNES DE ROALLY 2005

White | 2011 up to 2013   91

Exceptional finesse and purity, great length, a pinnacle of the vintage, without equal among the producers of this appellation.

Annual production: 450,000 bottles

DOMAINE VESSIGAUD

Hameau de Pouilly
71960 Solutré
Phone 00 33 3 85 35 81 18
Fax 00 33 3 85 35 84 29
contact@domainevessigaud.com
www.domainevessigaud.com

In just a few vintages, Pierre Vessigaud has made his name as one of the most stylish winemakers in his appellation. His very pretty, impeccably groomed vineyard produces grapes with all the character of their terroir, which he then turns into precisely made and very natural wines. The wines listed here are highly recommended.

Recently tasted

POUILLY-FUISSÉ VERS AGNIÈRES 2008
White | 2011 up to 2018   **88**

POUILLY-FUISSÉ VIEILLES VIGNES 2008
White | 2011 up to 2018   **88**

Older vintages

MÂCON-FUISSÉ LES TÂCHES 2007
White | 2011 up to 2013   **86**
Very fine, persistent nose. A simple, harmonious, quaffable wine.

POUILLY-FUISSÉ VERS AGNIÈRES 2006
White | 2011 up to 2014   **87**
Clean, fat, still fermentary, honest and well crafted; this is a wine that confirms this producer's skill and the quality of his terroirs.

POUILLY-FUISSÉ VERS POUILLY 2007
White | 2011 up to 2013   **87**
Very nice body and lively freshness that is nonetheless well balanced. A wine that is both unctuous and deep.

POUILLY-FUISSÉ VERS POUILLY 2006
White | 2011 up to 2014   **87**
A certain finesse that will grow with time, good style, ample, very natural.

POUILLY-FUISSÉ VIEILLES VIGNES 2007
White | 2011 up to 2015   **88**
Refined, well-integrated oak. Lively and fat on the palate, this is very balanced. A fine, tasty, refined wine.

POUILLY-FUISSÉ VIEILLES VIGNES 2006
White | 2011 up to 2016   **87**
Lots of oak here, but good length and energy, with racy terroir and a fine future ahead of it.

Red: 2.5 acres; gamay 100%. White: 24.7 acres; chardonnay 100%. Annual production: 80,000 bottles

DOMAINE AUBERT ET PAMÉLA DE VILLAINE

2, rue de la Fontaine
71150 Bouzeron
Phone 00 33 3 85 91 20 50
Fax 00 33 3 85 87 04 10
contact@de-villaine.com
www.de-villaine.com

Co-manager of Romanée-Conti Aubert de Villaine purchased this estate in 1971 and converted to organic methods in 1987. Since then, his wines have been staggeringly honest and natural—often delicious when tasted young but with the capacity to age superbly. Witness this unassuming aligoté Bouzeron 1998 that showed developed hints of fine Chablis. Our advice: don't drink these wines too young!

BOURGOGNE CÔTE CHALONNAISE LA DIGOINE 2007
Red | 2011 up to 2017   **91**
A more opulent fruit character than in La Fortune. The palate is fatter, with good, mellow tannins. More flesh; it finishes velvety and fresh.

BOURGOGNE CÔTE CHALONNAISE LA DIGOINE 2006
Red | 2011 up to 2016   **87**
Engaging fruit, mellow, tending toward red berries and spices. The palate is fleshy and balanced, with a fresh, luscious finish. Not very different from the 2007.

BOURGOGNE CÔTE CHALONNAISE LA FORTUNE 2007
Red | 2011 up to 2015   **89**
Clear fruit character, round. A voluptuous, radiant wine. Supple tannins, a charming wine that shows beautifully in its youth. Good, crisp balance for a difficult year.

BOURGOGNE CÔTE CHALONNAISE LA FORTUNE 2006
Red | 2011 up to 2014   **87**
A nice pinot noir, delicate and straightforward, rather concentrated, with nice tannins that are elegant and ripe. Full of charm.

BOURGOGNE CÔTE CHALONNAISE LES CLOUS 2007
White | 2011 up to 2017   **87**
The nose is in a reductive phase. Pure, straightforward, well defined. The opposite of the 2006. Taut, mineral. Long and fresh.

BOURGOGNE CÔTE CHALONNAISE LES CLOUS 2006
White | 2011 up to 2014   **87**
A chardonnay planted within the appellation of Bouzeron. A bit more dense than the Bouzeron, a little more perfumed.

Bouzeron 2007
White | 2011 up to 2017   89

Powerful floral notes. The palate is balanced, with less substance than in 2006. Well made for a difficult vintage, with a fresh finish.

Bouzeron 2006
White | 2011 up to 2021   88

Concentrated, pure, floral, expressive, and elegant. On the palate, an impressive fleshiness for this varietal, with great integrity. Long and fresh, it has evolved nicely. The absolute benchmark in aligoté, at a manageable price! And it ages very well.

Bouzeron 1998
White | 2011 up to 2013   91

Stunning! Notes of sunny Chablis. A complex nose, highly perfumed, with hints of herbal infusions, tea, and herbs. The palate is elegant, with very pure notes of honey. The finesse is magnificent, and the finish has a sumptuous purity (still with hints of honey), freshness, and harmony. A great wine! It would be impossible to know this is a Bouzeron in a blind tasting.

Mercurey Les Montots 2007
Red | 2011 up to 2017   88

A rather mineral nose, with ripe red berries. Good substance on the palate, with delicate tannins and a fleshy, appetizing finish. The most meaty of the estate's three red wines.

Mercurey Les Montots 2006
Red | 2011 up to 2016   88

A concentrated wine, mineral, rather taut. It needs to round off its tannins, which at this stage are a bit tight. Rich and chewy, with deep, intense red-berry notes.

Rully Les Saint-Jacques 2007
White | 2011 up to 2017   90

Delicate, mineral, all with great integrity. Elegant, the palate is pure; the end of the maturation phase will give it some extra flesh.

Rully Les Saint-Jacques 2006
White | 2011 up to 2016   88

A deeper nose with subtle aromas, an elegant palate. A refined wine, very pure, very natural. Good minerality on the finish.

Red: 15.1 acres; pinot noir 100%. White: 36.3 acres; aligoté 78%, chardonnay 22%. Annual production: 110,000 bottles

Bettane & Desseauve
Selections for Champagne

Champagne

The Champagne appellation extends over 81,000 acres planted to pinot noir (38 percent), pinot meunier (33 percent), and chardonnay (29 percent). The vineyards are spread over 319 towns (crus), making up four large areas: the Montagne de Reims, the Marne Valley, the Côte des Blancs, and the Côte des Bar. Around 350 million bottles are produced each year, which is relatively few when compared to the 4 billion bottles of sparkling wine produced worldwide. Alongside the bubbly, there are two other little-known appellations in the region that produce still wines: Coteaux Champenois (a red) and Rosé des Riceys (a rosé).

Champagne is by far the best example of what can be achieved when nature (the terroirs), climate, and human intervention come together. From a weather perspective, Champagne is one of the northernmost vineyards in the world; it is rare to find vines at a higher latitude. The climate is severe, with rain in the fall, very cold winters, cool springs, and temperate summers that are rarely very hot. These climatic conditions are far from ideal for winegrowing, as it is very difficult to properly ripen the grapes. Amazingly, the winemakers of Champagne have succeeded in overcoming these challenging weather conditions, even using their overly acidic grapes to their advantage.

The terroir in Champagne is primarily made up of limestone in very poor soil. In fact, that is the very reason that grape vines were planted here, the soil being too poor to grow wheat. Without human intervention, only barely ripe, superacidic grapes would be produced here. Thanks to ingenious winemakers, however, sparkling wines of rare elegance are produced throughout the region.

Vineyard Classifications

There are seventeen villages that are classified as "Grand Cru" and forty-four villages that are classified as "Premier Cru."

The Different Styles of Champagne

Non-Vintage

This style is referred to as "brut" and represents 80 percent of Champagne production. The wines are blends of several different vintages, usually primarily made up of wine from the most recent vintage. Many different types of grapes can go into these blends, but most often they are a blend of Chardonnay, Pinot Meunier, and Pinot Noir. Each Champagne producer has a unique house style. This type of Champagne is usually the least expensive in the range.

Vintage Champagnes

These are made from a single vintage, generally in an exceptional year. The decision to create a vintage bottling, which bears the mark of both the producer and the vintage, lies with each individual Champagne house. Some bottlings are sold ten years or more after they are made, and can be aged for even longer.

Prestige Cuvées

These limited-production cuvées may or may not be vintage dated. They are specially selected blends from the best suppliers or vineyards and are the prize bottles of the house. They are made to be aged and are often much more expensive than the brut cuvées.

Special Bottlings

From a specific vineyard or terroir, these are the specialties of wineries that vinify their own grapes.

Finally, there are also blanc de blancs, made exclusively from chardonnay, and blanc de noirs, made from pinot noir and/or pinot meunier.

Champagne Vineyards

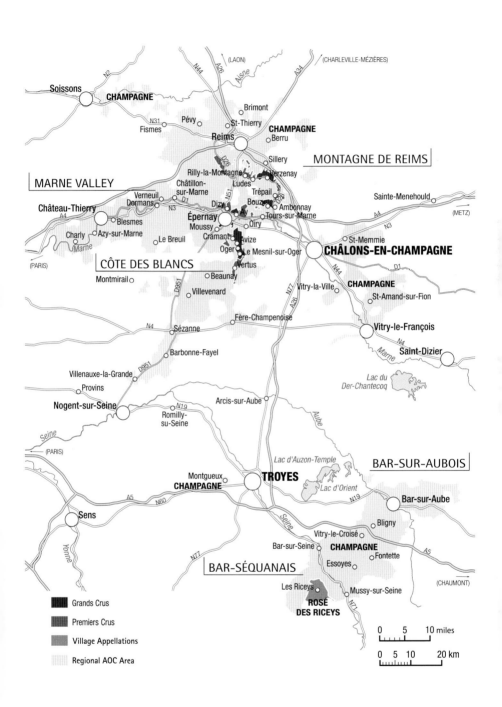

Soissons · CHAMPAGNE

(LAON) · (CHARLEVILLE-MÉZIÈRES)

Brimont

Pévy · St-Thierry · CHAMPAGNE
Fismes · Berru

Reims

Sillery · MONTAGNE DE REIMS

Rilly-la-Montagne · Verzenay
Châtillon-sur-Marne · Ludes
Verneuil · Trépail · Sainte-Menehould
Dormans · Dizy · Bouzy
Château-Thierry · Épernay · Ambonnay · (METZ)
Blesmes · Moussy · Tours-sur-Marne
Charly · Azy-sur-Marne · Oiry · St-Memmie · CHÂLONS-EN-CHAMPAGNE
Le Breuil · Cramant · Avize
Oger · Le Mesnil-sur-Oger

MARNE VALLEY

CÔTE DES BLANCS

Vertus

(PARIS)

Beaunay

Montmirail · Villevenard · Vitry-la-Ville · CHAMPAGNE
St-Amand-sur-Fion

Fère-Champenoise

Sézanne · Vitry-le-François

Barbonne-Fayel · Saint-Dizier

Villenauxe-la-Grande

Provins · Lac du Der-Chantecoq

Nogent-sur-Seine · Arcis-sur-Aube

Romilly-su-Seine

(PARIS) · Lac d'Auzon-Temple

BAR-SUR-AUBOIS

Montgueux · TROYES
CHAMPAGNE · Lac d'Orient

Sens · Bar-sur-Aube

Bligny

Vitry-le-Croisé

Bar-sur-Seine · CHAMPAGNE
Fontette

BAR-SÉQUANAIS · Essoyes

(CHAUMONT)

Les Riceys · Mussy-sur-Seine
ROSÉ DES RICEYS

■ Grands Crus

■ Premiers Crus

■ Village Appellations

Regional AOC Area

0   5   10 miles

0 5 10   20 km

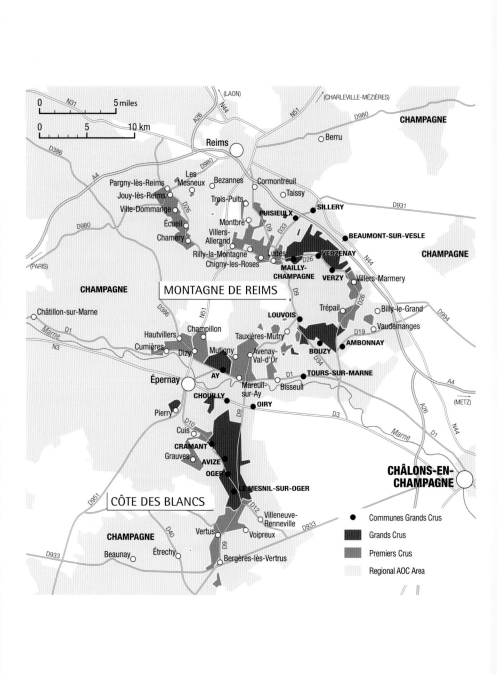

MONTAGNE DE REIMS

CÔTE DES BLANCS

CHAMPAGNE

Reims

Épernay

CHÂLONS-EN-CHAMPAGNE

(LAON)

(CHARLEVILLE-MÉZIÈRES)

(PARIS)

(METZ)

Scale markers:
0 · 5 miles
0 · 5 · 10 km

Legend:
● Communes Grands Crus
■ Grands Crus
■ Premiers Crus
□ Regional AOC Area

Communes and places:
Berru
Pargny-lès-Reims
Jouy-lès-Reims
Ville-Dommange
Les Mesneux
Bezannes
Cormontreuil
Taissy
Trois-Puits
PUISIEULX
SILLERY
Écueil
Chamery
Montbré
Villers-Allerand
Rilly-la-Montagne
Chigny-les-Roses
Ludes
MAILLY-CHAMPAGNE
VERZENAY
VERZY
BEAUMONT-SUR-VESLE
Villers-Marmery
Trépail
Billy-le-Grand
Vaudémanges
LOUVOIS
Châtillon-sur-Marne
Champillon
Hautvillers
Tauxières-Mutry
AMBONNAY
Cumières
Dizy
Mutigny
Avenay-Val-d'Or
BOUZY
AY
Mareuil-sur-Ay
Bisseuil
TOURS-SUR-MARNE
CHOUILLY
OIRY
Pierry
Cuis
CRAMANT
Grauves
AVIZE
OGER
LE MESNIL-SUR-OGER
Villeneuve-Renneville
Vertus
Voipreux
Bergères-lès-Vertus
Beaunay
Étrechy

Roads:
N31, A26, N44, N51, D980, D386, A4, D980, D26, D9, D33, D931, D994, D19, D34, D1, D10, D951, D40, D12, D933, N3, A26, D3, Marne

AGRAPART ET FILS

57, avenue Jean-Jaurès
51190 Avize
Phone 00 33 3 26 57 51 38
Fax 00 33 3 26 57 05 06
champagne.agrapart@wanadoo.fr
www.champagne-agrapart.com

To be based in Avize is always a good sign, and this first-rate "récoltant-manipulant" (grower-producer) does not disappoint. Agrapart et Fils is an excellent source of aperitif-style Champagnes, made from Côte des Blancs chardonnay. All of the range is precisely crafted, with just enough dosage to bring out the freshness and liveliness in the wines.

Recently tasted

BRUT GRAND CRU BLANC DE BLANCS
L'AVIZOISE 2004
Brut White | 2011 up to 2013   86

BRUT GRAND CRU MINÉRAL 2004
Brut White | 2011 up to 2013   88

BRUT GRAND CRU VÉNUS 2004
Brut White | 2011 up to 2014   86

Older vintages

BRUT GRAND CRU BLANC DE BLANCS
L'AVIZOISE 2002
Brut White | 2011 up to 2016   88
Austere and sharp with some bitterness, this wine has a lot of personality and absolutely must be held before drinking.

BRUT GRAND CRU MINÉRAL 2002
Brut White | 2011 up to 2013   90
Full, taut, ideal dosage, green olive notes typical of Avize. A purist's wine.

BRUT GRAND CRU VÉNUS 2001
Brut White | 2011 up to 2013   90
Fine terroir characteristics, ample and deep, with strong minerality and a smooth finish that makes this cuvée distinctly stand out from the rest of the range.

GRAND CRU BLANC DE BLANCS
EXTRA-BRUT 1996
Brut White | 2011 up to 2020   88
A linear, direct, and still very sharp Champagne, made to age slowly in the cellar.

TERROIRS
Brut White | 2011 up to 2014   88
Nervy, low dosage, clear terroir character, acidity still vivacious. Can be held three to four more years.

White: 23.7 acres; arbane 1%, chardonnay 97%, petit meslier 1%, pinot blanc 1%. **Annual production:** 90,000 bottles

AYALA

1, rue Edmond de Ayala
BP 6
51160 Aÿ
Phone 00 33 3 26 55 15 44
Fax 00 33 3 26 51 09 04
contact@champagne-ayala.fr
www.champagne-ayala.fr

This Aÿ-based Champagne house, founded in 1860, was taken over at the start of the new millennium by its neighbor Bollinger. Hervé Augustin, second in command at Bollinger, was appointed chief executive officer. He immediately set about producing wines as tasty as those of the illustrious parent house, building on the significant improvements achieved by his predecessors. In no time at all, this house has been revitalized, now turning out wines with real personality: honest, slender, and without a trace of heaviness. The Cuvée Zéro Dosage is the embodiment of that style. The nonvintage white and rosé cuvées are highly successful and, for the time being at least, more convincing than their vintage counterparts.

Recently tasted

BLANC DE BLANCS 2002
Brut White | 2011 up to 2016   91

PERLE D'AYALA NATURE 2002
Brut White | 2011 up to 2018   91

Older vintages

BLANC DE BLANCS 2000
Brut White | 2011 up to 2017   89
Sharp, straightforward, without being heavy-handed or fake, this is a successful Blanc de Blancs with lemon accents. Can be cellared longer.

BLANC DE BLANCS 1999
Brut White | 2011 up to 2013   86
A supple, tasty Blanc de Blancs, with somewhat pastry-like aromas.

BRUT MAJEUR
Brut White | 2011 up to 2013   90
Very straightforward and pure, a Champagne with no false pretenses, fairly well rounded, with citrus and white fruit aromas and a supple yet svelte constitution.

BRUT MILLÉSIMÉ 1999
Brut White | 2011 up to 2015   89
Now a mature wine, this powerful, well-built Champagne with its toasty notes is a fine success.

Brut Nature
Brut White | 2011 up to 2013   **91**
This non-dosage bottling is appealing in its purity and linearity. It's a very straightforward wine, made to drink before sitting down to dinner, or with shellfish, with which its minerality will pair wonderfully.

Perle d'Ayala 2001
Brut White | 2011 up to 2017   **88**
Markedly more vinous and intense than the previous vintage of this bottling (1999), this prestige cuvée is gradually finding its way, without truly being appealing yet.

Perle d'Ayala 1999
Brut White | 2011 up to 2013   **86**
Round, elegant Champagne that nonetheless lacks true intensity and personality.

Rosé Majeur
Brut Rosé | 2011 up to 2013   **87**
The strawberry aromas of this rosé are enticing, and its straightforward, direct simplicity on the palate completes that impression.

Rosé Nature
Brut Rosé | 2011 up to 2013   **90**
With no dosage, this very pure wine has great, imposing fullness in the mouth, along with a very dry, powerful, and dense character. A rosé with a lot of personality.

Annual production: 600,000 bottles

CHAMPAGNE BARNAUT

1, place André-Collard
BP 19
51150 Bouzy
Phone 00 33 3 26 57 01 54
Fax 00 33 3 26 57 09 97
contact@champagne-barnaut.fr
www.champagne-barnaut.com

Philippe Secondé is one of the most genial Bouzy producers we know: passionate about his terroir but eminently reasonable when it comes to price. His wines are energetic, sometimes slightly heavy and rustic but always sincere with, at their best, a very natural expression of this region's powerful pinot noir. Recent bottlings featured a still red and rosé wine that we found particularly impressive whereas the standard offerings lacked purity, with the exception of the NV Brut, which was delicious.

Recently tasted
Brut blanc de noirs grand cru
Brut White | 2011 up to 2014   **88**

Older vintages
Blanc de noirs
Brut White | 2011 up to 2050   **86**
Reductive, toasty, wild fermentation, mercaptans, grilled notes. Not our style.

Brut
Brut White | 2011 up to 2013   **84**
With strong bakery notes (toasted bread), this very seductive wine is easy but appealing.

Brut blanc de noirs grand cru
Brut White | 2011 up to 2013   **88**
Square-shouldered, powerful, with good expression of its terroir but lacking the complexity of the highest-level wines, and a bit tannic on the finish.

Brut grand cru 1999
Brut White | 2011 up to 2015   **91**
A nice nose with scents of wheat; vinous, elegant, typical of its roots but not as extraordinary as the rosé, as far as the fruit goes.

Grand cru Authentique Rosé
Brut Rosé | 2011 up to 2015   **95**
An extraordinary success, exquisitely fruity, great length, with the true spirit of the terroir and superior harmony. Bravo!

Red: 8.6 acres; pinot meunier 7%, pinot noir 93%. White: 32.1 acres; chardonnay 100%. **Annual production:** 100,000 bottles

FRANÇOISE BEDEL

71, Grande Rue
02310 Crouttes-sur-Marne
Phone 00 33 3 23 82 15 80
Fax 00 33 3 23 82 11 49
contact@champagne-bedel.fr
www.champagne-bedel.fr

This tiny property located practically on the outskirts of Paris practices idealistic and rigorous viticulture. With each passing year the Champagnes get better and better, truly showcasing their origins. The wines we tasted shone for their purity, their naturalness, and their true and subtle elegance. The minor oxidative flaws of the past are now but a memory.

Brut
Brut White | 2011 up to 2013   **88**
A Champagne from ultraripe grapes, with a caramel note that recalls the 2003s in style, this is full of fruit and character, ideally low in dosage, unique, made for the table.

Millésimé 1998
Brut White | 2011 up to 2013   **90**
A wine with great character and profound minerality. The flavors and mouthfeel show the depth of the mineral-rich soils the grapes are grown in. Savory and full-bodied.

Millésimé 1996
Brut White | 2011 up to 2013   **87**
With an evolved yet complex flavor, very natural, this is a less expressive bottle than the 1998, but it is drinking better than last year.

Prestige
Brut White | 2011 up to 2013   **89**
A perfect Champagne, complex, with a savory biscuit bouquet; long, honest, loyal and not for those who like more wiry, taut Champagnes.

Red: 17.8 acres; pinot meunier 100%. White: 2.7 acres; chardonnay 100%. Annual production: 55,000 bottles

BILLECART-SALMON

40, rue Carnot
51160 Mareuil-sur-Aÿ
Phone 00 33 3 26 52 60 22
Fax 00 33 3 26 52 64 88
billecart@champagne-billecart.fr
www.champagne-billecart.fr

This Champagne house in Mareuil-sur-Aÿ acquired an international reputation in the 1990s for its ethereal, refined Champagnes, based on an approach that relies partly on the house's own small vineyard, but mainly on the excellent quality of its purchased grapes. The rosé is a terrific ambassador for the range as a whole and has rightly risen to become a leader in its category. The great cuvées, such as the Nicolas-François Billecart and the Élisabeth Salmon (rosé), show an almost peerless refinement.

Recently tasted
ÉLISABETH SALMON ROSÉ 2000
Brut Rosé | 2011 up to 2018   **97**

NICOLAS-FRANÇOIS BILLECART 2000
Brut White | 2011 up to 2020   **95**

Older vintages
BLANC DE BLANCS
Brut White | 2011 up to 2013   **91**
This Blanc de Blancs is appealingly linear, with pretty aromatics and a palette of flavor ranging from fresh butter to citrus, capped off with superb mineral nuances.

BLANC DE BLANCS MILLÉSIME 1998
Brut White | 2011 up to 2017   **96**
Lively and refined, a very delicate Blanc de Blancs. An ultrasophisticated aperitif.

BRUT RÉSERVE
Brut White | 2011 up to 2013   **89**
A youthful but very tender Champagne without any aggressiveness. Made for parties and celebrations—in short, in the spirit of Champagne!

BRUT ROSÉ
Brut Rosé | 2011 up to 2013   **90**
Tender raspberry notes and a liveliness: an excellent Champagne that is refined, fruity, and immediately seductive.

CLOS SAINT-HILAIRE 1996
Brut White | 2011 up to 2017   **92**
Made from grapes grown in a small clos in Mareuil-sur-Aÿ, the Clos Saint-Hilaire shows firm terroir character, which has matured and been refined by the wine's lengthy aging. This is incontestably a Champagne to be enjoyed at the table.

ÉLISABETH SALMON ROSÉ 1998
Brut Rosé | 2011 up to 2015   99
A magnificent rosé with great delicacy in its texture and flavors, this opens up with finesse and aromatic charm on the palate without being heavy or aggressive.

GRANDE CUVÉE 1996
Brut White | 2011 up to 2020   96
With its delicate, appetite-whetting finesse as well as impressive length, here is an assuredly great Champagne that is at perfect maturity.

NICOLAS-FRANÇOIS BILLECART 1998
Brut White | 2011 up to 2018   96
A distinguished Champagne, very linear, long and pure, yet it has not lost the nimble spirit that characterizes the brand.

Red: 15.6 acres; pinot noir and pinot meunier 100%. White: 10.5 acres; chardonnay 100%. Annual production: 1,800,000 bottles

H. BLIN & CO

BP 3-5, rue de Verdun
51700 Vincelles
Phone 00 33 3 26 58 20 04
Fax 00 33 3 26 58 29 67
contact@champagne-blin.com
www.champagne-blin.com

H. Blin & Co is a medium-size cooperative winery (272 acres) in Vincelles, just outside Reims. A virtuoso of pinot meunier, it specializes in impeccably fresh, well-balanced wines with an airy character that makes them ideal as an aperitif—eminently affordable, too.

BLANC DE BLANCS
Brut White | 2011 up to 2013   87
A very clean wine, on the nose; frank, straightforward, very clean, impeccable dosage but with less tension than typical for a Champagne from the Côte des Blancs.

BRUT TRADITION
Brut White | 2011 up to 2013   90
Absolutely delicious: very pure on an aromatic level, round but without pronounced dosage, very ethereal bubbles. A remarkable pinot meunier blend.

Red: 27.2 acres; pinot meunier 100%. White: 244.6 acres; chardonnay 100%. Annual production: 700,000 bottles

BOIZEL

🍷🍷🍷🍷

46, avenue de Champagne
51200 Épernay
Phone 00 33 3 26 55 21 51
Fax 00 33 3 26 54 31 83
boizelinfo@boizel.fr
www.boizel.com

This family-run Champagne house has been part of Bruno Paillard's dynamic BCC group since the 1990s but is still managed by Évelyne Roques-Boizel and her husband. Their grape sources and winemaking principles also remain unchanged, though the range now includes an Extra-Brut Champagne called Ultime. The chardonnay is nothing special, but, that apart, the style of wine seems nicely homogeneous.

Recently tasted

BRUT JOYAU DE FRANCE 1996
Brut White | 2011 up to 2016   91

BRUT MILLÉSIMÉ 2000
Brut White | 2011 up to 2015   89

Older vintages

BRUT JOYAU DE FRANCE 1995
Brut White | 2011 up to 2013   90
A solid Champagne made for food, vinous and deep, with a somewhat evolved character whose spicy aromas will pair perfectly with roast poultry.

BRUT RÉSERVE
Brut White | 2011 up to 2013   85
A generous, well built Brut we wish were slightly less heavy on the finish, but with very honorable traits.

BRUT ROSÉ
Brut Rosé | 2011 up to 2013   86
Pretty pink-gold color, tender and delicate on the palate, with noticeable raspberry aromas and average length.

BRUT SOUS BOIS 1990
Brut White | 2011 up to 2015   94
Perfectly made, this Champagne for connoisseurs has now reached perfect maturity. It is vinous, savory, and intense.

BRUT ULTIME
Brut White | 2011 up to 2013   88
A solid, vinous Extra-Brut made for the table and poultry.

JOYAU DE FRANCE ROSÉ 2000
Brut Rosé | 2011 up to 2014   90
An excellent, rich, and mature rosé, with aromas that are both fruity and floral; an ample, perfectly structured body with good, fresh length. Superb dosage.

BOLLINGER

🍷🍷🍷🍷

16, rue Jules-Lobet
BP 4
51160 Aÿ
Phone 00 33 3 26 53 33 66
Fax 00 33 3 26 54 85 59
contact@champagne-bollinger.fr
www.champagne-bollinger.fr

This Aÿ-based Champagne house has remained a family-run business, home to what many wine lovers regard as the epitome of the purist's Champagne. Production relies on extensive plantings of exceptional vines, supplemented by grapes from carefully selected outside suppliers. Finely crafted from cask-fermented base wines, Bollinger Champagne is intensely vinous, honest, and deep, with that aromatic sparkle and freshness typical of noble pinot noir fruit. Every cuvée, including the Bollinger NV Brut Spécial Cuvée, is slowly matured in the house cellars prior to release. This gives them a wonderful purity of flavor, with no trace of rigidity or sharpness despite their terrific intensity. Strangers to the world of Bollinger should start with the near-perfect Spécial Cuvée, an uncompromising wine at a very affordable price. It sets the standard for the so-called "prestige" cuvées in this openly luxurious range, all of them with that honesty, purity, and depth that only good breeding can produce. R.D. Champagne is matured in the house cellars then disgorged immediately before release so as to retain maximum freshness. The Grande Année is an aristocratic vintage Champagne that usually ranks among the top Champagnes of the year.

Recently tasted

GRANDE ANNÉE 2000
Brut White | 2011 up to 2016   96

GRANDE ANNÉE ROSÉ 2002
Brut Rosé | 2011 up to 2016   98

R.D. 1997
Brut White | 2011 up to 2017   92

Older vintages

2003 BY BOLLINGER 2003
Brut White | 2011 up to 2018   98
Made from an extremely small harvest and consequently limited to a blend of three Grands Crus, this wine is a powerful testament to this extraordinary heat-wave vintage: the acidity is very low, but the wine has great freshness and is intense, very powerful, velvety, and long on the finish. A modern 1959!

Brut Grande Année 1999
Brut White | 2011 up to 2017   94

With a firmly vinous character, this is a great, intense, deep wine that demands to be served with good poultry. Very full and refined, with notes of nougatine, its freshness destines it for the table.

Brut Spécial Cuvée
Brut White | 2011 up to 2015   93

Great refinement and nice vigor: a perfect nonvintage Brut with flawless aperitif-style linearity.

Grande Année Rosé 1999
Brut Rosé | 2011 up to 2019   99

A wonderful rosé with a taffeta texture, an incredibly refined bouquet with red fruits and flowers, and magnificent length: a perfectly made rosé!

R.D. 1996
Brut White | 2011 up to 2030   97

A splendid Champagne that is vinous, demanding, and will absolutely age well: the aromatics are incredibly complex, a mix of fresh walnut and very fine pear notes; on the palate, it is exceptionally intense and long.

Red: 7.4 acres; pinot meunier 22%, pinot noir 78%. White: 395.4 acres; chardonnay 100%. Annual production: 2,500,000 bottles

BONNET GILMERT

Champagne Bonnet Gilmert
16, rue de la Côte
51190 Oger
Phone 00 33 3 26 59 49 47
Fax 00 33 3 26 59 00 17
contact@champagne-bonnet-gilmert.com
www.champagne-bonnet-gilmert.com

Here is yet another address for aperitif-like Blanc de Blancs. The vineyards of the town of Oger are contiguous to the famous Avize vineyards, which are without a doubt the most beautiful chardonnay terroirs of the entire Côte de Blancs, with the purest chalk soils in the area. This producer obviously pampers his reasonably priced nonvintage bottling, and more than deserves a place in this guide. Following in the footsteps of Sélosse, Sousa, or Larmandier, he may become a star of the "Côte," as he owns some superb vineyards in Oger and Le Mesnil.

Recently tasted

Cuvée de Réserve grand cru Millésime blanc de blancs 2004
Brut White | 2011 up to 2013   88

Millésime 2004
Brut White | 2011 up to 2014   88

Précieuse d'Ambroise
Brut White | 2011 up to 2013   90

Older vintages

Brut
Brut White | 2011 up to 2013   88

Deliciously fresh, appetite-whetting and mineral, with very refined bubbles; a very fine aperitif.

Cuvée de réserve Grand Cru blanc de blancs
Brut White | 2011 up to 2015   90

Pale, mineral nose; nice origins, with finesse, class, and an excellent finish. Bravo!

Cuvée de Réserve grand cru Millésime blanc de blancs 2002
Brut White | 2011 up to 2013   88

Slightly less clear-cut than others, this bottle has not completely integrated the oak, but it is still stylish and well bred.

Millésime 2002
Brut White | 2011 up to 2015   90

Great minerality, a full wine that gives an accurate picture of the best vines in Oger and Le Mesnil, with well-integrated oak. A wine to seek out.

White: 11.1 acres; chardonnay 100%. Annual production: 30,000 bottles

CÉDRIC BOUCHARD

4, rue du Creux-Michel
10110 Celles-sur-Ource
Phone 00 33 3 25 38 24 72
cbouchard@champagne-rosesdejeanne.com
www.champagne-rosesdejeanne.com

This handkerchief-size property makes a wine with exceptionally pure expression of terroir—a potential model for other Aube producers. The most recent bottling measures up to its predecessors: a complete wine, true to its roots.

ROSES DE JEANNE BLANC DE NOIRS
LES URSULES
Brut White | 2011 up to 2013   **90**
An interesting shade of light pink, great noble nose, pure, fruity, precise, ultraripe grapes, remarkable.

2.7 acres. **Red:** pinot noir 100%. **White:** chardonnay 100%.

GUY CHARLEMAGNE

4, rue de la Brèche-d'Oger
51190 Le Mesnil-sur-Oger
Phone 00 33 3 26 57 52 98
Fax 00 33 3 26 57 97 81
champagneguycharlemagne@orange.fr
www.champagne-guy-charlemagne.fr

This is one of the most serious-minded producers in Le Mesnil, making wines in an earlier-drinking style than most. Our favorites by far are the vintage cuvées, especially the celebrated and, at its best, sublimely refined Mesnillésime. The 2000 vintage is a little masterpiece of freshness, but we can recommend all the others too!

Recently tasted
MESNILLÉSIME GRAND CRU
BLANC DE BLANCS 2002
Brut White | 2011 up to 2014   **90**

RÉSERVE BRUT GRAND CRU BLANC DE BLANCS
Brut White | 2011 up to 2014   **87**

Older vintages
BRUT 2004
Brut White | 2011 up to 2014   **87**
A quaffable, very youthful wine with bubbles that are still somewhat forceful; good presence on the palate, no more apple notes, very crowd-pleasing in its roundness and precision.

BRUT ROSÉ
Brut Rosé | 2011 up to 2013   **88**
More complex and savory than the normal nonvintage Brut, this is tender, natural, easy to drink, light, perfect for an aperitif.

CUVÉE CHARLEMAGNE GRAND CRU
BLANC DE BLANCS 2004
Brut White | 2011 up to 2013   **86**
Very close to the Mesnillésime cuvée in all ways, this is savory, tender, complex, a little less appetite-whetting.

MESNILLÉSIME 2001
Brut White | 2011 up to 2015   **90**
With a very fine, spicy, mineral nose, this is slightly toasty, refined, and very chardonnay. Excellent style.

MESNILLÉSIME GRAND CRU
BLANC DE BLANCS 2000
Brut White | 2011 up to 2013   **95**
Very complex and evolved aromas of sweet spices and hazelnuts, with great finesse, verve, length, and very transparent terroir.

Red: 4.9 acres; pinot noir 100%. White: 32.1 acres; chardonnay 100%. Annual production: 150,000 bottles

CHARTOGNE-TAILLET

37 - 39, Grande Rue
51220 Merfy
Phone 00 33 3 26 03 10 17
Fax 00 33 3 26 03 19 15
chartogne.taillet@wanadoo.fr
www.chartogne-taillet.typepad.fr/france

Merfy, in the too-little-known Massif de Saint-Thierry, is home to some of the vineyards closest to Reims. Philippe Chartogne, his wife, Élisabeth, and their son, Alexandre, are among a handful of committed winegrowers who are steadily building an international reputation for artisan champagnes. Their wines are beautifully precise, with impeccable dosage and very subtle aromas. Alexandre is a fervent admirer of Anselme Selosse, and his first attempts at vinification in oak show great promise. This estate is sure to rise in our personal rankings. Don't expect the same vinosity as you would get on the Montagne de Reims—just finesse and a crispness that is never aggressive. The Cuvée Sainte-Anne and especially the Cuvée Fiacre deliver a flawless performance.

Recently tasted
MILLÉSIME 2002
Brut White | 2011 up to 2013   **91**

Older vintages
BRUT 2002
Brut White | 2011 up to 2013   **91**
Great aromatic clarity and precision, some toasty notes that should please connoisseurs, but fresher on the palate, with very fine, racy notes of hazelnut. Excellent overall impression.

BRUT 2000
Brut White | 2011 up to 2013   **89**
A nose that is pure but not neutral, ideally falling between reduction and oxidation, not very vinous but very fresh and pleasing. The prototype of good Champagnes from this area.

CUVÉE SAINTE-ANNE
Brut White | 2011 up to 2013   **89**
This blend of pinot and chardonnay is perfectly balanced, subtle, with imperceptible dosage and a great lingering aftertaste.

FIACRE
Brut White | 2011 up to 2015   **91**
The old vines of Chemin de Reims and Oriseaux have made the wine extremely vinous, very subtle and racy, with intelligent and tactful dosage.

White: 28.4 acres; chardonnay 100%. Annual production: 80,000 bottles

CHAMPAGNE ROGER COULON

12, rue de la Vigne-du-Roy
51390 Vrigny
Phone 00 33 3 26 03 61 65
Fax 00 33 3 26 03 43 68
contact@champagne-coulon.com
www.champagne-coulon.com

This is an exemplary grower for his precision and follow-through in the elaboration of his wines. The domaine's numerous tiny holdings are spread throughout Vrigny, just outside of Reims, one of the historic centers of Champagne production. A few of the vineyards are very old, even ungrafted, and their grapes make up the core of the prestige bottlings. The wines have panache and vinosity; the meticulous vineyard work really shows in the final product.

Recently tasted
BLANC DE NOIRS 2003
Brut White | 2011 up to 2013   **90**

ESPRIT DE VRIGNY
Brut White | 2011 up to 2013   **86**

LES COTEAUX DE VALLIER
Brut White | 2011 up to 2013   **91**

ROSÉ
Brut Rosé | 2011 up to 2013   **89**

Older vintages
GRANDE TRADITION
Brut White | 2011 up to 2013   **86**
A tight and savory wine, with citrus peel, smoke, and wild mushroom notes, somewhat like a fine Chablis, with a cutting, clean finish.

MILLÉSIME PREMIER CRU 2002
Brut White | 2011 up to 2013   **88**
Still some austerity, but nice integrity and character and ideal dosage.

RÉSERVE DE L'HOMMÉE
Brut White | 2011 up to 2013   **88**
A pleasurable wine that does justice to the pinot meunier of Vrigny, with accentuated pear flavors and, especially, a finish that is very appealing and smooth. It will be to everyone's taste.

Red: pinot meunier 57%, pinot noir 43%. White: chardonnay 100%. Annual production: 90,000 bottles

DE SOUSA

12, place Léon-Bourgeois
51190 Avize
Phone 00 33 3 26 57 53 29
Fax 00 33 3 26 52 30 64
contact@champagnedesousa.com
www.champagnedesousa.com

Eric de Sousa is one of the most brilliant and dynamic winegrowers on the Côte des Blancs. He has built up his family estate to quite a remarkable degree, optimizing production while continuing to offer old-vine Champagnes and vinifying in barrels as inspired by Anselme Selosse. Today all of his hard work has paid off although one senses that an extra one or two years "sur pointe" would have given his recent bottlings just a touch more smoothness.

Recently tasted

BRUT BLANC DE BLANCS GRAND CRU RÉSERVE
Brut White | 2011 up to 2013 **90**

CUVÉE DES CAUDALIES NON MILLÉSIMÉ
Brut White | 2011 up to 2013 **92**

GRAND CRU CAUDALIES 2002
Brut White | 2011 up to 2014 **95**

Older vintages

BRUT TRADITION
Brut White | 2011 up to 2013 **88**
Rounder but more open and subtle than the Réserve, both on the nose and on the palate, with slightly more noticeable but still reasonable dosage; ready to drink.

CUVÉE DES CAUDALIES NON MILLÉSIMÉ
Brut White | 2011 up to 2013 **93**
Quite mineral on the nose, splendid creamy foam, well-integrated oak, impeccable dosage: a great, classic wine that is long on the palate.

CUVÉE DES CAUDALIES ROSÉ
Brut Rosé | 2011 up to 2015 **93**
Salmon color, slightly oaky on the nose, a fairly sophisticated production, great complexity.

GRAND CRU CAUDALIES 2003
Brut White | 2011 up to 2018 **97**
Completely unique, a rare expressive force on the nose, monumental breadth of construction, a pure finish that is much lighter than the spirit and body of the wine. It will surprise more than one taster over the course of long aging! A standout for this so-called difficult vintage.

GRAND CRU CAUDALIES 2002
Brut White | 2011 up to 2020 **95**
This has a sumptuous nose that is typically Avize, with magnificent notes of green olive that only the chalk soil of that village can give. Great length.

GRAND CRU CAUDALIES 2000
Brut White | 2011 up to 2015 **94**
A typical Avize Grand Cru, with great delicacy in its bubbles and an obvious purity that is almost crystalline on the nose, with an ethereal finish. We like it.

ROSÉ
Brut Rosé | 2011 up to 2013 **91**
A remarkable bottling, this is a complete wine with a nose of great pinot noir (the red wine has obvious class) but with the freshness of a great Blanc de Blancs.

Red: 7.9 acres; pinot noir 75%, pinot meunier 25%. White: 14.3 acres; chardonnay 100%. Annual production: 90,000 bottles

DEHOURS ET FILS

2, rue de la Chapelle
51700 Cerseuil
Phone 00 33 3 26 52 71 75
Fax 00 33 3 26 52 73 83
champagne.dehours@wanadoo.fr
www.champagne-dehours.fr

Jérôme Dehours is one of the most imaginative and ambitious producers in the Cerseuil area, famous for his classy pinot meunier bottlings. They are made according to the compelling principles of single-vineyard vinification: the grapes are sourced from the best parcels of vines and then vinified separately in oak. The bottles are as elegantly styled as the wines, especially the exceptional Les Genevreaux. All of the current bottlings are very successful, the crème de la crème being the white Coteaux Champenois: a rare, genuine thoroughbred of a wine, like a great Chablis but with much more saline and mineral on the palate.

Recently tasted

COTEAUX CHAMPENOIS MAISONCELLE 2003
Brut White | 2011 up to 2015   **91**

COTEAUX CHAMPENOIS MAREUIL-LE-PORT
White | 2011 up to 2016   **92**

Older vintages

BLANC DE MEUNIER 2003
Brut White | 2011 up to 2013   **88**
Aged in oak, this is a very round, pleasant, balanced Champagne with vanilla, fine white fruit, and pear aromas that give it the charm of successful 2003s.

BRUT GRANDE RÉSERVE
Brut White | 2011 up to 2013   **88**
A very nice pinot meunier–based wine that is vinous and expressive, with remarkable dosage. A widely versatile wine, as an aperitif or at the table.

COTEAUX CHAMPENOIS LES RIEUX
White | 2011 up to 2013   **92**
One of the finest examples of this type of wine we have ever tasted. A very subtle iodine nose, generous body, extraordinary saline finish, appetite-whetting, with judiciously integrated oak.

EXTRA-BRUT LES GENEVREAUX
Brut White | 2011 up to 2013   **90**
Slightly oaky but vinous, strikingly energetic for a wine from this part of the region, this is complex and very recommendable, despite the slightly high price.

Annual production: 85,000 bottles

DELAMOTTE

7, rue de la Brèche-d'Oger
51190 Le Mesnil-sur-Oger
Phone 00 33 3 26 57 51 65
Fax 00 33 3 26 57 79 29
champagne@salondelamotte.com
www.salondelamotte.com

This unassuming wine house is part of the Laurent-Perrier Group and specializes in chardonnay-driven Champagnes that work particularly well as aperitifs. The range is deliberately limited (one Brut, one Blanc de Blancs, and one Vintage Champagne) and relies mainly on grapes from the Côte des Blancs. The aim is to create fresh, slender wines with supple character and a range of aromas highlighted by a crisp tang of citrus.

BLANC DE BLANCS
Brut White | 2011 up to 2013   **88**
Quite spirited, vivacious, and even spiritual: a very fine, appetite-whetting Blanc de Blancs. This is the brand's main bottling.

BLANC DE BLANCS MILLÉSIMÉ 1999
Brut White | 2011 up to 2013   **90**
Perfectly suited to the tender, appetite-whetting style of Delamotte, this 1999 adds qualities of intensity and depth. With its toasty aromas, this vintage is currently drinking well.

BRUT
Brut White | 2011 up to 2013   **87**
A tender, round bottling, very supple. The bubbles are discreet, not aggressive, accentuating its appetite-whetting freshness.

BRUT ROSÉ
Brut Rosé | 2011 up to 2013   **84**
Supple and pleasant, but with limited personality.

Red: 37.1 acres. White: 37.1 acres; chardonnay 100%.
Annual production: 700,000 bottles

PAUL DÉTHUNE

2, rue du Moulin
51150 Ambonnay
Phone 00 33 3 26 57 01 88
Fax 00 33 3 26 57 09 31
info@champagne-dethune.com
www.champagne-dethune.com

The Déthunes are one of the oldest families in the Grand Cru village of Ambonnay, and they continue to use time-honored practices—especially vinification in oak, either in barrels or in larger oak vats. Their Champagnes are a consistent expression of the charm and vinosity of the Ambonnay Grand Cru and are made in a style that ages very gracefully. The bottle labels may seem rather heavy by comparison, though they are actually quite collectible.

BLANC DE NOIRS
Brut White | 2011 up to 2013   **89**
Pinkish white-gold color, great noble nose, typical of the terroir, slightly oaky, a perfect example of this style of Champagne and its production; elegant, long, and stunning.

BRUT BLANC DE NOIRS GRAND CRU
Brut White | 2011 up to 2013   **90**
Vinified in large barrels, this is very successful, with complex, long, generous fruit. Made for the table.

BRUT BLANC DE NOIRS GRAND CRU
Brut White | 2011 up to 2013   **88**
A very classically made wine, round, fruity, balanced, crowd-pleasing, to be served either as an aperitif or with a meal. Could be slightly more vinous.

BRUT ROSÉ
Brut Rosé | 2011 up to 2014   **88**
A hunter's rosé with real character—gamey as a hare's belly! Nice length.

CUVÉE À L'ANCIENNE
Brut White | 2011 up to 2013   **92**
Great fruit ripened to full maturity, great length, a wine of great character but that should be reserved for knowing connoisseurs.

PRINCESSE DES THUNES
Brut White | 2011 up to 2013   **90**
A superb nose of honey, very typically Ambonnay; small and quickly dissipating bubbles, which make the wine particularly appetizing; savory, long on the palate; in the best tradition for this bottling.

Annual production: 55,000 bottles

DEUTZ

16, rue Jeanson
BP 9
51160 Aÿ
Phone 00 33 3 26 56 94 00
Fax 00 33 3 26 56 94 10
France@champagne-deutz.com
www.champagne-deutz.com

This very elegant Champagne house in Aÿ has gradually built up a now highly respectable range of wines—from its "Classic" NV Brut to its prestige cuvées, William Deutz (based on pinot noir and pinot meunier) and Amour de Deutz (pure chardonnay). Deutz Champagnes play neither on opulence nor heaviness—making them the perfect aperitif—but still have more than enough depth to hold their own with food.

Recently tasted
BLANC DE BLANCS 2004
Brut White | 2011 up to 2016   **91**

BRUT MILLÉSIMÉ 2004
Brut White | 2011 up to 2018   **92**

WILLIAM DEUTZ 1999
Brut White | 2011 up to 2015   **92**

Older vintages
AMOUR DE DEUTZ BLANC DE BLANCS 1999
Brut White | 2011 up to 2016   **94**
The aromatic palette of this wine has subtly evolved toward complex notes of flowers and candied fruit. A velvety, delicate, insinuating Champagne of great distinction.

BLANC DE BLANCS 2002
Brut White | 2011 up to 2018   **93**
With one more year of cellaring, this magnificent, very pure, intense Blanc de Blancs has started to develop all of its potential. Patient cellarers will wait on it a little more, because it truly has a great potential for developing further with age.

BRUT CLASSIC
Brut White | 2011 up to 2013   **92**
Vigorous, full, energetic, subtly aromatic (citrus zest), mineral, perfect dosage, very pure with great finesse: compliments rain down on this impeccable, high-class bottling.

BRUT MILLÉSIMÉ 2002
Brut White | 2011 up to 2020   **98**
A superbly vigorous, racy style, this offers great, remarkably expressive fruit and intensity and length on the palate. Almost perfect, and eminently cellar-worthy!

Brut Millésimé 2000
Brut White | 2011 up to 2017   **94**
The great vinous character of this Champagne comes through fully in this vintage. Very long on the palate and youthful.

Brut Rosé
Brut Rosé | 2011 up to 2013   **90**
Today this rosé has found its style: both refined and energetic, with very nice raspberry aromas and a vivacious, cheerful finish.

Millésimé demi-sec 2000
Semi-Dry White | 2011 up to 2017   **91**
A pretty Demi-Sec with perfectly integrated dosage and fine, deep length on the palate.

William Deutz 1998
Brut White | 2011 up to 2017   **96**
A great, full, intense Champagne that shows a rare sense of balance, with both a firmly vinous character and a splendid appetite-whetting freshness. Has reached full maturity.

William Deutz Rosé 1999
Brut Rosé | 2011 up to 2015   **92**
A nice, refined, full rosé with aromas of toast and red fruit, combining delicacy and intensity. But this is not the most impressive wine in the lineup.

Red: 72.6 acres. White: 31 acres. Annual production: 2,000,000 bottles

DOM PÉRIGNON

20, avenue de Champagne
51200 Épernay
Phone 00 33 3 26 51 20 00
Fax 00 33 3 26 54 84 23
sborde@mhdfrane.fr
www.domperignon.com

Moët & Chandon's legendary Dom Pérignon is not an estate in its own right, but it deserves a separate entry because it has the advantage of its own team and its own dedicated grape supply. The cuvée was first created by Robert de Vogüe in the prewar period, in homage to the eponymous monk who served as cellar master at the Abbey of Hautvillers. It was only produced when the vintage was good, originally at the rate of three or four every decade. As the market grew, so did supply and the 1990s alone saw seven Dom Pérignon vintages: 1990, 1992, 1993, 1995, 1996, 1998, and 1999! This was accompanied by a dramatic rise in sales, no doubt outselling any other prestige cuvée whatever the actual figures may be (Dom Pérignon output remains Moët & Chandon's most closely guarded secret). Success, however, did not spoil Dom Pérignon; quite the reverse. Having had the privilege to taste every vintage since the generous 1959, it is our considered opinion that "Dom Pé" today is as refined, beautifully constructed, and consistent as it ever was. First-class grapes have something to do with it, particularly since the addition of a large chunk of the former Pommery and Lanson vineyards, both exceptionally well situated. The other factor is the exacting level of craftsmanship applied by the winemaking team, headed by cellar master Richard Geoffroy, who is definitely one of the great names in contemporary Champagne making.

Dom Pérignon 2000
Brut White | 2011 up to 2019   **94**
Fine citrus notes and mineral nuances, deep but very elegant, nervy, upfront: a Champagne of great dimensions.

Dom Pérignon 1999
Brut White | 2011 up to 2019   **94**
Supple and delicate, this is a superb Champagne with very tiny bubbles and a taffeta-like body that exhales subtle aromas of citrus, toast, and red fruit. Perfectly worthy of its mythical status!

DOM PÉRIGNON 1996
Brut White | 2011 up to 2020   98

Long awaiting maturity, this vintage has started to open up after several years in the bottle and now appears to be one of the greatest successes of the decade. The wine is long, very pure, with remarkable finesse and texture.

DOM PÉRIGNON ROSÉ 2000
Brut Rosé | 2011 up to 2018   94

Very expressive fruit, fresh and tasty fullness, deeply linear: a very aristocratic rosé.

DOM PÉRIGNON ROSÉ 1996
Brut Rosé | 2011 up to 2017   100

Exquisitely refined, this wonderfully velvety, distinguished rosé is remarkable for its extremely delicate bouquet of raspberries and flowers, its unaggressive bubbles, and its soft and supple freshness. An absolute delight!

OENOTHÈQUE 1993
Brut White | 2011 up to 2017   94

With its Oenothèque line, the house offers connoisseurs several of its mature older vintages that have been aged in its cellars. The 1993 requires some time in the glass to fully open up, but its racy, mineral finesse and its delicate, very refined length are seductive.

OENOTHÈQUE 1990
Brut White | 2011 up to 2020   99

This wine has retained great freshness and imposes a remarkably ethereal, intense length. It's certainly one of the brand's great vintages.

PASCAL DOQUET

44, chemin du Moulin-de-la-Cense-Bizet
51130 Vertus
Phone 00 33 3 26 52 16 50
Fax 00 33 3 26 59 36 71
contact@champagne-doquet.com
www.champagne-doquet.com

This relatively young domaine is the result of the division of the holdings of Champagnes Douquet-Jeanmarie, a well-known family in Vertus, in the heart of the Côte des Blancs. Pascal Doquet had a clear vision of the wines he wanted to make, and the only way for him to do this was to set off on his own. An admirer of Selosse, Larmandier, Agrapart, and other famous organic vintners, he is trying to cultivate his vineyards as naturally as possible, and is vinifying each vineyard separately in order to reveal the individual characteristics of each terroir. His first wines are impressive, so keep a close eye on him.

BLANC DE BLANCS
Brut White | 2011 up to 2013   88

Very expressive on the nose, with fine malic notes of fresh apple that are part of the wine's charm, and tiny bubbles. A taut, saline wine that is faithful to its terroir.

MILLÉSIMÉ PREMIER CRU 2002
Brut White | 2011 up to 2014   90

An excellent vintage Champagne with very tiny bubbles, almost perfect yeast autolysis (neither reduction nor oxidation; an ideal balance between the two), great follow-through on the palate, finesse, and racy terroir.

MILLÉSIMÉ PREMIER CRU 1996
Brut White | 2011 up to 2014   90

Very typical of Vertus, this has fine tertiary notes, nice acidity, and a dosage that is more marked than in the 2002, but at the table it goes unnoticed, feeling long and racy.

ROSÉ
Brut Rosé | 2011 up to 2013   85

Less marked by the soil than the Blanc de Blancs, this is refined and clear-cut, but its crowd-pleasing side feels a bit standardized.

Red: 1.2 acres. White: 20 acres. Annual production: 80,000 bottles

DRAPPIER

Rue des Vignes
10200 Urville
Phone 00 33 3 25 27 40 15
Fax 00 33 3 25 27 40 15
info@champagne-drappier.com
www.champagne-drappier.com

This discreet Champagne house on the Côte des Bar relies on a ninety-one-acre sloping vineyard that is predominantly planted to pinot noir, with chardonnay plantings in Cramant and other pinot vines in Bouzy and Ambonnay. The top Champagne, Carte d'Or, is mainly made from pinot noir, while La Grande Sendrée, from a separate parcel of old vines, contains roughly equal quantities of chardonnay and pinot. All in all, if you like vinous Champagnes, Drappier is for you.

BRUT NATURE PINOT NOIR
Brut White | 2011 up to 2013   88
A successful attempt to produce a Champagne without added sulfur or any dosage, even if shipping may alter the purity of its aromas. A bottle in Épernay had oxidative tendencies; another on site was impeccable.

LA GRANDE SENDRÉE 2002
Brut Rosé | 2011 up to 2014   89
A vinous Champagne with character but discreet aromatic development.

LA GRANDE SENDRÉE 2000
Brut White | 2011 up to 2015   91
Elegant, racy bubbles, aromatic distinction, length and precision, great freshness on the finish, though lacking perfect velvetiness.

LA GRANDE SENDRÉE 2000
Brut Rosé | 2011 up to 2015   92
Deep color, red fruit (raspberry and gooseberry), lip-smacking and vinous, the red wine adds the voluptuousness that was lacking in the 2000 white.

LA GRANDE SENDRÉE 1996
Brut White | 2011 up to 2013   93
Very linear but also voluptuous, round, ripe; very fine notes of grain; long and refined with tension and harmony. But should be drunk now.

MILLÉSIME D'EXCEPTION 2000
Brut White | 2011 up to 2015   89
A powerful, vinous wine: fine pinot noir, taut, mineral, a bit austere, low dosage, nice character.

Annual production: 1,500,000 bottles

DUVAL-LEROY

69, avenue de Bammental
51130 Vertus
Phone 00 33 3 26 52 10 75
Fax 00 33 3 26 52 12 93
champagne@duval-leroy.com
www.duval-leroy.com

Quality at Duval-Leroy has soared since Carol Duval took control in 1991 and made a commitment to ever-higher standards of excellence. Located in Vertus, on the Côte des Blancs, the house offers a broad range of wines that all have lots of personality (such as a dessert Champagne called Lady Rose). Among them, the Brut Fleur de Champagne gets better all the time, and the intriguing single-parcel cuvées are very precisely and faithfully crafted.

Recently tasted
150 1999
Brut White | 2011 up to 2016   91

AUTHENTIS CLOS DES BOUVERIES 2004
Brut White | 2011 up to 2015   92

Older vintages
AUTHENTIS CLOS DES BOUVERIES 2002
Brut White | 2011 up to 2015   92
A fine, racy Champagne destined for aperitifs or a plate of oysters, in a pure, linear style with aromatic accents and the personality of a great chardonnay from the Côte des Blancs, in this case from Vertus. It is growing more powerful.

AUTHENTIS CUMIÈRES 2001
Brut White | 2011 up to 2016   92
A superb Blanc de Noirs that is both refined and intense, marked by notes of brilliant, persistent red fruit, with incredible length on the palate. It should be drunk now.

AUTHENTIS TRÉPAIL 1999
Brut White | 2011 up to 2016   90
Pure chardonnay, with low acidity and a finish that has good precision and undeniable character. Its hazelnut character will pair wonderfully with sole meunière.

AUTHENTIS TRÉPAIL 1998
Brut White | 2011 up to 2015   91
Pure chardonnay, this has absolutely refreshing acidity and is very stylish.

FEMME DE CHAMPAGNE 1996
Brut White | 2011 up to 2015   92
Refined, elegant, fine and creamy, this bottling—produced only in magnums—appeals with its racy, long, precise charm.

FLEUR DE CHAMPAGNE
Brut White | 2011 up to 2013   86
Contrary to many large house nonvintage bruts, the dosage is very subtle, here, and does not obscure the pure and nicely appetite-whetting character of the wine.

FLEUR DE CHAMPAGNE BLANC DE CHARDONNAY 1998
Brut White | 2011 up to 2013   89
The bubbles are very tiny and not aggressive, announcing a Champagne for the aperitif hour. It is tender but subtly constructed, with lemon zest on the finish.

FLEUR DE CHAMPAGNE PREMIER CRU
Brut White | 2011 up to 2013   90
Unquestionably savory and full, this is a success, with wonderful ripeness on the palate.

FLEUR DE CHAMPAGNE ROSÉ DE SAIGNÉE
Brut Rosé | 2011 up to 2013   87
A rosé with great personality and great finesse. Distinguished, with elegant acidity.

LADY ROSE
Brut Rosé | 2011 up to 2015   90
The high level of dosage, designed in collaboration with the pastry chef Pierre Hermé, makes it a striking, unexpected match for chocolate.

MILLÉSIMÉ 1996
Brut White | 2011 up to 2015   90
A vigorous Champagne from a prestigious vintage. Powerful, with a somewhat wild, untamed side to it.

Annual production: 5,500,000 bottles

EGLY-OURIET

9-15, rue de Trépail
51150 Ambonnay
Phone 00 33 3 26 57 82 26
Fax 00 33 3 26 57 06 52

Francis Egly sets the standard for winegrowers throughout the Champagne region, with his stringent work ethic, levels of stock that allow long fermentation on lees, and precise labeling that states the date of disgorgement and the duration of that fermentation on lees. The warm soils of Ambonnay bring the pinot noir to peak ripeness, maintaining a consistent level of quality in his grapes for the past ten years. Egly's two most outstanding cuvées are, first, the incredible, uniquely opulent nonvintage Blanc de Noirs; and the Coteaux Champenois, a wine made in pitifully small quantities but arguably the very best available in Champagne today. But even at entry level, the deliciously subtle, 100 percent pinot meunier Les Vignes de Vrigny puts on an exemplary performance. This is, in short, the most complete, homogeneous range of wines ever from this exceptional producer, who now boasts ultramodern facilities that should allow him to raise the bar even higher.

Recently tasted
BRUT BLANC DE NOIRS VIEILLES VIGNES GRAND CRU LES CRAYÈRES
Brut White | 2011 up to 2013   95

BRUT MILLÉSIMÉ 1999
Brut White | 2011 up to 2017   97

BRUT TERROIR DE VRIGNY
Brut White | 2011 up to 2014   90

COTEAUX CHAMPENOIS AMBONNAY 2007
Red | 2017 up to 2027   96

ROSÉ
Brut Rosé | 2011 up to 2014   90

Older vintages
BRUT BLANC DE NOIRS VIEILLES VIGNES GRAND CRU LES CRAYÈRES
Brut White | 2011 up to 2013   98
Kept for more than forty-eight months on its lees, this very golden wine is the apotheosis of pinot noir in Champagne, combining very fine red-fruit notes with extraordinary minerality from exceptional vines at the heart of a Grand Cru.

BRUT MILLÉSIMÉ 2000
Brut White | 2011 up to 2013   92
The amber color should not be considered worrisome, as the producer picks the pinot

noir ripe, which gives some color to the wine. The nose is reassuring, with the acacia honey notes typical of Ambonnay; the wine is admirable for its smoothness and class, even if its elegance is not on par with the 1996 or the 1999.

BRUT MILLÉSIMÉ 1999
Brut White | 2011 up to 2013 — 98
It is still uncertain when the producer will release magnums of this wine, which is absolutely stunning for the wonderful freshness of the pinot noir, which was retained by avoiding malolactic fermentation. In any case, those bottles will be severely rationed.

BRUT MILLÉSIMÉ 1996
Brut White | 2011 up to 2013 — 99
There may still be a few magnums left of this sumptuous wine, the perfect expression of its terroir and vintage.

BRUT TERROIR DE VRIGNY
Brut White | 2011 up to 2013 — 89
Superior balance, fine bakery notes, vinous, impeccable, imperceptible dosage, a strong terroir personality. The wine shows the potential of the oft-maligned pinot meunier.

COTEAUX CHAMPENOIS AMBONNAY 2006
Red | 2011 up to 2021 — 95
The oak is still too present, but the wine promises to equal or even better the finesse of the 2005. Nothing compares to the textural richness and nobility of this pinot noir bottling, which should be treated like a Grand Cru from the Côte de Nuits.

COTEAUX CHAMPENOIS AMBONNAY 2004
Red | 2011 up to 2019 — 94
An inimitable scent of peony rose that is superlatively fine, perceptible oak that is well integrated into the wine's texture and aromatic personality, and an amazingly racy finish. A brush with perfection.

GRAND CRU TRADITION
Brut White | 2011 up to 2013 — 90
A deep golden color, great verve on the nose, with nonoxidative honey notes that point to its terroir, and ideal ripeness, which is very rare in this category. This is long and complex, a true Grand Cru.

ROSÉ
Brut Rosé | 2011 up to 2013 — 91
A very successful wine with superb pinot noir aromas, elegant and vinous with perfect dosage; versatile.

Red: 22.2 acres; pinot 77.8%, pinot meunier 22.2%. White: 4.9 acres; chardonnay 100%. Annual production: 100,000 bottles

CHAMPAGNE FLEURY

43, Grande Rue
10250 Courteron
Phone 00 33 3 25 38 20 28
Fax 00 33 3 25 38 24 65
champagne@champagne-fleury.fr
www.champagne-fleury.fr

This is definitely the best producer in the Aube and a fervent pioneer of biodynamic viticulture. The wines it turns out today owe a lot to rigorous soil management, and are all precise, honest, and remarkably digestible.

Recently tasted
MILLÉSIME 1995
Brut White | 2011 up to 2013 — 87

Older vintages
BRUT ROSÉ
Brut Rosé | 2011 up to 2013 — 91
Floral, fruity, full of finesse, delicate, light and subtle: bravo! This is great viticulture, a marvelously thirst-quenching Champagne.

BRUT TRADITION CARTE ROUGE
Brut White | 2011 up to 2013 — 86
A round, fruity, pure wine that is slightly flabby on the finish, as though the grapes had not accepted the dosage. A year's cellaring should balance things out.

CUVÉE ROBERT-FLEURY 2000
Brut White | 2011 up to 2014 — 89
This wine has evolved a lot, but it has deepened its notes of fine mushroom and its minerality (tied to the terroir and the quality of the viticulture). A wine that should be served with food.

FLEUR DE L'EUROPE
Brut White | 2011 up to 2013 — 90
More finesse and class than the preceding vintage bottlings. A wine that typifies the house style: supple, pure, natural, wonderfully quaffable.

MILLÉSIME 1998
Brut White | 2011 up to 2014 — 90
Straw-colored with a subtle nose and very pure, natural floral and spicy notes, a delicate body and bubbles; this is soft, fully mature!

Red: 7.4 acres; pinot noir 100%. White: 27.2 acres; chardonnay 100%. Annual production: 200,000 bottles

GATINOIS

7, rue Marcel-Mailly
51160 Aÿ
Phone 00 33 3 26 55 14 26
Fax 00 33 3 26 52 75 99
champ-gatinois@hexanet.fr
www.champagne-gatinois.com

Pierre Cheval's small, highly reputed estate boasts the finest vineyards in Aÿ, the most famous of all the Champagne crus. Part of his crop has for many years been bought by neighbor Bollinger. The terroir comes through loud and clear in the nonvintage cuvées, particularly La Réserve (aged sur pointe, one year longer) but also the vintage wine and the Coteaux Champenois. Recent entries show a return to all the strength and fullness for which this producer is renowned. The exceptional 2002 represents a perfect specimen of great Aÿ wine.

BRUT GRAND CRU RÉSERVE
Brut White | 2011 up to 2050   **84**
The nose is too mature (apple notes), supple but not entirely convincing, and in line with the house's habitual style.

BRUT GRAND CRU TRADITION
Brut White | 2011 up to 2015   **90**
Light pink in color, this is wonderfully vinous, with great personality. Wait two or three years more.

BRUT ROSÉ
Brut Rosé | 2011 up to 2013   **88**
With nice aromatic precision, this is powerful but not heavy-handed, with style and raciness. Excellent dosage.

MILLÉSIMÉ 2002
Brut White | 2011 up to 2014   **95**
An admirable nose of red fruit and mineral notes; a magnificent body, ideal dosage, and a finish that is impressively taut and expressive: this is a true Grand Cru at its apogee.

Red: 16.1 acres; pinot noir 100%. White: 2.5 acres; chardonnay 100%. Annual production: 50,000 bottles

PIERRE GIMONNET ET FILS

1, rue de la République
51530 Cuis
Phone 00 33 3 26 59 78 70
Fax 00 33 3 26 59 79 84
info@champagne-gimonnet.com
www.champagne-gimonnet.com

This very large estate in the heart of the Côte des Blancs is now run by Olivier and Didier Gimonnet, who maintain a style of wine that will never go out of fashion: consistently good, with a focus on freshness and aromatic finesse. Recent vintages are among the most complete ever produced by these growers.

Recently tasted
PREMIER CRU ŒNOPHILE EXTRA-BRUT 2002
Brut White | 2011 up to 2013   **95**

Older vintages
BRUT BLANC DE BLANCS PREMIER CRU CUIS
Brut White | 2011 up to 2014   **88**
With the same technical mastery that gives the fruit exemplary cleanness, even if the wine is obviously not very complex.

BRUT BLANC DE BLANCS PREMIER CRU FLEURON 2004
Brut White | 2011 up to 2020   **90**
A perfect Blanc de Blancs with ethereal elegance and irresistible freshness, already perfectly drinkable, and completely in the producer's usual style.

BRUT BLANC DE BLANCS PREMIER CRU FLEURON 2002
Brut White | 2011 up to 2020   **90**
Lightly brioche-scented, clean, pure, chiseled, fairly ripe, straightforward, subtle.

BRUT VIEILLES VIGNES CHARDONNAY COLLECTION 1998
Brut White | 2011 up to 2015   **94**
Only available in magnum. Ideal purity and straightforwardness. Great wine that is drinking beautifully now, taut and elegant.

GASTRONOME 2004
Brut White | 2011 up to 2020   **90**
A fine chardonnay that is very round, with citrus notes. Accessible now, it is perfectly mouth-filling. Very appetizing, with perfect dosage. It would go perfectly with oysters.

GASTRONOME 2002
Brut White | 2011 up to 2020   **88**
A refined nose of fern, subtle, tender, pleasant, not very vinous.

GASTRONOME 1999
Brut White | 2011 up to 2017   **92**
The wine's tension has started to slacken in favor of a more mature character, with savory citrus notes. It is tasty, long on the palate, ideal paired with sole or line-caught turbot.

PREMIER CRU ŒNOPHILE EXTRA-BRUT 2000
Brut White | 2011 up to 2020   **93**
The essence of chalk-soil chardonnay, taut as an archery champion's bow, but without any sharp angles; incredibly pure. A model to follow for many growers in the region!

PREMIER CRU ŒNOPHILE EXTRA-BRUT 1999
Brut White | 2011 up to 2017   **93**
Ideal minerality, taut, clear-cut, ultra-precise, with wonderful balance.

PREMIER CRU SPÉCIAL CLUB BRUT 2002
Brut White | 2011 up to 2020   **93**
Great aromatic breeding, with lemon notes that are hard to equal in their finesse; strikingly vinous despite the apparent lightness of the bubbles; ideal dosage. A well-rounded wine.

PREMIER CRU SPÉCIAL CLUB BRUT 1999
Brut White | 2011 up to 2017   **93**
The same precision, the same freshness, and the same sense of balance as ever. An ideal aperitif.

White: 74.1 acres; chardonnay 100%. Annual production: 250,000 bottles

GONET-MÉDEVILLE

1, chemin de la Cavotte
51150 Bisseuil
Phone 00 33 6 07 19 66 78
Fax 00 33 3 26 57 75 60
gonet.medeville@wanadoo.fr

This estate was born of the marriage of the heirs to two great wine-growing families: Xavier Gonet (from Mesnil-sur-Oger) and Julie Médeville (from Preignac in the Sauternes area, most notably Château Gilette). Their impeccably tended vines are located in the superb sloping vineyards of Bisseuil, Ambonnay, and Mesnil-sur-Oger, with all three Champagne varietals featured. This gives the estate what it needs to produce well-blended Champagnes for every occasion, made with minimum dosage so as to highlight the purity of expression in each cuvée. The single-parcel Grand Cru bottlings and the blended cuvée Théophile are still undergoing aging. Of the wines currently for sale, the Blanc de Noirs bottling, Perle Noire, and the Perle Rosée are warmly recommended. Very honest, pure and refined, and very style-confident for such a young domaine!

Recently tasted
AMBONNAY LA GRANDE RUELLE 2002
Brut White | 2011 up to 2014   **93**

THÉOPHILE EXTRA BRUT GRAND CRU 2003
Brut White | 2011 up to 2013   **95**

TRADITION PREMIER CRU
Brut White | 2011 up to 2013   **87**

Older vintages
BLANC DE NOIRS
Brut White | 2011 up to 2013   **89**
Very light, pale pink color, very pure fruitiness, an ethereal, precise body, impeccably clean expression on the palate from beginning to end. This is one of the rare wines in this category that can be enjoyed from the start of the meal to the finish.

BLANC DE NOIRS PREMIER CRU
Brut White | 2011 up to 2015   **90**
Mineral on the nose and on the palate, linear, energetic, pure because there is almost no dosage, ideal for an aperitif.

BRUT ROSÉ
Brut Rosé | 2011 up to 2013   **91**
A pale rosé with a very fine nose of red fruit, this is very linear and ethereal in its bubbles, ideally appetite-whetting.

Brut Tradition
Brut White | 2011 up to 2013   **86**

A slight malic note (fresh apples) on the nose, light, easy-drinking, fresh, fruity, open, low dosage, a confirmed house style, somewhat simple.

Extra-brut
Brut White | 2011 up to 2013   **88**

A classic example of light, pure, appetite-whetting Champagne that makes no concessions, for true connoisseurs.

Extra-brut rosé
Brut Rosé | 2011 up to 2013   **91**

With a racy nose of small red fruit, this is a very well defined, taut, racy wine with ideal dosage, in a style made for the most demanding connoisseurs.

Grand cru blanc de noirs 2002
Brut White | 2011 up to 2016   **92**

With an ample nose of acacia honey and the terroir expression of Ambonnay, this is powerful, racy, long, ready to drink. A Champagne for the table.

Red: 12.4 acres. **White:** 12.4 acres. **Annual production:** 100,000 bottles

GOSSET

69, rue Jules-Blondeau
BP 7
51160 Aÿ
Phone 00 33 3 26 56 99 56
Fax 00 33 3 26 51 55 88
info@champagne-gosset.com
www.champagne-gosset.com

This very ancient Champagne house was acquired by celebrated Cognac family Cointreau in 1994. Since then it has been brilliantly revived by Béatrice Cointreau, who has now passed the baton to her brother. Gosset specializes in vinous, intense, powerful wines that are always better after a few years' cellaring—particularly the dazzling vintage cuvées and Cuvée Célébris. In 2007, the house introduced a new Blanc de Blancs cuvée that shows exceptional tautness and focus.

Célébris
Brut White | 2011 up to 2019   **92**

Deep and thick, this vinous Champagne has a complex bouquet of toasted grains and dark fruit but retains its vigor.

Célébris blanc de blancs
Brut White | 2011 up to 2017   **93**

Linear, pure, with great tension on the palate and aromas that display chalk and finely lemony notes, with great length. It can be enjoyed now with a plate of oysters, but the wine will develop with age.

Célébris Rosé 2003
Brut Rosé | 2011 up to 2013   **91**

This Extra-Brut rosé perfectly illustrates the character of the heat-wave 2003 vintage: taut, intense right up to the somewhat drying note on the finish, fresh but with low acidity. A nice fruity finish.

Grand Millésime 1999
Brut White | 2011 up to 2017   **90**

A harmonious, ripe Champagne with notes of torrefaction and hazelnut and average but appealing power. It is charming but lacks the intensity of the Célébris bottlings.

Grand Rosé
Brut Rosé | 2011 up to 2014   **90**

Pretty pale pink in color, refined and harmonious on the palate, this blossoms into a long, fruity finish.

Grande Réserve
Brut White | 2011 up to 2017   **90**

A fine, vigorous, fruity bottling that can easily be cellared, as its aging potential is forcefully apparent. A beautiful, vigorous finish with red-fruit notes.

Annual production: 1,200,000 bottles

CHARLES HEIDSIECK

12, allée du Vignoble
51100 Reims
Phone 00 33 3 26 84 43 00
Fax 00 33 3 26 84 43 49
www.charlesheidsieck.com

This old, established Champagne house is named after its ambitious and ingenious founder Charles Heidsieck, who in the nineteenth century conquered the entire American market virtually almost single-handedly. Strangely, it remains little known by wine lovers, which is unfair considering its long history as a producer of prestige cuvées with exquisite finesse and perfect maturity: Champagne Charlie (highly collectible) and especially the Blanc des Millénaires. Its nonvintage Brut is also particularly noted for its freshness and generous, aromatic flavors. The date of cellaring, though invaluable to any wine lover, no longer features on the bottle because it was too often mistaken for the vintage. All of the wines are stunningly consistent, supported by a smooth, instantly recognizable style with an irresistible whiff of hazelnuts. They are equally good on their own as an aperitif or to drink with a meal.

Recently tasted
MILLÉSIMÉ 2000
Brut White | 2011 up to 2015 **91**

ROSÉ RÉSERVE
Brut Rosé | 2011 up to 2013 **92**

Older vintages
BLANC DES MILLÉNAIRES 1995
Brut White | 2011 up to 2020 **99**
With its complex bouquet, fine texture, and infinite suaveness, the 1995 Blanc des Millénaires has exceptional finesse and magnificent subtlety.

BRUT RÉSERVE
Brut White | 2011 up to 2013 **92**
A Brut that is incredible for its softness and finesse, extremely smooth and deliciously round: certainly one of the best nonvintage Bruts from a large house.

CHAMPAGNE CHARLIE 1985
Brut White | 2011 up to 2030 **96**
A splendid example of the superb aging of great Champagnes, this has great freshness and aromas on the palate, a lot of generosity and verve, and very persistent, tiny bubbles.

Annual production: 1,000,000 bottles

HENRIOT

81, rue Coquebert
51100 Reims
Phone 00 33 3 26 89 53 00
Fax 00 33 3 26 89 53 10
contact@champagne-henriot.com
www.champagne-henriot.com

This family estate was the starting point for Joseph Henriot, who also owns Bouchard Père et Fils and the Domaine William Fèvre in Burgundy. It is run today by his son, Stanislas, who looks to make pure, svelte Champagnes with an airy finesse that makes them ideal aperitifs. The finest, most obvious expressions of that style are Henriot's pure chardonnay, Blanc Souverain, and the stunningly successful Cuvée des Enchanteleurs—not one disappointing vintage since it was first launched in 1985.

Recently tasted
BRUT MILLÉSIME 2000
Brut White | 2011 up to 2013 **89**

CUVÉE DES ENCHANTELEURS 1996
Brut White | 2011 up to 2014 **95**

Older vintages
BLANC SOUVERAIN
Brut White | 2011 up to 2013 **92**
A brilliant, elegant Blanc de Blancs with notes of citrus and toasted grains, this is deliciously refreshing on the palate, with ethereal length.

BRUT MILLÉSIME 1998
Brut White | 2011 up to 2015 **90**
A streamlined Champagne with fine, fresh butter notes in a refined style with no hard angles.

BRUT MILLÉSIME 1996
Brut White | 2011 up to 2016 **92**
Vinous and deep, this reflects its highly intense vintage: the 1996 does not have the ethereal subtlety of the rest of the lineup, but it is impressive in its straightforward style and perfect structure. The aromatic palette, with fine citrus and meringue notes, is also superb.

BRUT ROSÉ
Brut Rosé | 2011 up to 2013 **89**
A tender, raspberried rosé with perfect dosage and great finesse in its definition.

CUVÉE DES ENCHANTELEURS 1995
Brut White | 2011 up to 2015 **96**

Superb aromas of toast and dried fruits; ample, refined on the palate: a Champagne with great allure and perfect distinction.

Annual production: 1,300,000 bottles

JACQUESSON

68, rue du Colonel-Fabien
51530 Dizy
Phone 00 33 3 26 55 68 11
Fax 00 33 3 26 51 06 25
info@champagnejacquesson.com
www.champagnejacquesson.com

Jacquesson was founded in the late eighteenth century and enjoyed some success before fading from view in the first half of the twentieth century. For the past few decades it has been owned by the Chiquet family, who have gradually made this house the standard-bearer for the connoisseur's Champagne—a fabulously faithful expression of the terroir for which the name Jacquesson is renowned, thanks to minimum dosage and sufficient bottle aging prior to release. The result is wines of assertive character—sometimes surprisingly so—such as the lofty Dizy Corne-Bautray. Every batch of the nonvintage Brut is numbered: cuvée 731 mainly contains base wines from the 2003 vintage, 732 those from 2004, and so forth.

Recently tasted

CUVÉE 733
Brut White | 2011 up to 2013   **95**

DÉGORGEMENT TARDIF 1990
Brut White | 2011 up to 2020   **97**

DIZY TERRES ROUGES 2004
Brut Rosé | 2011 up to 2015   **93**

MILLÉSIME 2000
Brut White | 2011 up to 2015   **91**

Older vintages

AVIZE GRAND CRU BLANC DE BLANCS 1997
Brut White | 2011 up to 2017   **90**
Avize is a complex bottling, with an unctuous, intense character and aromas that are still fairly primary. It can be cellared for two or three years.

AVIZE GRAND CRU DÉGORGEMENT TARDIF 1996
Brut White | 2011 up to 2013   **94**
Absolutely delicate, perfectly pure, a Champagne of ethereal balance. Less intellectual than Corne-Bautray, but a must. Totally elegant.

CUVÉE 731
Brut White | 2011 up to 2015   **92**
Straw-colored with a superb cusp of tiny bubbles. The nose is intense, with notes of country-style bread and dried fruit; on the palate it is intense, brilliantly structured, with great finesse.

CUVÉE 732
Brut White | 2011 up to 2013   **91**
Complex notes of candied fruit and citrus; very dense and structured on the palate but at the same time showing great finesse: this is in the remarkable tradition of its antecedents.

DIZY PREMIER CRU CORNE-BAUTRAY 2000
Brut White | 2011 up to 2020   **95**
Made from a base of older chardonnays, this was made for those who love its exceptional terroir, which marks the wine with notes of fresh walnuts. It will please the most demanding connoisseurs. The very low dosage works because of the wine's exceptional ripeness.

MILLÉSIME 1996
Brut White | 2011 up to 2017   **98**
Very citrusy, with extraordinary potential in its primary aromatic palette, with grapefruit and orange notes. A great wine with immense personality.

Annual production: 350,000 bottles

JOSEPH PERRIER

69, avenue de Paris
BP 31
51016 Châlons-en-Champagne
Phone 00 33 3 26 68 29 51
Fax 00 33 3 26 70 57 16
contact@josephperrier.fr
www.josephperrier.com

This small wine house offers an impeccable range of wines, from its excellent NV Brut Royale to its ultra-refined prestige cuvée, Joséphine, which is only released after more than a decade's aging in bottle.

Recently tasted
JOSÉPHINE 2002
Brut White | 2011 up to 2015   **95**

Older vintages
CUVÉE ROYALE BRUT
Brut White | 2011 up to 2013   **90**
An appetizing, fatty, round Champagne with excellent ripeness and nice freshness. A very pleasant wine indeed.

CUVÉE ROYALE BRUT BLANC DE BLANCS
Brut White | 2011 up to 2013   **86**
Charming and tender, this is a nice Blanc de Blancs, even if it does not measure up to the personality of the house's best.

CUVÉE ROYALE ROSÉ
Brut Rosé | 2011 up to 2013   **90**
A vigorous, palate-whetting rosé that is appealing in its aromatic freshness and fine structure on the palate, very long but not at all rough or rustic.

CUVÉE ROYALE VINTAGE 1999
Brut White | 2011 up to 2018   **88**
Less freshness than the nonvintage bottlings, but more intensity.

JOSÉPHINE 1998
Brut White | 2011 up to 2018   **92**
Vinous, structured, still a little young to have the unctuousness of the great Joséphine vintages, but indisputably complete.

JOSÉPHINE 1995
Brut White | 2011 up to 2015   **97**
A superb bouquet of candied fruit and dried flowers; incomparable finesse and great freshness on the palate: an ample yet delicate vintage and a wonderful success.

Red: 46.9 acres; pinot noir 43%, pinot meunier 57%. White: 4.9 acres; chardonnay 100%. Annual production: 750,000 bottles

KRUG

5, rue Coquebert
51100 Reims
Phone 00 33 3 26 84 44 20
Fax 00 33 3 26 84 44 49
krug@krug.fr
www.krug.com

Champagne Krug was acquired by the luxury goods group LVMH in 1999 and is now under the direction of Olivier Krug, who succeeds his father, Henri, and uncle, Rémy. Krug remains a consummate master of Champagne blending, but its principles are quite unlike those of most, but not all, other Champagne houses. It is expert at juggling grape varieties (the much-maligned pinot meunier is on an equal footing here with the chardonnay and the pinot noir), vineyards (production relies on a wide range of crus, and not only the most famous ones), and especially vintages (the Grande Cuvée contains between 35 and 50 percent reserve wines, which clearly sets it apart from the other nonvintage Brut Champagnes on the market). Another characteristic feature of Krug style is the systematic use of barrel-aged base wines. All of this results in wines of pronounced character but with a particular style that takes some getting used to. In sharp contrast, Krug also makes a single-vineyard, single-varietal (chardonnay) Champagne: the deep, profoundly intense Clos du Mesnil.

BRUT GRANDE CUVÉE
Brut White | 2011 up to 2016   **94**
With its fine notes of hazelnut and candied fruit, this Champagne is fully mature. It is more of an aperitif wine than in the past, immediately tasty and appealing.

BRUT ROSÉ
Brut Rosé | 2011 up to 2016   **98**
A rosé that is very pale in color, pure and long, subtly constructed, full of finesse and great length, brilliant and distinguished.

CLOS DU MESNIL 1998
Brut White | 2011 up to 2018   **93**
Still very pale in color, discreet on the nose with fine notes of white flowers and a tiny hint of vanilla from barrel-aging, this is a wine with great tension and impeccable dosage, yet it is slightly less vinous than the greatest vintages of the Clos.

VINTAGE 1998
Brut White | 2011 up to 2023   98
This, the first vintage for cellar master Eric
Lebel, was a smashing success: very light
in color; a nose showing the archetypical
Krug style, a well-calibrated richness from
the yeasts, and an amazingly well-integrated
use of oak. The perfect blending of all three
grape varieties, with an exceptional 19 percent of pinot meunier, gives the wine a
greater purity and tension than in previous
vintages. This wine was only released for
sale at the end of 2008, and still needs several years of cellaring before reaching its
peak.

VINTAGE 1996
Brut White | 2011 up to 2030   95
Like many great 1996s right now, this vintage now seems rigorous, almost austere,
with its fruit and unctuousness taking the
fore only on the finish, which is a testament
to its great aging potential. It requires
patience.

VINTAGE 1995
Brut White | 2011 up to 2030   99
A magnificent Champagne with great length
and superlative finesse: the bouquet of candied fruit and nougatine is incredibly persistent, and the finesse and length are
endless.

BENOÎT LAHAYE

33, rue Jeanne-d'Arc
51150 Bouzy
Phone 00 33 3 26 57 03 05
Fax 00 33 3 26 52 79 94
lahaye.benoit@wanadoo.fr

This young but very serious-minded Bouzy
producer maintains high standards of
environmentally-friendly viticulture—without sacrificing his yields, as have some of
his more naïve colleagues. His wines
express their terroir perfectly—some
slightly rustic, some remarkably distinguished. All the latest editions of his Blanc
de Noirs, Rosé de Macération, and Brut
NV are proof that this is one of today's
most dependable producers of high-quality Bouzy wines. Sadly, production is very
limited.

Recently tasted
NATURESSENCE
Brut White | 2011 up to 2013   90

Older vintages
BLANC DE NOIRS PRESTIGE
Brut White | 2011 up to 2013   86
Pale pink in color, the same finesse, the same
freshness, stylish, round, natural, superb.

BRUT ESSENTIEL 2002
Brut White | 2011 up to 2013   90
Rich, powerfully marked by its pinot noir,
balanced well between the ripeness of the
grapes and the dosage, this is made for food
and is likely to please many people when
poured in that context.

BRUT ESSENTIEL
Brut White | 2011 up to 2013   91
Pale pink in color, very pure on the nose,
straightforward, fruity, refined, long on the
palate, with transparent terroir; delicious.
A good representation for organic winemakers.

BRUT NATURE
Brut White | 2011 up to 2013   86
Very powerful fruitiness and "traçant," as
they say in Champagne; that is, it is clearly
etched by its terroir. The fruit is ripe and on
the whole the wine is a little rustic, but very
natural.

COTEAUX CHAMPENOIS BOUZY 2003
Red | 2011 up to 2020   94
A great wine, exceptional terroir, exceptional
vintage, wonderful scents of cherries, splendid. Almost a giveaway, price-wise, for its
quality and potential.

Red: 17.3 acres. White: 93.9 acres. Annual
production: 40,000 bottles

LANCELOT PIENNE

1, place Pierre-Rivière
51530 Cramant
Phone 00 33 3 26 59 99 86
Fax 00 33 3 26 57 53 02
contact@champagnelancelotpienne.fr

This producer occupies the loveliest house in Cramant (once owned by Mumm) with fabulous views of the town's much-coveted sloping vineyards. Its wines are magnificently pure and dignified and were our Champagne find of the year—a tribute to their Grand Cru origins. There is a subtle mineral quality about a Cramant Grand Vin that is sure to delight oenophiles. The Cuvée de la Table Ronde (because Gilles Lancelot's wife was born a Perceval—nobody could make up a story like that) can easily compete with the celebrated Mumm de Cramant.

Older vintages
BRUT 2004
Brut White | 2011 up to 2014 **92**
Remarkable aromatic finesse, highly delicate bubbles, long and very promising, with the transparent, pure finish of vines grown on chalk soil; this is Cramant as we dream of it.

BRUT 2000
Brut White | 2011 up to 2050 **90**
A fine, stony, honeyed nose, with good finesse and cleanness—very much Champagne! Nice.

GRAND CRU BLANC DE BLANCS
CUVÉE DE LA TABLE RONDE 2002
Brut White | 2011 up to 2017 **96**
A splendid expression of the Cramant terroir, made from old vines in the most advantageous areas of La Goutte d'Or and Les Montaiguts. Crystalline purity, very reasonable dosage, superior minerality. Bravo! Alas, there is very little of it left.

GRAND CRU BLANC DE BLANCS
MARIE LANCELOT 2004
Brut White | 2011 up to 2014 **90**
Very pale, delicate, with rare purity and transparency, no aggressiveness. Delicious.

GRAND CRU BLANC DE BLANCS
MARIE LANCELOT 2000
Brut White | 2011 up to 2013 **92**
Another high-level Cramant, with a very subtle nose recalling the greatest bottlings from Mumm, with good freshness but also the start of classy tertiary notes of wild mushrooms.

Red: pinot meunier 75%, pinot noir 25%. White: chardonnay 100%. Annual production: 80,000 bottles

LANSON

66, rue de Cour-Lancy
51100 Reims
Phone 00 33 3 26 78 50 50
Fax 00 33 3 26 78 50 99
info@lansonpf.com
www.lanson.fr

In the grand tradition of Reims Champagne houses, Lanson has experienced a tumultuous existence since the eponymous family sold it in the 1970s. In the deal they lost their vineyards—some of the most beautiful in Champagne—which were acquired by LVMH but have recently been acquired by the BCC group, led by the ambitious team of Bruno Paillard and Philippe Baijot, and this has finally brought stability to the company. They block malolactic fermentation in all of their wines, including the NV Brut Black Label, which enables the wines to retain a wonderful liveliness, though it can sometimes be a bit harsh. This interesting technique also enables the wines to age particularly well.

Recently tasted
GOLD LABEL 1998
Brut White | 2011 up to 2018 **90**

Older vintages
BLACK LABEL
Brut White | 2011 up to 2013 **86**
A lively yet vigorous Champagne, frankly appetite-whetting, with good length.

GOLD LABEL 1997
Brut White | 2011 up to 2015 **86**
A supple, pleasant wine that is ready to drink but has limited personality.

IVORY LABEL
Semi-Dry White | 2011 up to 2013 **84**
A well-built dessert Champagne, but with limited personality.

NOBLE CUVÉE 1998
Brut White | 2011 up to 2018 **90**
Vinous yet streamlined, this is a nice, svelte and vigorous Champagne, with lively vivacity. It may be confidently cellared for several more years.

NOBLE CUVÉE 1995
Brut White | 2011 up to 2015 **91**
A refined, ample Champagne with excellent ripeness, perfectly ready to drink today. The bubbles are very fine.

NOBLE CUVÉE BLANC DE BLANCS 1998
Brut White | 2011 up to 2015   **88**
A fruity, loose-jointed chardonnay, vivacious and fairly vigorous, but without the elegance of the greatest expressions in its category.

NOBLE CUVÉE BLANC DE BLANCS 1996
Brut White | 2011 up to 2013   **88**
A supple, loose chardonnay with perhaps a little less presence than the 1995 Noble Cuvée, but indisputably deep, wiry, racy.

ROSÉ LABEL
Brut Rosé | 2011 up to 2013   **86**
This is elegant and very pale in color, with notes of dried flowers and wild strawberries, and tender and vivid on the palate. Appetite-whetting.

Annual production: 5,000,000 bottles

GUY LARMANDIER

30, rue du Général-Kœnig
51130 Vertus
Phone 00 33 3 26 52 12 41
Fax 00 33 3 26 52 19 38
guy.larmandier@wanadoo.fr
www.champagne-larmandier-guy.fr

Guy Larmandier has now handed over the reins to son François, whose influence is particularly noticeable in terms of better-integrated dosage. The wines come mainly from the famous vineyards of Cramant, Chouilly, and Vertus, boasting all the delicacy of their native terroirs—though not quite the definition and forcefulness one might hope for. The old-vine Cramant (made from very old vines indeed) is a remarkable vintage Blanc de Blancs—unbeatable value for money. The latest bottlings show signs of progress, which if it continues will definitely elevate these wines in our ratings.

Recently tasted
CRAMANT GRAND CRU 2002
Brut White | 2011 up to 2013   **88**

Older vintages
BRUT BLANC DE BLANCS GRAND CRU PERLÉE
Brut White | 2011 up to 2013   **88**
Frank, light; with a clear minerality that should please rock lovers and a restrained dosage, this is delicious as an aperitif.

BRUT GRAND CRU
Brut White | 2011 up to 2013   **89**
With a very clear-cut nose, this is a precise, pure wine that is moderately vinous but with transparent terroir in its minerality and finesse.

BRUT PREMIER CRU
Brut White | 2011 up to 2013   **88**
Fruity, pure, precise, with intelligent dosage, this is ready to drink, almost more vinous than the Grand Cru.

CRAMANT BRUT BLANC DE BLANCS GRAND CRU PRESTIGE 1999
Brut White | 2011 up to 2013   **90**
A remarkable Cramant wine, vinous, complex, worthy of the best cellars, but stocks are running low.

CRAMANT GRAND CRU 2002
Brut White | 2011 up to 2014   **92**
Complex, powerful, racy, with crowd-pleasing yet light-handed dosage, this is a wine of great character, worthy of its origins. Strongly recommended.

CRAMANT GRAND CRU 2000

Brut White | 2011 up to 2017   92

Cramant lace, supple, refined, ethereal, even if it does have a touch too much dosage: a clearly high-class terroir.

PREMIER CRU ROSÉ

Brut Rosé | 2011 up to 2013   86

Light color, showing excellently well-preserved freshness of the pinot noir fruit, simple but very pleasant.

Red: 1.7 acres; pinot 100%. White: 20.5 acres; chardonnay 100%. Annual production: 100,000 bottles

LARMANDIER-BERNIER
⚜ ⚜ ⚜ ⚜

19, avenue du Général-de-Gaulle
51130 Vertus
Phone 00 33 3 26 52 13 24
Fax 00 33 3 26 52 21 00
champagne@larmandier.fr
www.larmandier.fr

Pierre Larmandier is surely the most thoughtful winegrower in Vertus and the one who achieves the most precise expression of this terroir. His work is based on straightforward principles that are largely borrowed from Anselme Selosse: ecofriendly viticultural practices that are in advance of those generally accepted in Champagne, and a hands-off approach to vinification. The naturalness displayed by his Champagnes is exemplary but their popularity (though well deserved) does lead Larmandier to release them too early. Apart from his exceptional old-vines Cramant, his most emblematic wine is Terres de Vertus, a terroir Champagne with stunning finesse—though all of the recent bottlings seemed rather too "young." The red Coteaux Champenois surprises us with each new tasting: its beautiful aromas and finesse are unmatched by any Premier Cru available today!

Recently tasted
VIEILLE VIGNE DE CRAMANT GRAND CRU EXTRA-BRUT
Brut White | 2011 up to 2013   95

Older vintages
BLANC DE BLANCS PREMIER CRU EXTRA-BRUT
Brut White | 2011 up to 2013   94
Very fine, extremely pure and natural, this is a perfect example of "natural" yet masterfully produced Champagne. Wondrous elegance.

COTEAUX CHAMPENOIS VERTUS ROUGE 2005
Red | 2015 up to 2020   90
More robust than the famous 2002, as well as more tannic, denser, and without doubt less supremely elegant. A slight excess of somewhat astringent oakiness.

TERRE DE VERTUS PREMIER CRU NON DOSÉ
Brut White | 2011 up to 2013   92
With rare richness and aromatic complexity and an absolute purity in its expression, this is a wine of great character and great precision. A magnificent example of the superiority of honest winemaking.

TRADITION PREMIER CRU EXTRA-BRUT
Brut White | 2011 up to 2013   90
Fine color, very pure nose, pleasant fruitiness, ideal balance in acidity, very well-integrated dosage; it is hard to do better for an entry-level Champagne.

VIEILLE VIGNE DE CRAMANT GRAND CRU
EXTRA-BRUT 2003
Brut White | 2011 up to 2013   **92**
Extremely unusual due to its vintage and
oak aging, this Champagne drinks like a wine,
with striking richness on the palate and powerful autolysis. Destined for the table rather
than as an aperitif.

VIEILLE VIGNE DE CRAMANT GRAND CRU
EXTRA-BRUT 2002
Brut White | 2012 up to 2022   **90**
Still too young to express its origins; wait
three or four years.

Red: 4.9 acres; pinot noir 100%. White: 34.6 acres;
chardonnay 100%. Annual production: 130,000
bottles

LAURENT-PERRIER

32, Avenue de Champagne
51150 Tours-sur-Marne
Phone 00 33 3 26 58 91 22
Fax 00 33 3 26 58 77 29
al.domenichini@laurent-perrier.fr
www.laurent-perrier.fr

Laurent-Perrier remains largely family
owned despite its listing on the French
stock market. The house has seen spectacular growth since the 1950s, spurred on
by Bernard de Nonancourt, one of the
major players in the modern Champagne
industry. It was his idea to create a slender,
aperitif style of Champagne based on
chardonnay-driven blends. He was also
the first to spot the potential in rosé Champagne, launching what has since become
one of the company's leading products,
alongside the refined, ultrapure "Grand
Siècle." The first ever multivintage prestige cuvée, Grand Siècle is now once again
blended from several vintages following
an exceptional vintage-dated edition
(Grand Siècle Exceptionellement Millésimé). LP Brut is another of the company's mainstays and is now back on form
after its slightly shaky performance a few
years back: dynamic but slender character
and particularly notable for its well-judged
dosage.

BRUT L.P.
Brut White | 2011 up to 2013   **89**
Fairly vigorous and very direct, this is a good,
fresh, intense Champagne that will make
for a perfect aperitif. A very good Brut, appetite-whetting and refined.

BRUT ROSÉ
Brut Rosé | 2011 up to 2013   **89**
White gold, with scents of Reims cookies and
easy-drinking bubbles. An accessible, round,
fresh and balanced style. An enticing wine.

BRUT VINTAGE 1999
Brut White | 2011 up to 2015   **90**
Supple and suave, a tender, harmonious
Champagne with the freshness but also the
limitations of a vintage that lacks energy.

BRUT VINTAGE 1997
Brut White | 2011 up to 2015   **91**
This vintage develops perfectly in the house
style, i.e., refined, ethereal, very fresh, with
great aromatic charm punctuated by fine
citrus notes.

GRAND SIÈCLE

Brut White | 2011 up to 2017 — **96**

This Champagne, which is delicate and of great elegance, has very fine and particularly harmonious bubbles. It is brilliant for its perfect freshness.

GRAND SIÈCLE ALEXANDRA ROSÉ 1998

Brut Rosé | 2011 up to 2017 — **98**

The quintessence of Laurent-Perrier: pale in color, a delicate, brilliant aromatic palette, svelte length, intense, infinitely racy.

ULTRA BRUT

Brut White | 2011 up to 2013 — **91**

A taut, lively, and dynamic Champagne. The bubbles are tiny and quick, in the appetite-whetting style of the house.

Annual production: 9,000,000 bottles

MARIE-NOËLLE LEDRU

5, place de La Croix
51150 Ambonnay
Phone 00 33 3 26 57 09 26
Fax 00 33 3 26 58 87 61
info@champagne-mnledru.com

Marie-Noëlle Ledru operates a small artisan winery in Ambonnay. An exemplary winegrower, she makes wines in her own image—honest, robust, and sincere—that are sure to delight lovers of authentic Champagne. Price remains reasonable. The most recent bottlings are made in a style that has long been a favorite of ours, particularly Le Goulté, a Brut that perfectly expresses its classy origins.

Recently tasted

MILLÉSIME 2004

Brut White | 2012 up to 2015 — **84**

Older vintages

BRUT GRAND CRU

Brut White | 2011 up to 2013 — **86**

Simple but straightforward, clean, easy to drink. A little short and marked by the 2003 vintage.

CUVÉE DU GOULTÉ 2003

Brut White | 2011 up to 2013 — **89**

With a very aromatic, powerful nose, not at all unbalanced as its vintage might lead us to fear, this is a rich wine that is almost velvety, with an astonishingly straightforward finish. Truly well made.

CUVÉE DU GOULTÉ 2002

Brut White | 2011 up to 2050 — **88**

Mineral, classic, fairly vinous, savory, well-made.

EXTRA-BRUT GRAND CRU

Brut White | 2011 up to 2015 — **84**

Very straightforward and "radical" on the nose, this is strict, taut, made to please purist connoisseurs.

GRAND CRU CUVÉE DU GOULTÉ 2002

Brut White | 2011 up to 2014 — **90**

Very pale with a complex, pure nose, delicately honeyed, this is very Ambonnay: refined, linear, sincere.

MILLÉSIME 1999

Brut White | 2011 up to 2015 — **92**

A magnificent expression of this Grand Cru terroir, with notes of acacia, green olive, toasted hazelnut, very long and savory, and especially, absolutely straightforward. Perfect craftsmanship.

Red: 12.4 acres; pinot 100%. White: 2.5 acres; chardonnay 100%. Annual production: 25,000 bottles

LILBERT-FILS

223, rue du Moutier
BP 14
51530 Cramant
Phone 00 33 3 26 57 50 16
Fax 00 33 3 26 58 93 86
info@champagne-lilbert.com
www.champagne-lilbert.com

A tiny property wedded to rigorously styled wines with very low dosage plus a hint of rusticity that together accentuate the mineral character of the Cramant and Chouilly terroirs. The bulk of production goes to make the Cuvée Perle, usually blended from three vintages and flawlessly consistent. All of the wines will reward two to three years' bottle aging after purchase. The latest Perle is bursting with vitality and should reach its peak within two years.

Blanc de blancs Cramant 2002
Brut White | 2011 up to 2013   **93**
Ideally crystalline on the nose and on the palate. A wine of great nobility and exemplary evenhandedness, able to age a long time; the essence of the best Cramants on the Chouilly side, and vice versa.

Brut blanc de blancs grand cru Perle
Brut White | 2011 up to 2013   **90**
Pale, very pure, linear, mineral on the nose, impeccable dosage, exemplary lightness and faithfulness to the terroir; excellent.

Brut blanc de blancs grand cru Perle
Brut White | 2011 up to 2013   **88**
Cutting and pure, nice balance, ideally saline for an aperitif; a Champagne for connoisseurs.

White: 86.5 acres; chardonnay 100%. Annual production: 27,000 bottles

YVES LOUVET

21, rue du Poncet
51150 Tauxières
Phone 00 33 3 26 57 03 27
Fax 00 33 3 26 57 67 77
yves.louvet@wanadoo.fr
www.champagne-yves-louvet.com

Yves Louvet specializes in Champagne from the Tauxières Premier Cru, near Louvois and Bouzy. For years now, he has been turning out very vinous wines that offer good value for money. Recent bottlings show a tendency to heaviness, but the wines presented last year were faultless.

Brut Réserve
Brut White | 2011 up to 2013   **90**
Slightly amber in color, this is a magnificent expression of the Marne Valley, combining power, tension, complexity, and persistence; one of the best nonvintage Bruts in our tasting.

Brut Sélection
Brut White | 2011 up to 2013   **89**
Excellent, on the whole: powerful, vinous, very clean, very savory, with an ideal quality-price ratio.

Millésime 1999
Brut White | 2011 up to 2014   **88**
Very powerful, confirmed notes of honey and butter, a wine for the table, uncommonly broad; not for everyone.

Red: 17.3 acres; pinot 100%. White: 4.9 acres; chardonnay 100%. Annual production: 40,000 bottles

MAILLY GRAND CRU

🍷 🍷 🍷 🍷 🍷

28, rue de la Libération
51500 Mailly-Champagne
Phone 00 33 3 26 49 41 10
Fax 00 33 3 26 49 42 27
contact@champagne-mailly.com
www.champagne-mailly.com

Mailly Champagne stands out from other Champagne wine cooperatives by virtue of its comparatively small size and very consistent range of Champagnes. All of them are exclusively made from the local wines, Mailly Village, after which this cooperative is named, being a Grand Cru Classé. Thanks to the overall good quality of the grapes, Mailly can produce a range of wines with a remarkably uniform style, carefully supervised by gifted winemaker Hervé Dantan. Mailly Grand Cru wines are pinot noir–driven and are neither as powerful as those from Aÿ or Ambonnay nor as taut as those from Verzenay. But their finesse is more immediately obvious, supported by a particular balance that makes them very harmonious whatever the age of the wine. Those qualities are most stunningly expressed by Mailly's accomplished prestige cuvées which can easily rival the very best available in Champagne today.

Recently tasted
BLANC DE NOIRS
Brut White | 2011 up to 2013   **90**

LES ÉCHANSONS 1999
Brut White | 2011 up to 2015   **92**

Older vintages
BRUT MILLÉSIMÉ 2002

Brut White | 2011 up to 2014   **91**
With fine aromas of red fruit, this is deeply appetizing, with a balance falling between meaty and refined: a racy Champagne made for the table.

BRUT MILLÉSIMÉ 1999
Brut White | 2011 up to 2013   **90**
Very linear, powerful, deep, long, and elegant, marked by the pinot noir. A pretty wine with a fresh finish.

BRUT RÉSERVE
Brut White | 2011 up to 2013   **90**
A fine Champagne, well rounded and vinous yet refined and racy. A fine, distinguished, streamlined aperitif.

DEMI-SEC
Semi-Dry White | 2011 up to 2013   **88**
A good dessert Champagne, ample on the palate and fragrant with notes of meringue and pastry. Very well-integrated dosage.

EXTRA-BRUT
Brut White | 2011 up to 2013   **90**
With fine extract, great vigor, and heady aromas of red fruit that are deeply, authentically rooted, this is a superb aperitif Champagne.

L'INTEMPORELLE 2003
Brut White | 2011 up to 2013   **92**
Full, subtle, deep, without palpable acidity, this vintage is the opposite of a sharp Champagne, but its refined texture and fruity, smooth elegance are currently delicious.

L'INTEMPORELLE 2002
Brut White | 2011 up to 2014   **90**
A brilliant, refined Champagne. Pretty notes of red fruit, rich depth, and full body. A Champagne for the table, still young.

LE FEU 2000
Brut White | 2011 up to 2014   **91**
A Champagne with character, with aromas of fresh butter and toasted grain, long and ample on the palate, vigorous yet refined. Another year in the bottle will do it some good. With air, pleasant bitter orange notes emerge.

LES ÉCHANSONS 1998
Brut White | 2011 up to 2015   **91**
Les Échansons has a vinous, powerful style that benefits from long aging and is well suited to the table. This structured, solid vintage is a success, even if its aromatic character, slightly staler than that found in other bottlings in the lineup, might disturb those who are used to fruity, floral Champagnes.

Red: pinot noir 100%. White: chardonnay 100%.
Annual production: 500,000 bottles

MOËT & CHANDON

20, avenue de Champagne
51200 Épernay
Phone 00 33 3 26 51 20 00
Fax 00 33 3 26 54 84 23
contact@moet.fr
www.moet.com

The real professionals in Champagne venerate Moët & Chandon as the Grande Maison. Big it most certainly is, and not just because of its size. Historically speaking, Moët & Chandon has been the major player in Champagne since the eighteenth century. The first-ever modern prestige cuvée was invented by one of Moët's most emblematic owners, Count Robert de Vogüe, just before World War II. Though a heavyweight in economic terms, Moët & Chandon has never crushed the competition, especially not the growers with whom it has forged precious relationships over the years. Volume-wise, Moët is of course a giant, with an annual production of nearly thirty million bottles. It can cater to such gigantic demand thanks to house vineyards that have more than doubled in fifteen years (through the notable addition of Champagne Pommery) and thanks especially to long-term contracts with growers. Moët Champagne is always very consistently made, and all of the wines—from the Brut Impérial to the 2000 edition of the Vintage range—have displayed measurably more freshness in recent years under the inspiration of brilliant cellar master Benoît Gouez. The uneven 2003 vintage is very impressive here.

Brut Impérial
Brut White | 2011 up to 2013   **87**
Streamlined and more direct than in the past, the most frequently sold Champagne bottling in the world has a very appetite-whetting frankness to it.

Brut Impérial Rosé
Brut Rosé | 2011 up to 2013   **87**
A colorful, ample rosé with good balance and a round, straightforward style.

Brut Vintage 2003
Brut White | 2011 up to 2014   **92**
Brilliantly suave, ethereal and streamlined, tender without being soft, this is a splendid bottling from a complicated vintage: a great success.

Brut Vintage 2000
Brut White | 2011 up to 2014   **89**
This vintage affirms its personality, with very fruity aromas and great freshness on the palate.

Vintage Rosé 2003
Brut Rosé | 2011 up to 2014   **95**
Pure pleasure: soft aromas of wild strawberries, a slick, tender attack, great freshness despite very low acidity, velvety, aromatically persistent.

Vintage Rosé 2000
Brut Rosé | 2011 up to 2014   **90**
With a light and subtle tint and a round, savory body, this is very well constructed, with elegant raspberry aromas and delicate freshness.

Annual production: 29,700,000 bottles

PIERRE MONCUIT

11, rue Persault-Maheu
51190 Le Mesnil-sur-Oger
Phone 00 33 3 26 57 52 65
Fax 00 33 3 26 57 97 89
contact@pierre-moncuit.fr
www.pierre-moncuit.fr

This large estate always turns out very consistent Blanc de Blancs—somewhat more supple and forward than the majority of its peers, but with all the finesse and purity for which Mesnil is renowned. The cuvée Hugues de Coulmet comes from vines around Sézanne and shows real quality though not, of course, the same degree of finesse and class as the Grands Crus. A parcel of very old vines at the heart of Mesnil yields a tiny volume of one of the greatest Blanc de Blancs imaginable: the fabulous cuvée Nicole Moncuit.

Recently tasted

BLANC DE BLANCS GRAND CRU VIEILLES VIGNES NICOLE MONCUIT 1990
Brut White | 2011 up to 2013   **92**

MILLÉNAIRE 2002
Brut White | 2011 up to 2014   **88**

Older vintages

BLANC DE BLANCS GRAND CRU 2002
Brut White | 2011 up to 2017   **89**
Still a little young, this has a creamy body with some lactic notes that mask the terroir's minerality a bit, but savory, crowd-pleasing.

BLANC DE BLANCS GRAND CRU 1999
Brut White | 2011 up to 2019   **90**
Very good but still somewhat weighed down by its dosage; a lot of fruit, finesse, and length, however. Can still age longer.

BLANC DE BLANCS GRAND CRU 1996
Brut White | 2011 up to 2016   **94**
The ideal expression of the terroir, vinous, great style, a great vintage.

BLANC DE BLANCS GRAND CRU
Brut White | 2011 up to 2013   **86**
Great cleanness and straightforwardness on the nose, balanced on the palate, a somewhat simple finish for a Grand Cru and slightly too much dosage.

BLANC DE BLANCS GRAND CRU VIEILLES VIGNES NICOLE MONCUIT 1996
Brut White | 2011 up to 2016   **92**
A little more suave than the normal 1996, with immense finesse, this is a tender, refined wine with inimitable fruit.

White: 46.9 acres; chardonnay 100%. Annual production: 200,000 bottles

G.H. MUMM

29, rue du Champ-de-Mars
51100 Reims
Phone 00 33 3 26 49 59 69
Fax 00 33 3 26 40 46 13
mumm@mumm.com
www.mumm.com

In the 1980s, Mumm was the number-two Champagne brand. Now owned by the Pernod-Ricard Group, it is enjoying a comeback thanks to wines of more consistent quality—clean, supple, and immediately approachable. A sure sign of this revival is Mumm's new and long-awaited prestige cuvée, R. Lalou 1998, named in homage to Mumm chairman and winemaker René Lalou and the first prestige cuvée to be made under this label since 1985. The house now has the means, and certainly the ambition, to get back on top.

BRUT GRAND CRU
Brut White | 2011 up to 2013   **90**
More than any other, this bottling displays the craftsmanship and style of the house: it is full-bodied, ample, and tasty as well as supple and fresh, with delightful hazelnut notes.

CORDON ROUGE
Brut White | 2011 up to 2013   **87**
A supple, enjoyable Champagne; very clean, fruity, and versatile.

CORDON ROUGE MILLÉSIMÉ 1999
Brut White | 2011 up to 2014   **90**
Great precision and composition, a taut, appealing texture, linear without being heavy-handed, enticing aromatics with notes of fresh butter, toast, and hazelnuts.

CORDON ROUGE MILLÉSIMÉ 1998
Brut White | 2011 up to 2014   **90**
A solid, ample vintage with real vigor on the palate. This is a very successful cuvée.

MUMM DE CRAMANT GRAND CRU BRUT CHARDONNAY
Brut White | 2011 up to 2017   **92**
Delicious, suave expression of the great whites of Cramant, with a taffeta texture, ultrafine bubbles, and a happy combination of citrus zest and mineral nuances.

R. LALOU 1998
Brut White | 2011 up to 2013   **92**
With an additional year in the bottle, the first vintage of this prestige cuvée affirms its round, generous, instantly appealing character, which finishes with fresh, savory, toasty notes.

Red: 462.1 acres; pinot noir 97%, pinot meunier 3%.
White: 76.6 acres; chardonnay 100%. Annual production: 8,000,000 bottles

BRUNO PAILLARD

Avenue de Champagne
51100 Reims
Phone 00 33 3 26 36 20 22
Fax 00 33 3 26 36 57 72
info@brunopaillard.com
www.champagnebrunopaillard.com

Bruno Paillard is one of the very few native Champenois who has managed to craft a real entrepreneurial strategy within an ever more corporately controlled environment. Currently chief shareholder of the Boizel Chanoine Champagne Group, he also founded and runs this Champagne house, which offers a complete range from the impeccable NV Brut to the prestige cuvée, Nec Plus Ultra, as well as vintages with original labels, each one designed by a different artist.

ASSEMBLAGE 1999
Brut White | 2011 up to 2016   90
A vinous Champagne with much more character and fruit than most 1999s.

ASSEMBLAGE 1996
Brut White | 2011 up to 2014   91
This 1996 is a very vinous, intense, and powerful Champagne that is now blossoming into candied fruit and somewhat drier oaky notes. A fine Champagne for food.

BLANC DE BLANCS RÉSERVE PRIVÉE
Brut White | 2011 up to 2013   90
Elegant, fruity, straightforward, and appetite-whetting, a good, classic Blanc de Blancs with citrus and floral notes.

BRUT PREMIÈRE CUVÉE
Brut White | 2011 up to 2013   90
Low dosage, very appealing, expressing enticing citrus notes, yet finely ripe on the palate: an impeccable nonvintage Brut.

N.P.U. 1995
Brut White | 2011 up to 2020   94
NPU stands for "Nec Plus Ultra." The deliberately ambitious character of this wine justifies the name: aromas of candied fruits and torrefaction, a vinous yet unctuous expression on the palate, great balance, character, and depth. A brilliant and powerful success.

PREMIÈRE CUVÉE ROSÉ
Brut Rosé | 2011 up to 2013   89
Fruity, supple, straightforward, with perfect (that is to say, imperceptible) dosage, more lively than we remember it from our previous tastings.

Red: 39.5 acres; pinot noir 52%, pinot meunier 48%. White: 22.2 acres; chardonnay 100%. Annual production: 500,000 bottles

PALMER & CO

67, rue Jacquart
51100 Reims
Phone 00 33 3 26 07 35 07
Fax 00 33 3 26 07 45 24
champagne.palmer@wanadoo.fr

Palmer & Co is a discreet but very dependable Champagne cooperative, producing irresistibly fresh and expansive wines at every price point, from the impeccable Brut, to rare and venerable vintages that are worth knowing about even if they are difficult to get hold of. Perfect as a classy aperitif and flawlessly consistent for many years, thanks to rigorous grape selection using only the very best fruit available from co-op members.

Recently tasted
BLANC DE BLANCS 2004
Brut White | 2011 up to 2013   90

Older vintages
AMAZONE DE PALMER BRUT
Brut White | 2011 up to 2014   90
This prestige bottling has a great deal of intensity and generosity, but one might prefer the purity and direct nature of the house's 2002 Brut and Blanc de Blancs bottlings.

BLANC DE BLANCS 2002
Brut White | 2011 up to 2015   90
A very pure, linear, and racy Blanc de Blancs, brilliantly structured in its finesse and persistence.

BLANC DE BLANCS 2000
Brut White | 2011 up to 2015   92
Lively and very fruity, this energetic Blanc de Blancs has true distinction. A fine success.

BRUT
Brut White | 2011 up to 2013   86
Fat, ample, harmonious, and fresh, this is an excellent nonvintage Brut to drink as an aperitif. The prettily mineral finish is particularly enjoyable.

BRUT MILLÉSIMÉ 2002
Brut White | 2011 up to 2017   91
With good depth and body, this intense Champagne, with its aromas of small red fruits, is indisputably worth cellaring: its potential is remarkable.

BRUT MILLÉSIMÉ 1998
Brut White | 2011 up to 2014   86
With toasty aromas, this is a serious Champagne, though it is less appealing than the vintage Blanc de Blancs.

Red: pinot noir 84%, pinot meunier 16%. White: chardonnay 100%. Annual production: 3,000,000 bottles

PANNIER

23, rue Roger-Catillon
BP 300
02406 Château-Thierry cedex
Phone 00 33 3 23 69 51 30
Fax 00 33 3 23 69 51 31
champagnepannier@champagnepannier.com
www.champagnepannier.com

A very seriously run Champagne house, with vineyards somewhat off the beaten track for a producer of this standing. This is because in 1971 it was taken over by a wine co-op in Château Thierry, at the western tip of the AOC area and the Marne Valley vineyards. It nevertheless produces a range of wines that deliver a pure and honest expression of the Champagne appellation; the pinot-driven cuvées take terroir character to another dimension.

Recently tasted

ÉGÉRIE EXTRA-BRUT 2000
Brut White | 2011 up to 2013   89

ROSÉ VELOURS
Rosé | 2011 up to 2013   86

Older vintages

BRUT BLANC DE NOIRS LOUIS EUGÈNE 2002
Brut White | 2011 up to 2013   92
The best of this house can be found here: superbly vinous, impeccably fresh in its fruity aromas, with intense, svelte length. Magnificent!

BRUT BLANC DE NOIRS LOUIS EUGÈNE 1999
Brut White | 2011 up to 2013   89
A pretty Champagne with very present red-fruit aromas both on the nose and on the palate, structured, long, and straightforward.

BRUT MILLÉSIMÉ 2000
Brut White | 2011 up to 2020   89
An example of masterful dosage, this wine is very clean, without artifice and with good elegance.

BRUT ROSÉ
Brut Rosé | 2011 up to 2015   84
A fruity, supple rosé, pleasantly raspberried, but without great personality.

BRUT SÉLECTION
Brut White | 2011 up to 2013   87
A linear, straightforward Champagne of middling complexity, but immediately pleasant and extremely versatile.

ÉGÉRIE EXTRA-BRUT 1999
Brut White | 2011 up to 2013   91
Very fine aromas of lemon zest and candied orange and a velvety texture make this prestige bottling an elegant success.

ÉGÉRIE ROSÉ DE SAIGNÉE
Brut Rosé | 2011 up to 2013   90
Ample and well built, this healthy rosé has a very alluring bouquet of small red fruits and flowers, and a fresh intensity on the palate.

EXTRA-BRUT SÉLECTION
Brut White | 2011 up to 2013   88
A newcomer to the lineup, this nondosage bottling offers an excitingly straightforward, appetite-whetting, fruity character.

VINTAGE 2002
Brut White | 2011 up to 2015   90
A little less energetic than the Blanc de Noirs, but a fine, well-rounded wine, ample, with deep, intense fruit and definite length.

VINTAGE 2000
Brut White | 2011 up to 2014   88
Well-built and appetizing, this is a seriously structured Champagne, made for the start of a meal.

Red: 160.6 acres; pinot meunier 50%, pinot noir 50%. White: 12.4 acres; chardonnay 100%. Annual production: 600,000 bottles

PHILIPPONNAT

13, rue du Pont
51160 Mareuil-sur-Aÿ
Phone 00 33 3 26 56 93 00
Fax 00 33 3 26 56 93 18
commercial.france@
champagnephilipponnat.com
www.champagnephilipponnat.com

For many years the only really interesting thing about this Champagne house was its outstanding Clos des Goisses: an intensely vinous Champagne from a vineyard on a steep south-facing slope overlooking the Marne River. But following the takeover by Boizel Chanoine Champagne, director Charles Philipponnat, a distant relative of the founder, has been turning out a complete range of Champagne wines that get more interesting by the minute: generous and solid, with a mature, distinctive personality whatever the style.

Recently tasted
BRUT 1522 2002
Brut White | 2011 up to 2016   91

BRUT GRAND BLANC 2002
Brut White | 2011 up to 2013   90

CLOS DES GOISSES 2000
Brut White | 2012 up to 2022   95

ROYALE RÉSERVE NON DOSÉE
Brut White | 2011 up to 2013   90

Older vintages
BRUT 1522 2000
Brut White | 2011 up to 2013   89
In the house style, powerful, racy, and vinous, this dense Champagne is destined for the table, notably with poultry.

BRUT GRAND BLANC 1999
Brut White | 2011 up to 2013   89
An elegant, complex Champagne with fine, creamy bubbles.

BRUT PREMIER CRU ROSÉ 2000
Brut Rosé | 2011 up to 2013   90
A fine success: superb red-fruit aromas and remarkable fullness on the palate, with an energetic, ethereal style.

CLOS DES GOISSES 1997
Brut White | 2011 up to 2015   91
Very vigorous on the palate, this fine, vinous, straightforward Champagne, with an aromatic palette of red fruit and grain, will pair wonderfully with white meat.

CLOS DES GOISSES JUSTE ROSÉ 1999
Brut Rosé | 2011 up to 2013   91
The color is a delicate salmon shade; on the nose and on the palate is the powerful character of a specific terroir. This is a Champagne for the table, perfect with feathered game.

RÉSERVE MILLÉSIMÉE 1999
Brut White | 2011 up to 2013   88
A vinous Champagne with notes of toasted grain, appetizing and fleshy on the palate, fairly well rounded.

RÉSERVE ROSÉE
Brut Rosé | 2011 up to 2014   90
With notes of pastry and raspberry and firm bubbles, this is a delicate, fleshy wine with a middling finish and a fair amount of sweetness; a rosé for the table.

ROYALE RÉSERVE
Brut White | 2011 up to 2014   89
With ample mousse, this is a creamy, ripe Champagne with pear tart notes. Appetizing, with an ethereal, well-balanced finish.

SEC SUBLIME RÉSERVE
White | 2011 up to 2013   89
This is one of the best "Sec" Champagnes (i.e., sweet, as opposed to Brut) out there: the dosage works perfectly with the blend. Both vinous and ripe, the wine is drinking beautifully now.

Red: 48.2 acres; pinot noir 100%. White: 1.2 acres; chardonnay 100%. Annual production: 700,000 bottles

PIPER-HEIDSIECK

12, allée du Vignoble
51100 Reims
Phone 00 33 3 26 84 43 00
Fax 00 33 3 26 84 43 49
www.piper-heidsieck.com

Piper-Heidsieck is the number-two brand of French wines-and-spirits group Rémy-Cointreau. It is made by the same wine-making team as Charles Heidsieck, under guidance from the same cellar master. The style is nevertheless quite different, Piper being distinctly less complex and mature but fruity, approachable, and well-balanced. The NV Brut always used to strike us as inappropriately sweet; but now that they've eased up on the dosage, the entire range is eminently respectable.

BRUT MILLÉSIME 2000
Brut White | 2011 up to 2015   88
A good, solid, and fairly well-rounded Champagne, but in a somewhat heavy-handed style.

BRUT RÉSERVE
Brut White | 2011 up to 2013   88
Finesse and freshness in a Champagne with well-ministered dosage, elegant and refined: a bottling that is markedly improving.

BRUT SAUVAGE ROSÉ
Brut Rosé | 2011 up to 2013   88
Once you get used to the striking style and especially the very pronounced pink color of this Champagne, it quickly becomes one of those you're unlikely to forget, from its pretty strawberry aromas to its long, smooth finish.

RARE 1999
Brut White | 2011 up to 2019   95
An unctuous, refined Champagne with scents of fresh butter and brioche, remarkably savory and well rounded on the palate.

RARE 1988
Brut White | 2011 up to 2019   95
Piper commercializes some "collection" wines, including this magnificent, unctuous 1988, with its aromas of coffee liqueur and candied fruit, its calm but intense character, and its great, generous depth.

SUBLIME
Semi-Dry White | 2011 up to 2013   90
This bottling, with its delicate dosage, has remarkable balance between sweetness and elegance. An admirable Champagne for the end of a meal.

Annual production: 8,000,000 bottles

POL-ROGER

1, rue Henri-le-Large
BP 199
51206 Épernay cedex
Phone 00 33 3 26 59 58 00
Fax 00 33 3 26 55 25 70
polroger@polroger.fr
www.polroger.com

This medium-size house is still owned by its founding families. Pol-Roger made its name in the nineteenth century thanks to high-class vintages like the 1928, which placed it firmly among the elite of Champagnes. It also had a devoted customer, Winston Churchill, who made this brand his personal bedside choice. After a lackluster period a while back, the house has been back on track since the mid-1990s. All of the current cuvées are without exception superb, starting with the impeccable Brut Réserve.

BLANC DE BLANCS VINTAGE 1999
Brut White | 2011 up to 2015   97
Very fine, smooth and refined, a little more tender than the Vintage of the same year, but incomparably velvety. Amazingly classy.

BRUT CHARDONNAY
Brut White | 2011 up to 2015   96
Splendidly linear and deep, this is an intense, mineral chardonnay of remarkable length and great purity.

BRUT RÉSERVE
Brut White | 2011 up to 2013   88
Deep and ample, this is a very high-end non-vintage Brut. Connoisseurs will nonetheless prefer the lack of dosage in the Pure bottling.

ROSÉ VINTAGE 2000
Brut Rosé | 2011 up to 2013   92
The bouquet has great spirit and recalls the famous strawberry-flavored Reims biscuits; on the whole, it has great elegance and is well constructed and fresh.

SIR WINSTON CHURCHILL 1998
Brut White | 2011 up to 2020   97
We advise the fortunate owners of this wine to wait two or three more years before opening it: still very youthful, almost unbridled, this young Churchill is devilishly racy, with the combative, exuberant spirit of the man who inspired it.

SIR WINSTON CHURCHILL 1996
Brut White | 2011 up to 2020   95
Very refined, very pure, long and intense, perhaps less impressive at this point than the 1998 cuvées, yet brilliant for its superb elegance.

VINTAGE 1999
Brut White | 2011 up to 2016   96
Taffeta texture, unctuous and fresh, with great persistence on the palate: one of the best expressions of a 1999 vintage, rarely illustrated in Champagne with as much class.

VINTAGE 1998
Brut White | 2011 up to 2020   96
Very vinous and superbly pure: a long, powerful, intense Champagne that needs more time to open completely.

Red: 234.7 acres; pinot noir 33%, pinot meunier 67%. White: 222.4 acres; chardonnay 100%. Annual production: 1,600,000 bottles

POMMERY

5, place du Général-Gouraud
51100 Reims
Phone 00 33 3 26 61 62 56
Fax 00 33 3 26 61 62 96
domaine@vrankenpommery.fr
www.vrankenpommery.com

Pommery is one of the great historic brands of Champagne, heir to some of the most impressive and magnificent facilities in the entire region. Since the early 1980s the house has changed hands four times and had its fair share of ups and downs. Former owner, luxury goods group LVMH, kept hold of Pommery's 750-acre vineyard before selling the brand to Belgian Champagne magnate Paul-François Vranken. Now the flagship of the Vranken Group, Pommery has rediscovered its essential purpose. The standard of wine today seems very good across the board, epitomizing, in particular, that refined, fluid style much loved by generations of Pommery cellar masters.

Recently tasted
LOUISE 1999
Brut White | 2011 up to 2016   94

Older vintages
BRUT APANAGE
Brut White | 2011 up to 2013   86
Certainly more appropriate for connoisseurs than the house's classic Brut, here is a nice, svelte, slender Champagne with perfect dosage, very appetite-whetting.

BRUT GRAND CRU 1998
Brut White | 2011 up to 2013   91
Ready to drink now, this Champagne plays the power card more than the house's other bottlings; on the whole, it has character.

LOUISE 1998
Brut White | 2011 up to 2018   96
A magnificent Champagne, refined and intense, delicate and brilliant. The tiny red fruit aromas are infinitely delicate, and on the palate, the wine is tender and subtle, appealing yet long.

ROSÉ APANAGE
Brut Rosé | 2011 up to 2013   90
Fine fruit that is expressed well, supple and delicate; noticeable dosage but indisputably elegant character.

Red: 1,025.5 acres. White: 642.5 acres. Annual production: 4,500,000 bottles

ROEDERER

🍾 🍾 🍾 🍾

21, boulevard Lundy
51100 Reims
Phone 00 33 3 26 40 42 11
Fax 00 33 3 26 47 66 51
com@champagne-roederer.com
www.louis-roederer.com

Frédéric Rouzaud now succeeds his father, Jean-Claude, as head of this holding, which, together with Bollinger, is the most outstanding example of a Champagne house that has always been family-run. Despite the worldwide success of its prestige cuvée Cristal, Roederer has consistently refused to compete on quantity. It insists on retaining control of the grape supply, the bulk of its fruit coming from its own magnificent vineyards. The Roederer style is built on purity and honesty, producing Champagnes that can seem fairly simple in early youth but that always age with terrific finesse. Over the past twenty years, the family-owned Roederer group has diversified its portfolio, acquiring a constellation of wineries that include Ott in Provence, Ramos Pinto in Oporto, Pez and Pichon-Comtesse in the Médoc (particularly notable), and, of course, Deutz Champagne.

Recently tasted
BLANC DE BLANCS 2003
Brut White I 2011 up to 2015   **92**

CARTE BLANCHE
White I 2011 up to 2013   **91**

ROSÉ MILLÉSIMÉ 2004
Brut Rosé I 2011 up to 2015   **91**

Older vintages
BRUT PREMIER
Brut White I 2011 up to 2013   **90**
Ideally, this Brut should be cellared for a year or two so that its dosage can mesh perfectly with its slender, refined, and very linear body.

CRISTAL 2002
Brut White I 2011 up to 2020   **99**
Still very youthful and vivacious on the palate, this is a pure, intense Cristal, with a silky texture that is enlivened by tiny, quick bubbles. Great potential, such that it would be a shame to drink it now, given how promising its future is.

CRISTAL 2000
Brut White I 2011 up to 2016   **92**
Direct, pure, and svelte, the 2000 is entering its mature phase; this is a very complete Champagne.

ROSÉ MILLÉSIMÉ 2002
Brut Rosé I 2011 up to 2014   **93**
Very pure, delicate, but intensely fruity with its fine raspberry notes; a brilliant rosé, pale in color, with refined depth.

ROSÉ MILLÉSIMÉ 2000
Brut Rosé I 2011 up to 2013   **90**
Very pale pink gold in color, as the house prefers; a refined bouquet, tender on the palate, with a touch of subtle, deep vivacity, firmness, and delicacy.

VINTAGE 2002
Brut White I 2011 up to 2018   **93**
Great density and presence on the palate, intensely present fruit: undeniably, this vintage is a brilliant success.

Red: 333.6 acres; pinot noir 97%, pinot meunier 3%. White: 195.2 acres; chardonnay 100%. **Annual production:** 3,000,000 bottles

RUINART

4, rue des Crayères
BP 85
51053 Reims cedex
Phone 00 33 3 26 77 51 51
Fax 00 33 3 26 82 88 43
info@ruinart.com
www.ruinart.com

This Reims-based Champagne house is owned by parent company LVMH (Louis Vuitton Moët Hennessy) but retains its independence as a producer with a very distinctive style. Ruinart Champagnes tend to be chardonnay-driven and display delicately mineral character, hints of chalkiness subtly interweaving with floral and fruit aromas, with no trace of heaviness whatsoever—making them particularly ideal as an aperitif. Dom Ruinart, the house's white and rosé prestige cuvée, is now made in quite a clever, fresher style.

BLANC DE BLANCS
Brut White | 2011 up to 2014 **91**
In a style comparable to the Brut but with more defined subtlety and depth, this is a very fine Blanc de Blancs, deep and racy and wonderfully delicate.

BRUT
Brut White | 2011 up to 2013 **90**
One of the best current nonvintage Champagnes, with very fine notes of milky caramel and candied fruit. Perfect, i.e., "invisible," dosage and confirmed appetite-whetting character.

BRUT MILLÉSIMÉ 2000
Brut White | 2011 up to 2017 **92**
The house's mineral, ethereal style fully blossoms in this fine vintage, well-rounded, refined, with great length.

BRUT ROSÉ
Brut Rosé | 2011 up to 2013 **91**
The fruit is brilliant and delicate, with strawberry and raspberry notes; the body has great finesse: this is remarkably appetite-whetting.

DOM RUINART 1998
Brut White | 2011 up to 2015 **90**
Dense, deep, seriously built but less elegant than the wines of the previous decade.

DOM RUINART 1996
Brut White | 2011 up to 2020 **95**
Very linear, pure, mineral, racy, long and refined; the perfect illustration of a great Blanc de Blancs from a fine vintage.

Annual production: 3,000,000 bottles

SALON

5, rue de la Brèche-d'Oger
51190 Le-Mesnil-sur-Oger
Phone 00 33 3 26 57 51 65
Fax 00 33 3 26 57 79 29
champagne@salondelamotte.com
www.salondelamotte.com

The small Salon Champagne house was founded in the early twentieth century and now, as then, confines its production to a vintage Champagne exclusively made from chardonnay grapes grown in Le-Mesnil-sur-Oger—without doubt the most magnificent cru on the Côte des Blancs. Several of the vintages produced in the 1970s (1976) and 1980s (1982, 1988) are still proving this Champagne's terrific propensity for long and graceful aging. It has to be said, however, that Salon Champagne has never been better than it is now, under the inspired direction of the team in charge since Laurent-Perrier took over. Witness two recent vintages—the 1995 and 1996—both certainly the most precise and refined that the house has ever produced.

BRUT MILLÉSIMÉ 1997
Brut White | 2011 up to 2017 **94**
Refined, now entering a phase of full maturity, this Champagne elegantly expresses notes of toast and candied citrus zest. On the palate, this is a deep, brilliant, and elegant wine with an already tender finish.

BRUT MILLÉSIMÉ 1996
Brut White | 2011 up to 2020 **99**
To our taste, this is the greatest Salon in recent history, and certainly one of the greatest contemporary Champagnes. With phenomenal length, this wine ingeniously combines finesse and elegance, refinement and vivacity, and it ends with infinite notes of minerality and citrus zest.

BRUT MILLÉSIMÉ 1995
Brut White | 2011 up to 2025 **98**
A great Champagne that is deep and savory with blinding precision and definition and a personality that is as intense as but less round than the 1996.

BRUT MILLÉSIMÉ 1990
Brut White | 2011 up to 2025 **97**

An extremely refined, mineral style, with intense, svelte length: an incredibly racy affirmation of the Le Mesnil terroir.

Annual production: 60,000 bottles

JACQUES SELOSSE

22, rue Ernest-Vallé
51190 Avize
Phone 00 33 3 26 57 53 56
Fax 00 33 3 26 57 78 22
a.selosse@wanadoo.fr

Leading Côte des Blancs winemaker Anselme Selosse is an artist in his field and an inspiration to the new generation of idealistic winegrowers. His revolutionary approach to local viticulture is founded on biodynamic thinking, but all of his wines are still traditionally fermented in oak barrels. Their very assertive character is a tribute to the quality of Selosse's vineyards in Avize and Oger. Some batches do show signs of premature oxidation, but the vast majority of his Champagnes get a rave reception from even the most demanding connoisseurs. The most original wine from this estate—you either love it or hate it—is the Cuvée Substance. Known as a "solera" Champagne, it is made from more than ten different vintages that are raised together in the same cask—the idea being that the "oldest" brings on the "youngest." Not all of the wines undergo malolactic fermentation, and require slow aging to reach their peak. The crème de la crème are the rosé (sublimely complex nose), the Cuvée Contraste (pure Blanc de Noirs from Aÿ), and the 1988 vintage (available in pitifully small quantities only). Substance can vary from one bottle to another, as for instance in the otherwise exemplary Extra-Brut.

Recently tasted

CONTRASTE GRAND CRU
Brut White | 2011 up to 2016   94

INITIALE GRAND CRU
Brut White | 2011 up to 2015   92

Older vintages

BLANC DE BLANCS GRAND CRU 1998
Brut White | 2011 up to 2014   98
An incredibly racy wine, unfathomably complex and natural, this ideally expresses the best qualities of the vines at the heart of Avize's slopes. It is drinking beautifully now and demonstrates why this producer's vintage wines have earned cult status.

BLANC DE BLANCS GRAND CRU 1996
Brut White | 2011 up to 2016   99
Stocks of this are unfortunately depleted, but it is impossible not to recognize the eloquence and sublime aromatic complexity of this bottling, which brings to dazzling heights the expression of a vintage that is in all ways incomparable.

BRUT ROSÉ
Brut Rosé | 2011 up to 2015   92
A remarkable Ambonnay red is at the base of the magnificent rose aroma of this full-bodied rosé, which is refined and vinous and has an ideally minimal dosage.

CONTRASTE GRAND CRU
Brut White | 2011 up to 2014   94
A superb blend of fruit from Aÿ and Ambonnay, of fairly monumental structure, with rich flavors and ideal dosage. We are delighted to find in this rare bottling the precision and sure-handed vinification that made the producer famous.

INITIALE GRAND CRU
Brut White | 2011 up to 2015   90
A fine Blanc de Blancs, as creamy as one could wish, with fresh hazelnuts on the nose, opulence but perfect balance on the palate. A very complementary blend of the 2003, 2002, and 2001 vintages.

SUBSTANCE GRAND CRU
Brut White | 2011 up to 2015   90
This has a grandiose aromatic complexity derived from the beginnings of very elegant rancio notes that typify this bottling, which is constructed in the manner of an Andalusian solera and contains some ten (at least) vintages. A remarkably gastronomic wine, it is nonetheless not to be served to everyone.

VERSION ORIGINALE GRAND CRU
Brut White | 2011 up to 2015   92
This year we found the same slight flaw as last year, with a too-strong note of overripe apple. But that varies from bottle to bottle, because of the (excessive) risks taken.

Red: 2 acres; pinot 100%. White: 16.6 acres; chardonnay 100%. Annual production: 50,000 bottles

TAITTINGER

9, place Saint-Nicaise
51100 Reims
Phone 00 33 3 26 85 45 35
Fax 00 33 3 26 50 14 30
marketing@taittinger.fr
www.taittinger.com

The history of the great Champagne houses essentially dates back to the nineteenth century, when Champagne became famous worldwide and the all-conquering brand leaders established their reputation. This one is an exception, having only been founded by the celebrated Taittinger family in 1932. After the Taittinger Group was bought by an American company, the Champagne side of the business eventually reinstated part of the family, though Claude Taittinger preferred to pass the mantle to nephew Pierre-Emmanuel. Since then, the product range has remained basically unchanged, spearheaded as before by Taittinger's luxury bottling, the splendid Comtes de Champagne cuvée, one of the best of all the chardonnay-driven Champagnes and equally stunning in its pink incarnation. Another very lovely offering is Les Folies de la Marquetterie, a brilliant expression of Taittinger's historic Château de la Marquetterie vineyard.

Recently tasted
BRUT MILLÉSIMÉ 2004
Brut White | 2011 up to 2014   90

COMTES DE CHAMPAGNE ROSÉ 2004
Brut Rosé | 2011 up to 2016   96

Older vintages
BRUT MILLÉSIMÉ 2002
Brut White | 2011 up to 2014   88
A very enthusiastically fruity wine, with notes of raspberry and citrus, but, alas, marked by too-noticeable dosage, which uselessly weighs down the finish.

COMTES DE CHAMPAGNE BLANC DE BLANCS 1998
Brut White | 2011 up to 2018   95
With superb energy and elegance, this is certainly a very fine vintage Champagne for the star bottling of the house. A very classy aperitif.

COMTES DE CHAMPAGNE ROSÉ 2003
Brut Rosé | 2011 up to 2020   97
A delicate, deep wine with very tiny bubbles and low acidity, but without any softness; intense, finely aromatic, persistent, and extremely racy.

COMTES DE CHAMPAGNE ROSÉ 2002
Brut Rosé | 2011 up to 2020   98
The color is deep, the bouquet is superb, with notes of small, fresh red fruit; on the palate, it's ample, tasty, and extremely refined and suave, with a persistent, fresh finish: a work of art!

LES FOLIES DE LA MARQUETTERIE
Brut White | 2011 up to 2015   95
Produced from the Château de la Marquetterie vineyard, this bottling is brilliant in its refined texture, its fine and delicate vigorousness on the palate, and its refined, delicate aromas of meringue and citrus zest. This is a very distinguished Champagne.

PRÉLUDE GRANDS CRUS
Brut White | 2011 up to 2013   93
Made solely from Grands Crus, this Champagne seems deep, delicate, and distinguished all at once, with great length and undeniable class.

Annual production: 5,000,000 bottles

JEAN-LOUIS VERGNON

1, Grande Rue
51190 Le Mesnil-sur-Oger
Phone 00 33 3 26 57 53 86
Fax 00 33 3 26 52 07 06
contact@champagne-jl-vergnon.com
www.champagne-jl-vergnon.com

This small artisan winery in Mesnil has had its ups and downs over the past twenty years, but recent tastings indicate that production is now well up to the mark. The wines are pure and dynamic, made to deliver classic Côte des Blancs character rather than the most original (if not to say too original) expression of this celebrated terroir. The current nonvintage Brut is remarkable.

Recently tasted
BLANC DE BLANCS EXTRA-BRUT
Brut White | 2011 up to 2013   **86**

CONFIDENCE 2003
Brut White | 2011 up to 2013   **88**

Older vintages
BLANC DE BLANCS
Brut White | 2011 up to 2013   **88**
A true Le Mesnil wine, full, racy, with rare technical mastery. Highly recommended.

BLANC DE BLANCS EXTRA-BRUT
Brut White | 2011 up to 2013   **87**
A pure wine with a slight sulfur note on the nose, this is taut and balanced, with a slight bitterness that needs to smooth out; definitely an aperitif wine.

BLANC DE BLANCS GRAND CRU
Brut White | 2011 up to 2014   **86**
Fairly vinous and definitely of its terroir, but with perceptible bitterness and little elegance. Let it age a little more.

BRUT BLANC DE BLANCS MILLÉSIMÉ 2003
Brut White | 2011 up to 2013   **86**
A little heavier and more marked by its vintage than others, but rich in its extraction: it could come back into balance with age.

BRUT BLANC DE BLANCS MILLÉSIMÉ 2002
Brut White | 2011 up to 2013   **90**
Despite somewhat overbearing dosage, here is a fine Le Mesnil Champagne, vinous, taut, complex, very long, admirably made, to pair with lobster.

White: 13 acres; chardonnay 100%. Annual production: 50,000 bottles

VEUVE CLICQUOT-PONSARDIN

12, rue du Temple
51100 Reims
Phone 00 33 3 26 89 54 40
Fax 00 33 3 26 89 99 52
www.veuve-clicquot.com

Veuve Clicquot has plainly outstripped its competitors over the past twenty years. Production has more than doubled and in terms of image, Veuve Clicquot is now Champagne's most iconically glamorous brand. Despite this race for supremacy, the overall quality of production has never faltered, thanks to the talents and disciplined thinking of a brilliant winemaking team headed by cellar master Jacques Peters. The Brut Carte Jaune remains as supple and well built as ever; the new rosé is expertly put together and utterly seductive because of it; and the prestige Champagne cuvées, from the vintage cuvées to La Grande Dame, all show imposing, assertive personality.

Recently tasted
CAVE PRIVÉE 1990
Brut White | 2011 up to 2020   **96**

CAVE PRIVÉE 1980
Brut White | 2011 up to 2020   **95**

CAVE PRIVÉE ROSÉ 1989
Semi-Dry Rosé | 2011 up to 2020   **96**

Older vintages
BRUT CARTE JAUNE
Brut White | 2011 up to 2013   **86**
Perhaps less substantial than in the past, but still versatile: supple, balanced, fruity, perfect dosage.

BRUT ROSÉ
Brut Rosé | 2011 up to 2013   **88**
A supple, tender rosé with savory fruit and immediately appetite-whetting freshness.

DEMI-SEC
Semi-Dry White | 2011 up to 2013   **88**
A fine demi-sec, supple and balanced, with harmoniously integrated dosage.

LA GRANDE DAME 1998
Brut White | 2011 up to 2018   **98**
Light notes of small red fruits, long, ultra-refined, with superb elegance.

LA GRANDE DAME ROSÉ 1998
Brut Rosé | 2011 up to 2015   **95**
A remarkably elegant Champagne with a taffeta texture and very tiny bubbles. The bouquet, with pastry, wild strawberry and raspberry notes, is devilishly tempting.

Rare Vintage Reserve 1988
Brut White | 2011 up to 2030   **99**
On the nose and on the palate, the coffee and torrefaction notes are impressive. Total harmony, with a stunning sense of freshness.

Rare Vintage Reserve rosé 1985
Brut Rosé | 2011 up to 2020   **95**
This Champagne has great elegance and stunning freshness. It doesn't have the length of the 1988, but it remains tasty and immediately approachable.

Vintage 2002
Brut White | 2011 up to 2015   **88**
Supple, elegant, and fresh, this is an immediately appealing vintage wine, with straightforward, expressive red fruit aromas but not great intensity.

Vintage Rich 2002
Semi-Dry White | 2011 up to 2015   **90**
Deep, vinous, with well-integrated dosage; a fine success in its category.

Vintage rosé 2002
Brut Rosé | 2011 up to 2013   **92**
The great freshness and distinction of the fruit characterizes this long, vinous, light-footed, slender, brilliant rosé.

VILMART & CIE

4, rue de la République
51500 Rilly-La-Montagne
Phone 00 33 3 26 03 40 01
Fax 00 33 3 26 03 46 57
laurent.champs@champagnevilmart.fr
www.champagnevilmart.fr

Vilmart & Cie is a family estate that is much better known abroad than in France. It is painstakingly and lovingly tended by Laurent Champs, who takes great satisfaction in a job well done. The vines are planted in the Rilly-la-Montagne Premier Cru that provides ideal ripening conditions for all three approved Champagne varietals. We weren't especially impressed with the entry-level wines but the higher-end offerings made from seriously old vines are something else altogether. Traditionally matured in large wooden barrels, the Cuvée Grand Cellier d'Or and especially the Cœur de Cuvée achieve the utmost in complexity and aristocratic aromas. The Cœur de Cuvée 1999 is stunningly successful, a credit to venerable vines that deserve to become the mainstay of the house's future replantings.

Brut
Brut White | 2011 up to 2013   **88**
An entry-level wine: fresh, complex, impeccable dosage, slightly iodine on the finish, which will work well with shellfish.

Cœur de cuvée 2002
Brut White | 2011 up to 2017   **86**
The vanilla notes from the oak are still too present, but the body is full and balanced; this needs time.

Cœur de cuvée 1999
Brut White | 2011 up to 2014   **94**
A sumptuous bouquet with the force of character of very old vines that show the superiority of the plantings and rootstock of yore.

Grand Cellier d'Or 2000
Brut White | 2011 up to 2013   **92**
A wonderful Champagne with utter finesse, utterly delicate, ethereal, long, racy, worthy of the best prestige bottlings from the major houses.

Red: 10.9 acres; pinot noir 100%. White: 16.3 acres; chardonnay 100%. Annual production: 130,000 bottles

Bettane & Desseauve
Selections for Jura and Savoie

Jura and Savoie

Jura

The Jura region makes unusual reds and rosés from local grape varieties called poulsard (sometimes ploussard) and trousseau. The wines are lightly colored, rich in tannins with very unique flavors, sometimes softened by blending in a touch of pinot noir. In our opinion, though, the truly great wines from the region are white. Chardonnay, when vinified separately from certain areas near Arbois and in the southern part of the Côtes de Jura, can be quite expressive and flavorful, and the prices for these wines are often reasonable.

The star of the region is savagnin, an exceptional grape that is rich in sugar and high in acidity and has the amazing ability to grow a veil of yeast (*voile*). Savagnin is aged traditionally in oak barrels that aren't quite filled to the top; this allows the *voile* to grow on the surface of the wine, similar to the process in making Spanish sherry. This yeast protects the wine for six long years and allows the flavors to slowly deepen and become more complex. In other places this process would simply make vinegar, but here it makes Vin Jaune, with its inimitable flavor of walnuts and morel mushrooms, one of the most distinctive wines in the world.

The wines from the tiny Jura appellation have always had a loyal local following and have been consumed mostly in the region. This is starting to change, though, as many producers are breaking out and becoming well known throughout France and also to wine lovers internationally. The region produces unique wines with wonderfully individual personalities, and the new generation of winemakers has intelligently modernized the style of the wines. The dry whites made from chardonnay in the southern part of the appellation have set the tone, but the reds are following close behind, and the future lies with them.

Appellation Overview

• **Arbois and Arbois-Pupillin (a subdivision of the Arbois appellation):** The northern end of the Jura appellation, known for white, yellow, red, and rosé wines that are generously proportioned and have a rich bouquet but are rather delicate and "all-purpose" compared to other Jura wines. The most expressive savagnin wines come from the Pupillin area.

• **Côtes du Jura:** The appellation extends along the hillsides and ridges of the Jura wine zone as far as Burgundy. It represents many different expressions of terroir, most notably some exceptional savagnin-based white wines from the area around Voiteur.

• **Château-Chalon:** The village of Château-Chalon stands at the heart of this region, and is an appellation in its own right. Its impressive vineyards are dedicated to the production of a Vin Jaune ("yellow wine") that is slightly paler in color than elsewhere and is unequaled for aging potential (still drinkable after two hundred years!). Fully deserves its own appellation.

• **L'Étoile, near Lons-le-Saulnier:** The southern end of the appellation, specializing in exquisitely subtle whites, mostly vinified as sparkling wines, plus a tiny quantity of delicately aromatic Vins Jaunes.

Savoie

The Savoie region has a myriad of tiny appellations, essentially producing white wines that are light in alcohol and high in CO_2 content, giving them a slightly sparkling quality. Lively and acidic, these wines are a perfect complement to the hearty mountain cuisine of the region. It would be short sighted, though, to relegate the wines from the Savoie to a category of simple wines to accompany a hearty cheese fondue at the end of a long day of skiing.

The most elegant wines in the region are made in two areas: one from a grape called altesse, in the Roussette de Savoie appellation, and two from the roussanne grape, in the Chignin-Bergeron appellation. Some of these wines can compete with the best whites in France. But for many wine lovers, the greatest discovery comes in the form of reds made from the mondeuse grape, which could be compared with the wonderful syrahs from the northern Rhone. Deliciously thirst-quenching, they stand up in color and in elegance to good syrahs, with the same aromatic palette of spicy black pepper and red berries.

Appellation Overview

• **Vin de Savoie:** The principal Savoie appellation, famous for its perlant (slightly sparkling) wines. The wines from Ripaille, on the southeastern shore of Lake Geneva, are driven by the chasselas grape; those from Chautagne on Lake Bourget are based on gamay; those from Apremont and Abymes depend on the jaquère grape. Across the valley is Chignin, regarded by some as the top Savoie cru and particularly notable for its roussanne. It marks the start of a succession of vineyards in the Combe de Savoie. Along the river, the sunny slopes of the vineyards of Montmélian and Arbin provide ideal ripening conditions for the mondeuse grape.

• **Crépy:** A tiny, 200-acre appellation near Switzerland on the shores of Lake Geneva, dominated by the chasselas.

• **Roussette de Savoie:** The vineyards extend along the banks of the Rhone, from Frangy to Jongieux (Cru Marestel). Plantings are dominated by the altesse grape, and often blended with chardonnay. Wines that display the name of the commune on the label are exclusively produced from the altesse grape. These wines are more refined and longer on the palate than those made from chasselas.

• **Seyssel:** An enclave to the north of the roussette area, producing robust wines mainly driven by altesse.

Jura Vineyards

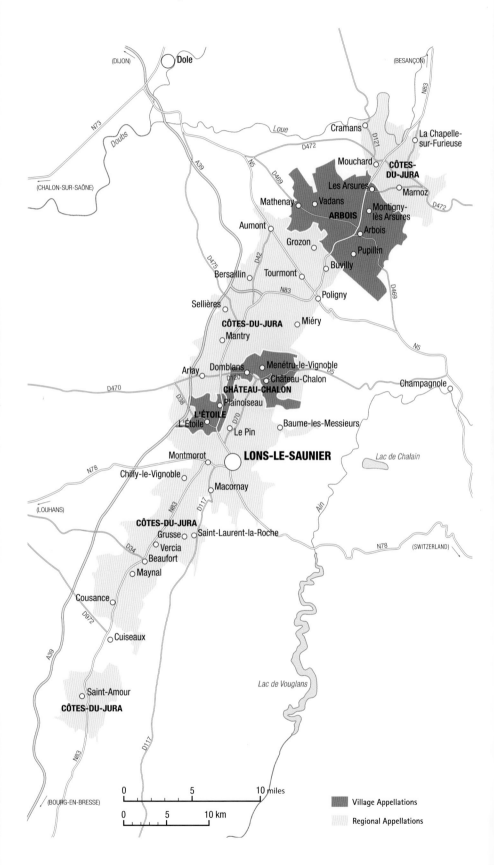

(DIJON)
Dole
(BESANÇON)

N73
Doubs
Loue
Cramans
La Chapelle-sur-Furieuse

(CHALON-SUR-SAÔNE)
D472
Mouchard
CÔTES-DU-JURA

N5
D469
Les Arsures
Marnoz
Mathenay
Vadans
Montigny-lès Arsures
D472
ARBOIS
Aumont
Grozon
Arbois
Pupillin
Buvilly
D475
D42
Bersaillin
Tourmont
N83
Poligny
Sellières
CÔTES-DU-JURA
Miéry
Mantry
N5
Arlay
Domblans
Menétru-le-Vignoble
Château-Chalon
Champagnole
D470
CHÂTEAU-CHALON
Plainoiseau
L'ÉTOILE
L'Étoile
Le Pin
Baume-les-Messieurs
Lac de Chalain

Montmorot
LONS-LE-SAUNIER

N78
Chilly-le-Vignoble
Macornay
Ain

(LOUHANS)
N83
D117
CÔTES-DU-JURA
Saint-Laurent-la-Roche
N78
(SWITZERLAND)
Grusse
D34
Vercia
Beaufort
Maynal
Cousance
D972
Cuiseaux

Lac de Vouglans

A39
Saint-Amour
CÔTES-DU-JURA
N83
D117

(BOURG-EN-BRESSE)

| 0 | 5 | 10 miles |
| 0 | 5 | 10 km |

Village Appellations

Regional Appellations

Savoie and Bugey Vineyards

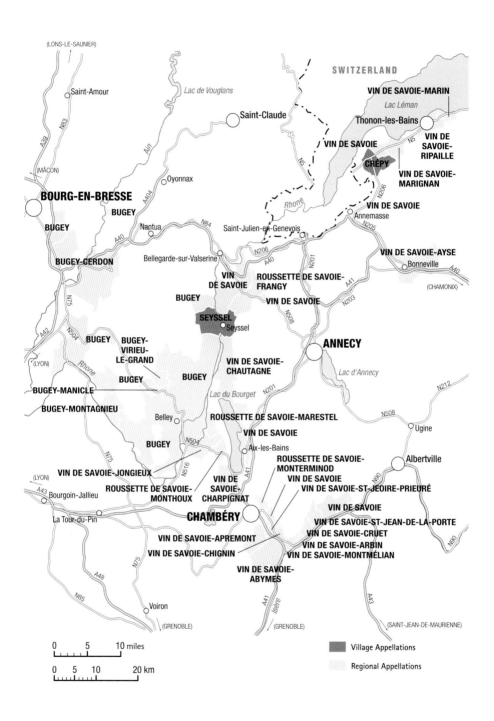

(LONS-LE-SAUNIER)

Saint-Amour

Lac de Vouglans

Saint-Claude

SWITZERLAND

VIN DE SAVOIE-MARIN

Lac Léman

Thonon-les-Bains

VIN DE SAVOIE-RIPAILLE

VIN DE SAVOIE

CRÉPY

VIN DE SAVOIE-MARIGNAN

Oyonnax

(MÂCON)

BOURG-EN-BRESSE

BUGEY

Nantua

Saint-Julien-en-Genevois

Annemasse

VIN DE SAVOIE

BUGEY

VIN DE SAVOIE-AYSE

Bonneville

(CHAMONIX)

BUGEY-CERDON

Bellegarde-sur-Valserine

Rhône

VIN DE SAVOIE

ROUSSETTE DE SAVOIE-FRANGY

BUGEY

VIN DE SAVOIE

SEYSSEL

Seyssel

BUGEY

BUGEY-VIRIEU-LE-GRAND

VIN DE SAVOIE-CHAUTAGNE

ANNECY

Lac d'Annecy

BUGEY

BUGEY

BUGEY-MANICLE

(LYON)

Rhône

BUGEY-MONTAGNIEU

Lac du Bourget

ROUSSETTE DE SAVOIE-MARESTEL

Ugine

Belley

VIN DE SAVOIE

Albertville

BUGEY

Aix-les-Bains

ROUSSETTE DE SAVOIE-MONTERMINOD

(LYON)

VIN DE SAVOIE-JONGIEUX

VIN DE SAVOIE

VIN DE SAVOIE-ST-JEOIRE-PRIEURÉ

Bourgoin-Jallieu

ROUSSETTE DE SAVOIE-MONTHOUX

VIN DE SAVOIE-CHARPIGNAT

VIN DE SAVOIE

La Tour-du-Pin

CHAMBÉRY

VIN DE SAVOIE-ST-JEAN-DE-LA-PORTE

VIN DE SAVOIE-CRUET

VIN DE SAVOIE-APREMONT

VIN DE SAVOIE-ARBIN

VIN DE SAVOIE-CHIGNIN

VIN DE SAVOIE-MONTMÉLIAN

VIN DE SAVOIE-ABYMES

Voiron

(GRENOBLE)

Isère

(GRENOBLE)

(SAINT-JEAN-DE-MAURIENNE)

| 0 | 5 | 10 miles |

| 0 | 5 | 10 | 20 km |

Village Appellations

Regional Appellations

CHÂTEAU D'ARLAY

Route de Saint-Germain
39140 Arlay
Phone 00 33 3 84 85 04 22
Fax 00 33 3 84 48 17 96
château@arlay.com
www.arlay.com

While many wineries are coming out with more and more single-vineyard bottlings, Château d'Arlay likes to keep its range short and traditional, producing just seven different wines over seventy-five acres of vineyards. The quality is homogeneous from vintage to vintage, and the long aging period makes for classic wines that are true to their origins. The "Vins de Paille" and the "Vins Jaunes" are excellent. These wines tend to age very well, and rather than enlarging the product line, Alain de Laguiche always has on hand between three and six vintages of each wine produced for sale at the winery. If you stop by the winery, you may also have a chance to visit the château.

Recently tasted
CÔTES DU JURA LES PAVILLONS
DU CHÂTEAU D'ARLAY 2007
Rosé | 2011 up to 2013   85

CÔTES DU JURA TRADITION 2004
White | 2011 up to 2019   89

CÔTES DU JURA VIN DE PAILLE 2005
Sweet White | 2011 up to 2025   90

CÔTES DU JURA VIN JAUNE 2002
White | 2011 up to 2022   91

CÔTES DU JURA VIN JAUNE 2000
White | 2011 up to 2030   93

CÔTES DU JURA VIN JAUNE 1998
White | 2011 up to 2030   92

Older vintages
CÔTES DU JURA 2003
Red | 2011 up to 2023   87
The domaine's red is a concentrated pinot noir with spicy aromas and rich, extracted flavors. Will age well.

CÔTES DU JURA TRADITION 2003
White | 2011 up to 2030   88
A blend of chardonnay and savagnin that is aged for more than four years in large, topped-off oak barrels, this is a very clean wine with spice and ripe fruit aromas. The palate is broad and very pure, with a long finish.

CÔTES DU JURA VIN DE PAILLE 2004
Sweet White | 2011 up to 2030   92
This has powerful, jammy yellow fruit aromas and a hint of chestnut. The sweet mouthfeel leads to candied fruit notes on the finish. Lovely complexity on the nose and palate. Quintessential Vin de Paille.

CÔTES DU JURA VIN DE PAILLE 2003
Sweet White | 2011 up to 2023   88
Powerful aromas of figs and chestnuts announce a very broad, sweet mouthfeel with nuts and candied fruit on the finish. Lovely complexity on both the nose and palate. Quintessential Vin de Paille.

CÔTES DU JURA VIN JAUNE 2001
White | 2011 up to 2030   92
This is already open, with complex aromas announcing an unctuous mouthfeel with refined acidity. The finish is long, with notes of curry and smoke.

CÔTES DU JURA VIN JAUNE 1999
White | 2011 up to 2050   90
A quintessential Vin Jaune with leather, walnut, and curry aromas leading to a lovely, clean mouthfeel with lots of concentration and finesse.

MACVIN DU JURA
Soft White | 2011 up to 2020   90
One of the appellation's references, displaying a rare combination of very pure fruit and elegant sweetness, and a long, complex finish.

MACVIN DU JURA
Soft Red | 2011 up to 2020   89
This easy-drinking, fresh red Macvin is an original from this domaine. It shows plenty of fresh red-fruit aromas. Its tannic structure alleviates the impression of sweetness.

Red: 39.5 acres; pinot noir 82%, poulsard 9%, trousseau 9%. White: 27.2 acres; chardonnay 49%, savagnin 51%. Annual production: 100,000 bottles

GILLES BERLIOZ

Le Viviers
73800 Chignin
Phone 00 33 4 79 28 00 51
Fax 00 33 4 79 71 58 80
domainegillesberlioz@wanadoo.fr

Gilles Berlioz and his wife took over the winery in the early 1990s, reducing the vineyard acreage and beginning a biodynamic conversion in 2001. Located in Chignin, the white wines have a crystalline purity; Berlioz adjusts his vinification and aging methods each year in order to enhance the character of each vintage.

Roussette de Savoie altesse 2007
White | 2011 up to 2013   88
A broad and creamy wine, this is very fine and deep in the mouth, with plenty of lovely, fresh fruit flavors.

Vin de Savoie Chignin 2007
White | 2011 up to 2013   87
This mouth-wateringly fresh wine made from the jacquère grape boasts an aromatic and citrusy palate and a refined, briny finish.

Vin de Savoie Chignin 2006
White | 2011 up to 2013   86
A well-balanced Jacquère, this has clean aromas of spring flowers and citrus, and dry, dense flavors carried on a creamy texture.

Vin de Savoie Chignin-Bergeron 2006
White | 2011 up to 2016   90
From very ripe grapes, this wine shows toasty, dried-apricot aromas and a broad, slightly sweet mouthfeel. A superb, slightly overripe Bergeron, this is worth cellaring for a few years.

Vin de Savoie Chignin-Bergeron 2005
White | 2011 up to 2020   91
After nearly two years of bottle-aging, this wine is already open, with very pleasant floral and honeyed aromas; a pure, well-balanced mouthfeel; and a long, floral and honeyed finish. A superb balance.

Vin de Savoie mondeuse 2003
Red | 2011 up to 2015   88
A superb, concentrated Mondeuse showing very pure, fruity aromas, a broad mouthfeel, and ripe black-currant aromas on the finish.

Red: 2 acres. White: 6.7 acres. Annual production: 20,000 bottles

DOMAINE BERTHET-BONDET

Rue de la Tour
39210 Château-Chalon
Phone 00 33 3 84 44 60 48
Fax 00 33 3 84 44 61 13
berthet-bondet@orange.fr
www.berthet-bondet.net

This property is ideally located at the heart of the Château-Chalon appellation, featuring some very steep parcels of chardonnay and savagnin vines. Jean Berthet-Bondet and his wife produce refined, unfailingly elegant wines that show masterful use of savagnin whatever the style.

Château-Chalon 2000
White | 2011 up to 2040   91
The nose is still closed, but the dense palate shows great finesse with very pure, classic Vin Jaune flavors and leads to a spicy finish with hints of lemon. Needs to be cellared.

Château-Chalon 1999
White | 2011 up to 2050   90
This quintessential, expressive Château-Chalon shows complex aromas and a precise, fluid, and long-lasting mouthfeel.

Côtes du Jura Alliance 2005
White | 2011 up to 2013   88
This blend of chardonnay and savagnin underwent a classic élevage in barrel and stainless steel. The wine is fresh and elegant with nutty and smoky aromas, and a broad and mineral mouthfeel with notes of cream.

Côtes du Jura Naturé 2006
White | 2011 up to 2013   88
This savagnin shows spicy, toasty aromas and a smooth, deep, and mineral palate. Its silky texture is very seductive.

Côtes du Jura Tradition 2003
White | 2011 up to 2015   88
This blend of chardonnay with one-third savagnin has been aged sous voile for two years. The wine shows great minerality with intense aromas of curry and apple, and a fluid mouthfeel finishing on sweet spice.

Côtes du Jura Vin de Paille 2002
Sweet White | 2011 up to 2025   91
The preponderance of white grapes (chardonnay and savagnin) in this blend has produced an atypical Vin de Paille with honey, spice, and yellow-fruit aromas and an unctuous, very pure mouthfeel that leads to an even fresher finish.

Red: 2.5 acres; pinot noir 10%, poulsard 50%, trousseau 40%. White: 22.2 acres; chardonnay 44%, savagnin 56%. Annual production: 50,000 bottles

DOMAINE GANEVAT

La Combe
39190 Rotalier
Phone 00 33 3 84 25 02 69
Fax 00 33 3 84 25 02 69

Following many years spent in Burgundy, Jean-François Ganevat took over this family estate in 1998 and set out to capture the truest expression of great wines from the Rotalier area. Ganevat practices organic viticulture and makes concentrated wines with great class and purity. He raises them on lees and uses the least amount of sulfur dioxide possible. His chardonnays are exclusively aged in topped-up barrels and sourced from vines that include very ancient plantings. Like the savagnins, they can take a few years in bottle to integrate their wood: these are wines that really go the distance but they do need time to find their balance. The reds are exceptionally pure and elegant—testament to assiduously maintained vineyards and tiny yields. The exemplary concentration and mineral content of the white wines meanwhile demonstrate that here, too, the Rotalier vineyard has the potential to produce great bottlings. Increasing fame and reasonable prices do have their downside, though: some of these wines are already highly allocated. Your chances of getting your hands on any bottles of the Vin de Paille or trousseau are extremely slim.

Recently tasted

CÔTES DU JURA CHARDONNAY CHALASSE VIEILLES VIGNES 2006
White | 2011 up to 2026   **96**

CÔTES DU JURA CHARDONNAY LES GRANDS TEPPES VIEILLES VIGNES 2006
White | 2012 up to 2026   **97**

CÔTES DU JURA CUVÉE MARGUERITE 2006
White | 2011 up to 2022   **92**

CÔTES DU JURA CUVÉE ORÉGANE 2006
White | 2011 up to 2021   **93**

CÔTES DU JURA PINOT NOIR CUVÉE JULIEN 2007
Red | 2011 up to 2022   **91**

CÔTES DU JURA PINOT NOIR CUVÉE Z 2007
Red | 2011 up to 2022   **92**

CÔTES DU JURA SAVAGNIN CUVÉE PRESTIGE 2004
White | 2011 up to 2024   **91**

CÔTES DU JURA SAVAGNIN LES CHALASSES MARNES BLEUES 2006
White | 2011 up to 2026   **95**

CÔTES DU JURA SOUS LA ROCHE CUVÉE Z 2005
Red | 2012 up to 2025   **95**

CÔTES DU JURA TROUSSEAU PLEIN SUD 2007
Red | 2011 up to 2017   **92**

CÔTES DU JURA VIN DE PAILLE 2005
Soft White | 2011 up to 2025   **95**

Older vintages

CÔTES DU JURA CHARDONNAY CHALASSE VIEILLES VIGNES 2005
White | 2011 up to 2025   **93**
Produced from century-old vines, this wine shows slightly oaky aromas with notes of butter and nuts. The broad, deep, and creamy palate is long-lasting and boasts a velvety texture that is typical of great marl terroirs. A wine to be cellared.

CÔTES DU JURA CHARDONNAY CUVÉE FLORINE 2005
White | 2011 up to 2015   **88**
Aged in foudres (large casks), this wine shows floral aromas and pure, clean, ripe fruit flavors. An elegant chardonnay.

CÔTES DU JURA CHARDONNAY LES GRANDS TEPPES VIEILLES VIGNES 2005
White | 2011 up to 2025   **96**
A wine of exceptional purity, this has nutty and toasty aromas and a broad, rich, very pure palate showing plenty of elegance. A perfect balance for this great wine from the Rotalier area.

CÔTES DU JURA PINOT NOIR CUVÉE JULIEN 2006
Red | 2011 up to 2013   **92**
Less than 1,000 bottles of this Julien were produced in 2006. With exemplary fresh black-fruit aromas and deep, vinous, and very concentrated flavors, this wine redefines the limits of pinot noir made in Jura. Everyone should taste this wine at least once to calibrate their palate.

CÔTES DU JURA PINOT NOIR CUVÉE Z 2006
Red | 2011 up to 2021   **89**
The nose is already expressive, with aromas of black fruit and hints of smoke. The broad, elegant palate shows remarkable purity and freshness and leads to a long-lasting finish of red and black fruit. A remarkable pinot noir.

CÔTES DU JURA POULSARD ENFANT TERRIBLE 2006
Red | 2011 up to 2026   **89**
This rare, fruity and very pure cuvée was produced from grapes that were destemmed by hand. The palate is dense and very vinous, with a long-lasting, spicy finish and dry tannins. Will age for many years.

Côtes du Jura savagnin cuvée Prestige 2003

White | 2011 up to 2020   **88**

A savagnin that was aged sous voile for four years, this shows spicy curry aromas and a broad, deep, and pure palate, with hints of cream to soften the finish. A wine to be cellared.

Côtes du Jura savagnin cuvée Privilège 2005

White | 2011 up to 2020   **91**

A perfumed savagnin aged in topped-off demi-muids, with spicy and slightly toasty aromas. The concentrated palate shows the classic structure and creaminess of savagnin and a long-lasting, spicy finish. A great savagnin.

Côtes du Jura trousseau Plein Sud 2006

Red | 2011 up to 2021   **91**

Produced from young vines planted on the hillside behind the domaine, this wine offers deep aromas of black fruit, white flowers, and cherries. The broad and intense palate shows power and great purity and leads to a long finish that lasts on a note of wild Morello cherries. A textbook trousseau on the same level as the fabulous 2005.

Côtes du Jura Vin de Paille 2002

Soft White | 2011 up to 2050   **95**

A blend of savagnin, poulsard and chardonnay, this wine shows deep and complex aromas of quince, fruit paste, and leather, and sweet, intense, and very pure flavors. A remarkably balanced Vin de Paille.

Côtes du Jura Vin Jaune 1999

White | 2011 up to 2030   **92**

To think that aging chardonnays in topped-off barrels are a detriment to wines aged sous voile is an error, as this cuvée, aged sous voile until December 2007, demonstrates. The nose is delicate, with aromas of fresh walnuts and crème fraîche; the palate is soft, with classic Vin Jaune flavors, and becomes drier as it evolves. The long-lasting finish is creamy with a note of nutmeg. A very impressive Vin Jaune, to age for many years.

Red: 7.4 acres; pinot noir 44%, poulsard 22%, trousseau 34%. White: 13.6 acres; chardonnay 73%, savagnin 27%. Annual production: 35,000 bottles

DOMAINE LABET

Place du Village
39190 Rotalier
Phone 00 33 3 84 25 11 13
Fax 00 33 3 84 25 06 75
domaine.labet@wanadoo.fr

Alain Labet now works with his son Julien, who since 1997 has vinified all the wines from the family estate in addition to developing his own holding. Wines from the southern part of the Jura may not be as typically regional as others but they do bring out the special qualities of marly and limestone soils, making for some outstandingly precise and mineral chardonnays. Fruit from ancient vines—more than fifty years old on average—reinforces this mineral character. A touch of oak from barrel aging adds extra complexity, though some of these wines may take a while to integrate their wood.

Recently tasted

Côtes du Jura chardonnay cuvée du Hazard 2005

White | 2011 up to 2020   **88**

Côtes du Jura chardonnay Fleur de Marne En Chalasse 2006

White | 2011 up to 2021   **91**

Côtes du Jura chardonnay Fleur de Marne La Bardette 2006

White | 2011 up to 2021   **92**

Côtes du Jura chardonnay Fleur de Marne La Beaumette 2006

White | 2011 up to 2022   **90**

Côtes du Jura chardonnay Fleur de Marne Le Montceau 2006

White | 2011 up to 2021   **90**

Côtes du Jura chardonnay Les Varrons 2006

White | 2011 up to 2021   **88**

Côtes du Jura chardonnay Les Varrons cuvée Julien 2006

White | 2011 up to 2021   **89**

Côtes du Jura Fleur de chardonnay 2007

White | 2011 up to 2017   **88**

Older vintages

CÔTES DU JURA CHARDONNAY
FLEUR DE MARNE EN CHALASSE 2005
White | 2011 up to 2020   **92**
Elegant, very pure nose with a hint of toast.
Broad, velvety, and concentrated flavors with
a menthol note on the finish.

CÔTES DU JURA CHARDONNAY
FLEUR DE MARNE LA BARDETTE 2005
White | 2011 up to 2020   **91**
Toasted sesame aromas lead to a powerful,
rich, and pure mouthfeel framed by lovely
acidity. It remains dominated by grilled flavors framed by an extensive structure and
has a long finish.

CÔTES DU JURA CHARDONNAY
FLEUR DE MARNE LA BEAUMETTE 2005
White | 2011 up to 2020   **90**
From deep gray-marl soils without limestone.
Lemon-drop aromas with a floral note
announce a fruity, broad palate with candied flavors and some creaminess. Slightly
overripe, but vibrant fruit.

CÔTES DU JURA CHARDONNAY
FLEUR DE MARNE LE MONTCEAU 2005
White | 2011 up to 2020   **89**
The slightly toasty, clean and intense aro-
mas of this wine announce a pure, mineral
palate with a velvety structure that is balanced by fine acidity.

CÔTES DU JURA FLEUR DE CHARDONNAY 2006
White | 2011 up to 2016   **88**
From mostly limestone soils, this wine is fresh
and sharp, with mineral aromas announcing
broad, very pure flavors with great definition.

CÔTES DU JURA FLEUR DE SAVAGNIN 2005
White | 2011 up to 2015   **88**
The barrels of savagnin were topped off here,
so this doesn't show any oxidative character. Instead it is ripe and spicy, with a broad,
fresh, and balanced palate. From older vines
(lieu-dit La Bardette) and with longer aging
than Domaine de Julien's version.

CÔTES DU JURA FLEURS 2006
White | 2011 up to 2016   **86**
A pleasant blend of chardonnay from several
marl-based soils dating back to the early Jurassic epoch, this offers floral aromas with hints
of candied fruit that persist on the palate.

CÔTES DU JURA PINOT NOIR 2005
Red | 2011 up to 2015   **86**
The clean cherry aromas lead to a dense,
pure mouthfeel showing plenty of fruit and
a perfumed, clean finish.

Red: 3.7 acres; pinot noir 25%, poulsard 50%,
trousseau 25%. White: 18.5 acres; chardonnay 82%,
savagnin 18%. Annual production: 50,000 bottles

DOMAINE JEAN MACLE

Rue de la Roche
39210 Château-Chalon
Phone 00 33 3 84 85 21 85
Fax 00 33 3 84 85 27 38
maclel@wanadoo.fr

This winery is now run by Laurent Macle,
who has taken over from his father, Jean, a
monumental presence in the Jura and in
Château-Chalon in particular. Laurent has
been making wines since 1995, producing
a small range based exclusively on chardonnay and savagnin. The flagship offering is the Château-Chalon Vin Jaune,
famous for its terrific purity and remarkable longevity and made from old vines
that include plantings in steep vineyard
plots directly beneath the village. Thanks
to aging in cool cellars, the wine retains a
moderate alcohol but low ethanol content
that produces a nose and palate of remarkable finesse. Equally compelling are the
Crémant du Jura and Côtes du Jura, both
leaders in their category and not to be
overlooked.

Recently tasted

CHÂTEAU-CHALON 2002
White | 2011 up to 2030   **92**

CÔTES DU JURA 2006
White | 2011 up to 2026   **88**

Older vintages

CHÂTEAU-CHALON 2000
White | 2011 up to 2050   **97**
The flagship wine of the domaine has become
more refined with time: the nose opens delicately, on aromas of curry and smoke, and
the palate has become very refined and elegant, with great concentration. The wine is
clean, streamlined, and very pure on the palate, leaving classic Vin Jaune flavors that are
at once delicate and profound. It shows disconcerting finesse, extraordinary depth, and
all of the magic of a great Château-Chalon.
It can be cellared for many years to gain even
more complexity.

CHÂTEAU-CHALON 1999
White | 2011 up to 2050   **97**
The nose is expressive and complex, with
the fruity notes of classic Vin Jaune. Supple
and elegant with plenty of depth, it evolves
into a very long-lasting, refined finish with
a hint of citrus. A superb wine!

CHÂTEAU-CHALON 1988
White | 2011 up to 2030   **92**
The wine has darkened to a deep gold color.
The nose is complex, with aromas of sweet
spice and crème fraîche. In the mouth, it

feels taut and very pure with good density, and it is evolving toward an intense balance paired with great finesse. This is a remarkably refined, mature Château-Chalon.

CHÂTEAU-CHALON MISE #2 2000
White | 2011 up to 2050   **95**
This second cuvée is from a second batch that was bottled one year after the first. It offers more expressive curry and morel-mushroom aromas, and more acidity on the straightforward, elegant palate. Very promising, it merits more time in bottle.

CÔTES DU JURA 2005
White | 2011 up to 2020   **90**
Produced from a majority of chardonnay and savagnin, aged eighteen months sous voile, this wine shows remarkable purity and finesse. It's very mineral and spicy on the nose, with a fresh mouthfeel structured by plenty of acidity. A complete wine that will gain even more complexity with time.

CÔTES DU JURA 2004
White | 2011 up to 2024   **90**
A blend of mostly chardonnay and savagnin that has been aged for two years sous voile, this wine shows remarkable purity and finesse with floral aromas, a broad and fruity palate, lovely acidity, and a long-lasting finish of fresh walnuts and morel mushrooms.

CÔTES DU JURA CHARDONNAY 2005
White | 2011 up to 2020   **92**
Made from 100 percent chardonnay from the Côtes du Jura that has been aged for eighteen months sous voile, this wine shows ripe and delicate aromas of curry and a pure, mineral, and deep mouthfeel. The classic Vin Jaune flavors have been well mastered, and will pair beautifully with monkfish in a curry sauce.

CRÉMANT DU JURA
Brut White sparkling | 2011 up to 2013   **88**
From Chardonnay harvested in 2004, aged for eighteen months on the lees and with a minimal dosage, this crémant shows elegant aromas and a very fresh, broad and fruity palate with compact bubbles.

MACVIN DU JURA
Soft White | 2011 up to 2020   **88**
With dried-fruit and quince aromas announcing sweet and very spicy flavors, this is a powerful Macvin showing great purity and a very long finish.

White: 29.7 acres; chardonnay 70%, savagnin 30%.
Annual production: 40,000 bottles

DOMAINE LOUIS MAGNIN

90, chemin des Buis
73800 Arbin
Phone 00 33 4 79 84 12 12
Fax 00 33 4 79 84 40 92
louis.magnin@wanadoo.fr
www.domainelouismagnin.fr

Louis and Béatrice Magnin enjoy a well-earned reputation as producers of top-notch Savoie wines that show dense, ripe, and especially consistent character vintage after vintage. Recognized by top restaurateurs and oenophiles the world over, Louis Magnin wines are the product of hard labor in the vineyards and long maturation. They often need several years in bottle to reveal their true colors.

Recently tasted
ROUSSETTE DE SAVOIE 2007
White | 2011 up to 2017   **88**

VIN DE SAVOIE ARBIN MONDEUSE 2007
Red | 2011 up to 2017   **88**

VIN DE SAVOIE ARBIN MONDEUSE LA BROVA 2006
Red | 2011 up to 2026   **93**

**VIN DE SAVOIE ARBIN MONDEUSE
VIEILLES VIGNES 2007**
Red | 2011 up to 2022   **90**

VIN DE SAVOIE CHIGNIN 2007
White | 2011 up to 2013   **86**

VIN DE SAVOIE CHIGNIN-BERGERON 2007
White | 2011 up to 2017   **89**

VIN DE SAVOIE CHIGNIN-BERGERON BAOBAB 2007
Soft White | 2011 up to 2017   **90**

VIN DE SAVOIE CHIGNIN-BERGERON VERTICALE 2007
White | 2011 up to 2017   **91**

Older vintages
ROUSSETTE DE SAVOIE 2006
White | 2011 up to 2016   **88**
A ripe Roussette, this offers elegant floral and ripe-fruit aromas and a sharp, taut, and briny palate with plenty of richness and candied fruit. Avoiding malolactic fermentation was the right decision for this 2006.

VIN DE SAVOIE ARBIN MONDEUSE 2006
Red | 2011 up to 2016   **88**
This well-structured Mondeuse shows well-managed oak aging with fruity aromas, a broad mouthfeel, and silky tannins.

Vin de Savoie Arbin mondeuse 2005
Red | 2011 up to 2013   **86**
A supple Mondeuse with black-fruit aromas, this has mouthwatering fruit flavors in lovely balance with the well-chiseled tannins.

Vin de Savoie Arbin mondeuse La Brova 2005
Red | 2011 up to 2025   **92**
This wine is still marked by its barrel aging, with plenty of smoke on its black-fruit aromas. The palate is rich and ample with great depth and high-quality tannins. The wine needs some time to fully integrate, but it already has great potential.

Vin de Savoie Arbin mondeuse La Rouge 2006
Red | 2011 up to 2026   **92**
Ripe, concentrated, and well structured, La Rouge is already very promising, with high-quality tannins that will fully integrate after several years of aging. A great wine for cellaring.

Vin de Savoie Arbin mondeuse La Rouge 2005
Red | 2011 up to 2020   **91**
2004 was the first vintage using the truncated, cone-shaped wood tank that is specially used for this cuvée, and the wine shows great balance with oaky overtones. The 2005 boasts exceptional balance and a deep mouthfeel framed by fat and polished tannins. A great Mondeuse.

Vin de Savoie Chignin-Bergeron 2006
White | 2011 up to 2016   **90**
This concentrated cuvée boasts fresh, floral aromas and a broad, pure, and very linear mouthfeel with plenty of richness. It will age well.

Vin de Savoie Chignin-Bergeron Grand Orgue 2006
White | 2011 up to 2016   **93**
The lovely 2006 vintage of this single-vineyard prestige cuvée shows perfectly ripe balance and has retained a good amount of acidity, considering the malolactic fermentation. The refined and mineral palate will improve in the next three years. Grand Orgue remains one of the greatest white wines of Savoie.

Red: 9.8 acres; gamay 100%. White: 8.6 acres; altesse 10%, mondeuse 50%, roussanne 40%. Annual production: 40,000 bottles

DOMAINE JACQUES PUFFENEY

11, rue de Saint-Laurent
39600 Montigny-les-Arsures
Phone 00 33 3 84 66 10 89
Fax 00 33 3 84 66 08 36
jacques.puffeney@wanadoo.fr

Jacques Puffeney is one of those winegrowers whose commitment to high standards is plainly visible in their vineyards. His wines are classically made and undergo long aging in large oak vats or barrels. The chardonnays show the balance characteristic of the Jura's Arbois appellation, while his savagnin sous-voile (aged under a veil or layer of yeast) achieves a precision that is rarely equaled by any wine. The Vins Jaunes boast remarkable finesse and a very precise mouthfeel. Other pleasures not to be missed are his Vins Jaunes from different bottling batches, some being aged for more than twelve years under the veil. His red wines are also masterfully crafted.

Recently tasted
Arbois chardonnay 2006
White | 2011 up to 2016   **89**

Arbois cuvée Sacha 2005
White | 2012 up to 2025   **90**

Arbois Naturé 2006
White | 2011 up to 2021   **90**

Arbois pinot noir 2007
Red | 2011 up to 2022   **88**

Arbois poulsard 2007
Red | 2011 up to 2017   **86**

Arbois trousseau Les Bérangères 2007
Red | 2011 up to 2017   **87**

Arbois Vin de Paille 2005
Soft White | 2011 up to 2030   **91**

Macvin du Jura
Sweet White | 2011 up to 2014   **90**

Older vintages
Arbois chardonnay 2005
White | 2011 up to 2020   **88**
Very ripe wine with fruit aromas that take on a note of white rum with air. The palate is ripe, broad, creamy, and pure, framed by fine minerality. A rich, already well-balanced wine.

Arbois Naturé 2005
White | 2011 up to 2020   **89**
From savagnin aged in large, topped-off oak barrels, the wine is expressive with rich, fine spice aromas and a dry, dense, and rich palate showing no oxidation.

ARBOIS PINOT NOIR 2006

Red | 2011 up to 2020   **91**

A deeply concentrated pinot noir with pure, very intense aromas of red fruit and cherries; rich, sappy, and deep flavors; and a long finish. It needs age to integrate the tannins. The 2006 is as concentrated as the very good 2005, but with more purity.

ARBOIS POULSARD 2006

Red | 2011 up to 2016   **87**

This wine is fruity on the nose and supple in the mouth, with plenty of richness. The finish is marked by the fine tannins.

ARBOIS SAVAGNIN 2004

White | 2011 up to 2024   **91**

Aged three years sous voile, this wine is clean on the nose, with aromas of spice and a hint of gentian, then dry and rich on the palate. The finish is long, lasting on notes of morel mushrooms.

ARBOIS TROUSSEAU 2006

Red | 2011 up to 2021   **88**

A promising trousseau with fresh, ripe black fruit and a rich, long-lasting mouthfeel. A well-structured wine to be cellared.

ARBOIS TROUSSEAU LES BÉRANGÈRES 2005

Red | 2011 up to 2020   **90**

Intense aromas with plenty of fresh, ripe red fruit announce a rich, broad, and vinous palate that lasts long on the finish. This trousseau is a reference for the region.

ARBOIS VIEILLES VIGNES 2005

Red | 2012 up to 2025   **90**

Produced from a field blend of old trousseau, poulsard, and pinot noir, this 2005 is supple and concentrated with already present fruit flavors that will become more expressive as the tannins integrate.

ARBOIS VIN JAUNE 2001

White | 2011 up to 2030   **93**

This wine shows notes of pomace and quince, and a creamy and powerful mouthfeel.

Red: 7.4 acres; pinot noir 23%, poulsard 36%, trousseau 41%. White: 8.2 acres; chardonnay 29%, savagnin 71%. Annual production: 40,000 bottles

DOMAINE ANDRÉ ET MICHEL QUÉNARD

Torméry
73800 Chignin
Phone 00 33 4 79 28 12 75
Fax 00 33 4 79 28 19 36
am.quenard@wanadoo.fr

This large family estate operates some lovely parcels on the steep slopes around Torméry in Chignin (Savoie), planted in ideal clayey-limestone terrain over limestone bedrock. For more than a decade now, the property has been assiduously managed by Michel Quénard, on the basis of sustainable viticulture and relentless soil management. The youngest vines have already come on stream, the bottles being released in the spring following harvest. The old-vines cuvées and wines raised in oak vats are matured until the fall; we recommend you wait for those.

Recently tasted

VIN DE SAVOIE CHIGNIN 2008
White | 2011 up to 2013   **85**

VIN DE SAVOIE CHIGNIN-BERGERON 2008
White | 2011 up to 2013   **86**

VIN DE SAVOIE CHIGNIN-BERGERON
LES TERRASSES 2008
White | 2011 up to 2013   **88**

VIN DE SAVOIE CHIGNIN MONDEUSE
VIEILLES VIGNES 2008
Red | 2011 up to 2015   **87**

VIN DE SAVOIE CHIGNIN VIEILLES VIGNES 2008
White | 2011 up to 2013   **88**

VIN DE SAVOIE LES ABYMES 2008
White | 2011 up to 2013   **87**

Older vintages

VIN DE SAVOIE CHIGNIN MONDEUSE
VIEILLES VIGNES 2007
Red | 2011 up to 2017   **88**

A silky mondeuse with fresh black-fruit and pepper aromas, this has an unctuous mouthfeel framed by rich tannins. This is promising, and worth waiting several years for it to become an even better wine.

VIN DE SAVOIE CHIGNIN MONDEUSE
VIEILLES VIGNES 2006
Red | 2011 up to 2015   **88**

An already expressive mondeuse with intense aromas, very pure, balanced flavors, and plenty of fresh black fruit on the finish.

VIN DE SAVOIE CHIGNIN-BERGERON
ÉLEVÉ EN FOUDRE DE CHÊNE 2007
White | 2011 up to 2017   **91**
Made from very ripe bergeron, this cuvée
has been aged in large oak casks for more
than a year. It gives a wine with apricot aromas and hints of smoke, a rich, honeyed,
concentrated palate and a long finish. A
lovely cuvée.

VIN DE SAVOIE CHIGNIN-BERGERON
LES ARPENTS D'ANTAN 2005
White | 2011 up to 2020   **91**
The grapes for this wine came from vines
more than seventy years old planted on a
steep slope. Picked late and aged in new
demi-muids, they have produced a concentrated and well-structured wine with plenty
of depth and great purity. The oaky notes
are still present, so aging is recommended,
and patience will be amply rewarded.

VIN DE SAVOIE CHIGNIN-BERGERON
LES TERRASSES 2007
White | 2011 up to 2013   **88**
From late-harvested grapes planted on the
steepest terraced parcels of the Torméry
hillside, this is a rich, fleshy wine with plenty
of depth, creamy flavors, and a long finish.

VIN DE SAVOIE CHIGNIN-BERGERON
LES TERRASSES 2006
White | 2011 up to 2015   **88**
The hillside's steepest parcels are terraced,
and the grapes are harvested late in the season in order to produce this fleshy, broad
and deep cuvée. It maintains an elegant
character with hints of flint on the finish.

Red: 14.8 acres; gamay 40%, mondeuse 40%, pinot
noir 20%. White: 44.5 acres; altesse 20%, bergeron
48%, jacquère 50%. Annual production: 180,000
bottles

LES FILS DE RENÉ QUÉNARD

Les Tours
Le Villard
73800 Chignin
Phone 00 33 4 79 28 01 15
Fax 00 33 4 79 28 18 98
fils.rene.quenard@wanadoo.fr
www.lesfilsderenequenard.com

Jacky and Georges Quénard manage a
large property, mainly planted to white
varietals. The jacquère wines develop fatness after aging on lees but the best wines
are made from the bergeron (aka roussanne), particularly the cuvée that sees
eighteen months in oak vats.

VIN DE SAVOIE CHIGNIN LA MARÉCHALE 2007
White | 2011 up to 2013   **84**
A Jacquère aged on the lees, this offers a
deep, briny palate with plenty of fat, and
lovely acidity on the finish.

VIN DE SAVOIE CHIGNIN MONDEUSE 2007
Red | 2011 up to 2017   **81**
A full-bodied wine with a smoky and peppery nose, a broad and powerful palate, and
a long-lasting, dry finish with aromas of violets. Still young, this is worth cellaring.

VIN DE SAVOIE CHIGNIN MONDEUSE 2006
Red | 2011 up to 2016   **89**
A lovely mondeuse showing silky fruit and
a vinous palate, with pure balance. Good
work in a tricky vintage has produced a wine
that's already open, ready to drink.

VIN DE SAVOIE CHIGNIN PINOT NOIR 2007
Red | 2011 up to 2013   **80**
An elegant pinot noir showing fruity aromas
with a hint of pepper and smoke, a pure palate, and a rich, spicy finish.

VIN DE SAVOIE CHIGNIN-BERGERON
LA BERGERONNELLE 2006
White | 2011 up to 2013   **88**
This amply fruited wine shows a fine bal-
ance held by its lovely acid structure.

VIN DE SAVOIE CHIGNIN-BERGERON
LA CIGALE 2006
White | 2011 up to 2016   **89**
A traditional, late-harvested Chignin-Bergeron
that has been aged in large, new oak "foudres" (casks) for eighteen months. It shows
ripe-apricot aromas, a broad, powerful, and
very ripe mouthfeel with well-integrated,
slightly oaky flavors, and a long-lasting finish.

Red: 84 acres. White: 261.9 acres. Annual
production: 140,000 bottles

DOMAINE JEAN-PIERRE ET JEAN-FRANÇOIS QUÉNARD

Caveau de la Tour Villard
73800 Chignin
Phone 00 33 4 79 28 08 29
Fax 00 33 4 79 28 18 92
j.francois.quenard@wanadoo.fr
www.jf-quenard.com

Jean-François Quénard now runs this estate, which has tripled in size since he took over from his father in 1987. He makes well-balanced wines from sustainably grown grapes, including a top-of-the-range offering that undergoes lengthy maturation on lees with frequent "bâton-nage" (stirring). The success of his 2005s has been a shot in the arm for the Chignin wine business. The superior quality of the wines is reflected in progressively climbing prices, but they remain reasonable compared with other regions.

Recently tasted

ROUSSETTE DE SAVOIE CUVÉE ANNE-SOPHIE 2007
White I 2011 up to 2017   **86**

VIN DE SAVOIE CHIGNIN ANNE DE LA BIGUERNE 2008
White I 2011 up to 2013   **87**

VIN DE SAVOIE CHIGNIN-BERGERON
VIEILLES VIGNES 2007
White I 2011 up to 2017   **89**

VIN DE SAVOIE LE BERGERON D'ALEXANDRA 2007
Sweet White I 2011 up to 2017   **90**

VIN DE SAVOIE MONDEUSE CUVÉE ÉLISA 2007
Red I 2011 up to 2015   **88**

Older vintages

VIN DE SAVOIE CHIGNIN-BERGERON
COMME AVANT 2006
White I 2011 up to 2016   **89**
The grapes were late-harvested and barrel-aged for a year to respect the ancient Chignin-Bergeron method. The 2006 follows the beautiful 2005 with some lingering oak notes, vivid and dense fruit flavors, and a long finish.

VIN DE SAVOIE CHIGNIN-BERGERON
VIEILLES VIGNES 2006
White I 2011 up to 2016   **88**
After nine months of aging, this old-vine cuvée shows some overripeness, with a note of smoke on the nose and a broad mouth-feel. It is ready to drink now but can also be cellared.

VIN DE SAVOIE LE BERGERON D'ALEXANDRA 2006
Sweet White I 2011 up to 2016   **90**
From Bergeron grapes late-harvested in mid-October, this sweet wine shows peach and apricot aromas and a broad, fresh palate leading to honey notes on the finish.

VIN DE SAVOIE MONDEUSE CUVÉE ÉLISA 2006
Red I 2011 up to 2026   **89**
Aged for a year in barrels and demi-muids, this wine shows intense fruit flavors and a powerful structure. It is ready to drink now, but can also be cellared.

VIN DE SAVOIE MONDEUSE CUVÉE ÉLISA 2005
Red I 2011 up to 2015   **90**
Produced from very ripe grapes aged in demi-muids, this supple wine shows ripe fruit aromas and a powerful and soft mouth-feel with creamy tannins on the finish.

Red: 7.4 acres; gamay 9%, pinot noir 9%, mondeuse 82%. White: 32.1 acres; jacquère 69%, roussanne 29%, rousette 2%. Annual production: 110,000 bottles

DOMAINE RIJCKAERT

Correaux
71570 Leynes
Phone 00 33 3 85 35 15 09
Fax 00 33 3 85 35 15 09
rijckaert.jean@orange.fr

Jean Rijckaert produces Viré-Clessé wines from the Mâconnais plus an array of wines from remote vineyards in the Jura that make him somewhat of an outsider as far as the locals are concerned. His twelve acres are planted almost exclusively to chardonnay, producing very sophisticated wines that are aged traditionally in wood. The oak is often perceptible but well integrated, adding to the sensation of purity in the wines. Aged in the same way as the chardonnays, the savagnins show magnificent clarity and richness, emphasizing the spicy character of the grape but avoiding the character of a Vin Jaune.

Recently tasted
ARBOIS CHARDONNAY EN PARADIS 2005
White | 2011 up to 2020   91

ARBOIS SAVAGNIN GRAND ÉLEVAGE 2006
White | 2011 up to 2021   91

CÔTES DU JURA CHARDONNAY LES SARRES 2007
White | 2011 up to 2017   86

CÔTES DU JURA SAVAGNIN LES SARRES 2006
White | 2011 up to 2021   89

Older vintages
ARBOIS CHARDONNAY EN CHANTE MERLE 2005
White | 2011 up to 2020   90
An intense wine with a nose of ripe fruit and white flowers, this presents a sumptuous, deep, and mineral palate with plenty of richness and lovely acidity. The wine needs time to integrate and achieve more finesse, but it is already delicious.

ARBOIS CHARDONNAY EN PARADIS 2006
White | 2011 up to 2016   88
An easy wine that still shows some oaky aromas, this feels fresh and pure.

ARBOIS CHARDONNAY EN PARADIS 2005
White | 2011 up to 2020   91
This remarkably balanced wine still shows some reserve, but it already boasts ripe, white-fleshed fruit and a mineral, very refined mouthfeel.

ARBOIS SAVAGNIN GRAND ÉLEVAGE 2005
White | 2011 up to 2020   90
Aged in topped-off barrels for twenty-three months, this savagnin shows ripe, fruity aromas, a broad and mineral palate with plenty of concentration and fat and a long-lasting, spicy finish. A great savagnin that does not have the traditional vin jaune flavors.

ARBOIS SAVAGNIN GRAND ÉLEVAGE 2004
White | 2011 up to 2020   90
Oak-aged for twenty-three months, this fruity savagnin shows citrus aromas and a concentrated, fresh, and mineral palate. The finish still shows some oaky flavors; cellar for several years.

CÔTES DU JURA CHARDONNAY LES SARRES 2006
White | 2011 up to 2016   88
A ripe chardonnay, still showing some oaky notes from aging, this has plenty of concentration, with a pure mouthfeel and candied fruit flavors.

CÔTES DU JURA CHARDONNAY LES SARRES 2005
White | 2011 up to 2015   88
This elegant and finely barrel-aged wine shows a deep and pure palate with great precision.

CÔTES DU JURA CHARDONNAY
VIGNE DES VOISES 2005
White | 2011 up to 2020   90
Refined aromas lead into a dense palate with plenty of finesse and minerality. A great wine to be cellared, and then decanted.

CÔTES DU JURA SAVAGNIN LES SARRES 2005
White | 2011 up to 2015   88
A savagnin aged in topped-off barrels, this wine shows straightforward, spicy aromas and savory, dense flavors with plenty of richness.

CÔTES DU JURA SAVAGNIN LES SARRES 2003
White | 2011 up to 2020   90
This complex and powerful savagnin is very spicy and a little oaky, but it lasts with plenty of minerality.

White: 12.5 acres; chardonnay 97%, savagnin 3%.
Annual production: 30,000 bottles

DOMAINE ROLET PÈRE ET FILS

Route de Dole
Lieu-dit Montesserin, BP 67
39600 Arbois
Phone 00 33 3 84 66 00 05
Fax 00 33 3 84 37 47 41
rolet@wanadoo.fr
www.rolet-arbois.com

This large, 160-acre family estate was started in the early 1940s by Désiré Rolet and continues to grow thanks to his children Bernard and Guy, who make the wines and manage the vineyards, and Pierre and Éliane, who take care of business. Their wines are internationally renowned but as time passes and retirement looms, the future of this estate looks a lot less certain than it was in Désiré's day. The Rolets make a wide variety of cuvées, almost half of them red, produced under the Arbois, Côtes du Jura, and L'Étoile appellations. All of them have good density, sometimes with a touch of rusticity but at no cost to great aging potential.

Recently tasted

ARBOIS TROUSSEAU 2006
Red | 2011 up to 2016   86

ARBOIS VIN JAUNE 2002
White | 2011 up to 2022   91

CÔTES DU JURA SAVAGNIN 2002
White | 2011 up to 2022   88

Older vintages

ARBOIS MÉMORIAL 2003
Red | 2011 up to 2023   90
The flagship cuvée of the domaine, this is a very elegant blend of trousseau and pinot noir. It is concentrated, rich, and broad, with a silky finish.

ARBOIS PINOT 2005
Red | 2011 up to 2020   88
A ripe and concentrated pinot noir showing straightforward red-fruit aromas, a broad and silky palate, and a long finish.

ARBOIS TROUSSEAU 2005
Red | 2011 up to 2020   86
An elegant trousseau with Morello cherry aromas, a rather light mouthfeel, and a finish with plenty of fine tannins.

ARBOIS VIN JAUNE 2000
White | 2011 up to 2030   90
This wine shows spicy and smoky aromas, a rich mouthfeel, and a curry finish.

ARBOIS VIN JAUNE 1999
White | 2011 up to 2050   88
A very spicy Vin Jaune showing intense walnut and leather aromas, a fresh and concentrated palate, and a spicy, leathery finish.

CÔTES DU JURA SAVAGNIN 2001
White | 2011 up to 2030   87
A well-balanced, spicy savagnin that is aged sous voile, this wine shows a dense palate with candied fruit and a finish with morel-mushroom overtones.

CÔTES DU JURA VIN DE PAILLE 2002
Sweet White | 2011 up to 2022   92
A great, concentrated and refined sweet Vin de Paille, this wine shows candied fruit aromas and a fresh, long-lasting finish of spices and stewed red fruit.

CRÉMANT DU JURA COEUR DE CHARDONNAY 2005
Brut White sparkling | 2011 up to 2013   88
The prestige cuvée of the domaine, this wine possesses plenty of ripeness, with a dry, concentrated, and balanced palate and a tight structure. Magnificent wine for the dinner table.

MACVIN DU JURA
Sweet White | 2011 up to 2020   86
A very powerful Macvin with spicy aromas, a sweet mouthfeel, and a warm finish.

Red: 64.2 acres: pinot noir 27%, poulsard 46%, trousseau 27%. White: 96.4 acres; chardonnay 58%, savagnin 42%. Annual production: 320,000 bottles

DOMAINE ANDRÉ ET MIREILLE TISSOT – STÉPHANE TISSOT

Quartier Bernard, BP 77
39600 Montigny-les-Arsures
Phone 00 33 3 84 66 08 27
Fax 00 33 3 84 66 25 08
stephane.tissot.arbois@wanadoo.fr
www.stephane-tissot.com

Winegrower Stéphane Tissot has an innovative approach to making Jura wines. He took the helm of this family estate more than ten years ago and has been shaking up traditions ever since. He has converted to biodynamics and brought change to the vineyard and cellars with an increasingly wide range of terroir-driven wines: chardonnays with unsurpassed mineral expression; reds that move into another dimension altogether; and a Vin Jaune that now ranks among the loftiest of all the regional bottlings. Stéphane also makes a range of sweet wines that are somewhat on the fringes of conventional notions of Vins de Paille (and indeed wine in the official sense). Known as "Moût de Raisin Partiellement Fermenté" (partially fermented grape juice), they are very pure, with an intensely raisined character. Stéphane's contagious enthusiasm is opening doors for him outside the region, especially in export markets where Tissot wines rank among the cream of French wines.

Recently tasted

ARBOIS CHARDONNAY 2007
White | 2011 up to 2017   **88**

ARBOIS CHARDONNAY LES GRAVIERS 2007
White | 2011 up to 2022   **91**

ARBOIS POULSARD VIEILLES VIGNES 2007
Red | 2011 up to 2017   **88**

ARBOIS TROUSSEAU SINGULIER 2007
Red | 2011 up to 2027   **90**

ARBOIS VIN JAUNE 2002
White | 2011 up to 2030   **93**

CÔTES DU JURA PINOT NOIR EN BARBERON 2007
Red | 2011 up to 2022   **89**

CRÉMANT DU JURA ROSÉ
Brut Rosé sparkling | 2011 up to 2013   **86**

VIN DE TABLE AUDACE 2006
Sweet Red | 2011 up to 2026   **90**

VIN DE TABLE PMG 2006
Sweet White | 2011 up to 2030   **92**

Older vintages

ARBOIS CHARDONNAY LA MAILLOCHE 2006
White | 2011 up to 2021   **91**
From unique soils dating back to the early Jurassic epoch that give this wine intense, toasty aromas. The remarkably elegant structure is straight as an arrow and shows fine, intense acidity. It is right on the mark; to be cellared.

ARBOIS CHARDONNAY LE CLOS DE LA TOUR DE CURON 2006
White | 2011 up to 2021   **94**
The third harvest from these young, densely planted vines on clay and limestone soil has produced a wine that gets better every year. It also exemplifies the sumptuous qualities of the best Jura whites in 2006. Elegant, pure aromas announce a dense palate with plenty of concentrated, creamy flavors that are framed by refined saline notes. The spicy finish is quintessential Arbois. Beautiful definition.

ARBOIS CHARDONNAY LES BRUYÈRES 2006
White | 2011 up to 2021   **90**
A broad and mineral wine that shows plenty of spicy and creamy character. Worth cellaring.

ARBOIS CHARDONNAY LES GRAVIERS 2006
White | 2011 up to 2021   **91**
The floral nose shows toasted notes, and the mouthfeel is concentrated, broad, and very pure, with plenty of finesse on the long finish. An elegant wine.

ARBOIS L'OPPORTUN 2006
Sweet White | 2011 up to 2016   **92**
Made with sun-dried trousseau, this floral and remarkably fresh wine shows red-fruit aromas, candied-fruit flavors, and a lovely finish full of wild strawberries.

ARBOIS PINOT NOIR 2005
Red | 2011 up to 2015   **90**
Made from grapes that come from a parcel of limestone soil below the Clos de la Tour de Curon, this wine is an original. The classic cherry nose is both clean and pure, while the concentrated, very sharp palate possesses a very Burgundian balance. A very well-made wine.

ARBOIS POULSARD LES BRUYÈRES 2005
Red | 2011 up to 2020   **90**
From old vines, this wine shows intense fruit aromas and a compact, concentrated, and very pure palate with fine tannins on the finish. It has remarkable balance and stability for a wine vinified without added sulfites.

ARBOIS TROUSSEAU SINGULIER 2006

Red | 2011 up to 2026   **92**

After sorting out the overripe grapes destined for the sweet cuvée L'Opportun, the healthy grapes have produced a remarkably pure, dense and deep wine with still-firm tannins. A great trousseau, and a reference in the 2006 vintage.

ARBOIS VIN DE PAILLE 2003

Soft White | 2011 up to 2030   **92**

The 2003 is a more quintessential Vin de Paille than the previous vintage, with typical "paille" aromas of leather and dry fruit. The sweet flavors show amazing freshness with plenty of red fruit. Long wild-raspberry finish.

ARBOIS VIN JAUNE 2001

White | 2011 up to 2050   **95**

A complete Vin Jaune with already precise, clean, and complex aromas, and a remarkably taut palate framed by lovely acidity. A very promising wine.

ARBOIS VIN JAUNE 111 1997

White | 2011 up to 2050   **95**

This Vin Jaune has been aged sous voile for 111 months and shows intense curry aromas and powerful, deep flavors. In spite of a high alcohol level, the wine boasts remarkable balance and magnitude. The subtly oxidative finish lingers on morel mushroom, smoke, and spice aromas.

CÔTES DU JURA CHARDONNAY EN BARBERON 2006

White | 2011 up to 2025   **90**

From marl soils dating back to the Early Jurassic epoch, this sulfite-free cuvée shows very pure, floral aromas and a broad, creamy palate leading to a mineral, long-lasting finish.

CÔTES DU JURA PINOT NOIR EN BARBERON 2006

Red | 2011 up to 2020   **90**

The expressive aromas of black-currant and spice announce a dense, rich, and fleshy palate framed by still-drying tannins. The 2006 surpasses the 2005 with its more supple balance, which allows the velvety texture characteristic of this cuvée to emerge.

CRÉMANT DU JURA EXTRA-BRUT

Brut White sparkling | 2011 up to 2013   **87**

From pinot noir and chardonnay grapes from the 2006 vintage, this is perfumed, clean, and fresh with fine bubbles. The dosage is minimal, and the wine is dry and taut.

SAVAGNIN 2004

White | 2011 up to 2024   **92**

A fresh, broad, and terrifically seductive savagnin that has undergone well-managed sous-voile aging. The nose shows plenty of fruit behind some oxidative notes, and the palate is very tender, smooth, rich, and long. A good example of Vin Jaune.

VIN DE TABLE AUDACE 2005

Sweet Red | 2011 up to 2030   **91**

Made like a Vin de Paille based on Poulsard, low in alcohol but with plenty of sweetness, this cuvée tastes like a sweet Morello cherry candy, framed by strong acidity.

VIN DE TABLE PMG 2005

Sweet White | 2011 up to 2013   **92**

PMG is a single-barrel cuvée that is low in alcohol, but extremely sweet (close to 450 grams per liter). It is made like a Vin de Paille with a base of poulsard and savagnin. Powerful aromas and very creamy yet clean texture. Drink with moderation.

Red: 37.3 acres; pinot noir 31%, poulsard 36%, trousseau 33%. White: 62.7 acres; chardonnay 64%, savagnin 36%. Annual production: 135,000 bottles

Bettane & Desseauve
Selections for Languedoc-Roussillon

Languedoc

The Languedoc, which we once called the "new French California," is no longer the latest trendy vineyard. It is now quite commonplace, with a two-tiered system, one that makes mass-produced simple wines, with an uncertain commercial future, and one that is made up of the elite wine-growers who are producing refined and expressive terroir-driven wines. They all make appealing, immediately pleasurable wines—and no one can complain about that.

Appellation Overview
Languedoc Appellations
• **Coteaux du Languedoc:** A huge appellation with much to recommend, especially in terms of red wines. The delimitation of appellations is currently underway. Some of the wines already display the name of the commune on the label, indicating a particular terroir and its potential. The appellation encompasses a broad range of terroirs, of which the most dependable producers are the Pic-Saint-Loup area (driven by syrah); the Terrasses du Larzac and the village of Montpeyroux (excellent blended wines with rich, generous character); and the La Clape (potentially a good source of white and rosé wines) and Pézenas areas.

• **Picpoul de Pinet:** A small coastal appellation making crisp, straightforward white wines—very pleasant, and perfect with oysters from the Mediterranean village of Bouzigues.

• **Saint-Chinian:** A region in the Upper Languedoc, built more on human effort than on the realities of the terroir, with schistose soils to the north and (to keep it simple) clay-limestone soils to the south. The north produces supple, tender red wines, including carignans made by carbonic maceration that consumers these days seem to love. Elevation to individual cru status is much more likely in the south, however, which is a source of dense, well-structured wines with more of the character expected of a delimited cru. Berlou and Roquebrun have been delimited production areas since 2004 (with no change in quality), and growers throughout the appellation are now entitled to produce white wines under the AOC Saint-Chinian label.

• **Faugères:** A potentially good source of red wines—unusually elegant for this region. The appellation continues to make great strides in blended wines that are often driven by syrah. Since 2004, white wines from this area may also be sold under the AOC Faugères label.

• **Minervois:** An area known for its traditional wineries, including some that are a cut above the rest. Recent years have seen plenty of good wines from this appellation, most notably from the village of La Livinière, which is packed with excellent producers.

• **Fitou:** One of the older appellations of the Languedoc. Fitou is divided into two geographically distinct sections (coastal and inland), which give it real potential as a producer of deep, well-structured red wines, made in a richly alcoholic Mediterranean style. Exceptions apart, overall quality remains quite consistent.

• **Corbières:** A huge appellation with plenty of wines to its name, but not necessarily very good ones. Plenty of dynamic producers nonetheless, turning out well-constructed red wines that avoid the rusticity of the average Corbières thanks to a lesser proportion of carignan. There's work being done to tighten up terroir boundaries, but for the time being the core areas (not necessarily mentioned on the label) are Boutenac, Lagrasse, and the Montagne d'Alaric. Note also the emerging vineyards at higher altitudes, producing white and rosé wines.

• **Muscat de Saint-Jean de Minervois and Muscat de Lunel:** Two appellations specializing in Vins Doux Naturels made from muscat grapes. Nothing special, except for those wines made by top producers.

Roussillon

The Roussillon is now producing ambitious, flavorful wines that are full of character, in keeping with the Catalan people who make them. Their only weakness is in the sweet wine category, where sales have proven difficult, which is particularly worrisome given that this is where you can find the most expressive wines of this wonderful region. It's up to you, the consumer, to save these complex wines, the loss of which would be irreplaceable.

Appellation Overview

• **Côtes du Roussillon and Côtes du Roussillon-Villages:** Very uneven quality, but the best of the red wines are well made and not overly heavy on alcohol. Thanks to a rich legacy of old grenache and carignan vines (left over from the days of sweet wine production), new producers soon manage to turn out wines with strong character. Wines on the rise include the white wines (driven by grenache gris and grenache blanc) from the limestone vineyards of Fenouillèdes in the northern Pyrénées-Orientales region.

• **Collioure:** Red and rosé wines from the vineyards of Banyuls. The reds are nicely balanced and quite delicate (if a bit too dry at times) and continue to improve. Prices can be a bit steep, though.

• **Banyuls and Banyuls Grand Cru:** Outstanding Vins Doux Naturels, some of which can rival the finest Ports. They come in two styles: traditional Banyuls, with the amber tones and elegant notes of rancio that come from several years aging in large oak casks; and vintage Banyuls (or Rimatges), a more brightly colored wine with aromas of black-skinned fruits.

• **Rivesaltes:** Another AOC for Vins Doux Naturels, but larger and less consistent than Banyuls. That said, the best of the traditional Rivesaltes are excellent and a far cry from the low-quality Rivesaltes that are often sold in French supermarkets.

• **Muscat de Rivesaltes:** When the wine retains a certain freshness on the palate, Muscat de Rivesaltes is a full-bodied, aromatic wine—ideal with fruit-based desserts.

• **Maury:** Vins Doux Naturels from the foothills of the Pyrenees. More fiery in style than a Rivesaltes and less complex than a Banyuls. Three or four really good producers at most.

Vins de Pays

This category is a real mixed bag, offering the best and the worst. For a start, it includes wines that are not entitled to AOC denomination, either because they come from areas outside the AOC area, or because growing practices don't follow the rules set by the appellation: certain popular varietals, such as cabernet and chardonnay for instance, are forbidden in AOC production. Also, scores of local producers find it more rewarding to make a Vin de Pays than an AOC wine of little or no reputation. Where the Languedoc-Roussillon is concerned, therefore, Vins de Pays are not necessarily inferior to their AOC counterparts—rather the reverse. But you do need to pick a good producer. Note, too, that many of the wines in this category (the most expensive ones) are made from a single, named grape variety but that some of them make a real mockery of the single-varietal style—starting with barrel-fermented chardonnay cuvées.

Languedoc Vineyards

(MILLAU)

COTEAUX DU LANGUEDOC
TERRASSES DU LARZA

Lodèv

CLAIRETTE DU LANGUEDOC

COTEAUX DU LANGUEDOC
TERRASSES DU LARZAC

Bédarieux

COTEAUX DU LANGUEDOC CABRIÈRES

Or   Faugères

FAUGÈRES

SAINT-CHINIAN
ROQUEBRUN   COTEA
                             LANGL
                             PÉZE

SAINT-CHINIAN
BERLOU   SAINT-
                CHINIAN

MUSCAT DE SAINT-JEAN-
DE-MINERVOIS   St-Chinian

SAINT
CHINIAN

COTEAUX DU LANGUED

Minerve

Caunes-
Minervois   MINERVOIS
                 LA LIVINIÈRE
                          MINERVOIS

CABARDÈS   Conques-sur-Orbiel   Olonzac

(TOULOUSE)
Montolieu   Béziers

N113

CARCASSONNE   MINERVOIS

Montréal   Lézignan-
                            Corbières   Narbonne   COTEAUX DU LANGUEDOC

MALEPÈRE   Capendu   COTEAUX DU
                                                     LANGUEDOC
                                                     LA CLAPE

Saint-Hilaire   Lagrasse   CORBIÈRES-
                                  BOUTENAC
                                                     Gruissan
Limoux
BLANQUETTE DE LIMOUX,   COTEAUX DU
CRÉMANT DE LIMOUX   LANGUEDOC
AND LIMOUX   CORBIÈRES   QUATOURZE

Cascatel-des-Corbières   Durban-
                          Corbières

FITOU   FITOU

Tuchan   Fitou   Leucate

                             Étang de Leucate

                     Salses-le-Château

0   5   10 miles

0 5 10   20 km

(PERPIGNAN)

Val
Pla

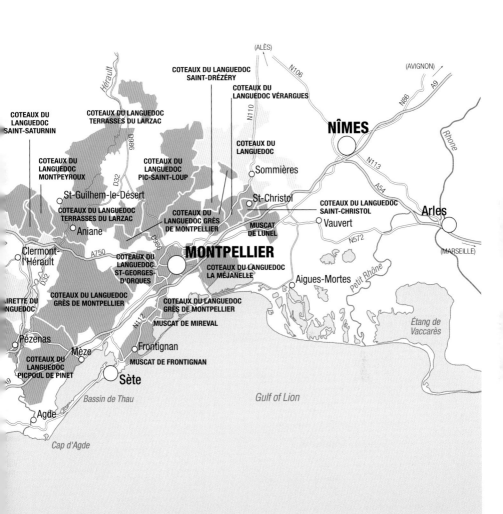

(ALÈS)

N106

(AVIGNON)

N86

A9

COTEAUX DU LANGUEDOC SAINT-DRÉZÉRY

COTEAUX DU LANGUEDOC VÉRARGUES

Hérault

N110

NÎMES

COTEAUX DU LANGUEDOC SAINT-SATURNIN

COTEAUX DU LANGUEDOC TERRASSES DU LARZAC

D986

COTEAUX DU LANGUEDOC

N113

Rhône

COTEAUX DU LANGUEDOC MONTPEYROUX

COTEAUX DU LANGUEDOC PIC-SAINT-LOUP

Sommières

A54

D32

St-Guilhem-le-Désert

COTEAUX DU LANGUEDOC TERRASSES DU LARZAC

COTEAUX DU LANGUEDOC GRÈS DE MONTPELLIER

St-Christol

COTEAUX DU LANGUEDOC SAINT-CHRISTOL

Arles

Aniane

D986

Vauvert

N572

(MARSEILLE)

Clermont-l'Hérault

A750

COTEAUX DU LANGUEDOC ST-GEORGES-D'ORQUES

MONTPELLIER

MUSCAT DE LUNEL

D32

COTEAUX DU LANGUEDOC GRÈS DE MONTPELLIER

COTEAUX DU LANGUEDOC LA MÉJANELLE

Aigues-Mortes

Petit Rhône

Étang de Vaccarès

IRETTE DU NGUEDOC

COTEAUX DU LANGUEDOC GRÈS DE MONTPELLIER

MUSCAT DE MIREVAL

N112

Pézenas

Mèze

Frontignan

COTEAUX DU LANGUEDOC PICPOUL DE PINET

MUSCAT DE FRONTIGNAN

9

Sète

Bassin de Thau

Gulf of Lion

Agde

Cap d'Agde

MEDITERRANEAN SEA

Village Appellations

Regional Appellations

Regional AOC Area

Roussillon Vineyards

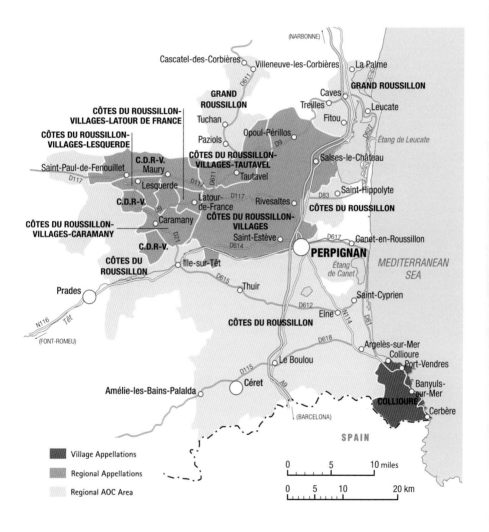

(NARBONNE)

Cascatel-des-Corbières · Villeneuve-les-Corbières · La Palme

GRAND ROUSSILLON

Caves · **GRAND ROUSSILLON**

GRAND ROUSSILLON

Treilles · Leucate

Fitou

CÔTES DU ROUSSILLON-VILLAGES-LATOUR DE FRANCE

Tuchan

CÔTES DU ROUSSILLON-VILLAGES-LESQUERDE

Paziols

Opoul-Périllos

Étang de Leucate

D9

CÔTES DU ROUSSILLON-VILLAGES-TAUTAVEL

Saint-Paul-de-Fenouillet

C.D.R-V. Maury

Salses-le-Château

D117

D611

Lesquerde

Tautavel

C.D.R-V.

Latour-de-France · Rivesaltes

Saint-Hippolyte

D117

D83

CÔTES DU ROUSSILLON

Caramany

CÔTES DU ROUSSILLON-VILLAGES-CARAMANY

D21

Caramany

CÔTES DU ROUSSILLON-VILLAGES

Saint-Estève

D617

Canet-en-Roussillon

C.D.R-V.

D614

PERPIGNAN

MEDITERRANEAN SEA

CÔTES DU ROUSSILLON

Ille-sur-Têt

Étang de Canet

D615

Thuir

Prades

Saint-Cyprien

N116 Têt

D612

Elne

N114

D81

(FONT-ROMEU)

CÔTES DU ROUSSILLON

D618

Argelès-sur-Mer

Collioure

Port-Vendres

Amélie-les-Bains-Palalda

D115

Le Boulou

Céret

A9

Banyuls-sur-Mer

COLLIOURE

Cerbère

(BARCELONA)

SPAIN

■ Village Appellations

■ Regional Appellations

▨ Regional AOC Area

0   5   10 miles

0   5   10   20 km

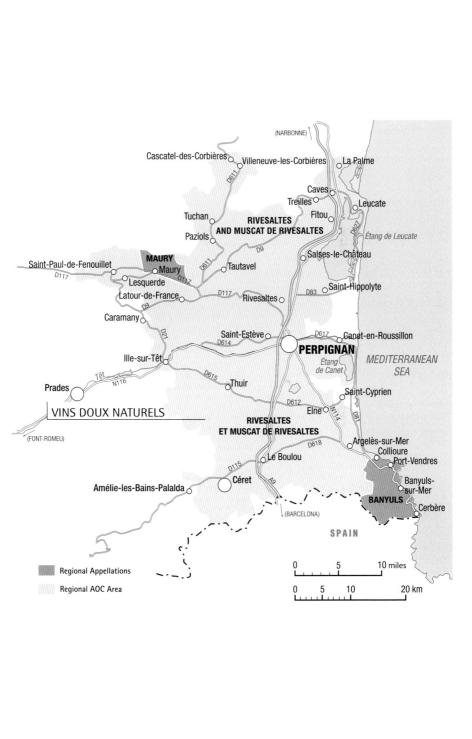

(NARBONNE)

Cascatel-des-Corbières   Villeneuve-les-Corbières   La Palme

Caves
Treilles   Leucate
Tuchan   **RIVESALTES**   Fitou
                AND MUSCAT DE RIVESALTES
Paziols   *Étang de Leucate*

                                D9
Saint-Paul-de-Fenouillet   **MAURY**   Salses-le-Château
            D117   Maury
        Lesquerde   Tautavel
        Latour-de-France   Saint-Hippolyte
                    D117   Rivesaltes   D83
    Caramany

            Saint-Estève   D617   Canet-en-Roussillon
            D614
    Ille-sur-Têt   **PERPIGNAN**   **MEDITERRANEAN**
                                                Étang   **SEA**
        Têt   *de Canet*
Prades   N116   Thuir
                                            Saint-Cyprien
VINS DOUX NATURELS
                        D612
(FONT-ROMEU)   Elne

                    RIVESALTES   Argelès-sur-Mer
                ET MUSCAT DE RIVESALTES   Collioure
                            D618   Port-Vendres
                    Le Boulou
            D115   Banyuls-
    Amélie-les-Bains-Palalda   Céret   sur-Mer
                                        BANYULS Cerbère

                    (BARCELONA)   **SPAIN**

            Regional Appellations   0   5   10 miles

            Regional AOC Area   0   5   10   20 km

LA CAVE DE L'ABBÉ ROUS

56, avenue Charles-de-Gaulle
66650 Banyuls-sur-Mer
Phone 00 33 4 68 88 72 72
Fax 00 33 4 68 88 30 57
contact@banyuls.com
www.abberous.com

The Cave de l'Abbé Rous is the business-oriented division of the Cellier des Templiers wine cooperative. It supplies wine merchants and restaurants with products of consistently high quality, all definitely worth seeking out. The Helyos and Christian Reynal cuvées are two benchmark examples of Banyuls style, with a palate that just goes on and on. The Cornet & Cie showcases the potential quality of the Collioure appellation and its grenache vines. The ultrarefined Cuvée Cyrcée relies on a blend of mourvèdre and syrah that rounds off the traditional mix of red varietals.

Recently tasted

COLLIOURE CORNET 2008
White | 2011 up to 2013   91

COLLIOURE CYRCÉE 2007
Red | 2011 up to 2013   95

Older vintages

BANYULS GRAND CRU CHRISTIAN REYNAL 1999
Sweet Red | 2011 up to 2013   94
A big Banyuls of cooked fruit, chocolate, and candied citrus flavors. The finish never ends.

BANYULS HELYOS 2003
Sweet Red | 2011 up to 2017   93
Cocoa and candied tangerine notes battle for dominance in this high-class Banyuls. Aristocratic and very elegant, this cuvée is held together by the vintage's powerful tannins.

COLLIOURE CORNET 2007
White | 2011 up to 2013   91
The magnificent grenache gris, too often overlooked, dominates the bouquet of this light and refreshing wine. It is lifted by rolle and rendered complex by other southern varieties. Savor the tropical notes and freshness.

COLLIOURE CYRCÉE 2005
Red | 2011 up to 2013   93
This wine has a bouquet that wouldn't be out of place among the great Médocs, and an absolutely refined texture. The oak in the finish is not yet integrated. Give it some time.

Red: 197.7 acres; carignan noir 12%, grenache gris 13%, grenache noir 63%, mourvèdre 6%, syrah 6%. White: 24.7 acres; grenache blanc 99%, vermentino 1%. Annual production: 670,000 bottles

CHÂTEAU D'AGEL

Les Crozes
34210 Agel
Phone 00 33 4 68 91 37 74
Fax 00 33 4 68 91 12 76
estelle.deheyer@châteaudagel.com
www.châteaudagel.com

The new team in charge here since 2003 has introduced a more modern style of wine and redesigned the labels to match: attractive graphics are now part of the tasting pleasure. The Vins de Pays d'Oc, marketed under the brand name Agellum, are as hedonistic as they come. Other wines include: Les Bonnes (Minervois), named after the vineyard and not the servants who once worked for the château ("bonnes" means servants in French); Caudios, a cask-matured range; and the In Extremis, a syrah-grenache blend produced only in good vintages. All very successful.

Recently tasted

MINERVOIS CAUDIOS 2007
White | 2011 up to 2013   88

MINERVOIS CAUDIOS 2007
Red | 2011 up to 2013   87

MINERVOIS LES BONNES 2007
White | 2011 up to 2013   86

Older vintages

MINERVOIS AGELLUM MUSCAT 2005
White | 2011 up to 2009   87
A delicate, dry and aromatic muscat, floral and elegant. A perfect before-dinner wine, not aggressive, very charming.

MINERVOIS CAUDIOS 2005
Red | 2011 up to 2013   88
This powerful wine is still marked by oak, with a spicy and delicious finish.

MINERVOIS IN EXTREMIS 2005
Red | 2011 up to 2013   89
The bouquet is strongly vanilla-scented with blackberry and dark berry notes. A touch of sweetness is perceptible in the finish, and the tannins are elegant and refined.

MINERVOIS LES BONNES 2006
Red | 2011 up to 2008   86
Relatively easy, with a limited structure, this is easy to drink, with fruit in the finish.

Red: 79.1 acres; carignan noir 26%, cinsault 1%, grenache noir 18%, mourvèdre 12%, syrah 43%. White: 14.8 acres; grenache blanc 5%, maccabeu 30%, muscat à petits grains 40%, roussanne 15%, vermentino 10%. Annual production: 190,000 bottles

DOMAINE DES AIRES HAUTES

Chemin des Aires
34210 Siran
Phone 00 33 4 68 91 54 40
Fax 00 33 4 68 91 54 40
gilles.chabbert@wanadoo.fr

Located on the Petit Causse, deep in the Minervois region, this Siran-based winery offers a range of skillfully crafted wines: from Vins de Pays with precise varietal expressions to the elegantly styled and tastefully tannic Clos de l'Escandil, alongside a supremely expressive Minervois-la-Livinière.

Recently tasted
MINERVOIS-LA-LIVINIÈRE 2007
Red | 2011 up to 2013　　　　　　　86

MINERVOIS-LA-LIVINIÈRE
CLOS DE L'ESCANDIL 2007
Red | 2011 up to 2013　　　　　　　90

MINERVOIS-LA-LIVINIÈRE
CLOS DE L'ESCANDIL 2006
Red | 2011 up to 2013　　　　　　　89

Older vintages
MINERVOIS 2005
Red | 2011 up to 2008　　　　　　　85
Fruity and round, expressive and easy to approach.

MINERVOIS-LA-LIVINIÈRE
CLOS DE L'ESCANDIL 2005
Red | 2011 up to 2013　　　　　　　88
This wine is marked by its oak, which will soften as it ages and reveals its elegant tannins. It has the potential to improve over the next few years.

MINERVOIS-LA-LIVINIÈRE
CLOS DE L'ESCANDIL 2004
Red | 2011 up to 2013　　　　　　　88
With its power, this wine is stamped by the terroir of La Livinière. It is deep and long with great density.

MINERVOIS-LA-LIVINIÈRE
CLOS DE L'ESCANDIL 2003
Red | 2011 up to 2008　　　　　　　87
Marked by its vintage, this wine shows its class in a remarkable mid-palate, but has disappointingly dry tannins that perturb its pleasurable finish.

Red: 69.2 acres; carignan 15%, grenache noir 20%, malbec 10%, mourvèdre 10%, syrah 45%. White: 4.9 acres; chardonnay 50%, sauvignon 50%. Annual production: 125,000 bottles

MAS AMIEL

Mas Amiel
66460 Maury
Phone 00 33 4 68 29 01 02
Fax 00 33 4 68 29 17 82
contact@lvod.fr
www.masamiel.fr

Mas Amiel was at the forefront of the qualitative and commercial revival of Maury wines. Since it was acquired by Olivier Decelle in 1997, this great domaine has rounded off its offerings with two new wines—Les Carérades (red) and Altaïr (white)—that complement its range of universally acclaimed Vins Doux Naturels. The Vintage Réserve wines, led by the Vintage Charles Dupuy, have been an oenophile's delight for ages, but there's plenty more to choose from in this range. A Maury aged in a reductive or oxidative environment is an awesome combination with any chocolate-based dish. All of the wines from this winery show great quality.

Recently tasted
MAURY VINTAGE 2007
Sweet Red | 2011 up to 2018　　　　　88

MAURY VINTAGE BLANC 2007
Sweet White | 2013 up to 2020　　　　90

Older vintages
CÔTES DU ROUSSILLON-VILLAGES
CARÉRADES 2006
Red | 2011 up to 2013　　　　　　　90
For this grenache, syrah, and carignan blend, 2006 was a good year. Still oaky, it has a refined tannic grain and a full-bodied finish.

CÔTES DU ROUSSILLON-VILLAGES CARÉRADES 2005
Red | 2011 up to 2013　　　　　　　89
Carérades is a wine of great density and depth. It lacks the freshness of Roussillon's biggest wines, but has a very delicate tannic grain. It shows how this domaine has progressed with its dry red wines.

MAURY VINTAGE CHARLES DUPUY 2006
Sweet Red | 2011 up to 2018　　　　　95
The Charles Dupuy cuvée is the quintessence of a reductively aged Maury. Its finesse is superlative, playing up the wine's dense and satiny body.

Red: 308.9 acres; carignan noir 13%, grenache noir 70%, syrah 17%. White: 61.8 acres; grenache blanc 29%, muscat à petits grains 64%, roussanne 7%. Annual production: 350,000 bottles

L'ANCIENNE MERCERIE

6, rue de l'Égalité
34480 Autignac
Phone 00 33 4 67 90 27 02
Fax 00 33 4 67 90 27 02
ancienne.mercerie@free.fr

This little-known property in the southern part of the Faugères AOC is home to Nathalie and François Caumette, trained bioengineers and enologists who make two irresistible cuvées from grapes that were planted by their forebears and are now vinified in what was once a notions store ("mercerie" in French). This is grand vin in every sense: the fabulous fruit in Les Petites Mains makes it more than just an entry-level wine, while the Cuvée Couture delivers freshness and delicacy from a blend of traditional varietals that marries one-third syrah with equal proportions of grenache, mourvèdre, and Carignan.

Recently tasted
COTEAUX DU LANGUEDOC 2008
Red | 2011 up to 2014   **88**

FAUGÈRES LES PETITES MAINS 2008
Red | 2011 up to 2013   **88**

Older vintages
FAUGÈRES COUTURE 2006
Red | 2011 up to 2014   **89**
Partially cask aged, this cuvée has a touch more complementary complexity due to its barrel time than the Petites Mains cuvée.

FAUGÈRES COUTURE 2005
Red | 2011 up to 2013   **91**
Vinified traditionally, this cuvée was partially cask aged. The élevage adds volume to the palate, which points up the freshness and delicacy this domaine obtains from the Faugères terroir.

FAUGÈRES LES PETITES MAINS 2007
Red | 2011 up to 2013   **90**
Delicacy in a bottle: red berry aromas open naturally with joyful freshness.

FAUGÈRES LES PETITES MAINS 2006
Red | 2011 up to 2013   **90**
With big and round tannins, this is dense yet silky and caressing.

Red: 39.5 acres; carignan noir 35%, cinsault 5%, grenache noir 25%, mourvèdre 10%, syrah 25%.
Annual production: 35,000 bottles

DOMAINE D'AUPILHAC

28, rue du Plô
34150 Montpeyroux
Phone 00 33 4 67 96 61 19
Fax 00 33 4 67 96 67 24
aupilhac@wanadoo.fr
www.aupilhac.com

Sylvain Fadat started out with a small family vineyard in 1988 and has since become a champion of the Montpeyroux terroir as well as a firm supporter of the much-maligned carignan grape. Some of his cuvées tend to show their animal side, but at their best they rank among the finest Languedoc offerings. His top-end wines come from Les Cocalières, terraced plots at a higher altitude, which sing loud and clear in his red, syrah-based wines; the 2006 was a knockout.

Recently tasted
COTEAUX DU LANGUEDOC LA BODA 2006
Red | 2011 up to 2017   **90**

COTEAUX DU LANGUEDOC LES COCALIÈRES 2007
White | 2011 up to 2013   **90**

COTEAUX DU LANGUEDOC LOU MASET 2008
Red | 2011 up to 2013   **86**

Older vintages
COTEAUX DU LANGUEDOC LA BODA 2005
Red | 2011 up to 2013   **89**
Beautiful aging and very unctuous tannins give charm to this wine made from very ripe grapes. The finish is very slightly dry.

COTEAUX DU LANGUEDOC
LES COCALIÈRES ROUGE 2005
Red | 2011 up to 2013   **89**
A wine of great power, just beginning to mature. The tannins are refined and roasted notes dominate the nose, especially coffee.

COTEAUX DU LANGUEDOC MONTPEYROUX 2006
Red | 2011 up to 2013   **86**
Lovely fruit and texture, with a slightly dry finish at this time; lightly animal.

VIN DE PAYS DU MONT BAUDILE LE CARIGNAN 2006
Red | 2011 up to 2013   **87**
Here's a lovely red, quite in line with its grape variety, with structure and lovely length.

Red: 64.2 acres; alicante 2%, aramon 2%, carignan noir 20%, cinsault 3%, grenache noir 15%, mourvèdre 30%, syrah 28%. White: 5.4 acres; chardonnay 10%, grenache blanc 15%, marsanne 30%, roussanne 15%, ugni blanc 15%, vermentino 15%. Annual production: 130,000 bottles

CHÂTEAU D'AUSSIÈRES

RD 613
11100 Narbonne
Phone 00 33 4 68 45 17 67
Fax 00 33 4 68 45 76 38
aussieres@lafite.com
www.lafite.com

When the Lafite branch of the Barons de Rothschild settled in Narbonne they brought their expertise with them. Since then, they have invested in the Corbières and Vins de Pays d'Oc regions, where they make wines that are the complete antithesis of the usual overextracted Languedoc wine. The aim here is to bring out the fruit and floral component in the red and white wines alike. Without slavishly copying Bordeaux, each one is matured in accordance with its own unique potential—and it shows.

VIN DE PAYS D'OC 2007
Red | 2011 up to 2013   **85**
Fifty percent cabernet franc and sauvignon, 10 percent merlot, with the rest made up of grenache and syrah, this is a blend of cultures. With Cabardès typicity, it is pleasant, simple, and precise.

VIN DE PAYS D'OC 2006
Red | 2011 up to 2013   **86**
The fruit quality is quite clear due to a remarkably precise vinification. The aging has preserved the extract and underlined it.

CORBIÈRES AUSSIÈRES ROUGE 2006
Red | 2011 up to 2013   **88**
Very beautiful material here, with nearly crunchy fruit. The finish is precise and very pure.

CORBIÈRES AUSSIÈRES ROUGE 2005
Red | 2011 up to 2013   **90**
This wine's floral finesse has been perfectly preserved. The vintner's performance is commendable, because he drew beautiful and flavorful elegance out of this Corbières.

CORBIÈRES BLASON D'AUSSIÈRES 2005
Red | 2011 up to 2013   **89**
The second wine of d'Aussières, this is delicate with beautiful freshness. It was not forced to give what it doesn't have. Rather, all that it is capable of offering has been delicately extracted and bottled.

Red: 395.4 acres; cabernet sauvignon 10%, carignan noir 11%, grenache noir 24%, mourvèdre 15%, syrah 30%, other 10%. White: 24.7 acres; chardonnay 100%.
Annual production: 500,000 bottles

MAS D'AUZIÈRES

22, rue de la Bénovie
Mas de Fontan
34270 Fontanes
Phone 00 33 4 67 85 39 54
Fax 00 33 4 67 85 39 54
irene@auzieres.com
www.auzieres.com

Irène Tolleret quit her job with the giant Val d'Orbieu cooperative in the Languedoc to set up this winery in the Coteaux du Languedoc AOC, north of Montpellier, probably set to become part of the Pic Saint-Loup appellation. With the help of her enologist husband, she cultivates a twenty-three-acre vineyard surrounded by pines and low vegetation. The range is small for the time being, but all of the wines share terrifically refined tannins. An estate to watch.

Recently tasted
COTEAUX DU LANGUEDOC LE BOIS DE PÉRIÉ 2006
Red | 2011 up to 2016   **90**
It's true that the notes of vanilla and fresh fruit dominate the nose, but the most interesting aspect of this wine is its structure and purity, which will enable it to age. The complex finish adds spice and an aromatic palate to an already well-endowed wine.

COTEAUX DU LANGUEDOC LES ÉCLATS 2007
Red | 2011 up to 2013   **90**
The fruit is magnificent. If 2006 is pleasant, 2007 is to die for. The texture is remarkable, diabolically precise. And that's not all!

Older vintages
COTEAUX DU LANGUEDOC LE BOIS DE PÉRIÉ 2005
Red | 2011 up to 2013   **91**
It required skill and precision to bring up the 2005s, to round out the slightly dry tannins of the vintage and to bring forth the depth of the exceptionally well-ripened grapes.

COTEAUX DU LANGUEDOC LES ÉCLATS 2005
Red | 2011 up to 2013   **88**
The year 2005 was clearly lacking in rainfall, but this domaine aimed for voluptuous tannins and has succeeded in gently extracting them. Lovely texture.

COTEAUX DU LANGUEDOC LES ÉCLATS 2004
Red | 2011 up to 2013   **88**
This Coteaux du Languedoc brings to mind the typicity of Pic-Saint-Loups in suppleness and density. The tannins are very delicate.

Annual production: 35,000 bottles

CLOS BAGATELLE

Clos Bagatelle
34360 Saint-Chinian
Phone 00 33 4 67 93 61 63
Fax 00 33 4 67 93 68 84
closbagatelle@wanadoo.fr
www.closbagatelle.com

Few wineries are as proficient in making and maturing wines as this one. Every one a winner: from the successful entry-level Cuvée Tradition, to the wickedly tempting Cuvée Mathieu et Marie, and the imposing Veillée d'Automne—which takes you into the realm of great wine—or the definitively pleasurable La Gloire de mon Père.

Recently tasted

SAINT-CHINIAN DONNADIEU
CAMILLE ET JULIETTE 2007
Red | 2011 up to 2013   **87**

SAINT-CHINIAN DONNADIEU MATHIEU ET MARIE 2007
Red | 2011 up to 2013   **88**
Syrah based, this really shows off the characteristics of the varietal, spices and black fruit. We want more!

SAINT-CHINIAN JE ME SOUVIENS 2007
Red | 2011 up to 2013   **91**

SAINT-CHINIAN LULU CARIGNAN 2008
Red | 2011 up to 2013   **89**

SAINT-CHINIAN TRADITION 2008
Red | 2011 up to 2013   **87**
From grapes grown on clayey-limestone soils, this is a charming, fruity, and spicy wine.

SAINT-CHINIAN VEILLÉE D'AUTOMNE 2007
Red | 2011 up to 2013   **90**

SAINT-CHINIAN VEILLÉE D'AUTOMNE 2006
Red | 2011 up to 2015   **90**

Older vintages

SAINT-CHINIAN DONNADIEU
CAMILLE ET JULIETTE 2006
Red | 2011 up to 2013   **85**
Powerful and friendly, this fruity wine would be even better with a touch more freshness.

SAINT-CHINIAN DONNADIEU
MATHIEU ET MARIE 2005
Red | 2011 up to 2013   **88**
Incredibly hedonistic, this wine has a nose of antique roses and licorice, with great fullness on the palate.

Red: 116.1 acres; carignan noir 15%, cinsault 5%, grenache noir 30%, mourvèdre 20%, syrah 30%. White: 24.7 acres; carignan blanc 5%, grenache blanc 10%, muscat à petits grains 75%, roussanne 10%. Annual production: 250,000 bottles

DOMAINE DE BARROUBIO

34360 Saint-Jean-de-Minervois
Phone 00 33 4 67 38 14 06
Fax 00 33 4 67 38 14 06
barroubio@barroubio.fr
www.barroubio.fr

This estate has been in the same family since the fifteenth century. It was originally famous for its Muscats de Saint Jean de Minervois, sourced from white limestone soils at the northern end of the Causse du Minervois. The red wines have improved significantly since then, now displaying delicate hints of flowers that make them surprisingly charming. The Cuvée Marie-Thérèse relies on the syrah while the carignan gives structure to the Cuvée Jean Miquel. A serious producer.

MINERVOIS 2006
Red | 2011 up to 2013   **88**
This cuvée exudes delicious red-berry flavor in a most natural way. Crisp and truly easy to drink.

MINERVOIS JEAN MIQUEL 2004
Red | 2011 up to 2013   **90**
Floral notes of lilies introduce this refined and delicate wine. Made mostly of carignan, it has a particularly elegant finish.

MINERVOIS MARIE-THÉRÈSE 2005
Red | 2011 up to 2013   **87**
What a shame that the oak is a bit too present, as the juice is remarkable. The flavorful finish lasts on leather, spices, and red berries.

MUSCAT SAINT-JEAN-DE-MINERVOIS 2006
Sweet White | 2011 up to 2013   **86**
The 2006s continue in the style of the 2005s: a fat and balanced muscat, intensely aromatic, finishing on good acidity.

MUSCAT SAINT-JEAN-DE-MINERVOIS 2005
Sweet White | 2011 up to 2009   **86**
Fat and balanced muscat, intensely scented, finishing on good acidity.

Red: 24.7 acres; carignan 32%, grenache 32%, syrah 36%. White: 42 acres; muscat à petits grains 100%. Annual production: 100,000 bottles

MAS BAUX

Voie des Coteaux
66140 Canet-en-Roussillon
Phone 00 33 4 68 80 25 04
Fax 00 33 4 68 80 25 04
contact@mas-baux.com
www.mas-baux.com

This winery, with its lovely parcels around Canet-en-Roussillon, was started by Gérard Baux after a career in the mining industry. The proximity of the Mediterranean (less than two miles away) allows Gérard to pamper his vines and leave them to get really ripe. He treats his wine cellar like a laboratory, looking to retain all the quality of the grape; and to judge by the quality of his red, white, and rosé wines, he succeeds. The Côtes du Roussillon Soleil red is a real winner and ages superbly. The Rivesaltes Tuilé is also definitely worth the trip.

Recently tasted
CÔTES DU ROUSSILLON SOLEIL ROUGE 2006
Red | 2011 up to 2014   88

VIN DE PAYS DES CÔTES CATALANES
SÉRIE B 2008
White | 2011 up to 2013   86

Older vintages
CÔTES DU ROUSSILLON SOLEIL ROUGE 2005
Red | 2011 up to 2013   89
Powerful yet with delicate tannins, this lovely Vin de Pays has dark-berry flavors and an elegant and refined finish.

CÔTES DU ROUSSILLON SOLEIL ROUGE 2004
Red | 2011 up to 2013   90
Mourvèdre and syrah are the principal varieties in this structured wine with beautiful finesse.

MUSCAT DE RIVESALTES L'ORIGINAL 2006
Sweet White | 2011 up to 2013   86
A lovely aromatic and taut muscat with pink grapefruit and menthol notes. It is perfectly dry, well adapted to enjoying before dinner, since it won't overtax the taste buds with excess sugar.

RIVESALTES GRAIN DE BEAUTÉ
Sweet Red | 2011 up to 2013   90
The lightly peppery finish in this lovely brick-colored gastronomic wine required more than six years in oak to achieve. Patience has been rewarded.

Red: 26.4 acres; cabernet sauvignon 11%, grenache noir 28%, mourvèdre 28%, syrah 33%. White: 4.7 acres; muscat à petits grains 100%. Annual production: 35,000 bottles

DOMAINE BELLES EAUX

Château Belles-Eaux
34720 Caux
Phone 00 33 4 67 09 30 96
Fax 00 33 4 67 90 85 45
contact@mas-belleseaux.com
www.château-belleseaux.com

This large property is located north of Pezenas. Surrounded by freshwater springs, which gave the winery its name, the vineyards extend over 250 acres around a whimsical nineteenth-century farmhouse. The domaine was acquired by AXA Millésimes portfolio in 2003, and since then they have made huge efforts to improve the brand. The product line includes Vin de Pays and Coteaux du Languedoc. The cuvée Sainte-Hélène brings together the best of what this winery has to offer. All of the wines are made in a dense, structured, resolutely modern style.

Recently tasted
LANGUEDOC LES COTEAUX 2006
Red | 2011 up to 2013   86

Older vintages
LANGUEDOC LES COTEAUX 2005
Red | 2011 up to 2013   86
From a gravel ridge, this wine is darkly colored, with simple tannins and a round finish. The 2005 will pair perfectly with grilled meats, enveloping them with its density.

LANGUEDOC SAINTE-HÉLÈNE 2005
Red | 2011 up to 2013   89
Made from syrah, grenache, and carignan, this wine's dark color announces a creamy red, concentrated and powerful with elegant tannins. Long on the palate, it finishes on vanilla, with a creamy texture.

Annual production: 200,000 bottles

GÉRARD BERTRAND

Château l'Hospitalet
Route de Narbonne-Plage
11100 Narbonne
Phone 00 33 4 68 45 36 00
Fax 00 33 4 68 45 27 17
vins@gerard-bertrand.com
www.gerard-bertrand.com

A broad range of wines from this enterprising winegrower, from the delicious and very successful Domaines de Villemajou and l'Hospitalet to the top-of-the-range La Forge, one of the most refined Corbières ever with an unbelievably velvety texture. The only snag is price, which already positions it among the prestige Languedoc cuvées. The equivalent Minervois offering is the Cuvée Le Viala, which may not be as sumptuously refined as La Forge but is fabulously charming nonetheless.

COTEAUX DU LANGUEDOC
CHÂTEAU L'HOSPITALET GRAND VIN 2005
Red | 2011 up to 2013   **92**
A remarkable and remarked wine. Aristocratic and very elegant, the tannins are very delicate with a touch of peonies and menthol. It is quietly maturing toward truffles.

COTEAUX DU LANGUEDOC
CHÂTEAU L'HOSPITALET LA RÉSERVE 2006
Red | 2011 up to 2013   **88**
A big wine marked by its terroir. Salty, powerful, and long.

MINERVOIS-LA-LIVINIÈRE
CHÂTEAU LAVILLE BERTROU 2006
Red | 2011 up to 2013   **90**
Explosively fresh, with surprisingly unctuous tannins. Bravo! The year 2006 marks a break in the style of this wine.

MINERVOIS-LA-LIVINIÈRE LE VIALA 2005
Red | 2011 up to 2013   **93**
A very big Minervois with surprisingly refined tannins. The freshness and finesse meet up in the finish!

VIN DE PAYS D'OC DOMAINE DE L'AIGLE 2007
Red | 2011 up to 2013   **89**
An aromatic explosion held together by light oak that makes a perfect before-dinner wine. Delicious and cajoling.

Red: 494.2 acres. White: 370.7 acres. Annual production: 400,000 bottles

DOMAINE BERTRAND-BERGÉ

38, avenue du Roussillon
11350 Paziols
Phone 00 33 4 68 45 41 73
Fax 00 33 4 68 45 03 94
bertrand-berge@wanadoo.fr
www.bertrand-berge.com

This domaine is now the model for the entire appellation thanks to the work and expertise put into these lovely vineyards in Paziols by owner-winemaker Jérome Bertrand. The entry-level reds are reasonably priced but definitely a cut above the usual Fitou. The creamy Cuvée Jean Sirven, so-called after the ancestor who was already working toward quality viticulture at the start of the last century, boasts all the breeding and density of the great, blue-blooded southern wines. The Muscat de Rivesaltes, in particular, serves as a benchmark for the entire appellation: not a trace of overblown sweetness, just that pure fruit expression that is the mark of great muscat wines. The vintage-type Vin Doux Naturel, Rivesaltes Tuilé "Ma Ga," is also right up there with the best of them.

Recently tasted
FITOU MÉGALITHES 2007
Red | 2011 up to 2013   **88**

FITOU ORIGINE 2007
Red | 2011 up to 2013   **89**

Older vintages
FITOU ANCESTRALE 2005
Red | 2011 up to 2013   **89**
The depth of this wine's aromas is amazing. It is absolutely delicious, with appetizing tannins. A well-rounded wine.

FITOU JEAN SIRVEN 2006
Red | 2011 up to 2017   **94**
The year 2006 holds consistently with this cuvée's history. The class and pedigree are there, brought by its exceptionally round and delicate tannins, lightly chocolaty. It's surely one of Languedoc's great wines.

FITOU MÉGALITHES 2006
Red | 2011 up to 2013   **90**
Yet again an amazing tour de force has been achieved in refining carignan, by far the dominant grape of this blend. The finish brings a hint of acidity and stunning roundness.

FITOU ORIGINE 2005
Red | 2011 up to 2013   **88**
If only all the introductory Languedoc-Roussillon AOC wines were at this level!

Muscat de Rivesaltes 2006
Sweet White | 2011 up to 2013   **93**
A pleasing muscat, very fresh and truly precise. Its subtle notes of peaches and exceptional length make it a point of reference.

Rivesaltes Tuilé Ma Ga 2006
Sweet Red | 2011 up to 2017   **93**
The refined, chocolaty notes will be in perfect communion with dessert.

Red: 71.7 acres; carignan noir 34%, grenache noir 30%, merlot 2%, mourvèdre 7%, syrah 27%. White: 9.8 acres; maccabeu 30%, muscat à petits grains 70%. Annual production: 100,000 bottles

BORIE DE MAUREL

Rue de la Sallèle
34210 Félines-Minervois
Phone 00 33 4 68 91 68 58
Fax 00 33 4 68 91 63 92
contact@boriedemaurel.fr
www.boriedemaurel.fr

Visionary esthete Michel Escande is one of the forerunners of the Minervois revival. Some may seem to have reached the high point of their career, but Escande is constantly looking to improve performance from his winery in Félines, noted for some of the best holdings in this area. Even his entry-level bottlings are plainly the work of a master winemaker. The peerlessly refined Sylla is one of the most outstanding of all the regional offerings. Carbonic maceration adds a particularly charming touch.

Recently tasted
Minervois Belle de Nuit 2007
Red | 2011 up to 2013   **87**

Minervois Esprit d'Automne 2007
Red | 2011 up to 2013   **84**

Minervois Sylla 2006
Red | 2011 up to 2013   **90**

Older vintages
Minervois Esprit d'Automne 2006
Red | 2011 up to 2013   **85**
With a bouquet of sous-bois and tobacco, this wine is well named. It is open and ready to drink.

Minervois Esprit d'Automne 2005
Red | 2011 up to 2013   **86**
With scents of sous-bois, this wine has earned its name. It is open and ready to drink. The tannic finesse of this introductory cuvée is a good introduction to the great wines of Minervois.

Minervois Sylla 2005
Red | 2011 up to 2013   **92**
The nose offers up notes of pink grapefruit, truffles, menthol, and black currants. It is charming, but 2005 wasn't a year that permitted going as far as other vintages in total complexity.

Minervois-La-Livinière La Féline 2005
Red | 2011 up to 2013   **86**
The terroir stamps its power on this wine with the tannins of 2005. Its fleshy volume should soften the tannins, if given the time. With a hint of truffles!

Red: 79.1 acres; carignan 46%, grenache 17%, syrah 33%, other 4%. White: 2.5 acres; marsanne 90%, muscat à petits grains 10%. Annual production: 140,000 bottles

BORIE LA VITARÈLE

Borie La Vitarèle
34490 Causses-et-Veyran
Phone 00 33 4 67 89 50 43
Fax 00 33 4 67 89 70 79
jf.izarn@libertysurf.fr
www.borielavitarele.fr

The surrounding woods shield this vineyard from the more environmentally intrusive methods used by its neighbors, making it an ideal place to experiment with biodynamics. The Terres Blanches is a refreshing entry-level wine, and we have to admit to a weakness for the refined cuvée Les Schistes. Jean-François Izarn is especially fond of Les Crès, because he has almost nothing to do in the vineyard. The vines there deliver naturally low yields, producing concentrated wines that age remarkably well—sure to appeal to those who want more structured Saint-Chinian wines with precise mineral flavors.

Recently tasted
SAINT-CHINIAN LES SCHISTES 2007
Red | 2011 up to 2013   91

SAINT-CHINIAN TERRES BLANCHES 2008
Red | 2011 up to 2013   88

VIN DE PAYS DES COTEAUX DE MURVIEL
LA COMBE 2007
Red | 2011 up to 2013   87

Older vintages
SAINT-CHINIAN LES CRÈS 2004
Red | 2011 up to 2013   89
A powerful wine with great aromatic depth. With a bit of time, all its potential charm will be realized. The mineral finish is tasty.

SAINT-CHINIAN LES SCHISTES 2006
Red | 2011 up to 2013   91
As always, this cuvée of grenache and syrah has absolutely refined tannins. Saint-Chinian's schist terroir is illuminated in this extremely aromatic and powerfully flavored wine.

SAINT-CHINIAN TERRES BLANCHES 2006
Red | 2011 up to 2013   88
An introductory Saint-Chinian, very straightforward with a deep and fleshy texture. The mineral and spicy finish is refreshing.

SAINT-CHINIAN TERRES BLANCHES 2005
Red | 2011 up to 2013   88
An introductory wine in Saint-Chinian. Very straightforward, with a deep and fleshy texture. The finish is mineral and refreshing.

Red: 37.1 acres; cabernet sauvignon 15%, carignan noir 2%, grenache noir 33%, merlot 5%, mourvèdre 5%, syrah 40%. **Annual production:** 60,000 bottles

CHÂTEAU LE BOUÏS

Route Bleue
11430 Gruissan
Phone 00 33 4 68 75 25 25
Fax 00 33 4 68 75 25 26
château.le.bouis@wanadoo.fr
www.châteaulebouis.fr

The whites and rosés from this winery in Gruissan are fairly unremarkable; the reds, on the other hand, display those impeccably refined tannins that make them classic examples of their type. The Arthur cuvée is dense, deep, and elegant with not a trace of that rusticity still seen in too many Corbières. The K lacks Arthur's immediate appeal but makes up for it with even greater long-term potential. The estate farms some beautifully located parcels in the foothills of the Massif de La Clape and along the coast. Sea spume and the constant wind that blows through Gruissan no doubt have something to do with the freshness of its reds.

Recently tasted
CORBIÈRES 2007
Red | 2011 up to 2013   90

Older vintages
CORBIÈRES 2006
Red | 2011 up to 2013   90
The nose bursts with pepper and dark berries, followed by magnificent palate expression. It is classy and delicious, with airy tannins. Beautiful work.

CORBIÈRES ARTHUR 2005
Red | 2011 up to 2013   92
With its refined tannins, yet still-rough finish, this wine asks only for a bit more time to soften.

CORBIÈRES K 2005
Red | 2011 up to 2013   95
The nose bluffs in its complexity. Its light texture is particularly classy. The lightly saline finish is exceptionally delectable. In its style, it is one of the great wines of the south.

CORBIÈRES ZOÉ 2006
Red | 2011 up to 2013   86
A joyous and elegant wine, dense, with a lovely mentholated and delicious finish.

Red: 49.4 acres; alicante 7%, carignan noir 25%, grenache noir 28%, mourvèdre 15%, syrah 25%. White: 12.4 acres; grenache blanc 35%, roussanne 41%, viognier 24%. **Annual production:** 30,000 bottles

MAS DES BROUSSES

2, chemin du Bois
34150 Puechabon
Phone 00 33 4 67 57 33 75
Fax 00 33 4 67 57 33 75
geraldine.combes@wanadoo.fr
www.masdesbrousses.fr

Géraldine Combes and Xavier Peyraud (originally from Domaine Tempier in Bandol) work about twenty acres in the Terrasses du Larzac appellation. They released their first-ever vintage in 1997 and now produce a merlot-grenache Vin de Pays and a high-flying Coteaux du Languedoc that ages exceptionally well. It is blended from syrah and mourvèdre wines that are matured in well-seasoned casks so as not to discolor the finished wine and to keep all of its staggering naturalness intact. Coming soon from this exceptional producer: a selection of white wines to round off the range.

Recently tasted
COTEAUX DU LANGUEDOC 2007
Red | 2011 up to 2015   **93**

COTEAUX DU LANGUEDOC MATARO 2007
Red | 2011 up to 2014   **91**

LE CHASSEUR DES BROUSSES 2008
Red | 2011 up to 2013   **88**

Older vintages
COTEAUX DU LANGUEDOC 2006
Red | 2011 up to 2013   **91**
More powerful and better dressed than the 2005, this new version of Mas des Brousses holds true to the refined, airy and silky texture we've become accustomed to, possible due to the high altitude of its parcel, and to the masterful technique of the vintner.

COTEAUX DU LANGUEDOC 2005
Red | 2011 up to 2013   **91**
What refined texture in this superlight, silky wine, all made possible by a high-altitude terroir and masterful technique.

LE CHASSEUR DES BROUSSES 2006
Red | 2011 up to 2013   **87**
A dense, powerful, and elegant Vin de Pays that will pair perfectly with Mediterranean dishes such as a daube. The finish is very fresh.

Red: 21 acres; carignan 7%, cinsault 10%, grenache 16%, merlot 16%, mourvèdre 18%, syrah 21%.
Annual production: 25,000 bottles

CHÂTEAU DE CABEZAC

16-18, hameau de Cabezac
11120 Bize-Minervois
Phone 00 33 4 68 46 23 05
Fax 00 33 4 68 46 21 93
info@châteaucabezac.com
www.châteaucabezac.com

The proprietor here is a businessman who specializes in gum arabic, a substance widely used in viticulture and commercial food production. The winery is located in Les Serres, a winegrowing region with a Mediterranean climate, planted on the stony Quaternary-period terraces of the Belvèze plateau and in favored plots on the Cazelles plateau higher up. As these newer plantings gradually come on stream, they should add even greater complexity to an estate that already boasts obvious technical expertise. The Carinu is an uncommonly delicious take on carignan and the top-end cuvées, Arthur and Belvèze, are testimony to first-rate winemaking skills.

Recently tasted
MINERVOIS LES CAPITELLES 2007
White | 2011 up to 2013   **86**

VIN DE PAYS DU VAL DE CESSE CARINU 2006
Red | 2011 up to 2013   **87**

Older vintages
MINERVOIS ARTHUR 2005
Red | 2011 up to 2013   **88**
The 2005 is a delight, with quality tannins that should soften the oak tannins. It feels airy, with a particularly aromatic finish.

MINERVOIS ARTHUR 2004
Red | Drink now   **88**
An ethereal wine, fruity with delicate tannins. The 2004 has now fully integrated its oak and has developed pleasantly spicy, truffle aromas.

Red: 135.9 acres; cabernet sauvignon 7%, carignan 32%, grenache noir 17%, mourvèdre 14%, syrah 30%.
White: 17.3 acres; grenache blanc 25%, maccabeu 19%, muscat 19%, roussanne 37%. Annual production: 180,000 bottles

MAS CAL DEMOURA

3A, Route de Saint-André
34725 Jonquières
Phone 00 33 4 67 44 70 82
Fax 00 33 4 67 88 59 35
info@caldemoura.com
www.caldemoura.com

This winery in Jonquières, in the Terrasses du Larzac appellation, was started by Jean-Pierre Jullien (father of Mas Jullien owner Olivier Jullien). When Jean-Pierre retired in 2004 the winery was taken over by former financial adviser Vincent Goumard, who has handled the delicate task of taking the winery forward while producing typically local wines with firm, powerful structure. Les Combariolles is dense and beautifully round, and L'Infidèle is a voluminous wine in the great Mediterranean tradition. The last few years have seen striking progress, with, in particular, a delightfully refreshing Vin de Pays called L'Étincelle—well worth "slumming it"!

Recently tasted

COTEAUX DU LANGUEDOC FEU SACRÉ 2006
Red | 2011 up to 2013   92
Engaging nose, with a wonderful finish of Morello cherries preserved in alcohol. A very welcoming wine, with charming tannins.

COTEAUX DU LANGUEDOC
LES COMBARIOLLES 2006
Red | 2011 up to 2014   90
Elegant aromas of smoke and ripe fruit thanks to the syrah. This is a complex, long wine, magnificent structure with the typical 2006 tannins on the finish.

COTEAUX DU LANGUEDOC L'INFIDÈLE 2006
Red | 2011 up to 2015   88
Elegant but powerful tannins, the quintessence of Jonquières wines. This is a charmer, carried by the tannic structure of 2006 and a touch of alcohol on the finish.

VIN DE PAYS DE L' HÉRAULT L'ÉTINCELLE 2008
White | 2011 up to 2013   88

Older vintages

COTEAUX DU LANGUEDOC L'INFIDÈLE 2005
Red | 2011 up to 2013   89
A lovely nose of truffles and a mineral palate, deep in flavor and strongly aromatic.

Red: 22.7 acres; carignan noir 15%, cinsault 10%, grenache noir 25%, mourvèdre 20%, syrah 30%.
White: 4.4 acres; chenin blanc 40%, grenache blanc 15%, muscat à petits grains 15%, roussanne 15%, viognier 15%. Annual production: 40,000 bottles

DOMAINE CALVET-THUNEVIN

Avenue Jean-Jaurès, Rond Point Est
66460 Maury
Phone 00 33 4 68 51 05 57
Fax 00 33 4 68 59 17 28
contact@thunevin-calvet.fr
www.thunevin-calvet.fr

Jean-Luc Thunevin burst upon the wine scene with the creation of Château Valandraud in Saint-Émilion. He then teamed up with Jean-Roger Calvet to start this enterprise, which is dedicated to those Roussillon wines that he likes so much. They are matured in good-quality oak and mainly built on power. The Hugo and Les Dentelles are blended from grenache, carignan, and syrah grapes that have spent eighteen months in new or almost-new barrels. Les Trois Marie relies solely on grenache, matured in new oak. All of the wines testify to a high level of technical expertise: very successfully crafted in an ultrapowerful style. Recently an extraordinary Maury vintage, made exactly like a Port wine and able to compare to the best, has been added to the red range.

Recently tasted

CÔTES DU ROUSSILLON-VILLAGES
CONSTANCE 2007
Red | 2011 up to 2013   88
The style is deep and intense, with notes of licorice and black fruit. A powerful wine with silky tannins.

CÔTES DU ROUSSILLON-VILLAGES HUGO 2006
Red | 2011 up to 2015   88
Generous, well made, super-concentrated, but still heavily marked by the oak, this succulent, fruit-filled wine needs time.

CÔTES DU ROUSSILLON-VILLAGES
LES DENTELLES 2007
Red | 2011 up to 2013   88

CÔTES DU ROUSSILLON-VILLAGES
LES TROIS MARIE 2006
Red | 2011 up to 2016   89

MAURY 2007
Sweet Red | 2011 up to 2028   90

Older vintages

CÔTES DU ROUSSILLON-VILLAGES
CONSTANCE 2006
Red | 2011 up to 2013   88
The style is intense and deep with notes of black licorice. It needs to soften, but the tannins are in place.

Côtes du Roussillon-Villages Hugo 2005
Red | 2011 up to 2013   **88**
A lovely and successful wine for this domaine, made with generous and well-aged material. Very concentrated, yet still marked by the oak. It finishes on delicious notes of dark berries.

Côtes du Roussillon-Villages
Les Trois Marie 2005
Red | 2011 up to 2014   **89**
A dense and structured red in which the dark-berry flavors are aligned with strong licorice and lozenge notes. It will please those who love wines that are powerful and expressive in both aroma and structure. The finish is flavorful.

Maury 2004
Sweet Red | 2011 up to 2013   **90**
A Maury vinified in a Bordeaux style and aged with great care. The toasted finish has creamy and smoky notes, with a finale of dark berries.

Red: 148.3 acres; carignan noir 10%, grenache noir 70%, mourvèdre 5%, syrah 15%. Annual production: 150,000 bottles

CAVE DE CAMPLONG

23, avenue de la Promenade
11200 Camplong-d'Aude
Phone 00 33 4 68 43 60 86
Fax 00 33 4 68 43 69 21
vignerons-camplong@wanadoo.fr
www.camplong.com

This cooperative winery in Lagrasse stands at the foot of the Alaric Mountain, named after the last king of the Visigoths. After some serious soul-searching, the owners called on Rhone merchant Michel Tardieu, in partnership with Burgundy négociant Dominique Laurent, to help rethink the cuvée C—which has since become a benchmark in regional winemaking. The Cuvée des Vignerons, matured like the C in 50 percent new oak, offers attractive value for money. So, too, does the entry-level Peyres Nobles—a good price even by the affordable standards of this area.

Recently tasted
Corbières La Cuvée des Vignerons 2006
Red | 2011 up to 2013   **85**

Corbières Le C de Camplong 2006
Red | 2011 up to 2013   **89**

Older vintages
Corbières Fontbories 2007
Red | 2011 up to 2013   **88**
This wine is cultivated on a minimally irrigated terroir at the base of the Alaric Mountain. The 2007 has finesse and light-handed tannins, flesh and pleasure.

Corbières La Cuvée des Vignerons 2005
Red | 2011 up to 2013   **87**
The wine has yet to find its harmony, but its attack is supple and it is easy to drink. A touch of alcohol in the finish shows the vintage's power, along with the noticeable tannins.

Corbières Le C de Camplong 2005
Red | 2011 up to 2013   **88**
C de Camplong is the cellar's top wine. With its full-bodied power, it is nearly wild. C will need a bit of time to become civilized.

Corbières Peyres Nobles 2007
Red | 2011 up to 2013   **87**
2007 shows all its sap, with astonishing fluidity and amazing charm for the price!

Red: 718.3 acres; cabernet 2%, carignan 38%, cinsault 6%, grenache 25%, mourvèdre 7%, syrah 22%. White: 11.1 acres. Annual production: 1,000,000 bottles

CANET-VALETTE

Route de Causses-et-Veyran
34460 Cessenon-sur-Orb
Phone 00 33 4 67 89 51 83
Fax 00 33 4 67 89 37 50
contact@canetvalette.com
www.canetvalette.com

Marc Valette makes wines in his own image: foursquare and obviously powerful. He uses organic methods and keeps yields to an absolute minimum. The cuvée Antonyme is the perfect wine to drink a toast to friends with after the rugby match. Ivresses is deep and structured and made in the style of Valette's top-end cuvée, the Maghani, a wine that ages remarkably well and becomes even more refined with time. The Une et Mille Nuits shows more immediate finesse and finishes on a bewitching note of exotic spice.

Recently tasted
SAINT-CHINIAN LE VIN MAGHANI 2005
Red | 2011 up to 2013   **88**

Older vintages
SAINT-CHINIAN ANTONYME 2006
Red | 2011 up to 2013   **86**
A rare blend of mourvèdre, which brings structure, and cinsault, which brings drinkability. A delicious wine for friends, with notes of rose petals.

SAINT-CHINIAN IVRESSES 2006
Red | 2011 up to 2013   **86**
Made with a majority of very ripe grenache, this fruity wine is powerful and deep and yet has kept a welcome freshness for 2006.

SAINT-CHINIAN IVRESSES 2005
Red | 2011 up to 2013   **88**
Made with a majority of very ripe grenache, this powerful cuvée is marked by heat. It is a hymn to the siesta.

SAINT-CHINIAN LE VIN MAGHANI 2004
Red | 2011 up to 2013   **88**
Powerfully flavored with strong notes of dark berries, smoky and deep, this wine has great length and marked tannins.

SAINT-CHINIAN UNE ET MILLE NUITS 2005
Red | 2011 up to 2013   **90**
Une et Mille Nuits shows finesse without departing from the powerful expression typical of the domaine's wines. Its name was well chosen, as notes of Asian spices, pepper, saffron, and curry carry the finish toward voluptuousness.

Red: 44.5 acres; carignan noir 15%, cinsault 10%, grenache noir 25%, mourvèdre 25%, syrah 25%.
Annual production: 75,000 bottles

DOMAINE DE CASENOVE

66300 Trouillas
Phone 00 33 4 68 21 66 33
Fax 00 33 4 68 21 77 81
château.la.casenove@wanadoo.fr

Étienne Montès left his job as a press photographer to take over the family domains Casenove and Saint-Luc. The core range of wines comprises the La Garrigue and Torrespeyres bottlings—both very approachable, with the 2004 Torrespeyres showing some particularly refined tannins. The Commandant-Jaubert is named after Étienne's seafaring great-great-uncle, who helped to build the domaine, and it is only produced in exceptional vintages. The Pla del Rey, which is the main focus of expertise at the Domaine Saint-Luc, has so far only been produced in 2000. Casenove production testifies to the variety and potential quality of Roussillon wines, with a range that aims more for drinkability than concentration and power.

RIVESALTES AMBRÉ 15/10 1998
Sweet Amber | 2011 up to 2018   **93**
A lovely sensation on the palate, very prune, candied apricot, walnut, and caramel in flavor. A moment of true pleasure.

VIN DE PAYS DES CÔTES CATALANES
COMMANDANT FRANÇOIS JAUBERT 2004
Red | 2011 up to 2013   **89**
This syrah-based red, selected from particular vineyard parcels and aged in used barriques (large wine barrels), is satiny, with fine yet still astringent tannins.

VIN DE PAYS DES CÔTES CATALANES
LA GARRIGUE 2005
Red | 2011 up to 2013   **88**
La Garrigue is an easy-to-drink wine of Mediterranean inspiration. The fresh finish ends on supple tannins.

VIN DE PAYS DES CÔTES CATALANES
TORRESPEYRES 2004
Red | 2011 up to 2013   **93**
The tannins need to soften a bit over the next few months, but there is great style in this surprisingly fresh wine, with its delicately expressed floral aromas. Bravo!

Red: 135.9 acres; carignan 44%, grenache noir 19%, mourvèdre 18%, syrah 19%. White: 37.1 acres; grenache blanc 38%, maccabeu 24%, muscat à petits grains 19%, muscat d'Alexandrie 19%. Annual production: 150,000 bottles

DOMAINE CAUSSE D'ARBORAS

477, rue Georges-Cuvier
Le Mas de Cazes
34090 Montpellier
Phone 00 33 6 11 51 08 41
Fax 00 33 4 67 04 11 40
causse-arboras@wanadoo.fr
www.causse-arboras.com

Jean-Louis Sagne's first-ever vintage in 2003 suffered from the notoriously hot summer, but he has made terrific strides since 2004. His two cuvées, Les Cazes and 3J, both show a welcome return to freshness thanks to Sagne's well-situated vineyard— a privileged terroir that comes through loud and clear in the wines. Les Cazes is his entry-level offering but was made with all the care of the 3J and tastes quite as good. The 2007 vintage is particularly tasty.

Coteaux du Languedoc Les 3 Jean 2004
Red | 2011 up to 2013   **90**
This wine beautifully expresses its terroir through delicate and refined tannins. The mineral finish is promising.

Coteaux du Languedoc Les Cazes 2007
Red | 2011 up to 2013   **90**
Bursting with fruit, the 2007 Cazes is made mostly of grenache, topped off with cinsault, syrah, and a touch of mourvèdre. Especially deep, it's a model of tasting pleasure.

Coteaux du Languedoc Les Cazes 2006
Red | 2011 up to 2013   **89**
This combines the freshness of 2004 with the fruit quality of 2006. The sweet spices render the finish more complex, lightly truffled and mentholated.

Coteaux du Languedoc Les Cazes 2005
Red | 2011 up to 2013   **90**
A thoroughbred, with depth and good balance. 2005 was a good year here, with maybe less freshness than 2004, but with superior density.

Red: 32.1 acres; cinsault 5%, grenache noir 50%, mourvèdre 15%, syrah 30%. Annual production: 30,000 bottles

CHÂTEAU DE CAZENEUVE

Cazeneuve
34270 Lauret
Phone 00 33 4 67 59 07 49
Fax 00 33 4 67 59 06 91
andre.leenhardt@wanadoo.fr
www.cazeneuve.net

André Leenhardt operates a sixty-four-acre vineyard in the Pic Saint-Loup area. He makes a very good roussanne-dominated white wine for gourmets that ages splendidly. The red wines are mainly based on syrah, supported by grenache and cinsault in Les Calcaires, and grenache and elegantly tannic mourvèdre in the Roc des Mates. Both cuvées are very successful and well worth buying. Le Sang du Calvaire, André's other offering, is entirely made from his much-cherished mourvèdre. Though brutally powerful when young, it loses its rough edges with a few years' aging and turns into a real thoroughbred.

Recently tasted
Coteaux du Languedoc 2007
White | 2011 up to 2013   **85**

Coteaux du Languedoc Pic Saint-Loup Le Roc des Mates 2006
Red | 2011 up to 2015   **88**

Coteaux du Languedoc Pic Saint-Loup Le Sang du Calvaire 2006
Red | 2011 up to 2013   **88**

Coteaux du Languedoc Pic Saint-Loup Les Calcaires 2007
Red | 2011 up to 2015   **88**

Older vintages
Coteaux du Languedoc Pic Saint-Loup Le Roc des Mates 2005
Red | 2011 up to 2014   **91**
The bouquet is peppery, powerful, and full-bodied, with delicately extracted tannins. A bit of cellaring would be marvelous for it.

Coteaux du Languedoc Pic Saint-Loup Le Sang du Calvaire 2004
Red | 2011 up to 2013   **88**
A wine with beautiful texture, yet for the moment it is under the stranglehold of the wood. The mourvèdre's class should win in the end.

Coteaux du Languedoc Pic Saint-Loup Les Calcaires 2006
Red | 2011 up to 2014   **89**
The texture is remarkable, tight yet dense, with refined tannins. It should be decanted to permit full expression of its potential.

Red: 64.2 acres. White: 14.8 acres. Annual production: 80,000 bottles

DOMAINE CAZES

4, rue Francisco-Ferrer
66602 Rivesaltes
Phone 00 33 4 68 64 08 26
Fax 00 33 4 68 64 69 79
info@cazes.com
www.cazes-rivesaltes.com

This estate raised a few eyebrows in 2004 by opting to sell its wines through wine négociant Jeanjean, leaving the owners to renew their focus on winemaking. They manage nearly 450 acres under vine, operated according to bold biodynamic principles that are helping to rebalance the soils. Following a bit of a rough patch, the 2007s came as a big relief, showing all the red-fruit expression expected of a winery that helped blaze the trail for good-quality Roussillon wines. Its particular specialty are naturally sweet wines (Vins Doux Naturels), which as ever deserve to be anthologized.

Recently tasted
CÔTES DU ROUSSILLON-VILLAGES EGO 2008
Red | 2011 up to 2013   89

Older vintages
CÔTES DU ROUSSILLON-VILLAGES EGO 2007
Red | 2011 up to 2013   87
After its vegetal bouquet, Ego is fleshy on the palate and has a pleasing fruitiness.

CÔTES DU ROUSSILLON-VILLAGES LE CREDO 2007
Red | 2011 up to 2013   90
Deep garnet color, a lively blend of blackberry, spice, and roasted coffee in the nose. On the palate the wine is full, ambitious, and generous. The wine is ripe and rich, but not flabby. The style is powerful and generous.

CÔTES DU ROUSSILLON-VILLAGES L'EXCELLENCE DE TRINIAC LATOUR DE FRANCE 2005
Red | 2011 up to 2013   86
Very Roussillon, deep and modern. Its delicate tannins will please many.

FITOU 2005
Red | 2011 up to 2013   87
A round and lovely modern Fitou, balanced and harmonious.

RIVESALTES 1990
Sweet Red | 2011 up to 2015   95
Patinaed by time, the tannins are still present and powerful in this Roussillon Vin Doux Naturel (fortified wine). It will pair nicely with spicy tajines, chocolate desserts, or curries. You could also drink it by itself, as one would a great Cognac, but it has less alcohol.

RIVESALTES AMBRÉ 1996
Sweet Amber | 2011 up to 2017   93
With notes of walnuts, rancio, figs, and dried fruits, this Ambré has real charm and will be much appreciated during late evenings by the fire.

Red: 269.3 acres; cabernet franc 1.5%, cabernet sauvignon 19.8%, carignan 2.2%, grenache 16.2%, merlot 14.7%, mourvèdre 7.4%, syrah 36%, tannat 2.2%. White: 175.4 acres; chardonnay 4.7%, maccabeu 9.3%, muscat 29.7%, muscat d'Alexandrie 46.9%, rolle 4.7%, viognier 4.7%. Annual production: 700,000 bottles

LA PRÉCEPTORIE DE CENTERNACH

1, route de Lansac
66220 Saint-Arnac
Phone 00 33 4 68 59 26 74
Fax 00 33 4 68 59 99 07
lapreceptorie@wanadoo.fr
www.la-preceptorie.com

The Préceptorie de Centernach is named after a preceptory (community) of the Knights Templar where pilgrims used to deposit their valuables. Located in Maury, it was started by the Parcé brothers to complement their range of Collioure and Banyuls wines from the Domaine de La Rectorie. They saw the potential in the Fenouillèdes region for elegant white wines based on varietals that were traditionally used to make Vins Doux Naturels. The red and rosé wines are often more powerful than those from La Rectorie but are made in an elegant style that retains all the quality of the fruit.

Recently tasted

CÔTES DU ROUSSILLON COUME MARIE 2007
Red | 2011 up to 2013   **88**

CÔTES DU ROUSSILLON TERRES NOUVELLES 2007
Red | 2011 up to 2013   **89**

CÔTES DU ROUSSILLON-VILLAGES
COUME MARIE 2008
White | 2011 up to 2013   **88**

CÔTES DU ROUSSILLON-VILLAGES
TERRES NOUVELLES 2007
White | 2011 up to 2013   **90**

MAURY AURÉLIE 2007
Sweet Red | 2011 up to 2027   **93**

MAURY T E 2007
Sweet Red | 2011 up to 2028   **90**

Older vintages

CÔTES DU ROUSSILLON COUME MARIE 2006
Red | 2011 up to 2013   **90**
This wine presents itself quite differently from the 2005. The tannins are nearly silky, with a finish of black licorice and impressive length.

MAURY AURÉLIE 2006
Sweet Red | 2011 up to 2020   **93**
In this Maury, the chocolate and very ripe fruit notes soften the powerful tannins. A very lovely wine to appreciate now, but it could wait a bit, too.

MAURY AURÉLIE 2005
Sweet Red | 2011 up to 2013   **93**
In this Maury, the chocolate and very ripe fruit notes soften the powerful tannins. A very lovely wine to appreciate now, but it could wait a bit, too.

MAURY HORS D'ÂGE
Sweet Red | 2011 up to 2017   **95**
A big Maury with wild color, this lasts on notes of bitter orange, cocoa, coffee, spices, and fresh figs. The finish never ends.

VIN DE PAYS DES CÔTES CATALANES
COUME MARIE 2007
White | Drink now   **89**
This is a Blanc de Noirs, a wine made with red grapes but vinified as a white. With great expression, it is developing astonishing harmony in a taut and refined style. The finish has great delicacy.

Red: 24.7 acres: carignan noir 12%, grenache gris 31%, grenache noir 49%, mourvèdre 4%, syrah 4%. White: 74.1 acres: carignan blanc 16%, maccabeu 52%, marsanne 16%, muscat 16%. Annual production: 75,000 bottles

CHÂTEAU CHAMP-DES-SŒURS

19, avenue des Corbières
11510 Fitou
Phone 00 33 4 68 45 66 74
Fax 00 33 4 68 45 66 74
châteauchampdessoeurs@orange.fr
www.champdessoeurs.fr

The Domaine Bertrand-Bergé leads the race for supremacy in Fitou production, but the outsider to watch is clearly this estate, Château Champ-des-Sœurs. Laurent Meynadier is a serious-minded, endlessly soul-searching producer whose commitment to progress will take him far. The domaine is located in the seacoast part of Fitou. It produces some well-made entry-level offerings and a wine named after Meynardier's in-laws, the Cuvée Bel Amant. There's also the Cuvée La Tina (which, as any linguist will tell you, means "tank/vat" in Occitan)—a pretty, exemplary Fitou for lovers of grand vin.

Recently tasted
FITOU 2007
Red | 2011 up to 2013   86

FITOU BEL AMANT 2007
Red | 2011 up to 2013   88

Older vintages
FITOU 2006
Red | 2011 up to 2013   87
An introductory wine with round tannins made to please right away. However, it lacks neither structure nor length.

FITOU BEL AMANT 2006
Red | 2011 up to 2013   88
With full-bodied power, the wine has round tannins and a bouquet of dark berries. Bel Amant is a charmer!

FITOU LA TINA 2007
Red | 2011 up to 2013   89
Lightly marked by vanilla, this wine's tannic finesse gives the finish delicacy and elegance. It has just a touch of comforting saltiness.

VIN ISSU DE RAISINS SURMŪRIS
Sweet White | 2011 up to 2015   93
A rare late-harvest roussanne. This little-known variety brings to this wine an elegant sweetness, powerful and spicy, with length. Harvested with a very low yield, there won't be much to go around.

Red: 22.2 acres; carignan noir 35%, grenache noir 40%, mourvèdre 15%, syrah 10%. White: 9.8 acres; grenache blanc 35%, muscat 35%, roussanne 30%.
Annual production: 35,000 bottles

MAS CHAMPART

Bramefan
Route de Villespassans
34360 Saint-Chinian
Phone 00 33 4 67 38 20 09
Fax 00 33 4 67 38 20 09
mas-champart@wanadoo.fr

This exemplary estate operates some lovely holdings south of Saint-Chinian, where it makes a very pure version of the regional wines. Taut and highly precise, the wines are fairly undemonstrative for the first few years, contrary to what you would expect from schistous soils. The Causse du Bousquet derives its refined structure from the dominant syrah; the Clos de la Simonette is fleshier and overwhelmingly mourvèdre-driven; the Côte d'Arbo and Vin de Pays d'Oc combine a delicate aromatic profile with respectable length. All in all, an attractive choice of wines at attractive prices.

Recently tasted
SAINT-CHINIAN CLOS DE LA SIMONETTE 2006
Red | 2011 up to 2015   91

SAINT-CHINIAN CÔTE D'ARBO 2007
Red | 2011 up to 2013   87

Older vintages
SAINT-CHINIAN 2006
White | 2011 up to 2013   89
This wine has true power on the palate and a complexity that will soon settle in.

SAINT-CHINIAN CAUSSE DU BOUSQUET 2006
Red | 2011 up to 2013   90
The depth and earthiness of Saint-Chinian's clay-limestone terroir is fully expressed here in the very mineral notes of this wine. The finish is remarkably precise, with unexpected freshness.

SAINT-CHINIAN CLOS DE LA SIMONETTE 2005
Red | 2011 up to 2013   93
A big, racy and deep wine, with remarkable tannins for the vintage. Its density and fullness are impressive.

SAINT-CHINIAN CÔTE D'ARBO 2006
Red | 2011 up to 2013   89
The violet scents of this delicate wine dominate in the bouquet. The palate then follows with mineral notes and a well-defined depth of terroir.

Red: 37.1 acres; cabernet franc 5%, carignan noir 10%, cinsault 6%, grenache noir 20%, mourvèdre 14%, syrah 45%. White: 3 acres; bourboulenc 20%, grenache blanc 40%, marsanne 20%, roussanne 20%.
Annual production: 40,000 bottles

DOMAINE DES CHÊNES

7, rue du Maréchal-Joffre
66600 Vingrau
Phone 00 33 4 68 29 40 21
Fax 00 33 4 68 29 10 91
domainedeschenes@wanadoo.fr

Alain Razungles is a professor of enology at Montpellier University and also runs this small family holding at the foot of the Cirque de Vingrau. All of his wines are beautifully turned out, entry-level offerings included. The white Les Magdaléniens are a credit to a blend of white grenache and roussanne grapes. The reds are all good; we have a particular weakness for the Ambré. This estate also produces a range of sometimes startling but always successful Vins Doux Naturels—definitely worth getting to know.

Recently tasted

CÔTES DU ROUSSILLON LES MAGDALÉNIENS 2006
White | 2011 up to 2015   88

CÔTES DU ROUSSILLON LES SORBIERS 2007
White | 2011 up to 2013   87

CÔTES DU ROUSSILLON-VILLAGES
LE MASCAROU 2005
Red | 2011 up to 2013   88

CÔTES DU ROUSSILLON-VILLAGES
TAUTAVEL LA CARISSA 2005
Red | 2011 up to 2014   92

Older vintages

CÔTES DU ROUSSILLON-VILLAGES
GRAND-MÈRES 2005
Red | 2011 up to 2013   87
Les Grand-Mères is a perfectly lovely introductory wine. It surprises with the length of its finish, with notes of tapenade and dark berries. In addition, this delight is priced reasonably.

MUSCAT DE RIVESALTES 2005
Sweet White | 2011 up to 2013   88
There is lots of yellow and candied fruit in this big muscat. Its flavors will go well with desserts in the same tonal range.

Annual production: 80,000 bottles

DOMAINE DU CLOS DES FÉES

69, rue du Maréchal-Joffre
66600 Vingrau
Phone 00 33 4 68 29 40 00
Fax 00 33 4 68 29 03 84
info@closdesfees.com
www.closdesfees.com

Hervé Bizeul acquired his seventy-five-or-so acres parcel by parcel. A former journalist, he attracted a few column inches by pricing his La Petite Sibérie cuvée at an unthinkable price for this region. It comes from a hillock around Calce, close to Gérard Gauby's vineyard, in a position that enjoys exceptionally cool conditions. Some might prefer the Clos des Fées, which is less powerful but possibly better behaved at table. Alongside these iconic wines the estate produces offerings at affordable prices, but still in line with the quality standards of this winery; the Cuvée Les Sorcières is a case in point. Hervé Bizeul also markets a range of wines called Walden, made from premium-quality grapes sourced from local producers.

Recently tasted

CÔTES DU ROUSSILLON LES SORCIÈRES 2008
Red | 2011 up to 2014   89

CÔTES DU ROUSSILLON-VILLAGES
DE BATTRE MON COEUR S'EST ARRÊTÉ 2008
Red | 2011 up to 2015   88

CÔTES DU ROUSSILLON-VILLAGES
LA PETITE SIBÉRIE 2007
Red | 2011 up to 2017   92

CÔTES DU ROUSSILLON-VILLAGES VIEILLES
VIGNES 2007
Red | 2011 up to 2013   92

Older vintages

CÔTES DU ROUSSILLON-VILLAGES
LA PETITE SIBÉRIE 2006
Red | 2011 up to 2017   92
The 2006 needs time to soften and assimilate its barrel aging, but the tannins are exceptional. The freshness of fruit typical of this cold and windy terroir has yet to come to the fore, but the finish's licorice and dark-berry notes are ravishing.

CÔTES DU ROUSSILLON-VILLAGES
LA PETITE SIBÉRIE 2005
Red | 2011 up to 2013   97
The quality of the tannins is superlative. The cold winds that blow over this cru bring exceptional freshness to this wine, filled with spice and licorice. The blackberry notes on the finish are stunning.

CÔTES DU ROUSSILLON-VILLAGES
LE CLOS DES FÉES 2006
Red | 2011 up to 2016   **92**
At the time of tasting, this wine had yet to
assimilate its oak notes, but, with its superb
texture, it will surely incorporate them and
come out on top.

CÔTES DU ROUSSILLON-VILLAGES
LE CLOS DES FÉES 2005
Red | 2011 up to 2013   **94**
This is very elegant and racy though muscular, with subtle tannins and a very classy
finish.

CÔTES DU ROUSSILLON-VILLAGES
VIEILLES VIGNES 2006
Red | 2011 up to 2014   **90**
For just a moment, spices and licorice dominate the fruit in this old-vine cuvée. It is as
concentrated as the 2005, and very ripe, with
silky and refined tannins.

CÔTES DU ROUSSILLON-VILLAGES
VIEILLES VIGNES 2005
Red | 2011 up to 2013   **93**
For just a moment, spices and licorice dom-
inate the fruit in this concentrated Vieilles
Vignes. The tannins are definitely refined.

Red: 66.7 acres; carignan noir 25%, grenache noir
35%, mourvèdre 10%, syrah 30%. White: 7.4 acres:
grenache blanc 100%. Annual production: 90,000
bottles

MAS CONSCIENCE

Mas Conscience
Route de Montpeyroux
34150 Saint-Jean-de-Fosse
Phone 00 33 4 67 57 77 42
Fax 00 33 4 67 57 77 42
mas.conscience@wanadoo.fr

This winery in Saint-Jean-de-Fosse is
named after one of the many potteries for
which this village was once renowned. It
was started by Geneviève and Laurent
Vidal, former owners of the Mas d'Auzières
(Pic Saint-Loup), who sold up in order to
return to their roots in the Terrasses du
Larzac appellation. They grow their vines
according to biodynamic principles and
released their first vintage in 2003. The
L'As is a Coteaux du Languedoc blended
from syrah, grenache, and carignan wines
that are raised in vats shaped like truncated cones. Le Cas, fermented in stainless-steel tanks, is made exclusively from
carignan, meaning it qualifies only for the
Vin de Pays designation. Production overall is of a high standard, making this young
winery one to watch.

Recently tasted
COTEAUX DU LANGUEDOC L'AS 2007
Red | 2011 up to 2013   **92**

COTEAUX DU LANGUEDOC
L'ESPRIT DE LA FONTAINE 2007
Red | 2011 up to 2013   **92**

Older vintages
COTEAUX DU LANGUEDOC L'AS 2006
Red | 2011 up to 2013   **92**
A superb Terrasses du Larzac, with exceptionally high-quality fruit. The tannins are
perfectly round and pleasing. This wine is
a model of its style.

VIN DE PAYS DE L' HÉRAULT LE CAS 2006
Red | 2011 up to 2013   **90**
This young property only presented two
wines, but it is already a point of reference.
Le Cas de Mas Conscience is a Vin de Pays
with lovely tannins. The finish is smooth and
well defined.

Red: 25.7 acres; carignan noir 20%, grenache noir
35%, mourvèdre 10%, syrah 35%. White: 4 acres;
grenache blanc 50%, rolle 25%, roussanne 22%,
viognier 3%. Annual production: 40,000 bottles

DOMAINE LE CONTE DES FLORIS

10, rue Alfred-Sabatier
34120 Pézenas
Phone 00 33 6 16 33 35 73
Fax 00 33 4 67 62 42 66
domaine.floris@gmail.com
www.domainelecontedesfloris.com

Daniel Le Conte des Floris recently quit his job as a wine journalist to settle here in Pézenas, deep in the Languedoc. His white wines are unusually deep but with the added acidity of white carignan—proving what a good idea it is in these hot regions to combine the latter with roussanne. The red wines are each named after a different type of subsoil: the Carbonifère, Basaltique, and Villafranchien. The 2002 Basaltique seemed the classiest of the three, and the 2002 Carbonifère was staggeringly fresh. An estate to watch for devotees of grand vin.

Recently tasted

COTEAUX DU LANGUEDOC ARÈS 2007
White | 2011 up to 2013   **87**

COTEAUX DU LANGUEDOC HOMO HABILIS 2005
Red | 2011 up to 2015   **89**

COTEAUX DU LANGUEDOC LUNE BLANCHE 2006
White | 2011 up to 2014   **89**

COTEAUX DU LANGUEDOC LUNE ROUSSE 2007
White | 2011 up to 2013   **88**

Older vintages

COTEAUX DU LANGUEDOC ARÈS 2006
White | 2011 up to 2013   **90**
Intensely aromatic and profoundly delectable, Arès is a wine with an irreproachably pure bouquet.

COTEAUX DU LANGUEDOC BASALTIQUE 2006
Red | 2011 up to 2013   **90**
A delicious Coteaux du Languedoc with very ripe fruit and red-berry notes and smooth and pleasing tannins. This terroir-marked wine has astonishingly airy volume and plenty of freshness.

COTEAUX DU LANGUEDOC CARBONIFÈRE 2004
Red | 2011 up to 2013   **88**
Clearly marked by the scent of black-currant buds, this wine's fluid texture offers an unusual sensation, and definite charm. We want more!

Red: 10.1 acres. White: 7.4 acres. Annual production: 22,000 bottles

DOMAINE LA CROIX CHAPTAL

Hameau de Cambous
34725 Saint-André-de-Sangonis
Phone 00 33 4 67 16 09 36
Fax 00 33 4 67 16 09 36
lacroixchaptal@wanadoo.fr
www.lacroixchaptal.com

After starting out in marketing with a major wine group, Charles Pacaud built up this estate with just one intention: to produce precise, very charming wines that defy convention. His white wines, though produced in small quantities, are one of France's purest expressions of the clairette grape. The rosé shows a vinous, claret-like style that likewise makes no concessions to fashion. The red wines are all very respectable. All of these wines are well worth trying because they go fabulously well with food.

Recently tasted

COTEAUX DU LANGUEDOC
TERRASSES DU LARZAC 2008
Red | 2011 up to 2013   **86**

Older vintages

CLAIRETTE DU LANGUEDOC CRU
CLAIRETTE—VIEILLES VIGNES 2005
White | 2011 up to 2013   **89**
Clairette is no longer a very fashionable variety due to its oxidative qualities. However, try it with food when it attains this level of purity, and it will demonstrate its ability to accompany and enhance even the most ambitiously gastronomic meal!

COTEAUX DU LANGUEDOC CHARLES 2005
Red | 2011 up to 2013   **90**
Densely textured and saline with very light tannins, this fleshy and powerfully flavored wine will be perfect with grilled beef.

COTEAUX DU LANGUEDOC
LES ORIGINES-DÉODOAT DE SÉVERAT 2005
Red | 2011 up to 2013   **89**
This has lovely delicate tannins, a silky texture and just the right amount of acidity to permit superlative pairings with North American cuisine.

COTEAUX DU LANGUEDOC LES SIGILLÉS 2005
White | 2011 up to 2013   **88**
Notes of menthol and rosemary emerge from this structured and aromatically charming wine. The tannins are supple, but not hollow.

Red: 5396.7 acres; aramon 5%, cabernet franc 5%, cabernet sauvignon 8%, carignan noir 13%, cinsault 5%, grenache noir 28%, merlot 5%, mourvèdre 9%, syrah 27%. White: 6.2 acres; clairette 80%, roussanne 20%. Annual production: 110,000 bottles

MAS DE DAUMAS-GASSAC

🦎🦎 🦎🦎 🦎🦎 🦎🦎

Mas de Daumas-Gassac
34150 Aniane
Phone 00 33 4 67 57 71 28
Fax 00 33 4 67 57 41 03
contact@daumas-gassac.com
www.daumas-gassac.com

There have been a lot of column inches devoted to Mas Daumas-Gassac, home of Aimé Guibert, who in the 1970s famously planted Bordeaux red varietals—predominantly cabernet sauvignon—around Aniane, deep in the Languedoc AOC. For the white wines, too, he chose to vinify a blend of chardonnay, viognier, and petit manseng, outside the rules for AOC classification. This means that the red and white wines alike may only be sold as Vins de Pays de l'Hérault—but at a price unheard of in this category. The white is matured in stainless-steel tanks, while the red undergoes partial aging in barrels. The reds can be exceptionally good in difficult years.

Recently tasted
VIN DE PAYS DE L'HÉRAULT 2008
White | 2011 up to 2013   88

Older vintages
VIN DE PAYS DE L'HÉRAULT 2007
White | 2011 up to 2013   87
This wine is pleasant to drink. Made from chardonnay, viognier, and petit manseng, it has a slightly short finish, bearing scents of undergrowth alongside fennel and anise.

VIN DE PAYS DE L'HÉRAULT 2006
Red | 2011 up to 2013   88
As is often the case, Daumas-Gassac first shows its power, masking the finesse of its finish. The 2006 follows suit, and deserves some time in bottle.

VIN DE PAYS DE L'HÉRAULT 2005
Red | 2011 up to 2013   90
The Daumas-Gassac 2005 red has a spicy finish with leather notes. It is not yet fully realized, but it is a civilized wine.

Red: 86.5 acres. White: 37.1 acres. Annual production: 200,000 bottles

DOMAINE DE L'ÈDRE

🦎🦎 🦎🦎 🦎🦎 🦎🦎

1, rue des Écoles
66600 Vingrau
Phone 00 33 6 08 66 17 51
Fax 00 33 4 68 54 65 18
contact@edre.fr
www.edre.fr

This domaine was founded in 2002 by Jacques Castany and Pascal Dieunidou. The reds are already among the benchmark Roussillon wines, and the whites are catching up quickly.

Recently tasted
CÔTES DU ROUSSILLON-VILLAGES CARRÉMENT ROUGE 2007
Red | 2011 up to 2013   90

CÔTES DU ROUSSILLON-VILLAGES L'ÈDRE 2007
Red | 2011 up to 2013   92

Older vintages
CÔTES DU ROUSSILLON-VILLAGES CARRÉMENT ROUGE 2006
Red | 2011 up to 2013   90
A very lovely wine kept taut by incredibly pleasing tannins. The chocolaty finish is full-bodied and charming. We want more!

CÔTES DU ROUSSILLON-VILLAGES L'ÈDRE 2006
Red | 2011 up to 2013   90
Delicious and full-bodied with strong licorice and dark-berry notes, this lightly jammy wine lacks only a hint of freshness. Very good work to obtain such delicious and pleasing tannins!

VIN DE PAYS DES CÔTES CATALANES CARRÉMENT BLANC 2007
White | 2011 up to 2013   90
Made with grenaches gris and blanc and a bit of maccabeu, this is a crystalline wine with finesse and astonishing aromatic precision. The pear-lemon finish is ravishing.

Red: 8.6 acres; carignan noir 10%, grenache noir 30%, mourvèdre 5%, syrah 55%. White: 3.7 acres; others 30%, grenache blanc 60%, roussanne 10%. Annual production: 10,000 bottles

CAVE D'EMBRES ET CASTELMAURE

4, route des Canelles
11360 Embres-et-Castelmaure
Phone 00 33 4 68 45 91 83
Fax 00 33 4 68 45 83 56
castelmaure@wanadoo.fr
www.castelmaure.com

The Embres et Castelmaure co-op has them all beat when it comes to technical and commercial clout. Not a boring wine in sight: every product is flawless, the price ultra-reasonable. We have a particular weakness for the Perpète, vinified using the Spanish solera system but with no obvious oxidation. The co-op's flagship cuvée is the Cave de Castelmaure No. 3, matured under the expert guidance of renowned Rhone and Burgundy growers Michel Tardieu and Dominique Laurent. If only more wine co-ops were like this one!

Recently tasted

CORBIÈRES LA POMPADOUR 2007
Red | 2011 up to 2013   88

CORBIÈRES N°3 DE CASTELMAURE 2007
Red | 2011 up to 2015   92

CORBIÈRES VENDANGES HUMAINES 2007
Red | 2011 up to 2013   88

Older vintages

CORBIÈRES A PERPÈTE
Red | 2011 up to 2013   90
Perpète is made with the solera technique, in which each new wine is added to a tank partially filled with the wine of earlier vintages. Each new batch is thus assimilated into the older wines. The result is very fresh, incredibly deep, with highly pleasing tannins, a bit patinaed by the age of the oldest vintages.

CORBIÈRES LA GRANDE CUVÉE 2007
Red | 2011 up to 2013   88
With linear and powerful tannins, this cuvée is taut, with a graphite, mineral finish.

CORBIÈRES LA POMPADOUR 2006
Red | 2011 up to 2013   87
Silky, powerful, but with round tannins, La Pompadour is quite a dependable bet in the cellar.

CORBIÈRES N°3 DE CASTELMAURE 2005
Red | 2011 up to 2013   91
The cuvée no. 3 is the cellar's star wine. It has a particularly refined style. The volume on the palate is impressive without renouncing either finesse or freshness.

Red: 840.1 acres. White: 24.7 acres. Annual production: 460,000 bottles

CHÂTEAU DE L'ENGARRAN

Château de l'Engarran
34880 Laverune
Phone 00 33 4 67 47 00 02
Fax 00 33 4 67 27 87 89
lengarran@wanadoo.fr
www.château-engarran.com

Diane Losfelt and her sister Constance Rerolle are the third generation of dynamic women to run this 123-acre estate, spread around a lovely eighteenth-century folly. The wines go from strength to strength, whether bottled as Vins de Pays d'Oc or as Coteaux du Languedoc. The Quetton Saint-Georges cuvée is remarkable for a freshness that the Saint-Georges d'Orques terroir seems to instill in its wines. The latest addition to the range is the grenache Majeur, a wine from the Grès de Montpellier area that is sure to get people talking.

Recently tasted

COTEAUX DU LANGUEDOC
CUVÉE SAINTE-CÉCILE 2007
Red | 2011 up to 2013   85

COTEAUX DU LANGUEDOC
QUETTON SAINT-GEORGES 2006
Red | 2011 up to 2015   90

VIN DE PAYS D'OC DOMAINE DE L'ENGARRAN 2008
White | 2011 up to 2013   88

Older vintages

COTEAUX DU LANGUEDOC
CHÂTEAU DE L'ENGARRAN 2006
Red | 2011 up to 2013   88
Dominated by syrah, this Grès de Montpellier sample is very promising, both round and powerful.

COTEAUX DU LANGUEDOC
CUVÉE SAINTE-CÉCILE 2006
Red | 2011 up to 2013   87
This has volume on the palate, filled with licorice and dark-berry flavor. It's a good representative of Languedoc, with an aromatic consistency in both bouquet and palate.

COTEAUX DU LANGUEDOC
GRENACHE MAJEUR 2006
Red | 2011 up to 2013   89
Just as delectable as its older brother, the 2006 overflows with fruit, carried by welcome freshness.

Red: 123.6 acres. White: 12.4 acres. Annual production: 220,000 bottles

CHÂTEAU DES ESTANILLES

Lentheric
34480 Cabrerolles
Phone 00 33 4 67 90 29 25
Fax 00 33 4 67 90 10 99
louison.estanilles@orange.fr
www.châteaudesestanilles.fr

Michel Louison's winemaking style grows more polished with every passing vintage. His white wines are purer and more precise; his mourvèdre rosé is more vinous than in the past, with none of that showiness that discouraged as many people as it attracted. The reds are increasingly refined and include an ever-more-precise syrah offering plus a new bottling, the Clos du Fou, that takes refinement to a whole new level. Proof that exemplary vineyard maintenance really does pay off.

Recently tasted
FAUGÈRES PRESTIGE 2005
Red | 2011 up to 2013   85

FAUGÈRES TRADITION 2006
Red | 2011 up to 2013   84

Older vintages
FAUGÈRES GRANDE CUVÉE SYRAH 2004
Red | 2011 up to 2013   90
With a base of voluptuous syrah, this cuvée has a refined structure and delicate aromas with saline notes.

FAUGÈRES LE CLOS DU FOU 2005
Red | 2011 up to 2013   89
This Estanilles cuvée allows the Faugères minerality to express itself in the finish, whereas the 2005 had more marked tannins.

FAUGÈRES LE CLOS DU FOU 2004
Red | 2011 up to 2013   91
This new wine from Estanilles shows improvements in tannin mastery, moving toward even more silkiness and roundness while maintaining the minerality lent by the Faugères terroir in the finish.

Red: 74.1 acres; carignan 10%, cinsault 10%, grenache 20%, mourvèdre 20%, syrah 40%. White: 12.4 acres: marsanne 65%, roussanne 25%, viognier 10%. Annual production: 200,000 bottles

CHÂTEAU L'EUZIÈRE

Ancien chemin d'Anduze
34270 Fontanès
Phone 00 33 4 67 55 21 41
Fax 00 33 4 67 56 38 04
leuziere@châteauleuziere.fr
www.châteauleuziere.fr

All of the wines from this estate in Fontanès (in the Pic Saint-Loup area) are a testament to careful winemaking. What they have in common are precise tannins plus a freshness that is this estate's leitmotif. The Tourmaline is made from a blend of grenache and syrah, supported by mourvèdre in the Almandin and the barrel-matured Les Escarboucles. Also definitely worth tasting is the white Grains de Lune Coteaux de Languedoc, made from roussanne and grenache blanc with a proportion of vermentino. Very well-crafted wines from an estate that is warmly recommended.

Recently tasted
COTEAUX DU LANGUEDOC PIC SAINT-LOUP L'ALMANDIN 2007
Red | 2011 up to 2013   86

COTEAUX DU LANGUEDOC PIC SAINT-LOUP LES ESCARBOUCLES 2007
Red | 2011 up to 2013   90

Older vintages
COTEAUX DU LANGUEDOC GRAINS DE LUNE 2007
White | 2011 up to 2013   88
Harvested at the right time, this wine has lively freshness with notes of citrus and pineapple.

COTEAUX DU LANGUEDOC PIC SAINT-LOUP-L'ALMANDIN 2006
Red | 2011 up to 2013   88
The 2006 version of L'Almandin showcases delicate and delicious fruit. It will be easy to drink.

COTEAUX DU LANGUEDOC PIC SAINT-LOUP LES ESCARBOUCLES 2006
Red | 2011 up to 2013   87
The style of this wine skews toward power, with demonstrative barrel and vanilla notes that mask the quality of the juice as well as its freshness.

COTEAUX DU LANGUEDOC TOURMALINE 2006
Red | 2011 up to 2013   86
The Tourmaline cuvée has lovely, delicious tannins with pretty fruit, but the finish is a bit dry at this time.

Red: 49.4 acres. White: 7.4 acres. Annual production: 60,000 bottles

DOMAINE FONTANEL

25, avenue Jean-Jaurès
66720 Tautavel
Phone 00 33 4 68 29 04 71
Fax 00 33 4 68 29 19 44
domainefontanel@hotmail.com
www.domainefontanel.com

Domaine Fontanel is a family-run business based in Estagel and Tautavel. The man in charge is the unassuming Pierre Fontanel, a foremost specialist in the Pyrénées-Orientales wine region. He is heir to some exceptional holdings of old vines, planted in a wide variety of soils. Every cuvée is true to its terroir and made from limited yields. Fontanel is a dependable producer with a real understanding of fruit ripeness, and his consistently made wines show good quality across the board.

Recently tasted

CÔTES DU ROUSSILLON-VILLAGES CISTES 2007
Red | 2011 up to 2013   **89**

MAURY 2006
Sweet Red | 2011 up to 2015   **90**

MUSCAT DE RIVESALTES L'ÂGE DE PIERRE 1999
Sweet White | 2011 up to 2013   **90**

Older vintages

CÔTES DU ROUSSILLON-VILLAGES CISTES 2006
Red | 2011 up to 2013   **88**
Les Cistes blends syrah, grenache, and mourvèdre. With strong notes of dark berries, it is long and strongly flavored.

CÔTES DU ROUSSILLON-VILLAGES LE PRIEURÉ 2006
Red | 2011 up to 2013   **91**
Strong licorice notes carry the other flavors in this wine. The tannins are elegant. Great freshness.

MAURY 2004
Sweet Red | 2011 up to 2013   **90**
What a charming bouquet and such a direct attack! The finish is fresh but not yet completely settled. It needs a bit more time.

RIVESALTES 1998
Soft Amber | 2011 up to 2017   **91**
The brick-orange color presages the tangerine, cinnamon, and dried fruits in the finish. Very fresh, the wine is incredibly long. It is clearly linked in style to the 1997.

Red: 69.2 acres; cabernet sauvignon 1%, carignan noir 12%, grenache noir 35%, merlot 1%, mourvèdre 11%, syrah 40%. White: 14.8 acres; grenache blanc 30%, maccabeu 5%, malvoisie 5%, muscat à petits grains 40%, roussanne 10%, viognier 10%. **Annual production:** 80,000 bottles

DOMAINE GARDIÈS

Chemin de Montpins
66600 Espira de l'Agly
Phone 00 33 4 68 64 61 16
Fax 00 33 4 68 64 69 36
domgardies@wanadoo.fr
www.domaine-gardies.fr

Domaine Gardiès made its name producing complex, powerfully structured red wines. It operates out of a pure limestone zone around Vingrau, where the property is based, planted to vines used for the Falaise cuvée. Jean Gardiès has also built ultra-modern facilities at Espira-de-l'Agly, near the Cirque de Vingrau, where his exceptional mourvèdre plantings yield La Torre, a wine unlike any other Roussillon bottling. The estate makes some superb dry white wines as well.

Recently tasted

CÔTES DU ROUSSILLON LES GLACIÈRES 2008
White | 2011 up to 2013   **91**

CÔTES DU ROUSSILLON-VILLAGES LA TORRE 2007
Red | 2011 up to 2017   **92**

CÔTES DU ROUSSILLON-VILLAGES
LES FALAISES 2007
Red | 2011 up to 2015   **94**

Older vintages

CÔTES DU ROUSSILLON-VILLAGES LA TORRE 2006
Red | 2011 up to 2014   **94**
This reserve is at the summit of the domaine's wines. The domaine's habitual power is here, but the dark-berry flavors are more refined, and the sweet spices give extra complexity. Mourvèdre has spoken!

CÔTES DU ROUSSILLON-VILLAGES
LES FALAISES 2006
Red | 2011 up to 2013   **92**
Particularly concentrated, here is a wine with high-class tannins and incomparable density.

CÔTES DU ROUSSILLON-VILLAGES
LES VIEILLES VIGNES 2006
Red | 2011 up to 2013   **91**
Vieilles Vignes climbs to a new level of concentration and freshness when compared to the Millères. It is dense with a rich and deep texture and a racy finish of extracted, dark-berry flavor.

Red: 61.8 acres. White: 37.1 acre. Annual production: 100,000 bottles

DOMAINE GAUBY

lieu-dit La Muntada
66600 Calce
Phone 00 33 4 68 64 35 19
Fax 00 33 4 68 64 41 77
domaine.gauby@wanadoo.fr
www.domainegauby.fr

This domaine has grown to be a full-time laboratory for the stylistic development of Roussillon wines. Once notorious for their very strong wines, Gérard Gauby and his son Lionel have since resolved to ease up on the alcohol content. The result is a fabulous increase in quaffability that makes up for any loss of flesh. The wines these days show a return to more substance but in a style geared toward aromatic freshness, avoiding the volatile acidity (caused by sloppy handling) that makes decanting essential. In the vineyard, the Gaubys always look to work in harmony with nature, applying organic principles that promise further progress in the tank room. The style of the famous Cuvée Muntada has changed slightly since the syrah was dropped from the mix of plantings; you could say that the carignan and grenache mark a return to its roots.

Recently tasted
CÔTES DU ROUSSILLON-VILLAGES
LA MUNTADA 2007
Red | 2011 up to 2016   92

CÔTES DU ROUSSILLON-VILLAGES
VIEILLES VIGNES 2007
Red | 2011 up to 2014   90

Older vintages
CÔTES DU ROUSSILLON-VILLAGES
LA MUNTADA 2005
Red | 2011 up to 2013   93
The 2005 Muntada is a pared-down wine with great subtlety, where eucalyptus, pine resin, and plant essences invite you to join them at a not-to-be-missed feast.

CÔTES DU ROUSSILLON-VILLAGES
LES CALCINAIRES 2006
Red | 2011 up to 2013   88
This wine, with its natural vibrancy, is not a monster of power. It is, to the contrary, quite drinkable.

CÔTES DU ROUSSILLON-VILLAGES
VIEILLES VIGNES 2005
Red | 2011 up to 2013   92
The immense quality of this wine's fruit is astonishing. Subtle and complex, its fleshy texture and its scents of mocha and chocolate are so delicious they're ready to bite into.

Annual production: 90,000 bottles

LA GRANGE DES PÈRES

34150 Aniane
Phone 00 33 4 67 57 70 55
Fax 00 33 4 67 57 32 04

Despite our repeated requests, we were not able to taste these wines in the context of our blind tastings, nor were we able to visit the winery. We regret that Laurent Vaillé systematically refuses to send us samples. In order to evaluate the wines we purchased these two at a large Paris wine shop. The 2004s were mixed. The white definitely figures among the best wines of the Languedoc. The red from the same vintage was showing some premature aging in both color and aromas. On the palate, the tannins were soothing, making the wine easy to drink.

VIN DE PAYS DE L' HÉRAULT 2004
White | 2011 up to 2013   92
This white is made from marsanne, roussanne, chardonnay and Gros manseng grown at high altitude, which gives the wine a fresh finish that underlines the quality of the fruit. It all comes together in a particularly complex wine with noble oak notes that place it in the pantheon of very great white wines.

VIN DE PAYS DE L'HÉRAULT 2004
Red | 2011 up to 2013   86
The bouquet is astonishing, although not particularly pleasant, and the color is evolving prematurely. On the palate, animal notes overlay the scents of the Mediterranean garrigue. The finish is racy, with well-wrapped tannins and a pleasant drinkability. Overall, the bouquet is not above reproach, but it has nobly structured tannins.

HAUTES TERRES DE COMBEROUSSE

Comberousse, route de Gignac
34660 Cournonterral
Phone 00 33 4 67 85 05 18
Fax 00 33 4 67 85 05 18
paul@comberousse.com
www.comberousse.com

Winegrower Paul Reder coaxes some of the Languedoc's most original white wines out of this Grès de Montpellier holding. No frills, no concessions to fashion, just very lightly oxidized whites that introduce one's taste buds to the ultimate in refinement. Honey, ginger, and nutmeg compete with candied fruit against a backdrop of impeccable dryness.

Recently tasted

COTEAUX DU LANGUEDOC ROUCAILLAT 2007
White | 2011 up to 2017   92

COTEAUX DU LANGUEDOC ROUCAILLAT 2006
White | 2011 up to 2015   88

COTEAUX DU LANGUEDOC SAUVAGINE 2008
White | 2011 up to 2013   86

Older vintages

COTEAUX DU LANGUEDOC ROUCAILLAT 2005
White | 2011 up to 2013   90
Lightly oxidative, this racy wine is dense and profound. It needs time to understand. Taste the 2000 to be convinced.

COTEAUX DU LANGUEDOC ROUCAILLAT 2000
White | 2011 up to 2013   92
This white is one of the most unusual in its area. The mineral bouquet is ravishing, and the palate, lightly oxidative, carries the taster toward ginger and candied fruit. It would make extraordinary pairings. Dare to try it!

COTEAUX DU LANGUEDOC SAUVAGINE 2006
White | 2011 up to 2013   86
Based on grenache and rolle, Sauvagine is an introductory wine, both round and marked with pleasant acidity that carries it far. Easy to drink, it is a superb introduction to the Roucaillat cuvée.

Red: 2.5 acres. White: 29.7 acres; chardonnay 15%, chasan 8%, clairette 6%, grenache blanc 29%, rolle 22%, roussanne 20%. Annual production: 20,000 bottles

HECHT ET BANNIER

3, rue Seguin
34140 Bouzigues
Phone 00 33 4 67 74 66 38
Fax 00 33 4 67 74 66 45
contact@hbselection.com
www.hechtbannier.com

Hecht et Bannier is a négociant business started by two young men passionate about wine, specializing in ambitious, original, high-quality wines from the Languedoc-Roussillon region. The real winners from this house are the Côtes de Roussillon-Villages, bursting with ultra-refined grenache expression, and also the Saint-Chinian and Minervois offerings. The rosé Vin de Pays des Côtes de Thau is the ultimate in wine pleasure: exquisitely tasty and thirst-quenchingly drinkable.

Recently tasted

CÔTES DU ROUSSILLON-VILLAGES 2006
Red | 2011 up to 2013   86

FAUGÈRES 2006
Red | 2011 up to 2013   86

LANGUEDOC 2007
Red | 2011 up to 2013   84

SAINT-CHINIAN 2006
Red | 2011 up to 2013   90

VIN DE PAYS D'OC SYRAH 2008
Rosé | 2011 up to 2013   86

Older vintages

COTEAUX DU LANGUEDOC 2003
Red | 2011 up to 2013   87
An explosively fruity wine with notes of black currants and a delicate texture. It is lightly marked by the vintage.

CÔTES DU ROUSSILLON-VILLAGES 2005
Red | 2011 up to 2013   87
The vintage has stamped these wines with slightly dry tannins. It has strong black-currant flavors and light, refined tannins.

MINERVOIS 2004
Red | 2011 up to 2013   88
This lovely Minervois has tannins that are just a touch dry and keep it from achieving the refinement of the 2003 Côtes du Roussillon-Villages.

Annual production: 200,000 bottles

DOMAINE DE L'HORTUS-VIGNOBLES ORLIAC

Domaine de l'Hortus
34270 Valflaunes
Phone 00 33 4 67 55 31 20
Fax 00 33 4 67 55 38 03
vins@vignobles-orliac.com
www.vignobles-orliac.com

This estate nestles at the foot of the impressive flanks of Mount Hortus. It produces wines under the Pic Saint-Loup appellation, plus a carefully crafted Vin de Pays du Val de Montferrand from the scenic highlands above the Buèges valley. The wines sometimes reveal a heavy hand, especially the whites, but the best of the reds are very sensitively made. The young wines tend to play down their Languedoc character and flirt quite successfully with Burgundy aromas.

Recently tasted
COTEAUX DU LANGUEDOC 2007
White | 2011 up to 2013   88

COTEAUX DU LANGUEDOC BERGERIE DE L'HORTUS ROSÉ DE SAIGNÉE 2008
Rosé | 2011 up to 2013   87

COTEAUX DU LANGUEDOC PIC SAINT-LOUP DOMAINE DE L'HORTUS GRANDE CUVÉE 2006
Red | 2011 up to 2013   88

Older vintages
COTEAUX DU LANGUEDOC CLOS DU PRIEUR 2004
Red | 2011 up to 2013   88
This offers noble, truffled aromas and a finish marked by the dry tannins of 2005. It is ready to drink.

COTEAUX DU LANGUEDOC PIC SAINT-LOUP BERGERIE DE L'HORTUS 2005
Red | 2011 up to 2013   87
Of finesse and fruit, balanced tannins and a harmonious finish.

VIN DE PAYS DU VAL DE MONTFERRAND BERGERIE DE L'HORTUS 2007
White | Drink now   90
This blend of chardonnay, viognier, sauvignon, and roussanne has surprising freshness and harmonious notes of fennel and garrigue. It is ready to drink now.

Red: 143.3 acres. White: 39.5 acres. Annual production: 370,000 bottles

MAS JULLIEN

Chemin du Mas Jullien
34725 Jonquières
Phone 00 33 4 67 96 60 04
Fax 00 33 4 67 96 60 50
masjullien@free.fr

Olivier Jullien combines the hypersensitivity of an artist with a commitment to humanist values that is increasingly rare these days. His wines are, like him, vibrant and energetic, thanks to a lively, distinctively tannin-driven profile that absolutely relies on pristine fruit and freshness. No overreliance on aging, just an abundance of civilized character that is definitely worth getting to know. Red wines don't get more quintessentially Languedoc than this. The Mas Jullien takes a few years to open. Olivier's latest creation, by contrast, the États d'Âme, is made in a more early-drinking style but with no loss of identity.

Recently tasted
COTEAUX DU LANGUEDOC 2006
Red | 2011 up to 2018   94

COTEAUX DU LANGUEDOC CARLAN 2007
Red | 2011 up to 2015   92

COTEAUX DU LANGUEDOC ÉTATS D'ÂME 2007
Red | 2011 up to 2015   89

Older vintages
COTEAUX DU LANGUEDOC 2005
Red | 2011 up to 2018   94
This vintage is more voluptuous and fruity than the 2004. The garrigue is here, followed on the palate by superlight tannins.

COTEAUX DU LANGUEDOC CARLAN 2006
Red | 2011 up to 2017   92
Still stamped by its cask aging, this wine's bouquet is nonetheless incredibly refined. This wine was made from a high-altitude parcel, resulting in a cuvée in which freshness dominates over alcohol. Its purity trumps the notion of varietals. The texture is complex, with dynamic and taut tannins.

COTEAUX DU LANGUEDOC ÉTATS D'ÂME 2006
Red | 2011 up to 2015   90
Etats d'Âme is a different wine each year, made in a more accessible style than the Mas Jullien. Its fullness, its natural personality, and its freshness are the stamp of its maker. The richness of 2006 is fully present here.

Red: 42 acres; carignan noir 28%, cinsault 4%, grenache noir 20%, mourvèdre 30%, syrah 18%. White: 7.4 acres. Annual production: 70,000 bottles

DOMAINE LACOSTE

Mas de Bellevue
34400 Saturargues
Phone 00 33 4 67 83 24 83
Fax 00 33 4 67 71 48 23
Rf.lacoste@gmail.com
www.domainelacoste.fr

Francis Lacoste remains one of the few winegrowers to fly the flag for Muscat de Lunel. He made his name as a producer of muscat wines with sharply defined aromas, a quality they owe to high standards of viticulture and winemaking. Once exclusively white, production now extends to red wines from several acres of plantings near Saint-Christol in the Coteaux du Languedoc appellation. These include some profoundly dark carignan vines that inspired the creation of the single-varietal Les Estivencs—really worth a look for any carignan devotee. The blended Clos des Estivencs is also very good.

Recently tasted

COTEAUX DU LANGUEDOC
CLOS DES ESTIVENCS 2006
Red | 2011 up to 2014   **87**

VIN DE PAYS DE L' HÉRAULT LES ESTIVENCS 2006
Red | 2011 up to 2013   **86**

Older vintages

COTEAUX DU LANGUEDOC
CLOS DES ESTIVENCS 2005
Red | 2011 up to 2013   **86**
With very ripe aromas, this wine offers hints of jamminess and lots of volume on the palate.

MUSCAT DE LUNEL CLOS BELLEVUE 2006
Sweet White | 2011 up to 2013   **89**
With its nuances of citrus and pineapple, this complex and precisely scented muscat is fresh on the palate. It finishes on light and ravishing smokiness.

VIN DE TABLE MUSCAT MOELLEUX 2007
Soft White | 2011 up to 2013   **88**
This wine's aromatic punch is piercing, with magnificent toastiness on the nose plus yellow fruit notes. The acidic palate supports the aromas.

Red: 8.9 acres; carignan noir 41%, grenache noir 34%, syrah 25%. White: 17.3 acres; muscat à petits grains 100%. Annual production: 38,000 bottles

DOMAINE J. LAURENS

Les Graimenous
Route de La Digne d'Amont
11300 La Digne-d'Aval
Phone 00 33 4 68 31 54 54
Fax 00 33 4 68 31 61 61
domaine.jlaurens@wanadoo.fr
www.jlaurens.com

A superb range of delicious sparkling wines: expressive blanquettes with pretty nuances of green apples and white flowers characteristic of mauzac fruit; chardonnay- and chenin-driven crémants steeped in refinement and subtlety. Not an undesirable aroma in sight, which is more than can be said about many of the wines we taste. Thanks to just the right amount of dosage and no heavy-handedness, all of the wines, even the demi-sec offering, finish very crisp and clean.

Recently tasted

CRÉMANT DE LIMOUX CLOS DES DEMOISELLES 2007
Brut White sparkling | 2011 up to 2013   **90**

CRÉMANT DE LIMOUX LES GRAIMENOUS 2007
Brut White sparkling | 2011 up to 2013   **89**

Older vintages

BLANQUETTE DE LIMOUX LE MOULIN
Brut White sparkling | 2011 up to 2013   **88**
This dynamic blanquette, vinous yet delicate, finishes very cleanly. It's a lovely, light-textured wine that has retained lots of freshness.

BLANQUETTE DE LIMOUX LE MOULIN
Semi-White sparkling | 2011 up to 2013   **87**
Even though it was made in the style of a demi-sec, this blanquette has a nervy and fresh finish. It is a perfect dessert wine for fruit tarts: it won't knock you out with sugar.

CRÉMANT DE LIMOUX CLOS DES DEMOISELLES 2005
Brut White sparkling | 2011 up to 2013   **90**
Racy bubbles, deep in flavor with no heaviness: we would love to find wines like this more often. Year after year, this wine confirms its class.

Red: 4.9 acres. White: 69.2 acres. Annual production: 135,000 bottles

MAS LUMEN

3, impasse du Lierre
34120 Cazouls-d'Hérault
Phone 00 33 6 70 71 41 30
Fax 00 33 4 67 90 13 66
maslumen@wanadoo.fr
www.maslumen.com

Former photographer Pascal Perret named this estate after a unit of luminous flux: lumen. It is located near Faugères and makes two wines, both with the same elegant feel: Prélude, a refined cuvée with graceful tannins; and La Sylve, a classy expression of the Coteaux du Languedoc, made in a deeper and more uncompromising style. The estate improved considerably in 2004, and the 2005 looks promising.

COTEAUX DU LANGUEDOC OFFRANDE 2005
Red | 2011 up to 2013   **76**
Sylve is a wine with powerful character and sap, with big length and refined, chocolaty tannins.

COTEAUX DU LANGUEDOC OFFRANDE 2004
Red | 2011 up to 2013   **88**
The cuvée's spirit is back in this 2004, with a finish marked by alcohol but also by the vintage's freshness. It has lovely tannins that have barely aged since last year's tasting!

COTEAUX DU LANGUEDOC PRÉLUDE 2005
Red | 2011 up to 2013   **90**
Has poorly matured, with notes from the lees that are a little unpleasant.

COTEAUX DU LANGUEDOC PRÉLUDE 2004
Red | 2011 up to 2013   **86**
Perturbing volatile notes.

COTEAUX DU LANGUEDOC PRÉLUDE 2003
Red | 2011 up to 2013   **84**
The vintage has dried out the wine. It presents notes of tobacco and cigars.

VIN DE PAYS DE CASSAN VIN DE TABLE ORPHÉE
White | 2011 up to 2013   **88**
This powerfully structured white will be a frequent dinner companion. Its vanilla notes and the depth of its flavors will beautifully complement seafood.

Red: 13.6 acres. White: 1.2 acres. Annual production: 12,000 bottles

BERNARD MAGREZ

Château Pape Clément
216, avenue du Docteur-Nancel-Pénard
33600 Pessac
Phone 00 33 5 57 26 38 38
Fax 00 33 5 57 26 38 39
château@pape-clement.com
www.bernard-magrez.com

In conjunction with his Bordeaux wineries, Bernard Magrez has both taken over and acquired several properties in the Languedoc and the Roussillon. The idea is the same as in Bordeaux, closely followed by Michel Rolland; the wines are divided between individual winery bottlings and "special cuvées." The powerful concentrated and ripe style of these southern wines is underscored by oak aging that doesn't try to outdo the substance of the wines.

Recently tasted
COLLIOURE L'EXCELLENCE DE MON TERROIR DE COLLIOURE 2007
Red | 2011 up to 2013   **89**

CÔTES DU ROUSSILLON GÉRARD DEPARDIEU EN ROUSSILLON 2006
Red | 2011 up to 2013   **89**

CÔTES DU ROUSSILLON MON SEUL RÊVE 2006
Red | 2011 up to 2013   **87**

CÔTES DU ROUSSILLON SI MON PÈRE SAVAIT 2006
Red | 2011 up to 2013   **88**

Older vintages
CÔTES DU ROUSSILLON GÉRARD DEPARDIEU EN ROUSSILLON 2005
Red | 2011 up to 2013   **88**
In a powerful style, this wine needs patience, but the quality of the tannins is impressive. The élevage was well done.

CÔTES DU ROUSSILLON LA PASSION D'UNE VIE 2005
Red | 2011 up to 2013   **90**
Powerful, dense, tight, and intense with serious flesh and a bouquet of dark berries and spices. Long.

CÔTES DU ROUSSILLON MON SEUL RÊVE 2005
Red | 2011 up to 2013   **87**
Fat, fleshy, and rich, with a touch of sugar. The finish is pointed and as a whole it is harmonious.

SAINT-CHINIAN EN SILENCE 2005
Red | 2011 up to 2013   **88**
A delicate wine, long, with beautiful and elegant tannins and a firm mineral character. The finish is precise.

Red: 74.1 acres; cabernet sauvignon 60%, merlot 40%. White: 4.9 acres; muscadelle 5%, sauvignon blanc 45%, sauvignon gris 5%, sémillon 45%. Annual production: 99,000 bottles

CHÂTEAU MANSENOBLE

11700 Moux
Phone 00 33 4 68 43 93 39
Fax 00 33 4 68 43 97 21
mansenoble@wanadoo.fr
www.mansenble.com

Mansenoble was bought up in 1994 by Belgian couple Guido and Marie-Annick Jansegers. As a seasoned wine connoisseur, Guido knew that, for Corbières winemakers in particular, the real Holy Grail is that elusive combination of aromatic freshness and tannic finesse. He therefore abandoned part of the vineyard and concentrated on about fifty-seven acres of vines, exclusively planted in the coolest terroirs. The result is taut, elegant Corbières, with a hint of smoke and menthol in every cuvée. Delicate as young wines, but built to age nonetheless.

CORBIÈRES 2005
Red | Drink now   84
This wine, after a lovely attack, follows on dry tannins that indicate it should be drunk quickly.

CORBIÈRES MARIE-ANNICK 2003
Red | Drink now   92
An exercise in elegance, smoky, deep, and joyous. Delicately cocoa-flavored, with stunning length and freshness. We recently tasted the 2001, and it has not aged a bit.

CORBIÈRES MONTAGNE D'ALARIC 2005
Red | 2011 up to 2013   87
A beautiful attack on dark-berry flavors, followed by licorice. The wine is fat and delicious, ready to drink.

CORBIÈRES MONTAGNE D'ALARIC 2004
Red | 2011 up to 2013   86
A round and fresh wine, with slightly dry tannins that evoke hay and black currants. Altogether quite elegant.

CORBIÈRES RÉSERVE 2005
Red | 2011 up to 2013   88
The climatic conditions of 2005 have translated into a touch of dryness in the finish. But, happily, it is well wrapped by richness and volume on the palate.

CORBIÈRES RÉSERVE 2004
Red | 2011 up to 2013   89
The style is aristocratic (as the domaine's name would lead one to believe), intensely deep, full-bodied, and fresh. A wine with great character, balance, and refinement.

Red: 56.8 acres; carignan 35%, grenache 32%, mourvèdre 6%, syrah 27%. Annual production: 80,000 bottles

CLOS MARIE

Route de Cazeneuve
34270 Lauret
Phone 00 33 4 67 59 06 96
Fax 00 33 4 67 59 08 56
clos.marie@orange.fr

Clos Marie, in the Pic Saint-Loup appellation, makes wines with a near-ideal Languedoc profile at every level. Christophe Peyrus developed a sense of "grand vin" by mixing with the best in his field. His biodynamic vineyard produces reds with very refined tannins and an uncanny, all-pervading impression of freshness.

Recently tasted
COTEAUX DU LANGUEDOC PIC SAINT-LOUP GLORIEUSES 2006
Red | 2011 up to 2013   92

COTEAUX DU LANGUEDOC PIC SAINT-LOUP L'OLIVETTE 2007
Red | 2011 up to 2013   89

COTEAUX DU LANGUEDOC PIC SAINT-LOUP MÉTAIRIE DU CLOS 2007
Red | 2011 up to 2013   88

COTEAUX DU LANGUEDOC PIC SAINT-LOUP SIMON 2007
Red | 2011 up to 2013   93

Older vintages
COTEAUX DU LANGUEDOC MANON 2006
White | 2011 up to 2013   92
Behind its lovely toasted notes, the traditional Languedoc grapes bring richness, pedigree, and freshness. A lesson for Languedoc regarding harvesting dates.

COTEAUX DU LANGUEDOC PIC SAINT-LOUP GLORIEUSES 2005
Red | 2011 up to 2013   90
Very precise. The bottle tasted had dry tannins. Needs to be tasted again.

COTEAUX DU LANGUEDOC PIC SAINT-LOUP GLORIEUSES 2004
Red | 2011 up to 2013   90
Fresh and intensely pleasurable with notes of garrigue and rosemary, this big wine finishes deliciously, with refinement in its delicate and present tannins.

Coteaux du Languedoc Pic Saint-Loup
L'Olivette 2006
Red | 2011 up to 2013   **88**
This basic cuvée is already notable for its honesty. The palate, marked by perceptible tannins, expresses red berries, garrigue, and spices.

Coteaux du Languedoc Pic Saint-Loup
Métairie du Clos 2006
Red | 2011 up to 2013   **89**
The dense texture of this wine is not in conflict with its elegance. The old-vine carignan is balanced with forty-year-old grenache, and completed with young syrah aromas. Its volume and largeness are impressive.

Coteaux du Languedoc Pic Saint-Loup
Simon 2006
Red | 2011 up to 2013   **90**
This wine pairs in equal parts grenache and syrah. Closed down for the moment, its power, and the fruitiness of its body, are more expressive on the attack than the finish, but time will correct this.

Coteaux du Languedoc Pic Saint-Loup
Simon 2005
Red | 2011 up to 2013   **91**
This wine pairs equal portions of grenache and syrah. The reduced yields carry this wine to a height of refinement and delicacy.

Red: 44.5 acres; carignan 10%, grenache rouge 40%, mourvèdre 10%, syrah 40%. White: 12.4 acres; clairette 20%, grenache blanc 30%, rolle 20%, roussanne 30%. Annual production: 85,000 bottles

MAS DE MARTIN

Route de Carnas
34160 Saint-Bauzille-de-Montmel
Phone 00 33 4 67 86 98 82
Fax 00 33 4 67 86 98 82
masdemartin@wanadoo.fr
www.masdemartin.info

Christian Mocci left his native Corsica and a career in teaching to devote himself to this small estate in the Coteaux de Languedoc appellation. The wines he produces there testify to his discerning palate and fascination with Grand Vin, all summed up in two words: aromatic charm. The Cuvée Vénus is devastatingly seductive and sure to be the downfall of mere mortals like us. The Cinarca, also made from the syrah and grenache, and the Ultreia, which includes some mourvèdre, both display those refined tannins typical of modern-style Languedoc wines. These are intensely pleasurable wines, intended for immediate enjoyment but equally capable of impressive aging.

Recently tasted
Coteaux du Languedoc Cinarca 2007
Red | 2011 up to 2013   **88**

Coteaux du Languedoc Ultreia 2007
Red | 2011 up to 2013   **90**

Coteaux du Languedoc Vénus 2007
Red | 2011 up to 2013   **87**

Older vintages
Coteaux du Languedoc Cinarca 2006
Red | 2011 up to 2013   **90**
Beautifully racy, this is a red with toasty notes and a velvety, mineral texture. Great length.

Coteaux du Languedoc Ultreia 2006
Red | 2011 up to 2013   **90**
When we tasted this wine, it hadn't yet assimilated its barrel-aging notes. It deserves to be tasted a bit later because the potential is quite clearly there. It has perceptible class and pedigree.

Coteaux du Languedoc Vénus 2006
Red | 2011 up to 2013   **86**
Powerful and ripe, this red has notes of torrefaction and is long on the palate. The finish has a hint of sweetness.

Red: 44.5 acres; cabernet franc 5%, cabernet sauvignon 5%, grenache noir 20%, merlot 5%, mourvèdre 10%, syrah 50%, tannat 5%. Annual production: 55,000 bottles

DOMAINE DU MAS BLANC

9, avenue du Général-de-Gaulle
66650 Banyuls-sur-Mer
Phone 00 33 4 68 88 32 12
Fax 00 33 4 68 88 72 24
domainemasblanc@free.fr
www.domainedumasblanc.com

The Mas Blanc maintains the momentum that was inspired by famous Collioure advocate, the late Dr. André Parcé. The dry, white "Collioure Signature" is made in a typically southern style but retains all of that precious acidity that is sometimes lacking in Languedoc-Roussillon wines. The red Collioure cuvées are off the popular radar, with salty, iodized notes that give them a character all of their own; nowhere can you taste the sea spray more than here. The magnificent Vins Doux Naturels, meanwhile, are unsurpassed: quite simply transcendent.

Recently tasted
BANYULS VIEILLES VIGNES 2000
Sweet Red | 2011 up to 2028   **94**

COLLIOURE LES JUNQUETS 2006
Red | 2011 up to 2015   **88**

COLLIOURE RÉVÉRENCE 2007
Red | 2011 up to 2015   **90**

Older vintages
BANYULS EXCELLENCE 2000
Sweet Red | 2011 up to 2013   **93**
Caramelized sugar, mocha, cocoa, and bitter orange are the aromatic vectors for this marvelous, subtle, and tempting wine.

COLLIOURE CLOS DU MOULIN 2005
Red | 2011 up to 2013   **91**
The maritime influence is clearly perceptible in the saline notes on the finish. This is an elegant and carefully constructed wine. It is already drinkable, but it will pass its cellar neighbors in fullness with time.

COLLIOURE COSPRONS LEVANTS 2005
Red | 2011 up to 2013   **91**
With very powerful aromas marked by sea spray, this 2005 shows stunning complexity. It is currently more open than either Les Junquets or Clos du Moulin.

COLLIOURE LES JUNQUETS 2005
Red | 2011 up to 2013   **91**
This Collioure exudes its maritime influence with its delicately salty notes. Seaweed notes render even more complexity in its blackcurrant bouquet. Very long.

Red: 46.9 acres; grenache 90%, mourvèdre 5%, syrah 5%. White: 2.5 acres; grenache 80%, muscat d'Alexandrie 20%. Annual production: 55,000 bottles

DOMAINE DE MONTCALMÈS

Chemin du Cimetière
34150 Puéchabon
Phone 00 33 4 67 57 74 16
Fax 00 33 4 67 57 74 16
gaecbh@wanadoo.fr

You have to have a real curiosity about grand vin to make it yourself. Frédéric Pourtalié and his cousin Vincent Guizard previously made wines for the Grange des Pères, Olivier Jullien and Alain Graillot. In 1999 they established this winery in Puéchabon, in the Terrasses du Larzac area of the Coteaux du Languedoc appellation. The red wine is noted for its velvety, ultra-refined tannins. Thanks to exceptional fruit, it combines all the tranquility of grand vin with a supremely natural style that is absolutely the real thing.

Recently tasted
COTEAUX DU LANGUEDOC 2006
Red | 2011 up to 2018   **94**

Older vintages
COTEAUX DU LANGUEDOC 2005
Red | 2011 up to 2013   **96**
Overflowing with fruit, transcending its grape varieties, this 2005 is the incarnation of Languedoc finesse.

COTEAUX DU LANGUEDOC 2005
White | 2011 up to 2013   **92**
This full-bodied white made from marsanne and roussanne openly expresses its spice and complexity, while preserving its aromatic freshness.

COTEAUX DU LANGUEDOC 2004
Red | 2011 up to 2013   **93**
This cuvée is not deeply colored, but the fruit quality is confounding. Everything is there: a successful, grand Languedoc wine.

COTEAUX DU LANGUEDOC 2003
Red | 2011 up to 2013   **93**
This absolutely fresh and very elegant 2003 is quite different from the 2003s with dry tannins that abound. Only a hint of jamminess reminds us of the year's heat wave.

Red: 39.5 acres; grenache noir 25%, mourvèdre 25%, syrah 50%. White: 7.4 acres; marsanne 50%, roussanne 50%. Annual production: 35,000 bottles

CHÂTEAU DE NOUVELLES

SCEA R. Daurat-Fort
Château de Nouvelles
11350 Tuchan
Phone 00 33 4 68 45 40 03
Fax 00 33 4 68 45 49 21
daurat-fort@terre-net.fr
www.châteaudenouvelles.com

This somewhat remote winery in Tuchan was at the forefront of the Fitou revival: current owner Jean Daurat has been the region's most vocal and indefatigable proponent for decades. Originally famous for its Vins Doux Naturels, Château de Nouvelles still makes a range of offerings that enjoy particular success with VDN devotees (like us, for instance), even if they have gone out of fashion. The reds improve all the time and range from wines with animal notes that go best with game and meat sauces, to others with much fresher, wonderfully savory aromas. Jean Daurat is now joined by his son Jean-Rémy.

Recently tasted

FITOU GABRIELLE 2007
Red | 2011 up to 2013   90

FITOU VIEILLES VIGNES 2006
Red | 2011 up to 2013   90

MUSCAT DE RIVESALTES PRESTIGE 2008
Sweet White | 2011 up to 2013   94

RIVESALTES HORS D'ÂGE 1985
Sweet Amber | 2011 up to 2015   94

Older vintages

FITOU CANTOREL 2006
Red | 2011 up to 2013   89
A lovely salty and delicate palate with very refined tannins. It is powerfully flavored, ideal for grilled meats.

FITOU VIEILLES VIGNES 2000
Red | 2011 up to 2008   92
This top-level red has the finesse we expect from this beautiful domaine. It has no harshness, just an elegant and harmonious palette of flavors.

RIVESALTES 1996
Sweet Red | Drink now   90
This Ambré will encourage unusual pairings with Asian cuisines. With the elegance of 1996, with notes of rancio and walnuts, it should be a frequent guest at the table.

Red: 103.8 acres; carignan noir 35%, grenache noir 35%, syrah 30%. White: 66.7 acres; grenache blanc 20%, maccabeu 10%, muscat à petits grains 35%, muscat d'Alexandrie 35%. Annual production: 140,000 bottles

DOMAINE OLLIER-TAILLEFER

Route de Gabian
34320 Fos
Phone 00 33 4 67 90 24 59
Fax 00 33 4 67 90 12 15
ollier.taillefer@wanadoo.fr
www.olliertaillefer.com

Françoise Ollier and brother Luc took over their family estate a few years back. Their wines are rich with a sense of naturalness without ever showing off. The white Cuvée Allegro brings out the essence of the roussanne and the rolle, unaided by oak. The Grande Réserve is a refined red wine that is produced in large volumes so there is always enough to go around. The Castel Fossibus (Occitan for "Fos Castle") draws on the exquisite fruit of the syrah, grenache, and mourvèdre, displaying a delicate substance untainted by new oak, which wisely accounts for just 10 percent of barrels. A homogeneous range of wines and, so far at least, very affordable.

Recently tasted

FAUGÈRES ALLEGRO 2008
White | 2011 up to 2013   88

FAUGÈRES CASTEL FOSSIBUS 2006
Red | 2011 up to 2013   92

FAUGÈRES GRANDE RÉSERVE 2007
Red | 2011 up to 2014   90

Older vintages

FAUGÈRES ALLEGRO 2007
White | 2011 up to 2013   91
Grand style. A superb finish of fresh pineapple flavor follows the delicate and truly refined aromas.

FAUGÈRES CASTEL FOSSIBUS 2005
Red | 2011 up to 2013   92
Smoke and licorice: this beautiful expression of the terroir of Faugères has remarkably refined tannins on the finish.

FAUGÈRES GRANDE RÉSERVE 2006
Red | 2011 up to 2013   90
This velvety Faugères, blended from traditional Languedoc varieties, has delicate tannins and aromas that come directly from the schist.

FAUGÈRES LES COLLINES 2006
Red | 2011 up to 2013   86
This fresh and thirst-quenching wine finishes with minerality. Charming.

Red: 66.7 acres. White: 7.4 acres. Annual production: 140,000 bottles

L'OSTAL CAZES

Tuilerie Saint-Joseph
34210 La Livinière
Phone 00 33 4 68 91 47 79
Fax 00 33 4 68 91 47 79
lostalcazes@aol.com
www.lostalcazes.com

Jean-Michel Cazes, who also owns Château Lynch Bages in Pauillac, created this
estate by combining two old and reputable
domains that he acquired in 2002. He then
handed the reins to son Jean-Charles,
whose duty it now is to build up an estate
that justifies the considerable investment
so far. Improvements include a high-flying
technical team that clearly aims to steer the
wines toward ever-greater finesse and tannic elegance. The Cuvée Estibals isn't quite
there yet but the Minervois-la-Livinière is
already an appellation front-runner. We
look forward to seeing how future vintages
develop.

Minervois Estibals 2005
Red | 2011 up to 2013   85
There is lovely fruit on the attack, and a finish of slightly dry tannins due to the 2005
vintage.

Minervois-La-Livinière 2005
Red | 2011 up to 2013   88
Quite in line with its terroir, with a hint of
lightly cooked aromas brought about by the
drought of 2005. The quality of the tannins
is impressive. The saline finish is especially
long and elegant.

Minervois-La-Livinière 2004
Red | 2011 up to 2013   90
A linear wine, aged with care, this cuvée
has tannins that are a hint dry, yet refined
and classy. After a very ripe bouquet, the
palate finishes on peppers and salty notes,
nicely fresh. The masterful élevage is a
model of style.

Minervois-La-Livinière 2003
Red | 2011 up to 2013   86
The drought of 2003 has marked this wine,
but its richness has managed to soften and
envelop it nicely.

Red: 148.3 acres; carignan 13%, grenache 12%,
mourvèdre 10%, syrah 65%. Annual production:
200,000 bottles

DOMAINE L'OUSTAL BLANC

4 bis, avenue de la Source
34370 Creissan
Phone 00 33 4 67 93 68 47
Fax 00 33 4 67 93 68 47
earl.fonquerle@wanadoo.fr
www.oustal-blanc.com

Former Châteauneuf-du-Pape rugby players Claude Fonquerle and Philippe Cambie started this Minervois winery in 2002.
Claude takes care of day-to-day management, while Philippe is in Châteauneuf,
where he continues to advise on winemaking. In just a few years, Oustal Blanc has
wowed leading restaurateurs with its precise, fresh, and thoroughbred range of
wines. The table wines, unfettered by
AOC regulations, allow themselves a few
tasty deviations—a demonstration of
impressive skills that we see transformed
in the AOC offerings.

Recently tasted
Minervois Maestoso 2006
Red | 2011 up to 2013   90

Minervois-La-Livinière Prima Donna 2006
Red | 2011 up to 2013   91

Vin de table Naïck 6
Red | 2011 up to 2013   88

Vin de table Naïck 7
White | 2011 up to 2013   92

Older vintages
Minervois Giocoso 2006
Red | 2011 up to 2013   90
Rigorous work in the vineyard has brought
to life this distinguished and brilliant wine,
with its elegant and precise tannins. The
finish is flavorful, with undeniable aromatic
charm.

Minervois Maestoso 2005
Red | 2011 up to 2013   90
The tannins from this luxuriously matured
wine are refined. It is highly seductive!

Minervois-La-Livinière Prima Donna 2005
Red | 2011 up to 2013   92
The La Livinière terroir has given this 2005
astonishingly high-quality fruit. The finish
is exceptionally dense and long.

Red: 23.5 acres; carignan 29%, cinsault 10%,
grenache 51%, syrah 10%. White: 3 acres; maccabeu
100%. Annual production: 40,000 bottles

DOMAINE DU PAS DE L'ESCALETTE

Le Champ de Peyrottes
34700 Poujols
Phone 00 33 4 67 96 13 42
contact@pasdelescalette.com
www.pasdelescalette.com

Zernott and Delphine Rousseau bought this estate in 2002: a twenty-four-acre terraced vineyard with dry-stone retaining walls known as "clapas," standing some 1,050 feet above the Larzac plateau on a limestone scree slope. Viticulture and soil management are largely organic and the grapes are manually harvested and handled with the utmost care. This sort of work and the thinking behind it produces cuvées with a refined, almost fragile mouthfeel. We particularly liked their delicate and subtle substance.

Recently tasted

COTEAUX DU LANGUEDOC LE GRAND PAS 2007
Red | 2011 up to 2015   **89**

COTEAUX DU LANGUEDOC LES CLAPAS 2007
Red | 2011 up to 2014   **88**

COTEAUX DU LANGUEDOC LES PETITS PAS 2008
Red | 2011 up to 2014   **86**

Older vintages

COTEAUX DU LANGUEDOC LE GRAND PAS 2006
Red | 2011 up to 2013   **89**
This wine enjoys beautiful primary matter. It is delicate, nearly fragile in its balance, with very streamlined tannins.

COTEAUX DU LANGUEDOC LES CLAPAS 2004
Red | 2011 up to 2013   **88**
The terroir of Terrasses du Larzac cuvée gives its refined juice more depth than the classic Coteaux du Languedoc.

COTEAUX DU LANGUEDOC LES PETITS PAS 2006
Red | 2011 up to 2013   **86**
A lovely wine for friends. It will be perfect with charcuterie or even on its own, contributing ambiance to an evening party.

VIN DE PAYS DE L'HÉRAULT LES CLAPAS 2007
White | 2011 up to 2013   **86**
Lively and fresh, carried by notes of lemon and oranges.

Red: 22.2 acres; carignan noir 30%, cinsault 10%, grenache noir 40%, syrah 20%. **White:** 2.4 acres; carignan blanc 40%, grenache blanc 20%, terret bourret 40%. **Annual production:** 60,000 bottles

CHÂTEAU DE PENNAUTIER

Vignobles Lorgeril
BP 4
11610 Pennautier
Phone 00 33 4 68 72 65 29
Fax 00 33 4 68 72 65 84
contact@lorgeril.com
www.lorgeril.com

Château de Pennautier is located in Cabardès, where the Atlantic influence meets the Mediterranean weather system and Bordeaux varietals make way for those of the Languedoc. At first glance, this historic estate (part of Vignobles Lorgeril) looks like a bastion of traditional values in an appellation awash with young talent. Closer inspection reveals a winery feeling its way toward modern, irresistible Cabardès wines, marketed under the Pennautier-Lorgeril banner. Vignobles Lorgeril also makes Domaine de la Borie Blanche, from its Minervois estate.

Recently tasted

CABARDÈS 2008
Red | 2011 up to 2013   **88**

CORBIÈRES DOMAINE DES CROUZETS 2007
Red | 2011 up to 2013   **86**

MINERVOIS LA BORIE BLANCHE 2008
Red | 2011 up to 2013   **88**

SAINT-CHINIAN MOULIN DE CIFFRE 2008
Red | 2011 up to 2013   **88**

Older vintages

CABARDÈS 2005
Red | 2011 up to 2013   **87**
The 2005 has power in its notable tannins and a very precise structure. A little patience is recommended to allow this red to deliver on its aromatic potential.

CORBIÈRES LES COMBES DES OLIVIERS 2006
Red | 2011 up to 2013   **86**
A strong predominance of mourvèdre brings structure, but this wine is, above all, approachable and easy to drink. It offers pleasant aromas of garrigue.

MINERVOIS LA BORIE BLANCHE 2006
Red | 2011 up to 2013   **86**
The red fruit notes that come from schist soils come through clearly in this cuvée, even though they make up only a small portion of the blend. It is a wine that's easy to drink.

Red: 479.4 acres; cabernet sauvignon 18%, cinsault 9%, côt 3%, grenache 8%, merlot 30%, syrah 32%. **White:** 54.4 acres; chardonnay 100%. **Annual production:** 2,500,000 bottles

DOMAINE DU PETIT CAUSSE

De la Sallèle
34210 Félines-Minervois
Phone 00 33 4 68 91 66 12
Fax 00 33 4 68 91 66 12
chabbert-philippe@orange.fr
www.domaine-du-petit-causse.
www.leminervois.com

This estate is located in the village of Félines-Minervois, in an area known as the Petit Causse, from which it takes its name. Formerly part of the village co-op, the winery now goes it alone, producing deliciously fruity wines with a naturalness that makes them hugely quaffable—a combination of refinement and simplicity that is a real tour de force. The Cuvée Andréa brings a touch more finesse to a range that is already superbly polished. The estate has picked up speed in recent years and is definitely now a winery worth watching—particularly since prices remain sensible.

Recently tasted
MINERVOIS 2007
Red | 2011 up to 2013   87

MINERVOIS GRIOTTE DE VENTAJOUX 2007
Red | 2011 up to 2013   89

MINERVOIS-LA-LIVINIÈRE ANDRÉA 2007
Red | 2011 up to 2013   87

Older vintages
MINERVOIS 2006
Red | 2011 up to 2013   87
Very clean aromatically, this introductory red wine is sufficiently powerful and fleshy, with a mentholated finish.

MINERVOIS GRIOTTE DE VENTAJOUX 2006
Red | 2011 up to 2013   89
The black marble of Félines is called "la griotte," due to its red, cherry-shaped incrustations. Aged in tank, this is a delicate, delectable, and charming cuvée enhanced by lovely red-berry scents.

MINERVOIS-LA-LIVINIÈRE ANDRÉA 2005
Red | 2011 up to 2013   89
This cuvée bears the name of the grandmother who owned the vineyards. You can sense magnificent red berries and quality tannins, but the oak is still quite present. A more discreet élevage might be better adapted to the great quality of this cuvée's fruit.

Red: 48.9 acres; grenache 20%, carignan 20%, cabernet sauvignon 10%, merlot 10%, syrah 40%.
Annual production: 15,000 bottles

DOMAINE PEYRE ROSE

34230 Saint-Pargoire
Phone 00 33 4 67 98 75 50
Fax 00 33 4 67 98 71 88
peyrerose@orange.fr

In 1983 Marlène Soria abandoned a budding career in real estate to devote herself to clearing and planting an isolated property completely surrounded by garrigue. What we see there today is a remote but biodynamically cultivated vineyard that is meticulously managed to keep yields extremely low. The domaine produces two red, syrah-driven cuvées: Clos des Cistes and Syrah Léone. The first is the more acidic of the two and comes from the stony, very dry soils in the upper part of the vineyard. The Syrah Léone comes from a more friable, rocky parcel that is readily permeable to water. All of the wines from this estate rank among the cream of the Languedoc: fabulously complete and built on aromatic sensibilities and naturalness. No other estate, for sure, produces wines that so faithfully mirror their respective vintages. The 2002 saw a slight change in style with some of the wines being matured in large oak vats—improvement worth pursuing, since it adds extra depth. Let's hear it, too, for the white wine, a blend of rolle, roussanne, and viognier grapes that also plays on the exceptional. Sure to delight those of us who love vins de voile (referring to a vinification technique in which a yeasty layer is allowed to form on the surface of the wine during aging).

Recently tasted
COTEAUX DU LANGUEDOC MARLÈNE N°3 2003
Red | 2011 up to 2017   90

Older vintages
COTEAUX DU LANGUEDOC CISTES 2003
Red | 2011 up to 2018   93
This 2003 has matured toward lightly jammy notes. The tannins have a hint of dryness, typical of the vintage, requiring a bit more time to develop a patina.

COTEAUX DU LANGUEDOC CISTES 2002
Red | 2011 up to 2017   93
A third of this cuvée passed through oak, lightly tinting the wine. With such deep and rich juice, it has taken on a very velvety texture. We can only lavish superlatives on it.

COTEAUX DU LANGUEDOC CISTES 1998
Red | 2011 up to 2014   93
This big wine has tannins a touch dryer than those of the 1998 Léone. It is deep, black, and very peppery, with elevated alcohol. It is similar in style to the 1994 and 1995.

COTEAUX DU LANGUEDOC CISTES 1996
Red | 2011 up to 2015   **97**
Cistes 1996 has never touched wood. Its exceptional freshness has no equal other than its own luminous fruit. Top of the game!

COTEAUX DU LANGUEDOC ORO 1997
White | 2011 up to 2017   **97**
Those who don't appreciate vins de voile can continue on their way. Lovers of the great yellow wines of Jura and the best Fino Sherries will have a pleasant gustatory shock with this 1997 white.

COTEAUX DU LANGUEDOC ORO 1996
White | 2011 up to 2017   **93**
The 1996 is nothing like the others. Halfway between a dry Languedoc white and a big Fino Sherry, it is atypical, designed for those who appreciate big oxidative and absolutely delicious wines.

COTEAUX DU LANGUEDOC SYRAH LÉONE 2003
Red | 2011 up to 2013   **93**
Intensely scented, with great depth, this 2003 is stamped by its vintage. Profound, very Peyre Rose.

COTEAUX DU LANGUEDOC SYRAH LÉONE 2002
Red | 2011 up to 2015   **98**
Explosive and fabulous, the 2002 Léone is a pure expression of a nearly perfect southern wine.

COTEAUX DU LANGUEDOC SYRAH LÉONE 1998
Red | 2011 up to 2013   **96**
This high-class, structured wine is deep and velvety. It borrows Mediterranean garrigue accents from Bandol.

COTEAUX DU LANGUEDOC SYRAH LÉONE 1996
Red | 2011 up to 2015   **97**
There is extraordinary freshness in this luminous and deep wine. Its scents evoke great Burgundian pinots noir. This unexpected aromatic similarity only reinforces this wine's exceptional fullness.

COTEAUX DU LANGUEDOC SYRAH LÉONE 1995
Red | 2011 up to 2015   **95**
Even more languorous than the 1995 Cistes, Léone climbs a notch in voluptuousness. This very Mediterranean cuvée has more velvet and depth, whereas its alter ego had more tension in the finish.

Red: 51.9 acres; carignan noir 5%, grenache noir 15%, mourvèdre 10%, syrah 70%. White: 4.9 acres; others 10%, rolle 50%, roussanne 40%. Annual production: 35,000 bottles

DOMAINE POUDEROUX

2, rue Émile-Zola
66460 Maury
Phone 00 33 4 68 57 22 02
Fax 00 33 4 68 57 11 63
domainepouderoux@orange.fr
www.domainepouderoux.fr

Robert and Catherine Pouderoux operate a forty-two-acre estate in Corneilla-de-la-Rivière and Maury, planted in black schists and schistose marls. They plow their vineyards and have stopped using chemical fertilizers. The bulk of production is geared toward vintage-style Vins Doux Naturels. The estate's top offering is La Mouriane, made from old syrah and very old grenache vines.

Recently tasted
CÔTES DU ROUSSILLON-VILLAGES
LA MOURIANE 2006
Red | 2011 up to 2014   **90**

CÔTES DU ROUSSILLON-VILLAGES
TERRE BRUNE 2006
Red | 2011 up to 2013   **87**

MAURY VENDANGE 2007
Sweet Red | 2011 up to 2018   **88**

MAURY VENDANGE MISE TARDIVE 2004
Sweet Red | 2011 up to 2018   **90**

Older vintages
CÔTES DU ROUSSILLON-VILLAGES
LA MOURIANE 2005
Red | 2011 up to 2013   **92**
A big, refined wine, with full-bodied tannins. There is no roughness; it is all finesse. The notes of fruit in eau-de-vie that fill the incredibly long finish are impressive.

CÔTES DU ROUSSILLON-VILLAGES
TERRE BRUNE 2005
Red | 2011 up to 2013   **88**
Full-bodied and refined with cocoa notes, this cuvée will age very well.

MAURY HORS D'ÂGE
Sweet Red | 2011 up to 2017   **93**
Schist terroir, very old grenache, and fifteen years of patience have created this perfectly balanced wine, with notes of caramel, figs, and sweet spices.

Red: 37.1 acres; carignan noir 10%, grenache noir 65%, mourvèdre 10%, syrah 15%. White: 4.9 acres; grenache blanc 85%, maccabeu 8%, muscat à petits grains 7%. Annual production: 60,000 bottles

DOMAINE DE LA PROSE

🍷🍷🍷🍷

Domaine de la Prose
34570 Pignan
Phone 00 33 4 67 03 08 30
Fax 00 33 4 67 03 48 70
domaine-de-la-prose@wanadoo.fr
www.laprose.com

Saint-Georges d'Orques stands at the gateway to Montpellier, fanned by cooling, on-shore breezes that lend a saline complexity to the local wines. The red wines are powerful and angular and unbelievably refined and the white wines can also be quite delicate. The Domaine de la Prose is named after the lieu-dit of La Prose, not prose literature; its wines are an ode to civilization nonetheless. Sourced locally and from vineyards around the Grès de Montpellier area, these are wines stripped of all unnecessary pretense—every one terrifically pure.

Recently tasted

COTEAUX DU LANGUEDOC
GRANDE CUVÉE SAINT-GEORGES 2006
Red | 2011 up to 2014   **88**

COTEAUX DU LANGUEDOC LES CADIÈRES 2008
White | 2011 up to 2013   **88**

COTEAUX DU LANGUEDOC LES CADIÈRES 2007
Red | 2011 up to 2013   **86**

COTEAUX DU LANGUEDOC LES EMBRUNS 2007
Red | 2011 up to 2013   **90**

Older vintages

COTEAUX DU LANGUEDOC GRANDE CUVÉE
SAINT-GEORGES 2005
Red | 2011 up to 2013   **90**
This Saint-Georges d'Orques is a model of a style that balances density and refined tannins. It is perfectly honed.

COTEAUX DU LANGUEDOC LES CADIÈRES 2006
Red | 2011 up to 2013   **89**
Aged in cement tanks, Les Cadières is elegant, nervy on the finish, natural, pure, saline, and always very fresh. It could be enjoyed from the beginning to the end of an evening without growing tiresome. The 2006 is showing well.

Red: 34.8 acres; cinsault 25%, grenache noir 21%, mourvèdre 14%, syrah 40%. White: 8.4 acres; grenache blanc 35%, roussanne 30%, vermentino 35%. Annual production: 60,000 bottles

DOMAINE DE LA RECTORIE

🍷🍷🍷🍷

65, avenue du Puig-Delmas
66650 Banyuls-sur-Mer
Phone 00 33 4 68 88 13 45
Fax 00 33 4 68 81 02 42
larectorie@wanadoo.fr
www.la-rectorie.com

The Domaine de La Rectorie is named after the hamlet that is home to its vineyards. Marc and Pierre Parcé market the wines and Thierry crafts them. Their specialty is a selection of great Banyuls and Collioure wines in all three colors, with that slightly saline, iodized taste that comes from vines kissed by sea spray. All of these wines deliver on quality: no monstrous power, just balance and delicacy every time.

Recently tasted

BANYULS LÉON PARCÉ 2007
Sweet Red | 2011 up to 2027   **93**

BANYULS PARCÉ FRÈRES 2007
Sweet Red | 2011 up to 2028   **92**

COLLIOURE CÔTÉ MER 2007
Red | 2011 up to 2013   **90**

COLLIOURE L'ARGILE 2008
White | 2011 up to 2013   **90**

Older vintages

BANYULS PARCÉ FRÈRES 2006
Sweet Red | 2011 up to 2018   **91**
The marked tannins of this powerful Banyuls are a sign of its great aging potential, but this sweet red can also be enjoyed now for the immediate charm of its red-berry flavors.

COLLIOURE CÔTÉ MER 2006
Red | 2011 up to 2013   **90**
A delicate, fresh, and harmonious red with tannic power in its finish, with a light and tasty saltiness.

COLLIOURE CÔTÉ MONTAGNE 2006
Red | 2011 up to 2013   **89**
A blend of grenache, carignan, syrah, and mourvèdre, this is powerful and tannic, yet refined, unusual and truly long.

VIN DE LIQUEUR
Sweet Amber | 2011 up to 2018   **94**
Fortified before fermentation, this liquorous wine has exceptional length, with walnuts, curry, dried fruits, and sweet spices. Its subtlety is exceptional, and its length no less. It is equally beautiful, with a color somewhere between pale orange and onion skin.

Red: 46.9 acres; carignan 10%, grenache 80%, syrah 10%. White: 19.8 acres; grenache 10%, grenache gris 90%. Annual production: 100,000 bottles

DOMAINE RIMBERT

Place de l'Aire
34360 Berlou
Phone 00 33 4 67 89 74 66
Fax 00 33 4 67 89 73 98
domaine.rimbert@wanadoo.fr
www.domainerimbert.com

Jean-Marie Rimbert settled in Berlou in 1994 and is one of the winemakers who brings out the best in this little-known schistose corner of the Saint-Chinian appellation. The carignan grape coaxes out the acidity it needs to prove its worth in El Carignator; the Travers de Marceau, Mas au Schiste, and Berlou all likewise celebrate the qualities of schist. All of them possess a hint of antique rose that says a lot about the strides made by this estate to keep such delicate aromas intact.

Recently tasted
SAINT-CHINIAN 2007
White | 2011 up to 2013   **84**

SAINT-CHINIAN LES TRAVERS DE MARCEAU 2007
Red | 2011 up to 2013   **88**

Older vintages
SAINT-CHINIAN BERLOU VILLAGE 2004
Red | 2011 up to 2009   **89**
This cuvée was harvested on the Berlou schists. It has silky tannins and a velvety texture superior even to the domaine's other wines. Deeply flavored, with a finish of red berries, it will delight lovers of schist-grown wines. Drink soon.

SAINT-CHINIAN LE MAS AU SCHISTE 2005
Red | 2011 up to 2013   **91**
The northern portion of Saint-Chinian is constituted of schist, which here, year after year, give notes of peonies, antique roses, and smoke to this delicious wine.

SAINT-CHINIAN LES TRAVERS DE MARCEAU 2006
Red | 2011 up to 2013   **86**
This wine, with notes of black-currant buds and great lightness, seeks to be consumed easily and pleasurably.

VIN DE TABLE EL CARIGNATOR
Red | 2011 up to 2013   **86**
This wine, made in honor of the carignan grape, has a delicious palate, lightly mature with racy tannins. It's evolving toward flavors of fruit in eau-de-vie.

Red: 59.3 acres. White: 9.8 acres. Annual production: 90,000 bottles

DOMAINE LE ROC DES ANGES

2, place de l'Aire
66720 Montner
Phone 00 33 4 68 29 16 62
Fax 00 33 4 68 29 45 31
rocdesanges@wanadoo.fr
www.rocdesanges.com

Marjorie Gallet makes trail-blazing Roussillon wines from vines planted in dark gray schists around Tautavel. Her dry white wine gets the best out of the grenache gris, a grape with the potential for greatness when carefully vinified. Her newly revived ancient parcels produce red wines with surprisingly good tannins and great elegance. Add to that the freshness of grapes from ideally exposed vineyards and you have an outstanding range of wines across the board—whether red or white, Vin de Pays or AOC.

Recently tasted
CÔTES DU ROUSSILLON-VILLAGES SEGNA DE COR 2006
Red | 2011 up to 2013   **91**

PASSERILLÉ 2008
Sweet White | 2011 up to 2015   **90**

VIN DE PAYS DES PYRÉNÉES-ORIENTALES 1903 2008
Red | 2011 up to 2013   **92**

VIN DE PAYS DES PYRÉNÉES-ORIENTALES VIEILLES VIGNES 2007
Red | 2011 up to 2013   **92**

Older vintages
CÔTES DU ROUSSILLON-VILLAGES SEGNA DE COR 2005
Red | 2011 up to 2013   **90**
Tank-aged, this wine has refined and delicious tannins. Voluptuous and tempting, the finish is peppery, rapid, and flavorful.

VIN DE PAYS DES PYRÉNÉES-ORIENTALES 1903 2006
Red | 2011 up to 2013   **88**
The 2006 looks to be remarkable. Powerful enough for the moment, the wine has pure expression and rare balance that does much to honor carignan.

VIN DE PAYS DES PYRÉNÉES-ORIENTALES 1903 2005
Red | 2011 up to 2013   **90**
Old-vine carignan from a parcel planted in 1903 made for a refined and delicious wine that is maturing very well. The freshness is comforting.

VIN DE PAYS DES PYRÉNÉES-ORIENTALES VIEILLES VIGNES 2006

White | 2011 up to 2013   **88**

Still not completely integrated, this wine is slowly but surely settling into place, and at this time it amazes more by its delicious depth than by its freshness.

VIN DE PAYS DES PYRÉNÉES-ORIENTALES VIEILLES VIGNES 2005

White | 2011 up to 2013   **92**

Grenache gris is dominant in this cuvée, lightened by maccabeu. The aromas are nearly irresistible, and the refined finish maintains its structure.

VIN DE PAYS DES PYRÉNÉES-ORIENTALES VIEILLES VIGNES 2005

Red | 2011 up to 2013   **92**

Excellent wine, with extraordinarily refined tannins. Great style!

VIN DE PAYS DES PYRÉNÉES-ORIENTALES VIEILLES VIGNES 2004

Red | 2011 up to 2013   **92**

This Vieilles Vignes cuvée is an earthly translation of velvet.

Red: 34.6 acres; carignan noir 50%, grenache noir 25%, syrah 25%. White: 19.8 acres; grenache gris, carignan blanc, maccabeu. Annual production: 45,000 bottles

PRIEURÉ DE SAINT-JEAN DE BÉBIAN

Route de Nizas
34120 Pézenas
Phone 00 33 4 67 98 13 60
Fax 00 33 4 67 98 22 24
info@bebian.com
www.bebian.com

After a career in the specialist wine press, Chantal Lecouty and Jean-Claude Le Brun had fairly clear ideas about how to make a grand vin—the French term for a house's benchmark wine. They bought this Pézenas property in 1994 and have been improving it ever since. Even their second wine, La Chapelle, now ranks alongside the finest Languedoc wines. Its creation served to focus attention on the grand vin, Bébian, a rare expression of classically Languedoc style: generous and refined but also capable of graceful aging. Recent vintages of the heavily roussanne-driven white wine have been made to the same lofty standards as the reds. The property has just been sold.

Recently tasted

COTEAUX DU LANGUEDOC 2007
White | 2011 up to 2015   **91**

COTEAUX DU LANGUEDOC LA CHAPELLE DE BÉBIAN 2008
White | 2011 up to 2013   **88**

COTEAUX DU LANGUEDOC LA CHAPELLE DE BÉBIAN 2007
Red | 2011 up to 2014   **90**

Older vintages

COTEAUX DU LANGUEDOC 2005
Red | 2011 up to 2013   **94**

The terroir's pedigree is clearly expressed in this very ripe, spicy, high-class wine. The rebellious tannins of 2005 are softening into a full-bodied finish, and the wine is beginning to take flight.

COTEAUX DU LANGUEDOC LA CHAPELLE DE BÉBIAN 2006
Red | 2011 up to 2013   **87**

Vintage after vintage La Chapelle champions its style of wine with complex red fruit, a slight touch of tannins softened by leather and spice. Delicate notes of anise complete the aromatic finish.

Red: 66.7 acres; carignan noir 5%, cinsault 10%, grenache noir 35%, mourvèdre 20%, syrah 30%. White: 14.8 acres; clairette 10%, grenache blanc 20%, picpoul 10%, roussanne 60%. Annual production: 120,000 bottles

DOMAINE SARDA-MALET

Mas Saint-Michel
Chemin de Sainte-Barbe
66000 Perpignan
Phone 00 33 4 68 56 72 38
Fax 00 33 4 68 56 47 60
sardamalet@wanadoo.fr
www.sarda-malet.com

Good-quality fruit is a Malet family tradition. Jérôme Malet works in one of the last surviving agricultural districts around Perpignan. The wines he makes there belong to an elite group of Roussillon wines, made in a style that relies on refinement rather than that monstrous concentration that always palls in the end. Jérôme's top-of-the-range cuvée is his dry red or white Terroir de Mailloles. La Réserve is certainly more modest but a perfect wine for any occasion. The muscat is savory, while La Carbasse (Rivesaltes Vin Doux Naturel) is near exceptional and simply defies time.

Recently tasted
RIVESALTES LE SERRAT 2000
Sweet Amber | 2011 up to 2028   92

Older vintages
CÔTES DU ROUSSILLON LE SARDA 2007
Red | 2011 up to 2013   88
With power, lovely fruit, and freshness, this introductory wine is pleasant and friendly.

CÔTES DU ROUSSILLON RÉSERVE 2005
Red | 2011 up to 2013   89
With stone fruit, garrigue, fig, and blackberry flavors and supple tannins, this full-bodied wine is quite delectable.

CÔTES DU ROUSSILLON TERROIR DE MAILLOLES 2005
Red | 2011 up to 2013   91
A big, refined wine whose élevage is well assimilated in its full-bodied texture. It has remarkable finesse with racy tannins. The most Bordeaux-like of the big Roussillon wines?

MUSCAT DE RIVESALTES 2006
Sweet White | 2011 up to 2013   90
Candied peaches and apricots dominate in this muscat's aromas. It is built on power, yet retains finesse.

RIVESALTES LA CARBASSE 2006
Sweet Red | 2011 up to 2027   90
Full-bodied and nearly wild, this wine has notes of stone fruit and prunes and slightly rebellious tannins. It would wake up a chocolate dessert.

Red: 96.4 acres. White: 29.7 acres. Annual production: 130,000 bottles

DOMAINE DES SCHISTES

1, avenue Jean-Lurçat
66310 Estagel
Phone 00 33 4 68 29 11 25
Fax 00 33 4 68 29 47 17
sire-schistes@wanadoo.fr
www.domaine-des-schistes.com

This estate in the foothills of the Massif des Corbières operates north- and southwest-facing vineyards planted in a mixture of gray and black schists and limestone scree. Owner Jacques Sire is a discerning taster and is now supported by his son Mickael.

Recently tasted
CÔTES DU ROUSSILLON-VILLAGES
LES TERRASSES 2007
Red | 2011 up to 2015   91

MUSCAT DE RIVESALTES 2007
Sweet White | 2011 up to 2016   90

Older vintages
CÔTES DU ROUSSILLON-VILLAGES
LA COUMEILLE 2005
Red | 2011 up to 2013   91
This top-level cuvée was made with care. The oak underlines the juice without dominating it, leaving it voluptuous, airy, and very delicate.

CÔTES DU ROUSSILLON-VILLAGES
LES TERRASSES 2006
Red | 2011 up to 2013   90
This velvety wine has smooth and round tannins. It finishes delightfully with truly delectable, great, racy length.

CÔTES DU ROUSSILLON-VILLAGES TRADITION 2006
Red | 2011 up to 2013   88
Marked by black currants and dark berries, this tank-aged wine is very pleasant to drink now.

MAURY LA CERISAIE 2006
Sweet Red | 2011 up to 2017   92
This domaine's Maury always exudes lots of elegance, with its dried-fruit, cocoa, and refined spice notes. The finish is charmingly light.

RIVESALTES SOLERA
Sweet Amber | 2011 up to 2027   94
This solera is a Rivesaltes made in the spirit of Andalusian Jerez. The finish of walnuts, bitter orange, dried figs, and blond tobacco is exceptional and very delicate.

Red: 69.2 acres; carignan noir 26%, grenache noir 37%, syrah 30%, other 7%. White: 49.4 acres; grenache blanc 41%, maccabeu 27%, muscat à petits grains 21%, muscat d'Alexandrie 11%. Annual production: 85,000 bottles

DOMAINE JEAN-BAPTISTE SÉNAT

12, rue de l'Argen-Double
11160 Trausse-Minervois
Phone 00 33 4 68 78 38 17
Fax 00 33 4 68 78 26 61
jbsenat@terre-net.fr

Jean-Baptiste Sénat, a talented and perfectionist winemaker, never stops evolving. He farms forty-four acres in Trausse, located in the Aude region, right in the center of the Minervois appellation—not the hottest area, but certainly the driest. The wines are made to be more drinkable than prize-winning. They are never better than when enjoyed among friends, where they will inspire animated and heartfelt conversations!

Recently tasted

MINERVOIS LA NINE 2007
Red | 2011 up to 2013   89

MINERVOIS LE BOIS DES MERVEILLES 2007
Red | 2011 up to 2013   91

MINERVOIS MAIS OÙ EST DONC ORNICAR 2008
Red | 2011 up to 2013   88

Older vintages

MINERVOIS LA NINE 2006
Red | 2011 up to 2013   89
Harmonious, with very elegant, fleshy, and particularly delicious tannins. La Nine is named after the vineyard parcel whence it comes.

MINERVOIS LE BOIS DES MERVEILLES 2006
Red | 2011 up to 2013   90
With notes of licorice, this Bois de Merveilles concentrates on beautiful mourvèdre and grenache. The texture is refined, elegant, and light. A little patience is nonetheless necessary.

MINERVOIS MAIS OÙ EST DONC ORNICAR 2007
Red | 2011 up to 2013   88
Vintage after vintage, this is the prototype of a vin gourmand, with fleshy fruit. Harmonious and well balanced, it's to be shared with good friends.

Red: 44.5 acres: carignan 30%, cinsault 5%, grenache 30%, merlot 10%, mourvèdre 10%, syrah 5%. Annual production: 45.000 bottles

DOMAINE LA TOUR BOISÉE

1, rue du Château-d'Eau
11800 Laure-Minervois
Phone 00 33 4 68 78 10 04
Fax 00 33 4 68 78 10 98
info@domainelatourboisee.com
www.domainelatourboisee.com

The revival of Minervois wines owes a lot to this estate, which continues to make progress today thanks to prominent Minervois personality Jean-Louis Poudou. The vineyard is located in Laure, planted in a mixture of sandstone and marly sandstone. The top-of-the-range offering is Jardin Secret, a cuvée with refined tannins and first-class aging potential that showcases Poudou's savoir-faire. The white incarnation of the Cuvée à Marie-Claude, made in a Mediterranean style that just begs to go with food, won't leave you cold either.

Recently tasted

MINERVOIS JARDIN SECRET 2003
Red | 2011 up to 2014   88

Older vintages

MINERVOIS À MARIE-CLAUDE 2005
Red | 2011 up to 2015   87
This distinguished wine has deep tannins and velvety length. Its density is joyous in its lack of heaviness.

MINERVOIS À MARIE-CLAUDE 2004
Red | 2011 up to 2013   86
The attack is elegant and round, with animal notes. It finishes on autumnal scents, lightly dry.

MINERVOIS JARDIN SECRET 2002
Red | 2011 up to 2013   90
There is great finesse and true harmony in this tender and deep wine. It finishes on perfectly silky tannins, with scents of truffles and meat juices.

MINERVOIS JARDIN SECRET 2001
Red | 2011 up to 2013   90
This tender, deep wine has lots of harmony and a finish with good intensity, with notes of meat juices and sweet spices.

MINERVOIS MARIELLE ET FRÉDÉRIQUE 2003
Red | 2011 up to 2013   85
A serious and well-made Minervois, this will need some time to allow the tannins to soften.

Red: 173 acres. White: 29.7 acres. Annual production: 400,000 bottles

DOMAINE LA TOUR VIEILLE

12, route de Madeloc
66190 Collioure
Phone 00 33 4 68 82 44 82
Fax 00 33 4 68 82 38 42
contact@latourvieille.fr

The Domaine La Tour Vieille was created in 1982 with the joining of two family properties, one in Collioure, one in Banyuls. Jean Baillis recently added his vines to the mix to complement the range of the winery. Planted in clay and schist soils, the vineyards are essentially located on steep hillsides, overlooking the Mediterranean, where the nuances come from the exposition, the altitude, and the winds. The 2006 dry whites and reds that we tasted were all of good quality. The sweet wine, Banyuls Reserva, was quite a beauty.

Recently tasted

COLLIOURE LA PINÈDE 2007
Red | 2011 up to 2013   88

COLLIOURE LES CANADELLS 2008
White | 2011 up to 2013   89

COLLIOURE PUIG AMBEILLE 2007
Red | 2011 up to 2013   87

COLLIOURE PUIG ORIOL 2007
Red | 2011 up to 2013   90

COLLIOURE ROSÉ DES ROCHES 2008
Rosé | 2011 up to 2013   88

Older vintages

BANYULS RESERVA
Sweet Red | 2011 up to 2017   91
A lovely Banyuls with delicate and refined tannins. The finish is especially aromatic, long, and elegant.

COLLIOURE LES CANADELLS 2007
White | 2011 up to 2013   90
This fat and subtle Collioure, influenced by the sea, has notes of iodine and salt in a long and refined finish. The terroir is one of Roussillon's most interesting when cultivated by a gifted winegrower. The finish is especially refreshing.

COLLIOURE PUIG AMBEILLE 2006
Red | 2011 up to 2013   90
A classy wine, salty and deep with powerful tannins.

Red: 22.2 acres. White: 8.6 acres. Annual production: 55,000 bottles

CHÂTEAU DE VAUGELAS

11200 Camplong-d'Aude
Phone 00 33 4 68 43 68 41
Fax 00 33 4 68 43 57 43
châteauvaugelas@wanadoo.fr
www.château-vaugelas.com

The Bonfils family estate is home to some particularly delicate red wines, sold under the Château de Vaugelas and Cuvée Le Prieuré labels. Thanks to expertise and high standards, this estate now ranks among the top Corbières properties. Despite a difficult, pebbly terroir ("galets roulés") on the borders of the Orbieu River, the wines are utterly charming with no trace of grating tannins. Well worth seeking out.

Recently tasted

CORBIÈRES CHÂTEAU VAUGELAS 2006
Red | 2011 up to 2013   89

CORBIÈRES FÛTS DE CHÊNE 2007
Red | 2011 up to 2013   87

CORBIÈRES LE PRIEURÉ 2007
Red | 2011 up to 2013   87

Older vintages

CORBIÈRES CHÂTEAU VAUGELAS 2005
Red | 2011 up to 2013   90
A refined and elegant Corbières with a velvet texture, subtle graphite note, and a lovely fresh finish with savory hints of salt.

CORBIÈRES CHÂTEAU VAUGELAS 2004
Red | 2011 up to 2013   88
A very open bouquet and a long finish on fruit eau-de-vie flavors define this 2004. A few rancio notes make it quite unusual.

CORBIÈRES CHÂTEAU VAUGELAS 2003
Red | 2011 up to 2008   88
With leather and spice-cake notes, this wine is clearly marked by its vintage. Its refined tannins are beginning to mature.

CORBIÈRES LE PRIEURÉ 2006
Red | 2011 up to 2013   88
This wine has very refined tannins, with notes of caramel, licorice, and lightly jammy fruits. The style is appetizing.

CORBIÈRES PRESTIGE 2006
Red | 2011 up to 2013   87
Superripe, with lovely body, this wine has a lightly jammy finish, but lacks the expected freshness.

Annual production: 650,000 bottles

CHÂTEAU VILLERAMBERT-JULIEN

D620
11160 Caunes-Minervois
Phone 00 33 4 68 78 00 01
Fax 00 33 4 68 78 05 34
contact@villerambert-julien.com
www.villerambert-julien.com

Caunes-Minervois is famous for being the source of the pink marble used to build the Grand Trianon and the Opéra Garnier. It is also home to this estate, one of the region's most dependable producers. Its syrah bottling offers the perfect introduction for complete novices; its château-bottled Minervois is well structured, with all the characteristic finesse to be expected of this lovely appellation; and the Ourdivieille, having absorbed its oak, unveils that extraordinary complexity of old grenache vines. A surefire producer.

Recently tasted
MINERVOIS L'OPÉRA 2006
Red | Drink now   86

MINERVOIS LA SYRAH 2006
Red | Drink now   85

Older vintages
MINERVOIS 2007
White | 2011 up to 2013   85
A white wine with scents of yellow peaches and citrus, and imposing power.

MINERVOIS L'OPÉRA 2005
Red | 2011 up to 2009   87
This cuvée was the second wine of Villerambert-Julien, but it is now beginning to go its own way. It is easy to drink, with supple tannins, a bouquet of cooked red berries, and a finish that is beginning to mature toward notes of almonds and spices.

MINERVOIS LA SYRAH 2005
Red | 2011 up to 2013   87
The year's vintage dominates the traditional varietal expression in this cuvée. With darkberry and spice notes, it has an ample and vanilla-flavored finish.

MINERVOIS OURDIVIEILLE 2004
Red | 2011 up to 2013   90
This wine expresses floral notes of peonies, with a licorice finish. The especially powerful tannins deserve patience.

Red: 189 acres. White: 8.6 acres. Annual production: 370,000 bottles

CHÂTEAU LA VOULTE-GASPARETS

Rue des Corbières
11200 Boutenac
Phone 00 33 4 68 27 07 86
Fax 00 33 4 68 27 41 33
châteaulavoulte@wanadoo.fr

Patrick Reverdy and son Laurent are very fond of their carignan vines, now a specialty of the Corbières-Boutenac area. The Romain-Pauc cuvée, so named after a family ancestor, marries old-vine carignan and grenache (forty-plus years) with grapes from younger syrah and mourvèdre vines. Always very dependable, the wine possesses a deep and mineral character that makes it a benchmark example of Languedoc style—a standard for any new Corbières producer to follow.

Recently tasted
CORBIÈRES-BOUTENAC ROMAIN PAUC 2007
Red | 2011 up to 2013   90

Older vintages
CORBIÈRES CUVÉE RÉSERVÉE 2006
Red | 2011 up to 2013   88
Behind its classic bouquet of dark berries, the tannic quality is clear in what is essentially this domaine's primary red. The very ripe carignan shows its power on the palate and in the wine's roundness.

CORBIÈRES-BOUTENAC ROMAIN PAUC 2006
Red | 2011 up to 2014   88
The oak is still noticeable, but the flavor of the high-quality juice is gradually emerging as it ages. The nose recalls flowering Scotch broom, and the finish is harmonious and long. This wine proves what it was possible to achieve in this difficult but potentially high-quality vintage.

CORBIÈRES-BOUTENAC ROMAIN PAUC 2005
Red | 2011 up to 2013   90
The extract is refined, with a hint of carignan's animal notes. The tannins are truly flavorful. No worries about this wine's maturation: it will cellar well.

CORBIÈRES-BOUTENAC ROMAIN PAUC 2004
Red | 2011 up to 2013   91
The Romain Pauc cuvée was one of the first high-level cuvées to come out of Corbières. Over time, it has become one of the appellation's sure values. Its quality has never slipped. With graceful simplicity, it expresses its vintage well, and 2004 is one of its best years, alongside the sumptuous 1998.

Red: 145.8 acres . White: 9.8 acres. Annual production: 240,000 bottles

Bettane & Desseauve
Selections for the Loire Valley

Loire Valley

The vineyards of the Loire Valley meander along the entire length of France's longest river. The Loire extends from its source at the edge of the Rhone region all the way to the Atlantic Ocean, even including a short section that crosses into Burgundy in Pouilly-sur-Loire. Every type of wine is made here (red, white, sparkling, and dessert), with very elegant examples of several different grape varieties.

Near Nantes, with the influence of the Atlantic, the dry, light whites take on notes of saline and iodine and are a wonderful match with oysters, shellfish, and seafood. These wines can be drunk young, but the very best producers will surprise you with wines that are amazing after ten to fifteen years in bottle.

Sunshine is the key in the Anjou and Saumur regions; a surprisingly hot climate makes for explosively fruity whites in Anjou. The region has the ability to produce fairly large amounts of high-quality sweet wines, if there were a market for them. The reds have improved greatly over the past few years and are the most robust in the Loire.

The wines of the Touraine region are graceful and airy while remaining quite powerful, often achieving perfect balance between alcohol, acidity, and tannins. The quality, however, is completely dependent on the vintage and the varying talents of the winemakers. In the Center-Loire, very old limestone soils, like those found in Champagne and Chablis, are perfectly suited to the sauvignon blanc grape, producing the most elegant but also the most minerally, lively whites. Global warming is allowing for riper pinot noir and reds that are getting better and better.

Appellation Overview

The Loire Valley vineyards are some of the most complex in France in terms of terroir and grape variety, and the appellation system was introduced there to try to make sense of it all. The best way to comprehend it is to follow the course of the Loire River and discover the appellations, grapes and wines along the way.

The Pays Nantais

• **Muscadet Sèvre-et-Maine, Muscadet-Coteaux de la Loire, Muscadet–Côtes de Grandlieu, and Muscadet:** Four closely related AOCs making light, dry, often slightly sparkling white wines, based on the melon de bourgogne variety, known locally as the Muscadet. The first of the four is by far the largest and, in principle at least, represents the best of the Muscadets. In fact, as is always the case in France, there are plenty of exceptions. All of the wines are made in an early-drinking style, and given that the price is delightfully modest, they can be enjoyed often. Also from the Nantes region comes the Gros-Plant, a dry white wine of lesser stature made from a grape called folle blanche.

Anjou

Heir to a rich legacy of vines, the Anjou region makes wines of every style: white, red, rosé, dry, demi-sec, sweet, still, and effervescent.

• **Anjou, Anjou-Villages, and Anjou-Villages Brissac:** The first of the three is the largest appellation in the Maine-et-Loire department and applies to dry, chenin blanc–driven white wines; light, dry rosés based on grolleau; and reds that are generally quite simple, made from cabernet franc and gamay. Demi-sec rosés made from cabernet franc may be labeled Cabernet d'Anjou. The second appellation is reserved for red wines from the best terroirs (usually schistose), made from cabernet franc and cabernet sauvignon. The last of the three appellations, Anjou-Villages Brissac, applies exclusively to ten villages between the rivers Loire and Layon, famous for reds that are made for laying down. To the west of Angers, the privileged Savennières AOC yields robust, magnificently age-worthy dry white wines (and a few demi-secs) made from chenin. Within Savennières, two vineyards hold cru status: Roche-aux-Moines and

Coulée-de-Serrant, both owned by the same producer. Traditionally much sought after, these wines now face stiff competition from the new generation of ambitiously made white Anjou wines.

• **Coteaux de l'Aubance, Coteaux du Layon, Coteaux du Layon Villages (six villages), Bonnezeaux, and Quarts de Chaume:** The sweet wine appellations of Anjou. When properly made, Anjou dessert wines can be sumptuously fragrant, with an infinite variety of nuances depending on where they come from and who makes them—a real delight for the curious enthusiast.

The Saumur Region
• **Saumur:** An appellation for white chenin-based wines, from limestone soils. A Saumur is lighter and more refined than an Anjou, and unbeatable value for the money. Red Saumur tends to lack depth (with the exception of wines made by a few producers, most notably in Puy-Notre-Dame).

• **Saumur-Champigny:** No lack of depth here, thanks to a sunnier terroir that is richer in clay, managed by a new generation of passionate winegrowers.

• **Coteaux de Saumur:** An appellation for extremely rare sweet wines, some of them quite extraordinary.

• **Saumur Mousseux and Crémant de Loire:** The first of these has a long-standing tradition of sparkling wines that made the fortunes of certain wine merchants. The Crémant de Loire AOC is a more general (and increasingly popular) appellation, using grapes from all areas of the Loire Valley.

The Touraine Region
These three groups of appellations, nestled in the heart of the Loire Valley, are a an excellent example of this area's versatility.

• **Touraine:** An appellation for early-drinking red wines made from gamay; other red wines for short-term cellaring that also contain a proportion of cabernet and malbec (known locally as the cot); white sauvignon- and chenin-based wines; and rosés blended from pineau d'aunis, gamay, pinot gris, and pinot noir. The subdivisions of Amboise and Mesland enjoy a more established reputation.

• **Chinon, Bourgueil, and Saint-Nicolas-de-Bourgueil:** Communal appellations with the capacity for greatness in good vintages. These are mainly supple, fruity red wines made from cabernet franc, suitable for medium-term cellaring.

• **Montlouis and Vouvray:** Two appellations exclusively for white wines, made from chenin blanc in all its various manifestations—from sparkling to dessert wines, some of which, depending on the vintage, are legendary.

The Centre Region
The magnificent sloping vineyards of Sancerre, Morogues, and Pouilly-sur-Loire are exclusively planted to sauvignon blanc, which can take on exceptional finesse in this marly-limestone terrain—providing, of course, that the fruit is allowed to ripen properly.

Certain microclimates here are good for pinot noir. This can be a source of red wines that are lighter than on the Côte d'Or but much more accomplished than those of the Yonne or Champagne. As for the white wines, the best *lieux-dits* are long overdue for promotion to premier cru status.

Loire Valley Vineyards

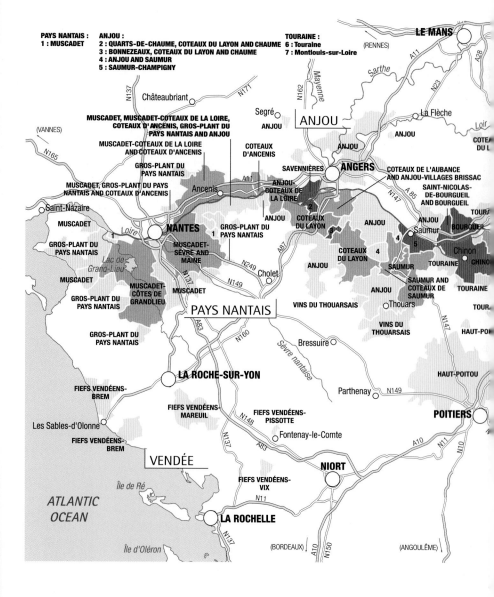

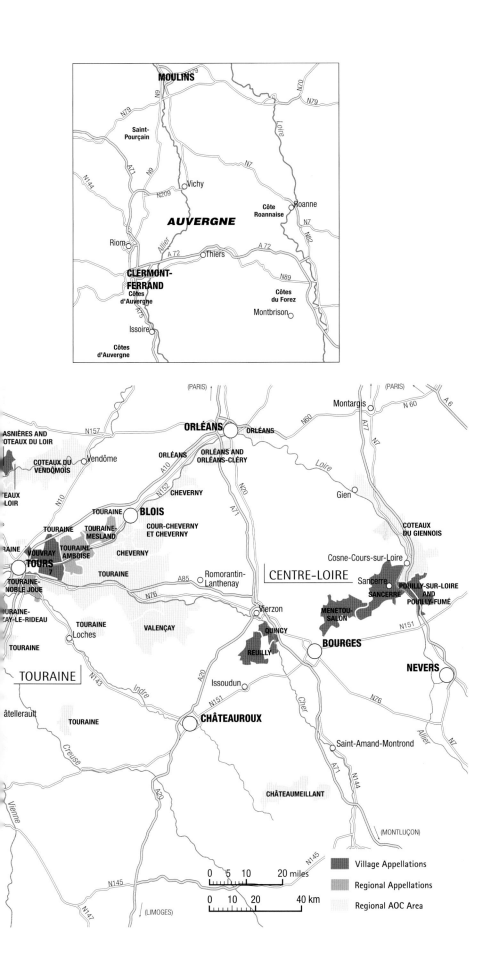

DOMAINE PHILIPPE ALLIET

Briançon, Départementale 8
37500 Cravant-les-Coteaux
Phone 00 33 2 47 93 17 62
Fax 00 33 2 47 93 17 62
philippe.alliet@wanadoo.fr

Husband-and-wife team Claude and Philippe Alliet are joint owners of this cabernet franc estate and added to their family L'Huisserie, a sloping parcel of very young vines on a clay-silica site. The Chinon Vieilles Vignes is sourced from vines planted in gravel and sand and grows more distinctive every year. The Coteau de Noiré today ranks as a reference point for Chinon wines from clay-limestone terroirs—deep, with a precise nose and utterly compelling.

CHINON COTEAU DE NOIRÉ 2007
Red | 2011 up to 2030   **94**
This wine shows great volume, deep floral overtones, and mouth-watering, taut tannins.

CHINON COTEAU DE NOIRÉ 2006
Red | 2011 up to 2015   **94**
One of the top Coteaux de Noiré of the domaine. This immensely deep wine displays stone-fruit overtones, a remarkable texture, and incredibly seductive aromas.

CHINON L'HUISSERIE 2007
Red | 2011 up to 2015   **90**
The initial floral notes lead to a fleshy, complex finish with hints of tobacco and spices. A refined, mouth-watering wine.

CHINON L'HUISSERIE 2006
Red | 2011 up to 2013   **90**
This great wine displays textbook tannins and a floral, intensely fruity, and refined character.

CHINON VIEILLES VIGNES 2007
Red | 2011 up to 2015   **92**
This great wine displays a remarkable freshness with black-fruit overtones. Refined tannins have a touch of electric acidity on the finish.

Red: 38.3 acres. Annual production: 90,000 bottles

DOMAINE YANNICK AMIRAULT

5, pavillon du Grand-Clos
37140 Bourgueil
Phone 00 33 2 47 97 78 07
Fax 00 33 2 47 97 94 78
info@yannickamirault.fr
www.yannickamirault.fr

Perfectionist winemaker Yannick Amirault sets the pace for Bourgueil and Saint-Nicolas-de-Bourgueil wines thanks to his privileged heritage of old vines. A born worrier, Amirault tends his vines assiduously and vinifies the grapes from each parcel separately. The wines are raised in demi-muids of different origin, except for La Coudraye, which sees oak (exceptionally good value for a Val de Loire wine). The Quartiers reflects the elegance characteristic of Bourgueil's limestone soils, displaying a tannin profile that grows ever more precise vintage after vintage. All of the cuvées are bottled unfined and unfiltered and show beautifully ripe fruit, with that combination of silky-textured tannins, smooth palate, and long, fresh finish that comes from masterful aging. These wines, which can be around twenty dollars a bottle, are a steal!

Recently tasted
BOURGUEIL LA COUDRAYE 2008
Red | 2011 up to 2013   **88**

BOURGUEIL LA PETITE CAVE 2007
Red | 2011 up to 2018   **93**

SAINT-NICOLAS-DE-BOURGUEIL LA SOURCE 2007
Red | 2011 up to 2013   **88**

SAINT-NICOLAS-DE-BOURGUEIL LES MALGAGNES 2006
Red | 2011 up to 2019   **90**

Older vintages
BOURGUEIL LA COUDRAYE 2005
Red | 2011 up to 2015   **89**
This wine has it all: concentration, maturity, freshness, and well-chiseled tannins. One of the Loire's best values.

BOURGUEIL LA PETITE CAVE 2006
Red | 2011 up to 2019   **93**
The suave, fleshy mouthfeel shows plenty of blueberries, as well as great magnitude and promise.

SAINT-NICOLAS-DE-BOURGUEIL LA MINE 2006
Red | 2011 up to 2020   **92**
This vibrant wine displays licorice and fresh black-fruit flavors that support a silky, very promising mouthfeel.

SAINT-NICOLAS-DE-BOURGUEIL
LES MALGAGNES 2006
Red | 2011 up to 2013   **90**
Predominant aromas of spice and licorice open to a promising, full-bodied, and soft palate, reminiscent of the great 1996.

Red: 46.9 acres; cabernet franc 100%. Annual production: 90,000 bottles

DOMAINE BERNARD BAUDRY

9, coteau de Sonnay
Cravant-les-Coteaux
37500 Chinon
Phone 00 33 2 47 93 15 79
Fax 00 33 2 47 98 44 44
bernard-baudry@chinon.com
www.chinon.com/vignoble/
bernardbaudry

Bernard Baudry now works with his son Matthieu; together they built their reputation on Chinons that are concentrated and tannic, made to age. The cuvées are named after the terroirs that give them their unique characteristics. Les Granges is made for early drinking from grapes that come from gravel and clay soils, which make a supple and lively wine. Les Grézeaux, grown on clay and silica soils, has wonderful finesse and a structure that enables it to age well (the 1989 is still in great shape). The most intense, La Croix Boisée, from clayey-limestone soils, is more solidly built. Finally, the Clos Guillot, made from ungrafted vines, makes a rich, full, and suave wine. There is also a small amount of melodious chenin blanc.

Recently tasted
CHINON 2007
Red | 2011 up to 2013   **88**

CHINON LE CLOS GUILLOT 2007
Red | 2011 up to 2020   **92**

Older vintages
CHINON LA CROIX BOISSÉE 2007
White | 2011 up to 2020   **89**
A well-made Chinon with powerful, long-lasting aromas, and notes of pears and white flowers, this wine will age well.

CHINON LE CLOS GUILLOT 2006
Red | 2011 up to 2014   **88**
Powerful and structured, but with an imprecise, indistinct aromatic definition. Worth retrying, as the wine was bottled shortly before our tasting.

CHINON LES GRANGES 2007
Red | 2011 up to 2013   **87**
With a hint of vegetal on the finish, this well-made wine pairs nicely with roast pork.

CHINON LES GRÉZEAUX 2007
Red | 2011 up to 2013   **89**
Voluptuous wine with a sharp, precise profile and fleshy tannins.

Red: 69.2 acres; cabernet franc 100%. White: 4.9 acres. Annual production: 130,000 bottles

DOMAINE DES BAUMARD

8, rue de l'Abbaye
49190 Rochefort-sur-Loire
Phone 00 33 2 41 78 70 03
Fax 00 33 2 41 78 83 82
contact@baumard.fr
www.baumard.fr

Florent Baumard is based in Rochefort near Savennières, where the soils are a mixture of schist, sandstone, and sand. The goal here is to get the best out of the vines, without overextraction, focusing on naturalness and the quality of the fruit. The red Clos de la Folie is made in an easy, appealing style. The white Clos du Papillon sends you reeling with its purity, and the sweet white Coteaux Layon Cuvée Le Paon is most heartily recommended.

Recently tasted
CRÉMANT DE LOIRE CARTE TURQUOISE
Brut White sparkling | 2011 up to 2013   **86**

QUARTS-DE-CHAUME 2007
Sweet White | 2011 up to 2013   **94**

SAVENNIÈRES CLOS DU PAPILLON 2007
White | 2011 up to 2013   **92**

Older vintages
ANJOU CLOS DE LA FOLIE 2005
Red | 2011 up to 2013   **88**
Unlike the original label that shows a collection of quotes about insanity, this wine is as easy to read as it is to enjoy. It has a flattering, velvety nose and a deep structure.

COTEAUX DU LAYON LE PAON 2005
Sweet White | 2011 up to 2025   **91**
This "simple" yet well-made Layon is impressively pure and balanced.

QUARTS-DE-CHAUME 2006
Sweet White | 2011 up to 2013   **88**
This is a delicate Quarts-de-Chaume, with a less dynamic structure than usual, reflecting this difficult vintage.

SAVENNIÈRES CLOS DU PAPILLON 2006
White | 2011 up to 2013   **90**
With a rich nose of caramel, a full mouthfeel, and a harmonious finish, this wine is an honest expression of the terroir.

Red: 37.1 acres; grolleau 13%, cabernet franc 75%, cabernet sauvignon 12%. White: 49.4 acres; chenin blanc 83%, chardonnay 17%. Annual production: 150,000 bottles

CHÂTEAU BELLERIVE

49190 Rochefort-sur-Loire
Phone 00 33 2 41 78 33 66
Fax 00 33 2 41 78 68 47
info@vignobles-alainchâteau.com
www.domaine-belle-rive.com

Alain Château owns several vineyards in Anjou, Château Bellerive being the most famous. Naturally sweet wines are his forte and we were particularly struck by the Château Bellerive Quarts-de-Chaume and the Château de la Guimonière Coteaux du Layon Chaume: the 2005 vintage has done them proud. Alongside the sweet wines, Bellerive's Rosé de Loire is anything but boring and the Château de Varennes (Savennières) is entirely pleasing.

Recently tasted
ANJOU CHÂTEAU DE LA GUIMONIÈRE 2008
White | 2011 up to 2013   **87**

QUARTS-DE-CHAUME 2007
Sweet White | 2011 up to 2019   **90**

SAVENNIÈRES CHÂTEAU DE VARENNES 2008
White | 2011 up to 2013   **88**

SAVENNIÈRES CHÂTEAU DE VARENNES 2007
White | 2011 up to 2015   **84**

Older vintages
COTEAUX DU LAYON
CHÂTEAU DE LA GUIMONIÈRE 2005
Sweet White | 2011 up to 2025   **84**
The 2005 is a very successful vintage. Powerful yet refined. An admirable effort!

QUARTS-DE-CHAUME 2005
Sweet White | 2011 up to 2025   **91**
With beautiful balance and freshness, this cuvée boasts aromas that are more reminiscent of a Bonnezeaux than a Quarts-de-Chaume.

White: 29.7 acres; chenin 91%. Annual production: 30,000 bottles

DOMAINE DE BELLIVIÈRE

Bellivière
72340 Lhomme
Phone 00 33 2 43 44 59 97
Fax 00 33 2 43 79 18 33
info@belliviere.com
www.belliviere.com

Eric Nicolas is changing the way people think about wines from the Sarth. This master of chenin blanc has returned to massal selection, and his farming methods are impeccable year after year: the 2006 completely convinced us of the quality of wines he is now making. The vinifications are exemplary, and the wines perfectly express their terroir: the Coteaux-du-Loir has a wonderful presence, and the Jasnières a depth and refinement that are unique in the region. You just need to decant them a few hours before serving. They also make a delicious red called Rouge Gorge from the pineau d'aunis grape.

Recently tasted
COTEAUX DU LOIR L'EFFRAIE 2007
White | 2011 up to 2019   90

COTEAUX DU LOIR ROUGE-GORGE 2007
Red | 2011 up to 2013   87

Older vintages
COTEAUX DU LOIR L'EFFRAIE 2006
White | 2011 up to 2016   89
A classy wine with good minerality. The taut mouthfeel is already very pleasant, and is framed by an enticing freshness.

COTEAUX DU LOIR ROUGE-GORGE 2006
Red | 2011 up to 2013   86
Full of red-fruit flavors, this spicy wine can be enjoyed now with grilled chicken.

COTEAUX DU LOIR VIEILLES VIGNES 2006
White | 2011 up to 2015   91
Almond, licorice, and white-peach flavors, and a delicate and refined structure framed by lots of minerality.

JASNIÈRES CALLIGRAMME 2006
White | 2011 up to 2017   90
Intense and long-lasting minerality. Will develop even more complexity with age.

JASNIÈRES LES ROSIERS 2006
White | 2011 up to 2013   90
This is a delicate wine that boasts fresh minerality and 7 grams per liter of residual sugar.

Red: 9.8 acres. White: 22.2 acres. Annual production: 43,000 bottles

DOMAINE GÉRARD BOULAY

Le Cul de Beaujeu
Chavignol
18300 Sancerre
Phone 00 33 2 48 54 36 37
Fax 00 33 2 48 54 30 42
boulayg-vigneron@wanadoo.fr

Gérard Boulay makes wines that are now more precise than ever thanks to his policy of keeping each individual plot strictly separate—sure to delight lovers of taut, mineral sauvignon. The cuvée Tradition shows pretty fruit; the salty Monts Damnés is true to its terroir; and the Clos de Beaujeu is a little gem: more crystalline than the others and boldly assertive after five years' aging (and when served with lobster and truffles!). The exquisitely rare, powerfully mineral cuvée Comtesse is rich with promise.

Recently tasted
SANCERRE 2008
White | 2011 up to 2013   88
A great entry-level wine with a mineral acidity and harmonious length.

SANCERRE 2007
White | 2011 up to 2016   90
The chalky terroir really shows through on the nose, and the structure is imposing on the palate, with the characteristic minerality of Chavignol.

SANCERRE CLOS DE BEAUJEU 2008
White | 2011 up to 2017   92
With superb structure and explosive minerality, this wine is wonderfully full!

SANCERRE CLOS DE BEAUJEU 2007
White | 2011 up to 2019   92
With wonderful citrus flavors in the nose, slightly salty, edgy, and long in the mouth, this is one of the best Sancerres.

SANCERRE COMTESSE 2007
White | 2011 up to 2019   91

SANCERRE MONTS DAMNÉS 2008
White | 2011 up to 2017   90

Older vintages
SANCERRE 2006
White | 2011 up to 2020   88
With plenty of mineral potential, this sharp wine is beginning to show a lovely, confident maturity.

SANCERRE CLOS DE BEAUJEU 2006
White | 2011 up to 2015   92
Along with lovely minerality, this sharp wine fully expresses the Chavignol terroir. Pair with lobster and truffles.

Sancerre Comtesse 2006
White | 2011 up to 2017   **90**
Exotic fruits and fresh minerality create a multidimensional flavour with a slight amount of residual sugar. Will become even more expressive with time.

Sancerre Monts Damnés 2006
White | 2011 up to 2015   **90**
The intense aromas of citrus and mineral overtones persist through the balanced mouthfeel.

Red: 4.9 acres. White: 22.2 acres. Annual production: 50,000 bottles

DOMAINE HENRI BOURGEOIS

Chavignol
18300 Sancerre
Phone 00 33 2 48 78 53 20
Fax 00 33 2 48 54 14 24
domaine@henribourgeois.com
www.henribourgeois.com

The best wines from Henri Bourgeois are now moving into the elite Sancerre category. We particularly appreciate the subtlety of the Chapelle des Augustins and the consistency of the Monts Damnés, both characterized by an elegant, mineral note. The depth of the Cuvée d'Antan is a hymn of praise to great sauvignon wines, and the La Bourgeoise is always up there with the best of them.

Recently tasted
Sancerre Chapelle des Augustins 2007
White | 2011 up to 2013   **87**
With a discreet but elegant nose, this wine is a bit tight on the palate, kind of like biting into a piece of fruit.

Sancerre d'Antan 2007
White | 2011 up to 2016   **92**
Edgy and ripe, this wine is quite lively, very well balanced, and pure, with a good minerality.

Sancerre Monts Damnés 2007
White | 2011 up to 2015   **90**
Chalky on the nose, this wine is unquestionably from Chavignol.

Older vintages
Pouilly-Fumé La Demoiselle 2006
White | 2011 up to 2015   **89**
The nose of mineral-saline and citrus overtones leads to a fresh, slender mouthfeel. An elegant wine.

Sancerre Chapelle des Augustins 2006
White | 2011 up to 2013   **87**
Saline-mineral aromas are dominated by lemon verbena, lime overtones, and hints of flowers.

Sancerre d'Antan 2006
White | 2011 up to 2017   **92**
Near crystalline purity with hints of citrus. Once again, one of the vintage's top achievers.

Sancerre Jadis 2007
White | 2011 up to 2019   **93**
Abundant with style, this wine combines power, elegance, and fresh minerality.

SANCERRE LA BOURGEOISE 2006
White | 2011 up to 2013   **87**
The grapefruit notes on the nose persist
through a fresh and slender mouthfeel.

SANCERRE MONTS DAMNÉS 2006
White | 2011 up to 2013   **90**
Once bottled, this wine became more integrated. It now shows an accomplished balance of fresh minerality and lovely maturity.

Red: 29.7 acres; pinot noir 100%. White: 148.3 acres;
sauvignon blanc 100%. Annual production: 2,300,000
bottles

DOMAINE BRÉGEON

5, Les Guisseaux
44190 Gorges
Phone 00 33 2 40 06 93 19
Fax 00 33 2 40 06 95 91

A firm believer in hand picking, as opposed
to machine harvesting, all of his grapes,
Michel Brégeon presses the grapes slowly
and then ages his muscadets with the fine
lees for two to five years. Yields are
between 316 and 528 gallons per acre,
which allows Brégeon to get the best out
of his 14.8 acres located on the Gorges terroir. The terroir is largely made up of volcanic rock called "le gabbro," which is even
harder than granite. He is currently
focused on making age-worthy wines and
his offerings show surprising youth with a
pronounced mineral character. The cuvée
Gorgeois, from a five-acre vineyard with
vines that are over fifty years old, simply
soars, and is one of the best wines of the
appellation, even resembling a Grand Cru
Burgundy. These are wines that, contrary
to popular belief, benefit from a bit of age.
They are an absolute favorite of ours.

Recently tasted
MUSCADET SÈVRE-ET-MAINE GORGEOIS 1996
White | 2011 up to 2017   **92**

MUSCADET SÈVRE-ET-MAINE GORGEOIS 1993
White | 2011 up to 2016   **93**

MUSCADET SÈVRE-ET-MAINE SUR LIE 2007
White | 2011 up to 2019   **91**
This wine's peppery, smoky nose, and amazing structure on the finish give an indication
of its aging potential.

Older vintages
MUSCADET SÈVRE-ET-MAINE 2003
White | 2011 up to 2019   **91**
Citrus aromas with a hint of minerality, and
a taut, saline mouthfeel. What a lively wine!

MUSCADET SÈVRE-ET-MAINE GORGEOIS 1999
White | 2011 up to 2017   **91**
Orange-peel aromas give way to nice minerality. With a beautiful balance of citrus
and delicate, fresh minerality, this is one of
the best cuvées of the area.

White: 14.8 acres. Annual production: 35,000 bottles

DOMAINE DU CARROU

7, place du Carrou
18300 Bué
Phone 00 33 2 48 54 10 65
Fax 00 33 2 48 54 38 77
contact@dominique-roger.fr
www.dominique-roger.fr

Star of the 2008 edition, Dominique Roger continues to turn out beautifully precise wines. His whites are now up to the standard of the reds and since 2006 include a lovely cuvée, the Chêne Marchand. Dominique is a meticulous grower with great respect for the specific character of each terroir. His wines are flawlessly consistent, with the past five vintages sappier than ever. Pinot noir accounts for some 35 percent of plantings. The old-vines La Jouline, dedicated to Dominique's great-grandfather, is a glorious, irresistible Sancerre—silky on the attack, with enduring aromas and a lovely edge to the finish—but it does need at least five years to achieve full expression. The old vines in question are located in Crézancy, Bué, and Sancerre, planted half in caillotes (chalky soils that give the wine elegance) and half in terres blanches (clay and limestone soils that add strength). The white La Jouline boasts the same combination of ripeness and minerals as the red. Following bottling, the 2006 confirmed our excellent impression of the wine at the start of maturation and the 2007 is rich with promise. As always, the Cuvées Domaine offer good value for the money.

Recently tasted

SANCERRE 2008
White | 2011 up to 2013   **89**

SANCERRE LA JOULINE 2008
Red | 2011 up to 2022   **93**

Older vintages

SANCERRE CUVÉE CHÊNE MARCHAND 2007
White | 2011 up to 2015   **91**
With a perfect combination of white-peach and iodine flavors, this wine is elegant and deliciously balanced.

SANCERRE CUVÉE DOMAINE DU CARROU 2006
Red | 2011 up to 2013   **91**
This juicy wine boasts delicious, fresh cherry flavors. It will become smoother over time.

SANCERRE LA JOULINE 2007
Red | 2011 up to 2017   **92**
Demonstrating superlative purity of fruit, this wine has fleshy, cherry overtones that are framed by refined tannins, which are both slender and intense.

SANCERRE LA JOULINE 2007
White | 2011 up to 2017   **91**
Fleshy apricot notes laced with fresh minerality lead to a wonderful, vibrant mouthfeel.

SANCERRE LA JOULINE 2005
Red | 2011 up to 2020   **92**
A magnificent cuvée framed by velvety tannins that give structure and volume to the wine. Cellar it for three to five years.

Red: 7.4 acres; pinot noir 100%. White: 17.3 acres; sauvignon blanc 100%. Annual production: 60,000 bottles

DOMAINE DE LA CHEVALERIE

7-14, rue du Peu-Muleau
37140 Restigné
Phone 00 33 2 47 97 46 32
Fax 00 33 2 47 97 45 87
caslot@wanadoo.fr
www.domainedelachevalerie.fr

The chalk cave at Domaine de la Chevalerie is one of the most beautiful in the Loire Valley, and their recent vintages truly resonate. In 2004 Stéphanie Caslot returned to the family winery to work alongside her brother Emmanuel and father Pierre. The wines here are lively and fresh, clearly expressing the terroir of the eighty-two-acre vineyard that is in one single block. We were pleasantly surprised by the evolution of the 1991s and 1994s opened for our recent tastings. The wines age remarkably well.

Recently tasted
BOURGUEIL BUSARDIÈRES 2008
Red | 2011 up to 2030   92

BOURGUEIL BUSARDIÈRES 2007
Red | 2011 up to 2030   92

BOURGUEIL CHEVALERIE 2007
Red | 2011 up to 2030   89

BOURGUEIL GALICHETS 2008
Red | 2011 up to 2030   90

Older vintages
BOURGUEIL BINETTE 2007
Red | 2011 up to 2013   86
Easygoing and showing lovely fruit, this is a wine to share with friends.

BOURGUEIL BUSARDIÈRES 2006
Red | 2011 up to 2025   91
The limestone soil always brings elegance and a unique complexity. This wine has great potential.

BOURGUEIL CHEVALERIE 2006
Red | 2011 up to 2025   88
A nicely structured, elegant wine. Taut with fresh tannins and lovely floral notes on the finish.

BOURGUEIL CHEVALERIE 2005
Red | 2011 up to 2015   91
Amazing, multidimensional flavors, with some dominant notes of blueberries and eucalyptus.

BOURGUEIL GALICHETS 2006
Red | 2011 up to 2013   89
From sandy clay soil, Galichets is concentrated with lovely refined tannins.

BOURGUEIL GALICHETS 2005
Red | 2011 up to 2015   91
Crushed strawberry and spice flavors are backed by beautifully drawn tannins.

BOURGUEIL PEU MULEAU 2007
Red | 2011 up to 2015   87
This wine has a taut, fresh mouthfeel with lots of red-fruit flavors.

BOURGUEIL PEU MULEAU 2006
Red | 2011 up to 2015   88
Fresh black fruit and an opulent and elegant structure are framed by well-proportioned tannins.

Red: 81.5 acres; cabernet franc 100%. **Annual production:** 90,000 bottles

DOMAINE FRANÇOIS CHIDAINE

5, Grand Rue
37270 Montlouis-sur-Loire
Phone 00 33 2 47 45 19 14
Fax 00 33 2 47 45 19 08
francois.chidaine@wanadoo.fr
www.cave-insolite-chidaine.com

François Chidaine preceded the new wave of passionate young winemakers in Montlouis by a few years. The wines he makes are stylish and dynamic and say a lot about his approach to farming. Having converted to biodynamics, Chidaine's guiding principle today is to leave the smallest footprint possible on the environment. His Vouvrays show the same brio as his Montlouis and are made to the same consistently high standards. To enjoy them at a young age, the wines must be decanted in order for them to truly open up. This is a producer that true oenophiles should seek out.

Recently tasted

Montlouis-sur-Loire Clos Habert 2007
Semi-Dry White | 2012 up to 2023   **90**
There's true potential here in this finely structured wine. The aromas are currently showing mango and pineapple. The texture is round in the middle and followed by a bitter note that balances the wine.

Montlouis-sur-Loire Clos du Breuil 2007
Semi-Dry White | 2011 up to 2015   **89**
From the first whiff, you can smell the minerality, which is quite present in the mouth. For the moment the wine is rather closed.

Vouvray Clos Baudoin 2007
White | 2013 up to 2030   **90**

Vouvray Les Argiles 2007
White | 2011 up to 2019   **91**

Older vintages

Montlouis-sur-Loire Choisilles 2006
Brut White sparkling | 2011 up to 2015   **89**
With its vibrant dimension, this intense and fruit-forward Choisilles is framed by fresh minerality.

Montlouis-sur-Loire Clos du Breuil 2007
White | 2011 up to 2015   **89**
This wine tastes perfectly dry despite five grams of residual sugar. The aromas are not very expressive, but the wine boasts amazing natural energy and tension.

Montlouis-sur-Loire Clos Habert 2006
Semi-Dry White | 2011 up to 2017   **91**
Balanced, with an abundance of ripe fruit and dried apricot on the mid-palate, this wine is seductive and fresh.

Montlouis-sur-Loire Les Bournais 2007
Sweet White | 2011 up to 2017   **86**
Les Bournais is a Montlouis moelleux on the sweeter side, with remarkable aromatic purity.

Vouvray Clos Baudoin 2006
White | 2011 up to 2015   **90**
Although not yet fully integrated, this wine shows typical demi-sec balance, and combines great fruit with outstanding energy.

Vouvray Le Bouchet 2006
Semi-Dry White | 2011 up to 2013   **87**
Lovely upon first impression, this wine lacks a harmonious and precise finish.

Vouvray Les Argiles 2006
White | 2011 up to 2015   **89**
A full-bodied wine, with balanced, candied-fruit overtones. Its subtle minerality provides nice structure.

White: 74.1 acres; chenin 98%, sauvignon 2%.
Annual production: 120,000 bottles

DOMAINE STÉPHANE COSSAIS

12 bis, route de Saint-Aignan
37270 Montlouis-sur-Loire
Phone 00 33 6 63 16 21 91
stephanecossais@neuf.fr

Stéphane Cossais started out in the world of classical music then moved here in 2001 to indulge his passion for great chenin wines from Montlouis. Penniless but talented, he farms 7.4 acres of this lovely terroir, producing only white wines and exclusively dry ones at that. The La Maison Marchandelle and the Volagré are astonishingly classy from the first whiff.

Recently tasted
Montlouis-sur-Loire Le Volagré 2006
White | 2011 up to 2030   92

Older vintages
Montlouis-sur-Loire Cloclote 2003
Sweet White | 2011 up to 2013   88
Cloclote has benefited from the vintage's generosity: its lush mouthfeel finishes with hints of lemon zest and candied fruit.

Montlouis-sur-Loire Le Volagré 2005
White | 2011 up to 2013   92
This wine has impressively pure aromas and shows great class and depth.

Montlouis-sur-Loire Le Volagré 2004
White | 2011 up to 2013   90
This fairly difficult vintage has produced a taut, very linear wine that is beginning to evolve toward tertiary notes of underbrush. Quite an achievement.

Montlouis-sur-Loire
Maison Marchandelle 2006
White | 2011 up to 2015   91
An elegant cuvée boasting some incredible aromas and amazing energy.

Montlouis-sur-Loire
Maison Marchandelle 2004
White | 2011 up to 2013   88
Montlouis suffered in 2004. However, Stéphane Cossais has succeeded in preserving a quintessential Loire finish, full of complexity.

White: 7.4 acres; chenin blanc 100%. **Annual production:** 10,000 bottles

DOMAINE PASCAL COTAT

98, chemin des Grous
18300 Sancerre
Phone 00 33 2 48 54 14 00
Fax 00 33 2 48 54 14 00

Francis Cotat's memory is everywhere here but he has now passed the flame to his son Pascal, an exact replica of his father. Time seems to have no hold on this family, whose history is dotted with legendary white Sancerres: wines made from perfectly ripe fruit that can age gracefully for ten, twenty, or forty-plus years. The citrus flavors and touches of chalk vary depending on the cuvée, supported by distinctive nuances of truffle. Monts Damnés and La Grande Côte are sure to tickle the palate of all lovers of great sauvignons, and the rosé is almost beyond description: fabulously fresh flavors of red fruits and rosés even after twenty years!

Recently tasted
Sancerre La Grande Côte 2007
White | 2013 up to 2022   90
There's great potential here, but for the moment the wine is showing only its structure and richness; it needs time.

Older vintages
Sancerre 2005
Rosé | 2011 up to 2013   88
Several years from now, the red fruit and spicy overtones of this rosé will overshadow the tasty 1989, which remains in great shape today.

Sancerre La Grande Côte 2001
White | 2011 up to 2020   91
This wine is a marvel of vibrant minerality. Enjoy it with grilled prawns.

Sancerre La Grande Côte 1995
White | 2011 up to 2015   90
The round 1995 vintage is still remarkably fresh, and it would happily complement prawns with foie gras.

Sancerre La Grande Côte 1990
White | 2011 up to 2015   88
This wine is still vibrant with delicious truffle notes. It has gained complexity with age.

Sancerre Monts Damnés 2005
White | 2011 up to 2020   91
This powerful, mineral wine has great potential and is best suited for aging.

Red: ,2 acres; pinot 100%. **White:** 5.9 acres; sauvignon 100%. **Annual production:** 14,800 bottles

DOMAINE FRANÇOIS COTAT

18300 Chavignol
Phone 00 33 2 48 54 21 27
Fax 00 33 2 48 78 01 41
valerie.cotat@free.fr

There were once two brothers, Francis and Paul Cotat, who owned three vineyards in Chavignol that they tended with the greatest of care: the Monts Damnés, Grande Côte, and Cul de Beaujeu. In the mid 1990s, they divided the estate between their respective sons, Pascal and François. This is François's property: the same terroirs as Pascal's but with a portfolio that also features some delightfully mineral Culs de Beaujeu. The philosophy remains the same on both properties: making creamy wines, usually containing small amounts of residual sugar, from late-harvested, overripe grapes. Cotat wines can easily last for decades, and they belong in the legendary category of great Sancerre wines.

Recently tasted

SANCERRE GRANDE CÔTE 1995
White | 2012 up to 2024 **89**

SANCERRE MONTS DAMNÉS 2007
White | 2013 up to 2024 **90**
Well structured, this wine will evolve until around 2013 and will then show notes of chalk, citrus, and mint.

Older vintages

SANCERRE CUL DE BEAUJEU 1998
White | 2011 up to 2015 **91**
This 1998 keeps delighting us with its grapefruit flavors and subtle minerality. It gets richer and more complex in the glass.

SANCERRE GRANDE CÔTE 2001
White | 2011 up to 2020 **88**
A sharp wine with lemon overtones, it pairs well with lobster.

SANCERRE GRANDE CÔTE 1986
White | 2011 up to 2013 **91**
With delicious truffle overtones, this full-bodied 1986 has an unctuous palate with a hint of minerality.

SANCERRE MONTS DAMNÉS 2005
White | 2011 up to 2020 **90**
The structure of this wine currently outweighs its aromas. It would pair well with mushrooms and poached sea snails dressed in a citrus-and-hazelnut vinaigrette.

White: 10.4 acres. Annual production: 30,000 bottles

DOMAINE DE LA COTELLERAIE

2, La Cotelleraie
37140 Saint-Nicolas-de-Bourgueil
Phone 00 33 2 47 97 75 53
Fax 00 33 2 47 97 85 90
gerald.vallee@wanadoo.fr

Gérard Vallée has now taken over his family winery with vineyards in Saint-Nicolas-de-Bourgueil. The soils are tilled and the vineyards farmed organically. The grapes are hand harvested. The range of wines is wonderful; they are silky and refined. This is a winery to watch closely.

Recently tasted

SAINT-NICOLAS-DE-BOURGUEIL LA CROISÉE 2008
Red | 2011 up to 2013 **89**

SAINT-NICOLAS-DE-BOURGUEIL LE VAU JAUMIER 2007
Red | 2011 up to 2017 **92**
Long and silky, with marvelously defined tannins; this wine has great potential.

SAINT-NICOLAS-DE-BOURGUEIL LES PERRUCHES 2007
Red | 2011 up to 2014 **91**
Silky textured, with ripe fruit and luscious tannins, this is truly one of the best wines from the Loire!

Older vintages

SAINT-NICOLAS-DE-BOURGUEIL 2006
Red | 2011 up to 2013 **87**
An easy-drinking, floral, and well-structured red, this is a well-made, entry-level wine.

SAINT-NICOLAS-DE-BOURGUEIL L'ENVOLÉE 2006
Red | 2011 up to 2015 **92**
The sixty-plus-year-old vines planted in clay and flint soil have produced greatly refined tannins and velvety structure.

SAINT-NICOLAS-DE-BOURGUEIL L'ENVOLÉE 2005
Red | 2011 up to 2013 **93**
This cuvée reaches its potential after a few years of aging, producing a smoother wine that reinforces its pure mineral expression.

SAINT-NICOLAS-DE-BOURGUEIL LE VAU JAUMIER 2006
Red | 2011 up to 2015 **91**
From clay and limestone soil on the slopes of Saint Nicolas, this velvety wine has the texture of taffeta, an amazing magnitude, and high-quality tannins. The oaky notes will become better incorporated with time.

SAINT-NICOLAS-DE-BOURGUEIL LES PERRUCHES 2006
Red | 2011 up to 2015 **90**
From clay and flint soil, this elegant wine is lifted by fine minerality and framed by incredibly intense fruit.

Red: 66.7 acres. Annual production: 130,000 bottles

LES FRÈRES COUILLAUD

Château de la Ragotière
44330 La Regrippière
Phone 00 33 2 40 33 60 56
Fax 00 33 2 40 33 61 89
freres.couillaud@wanadoo.fr
www.freres-couillaud.com

The Couillaud brothers' estate has 180 acres of vines, planted in lovely soils of schist and mica-schist. All of the cuvées display an honest, accurate expression entirely in keeping with this appellation. The same goes for the Vins de Pays, which are accomplished expressions of their varietals. The viognier bottling (not included here) is particularly charming in hot years.

Recently tasted

MUSCADET SÈVRE-ET-MAINE
CHÂTEAU DE LA RAGOTIÈRE VIEILLES VIGNES 2008
White | 2011 up to 2014   86

MUSCADET SÈVRE-ET-MAINE
CHÂTEAU DE LA RAGOTIÈRE VIEILLES VIGNES 2007
White | 2011 up to 2017   87

MUSCADET SÈVRE-ET-MAINE
CHÂTEAU LA MORINIÈRE 2007
White | 2011 up to 2019   89

MUSCADET SÈVRE-ET-MAINE
CLOS DU PETIT CHÂTEAU 2007
White | 2011 up to 2013   83

VIN DE PAYS DU JARDIN DE LA FRANCE
COLLECTION PRIVÉE PETIT MANSENG 2007
White | 2011 up to 2013   82

Older vintages

MUSCADET SÈVRE-ET-MAINE
CHÂTEAU DE LA RAGOTIÈRE VIEILLES VIGNES 2006
White | 2011 up to 2013   86
A lively and remarkably agile Muscadet, with notes of grapefruit on the entry leading to a fresh and elegant finish.

MUSCADET SÈVRE-ET-MAINE
CHÂTEAU LA MORINIÈRE 2006
White | 2011 up to 2016   86
This smooth wine displays a lovely expression of fresh fruit and hints of lemon flavors.

MUSCADET SÈVRE-ET-MAINE
CLOS DU PETIT CHÂTEAU 2006
White | 2011 up to 2017   87
A floral and lively wine, with a straight-as-an-arrow style that will pair well with shellfish.

White: 180.4 acres; chardonnay 34%, fié Gris (sauvignon gris) 1%, malvoisie 1%, melon de Bourgogne 61%, muscat à petits grains 1%, petit manseng 1%, viognier 1%.
Annual production: 500,000 bottles

DOMAINE LUCIEN CROCHET

Place de l'Église
18300 Bué
Phone 00 33 2 48 54 08 10
Fax 00 33 2 48 54 27 66
contact@lucien-crochet.fr
www.lucien-crochet.fr

Gilles Crochet, like his father, Lucien, has always had an instinct for elegant wine. His Sancerre Le Chêne comes from pebbly limestone soils ("caillottes") and shows classy mineral character. The Prestige cuvée is deliciously concentrated and blends fruit from some of the oldest vines in the vineyard; give it at least five years to express itself properly. The cuvée made with later-harvested, overripe fruit (picked in mid-October) has a soft, fresh sweetness. The red offerings feature the Croix du Roy, a wine from those great terrroirs in Bué that add charm and distinction to pinot noir. Deliciously fruity as a young wine, it takes on another dimension altogether after five or six years' bottle aging.

Recently tasted

SANCERRE CROIX DU ROY 2005
Red | 2011 up to 2017   91

SANCERRE CUVÉE PRESTIGE 2005
Red | 2011 up to 2013   92
The smooth tannic grain here is unique to Sancerre. Fruit-forward, with stylish elegance, this should serve as a model for all Loire Valley pinot noirs.

SANCERRE CUVÉE PRESTIGE 2005
White | 2011 up to 2013   90

SANCERRE LE CHÊNE MARCHAND 2008
White | 2011 up to 2014   90

SANCERRE LE CHÊNE MARCHAND 2007
White | 2011 up to 2013   90
Notes of yellow fruit on the nose, a touch of minerality, and elegant citrus flavors on the palate.

SANCERRE VENDANGE DU 10 OCTOBRE 2006
White | 2011 up to 2015   90
This late-harvest wine is particularly good, with mango on the nose and forward notes of tropical fruit on the palate, and above all a wonderful acidity on the finish.

Older vintages

SANCERRE CUVÉE PRESTIGE 2003
White | 2011 up to 2013   88
The pineapple nose announces an unctuous mouthfeel. The finish is taut, and displays notes of saline.

SANCERRE LE CHÊNE MARCHAND 2007
White | 2011 up to 2017 **90**
This wine boasts a lovely floral nose with hints of apricots, and an elegant, very slender mouthfeel.

SANCERRE LE CHÊNE MARCHAND 2005
White | 2011 up to 2013 **85**
A delicious and distinguished sauvignon blanc with delicate minerality.

Red: 22.2 acres; pinot noir 100%. White: 70.4 acres; sauvignon blanc 100%. Annual production: 300,000 bottles

DOMAINE DIDIER DAGUENEAU

Le Bourg
58150 Saint-Andelain
Phone 00 33 3 86 39 15 62
Fax 00 33 3 86 39 07 61
silex@wanadoo.fr

When it comes to quality, the late Didier Dagueneau was an extremist. Killed in a plane crash in September 2008, Dagueneau was an extraordinary man and an exceptional winemaker. His soil-working methods and respect for the environment produced wines whose rich aromas and honest terroir expression brought the sauvignon blanc and the Pouilly crus to an entirely new level. His white wines have been rightly sought after by wine lovers worldwide for their pure, brilliant, uncompromising character. His son Benjamin has stepped up to ensure the continuity of the domaine and has shown that he is up to the task. The 2007s are exceptional in their crystalline purity, which is reflected in each and every cuvée. Be sure to decant these wines at least two hours ahead of time in order to fully enjoy their brilliance.

POUILLY-FUMÉ 2007
White | 2011 up to 2022 **96**
A subtle combination of power and elegance paired with citrus overtones, the sharp minerality expected from this terroir shines through. This is a highly refined wine that competes with the best white wines in the world.

POUILLY-FUMÉ 2006
White | 2011 up to 2017 **96**
Made from ungrafted vines, this vibrant, crystalline wine shows superlative structure and purity.

POUILLY-FUMÉ 2002
White | 2011 up to 2017 **96**
Phenomenal aromas of apricots and yellow peaches, with spicy and mineral hints that persist through an elegant, slender mouthfeel.

POUILLY-FUMÉ BLANC FUMÉ DE POUILLY 2007
White | 2011 up to 2013 **90**
A sharp wine with predominant citrus flavors, this sets the tone for a particularly successful vintage for the domaine. Mouth-watering minerality.

POUILLY-FUMÉ BUISSON RENARD 2007
White | 2011 up to 2017 **94**
The delicious notes of apricot and white peach on the nose persist through the fresh mouthfeel. This expression of terroir gets more and more dynamic with every year.

POUILLY-FUMÉ PUR SANG 2007
White | 2011 up to 2017   **92**
With gooseberry overtones and hints of minerals, this wine should evolve beautifully.

POUILLY-FUMÉ SILEX 2006
White | 2011 up to 2020   **96**
There is plenty of pure mineral fruit and nervosity in the 2006, and its structure had developed when we tasted it in March 2007. There will be heavy competition for the 2005.

POUILLY-FUMÉ SILEX 2002
White | 2011 up to 2015   **95**
A striking combination of mineral purity and citrus flavors.

POUILLY-FUMÉ SILEX 1986
White | 2011 up to 2013   **90**
With great structure and plenty of purity, this is a crisp, sharp wine that will pair especially well with the richness of a truffle millefeuille.

SANCERRE LE MONT DAMNÉ 2007
White | 2011 up to 2017   **97**
Boasting almost crystalline minerality and staggering balance, this wine is made from young vines. Bravo, Didier Dagueneau!

White: 28.4 acres. Annual production: 50,000 bottles

DOMAINE PHILIPPE DELESVAUX
🦂🦂🦂🦂

Les Essards-Lahaielongue
La Haie-Longue
49190 Saint-Aubin-de-Luigné
Phone 00 33 2 41 78 18 71
Fax 00 33 2 41 78 68 06
dom.delesvaux.philippe@wanadoo.fr

Philippe Delesvaux started this estate in 1978, gambling that he could become one of the few producers to concentrate mainly on dessert wines. The vineyard is located on the Corniche Angevine, a hillside undercut by the Layon River, and is cultivated according to biodynamic methods. A small quantity of red cabernet sauvignon is also produced from holdings in the Montée de l'Épine. Delesvaux was one of the first Anjou producers to offer a Sélection de Grains Nobles—and his are definitely worth the trip.

Recently tasted
ANJOU AUTHENTIQUE 2007
Semi-Dry White | 2011 up to 2013   **87**

ANJOU FEUILLE D'OR 2007
White | 2011 up to 2013   **88**

ANJOU LA MONTÉE DE L'ÉPINE 2008
Red | 2011 up to 2013   **88**

COTEAUX DU LAYON SÉLECTION DE GRAINS NOBLES 2007
Sweet White | 2011 up to 2027   **90**

COTEAUX DU LAYON SÉLECTION DE GRAINS NOBLES 2006
Sweet White | 2011 up to 2016   **90**

Older vintages
ANJOU AUTHENTIQUE 2006
Semi-Dry White | 2011 up to 2015   **86**
Philippe Delesvaux produces this Authentique, a smooth Anjou blanc with iodine overtones and some slight residual sugar. Perfect with fish and white meats.

ANJOU FEUILLE D'OR 2006
White | 2011 up to 2015   **88**
A beautiful Anjou blanc displaying lovely volume and a powerful, promising mouthfeel.

ANJOU LA MONTÉE DE L'ÉPINE 2005
Red | 2011 up to 2013   **87**
The Anjou rouge from this producer, who is better known for his late-harvest wines, displays a round, mouth-watering body, but needs more time to develop the finish.

COTEAUX DU LAYON 2006
Sweet White | 2011 up to 2013   **86**
This Coteaux du Layon shows initial hints
of wax, iodine, and yellow fruit on the palate, balanced by bright acidity.

Red: 9.8 acres; cabernet franc 57%, cabernet
sauvignon 43%. White: 24.7 acres; chenin 100%.
Annual production: 30,000 bottles

DOMAINE PIERRE-JACQUES DRUET

7, rue de la Croix-Rouge
Le Pied-Fourrier
37140 Benais
Phone 00 33 2 47 97 37 34
Fax 00 33 2 47 97 46 40
pjdruet@wanadoo.fr

Because tasters criticize Loire cabernet
wines for reeking of green peppers, many
estates tend to go for excessive extraction,
often overly oaked. These producers are
always ready to heap scorn on Pierre-
Jacques Druet's wines, but one taste of his
cuvées Grand Mont and Vaumoreau is
enough to whet your palate for more. In
fact, our only complaint is that the bottles
are too small: masterpieces like this can
dare to be served in magnums! In 2003,
these bottlings ranked among the freshest, most distinguished of all the Loire
wines.

Recently tasted

BOURGUEIL CENT BOISSELÉES 2008
Red | 2011 up to 2013   **88**

BOURGUEIL VAUMOREAU 2005
Red | 2013 up to 2030   **94**

CHINON 2001
Red | 2011 up to 2016   **88**

Older vintages

BOURGUEIL CENT BOISSELÉES 2005
Red | 2011 up to 2013   **86**
This mouth-watering wine displays red-fruit
overtones. Ready to drink now.

BOURGUEIL GRAND MONT 2005
Red | 2014 up to 2027   **91**
With a taut mouthfeel framed by fresh tannins typical of the domaine, this wine is made
for aging.

BOURGUEIL GRAND MONT 2003
Red | 2011 up to 2015   **88**
Elegant and fresh with a quintessential Loire
structure. Perfect with veal chops.

BOURGUEIL VAUMOREAU 2003
Red | 2011 up to 2020   **90**
Everything in the right amount! A perfect
balance of tannins. On every level, this subtle wine is of the vintage's best.

Red: 54.4 acres. Annual production: 100,000 bottles

DOMAINE DE L'ÉCU

La Bretonnière
44430 Le Landreau
Phone 00 33 2 40 06 40 91
Fax 00 33 2 40 06 46 79
bossard.guy.muscadet@wanadoo.fr

Manual harvests, horse-drawn plows, and biodynamic vines: Guy Bossard's estate certainly stands out in a winegrowing area that is otherwise one of the most mechanized in France. His wines likewise depart sharply from the classical wines of their appellation. Surprisingly austere when young (especially for the uninitiated), they more than make up for it after a few years' aging. Expression d'Orthogneiss and Expression de Gneiss are textbook expressions of their terroirs, as attested by their geological names. Expression de Granite is particularly classy, coming from a vineyard with nothing but a thin layer of soil between it and the underlying rock.

Recently tasted

MUSCADET SÈVRE-ET-MAINE
EXPRESSION D'ORTHOGNEISS 2008
White | 2011 up to 2013   **90**

MUSCADET SÈVRE-ET-MAINE
EXPRESSION DE GNEISS 2008
White | 2011 up to 2013   **91**

MUSCADET SÈVRE-ET-MAINE
EXPRESSION DE GRANITE 2008
White | 2011 up to 2017   **93**

Older vintages

MUSCADET SÈVRE-ET-MAINE
EXPRESSION D'ORTHOGNEISS 2007
White | 2011 up to 2017   **91**
With delicious saline notes, this cuvée has great potential that will express itself fully in a few years.

MUSCADET SÈVRE-ET-MAINE
EXPRESSION DE GNEISS 2007
White | 2011 up to 2016   **90**
Already showing great potential—with minerality, freshness, and good structure—this cuvée will get even better with time.

MUSCADET SÈVRE-ET-MAINE
EXPRESSION DE GRANITE 2007
White | 2011 up to 2013   **93**
Sharp and well-structured, this wine shows obvious potential.

VIN DE PAYS DU JARDIN DE LA FRANCE
CABERNET FRANC 2006
Red | 2011 up to 2013   **88**
This medium-bodied cabernet shows a subtle red-fruit nose, and a fresh, crisp mouthfeel backed by some pleasant tannins. Pair this with charcuterie.

VIN DE PAYS DU JARDIN DE LA FRANCE CUVÉE
LUDWIG HAHN RD
Brut White sparkling | 2011 up to 2013   **89**
Recently disgorged, this wine shows finesse and subtle purity.

Red: 4.9 acres; cabernet franc 50%, cabernet sauvignon 50%. **White:** 49.4 acres; chardonnay 9%, folle blanche 8%, melon de Bourgogne 83%. **Annual production:** 125,000 bottles

CHÂTEAU DE FESLES

Château de Fesles
49380 Thouarcé
Phone 00 33 2 41 68 94 08
Fax 00 33 2 41 68 94 30
sauvion@sauvion.fr

Present owner Bernard Germain has restored this château's reputation over the past ten years after its wines were popularized by former owner, pastry chef Gaston Lenôtre. Château de Fesles is now the reference point for Anjou wines. The purity of the Anjou Blanc has to be tasted; it constitues an unbridled expression of the delicacy and breeding of the Chenin. The Anjou Rouge shows exemplary expression of local cabernet franc. The Bonnezeaux in good vintages shows pure, poetic balance.

Recently tasted

ANJOU VIEILLES VIGNES 2006
Red | 2011 up to 2013   88

BONNEZEAUX 2007
Sweet White | 2011 up to 2019   93

BONNEZEAUX 2006
Sweet White | 2011 up to 2015   86

ROSÉ D'ANJOU LE JARDIN 2008
Semi-DryRosé | 2011 up to 2013   89

Older vintages

ANJOU 2006
White | 2011 up to 2013   87
We were surprised by the purity of this entry-level wine. Rich, with nice minerality, and hints of lemon and white flowers.

ANJOU LA CHAPELLE 2006
White | 2011 up to 2013   89
Aged in oak, the structure of this wine needs further aging to reveal its complexity. Slightly briny aromas with hints of lemon.

ANJOU VIEILLES VIGNES 2006
Red | 2011 up to 2013   90
This 2006 is nicely structured with a soft but intense fruit and a long, refined mineral finish.

BONNEZEAUX 2005
Sweet White | 2011 up to 2027   93
A very pure Bonnezeaux with complex aromas of peach, apricots, and spices. Intense, yet beautifully balanced and delicate. An impressive wine.

Red: 556 acres: cabernet franc 83%, cabernet sauvignon 7%. White: 49.4 acres; chenin blanc 100%. Annual production: 220,000 bottles

DOMAINE FL (FORMERLY DOMAINE JO PITHON)

Les Bergères
49750 Saint-Lambert-du-Lattay
Phone 00 33 2 41 77 20 04
Fax 00 33 2 41 78 46 3
commercial@domainefl.com
www.domainefl.com

Jo Pithon operates some thirty acres at the heart of the Coteaux du Layon appellation, most of them planted to organically grown chenin. The dessert wines made the reputation of the dry white wines, which are all very successful. The Les Pépinières and Les Bergères are deliciously lush but we have a particular weakness for the Les Treilles, a crisply acidic wine from a sloping vineyard that ceased production in the mid-twentieth century and was replanted in 2000. Of the dessert wines, the 4 Villages demonstrates all the savoir-faire of this estate; the Quarts-de-Chaume Les Varennes won't leave you unmoved either.

Recently tasted

ANJOU LE CHENIN 2007
White | 2011 up to 2013   88

COTEAUX DU LAYON 4 VILLAGES 2007
Sweet White | 2011 up to 2015   86

SAVENNIÈRES LE PARC 2007
White | 2011 up to 2013   89

Older vintages

ANJOU CABERNETS 2006
Red | 2011 up to 2013   90
A wonderful, finely-grained cuvée of cabernet franc. Plenty of deep fruit and very well-chiseled tannins.

ANJOU LES BLANCHES BERGÈRES 2006
White | 2011 up to 2013   89
This barrel-fermented cuvée is fresh and elegant, framed by fresh minerality, and delicately textured.

ANJOU LES TREILLES 2006
White | 2011 up to 2013   90
This is a lovely, pure chenin blanc showing great precision of aromas and texture. Unlike many chenin blancs, it is ready to drink now.

COTEAUX DU LAYON 4 VILLAGES 2006
Sweet White | 2011 up to 2013   88
The 4 Villages cuvée is a blend of grapes primarily from Saint-Aubin and Chaume, but also includes some from Beaulieu and Saint-Lambert. This is a pleasant wine, given the late-harvest vintage.

QUARTS-DE-CHAUME LES VARENNES 2005
Sweet White | 2011 up to 2013   88
This amber-colored cuvée, reminiscent of a great rancio from the south, shows rich notes of dried currants. This is a pleasant, yet atypical and original style for the region.

Red: 9.8 acres; cabernet franc 66%, cabernet sauvignon 34%. White: 89 acres; chenin 100%.

DOMAINE GADAIS PÈRE ET FILS

Les Perrières
44690 Saint-Fiacre-sur-Maine
Phone 00 33 2 40 54 81 23
Fax 00 33 2 40 36 70 25
musgadais@wanadoo.fr
www.gadaispereetfils.fr

Christophe Gadais's estate encompasses numerous parcels around Saint-Fiacre. His thirty-year-old vines are the raw material for a range of Muscadets that are expressive as young wines—clean, harmonious, and well balanced. His cuvées have a lovely delicacy on the finish. We particularly liked the cuvée aux Avineaux and the Grande Réserve du Moulin, both very reasonably priced. The Vieilles Vignes is somewhat pricier and more of a gastronomic Muscadet.

Recently tasted
MUSCADET SÈVRE-ET-MAINE
GRANDE RÉSERVE DU MOULIN 2008
White | 2011 up to 2013   90

MUSCADET SÈVRE-ET-MAINE
LE MUSCADET AUX AVINEAUX 2008
White | 2011 up to 2013   88

Older vintages
MUSCADET SÈVRE-ET-MAINE
GRANDE RÉSERVE DU MOULIN 2005
White | 2011 up to 2017   91
This very promising wine displays superb balance with saline overtones. The refined and elegant 2000 shows mushroom overtones, while the elegant and fresh 2001, sharp with hints of iodine, begs to be paired with shellfish.

MUSCADET SÈVRE-ET-MAINE
LE MUSCADET AUX AVINEAUX 2007
White | Drink now   84
A straightforward, easygoing wine with plenty of freshness.

MUSCADET SÈVRE-ET-MAINE
VIEILLES VIGNES 2002
White | Drink now   90
This 2002, which has developed delicate notes of forest undergrowth, is a harmonious and refined wine.

White: 98.8 acres; melon de Bourgogne 100%.
Annual production: 260,000 bottles

DOMAINE LES GRANDES VIGNES

Lieu-dit La Roche Aubry
49380 Thouarcé
Phone 00 33 2 41 54 05 06
Fax 00 33 2 41 54 08 21
vaillant@domainelesgrandesvignes.com
www.domainelesgrandesvignes.com

The Domaine Les Grandes Vignes has stood at the heart of the Layon winegrowing area for four centuries. Owner Jean-François Vaillant turns out stylish Loire wines of every kind, though he is particularly passionate about his reds, giving them a fleshy, rounded quality too often lacking in the reds from this region. We were equally impressed by his dry whites, to say nothing of his vertical collection of dessert wines. Few estates at this level boast such stunning sweet wines. All in all a very highly recommended producer.

Recently tasted

ANJOU LA VARENNE DE COMBRE 2007
White | 2011 up to 2015   89

ANJOU LA VARENNE DE POIRIER 2007
White | 2011 up to 2013   87

BONNEZEAUX LE MALABÉ 2007
Sweet White | 2011 up to 2027   90

COTEAUX DU LAYON LE PONT MARTIN 2007
Sweet White | 2011 up to 2017   90

Older vintages

ANJOU LA VARENNE DE POIRIER 2005
White | 2011 up to 2015   91
This Anjou boasts a great personality with hints of pear and a remarkable body that shows great pedigree.

ANJOU-VILLAGES COCAINELLES 2005
Red | 2011 up to 2013   88
This dense and powerful red shows an impressively fleshy yet balanced body that will become more refined with time.

BONNEZEAUX LE MALABÉ 2006
Sweet White | 2011 up to 2013   88
Bonnezeaux late-harvest wines are enticing, with original hints of acacia gum aromas. This wine is pleasant, despite the difficult vintage.

COTEAUX DU LAYON LE PONT MARTIN 2006
Sweet White | 2011 up to 2016   88
2006 was well managed, and the wine is an accurate expression of the vintage. Not much power, but well balanced.

Red: 86.5 acres; cabernet franc 61%, cabernet sauvignon 15%, gamay 6%, grollau 18%. White: 49.4 acres; chenin 100%. Annual production: 200,000 bottles

DOMAINE LA GRANGE TIPHAINE

La Grange Tiphaine
37400 Amboise
Phone 00 33 9 64 04 32 09
Fax 00 33 2 47 57 39 49
lagrangetiphaine@wanadoo.fr
www.lagrangetiphaine.com

Damien Delecheneau took over the family estate after training as an enologist in both France and the New World. Heir to plantings of old vines in Montlouis and Touraine-Amboise, he always insists on the best. Unlike so many of his neighbors, he has not gone for wines that sell well to local tourist restaurants. All of his cuvées show off his talents. He is also a passionate clarinetist and often picks wine names with musical connotations. His latest bottling—a naturally sparkling, non-dosed wine called the Nouveau Nez—also deserves serious attention.

Recently tasted

MONTLOUIS-SUR-LOIRE NOUVEAU NEZ 2007
White sparkling | 2011 up to 2013   87

TOURAINE AMBOISE CLEF DE SOL 2007
Red | 2011 up to 2013   86

Older vintages

MONTLOUIS-SUR-LOIRE CLEF DE SOL 2007
White | 2011 up to 2013   86
Although the alcohol-fermentation is not yet complete, the wine shows predominant citrus aromas.

MONTLOUIS-SUR-LOIRE L'ÉQUILIBRISTE 2005
White | 2011 up to 2015   91
Remarkably fresh aromas with floral overtones—a very promising cuvée.

MONTLOUIS-SUR-LOIRE LES GRENOUILLÈRES 2006
White | 2011 up to 2013   90
This demi-sec displays impressively pure aromas and a long-lasting finish.

TOURAINE AMBOISE BÉCARRE 2007
Red | 2011 up to 2013   86
It is difficult to resist the seductive mouthfeel of this Touraine-Amboise. The palate of explosive fruit is backed by a mouth-wateringly refined body.

TOURAINE AMBOISE CLEF DE SOL 2005
Red | 2011 up to 2013   89
This wine is the Loire equivalent of taffeta. The vigneron has successfully preserved all of the fruit of the cuvée, and coupled it with remarkable length and tension.

Red: 17.3 acres; cabernet franc 35%, côt 35%, gamay 30%. White: 14.8 acres; chenin blanc 92%, sauvignon blanc 8%. Annual production: 55,000 bottles

DOMAINE GUIBERTEAU

3, impasse du Cabernet
Mollay
49260 Saint-Just-sur-Dive
Phone 00 33 2 41 38 78 94
Fax 00 33 2 41 38 56 46
domaine.guiberteau@wanadoo.fr

Young Romain Guiberteau certainly hasn't been slow to make his mark. His wines positively radiate serenity, probably because they come from organically grown vines. The whites have obvious class and demonstrate all the potential for white-wine production in Saumur. The reds, not to be outdone, capture a unique expression of cabernet franc that surpasses all expectations. This is a departure from the real or supposed spirit of Saumur, with a quality of fruit that places them alongside the greatest wines in France, be they from Burgundy, the Languedoc, or Bordeaux.

Recently tasted

COTEAUX DE SAUMUR BRÉZÉ 2003
Sweet White | 2011 up to 2017   92

SAUMUR BRÉZÉ 2006
White | 2011 up to 2017   94

SAUMUR DOMAINE 2007
White | 2011 up to 2013   91

SAUMUR LES ARBOISES 2005
Red | 2011 up to 2014   88

SAUMUR LES MOTELLES 2005
Red | 2011 up to 2016   92

Older vintages

SAUMUR DOMAINE 2005
White | 2011 up to 2014   90
Balance comes first in this deep, round, and mouth-watering Saumur blanc. Its woody overtones from oak aging will soften with time.

SAUMUR DOMAINE 2005
Red | 2011 up to 2015   90
Vibrant fruit and a soothing, natural impression frame this Saumur. The Tuffeau soil gives the wine beautiful minerality.

SAUMUR LES ARBOISES 2004
Red | 2011 up to 2013   92
The natural taste of pure, bright fruit leaves you with an exhilarating impression. Those who can stand to wait will be rewarded for their patience.

SAUMUR LES ARBOISES 2003
Red | 2011 up to 2013   92
Showing magnitude and technical achievement, this wine has been successfully polished by time. The leathery and spicy round finish leaves an exhilarating impression.

SAUMUR LES CLOS 2004
White | 2011 up to 2015   91
Les Clos is a parcel of land on the Côte de Brézé that is capable of producing rich wines with nutty overtones. That's the case here.

SAUMUR LES MOTELLES 2004
Red | 2011 up to 2015   92
Powerful and mouth-watering with a long finish, this dense yet very natural and pure wine is made from grapes native to Montreuil-Bellay. A very promising wine.

Red: 12.4 acres; cabernet franc 100%. **White:** 12.4 acres; chenin blanc 100%. **Annual production:** 30,000 bottles

DOMAINES VÉRONIQUE GÜNTHER-CHÉREAU

Château du Coing de Saint-Fiacre
La Bourchinière
44690 Saint-Fiacre-sur-Maine
Phone 00 33 2 40 54 85 24
Fax 00 33 2 51 71 60 96
contact@château-du-coing.com
www.château-du-coing.com

With her charming voice, Véronique Günther-Chéreau explains that she began making wine with the extraordinary 1989 vintage: "With time I have realized how good it was, and so far no other vintage has surpassed it." Despite this fact, we can sing the praises of her 2004s, as well as the 1993, 1994, and 1995 trilogy, all still drinking well today. If you enjoy older Muscadets, a few precious bottles can still be purchased at the winery; but don't forget the most recent vintages—they are truly wonderful.

Recently tasted
MUSCADET SÈVRE-ET-MAINE
CHÂTEAU DE LA GRAVELLE, GORGEOIS 2004
White | 2011 up to 2023   90

MUSCADET SÈVRE-ET-MAINE CHÂTEAU
DU COING MONNIÈRES-SAINT-FIACRE 2004
White | 2011 up to 2017   90

Older vintages
MUSCADET SÈVRE-ET-MAINE
CHÂTEAU DE LA GRAVELLE 2005
White | Drink now   87
This terroir wine has a precise, straight-as-an-arrow finish.

MUSCADET SÈVRE-ET-MAINE
CHÂTEAU DU COING DE SAINT-FIACRE 2006
White | 2011 up to 2013   89
This promising wine delivers some delicious iodine flavors with lovely shades of citrus.

MUSCADET SÈVRE-ET-MAINE
GRAND FIEF DE LA CORMERAIE 2007
White | 2011 up to 2013   88
Fresh with hints of iodine, this is a great aperitif wine.

MUSCADET SÈVRE-ET-MAINE
GRAND FIEF DE LA CORMERAIE 2006
White | 2011 up to 2013   88
A fresh and easygoing wine that pairs especially well with seafood.

White: 160.6 acres; chardonnay 3%, folle blanche 2%, melon de Bourgogne 95%. **Annual production:** 400,000 bottles

DOMAINE DES GUYONS

7, rue Saint-Nicolas
49260 Le Puy-Nôtre-Dame
Phone 00 33 2 41 52 21 15
Fax 00 33 2 41 38 88 24
domainedesguyons@wanadoo.fr

Franck and Ingrid Bimond's white wines from Puy-Nôtre-Dame are growing to be a reference for the entire Saumur appellation. Vent du Nord is their deliciously lush and distinguished entry-level wine. L'Ardile, named after the clay parcel from which it originates, achieves peerless finesse and naturalness. L'Ydill d'Ingrid, bottled under the Cabernet de Saumur AOC, was love at first sight. What's new about this estate is the improvement in the reds—not yet as outstanding as the white wines but certainly promising to be so.

Recently tasted
SAUMUR L'ARDILE 2008
White | 2011 up to 2015   90

SAUMUR MURMURE 2008
Red | 2011 up to 2013   88

SAUMUR ODYSSÉE 2008
Red | 2011 up to 2015   90

SAUMUR VENT DU NORD 2008
White | 2011 up to 2013   91

Older vintages
CABERNET D'ANJOU FREE VOL 2007
Semi-Dry Rosé | 2011 up to 2013   90
A delicate nose of raspberry and peach precedes a mouthfeel that is alluringly silky and velvety.

CABERNET DE SAUMUR YDILL D'INGRID 2007
Rosé | Drink now   87
Although it is a little-known appellation, the Cabernet de Saumur produces a pleasant and very delicate rosé.

CABERNET DE SAUMUR YDILL D'INGRID 2006
Rosé | Drink now   88
Here is a delicate, nonaggressive Cabernet de Saumur with a perfect, velvety finish.

SAUMUR L'ARDILE 2006
White | 2011 up to 2013   88
The 2006 won't be as fruit-forward as the 2005. However, this is a lovely, delicate, and easy-drinking Saumur.

SAUMUR MURMURE 2007
Red | 2011 up to 2013   88
In this atypical vintage, this smooth and fleshy Saumur rouge is lovely and seductive, yet not over the top. A total success.

SAUMUR ODYSSÉE 2006

Red | 2011 up to 2013   **88**

This wine is evolving well. It has a nice, mineral palette and finishes with fresh and silky tannins.

SAUMUR VENT DU NORD 2007

White | 2011 up to 2013   **90**

Lovely, very aromatic fruit. Powerful, with 13.75% alcohol, yet a well-balanced wine. A very good value.

SAUMUR VENT DU NORD 2006

White | 2011 up to 2013   **90**

The cuvée Vent du Nord doesn't lack freshness in 2006. It shows superlative richness, structure, and length.

Red: 22.2 acres; cabernet franc 95%, cabernet sauvignon 5%. **White:** 27.2 acres; 89%, chardonnay 11%. **Annual production:** 50,000 bottles

DOMAINE HUET

11-13, rue de la Croix-Buisée
37210 Vouvray
Phone 00 33 2 47 52 78 87
Fax 00 33 2 47 52 66 74
contact@huet-echansonne.com
www.huet-echansonne.com

The Vouvray appellation is blessed with a few flagship domains that shine in even the most difficult periods. No bells, no whistles, just first-class results that prove how great Vouvray can be. The Domaine Huet is a good example: vines and wines that bear testament to Noël Pinguet's supreme experience, based on principles that stay as close to nature—and perfection—as possible. Words cannot do justice to the exquisite purity of these cuvées, each one named after the vineyard of origin: Le Mont (mineral elegance), Haut-Lieu (suppleness plus a tender side), and Clos du Bourg (the most structured of the three). Half the 2006 harvest was eliminated, with superb results: chenin purists couldn't ask for more!

Recently tasted

VOUVRAY HAUT-LIEU 2008
Sweet White | 2011 up to 2030   **90**

VOUVRAY HAUT-LIEU 2007
White | 2011 up to 2030   **92**

VOUVRAY HAUT-LIEU 2007
Semi-Dry White | 2011 up to 2030   **95**

VOUVRAY LE MONT 2008
Semi-Dry White | 2011 up to 2023   **96**

VOUVRAY LE MONT 2007
White | 2011 up to 2030   **97**

VOUVRAY LE MONT PREMIÈRE TRIE 2008
Sweet White | 2011 up to 2030   **92**

Older vintages

VOUVRAY CLOS DU BOURG 2007
Sweet White | 2011 up to 2017   **96**

Great precision with good ripeness and a crystalline, perfectly clean mouthfeel. A lively wine!

VOUVRAY CLOS DU BOURG 2006
Sweet White | 2011 up to 2020   **98**

Almond and apricot flavors are framed in fresh minerality. An impressively fresh and long-lasting mouthfeel.

VOUVRAY CLOS DU BOURG PREMIÈRE TRIE 2005
Sweet White | 2011 up to 2020   **99**

Pleasant lime-flower, tea, and citrus overtones framed by a superbly rich, taut, and refined palate.

Vouvray Haut-Lieu 2007
Sweet White | 2011 up to 2017   **96**
The finish is incredibly precise, taut, and
mouth-watering. A very promising wine.

Vouvray Haut-Lieu 2006
White | 2011 up to 2020   **96**
A very sharp wine with quintessential minerality and notes of floral and saline.

Vouvray Le Mont 2006
White | 2011 up to 2020   **99**
Although it possesses an abundance of fresh
mineral structure, the nose is still a bit
closed.

Vouvray Pétillant 2001
Brut White sparkling | 2011 up to 2013   **89**
A well-made, dry chenin blanc with hints
of brioche and candied fruit, this lovely sparkling wine has benefited from long maturation.

White: 86.5 acres; chenin blanc 100%. Annual
production: 150,000 bottles

CHÂTEAU DU HUREAU

Le Hureau
49400 Dampierre-sur-Loire
Phone 00 33 2 41 67 60 40
Fax 00 33 2 41 50 43 35
philippe.vatan@wanadoo.fr
www.domaine-hureau.fr

Philippe Vatan has become something of
an authority on Saumur-Champigny since
he settled here in 1987. An agronomical
engineer by profession, he takes a very
methodical approach to winemaking, looking to make refreshing, mouth-filling reds
that avoid aggressive tannins. His entry-
level Saumur-Champigny is exemplary;
the Lisagathe is a pretty, well-structured
wine from clayey parcels, made for laying
down; and the Fevettes, named after the
parcel of origin, is delicate but ages very
gracefully, developing elegant notes of
peonies. The white Saumur and Coteaux
de Saumur are both good quality. All in all,
a delicious assortment!

Recently tasted
Saumur-Champigny Fours à Chaux 2008
Red | 2011 up to 2017   **88**

Saumur-Champigny Fours à Chaux 2007
Red | 2011 up to 2015   **88**

Saumur-Champigny Lisagathe 2008
Red | 2011 up to 2015   **88**

Older vintages
Coteaux de Saumur 2005
Sweet White | 2011 up to 2025   **90**
Very well balanced with hints of candied
oranges and tangerine intertwined with a
fresh acidity.

Saumur 2005
Red | 2011 up to 2013   **88**
Young, yet very soft, this wine is refined and
elegant with lots of freshness.

Saumur-Champigny Lisagathe 2006
Red | 2011 up to 2013   **88**
The name of this cuvée is a contraction of
the vigneron's daughters' names. Velvety
and very well balanced, this cuvée will get
even better with age.

Saumur-Champigny Tuffe 2006
Red | 2011 up to 2013   **87**
A pleasant Saumur-Champigny, round with
a ripe finish. Perfect with roasted duck
breast.

Red: 44.5 acres; cabernet franc 100%. White: 3.7
acres; chenin blanc 100%. Annual production:
130,000 bottles

DOMAINE CHARLES JOGUET

La Dioterie
37220 Sazilly
Phone 00 33 2 47 58 55 53
Fax 00 33 2 47 58 52 22
contact@charlesjoguet.com
www.charlesjoguet.com

Charles Joguet is to Chinon wines what Henri Jayer is to Burgundy. The man was a master of cabernet franc: his 1986, 1988, 1989, and 1990 vintages display a silkiness and sensuality unique among Loire wines. After his retirement in the early 1990s, oenophiles rather missed that great Loire style, even if some of the Dioterie and Chêne Vert vintages did occasionally stand out in tastings. The 2002 vintage, however, marked a return to that peerless fruit and satiny texture for which Jonguet was renowned. All of the 2005s were top performers. If you see one, make sure you grab it—though there would be no harm in settling for a more recent vintage either.

Recently tasted

CHINON CLOS DE LA DIOTERIE 2007
Red | 2011 up to 2022   **92**

CHINON CLOS DU CHÊNE VERT 2007
Red | 2012 up to 2023   **92**

CHINON CUVÉE DE LA CURE 2007
Red | 2011 up to 2013   **86**

CHINON CUVÉE TERROIR 2008
Red | 2011 up to 2013   **88**

CHINON LES VARENNES
GRAND CLOS FRANC DE PIED 2007
Red | 2011 up to 2013   **89**

Older vintages

CHINON CLOS DE LA DIOTERIE 2006
Red | 2011 up to 2017   **90**
Right now, the Clos de la Dioterie shows rough tannins and sharp acidity, but time is on its side.

CHINON CLOS DE LA DIOTERIE 2005
Red | 2011 up to 2015   **91**
A sensual wine that shows refined tannins, it is reminiscent of the legendary 1989.

CHINON CLOS DU CHÊNE VERT 2006
Red | 2011 up to 2017   **90**
A pure expression of the terroir, with intense and deep aromas, this will age well.

CHINON CLOS DU CHÊNE VERT 2005
Red | 2011 up to 2020   **90**
Notes of eucalyptus and blueberries characterize this promising wine.

CHINON CUVÉE DE LA CURE 2005
Red | 2011 up to 2015   **87**
Shows more structure than fruit right now. The tannins have smoothed out since bottling.

CHINON LES PETITES ROCHES 2005
Red | 2011 up to 2013   **86**
Plump black fruit with spicy notes and silky tannins. Very easy-drinking.

CHINON LES VARENNES DU GRAND CLOS 2006
Red | 2011 up to 2013   **87**
Packed with aromas of charred wood and tar, the cuvée boasts refined tannins and a long-lasting finish.

CHINON LES VARENNES
GRAND CLOS FRANC DE PIED 2006
Red | 2011 up to 2015   **90**
The best made since 1989, this is excellent now that the tannins have rounded out.

Red: 91.4 acres: cabernet franc 100%. White: 7.4 acres; chenin blanc 100%. Annual production: 180,000 bottles

DOMAINES JOSEPH LANDRON

Les Brandières
44690 La Haye-Fouassières
Phone 00 33 2 40 54 83 27
Fax 00 33 2 40 54 89 82
domaines.landron@wanadoo.fr
www.domaines-landron.com

Joseph Landron is entitled to twirl his mustache as he reflects on what he's accomplished—and the move toward biodynamics should make his terroirs even more expressive. The range may be extensive, but every cuvée is nonetheless impeccable. The Cuvée Haute Tradition proves that it is possible to make a very great, gourmet style of Muscadet.

Recently tasted
MUSCADET SÈVRE-ET-MAINE AMPHIBOLITE 2008
White | 2011 up to 2013 **92**

MUSCADET SÈVRE-ET-MAINE
DOMAINE DE LA LOUVETRIE 2008
White | 2011 up to 2017 **89**

MUSCADET SÈVRE-ET-MAINE
CLOS LA CARIZIÈRE 2008
White | 2011 up to 2017 **92**
This 2008, with a wonderfully elegant vein, seems ready for the long haul.

MUSCADET SÈVRE-ET-MAINE HERMINE D'OR 2008
White | 2011 up to 2015 **90**
The wine is tight, with elegant notes of preserved lemon on the finish and beautiful purity.

Older vintages
MUSCADET SÈVRE-ET-MAINE AMPHIBOLITE 2007
White | Drink now **90**
Fresh with delicious iodine flavors, this cuvée will pair well with oysters.

MUSCADET SÈVRE-ET-MAINE
CHÂTEAU LA CARIZIÈRE 2007
White | 2011 up to 2017 **91**
Classy, sharp, and long-lasting, this wine has a superlative nervy finish with a great pedigree.

White: 111.2 acres; folle blanche 3%, melon de Bourgogne 95%. Annual production: 300,000 bottles

LANGLOIS-CHÂTEAU

3, rue Léopold-Palustre
BP 57
49400 Saint-Hilaire-Saint-Florent
Phone 00 33 2 41 40 21 40
Fax 00 33 2 41 40 21 49
contact@langlois-château.fr
www.langlois-château.fr

Langlois-Château has belonged to foremost Champagne house Bollinger since 1976. It was founded near Saumur almost a century ago and offers good-quality bottlings from across the Loire, many of them sourced from its own vines. The still wines revolve around red and white Saumurs, the top white being the Saumur Blanc Vieilles Vignes. But the estate's real forte, as you might expect given its connections, is sparkling-wine production. Its range of Crémant de Loire wines is impeccable across the board, with the prestige cuvée Quadrille representing a quality unmatched by any other Loire wine.

Recently tasted
CRÉMANT DE LOIRE QUADRILLE 2002
Brut White sparkling | 2011 up to 2013 **90**

Older vintages
CRÉMANT DE LOIRE
Brut White sparkling | 2011 up to 2013 **89**
This blend from chardonnay, chenin blanc, and cabernet franc produces the richness you expect from a good crémant.

CRÉMANT DE LOIRE
Brut Rosé sparkling | 2011 up to 2013 **88**
A lovely raspberry and Morello cherry nose opens to a broad mouthfeel with perceptible dosage. Perfect as an aperitif, or paired with grilled salmon

CRÉMANT DE LOIRE QUADRILLE 2001
Brut White sparkling | Drink now **88**
This cuvée made from four different terroirs consists of four grapes: chenin blanc, cabernet sauvignon, cabernet franc, and chardonnay. The wine shows notes of honey, and is ready to drink now.

SAUMUR 2007
White | 2011 up to 2013 **88**
A smooth texture leads to citrus notes and a remarkable, fruit-forward finish.

SAUMUR 2007
Red | 2011 up to 2013 **87**
An easygoing, Morello cherry–colored wine, it balances fruit and freshness and is quintessential of the Loire.

Red: 111.2 acres; cabernet franc 100%. White: 69.2 acres. Annual production: 450,000 bottles

DOMAINE DAMIEN LAUREAU

Chemin du Grand Hamé, Epiré
49170 Savennières
Phone 00 33 9 64 37 02 57
Fax 00 33 2 41 72 87 39
damien.laureau@orange.fr
www.damien-laureau.fr

In 1999 young Damien Laureau took over a family estate planted with fruit trees and vines, but he recently opted to drop the former in favor of the latter. We tasted his two prettily made Savennières offerings, the Les Genêts and Le Bel Ouvrage. The grand vin would seem to hail from the Clos Fremur, an ancient parcel at the entrance to Angers that has been renowned since medieval times. The red is blended from the cabernet franc and sauvignon, and, unusually for an Anjou wine, is a tad better than the chenin. An estate with an exciting future and, who knows, perhaps even greatness ahead.

Recently tasted

SAVENNIÈRES-ROCHE AUX MOINES 2007
White | 2011 up to 2017   **95**

SAVENNIÈRES LE BEL OUVRAGE 2007
White | 2011 up to 2019   **91**

SAVENNIÈRES LES GENÊTS 2007
White | 2011 up to 2017   **88**

Older vintages

ANJOU CLOS FREMUR 2006
Red | 2011 up to 2013   **92**
This wine has a great pedigree, a superb nose of violets, and delicate, long-lasting saline flavors. With fine tannins on the finish, it will age well, but the wine is so pleasant now that we might have a hard time waiting.

ANJOU CLOS FREMUR 2005
White | 2011 up to 2015   **90**
The Clos Fremur terroir adds some delicate salty notes to the chenin blanc. The finish is a striking marriage of minerality and freshness.

ANJOU CLOS FREMUR 2005
Red | 2011 up to 2013   **92**
This is an exceptional wine for Anjou, made with 30 percent cabernet sauvignon and 70 percent cabernet franc. It has great class and a slightly saline length.

SAVENNIÈRES LE BEL OUVRAGE 2005
White | 2011 up to 2015   **88**
The wine's lovely structure is a bit overwhelmed by the oak aging, but it will get more expressive with time.

SAVENNIÈRES LES GENÊTS 2005
White | 2011 up to 2015   **88**
This classic Savennières was a bit austere in its youth—it just needed some time to open.

Red: 9.6 acres; cabernet franc 85%, cabernet sauvignon 15%. White: 14.9 acres; chenin blanc 100%. Annual production: 38,000 bottles

DOMAINE RICHARD LEROY

52, Grande Rue
49750 Rablay-sur-Layon
Phone 00 33 2 41 78 51 84
Fax 00 33 2 41 78 51 84
sr.leroy@wanadoo.fr

Young winegrower Richard Leroy came to Anjou determined to make gourmet wines that brought out the best in the local terroirs. Passionate about wine, he used his tasting skills to put together a consistent range of wines, all of them eminently suited to supply some delightful drinking—hugely round, but never flabby. The Le Clos des Rouliers belongs among the loveliest of the Loire chenins and the Les Noëls de Montbenault—especially perhaps in its sweet incarnation—displays a class that comes close to grand vin.

Anjou Clos des Rouliers 2006
White | 2011 up to 2013   84
The lovely, well-vinified structure of this wine is currently overpowered by the oak. Will it become more balanced with time? Let's wait and see.

Anjou Clos des Rouliers 2005
White | 2011 up to 2015   89
This chenin blanc was vinified to produce a round wine with citrus and candied lemon overtones. It is harmonious and delicious.

Anjou Noëls de Montbenault 2005
White | 2011 up to 2015   89
Although slightly over-oaked, this cuvée has more character than the Clos des Rouliers, and its elegant finish leaves the palate quite satisfied.

Coteaux du Layon Faye-d'Anjou Noëls de Montbenault 2003
Sweet White | 2011 up to 2020   90
This Layon Faye-d'Anjou offers some powerful sweetness with nuances of peaches and candied apricots on the finish, and has balanced acidity.

White: 6.7 acres; chenin 100%. **Annual production:** 7,000 bottles

DOMAINE PIERRE LUNEAU-PAPIN

La Grange
44430 Le Landreau
Phone 00 33 2 40 06 45 27
domaineluneaupapin@wanadoo.fr
www.domaineluneaupapin.com

This winery prefers to vinify its different terroirs separately, making clean and focused wines with lots of character. The cuvée L d'Or, made from grapes grown on granitic soils, has that iodine character that is found in the best wines from this area. The cuvée Excelsior, grown on local schist, has a noble minerality. These wines evolve well and are made to be aged. The other wines are less ambitious, but they have style and are the perfect match for seafood dishes.

Recently tasted
Muscadet Sèvre-et-Maine Clos des Allées 2008
White | 2011 up to 2013   87

Muscadet Sèvre-et-Maine Clos des Pierres Blanches, Vieilles Vignes 2007
White | 2011 up to 2015   88

Muscadet Sèvre-et-Maine Domaine Pierre de La Grange, Vieilles Vignes 2007
White | 2011 up to 2016   86

Muscadet Sèvre-et-Maine L d'Or 2008
White | 2011 up to 2018   91

Muscadet Sèvre-et-Maine L d'Or 2007
White | 2011 up to 2017   90

Older vintages
Muscadet Sèvre-et-Maine Clos des Allées 2007
White | 2011 up to 2013   87
Lovely grapefruit nuances with hints of iodine, and a balanced mouthfeel.

Muscadet Sèvre-et-Maine Clos des Pierres Blanches 2007
White | 2011 up to 2013   85
With a texture like satin and a fresh salinity, this wine would be exceptional with oysters.

Muscadet Sèvre-et-Maine L d'Or 2005
White | 2011 up to 2020   90
This promising cuvée is full of minerality, and is framed by power and elegance. A vertical tasting from 2006 to 1976 allows for a good understanding of Muscadets worth cellaring. The 1997s, 1999s, and 2000s are delicious. If you find a 1976, enjoy!

Red: 12.4 acres. White: 111.2 acres. **Annual production:** 220,000 bottles

DOMAINE FRÉDÉRIC MABILEAU

6, rue du Pressoir
37140 Saint-Nicolas-de-Bourgueil
Phone 00 33 2 47 97 79 58
Fax 00 33 2 47 97 45 19
contact@fredericmabileau.com
www.fredericmabileau.com

Fréderic Mabileau makes his wines in a floral and fresh style, and that's all the better since this is exactly what we expect from a Saint-Nicolas-de-Bourgueil. Mabileau took over the domaine in 2003 and since has planted grass between the rows of vines; he tills the soil and hand harvests with small crates. There is a good range here, with entry-level wines that are superbly drinkable!

Recently tasted
ANJOU 2007
Red | 2011 up to 2017   86

SAINT-NICOLAS-DE-BOURGUEIL RACINES 2007
Red | 2011 up to 2016   90

Older vintages
BOURGUEIL RACINES 2007
Red | 2011 up to 2017   92
A very fruity, pleasant wine with subtle depth, it has the capacity to age well.

SAINT-NICOLAS-DE-BOURGUEIL COUTURES 2007
Red | 2011 up to 2013   90
With a powerful mouthfeel and a palate of peony and floral overtones, this wine will gain in complexity and reward patient aficionados.

SAINT-NICOLAS-DE-BOURGUEIL ÉCLIPSE 2007
Red | 2011 up to 2013   90
Eclipse is the domaine's most ambitious cuvée, well structured and powerful.

SAINT-NICOLAS-DE-BOURGUEIL
LES ROUILLÈRES 2007
Red | 2011 up to 2013   86
A thirst-quenching, round, and fruit-forward wine that is easy to drink.

SAINT-NICOLAS-DE-BOURGUEIL
LES ROUILLÈRES 2006
Red | 2011 up to 2013   85
This easygoing wine shows red-fruit flavors framed by a fresh and elegant mouthfeel.

SAINT-NICOLAS-DE-BOURGUEIL RACINES 2006
Red | 2011 up to 2013   90
A balanced nose and mouthfeel are framed by lovely, fresh tannins.

Red: 66.7 acres; cabernet franc 95%. cabernet sauvignon 5%. White: 37.1 acres; chenin blanc 100%.
Annual production: 150,000 bottles

HENRY ET JEAN-SEBASTIEN MARIONNET

La Charmoise
41230 Soings
Phone 00 33 2 54 98 70 73
Fax 00 33 2 54 98 75 66
henry@henry-marionnet.com
www.henry-marionnet.com

Only a complete Philistine would find this place boring. Every wine has a story to tell and many ancient varieties have been preserved for posterity; future scientists who study wine grapes and their origins are sure to be truly grateful. Henry Marionnet even dares to plant own-rooted vines—not grafted on the phylloxera-resistant rootstock that was introduced in the wake of the nineteenth-century plague that devastated French vineyards. The product is a wine of great quality, though it receives only grudging recognition. Fact is, it shows just how much harmonious flavor was sacrificed to the ravaging pest.

Recently tasted
TOURAINE CÔT VINIFERA FRANC DE PIED 2007
Red | 2011 up to 2017   94

TOURAINE DOMAINE DE LA CHARMOISE 2007
Red | 2011 up to 2013   89

TOURAINE PREMIÈRE VENDANGE 2008
Red | 2011 up to 2013   90

TOURAINE SAUVIGNON VINIFERA FRANC DE PIED 2008
White | 2011 up to 2015   90

VIN DE PAYS DU JARDIN DE LA FRANCE BOUZE 2008
Red | 2011 up to 2017   92

VIN DE PAYS DU JARDIN DE LA FRANCE
PROVIGNAGE 2008
White | 2011 up to 2018   92

Older vintages
TOURAINE CÔT VINIFERA FRANC DE PIED 2006
Red | 2011 up to 2016   94
This cuvée has evolved perfectly with time. The tannins have become silky and the fruit remains fresh. This 2006 is promising and should evolve like the wonderful 2002.

TOURAINE M DE MARIONNET 2005
White | 2011 up to 2017   89
The M de Marionnet is made from very ripe sauvignon blanc grapes. It shows a great balance between richness and acidity, which allows its true character to shine. The 1995 vintage is still in great shape: an unctuous sense of orange peel and spice aromas leads to a fresh, rich mouthfeel.

TOURAINE PREMIÈRE VENDANGE 2006

Red | 2011 up to 2013   **90**

This wine shows plenty of black cherry and mouth-watering purity.

TOURAINE SAUVIGNON 2007

White | Drink now   **87**

A saline and floral cuvée backed by a juicy, fresh texture that works wonders with goat cheese from Pouligny.

TOURAINE SAUVIGNON VINIFERA FRANC DE PIED 2006

White | 2011 up to 2015   **89**

Lovely fruit purity with floral notes and a dynamic mouthfeel characterize this wine.

VIN DE PAYS DU JARDIN DE LA FRANCE BOUZE 2007

Red | 2011 up to 2013   **92**

Full of fresh black fruit, this wine shows amazing, mouth-watering purity. One of the vintage's best wines. Drink it now.

Red: 98.8 acres; côt 10%, gamay 90%. White: 49.4 acres; chenin blanc 2%, romorantin 2%, sauvignon blanc 96%. Annual production: 400,000 bottles

DOMAINE ALPHONSE MELLOT

3, rue Porte-César BP 18
18300 Sancerre
Phone 00 33 2 48 54 07 41
Fax 00 33 2 48 54 07 62
alphonse@mellot.com
www.mellot.com

The current Alphonse is the nineteenth generation to bear the name Alphonse Mellot—better known as Junior to distinguish him from his father, whose work he continues, proving a worthy successor and even accomplice from time to time. In addition to his enological and cultural skills, Alphonse Junior boasts a creative genius that never lets him down: his wines are altogether sumptuous and deliciously quaffable. The whites start with the delightful Cuvée La Moussière, a well-crafted entry-level wine that paves the way for the almost crystalline Cuvée Générations white—iodized, with a sweep of salinity and exceptional purity and precision. The reds follow suit, fruity with a sensuality and refinement to die for. The Demoiselle is very focused, the Grands-Champs all velvet, and the Cuvée Générations red is almost beyond words: so awesomely complete and refined that it is still delicious seventy-two hours after opening—like most of the wines from this estate, all of which rank among the very greatest wines ever produced.

Recently tasted

SANCERRE EDMOND 2007
White | 2012 up to 2019   **96**

SANCERRE EN SATELLITE 2008
White | 2011 up to 2016   **91**

SANCERRE GÉNÉRATIONS 2008
White | 2011 up to 2019   **96**

SANCERRE LA DEMOISELLE 2008
White | 2011 up to 2019   **90**

SANCERRE LA MOUSSIÈRE 2008
White | 2011 up to 2016   **90**

SANCERRE LA MOUSSIÈRE 2008
Red | 2011 up to 2013   **90**

SANCERRE LES ROMAINS 2008
White | 2011 up to 2014   **89**

VIN DE PAYS DES COTEAUX CHARITOIS 2007
Red | 2011 up to 2013   **89**

Older vintages
SANCERRE EDMOND 2006
White I 2011 up to 2022   **98**
Great fruit and superb minerality shine in this cuvée. Expressive, rich, and perfectly balanced, this 2006 shows great potential. The 2005 shows a perfect structure with an opulent profile, rich aromas of citrus, and a remarkable energy. This wine improves gradually, and remains a benchmark of the appellation.

SANCERRE GÉNÉRATIONS 2007
White I 2011 up to 2018   **98**
A very crystalline wine with great harmonious tension and remarkable precision both in structure and aromatic definition.

SANCERRE GÉNÉRATIONS 2006
Red I 2011 up to 2020   **96**
This intensely fruity wine has power, elegance, and fine tannins in a well-chiseled structure. It will pair particularly well with venison loin.

SANCERRE GRANDS-CHAMPS 2007
Red I 2011 up to 2020   **92**
Very elegant, with fresh, ripe fruit, this wine is likely to gain power and harmony with age. Sure to please.

SANCERRE LA DEMOISELLE 2006
Red I 2011 up to 2015   **92**
Full of black cherries, well rounded and integrated, this wine shows great silky tannins from the first taste.

SANCERRE LA MOUSSIÈRE 2007
Red I 2011 up to 2013   **90**
Full of citrus flavors with a hint of saline, this wine shows great precision.

SANCERRE LES ROMAINS 2007
White I 2011 up to 2015   **92**
White peach and saline flavors glide through the nose and create a sharp, yet opulent mouthfeel.

Red: 19.8 acres; pinot noir 100%. White: 98.8 acres; sauvignon blanc 100%. Annual production: 330,000 bottles

DOMAINE ALBANE ET BERTRAND MINCHIN

Saint-Martin
18340 Crosses
Phone 00 33 2 48 25 02 95
Fax 00 33 2 48 25 05 03
tour.saint.martin@wanadoo.fr

Vigneron Bertrand Minchin switched from growing grains to vines in the late 1980s—a wise decision, as it turns out. He settled in Morogues, in the Menetou-Salon appellation, diligently applying viticultural principles that he borrowed from his friend Alphonse Mellot "Junior." His style has grown more refined with every passing vintage, and his now handpicked reds rank among the finest offerings of the region. The white wines, also increasingly precise, are beautifully structured—witness the superb 2006s. Wines like these grow more complex with time. Since 2004, Minchin has produced a fine succession of bottlings from newly acquired parcels in Valençay. Convinced that his terroirs can bring out 100 percent expression in sauvignon, he rarely blends it with chardonnay (2006 was an exception): less rounded but more mineral, his sauvignon strongly reflects its origins around Selles-sur-Cher.

Recently tasted
MENETOU-SALON 2008
Red I 2011 up to 2015   **88**

MENETOU-SALON MOROGUE 2008
White I 2011 up to 2016   **89**

TOURAINE FRANC DU CÔT LIÉ 2008
Red I 2011 up to 2017   **91**

TOURAINE FRANC DU CÔT LIÉ 2007
Red I 2011 up to 2016   **91**

TOURAINE HORTENSE 2008
White I 2011 up to 2013   **89**

VALENÇAY CLAUX DELORME 2008
Red I 2011 up to 2013   **90**

VALENÇAY CLAUX DELORME 2008
White I 2011 up to 2013   **89**

Older vintages
MENETOU-SALON CÉLESTIN 2008
Red I 2011 up to 2019   **90**
Velvety, powerful, and precise tannins are proof of the great style of this wine, which can be cellared for many years.

MENETOU-SALON CÉLESTIN 2006
Red | 2011 up to 2015   90
Delightful, luminous, and silky, this Menetou shows good structure and spiciness, along with some black-cherry notes. When it reaches maturity, in a few years it will pair nicely with venison.

MENETOU-SALON HONORINE 2006
White | 2011 up to 2013   91
With an unctuous mouthfeel backed by some obvious citrus notes and fresh minerality, this wine pairs very nicely with lobster and truffles.

MENETOU-SALON MOROGUE 2007
White | 2011 up to 2015   89
Beautiful tension for this cuvée, which shows an elegant minerality.

TOURAINE FRANC DU CÔT LIÉ 2006
Red | 2011 up to 2015   90
This blend of côt and cabernet has great depth and a bright future, with firm, silky, and well-coated tannins. It will partner well with rabbit stew.

TOURAINE HORTENSE 2007
White | 2011 up to 2013   88
Beautiful definition for this saline and fresh white, which pairs well with mild goat cheese.

VALENÇAY CLAUX DELORME 2006
Red | 2011 up to 2015   90
This is the most accomplished of red Valençay cuvées. The silky and powerful mouthfeel has gained in complexity since bottling. Decant one hour before serving. Great with duck confit.

Red: 39.5 acres. White: 37.1 acres. Annual production: 200,000 bottles

DOMAINE DU CLOS NAUDIN
Ƶ Ƶ Ƶ Ƶ Ƶ

14, rue de la Croix-Buisée
37210 Vouvray
Phone 00 33 2 47 52 71 46
Fax 00 33 2 47 52 73 81
leclosnaudin.foreau@orange.fr

Philippe Foreau is a seasoned food and wine critic with a very discerning palate. He likes to chew over his opinions while savoring Jacky Dallais's refined cooking at the Petit-Pressigny restaurant. His acumen in matters of taste explains his exacting approach to grape growing and painstaking winemaking sensibilities. The Vouvrays he conjures out of the celebrated Les Perruches vineyard show deliciously fresh fruit and may be aged for decades. His wines are extraordinarily pure and an asset to any eminent dish, thanks to a hint of citrus zest that keeps things lively on the finish.

Recently tasted
VOUVRAY 2008
White | 2011 up to 2030   92

VOUVRAY 2008
Sweet White | 2011 up to 2030   95

Older vintages
VOUVRAY 2007
White | 2014 up to 2030   90
An austere yet promising wine that will improve with cellaring. Or drink it now with prawns.

VOUVRAY 2005
Sweet White | 2011 up to 2020   95
A lush nose of dried apricots and saffron gives way to a suave mouthfeel, backed by apricot overtones and fresh minerality. A radiant wine with exceptional structure.

VOUVRAY RÉSERVE 2005
Sweet White | 2011 up to 2020   96
The pure nose of candied apricots and gooseberries persists through a finely structured, opulent mouthfeel, framed by superlative freshness. This could rival the 1945 vintage.

White: 29.7 acres. Annual production: 55,000 bottles

DOMAINE OGEREAU

44, rue de la Belle-Angevine
49750 Saint-Lambert-du-Lattay
Phone 00 33 2 41 78 30 53
Fax 00 33 2 41 78 43 55
contact@domaineogereau.com
www.domaineogereau.com

This family estate is run today by Vincent Ogereau, whose cellars are located in the village of Saint-Lambert, opposite the museum of vines and wine. He owns holdings in three particularly fine vineyards: the Clos du Grand Beaupréau for Savennières; the Côte de la Houssaye for Anjou-Villages; and the Clos des Bonnes Blanches for Coteaux du Layon. This last site overlooks Saint-Lambert on the north bank of the River Layon and, vintage permitting, yields great dessert wines as in 2005. For the wine lover, a tour of Vincent Ogereau's cellars is like visiting Anjou in miniature, homing in on its finest crus.

Recently tasted

ANJOU PRESTIGE 2007
White | 2011 up to 2013   **87**

ANJOU-VILLAGES 2007
Red | 2011 up to 2013   **86**

ANJOU-VILLAGES CÔTE DE LA HOUSSAYE 2007
Red | 2011 up to 2013   **88**

COTEAUX DU LAYON SAINT-LAMBERT
CLOS DES BONNES BLANCHES 2007
Sweet White | 2011 up to 2017   **90**

SAVENNIÈRES CLOS DU GRAND BEAUPRÉAU 2007
White | 2011 up to 2014   **89**

Older vintages

ANJOU PRESTIGE 2006
White | 2011 up to 2013   **88**
This Anjou shows a well-balanced minerality and a smooth mouthfeel. The bitterness that is sometimes characteristic of chenin blanc is absent here. Fans will be delighted by this well-chiseled expression of the grape.

ANJOU-VILLAGES 2006
Red | 2011 up to 2013   **86**
With an initial impression of finesse, the fine tannins lead to a slightly narrow finish. This wine will benefit from further age. A pretty, seductive red!

COTEAUX DU LAYON SAINT-LAMBERT
CLOS DES BONNES BLANCHES 2005
Sweet White | 2011 up to 2025   **90**
This Coteaux du Layon is very sweet, but doesn't lack acidity. It is elegant and deep with tasty notes of roasted fruit. Enjoy it now, or cellar it for later.

SAVENNIÈRES CLOS DU GRAND BEAUPRÉAU 2006
White | 2011 up to 2015   **90**
This well-rounded Savennières shows no hardness. It expresses the fine pedigree of both the grape and the terroir with lovely notes of white flowers and beeswax. The 2006 displays soft fruit with fresh minerality.

Red: 31.9 acres; cabernet 92%, gamay 8%. **White:** 30.6 acres; chardonnay 2%, chenin 86%, grollau 11%, sauvignon blanc 1%. **Annual production:** 70,000 bottles

DOMAINE HENRY PELLÉ

Route d'Aubinges
18220 Morogues
Phone 00 33 2 48 64 42 48
Fax 00 33 2 48 64 36 88
info@henry-pelle.com
www.henry-pelle.com

Anne Pellé has run this estate since her husband's death in 1995. Ably supported by ebullient enologist Julien Zernott, she maintains high standards of viticulture and winemaking that make for a genuine selection of terroir-driven wines—witness the pronounced differences in expression among the whites. The Morogues is deliciously feisty while the Clos de Ratier, from the vineyard that made the reputation of Morogues, will develop more complexity as the vines grow older. Most of them date from the replanting of 1988, but some were replaced as recently as 2003. This is Kimmeridgian limestone par excellence, home to wines with a characteristic whiff of iodine. Clos des Blanchais remains a benchmark sauvignon, with an expansive mineral quality that will blow you away after three years' aging.

Recently tasted

MENETOU-SALON 2008
White | 2011 up to 2013   87

MENETOU-SALON CLOS DE RATIER 2008
White | 2011 up to 2014   91

MENETOU-SALON CLOS DES BLANCHAIS 2007
White | 2011 up to 2015   88

Older vintages

MENETOU-SALON CLOS DE RATIER 2006
White | 2011 up to 2015   89
The nose of saline-mineral notes persists through a sharp, linear mouthfeel. Wonderful paired with cod.

MENETOU-SALON CLOS DES BLANCHAIS 2006
White | 2011 up to 2015   90
A superb balance between white-peach flavors, pepper, and fresh minerality. The mouthfeel is taut and smooth at first taste, and finishes with a hint of saline.

MENETOU-SALON Z CŒUR DE CRIS 2006
Red | 2011 up to 2015   88
The structure of this wine outweighs its aromas. On the shy side for now, it will blossom with time.

Red: 29.7 acres; pinot 100%. White: 74.1 acres; sauvignon 100%. Annual production: 350,000 bottles

DOMAINE DU PETIT MÉTRIS

13, chemin de Treize Vents
Le Grand Beauvais
49190 Saint-Aubin-de-Luigné
Phone 00 33 2 41 78 33 33
Fax 00 33 2 41 78 67 77
domaine.petit.metris@wanadoo.fr
www.domaine-petit-metris.com

Domaine du Petit Métris is located in Saint-Aubin, planted in predominantly schistose soils that extend into three appellations: Coteaux du Layon, Chaume, and Quarts-de-Chaume. The property is run today by Hervé and Pascal Renou, whose family has owned this estate for nearly three hundred years. Half of their production goes into making dessert wines. The Les Tétuères parcel in the Chaume AOC produces wines that are fairly unapproachable when young and therefore grow that much more complex as they age.

Recently tasted

CHAUME LES TÉTUÈRES 2007
Sweet White | 2011 up to 2026   91

COTEAUX DU LAYON SAINT-AUBIN
CLOS DE TREIZE VENTS 2007
Sweet White | 2011 up to 2016   87

QUARTS-DE-CHAUME LES GUERCHES 2007
Sweet White | 2011 up to 2018   89

Older vintages

CHAUME 2005
Sweet White | 2011 up to 2025   86
This is a pleasant late-harvest wine with a balance of sugar and acidity; try it as an aperitif.

CHAUME LES TÉTUÈRES 2005
Sweet White | 2011 up to 2013   86
This pleasant cuvée displays very ripe yellow fruit and white-flower overtones. It would pair very well with a fruit tart.

CHAUME LES TÉTUÈRES 1997
Sweet White | 2011 up to 2030   92
1997 was a great vintage for the sweet wines of Anjou. It produced a supremely balanced, graceful Tétuères, with no cloying heaviness. It's nearing maturity, but your grandchildren will be able to enjoy it too.

QUARTS-DE-CHAUME LES GUERCHES 2006
Sweet White | 2011 up to 2017   88
This rather rich Quarts-de-Chaume is balanced by a bright, acidic finish.

Red: 19.8 acres; cabernet franc 65%, gamay 3%, grolleau 32%. White: 49.4 acres; chardonnay 1%, chenin blanc 99%. Annual production: 80,000 bottles

DOMAINE DES PETITS QUARTS

CA Douve
49380 Faye-d'Anjou
Phone 00 33 2 41 54 03 00
Fax 00 33 2 41 54 25 36

Jean-Pascal Godineau inherited his passion for sweet wines, thus three-quarters of his acreage are dedicated to making just that. In the vineyards he took a page from Henri Ramonteau's book, thinning the leaves and using similar methods of farming. The Bonnezeaux wines are of a stunning purity and richness, the cuvée Malabé being a touch more refined than the others.

Recently tasted

BONNEZEAUX LE MALABÉ 2007
Sweet White | 2011 up to 2018　　　　**95**

BONNEZEAUX LES MÉLERESSES 2007
Sweet White | 2011 up to 2026　　　　**94**

BONNEZEAUX LES MÉLERESSES 2005
Sweet White | 2011 up to 2026　　　　**92**

BONNEZEAUX VENDANGÉ GRAIN PAR GRAIN 2007
Sweet White | 2011 up to 2026　　　　**91**

Older vintages

BONNEZEAUX 2005
Sweet White | 2011 up to 2027　　　　**93**
This classic Bonnezeaux has lovely roasted-fruit notes and thick yet balanced sweetness.

BONNEZEAUX ÉLEVÉ EN FÛTS DE CHÊNE 2007
Sweet White | 2011 up to 2017　　　　**88**
This 2007 boasts notes of roasted fruit and intense aromas of dried currants.

BONNEZEAUX LE MALABÉ 2005
Sweet White | 2011 up to 2027　　　　**94**
Compared to the other Bonnezeaux, this 2005 has great sweetness with added finesse and freshness. Lots of caramel flavors lead to a staggeringly long finish.

BONNEZEAUX LE MALABÉ 1997
Sweet White | 2011 up to 2027　　　　**97**
An exceptional wine. The fruit aromas have become polished with time, allowing the emergence of caramel notes. A glorious, fresh finish, with pineapple and grapefruit overtones.

BONNEZEAUX VENDANGÉ GRAIN PAR GRAIN 2005
Sweet White | 2011 up to 2027　　　　**93**
Sweeter than the basic Bonnezeaux, with predominant aromas of caramel, quince, and candied fruit. Those who favor freshness will prefer the basic cuvée.

COTEAUX DU LAYON FAYE-D'ANJOU 2005
Sweet White | 2011 up to 2025　　　　**91**
The label may be a bit old-fashioned, but this wine is remarkable and very well-balanced.

Red: 37.1 acres; grolleau 33%, other 67%. **White:** 74.1 acres; chenin 100%. **Annual production:** 40,000 bottles

CHÂTEAU PIERRE-BISE

Château Pierre-Bise
49750 Beaulieu-sur-Layon
Phone 00 33 2 41 78 31 44
Fax 00 33 2 41 78 41 24
châteaupb@hotmail.com

Can you detect human feelings in wines? There is something particularly serene about this château's offerings, as if they reflect the spirit of their maker, Claude Papin, a man whose labors have created a vineyard in harmony with its biotope. A tasting at Château Pierre-Bise is always a sensation: such natural, precise wines, so entirely in tune with their terroir. The range is vast but infinitely recommended.

Recently tasted
ANJOU HAUT DE LA GARDE 2007
White | 2011 up to 2015   **89**

COTEAUX DU LAYON L'ANCLAIE 2007
Sweet White | 2011 up to 2017   **92**

COTEAUX DU LAYON LES ROUANNIÈRES 2007
Sweet White | 2011 up to 2018   **93**

QUARTS-DE-CHAUME 2007
Sweet White | 2011 up to 2028   **96**

SAVENNIÈRES CLOS LE GRAND BEAUPRÉAU 2007
White | 2011 up to 2018   **93**

SAVENNIÈRES LA ROCHE AUX MOINES 2007
White | 2011 up to 2016   **88**

Older vintages
ANJOU 2007
White | 2011 up to 2013   **88**
Made of chardonnay, sauvignon blanc, and chenin blanc; the linear and precise structure gives way to a pleasant, fresh finish. Great value!

COTEAUX DU LAYON 2007
Sweet White | 2011 up to 2017   **88**
Not yet integrated on the nose, but the structure is precise and dynamic, backed by supple body and beautiful fruit.

COTEAUX DU LAYON BEAULIEU
CLOS DE LA SOUCHERIE 2005
Sweet White | 2011 up to 2017   **92**
Made from a single picking. There are delicate notes of dried currants and spices on the finish. Harmonious overall.

COTEAUX DU LAYON CHAUME 2005
Sweet White | 2011 up to 2025   **95**
An exceptional Chaume, syrupy yet balanced by racy acidity. Notes of candied fruit give it complexity and magnitude.

QUARTS-DE-CHAUME 2005
Sweet White | 2011 up to 2017   **96**
An exuberant nose full of fresh fruits, pineapple, and citrus leads to a never-ending, deeply velvety and silky finish. A great dessert wine!

SAVENNIÈRES CLOS LE GRAND BEAUPRÉAU 2006
White | 2011 up to 2017   **90**
With more aromatic precision and acidic tension than the Clos de Coulaine from the same soil, this wine has lots of finesse.

SAVENNIÈRES LA ROCHE AUX MOINES 2006
White | 2011 up to 2013   **91**
Less vibrant than the Grand Beaupréau, this wine offers great magnitude backed by ultra-fine acidity. A pleasant bitterness boosts the finish.

SAVENNIÈRES LE CLOS DE COULAINE 2006
White | 2011 up to 2013   **89**
From deep, sandy soils, this 2006 has a full-bodied, velvety texture, with a well-defined aromatic expression.

Red: 44.5 acres; cabernet franc 50%, cabernet sauvignon 50%. White: 91.4 acres; chenin blanc 100%. Annual production: 150,000 bottles

DOMAINE VINCENT PINARD

42, rue Saint-Vincent
18300 Bué
Phone 00 33 2 48 54 33 89
Fax 00 33 2 48 54 13 96
vincent.pinard@wanadoo.fr

Specializing in reds, this domaine delivers some amazingly substantive wines. Pinot noir lovers will adore the cuvée Charlouise, made from very old vines; it has wonderful depth and exudes more black fruit than red. It is recommended that you wait at least five years from the vintage date so that the oak has time to integrate. The cuvée Domaine is more immediately accessible and is truly a pleasure. For the whites, the cuvée Florès is a springtime sauvignon blanc with floral notes and wonderful subtlety. The Nuance is aromatic and seductive with hints of white fruit.

Recently tasted

SANCERRE CHÊNE MARCHAND 2008
White | 2011 up to 2016   90

SANCERRE CUVÉE CHARLOUISE 2008
Red | 2011 up to 2017   92

SANCERRE FLORÈS 2008
White | 2011 up to 2013   90

SANCERRE VENDANGES ENTIÈRES 2008
Red | 2011 up to 2017   93

Older vintages

SANCERRE CHÊNE MARCHAND 2007
White | 2011 up to 2015   90
For the first time, the domaine has produced a cuvée from the mythical terroir of Bué. Citrus flavors open to a lovely balance and finish with notes of iodine.

SANCERRE CUVÉE CHARLOUISE 2006
Red | 2011 up to 2019   91
A delicious, fresh cherry nose with a deep, well-structured, and fleshy mouthfeel.

SANCERRE CUVÉE NUANCE 2007
White | 2011 up to 2013   88
A rich and unctuous wine with predominant exotic fruits.

SANCERRE FLORÈS 2006
White | 2011 up to 2013   88
A fresh, mouth-watering cuvée, with aromas of white flowers and hints of citrus. .

SANCERRE HARMONIE 2006
White | 2011 up to 2015   91
The predominant aromas of mango, cumin, and minerals are still very expressive and persist through the pure and soft, long-lasting palate, which has only refined with time.

SANCERRE PETIT CHEMARIN 2007
White | 2011 up to 2016   92
From limestone soils, this wine shows tremendous style with a vibrant crystalline structure, and would go nicely with toasted baguette and truffles.

SANCERRE VENDANGES ENTIÈRES 2006
Red | 2011 up to 2020   95
The superb structure of this wine currently outweighs the aromas, but it has incredible potential for aging.

Red: 11.1 acres; pinot noir 100%. **White:** 28.4 acres; sauvignon blanc 100%. **Annual production:** 100,000 bottles

MICHEL REDDE ET FILS

La Moynerie
58150 Saint-Andelain
Phone 00 33 3 86 39 14 72
Fax 00 33 3 86 39 04 36
thierry-redde@michel-redde.com
www.michel-redde.com

Thierry Redde still grows a few acres of Chasselas vines in memory of his great-grandfather Gustave Daudin. Chasselas was the traditional varietal used for Pouilly-sur-Loire wines and was notable for a fruit-iness that goes perfectly with cheese. Thierry also has his eye on the future, par-ticularly since son Sébastien arrived on the scene in 2005 and began to craft sharply focused, terroir-driven wines. Les Champs des Billons comes from Tracy sur Loire, reflecting all the elegance of clay and limestone soils known locally as "cail-lotes." The Les Cornets is sourced from Pouilly's Kimmeridgian marls ("terres blanches") that yield more opulent wines. Les Bois de Saint-Andelain comes from flint-clay soils and allies freshness with quite a soft mineral quality. The blended cuvée, La Moynerie, has a saline finish and is very drinkable.

Recently tasted

POUILLY-FUMÉ LES BOIS DE SAINT-ANDELAIN 2006
White | 2011 up to 2015   **88**

POUILLY-FUMÉ LES CHAMPS DES BILLONS 2006
White | 2011 up to 2014   **88**

POUILLY-FUMÉ LES CORNETS 2006
White | 2011 up to 2013   **86**

POUILLY-FUMÉ PETIT FUMÉ 2008
White | 2011 up to 2013   **88**

Older vintages

POUILLY-FUMÉ LA MOYNERIE 2006
White | 2011 up to 2013   **88**
A straightforward wine with predominant citrus and iodine flavors. It has already reached its peak and is best paired with shellfish.

POUILLY-FUMÉ LES BOIS DE SAINT-ANDELAIN 2005
White | 2011 up to 2015   **88**
The fresh mouthfeel becomes more asser-tive over time, showing saline minerality and white-peach flavors.

POUILLY-FUMÉ LES CHAMPS DES BILLONS 2005
White | 2011 up to 2015   **90**
This wine displays floral and mineral over-tones with an elegant, linear and clean struc-ture.

POUILLY-FUMÉ LES CORNETS 2005
White | 2011 up to 2013   **87**
This richer wine displays citrus overtones and will pair well with creamy chicken dishes.

POUILLY-FUMÉ MAJORUM 2005
White | 2011 up to 2015   **91**
With a few years in bottle, the rich and min-eral structure of this promising wine pairs beautifully with lobster.

POUILLY-FUMÉ PETIT FUMÉ 2007
White | 2011 up to 2013   **87**
Brimming with yellow-peach and iodine fla-vors, this wine is pure pleasure.

POUILLY-SUR-LOIRE GUSTAVE DAUDIN 2005
White | 2011 up to 2013   **87**
A well-made, sharp, and unctuous chasselas.

White: 97.6 acres; chasselas 3%, sauvignon blanc 97%. Annual production: 240,000 bottles

DOMAINE RICHOU

Chauvigné
49610 Mozé-sur-Louet
Phone 00 33 2 41 78 72 13
Fax 00 33 2 41 78 76 05
domaine.richou@wanadoo.fr
www.domainerichou.fr

Domaine Richou lies at the western end of the Aubance River, planted in sandstone and schistose soils that are worked to produce fresh and elegant wines. The Crémant Dom Nature is an agreeable aperitif and the Cuvée Rogeries is a fine expression of the Chenin grape. The Anjou-Villages Brissac is pure charm, and a far cry from those hard reds you sometimes find in these parts. The Les Violettes Coteaux de l'Aubance is the epitome of style—an inspiration perhaps for an appellation that is still in search of its identity.

Recently tasted

ANJOU LE CHAMP DE LA PIERRE 2008
Red | 2011 up to 2015   86

ANJOU-VILLAGES BRISSAC 2007
Red | 2011 up to 2015   88

COTEAUX DE L'AUBANCE LES VIOLETTES 2007
Sweet White | 2011 up to 2013   84

CRÉMANT DE LOIRE DOM NATURE 2005
Brut White sparkling | 2011 up to 2013 84

Older vintages

ANJOU GAMAY CHATELIERS 2007
Red | Drink now   84
This light gamay is easy to drink and pairs well with charcuterie.

ANJOU GAMAY CHATELIERS 2006
Red | 2011 up to 2013   84
Although smooth and fresh, this wine shows a bit of hardness for the moment.

ANJOU LES ROGERIES 2006
White | 2011 up to 2015   87
Framed by an acidity that carries through to a precise finish, this wine will gain in complexity with time.

ANJOU-VILLAGES BRISSAC 2005
Red | 2011 up to 2013   90
There are no hard tannins here, but an abundance of fruit, freshness, and elegance. This well-made red wine is worthy of imitation. Bravo!

ANJOU-VILLAGES GRANDES ROGERIES 2007
Semi-Dry White | 2011 up to 2013   87
This chenin blanc is intensely floral and fruity with a light, demi-sec sort of sweetness, which makes it very versatile with food. A precise finish with lemon overtones.

COTEAUX DE L'AUBANCE LES TROIS DEMOISELLES 2005
Sweet White | 2011 up to 2013   88
Nuances of quince and very ripe pear on the nose. The finish is typical of the Coteaux de l'Aubance: reasonably sweet and well balanced.

COTEAUX DE L'AUBANCE LES VIOLETTES 2005
Sweet White | 2011 up to 2025   91
A very pure Coteaux de l'Aubance with vibrant fruit, reasonable sweetness, and superlative balance.

CRÉMANT DE LOIRE DOM NATURE 2004
Brut White sparkling | 2011 up to 2013 86
Dom Nature is a reference to an even better-known Dom. Showing chenin character, without being aggressive, this refreshing sparkling wine shows some good volume on the palate.

Red: 32.1 acres; cabernet franc 57%, cabernet sauvignon 43%. **White:** 46.9 acres; chardonnay 20%, chenin 80%. **Annual production:** 130,000 bottles

CLAUDE RIFFAULT

Maison Sallé
18300 Sury-en-Vaux
Phone 00 33 2 48 79 38 22
Fax 00 33 2 48 79 36 22
claude.riffault@wanadoo.fr

Claude and Stéphane Riffault make text-book examples of white Sancerre: Les Chasseignes expresses all the mineral elegance of the clay and limestone soils ("cail-lotes") in the upper part of the slope. Les Boucauds is a powerful, splendidly mineral wine from southeast-facing Kimmeridgian marls ("terres blanches") farther down the slope, while the cuvée Les Pierrotes is sharper and comes from flinty soils. The unfined and unfiltered Antique boasts a deliciously rich constitution and originates from a limestone terroir very like the terres blanches. The red wines are also beautiful examples of Sancerre.

Recently tasted

SANCERRE ANTIQUE 2008
White | 2011 up to 2019   93

SANCERRE LES BOUCAUDS 2008
White | 2011 up to 2013   87

SANCERRE LES CHASSEIGNES 2008
White | 2011 up to 2014   90

Older vintages

SANCERRE ANTIQUE 2007
Red | 2011 up to 2015   90
Lovely fruit flavors are framed by tannins that have smoothed out nicely.

SANCERRE ANTIQUE 2007
White | 2011 up to 2015   92
This cuvée has beautiful structure that marries power and freshness.

SANCERRE LA NOUE 2007
Red | 2011 up to 2013   88
Along with precise aromas, this cuvée boasts complex red-fruit flavors.

SANCERRE LES CHASSEIGNES 2006
White | 2011 up to 2015   89
Mango and mineral notes glide through an exceptionally pure mouthfeel. Great balance of power and finesse.

SANCERRE LES PIERROTES 2007
White | 2011 up to 2015   90
Full of citrus and refreshing minerality.

Red: 8.6 acres; pinot noir 100%. White: 24.7 acres; sauvignon blanc 100%. Annual production: 90,000 bottles

DOMAINE DES ROCHELLES

Domaine Jean-Yves Lebreton
49320 Saint-Jean-des-Mauvrets
Phone 00 33 2 41 91 92 07
Fax 00 33 2 41 54 62 63
jy.a.lebreton@wanadoo.fr
www.domainedesrochelles.com

Jean-Yves Lebreton, now joined by son Jean-Hubert, operates a vineyard to the east of the Coteaux de l'Aubance appellation. Soils made of composed schists produce La Croix de Mission (tank-matured) and Les Millerits (wood-matured). Cabernet sauvignon is in its element here, regularly delivering mellow, ripe wines that lean toward great Médoc wines. On the dessert-wine side, the estate produces excellent Coteaux de l'Aubance that are a credit to the appellation. Bravo!

ANJOU-VILLAGES BRISSAC CROIX DE MISSION 2006
Red | 2011 up to 2013   88
The Brissac appellation produces structured reds, and this one is no exception. Although it is well balanced, it is worth holding onto a bit for greater enjoyment.

ANJOU-VILLAGES BRISSAC CROIX DE MISSION 2005
Red | 2011 up to 2013   90
2005 was a successful year. This is a highly linear, elegant wine, with a finish of fresh, pleasant tannins.

ANJOU-VILLAGES BRISSAC LES MILLERITS 2005
Red | Drink now   91
An elegant red, this 2005 is ripe, without showing any heaviness. Seductive, fine tannins lead to a finish of delicate stone-fruit notes.

COTEAUX DE L'AUBANCE 2005
Sweet White | 2011 up to 2025   90
This elegant and fresh Coteaux de l'Aubance shows an indisputable finesse without any heaviness. Medium-sweet, it pairs well with white meats or, even better, desserts.

COTEAUX DE L'AUBANCE AMBRE DE ROCHES 2005
Sweet White | 2011 up to 2025   92
This Coteaux de l'Aubance is reminiscent of a late-harvest wine. Notes of pure and intense roasted fruit are balanced by fresh minerality.

Red: 89 acres; cabernet 79%, grollau 10%, sauvignon 11%. White: 39.5 acres; chardonnay 16%, chenin 84%. Annual production: 150,000 bottles

DOMAINE DU ROCHER DES VIOLETTES

38, rue Rocher-des-Violettes
37400 Amboise
Phone 00 33 2 47 23 57 82
Fax 00 33 2 47 23 57 82

Xavier Weisskopf cut his teeth in one of the foremost Gigondas properties, the dynamic Château Saint-Cosme. He then settled near Amboise, where he now grows twenty acres of chenin and two acres of red varietals. All of his parcels are planted to ancient vines that were developed by massal selection. The 2005 was only his second vintage from this estate, but the white wines are already impressive and the red is extremely delicate. The fact that the vineyard is impeccably kept has a lot to do with it.

Recently tasted

MONTLOUIS-SUR-LOIRE TOUCHE-MITAINE 2007
White | 2011 up to 2021   **90**

TOURAINE 2007
Red | 2011 up to 2018   **88**

Older vintages

MONTLOUIS-SUR-LOIRE 2007
Sweet White | 2011 up to 2025   **92**
This lovely wine shows less precision than the dry whites from the same domaine, and its mineral structure lacks purity.

MONTLOUIS-SUR-LOIRE LA NÉGRETTE 2006
White | 2013 up to 2030   **91**
This classic Montlouis shows delicate floral overtones and a strikingly complex finish. A delicious wine made from seventy-year-old vines on clay and limestone soil.

MONTLOUIS-SUR-LOIRE PÉTILLANT NATUREL
Brut White sparkling | 2011 up to 2013   **88**
This lovely sparkling wine shows hints of biscuit and plenty of purity and grace.

MONTLOUIS-SUR-LOIRE TOUCHE-MITAINE 2006
White | 2011 up to 2013   **90**
This cuvée is produced from forty-year-old vines that are situated on clay and silica soil. This perfectly dry, sharp Montlouis displays lemon flavors framed by crystalline purity.

TOURAINE 2006
Red | 2011 up to 2013   **91**
This elegant, light red is well balanced and boasts a refined and delicate floral signature.

DOMAINE DES ROCHES NEUVES

56, boulevard Saint-Vincent
49400 Varrains
Phone 00 33 2 41 52 94 02
Fax 00 33 2 41 52 49 30
thierry-germain@wanadoo.fr
www.rochesneuves.com

Passionate, headstrong winegrower Thierry Germain has been working on the potential in this terroir since 1992. The vineyard is dedicated to the production of white Saumur and Saumur-Champigny wines, sourced from vines planted in tuffeau-based clay and limestone soils. Viticulture is now fully biodynamic. An energetic performance overall, aimed at freshness and peak ripeness.

Recently tasted

SAUMUR INSOLITE 2008
White | 2011 up to 2016   **92**

SAUMUR-CHAMPIGNY 2008
Red | 2011 up to 2017   **89**

SAUMUR-CHAMPIGNY FRANC DE PIEDS 2008
Red | 2011 up to 2016   **91**

SAUMUR-CHAMPIGNY TERRES CHAUDES 2008
Red | 2011 up to 2018   **90**

Older vintages

SAUMUR INSOLITE 2007
White | 2011 up to 2015   **92**
Plenty of elegance in this complex and refined cuvée. The Insolite has a fresh, mineral finish and is ready to drink now—although it will become softer and more voluptuous with age.

SAUMUR-CHAMPIGNY 2006
Red | 2011 up to 2013   **89**
Pleasant, with notes of red fruit, this Saumur-Champigny is fleshy and balanced. Ready to drink now.

SAUMUR-CHAMPIGNY MARGINALE 2006
Red | 2011 up to 2016   **92**
The 2006 Marginale is creamy, round, and very easy drinking. It has a fresh, precise finish that is very typical of Loire Valley wines.

SAUMUR-CHAMPIGNY TERRES CHAUDES 2007
Red | 2011 up to 2014   **90**
With a high level of consistency from year to year, this perfectly ripe 2007 shows a precise structure, a taut mouthfeel, and a delightfully fruity finish.

Red: 46.9 acres; cabernet franc 100%. White: 7.4 acres; chenin 100%. Annual production: 120,000 bottles

CLOS ROUGEARD

15, rue de L'Église
49400 Chacé
Phone 00 33 2 41 52 92 65
Fax 00 33 2 41 52 98 34

The village of Chacé is home to the twinkle-eyed, mustachioed Foucault brothers, producers of the best cabernet franc in the world, worthy of the very greatest Bordeaux. The vineyards are meticulously tended, the soils are tilled to perfection, and the pruning is exceptionally strict. Biodynamics seems to be in the genes here—something that happens unconsciously—and, despite partial aging in new barrels, the wines possess a legendary capacity for aging. The making of Rougeard's reputation is Les Poyeux, a seven-and-a-half-acre parcel of silica and limestone soils that produced the eponymous 1934 and 1937 vintages—intensely tannic wines that are still going strong today. Those intense tannins provide elegant sustenance for the wine's body while creating a sense of refinement that helps to bring out the aromas. The Clos du Bourg (vinified separately since 1988) is two and a half acres of clay-limestone soils planted to seventy-five-year-old vines. Aged in 100-percent new barrels, its wine combines strength with litheness and develops a lovely energy with precise, distinguished tannins. The other clay-limestone parcels account for a further eleven-acre area and supply the grapes for the Clos Rougeard, a wine of measured strength but with a structure that keeps it tightly wound. Rougeard white wines come from a three-acre area, the dry wines being considered the reference point for chenin blanc. Their mineral quality has a refinement that is revealed with age.

Recently tasted
SAUMUR BRÉZÉ 1999
White | 2011 up to 2030   **94**

SAUMUR-CHAMPIGNY CLOS DU BOURG 2006
Red | 2017 up to 2060   **95**

SAUMUR-CHAMPIGNY POYEUX 2007
Red | 2015 up to 2040   **93**

SAUMUR-CHAMPIGNY POYEUX 2004
Red | 2015 up to 2030   **93**

Older vintages
SAUMUR BRÉZÉ 2004
White | 2011 up to 2020   **94**
With notes of caramel and sweet cream butter, this is a great full-bodied wine with spicy notes and a long finish.

SAUMUR-CHAMPIGNY CLOS DU BOURG 2005
Red | 2015 up to 2030   **97**
Everything is harmonious here. The opulent flesh, paired with well-integrated tannins, leaves an impression of elegance and character.

SAUMUR-CHAMPIGNY CLOS DU BOURG 2004
Red | 2011 up to 2020   **94**
Black-fruit aromas laced with a very pure minerality, reminiscent of the 2002.

SAUMUR-CHAMPIGNY CLOS ROUGEARD 2003
Red | 2011 up to 2015   **89**
A straightforward, full-bodied wine with lots of freshness in the finish.

SAUMUR-CHAMPIGNY POYEUX 2006
Red | 2011 up to 2020   **93**
A slender ballerina of a wine, supported by great black-fruit intensity and beautifully drawn tannins.

SAUMUR-CHAMPIGNY POYEUX 2005
Red | 2012 up to 2050   **97**
Silky and taut, this 2005 is a successful balance of finesse and power.

CHÂTEAU DE LA ROULERIE

49190 Saint-Aubin-de-Luigne
Phone 00 33 2 41 54 88 26
Fax 00 33 2 41 68 94 01
philippemile.germain@wanadoo.fr
www.germain-saincrit.fr

Philippe Germain works some fifty acres of vines in Saint-Aubin, planted in gravelly clays over a schistose subsoil. What we have here is a coherent selection of good-quality wines at every price point. The entry-level chenin has the purity and profile expected of a well-made Anjou white wine. The Terrasses is rather more ambitious and captures the mineral expression of chenin grapes from this particular terroir. The reasonably priced Anjou red delivers a lushness that is sure to delight even the most demanding oenophile. The Chaume is a very well crafted dessert wine that does credit to the entire appellation.

Anjou 2006
White I 2011 up to 2013 **86**
A fresh Anjou blanc with a pure definition. Notes of citrus carry the finish.

Anjou 2006
Red I 2011 up to 2013 **88**
With everything you look for in a good Anjou, this 2006 is medium-bodied, fruit-forward, and has round and soft tannins.

Anjou Les Terrasses 2006
White I 2011 up to 2014 **88**
With lots of minerality and pure aromas, this chenin blanc is ready to drink now but has enough structure to age well.

Anjou Les Terrasses 2005
White I 2011 up to 2015 **90**
Aged in oak. Clean, with notes of cream and spices. Will pair well with Asian food.

Coteaux du Layon 2007
White I 2011 up to 2017 **89**
With notes of lemon and grapefruit intertwined with a sharp acidity, this Layon will age beautifully.

Coteaux du Layon Chaume 2005
Sweet White I 2011 up to 2025 **90**
Pure and powerful at once—textbook Chaume!

Red: 9.8 acres; cabernet franc 100%. White: 44.5 acres; chenin 100%. Annual production: 120,000 bottles

DOMAINE DE SAINT-JUST

Mollay
12, rue de la Prée
49260 Saint-Just-sur-Dive
Phone 00 33 2 41 51 62 01
Fax 00 33 2 41 67 94 51
infos@st-just.net
www.st-just.net

This Saumur-Champigny property in Saint-Just was started in 1996 by financier-turned-winegrower Yves Lambert and is now run by his son Arnaud, who previously worked for a famous cooper. It wasn't easy choosing among the different samples submitted because the entire range of wines is flawless. The exquisitely refined whites are a paean to delicacy, and the reds are made to the same high standard. Seriously old vines have a lot to do with it—so does talent.

Recently tasted

Saumur Coulée de Saint-Cyr 2007
White I 2011 up to 2015 **92**

Saumur Les Perrières 2008
White I 2011 up to 2015 **88**

Saumur-Champigny Clos Moleton 2007
Red I 2011 up to 2015 **90**

Saumur-Champigny Terres Rouges 2008
Red I 2011 up to 2013 **89**

Older vintages

Coteaux de Saumur Valboisière 2005
Sweet White I 2011 up to 2015 **92**
This sweet Coteaux de Saumur shows classic, chalky minerality. It's a lovely, fruit-forward wine.

Saumur Coulée de Saint-Cyr 2006
White I 2011 up to 2013 **92**
This is one of the best examples of Saumur blanc, with a velvety nose and a delicate, refined structure. It has been gracefully aged in oak, and shows great complexity with wonderful grapefruit aromas.

Saumur Coulée de Saint-Cyr 2005
White I 2011 up to 2015 **92**
With a velvety nose and a delicate, refined structure, this chenin blanc has begun to evolve and is reminiscent of a middle-aged sauvignon blanc.

Saumur Les Perrières 2007
White I 2011 up to 2013 **90**
Full of finesse and elegance, this Saumur has a taut, very pure structure with hints of citrus.

Saumur-Champigny Clos Moleton 2006
Red | 2011 up to 2015   **91**

This cuvée bears the name of the land parcel, and is also named Coulée de Saint-Cyr in its white version. Although cabernet franc often produces hard wines with pepper aromas, here the structure is silky and refined, with plenty of minerality in the 2007, which adds nice complexity. Will improve with some age.

Saumur-Champigny Clos Moleton 2005
Red | 2011 up to 2013   **92**

This cuvée bears the name of the land parcel. Although it often produces hard wines with pepper aromas, here the structure is silky and refined.

Saumur-Champigny Montée des Roches 2007
Red | 2011 up to 2013   **91**

This wine boasts a very refined structure, with velvety and elegant tannins, and with marked minerality showing in the 2007 vintage. Silky and delicate mouthfeel that will gain in complexity with age.

Red: 74.1 acres; cabernet franc 100%. White: 24.7 acres; chardonnay 40%, chenin blanc 60%. Annual production: 140,000 bottles

DOMAINE SAINT-NICOLAS

11, rue des Vallées
85470 Brem-sur-Mer
Phone 00 33 2 51 33 13 04
Fax 00 33 2 51 33 18 42
contact@domainesaintnicolas.com
www.domainesaintnicolas.com

It takes real talent and considerable effort to produce such great biodynamic wines from these difficult, unfertile soils near Les Sables d'Olonne. Price is high for the region; but then, in a blind tasting, the pinot noir could easily be mistaken for a Burgundy, the chenin could humble many a white Anjou, and the négrette could more than hold its own against a Fronton. When you have wines of this standard, price comparisons with other Fiefs Vendéens VDQS are hardly relevant.

Recently tasted
Fiefs Vendéens La Grande Pièce 2006
Red | 2011 up to 2015   **89**

Fiefs Vendéens Le Haut des Clous 2006
White | 2011 up to 2014

Fiefs Vendéens Le Poiré 2007
Red | 2011 up to 2013   **89**

Fiefs Vendéens Plante Gâte 2006
Red | 2011 up to 2013   **90**

Older vintages
Fiefs Vendéens Cabaret 2006
Red | 2011 up to 2013   **87**

This wine, full of red fruit, has a predominant flavor of cherries and a lovely freshness.

Fiefs Vendéens Jacques 2006
Red | 2011 up to 2013   **89**

Jacques was made from a combination of pinot noir and cabernet franc. The lovely Morello cherry and red-fruit nose leads to a powerful structure.

Fiefs Vendéens Le Poiré 2005
Red | 2011 up to 2013   **91**

Le Poiré is made from 100 percent négrette, a high-quality grape that is only grown in Fronton. Red-fruit and juniper berry characteristics in this refined, full-bodied wine are framed by lovely tannins.

Fiefs Vendéens Plante Gâte 2005
Red | 2011 up to 2013   **90**

The spice and black-cherry nose opens to a voluptuous and silky palate full of fresh, pure fruits.

Red: 61.8 acres; cabernet franc 10%, gamay 19%, négrette 6%, pinot noir 65%. White: 29.7 acres; chardonnay 37%, chenin blanc 47%, others 16%. Annual production: 80,000 bottles

DOMAINE DE LA SANSONNIÈRE

La Sansonnière
49380 Thouarcé
Phone 00 33 2 41 54 08 08
Fax 00 33 2 41 54 08 08

Wines often reveal the winegrowing sensibilities of their makers, and this one is a good example. Mark Angeli is a firm believer in biodynamics, and his wines boast a natural expression that is unequaled in the Loire. His cuvées are largely unsulfured so as to retain all of their luscious fruit, thus they should not be exposed to warm weather conditions. Knowing that the ultimate harmony between a vineyard and its surrounding biotope depends on human intervention, Angeli has created a breeding ground for fellow biodynamic believers, helping young and talented winegrowers to get started.

Recently tasted

VIN DE TABLE LA LUNE 2007
White | 2011 up to 2013   88

VIN DE TABLE LES VIEILLES VIGNES DES BLANDERIES 2007
White | 2011 up to 2013   86

VIN DE TABLE ROSÉ D'UN JOUR 2008
Sweet Rosé | 2011 up to 2013   86

Older vintages

LES FOUCHARDES 2006
Semi-Dry White | 2011 up to 2013   88
A classy and mineral Anjou Blanc, softened by some pleasant residual sugar. Think "demi-sec" when pairing with food.

MPF COTEAU DU HOUET 2006
Sweet White | 2011 up to 2013   88
Leaning toward a late-harvest wine, with honey, peach, apricot, and spicy notes on the finish.

MPF COTEAU DU HOUET 2005
Sweet White | 2011 up to 2025   89
Because it doesn't exceed 6.5° alcohol, this 2005 doesn't qualify as wine. It has a sweet wine profile with pear flavors on the finish.

VIN DE TABLE LA LUNE 2005
White | 2011 up to 2015   91
This dry-fermented Anjou Blanc shows a lovely volume. Classy wine with spicy, plump overtones. Recently, we had a 1997 that still tasted very fresh.

Red: 4.2 acres; cabernet sauvignon 100%. White: 8.2 acres; chenin 80%, grolleau gris 20%. Annual production: 15,000 bottles

COULÉE DE SERRANT

Château de la Roche-aux-Moines
49170 Savennières
Phone 00 33 2 41 72 22 32
Fax 00 33 2 41 72 28 68
coulee-de-serrant@wanadoo.fr
www.coulee-de-serrant.com

The Coulée de Serrant vineyard occupies a schistose headland on the northern bank of the Loire River, some eight miles from Angers. French writer Curnonsky, known as the prince of the gastronomes, ranked it among the five greatest wines in France. The vineyard has been fully biodynamic since 1980 and produces a wine that is difficult to appreciate when young since it takes time for this terroir to assert all of its character. Nicolas Joly, the proprietor, also makes the Savennières Les Vieux Clos and the Savennières–Roche aux Moines Le Clos de la Bergerie—both great wines built to last and worth waiting for. The quality of wines from the same vintage is still not as consistent as it should be.

Recently tasted

SAVENNIÈRES-COULÉE DE SERRANT 2007
White | 2011 up to 2025   97

SAVENNIÈRES-ROCHE AUX MOINES LE CLOS DE LA BERGERIE 2007
White | 2011 up to 2017   95

Older vintages

SAVENNIÈRES-COULÉE DE SERRANT 2006
White | 2011 up to 2018   88
With intense oak, oxidation and notes of baked apple, this 2006 shows much dry extract and lacks purity.

SAVENNIÈRES-COULÉE DE SERRANT 2005
White | 2011 up to 2028   91
Full-bodied, with ample structure, this wine is high in alcohol and powerful, with some creamy notes. It will be worthy of a better review in ten years' time.

SAVENNIÈRES-COULÉE DE SERRANT 2004
White | 2011 up to 2027   95
This great Coulée de Serrant is a quintessential expression of the grape and terroir. Its finish is remarkably long and lively.

SAVENNIÈRES-COULÉE DE SERRANT 2003
White | 2011 up to 2027   97
With a great honeyed texture and exceptional ripeness, this electric wine expresses bright fruit as well as terroir.

SAVENNIÈRES-COULÉE DE SERRANT 2002
White | 2011 up to 2015   88
A powerful, full-bodied wine, but lacking the freshness and energy of the 2003 or 2004.

SAVENNIÈRES-COULÉE DE SERRANT 1999
White | 2011 up to 2017   **88**
This wine has a lively mouthfeel, notes of
iodine and clove, and hints of botrytis concentration in the finish.

SAVENNIÈRES-ROCHE AUX MOINES LE CLOS DE
LA BERGERIE 2005
White | 2011 up to 2015   **90**
Behind the oaky notes are beautiful floral
aromas that suggest the presence of terroir
and leave you with a superlative impression.

SAVENNIÈRES LES VIEUX CLOS 2007
White | 2011 up to 2015   **88**
A very terroir-driven wine with an intense
mineral backbone and a lot of character.
Despite slightly neutral aromas, its broad
structure will develop and become more
complex.

White: 39.2 acres; chenin 100%. Annual production:
32,000 bottles

DOMAINE DE LA TAILLE AUX LOUPS

8, rue des Aitres
Husseau
37270 Montlouis-sur-Loire
Phone 00 33 2 47 45 11 11
Fax 00 33 2 47 45 11 14
latailleauxloups@jackyblot.fr
www.jackyblot.fr

The new generation of Montlouis owe a lot
to Jacky Blot. For nearly twenty years now
he has been building up the reputation of
an appellation that tends to languish in the
shadow of its more illustrious neighbor
Vouvray—but that nevertheless turns out
some surprisingly good wines. Jacky is still
hard at it today, looking to refine his style.

Recently tasted
MONTLOUIS-SUR-LOIRE 2007
Semi-Dry White | 2011 up to 2019   **87**

VOUVRAY CLOS DE VENISE 2007
Sweet White | 2011 up to 2025   **89**

Older vintages
MONTLOUIS-SUR-LOIRE 2005
Sweet White | 2011 up to 2025   **90**
This deep yet balanced Cuvée des Loups
marries sweetness and minerality, elegance
and charm.

MONTLOUIS-SUR-LOIRE LES DIX ARPENTS 2007
White | 2011 up to 2015   **89**
With sharp minerality and a precise finish,
this wine should soften up soon.

MONTLOUIS-SUR-LOIRE LES DIX ARPENTS 2005
White | 2011 up to 2015   **91**
A deep and opulent dry Montlouis, extremely
versatile with fish and white meat.

MONTLOUIS-SUR-LOIRE REMUS 2007
White | 2011 up to 2013   **90**
The nose and the mouthfeel are coherent,
with harmonious minerality backed by
appealing citrus overtones.

MONTLOUIS-SUR-LOIRE REMUS 2005
White | 2011 up to 2015   **90**
Although there isn't any residual sugar in
this Montlouis, the vanilla, caramel, and spicy
aromas leave you with a pleasant, opulent
impression.

MONTLOUIS-SUR-LOIRE ROMULUS 2005
Sweet White | 2011 up to 2025   **87**
A honey nose with hints of candied ginger,
followed by a voluptuous mouthfeel.

Montlouis-sur-Loire Triple Zéro
Brut White sparkling | 2011 up to 2013   **89**
Triple Zéro beats expectations. No chaptalization, no "liqueur de tirage" or "liqueur d'expédition." Refreshing, with slight toasted notes, and a free spirit.

Vouvray Tradition
Brut White sparkling | 2011 up to 2013   **90**
A great Loire Valley sparkling wine, this is seductive, refined, and lifted by lots of minerality.

White: 69.2 acres; chenin blanc 100%. Annual production: 140,000 bottles

DOMAINE VACHERON

1, rue du Puits-Poulton BP 49
18300 Sancerre
Phone 00 33 2 48 54 09 93
Fax 00 33 2 48 54 01 74
vacheron.sa@wanadoo.fr

This family domaine is jointly run by brothers Denis and Jean-Louis and their sons Jean-Dominique and Jean-Laurent. Close attention to viticulture is really paying off here. The first-class whites include the flagship cuvée, Les Romains, from one of the best-exposed sites in this appellation. The reds are as exemplary as ever and are particularly good with a meal if decanted beforehand.

Recently tasted
Sancerre 2008
White | 2011 up to 2013   **90**

Sancerre 2007
Red | 2011 up to 2014   **88**

Sancerre La Belle Dame 2008
Red | 2011 up to 2017   **93**

Sancerre Les Romains 2007
White | 2012 up to 2016   **90**

Older vintages
Sancerre 2005
Red | 2011 up to 2013   **88**
A mouth-watering, fruity wine—pure pleasure.

Sancerre 2007
White | 2011 up to 2013   **88**
Plenty of white peaches and iodine show in this easygoing, delicious cuvée.

Sancerre 2006
Red | 2011 up to 2013   **89**
A smooth and distinguished palate with plenty of red fruit mark this delectable wine.

Sancerre La Belle Dame 2007
Red | 2012 up to 2020   **92**
The tasty and deep tannins display the typical silkiness of the vintage's great reds. This wine has gained in magnitude.

Sancerre Les Romains 2006
White | 2011 up to 2020   **92**
The mineral flavors and the sharp mouthfeel of this wine make it one of the vintage's best reference points. A pure expression of this great terroir, it will develop complexity with time.

Red: 26.6 acres; pinot noir 100%. White: 84.6 acres; sauvignon blanc 100%. Annual production: 200,000 bottles

CHÂTEAU LA VARIÈRE

49320 Brissac
Phone 00 33 2 41 91 22 64
Fax 00 33 2 41 91 23 44
beaujeau@wanadoo.fr
www.châteaulavariere.com

This leading domaine in Brissac produces wines that are sometimes overly oaked; but its red wines, sourced from cabernet sauvignon plantings in the Clos de Boujets, are excellent. The Coteaux de l'Aubance, Quarts-de-Chaume, and Bonnezeaux are vinified in the same style so as to let the terroir show through. Tasting the three wines side by side is a good way to understand the subtle distinctions between them. All of these offerings are very well made, with the look and feel of great dessert wine thanks to pure, accomplished fruit expression.

Recently tasted

ANJOU-VILLAGES BRISSAC 2007
Red | 2011 up to 2013 **87**

BONNEZEAUX MELLERESSES 2007
Sweet White | 2011 up to 2026 **92**

COTEAUX DE L'AUBANCE CLOS DE LA DIVISION 2007
Sweet White | 2011 up to 2017 **90**

QUARTS-DE-CHAUME LES GUERCHES 2007
Sweet White | 2011 up to 2026 **92**

Older vintages

BONNEZEAUX MELLERESSES 2003
Sweet White | 2011 up to 2020 **92**
This Bonnezeaux is more expressive and ready to drink than the Quarts-de-Chaume. Fruit-forward, yet very complex.

COTEAUX DE L'AUBANCE CLOS DE LA DIVISION 2005
Sweet White | 2011 up to 2025 **91**
Notes of candied fruit and quince are perfectly balanced, with no overextraction.

COTEAUX DU LAYON CLOS DU SAVETIER 2005
Sweet White | 2011 up to 2013 **92**
This wine has great richness, a texture like satin, pretty fresh-fruit aromas, and a long finish.

QUARTS-DE-CHAUME LES GUERCHES 2005
Sweet White | 2011 up to 2017 **92**
An excellent fruit-forward Quarts-de-Chaume with a dense and velvety mouthfeel. Notes of fresh and candied apricots carry the finish.

Red: 168 acres; cabernet franc 70%, cabernet sauvignon 30%. White: 54.4 acres; chenin 100%. Annual production: 500,000 bottles

CHÂTEAU DE VILLENEUVE

Château de Villeneuve
3, rue Jean-Brevet
49400 Souzay-Champigny
Phone 00 33 2 41 51 14 04
Fax 00 33 2 41 50 58 24
jpchevallier@château-de-villeneuve.com
www.château-de-villeneuve.com

The vineyard here is planted in chalk, on a hillside in Souzay just south of the Loire River. Enologist Jean-Pierre Chevallier's so-called basic cuvées are always deliciously approachable. Les Cormiers is an exemplary white Saumur. The Vieilles Vignes is often closed as a young wine but remained accessible in 2005 thanks to the quality of the fruit that year. The linchpin to this domain's success is the Grand Clos, which needs to sit in the cellar for a while. A dependable producer of good-quality Saumur-Champigny wines.

Recently tasted

SAUMUR 2008
White | 2011 up to 2013 **88**

SAUMUR-CHAMPIGNY 2007
Red | 2011 up to 2013 **88**

SAUMUR-CHAMPIGNY GRAND CLOS 2006
Red | 2011 up to 2017 **91**

Older vintages

SAUMUR 2007
White | 2011 up to 2013 **90**
Gourmands won't want to wait for this great chenin blanc with spices and minerality, but patience will be rewarded too.

SAUMUR LES CORMIERS 2005
White | 2011 up to 2015 **91**
A fresher and more complex style than the cuvée du château, with a clean and pure finish.

SAUMUR-CHAMPIGNY 2006
Red | 2011 up to 2013 **88**
A classic Saumur-Champigny with minerality, intensity, and sweet tannins. Deeply textured.

SAUMUR-CHAMPIGNY GRAND CLOS 2005
Red | 2011 up to 2013 **91**
A dense and deep Saumur-Champigny that will reach its peak in a few years.

SAUMUR-CHAMPIGNY VIEILLES VIGNES 2006
Red | 2011 up to 2016 **90**
This cuvée is denser than the domaine cuvée, with velvety fruit and lots of minerality.

Red: 56.8 acres; cabernet franc 100%. White: 12.4 acres; chenin blanc 100%. Annual production: 150,000 bottles

CHÂTEAU YVONNE

12, rue Antoine Cristal
49730 Parnay
Phone 00 33 2 41 67 41 29
Fax 00 33 2 41 67 41 29
château.yvonne@wanadoo.fr

Château Yvonne is a small estate, equally divided between white plantings in Saumur and red plantings in Saumur-Champigny. The vines are organically grown and lovingly tended. White and red wine alike are made in a modern style, fermented and raised in large, new (or almost new) barrels, then tanked and bottled without filtration. The white wine is luxuriously but precisely matured and very fat. The red wine is nicely restrained, making do with what nature provides rather than aiming for excessive concentration. What they have in common is a crisp, invigorating finish.

Recently tasted
SAUMUR 2007
White | 2011 up to 2016   **92**
This is a great Saumur—impressively powerful in the mouth, with the typical chenin bitterness on the finish, and the underlying distinction of the terroir throughout.

SAUMUR-CHAMPIGNY CHÂTEAU YVONNE 2006
Red | 2011 up to 2016   **92**

Older vintages
SAUMUR 2005
White | 2011 up to 2015   **91**
The 2005 is strikingly more mineral than the 2004. A very structured wine; the fruit and wood are better integrated here. Overall, it leaves a surprisingly dynamic impression.

SAUMUR-CHAMPIGNY CHÂTEAU YVONNE 2005
Red | 2011 up to 2013   **92**
Quite powerful overall. No hardness or rough tannins here. Tasty, deep fruit overlays voluptuous tannins. A hit by the new generation of winemakers.

SAUMUR-CHAMPIGNY LA FOLIE 2007
Red | 2011 up to 2013   **89**
You might need to decant this wine in order to release some remaining effervescence. Wonderful, opulent, and silky fruit is backed by refined tannins. Among the high achievers of the appellation.

Red: 17.3 acres; cabernet franc 100%. White: 7.4 acres; chenin blanc 100%. Annual production: 30,000 bottles

Bettane & Desseauve
Selections for Provence and Corsica

Provence and Corsica

Provence

Historically wines from Provence have not been taken very seriously, largely because the bulk of their production consists of easy-drinking fruity rosés. The region's image has changed recently due to improved quality and the rosés' appeal to a large public. This should, as a result, draw more attention to their whites and reds, which are often unique expressions of little-known grape varieties (rolle and mourvèdre) and very elegant wines.

Appellation overview

• **Coteaux d'Aix, Coteaux des Baux, and Coteaux Varois:** Winemaking potential and style seem to depend more on the individual producer than on the characteristics of the appellations themselves. Some very interesting wines, but prices can be steep. Choose carefully.

• **Côtes de Provence:** A huge appellation producing wines that vary in quality and price. The 2004 vintage saw the arrival of the Côtes de Provence Sainte-Victoire AOC, covering an area with a particular terroir and climate that fully deserves its own appellation. The best Côtes de Provence tend to be white and rosé wines; too few of the reds show any real style to speak of. That said, the average quality of the wines has improved significantly over the past fifteen years.

• **Palette:** A tiny appellation near Aix-en-Provence—just two producers, but home to the classiest white and rosé wines in Provence.

• **Cassis:** A coastal appellation with the potential to produce delicately aromatic white wines. The best of them are well balanced and deliciously crisp, but performance across the board is very uneven.

• **Bandol:** The most qualitative of the Provence vineyards, especially for red wines. Mainly based on mourvèdre, Bandol reds are powerful and well structured with an elegant, delicately spicy, peppery nose—admirably age-worthy, too. The rosés are also increasingly well made, but the white wines, with some exceptions, are nothing special. The overall quality of the wines is generally improving and quite consistent across the appellation.

• **Bellet:** Another tiny appellation, this one in the highlands around Nice. Some of the whites are worth a look.

Corsica

With each new vintage we are reminded of the enormous potential of Corsican wines and the talent of their young, and not so young, winemakers, including more and more passionate, ambitious women. They are making elegant expressions of the sun-drenched local grape varieties; among the most eloquent examples—well worth seeking out—are sciacarello-based rosés and vermentino-based whites.

• **Patrimonio:** An appellation at the foot of the Cap Corse, concentrated around limestone slopes that mainly yield fat, complex white wines that bring out all the power and delicacy in the red nielluccio grape—more so than anywhere else on the island. The vineyards in the valley produce lighter wines.

• **Ajaccio:** A source of sciacarello-based red wines with a very distinctive expression in good vintages. The whites are improving.

• **Vin de Corse:** A generic AOC covering a wide variety of terroirs. There's still hugely underexploited potential in the narrow "pieves" (coastal valleys) of Calvi, with their granitic and clay-limestone sub-soils. Likewise, Porto Vecchio has too few producers to assert any real identity. By contrast, the vineyards of Figari in the wild, windswept south of the island are now enjoying a revival.

• **Muscat du Cap Corse:** Vineyards to the north of the island (including in Patrimonio), producing harmonious muscats noted for their perfume, good balance, and finesse.

• **Vins de Pays de l'Île de Beauté:** This is the Corsican Vins de Pays classification. The huge coastal plain that runs from Bastia to the south of Aléria has now been reorganized as a Vins de Pays zone, focusing on fashionable varietals such as the merlot, cabernet, and chardonnay. The chardonnays suffer from none of those heavy, buttery characteristics seen in too many of their southern French counterparts—suggesting that this grape must enjoy the windy, sunny climate here.

Provence Vineyards

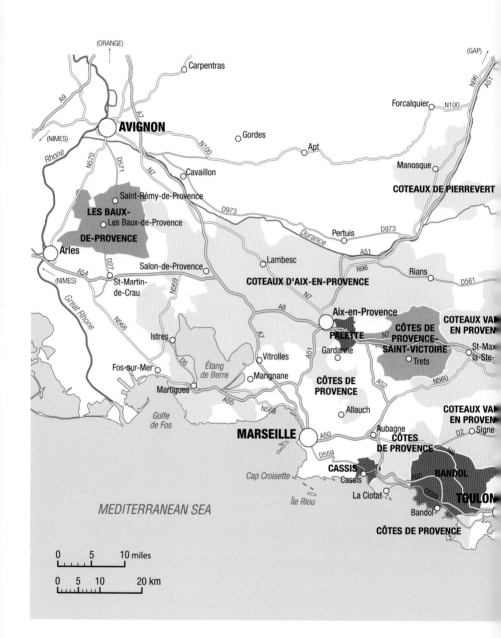

(ORANGE)

Carpentras

(GAP)

Forcalquier — N100

AVIGNON

(NIMES)

Rhone

Gordes

Apt

Manosque

COTEAUX DE PIERREVERT

Cavaillon

Saint-Rémy-de-Provence

LES BAUX-
Les Baux-de-Provence

DE-PROVENCE

Arles

Durance

Pertuis

D973

Salon-de-Provence

Lambesc

Rians

COTEAUX D'AIX-EN-PROVENCE

St-Martin-
de-Crau

(NIMES)

Great Rhone

A8

Aix-en-Provence

COTEAUX VA
EN PROVEN

Istres

PALETTE

CÔTES DE
PROVENCE-
SAINT-VICTOIRE

St-Max
la-Ste-

Fos-sur-Mer

Étang
de Berre

Vitrolles

Gardanne

Trets

Marignane

CÔTES DE
PROVENCE

Martigues

COTEAUX VA
EN PROVEN

Golfe
de Fos

Allauch

MARSEILLE

Aubagne

CÔTES
DE PROVENCE

Signe

Cap Croisette

CASSIS

Cassis

BANDOL

Île Riou

La Ciotat

TOULON

MEDITERRANEAN SEA

Bandol

CÔTES DE PROVENCE

0   5   10 miles

0   5   10   20 km

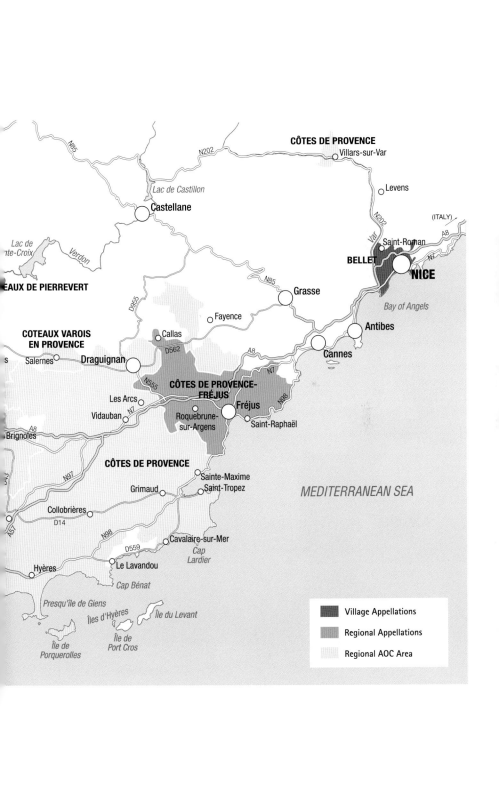

CÔTES DE PROVENCE
Villars-sur-Var

Levens

Lac de Castillon

Castellane

Verdon

(ITALY)

Lac de
nte-Croix

EAUX DE PIERREVERT

Var

Saint-Roman

BELLET

NICE

Grasse

Bay of Angels

Fayence

COTEAUX VAROIS
EN PROVENCE

Callas

Antibes

Salernes

Draguignan

Cannes

CÔTES DE PROVENCE-
FRÉJUS

Les Arcs

Vidauban

Fréjus

Brignoles

Roquebrune-
sur-Argens

Saint-Raphaël

CÔTES DE PROVENCE

Sainte-Maxime

Grimaud

Saint-Tropez

MEDITERRANEAN SEA

Collobrières

Cavalaire-sur-Mer

Cap
Lardier

Hyères

Le Lavandou

Cap Bénat

Presqu'île de Giens

Îles d'Hyères

Île du Levant

Île de
Porquerolles

Île de
Port Cros

	Village Appellations
	Regional Appellations
	Regional AOC Area

Corsica Vineyards

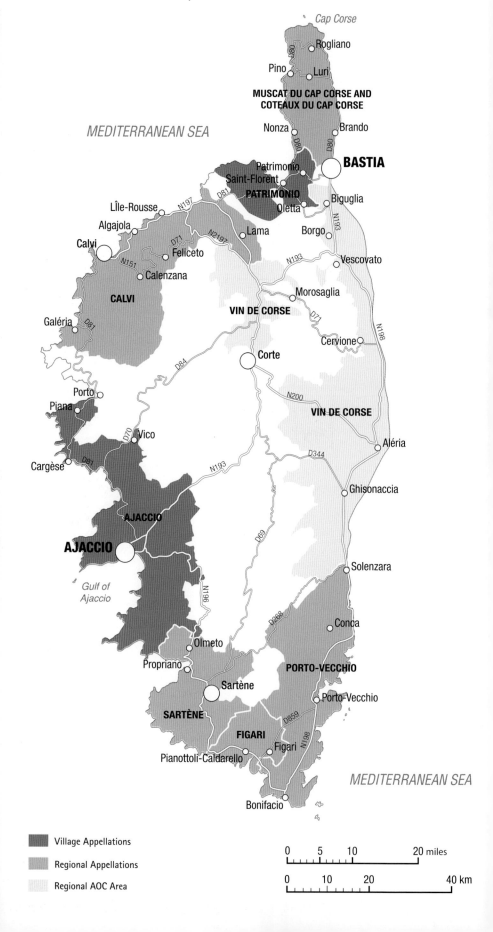

Cap Corse

Rogliano

Pino   Luri

**MUSCAT DU CAP CORSE AND
COTEAUX DU CAP CORSE**

MEDITERRANEAN SEA

Nonza   Brando

Patrimonio

BASTIA

Saint-Florent

PATRIMONIO

Oletta   Biguglia

L'Île-Rousse

Algajola   Lama   Borgo

Calvi

Feliceto   Vescovato

Calenzana

CALVI

Morosaglia

VIN DE CORSE

Galéria

Cervione

Porto   Corte

Piana

Vico

VIN DE CORSE

Cargèse

Aléria

AJACCIO

Ghisonaccia

AJACCIO

*Gulf of
Ajaccio*

Solenzara

Olmeto   Conca

Propriano

PORTO-VECCHIO

Sartène

Porto-Vecchio

SARTÈNE

FIGARI

Pianottoli-Caldarello   Figari

MEDITERRANEAN SEA

Bonifacio

Village Appellations

Regional Appellations

Regional AOC Area

0   5   10   20 miles

0   10   20   40 km

DOMAINE COMTE ABBATUCCI

Lieu-dit Chiesale
20140 Casalabriva
Phone 00 33 4 95 74 04 55
Fax 00 33 4 95 74 26 39
dom-abbatucci@wanadoo.fr
www.domaine-comte-abbatucci.com

This historic vineyard in the Ajaccio AOC boasts a unique collection of old, white local varietals that we hope may shortly help to increase the variety of vines in Corsica. Jean-Charles Abbatucci works the vineyard according to strict biodynamic principles, and the results are flawless. Recent bottlings are as supple, natural, and sleek as you would expect of a winemaker who leaves nothing to chance.

Recently tasted
CORSE COLLECTION 2006
White | 2011 up to 2013   88

Older vintages
AJACCIO FAUSTINE 2006
Red | 2011 up to 2014   90
Notes of stewed fruits on the nose, lovely sap, tasty, quite velvety tannins, complex, very original and interesting.

CORSE 2005
White | 2011 up to 2009   90
Fruity with ample citrus flavors, this is pure, long, very "terroir." Another wine, Confidentielle, is made from all the native varieties of the domaine, but the blend doesn't feel like all of the elements have completely fused.

CORSE FAUSTINE 2007
White | 2011 up to 2013   87
Pure, very subtle, but at the limit (not over) of oxidative character, with a light note of flor in the fashion of Manzanilla. It is a balanced, long, handsome gastronomical wine, very natural in its expression of terroir.

CORSE FAUSTINE 2007
Rosé | Drink now   85
Pale pink, very pure nose. A soft wine, very natural with little vatting, this has the finesse of a white, but drink it quite soon.

DOMAINE D'ALZIPRATU

20214 Vilia
Phone 00 33 4 95 62 75 47
Fax 00 33 4 95 60 32 16
alzipratu@wanadoo.fr

This excellent property is intelligently run by Pierre Acquaviva and takes its name from the superb convent of Alzipratu, known for its music festival launched by foremost Mahler specialist Baron Henry Louis de la Grange. The rather cool, hilly microclimate here, tempered by sea spray from the nearby Mediterranean, produces nervous, subtle wines—more incisive than most but less harmonious than those of the Clos Culombu run by Pierre's friend Étienne Suzzoni.

Recently tasted
CORSE-CALVI PUMONTE 2008
White | 2011 up to 2013   90

CORSE-CALVI PUMONTE 2007
Red | 2012 up to 2017   87

CORSE FIUME SECCU 2008
Rosé | 2011 up to 2013   86

Older vintages
CORSE-CALVI FIUME SECCU 2007
White | 2011 up to 2013   89
With light reduction and subtle aromas of pine and citron very typical of Balagne, this is complex and elegant with excellent freshness. Impeccable winemaking!

CORSE-CALVI FIUME SECCU 2006
White | 2011 up to 2013   90
Nice aromas of flowers and lemon, very classic in this area; balanced body, tasty, clean. Very successful.

CORSE FIUME SECCU 2007
Rosé | Drink now   85
Fruity, supple, very pleasant in the absence of strong terroir character. Nice summer quaffing wine!

CORSE FIUMI SECCU 2006
Red | 2011 up to 2013   86
Delicate color, nose of aromatic garrigue herbs, true to type, long, not too dry in its tannins, deft, quite long; well done!

Red: 86.5 acres. White: 12.4 acres. Annual production: 80,000 bottles

DOMAINE ANTOINE ARENA

20253 Patrimonio
Phone 00 33 4 95 37 08 27
Fax 00 33 4 95 37 01 14
antoine.arena@wanadoo.fr
www.antoine-arena.fr

Of all the Corsican winemakers, Antoine Arena was always the most determined to get his wines known outside the island itself—and so he should be. His white vermentinu, muscat, and bianco gentile wines, whether dry or late-harvested, are the work of an artist and count among our personal benchmarks. There aren't many Mediterranean wines that can boast such splendid aromas or forceful character. We are glad to see today that Antoine's sons share their father's ideals!

Recently tasted

PATRIMONIO CARCO 2008
White | 2011 up to 2016   92

PATRIMONIO HAUTS DE CARCO 2008
White | 2011 up to 2016   95

Older vintages

CORSE BIANCO GENTILE 2007
White | 2011 up to 2013   90
Magnificent extract, nose of flower honey, general sensation of superior harmony, although a little less nervy and bright on the finish than the vermentino.

MUSCAT DU CAP CORSE 2007
White | 2011 up to 2013   89
Golden color, very rich nose, harmonious, candied citrus fruit, unctuous and long: this is very successful in its balance, but one would have imagined something more grandiose, with more superripe, dried grape character, in the fashion of Nicrosi Muscatellu, for the glory of this domaine. This bottling may still exist but not on the market!

PATRIMONIO CARCO 2007
White | 2011 up to 2013   95
Very pale color, nose of vine flowers. Gracious, crystalline, and long; one senses this was made with exceptional grapes and underwent a vinification worthy of the wine. It has a terroir expression more common to vermentino! An exceptional wine.

PATRIMONIO CARCO 2007
Red | 2011 up to 2017   92
This has a generosity of fruit that is more classic for the appellation than Morta Maïo's, this time with the traditional notes of rabbit fur and hide that give this wine its reputation, but very balanced with aromas of red fruit and the aromatic herbs of Corsica's maquis. Complete and very promising, one of the most elegant wines ever vinified by Antoine Arena.

PATRIMONIO CARCO 2006
Red | 2011 up to 2013   90
Magnificent bouquet of citron, imposing body, exemplary purity and finesse of terroir expression, high grape maturity.

PATRIMONIO GROTTE DE SOLE 2007
White | 2011 up to 2013   92
Pale color, stunning nose of white fruit, very voluptuous texture without heaviness, stunning, natural, with an authoritative finish: a marvelously produced wine and highly recommended!

PATRIMONIO GROTTE DE SOLE 2005
White | 2011 up to 2013   92
Ultraripe grapes, ample nose, generous, almost roasted, majestic constitution: this is a wine of great personality that might displease some.

PATRIMONIO GROTTE DI SOLE 2007
Red | 2011 up to 2019   90
A red as personal as the white (not a surprise), with a solid structure and almost excessively strong aromas and tannic mass. This confirms the value of the vintage.

PATRIMONIO MORTA MAÏO 2007
Red | 2011 up to 2017   90
With a dark color and pure, magnificent redberry nose, this is showing incredibly in the glass, the tannins energetic but not harsh, the fruit exceptionally pure.

Red: 11.1 acres; nielluccio 100%. White: 23.5 acres; muscat petits grains 35%, vermentino 65%. Annual production: 50,000 bottles

DOMAINE DE LA BÉGUDE

La-Cadière-d'Azur
83330 Le Camp-du-Castellet
Phone 00 33 4 42 08 92 34
Fax 00 33 4 42 08 27 02
domaines.tari@wanadoo.fr
contact@domainedelabegude.fr
www.domainedelabegude.fr

The owners of this immense estate (upwards of 1,250 acres, of which only forty-three are under vine and including a large olive grove) were once famous throughout Bordeaux for their decades-long ownership of Château Giscours. The property has been restored since its acquisition by Guillaume Tari in 1996, and the improvement is noticeable in red and rosé wines alike.

Recently tasted
BANDOL 2006
Red | 2012 up to 2018   88

BANDOL LA BRULADE 2006
Red | 2011 up to 2018   86

BANDOL LA BRULADE 2005
Red | 2011 up to 2013   86

Older vintages
BANDOL 2007
Rosé | Drink now   88
A great, elegant wine, powerful, balanced and profoundly Bandol. What charm, in a salty style that is as suited to the aperitif hour as it is the dinner table!

BANDOL 2005
Red | 2011 up to 2017   93
Deeply colored, this wine offers a powerful bouquet combining quality oak and intensely fruity notes. Great, enveloping wine, brilliantly constructed with perfectly ripe tannins, emphasizing what could be done well in 2005. Long, spicy finish.

BANDOL 2004
Red | 2011 up to 2018   92
Deeply colored, this wine expresses itself with a powerful bouquet, linking quality oak and intensely fruity notes. It is enveloping and high-class, brilliantly structured with perfectly ripe tannins and a long and peppery finish. Grand future, grand wine.

BANDOL LA BRULADE 2004
Red | 2011 up to 2017   93
Fiery with intense black fruits, this wine's length is stunning. The tannins are charming and profound, and the finish is long.

Annual production: 65,000 bottles

CHÂTEAU DE BELLET

440, chemin de Saquier
06200 Nice
Phone 00 33 4 93 37 81 57
Fax 00 33 4 93 37 93 83
châteaudebellet@aol.com

This winery and its Renaissance château have been in the same family since the fifteenth century. Located in Séoules, on the steep hillsides above Nice, the vineyards benefit from the sea spray that tempers the summer heat. The Baron G. bottlings in white and red showcase the savoir-faire of the property. The white is made from vermentino with a bit of chardonnay, the red from the braquet and folle noir grape varieties with a little grenache added in. Whether white or red, both wines are of exceptional quality and are the wines of choice in the mansions of the Côte d'Azur. The rosé is one of the most original ever. This domaine is clearly at the top of its game.

BELLET BARON G. 2007
White | 2011 up to 2013   91
A rolle-based wine of stunning purity. The aromas are very noble with notes of white flowers, apricots, and violets. When the wood on the finish integrates, this will become one of the great white wines of the south.

BELLET BARON G. 2005
White | 2011 up to 2013   95
An exceptional wine based on rolle, with perfect purity and noble and distinct aromas of white flowers, apricot, bergamot, and violets. It recalls Condrieu a bit, though with no trace of viognier here. Aristocratic finish.

BELLET CHÂTEAU DE BELLET 2005
Rosé | 2011 up to 2013   90
Pale gold in color and scented with fruit and flowers, this is rich, savory, balanced, ripe and fresh on the palate, with volume.

BELLET ROSE DE BELLET 2006
Red | 2011 up to 2015   95
With very refined tannins and aromatic freshness, this wine justifies having protected these slopes from real estate development. It exhales notes of garrigue, lavender, and a lovely bouquet of red fruits. An extraordinary expression of naturalness and simplicity. The structure is a little reminiscent of great Burgundy in texture. Bravo!

Red: 7.4 acres; braquet 10%, folle noire 60%, grenache noir 30%. White: 7.4 acres; chardonnay 10%, rolle 90%. Annual production: 18,000 bottles

CLOS CANARELLI

Tarabucetta
20114 Figari
Phone 00 33 4 95 71 07 55
Fax 00 33 4 95 71 07 55
closcanarelli2a@orange.fr

Yves Canarelli caused a stir in the small winemaking community of Figari when he introduced the methods employed by top winemakers and commenced fermenting his white wines in oak. The style at the start was similar to famous Bandol producer Domaine OTT, but results today justify a level of skill that is unique in Corsica. Kudos in particular to Yves Canarelli for vinifying his wines in borrowed facilities, pending the building of his own cellars.

Recently tasted
CORSE-FIGARI 2008
White | 2011 up to 2013   92

CORSE-FIGARI 2008
Rosé | 2011 up to 2013   90

CORSE-FIGARI 2007
Red | 2011 up to 2017   87

Older vintages
CORSE-FIGARI 2007
White | 2011 up to 2013   95
Once again, the top wine and the model! Perfect integration of wood, controlled oxygenation yielding the finest notes of acacia flowers and lemon tree; this is ethereal, elegant, perfection from the tip of the tongue to the middle of the palate: a rapture! Be careful not to "shock" the wine and serve at 55 to 57°, no colder.

CORSE-FIGARI 2007
Rosé | Drink now   88
Pale color, clean nose, precise, delicate, smooth on the palate, but without the raciness and complexity of vermentino! Nice quaffing wine, but the producer could still give it more personality.

CORSE-FIGARI 2006
White | 2011 up to 2013   97
Wonder of wonders! And to imagine how a wine so elegant, ethereal, and refined could be produced in the furnacelike climate of Figari. A model for all of the south of France.

CORSE-FIGARI 2006
Rosé | Drink now   90
A treat: a smooth wine, velvety, full of red-fruit flavor but without exaggeration and very pure on the finish; this bottle will be easy to finish!

CORSE-FIGARI 2006
Red | 2011 up to 2014   88
This has a deep color, notes of bay leaf but, alas, also fox and fur on the nose, and an imposing body with assertive tannins. It is a wine of style and character, if certain undesirable yeasts do not intrude. Store the bottle in a cool cellar.

CORSE-FIGARI 2005
Red | 2011 up to 2015   87
Drier and less velvety than the 2006, but cleaner on the nose, tannins a little drying. One senses the terroir and quality fruit, but the élevage did not bring the wine to the peak of its potential.

VIN DE TABLE DE FRANCE
Rosé | 2011 up to 2013   88
Nonvintage due to local wine rules, but coming from the 2007 vintage, this is quite powerful, made from ripe grapes, with a dry character. We don't understand what turned off local tasters to this wine. But the Clos has more finesse and personality in its balance of maturity and élevage. A sweet version of this cuvée is less convincing.

Red: 54.4 acres; grenache 8%, nielluccio 46%, sciacarello 25%, syrah 21%. White: 14.8 acres; vermentino 100%. Annual production: 100,000 bottles

CLOS CAPITORO

Pisciatella (route se Sartène)
20166 Porticcio
Phone 00 33 4 95 25 19 61
Fax 00 33 4 95 25 19 33
info@clos-capitoro.com
www.clos-capitoro.com

Ajaccio's granitic hillsides are likely the most unique in Corsica, in that they are ideally adapted to the king of the indigenous red grapes, the sciacarello. This is a grape capable of expressing aromas of both aromatic herbs from the Corsican countryside "maquis" and the iodine notes of the Mediterranean sea spray. But this variety is unpredictable and difficult to vinify with modern equipment (destemmers and pumps, which tend to damage the grapes and bring out the drying tannins) and above all, it doesn't make deeply colored wines. It is therefore necessary to be part artist and willing to go against the grain of current fashions to believe in it: Clos Capitoro, having a very complex terroir, excels in making red and rosé sciacarello. Only the whites, though very pure, are not yet complex enough to measure up to the best.

Recently tasted
AJACCIO 2008
White I 2011 up to 2013   86

AJACCIO 2007
Red I 2011 up to 2015   85

Older vintages
AJACCIO 2007
White I 2011 up to 2013   85
Pale, very slightly reduced on the nose, very clean, fine aromatics, nice saline tension, finish still reserved with the bitterness of youth. To drink in a year.

AJACCIO 2007
Rosé I Drink now   84
A bright pink-fuchsia color, this is technically fruity with red-currant flavors. It is well-made, but offers little terroir character.

AJACCIO 2006
Red I 2011 up to 2013   84
Quite full, spicy, soft and clean, but this could have more diversity of fruit.

AJACCIO GRANDE RÉSERVE 2005
Red I 2011 up to 2015   88
Nice fullness, firm tannins, much more "proper" on the nose than those from Ajaccio. Long, classic.

Red: 86.5 acres; grenache 20%, nielluccio 16%, sciacarello 64%. White: 37.1 acres; vermentino 100%.
Annual production: 150,000 bottles

DOMAINE DE LA COURTADE

83400 Île de Porquerolles
Phone 00 33 4 94 58 31 44
Fax 00 33 4 94 58 34 12
domaine@lacourtade.com
www.lacourtade.com

La Courtade is one of the few Porquerolles wineries that really do fly the flag for Provence. The L'Alycastre cuvée, whether rosé or white, is a wine lover's delight at a reasonable price. The château-labeled bottles develop greater depth of flavor thanks to more concentrated substance but do take a while to show their stuff. La Courtade is a quality-driven estate that knows how to get the best out of schistose terroirs and sea mists, which join together here to add a refreshing mineral quality.

Recently tasted
CÔTES DE PROVENCE 2006
White I 2011 up to 2013   89

CÔTES DE PROVENCE L'ALYCASTRE 2008
White I 2011 up to 2013   86

CÔTES DE PROVENCE L'ALYCASTRE 2008
Rosé I 2011 up to 2013   84

Older vintages
CÔTES DE PROVENCE 2007
Rosé I Drink now   91
White gold, nodding toward onion-skin in color. Complex on the nose with lots of charm on the palate, this is long, with a suave, rich character.

CÔTES DE PROVENCE 2004
Red I 2011 up to 2013   89
Soft in texture, this elegant red doesn't lack charm, with long, profound tannins.

CÔTES DE PROVENCE L'ALYCASTRE 2007
Rosé I Drink now   88
White gold, lightly salmon-hued. Very expressive, this wine is delicate with a refined, rich finish.

CÔTES DE PROVENCE L'ALYCASTRE 2006
White I 2011 up to 2013   90
This very refreshing white is rich, with delicate anise notes and charming length.

Red: 42 acres; mourvèdre 97%, syrah 3%. White: 32.1 acres; rolle 100%.

DOMAINE CULOMBU

Chemin San-Petru
20260 Lumio
Phone 00 33 4 95 60 70 68
Fax 00 33 4 95 60 63 46
culombu.suzzoni@wanadoo.fr
www.closculombu.fr

Little by little the superb 210-acre vineyard, which is spread over many different types of soils, is becoming a winery not to be missed. Étienne Suzzoni makes wines with flair, whether white, red, or rosé, all made with the same clean fruit expression, the same elegance, and the same purity, which for the reds wasn't necessarily easy. The 2006 reds are exceptional, among the most balanced ever made here.

Recently tasted
CORSE CLOS CULOMBU 2008
White | 2011 up to 2014   **92**

CORSE RIBBE ROSSE 2008
White | 2011 up to 2013   **85**

Older vintages
CORSE 2007
White | 2011 up to 2013   **90**
With delicate citrus fruit aromas, transparent and crystalline, this is a triumph of the granitic soils. It has great length on magnificent notes of citrus fruit. The modern vinification resulted in a bitterness that is well controlled and softened. Superb.

CORSE 2006
Red | 2011 up to 2013   **87**
Again a beautifully fruity wine, velvety and complex with tannins adapted to the style of the day, and good flavor that favors pleasure over austerity. Quite long, with successful use of oak.

CORSE CLOS CULOMBU 2007
White | 2011 up to 2013   **91**
Color a little more pronounced; irresistable aromas of candied citron. A wine of texture, one of the greatest expressions of Vermentino in the world.

CORSE CLOS CULOMBU RIBBE ROSSE 2006
Red | 2011 up to 2013   **88**
Magnificient fruitiness, unctuous texture, deep licorice and anise flavor, integrated tannins, civilized: this is an example of the direction the local reds should follow.

Annual production: 200,000 bottles

DUPÉRÉ-BARRERA

254, rue Robert-Schumann
83130 La Garde
Phone 00 33 4 94 23 36 08
Fax 00 33 4 92 94 77 63
vinsduperebarrera@hotmail.com
www.duperebarrera.com

The young couple Emmanuelle Dupéré and Laurent Barrera have launched into high-class Provence and Rhone wines with all the care of a pair of haute-couture designers. Owners of their own vineyard, they also buy grapes from handpicked suppliers and produce fabulously natural wines. Their Nowat (hear "No watt") bottlings, for instance, are handmade using no electricity, from handpicked, foot-trodden, basket-pressed grapes. No added yeast, no chaptalization, no acidification, no fining, and no filtration! A stunning range of wines from a brilliant newcomer to the world of Provence wines.

Recently tasted
CÔTES DE PROVENCE NOWAT 2006
Red | 2011 up to 2013   **88**

CÔTES DE PROVENCE TRÈS LONGUE MACÉRATION 2006
Red | 2011 up to 2013   **91**

Older vintages
BANDOL INDIA 2005
Red | 2011 up to 2013   **89**
A pleasant Bandol, this has a refined texture and aromas of stone fruits. The tannins are fine and intensely rich.

CÔTES DE PROVENCE LA PROCURE LES VIGNES DE SAINT-SAUX 2006
Red | 2011 up to 2013   **88**
This 2006 was produced from 100 percent cinsault. The fruit is very pleasant. A successful, jovial wine ready to drink now, with a full, long finish.

CÔTES DE PROVENCE NOWAT 2005
Red | 2011 up to 2013   **89**
Produced without electrical equipment, Nowat is a blend of old-vine syrah, cabernet sauvignon, carignan, and mourvèdre. It displays structure and great promise, with a full finish and quite refined tannins.

CÔTES DE PROVENCE TRÈS LONGUE MACÉRATION 2004
Red | 2011 up to 2013   **89**
The depth demonstrates that there is more than just power in this very clean wine. It is still closed but the potential is great.

Red: 16.1 acres; carignan 13%, cinsault 13%, grenache 37%, mourvèdre 37%. White: 1.2 acres; ugni blanc 100%. Annual production: 30,000 bottles

DOMAINE DE GAVOTY

Le Grand Campdumy
83340 Cabasse
Phone 00 33 4 94 69 72 39
Fax 00 33 4 94 59 64 04
domaine.gavoty@wanadoo.fr
www.gavoty.com

Domaine Gavoty is located in Cabasse, deep in the heart of Provence. It makes remarkable red, white, and rosé wines, our particular favorites being the rosés, though we also have a weakness for the whites. The most accomplished offerings are those named after French music critic Bernard Gavoty's nom de plume: Clarendon. The delectably soft Clarendon rosé possesses a finesse rarely seen in Provence. Note that the estate still has a few old vintages in stock.

Recently tasted

CÔTES DE PROVENCE CLARENDON 2008
Rosé | 2011 up to 2014   **92**

CÔTES DE PROVENCE CLARENDON 2008
White | 2011 up to 2015   **92**

Older vintages

CÔTES DE PROVENCE CLARENDON 2007
White | 2011 up to 2014   **92**
The fresh pineapple, grapefruit, and lemon notes are inviting in this tasty Côtes de Provence. The purity is crystalline. What a finish, of a precision that could well provide inspiration in Provence!

CÔTES DE PROVENCE CLARENDON 2007
Rosé | 2011 up to 2013   **91**
The Clarendon bottling always displays a more velvety character than the basic bottling. The toughest rosé critics will be astonished by a wine with so much sincerity and grace.

CÔTES DE PROVENCE TRADITION 2007
White | 2011 up to 2013   **88**
Pretty nuances of pineapple and grapefruit very much pleased us in this basic cuvée. It is fresh and pure, very correct.

CÔTES DE PROVENCE TRADITION 2007
Rosé | Drink now   **87**
This elegant rosé is pleasant in the mouth. It offers pretty, delicate extract that yields a wine that is easy to drink yet elegant.

Red: 86.5 acres. White: 24.7 acres. Annual production: 230,000 bottles

DOMAINE DE GIOIELLI

20248 Macinaggio
Phone 00 33 4 95 35 42 05
Fax 00 33 4 95 35 36 97

This is the heart of traditional Corsica, home to wines that perfectly express the particular climate of the Cap Corse. The muscats are triumphant, but even more original is the celebrated Rappu, a Vin Doux Naturel, originally from the Island of Elba—one of the classiest aperitifs we know of. Blended from muscat and the rare aleatico varietal, Rappu is cask-matured for seven years. This one is as remarkable as ever, but so, too, are the flawlessly classical muscats!

Recently tasted

CORSE-COTEAUX DU CAP CORSE 2008
White | 2011 up to 2013   **86**

CORSE RAPPU
Soft Amber | 2011 up to 2013   **92**

Older vintages

CORSE 2007
Rosé | Drink now   **87**
Pale color. This is a powerful wine, ripe, ample, and harmonious, with a strong personality leaning toward the candy style, but without heaviness. Wine of character.

CORSE-COTEAUX DU CAP CORSE 2007
White | 2011 up to 2013   **88**
Fat, powerful, unctuous, ripe grape maturity, very marked terroir, made for aging.

CORSE RAPPU
Soft Amber | 2011 up to 2050   **90**
Again an exceptional Rappu, with the perfect rancio notes of walnuts, with just the right bitterness to balance the sugar. An inimitable speciality.

MUSCAT DU CAP CORSE MUSCAT 2006
Sweet White | 2011 up to 2013   **90**
Great, sweet richness, profound aromas of honey and citron, great length; sumptuous!

Red: 6.2 acres. White: 6.2 acres. Annual production: 55,000 bottles

DOMAINE DU JAS D'ESCLANS

3094, route de Callas
83920 La-Motte-en-Provence
Phone 00 33 4 98 10 29 29
Fax 00 33 4 98 10 29 28
mdewulf@terre-net.fr
www.jasdesclans.fr

This vineyard looks out over the Mediterranean and is named after the "jas" (sheepfold, in local patois) that once stood here. Vines kissed by sea spray yield a basic cuvée in three colors that does more than hold its own. The special selection Cuvée de Loup was created by the estate's latest owners, Matthieu and Gwenaëlle de Wulf, a genial couple who took over in 2002 and introduced organic farming methods. Named a Provence classified growth in 1955, this estate continues to perform at the level appropriate to its status.

Recently tasted

CÔTES DE PROVENCE 2008
White | 2011 up to 2013   87

CÔTES DE PROVENCE COUP DE FOUDRES 2004
Red | 2011 up to 2013   86

CÔTES DE PROVENCE CUVÉE DU LOUP 2008
White | 2011 up to 2013   90

CÔTES DE PROVENCE CUVÉE DU LOUP 2008
Rosé | 2011 up to 2013   86

CÔTES DE PROVENCE CUVÉE DU LOUP 2007
Red | 2011 up to 2013   84

Older vintages

CÔTES DE PROVENCE 2007
White | Drink now   90
As in 2006, this wine's Provençal origin seems to flirt with the sauvignons of Pessac-Léognan. This elegant wine will please many, thanks to the subtle notes of fresh pineapple that suit its charm. It does not have the depth of the Loup cuvée, but its freshness is brilliant.

CÔTES DE PROVENCE 2007
Rosé | Drink now   87
This rosé is not without similarities to the white cuvées, with their brilliant fruit. An aromatic bomb, it will please everyone, including those who regard rosés with polite condescension.

CÔTES DE PROVENCE 2007
Red | 2011 up to 2013   86
Intensely aromatic, this fruity, vanilla-toned red displays immediate charm.

CÔTES DE PROVENCE CUVÉE DU LOUP 2007
White | 2011 up to 2013   90
The Loup cuvée is produced in the same spirit as the domaine bottling. Smoky and fresh pineapple notes suit its charm.

CÔTES DE PROVENCE CUVÉE DU LOUP 2007
Rosé | 2011 up to 2013   82
Very mango and candied fruit on the nose, refined in body, with stunning length. Fine work.

CÔTES DE PROVENCE CUVÉE DU LOUP 2006
White | 2011 up to 2013   88
Again a little marked by the wood, this wine's Provençal origin seems to flirt with the sauvignons of Pessac-Léognan. This wine will please many thanks to the subtle notes of fresh pineapple that suit its charm.

CÔTES DE PROVENCE CUVÉE DU LOUP 2006
Red | 2011 up to 2013   86
With vanilla, butter, and black-fruit notes, this wine offers a texture that is a bit candied, but profound.

CÔTES DE PROVENCE CUVÉE DU LOUP 2005
Red | 2011 up to 2013   90
2005 produced here an appetizing and flavorful red that still retains fresh butter aromas. With deep black-fruit flavors, its texture is velvety and ethereal.

Red: 98.8 acres. White: 19.8 acres. Annual production: 250,000 bottles

YVES LECCIA

Morta Piana
20232 Poggio-d'Oletta
Phone 00 33 4 95 30 72 33
Fax 00 33 4 95 30 72 33
leccia.yves@wanadoo.fr
www.yves-leccia.com

Yves Leccia left the family estate in 2005 (it has since been taken over by his sister Annette) but he retained holdings in the most schistose part of E Crocce. Yves remains uniquely talented among Corsican winemakers, turning out wines with much more modern labels that bear his name. All of them showed exceptional finesse and full body.

Recently tasted
PATRIMONIO O 2008
Rosé | 2011 up to 2013   **90**

Older vintages
PATRIMONIO 2007
Rosé | Drink now   **88**
Nice, classic color, remarkable fruit. This has an angelic character and the vivaciousness and richness of a true Patrimonio.

PATRIMONIO 2007
Red | 2011 up to 2017   **92**
Remarkable aromatic complexity: citron, fennel, mint. A full-bodied, accomplished style, and a model for all young Corsican winegrowers.

PATRIMONIO 2006
White | 2011 up to 2013   **92**
With a handsome, spicy nose of overripe fruit, this is rich, unctuous, and long, with the power of northern Corsican terroirs!

PATRIMONIO 2005
Red | 2011 up to 2013   **87**
Deeply colored, long and supple despite its power, this has fine tannins and less aromatic nuances than Clos Teddi 2006, still needing time to evolve. Very pleasant texture.

VIN DE PAYS DE L'ILE DE BEAUTÉ Y.L. 2007
Red | 2011 up to 2013   **86**
Very fruity and fat with notes of prune, violet, and licorice, this was very well vinified, demonstrating generosity without aggressiveness, which is the way of the future for Corsican wines.

Red: 29.7 acres. White: 7.4 acres. Annual production: 70,000 bottles

DOMAINE LECCIA – ANNETTE LECCIA

Morta Piana
20232 Poggio d'Oletta
Phone 00 33 4 95 37 11 35
Fax 00 33 4 95 37 17 03
domaine.leccia@wanadoo.fr
www.domaineleccia.fr

Annette Leccia took over this family estate after her brother's departure, retaining the bulk of the magnificent limestone terroirs (the famous Petra Bianca) at the heart of Patrimonio. The red wines always were particularly good from this producer, and they remain that way today. The muscats owe a lot to precise vinification, boasting exceptional radiance and aromatic purity. The wines are as technically well made as ever but the aromas and texture are just a shade more impersonal than before. That said, they still rank among the best on the island!

Recently tasted
MUSCAT DU CAP CORSE 2008
Sweet White | 2011 up to 2013   **86**

Older vintages
MUSCAT DU CAP CORSE 2007
Sweet White | 2011 up to 2013   **86**
A technological wine, clean and elegant with precise floral aromas, but without really enough super-ripeness to provoke emotion.

PATRIMONIO 2007
White | 2011 up to 2013   **85**
Very ripe and spicy, this has quite marked lactic notes, to the detriment of the fruit, but it is fat, long, and rich.

PATRIMONIO 2007
Rosé | Drink now   **86**
Showing excellent winemaking, this is delicately fruity, pure, clean, and flavorful.

PATRIMONIO 2006
White | 2011 up to 2013   **92**
Nice, complex aroma, with the notes of citrus one would expect; very pure, long, elegant body. Remarkably masterful winemaking.

Red: 20 acres. White: 12.1 acres. Annual production: 60,000 bottles

CHÂTEAU MINUTY

Route de la Berle
83580 Gassin
Phone 00 33 4 94 56 12 09
Fax 00 33 4 94 56 18 38
infominuty@orange.fr
www.châteauminuty.com

Château Minuty once formed part of nearly 5,000 acres of vines that blanketed the Saint-Tropez peninsula more than a century ago. But time took its toll, and the vineyard had virtually disappeared by the time Jean-Étienne and François Matton bought the Napoleon III château and its chapel in 1936. They painstakingly rebuilt a 185-acre vineyard, planted in clay and mica-schist soils. The estate was awarded classed status in 1955—a position it retains to this day, thanks to its consistently good Provence wines.

Recently tasted
CÔTES DE PROVENCE PRESTIGE 2008
Rosé I 2011 up to 2013   87

CÔTES DE PROVENCE PRESTIGE 2007
Red I 2011 up to 2013   87

Older vintages
CÔTES DE PROVENCE PRESTIGE 2007
Rosé I Drink now   89
This rich, racy rosé, primarily grenache blended with a bit of tibouren, is velvety with a hedonistic, sensual finish.

CÔTES DE PROVENCE PRESTIGE CUVÉE M 2005
Red I 2011 up to 2013   88
Refined and reserved in aromas, Minuty's red is a profound, velvety wine that is lightly tannic but round, expressing a Provençal charm. This Cuvée M is 90 percent mourvèdre.

CÔTES DE PROVENCE PRESTIGE CUVÉE M 2004
Red I 2011 up to 2013   88
With a tight, dominant structure of spices and black fruit, this is a wine to age.

VIN DE PAYS DU VAR BLANC ET OR 2007
White I 2011 up to 2013   87
Blanc et Or blends sauvignon blanc, viognier, and roussanne. Very aromatic and flattering, it is to be drunk for its fruit, which is prolonged by its minerality.

Red: 148.3 acres; cabernet sauvignon 10%, carignan 5%, cinsault 5%, grenache 40%, mourvèdre 5%, syrah 15%, tibouren 20%. White: 37.1 acres; clairette 5%, rolle 40%, sémillon 35%, ugni 20%. Annual production: 500,000 bottles

DOMAINE ORENGA DE GAFFORY

Morta Majo
20253 Patrimonio
Phone 00 33 4 95 37 45 00
Fax 00 33 4 95 37 14 25
domaine.orenga@wanadoo.fr
www.domaine-orengadegaffory.com

This domaine is by far the largest producer in Patrimonio, with vineyards in the village as well as on the Conca d'Oro including the Clos San-Quilico vineyard. Due to the size of the property, inevitable compromises have been made that don't allow for the purest expression of terroir, but the wines are always very well made, focused, balanced, and widely available.

Recently tasted
CORSE-COTEAUX DU CAP CORSE 2008
Sweet White I 2011 up to 2013   90

CORSE RAPPO
Soft Red I 2011 up to 2013   88

MUSCAT DU CAP CORSE IMPASSITO 2008
Syrupy White I 2011 up to 2013   87

PATRIMONIO 2008
Rosé I 2011 up to 2013   86

PATRIMONIO FELICE 2007
White I 2011 up to 2013   90

Older vintages
MUSCAT DU CAP CORSE IMPASSITO 2006
Sweet White I 2011 up to 2013   90
A splendid "passito" of superripe, dried fruit, this is rich, candied, long and complex, supported by a magnificent acidity.

PATRIMONIO FELICE 2006
White I 2011 up to 2013   87
Straw color. Light evolution toward petrol, classic to wines aged to adequate maturity. Tender, fine, quite long, true to type—and ready to drink.

PATRIMONIO FELICE 2006
Red I 2011 up to 2015   85
Spicy nose, firm wine, straightforward, articulated with precise tannins: this is not excessively fruity or complex, but it is solid and well-made.

Red: 89 acres; grenache 10%, niellucio 90%. White: 46.9 acres; muscat 25%, vermentino 75%. Annual production: 300,000 bottles

DOMAINE DU COMTE PERALDI

Chemin du Stiletto
20167 Mezzavia
Phone 00 33 4 95 22 37 30
Fax 00 33 4 95 20 92 91
info@domaineperaldi.com
www.domaineperaldi.com

This leading Ajaccio estate has never looked better: having rethought its wine-making processes, it now produces red, white, and rosé wines that are supremely refined—with all the elegance to be expected of their plainly Burgundy-styled bottles. We thought the Clos du Cardinal 2003 and 2005, along with the basic blend, were highly accomplished expressions of the famous sciacarello grape. Not much color here, but the texture has a refinement strongly reminiscent of good pinot noir.

Recently tasted
AJACCIO 2007
Red | 2011 up to 2015   88

CORSE 2008
Rosé | 2011 up to 2013   88

Older vintages
AJACCIO 2007
White | 2011 up to 2013   86
Supple but rich and strong with a pleasant delicacy in its citron aromas, this is round, balanced, and clean.

AJACCIO 2007
Red | Drink now   84
Orange-rose, handsome fruit, quite rich but finishes on a lightly sweet note. A shame! But many will like it.

AJACCIO 2006
Red | Drink now   88
Balanced, impeccable, and fresh, with finesse, clarity, and a moderate sensation of alcohol, this is a nice quaffing wine.

AJACCIO 2005
Red | 2011 up to 2013   90
Not very dark but very pure on the nose, with subtle notes of aromatic herbs. On the palate it is soft and refined, the opposite of what many imagine!

AJACCIO CLOS DU CARDINAL 2003
Red | 2011 up to 2018   88
Clear color, open nose, spicy, elegant, soft but unctuous texture: here is a generous wine with finesse. Its unique balance is due to its producer and to sciacarello.

Red: 98.8 acres; carignan 10%, cinsault 12%, grenache 3%, nielluccio 7%, sciacarello 68%. White: 24.7 acres; vermentino 100%. Annual production: 250,000 bottles

CHÂTEAU DE PIBARNON

410, chemin de la Croix-des-Signaux
83740 La Cadière-d'Azur
Phone 00 33 4 94 90 12 73
Fax 00 33 4 94 90 12 98
contact@pibarnon.fr
www.pibarnon.fr

Château de Pibarnon is an eighteenth-century Provençal farmhouse, set at an altitude of 900 feet in an amphitheater of vines that face the Mediterranean—conditions that perfectly suit the capricious mourvèdre and bring out all of its finesse. Created by geological upheaval, this valuable and very ancient terroir was snapped up by the count Saint-Victor in 1978. Since then it has grown from twelve to roughly 120 acres and continues to improve under the count's son, Éric. The rosé is unfailingly one of the most savory in Provence. The red wine is robust when young but develops a range of subtle, typically Mediterranean aromas, together with a tannic quality that places it among the greatest of all the French wines.

Recently tasted
BANDOL 2008
Rosé | 2011 up to 2013   92

BANDOL 2007
Red | 2011 up to 2016   90

Older vintages
BANDOL 2007
Rosé | 2011 up to 2013   87
Elegant but lacking the exceptional dynamics of the 2006, this Pibarnon offers breadth and richness on the palate. The mourvèdre requires a little patience, ideally.

BANDOL 2006
White | 2011 up to 2013   86
The white 2006 is a honeyed wine with volume. Quite elegant, it shows velvety softness.

BANDOL 2005
Red | 2011 up to 2017   93
Racy and full-bodied, this elegant Bandol is still in its infancy yet exhibits a rare harmony. The finish combines intense pleasure with finesse.

BANDOL 2004
Red | 2011 up to 2015   90
The aromas of black fruit, spice, resin, and garrigue carry this powerful 2004. The enveloping tannins merit a little patience.

Red: 108.7 acres; grenache noir 10%, mourvèdre 90%. White: 9.8 acres; bourboulenc 40%, clairette 50%, others 10%. Annual production: 180,000 bottles

DOMAINE PIERETTI

Santa-Severa
20228 Luri
Phone 00 33 4 95 35 01 03
Fax 00 33 4 95 35 01 03
domainepieretti@orange.fr

This one was the guide's big surprise from Corsica. Red, white, or rosé, Lina Venturi's wines mark him out as one of the greatest stylists on the island. His wines are exquisitely formed, especially the reds, with an old-vines bottling that achieves some of the most staggeringly refined tannins we have ever tasted! What Venturi coaxes out of this coastal, schistose terroir can equal and even surpass the best Patrimonios. His delicately aromatic whites are just as delicious. Corsican winemakers have plainly got the wind behind them now!

Recently tasted

CORSE-COTEAUX DU CAP CORSE 2008
White | 2011 up to 2013   90

CORSE-COTEAUX DU CAP CORSE
SÉLECTION VIEILLES VIGNES 2007
Red | 2011 up to 2013   87

MUSCAT DU CAP CORSE 2008
Sweet White | 2011 up to 2013   86

Older vintages

CORSE A MURTETA 2006
Red | 2011 up to 2013   90
With better color than the normal red and excellent body and complexity of fruit, this shows successful winemaking. It is a quality red without rusticity.

CORSE-COTEAUX DU CAP CORSE 2007
White | 2011 up to 2014   86
Very pale and smooth, with nice, natural malic acidity, subdued fruit, and pleasant aperitif-like notes of mint. It is relaxed, and slightly lacking richness.

CORSE-COTEAUX DU CAP CORSE
VIEILLES VIGNES 2004
Red | 2011 up to 2014   92
This has a stunning fullness and especially silky tannins, extremely rare in Corsica, and proper for well-ripened grenache.

Red: 8.6 acres; grenache 35%, niellucio 65%. White: 6.8 acres; muscat à petits grains 45%, vermentino 55%. Annual production: 45,000 bottles

CHÂTEAU PRADEAUX

676, chemin des Pradeaux
83270 Saint-Cyr-sur-Mer
Phone 00 33 4 94 32 10 21
Fax 00 33 4 94 32 16 02
châteaupradeaux@wanadoo.fr
www.château-pradeaux.com

Figurehead of the appellation, this winery has been in Cyrille Portalis' family since 1752. The property only produces one red and one white, under the name of the château. Mourvèdre dominates here as it accounts for nearly 90 percent of the red-grape plantings. There is a bit less in the rosé, where they also blend in cinsault. The wines are often quite austere when young, but numerous older vintages show surprising similarities to great Bordeaux bottles, even though they share neither similar climates, grapes, nor terroirs.

Recently tasted

BANDOL 2008
Rosé | 2011 up to 2013   85

BANDOL 2005
Rosé | 2011 up to 2013   84

Older vintages

BANDOL 2007
Rosé | 2011 up to 2013   88
Profound and long in the mouth, this is a rosé of character, vinous and requiring a little patience. One must wait for this wine.

BANDOL 2004
Red | 2011 up to 2020   89
At this stage, the tannins of this red are more approachable than those of the 2003, with a complement of freshness on the palate.

BANDOL 2003
Red | 2011 up to 2020   86
The year 2003, marked by a particularly warm summer, yielded a profound red with lightly dry tannins. Guaranteed to age well and stun in a few years.

BANDOL 2002
Red | 2011 up to 2013   87
This is a challenging red. The body is unctuous and refined for a difficult vintage but the élevage doesn't seem beyond reproach. Time will permit the wine to express itself. We will wait impatiently for other Pradeaux vintages.

Red: 51.9 acres; grenache noir 5%, mourvèdre 95%. Annual production: 50,000 bottles

DOMAINE BERNARD RENUCCI

20225 Feliceto
Phone 00 33 4 95 61 71 08
Fax 00 33 4 95 38 28 74
domaine.renucci@wanadoo.fr
www.domaine-renucci.com

Bernard Renucci is the rising star of the Calvi winegrowing area. His well-groomed vineyard is planted to an ideal mix of niellucio and sciacarello, and he handles vinification exceptionally well. All of his wines (red, white, and rosé) exhibit admirable finesse and purity of aroma, with the Vignola wines squeezing out a touch more vinosity from these granitic soils. Prices are surprisingly reasonable.

Recently tasted
CORSE-CALVI 2008
Rosé I 2011 up to 2013   88

CORSE-CALVI CUVÉE VIGNOLA 2008
White I 2011 up to 2013   84

Older vintages
CORSE-CALVI 2007
Rosé I 2011 up to 2013   84
With very pronounced color, powerful red-fruit aromas, and a finish rich in alcohol but with a sensation of strawberries, this is a bit sweeter than expected, given the local granite. Excessive wine.

CORSE-CALVI CUVÉE VIGNOLA 2007
White I 2011 up to 2013   88
Remarkable aromatic freshness. Nervy wine, clean, spicy, long; very well done.

CORSE-CALVI CUVÉE VIGNOLA 2006
White I 2011 up to 2013   93
This has a big nose, subtly floral, and a marvelously balanced body with exquisite fruitiness. It shows all the aristocratic charm and delicacy of great vermentinos and will be a revelation for those who don't know them.

CORSE VIGNOLA 2006
Red I 2011 up to 2013   85
Lovely color, supple wine, fruity, nimble, tannins without dryness, pleasant finish but far from having the complexity of the whites and rosés.

VIN DE TABLE-VIN DOUX 2006
Sweet White I 2011 up to 2013   91
A remarkable dessert wine with generous fruit and notes of candied apricot, long and complex, demonstrating admirable vinification.

Red: 32.1 acres. White: 9.8 acres. Annual production: 80,000 bottles

DOMAINE DE RIMAURESQ

Route de Notre-Dame-des-Anges
BP 26
83790 Pignans
Phone 00 33 4 94 48 80 45
Fax 00 33 4 94 33 22 31
rimauresq@wanadoo.fr
www.rimauresq.fr

Located near the highest point of the Massif des Maures, the layers of schist and quartz that make up the Rimauresq terroirs enable them to make very complete wines. Two wines are produced here; one bears the name of the château, and the other, labeled R de Rimauresq, is a blend of the best terroirs and has slightly more density. They have recently made efforts to raise the quality of the entry-level wines, and the line-up is now homogeneous in all three colors, which is rare!

Recently tasted
CÔTES DE PROVENCE 2008
Rosé I 2011 up to 2013   90

CÔTES DE PROVENCE 2008
Red I 2011 up to 2013   89

CÔTES DE PROVENCE QUINTESSENCE 2006
Red I 2012 up to 2019   90

CÔTES DE PROVENCE R 2008
Red I 2011 up to 2013   88

Older vintages
CÔTES DE PROVENCE 2007
Rosé I 2011 up to 2013   89
Straight, pure, and lightly smoky, this is a rosé of grand elegance.

CÔTES DE PROVENCE 2007
Red I Drink now   90
Very pretty rosé, with a silky texture and delicate, harmonious finish. A model rosé!

CÔTES DE PROVENCE 2006
Red I Drink now   89
This white-gold rosé is pleasant, fine, and well balanced, with a harmonious finish.

CÔTES DE PROVENCE QUINTESSENCE 2005
Red I 2011 up to 2013   90
A red of profound, powerful character, with a lovely quality of fruit. The tannins are delicate.

CÔTES DE PROVENCE R 2007
Red I 2011 up to 2013   90
A great white of immense delicacy on the palate, this is fine, long, and intensely citrus.

Annual production: 300,000 bottles

CHÂTEAU SAINTE-ROSELINE

83460 Les Arcs-sur-Argens
Phone 00 33 4 94 99 50 30
Fax 00 33 4 94 47 53 06
contact@sainte-roseline.com
www.sainte-roseline.com

Sainte-Roseline is entombed in the châ-teau chapel, watching over this great estate for nearly seven centuries. In 1994 it was acquired by Bernard Teillaud, who has spared no expense in equipping the vineyards and winery with state-of-the art facilities. All that hard work is starting to pay off and Sainte-Roseline today fully deserves its status as a Provence Cru Classé. The entry-level offering is a red, white, or rosé wine called the Cuvée Lampe de Méduse while the top-of-the-range wine is an oenophile's delight called the Cuvée Prieuré. The white incarnation of the Cuvée La Chapelle was having trouble integrating its wood when we last tasted it but the red definitely ranked as one of the very great Provence wines

Recently tasted

CÔTES DE PROVENCE LA CHAPELLE 2008
White | 2011 up to 2017   92

CÔTES DE PROVENCE LA CHAPELLE 2007
White | 2011 up to 2013   90

CÔTES DE PROVENCE LAMPE DE MÉDUSE 2008
White | 2011 up to 2013   90

CÔTES DE PROVENCE LAMPE DE MÉDUSE 2008
Rosé | 2011 up to 2013   90

CÔTES DE PROVENCE PRIEURÉ 2008
Rosé | 2011 up to 2013   91

CÔTES DE PROVENCE PRIEURÉ 2007
Rosé | 2011 up to 2017   93

Older vintages

CÔTES DE PROVENCE LA CHAPELLE 2004
Red | 2011 up to 2013   90
A very pretty red from quality grapes. The palate is rich with fine, elegant tannins and concludes with a fresh finish.

CÔTES DE PROVENCE LAMPE DE MÉDUSE 2007
White | 2011 up to 2013   84
Pleasant white, with richness and average length. It would be charming with grilled fish.

CÔTES DE PROVENCE LAMPE DE MÉDUSE 2006
White | Drink now   84
This fat white, marked by fennel and spicy anise on this finish, lacks precision.

CÔTES DE PROVENCE LAMPE DE MÉDUSE 2006
Red | 2011 up to 2013   86
This red has tension and integration. With red-fruit flavors, it is long and has preserved its freshness.

CÔTES DE PROVENCE PRIEURÉ 2007
Rosé | 2011 up to 2013   87
Vanilla, pretty fruit, and a smoky note. This rosé is almost tannic. Open as an aperitif: it will hold well at the table.

CÔTES DE PROVENCE PRIEURÉ 2006
Rosé | Drink now   85
This dense rosé is powerful. It will pair well at the table with an array of Mediterranean or Asian dishes.

CÔTES DE PROVENCE PRIEURÉ 2006
Red | 2011 up to 2013   89
Prieuré 2006 evolves toward Mediterranean notes of garrigue, rosemary, and lavender. We welcome the evolution toward a pure style. Ideally, the tannic power would need a little time to refine itself.

CÔTES DE PROVENCE PRIEURÉ 2005
Red | 2011 up to 2013   88
The Prieuré 2005 is a powerful, chocolaty red with elegant tannins. The finish brings the taster toward Mediterranean notes of garrigue, rosemary, and lavender.

CÔTES DE PROVENCE PRIEURÉ 2000
Red | 2011 up to 2013   90
The domaine still has some Prieuré 2000s. We tasted them from magnums, where they had developed pleasant notes that will move truffle lovers. Evolved and lightly animal, this wine has a spicy, aromatic finish, complex and savory.

Red: 217.4 acres; cabernet sauvignon 20%, grenache 10%, mourvèdre 20%, syrah 50%. White: 29.7 acres; rolle 90%, sémillon 10%. Annual production: 1,400,000 bottles

CHÂTEAU SIMONE

13590 Meyreuil
Phone 00 33 4 42 66 92 58
Fax 00 33 4 42 66 80 77
mail@château-simone.fr
www.château-simone.fr

Château Simone is tucked between Aix-en-Provence and the Montagne Sainte-Victoire, and is the foremost representative of the small Palette AOC. The vines are planted some 600 feet above sea level, on a north-facing slope that protects them from the fierce Provençal sun. The estate has been owned by the Rougier family for nearly two hundred years, and vine management and winemaking are strictly traditional. The wines are matured in vaulted, multistory cellars, carved out of the rock in the sixteenth century by the monks of the Order of the Grands Carmes in Aix. The rosé and red wines rely on the grenache and mourvèdre, supported by the syrah and several subsidiary Provençal grape varieties. But what really gives Château Simone extra dimension is the white wine. This is distinguished by a composition essentially based on the clairette, with a capacity for graceful aging that destines it to greatness among Provence wines.

PALETTE 2006

Rosé | 2011 up to 2013   **87**
The wine is produced in an old-fashioned style, with mature notes of leather and spice that make it unclassifiable. It will displease some, but others will appreciate it for its capacity at the table.

PALETTE 2005

White | 2011 up to 2013   **89**
Gold color, fat florals and mimosa on the nose. The palate is dense, floral, and a little disjointed at the moment, but it will come together over time.

PALETTE 2004

White | 2011 up to 2015   **90**
Palette knows how to produce great white wines based on clairette. The aromatic palette is complex, with notes of herb, butter, and fresh honey. This is a wine of great refinement.

PALETTE 2004

Red | 2011 up to 2015   **86**
The year 2004 produced a wine with firm tannins that needed to age. Produced in a traditional style, it is made for the long term, which will make it possible for the terroir to be fully expressed.

Red: 29.7 acres. White: 22.2 acres. Annual production: 100,000 bottles

DOMAINE TEMPIER

Le Plan du Castellet
83330 Le Castellet
Phone 00 33 4 94 98 70 21
Fax 00 33 4 94 90 21 65
info@domainetempier.com
www.domainetempier.com

The Domaine Tempier is an old, established winery that has been in the same family since the early nineteenth century. Today Jean-Marie and François Peyraud, Tempiers on their mother's side, watch over the destinies of a vineyard that extends over the villages of Le Beausset, Le Castellet, and La Cadière, where some of the vines grow on terraced hillsides with traditional drystone walls "restanques" facing the sea. Tempier offers a quality basic cuvée plus three other wines: Cabassaou (the most Provençal), La Migoua (the freshest), and La Tourtine (the densest).

BANDOL 2007

Rosé | Drink now   **88**
Of great intensity, this is saline, long and very precise; a rosé of character, anchored in the typicity of Bandol rosé.

BANDOL 2006

Red | 2011 up to 2015   **91**
This basic Bandol is powerful with a strong perfume of garrigue, almost wild but very appetizing.

BANDOL CABASSAOU 2006

Red | 2011 up to 2016   **92**
This volumptuous wine, very mourvèdre, offers ethereal tannins that will charm aficionados of red Bandol. The depth is remarkable.

BANDOL LA MIGOUA 2006

Red | 2011 up to 2015   **91**
This wine, made partially from cinsault, is dense and structured, with a long, velvety finish.

BANDOL LA TOURTINE 2006

Red | 2011 up to 2017   **95**
A grand Bandol, voluminous and racy, with appetizing, refined tannins. The finish is full and notably refined and long.

Red: 79.1 acres; carignan 4%, cinsault 10%, grenache 20%, mourvèdre 65%, syrah 1%. White: 2.5 acres. Annual production: 120,000 bottles

DOMAINE DE TORRACCIA

Lecci
20137 Porto-Vecchio
Phone 00 33 4 95 71 43 50
Fax 00 33 4 95 71 50 03
torracciaoriu@wanadoo.fr

This little piece of heaven wrested from the brambles is mainly famous as a mecca of Corsican viticulture. Christian Imbert makes wines with the least intervention possible—the kind of hypernatural wines he likes. But that's not all. As founder and director of a dynamic collective of producers called UVA, he also devoted himself to the protection and promotion of local viticulture in countries throughout Europe. His top wine is the Porto-Vecchio Oriu, a red wine with a subtle garrigue nose that is slow to develop but once sniffed is never forgotten!

Recently tasted
CORSE ORIU 2005
Red | 2011 up to 2015   90

Older vintages
CORSE ORIU 2007
White | 2011 up to 2013   85
Clean, finely lemony and supple, this shows the light bitterness of youth. Lively wine, but a bit simple.

CORSE ORIU 2007
Rosé | 2011 up to 2013   87
Classic rosé, very spicy, showing ripe grapes and marked terroir character. Very pleasant and uniform in the mouth from start to finish.

CORSE ORIU 2004
Red | 2011 up to 2013   90
Burnished color. Marvelous aromatic expression on the nose, with notes of violet and coffee. Very refined in its tactile sensations, natural. This is the opposite of the rustic wines of some local traditionalists, for this is the best of the local tradition. A model of style for the region.

CORSE-PORTO-VECCHIO ORIU 2006
Rosé | Drink now   88
The first Oriu rosé in history, this is very tasty, spicy and soft, showing reductive vinification and a very clean finish.

Red: 84 acres. White: 22.2 acres; vermentino 100%.
Annual production: 200,000 bottles

DOMAINE DE TRÉVALLON

13103 Saint-Étienne-du-Grès
Phone 00 33 4 90 49 06 00
Fax 00 33 4 90 49 02 17
info@domainedetrevallon.com
www.domainedetrevallon.com

Eloi Dürrbach downgraded his wines so as to avoid AOC regulations forbidding him from making red wines based on equal quantities of the cabernet sauvignon and the syrah. Regardless of the label, this is a Grand Vin that owes a lot to precise extraction and maturation. His white wine is mainly based on the marsanne and the roussanne. The mix of vines is more typical of the northern Rhone Valley and produces a range of aromas not unlike those in the great Châteauneuf-du-Pape wines. What you also get, thanks to 10 percent chardonnay, is a delicate, Burgundy-like touch of butter on the finish. Holding it all together is a terroir steeped in Mediterranean scents that add even greater complexity.

Recently tasted
VIN DE PAYS DES BOUCHES-DU-RHONE 2006
Red | 2013 up to 2023   91

VIN DE PAYS DES BOUCHES-DU-RHONE 1999
Red | 2011 up to 2020   95

VIN DE PAYS DES BOUCHES-DU-RHONE 1995
Red | 2011 up to 2015   93

Older vintages
VIN DE PAYS DES BOUCHES-DU-RHONE 2007
White | 2013 up to 2023   91
Generous and rich, this white, based on roussanne and marsanne, is produced in the spirit of the greats of the Rhone. The texture is that of a wine of noble descent, with a buttery finish that will develop complexity. Patience will be rewarded but those in a hurry will equally enjoy the wine.

VIN DE PAYS DES BOUCHES-DU-RHONE 2006
White | 2011 up to 2017   90
Although tasted just after a roussanne from Château Beaucastel, this blend of roussanne and marsanne, vinified in the spirit of the great whites of the Rhone, was not compromised. It truly deserves time to amplify the potential of everything perceived on the finish.

VIN DE PAYS DES BOUCHES-DU-RHONE 2005
Red | 2011 up to 2015   91
As is common in young wines, the syrah and cabernet sauvignon have not yet completely integrated but the body has a delightful fluidity without being thin. Very

noble, very pure, and with great freshness, this red was produced without conceding to stereotypical modern tastes. It will simply require a bit of time to soften the tannins on the finish.

Vin de pays des Bouches-du-Rhone 2004
Red | 2011 up to 2013   **91**
The syrah and cabernet sauvignon have not yet completely integrated but the body has a delightful fluidity without being thin. Very noble, very pure, and with great freshness, this red was produced without conceding to stereotypical modern tastes. It will simply require a bit of time to soften the tannins on the finish.

Red: 37.1 acres; cabernet sauvignon 50%, syrah 50%. White: 4.9 acres; chardonnay 10%, marsanne 45%, roussanne 45%. Annual production: 55,000 bottles

CHÂTEAU VANNIÈRES

Chemin Saint-Antoine
83740 La Cadière d'Azur
Phone 00 33 4 94 90 08 08
Fax 00 33 4 94 90 15 98
info@château vannieres.com
www.château vannieres.com

Located between the towns of La Cadière d'Azur and Saint-Cyr-sur-Mer, Château Vannières has some eighty acres of vineyards exposed to the south and west on a shale and limestone terroir. Made from grapes picked by hand, the wines are among the best Bandols produced. Made in a classic style, the reds have great aging potential, rather quickly taking on notes of tobacco and leather that soften with time. Wine enthusiasts will find wonderful wines here to fill their cellars since the winery tends to hold some bottlings back for later release.

Recently tasted
Bandol 2008
White | 2011 up to 2013   **89**

Bandol 2007
Red | 2011 up to 2016   **89**

Bandol 2006
Red | 2011 up to 2018   **95**

Bandol 1983
Red | 2011 up to 2015   **96**

Older vintages
Bandol 2007
Rosé | Drink now   **88**
Gray-salmon in color, this wine is refined and correct in its aromas.

Bandol 2005
Red | 2011 up to 2020   **91**
Garrigue, profoundly Mediterranean in its scents. This wine is not very concentrated but it is deliciously long, with iodine notes and undeniable character.

Bandol 2004
Red | 2011 up to 2018   **91**
The tannins display the dryness typical of this domaine. It has evolved very well, becoming more polished over time. It finishes long, on stone fruit flavors.

Red: 76.6 acres. White: 2.5 acres. Annual production: 160,000 bottles

CLOS VENTURI

Route de Calvi
20218 Ponte-Leccia
Phone 00 33 4 95 47 61 35
Fax 00 33 4 95 30 85 57
domaine.vico@orange.fr
www.domainevico.com

The Clos Venturi is named after Jean-Marc Venturi, a remarkable Corsican enologist who for many years ran UVIB, the Corsican grape growers' association started by the two cooperative wineries in Aleria in 1976. Today, Venturi devotes himself to his vineyards at Domaine Vico and has just released this label, which has set out to capture the most perfect expression possible of the vermentinu grape. It does. What we have here is the most complete Corsican dry white wine we have ever tasted—the island's equivalent of Montrachet! Dazzlingly classy, fabulously big, and sure to be a smash hit with all the leading restaurants on the Island of Beauty.

Recently tasted
CORSE 2008
White | 2011 up to 2016   92

CORSE 2008
Rosé | 2011 up to 2013   89

Older vintages
CORSE 2007
White | 2011 up to 2013   92
With great aromas of spice and pine, this is fat and powerful yet streamlined and perfectly dry, with great purity and noble bitterness. It is long and suberbly made, once again.

CORSE 2005
Red | 2011 up to 2013   87
Showing excellent grape ripeness, this is fleshy wine. Good élevage refined the firm tannins from the start. Not to say too little—it's well made and delicious—but it is not as accomplished, original, and racy as the white.

Red: 14.8 acres; niellucio 70%, syrah 30%. White: 4.9 acres; vermentino 100%. Annual production: 20,000 bottles

DOMAINE VICO

Route de Calvi
20218 Ponte-Leccia
Phone 00 33 4 95 36 51 45
Fax 00 33 4 95 36 50 26
domaine.vico@orange.fr
www.domainevico.com

Domaine Vico is home to one of the largest mid-slope vineyards in the whole of Corsica. The owner is particularly serious about vineyard maintenance and stocks a complete mix of vines so as to produce a wide range of wines. All of them are impeccably made, in a style that is unmistakably Jean-Marc Venturi. The vines have now reached a respectable age, producing wines that are surprisingly expressive of their terroir.

CORSE 1769 2007
White | 2011 up to 2013   88
Very aromatic and "technical" with fine citron aromas, this tastes like the grapes were harvested at optimal maturity to preserve its energy. It is very pure, complex, and subtle, well within the spirit of this remarkable domaine.

CORSE 1769 2007
Rosé | Drink now   88
A technical model of a modern rosé, this is fuchsia in color, fruity but not candied on the nose, balanced and ripe. Guarantees lots of pleasure.

CORSE 1769 2006
Red | 2011 up to 2013   85
Spicy on the nose, full, rich, tannins as spicy as one could expect, of character but still very reserved.

CORSE COLLECTION 2007
Rosé | 2011 up to 2013   86
A technical rosé but impeccable, with precise fruit and a flavorful, clean finish, to drink all summer—with moderation, all the same.

CORSE MOROSAGLIA 2006
White | 2011 up to 2013   88
Pale color, clean and pure nose combining power and freshness, remarkable technique but dedicated to the expression of a certain vermentino ideal.

Red: 64.2 acres. White: 37.1 acres. Annual production: 350,000 bottles

CHÂTEAU VIGNELAURE

Route de Jouques
83560 Rians
Phone 00 33 4 94 37 21 10
Fax 00 33 4 94 80 53 39
info@vignelaure.com
www.vignelaure.com

This property, in the northeast of the appellation, was discovered by former Château La Lagune owner Georges Brunet. He realized that the gravelly, clay-limestone soils here were not unlike those in the Médoc Cru Classé that he had just sold. The estate then enjoyed varying degrees of success, subsequently belonging to Irish enologist David O'Brien and now owned by Danish couple Bength and Mette Sundström. The red wines share a common mineral edge. The Colline de Vignelaure is a powerfully built prestige cuvée made from Bordeaux grape varieties, and the Cuvée du Château is one of the great wines of Provence.

Recently tasted

COTEAUX D'AIX-EN-PROVENCE 2008
Rosé | 2011 up to 2013   **88**

COTEAUX D'AIX-EN-PROVENCE 2006
Red | 2011 up to 2019   **89**

COTEAUX D'AIX-EN-PROVENCE 2005
Red | 2011 up to 2013   **87**

Older vintages

COTEAUX D'AIX-EN-PROVENCE 2007
Rosé | Drink now   **88**
Dense with a coral hue, this wine has a very beautiful, deep body, in a style of claret.

COTEAUX D'AIX-EN-PROVENCE 2004
Red | 2011 up to 2013   **88**
The tannins lack fullness, but the body of this 2004 is dense and silky.

COTEAUX D'AIX-EN-PROVENCE 2003
Red | 2011 up to 2013   **89**
The tannins are more polished than in the previous two vintages, making for a wine that's more open and ready to drink. The freshness is stunning for this dry vintage. What finesse of tannins!

COTEAUX D'AIX-EN-PROVENCE 2002
Red | Drink now   **88**
Again lightly marked by wood, the body of this nice red is rich and refined. Ready to drink.

COTEAUX D'AIX-EN-PROVENCE 2001
Red | 2011 up to 2014   **91**
This 2001 is powerful and soft in its structure. It is approaching its peak, with reserved tannins.

VIN DE PAYS DES COTEAUX DU VERDON
LA COLLINE DE VIGNELAURE 2001
Red | 2011 up to 2013   **87**
This premium cuvée is produced from merlot and cabernet sauvignon. Deep and powerful, it lacks neither raciness nor length, and has very streamlined tannins.

VIN DE PAYS DES COTEAUX DU VERDON
LA COLLINE DE VIGNELAURE 2000
Red | 2011 up to 2013   **88**
A wine of great power. Time has softened the still-present tannins, and the finish is full, not lacking style. Altogether, it is very explicit in its classic Mediterranean aromas.

Red: 143.3 acres; cabernet sauvignon 46%, carignan noir 3%, cinsault 3%, grenache noir 20%, merlot 5%, syrah 23%. **Annual production:** 250,000 bottles

Bettane & Desseauve
Selections for the Rhone Valley

Rhone Valley

There are two very distinct areas in this region, which is at the height of its popularity. A pocket-size strip of vineyards between Vienne and Valence is still influenced by the weather of the Massif Central, and a sea of sun-soaked vineyards south of Montelimar is influenced by the Provençal weather patterns. The style of the wines in the south is generous, sometimes overblown.

The northern Rhone specializes in finely made cuvées, produced in small quantities with precise winemaking skills. The reds are made from syrah and the whites from viognier, marsanne, and roussanne. These wines are uniquely crafted, often exceptional. Grenache is the principal grape in the southern Rhone, often blended with a symphony of other red grapes. The wines are full-bodied, velvety, and smooth and are appreciated throughout the world.

Appellation Overview
Two Regional Appellations
• **Côtes du Rhône:** The basic appellation for red, white, and rosé wine, exclusively used in the south of the region. Performance is very uneven and quality is average, but wines from reputable producers are worth a look.

• **Côtes du Rhône-Villages:** Reserved for specific terroirs in sixteen villages of the departments of the Gard, Vaucluse, and Drôme. The rules of production are stricter than for Côtes du Rhône wines, and, quality can be exceptional. Wines from the following areas often represent particularly good value for the money: Cairanne, Rasteau, Sablet (Vaucluse), Vinsobres (Drôme), and Laudun (Gard).

Crus of the Northern Rhone Valley
Between Vienne and Valence, on the Banks of the Rhone
• **Côte Rôtie:** Red wines made from syrah (and, to a lesser extent, viognier), grown on the steep hillsides overlooking Ampuis, on the right bank of the Rhone. These are great, sometimes exceptional, wines, made in a powerful but smooth style.

• **Condrieu:** A wine region neighboring Côte Rôtie, producing whites made exclusively from viognier. Very aromatic, fat but crisp, made in a lush style suitable for early drinking. Condrieu wines are currently enjoying a comeback and prices are skyrocketing, with some wines carrying outrageous price tags.

• **Château-Grillet:** The only wine to be awarded AOC status in its own right. The vineyard is devoted to the viognier, like its neighbor Condrieu, and yields a wine that needs long cellaring to display its true potential.

• **Saint-Joseph:** An appellation nearly fifty miles long, extending from the tip of the Condrieu AOC area to within a few miles of Cornas, and almost entirely located on the steep slopes bordering the right bank of the Rhone. It produces quite firm red wines (syrah) and white wines (marsanne, sometimes with a touch of roussanne) that can be of very good quality. But performance does vary depending on the producer, so choose carefully.

• **Crozes-Hermitage:** The largest of the northern appellations and one of only two (along with Hermitage) on the left bank of the Rhone. Thanks to several talented producers, this appellation has come on nicely in recent years. The red wines are for medium-term cellaring; so far, the white wines are less interesting.

• **Hermitage:** Without a doubt, one of France's most exceptional wines, thanks to a remarkable terroir with a highly privileged exposition. The red wines are made from syrah and built for long-term aging. The lesser-known white wines also depend on long cellaring to reveal the fullness of their aromas. Performance overall is of a high standard and prices tend to reflect this quality.

Southern Vineyards
From Bollène to the South of Avignon

• **Costières de Nîmes, Coteaux du Tricastin, Côtes du Luberon, and Côtes du Ventoux:** Appellations with administrative links to the Rhone Valley wine region. These appellations have made huge strides recently and the quality here is very high. With the exception of Costières de Nîmes, the wines from these appellations are fresh and lively, often better balanced than their counterparts in the vast sea of Côtes du Rhône wines. Prices are more than reasonable.

• **Tavel:** vineyards on the right-bank of the Rhone, opposite Châteauneuf-du-Pape, devoted to the production of vinous, fleshy, aromatic rosés. Pleasant wines all in all, but quality does vary.

• **Lirac:** Vineyards in the Gard region, next to Tavel, that make quite refined red wines, rosés very like Tavel, and white wines that can be remarkable—often with a competitive price tag.

• **Gigondas:** A terroir made for the grenache, with sunny vineyards on rolling hills that slope gently down to the plain. Gigondas is the archetypal wine for laying down: powerful and packed with character. Price is very affordable for wines with such great potential.

• **Vacqueyras:** Comparable to Gigondas in terms of climate, blend and style of wine. This is an appellation that is home to some exceptional wines and getting better with each passing vintage.

• **Châteauneuf-du-Pape:** A very extensive appellation, encompassing five communes and a wide variety of terrain. The quality varies accordingly, made more complicated by differences in winemaking style and aging techniques. The best estates produce red wines of exceptional richness that will reward patient cellaring: old age suits them splendidly (even better than some Bordeaux). Wines like these are a far cry from those alcoholic fruit bombs that people tend to associate with Châteauneuf-du-Pape made in a modern, international style. The white wines have improved a lot in recent years, but are still not up to the standard of the reds.

• **Beaumes de Venise:** An appellation renowned for its sweet white muscat wines. It was promoted to cru status in 2005, but only for its lesser-known red wines, which have made steady progress the past few years.

• **Vinsobres:** Another appellation promoted to cru status in 2005. It produces fresh, rich, ample wines, usually with a higher proportion of syrah, which performs very well in this appellation.

Northern Rhone Vineyards

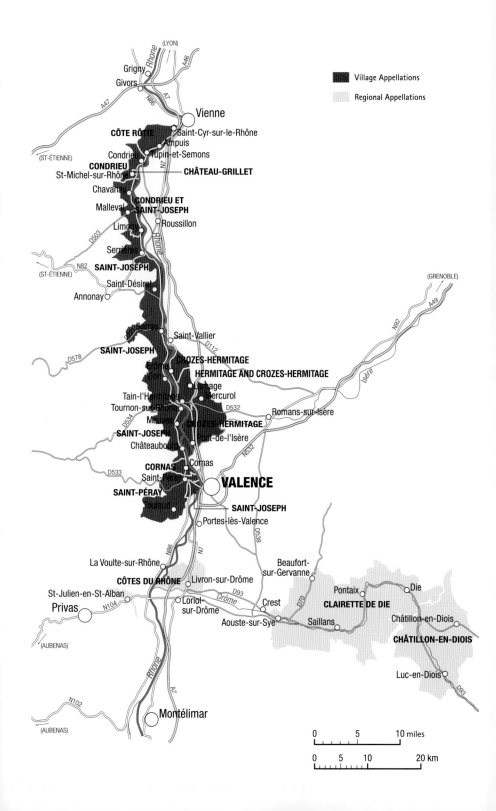

Village Appellations

Regional Appellations

(LYON)

Grigny

Givors

Vienne

CÔTE RÔTIE
Saint-Cyr-sur-le-Rhône
Ampuis
Condrieu Tupin-et-Semons

(ST-ÉTIENNE)

CONDRIEU
St-Michel-sur-Rhône

CHÂTEAU-GRILLET

Chavanay

Malleval

**CONDRIEU ET
SAINT-JOSEPH**

Limony Roussillon

Serrières

SAINT-JOSEPH

Saint-Désirat

Annonay

(ST-ÉTIENNE)

Sarras

Saint-Vallier

SAINT-JOSEPH

CROZES-HERMITAGE

Drôme
Glun

HERMITAGE AND CROZES-HERMITAGE

Gervans
Mercurol

Tain-l'Hermitage

Tournon-sur-Rhône

Romans-sur-Isère

Mauves

CROZES-HERMITAGE

SAINT-JOSEPH

Pont-de-l'Isère

Châteaubourg

CORNAS Cornas

Saint-Péray

VALENCE

SAINT-PÉRAY

Toulaud

SAINT-JOSEPH

Portes-lès-Valence

La Voulte-sur-Rhône

CÔTES DU RHÔNE Livron-sur-Drôme

Beaufort-
sur-Gervanne

St-Julien-en-St-Alban

Privas

Loriol-
sur-Drôme

Drôme

Crest

Pontaix

Die

CLAIRETTE DE DIE

Aouste-sur-Sye

Saillans

Châtillon-en-Diois

(AUBENAS)

CHÂTILLON-EN-DIOIS

Luc-en-Diois

Montélimar

(AUBENAS)

| 0 | 5 | 10 miles |

| 0 | 5 | 10 | 20 km |

DOMAINE THIERRY ALLEMAND

22, impasse des Granges
07130 Cornas
Phone 00 33 4 75 81 06 50
Fax 00 33 4 75 81 06 50

Thierry Allemand opened for business in 1982 at a time when more people were turning away from viticulture than toward it. His small vineyard holding produces just two or three cuvées, sometimes only one when the vintage is unsuitable for volume production (as in 2002 and 2003). His two traditional cuvées are Les Chaillots (young vines) and Reynard (old vines, forty-plus years), both vinified with no added sulfur. Very consistent quality—a must-have for Cornas enthusiasts.

CORNAS CHAILLOT 2006
Red | 2011 up to 2015   **88**
As always, this cuvée shows concentrated fruit, dense and chewy in the mouth.

CORNAS CHAILLOT 2005
Red | 2011 up to 2015   **89**
Ink colored. The fruit is concentrated, all blueberry and graphite. On the palate, the tannins are supple and evident. It finishes with concentration and firm tannins. It's a big wine with a beautiful future.

CORNAS REYNARD 2006
Red | 2011 up to 2015   **89**
Very aromatic, with a licorice finish, this wine is smooth and unctuous. It would be a pleasure to enjoy right now.

CORNAS REYNARD 2005
Red | 2011 up to 2015   **91**
A wine with dense and refined juice, this feels velvety on the palate, with concentrated fruit. It is subtle and elegant, with beautiful tension in the finish. Very beautiful, chewy texture.

Red: 8.4 acres; syrah 100%. Annual production: 12,000 bottles

DOMAINE BELLE

Quartier les Marsuriaux
26600 Larnage
Phone 00 33 4 75 08 24 58
Fax 00 33 4 75 07 10 58
domaine.belle@wanadoo.fr

Philippe Belle manages a fifty-acre domaine in the town of Larnage. The farming has been "reasoned" (with little use of chemicals) since 2002, but 2008 saw the first experiments with fully organic practices. If the results are conclusive, the entire property will be converted. Following this logic, the grapes have been manually harvested since the difficult 2002 vintage when they had no choice due to heavy rains; this has definitely increased the quality of the wines. All of the wines are vinified in barrel, but from six different coopers, with wood from two different forests, so that the oak doesn't overpower the wine. Each vineyard is vinified separately, thus they produce seven different bottlings in the appellations of Crozes-Hermitage, Hermitage, and Saint-Joseph. The Hermitage wines are very good in both red and white, though not the most accomplished of the appellation, and the Crozes-Hermitages are of high quality, especially the Louis Belle and Roche Pierre—a new cuvée, first produced in 2007.

Recently tasted

CROZES-HERMITAGE CUVÉE LOUIS BELLE 2007
Red | 2011 up to 2014   **88**

CROZES-HERMITAGE LES PIERRELLES 2007
Red | 2011 up to 2013   **86**

CROZES-HERMITAGE LES TERRES BLANCHES 2007
White | 2011 up to 2013   **89**

CROZES-HERMITAGE ROCHE PIERRE 2007
Red | 2011 up to 2014   **89**

HERMITAGE 2006
White | 2011 up to 2016   **89**

HERMITAGE 2006
Red | 2011 up to 2016   **89**

Older vintages

CROZES-HERMITAGE CUVÉE LOUIS BELLE 2006
Red | 2011 up to 2016   **88**
Mineral, a bit reserved, but this is still very young. The palate is taut, with tight yet ripe tannins. The finish feels corseted, suggesting that this is a wine that requires a patient wait. The white clay-limestone terroir of Larnage produces wines that age well.

CROZES-HERMITAGE LES PIERRELLES 2006
Red | 2011 up to 2013   85
Dark fruit, delicious and tasty, with round tannins. Medium concentration, yet balanced and fruity. A touch of minerality in the finish.

CROZES-HERMITAGE ROCHE PIERRE 2006
Red | 2011 up to 2016   90
Tight, dense, this has great tension in the mouth. The minerality of the terroir is present, and the tannins are well enrobed due to the wine's élevage. The wine is already superb, but it would be best to wait longer. The finish is spicy and mineral. Elegant and refined.

HERMITAGE 2005
Red | 2011 up to 2020   91
Taut, with firm yet very ripe tannins. This is in a closed-down phase, but it is linear, mineral, and concentrated on the palate. Powerful, very honest.

HERMITAGE 2005
White | 2011 up to 2020   89
Toasty, delicate, elegant, a wine that starts out discreetly but will age well. Balanced and classic.

HERMITAGE 2004
Red | 2011 up to 2013   87
Medium-intense color. Fresh fruit, somewhat frank, with delicate oak. Clean on the palate, fruity and taut, but with little power.

Red: 44.5 acres; syrah 100%. White: 4.9 acres; marsanne 70%, roussanne 30%. Annual production: 110,000 bottles

DOMAINE PATRICK ET CHRISTOPHE BONNEFOND

Mornas
69420 Ampuis
Phone 00 33 4 74 56 12 30
Fax 00 33 4 74 56 17 93
gaec.bonnefond@terre-net.fr

Christophe Bonnefond takes a very disciplined approach to the management of his family estate. The vineyards are located on the Côte Rôtie in the northern Rhone (with a particularly fine parcel on the Côte Rozier). They produce balanced wines, with well-integrated oak and the potential to age gracefully; powerful and fat, but always with a fresh, irresistible finish and a modern but seductive style that suits this appellation. A dependable producer, vintage after vintage.

CONDRIEU 2007
White | 2011 up to 2015   87
Lively, fresh and ripe, fresher than the 2006 (14° alcohol). It's better balanced and has found its length again!

CONDRIEU 2006
White | 2011 up to 2014   86
Highly refined, quite elegant. Delicate notes of ripe lemons. Fat on the palate, delectable, without any heaviness. Subtle, elegant, and fresh. A bit hot, high in alcohol (15°).

CÔTE RÔTIE 2007
Red | 2011 up to 2017   89
Very dark in color. Straightforward and concentrated on the palate, with good, firm tannins. Very beautiful dark-berry juice, with a mineral finish.

CÔTE RÔTIE 2006
Red | 2011 up to 2021   89
Open and seductive, with round and ripe fruit, this wine shows firm but fat tannins. Good élevage: the wood is well integrated into this harmonious wine. Very balanced and seductive.

CÔTE RÔTIE 2005
Red | 2011 up to 2020   90
With ravishing fruit, concentrated and licorice-tinged, this wine is delicious. The palate is seductive, fat, and ripe, with good tannic structure and a long and very fresh finish. It will close down, but it is already delicious today! The licorice finish is quite long-lasting.

CÔTE RÔTIE CÔTE ROZIER 2007

Red | 2011 up to 2014   **88**

More floral and fresher than the introductory cuvée. Softer on the palate and chewier, but also longer. One could wait a long time for this. Tight and dense, it has a bitter note in the finish. (This parcel was hit by hail.)

CÔTE RÔTIE CÔTE ROZIER 2006

Red | 2011 up to 2021   **91**

The flavors are more concentrated and denser than in the simple Côte Rôtie. It's rich in tannins, fat, with a balanced and nervy finish. Good volume.

CÔTE RÔTIE CÔTE ROZIER 2005

Red | 2011 up to 2025   **93**

The nose is very fresh: eucalyptus, dark fruit. Flavorful on the palate, ripe and unctuous, with juicy, sweetened dark-berry flavor and fat, well-enrobed tannins. A long, intense, and fresh wine, both aromatic and seductive.

CÔTE RÔTIE CÔTE ROZIER 2003

Red | Drink now   **90**

The nose is concentrated and ripe, though still closed and a bit austere at this point. The palate is ripe, with beautiful firm tannins. Good concentration and good length. The wood is balanced.

CÔTE RÔTIE LES ROCHAINS 2007

Red | 2011 up to 2017   **88**

The hail has affected the palate, hardening the tannins a bit and bringing a touch of bitterness to the finish. Yet it is still dense, mineral, and intensely juicy. It has great structure but absolutely requires time.

CÔTE RÔTIE LES ROCHAINS 2006

Red | 2011 up to 2021   **91**

More intense and mineral than the Côte Rozier. Edgier, with a mineral and streamlined finish that is more truly representative of the Côte Brune (schist soils). A touch saline in the finish, with fat and well-integrated tannins.

CÔTE RÔTIE LES ROCHAINS 2005

Red | 2011 up to 2025   **94**

More reserved in bouquet, but also more concentrated, than the Côte Rozier. It's also edgier on the palate, with a bit more minerality and firm tannins. It is a long, nervy, thoroughbred wine with an impressively chewy texture. Finishes on notes of brown tobacco.

CÔTE RÔTIE LES ROCHAINS 2003

Red | 2011 up to 2022   **90**

Very woody. The aromas are rather austere at this point; the wine is closing down. On the palate, the wine is firm and chewy, even if some of the tannins are a bit stiff. Not completely open.

CHAPOUTIER

18, avenue du Docteur-Paul-Durand
26600 Tain-l'Hermitage
Phone 00 33 4 75 08 28 65
Fax 00 33 4 75 08 81 70
chapoutier@chapoutier.com
www.chapoutier.com

Chapoutier is now firmly established as a domaine with an influential presence throughout the southern French vineyards and a commitment to biodynamic farming in its own holdings. Quietly but steadily, it has crossed that line that separates great but surprisingly inconsistent producers from those who always deliver results whatever the style of wine. Its single-vintage Hermitage cuvées have been top performers for some years now, and all of its northern Rhone wines are doing better than ever before, particularly the more widely available offerings such as Les Crozes, Saint-Joseph, and L'Hermitage Chante-Alouette. There is more precision and balance in the whites, too, but with an incredible opulence; we still tend to favor the mineral freshness of the basic cuvées over the opulence of their prestige counterparts. One of this estate's latest strengths is certainly its wines from farther afield, whether the high-volume but impeccable Belleruche Côtes du Rhône or the original Bila-Haut Côtes du Roussillon.

Recently tasted

CHÂTEAUNEUF-DU-PAPE LA BENARDINE 2007
White | 2011 up to 2015   **88**

CONDRIEU INVITARE 2007
White | 2011 up to 2015   **90**

CÔTE RÔTIE LA MORDORÉE 2006
Red | 2011 up to 2016   **92**

CROZES-HERMITAGE LA PETITE RUCHE 2007
Red | 2011 up to 2013   **86**

ERMITAGE DE L'ORÉE 2007
White | 2011 up to 2025   **98**

Pretty spices with a slight touch of smoked tea; the finish more vibrant with hints of honeysuckle; immense volume on the palate.

ERMITAGE DE L'ORÉE 2006
White | 2011 up to 2026   **99**

ERMITAGE L'ERMITE 2007
White | 2011 up to 2025   **98**

The purest, the most linear, the most distinguished, even in this stunning vintage.

ERMITAGE L'ERMITE 2006
White | 2011 up to 2026   **100**
The texture is svelte, with notes of cassis, of indescribably beautiful black fruit. Almost perfect!

ERMITAGE LE MÉAL 2007
Red | 2015 up to 2035   **97**
Noble notes of black pepper, complete, incomparably elegant tannins.

ERMITAGE LE MÉAL 2007
White | 2011 up to 2020   **95**
Wonderfully elegant notes of flowery honey, slightly smoky, amazing length.

ERMITAGE LE MÉAL 2006
White | 2011 up to 2026   **97**
The same core as Greffieux, but with a more velvety texture, refined and pure in all aspects.

ERMITAGE LES GREFFIEUX 2007
Red | 2015 up to 2025   **95**
Surgically precise aromas, but sensual at the same time, with ultra-focused tannins. Yet another marvel.

ERMITAGE LES GREFFIEUX 2006
Red | 2011 up to 2026   **96**
Captivating aromas, amazingly elegant, expert barrel aging. An absolute benchmark where perfect grapes, vinification, and aging are concerned.

ERMITAGE LE PAVILLON 2007
Red | 2015 up to 2035   **97**
A wine with grand nobility and a timeless classicism in body and texture.

ERMITAGE LE PAVILLON 2006
Red | 2011 up to 2025   **97**
This wine has the classic graphite mark typical of the granite terroir, which shines through with its flavors of "eau de roche." Power, elegance, length—it's all here, and it's built to last.

GIGONDAS 2007
Red | 2011 up to 2017   **90**

SAINT-JOSEPH DESCHANTS 2007
White | 2011 up to 2014   **88**

SAINT-PÉRAY PIC ET CHAPOUTIER 2007
White | 2011 up to 2015   **88**

VIN DE PAYS DES COTEAUX DE L'ARDÈCHE LES GRANGES DE MIRABEL 2007
White | 2011 up to 2013   **88**

Older vintages

CHÂTEAUNEUF-DU-PAPE 2004
Red | 2011 up to 2020   **89**
Deeply colored, dark-berried, unctuous and intense, with beautiful deep volume. The finish lacks voluptuousness, but it is very spicy.

CHÂTEAUNEUF-DU-PAPE 2003
Red | 2011 up to 2013   **86**
This is a wine with a medium-deep color, expressing fruity notes of raspberry and strawberry. It has good balance on the palate, supple and soft. It is not very intense but is well balanced.

CHÂTEAUNEUF-DU-PAPE BARBE RAC 2006
Red | 2011 up to 2026   **93**
A powerful and rich wine with fat, rich texture. The bouquet is a bit cooked. The wine is lacking in balance due to its high alcohol content.

CHÂTEAUNEUF-DU-PAPE BARBE RAC 2004
Red | 2011 up to 2020   **87**
A powerful and ripe wine, with a finish that is a touch hot (it is about 16° alcohol).

CHÂTEAUNEUF-DU-PAPE BARBE RAC 2003
Red | 2011 up to 2020   **89**
The color is lively and medium-intense. The expressive bouquet brings together red-berry and dried-herb notes with a touch of acidity. The palate is rather delicate, emphasizing length more than density. It absolutely needs time in the cellar.

CHÂTEAUNEUF-DU-PAPE CROIX DE BOIS 2006
Red | 2011 up to 2021   **90**
Lightly colored, fruity, soft, defined more by its freshness than its length. Yet the length has depth and delicacy.

CHÂTEAUNEUF-DU-PAPE CROIX DE BOIS 2003
Red | 2011 up to 2017   **88**
This wine expresses itself in a more powerful register than the house's other Châteauneufs. Crafted in a more generous, oaked style, it is very full on the palate, with length and tannins that should soften over time.

CONDRIEU IN VITARE 2006
White | 2011 up to 2016   **89**
A lovely Condrieu, which defines itself in opposition to the very rich and somewhat heavy style of many rivals in the appellation. This wine is sober, with delicate lemony notes paired with a very mineral character. Undeniably distinguished, it has elegance and delicate depth. It is a wine to wait for.

CORNAS LES ARÈNES 2006
Red | 2011 up to 2018   **90**
Deeply colored, with a black-currant nose. The attack is supple, but the wine then unfurls on the palate to impose its long, deep, and brilliantly persistent character.

CÔTE RÔTIE LA MORDORÉE 2005
Red | 2011 up to 2018   **90**
A supple wine with length, elegance, and well-crafted notes of red and dark berries. The tannins are very delicate and have a little less energy than those of some of this vintage's bigger Côtes Rôties.

CÔTE RÔTIE LA MORDORÉE 2004
Red | 2011 up to 2013   **85**
A powerful and massive wine, with expressive and spicy tannins, but a bit overextracted. Light dryness in the finish.

CÔTE RÔTIE LES BÉCASSES 2006
Red | 2011 up to 2015   **88**
An elegant wine, very black-currant, this is harmonious and fruity on the palate and blessed with a supple finish. This is a Côte Rôtie you could drink now, but it will cellar well, too.

CÔTES DU RHÔNE BELLERUCHE 2007
Red | 2011 up to 2013   **86**
A classic Côtes du Rhône, with a bouquet of red berries and garrigue. Round and approachable, a bit hot in the finish but undeniably flavorful.

CÔTES DU RHÔNE-VILLAGES RASTEAU 2007
Red | 2011 up to 2013   **85**
Beautiful texture, fresh on the palate, with scents of wild blackberries and garrigue. This is well married to its structure, with tannins that are perceptible but not too aggressive.

CÔTES DU ROUSSILLON-VILLAGES DOMAINE DE BILA-HAUT CUVÉE OCCULTUM LAPIDEM 2005
Red | 2011 up to 2013   **85**
A concentrated and spicy bouquet dominated by dark berries and herbes de Provence. The palate is rich and tannic, but it is not too open.

CROZES-HERMITAGE LA PETITE RUCHE 2007
White | 2011 up to 2014   **88**
A perfumed nose of yellow fruit, herbal tea, and wild herbs. The palate is rich, but with neither the freshness nor the balance of Belleruche.

CROZES-HERMITAGE LES MEYSONNIERS 2007
White | 2011 up to 2017   **89**
A delicate and fresh bouquet. The palate is rich and fat with good balance. It is rich but stays pleasing and nicely fresh.

CROZES-HERMITAGE VARONNIERS 2006
Red | 2011 up to 2016   **93**
The fruit is concentrated, ripe, dark. The tannins are ripe and fat. This wine is assured a lovely future.

CROZES-HERMITAGE VARONNIERS 2004
Red | 2011 up to 2013   **90**
An intense, fruity, spicy, and velvety bouquet. The palate is rich and unctuous, with a superb touch of elegance, smooth and mineral. Perfumed and open.

ERMITAGE DE L'ORÉE 2005
White | 2011 up to 2022   **92**
Golden in color, with strong notes of acacia honey. Rich, even opulent, as is typical for this wine. It finishes long, with lots of depth, definition, and elegance. Cellar it.

ERMITAGE DE L'ORÉE 2004
White | 2011 up to 2013   **95**
A complete and open wine, elegant, smooth, rich, and complex. Superb juice on the palate. A very big wine, subtle and mineral.

ERMITAGE L'ERMITE 2007
Red | 2011 up to 2035   **98**
Admirably constructed in the mouth, with admirable precision.

ERMITAGE L'ERMITE 2006
Red | 2011 up to 2026   **97**
A direct and streamlined wine. Very pure, very elegant. The palate is subtle, chiseled. It is a big wine, with subtle mineral notes that balance the finish.

ERMITAGE L'ERMITE 2005
Red | 2011 up to 2013   **94**
A dense and concentrated wine. The juice on the palate is rich with firm and ripe tannins and beautifully expressed notes of dark berries and spices. It will mature slowly.

ERMITAGE L'ERMITE 2004
Red | 2011 up to 2013   **94**
A wine with dense and concentrated juice, beautifully elegant on the palate. Its texture is unctuous and delicate.

ERMITAGE LE MÉAL 2006
Red | 2011 up to 2026   **94**
Remarkably ample, muscled, velvety, and deep, with beautiful mineral notes, very silky tannins, lots of finesse, and flavorful length. It will cellar well.

ERMITAGE LE MÉAL 2005
White | 2011 up to 2013   **93**
Rich and powerful, this is a complex and deep wine, but the finish lacks a touch of freshness. Lots of fat.

ERMITAGE LE MÉAL 2004
White | 2011 up to 2013   93
A delicate and fresh nose with pleasant notes of ripe grapes, apricots, and yellow fruit. The palate is very honeyed. Balanced and refined, in a powerful style.

ERMITAGE LE MÉAL 2004
Red | 2011 up to 2013   95
A fat and perfumed wine. The tannins are rich and well enrobed. The palate is expressive, with notes of dark berries and licorice.

ERMITAGE LE PAVILLON 2006
Red | 2011 up to 2026   94
Incontestably the most thoroughbred Hermitage of this house in this vintage, this wine has tannic finesse and svelte and refreshing depth. It has superb mineral notes, and even a touch of menthol in the finish. Great length and persistence.

ERMITAGE LE PAVILLON 2004
Red | 2011 up to 2013   95
A fruity and velvety wine, elegant, smooth, and highly perfumed. The palate is rich, the tannins well enrobed, and the palate definition magnificent. It is long and fresh.

HERMITAGE CHANTE-ALOUETTE 2006
White | 2011 up to 2016   90
Golden colored, with a lovely bouquet of white fruits and candied pineapple. The palate is ample, fleshy, and structured without being heavy. Beautiful length.

HERMITAGE CHANTE-ALOUETTE 2005
White | 2011 up to 2013   91
A refined and perfumed wine. The palate is delicate, sculpted, quite streamlined and pure. Very elegant.

HERMITAGE CHANTE-ALOUETTE 2004
White | 2011 up to 2013   90
An intense and delicate bouquet with subtle toasted notes. Perfumed and elegant. The palate is rich, with a delicate bitterness in the finish.

HERMITAGE LES GREFFIEUX 2005
Red | 2011 up to 2013   92
Syrah's character is still dominant in this young wine, with its very present blackcurrant notes. It is ample and flavorful, with tannins a touch more rustic than in Le Méal and Le Pavillon.

HERMITAGE LES GREFFIEUX 2004
Red | 2011 up to 2013   92
A wine with dense and concentrated juice. Licorice, raisins, dark berries on the nose. The palate has spicy, ripe tannins, well enrobed.

HERMITAGE MONIER DE LA SIZERANNE 2006
Red | 2011 up to 2016   90
A dense Hermitage, rich and deep with beautiful prune and white peppercorn scents. It has generous length and a ripe, powerful, and smooth tannic structure.

HERMITAGE MONIER DE LA SIZERANNE 2005
Red | 2011 up to 2013   89
A straightforward wine, with delicate and ripe tannins. At this point, it is a little tight, but it has great style. Concentrated and direct.

HERMITAGE MONIER DE LA SIZERANNE 2004
Red | 2011 up to 2013   88
An intense, delicate, and concentrated bouquet. The palate is rich and smooth. The tannins are delicate. It is limited only by its aromas, which are not quite fully expressed.

SAINT-JOSEPH DESCHANTS 2007
Red | 2011 up to 2013   88
Svelte, deep, taut, mineral, ready to drink but with the true character of the granite soils of Saint-Joseph.

SAINT-JOSEPH DESCHANTS 2005
Red | 2011 up to 2013   87
A straightforward wine, with firm and tight tannins. Good structure on the palate, in a mineral style, a bit austere. It will age slowly.

SAINT-JOSEPH LES GRANITS 2005
White | 2011 up to 2013   93
A refined and sculpted wine, all about minerality, with stature. It's delicate and elegant. It will go far!

SAINT-JOSEPH LES GRANITS 2005
Red | 2011 up to 2016   88
Deeply colored, a bit heavy on scents of dark berries. The palate is ample and fleshy, but without the finesse and the svelte depth we have come to expect in this cuvée.

Red: 190.3 acres; syrah 100%. White: 19.8 acres; marsanne 93%, viognier 7%. Annual production: 330,000 bottles

DOMAINE JEAN-LOUIS CHAVE

37, avenue du Saint-Joseph
07300 Mauves
Phone 00 33 4 75 08 24 63
Fax 00 33 4 75 07 14 21

Jean-Louis Chave now runs this estate, having taken over from his father, Gérard, a keen-witted man with an admirable sense of balance, and a fervent champion of L'Hermitage. Jean-Louis fully understands his duty toward this exceptional terroir, home to one of the longest surviving family estates in the business. He is a perfectionist to the core and focuses on taking care of detail at every stage of the production process, from farming, through fermentation and aging. Blending and selection of the base wines remain painstakingly precise (a significant proportion of wines are now eliminated from the cuvée Cathelin, an exceptional cuvée made only in great vintages). Chave Hermitage wines exhibit all the nuances of this celebrated hillside where the family owns vines in several vineyards (including Beaumesommes, Péléat, Les Rocoules, L'Ermite, Le Méal, and Les Bessards). The white wines showed continuous improvement throughout the 1990s and now achieve a balance, finesse, and length that leave all other wines behind. The red wines remain elegantly deep and unrivaled for sheer finesse of texture—in our opinion, the absolute benchmark for great wine.

Recently tasted

HERMITAGE 2006
White | 2011 up to 2026　　　　　95

HERMITAGE 2006
Red | 2011 up to 2026　　　　　97

Older vintages

HERMITAGE 2005
White | 2011 up to 2025　　　　　98
This is a very rich and ample wine, nearly tannic in its tactile presence, but imposing finesse quickly follows, the wine coming together on a slightly bitter finish that brings welcome freshness. A wine to cellar.

HERMITAGE 2005
Red | 2011 up to 2030　　　　　97
A big and powerful wine, less "artistic" in style and balance than usual. Yet the tannins are perfectly ripe and tight. Altogether, it's a very deep wine with lots of personality.

HERMITAGE 2004
White | 2011 up to 2024　　　　　95
Ample and very open, with a luscious body, subtle honeyed scents, and a pure, fresh finish.

HERMITAGE 2004
Red | 2011 up to 2024　　　　　95
The fruit is highly expressive and pairs delicate notes of prunes with sweet spices. Long and intense, it makes its mark without being heavy. It has a silky and refined structure.

HERMITAGE 2003
White | 2011 up to 2018　　　　　93
The honey and licorice notes are very present in this round and super-lush wine. Even with its low acidity, this wine has a delicious freshness.

HERMITAGE 2003
Red | 2011 up to 2023　　　　　95
Velvety and firm, more classic than the Cathelin, but equally brilliant in its textural finesse and its round, smooth finish.

HERMITAGE 2002
White | 2011 up to 2017　　　　　90
Softer than the two vintages that followed, this wine has racy suppleness and is balanced with great freshness.

HERMITAGE 2002
Red | 2011 up to 2017　　　　　90
Svelte and light, ready to drink, this wine expresses delicate and pure fruit.

HERMITAGE 1998
White | 2011 up to 2018　　　　　98
This wine is now approaching its peak: it exudes notes of decadent candied tangerine with purity and fullness on the palate. Dense, unctuous, with an infinite finish.

HERMITAGE CATHELIN 2003
Red | 2011 up to 2013　　　　　99
This has great richness and extraordinary aromatic intensity. More powerful than what we've been accustomed to, it has great freshness in the tannins. It's an incredible wine that should immediately enter the ranks of legendary Hermitage wines.

HERMITAGE CATHELIN 1998
Red | 2011 up to 2030　　　　　98
Inky color. Even after thirteen years, this wine remains very young, with a pure and mineral bouquet. Deep and intense on the palate, with great length. The wine seems to have eternal youth!

SAINT-JOSEPH 2005
Red | 2011 up to 2017　　　　　92
Very pure, deep and supple in the finish, this Saint-Joseph is not in the least heavy. It is muscular with great balance.

Red: 24.7 acres; syrah 100%. **White:** 12.4 acres; marsanne 80%, roussanne 20%. **Annual production:** 48,000 bottles

DOMAINE YANN CHAVE

🦎 🦎 🦎 🦎 🦎

La Burge
26600 Mercurol
Phone 00 33 4 75 07 42 11
Fax 00 33 4 75 07 47 34
chaveyann@yahoo.fr

Yann Chave (no relation to the owners of Domaine Jean-Louis Chave) took over the family estate in 1996 and immediately started to make and sell wines using grapes that up until then had been sent off to the Tain co-op. The breakthrough came in 2003, particularly in terms of improved physiological ripening. The oaky bottlings benefit from refined, well-integrated wood aging. This estate has definitely reached a new level!

Recently tasted
CROZES-HERMITAGE 2007
Red | 2011 up to 2013   **87**

CROZES-HERMITAGE LE ROUVRE 2007
Red | 2011 up to 2015   **88**

HERMITAGE 2007
Red | 2011 up to 2017   **88**

Older vintages
CROZES-HERMITAGE 2007
White | 2011 up to 2013   **86**
Elegant, fruity, refined, with beautiful floral notes. Nicely fresh on the palate. A gastronomic wine with a lemony finish.

CROZES-HERMITAGE LE ROUVRE 2006
Red | 2011 up to 2016   **88**
Rich in texture, this is a straightforward and concentrated wine with firm tannins. Firm but ripe.

CROZES-HERMITAGE LE ROUVRE 2005
Red | 2011 up to 2013   **87**
A solid wine, built on a ripe, tannic framework. The finish is long and fresh. The fruit isn't very expressive, but it should age well.

HERMITAGE 2006
Red | 2011 up to 2016   **89**
A richly oaked wine, delectable and unctuous. Good texture, balanced and refined. It still needs to soften a bit.

HERMITAGE 2004
Red | 2011 up to 2013   **89**
The body is deep and tight, the tannins firm. This Hermitage is characterized by excellent, fresh length, with no astringency.

Red: 38.8 acres; syrah 100%. White: 2.5 acres; marsanne 70%, roussanne 30%. Annual production: 90,000 bottles

DOMAINE AUGUSTE CLAPE

🦎 🦎 🦎 🦎 🦎

146, avenue Colonel-Rousset
07130 Cornas
Phone 00 33 4 75 40 33 64
Fax 00 33 4 75 81 01 98

You can't think of Cornas without thinking of August Clape. This iconic producer started the winery in 1956, in 1990 his son Pierre took over, and now Pierre's son Olivier is starting to learn the ropes. This is truly a family-run domaine. Four wines are produced here, one white and three reds, two of which are Cornas. The cuvée Renaissance is a young-vine Cornas, while the "grande" cuvée doesn't have a special name, it's simply Clape Cornas. The reds are vinified in small concrete tanks, and then aged in very old large oak casks. There's no chance of finding an over-oaked wine here! Black in color, the wines show pronounced minerality, while maintaining fresh fruit and a lot of substance; and, of course, they age magnificently. The 2005s are superconcentrated, the 2006 is well balanced but a notch below, and the 2007s show great potential. Victim of their own success, the winery no longer accepts new clients, so you'll have to seek these wines out at your local wine store or in very good restaurants.

Recently tasted
CORNAS 2007
Red | 2013 up to 2022   **93**

CORNAS RENAISSANCE 2007
Red | 2011 up to 2017   **90**

Older vintages
CORNAS 2006
Red | 2011 up to 2021   **93**
More mineral than the Renaissance, with spicier tannins. Greater depth on the palate, with a good, full-bodied finish.

CORNAS 2005
Red | 2011 up to 2025   **93**
Concentrated, ripe, with dark berries and licorice. Fat in the mouth, rich in enrobed tannins, with a finish both mineral and mouth-watering. A great future ahead.

CORNAS 2004
Red | 2011 up to 2014   **89**
Lighter in color and less concentrated in fruit than the 2005. Elegant and smooth on the palate, with lots of fruity charm and a licorice finish. But not up to the level of the 2005.

CORNAS 2000
Red | 2011 up to 2015   **91**
The bouquet opens well, on red berries with a few tertiary touches (leather in particular). It is concentrated and mineral on the palate, with a good return of aromatic freshness on the finish and mentholated notes. Harmonious.

CORNAS RENAISSANCE 2006
Red | 2011 up to 2016   **88**
Fleshy body, very mouth-watering red and black fruit flavors.

CORNAS RENAISSANCE 2005
Red | 2011 up to 2015   **90**
Good, intense fruit. An honest and concentrated palate. The minerality is just beginning to appear.

CORNAS RENAISSANCE 2004
Red | 2011 up to 2013   **91**
Beautiful notes of red berries (cherries), velvety tannins. Delicate and refined on the palate. At this stage, it tastes better than the Cornas.

Red: 17.5 acres; syrah 100%. White: 1 acre; marsanne 100%. Annual production: 30,000 bottles

DOMAINE CLUSEL-ROCH

15, route du Lacat
Verenay
69420 Ampuis
Phone 00 33 4 74 56 15 95
Fax 00 33 4 74 56 19 74
contact@domainecluselroch.fr
www.domaine-clusel-roch.fr

This tiny estate is named after the two people who run it, Gilbert Clusel and his wife, Brigitte Roch. Annual production amounts to just 17,000 to 18,000 bottles of wine from organically farmed vineyards on the Côte Rôtie (about nine acres) and Condrieu (one acre). The owners are experts in the diversity of terroirs in this appellation and look to highlight the differences in their cuvées. Their Côte Rôtie bottlings focus more on finesse and elegance than power and concentration and are often underestimated in blind tastings. Though discreet as young wines, they actually age very nicely, developing a pure and elegant palate that always finishes fresh and well balanced. The Condrieu bottling plays on the same style, the aromas growing more expressive as the tasting proceeds.

CONDRIEU VERCHERY 2006
White | 2011 up to 2014   **84**
A bit hot on the nose. Yellow fruit. Generous on the palate, but a bit heavy in its alcohol-rich finish. Still, the aromas are pure.

CONDRIEU VERCHERY 2004
White | 2011 up to 2013   **90**
Mineral and toasty. Refined on the palate, with charm. Lovely length. Not opulent, but fine and delicate. The finish is pure. Superb elegance. A wine that will improve as it opens.

CÔTE RÔTIE 2006
Red | 2011 up to 2014   **88**
Straightforward, with firm tannins. This is fruity and elegant with medium concentration.

CÔTE RÔTIE 2005
Red | 2011 up to 2015   **86**
Some discreet hints of dark berries. Tannic on the tongue, with a minerality that grows in power in the mid-palate and at the finish. A rich and sufficiently concentrated wine.

CÔTE RÔTIE 2004
Red | 2011 up to 2017   **90**
Tea and very ripe red berries on the nose. Lots of spice (cinnamon, pepper). The texture is appetizing and tender, with supple tannins. This is an elegant wine, sufficiently linear without being austere.

CÔTE RÔTIE 2003
Red | 2011 up to 2013   **92**
A fresh bouquet of very forward fruit. Suave
and soft on the tongue, delicious and pleasing. Good freshness on the finish (strawberry syrup).

CÔTE RÔTIE LA PETITE FEUILLE 2006
Red | 2011 up to 2013   **85**
Supple, tender. These young vines don't yet
give the concentration of the old vines, but
the fruit is elegant. To enjoy for its youthful
aromas.

CÔTE RÔTIE LES GRANDES PLACES 2006
Red | 2011 up to 2016   **89**
More concentrated and longer on the palate than the introductory cuvée.

CÔTE RÔTIE LES GRANDES PLACES 2005
Red | 2011 up to 2015   **87**
Concentrated dark berries in the bouquet.
The attack in the mouth is saline. Good structure, with firm tannins. Nice length, with a
finish both mineral and direct. The old vines
played their part in giving this juice its perfume and concentration.

CÔTE RÔTIE LES GRANDES PLACES 2004
Red | 2011 up to 2013   **90**
More fine and concentrated on the nose than
the "simple" cuvée, this has great purity and
very delicate barrel notes, the aromas holding to fresh fruits and almond notes. On the
palate it is chewier and firmer, but the tannins are still as soft.

Red: 8.6 acres; syrah 100%. White: 1.2 acres; viognier
100%. Annual production: 17,000 bottles

JEAN-LUC COLOMBO

Les Eygas
07130 Cornas
Phone 00 33 4 75 84 17 10
Fax 00 33 4 75 84 17 19
www.vinsjlcolombo.com

Smooth-talking, larger-than-life Jean-Luc
Colombo is one of the most lovable personalities in the wine world today—a man with
big ideas and a genius for making them
happen. His greatest asset is a superb vineyard that features an impossibly steep hillside parcel known as Les Ruchets—a
dramatic site even for a winegrowing region
as spectacular as this one. Since the late
1980s, this has been the showcase for
Colombo's talents as a winegrower and
winemaker. Thanks to him, the Cornas
appellation now boasts silky tannins and
elegant aging potential that at last do justice to its exceptional terroirs. Colombo
started out as a wine consultant and
remains in high demand, having built up a
range of négociant wines that get better
every year (with appellations throughout
the northern Rhone). Other wines include
an agreeable Côtes du Rhône (red and
white) and selected Vins de Pays. His latest
coup is Les Pins Couchés, a wine from the
heavily limestone coastal area of Carry-le-
Rouet, near Colombo's native Marseilles,
where he has holdings in the prettily named
Côte Bleue district.

Recently tasted

CHÂTEAUNEUF-DU-PAPE LES BARTAVELLES 2006
Red | 2011 up to 2016   **89**

CONDRIEU AMOUR DE DIEU 2007
White | 2011 up to 2015   **89**

CORNAS LES MÉJEANS 2007
Red | 2011 up to 2014   **89**

CORNAS LES RUCHETS 2006
Red | 2011 up to 2016   **95**

CÔTE RÔTIE LA DIVINE 2006
Red | 2011 up to 2016   **89**

CÔTES DU RHÔNE LA REDONNE 2007
White | 2011 up to 2014   **90**

CÔTES DU RHÔNE LES ABEILLES 2007
White | 2011 up to 2013   **86**

CÔTES DU RHÔNE LES ABEILLES 2006
Red | 2011 up to 2013   **87**

CÔTES DU RHÔNE LES FOROTS 2006
Red | 2011 up to 2013   **88**

CÔTES DU RHÔNE-VILLAGES 2006
Red | 2011 up to 2013   87

CROZES-HERMITAGE LES FÉES BRUNES 2006
Red | 2011 up to 2013   88

CROZES-HERMITAGE LES GRAVIÈRES 2007
White | 2011 up to 2014   87

SAINT-JOSEPH LES LAUVES 2006
Red | 2011 up to 2013   88

SAINT-PÉRAY LA BELLE DE MAI 2007
White | 2011 up to 2014   88

VIN DE PAYS D' OC VIOGNIER LA VIOLETTE 2008
White | 2011 up to 2013   86

Older vintages

CONDRIEU AMOUR DE DIEU 2005
White | 2011 up to 2013   84
Round and mellow, yet limited in personality.

CORNAS LA LOUVÉE 2006
Red | 2011 up to 2016   92
Big and unctuous, with superbly silky tannins, a harmonious texture, and very delicate fruit: a great success.

CORNAS LA LOUVÉE 2005
Red | 2011 up to 2017   92
In a more suave and unctuous style than Les Ruchets, this splendid cuvée reveals itself to be both refined and full of energy, perfectly enhanced by its excellent élevage.

CORNAS LES RUCHETS 2006
Red | 2011 up to 2018   91
Deep and intense, a bit more austere at this time than La Louvée, but with tannins that are just as precise. A wine to be cellared.

CORNAS LES RUCHETS 2005
Red | 2011 up to 2020   96
A wine of great fullness, superbly made and showing a magnificently chiseled body: this wine shines in its unctuous definition. Its bouquet of ripe, dark berries is completed by very refined torrefacted notes. Splendid.

CORNAS TERRES BRÛLÉES 2006
Red | 2011 up to 2013   88
A Cornas with delicate texture but direct style, with its fruity scents and unctuous length.

CÔTE RÔTIE LA DIVINE 2005
Red | 2011 up to 2017   86
Solid but without the refinement of Cornas, this wine has good base structure. It could assuredly be cellared for several years to give it a chance to realize its spicy and fleshy potential.

COTEAUX D'AIX-EN-PROVENCE CÔTE BLEUE LES PINS COUCHÉS 2005
Red | 2011 up to 2014   88
A beautiful, unctuous, and full wine with no heaviness, amply proving the potential of this coastal terroir.

CÔTES DU RHÔNE LA REDONNE 2006
White | 2011 up to 2013   90
A very seductive white, combining lots of freshness and a profusion of apricot and floral notes from the roussanne and viognier. Balanced, with superb freshness.

CÔTES DU RHÔNE LES ABEILLES 2006
White | 2011 up to 2013   84
Fruity, round, pleasant, light.

CÔTES DU RHÔNE LES ABEILLES 2005
Red | 2011 up to 2013   88
Fruity and mellow, this is a ready-to-drink Côtes du Rhône, perfectly balanced and very direct.

CÔTES DU RHÔNE LES FOROTS 2005
Red | 2011 up to 2013   90
The bouquet of blackberries and the unctuous and refined texture bear witness to the superior pedigree of this Côtes du Rhône grown at the foot of the Cornas hills.

CROZES-HERMITAGE LES FÉES BRUNES 2005
Red | 2011 up to 2013   86
The fruit expresses itself very freely in this light and fresh wine. Ready to drink.

SAINT-JOSEPH LES LAUVES 2006
Red | 2011 up to 2013   90
You can smell the granite! An excellent Saint-Joseph, taut, deep, with pure fruit and no heaviness.

SAINT-JOSEPH LES LAUVES 2005
Red | 2011 up to 2013   84
This Saint-Joseph is well structured and well made, but it lacks a defined personality.

SAINT-PÉRAY LA BELLE DE MAI 2007
White | 2011 up to 2013   88
The scents of white peaches are expressive in this fat, fleshy, and flattering wine with good balance.

DOMAINE COMBIER

⚏ ⚏ ⚏ ⚏ ⚏

26600 Pont-de-l'Isère
Phone 00 33 4 75 84 61 56
Fax 00 33 4 75 84 53 43
domaine-combier@wanadoo.fr

This is one of the few properties that still has a significant quantity of fruit trees as well as vineyards. Laurent Combier, a third-generation farmer, was behind the development of the winemaking activities, which he began in 1989. Certified organic since 1970 (the domaine is a pioneer in the region), they now have fifty-eight acres of vines. Six different bottlings are produced: five Crozes-Hermitages and one Saint-Joseph. All of the wines see some time in barrel; the Clos des Grives spends a fair amount of time in new oak. A vertical tasting of recent vintages confirms the excellent quality of the wines, as well as their ability to age, for ten years or more in good vintages. The only problem is, the wines are so good that it has become difficult to get hold of them!

Recently tasted
Crozes-Hermitage 2008
Red | 2011 up to 2013   86

Crozes-Hermitage cuvée L. 2008
Red | 2011 up to 2013   84

Older vintages
Crozes-Hermitage 2007
Red | 2011 up to 2013   87
More concentrated and spicy than the cuvée L. Good texture, velvety, with refined and concentrated fruit. Elegant.

Crozes-Hermitage Clos des Grives 2007
White | 2011 up to 2017   90
Beautifully rich in texture and elegantly made, this is a fat wine with very beautiful extract, richly juicy yet plenty fresh on the finish.

Crozes-Hermitage Clos des Grives 2006
White | 2011 up to 2016   90
The nose is rich, still showing hints of wood. Fat in the mouth yet elegant, this still needs a bit of time. It's a ripe and civilized wine, and well balanced.

Crozes-Hermitage Clos des Grives 2007
Red | 2011 up to 2017   89
A wine with delicate and fat tannins, good extract, and delicious length. Fleshy and fresh.

Crozes-Hermitage Clos des Grives 2006
Red | 2011 up to 2015   88
Elegant, very ripe, with a round and delectable texture. The tannins caress. A fresh finish.

Crozes-Hermitage Clos des Grives 2005
Red | 2011 up to 2015   90
Refined and balanced, with good presence on the palate, streamlined and fresh. Good, flavorful length.

Crozes-Hermitage Clos des Grives 2004
Red | 2011 up to 2014   89
This is beginning to evolve. Round, tasty, with delicate tannins, good acidity. Balanced, straightforward, and fresh. Spicy and mentholated notes on the finish.

Crozes-Hermitage Clos des Grives 1997
Red | 2011 up to 2013   88
This has a beautiful aromatic range, concentrating on licorice and dark berries. Good freshness. The flavors are pleasing, the tannins tender, the finish spicy. It is perfectly ready.

Red: 54.4 acres; syrah 100%. White: 3.7 acres; marsanne 80%, roussanne 20%. Annual production: 130,000 bottles

DOMAINE PIERRE ET JÉRÔME COURSODON

3, place du Marché
07300 Mauves
Phone 00 33 4 75 08 18 29
pierre.coursodon@wanadoo.fr

This domaine is one of the benchmark wineries in the Saint-Joseph appellation. This is a family enterprise, run today by Pierre Coursodon's son Jérôme, whose drive and enthusiasm have taken the wines toward purer fruit and more freshness (for the white wines) and mainly sleeker, silkier tannins (for the reds). All of the wines age as gracefully as ever but are now more supple and approachable when young—definitely a sea change for this producer! Jérôme even rethought the somewhat tired-looking labels: since 2006, the former cuvée domaine has been known as the Silice.

Recently tasted
SAINT-JOSEPH SILICE 2008
White | 2011 up to 2013   **86**

Older vintages
SAINT-JOSEPH L'OLIVAIE 2007
Red | 2011 up to 2015   **88**
Very hedonistic, with notes of dark berries and cocoa. The tannins are linear with good tension on the palate; the finish is flavorful and fresh, racy and lightly peppery. Very elegant.

SAINT-JOSEPH L'OLIVAIE 2006
Red | 2011 up to 2016   **88**
More concentrated and stronger in aroma than Silice, with notes of stewed red berries and sweet spices. It is delicious and charming, with a tasty and fresh finish.

SAINT-JOSEPH LA SENSONNE 2006
Red | 2011 up to 2016   **89**
The nose reveals new oak aging, but the style is appetizing. The palate is spicy and lightly peppery, with fine tannins and a tight, concentrated finish.

SAINT-JOSEPH LE PARADIS SAINT-PIERRE 2007
White | 2011 up to 2014   **88**
A fat wine with a beautifully expressive palate, both floral and elegant. It has beautiful, mouth-watering bitterness in the finish.

SAINT-JOSEPH LE PARADIS SAINT-PIERRE 2007
Red | 2011 up to 2016   **89**
Rich and taut, this is an honest and concentrated wine that will offer itself more freely after a few years of cellaring. The finish offers up spicy tannins.

SAINT-JOSEPH LE PARADIS SAINT-PIERRE 2006
White | 2011 up to 2013   **92**
Persistent and long, this is a great white wine. Superb! It can be appreciated right now, but it will undoubtedly improve over the next few years.

SAINT-JOSEPH LE PARADIS SAINT-PIERRE 2006
Red | 2011 up to 2016   **89**
Fruitier and fleshier than the Sansonne, this has a velvet palate, balanced and fresh. It showcases the grape's natural fruit flavors better since the élevage was less intense.

SAINT-JOSEPH LE PARADIS SAINT-PIERRE 2005
White | 2011 up to 2013   **88**
Still youthful, but with beautiful fruit and floral scents. The finish is tense and precise, the sign of good terroir.

SAINT-JOSEPH SILICE 2007
Red | 2011 up to 2013   **87**
Fleshy, good red fruit and sweet spice. A delicious wine with well-enrobed tannins and a fresh finish.

SAINT-JOSEPH SILICE 2006
White | 2011 up to 2013   **90**
Here is a beautiful expression of granite terroir. This wine blends richness and minerality, all at once fresh and ample, all the while retaining great purity.

Red: 32.1 acres; syrah 100%. White: 4.9 acres; marsanne 95%, roussanne 5%. Annual production: 60,000 bottles

DOMAINE YVES CUILLERON

🦐 🦐 🦐 🦐 🦐

59 RN 86 Verlieu
42410 Chavanay
Phone 00 33 4 74 87 02 37
Fax 00 33 4 74 87 05 62
cave@cuilleron.com
www.cuilleron.com

Yves Cuilleron is the second largest Condrieu producer after Guigal, with enough holdings to showcase his different terroirs in the Côte Rôtie, Saint-Joseph, and Condrieu. He makes an impressive variety of wines, all with a certain family resemblance. The reds display spicy, savory power thanks to ripe, concentrated juice that culminates in a taut finish. The wood influence is quite distinct in the young wine but eventually fades after four to five years in the bottle. The white wines play on fatness and volume but always finish fresh and balanced, with a terrifically pure nose and pronounced, mature notes of fruit and flowers. Production is very consistent whatever the wine or vintage—which is particularly admirable from a winery that always makes enough to go around!

Recently tasted

CONDRIEU LES AYGUETS 2007
White | 2011 up to 2017   89

CORNAS LES VIRES 2007
Red | 2011 up to 2017   89

CÔTE RÔTIE LES TERRES SOMBRES 2007
Red | 2011 up to 2017   90

CÔTE RÔTIE MADINIÈRE 2007
Red | 2011 up to 2015   89

SAINT-JOSEPH L'AMARYBELLE 2007
Red | 2011 up to 2013   88

Older vintages

CONDRIEU LES CHAILLETS VIEILLES VIGNES 2005
White | 2011 up to 2013   88
A very ripe Condrieu, rich in alcohol, this is more powerful than refined, but the quality of the base material is incontestable.

CONDRIEU VERTIGE 2006
White | 2011 up to 2016   90
A powerful and rich wine, lightly lactic, but delicious and flavorful. Its richness is balanced.

CORNAS LES VIRES 2006
Red | 2011 up to 2016   88
Ripe and concentrated, with a touch of minerality in the bouquet. The palate is pleasing, the tannins well dressed, balanced, and fresh. A rich and unctuous Cornas that doesn't deny its roots!

CÔTE RÔTIE BASSENON 2004
Red | 2011 up to 2015   90
Lightly smoky and velvety on the nose. Hints of tea and ripe herbs. Ample and ripe, with beautiful aromatic largesse. The palate is rich, with a bit of rigidity typical of this vintage, but the tannins are nonetheless nicely enrobed. It is honest and somewhat fruity. A tense wine, with a good, straightforward finish.

CÔTE RÔTIE LES TERRES SOMBRES 2005
Red | 2011 up to 2025   91
Ripe and intense fruit. Concentrated on the palate, honest and elegant, with great maturity, this is a pure, rich wine with a long and fresh finish. Flavorful.

CÔTE RÔTIE LES TERRES SOMBRES 2004
Red | 2011 up to 2015   92
A wine with impeccable definition on the palate: long and streamlined, with beautiful, fat tannins, firm and smooth. Superb finesse.

CÔTE RÔTIE LES TERRES SOMBRES 2003
Red | 2011 up to 2015   91
The bouquet is complex and velvety. Hints of tea and strong fruit notes, lightly cooked. Firm and dense tannins. A smooth finish, just a little short. Beautiful aromatic depth. A dense wine that will age well, this is in a closed phase right now.

CÔTE RÔTIE MADINIÈRE 2004
Red | 2011 up to 2013   89
Open on the nose, with a diverse bouquet. The palate is smooth and nicely concentrated, but the youth of the vines is detectable, with a small dip in the mid-palate. The finish is dense and precise. This will mature rather quickly.

SAINT-JOSEPH L'AMARYBELLE 2004
Red | 2011 up to 2013   90
A very open bouquet, nearly opulent: tea and red berries, a touch buttery. Delicious and flattering, well structured. The tannins are firm. It's a ripe wine that could be enjoyed young, but it will mature well over the next few years.

SAINT-JOSEPH LES SERINES 2005
Red | 2011 up to 2015   89
Hot and fruity, pretty powerful. The palate is velvety, the fruit ripe, the finish aromatic and fresh (eucalyptus). A fat and aromatic wine, balanced and fresh.

Red: 61.8 acres; syrah 100%. White: 49.4 acres; marsanne 23%, roussanne 15%, viognier 62%.
Annual production: 250,000 bottles

DELAS

ZA de l'Olivet
07300 Saint-Jean-de-Muzols
Phone 00 33 4 75 08 60 30
Fax 00 33 4 75 08 53 67
france@delas.com

Delas, now owned by Deutz Champagne, is an ancient, traditional wine house offering a broad selection of wines from all areas of the Rhone Valley. Quality does vary depending on the cuvée—many of the entry-level offerings tend to lack depth—but the good bottlings are very good indeed, as demonstrated by the Marquise de la Tourette Hermitage.

Recently tasted

CONDRIEU CLOS BOUCHER 2007
White | 2011 up to 2017   90

CONDRIEU LA GALOPINE 2007
White | 2011 up to 2015   89

CORNAS CHANTE-PERDRIX 2006
Red | 2011 up to 2016   90

CÔTE RÔTIE LA LANDONNE 2006
Red | 2011 up to 2021   93

COTEAUX DU TRICASTIN 2007
Red | 2011 up to 2013   89

CÔTES DU RHÔNE SAINT-ESPRIT 2007
Red | 2011 up to 2013   90

CÔTES DU VENTOUX 2007
Red | 2011 up to 2013   87

CROZES-HERMITAGE LE CLOS 2006
Red | 2011 up to 2016   91

CROZES-HERMITAGE LES LAUNES 2007
Red | 2011 up to 2015   88

HERMITAGE MARQUISE DE LA TOURETTE 2006
Red | 2011 up to 2021   92

HERMITAGE MARQUISE DE LA TOURETTE 2006
White | 2011 up to 2021   93

Older vintages

CONDRIEU CLOS BOUCHER 2006
White | 2011 up to 2013   90
Rich and fat, fully open, with ample length and beautiful generosity.

CONDRIEU LA GALOPINE 2006
White | 2011 up to 2013   87
Mild fruit, deliciously pleasing length. Quite well done even if lacking intensity.

CORNAS CHANTE-PERDRIX 2005
Red | 2011 up to 2013   90
Fat and supple with honest fruit, this is elegant and tender, finishing on fruit.

CÔTE RÔTIE LA LANDONNE 2005
Red | 2011 up to 2016   92
Straightforward, deep, rather austere. Long.

CÔTE RÔTIE SEIGNEUR DE MAUGIRON 2006
Red | 2011 up to 2016   92
Smooth and fat with mellow, ripe fruit and supple length, but lacking a bit of energy.

CÔTES DU RHÔNE SAINT-ESPRIT 2006
Red | 2011 up to 2013   89
With a majority of syrah, this is a fat and deep wine with generous dark-berry scents. Long.

CROZES-HERMITAGE
DOMAINE DES GRANDS CHEMINS 2006
Red | 2011 up to 2016   89
A full wine with a fruity bouquet, this is generous, svelte, and long. Excellent.

CROZES-HERMITAGE LE CLOS 2005
Red | 2011 up to 2013   88
A special selection from vines on alluvial gravel: a good, rich wine, supple, harmonious, well built but with medium density.

CROZES-HERMITAGE LES LAUNES 2006
Red | 2011 up to 2013   88
Supple and honest fruit, with lots of energy and freshness. Frank length.

HERMITAGE BESSARDS 2006
Red | 2011 up to 2023   95
Black in color. Deep fruit, great flavors, and impressive length, force, and intensity. A great wine, true to its region.

HERMITAGE MARQUISE DE LA TOURETTE 2005
Red | 2011 up to 2016   93
Deep, racy, long, and flavorful, with minerality and length. A thoroughbred.

HERMITAGE MARQUISE DE LA TOURETTE 2005
White | 2011 up to 2018   90
Golden. Almond bouquet. Fat and intense, with bitterness in the finish. It has potential.

SAINT-JOSEPH SAINTE-ÉPINE 2006
Red | 2011 up to 2016   88
A splendid Saint-Joseph: supple, elegant, mineral, and deep, with an elegant structure and brilliant fruit.

Annual production: 1,500,000 bottles

FERRATON PÈRE & FILS

13, rue de la Sizeranne
26600 Tain-l'Hermitage
Phone 00 33 4 75 08 59 51
Fax 00 33 4 75 08 81 59
ferraton@ferraton.fr
www.ferraton.fr

This is a small but admirably located estate with holdings in Hermitage, Crozes, and Saint-Joseph. It is now almost wholly owned by Maison Chapoutier (with which it already worked in partnership) but remains independently run. Rather more interesting, Ferraton Père & Fils has retained a very specific style and recently opened up a small wine business, specializing in its entry-level offerings (Côtes du Rhône, Ermitage Le Reverdy, and Crozes-Hermitage La Matinière). Recent vintages have improved dramatically under the brilliant tutelage of Ferraton's present director: some of these wines are among the most attractive of all the appellation offerings.

Recently tasted

Côtes du Rhône-Villages Plan de Dieu 2007
Red | 2011 up to 2013   89

Ermitage Le Méal 2007
Red | 2012 up to 2022   97

Ermitage Le Reverdy 2007
White | 2011 up to 2022   90

Ermitage Les Dionnières 2007
Red | 2012 up to 2022   95

Saint-Joseph Les Oliviers 2007
White | 2011 up to 2017   89

Older vintages

Châteauneuf-du-Pape Le Parvis 2005
Red | 2011 up to 2013   86
A classically structured Châteauneuf, yet without particular depth. Its bouquet of spice and meat juices and its rather remarkable suppleness make it a good wine for restaurants.

Côtes du Rhône Samorëns 2007
White | 2011 up to 2013   87
A very good white Côtes du Rhône, both firm and flavorful, with beautiful almond aromas blended with notes of white fruit. Generous length, with truly fresh and intense persistence.

Côtes du Rhône Samorëns 2006
Red | 2011 up to 2013   88
A taut, svelte Côtes du Rhône with notes of dark berries and pain au chocolat, lifted by a nuance of minerality. Straightforward and pleasing on the palate, it's very flavorful, a perfect wine to accompany red meat.

Crozes-Hermitage La Matinière 2007
White | 2011 up to 2013   88
A lithe wine with fruit enlivened by a light salinity and a good, precise, and clean finish.

Crozes-Hermitage La Matinière 2006
Red | 2011 up to 2013   84
A light and svelte wine, but with less character than the Saint-Joseph La Source.

Crozes-Hermitage La Matinière 2005
Red | 2011 up to 2013   88
The nose is concentrated and mineral. The palate is suave and elegant, with beautiful, silky, refined tannins. It's a structured wine with a spicy finish.

Crozes-Hermitage Le Grand Courtil 2007
Red | 2011 up to 2017   90
From estate vineyards, this Crozes has lots of body, character, and depth. It's a pedigreed wine, intense with elegant yet firm tannins and generous, flavorful length.

Crozes-Hermitage Le Grand Courtil 2006
Red | 2011 up to 2018   91
Very full, tasty, deep, and intense, this has a superb range on the nose, from white peppercorns to tiny black and red berries and a touch of minerality in the finish.

Ermitage Le Méal 2006
Red | 2011 up to 2022   95
More delicately mineral in character than Les Dionnières, this has intense length and a smooth finish. The texture is elegant, with silky tannins. An absolutely remarkable wine.

Ermitage Le Méal 2005
Red | 2011 up to 2022   95
Despite strong notes of ultraripe black currants, this wine has no heaviness but instead comes across as very rich and fleshy, with great freshness. Lots of elegance, finesse, and depth.

Ermitage Le Reverdy 2006
White | 2011 up to 2016   89
Amply structured, but a little less energetic than the 2005, this 2006 Hermitage is golden-hued, generous, and full. The finish is still a bit heavy and requires a few years to become more refined.

ERMITAGE LE REVERDY 2005
White | 2011 up to 2018 **90**
This wine from the Ferraton domaine offers remarkable depth lifted by the scents of toasted almonds and very mineral notes. It is ample, long, and persistent, undeniably a choice for cellaring.

ERMITAGE LES DIONNIÈRES 2006
Red | 2011 up to 2020 **92**
This wine is ample, warm, and deep, rich in dark-berry flavor and expanding on velvety length. It's delicious, with great intensity, simultaneously demonstrative and refined.

ERMITAGE LES DIONNIÈRES 2005
Red | 2011 up to 2022 **95**
Totally opaque in color, a deep garnet. Magnificent nose of very ripe black currants. Big, fleshy, deep, and pedigreed, with very silky tannins and beautiful freshness in the finish.

HERMITAGE LES MIAUX 2007
White | 2011 up to 2017 **88**
Golden in color, this has aromas of salted caramel and white fruit. On the palate, it's mellow yet long, and well structured. To be enjoyed soon.

HERMITAGE LES MIAUX 2006
Red | 2011 up to 2016 **88**
A beautiful, fat Hermitage, this is delicious and deep, with a richly berried bouquet and a delectable, full body. It could be cellared for a few years.

HERMITAGE LES MIAUX 2005
Red | 2011 up to 2018 **90**
Deep and pedigreed, this is a very elegant Hermitage with delicate notes of small red berries and svelte length. Intense and full of energy.

SAINT-JOSEPH LA SOURCE 2007
White | 2011 up to 2014 **87**
A simple and sapid Saint-Joseph with mineral freshness and good suppleness—yet it is undeniably less tasty than the Côtes du Rhône.

SAINT-JOSEPH LES OLIVIERS 2007
White | 2011 up to 2013 **87**
Remarkably fat with scents of pêche de vigne and apricot, this is ample and immediately tasty. You could drink it right now, but it could also be cellared for two to three years.

Red: 15.6 acres; syrah 100%. White: 2.5 acres; marsanne 50%, roussanne 50%. Annual production: 35,000 bottles

DOMAINE PIERRE GAILLARD

Lieu-dit Chez Favier
42520 Malleval
Phone 00 33 4 74 87 13 10
Fax 00 33 4 74 87 17 66
vinsp.gaillard@wanadoo.fr
www.domainespierregaillard.com

You can't miss Pierre Gaillard's wines: just look for the bottles with the brightly colored labels. The estate itself is lovely and mainly famous for its splendid Côte Rôtie bottlings: unfailingly creamy, perfumed wines that are delicious when young but equally capable of graceful aging. In addition, Gaillard also makes a slightly sweet Condrieu that remains fresh and balanced despite a phenomenally high sugar concentration. The wine is a real stunner and sure to fool more than one oenophile in a blind tasting of great sweet wines. Gaillard's other winemaking ventures include the highly original Maison des Vins de Vienne that he started with François Villard and Yves Cuilleron.

Recently tasted
CONDRIEU 2007
Sweet White | 2011 up to 2013 **88**

CORNAS 2007
Red | 2011 up to 2017 **89**

CÔTE RÔTIE 2007
Red | 2011 up to 2017 **89**

CÔTES DU RHÔNE 2007
White | 2011 up to 2013 **87**

SAINT-JOSEPH CLOS DE CUMINAILLE 2007
Red | 2011 up to 2017 **90**

SAINT-JOSEPH LES PIERRES 2007
Red | 2011 up to 2017 **91**

VIN DE PAYS DES COLLINES RHODANIENNES
ASIATICUS 2007
Red | 2011 up to 2017 **89**

Older vintages
CONDRIEU FLEURS D'AUTOMNE
VENDANGES TARDIVES 2005
Sweet White | 2011 up to 2013 **97**
The saturated golden color indicates a strong maturity. On the nose, the candied aromas are absolutely beautiful: apricot, peach, the whole range of yellow fruit with a few hints of tropical fruit, fruit jellies, and jams. The palate is unbelievably pure, with great, sweet richness. The acidity is superb, striking the sort of balance found only in the greatest wines.

CORNAS 2006
Red | 2011 up to 2021   **88**

Powerful and intense, a Cornas with well-presented wood notes. The base material is ripe, the finish saline, the tannins firm. It needs more time. A civilized Cornas.

CÔTE RÔTIE 2006
Red | 2011 up to 2021   **89**

Concentrated dark-fruit aromas. On the palate, this is a wine with tight flavors, dense and beautifully mineral in the finish. It's very taut.

CÔTE RÔTIE 2004
Red | 2011 up to 2015   **90**

A very lovely buttery bouquet, spicy and very smooth. It is fleshy on the palate, fat and balanced, with skillful aging that underscores the wine without hardening it. Good length. A balanced and dense wine.

CÔTE RÔTIE 2003
Red | 2011 up to 2013   **90**

The nose is very ripe dominated by black olives and licorice. Delicious and seductive, long on the palate, fat and rich with a superbly fresh finish. Good balance.

CÔTE RÔTIE ROSE POURPRE 2004
Red | 2011 up to 2013   **95**

A Côte Rôtie with delicate and direct aromas, this is velvety in texture, with a superb soft finish. A true delight.

SAINT-JOSEPH CLOS DE CUMINAILLE 2006
Red | 2011 up to 2016   **89**

Spicy, fruity, and flavorful, this feels mellow on the palate, round, smooth, and charming. Very beautiful balance. Needs time to integrate the effects of its barrel aging.

Red: 27.2 acres; syrah 100%. White: 14.8 acres; roussanne 25%, viognier 75%. Annual production: 85,000 bottles

DOMAINE GANGLOFF

2, rue Garenne
69420 Gondrieu
Phone 00 33 4 74 59 57 04

Yves Gangloff is a fifty-year-old wine-grower with a head full of ideas: one of them is this winery that he started from scratch some twenty years ago. Gangloff's casual demeanor looks a bit out of place in this somewhat traditional, conservative winegrowing community. So do his wines: honest-tasting, very pure, with real palate expression and good concentration, made to drink fairly young. The consistent quality of the red and white wines alike says a lot about Gangloff's meticulous attention to viticulture. The attractive labels on some of his wines are an added sensual pleasure!

CONDRIEU 2004
White | 2011 up to 2013   **90**

Very pure in fruit aromas. Fat in the mouth, very rich, very ripe, with generous alcohol and a spicy finish. Altogether well balanced.

CONDRIEU COTEAU DE CHERY 2005
White | 2011 up to 2013   **90**

Tasted while still fermenting, this is pure, complete, fat, and quite delicious.

CÔTE RÔTIE LA BARBARINE 2005
Red | 2011 up to 2015   **90**

Powerful, very tannic. A massive wine. Nicely matured and well made. It has a spicy, highly seasoned finish.

CÔTE RÔTIE LA BARBARINE 2004
Red | 2011 up to 2015   **89**

Very fresh fruit (strawberry), with vegetal notes typical of the vintage. The tannins are delicate, and the length is nicely present. The freshness returns in the finish.

CÔTE RÔTIE LA BARBARINE 2003
Red | 2011 up to 2014   **88**

The nose is very ripe, with prune aromas. Powerful. The palate remains fresh, with density. A little volatile. It should mature rather quickly, but is pleasant now. The tannins are fresh and sufficiently fat.

CÔTE RÔTIE LA SEREINE NOIRE 2004
Red | 2011 up to 2015   **91**

The bouquet is voluptuous, the attack on the palate fleshy. The mineral notes and tension take over on the palate. It has a lightly smoky finish and beautiful concentration. A powerful wine, yet very pleasant to drink.

DOMAINE JEAN-MICHEL GERIN

ɪɪɪ ɪɪ

19, rue de Montmain
Verenay
69420 Ampuis
Phone 00 33 4 74 56 16 56
Fax 00 33 4 74 56 11 37
gerin.jm@wanadoo.fr
www.domaine-gerin.fr

Jean-Michel Gerin's first-class estate is certainly one of the top sources for excellent Côte Rôtie and makes three quite different wines: Champin le Seigneur is the most widely distributed offering and is made in a readily approachable, irresistible style; Les Grandes Places shows slightly more depth; and La Landonne boasts an unfailingly precise, rigorously defined palate. Overall quality is flawless and has been for many years, always delivering those ripe, fat, palate-coating tannins. Jean-Michel Gerin and a few friends have recently opened a bar in the village square in Ampuis: another address worth noting.

Recently tasted

CONDRIEU LA LOYE 2007
White | 2011 up to 2014   **89**

CÔTE RÔTIE CHAMPIN LE SEIGNEUR 2007
Red | 2011 up to 2017   **90**

CÔTE RÔTIE LA LANDONNE 2007
Red | 2012 up to 2027   **95**

CÔTE RÔTIE LES GRANDES PLACES 2007
Red | 2014 up to 2027   **94**

SAINT-JOSEPH 2007
Red | 2011 up to 2017   **90**

Older vintages

CONDRIEU LA LOYE 2006
White | 2011 up to 2016   **87**
With a highly refined and elegant bouquet and great purity of palate, this has a beautiful range of fruit (ripe apricots, honey). It's balanced and rich, yet fresh in the mouth, with a correct and concentrated finish. The high alcohol is well handled. Savory and elegant.

CÔTE RÔTIE CHAMPIN LE SEIGNEUR 2006
Red | 2011 up to 2016   **89**
Delectable and elegant, this is a charming, pleasing, and round wine, fruity on the palate with a touch of minerality (salty finish). Ideal for restaurants, as it can be enjoyed young.

CÔTE RÔTIE CHAMPIN LE SEIGNEUR 2005
Red | 2011 up to 2020   **90**
Fruity, open, and generous, with a refined and noble bouquet of raisins and tobacco, this is delicious and appetizing. Very velvety, with superb texture on the palate, it caresses the mouth suavely. The finish is long and aromatic. Already very seductive, it will get even better with time. Well done in the style of its vintage.

CÔTE RÔTIE LA LANDONNE 2006
Red | 2011 up to 2026   **93**
A linear, intense, and very elegant bouquet, with superbly concentrated and refined juice. The finish is all purity and honesty, while the aging brings it nobility. Very flattering.

CÔTE RÔTIE LES GRANDES PLACES 2006
Red | 2011 up to 2026   **93**
More linear and tight than La Landonne, with less volume and more length and minerality. It will age beautifully as well. Taut, classy, long, and fresh.

Red: 19.8 acres; syrah 100%. White: 4.9 acres; viognier 100%. Annual production: 100,000 bottles

DOMAINE PIERRE GONON

🙐 🙐 🙐 🙐 🙐

34, avenue Ozier
07300 Mauves
Phone 00 33 4 75 08 45 27
Fax 00 33 4 75 08 65 21
gonon.pierre@wanadoo.fr

Domaine Gonon is a very small estate in Saint-Joseph. All of its wines are refined and honest, though we do have to admit a preference for the reds: solid, with firm tannins and honest expression of fruit. Among the whites, the Cuvée Les Oliviers shows sincerity but not always enough freshness. Kudos to this estate for its adroit handling of recent vintages, especially the 2005 and 2006. This is certainly one of the most reliable Saint-Joseph estates.

SAINT-JOSEPH 2007
Red | 2011 up to 2017   **90**
Fleshy and elegant, with good, ripe, delicious fruit, this is a refined wine, rich in good tannins, dense and fresh.

SAINT-JOSEPH 2006
Red | 2011 up to 2014   **90**
Quite ripe, with notes of dark berries and peppery spices, this is a linear, concentrated wine, refined and fresh, a thoroughbred. The finish is flavorful. The minimal destemming gives it a more austere side.

SAINT-JOSEPH 2005
Red | 2011 up to 2013   **90**
Very good, with a very pleasant expression of fruit and a great, forthright structure.

SAINT-JOSEPH 1998
Red | 2011 up to 2013   **90**
Nicely open, with expressive red fruit and floral scents as well as tertiary notes (leather). Elegant on the palate, with silky tannins and delicate extract. The finish is flavorful, complex, and expressive, with very fresh aromas. This is not in any way past its prime! Good aromatic persistence.

SAINT-JOSEPH LES OLIVIERS 2007
White | 2011 up to 2014   **88**
Very lovely richness on the palate. Complex, refined, subtle, elegant. The finish is fresh and flavorful.

SAINT-JOSEPH LES OLIVIERS 2006
White | 2011 up to 2014   **90**
Ripe and perfumed, this is a refined and delicate wine with a pleasant aromatic palette. Good richness on the palate, with a tasty and long finish.

SAINT-JOSEPH LES OLIVIERS 2005
White | 2011 up to 2013   **86**
Pleasant, but this wine lacks freshness and a touch of finesse.

SAINT-JOSEPH LES OLIVIERS 2001
White | 2011 up to 2013   **90**
This wine is evolving with notes of flowers and herbal tea. Refined and classy, very elegant, it is rich and flavorful on the palate with a finish of dried fruits and raisins. Even the white wines age very well here!

VIN DE PAYS DE L'ARDÈCHE LES ÎLES FERAY 2007
Red | 2011 up to 2013   **86**
A spicy syrah with good fruit. It's fleshy and delicious, very supple, with beautiful elegance.

Red: 13.6 acres; syrah 100%. White: 4.9 acres; marsanne 75%, roussanne 25%. Annual production: 29,000 bottles

DOMAINE ALAIN GRAILLOT

🍷🍷🍷🍷🍷

Les Chênes Verts
26600 Pont-de-l'Isère
Phone 00 33 4 75 84 67 52
Fax 00 33 4 75 84 79 33
graillot.alain@wanadoo.fr

It is winegrowers like Alain Graillot who have made Crozes-Hermitage the dynamic appellation it is today. Witness his red Crozes: among the finest, most harmonious syrah-based wines in all of the Rhone Valley. Oenophiles will be glad to know that despite this winery's leading reputation, it is still accepting new customers (simply get in touch by December 1 in the year following the harvest). Viticulture here is not organic but very soil-friendly nonetheless. The wines are fruity and honest, with ripe, tannic reds that make excellent Crozes for drinking young or not so young—the La Guiraude, for instance. The whites are more straightforward but equally recommended.

Recently tasted

CROZES-HERMITAGE LA GUIRAUDE 2007
Red | 2011 up to 2017   **91**

SAINT-JOSEPH 2007
Red | 2011 up to 2017   **90**

Older vintages

CROZES-HERMITAGE 2007
White | 2011 up to 2013   **85**
Delicate fruit, light on the palate, taut, with beautiful aromatic expression. To be enjoyed young.

CROZES-HERMITAGE 2007
Red | 2011 up to 2015   **89**
Powerful and full-bodied, this is a dense and flavorful wine.

CROZES-HERMITAGE 2006
White | 2011 up to 2013   **87**
A fruity nose, full of honey and yellow fruit. It feels fat in the mouth, rich and already open.

CROZES-HERMITAGE 2006
Red | 2011 up to 2014   **89**
Elegant, ripe fruit. Concentrated on the palate, honest. A concentrated and lively finish. Very good.

CROZES-HERMITAGE 2005
Red | 2011 up to 2013   **89**
The nose is refined and elegant. The palate is unctuous, with great depth and a touch of delicacy. The tannins are fat. The finish is long, perfumed, fresh, and balanced.

CROZES-HERMITAGE LA GUIRAUDE 2006
Red | 2011 up to 2016   **90**
Elegant and spicy. Straightforward on the palate, taut, and fresh. A Crozes with a tight and concentrated finish.

CROZES-HERMITAGE LA GUIRAUDE 2005
Red | 2011 up to 2013   **92**
A refined and velvety wine, well concentrated in its dark-berry and tapenade notes. It is rich and powerful yet fresh and balanced. Subtle and refined.

CROZES-HERMITAGE LA GUIRAUDE 1996
Red | 2011 up to 2013   **91**
Open, fully formed, complex, with a beautiful aromatic range of red and black berries and spice as well as impressive aromatic freshness. Straightforward on the palate and long, with a lively and taut finish. Delicately full-bodied. It is ready. Good Crozes do age well!

SAINT-JOSEPH 2006
Red | 2011 up to 2013   **84**
Seductive fruitiness in the mouth, with round tannins. This lacks structure (young vines), but its fruity character is pleasing. Supple.

Red: 42 acres; syrah 100%. White: 7.4 acres; marsanne 80%, roussanne 20%. Annual production: 100,000 bottles

CHÂTEAU GRILLET

🍃 🍃 🍃 🍃 🍃

42410 Verin
Phone 00 33 4 74 59 51 56
Fax 00 33 4 78 92 96 10

In the first half of the twentieth century, French writer and gastronome Curnonsky (aka the "prince of the gastronomes") placed this cru among the five greatest white wines in France. Today's owner, Isabelle Canet-Baratin, is fiercely determined to restore that reputation. Château Grillet is an enclave with its own AOC within the Condrieu AOC. Both are exclusively planted to viognier, but otherwise the Grillet vineyards are distinguished by their southern aspect (unlike the slopes bordering the Rhone, which face mostly east) and especially by their extraordinary, almost sandy soils derived from decomposed granite. The wines show none of the exuberance of a Condrieu but on the contrary exhibit an immense finesse that settles on the palate in layers of refined, lively, velvety depth. Château Grillet wines age magnificently but are also accessible when young (in which case, best to decant them several hours before serving).

Recently tasted
CHÂTEAU-GRILLET 2007
White | 2011 up to 2022   92

Older vintages
CHÂTEAU-GRILLET 2006
White | 2011 up to 2021   91
With purity and intense stature, this is a flavorful and refined wine. Even though it's young, it still manages to express its superior terroir. Charming and delicate.

CHÂTEAU-GRILLET 2005
White | 2011 up to 2025   96
An intense and complex wine with subtle floral and toasted notes. It feels rich, but the wine is still young, with superb acidity in the finish. Very delicate and pure, this wine has a long and radiant future ahead.

CHÂTEAU-GRILLET 2004
White | 2011 up to 2020   92
Less complex than the 2005, this is a delicate wine with subtle toast and yellow-fruit notes. The balance isn't quite there yet, but it has good acidity and a refreshing finish. Best to wait a bit, even though it seems supple.

CHÂTEAU-GRILLET 2003
White | 2011 up to 2020   96
The flavors are rich, with superb balance, finishing with a pleasant bitterness and delicate lemon notes. The wine seems powerful, but lacks a little maturity and volume in the mouth. Still, it maintains a certain freshness and balance. Atypical for this producer, but a very great wine! Unctuous and sensual in the mouth.

DOMAINE BERNARD GRIPA

5, avenue Ozier
07300 Mauves
Phone 00 33 4 75 08 14 96
Fax 00 33 4 75 07 06 81
gripa@wanadoo.fr

Fabrice Gripa belongs to the same generation as Jérôme Coursodon and, like him, has also returned to the family holdings, mainly located in Saint-Joseph. His style of wine is, however, quite different. Gripa white wines are fat and ripe, with pure, honest floral notes, while the reds are more traditional in style, with quite pronounced tannins. Red and white alike can stand moderate cellaring.

Recently tasted

SAINT-JOSEPH LE BERCEAU 2007
Red | 2011 up to 2013   86

SAINT-JOSEPH LE BERCEAU 2007
White | 2011 up to 2013   84

SAINT-PÉRAY LES PINS 2007
White | 2011 up to 2013   85

Older vintages

SAINT-JOSEPH 2006
White | 2011 up to 2013   84
Fat and toasty, with a medium-long finish. Pleasant.

SAINT-JOSEPH 2006
Red | 2011 up to 2013   84
Medium concentration. Fruity, rather light, and ready to drink. A bit short.

SAINT-JOSEPH LE BERCEAU 2006
White | 2011 up to 2014   87
Fat, with refined bitterness on the palate, this wine is elegant and delicious.

SAINT-JOSEPH LE BERCEAU 2006
Red | 2011 up to 2014   87
The nose is open; the palate is fruity with hints of spices. An elegant, rather charming wine with a linear finish.

SAINT-JOSEPH LE BERCEAU 2005
White | 2011 up to 2013   88
Richly oaked but with ripe fruit, this is a fat, ambitious wine, well done in a modern style. The butter and vanilla overwhelm the other aromas for the moment.

SAINT-JOSEPH LE BERCEAU 2005
Red | 2011 up to 2013   90
Beautiful and deep in color. A serious wine, long and filled with sap. The tannins are firm yet refined, with length.

SAINT-PÉRAY LES FIGUIERS 2006
White | 2011 up to 2013   86
Very ripe, notes of yellow fruit (peaches). Delicious oak. Rich, round, and elegant on the palate, with the barrel notes just lightly perceptible at this time.

SAINT-PÉRAY LES FIGUIERS 2005
White | 2011 up to 2013   90
Pale gold in color. Vanilla oak. A floral wine, fat and subtle, long and brilliant.

SAINT-PÉRAY LES PINS 2006
White | 2011 up to 2013   84
Fat, floral, medium concentration. Notes of yellow fruit on the palate.

Red: 19.8 acres; syrah 100%. **White:** 14.8 acres; marsanne 75%, roussanne 25%. **Annual production:** 60,000 bottles

E. GUIGAL

🍷🍷🍷🍷

Château d'Ampuis
69420 Ampuis
Phone 00 33 4 74 56 10 22
Fax 00 33 4 74 56 18 76
contact@guigal.com
www.guigal.com

You have only to cross the village of Ampuis, home of this domaine, to realize the fantastic progress made by Guigal over the past ten years. But the indefatigable Marcel Guigal is by no means resting on his laurels. Now partnered full-time with his son Philippe, the spitting image of his father, Marcel is ever ready to give his business what it needs to go even farther. He has expanded his business through the purchase of new vineyard holdings, some now incorporated within this domaine (notably De Vallouit and Grippat, keys to the creation of great Saint-Joseph and Hermitage cuvées), others remaining domaines in their own right (such as the Domaine de Bonserine, on the Côte Rôtie). Then there is the acquisition of Ampuis castle and, most notably, the impressive expansion of the fermenting room and aging cellars. Such are the assets that have given this astonishing family the means to make continuous progress. The last example is particularly significant because it now allows the Guigals to grow and blend all of their négociant wines themselves, including the Côtes du Rhône, which Ampuis produces to the tune of several million bottles. It isn't every producer who can deliver such magisterial Côte Rôtie wines as the mythical La Mouline, La Landonne, or La Turque; but it is even more difficult to make a Côtes du Rhône of such impressive consistency and quality!

Recently tasted

CHÂTEAUNEUF-DU-PAPE 2004
Red | 2011 up to 2019   90

CONDRIEU 2007
White | 2011 up to 2013   88

CONDRIEU LA DORIANE 2007
White | 2011 up to 2017   91

CÔTE RÔTIE CHÂTEAU D'AMPUIS 2005
Red | 2012 up to 2025   92

CÔTE RÔTIE LA BRUNE ET LA BLONDE 2005
Red | 2011 up to 2015   88

CÔTE RÔTIE LA LANDONNE 2005
Red | 2014 up to 2025   98

CÔTE RÔTIE LA MOULINE 2005
Red | 2012 up to 2025   97

CÔTE RÔTIE LA TURQUE 2005
Red | 2012 up to 2025   99

CÔTES DU RHÔNE 2007
White | 2011 up to 2013   87

SAINT-JOSEPH 2005
Red | 2011 up to 2015   90

SAINT-JOSEPH LE SAINT-JOSEPH 2007
White | 2011 up to 2017   90

SAINT-JOSEPH LE SAINT-JOSEPH 2006
Red | 2011 up to 2016   90

SAINT-JOSEPH VIGNES DE L'HOSPICE 2006
Red | 2011 up to 2016   92

Older vintages

CHÂTEAUNEUF-DU-PAPE 2003
Red | 2011 up to 2020   92
A concentrated wine with superb expression and good minerality on the palate. The tannins are delicate. It's a big wine that will age slowly. Soft and delicious. The finish is classy.

CONDRIEU 2006
White | 2011 up to 2013   90
Delicately floral and fruity without being heavy. Delicious length, airy and fresh. Precise and pure.

CONDRIEU 2005
White | 2011 up to 2013   91
Concentrated and mineral at this point, this is a rich wine with clean scents of almonds and flowers. The balance is as delicate as lace.

CONDRIEU LA DORIANE 2005
White | 2011 up to 2015   93
A refined and delicate wine, rich and fat on the palate, with superb mineral tension in the finish and beautiful notes of bitters. Pure, fresh, long, and highly pedigreed.

CÔTE RÔTIE CHÂTEAU D'AMPUIS 2004
Red | 2011 up to 2018   92
With a brilliant bouquet of berries, this is ample and velvety on the palate, yet fresh. Most of all, it has well-structured, refined tannins that are characteristic of this harmonious and complete Côte Rôtie.

CÔTE RÔTIE CHÂTEAU D'AMPUIS 2003
Red | 2011 up to 2020   94
A concentrated and refined bouquet. Velvety on the palate, with fat, well-integrated tannins and a fresh and harmonious finish, this will age very well. The aromatic subtlety is remarkable.

CÔTE RÔTIE LA BRUNE ET LA BLONDE 2004
Red | 2011 up to 2014   **86**
An elegant and harmonious wine, very supple. In the end, the cuvée is pleasant and ready to drink, but it lacks the strong personality that used to characterize it.

CÔTE RÔTIE LA BRUNE ET LA BLONDE 2003
Red | 2011 up to 2015   **89**
Subtle, refined, pleasing. The flavor on the palate is delicate and long, with beautiful aromas of dark berries and licorice. It finishes fresh.

CÔTE RÔTIE LA LANDONNE 2004
Red | 2011 up to 2022   **94**
Structured, firm, and deep, this is clearly destined for the cellar. It has the austerity of the vintage, but its length guarantees a beautiful future.

CÔTE RÔTIE LA LANDONNE 2003
Red | 2011 up to 2020   **98**
An edgier wine than La Mouline or La Turque. The bouquet is more floral, the palate more linear. It is a tight wine, yet it also will have a magnificent future.

CÔTE RÔTIE LA MOULINE 2004
Red | 2011 up to 2020   **96**
Both seductive and deep, this wine has superbly fine tannins linked to an unctuous and fleshy body. The fruit is pure and precise.

CÔTE RÔTIE LA MOULINE 2003
Red | 2011 up to 2025   **97**
The texture on the palate is silky; the tannins are integrated and fresh; the finish is velvety and delectable. This is a great wine, unctuous, classy, superbly elegant.

CÔTE RÔTIE LA TURQUE 2004
Red | 2011 up to 2020   **96**
Very expressive aromas of blackberries. Ample and velvety body, immediately seductive. A beautiful wine with a silky and soft texture.

CÔTE RÔTIE LA TURQUE 2003
Red | 2011 up to 2020   **98**
More powerful on the nose than La Mouline. The palate is even more concentrated, with dark-berry flavor and licorice notes. The gentleness of the finish is remarkable, with a finale of tobacco. Enormous! It will age very well.

CÔTES DU RHÔNE 2005
Red | 2011 up to 2013   **90**
Here is certainly the greatest Côte du Rhône offered by this domaine. It is also the first to be made in the new facility in Ampuis. Very rich yet splendidly balanced, it is a complete wine, redolent of plums, blackberries, and delicate spices. It's ample in body and has an unctuous, long, and fresh finish.

CROZES-HERMITAGE 2006
White | 2011 up to 2013   **88**
Fat, rich, and nicely ripe, this is a complete and delicious wine with beautiful fruity aromas and a pleasing buttery note. Balanced and fresh.

CROZES-HERMITAGE 2006
Red | 2011 up to 2013   **86**
A delicious and supple wine, a good example and perfectly representative of the fresh and honest fruit of the appellation.

GIGONDAS 2005
Red | 2011 up to 2020   **90**
Excellent Gigondas, consistent, structured, and full, yet without any tannic hardness or alcoholic heaviness.

HERMITAGE 2005
White | 2011 up to 2020   **93**
Powerfully built, intense, and deep, this is incontestably a wine to be cellared, neither heavy nor flabby.

HERMITAGE 2003
White | 2011 up to 2015   **90**
The nose is powerful and rich, grapey and fruity. The palate is rich with good volume, subtle and delicately balanced.

HERMITAGE 2003
Red | 2011 up to 2018   **91**
A correct and concentrated wine, this has superbly expressive and concentrated juicy flavor. The finish is fresh and soft. It's a rich and powerful wine, high in alcohol, yet perfectly balanced.

HERMITAGE EX-VOTO 2003
White | 2011 up to 2018   **96**
The nose is complex, refined, and classy. The palate is subtle, with a superb mineral grain in the finish. Balanced, delicate, and fresh, this is a powerful wine in the spirit of 2003, but with good freshness and excellent balance.

SAINT-JOSEPH VIGNES DE L'HOSPICE 2005
Red | 2011 up to 2018   **96**
Profound, highly structured, intense, and svelte, this Saint-Joseph comes from a spectacularly exposed hillside overlooking Tournon. It has extraordinary finesse in its tannins. Great class.

Red: 111.2 acres; syrah 100%. White: 24.7 acres: marsanne 60%, roussanne 7%, viognier 33%. Annual production: 6,000,000 bottles

DOMAINES PAUL JABOULET AÎNÉ

8, rue Monier
26600 Tain-l'Hermitage
Phone 00 33 4 75 84 68 93
info@jaboulet.com
www.jaboulet.com

This famous traditional négociant in Tain l'Hermitage no longer belongs to the Jaboulet family. The Jaboulets sold it to the Frey Champagne company, also owner of Château la Lagune in the Médoc. The world-beloved Hermitage la Chapelle and other great Rhone red cuvées needed this change because they had lost character between 1996 and 2004. The changes were drastic in the cultivation: now the entire vineyard shows better vines. Denis Dubourdieu, master of the Bordeaux enology, was hired to give an up-to-date style and constancy to the reds and the whites. The first vintage to emerge was the 2006, and it shows the positive direction of the new owners.

Recently tasted

CORNAS DOMAINE DE SAINT-PIERRE 2007
Red | 2011 up to 2017   **90**

CÔTE RÔTIE LES JUMELLES 2007
Red | 2011 up to 2017   **90**

CROZES-HERMITAGE DOMAINE DE ROURE 2007
Red | 2011 up to 2017   **90**

CROZES-HERMITAGE DOMAINE DE ROURE 2007
White | 2011 up to 2017   **91**

CROZES-HERMITAGE DOMAINE DE THALABERT 2007
Red | 2011 up to 2015   **89**

CROZES-HERMITAGE DOMAINE LA MULE
BLANCHE 2007
White | 2011 up to 2014   **88**

HERMITAGE CHEVALIER DE STERIMBERG 2007
White | 2012 up to 2022   **95**

HERMITAGE LA CHAPELLE 2007
Red | 2012 up to 2027   **95**

Older vintages

CHÂTEAUNEUF-DU-PAPE LES CÈDRES 2006
White | 2011 up to 2013   **88**
Fat and round, pure enough, delicious and full-bodied, yet with excellent freshness in the finish.

CHÂTEAUNEUF-DU-PAPE LES CÈDRES 2006
Red | 2011 up to 2015   **86**
Classically built but not very refined, with solid length but little finesse.

CHÂTEAUNEUF-DU-PAPE LES CÈDRES 2005
Red | 2011 up to 2013   **84**
A ripe bouquet, on notes of dark berries and herbes de Provence. The palate dips. A bit short, but elegant and fruity.

CONDRIEU LES CASSINES 2007
White | 2011 up to 2013   **87**
Light fruit, soft length, zest. A friendly and light Condrieu with limited presence.

CONDRIEU LES CASSINES 2005
White | 2011 up to 2013   **85**
Rich, but without much personality. Pleasant, well done, but lacking character.

CORNAS DOMAINE DE SAINT-PIERRE 2006
Red | 2011 up to 2018   **89**
Solid wine with lots of structure and serious personality, yet again not nuanced. Definitely a wine to be cellared, but it hasn't yet developed true complexity.

CORNAS LES GRANDES TERRASSES 2006
Red | 2011 up to 2015   **86**
Fruity, solidly built, with a tannic finish, this has limited personality even if it will mature into a classic and well-structured wine.

CÔTE RÔTIE LES JUMELLES 2006
Red | 2011 up to 2018   **90**
Dark berries and mineral nuances. A svelte and taut wine, very mineral, this has true character without flab. Has length and class.

CROZES-HERMITAGE DOMAINE DE ROURE 2006
White | 2011 up to 2015   **90**
Fat and structured, this has the minerality typical of the cru, and good length. It's svelte and taut, refined, pedigreed. It needs a bit of cellaring.

CROZES-HERMITAGE DOMAINE DE ROURE 2006
Red | 2011 up to 2015   **90**
Beautiful, racy bouquet, silky tannins. This is profound and complete, without any faults, and with granite notes in the finish.

CROZES-HERMITAGE DOMAINE DE THALABERT 2005
Red | 2011 up to 2013   **88**
The oak is powerful, but the tannins are fat and silky. This is a rich wine, supple and elegant. The aromas are delicious.

CROZES-HERMITAGE
DOMAINE LA MULE BLANCHE 2006
White | 2011 up to 2013   **89**
From a small domaine of 7.5 acres, and 100 percent vinified in barriques. Fat, round, solid, and velvety. Beautiful pure and precise vinification. Long and harmonious. Definite density and persistence.

CROZES-HERMITAGE THALABERT 2006
Red | 2011 up to 2015   **88**
This is a deeply colored wine with a bouquet of wood and dark berries. It's fat and structured, very precise, with more finesse and definition than the preceding vintages. To cellar with confidence.

CROZES-HERMITAGE THALABERT 2005
Red | 2011 up to 2015   **87**
Fleshy, solid, but without complex flavors; a finish of plums and dark-berry jam.

GIGONDAS PIERRE AIGUILLE 2005
Red | 2011 up to 2013   **86**
Solid, with powerful tannins and spices, this is a complete wine that will come into its own slowly.

HERMITAGE CHEVALIER DE STERIMBERG 2006
White | 2011 up to 2021   **92**
Classy. Beautifully golden. Mineral and zest notes; deep and refined length. Pure, not a hint of oversweetness, with brilliant length. Clearly superior to all the Sterimbergs of the past fifteen years.

HERMITAGE CHEVALIER DE STERIMBERG 2004
White | 2011 up to 2013   **87**
This wine has less body and volume than the 2005. Refined and fresh, it has a shorter finish. It nonetheless offers beautiful aromas of very pure fruit.

HERMITAGE LA CHAPELLE 2006
Red | 2011 up to 2023   **93**
A very solid wine, long, svelte, structured and deep, with beautiful, pure fruit. It's masculine, rigorous, not "artistic" but of its terroir. A beautiful, complete wine.

HERMITAGE LA CHAPELLE 2005
Red | 2011 up to 2020   **90**
Linear, firm, few nuances, and much akin to the Petite Chapelle in its definition (whereas in 2006 they were very different), only the depth in the finish defines the hierarchy. This one seems, however, quite tight.

HERMITAGE LA CHAPELLE 2004
Red | 2011 up to 2013   **89**
This has tension on the palate and a delicate juiciness, with spicy licorice and dark-berry notes. Similar to the 2005 but without the depth.

HERMITAGE LA PETITE CHAPELLE 2006
Red | 2011 up to 2015   **89**
Petite Chapelle is a true second wine, representing 60 percent of the house's production. It's a refined wine, fruity, soft, and very elegant, with lovely definition.

HERMITAGE LA PETITE CHAPELLE 2005
Red | 2011 up to 2015   **88**
A stripped-down wine, lean, without roundness, yet structured and deep enough, with real length on stone-fruit flavors.

HERMITAGE LA PETITE CHAPELLE 2004
Red | 2011 up to 2013   **87**
Already open, this is a light and perfumed wine. It has notes of licorice, dark berries, and flowers. It doesn't match the personality or the length of the 2005.

SAINT-JOSEPH LE GRAND POMPÉE 2006
Red | 2011 up to 2013   **85**
A wine to decant. Fleshy, dark fruit, deep enough but still tight. The length is firm.

SAINT-JOSEPH LE GRAND POMPÉE 2006
White | 2011 up to 2013   **86**
The color is marked, mellow to the point of lacking a little liveliness. It is concentrated but minimally mineral. Nonetheless, it has supple length.

SAINT-PÉRAY LES SAUVAGÈRES 2007
White | 2011 up to 2013   **89**
Fatter, more flavorful and refined. Beautiful and very pure floral aromas. Honest, precise, approachable, and vibrant.

Red: 207.6 acres; syrah 100%. White: 39.5 acres; marsanne 64%, roussanne 29%, viognier 7%. Annual production: 396,000 bottles

DOMAINE JAMET

Le Vallin
69420 Ampuis
Phone 00 33 4 74 56 12 57
Fax 00 33 4 74 56 02 15
domainejamet@wanadoo.fr

Jean-Paul Jamet and his brother run one of the finest domains in the Côte Rôtie appellation. Jean-Paul offers just two cuvées: a "classical" blend, drawn from vineyard plots throughout the appellation; and the selectively blended Côte Brune, always tauter, more precise, and of course more expensive. Both wines age superbly, retaining all of their dense, mineral expression and palpably fat tannins; and most especially, that uncannily precise palate for which they are renowned. Every vintage has been superb, even the most complicated ones (for which, read the 2002).

Recently tasted

CÔTE RÔTIE 2007
Red | 2012 up to 2022   92

CÔTE RÔTIE 2006
Red | 2011 up to 2021   90

CÔTE RÔTIE CÔTE BRUNE 2007
Red | 2012 up to 2027   97

CÔTE RÔTIE CÔTE BRUNE 2006
Red | 2011 up to 2026   94

Older vintages

CÔTE RÔTIE 2005
Red | 2011 up to 2025   92
Very ripe bouquet (spices, incense, dark berries); opulent, intense. The palate is smooth, with a huge tannic richness, built especially on refined, fat tannins. The finish is fresh. It's a rich and structured wine that requires at least eight years in the bottle, and no doubt more. It is closed at this time.

CÔTE RÔTIE 2004
Red | 2011 up to 2019   91
The nose is fresh and fine, floral and elegant, very pure, with notes of tobacco. The palate is concentrated with a touch of smoky minerality in the finish. The tannins are ripe, a bit less fat than the 2005. It's a pleasing and charming wine from a classic, elegant, and pedigreed vintage.

CÔTE RÔTIE 2003
Red | 2011 up to 2015   95
Beautiful strawberry aromas (strawberry jam). On the palate the tannins are quite pleasurable. This is a smooth wine, soft in the mouth, with a delightful peppery finish.

CÔTE RÔTIE CÔTE BRUNE 2005
Red | 2011 up to 2030   94
The nose is intense and perfumed with notes of very ripe dark berries. It's concentrated on the palate with a great, fresh finish. The tannins are well integrated, making it feel like a fat wine despite its structure. Here too, wait a bit.

CÔTE RÔTIE CÔTE BRUNE 2004
Red | 2011 up to 2018   93
Seductive, with pleasing length, this stays fresh and expresses a highly perfumed personality, with a beautiful, smoky finish. One can clearly feel the schist in the finish (tension, smoky notes).

CÔTE RÔTIE CÔTE BRUNE 2003
Red | 2011 up to 2018   97
Fat in the mouth and fresh, with magnificent length. Complex and smooth, this wine has great stature in a vintage of extreme ripeness, which has been elevated by skillful élevage. Almost perfect!

CÔTE RÔTIE ÉLÉGANCE 2006
Red | 2011 up to 2014   88
Crisp fruit. A fleshy wine, ripe, with well-rounded tannins. Seductive, with hedonistic aromas, it is already a pleasure, but it could be cellared a bit.

Red: 16.1 acres; syrah 100%. Annual production: 25,000 bottles

DOMAINE JASMIN

🎜🎜 🎜🎜 🎜🎜 🎜🎜

14, rue des Maraîchers
69420 Ampuis
Phone 00 33 4 74 56 16 04
Fax 00 33 4 74 56 01 78
jasmin.pa@wanadoo.fr

This small Côte Rôtie estate is a regular source of well-made wines: powerful and rich with lovely floral expressions.

Recently tasted
VIN DE PAYS DES COLLINES
RHODANIENNES 2007
Red | 2011 up to 2013   **88**

Older vintages
CÔTE RÔTIE 2007
Red | 2011 up to 2022   **90**
Always stylish, silky, and refined, this has beautiful, ripe fruit. It is an elegant and balanced wine from a vintage affected by hail.

CÔTE RÔTIE 2006
Red | 2011 up to 2021   **90**
Very floral, open, delicate, and supple, this is a sensual Côte Rôtie, with well-integrated tannins. It will be enjoyable soon.

CÔTE RÔTIE 2005
Red | 2011 up to 2020   **89**
The nose is very dense and black in fruit. Mineral (graphite, tobacco) and licorice. Concentrated and dense, it is in the process of closing down. The palate is structured, with tannins that are firm yet silky and elegant. The finish is dense and taut. It would be best to wait a bit.

Red: 9.8 acres. **Annual production:** 15,000 bottles

DOMAINE DU MONTEILLET

🎜🎜 🎜🎜 🎜🎜 🎜🎜

Le Montelier
42410 Chavanay
Phone 00 33 4 74 87 24 57
Fax 00 33 4 74 87 06 89
stephanemontez@aol.com

At the helm of this historic estate today is tenth-generation Montez Stéphane, a talented young winegrower with a solid track record for his age. He vinified his first wines in 1997 and has not looked back since. An ambitious thinker, Stéphane is constantly trying out new methods of vinification: varying the size of barrel according to the degree of physiological ripeness, for instance; or prolonging the maturation time (up to fifty-four months in some cases!). His aim is to capture the precise flavors of every vintage—and he does. His red wines are already a bit on the expensive side, the price of success, no doubt, with a fatness and tannic chewiness that make for some succulent, velvety drinking. Definitely a winegrower to watch!

Recently tasted
SAINT-JOSEPH CUVÉE DU PAPY 2007
Red | 2011 up to 2014   **87**

Older vintages
CONDRIEU 2005
White | 2011 up to 2013   **88**
A balanced wine, very pure, with beautiful floral scents and a crystalline palate. It will be ready to drink soon.

CONDRIEU GRAIN DE FOLIE 2004
White | 2011 up to 2013   **90**
Amber color. Evidently, a well-matured wine. The scents are roasted—caramel and apricot. Ample on the palate, with a beautiful, sweet richness.

CÔTE RÔTIE FORTIS 2005
Red | 2011 up to 2015   **89**
Ripe with very present wood, good concentration, and fat tannins, this is smooth on the palate, very seductive.

CÔTE RÔTIE LES GRANDES PLACES 2005
Red | 2011 up to 2018   **93**
Violets and red berries in the bouquet. The scents are pure and taut, with magnificent precision. This is a very great Côte Rôtie, balanced and fresh, with no heaviness.

CÔTE RÔTIE LES GRANDES PLACES 2004
Red | 2011 up to 2015   **90**
Still very young, this wine is powerful in the mouth. It nonetheless has solid potential. The aromas are direct and very pure.

DOMAINE MICHEL ET STÉPHANE OGIER

3, chemin du Bac
69420 Ampuis
Phone 00 33 4 74 56 10 75
Fax 00 33 4 74 56 01 75
sogier@domaine-ogier.fr

Stéphane took over from his father, Michel, in 1997, and has quickly enlarged the domaine, taking it from seven acres to thirty-one, essentially planted to red grapes. He is a young, dynamic winemaker who keeps moving forward: replanting the historic Seyssuel vineyard, enlarging the vinification cellars, doing a bit of négociant work on the side. But he never forgets the most essential aspects of his job. He started to till the soils again, and now uses only plant-based fertilizer. After careful sorting, the grapes are destemmed for the most part, the wines are not yeasted, and the skin contact is rather short for the region. The wines are aged in Burgundy barrels for between eighteen and thirty months depending on the vintage and the wine (with 30 percent new oak for the Côte Rôties). The Côte Rôtie Reserve du Domaine is produced in the largest quantities; it is ripe and fruity, with round tannins. The single-vineyard bottlings—Lancement in the Côte Blonde, and Belle Hélène in the Côte Rozier—are both more expressive and concentrated than the first wine. The wines produced here are a sure bet when it comes to quality.

Recently tasted

CONDRIEU 2007
White | 2011 up to 2013   87

CÔTE RÔTIE LA BELLE HÉLÈNE 2007
Red | 2011 up to 2017   90

CÔTE RÔTIE LANCEMENT 2007
Red | 2011 up to 2017   90

CÔTE RÔTIE RÉSERVE DU DOMAINE 2007
Red | 2011 up to 2015   88

VIN DE PAYS DES COLLINES RHODANIENNES
L'ÂME SOEUR 2007
Red | 2011 up to 2013   86

VIN DE PAYS DES COLLINES RHODANIENNES
LA ROSINE 2007
Red | 2011 up to 2013   87

VIN DE PAYS DES COLLINES RHODANIENNES
LE VIOGNIER DE ROSINE 2007
White | 2011 up to 2013   86

Older vintages

CÔTE RÔTIE LA BELLE HÉLÈNE 2006
Red | 2011 up to 2021   90
An open bouquet of red berries and spice (cinnamon). More edgy on the palate than the Lancement, it has good tannic structure. It's a mineral wine, but it remains charming and fresh in the finish, with tobacco notes at the very end. It is a touch above the Lancement. The tannins are a little spicier.

CÔTE RÔTIE LA BELLE HÉLÈNE 2005
Red | 2017 up to 2025   92
Straight and mineral in the bouquet, with tobacco and graphite notes. Extremely tense on the palate, with very lovely and ripe tannins, which for the moment are tightening on the finish. This will be a very lovely bottle, but it needs a minimum of ten years.

CÔTE RÔTIE LANCEMENT 2006
Red | 2011 up to 2021   89
A deep, charming, and intense bouquet of candied fruit, red berries, and hints of herbal tea. Very ripe on the palate, very velvety, this is truly sensual on the tongue, with a pure, aromatic finish. Beautiful finesse.

CÔTE RÔTIE LANCEMENT 2005
Red | 2015 up to 2025   90
An intense bouquet, very fruity. On the palate, it has great tannic structure, richness, and concentration. It tightens in the finish, but the tannins are fat. It's a wine to leave in the cellar for a long time.

CÔTE RÔTIE RÉSERVE DU DOMAINE 2006
Red | 2011 up to 2016   87
Fruity, expressive, delicately mineral and smoky. Fresh red berries. Ripe and round on the palate with silky tannins. Caressing, it is easy to appreciate already.

CÔTE RÔTIE RÉSERVE DU DOMAINE 2005
Red | 2013 up to 2020   88
A concentrated and lightly mineral bouquet. Round on the palate, with spicy tannins. Good and chewy, with a fresh finish. A concentrated wine. Cellar it and wait.

CÔTE RÔTIE RÉSERVE DU DOMAINE 2004
Red | 2011 up to 2015   91
Powerful and voluptuous on the nose. A pleasant, nimble wine with fresh menthol aromas, this is already very attractive, but it will age very well.

Red: 23.5 acres; syrah 100%. White: 7.4 acres; viognier 100%. Annual production: 80,000 bottles

DOMAINE ANDRÉ PERRET

17, route nationale 86
42410 Chavanay
Phone 00 33 4 74 87 24 74
Fax 00 33 4 74 87 05 26
andre.perret@terre-net.fr
www.andreperret.com

André Perret's lovely Rhone Valley estate boasts vines in Condrieu and Saint-Joseph, planted on steep slopes that make for challenging growing conditions. The Clos Chanson is certainly very interesting, but the estate's flagship Condrieu bottling is plainly the Coteaux de Chéry, an unfailingly rich and exuberant wine that achieved a fabulous crystalline purity in 2005. We particularly recommend this estate for its white wines, though it also does a good job with some of its reds.

Recently tasted
CONDRIEU 2007
White | 2011 up to 2013   86

CONDRIEU CHÉRY 2007
White | 2011 up to 2017   90

CONDRIEU CLOS CHANSON 2007
White | 2011 up to 2017   89

SAINT-JOSEPH 2007
White | 2011 up to 2013   87

SAINT-JOSEPH 2007
Red | 2011 up to 2014   87

SAINT-JOSEPH LES GRISIÈRES 2007
Red | 2011 up to 2017   88

VIN DE PAYS DES COLLINES RHODANIENNES
MARSANNE 2007
White | 2011 up to 2013   90

Older vintages
CONDRIEU 2006
White | 2011 up to 2013   86
Delicate, lightly mineral. Fruit and mineral notes on the palate. Elegant, fresh.

CONDRIEU CHÉRY 2006
White | 2011 up to 2014   87
In the past this was called Coteaux de Chéry. It is delicious and ripe on the palate, a rich, well-rounded wine with frank scents of yellow fruit.

CONDRIEU CHÉRY 2005
White | 2011 up to 2014   86
A refined and balanced wine. In the mouth it has a crystalline purity and a superbly long finish. Very harmonious and fresh.

CONDRIEU CHÉRY 2004
White | 2011 up to 2013   89
There is good freshness in this delicate and floral wine. It's blessed with a light, mineral bitterness in the finish. Complete and elegant.

CONDRIEU CLOS CHANSON 2006
White | 2011 up to 2014   88
Beautiful elegance, straightforward and refined. Delicate on the palate with a lightly mineral finish. It offers more finesse and elegance than the Chéry.

SAINT-JOSEPH 2006
White | 2011 up to 2013   84
Floral on the nose. The attack is a little soft. It is not very nervy, but it is ripe, with honest flavor. Not much length.

SAINT-JOSEPH 2006
Red | 2011 up to 2013   86
Fruity, with enrobed tannins, this is a supple wine with a mineral finish. Round and elegant.

SAINT-JOSEPH 2005
White | 2011 up to 2013   84
Light and supple, perhaps a bit too much so. But delicate and pleasant nonetheless.

SAINT-JOSEPH 2004
White | 2011 up to 2013   83
In a light style, this is a ripe wine. It is just a bit short in the finish.

SAINT-JOSEPH LES GRISIÈRES 2006
Red | 2011 up to 2016   88
This is more concentrated in aromas and more mineral than the Saint-Joseph. In the mouth, it is structured with refined tannins. An elegant and well-balanced wine, tight in the finish.

SAINT-JOSEPH LES GRISIÈRES 2005
Red | 2011 up to 2013   89
Brilliant garnet in color. The wood is chic. It's a modern and long wine. Good balance, frank and pleasing.

SAINT-JOSEPH LES GRISIÈRES 2004
Red | 2011 up to 2013   84
An honest and solid wine with good fruit, but altogether rather lackluster.

Red: 14.5 acres; merlot 10%, syrah 90%. White: 14.2 acres; marsanne 10%, roussanne 10%, viognier 80%.

DOMAINE DES REMIZIÈRES

26600 Mercurol
Phone 00 33 04 75 07 44 2
Fax 00 33 4 75 07 45 87
contact@domaineremizieres.com

Philippe Desmesure took over the family winery in 1978 and brought it to another level, increasing the holdings from ten to seventy-five acres. The domaine makes Crozes-Hermitage, Hermitage, and Saint-Joseph, with many different bottlings. They are conducting trials in the vineyards with organic farming, which tends to give these wines a fresh and flavorful character. All of the wines are aged in oak barrels, of various ages, with a percentage of new oak each year. The Autrement bottlings in Croze-Hermitage and Hermitage are exercises in extraction and style produced in very limited quantities—only 1,500 bottles. These wines are powerful, concentrated, fleshy, and flavorful. The rest of the wines are more accessible (especially where price is concerned) and always impeccable, straightforward, fresh, and balanced.

Recently tasted

CROZES-HERMITAGE AUTREMENT 2007
Red | 2011 up to 2017   91

CROZES-HERMITAGE CUVÉE CHRISTOPHE 2007
White | 2011 up to 2017   89

CROZES-HERMITAGE CUVÉE CHRISTOPHE 2007
Red | 2011 up to 2017   89

CROZES-HERMITAGE CUVÉE PARTICULIÈRE 2007
Red | 2011 up to 2013   87

HERMITAGE AUTREMENT 2007
Red | 2012 up to 2022   93

HERMITAGE CUVÉE ÉMILIE 2007
White | 2011 up to 2022   90

HERMITAGE CUVÉE ÉMILIE 2007
Red | 2012 up to 2022   91

SAINT-JOSEPH 2007
Red | 2011 up to 2014   88

Older vintages

CROZES-HERMITAGE AUTREMENT 2006
Red | 2011 up to 2016   91
Rich, pleasing, fleshy, with rich blackberries on the palate. Round, nearly opulent, but fresh and well balanced. The substantial juice supports the new oak. Very beautiful wine.

CROZES-HERMITAGE CUVÉE CHRISTOPHE 2006
Red | 2011 up to 2016   88
With a delicate bouquet, this is rich on the palate with fat tannins and good acidity. An honest, fresh, and balanced wine with delicious length.

CROZES-HERMITAGE CUVÉE CHRISTOPHE 2006
White | 2011 up to 2014   88
Beautiful toasty notes on the nose. Elegant, pedigreed, refined. The palate is fat, with good volume. The finish is balanced and very pleasing, with notes of almond paste.

HERMITAGE AUTREMENT 2006
Red | 2011 up to 2016   90
A very powerful bouquet with strong notes of dark berries and spices (the fruit is a bit cooked). It's rich on the palate, structured, with firm, well-enrobed tannins and a cocoa finish. Huge phenolic maturity.

HERMITAGE CUVÉE ÉMILIE 2006
Red | 2011 up to 2016   89
The bouquet is more reserved, more concentrated than the Crozes. The sensation on the palate is fat; the tannins are spicy, and the finish is fresh and tense. It's less opulent and fleshy than the Crozes Autrement.

HERMITAGE CUVÉE ÉMILIE 2006
White | 2011 up to 2016   89
Noticeable wood at this point, but the fruit is good, rich and ripe. It's a powerful wine, very rich on the palate, with a tasty finish. Best to wait until it finds its balance.

DOMAINE GILLES ROBIN

Les Chassis Sud
26600 Mercurol
Phone 00 33 4 75 08 43 28
Fax 00 33 4 75 08 43 64
gillesrobin@wanadoo.fr

Fourth-generation winegrower Gilles Robin took over this family estate in 1996. Since then it has grown to cover a thirty-acre area in the Crozes-Hermitage and Saint-Joseph appellations, with red Crozes-Hermitage wines accounting for the bulk of production. The Papillon is a supple, fruity wine, bottled in the spring following tank fermentation. The Albéric Bouvet, dedicated to Gilles's grandfather, is made from vines aged fifty-plus years and raised in wood. The result is an unfailingly fresh and concentrated wine with spicy tannins and a salty finish.

Recently tasted

CROZES-HERMITAGE 1920 2005
Red | 2011 up to 2020   **91**

CROZES-HERMITAGE ALBÉRIC BOUVET 2007
Red | 2011 up to 2017   **89**

CROZES-HERMITAGE LES MARELLES 2007
White | 2011 up to 2015   **89**

CROZES-HERMITAGE PAPILLON 2007
Red | 2011 up to 2013   **89**

SAINT-JOSEPH ANDRÉ PÉALAT 2007
Red | 2011 up to 2017   **89**

Older vintages

CROZES-HERMITAGE ALBÉRIC BOUVET 2006
Red | 2011 up to 2014   **88**
The bouquet is concentrated and refined, even if a bit closed right now. The palate is rich, the tannins well integrated. Beautiful tannic structure. Balanced and flavorful.

CROZES-HERMITAGE ALBÉRIC BOUVET 2005
Red | 2011 up to 2013   **90**
An unctuous, refined, and complete wine, this is built on high-quality, perfectly ripe grapes and careful aging. It possesses a particularly harmonious balance, delicious and fresh. Its length seduces.

CROZES-HERMITAGE ALBÉRIC BOUVET 2003
Red | 2011 up to 2013   **88**
Closed down, a bit reduced; best if decanted. Delicious, nicely ripe red berries (strawberries!), typical of the vintage. Delicate tannins.

CROZES-HERMITAGE PAPILLON 2006
Red | 2011 up to 2013   **86**
Deliciously fruity, like biting into a red berry. The palate is round, the tannins ripe, the finish balanced and fresh.

CROZES-HERMITAGE PAPILLON 2005
Red | 2011 up to 2013   **89**
A seductive and delicious Crozes with delicate aromas of cocoa and dark berries. It is ample and flavorful on the palate, perfectly structured with silky tannins.

SAINT-JOSEPH ANDRÉ PÉALAT 2006
Red | 2011 up to 2014   **88**
Very linear, pure, and delicate on the palate. The finish is nervy and quite streamlined. Racy.

Red: 28.4 acres; syrah 100%. **White:** 1.2 acres; marsanne 75%, roussanne 25%. **Annual production:** 50,000 bottles

DOMAINE MARC SORREL

128 bis, avenue Jean-Jaurès
26600 Tain-l'Hermitage
Phone 00 33 4 75 07 10 07
Fax 00 33 4 75 08 75 88
marc.sorrel@wanadoo.fr
www.marcsorrel.com

Marc Sorrel is one of the great names of Tain l'Hermitage, and his wines show enormous potential to improve over the years. He is particularly notable among the coterie of Hermitage producers for calling his top red cuvée "Gréal," a witty contraction of Méal and Greffieux, the two lieux-dits of origin. His white Rocoules is always fat but delicate on the palate, with fresh, elegant length.

Recently tasted

CROZES-HERMITAGE 2007
White | 2011 up to 2017   89

CROZES-HERMITAGE 2007
Red | 2011 up to 2013   87

HERMITAGE 2007
White | 2011 up to 2017   89

HERMITAGE 2007
Red | 2011 up to 2017   89

HERMITAGE LE GRÉAL 2007
Red | 2012 up to 2027   94

HERMITAGE LES ROCOULES 2007
White | 2012 up to 2022   95

Older vintages

CROZES-HERMITAGE 2006
White | 2011 up to 2016   90
Frank and delicious scents of apples and honey. Linear on the palate and lively, with an edgy and tasty finish.

CROZES-HERMITAGE 2006
Red | 2011 up to 2013   87
Fruity, spicy, a soft and delectable wine with full-bodied fruit. Elegant, to drink for the pure pleasure of it.

CROZES-HERMITAGE 2005
Red | 2011 up to 2013   82
A rather vibrant Crozes, simple but with good length. Edgy.

HERMITAGE 2006
White | 2011 up to 2021   91
Refined, elegant, concentrated. Richly expressive on the palate.

HERMITAGE 2006
Red | 2011 up to 2021   89
Concentrated, ripe, and hedonistic, this is fat on the palate, with spicy yet well-integrated tannins. The finish is fruity and flavorful, round and ripe.

HERMITAGE 2005
White | 2011 up to 2013   87
Fat, honeyed, long, but with medium finesse, this wine lacks grace but not volume.

HERMITAGE 2005
Red | 2011 up to 2018   90
Very beautiful and unctuous in texture. Mineral. We'd certainly like to see it a bit more refined by a more precise élevage, but the wine will reveal its grace and class over time.

HERMITAGE LE GRÉAL 2006
Red | 2011 up to 2026   95
Concentrated, full-bodied, and delectable. The tannins are quite delicate, the finish tense and tasty.

HERMITAGE LE GRÉAL 2005
Red | 2011 up to 2020   92
This wine is impressive in its no-holds-barred mineral depth, but also in its voluptuous texture. Great future.

HERMITAGE LE GRÉAL 2004
Red | 2011 up to 2013   88
Woody, with clean fruit. This is made in a modern style, but it's well done. Beautiful depth and volume. The finish is lively and persistent.

HERMITAGE LES ROCOULES 2006
White | 2011 up to 2026   95
Opulent, very floral. A rich and powerful wine, generous on the palate, but still elegant and balanced in spite of its high alcohol content.

HERMITAGE LES ROCOULES 2005
White | 2011 up to 2015   88
Ample and deep, this wine has big potential. Best to wait quietly for this bottle to mature.

HERMITAGE LES ROCOULES 2004
White | 2011 up to 2013   88
Golden and sheer, this is a long and deep wine.

Red: 6.9 acres; syrah 100%. White: 3 acres; marsanne 90%, roussanne 10%. Annual production: 20,000 bottles

DOMAINE JEAN-MICHEL STEPHAN

1, ancienne route de Semons
69420 Tupin-Semons
Phone 00 33 4 74 56 62 66
Fax 00 33 4 74 56 62 66
jean-michel.stephan3@wanadoo.fr

Jean-Michel Stephan's property is in Tupin-Semons, in the south of the appellation. Stephan only makes red wines and, with the exception of his Vin de Pays, all of them are Côte Rôtie bottlings. What they have in common is the fragrant juiciness of dark fruit, dotted with notes of graphite and licorice. His Vieilles Vignes (old vines) cuvée is an outstanding expression of the illustrious and hugely expensive Côte Rôtie—pricey but well worth it when you think of what it means to be a winegrower on these precipitous slopes.

CÔTE RÔTIE 2005
Red | 2011 up to 2025   **88**
Powerful, rich in tannins, delicious in its notes of dark berries and firm tannins. The finish is linear and taut. Wait a bit.

CÔTE RÔTIE CÔTE DE TUPIN 2005
Red | 2011 up to 2013   **91**
Powerful, mineral, deep, and complex. Dense on the palate, with very ripe tannins. The tension in the finish is superb, with notes of minerals (graphite) and dark berries.

CÔTE RÔTIE COTEAUX DE BASSENON 2007
Red | 2011 up to 2017   **89**
Fat, rich, aromatic—you can feel the viognier (that touch of apricot!). It is seductive thanks to its fleshy and fruity flavor.

CÔTE RÔTIE COTEAUX DE BASSENON 2006
Red | 2011 up to 2021   **89**
Here, too, the viognier comes through. Charming, a wine that shines with brilliance on the palate. Seductive.

CÔTE RÔTIE COTEAUX DE TUPIN 2007
Red | 2012 up to 2022   **92**
More concentrated and tighter than the Coteaux de Bassenon. A wine with lovely grain: concentrated, dense, balanced, and refined.

CÔTE RÔTIE COTEAUX DE TUPIN 2006
Red | 2011 up to 2021   **91**
More mineral than the Bassenon, this is also nervier and a bit tight, but the finish has beautiful length, fresh and taut.

CÔTE RÔTIE COTEAUX DE TUPIN 2005
Red | 2011 up to 2025   **91**
The most open of the three 2005s. The bouquet has notes of dark berries and graphite. On the palate, it is full-bodied yet elegant and well supported. Straight and firm. Worth waiting for patiently.

CÔTE RÔTIE VIEILLES VIGNES 2006
Red | 2011 up to 2021   **90**
Tighter and more concentrated than the Coteaux de Bassenon, this is an elegant cuvée with lots of distinction.

CÔTE RÔTIE VIEILLES VIGNES 2005
Red | 2011 up to 2025   **91**
Round and generous, with notes of chocolate and dark berries. Big tannins and structure. Definitely to be cellared; it is closing down at this time. Good length.

CÔTE RÔTIE VIEILLES VIGNES 2004
Red | 2011 up to 2013   **95**
An intense mineral bouquet, refined and complex. Expressive on the palate, with spicy and refined tannins. Superb body. The aromatic stamp is simply beautiful. It finishes on mineral and tobacco notes. A thoroughbred. It will mature well, but is already very tempting.

DOMAINE DU TUNNEL

🍷🍷🍷🍷🍷

20, rue de la République
07130 Saint-Péray
Phone 00 33 4 75 80 04 66
Fax 00 33 4 75 80 06 50
domaine-du-tunnel@wanadoo.fr

Domaine du Tunnel is a tiny estate but home to a respectable range of cuvées from various appellations in the Northern Rhone Valley (Saint-Péray, Cornas, and Saint-Joseph). The wines are always honest and well balanced, with pleasing, charming fruit that makes them approachable at an early stage. The Cornas Vin Noir shows real personality even if it does seem a bit overblown at times.

Recently tasted

Cornas 2007
Red | 2011 up to 2013   87

Cornas Vin Noir 2007
Red | 2011 up to 2015   89

Saint-Joseph 2007
Red | 2011 up to 2013   87

Saint-Péray Prestige 2007
White | 2011 up to 2014   88

Saint-Péray roussanne 2007
White | 2011 up to 2013   87

Older vintages

Cornas 2006
Red | 2011 up to 2013   87
Concentrated dark-berry flavor, nervy on the palate, straightforward, with good mineral tension and expressive licorice notes on the finish. Round and flavorful.

Cornas 2005
Red | 2011 up to 2015   88
Deeply colored. Good wood. A solid and ripe wine, with flavorful length and persistence.

Cornas Pur Noir 2006
Red | 2011 up to 2016   89
Concentrated, with dark-berry scents. The tannins are fat, the finish well padded. More substance and finesse than the Vin Noir.

Cornas Vin Noir 2006
Red | 2011 up to 2016   88
Black in color: the wine deserves its name! The nose is concentrated: dark berries, licorice, sweet spice. On the palate it is fleshy, tannic, and concentrated. It finishes fresh and nervy.

Cornas Vin Noir 2005
Red | 2011 up to 2017   86
Deeply colored, this is dense on the palate but the wood is a touch drying. The finish is firm but lacks suppleness.

Saint-Joseph 2006
Red | 2011 up to 2013   86
Ripe fruit. A spicy wine, round, delicious, and charming.

Saint-Joseph 2005
Red | 2011 up to 2013   84
Deeply colored. The fruit is vibrant, rather linear, yet full.

Saint-Péray Prestige 2005
White | 2011 up to 2013   89
A good, oaked Saint-Péray: fat, ambitious, and well done.

Saint-Péray roussanne 2006
White | 2011 up to 2013   85
Fat, round, medium length, good maturity (a comfortable degree of alcohol), balanced. To be enjoyed young.

DOMAINE GEORGES VERNAY

𐂏 𐂏 𐂏 𐂏 𐂏

1, route Nationale
69420 Condrieu
Phone 00 33 4 74 56 81 81
Fax 00 33 4 74 56 60 98
pa@georges-vernay.fr
www.georges-vernay.fr

This domaine is the outright leader in Condrieu production, internationally acclaimed for wines that Georges Vernay restored to greatness in the 1960s and 1970s. These days his daughter Christine carries on his good work, showing herself to be quite as spirited and at least as talented as her winemaker father. Her impeccable Condrieu bottlings show superbly nuanced expressions from one cuvée to another—the complete antithesis of flabby viogniers bogged down in stewed apricots. The wines are refined, elegant, and gracefully aged with a taut, mineral finish. Also from this winery, some delicate, fragrant Côte Rôties with pure, velvety juice. Recent vintages have been unfailingly flawless.

Recently tasted

CONDRIEU COTEAU DE VERNON 2007
White I 2011 up to 2022   95

CONDRIEU LES CHAILLÉES DE L'ENFER 2007
White I 2011 up to 2022   91

CÔTE RÔTIE LA MAISON ROUGE 2006
Red I 2011 up to 2021   90

CÔTES DU RHÔNE SAINTE-AGATHE 2007
Red I 2011 up to 2013   89

SAINT-JOSEPH 2007
Red I 2011 up to 2013   88

SAINT-JOSEPH LA DAME BRUNE 2006
Red I 2011 up to 2016   90

Older vintages

CONDRIEU COTEAU DE VERNON 2006
White I 2011 up to 2016   91
Beautiful, fresh, and refined fruit. An elegant and delicately perfumed wine. Subtle aromatic palette. Very pure. It is more balanced and fresher than the Chaillées. Beautiful bitter notes on the finish. Very elegant.

CONDRIEU COTEAU DE VERNON 2005
White I 2011 up to 2015   95
A very beautiful Condrieu, ripe and adroitly vinified. Delicate and light, it is superbly balanced.

CONDRIEU COTEAU DE VERNON 2004
White I 2011 up to 2015   96
The nose is profound, balanced with toasted notes. The palate is very pure and correct. The wood has a fine grain. The finish is delicate, precise, and toasted. Very noble.

CONDRIEU LES CHAILLÉES DE L'ENFER 2006
White I 2011 up to 2016   89
A refined and powerful wine, very pure. The cask aging is nicely integrated. The palate is fat and delicious, with juicy white and yellow fruit. Fleshy. A true gastronomic wine! Quite rich.

CONDRIEU LES CHAILLÉES DE L'ENFER 2005
White I 2011 up to 2015   96
A quality oaked wine. The balance is perfect, the aromas very pure. The sensation on the palate is crystalline. Magnificent.

CONDRIEU LES CHAILLÉES DE L'ENFER 2004
White I 2011 up to 2015   92
The bouquet is more about fruit than the Terrasses de l'Empire; it's deeper, more delectable, and riper. Honey and yellow fruit, with hints of tropical fruit (banana). The palate is fat, very ripe, and rich. The impact from the oak is perceptible. A balanced and suave wine.

CONDRIEU LES TERRASSES DE L'EMPIRE 2007
White I 2011 up to 2015   88
Refined and elegant notes: anise, white flowers, pêche de vigne. The palate is delicate and pure, honest and fresh, with good balance in the finish.

CONDRIEU LES TERRASSES DE L'EMPIRE 2006
White I 2011 up to 2015   86
Ripe, concentrated, and rich, this is a rather powerful wine with notes of yellow fruit. The palate is somewhat vibrant, with a comfortable level of alcohol. It finishes fresh, on a more powerful and richer register than the 2007.

CONDRIEU LES TERRASSES DE L'EMPIRE 2005
White I 2011 up to 2015   95
Great purity. The wine is still young, but the minerality in the finish is very elegant and pure.

CONDRIEU LES TERRASSES DE L'EMPIRE 2004
White I 2011 up to 2015   95
Floral, intense, and perfumed, this is a complex wine, pure on the palate with a clean attack. The alcohol is rather high, but the structure of the wine can handle it. A gastronomic thoroughbred. Classy and perfumed.

CÔTE RÔTIE BLONDE DU SEIGNEUR 2006
Red | 2011 up to 2016   **88**
Perfumed, very floral, elegant. The palate
is ripe, the tannins well enrobed. It is not
very expressive at this time.

CÔTE RÔTIE BLONDE DU SEIGNEUR 2004
Red | 2011 up to 2018   **93**
Powerful bouquet, hot, spicy, velvety. The
scents are straightforward and seductive,
with the appellation's warm-hearted generosity. Fat and velvety on the palate. Beautiful freshness.

CÔTE RÔTIE LA MAISON ROUGE 2004
Red | 2011 up to 2018   **95**
A ripe wine, rich with fat tannins. Rich
extract on the palate. Irresistibly charming
and delicious.

CÔTES DU RHÔNE SAINTE-AGATHE 2006
Red | 2011 up to 2013   **87**
Concentrated, ripe, and rich, with fine,
streamlined tannins. Beautifully balanced
on the palate, this is a fleshy, highly concentrated wine.

SAINT-JOSEPH 2006
Red | 2011 up to 2014   **87**
Tense, concentrated. The palate is correct,
the tannins refined. It's a serious wine with
firm tannins that require a bit of a wait.

VIN DE PAYS DES COLLINES RHODANIENNES
LE PIED DE SAMSON 2007
White | 2011 up to 2013   **86**
Ripe and refined, this is a balanced and delicate viognier. Delicious, it finishes fresh and
refined, without any heaviness. Frank scents
of white fruit (white peach).

VIN DE PAYS DES COLLINES RHODANIENNES
SYRAH 2007
Red | 2011 up to 2013   **85**
Fruity, with some mineral and smoky notes.
The palate is rich, with delicate tannins.
Pure, streamlined, very pleasing. The finish
is lightly spicy.

Red: 19.8 acres; syrah 100%. White: 24.7 acres;
viognier 100%. Annual production: 100,000 bottles

VIDAL-FLEURY

Lieu-dit Tupin RD 386
69420 Tupin-et-Semons
Phone 00 33 4 74 56 10 18
Fax 00 33 4 74 56 19 19
vidal-fleury@wanadoo.fr

Though owned by Marcel Guigal, this venerable wine house in Ampuis continues to
operate as a separate business and maintains it own individual style. It offers a wide
range of Rhone wines, from the solid and
complete Côtes du Rhône, to the very tasty
Muscat de Beaumes de Venise (the
house's specialty) and the Châtillonne
Côte Rôtie. A huge new winemaking and
aging cellar was just opened and should
mark a new turning point in performance.

Recently tasted

CHÂTEAUNEUF-DU-PAPE 2008
White | 2011 up to 2014   **87**

CHÂTEAUNEUF-DU-PAPE 2006
Red | 2011 up to 2014   **86**

CONDRIEU 2006
White | 2011 up to 2013   **88**

CORNAS 2006
Red | 2011 up to 2014   **86**

CÔTE RÔTIE BRUNE ET BLONDE 2004
Red | 2011 up to 2014   **87**

CÔTE RÔTIE CÔTE BLONDE LA CHÂTILLONNE 2004
Red | 2011 up to 2014   **89**

CÔTES DU RHÔNE 2008
White | 2011 up to 2013   **87**

CÔTES DU RHÔNE 2007
White | 2011 up to 2013   **85**

CÔTES DU RHÔNE 2007
Red | 2011 up to 2013   **86**

CÔTES DU RHÔNE-VILLAGES 2007
Red | 2011 up to 2013   **87**

CÔTES DU RHÔNE-VILLAGES CAIRANNE 2007
Red | 2011 up to 2013   **87**

CROZES-HERMITAGE 2007
White | 2011 up to 2013   **87**

CROZES-HERMITAGE 2007
Red | 2011 up to 2013   **86**

GIGONDAS 2007
Red | 2011 up to 2015   **88**

GIGONDAS 2006
Red | 2011 up to 2014   87

MUSCAT DE BEAUMES-DE-VENISE 2007
Sweet White | 2011 up to 2015   89

SAINT-JOSEPH 2007
White | 2011 up to 2013   87

VACQUEYRAS 2007
Red | 2011 up to 2014   88

Older vintages
CONDRIEU 2005
White | 2011 up to 2013   89
A seductive and rather delicate nose, with notes of toast, herbal tea, and melted butter. Very pleasing aromas. The palate is rich, with a finish of dried apricots. Charming.

CONDRIEU 2005
White | 2011 up to 2013   87
Refined, elegant, and ripe, this is a well-sculpted wine, pure and tight, fresh and flavorful.

CÔTE RÔTIE BRUNE ET BLONDE 2003
Red | 2011 up to 2018   89
Good concentrated fruit, very ripe, yet fresh in aromas. The palate is fleshy, pleasing. It's a suave and charming wine with ripe tannins. Very beautiful vintage.

CÔTE RÔTIE CÔTE BLONDE LA CHÂTILLONNE 2003
Red | 2011 up to 2018   91
More concentrated than the Brune et Blonde, more voluptuous. Refined and integrated tannins. Very elegant. Superb!

CÔTE RÔTIE CÔTES BRUNE ET BLONDE 2003
Red | 2011 up to 2015   88
A wine with smooth and perfumed juice, with pleasant notes of dark berries and licorice. The palate isn't too alcoholic and the tannins are rather silky. It is pleasing and delicious.

CÔTE RÔTIE LA CHÂTILLONNE 2001
Red | 2011 up to 2015   90
A rich wine with refined and elegant juiciness. The expression on the palate is voluptuous and delicate. It is very seductive, ready to be appreciated.

CÔTES DU RHÔNE 2006
Red | 2011 up to 2013   85
Ripe and frank, this is a solid Côtes du Rhône that rests on its grenache, expressing dark berry and cocoa notes. Powerful tannic grain.

CROZES-HERMITAGE 2006
White | 2011 up to 2013   86
A fat and supple wine, already open. Beautiful notes of yellow fruit. Ready to drink.

CROZES-HERMITAGE 2006
Red | 2011 up to 2013   85
Fresh fruit. A ripe and fleshy wine. Delicious, refined, and fresh.

CROZES-HERMITAGE 2005
Red | 2011 up to 2013   83
A ripe wine, yet light on the palate, with a slight dip in mid-palate. It's well done, but short.

HERMITAGE 1999
Red | 2011 up to 2013   88
A complete and direct wine, with firm tannins. The palate is well structured. It's beginning to take on tertiary notes (asphalt). Elegant and pedigreed.

MUSCAT DE BEAUMES-DE-VENISE 2005
Sweet White | 2011 up to 2013   93
A pretty Muscat with brilliant fruit, this is so fresh it's like biting into a grape. Truly delicious, it is a delight, a dessert all by itself. The balance of the sugar, alcohol, acidity, and fruit is perfect! A wine that must be tasted! Do observe the serving temperature (53°F/12°C is perfect).

SAINT-JOSEPH 2005
Red | 2011 up to 2013   87
Mineral, a linear Saint-Joseph, pleasantly concentrated, taut, quite correct. Pretty.

Red: 29.7 acres; syrah 100%. Annual production: 1,200,000 bottles

DOMAINE FRANÇOIS VILLARD

Montjoux
42410 Saint-Michel-sur-Rhone
Phone 00 33 4 74 56 83 60
Fax 00 33 4 74 56 87 78
vinsvillard@aol.com

Bold and always ready for a new adventure, François Villard has remained as fresh and enthusiastic as he was in the early 1990s when he made just a few barrels of wine from the tiny Condrieu vineyard De Poncins. This is still his benchmark wine, though it is now joined by the more mineral, but wonderful, Terrasses du Palat. They are wonderful wines for aging (Poncins 2001 and 1996 are extraordinary), combining a full body and distinguished length. The red Côte Rôtie La Brocarde and the Saint-Joseph Reflet are at their best when young and full of fruit.

Recently tasted
CONDRIEU DE PONCINS 2007
White | 2011 up to 2017   90

CÔTE RÔTIE LA BROCARDE 2007
Red | 2011 up to 2017   91

CÔTE RÔTIE LE GALLET BLANC 2007
Red | 2011 up to 2017   88

SAINT-JOSEPH GRAND REFLET 2007
Red | 2011 up to 2019   93

SAINT-JOSEPH REFLET 2007
Red | 2011 up to 2017   90

SAINT-PÉRAY VERSION 2007
White | 2011 up to 2013   86

VIN DE PAYS DES COLLINES RHODANIENNES
GRANDE GRUE GLACÉE 2007
Red | 2011 up to 2014   88

VIN DE PAYS DES COLLINES RHODANIENNES
TERRES DE VIENNAE SEUL EN SCÈNE 2007
Red | 2011 up to 2013   88

Older vintages
CONDRIEU DE PONCINS 2006
White | 2011 up to 2016   90
Delicious on the attack. Rich, flavorful, with fat and round expressiveness on the palate. Fresh finish. Good minerality, which gives an edge to the palate.

CONDRIEU LE GRAND VALLON 2006
White | 2011 up to 2014   89
The nose is a bit more reserved than the Terrasses du Palat, but also more concentrated. Pure on the palate, chiseled, less rich but quite correct.

CONDRIEU LES TERRASSES DU PALAT 2006
White | 2011 up to 2014   88
A clean attack, rich and direct. Refined, elegant, and very rich on the palate. Honest and pure, with superb freshness on the finish.

CONDRIEU LES TERRASSES DU PALAT 2005
White | 2011 up to 2013   96
A great, classy wine, in which the minerality of the terroir marries perfectly with its ripe fruit without any softness. Streamlined, deep, and cutting, the wine lacks neither substance nor intensity.

CÔTE RÔTIE LA BROCARDE 2006
Red | 2011 up to 2021   91
Aromatic and very ripe, with juicy fruit on the palate. Pure and delicious, with superb fruit elegance.

CÔTE RÔTIE LA BROCARDE 2003
Red | 2011 up to 2015   92
A rich and dense wine with beautiful minerality, an unctuous body, and tannins that are gripping but not green. Altogether, it is very concentrated, with a strong personality.

CÔTE RÔTIE LA BROCARDE 2000
Red | 2011 up to 2013   90
Fleshy and very structured, this wine has fullness and depth, with a smoky mineral character that marries well with its very expressive, perfectly ripe fruit.

CÔTE RÔTIE LA BROCARDE 1999
Red | 2011 up to 2013   88
This has a beautifully deep color and strong notes of blackberry and black-currant jam both on the nose and on the palate. This aromatic persistence gives the wine exuberance, flesh, and a nearly exotic charm.

CÔTE RÔTIE LE GALLET BLANC 2006
Red | 2011 up to 2021   90
Tasty, fleshy, pleasing. Rich on the palate, ripe, with well-padded tannins. The finish is lightly nervy, with notes of licorice.

SAINT-JOSEPH FRUIT D'AVILLERAN 2006
White | 2011 up to 2013   85
Floral, elegant, less rich than the Saint-Péray Version. Lacking a bit of freshness.

SAINT-JOSEPH MAIRLANT 2006
White | 2011 up to 2013   87
Ripe, with a very pretty expression on the palate. Fat, but very fresh in the finish. Delicious and long. It is longer and fresher than the Fruit d'Avilleran. Flavorful.

SAINT-JOSEPH MAIRLANT 2006
Red | 2011 up to 2014   **87**
Spicy, straightforward, and mineral on the palate. A wine that keeps its freshness and tension, with a delicious finish.

SAINT-JOSEPH REFLET 2006
Red | 2011 up to 2016   **90**
Tense and highly concentrated, this has rich, ripe flavors of dark berries, olives, and licorice. Rich and tasty, it stays fresh.

SAINT-PÉRAY VERSION 2006
White | 2011 up to 2013   **86**
Fat, ripe, perfumed, and fresh, this is a tasty wine with a light bitterness that enlivens the finish.

SAINT-PÉRAY VERSION LONGUE 2006
White | 2011 up to 2016   **89**
Ripe and powerful, the attack is rich and delicious. The flavorful finish tastes of raisins and herbal tea. Twenty months in oak barrels has given it power, but it's also retained balance and freshness.

Red: 11.1 acres. White: 11.1 acres

LES VINS DE VIENNE

Bas Seyssuel
38200 Seyssuel
Phone 00 33 4 74 85 04 52
Fax 00 33 4 74 31 97 55
vdv@lesvinsdevienne.fr
www.vinsdevienne.com

Vins de Vienne is the name of a small business set up by winemakers François Villard, Yves Cuilleron, and Pierre Gaillard as a sideline to their own (famous) estates. The idea was to resurrect a long-neglected vineyard in the granitic hills of Seyssuel. Now fully operational, the domaine turns out ambitious, rich, and powerful wines with none of that overblown character noticed in the past. The négociant side of the business meanwhile specializes in wines from the northern Rhone.

Recently tasted
CONDRIEU LA CHAMBÉE 2007
White | 2011 up to 2013   **86**

CORNAS LES BARCILLANTS 2007
Red | 2011 up to 2017   **88**

CÔTE RÔTIE LES ESSARTAILLES 2007
Red | 2011 up to 2017   **89**

CÔTES DU RHÔNE LES CRANILLES 2007
Red | 2011 up to 2013   **87**

CROZES-HERMITAGE LES PALIGNONS 2007
Red | 2011 up to 2013   **87**

SAINT-JOSEPH 2007
Red | 2011 up to 2013   **87**

SAINT-JOSEPH L'ARZELLE 2007
Red | 2011 up to 2015   **88**

SAINT-JOSEPH LES ARCHEVÊQUES 2007
Red | 2011 up to 2017   **90**

VIN DE PAYS DES COLLINES RHODANIENNES
HELUICUM 2007
Red | 2011 up to 2013   **86**

VIN DE PAYS DES COLLINES RHODANIENNES
SOTANUM 2007
Red | 2011 up to 2013   **87**

VIN DE PAYS DES COLLINES RHODANIENNES
TABURNUM 2007
White | 2011 up to 2013   **87**

Older vintages

CONDRIEU LA CHAMBÉE 2006
White | 2011 up to 2016   **88**
Refined, with ripe yellow fruit. The palate is fat. The oak is delicate and discreet. This is a Condrieu with typicity and elegance. It stays fresh in spite of its richness, in a particularly hot vintage.

CONDRIEU LA CHAMBÉE 2005
White | 2011 up to 2013   **91**
This Condrieu has a strong personality. Beautiful aromas of toasted almonds fill the palate. The finish is mineral and tense.

CORNAS LES BARCILLANTS 2006
Red | 2011 up to 2016   **87**
Mineral and tense bouquet. Good stature, with length and a good return of mineral in the mid-palate. Good tannins. Wait a bit.

CORNAS LES BARCILLANTS 2004
Red | 2011 up to 2013   **88**
Nice color. The wood is light, the palate honest and full. It is mouth-filling, with pleasant, fruity length (blackberries).

CÔTE RÔTIE LES ESSARTAILLES 2006
Red | 2011 up to 2016   **87**
A dense, smoky, and concentrated bouquet. Long on the palate, balanced, with fat tannins. Mineral and compact, the palate is fleshy and finishes fresh and flavorful.

HERMITAGE LES CHIRATS DE SAINT-CHRISTOPHE 2006
Red | 2011 up to 2021   **88**
Powerful, a little rich in alcohol on the nose, and marked by black and red fruit. The palate is powerful, but the terroir gives it a freshness that lengthens the wine. Generous and rich.

HERMITAGE LES CHIRATS DE SAINT-CHRISTOPHE 2004
Red | 2011 up to 2013   **88**
Beautiful color. The wood is light, the fruit forward. It's a streamlined and elegant wine, very well made, but lacking that extra dimension that would make it extraordinary.

SAINT-JOSEPH LES ARCHEVÊQUES 2006
Red | 2011 up to 2016   **87**
The bouquet is concentrated, fruity. Quite tense on the palate. It's a structured, dense wine with firm yet ripe tannins. Elegant.

SAINT-PÉRAY LES ARCHEVÊQUES 2007
White | 2011 up to 2015   **90**
The oak is still very perceptible. The palate is rich and concentrated, but a bit unbalanced at this stage by its aging.

SAINT-PÉRAY LES BIALÈRES 2007
White | 2011 up to 2013   **87**
Generally woody, but the juice handles it well. This is a rich and powerful wine, very civilized, with a balanced palate, long and fresh.

SAINT-PÉRAY LES BIALÈRES 2005
White | 2011 up to 2013   **89**
Golden, with toasted oak notes, this is a full wine, smooth and fat, with beautiful length.

VIN DE PAYS DES COLLINES RHODANIENNES SOTANUM 2006
Red | 2011 up to 2016   **87**
Deep and intense fruit. Mineral notes. Rich and powerful on the palate, with velvety tannins. It's a powerful wine (more so than the Côte Rôtie!) with a generous finish, even a little warm.

VIN DE PAYS DES COLLINES RHODANIENNES TABURNUM 2006
White | 2011 up to 2016   **89**
A beautiful wine, fresh and taut, with tender and unaggressive aromas. Rich without being heavy, it's a wine made for the dinner table, not as an aperitif. The serving temperature should be carefully respected.

Red: 34.6 acres; syrah 100%. **White:** 9.8 acres; marsanne 40%, roussanne 10%, viognier 50%. **Annual production:** 300,000 bottles

DOMAINE ALAIN VOGE

🍇🍇🍇🍇

4, impasse Equerre
07130 Cornas
Phone 00 33 4 75 40 32 04
Fax 00 33 4 75 81 06 02
contact@alain-voge.com
www.alain-voge.com

Alain Voge recently celebrated the fiftieth anniversary of his winery. Now partnered with Albéric Mazoyer, former technical director of Chapoutier, he is slowly stepping back from daily operations. With thirty acres of vineyards, this winery makes nine different wines, Saint-Péray whites and Cornas reds being their specialties. Only the Saint-Péray Harmonie is aged in tank; the rest are aged in barrel, for extended periods of time, with up to 30 percent new oak. The two old-vines bottlings, Fleur de Crussol in Saint-Péray and Les Vieilles Fontaines in Cornas, are often the best wines produced here.

Recently tasted

Cornas Les Chailles 2007
Red | 2011 up to 2017   **90**

Cornas Les Vieilles Vignes 2007
Red | 2011 up to 2017   **91**

Saint-Péray Fleur de Crussol 2007
White | 2011 up to 2017   **91**

Saint-Péray Terres Boisées 2007
White | 2011 up to 2017   **90**

Older vintages

Cornas Les Chailles 2006
Red | 2011 up to 2016   **88**
Very spicy, with notes of ripe black olives. Racy terroir character. Tight and tasty, with a streamlined, mineral finish.

Cornas Les Chailles 2005
Red | 2011 up to 2015   **88**
Very ripe fruit, concentrated and black. Fat on the palate, with well-enrobed tannins. A very pleasing wine with a bit of licorice in the finish.

Cornas Les Vieilles Fontaines 2006
Red | 2011 up to 2021   **93**
Very full-bodied and concentrated, this is a long and flavorful wine that must absolutely be cellared. The finish is fruity, with well-ripened cherry notes.

Cornas Les Vieilles Fontaines 2005
Red | 2011 up to 2020   **91**
Ripe and seductive, this is a concentrated and fleshy wine that stays fresh. The tannins are enrobed. It finishes on candied dark berries and black olives. Typical of its vintage.

Cornas Les Vieilles Vignes 2006
Red | 2011 up to 2016   **90**
Very pure fruit. An elegant and honest wine, with delicate and fresh tannins. The finish is mineral and pleasing. Very beautiful juice.

Cornas Les Vieilles Vignes 2005
Red | 2011 up to 2015   **90**
This wine starts out rather discreetly, but the tension mounts little by little. It is delicate, fresh, and tasty, with licorice tannins in the finish.

Saint-Péray Fleur de Crussol 2006
White | 2011 up to 2014   **89**
Elegant, flavorful, honest. It finishes fine and fresh. Very harmonious.

Saint-Péray Fleur de Crussol 2005
White | 2011 up to 2013   **89**
Floral, pure, delicate, this is a powerful wine, very sunny and rich (it's the vintage), but elegant. The seventy-year-old vines have managed to retain their freshness.

Saint-Péray Harmonie 2007
White | 2011 up to 2014   **88**
Very ripe, with seductive floral notes. This is delicate and balanced.

Saint-Péray Terres Boisées 2006
White | 2011 up to 2014   **89**
Fresher, more delicate than the 2005, this is quite elegant, subtle, and refined. It finishes with delicate minerality.

Saint-Péray Terres Boisées 2005
White | 2011 up to 2013   **88**
Fat, long, and rich. A beautiful aromatic palette of flowers and honey, strong but delicate. It is fresh despite its richness.

Red: 19.8 acres. White: 9.8 acres. Annual production: 55,000 bottles

Southern Rhone Vineyards

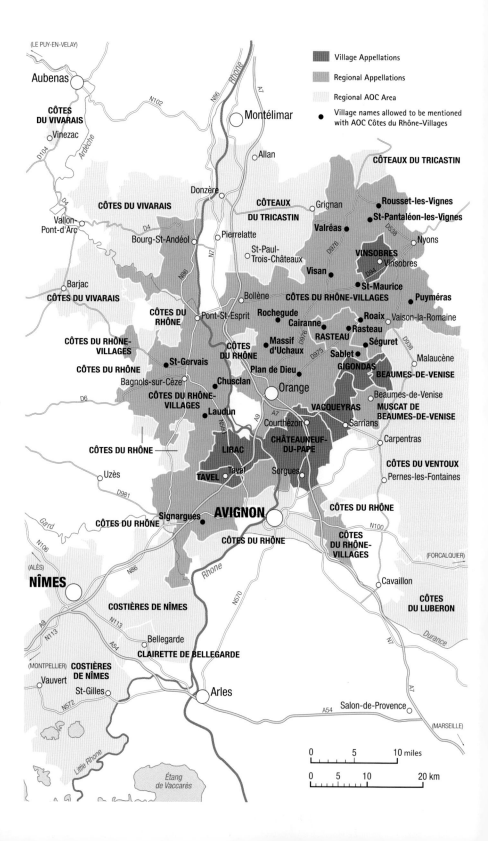

Legend:
- Village Appellations
- Regional Appellations
- Regional AOC Area
- Village names allowed to be mentioned with AOC Côtes du Rhône-Villages

(LE PUY-EN-VELAY)

Aubenas

CÔTES DU VIVARAIS

Vinezac

Montélimar

Allan

CÔTEAUX DU TRICASTIN

Donzère

CÔTES DU VIVARAIS

Vallon-Pont-d'Arc

Bourg-St-Andéol

Pierrelatte

CÔTEAUX DU TRICASTIN

Grignan

Rousset-les-Vignes

St-Pantaléon-les-Vignes

Valréas

Nyons

St-Paul-Trois-Châteaux

VINSOBRES

Visan

Vinsobres

Barjac

CÔTES DU VIVARAIS

Bollène

St-Maurice

CÔTES DU RHÔNE-VILLAGES

Puyméras

CÔTES DU RHÔNE

Pont-St-Esprit

Rochegude

Cairanne

Roaix

Vaison-la-Romaine

CÔTES DU RHÔNE-VILLAGES

St-Gervais

Massif d'Uchaux

RASTEAU

Rasteau

Séguret

Malaucène

CÔTES DU RHÔNE

Plan de Dieu

Sablet

GIGONDAS

BEAUMES-DE-VENISE

CÔTES DU RHÔNE-VILLAGES

Bagnols-sur-Cèze

Chusclan

Orange

Beaumes-de-Venise

VACQUEYRAS

MUSCAT DE BEAUMES-DE-VENISE

Laudun

Courthézon

Sarrians

Carpentras

CÔTES DU RHÔNE

CHÂTEAUNEUF-DU-PAPE

CÔTES DU VENTOUX

Uzès

LIRAC

Tavel

Sorgues

Pernes-les-Fontaines

TAVEL

Signargues

AVIGNON

CÔTES DU RHÔNE

(FORCALQUIER)

CÔTES DU RHÔNE

CÔTES DU RHÔNE-VILLAGES

Cavaillon

NÎMES

CÔTES DU LUBERON

COSTIÈRES DE NÎMES

Bellegarde

CLAIRETTE DE BELLEGARDE

(MONTPELLIER) **COSTIÈRES DE NÎMES**

Vauvert

St-Gilles

Arles

Salon-de-Provence

(MARSEILLE)

Étang de Vaccarès

| 0 | 5 | 10 miles |
| 0 | 5 | 10 | 20 km |

DOMAINE ALARY

Route de Rasteau
La Font d'Estevénas
84290 Cairanne
Phone 00 33 4 90 30 82 32
Fax 00 33 4 90 30 74 71
alary.denis@wanadoo.fr

Cairanne is certainly blessed when it comes to talented winemakers, but Daniel and Denis Alary stand out for their discreet style, relying simply on the true expression of their terroirs. The wines here are serious, not flashy, with distinct personalities that tend to age very well. Above all these are wines to be enjoyed with a meal; they just keep getting better and better throughout the evening.

CÔTES DU RHÔNE LA GERBAUDE 2007
Red | 2011 up to 2013   **87**
Fruit-filled and succulent, with notes of cassis and blackberry; the tannins are round and smooth.

CÔTES DU RHÔNE-VILLAGES CAIRANNE 2007
Red | 2011 up to 2013   **89**
Filled with personality, fruit forward but with a fresh, savory streak. The concentration is superb!

CÔTES DU RHÔNE-VILLAGES CAIRANNE LA FONT D'ESTEVÉNAS 2007
Red | 2011 up to 2014   **89**
A bit less concentrated, but this wine has lots of character; complex, not simply fruit forward, it's deep with a touch of pleasant bitterness. Brambly and wild on the palate, with a full and refined texture. Delicious.

CÔTES DU RHÔNE-VILLAGES CAIRANNE LA JEAN DE VERDE 2006
Red | 2011 up to 2016   **90**
Intense and seriously built, concentrated with perfectly ripe fruit and a nice texture, but still a bit closed. The tannins are tight, but well integrated. Cellar for a few years.

DOMAINE PIERRE ANDRÉ

30 Faubourg Saint-George
84350 Courthézon
Phone 00 33 4 90 70 81 14
Fax 00 33 4 90 70 75 73
domaine.pierre.andre@wanadoo.fr

Owner Jacqueline André manages this small estate very sensibly. The grapes have been organically grown for decades and are very precisely vinified under pristine conditions. A very dependable producer vintage after vintage, of wines that won't break the bank.

CHÂTEAUNEUF-DU-PAPE 2006
White | 2011 up to 2013   **88**
A supple and soft wine, lightly anise-scented, with no artifice. Honest, pure, and very balanced.

CHÂTEAUNEUF-DU-PAPE 2005
Red | 2011 up to 2019   **89**
Garnet in color, very fat, this is balanced, with a touch of bitterness in the finish in spite of its velvet texture and fruit. Nevertheless, it's quite convincing and undeniably energetic.

CHÂTEAUNEUF-DU-PAPE 2004
Red | 2011 up to 2017   **88**
This good wine, with deep color and clean fruit, has body and volume. It has depth, with notes of blackberry jam on the palate, and a seriously structured finish.

CHÂTEAUNEUF-DU-PAPE 2003
Red | 2011 up to 2018   **90**
A very well structured wine, silky and deep. It expresses superb long and racy tannins. A lovely and complete modern wine.

CHÂTEAUNEUF-DU-PAPE 2001
Red | 2011 up to 2015   **86**
Full color with mahogany tones, with a cashew hue, suggesting a certain evolution that's confirmed on the nose, with its scents of fruit in eau-de-vie. The palate is supple and grand, in a languid style, ready to drink.

CHÂTEAUNEUF-DU-PAPE 1999
Red | 2011 up to 2013   **86**
Good color. A slight dip in the mid-palate, but altogether, very soft with notes of prunes. Charming.

Red: 43.2 acres: grenache 80%, mourvèdre 8%, syrah 10%. **White:** 1.2 acres: bourboulenc 30%, clairette 40%, grenache blanc 10%, roussanne 20%. **Annual production:** 30,000 bottles

CHÂTEAU D'AQUÉRIA

Route de Roquemaure
30126 Tavel
Phone 00 33 4 66 50 04 56
Fax 00 33 4 66 50 18 46
contact@aqueria.com
www.aqueria.com

This large domaine is unique in owning the only single-block vineyard that straddles both the Tavel and Lirac appellations. Its wines are quite refreshing thanks to a blanket of rounded pebbles over a sand-and-clay subsoil that protects the vines from the fierce heat seen elsewhere in this appellation. The Tavel d'Aquéria contains eight of the nine approved appellation varietals.

Recently tasted

LIRAC CHÂTEAU D'AQUÉRIA 2007
Red | 2011 up to 2015   88

TAVEL CHÂTEAU D'AQUÉRIA 2008
Rosé | 2011 up to 2013   92

Older vintages

LIRAC CHÂTEAU D'AQUÉRIA 2006
Red | 2011 up to 2013   88
Pure and precise, with an aromatic palette that ranges from dark berries to sweet spice, with a touch of pepper in the finish. It's concentrated without being heavy, with perfectly worked tannins. Superb texture.

LIRAC CHÂTEAU D'AQUÉRIA 2005
Red | 2011 up to 2013   87
Smooth on the palate, this wine offers candied-fruit notes carried on a soft texture, yet the tannins are tight. On the whole, it doesn't lack acidity, and it has a very balanced character.

LIRAC HÉRITAGE D'AQUÉRIA 2005
Red | 2011 up to 2015   88
Quite complex, with scents of tobacco, licorice, and spices and a fine tannic structure. It could be briefly cellared to allow the oak notes more time to meld.

TAVEL CHÂTEAU D'AQUÉRIA 2007
Rosé | 2011 up to 2013   90
Dark pink in color, unctuous and smooth in body, this has intense scents of red berries and spices. Elegant and balanced, this wine has all that you could want from a great Tavel.

Red: 148.3 acres; cinsault 5%, grenache noir 45%, mourvèdre 25%, syrah 25%. White: 98.8 acres; bourboulenc 35%, clairette 45%, grenache blanc 12%, viognier 3%. Annual production: 380,000 bottles

DOMAINE PAUL AUTARD

Route de Châteauneuf
84350 Courthézon
Phone 00 33 4 90 70 73 15
Fax 00 33 4 90 70 29 59
jean-paul.autard@wanadoo.fr
www.paulautard.com

This domaine had the use of a lovely old stone farmhouse until the local city hall asked for it back. Since then, the domaine has occupied new, high-performance installations that make for increasingly refined and skillful vinification. That, and destemmed grapes from a sixty-acre vineyard between Courthézon and Bédarrides, produce wines with very distinctive smoothness—such as the modern but also remarkably mellow cuvée La Côte Ronde listed here.

Recently tasted

CHÂTEAUNEUF-DU-PAPE 2007
Red | 2011 up to 2016   92

CHÂTEAUNEUF-DU-PAPE 2007
White | 2011 up to 2015   88

CHÂTEAUNEUF-DU-PAPE
CUVÉE LA CÔTE RONDE 2007
Red | 2012 up to 2022   94

CHÂTEAUNEUF-DU-PAPE
CUVÉE LA CÔTE RONDE 2006
Red | 2013 up to 2020   90

Older vintages

CHÂTEAUNEUF-DU-PAPE
CUVÉE LA CÔTE RONDE 2005
Red | 2011 up to 2020   95
This wine is now revealing all the facets of its personality, with lots of charm and seductiveness. It is brilliant and dark in color, scented with fresh, ripe dark berries, and it's ample, silky, and velvety on the palate. It's softly full-bodied, but doesn't lack freshness.

CHÂTEAUNEUF-DU-PAPE
CUVÉE LA CÔTE RONDE 2004
Red | 2011 up to 2017   94
Deeply colored, with a racy bouquet of black olives and bay laurel, this is fat on the palate, fleshy, and unctuous, with superb and refined volume. A great thoroughbred.

CHÂTEAUNEUF-DU-PAPE
CUVÉE LA CÔTE RONDE 2003
Red | 2011 up to 2015   84
Deeply colored, this sticks to a rather simple register of fruitiness. It's supple and fat, not very expressive.

CHÂTEAUNEUF-DU-PAPE
CUVÉE LA CÔTE RONDE 2001
Red | 2011 up to 2015   **86**
The color is intense. The wine expresses its
suppleness in a soft raspberry register. Quite
precise, with smooth length.

CHÂTEAUNEUF-DU-PAPE
CUVÉE LA CÔTE RONDE 1999
Red | 2011 up to 2013   **88**
Full on the attack, but otherwise of medium
depth, with scents of blackberry jam and
prunes paired with more smoky notes.

Red: 54.4 acres. White: 4.9 acres. **Annual production:** 120,000 bottles

DOMAINE DE LA BARROCHE

19, avenue des Bosquets
84230 Châteauneuf-du-Pape
Phone 00 33 6 83 85 72 04
Fax 00 33 04 90 83 71 9
julien@domainelabarroche.com
www.domainelabarroche.com

Like many Châteauneuf estates, this one
used to sell all of its production to négociants and has only been bottling its own
wines since Julien Barrot took over in 2002.
The strength of this estate resides in its
very old vineyards, mainly located in the
north and northeast of the appellation: the
average age of the vines is sixty years, with
a third of plantings aged one hundred
years and more. Barrot produces two
cuvées: La Fiancée, a remarkable blend of
young syrah and very old grenache; and
Pure, exclusively made from hundred-
year-old grenache, planted in sandy soils.
The winemaking is precise and carefully
controlled for this rising star in the world of
Châteauneuf.

Recently tasted
CHÂTEAUNEUF-DU-PAPE 2007
Red | 2011 up to 2015   **89**

Older vintages
CHÂTEAUNEUF-DU-PAPE 2005
Red | 2011 up to 2015   **88**
Beautiful color, with the supple fruitiness
of ripe grenache, this is expansive in a delicious and refined style.

CHÂTEAUNEUF-DU-PAPE 2004
Red | 2011 up to 2015   **88**
Deeply colored, with a lovely bouquet of dark
berries and plums, this is smooth and long,
finely structured and expansive.

CHÂTEAUNEUF-DU-PAPE LA FIANCÉE 2006
Red | 2012 up to 2017   **89**
Garnet-hued. Scents of plums. Rich body,
medium-fine tannins, definite volume.

CHÂTEAUNEUF-DU-PAPE LA FIANCÉE 2005
Red | 2011 up to 2017   **91**
Beautifully made: deep color, harmonious
body, very delicate and racy tannins, unctuous length, and wonderful flavor.

CHÂTEAUNEUF-DU-PAPE LA FIANCÉE 2004
Red | 2011 up to 2015   **89**
Deeply colored; beautiful spicy bouquet;
generous volume filled with persistent notes
of chocolate. It is not as intense as the initial attack would suggest, but it has quite a
lovely voluptuousness.

CHÂTEAUNEUF-DU-PAPE PURE 2006
Red | 2012 up to 2017   90
Seductive and expressive aromas of strawberries; fat and long, with beautiful flavor.

CHÂTEAUNEUF-DU-PAPE PURE 2005
Red | 2011 up to 2018   94
Soft color, this is smooth and expansive grenache, supple and deep in volume and very persistent, with no roughness. A beautiful thoroughbred.

CHÂTEAUNEUF-DU-PAPE PURE 2004
Red | 2011 up to 2017   89
This wine expresses smooth notes of spices and black olives with a sunny constitution and beautiful balance. Supple and fat in length.

Red: 29.7 acres; cinsault 5%, grenache 70%, mourvèdre 14%, syrah 10%. Annual production: 40,000 bottles

CHÂTEAU DE BEAUCASTEL

Chemin de Beaucastel
84350 Courthézon
Phone 00 33 4 90 70 41 00
Fax 00 33 4 90 70 41 19
contact@beaucastel.com
www.beaucastel.com

What we have here is a single-block vineyard planted in a spectacular blanket of rounded stones ("galets roulés"), on a very clayey subsoil (useful for preventing drought stress) that extends throughout the northeast of the appellation, around the Coudoulet lieu-dit. This is Château de Beaucastel, rebuilt in the early twentieth century, first by the Tramier family then by the Perrin family, and since that time it has been one of the most innovative and exceptional of the Châteauneuf estates. It produces two red and two white wines, plus a Côtes du Rhône, the Coudoulet de Beaucastel, which is made with fruit from adjacent vineyards. Roussanne is the dominant grape in the white classic cuvée, and is the only grape in the Vieilles Vignes. The red wines are heavily based on mourvèdre, which accounts for roughly a third of plantings along with grenache. Syrah and cinsault as well as counoise and other permitted varietals make up the remaining two-thirds. The Hommage à Jacques Perrin is made almost entirely from ancient mourvèdre vines.

Recently tasted
CHÂTEAUNEUF-DU-PAPE 2007
White | 2011 up to 2017   95
A perfect nose laced with scents of acacia honey, wonderfully fine texture, splendidly smooth and fresh, remarkable length: a stunning wine.

CHÂTEAUNEUF-DU-PAPE 2007
Red | 2011 up to 2018   92
This wine shows beautiful power, structure, and intensity, revealing more aromatic intensity on the palate. The volume is impressively long on the finish.

CHÂTEAUNEUF-DU-PAPE ROUSSANNE
VIEILLES VIGNES 2007
White | 2011 up to 2018   97
A dazzling aromatic palette showing notes of dried apricots, sweet spices, and candied fruit. With an almost sweet length and layered depth, this is truly a great wine, radiant, and with clear aging potential.

CÔTES DU RHÔNE COUDOULET 2007
White | 2011 up to 2013   89

Older vintages
CHÂTEAUNEUF-DU-PAPE 2006
Red | 2011 up to 2025   95
A very pure wine, precise and direct: the bouquet is fresh and complex, with fullness and beautifully present structure. The combination is supple, with no stiffness. Great potential.

CHÂTEAUNEUF-DU-PAPE 2005
White | 2011 up to 2025   92
A generous and intense wine, yet very fresh. Beaucastel whites uniquely succeed in marrying freshness and richness!

CHÂTEAUNEUF-DU-PAPE 2005
Red | 2011 up to 2025   96
The bouquet reflects the vintage with notes of fig and spice. It is very intense on the palate, with great energy and a subtly present tannic structure. A thoroughbred, it will reveal itself after long cellaring.

CHÂTEAUNEUF-DU-PAPE 2004
Red | 2011 up to 2020   92
A long body, pure and streamlined, with impressive balance. No bluffing; a thoroughbred vintage.

CHÂTEAUNEUF-DU-PAPE 2003
White | 2011 up to 2015   90
From a year as marked by a heat wave as 2003, we're amazed and delighted by the freshness of this ample, profound, and deep wine, with its delicate floral and white-fruit aromas.

CHÂTEAUNEUF-DU-PAPE 2003
Red | 2011 up to 2020   93
A great wine. Its smooth and velvety texture doesn't mask its depth and classic tannic structure. Great potential.

CHÂTEAUNEUF-DU-PAPE 2001
Red | 2011 up to 2020   97
Great vintage. The elegant texture and bouquet pair beautifully with its impressive energy. In our opinion it's one of the greatest Beaucastels in fifteen years.

CHÂTEAUNEUF-DU-PAPE
HOMMAGE À JACQUES PERRIN 2005
Red | 2011 up to 2030   98
A great, taut wine, deep, well structured, but never massive. Unctuous and refined texture; good, dynamic length.

CHÂTEAUNEUF-DU-PAPE
HOMMAGE À JACQUES PERRIN 2004
Red | 2011 up to 2020   96
The mourvèdre brings delicate notes of white pepper that pair with the intense fruit, creating an unctuous and deep wine. Great character.

CHÂTEAUNEUF-DU-PAPE ROUSSANNE
VIEILLES VIGNES 2005
White | 2011 up to 2025   92
In a rather more overripe style than the classic cuvée, this is a very fat, ultrarich wine, with great generosity.

CHÂTEAUNEUF-DU-PAPE ROUSSANNE
VIEILLES VIGNES 2003
White | 2011 up to 2017   95
Very rich, fat, dense and profound, with a stunning and filling bouquet, this is a wine with impressive length, allied with a rare combination of richness and freshness.

Red: 222.4 acres; cinsault 5%, counoise 10%, grenache noir 30%, mourvèdre 30%, syrah 10%, others 15%. **White:** 24.7 acres; others 5%, grenache blanc 15%, roussanne 80%. **Annual production:** 33,5000 bottles

DOMAINE DE BEAURENARD

🍇 🍇 🍇 🍇 🍇

SCEA Paul Coulon et Fils
10, avenue Pierre de Luxembourg
84230 Châteauneuf-du-Pape
Phone 00 33 4 90 83 71 79
Fax 00 33 4 90 83 78 0
paul.coulon@beaurenard.fr
www.beaurenard.fr

Beaurenard has long been one of the great classics of Châteauneuf-du-Pape thanks to an impressive heritage of vines that are expertly farmed by brothers Daniel and Frédéric Coulon. The domaine owns eighty acres of plantings in Châteauneuf-du-Pape and sixty-two in Rasteau in the Côtes du Rhône appellation. All of the wines, including the classical and the prestige cuvées (the latter christened Boisrenard) are made in a powerful style that can make them seem slightly abrupt when young. Potentially very long-lived—which means they do need time in the cellar to show their best.

Recently tasted

CHÂTEAUNEUF-DU-PAPE BOISRENARD 2007
White | 2011 up to 2013   86
Golden color, fat and supple, expansive, but a bit flabby.

CHÂTEAUNEUF-DU-PAPE BOISRENARD 2007
Red | 2014 up to 2024   90
Currently this wine is overpowered by vanilla-oak flavors, but there is amazing substance. Patience is required for this powerfully structured wine.

CÔTES DU RHÔNE-VILLAGES 2008
Red | 2011 up to 2014   87

Older vintages

CHÂTEAUNEUF-DU-PAPE BOISRENARD 2006
White | 2011 up to 2015   91
Ambitious yet without the demonstrative heaviness that characterized earlier versions of this cuvée, this is a deep and intense wine. It is less ethereal than the classic cuvée, but it has great potential.

CHÂTEAUNEUF-DU-PAPE BOISRENARD 2006
Red | 2012 up to 2017   90
In line with the 2005s, this is a wine of deep color and magnificent texture, unctuous and sappy. Racy, knit together on delicate tannins.

CHÂTEAUNEUF-DU-PAPE BOISRENARD 2005
Red | 2011 up to 2025   96
The best Boisrenard in history, and one of the great wines of the vintage: this is splendidly suave and complex, with notes of red berries, delicate spices, and young leather and a great velvety texture.

CHÂTEAUNEUF-DU-PAPE BOISRENARD 2003
Red | 2011 up to 2022   91
Garnet in color, nearly opaque. An expressive bouquet of black cherries and kirsch. Intense, generous, and deep on the palate. Still rather blocky, but has lots of volume and balance. It is long and sure to age well in the cellar.

CHÂTEAUNEUF-DU-PAPE BOISRENARD 2001
Red | 2011 up to 2025   92
The color is nearly black and the oak still overt, paired with notes of dark berry jam and cocoa. It's an ultrarich wine, aromatically heady, but with great length.

CHÂTEAUNEUF-DU-PAPE BOISRENARD 1999
Red | 2011 up to 2013   95
At its best now: great color, notes of leather and flesh ("l'épaule d'agneau," or lamb shoulder), unctuous and deep, with great potential. A great Châteauneuf.

CHÂTEAUNEUF-DU-PAPE BOISRENARD 1998
Red | 2011 up to 2022   96
Intense and black, still very young, with a bouquet as delicious as its palate. It's rich, spicy, and hugely unctuous, unfurling notes of bay laurel in a long and persistent finish.

CHÂTEAUNEUF-DU-PAPE BOISRENARD 1995
Red | 2011 up to 2018   91
More mineral in the bouquet, this is a very concentrated wine, a touch austere, but with great depth and good length.

CHÂTEAUNEUF-DU-PAPE BOISRENARD 1990
Red | 2011 up to 2017   94
The tannins are fresh with not a bit of dryness. The flavors unfurl delicate notes of bay laurel and spices, with beautiful and smooth length.

CÔTES DU RHÔNE-VILLAGES 2006
Red | 2011 up to 2014   91
Very subtly built, fleshy and long, expressing delicate notes of apricots and pêche de vigne, this is fat yet fresh, and immediately seductive.

CÔTES DU RHÔNE-VILLAGES
LES ARGILES BLEUES 2006
Red | 2011 up to 2016   90
Refined, fat, very unctuous and long, this is a beautiful wine with delicate tannins.

Red: 138.4 acres; cinsault 8%, grenache noir 70%, mourvèdre 10%, syrah 10%, others 2%. White: 9.8 acres; bourboulenc 25%, clairette 30%, grenache blanc 20%, picpoul 3%, roussanne 22%. Annual production: 200,000 bottles

DOMAINE DES BERNARDINS

Route de Lafare
84190 Beaumes-de-Venise
Phone 00 33 4 90 62 94 13
Fax 00 33 4 90 65 01 42
contact@domaine-des-bernardins.com
www.domaine-des-bernardins.com

The reds wines from this attractive Beaumes de Venise property are sometimes less than convincing, but its Muscat is one of the finest sweet wines in France: a delicious balance of refined aromas, lushness, and, most especially, peerless freshness on the palate. A brilliantly natural expression of joyful fruit—ideal as a dessert wine but equally memorable as an aperitif.

Recently tasted

BEAUMES DE VENISE 2007
Red | 2011 up to 2013   86

CÔTES DU RHÔNE LES BALMES 2006
Red | 2011 up to 2013   85

MUSCAT DE BEAUMES-DE-VENISE 2008
Soft White | 2011 up to 2018   92

MUSCAT DE BEAUMES-DE-VENISE HOMMAGE
Soft White | 2011 up to 2020   95

Older vintages

BEAUMES DE VENISE 2006
Red | 2011 up to 2013   87
A true accomplishment! The wine—floral with notes of lavender and wildflowers—shines in its freshness, its elegant fruit, and its well-integrated, supple tannins.

MUSCAT DE BEAUMES-DE-VENISE 2007
Soft White | 2011 up to 2013   93
Quite finely perfumed, round and velvety, this wine is an outstanding example of the genius that can be found in a grand Muscat Vin Doux Naturel. The finish is marvelously fresh and the sweetness is perfectly integrated.

Red: 13.6 acres. White: 43.2 acres. Annual production: 100,000 bottles

DOMAINE HENRI BONNEAU

Rue Joseph-Ducros
84230 Châteauneuf-du-Pape
Phone 00 33 4 90 83 73 08
Fax 00 33 4 90 83 73 08
le.ballon.rouge@wanadoo.fr

Henri Bonneau is legendary in Châteauneuf-du-Pape as the maker of some of the most astonishing wines of the past three decades. His cellar perches at the top of the village, full of tiny recesses packed with ancestral casks of different sizes, all practically fossilized through use. This is where the jovial but cunning Bonneau leaves his treasures from the Crau plateau to slumber for as long as it takes (often more than six years) and only bottles them when desire or necessity dictates. His nectar-like wines are stunningly natural and sappy with endless depth and an incredibly refined texture—particularly the Réserve des Célestins.

CHÂTEAUNEUF-DU-PAPE
MARIE BEURRIER 2003
Red | 2011 up to 2020   91
Tasted before bottling, this is a beautiful, ample wine, long and not flabby, all finesse.

CHÂTEAUNEUF-DU-PAPE
MARIE BEURRIER 2001
Red | 2011 up to 2025   90
This luscious and refined cuvée expresses profound charm with great freshness and finesse.

CHÂTEAUNEUF-DU-PAPE
RÉSERVE DES CÉLESTINS 2004
Red | 2014 up to 2024   92
Tasted before bottling, the wine is intense and deep, with a finish both persistent and delicate.

CHÂTEAUNEUF-DU-PAPE
RÉSERVE DES CÉLESTINS 2001
Red | 2011 up to 2025   92
This wine has depth, true length, and beautiful intensity. Its tannins are undeniably refined. Great aging potential.

CHÂTEAUNEUF-DU-PAPE
RÉSERVE DES CÉLESTINS 2000
Red | 2011 up to 2025   94
Impressive in its freshness and finesse, this has an aromatic character reminiscent of a great Porto, yet with elegance and a magnificent texture.

CHÂTEAUNEUF-DU-PAPE SPÉCIALE 1998
Red | 2011 up to 2025   **92**

At 16.7° alcohol, this is quite obviously a "special" wine. Yet it still has incredible balance. Aromatically and gustatorially, the wine comes close to the style of a vintage Porto, without fortification. Astonishing!

VIN DE TABLE LES ROULLIERS
Red | 2011 up to 2013   **86**

Delicious, light, long, and rather charmingly rustic.

Red: 21 acres. Annual production: 5,000 bottles

DOMAINE BOSQUET DES PAPES

18, route d'Orange
BP 50
84230 Châteauneuf-du-Pape Cedex
Phone 00 33 4 90 83 72 33
Fax 00 33 4 90 83 50 52
bosquet.des.papes@orange.fr

This domaine has been bottling its own wines for at least forty years now and is particularly renowned for its cuvée Chante Le Merle, an old-vines bottling of three quarters grenache and one quarter black-skinned grapes. The latest offering is the Gloire de Mon Grand-Père, made from 98 percent grenache. Both wines show appealing depth of character, though the break with the cuvée Tradition is more sharply evident than it was a few years back. The whites could still benefit from a little more personality.

Recently tasted
CHÂTEAUNEUF-DU-PAPE CHANTE LE MERLE 2006
Red | 2012 up to 2017   **88**

CHÂTEAUNEUF-DU-PAPE LA FOLIE 2007
Red | 2012 up to 2017   **89**

Older vintages
CHÂTEAUNEUF-DU-PAPE 2005
Red | 2011 up to 2015   **86**

A solid wine, classically made but with rather rustic tannins.

CHÂTEAUNEUF-DU-PAPE 2004
White | 2011 up to 2013   **82**

A pale wine with rather heavy apricot aromas, this is generous on the attack but seriously lacks structure.

CHÂTEAUNEUF-DU-PAPE 2003
Red | 2011 up to 2013   **85**

Medium-intense in color, with notes of strawberries and kirsch in the bouquet. This is an unctuous and balanced wine, but it is clearly more limited than the domaine's other cuvées.

CHÂTEAUNEUF-DU-PAPE 2001
Red | 2011 up to 2013   **86**

Beautifully ruby-colored, this is discreet on the nose but generous in style and character on the palate. The finish is supple but not rustic.

CHÂTEAUNEUF-DU-PAPE CHANTE LE MERLE 2005
Red | 2011 up to 2018   **90**

This wine is more pleasing today than it was in its youth: it is fat and velvety with beautiful, smooth length. Very grenache, with ample volume.

CHÂTEAUNEUF-DU-PAPE CHANTE
LE MERLE 2003
Red | 2011 up to 2018   89
An ample wine, very fat, generous in alcohol, fleshy, tannic, finishing on fruit.

CHÂTEAUNEUF-DU-PAPE CHANTE
LE MERLE 2001
Red | 2011 up to 2015   88
Sunny and ample. A very traditional Châteauneuf with serious structure.

CHÂTEAUNEUF-DU-PAPE
GLOIRE DE MON GRAND-PÈRE 2007
Red | 2011 up to 2015   88
A wine of lovely dimensions, intense and generous, with smooth and spicy length and notes of black olives.

CHÂTEAUNEUF-DU-PAPE
GLOIRE DE MON GRAND-PÈRE 2003
Red | 2011 up to 2020   92
The bouquet is very expressive, in a Mediterranean register of spice and black olives. Its evolved character fully expresses itself in the wine's unctuous texture. It is neither heavy nor rough, yet it is assuredly deep.

Red: 63 acres. White: 3.7 acres. Annual production: 60,000 bottles

DOMAINE DES BOSQUETS

84190 Gigondas
Phone 00 33 4.90.83.70.31
Fax 00 33 4.90.83.51.97
contact@famillebrechet.fr
www.domainedesbosquets.com

The Brechet family has the good fortune of running this fairly large winery, with sixty-five acres of Gigondas. Grenache makes up two-thirds of the plantings and the wines are vinified using indigenous yeasts when possible, in the traditional concrete tanks of the region. Care is taken not to push the extraction too far, as the terroir here has a natural tendency toward hard tannins. The wines are structured showing grace and finesse, and tend to age marvelously.

Recently tasted
CÔTES DU RHÔNE-VILLAGES
DOMAINE DE LA JÉRÔME 2007
Red | 2011 up to 2014   87

GIGONDAS 2007
Red | 2012 up to 2017   89
Opaque, it is rich and jammy with a nice acidity bringing balance to the palate, with just a touch of oak that adds elegance. The tannins are young and quite powerful on the finish. This is a wine you can hold on to for several years.

Older vintages
GIGONDAS 2006
Red | 2011 up to 2016   88
This wine is astonishing: it is hefty in structure and saturated flavor; yet, at the same time, it's silky on the palate, with firm and perfectly integrated tannins. It finishes on notes of wild fruit, orange peel, and cedar.

GIGONDAS 2005
Red | 2011 up to 2013   88
A potent, peppery bouquet. A rich palate with beautiful, silky tannins. This is complex and well structured, with nicely assimilated alcohol (14.8°).

GIGONDAS 2004
Red | 2011 up to 2013   90
A deep and dense bouquet with notes of hot chocolate. The alcohol is perceptible (15°) but well paired to the pleasant fruit notes. The attack is clean, the mid-palate is nicely straightforward, and the finish is mineral and tense, with a nice tannic grain. It is a dense, structured, and firm wine, ready to drink.

Red: 64.2 acres; cinsault 5%, grenache noir 70%, mourvèdre 5%, syrah 20%. Annual production: 50,000 bottles

DOMAINE DE LA BOUÏSSIÈRE

Rue du Portail
84190 Gigondas
Phone 00 33 4 90 65 87 91
Fax: 00 33 4 90 65 82 16
labouissière@aol.com
www.bouissiere.com

La Bouissière is a tiny Gigondas property of only twenty-one acres. Gilles and Thierry Faravel manage the domaine with passion and wisdom, making sumptuous wines with elegant tannins. Most of the vineyards are located in the Dentelles de Montmirail between 1,100 and 1,300 feet altitude, which enables them to push the grapes to perfect ripeness, often harvesting the grapes in mid-October. They also have six acres of Vacqueyras; the wines are just as good, but the quantities are minuscule!

GIGONDAS CUVÉE PRESTIGE "LE FONT DE TONIN" 2007
Red | 2015 up to 2020 **93**
An intense and profound wine made from perfectly ripe grapes. Notes of tobacco, prunes, eau-de-vie, caramel, and figs. Barrel aged to perfection, with powerful but perfectly balanced tannins.

GIGONDAS CUVÉE TRADITIONELLE 2007
Red | 2012 up to 2020 **90**
Impressive for its concentration but also for its ethereal style. Notes of tea and raisins; it almost seems Port-like, but it's completely dry on the palate. Complex and long, this is not a shy wine. Cellar it for a few years.

VACQUEYRAS 2007
Red | 2012 up to 2020 **90**
Notes of raisins, sun-dried figs, orange peel, and gingerbread, with surprising precision and concentration. This is a powerful wine with an assertive character and powerful tannins.

CLOS DU CAILLOU

1600, chemin Saint-Dominique
84350 Courthézon
Phone 00 33 4 90 70 73 05
Fax 00 33 4 90 70 76 47
closducaillou@wanadoo.fr
www.closducaillou.com

With an efficient and well-adapted cellar, Sylvie Vacheron relies on vineyards located in the northeastern part of the appellation, parts of which produce excellent Côtes du Rhônes. In Châteauneuf-du-Pape she makes concentrated and modern wines, fruit-filled and flavorful, but they can be a bit on the hot side. All in all the wines are highly recommended.

CHÂTEAUNEUF-DU-PAPE LES QUARTZ 2007
Red | 2012 up to 2017 **87**
Very dark in color, powerful notes of kirsch, good volume, hot and slightly heady, it needs a bit of time to settle in.

CHÂTEAUNEUF-DU-PAPE LES QUARTZ 2007
White | 2011 up to 2013 **84**
With notes of lemon and apricot, this wine is simple and balanced but seems to lack vitality.

CHÂTEAUNEUF-DU-PAPE LES QUARTZ 2006
Red | 2012 up to 2017 **89**
A solid wine with notes of kirsch, but the tannins are elegant and the palate unctuous. Clear potential.

CHÂTEAUNEUF-DU-PAPE LES SAFFRES 2007
Red | 2012 up to 2020 **86**
Pretty ruby color, plum and cherry eau-de-vie in the nose, young and acidic in the mouth, soft on the finish. It needs time.

CHÂTEAUNEUF-DU-PAPE RESERVE 2007
Red | 2012 up to 2017 **88**
Dark color, with notes of kirsch, unctuous on the palate, generous personality, warm and flavorful.

CHÂTEAUNEUF-DU-PAPE RÉSERVE 2006
Red | 2012 up to 2017 **88**
A solid wine with notes of black cherry, elegant tannins, and unctuous mouthfeel. Definite potential.

LES CAILLOUX – ANDRÉ BRUNEL

6, chemin du Bois-de-la-Ville
84230 Châteauneuf-du-Pape
Phone 00 33 4 90 83 72 62
Fax 00 33 4 90 83 51 07

Former-teacher-turned-winegrower André Brunel has spent the past few decades making a name for himself as a benchmark producer of Châteauneuf-du-Pape. He owes his success to a very personal sense of balance, producing wines that combine palpable generosity and opulent body with real finesse and a tangibly fresh mouthfeel. The scattered vineyards include parcels in practically every Châteauneuf terroir, the dominant feature being of course the famous rounded stones after which this estate is named. Grenache fruit prevails in the red wine, nicely backed up by the mourvèdre, while the clairette takes the leading role in the deliciously refined white wine. La Centenaire, a rare and exceptional cuvée first created by Brunel in the 1990s, is made from ancient grenache vines planted on the Mont-Redon plateau.

Recently tasted

CHÂTEAUNEUF-DU-PAPE 2007
Red | 2011 up to 2015   **88**
Full-bodied, fat and dense, black fruit, quite supple on the finish.

CHÂTEAUNEUF-DU-PAPE CENTENAIRE 2007
Red | 2012 up to 2017   **91**
A generous and spicy personality, rich volume, dense, tightly wound at this stage.

Older vintages

CHÂTEAUNEUF-DU-PAPE 2007
White | 2011 up to 2015   **91**
Beautiful golden green in color, this has delicate floral and honeyed notes and a very elegant palate. It is delicious and persistent, suave in the finish.

CHÂTEAUNEUF-DU-PAPE 2006
White | 2011 up to 2015   **90**
Floral and mineral, this wine shines with its largesse and its freshness: it has not a trace of heaviness. The style is light and delicately perfumed.

CHÂTEAUNEUF-DU-PAPE 2006
Red | 2011 up to 2016   **90**
Supple color; dark berries and plums in the bouquet; round and harmonious with no heaviness on the palate, with a fresh finish. Beautiful balance overall.

CHÂTEAUNEUF-DU-PAPE 2005
Red | 2011 up to 2020   **92**
With a lovely floral bouquet, this is rich on the palate, mellow and elegant, with notes of chocolate and tobacco. Opulent.

CHÂTEAUNEUF-DU-PAPE 2004
White | 2011 up to 2013   **92**
A finely floral wine, very ample but with no heaviness. It's edgy, refined, long, and brilliantly refreshing—a quality not often found in Châteauneuf.

CHÂTEAUNEUF-DU-PAPE 2004
Red | 2011 up to 2020   **90**
A beautiful, classy and harmonious wine with a precise and delicate tannic structure. Very sunny, the wine expresses itself with finesse and elegance.

CHÂTEAUNEUF-DU-PAPE 2003
Red | 2011 up to 2018   **95**
The great artists of the wine world know how to transcend a difficult year. This is the case for Brunel, who has produced a wine of astonishing finesse that, in spite of its depth, its sap, its aromatic intensity, and its strong tannic structure, flows over the tongue, leaving a graceful and supremely light impression. It's proof of the wine's amazing class and pedigree.

CHÂTEAUNEUF-DU-PAPE CENTENAIRE 2006
Red | 2011 up to 2022   **92**
A very deep wine, this exhales notes of blackberry jam, bay leaf, and delicate spices. It's ample and generous, with no heaviness.

CHÂTEAUNEUF-DU-PAPE CENTENAIRE 2005
Red | 2011 up to 2025   **96**
With a production of only 4,000 bottles, this wine has attained mythical status. It is broad with no hardness; a thoroughbred, long and refined.

Red: 46.9 acres; grenache 65%, mourvèdre 20%, syrah 10%, others 5%. **White:** 4.9 acres; bourboulenc 10%, clairette 20%, grenache 20%, roussanne 50%.
Annual production: 80,000 bottles

DOMAINE DE LA CHARBONNIÈRE

26, route de Courthézon
84230 Châteauneuf-du-Pape
Phone 00 33 4 90 83 74 59
Fax 00 33 4 90 83 53 46
maret-charbonniere@club-internet.fr
www.domainedelacharbonniere.com

Michel Maret takes a wise but very firm approach to the running of this family estate, which in all its long history has never been in better shape than it is today. Production includes a very comprehensive range of Châteauneuf-du-Pape wines and even extends into the neighboring Vacqueyras region. Recent years have brought significant improvements, thanks in particular to a variety of highly characteristic cuvées sourced from assiduously selected terroirs. The Hautes-Brusquières and the white wine come from a lieu-dit (single vineyard) on the Mont-Redon plateau. The 100-percent-grenache Vieilles Vignes comes from La Charbonnière lieu-dit on the east-facing slopes of the Crau plateau; so, too, does the Mourre des Perdrix. The wines offer plenty of sap and are very elegantly matured.

Recently tasted

CHÂTEAUNEUF-DU-PAPE 2008
White | 2011 up to 2013   84

CHÂTEAUNEUF-DU-PAPE HAUTES-BRUSQUIÈRES 2007
Red | 2011 up to 2015   88

CHÂTEAUNEUF-DU-PAPE MOURRE DES PERDRIX 2007
Red | 2011 up to 2015   90

CHÂTEAUNEUF-DU-PAPE VIEILLES VIGNES 2007
Red | 2012 up to 2017   89

Older vintages

CHÂTEAUNEUF-DU-PAPE 2006
White | 2011 up to 2014   90
Very pale-hued, with lovely notes of almonds and dried apricots. Harmonious and persistent in length, with beautiful finesse. As is often the case here, this is a remarkable white wine.

CHÂTEAUNEUF-DU-PAPE 2005
Red | 2011 up to 2015   91
Beautiful, deep color; delicate fruit and softened tannins; unctuous, long, and smooth. A beautiful wine of the region.

CHÂTEAUNEUF-DU-PAPE 2004
White | 2011 up to 2013   90
A very lovely white Châteauneuf, fat, perfumed, tasty, and fruity, with remarkable length.

CHÂTEAUNEUF-DU-PAPE 2003
Red | 2011 up to 2015   90
A beautiful and unctuous wine, silky yet not heavy, with good maturity, finishing with a length both harmonious and mellow.

CHÂTEAUNEUF-DU-PAPE MOURRE DES PERDRIX 2006
Red | 2011 up to 2017   90
A fat wine, powerful, chocolaty, rich and long, this finishes on generous notes of blackberries.

CHÂTEAUNEUF-DU-PAPE MOURRE DES PERDRIX 2005
Red | 2011 up to 2020   90
Color as it should be. After a light attack of soft fruit with strawberry notes, this wine lengthens gently, and yet with depth.

CHÂTEAUNEUF-DU-PAPE VIEILLES VIGNES 2006
Red | 2011 up to 2020   92
An unctuous wine, very dense, with great richness of flavor and remarkable length.

CHÂTEAUNEUF-DU-PAPE VIEILLES VIGNES 2005
Red | 2011 up to 2020   92
A thoroughbred cuvée, long and flavorful, intense, deep.

CHÂTEAUNEUF-DU-PAPE VIEILLES VIGNES 2001
Red | 2011 up to 2017   90
Soft and generous, suave and long. Here is a very flavorful Châteauneuf, very classic, in a traditional register. It's more classic than the domaine's other cuvées.

CHÂTEAUNEUF-DU-PAPE VIEILLES VIGNES 1998
Red | 2011 up to 2015   90
The tannins are a bit tired now, but this is a noble Châteauneuf, smooth and languorous.

Red: 58.1 acres; cinsault 2%, grenache 68%, mourvèdre 10%, syrah 19%, other 1%. White: 1.2 acres; bourboulenc 5%, clairette 15%, grenache 40%, roussanne 40%. Annual production: 70,000 bottles

DOMAINE CHARVIN

Chemin de Maucoil
84100 Orange
Phone 00 33 4 90 34 41 10
Fax 00 33 4 90 51 65 59
domaine.charvin@free.fr
www.domaine-charvin.com

This estate lies in the north of the appellation, going toward Orange, planted in generous clay and limestone soils that have never really been made the most of until now. Many of these bottlings come under the Côtes du Rhône appellation and are actually well worth a look. Thanks to Laurent Charvin's meticulous, no-nonsense approach (no destemming and especially no filtration), this estate is now warmly recommended. The Châteauneufs are honest, intense, and sincere, with just an occasional hint of rusticity.

Recently tasted
CHÂTEAUNEUF-DU-PAPE 2007
Red | 2011 up to 2017   89

Older vintages
CHÂTEAUNEUF-DU-PAPE 2005
Red | 2011 up to 2016   90
A fleshy wine with a very natural build, this smells of red berries and feels rich and generous but not heavy. Altogether a very seductive wine that will age well.

CHÂTEAUNEUF-DU-PAPE 2004
Red | 2011 up to 2018   86
Good intensity of color and somewhat reduced bouquet. Supple, refined, and light on the tongue, with smooth length.

CHÂTEAUNEUF-DU-PAPE 2001
Red | 2011 up to 2014   88
The color is deep and alive; the bouquet is spicy and peppery with a slight hint of animal. On the palate it is assured and solid, suave and long. Still a bit reduced.

Red: 59.3 acres; grenache 82%, mourvèdre 5%, syrah 8%, vaccarèse 5%. **Annual production:** 100,000 bottles

DOMAINE DE LA CITADELLE

Route de Cavaillon
84560 Ménerbes
Phone 00 33 4 90 72 41 58
Fax 00 33 4 90 72 41 59
contact@domaine-citadelle.com
www.domaine-citadelle.com

Successful movie producer Yves Rousset-Rouard bought this estate in 1989 when it represented just twenty acres of plantings. That was the start of a love affair with the Luberon that led to his election as mayor of the delightful village of Ménerbes, while also working to rebuild his vineyard. He added another seventy-five acres and built a winemaking facility that is now run by his son Alexis. The vines are planted on the Mistral-swept northern flank of the Luberon mountains, producing a broad range of wines with a very fresh expression. Well made across the board, though the appellation wines are a definite cut above the Vins de Pays.

Recently tasted
CÔTES DU LUBERON GOUVERNEUR
SAINT-AUBAN 2007
Red | 2012 up to 2017   91

CÔTES DU LUBERON LES ARTÈMES 2007
Red | 2011 up to 2015   89

Older vintages
CÔTES DU LUBERON GOUVERNEUR
SAINT-AUBAN 2005
Red | 2011 up to 2017   90
Old-vine syrah makes up the majority of this high-end cuvée from Citadelle. Oak barrel aging renders it suave and velvety, with good extract on the palate without being heavy. The high altitude of the vines gives the wine good freshness and renders it harmonious.

CÔTES DU LUBERON LE CHÂTAIGNIER 2008
White | 2011 up to 2013   88
A wonderful expression of clairette, fresh and balanced on the palate, elegantly made with soft floral notes on the finish.

CÔTES DU LUBERON LE CHÂTAIGNIER 2007
Red | 2011 up to 2013   88
Flavorful and well balanced, this wine is a good example of the delicious 2007 vintage. Very ripe, wild, dark fruit; superb texture on the palate; round and supple tannins.

Annual production: 195,000 bottles

DAUVERGNE & RANVIER

Château Saint-Maurice
Route nationale 580
30290 Laudun l'Ardoise
Phone 00 33 4 66 82 96 59
Fax 00 33 4 66 82 96 58
contact@dauvergne-ranvier.com
www.dauvergne-ranvier.com

François Dauvergne and Jean-François Ranvier belong to a new generation of Rhone Valley wine merchants who believe in teamwork. They support their winegrowing friends all year, providing advice on techniques and usually retaining the producers' own labels so as to bring their terroir to the fore. They handle from twenty to thirty properties, focusing on Côtes du Rhône and Côtes du Rhône-Villages from the Ardèche, Gard, and Vaucluse. Other wines include a Gigondas, Châteauneuf-du-Pape, and even a Côte Rôtie. The wines are made in a fruit-forward, ripe style, supported by careful growing and maturation.

Recently tasted

CÔTE RÔTIE 2007
Red | 2011 up to 2016   89
An aromatic nose with notes of violets and leather, the wine is tight on the palate and still young; a nice touch of oak, but it needs time.

CÔTES DU RHÔNE 2007
Red | 2011 up to 2014   87
A lovely dense and silky texture, perfectly ripened grapes, nicely balanced on the palate with smooth tannins and an elegant touch of oak on the finish.

CÔTES DU RHÔNE-VILLAGES 2007
Red | 2011 up to 2014   86
Notes of black cherry and concentrated fruit. Quite tannic for the time being; it needs a bit of time to integrate the oak.

CÔTES DU RHÔNE-VILLAGES
CHÂTEAU SAINT-MAURICE 2007
Red | 2011 up to 2013   87
Pretty, fresh, and succulent on the palate, with notes of brambly black fruit and wild blackberries, and nice round, flavorful tannins.

CROZES-HERMITAGE 2007
Red | 2011 up to 2013   88
Focused and linear with ripe black fruit, suave but restrained, with nice acidity on the finish.

GIGONDAS 2007
Red | 2011 up to 2015   88
A complex and deep nose of wild blackberries, wonderfully dense texture in the mouth, suave and elegant, perfectly oaked with smooth tannins, just a touch hot on the finish.

Annual production: 400,000 bottles

DOMAINE PAUL DURIEU

27, avenue Pasteur
84850 Camaret
Phone 00 33 4 90 37 28 14
Fax 00 33 4 90 37 76 05
domaine-durieu@hotmail.fr

All of the entries from this young Châteauneuf-du-Pape estate were irresistible: mouth-filling, with velvety roundness and stunning aromas. Definitely one to watch!

CHÂTEAUNEUF-DU-PAPE 2006
Red | 2011 up to 2013   88
Powerful and intense, with very rich volume that should please.

CHÂTEAUNEUF-DU-PAPE 2005
Red | 2011 up to 2020   90
Very rich and unctuous, full and classy, with beautiful scents of black olives and smooth depth. This wine needs more aging in order to integrate its uncontestably generous alcohol.

CHÂTEAUNEUF-DU-PAPE 2004
Red | 2011 up to 2020   92
Highly colored, this fleshy wine, scented with chocolate and spice, is unctuous on the palate, refined and fat, developing a rich, suave volume.

CHÂTEAUNEUF-DU-PAPE LUCILLE AVRIL 2006
Red | 2011 up to 2020   88
Very rich, maybe a bit too much so, with overt and generous alcohol and notes of dried currants.

CHÂTEAUNEUF-DU-PAPE LUCILLE AVRIL 2005
Red | 2011 up to 2025   91
Deep and opaque in color, scented with black-fruit jam and blackberry brambles, this is fat and velvety on the palate with intense volume and very generous alcohol. It must be cellared.

Red: 61.8 acres.

DOMAINE DES ESCARAVAILLES

84110 Rasteau
Phone 00 33 4 90 46 14 20
Fax: 00 33 4 90 46 11 45
Domaine.escaravailles@rasteau.fr

Gilles Ferran took over the 150-acre family domaine in the late 1990s. With vineyards in Rasteau, Cairanne, and Roaix, he makes elegant wines in a region where extraction is the norm. The winery has been adapted in order to vinify each appellation separately, according to the style of the domaine.

Côtes du Rhône Les Antimagnes 2007
Red | 2011 up to 2014   **88**
Scents of blackberry and cassis on the nose, with hints of orange peel and cloves. Smooth on the palate with impressive density and concentrated fruit, without overextraction.

Côtes du Rhône-Villages la Boutine 2007
Red | 2011 up to 2016   **90**
A touch of oak on the nose, ripe, brambly fruit, a touch of bitterness that enlivens the core, nice tannic structure and good length.

Côtes du Rhône-Villages Rasteau 2007
Red | 2011 up to 2013   **88**
Wonderfully silky and elegant texture, ripe, rich fruit, well made with smooth, well-integrated tannins.

Côtes du Rhône-Villages Rasteau La Ponce 2007
Red | Drink now   **88**
Perfectly ripe fruit on the nose and palate, modern and fruity in style, with savory, soft, and spicy tannins.

Côtes du Rhône-Villages Rasteau Ventabren 2007
Red | Drink now   **88**
Rich, fat, and tasty, with nicely wrought, powerful tannins.

DOMAINE DE FONDRÈCHE

84380 Mazan
Phone 00 33 4 90 69 61 42
Fax 00 33 4 90 69 61 18
contact@fondreche.com
www.fondreche.com

This premium winery is a reliable source for Côtes du Ventoux production. Its wines have been exceptionally consistent for the past decade: fleshy and balanced but always with plenty of finesse thanks to a vineyard planted mainly on the plain, in clay and limestone soils. The wines are very carefully made, with differences in maturation depending on the bottling, but always masterfully oaked. The result is a well-made range across the board, from the simplest offering to the ambitious Persia cuvée.

Recently tasted
Côtes du Ventoux L'Éclat 2008
White | 2011 up to 2013   **86**

Côtes du Ventoux Nadal 2007
Red | 2011 up to 2016   **87**

Côtes du Ventoux Nature 2008
Red | 2011 up to 2013   **86**

Côtes du Ventoux Persia 2007
Red | 2011 up to 2013   **87**

Older vintages
Côtes du Ventoux Fayard 2006
Red | 2011 up to 2014   **87**
Expressive with a bouquet of dark berries and wild herbs, this is round and ample, a little hot. Good acidity lifts the finish on softened tannins.

Côtes du Ventoux Nadal 2006
Red | 2011 up to 2015   **88**
The wood tannins dominate this wine and render it a little hard. That said, it has a very good extract behind it, with notes of black olives, tobacco, and spices. It just needs a year or two in the bottle. With a bit of patience, it will certainly have a lovely future.

Côtes du Ventoux Persia 2006
Red | 2011 up to 2015   **90**
The black fruit and the beautiful freshness reveal the dominance of syrah in this cuvée. The intensity of the fruit and the texture on the palate finish with well-mastered wood nuances.

Red: 74.1 acres. White: 12.4 acres. Annual production: 200,000 bottles

CHÂTEAU DE FONSALETTE

Château Rayas
84230 Châteauneuf-du-Pape
Phone 00 33 4 90 83 73 09
Fax 00 33 4 90 83 51 17
www.châteaurayas.fr

This small but famous property is run by Emmanuel Reynaud, who vinifies and ages wines in much the same style as those of Rayas. The grenache may only account for half of the red plantings but, as in Rayas, it is the signature varietal, except in the often-excellent syrah-based cuvée. Fonsalette, like all Reynaud's wines, needs time to firm up in the bottle because it doesn't play on luscious roundness and exuberant fruit. What you get instead is depth, exquisitely refined texture, and an abundance of class. The whites have improved enormously.

Recently tasted
CÔTES DU RHÔNE 2006
Red | 2011 up to 2013   92

Older vintages
CÔTES DU RHÔNE 2007
White | 2011 up to 2015   88
Rich and fat, with more candied-fruit notes than in previous vintages.

CÔTES DU RHÔNE 2006
White | 2011 up to 2013   92
Fat, deep, pure: an ideal white!

CÔTES DU RHÔNE 2005
White | 2011 up to 2013   90
Astonishing and seductive notes of star anise. Full and seductive. Very pleasing.

CÔTES DU RHÔNE 2005
Red | 2011 up to 2015   91
Great color, supple and very fat, with beautiful structure. Can be cellared still.

CÔTES DU RHÔNE 2004
White | 2011 up to 2013   88
The bouquet is quite discreet at this time, but the wine, both ample and fresh, is complete.

CÔTES DU RHÔNE 2004
Red | 2011 up to 2013   92
Fat, delicious, and complete, this is a very seductive wine, expressing pure fruit.

CÔTES DU RHÔNE 2003
Red | 2011 up to 2013   90
Very ripe on the nose and palate, with notes of blackberry jam. It is immediately open, flavorful, full and velvety.

Red: 14.8 acres. White: 4.9 acres.

DOMAINE FONT DE MICHELLE

14, impasse des Vignerons
84370 Bédarrides
Phone 00 33 4 90 33 00 22
Fax 00 33 4 90 33 20 27
egonnet@terre-net.fr
www.font-de-michelle.com

The place name here dates back a very long way—you won't find any "Michelle" among recent generations of the Gonnet family. The vineyard lines the slope leading up to the Crau plateau, west of the village of Bédarrides. Ancient plantings largely dominated by grenache represent the backbone of the Gonnets' wines, which are made from partially destemmed grapes. The grenache is fermented and raised in large oak vats for as long as it takes; barrels are used for the other varietals. These are powerful wines built for cellaring. The white wines are refined and deep and mainly blended from grenache, roussanne, and clairette.

Recently tasted
CHÂTEAUNEUF-DU-PAPE 2008
White | 2011 up to 2014   90

CHÂTEAUNEUF-DU-PAPE ÉLÉGANCE DE JEANNE 2007
Red | 2012 up to 2017   88

CHÂTEAUNEUF-DU-PAPE ÉTIENNE-GONNET 2006
Red | 2011 up to 2016   92

Older vintages
CHÂTEAUNEUF-DU-PAPE 2007
White | 2011 up to 2014   90
A fleshy and elegant wine, very pleasing with its white-fruit scents and beautiful freshness.

CHÂTEAUNEUF-DU-PAPE 2005
Red | 2011 up to 2013   92
This wine is tasting much better now than it was last year: it is an ample and generous wine with good structure, pepper and spice. Generous and balanced.

CHÂTEAUNEUF-DU-PAPE 2004
White | 2011 up to 2013   90
A lovely wine without any artifice. Pale, with delicate notes of fennel, it is long and streamlined on the palate. Very racy; it will age well.

CHÂTEAUNEUF-DU-PAPE 2003
Red | 2011 up to 2020   87
Nicely colored, with notes of kirsch and chocolate in the bouquet. The attack is rather heavy and dominated by relatively dry tannins and strong alcohol. There is lots of material here. In the end, however, it is tiring, quite marked by its vintage.

CHÂTEAUNEUF-DU-PAPE 2001
Red | 2011 up to 2020   **86**
This wine is passing through a closed-down phase. It has medium-dense color and seems somewhat linear, with a minimally expressive structure at this point.

CHÂTEAUNEUF-DU-PAPE ÉTIENNE-GONNET 2007
Red | 2011 up to 2022   **89**
Not particularly luminous color. Nose of stone fruit. Rustic tannins, alcohol, and flesh: this is an old-style wine, voluminous without actually being spectacular.

CHÂTEAUNEUF-DU-PAPE ÉTIENNE-GONNET 2003
Red | 2011 up to 2020   **89**
Beautiful garnet in color, with good depth. Its chocolate bouquet prepares the taster for its powerfully fleshy and spicy palate. The tannins are medium-fine, but with very great volume.

CHÂTEAUNEUF-DU-PAPE ÉTIENNE-GONNET 2001
Red | 2011 up to 2020   **92**
A fat and powerful wine, with lots of body and structure that reflect the perfect maturity of its thoroughbred grenache.

Annual production: 200,000 bottles

CHÂTEAU FORTIA

Route de Bédarrides BP 13
84231 Châteauneuf-du-Pape
Phone 00 33 4 90 83 72 25
Fax 00 33 4 90 83 51 03
fortia@terre-net.fr
www.château-fortia.com

Wineries don't get much more historic than this one: Fortia once belonged to Baron Le Roy, who laid the foundation of the AOC system. The domaine lies on the edge of the village of Châteauneuf and is certainly one of the oldest in the eponymous appellation. The mix of vine varieties is entirely classical. Roussanne may be by far the most dominant white varietal, but grenache makes up for it among the reds with support from syrah (24 percent) and minor plantings of the mourvèdre and counoise. The wines show real class with age, particularly the cuvée du Baron.

Recently tasted
CHÂTEAUNEUF-DU-PAPE CUVÉE DU BARON 2007
Red | 2012 up to 2017   **90**

CHÂTEAUNEUF-DU-PAPE TRADITION 2007
Red | 2011 up to 2015   **86**

Older vintages
CHÂTEAUNEUF-DU-PAPE 2006
White | 2011 up to 2013   **86**
A supple and elegantly built wine, yet limited in intensity.

CHÂTEAUNEUF-DU-PAPE 2004
White | 2011 up to 2013   **88**
Beautiful nuanced aromas with floral touches and notes of apricot and citrus zest. On the palate, it is elegant and harmonious. Medium intensity.

CHÂTEAUNEUF-DU-PAPE CUVÉE DU BARON 2006
Red | 2011 up to 2025   **90**
Rather deep in color, fat, unctuous, with beautiful depth. Classic.

CHÂTEAUNEUF-DU-PAPE CUVÉE DU BARON 2005
Red | 2011 up to 2025   **92**
A beautiful, classic, and elegant wine: deep ruby in color, long and supple, almost delicate, with good balance without being too powerful. Harmonious without heaviness.

CHÂTEAUNEUF-DU-PAPE CUVÉE DU BARON 2004
Red | 2011 up to 2025   **90**
The balance is very harmonious, with freshness, generosity, and lots of persistence.

CHÂTEAUNEUF-DU-PAPE RÉSERVE 2006
Red | 2012 up to 2017   85
Deeply colored, opaque. Powerful, with
chocolate and spices, yet the tannins are
delicate. Lots of texture. Excellent, in a register distinct from the domaine's other
cuvées.

CHÂTEAUNEUF-DU-PAPE TRADITION 2006
Red | 2011 up to 2018   89
Very grenache, with notes of strawberries.
Its fullness is tender but delicate, not in-
your-face. Beautiful length.

CHÂTEAUNEUF-DU-PAPE TRADITION 2005
Red | 2011 up to 2018   89
Supple body. A lovely, fine, and elegant wine
with medium depth. Refined.

CHÂTEAUNEUF-DU-PAPE TRADITION 2004
Red | 2011 up to 2018   87
Built more on its finesse than on its power,
this wine has lovely scents of strawberries
and raspberries. On the palate, the tannins
are light. The overall sensation is fresh.

CHÂTEAUNEUF-DU-PAPE TRADITION 2003
Red | 2011 up to 2018   89
With notes of figs and nearly candied berries as well as delicate spices, this is a thoroughbred wine. It's ample although only of
medium depth.

Annual production: 100,000 bottles

MOULIN DE LA GARDETTE

Place de la Mairie
84190 Gigondas
Phone 00 33 4 90 65 81 51
Fax 00 33 4 90 65 86 80
moulingardette@wanadoo.fr
www.moulindelagardette.com

Since 1988 Jean-Baptiste Meunier has
been in charge of this wonderful family
winery, which has twenty-four acres
entirely in the Gigondas appellation. His
farming practices lean toward organic,
although not certified; he hasn't used
weed killer in the vineyards since 1999. The
yeasts here are wild, and sulfur additions
are extremely limited. In the bottle the two
wines produced here show remarkably
pure and natural fruit expression, and they
age particularly well. Meunier even experi-
mented with a 1998 solera-style Gigondas
that he didn't bottle until 2006! Quite
unique, it's a wine that you initially taste
with curiosity, and then drink with pleasure. La Petite Gardette is also not to be
missed; it's a young-vines Gigondas that is
pure pleasure in the glass!

Recently tasted
GIGONDAS LA PETITE GARDETTE 2007
Red | 2011 up to 2013   88

GIGONDAS TRADITION 2007
Red | 2012 up to 2016   88

GIGONDAS VENTABREN 2007
Red | 2012 up to 2017   89

GIGONDAS ZOÉ 2001
Red | 2011 up to 2013   90

Older vintages
GIGONDAS LA PETITE GARDETTE 2006
Red | 2011 up to 2013   88
Fresh and quaffable, this is vinified in the
same style as the domaine's other wines,
but it's more focused on the fruit. Half grenache, half young-vine syrah, it's a charming, honest, and natural wine. Beautiful
balance in the finish.

GIGONDAS TRADITION 2005
Red | 2011 up to 2014   89
Lots of character, expressive and refined,
with svelte and ripe tannins. The bouquet
has hints of prunes and raisins mixed with
sweet spices and tobacco. Ample and generous on the palate.

GIGONDAS TRADITION 2004
Red | 2011 up to 2013   90
A very powerful bouquet, hot, with notes of
cocoa, hints of artichoke and freshly cut hay,

and candied cherries. Pleasing and refined. The palate is structured and rich, with a beautiful aromatic range and a pleasant freshness in the finish.

GIGONDAS VENTABREN 2005
Red | 2011 up to 2016   **91**

Truly of the region, this has a deep and intense bouquet, with dried herbs and candied fruit. Impressive texture on the palate, suave and refined, with good tannins. Beautiful cellaring potential.

GIGONDAS VENTABREN 2004
Red | 2011 up to 2013   **93**

Deeper and more candied on the nose, with more fruit. A hint of pineapple in juice. Quite astonishing! Lots of sweet spices (cinnamon). The palate is unctuous and quite smooth, with truly pleasing charm. Long and complex. A very refined wine, already very tempting to drink. Its 15.4° of alcohol are well integrated. Hugely rich texture.

Red: 22.2 acres; cinsault 7%, grenache noir 70%, mourvèdre 6%, syrah 17%. **Annual production:** 30,000 bottles

CHÂTEAU DE LA GARDINE

Route de Roquemaure BP 35
84231 Châteauneuf-du-Pape Cedex
Phone 00 33 4 90 83 73 20
Fax 00 33 4 90 83 77 24
château@gardine.com
www.gardine.com

Château La Gardine is one of the great classics of this appellation. It comes from a single-block vineyard on the northwestern border of Châteauneuf-du-Pape, part of holdings that also include a handsome vineyard in Rasteau and an estate in Lirac (Château Saint-Roch). La Gardine's classical offering is flawlessly consistent. Other wines include the white and red cuvée Les Générations special bottlings—very powerful; need a few years' cellaring to lose their rough edges—and a wine made without sulfur dioxide called Peur Bleue.

Recently tasted
CHÂTEAUNEUF-DU-PAPE 2008
White | 2011 up to 2015   **89**

CHÂTEAUNEUF-DU-PAPE 2007
Red | 2011 up to 2015   **88**

CHÂTEAUNEUF-DU-PAPE IMMORTELLE 2007
Red | 2013 up to 2023   **91**

CHÂTEAUNEUF-DU-PAPE LES GÉNÉRATIONS 2007
Red | 2012 up to 2017   **90**

CHÂTEAUNEUF-DU-PAPE LES GÉNÉRATIONS 2007
White | 2011 up to 2013   **88**

CHÂTEAUNEUF-DU-PAPE PEUR BLEUE 2007
Red | 2012 up to 2017   **87**

Older vintages
CHÂTEAUNEUF-DU-PAPE 2006
Red | 2011 up to 2016   **90**

Young and deeply colored. A classic bouquet. Elegant, supple, harmonious, with beautiful and delicate fruit.

CHÂTEAUNEUF-DU-PAPE 2005
Red | 2011 up to 2020   **90**

Youthful and full in color, unctuous and refined on the palate, with flavorful length and lovely strawberry notes, this wine is opening up.

CHÂTEAUNEUF-DU-PAPE 2004
Red | 2011 up to 2017   **90**

A lovely Châteauneuf, harmonious and balanced, with deep color and a delicate bouquet of chocolate and beautiful licorice notes. It's elegant on the palate, silky, with good length, not in any way seeming unduly intense.

CHÂTEAUNEUF-DU-PAPE 2003
Red | 2011 up to 2020   90
This is a good illustration of a 2003. In its power, it easily carries its sunny character: beautiful scents of bay laurel, garrigue, and black olives; a generous fullness and mellow finish.

CHÂTEAUNEUF-DU-PAPE 1998
Red | 2011 up to 2018   88
Still very young, dense and chocolaty, fat and powerful. Why not wait a bit?

CHÂTEAUNEUF-DU-PAPE IMMORTELLE 2005
Red | 2011 up to 2025   93
Dense and tannic in the mouth, this is very full and highly expressive, with notes of black fruit and great intensity. It's certain to age well.

CHÂTEAUNEUF-DU-PAPE LES GÉNÉRATIONS 2006
Red | 2013 up to 2023   90
Opaque garnet in color; scents of blackberries and black currants; powerful body, dense, with good length, profound.

CHÂTEAUNEUF-DU-PAPE LES GÉNÉRATIONS 2005
Red | 2011 up to 2025   91
Dense in color, good and intense volume, solid and rich, in a powerful style.

CHÂTEAUNEUF-DU-PAPE LES GÉNÉRATIONS 2004
Red | 2011 up to 2020   90
Consistently round in the mouth, with softened, well-integrated tannins, this is an ample wine expressing intense notes of licorice and tobacco.

CHÂTEAUNEUF-DU-PAPE LES GÉNÉRATIONS 2004
White | 2011 up to 2015   90
Very golden in color and rich in the mouth, this tastes caramelized and buttery, long but not too soft. It has stunning potential in spite of its opulence.

CHÂTEAUNEUF-DU-PAPE PEUR BLEUE 2004
Red | 2011 up to 2013   89
The color lacks brilliance. The nose expresses notes of very fresh dark fruit. The body is powerful and straightforward, with a palpable tannic structure.

Red: 121.1 acres; grenache 60%, mourvèdre 20%, syrah 18%. White: 12.4 acres. Annual production: 210,000 bottles

DOMAINE GIRAUD

19, Le Bois de la Ville
84320 Châteauneuf-du-Pape
Phone 00 33 4 90 83 73 49
Fax 00 33 4 90 83 52 05
contact@domainegiraud.fr
www.domainegiraud.fr

The fifty-four acres of Domaine Giraud are located at the southern end of the appellation, notably in the sector called Gallimardes, from which they take the name of the reserve bottling. They also make a remarkable cuvée. Grenaches de Pierre from hundred-year-old grenache vines planted on compacted sand soils locally known as "safres." All of the wines produced here are of excellent quality.

Recently tasted
CHÂTEAUNEUF DU PAPE LES GALLIMARDES 2008
White | 2011 up to 2015   86
Tasted before bottling, this rich and ample wine doesn't lack potential.

CHÂTEAUNEUF-DU-PAPE LES GALLIMARDES 2007
Red | 2011 up to 2015   90
Deeply colored with notes of cherry and blackberry, wonderful definition, in a modern style, but balanced with nice tannins.

CHÂTEAUNEUF-DU-PAPE GRENACHE DE PIERRE 2007
Red | 2012 up to 2017   90
Beautifully full color, rich and balanced, the wine is round, smooth, and spicy.

Older vintages
CHÂTEAUNEUF-DU-PAPE GRENACHE DE PIERRE 2006
Red | 2012 up to 2017   90
Deep color, pretty notes of strawberry; on the palate it has a wonderful sucrosity, generous but well balanced.

CHÂTEAUNEUF-DU-PAPE LES GALLIMARDES 2006
Red | 2012 up to 2017   88
Dark color, notes of leather and red fruit, savory length.

DOMAINE LES GOUBERT

84190 Gigondas
Phone 00 33 4 90 65 86 38
Fax 00 33 4 90 65 81 52
jpcartier@lesgoubert.fr
www.lesgoubert.fr

You really can't go wrong with the wines of this well-known property, which owns fifty-seven acres, twenty-five of them in Gigondas. Harvested by hand or machine, depending on the weather, the grapes are almost entirely destemmed, with long fermentations, and the wines are then aged for ten months, partially in oak barrels. Vintage after vintage the cuvée Florence is a powerful but balanced expression of the terroir, but you have to be a fan of new oak.

Recently tasted

BEAUMES DE VENISE 2007
Red | 2011 up to 2014   88

CÔTES DU RHÔNE 2007
Red | 2011 up to 2013   85

CÔTES DU RHÔNE-VILLAGES SABLET 2007
Red | 2011 up to 2013   86

GIGONDAS 2006
Red | 2011 up to 2016   87

Older vintages

BEAUMES DE VENISE 2005
Red | 2011 up to 2013   89
Solid, spicy. Very beautiful fruit. Complete and as it should be.

CÔTES DU RHÔNE 2005
Red | 2011 up to 2013   87
Balanced and fresh, here's a wine that has good tannins.

CÔTES DU RHÔNE LES FAVORIS 2007
White | 2011 up to 2013   88
A beautiful white wine. Generous and fully expressed, with notes of wax and vanilla oak.

CÔTES DU RHÔNE-VILLAGES SABLET 2007
White | 2011 up to 2013   88
Rich and expansive on the palate, with honeysuckle and pears in the bouquet. Spicy and round, with beautiful balance.

GIGONDAS 2005
Red | 2011 up to 2013   87
A linear and ephemeral wine. Nearly transparent, with subtle tannins.

Red: 50.5 acres; carignan noir 2%, cinsault 4%, grenache noir 63%, mourvèdre 6%, syrah 18%, others 7%. White: 6.6 acres; bourboulenc 10%, clairette 33%, roussanne 14%, viognier 43%. Annual production: 70,000 bottles

DOMAINE GOURT DE MAUTENS

Route de Cairanne
84110 Rasteau
Phone 00 33 4 90 46 19 45
Fax 00 33 4 90 46 18 92
info@gourtdemautens.com
www.gourtdemautens.com

Why the INAO did not classify Rasteau as an AOC in its own right, rather than Beaumes de Venise, is anybody's guess. Local boy Jérôme Bressy knew from the start that Rasteau was the most underestimated terroir in the Vaucluse and immediately set out to prove it by his fastidious approach to viticulture. His red wines are intense and deep, combining thoroughbred focus with a characteristic bouquet of black olives and black and red berries. His white wines are full-bodied but always very fresh. All of these wines are definitely a cut above the usual Côtes du Rhône-Villages.

Recently tasted

RASTEAU 2006
Red | 2012 up to 2019   92

RASTEAU VIN DOUX NATUREL 2006
Red | 2016 up to 2030   96

Older vintages

RASTEAU 2006
White | 2011 up to 2016   91
Very ample yet equally natural and remarkably balanced, this big, sappy white pairs corpulence and agility. It's full of energy, subtly aromatic, and has a great future.

RASTEAU 2005
Red | 2011 up to 2018   95
This majestic, profound wine is beginning to reveal the true extent of its potential. Highly structured yet equally silky, it expresses as few others can the intensity inherent in a pedigreed wine from a great, sunny terroir.

RASTEAU 2004
Red | 2011 up to 2013   90
With an ambitious élevage, and still very oaky on the nose and palate, this is concentrated and silky, with scents of menthol, wild herbs, chocolate, and licorice. It has great potential.

Red: 29.7 acres. White: 2.5 acres. Annual production: 23,000 bottles

DOMAINE DE LA JANASSE

🍷🍷🍷🍷🍷

27, chemin du Moulin
84350 Courthézon
Phone 00 33 4 90 70 86 29
Fax 00 33 4 90 70 75 93
lajanasse@free.fr
www.lajanasse.com

This is certainly the estate that has improved the most since the early 1990s, rising to become one of the most consistently excellent producers of Châteauneuf-du-Pape. Its 100 percent grenache wine, the cuvée Chaupin, comes from those impressive deposits of rolled stones (Alpine diluvium) to the northwest of Courthézon. It contains 80 percent destalked grapes and is raised in barrels (some made of new oak) and larger oak vats. Its old-vines wine comes from Chaupin and three other areas with different soils. Vinification and maturing are the same, but the wines also include small quantities of the syrah and mourvèdre. All of these wines, including the Côtes du Rhône, are made to a very high standard.

Recently tasted

CHÂTEAUNEUF-DU-PAPE 2008
White | 2011 up to 2014   86

CHÂTEAUNEUF-DU-PAPE 2007
Red | 2011 up to 2015   89

CHÂTEAUNEUF-DU-PAPE PRESTIGE 2007
White | 2011 up to 2015   90

CHÂTEAUNEUF-DU-PAPE VIEILLES VIGNES 2007
Red | 2012 up to 2017   90

Older vintages

CHÂTEAUNEUF-DU-PAPE 2006
Red | 2011 up to 2020   91
Splendid, vibrant and brilliant color; melt-in-the-mouth fruit. This is delicious, velvety and fresh, with a good tannic weave.

CHÂTEAUNEUF-DU-PAPE 2005
Red | 2011 up to 2020   91
Grandiose, ample flavor, velvety and superb in texture. Brilliant and deep length. Excellent potential.

CHÂTEAUNEUF-DU-PAPE 2004
Red | 2011 up to 2020   90
An elegant wine, deep and racy, with sufficient acidity to bring it all into balance.

CHÂTEAUNEUF-DU-PAPE CHAUPIN 2006
Red | 2012 up to 2017   91
Beautiful and deep in color, ultra-mellow, languid and suave in texture, this is very long, opulent, and refined.

CHÂTEAUNEUF-DU-PAPE CHAUPIN 2005
Red | 2011 up to 2025   95
This wine expresses remarkable refinement with a smooth, velvety, and intense body, hugely unctuous. A crème de grenache!

CHÂTEAUNEUF-DU-PAPE CHAUPIN 2004
Red | 2011 up to 2020   92
Tannic and serious, with overt wood. A wine with great potential.

CHÂTEAUNEUF-DU-PAPE CHAUPIN 2003
Red | 2011 up to 2018   88
This wine seems caught in a rather heavy and generous matrix, certainly large and spicy, but lacking a note of finesse. Nevertheless, it can be cellared with confidence.

CHÂTEAUNEUF-DU-PAPE CHAUPIN 2001
Red | 2011 up to 2018   95
Superbly deep ruby in color, this has a magnificently expressive bouquet blending dark berries, tapenade, and raspberries. It has fleshy length, developing a grand, racy volume. Splendid wine, expressive and long.

CHÂTEAUNEUF-DU-PAPE CHAUPIN 1999
Red | 2011 up to 2015   90
An unctuous and fat wine, suave, with less delicate tannins than the young vintages, yet intense and warm.

CHÂTEAUNEUF-DU-PAPE CHAUPIN 1998
Red | 2011 up to 2018   95
This offers a great, languid style. It's a bit less intense than the old-vine cuvée in this vintage, but what smoothness, what unctuousness and, most of all, what persistence!

CHÂTEAUNEUF-DU-PAPE VIEILLES VIGNES 2006
Red | 2011 up to 2025   95
Intense in color. Blackberries and wild strawberries. A brilliant and unctuous body; delicious length.

CHÂTEAUNEUF-DU-PAPE VIEILLES VIGNES 2005
Red | 2011 up to 2025   94
Imposing, powerful, and opulent, this is a touch closed right now, but has great intensity. Wait for it.

CHÂTEAUNEUF-DU-PAPE VIEILLES VIGNES 2004
Red | 2011 up to 2020   91
Chocolaty and fruity, very dense, very powerful. Just a touch more elegant than the Chaupin.

CHÂTEAUNEUF-DU-PAPE VIEILLES VIGNES 2001
Red | 2011 up to 2018   93
Garnet in color, this offers chocolate and woody notes on the nose, yet it isn't heavy. It is powerful, dense, and generous, with a soft, unctuous texture. Assuredly a profound wine, to be cellared.

Châteauneuf-du-Pape Vieilles Vignes 1999
Red | 2011 up to 2016   **91**
Youthful color; notes of café au lait; balanced flavors with delicate spice in the finish; long.

Châteauneuf-du-Pape Vieilles Vignes 1998
Red | 2011 up to 2018   **94**
A great, classic Châteauneuf, both open and structured. It has a very complex bouquet of red berries in eau-de-vie, chocolate, spices, and leather. Great persistence.

Côtes du Rhône-Villages Les Garrigues 2006
Red | 2011 up to 2013   **88**
Superb balance, rich and extracted in the mouth, with jammy and sugary fruit and notes of sweet spices. The tannins are hefty, but there is class in the finish.

Côtes du Rhône-Villages
Terres d'Argile 2006
Red | 2011 up to 2013   **88**
A straightforward and honest wine in the modern style, this is dense and concentrated, with lightly drying tannins in the finish.

Red: 133.4 acres. White: 14.8 acres. Annual production: 200,000 bottles

DOMAINE LAFOND ROC-ÉPINE

Route des Vignobles
30126 Tavel
Phone 00 33 4 66 50 24 59
Fax 00 33 4 66 50 12 42
lafond@roc-epine.com
www.roc-epine.com

This large family estate is located in Tavel, but its 200-acre vineyard extends into the commune of Lirac, too. Since 2001, it has also included a few small parcels in Châteauneuf-du-Pape. Jean-Pierre and Pascal Lafond have worked hard to raise the quality of their wines over the past ten years. They now make very balanced and increasingly classy wines: very clean, extremely natural, and with an honest, straightforward style.

Recently tasted
Châteauneuf-du-Pape 2006
Red | 2011 up to 2017   **88**

Lirac 2008
White | 2011 up to 2013   **84**

Lirac La Ferme Romaine 2006
Red | 2011 up to 2016   **90**

Tavel 2008
Rosé | 2011 up to 2013   **86**

Older vintages
Châteauneuf-du-Pape 2005
Red | 2011 up to 2016   **89**
A dense and serious Châteauneuf with beautiful texture on the palate. The tannins are refined and svelte, finishing on notes of bay laurel, tobacco, and undergrowth. A very beautiful wine that will mature well.

Lirac 2007
White | 2011 up to 2013   **87**
The Lafond Roc-Épine white is always a sure value. With a rare finesse for the region, this blend of grenache blanc, viognier, and roussanne is remarkably fresh and balanced on the palate. With its white flower and citrus notes and its beautiful acidity, it's a wine that would be as delightful before dinner as with the meal.

Lirac 2006
Red | 2011 up to 2013   **88**
Very seductive on the nose, rich and fruity on the palate. Lightly spicy, the tannins are firm and young. The finish is fresh.

LIRAC LA FERME ROMAINE 2005
Red | 2011 up to 2015   89

One of the characteristics of this domaine is its ability to produce balanced wines without heaviness, in spite of the higher and higher temperatures in the region. The Ferme Romaine is a beautiful example of this harmony. Culled from a special section of the vineyard and barrel aged, it is a powerful and marvelously built wine, without the slightest hint of heat or overripeness.

TAVEL 2007
Rosé | 2011 up to 2013   87

Round and flattering on the palate, with floral and red-berry notes, this wine is ample and generous, with beautiful freshness in the finish.

Red: 192.7 acres; carignan noir 5%, cinsault 10%, grenache noir 60%, syrah 25%. White: 9.8 acres; clairette 10%, grenache blanc 30%, roussanne 30%, viognier 30%. Annual production: 400,000 bottles

DOMAINE DE MARCOUX

Chemin de la Gironde
84100 Orange
Phone 00 33 4 90 34 67 43
Fax 00 33 4 90 51 84 53
info@domaine-marcoux.com

This estate was one of the forerunners of the biodynamic movement. It is located in the north of the appellation but also boasts extensive holdings in the southern (Gallimardes) and eastern (La Crau) parts of Châteauneuf-du-Pape. Domaine de Marcoux is one of the greatest success stories of recent years: the wines are ambitiously crafted by Sophie Armenier, with a particularly sensational, barrel-matured old-vines bottling that demonstrates just how far this estate has come since 2000.

Recently tasted
CHÂTEAUNEUF-DU-PAPE 2008
White | 2011 up to 2013   90

CHÂTEAUNEUF-DU-PAPE 2007
Red | 2012 up to 2017   93

CHÂTEAUNEUF-DU-PAPE VIEILLES VIGNES 2007
Red | 2012 up to 2017   96

Older vintages
CHÂTEAUNEUF-DU-PAPE 2006
White | 2011 up to 2015   90

Elegant, fat, and refined, this very successful wine expresses very pretty notes of toasted almonds on a smooth, long finish.

CHÂTEAUNEUF-DU-PAPE 2006
Red | 2011 up to 2016   89

Spicy, deeply colored, fat, with good length and a strong, clearly expressed personality.

CHÂTEAUNEUF-DU-PAPE 2005
Red | 2011 up to 2020   90

Deepy colored, fat, smooth, unctuous, and velvety, this expresses beautiful scents of black olives and sweet spice. Good length.

CHÂTEAUNEUF-DU-PAPE 2004
Red | 2011 up to 2015   88

A very pretty wine showing yet again the harmony of this vintage. The bouquet is already quite open, with very seductive notes of dark berries and plums that continue on the generous palate, dense and deep. The tannins are not as delicate as one might wish, but it has a remarkable generosity and a freshness that will permit it to age well.

CHÂTEAUNEUF-DU-PAPE VIEILLES VIGNES 2006
Red | 2011 up to 2020   93

Highly colored. Stone fruits in the bouquet. Intense and fat, with good, unctuous volume.

CHÂTEAUNEUF-DU-PAPE VIEILLES VIGNES 2005
Red | 2011 up to 2025   92
Highly colored, with a bouquet of stone fruit
and delicate spice. An intense and fat body.
Beautiful, deep volume.

CHÂTEAUNEUF-DU-PAPE VIEILLES VIGNES 2004
Red | 2011 up to 2020   92
An intense and vigorous wine with great,
sappy generosity and brilliant length.

CHÂTEAUNEUF-DU-PAPE VIEILLES VIGNES 2003
Red | 2011 up to 2020   92
This intensely structured wine fully lives up
to its vintage, both with its bouquet of bay
laurel, spice, black olive, and candied citrus
zest, and with its ample and rich flavors.

CHÂTEAUNEUF-DU-PAPE VIEILLES VIGNES 1998
Red | 2011 up to 2015   90
Deeply colored and very rich and generous,
this has powerful tannins. Ample and long.

Red: 49.4 acres; grenache 85%, mourvèdre 7%, syrah
8%. White: 2.5 acres. Annual production: 40,000
bottles

DOMAINE DE LA MONARDIÈRE

La Monardière
84190 Vacqueyras
Phone 00 33 4 90 65 87 20
Fax 00 33 4 90 65 82 01
info@monardiere.com
www.monardiere.fr

This estate has been one of Vacqueyras's
star performers for several years. Christian and Martine Vache, now joined by son
Damien, together turn out well-balanced
wines with unmistakable personality plus
that particular combination of finesse and
power that is typical of southern grapes.
The grapes are sourced from two terroirs,
one with clay-sandy soils, the other planted
in clay and limestone. The wines are traditionally vinified in concrete tanks, then
matured in tanks, barrels, or tuns depending on the cuvée. Les Deux Monardes and
the Vieilles Vignes regularly win acclaim
for their textbook Vacqueyras style.

Recently tasted
VACQUEYRAS LE ROSÉ 2008
Rosé | 2011 up to 2013   86

VACQUEYRAS LES DEUX MONARDES 2007
Red | 2011 up to 2013   88

VACQUEYRAS VIEILLES VIGNES 2007
Red | 2011 up to 2015   87

Older vintages
VACQUEYRAS LES CALADES 2008
Red | 2011 up to 2013   86
The aromatic palette is rich, with notes of
cherry jam and light nuances of smoke,
tobacco, and red berries on the palate. It is
dense and seriously structured, with still-
strong tannins.

VACQUEYRAS LES DEUX MONARDES 2006
Red | 2011 up to 2015   88
A lovely style, representative of the 2006 vintage, with scents of prunes, kirsch, and
tobacco, followed on the palate by a beautiful and concentrated tannic structure.

VACQUEYRAS VIEILLES VIGNES 2005
Red | 2011 up to 2015   90
Very rich, this is an intense and concentrated
wine. The bouquet ranges from black cherries and prunes to cocoa and cinnamon. The
wood notes have been integrated into the
ensemble. The wine is gaining in harmony,
but it could be cellared for a few more years.

Red: 46.9 acres; cinsault 5%, grenache noir 65%,
mourvèdre 10%, syrah 20%. White: 2.5 acres;
clairette 10%, grenache blanc 25%, roussanne 50%,
viognier 15%. Annual production: 75,000 bottles

CLOS DU MONT-OLIVET

15, avenue Saint-Joseph
84230 Châteauneuf-du-Pape
Phone 00 33 4 90 83 72 46
Fax 00 33 4 90 83 51 75
clos.montolivet@wanadoo.fr
clos-montolivet.com

A "clos" is usually a walled vineyard, but this one is in fact parceled out into multiple plots of clay-limestone and clayey-sandy soils (source of the cuvée du Papet in particular). Planted by the Sabon family more than a century ago, the vineyard yields ultra-traditional wines, sometimes austere and curiously evanescent as young wines, but with great aging potential. Some of the 1978s and 1981s are still going strong, proving that good things come to those who wait!

Recently tasted
CHÂTEAUNEUF-DU-PAPE
CLOS DU MONT-OLIVET 2007
Red | 2012 up to 2017   84

CHÂTEAUNEUF-DU-PAPE CUVÉE DU PAPET 2007
Red | 2012 up to 2017   87

Older vintages
CHÂTEAUNEUF-DU-PAPE
CLOS DU MONT-OLIVET 2006
White | 2011 up to 2013   86
A classic and precise wine with light floral scents and a true freshness on the palate. Ready to drink.

CHÂTEAUNEUF-DU-PAPE
CLOS DU MONT-OLIVET 2006
Red | 2011 up to 2016   86
Light, simple fruit. This grenache is still very young and of medium depth, but it has a pleasantly tender texture.

CHÂTEAUNEUF-DU-PAPE
CLOS DU MONT-OLIVET 2005
Red | 2011 up to 2020   86
Round, supple, almost silky but minimally expressive. Check back in a few years.

CHÂTEAUNEUF-DU-PAPE
CLOS DU MONT-OLIVET 2003
Red | 2011 up to 2015   86
Full in color, with a simple raspberry scent, this feels round and supple in the mouth, but, alas, lacks much tannic finesse.

CHÂTEAUNEUF-DU-PAPE CUVÉE DU PAPET 2006
Red | 2012 up to 2017   86
Deep color. A classic, unpretentious wine, yet intense and voluminous, with good persistence.

CHÂTEAUNEUF-DU-PAPE CUVÉE DU PAPET 2005
Red | 2011 up to 2018   85
The 2005 vintage is very enigmatic here, and that includes the cuvée du Papet: it's a fat wine, supple, with medium but real intensity. Good length, but little true personality.

CHÂTEAUNEUF-DU-PAPE CUVÉE DU PAPET 2003
Red | 2011 up to 2023   91
Beautifully deep ruby color; unctuous, generous, and fleshy texture. The flavors on the palate evoke the bouquet's dark berries. The tannins are well padded and give the wine an immediately seductive personality.

Red: 102.5 acres; cinsault 4%, grenache noir 80%, mourvèdre 6%, syrah 10%. White: 6.2 acres; bourboulenc 30%, clairette 30%, grenache blanc 13%, picardan 1%, picpoul 1%, roussanne 25%.
Annual production: 200,000 bottles

CHÂTEAU MONT-REDON

BP 10
84231 Châteauneuf-du-Pape
Phone 00 33 4 90 83 72 75
Fax 00 33 4 90 83 77 20
contact@châteaumontredon.fr
www.châteaumontredon.fr

This huge property covers a total of 370 acres (250 dedicated to the Châteauneuf-du-Pape appellation). The bulk of the vineyard is planted in the Alpine diluvium (composed of rounded stones) of the Mont-Redon plateau. The Abeille-Fabre family has always eschewed the fashion for prestige cuvées, preferring to produce a single wine, representative of the estate as a whole. Château Mont-Redon boasts a quiet fullness and, though not as spectacular as some in this appellation, actually ages extremely well. The family also produces good-quality whites, several Côtes du Rhône, and owns another property in Lirac.

Recently tasted
CHÂTEAUNEUF-DU-PAPE 2008
White | 2011 up to 2014   **86**

CHÂTEAUNEUF-DU-PAPE 2007
Red | 2012 up to 2020   **89**

CHÂTEAUNEUF-DU-PAPE 2007
White | 2011 up to 2013   **90**

Older vintages
CHÂTEAUNEUF-DU-PAPE 2006
White | 2011 up to 2013   **88**
Lovely lemon notes, long and balanced on the palate. Good freshness. This is not the most complex white Châteauneuf, but it is certainly one of the most pleasant to drink right now.

CHÂTEAUNEUF-DU-PAPE 2005
Red | 2011 up to 2018   **89**
Medium-dense color, fruity, lifted by its delicate oak character. Full-bodied, smooth, soft. A very accessible style, yet sufficiently long and persistent. It will age well.

CHÂTEAUNEUF-DU-PAPE 2003
Red | 2011 up to 2018   **90**
Fat, ample, smooth, and generous, this possesses real volume and, in spite of its demonstrative aromas, bears witness to true potential. Mont-Redon's exceptional terroir has been particularly brought to the fore in this difficult year.

CHÂTEAUNEUF-DU-PAPE 1999
Red | 2011 up to 2015   **90**
A beautiful, spicy, and palate-pleasing wine, supple but complete, delicious to drink right away.

CHÂTEAUNEUF-DU-PAPE 1998
Red | 2011 up to 2020   **90**
With a beautiful, youthful color, this is a warm-hearted wine, ample and fat, that's just beginning to integrate its great texture and generous alcohol.

LIRAC 2005
Red | 2011 up to 2013   **87**
A classic for this major Châteauneuf house, this Lirac is honest and natural, immediately drinkable, with notes of candied fruit, kirsch, and tobacco. Long, with rounded tannins.

Red: 321.2 acres. White: 49.4 acres. Annual production: 700,000 bottles

DOMAINE DE LA MORDORÉE

Chemin des Oliviers
30126 Tavel
Phone 00 33 4 66 50 00 75
Fax 00 33 4 66 50 47 39
info@domaine-mordoree.com
www.domaine-mordoree.com

The Delorme brothers are still relative youngsters, but for nearly two decades now they have been the unchallenged standard-bearers of the Lirac appellation, producing wines that set new benchmarks for quality. Thanks to modern vinification and maturation processes, the wines show forceful, assertive character—slender, refined, and subtly fragrant (especially the white wines)—but not a trace of rusticity. The Delormes' Châteauneuf-du-Pape offerings reflect the same drive for excellence. Over the past ten years their Reine des Bois cuvée (now joined by the very impressive Plume du Peintre) has been consistently rated as one of the most exemplary expressions of Châteauneuf-du-Pape.

Recently tasted

Lirac La Reine des Bois 2008
White | 2011 up to 2013   88

Lirac La Reine des Bois 2007
Red | 2012 up to 2020   92

Tavel 2008
Rosé | 2011 up to 2013   89

Older vintages

Châteauneuf-du-Pape La Reine des Bois 2007
Red | 2014 up to 2024   93
Ink-dark, imposing wood, expressive scents of dark berries. Fat and powerful, with great sappiness. The alcohol is rather abrupt in the finish, but this has undeniable potential in a super-powerful style.

Châteauneuf-du-Pape La Reine des Bois 2003
Red | 2011 up to 2020   95
This micro-cuvée (1,500 bottles) is extremely impressive in its richness and the extremely high quality of all its parts. But it is possible that this is a splendid exercise in style without necessarily attaining the exquisite balance of a normal vintage.

Lirac 2007
Red | 2011 up to 2015   90
This exemplary cuvée, the star of the appellation, is rich and generous on the palate, with very intense dark fruit flavor. The oak barrel aging adds tight tannins. Still quite youthful, this is a great wine for the cellar, from an often under-appreciated terroir.

Lirac La Reine des Bois 2006
Red | 2011 up to 2025   89
Very ripe, rich, concentrated and oaked, this is an intensely fruity wine that demands cellaring.

Lirac La Reine des Bois 2003
Red | 2011 up to 2020   95
A superlative wine in all aspects: the color is a garnet so dark it's nearly black; the wood is imposing and yet it melts in perfectly with the more delicate notes of spices and blackberries. On the palate, it has great volume, powerfully built but also extremely silky, with a refined density, incontestable extract, and generous length. It is a wine of great class and great potential that skillfully pairs power and silky tannins as few others have achieved.

Lirac La Reine des Bois 2001
Red | 2011 up to 2020   94
A great success, very deep garnet in color, with a seductive and modern bouquet marrying oak with notes of blackberries and raspberries. On the palate, the super-full body and the silky tannins are impressive. The wine is magnificently balanced, full of promise and intensity. This one will go far.

Tavel 2007
Rosé | 2011 up to 2013   89
Rich and fruity with notes of strawberries, this wine has stunning textural finesse. A harmonious wine.

Red: 143.3 acres; cinsault 5%, counoise 5%, grenache 70%, mourvèdre 10%, syrah 5%, vaccarèse 5%. White: 9.8 acres Annual production: 260,000 bottles

CHÂTEAU MOURGUES DU GRÈS

Route de Bellegarde - D 38
30300 Beaucaire
Phone 00 33 4 66 59 46 10
Fax 00 33 4 66 59 34 21
château@mourguesdugres.com
www.mourguesdugres.com

Château Mourgues du Grès stands at the forefront of the Rhone Valley's quality revolution, playing on its variety of terroirs to produce blended wines with just the right balance of finesse and structure. The prestige cuvées spend time in oak barrels prior to blending, and all of the wines (red, white, and rosé) deliver immediate flavor but without a trace of heaviness or wateriness. Kudos to Anne and François Collard for creating a fleshy style of red wine with silky fruit but no loss of refined, well-integrated tannins.

Recently tasted

COSTIÈRES DE NÎMES
CAPITELLES DE MOURGUES 2008
Rosé | 2011 up to 2013   **87**

COSTIÈRES DE NÎMES
CAPITELLES DES MOURGUES 2007
Red | 2011 up to 2016   **88**

COSTIÈRES DE NÎMES FLEUR D'ÉGLANTINE 2008
Rosé | 2011 up to 2013   **86**

COSTIÈRES DE NÎMES TERRE D'ARGENCE 2007
Red | 2011 up to 2015   **88**

COSTIÈRES DE NÎMES TERRE DE FEU 2007
Red | 2011 up to 2014   **88**

VIN DE PAYS DU GARD TERRE D'ARGENCE 2007
White | 2011 up to 2013   **88**

Older vintages

COSTIÈRES DE NÎMES
CAPITELLES DE MOURGUES 2007
Rosé | 2011 up to 2013   **88**
A completely surprising rosé. Principally mourvèdre, with a bit of syrah and grenache, this wine is both fermented and aged in barrels. It's very sensual and expressive on the palate. One senses the wood, but it is perfectly integrated into the wine's extract and body.

COSTIÈRES DE NÎMES
CAPITELLES DES MOURGUES 2006
Red | 2011 up to 2017   **90**
Still quite young and marked by oak, this wine is intensely colored and full of extract.

COSTIÈRES DE NÎMES LES GALETS ROUGES 2007
Red | 2011 up to 2013   **88**
Filled with ripe fruit, the aromas jump out of the glass and make you want to taste this domaine's first 2007. Intensely colored, with fresh stone-fruit flavors, yet not in the least hot in the mouth. There's lots of pleasure in this bottle.

COSTIÈRES DE NÎMES TERRE DE FEU 2006
Red | 2011 up to 2013   **88**
Floral, with notes of violets on the nose. Generous and round on the palate. With very ripe, dark-fruit flavors, this is a charming wine with volume that finishes on smooth and elegant tannins.

Red: 135.9 acres. White: 32.1 acres. Annual production: 320,000 bottles

CROS DE LA MÛRE

84430 Mondragon
Phone 00 33 4 90 30 12 40
Fax 00 33 4 90 30 46 58
crosdelamure@wanadoo.fr

Most of this vineyard (but not all) is located around Mondragon in the Vaucluse. Owner Éric Michel makes very tasty wines with great character and is currently seeking organic certification. His vineyard is planted with very low-yield vines, in clay and limestone soils with silica-sandstone and silica-limestone subsoils that give the wines their pronounced mineral quality. Traditional vinification in concrete vats brings out their honest, natural character, supported by very intense fruit as well as firm tannins. Éric also owns small plots in the hills of Uchaux, in Gigondas, and in Châteauneuf-du-Pape. This now gives him the potential to produce a complete range of very good quality wines.

CHÂTEAUNEUF-DU-PAPE 2006
Red | 2011 up to 2015   86
A solid yet rather simple wine: garnet in color, scents of black currants and blackberries, powerful, persistent alcohol.

CHÂTEAUNEUF-DU-PAPE 2004
Red | 2011 up to 2016   91
Deeply colored. Discreet notes of black fruit, cedar, and pale, fine tobacco. Unctuous on the palate, smooth and velvety, with delicate oak. Fat and long, it's a lovely, modern wine, with a harmonious and generous finish.

CÔTES DU RHÔNE 2007
Red | 2011 up to 2013   88
Impressive in its concentration of ripe and sweet fruit, with notes of eucalyptus and undergrowth. It is rich and round, with elegant and refined tannins.

CÔTES DU RHÔNE-VILLAGES MASSIF D'UCHAUX 2005
Red | 2011 up to 2013   86
An honest wine, very dense, long in the mouth, expressing fresh fruit notes and tannins that haven't yet softened.

GIGONDAS 2005
Red | 2011 up to 2013   90
Healthy and ripe berries, deep length. Generous without being heavy; firm tannins and great depth of texture. The signs of a very well made wine.

Red: 45.7 acres; carignan 1%, cinsault 4%, grenache 62%, mourvèdre 8%, syrah 20%. White: 3.7 acres.
Annual production: 40,000 bottles

CHÂTEAU LA NERTHE

Route de Sorgues
84232 Châteauneuf-du-Pape
Phone 00 33 4 90 83 70 11
Fax 00 33 4 90 83 79 69
contact@châteaulanerthe.fr
www.châteaulanerthe.fr

This is one of the foremost historic domains in the Châteauneuf-du-Pape appellation, especially famous as the place where Commander Joseph Ducos established the traditional canons of Châteauneuf production in the nineteenth-century. The cru has belonged to the Richard family (wine and coffee specialists supplying the restaurant trade) since 1895 and is now in the expert hands of Alain Dugas. The 227-acre vineyard is located around the château, in the southern part of the appellation, and includes substantial plantings (sixty-two acres) on the Crau plateau. Lovely pebble-covered terraces and beautifully maintained, organically certified vines are the basis for ambitiously made red and white cuvées. The cuvée Les Cadettes is made from roughly equal quantities of barrel-aged grenache, syrah, and mourvèdre, while the classical, extremely interesting white offering is a blend of four varietals. Red and white wines alike show a distinctive personality quite unlike the usual sunny, rustic Châteauneufs. That said, among the red wines, there is a big difference between Les Cadettes and the classic cuvée.

Recently tasted
CHÂTEAUNEUF-DU-PAPE 2008
White | 2011 up to 2013   86

CHÂTEAUNEUF-DU-PAPE 2007
Red | 2011 up to 2020   89

CHÂTEAUNEUF-DU-PAPE CLOS DE BEAUVENIR 2007
White | 2011 up to 2013   82

Older vintages
CHÂTEAUNEUF-DU-PAPE 2006
White | 2011 up to 2013   91
Suave, velvety, and elegant, this is a beautiful Châteauneuf, refined with no heaviness. It shows splendid savoir-faire.

CHÂTEAUNEUF-DU-PAPE 2006
Red | 2011 up to 2020   90
A great wine with beautiful color and harmonious style, this is fruity and delicate, classy.

CHÂTEAUNEUF-DU-PAPE 1999
Red | 2011 up to 2016　　　　　　**90**
Remarkable youthfulness: whole, big, refined and balanced, with velvety length.

CHÂTEAUNEUF-DU-PAPE 1998
Red | 2011 up to 2016　　　　　　**94**
Beautiful, youthful color. Stone fruits, brilliant length, great flavor, and remarkable balance: a great wine at its best!

CHÂTEAUNEUF-DU-PAPE LES CADETTES 2006
Red | 2012 up to 2022　　　　　　**90**
Ambitious wood, still young and rather blocky, but great style both rich and dense.

CHÂTEAUNEUF-DU-PAPE LES CADETTES 2005
Red | 2011 up to 2025　　　　　　**95**
Ample wood, great generosity, suave depth, great pedigree.

CHÂTEAUNEUF-DU-PAPE LES CADETTES 2003
Red | 2011 up to 2020　　　　　　**92**
Aromas of stone fruits, black olives, and spices. Good character on the palate, refined structure. Silky and pedigreed, with great length.

CHÂTEAUNEUF-DU-PAPE LES CADETTES 2001
Red | 2011 up to 2025　　　　　　**92**
This wine has lots of color and a powerful bouquet, still very youthful, with notes of blackberries and oak. There is alcohol, a fat body, richness, power, and a slight lack of freshness, but it has strong potential; one simply needs to wait quietly for it.

CHÂTEAUNEUF-DU-PAPE LES CADETTES 1999
Red | 2011 up to 2016　　　　　　**92**
The oak is still highly present, but the wine has developed grand and brilliant length, with ultra-racy flavor.

CHÂTEAUNEUF-DU-PAPE LES CADETTES 1998
Red | 2011 up to 2018　　　　　　**97**
Great, harmonious texture, smooth length, impressive sweetness. A shame the wood is still a bit demonstrative. But what a wine!

Red: 202.6 acres; cinsault 5%, grenache noir 50%, mourvèdre 12%, syrah 31%. White: 24.7 acres; bourboulenc 5%, clairette 12%, grenache blanc 41%, roussanne 42%. Annual production: 280,000 bottles

DOMAINE DE L'ORATOIRE SAINT-MARTIN

84290 Cairanne
Phone 00 33 4 90 30 82 07
Fax 00 33 4 90 30 74 27
falary@wanadoo.fr
www.oratoiresaintmartin.com

In just under twenty years, Frédéric and François Alary have turned this estate into one of the most powerful and trusted ambassadors for Côtes du Rhône wines. Their red wines always show solid structure but with no trace of harsh tannins, plus well-defined expression of ripe but never overripe fruit and well-integrated alcohol. They are not as immediately lush as a Richaud but impeccably put together and particularly good after one to three years' cellaring, depending on the cuvée and the vintage.

Recently tasted
CÔTES DU RHÔNE 2008
Red | 2011 up to 2013　　　　　　**86**

CÔTES DU RHÔNE-VILLAGES CAIRANNE CUVÉE PRESTIGE 2007
Red | 2011 up to 2015　　　　　　**90**

CÔTES DU RHÔNE-VILLAGES CAIRANNE HAUT COUSTIAS 2006
Red | 2011 up to 2016　　　　　　**90**

CÔTES DU RHÔNE-VILLAGES RÉSERVE DES SEIGNEURS 2007
Red | 2011 up to 2014　　　　　　**88**

Older vintages
CÔTES DU RHÔNE 2007
Red | 2011 up to 2013　　　　　　**90**
A model Côtes du Rhône, delicious and fresh with notes of dark berries (blueberries). The tannins are present but not hard.

CÔTES DU RHÔNE-VILLAGES CAIRANNE HAUT COUSTIAS 2005
Red | 2011 up to 2015　　　　　　**90**
Made from a majority of old-vine mourvèdre, this is a powerful and consistent wine with aromas of red fruit and wild strawberries. Rather ambitiously oaked, it requires a few more years of age.

CÔTES DU RHÔNE-VILLAGES RÉSERVE DES SEIGNEURS 2006
Red | 2011 up to 2015　　　　　　**92**
Full and deep, rich in candied dark-berry flavors without being too sweet. Elegant in texture, and perfectly enhanced by a precise and mastered élevage.

Annual production: 100,000 bottles

DOMAINE LES PALLIÈRES

Route d'Ancieu
84190 Gigondas
Phone 00 33 4 90 33 00 31
Fax 00 33 4 90 33 18 47
vignobles@brunier.fr
www.les-pallieres.com

This large property (325 acres, sixty-two of which are planted in vines) has benefited from a solid reputation for many years now. In 1998 it was purchased by the Brunier family (Vieux Télégraphe-Châteauneuf) and the American wine importer Kermit Lynch, with the firm intention to make a wine that truly expresses the terroir that is unique to Gigondas. In 2007 they decided for the first time to bottle two different wines, from two distinctly different origins. The Terrasse du Diable bottling is made from the property's younger vines (forty-five years young!) planted on terraces situated between 820 and 1,312 feet in altitude. The cuvée Originé is made from the oldest vines of the property that surround the old farmhouse and winery. The wines made here are powerful and chewy and need a few years in bottle to be fully appreciated.

Recently tasted

GIGONDAS TERRASSE DU DIABLE 2007
Red | 2012 up to 2017   90

GIGONDAS ORIGINES 2007
Red | 2012 up to 2020   90

Older vintages

GIGONDAS 2006
Red | 2011 up to 2015   90
Les Pallières is playing the elegance card, with this refined and subtle wine. Notes of ripe cherries and a touch of caramelized wood blend with the perfectly integrated tannins, creating a lovely whole.

GIGONDAS 2005
Red | 2011 up to 2016   90
The nose is powerful, nicely peppery. The palate is fat and ripe with well-enrobed, smooth tannins. Delicious. It will mature well over time.

GIGONDAS 2004
Red | 2011 up to 2015   89
A powerful bouquet dominated by peonies and pepper. Dense on the palate, with tight tannins; very pleasingly chewy. A solid wine, with a beautiful, smooth roundness in the finish. It promises a beautiful future.

Red: 61.8 acres; cinsault 5%, grenache 85%, mourvèdre 5%, syrah 5%. **Annual production:** 80,000 bottles

CLOS DES PAPES

13, avenue Pierre-de-Luxembourg
BP 8
84231 Châteauneuf-du-Pape
Phone 00 33 4 90 83 70 13
Fax 00 33 4 90 83 50 87
clos-des-papes@clos-des-papes.com

The Clos des Papes, whatever its name may suggest, actually relies on twenty-four vineyard plots spread across virtually every kind of terroir (though seven on the Crau plateau). It is one of the great classics of Châteauneuf: barely a single disappointing vintage in the past twenty years. Growing standards are exacting, and vinification is classical, with total destemming (except for the grenache) and no punching down. This delicate handling shows in the style of the wines—definitely the most balanced and harmonious of all the appellation wines. Distinctively full-bodied, too, thanks to the Avril family having resisted the trend toward cuvées spéciales. Balance and freshness are also the keys to the quality of the whites, which are certainly not to be ignored and account for a generous tenth of the planting area.

Recently tasted

CHÂTEAUNEUF-DU-PAPE 2007
Red | 2012 up to 2025   98

Older vintages

CHÂTEAUNEUF-DU-PAPE 2005
Red | 2012 up to 2022   97
A remarkable achievement of depth and intensity, this has brilliantly elegant tannins and nearly perfect balance on the palate.

CHÂTEAUNEUF-DU-PAPE 2004
White | 2011 up to 2015   92
A highly perfumed wine, dense, with good length and full body, this pairs a velvety roundness with a definite freshness. Perfectly balanced, this is a very beautiful expression of the appellation in white.

CHÂTEAUNEUF-DU-PAPE 2004
Red | 2011 up to 2018   92
Beautifully alive in color; dark berries and herbs in the bouquet; rich roundness. Good fruit in the mouth, deep body, with no tannic roughness or alcoholic heaviness. Great freshness in the velvety finish.

CHÂTEAUNEUF-DU-PAPE 2003
Red | 2011 up to 2018   94
Its open style and aromatic accents do not prevent the wine from also showing concentrated depth. It is particularly harmonious and balanced.

CHÂTEAUNEUF-DU-PAPE 2001
White | 2011 up to 2017   **97**

Superb almond bouquet, fresh, fat, long, racy, all while maintaining a svelte body and pleasing freshness. A model of balance for this appellation and for southern French white wines in general.

CHÂTEAUNEUF-DU-PAPE 2001
Red | 2011 up to 2021   **94**

Long, full, silky. Great aging potential.

CHÂTEAUNEUF-DU-PAPE 2000
White | 2011 up to 2015   **95**

A bouquet of delicate honey and almonds. Wonderfully unctuous, slippery on the tongue. A refined, supple texture.

CHÂTEAUNEUF-DU-PAPE 2000
Red | 2011 up to 2013   **93**

A wine of great finesse, elegant and easy to drink, less intense than the 2001 and the preceding vintages. The aromas are fresh, with licorice notes. Lots of style.

Red: 71.7 acres; grenache 65%, mourvèdre 20%, syrah 10%, others 5%. White: 7.4 acres. Annual production: 110,000 bottles

DOMAINE DU PEGAU

15, avenue Impériale
84230 Châteauneuf-du-Pape
Phone 00 33 4 90 83 72 70
Fax 00 33 4 90 83 53 02
pegau@pegau.com
www.pegau.com

Laurence Féraud and her father have made this Châteauneuf-du-Pape property the home of a powerfully structured and generously aromatic wine that is a model for its appellation. Pegau's basic wine is the classically generous but sometimes rustic Réservée cuvée. Next comes the middle-of-the-range Laurence: barrel-raised, beautifully consistent, and noted for its generous, spicy profile. The top wine is the Da Capo, made only in the best vintages from selected wines sourced from the oldest parcels in Châteauneuf and set aside for aging in new oak—definitely one of the most stunning Châteauneufs available today.

Recently tasted
CHÂTEAUNEUF-DU-PAPE RÉSERVÉE 2007
Red | 2012 up to 2020   **90**

CHÂTEAUNEUF-DU-PAPE RÉSERVÉE 2006
Red | 2011 up to 2018   **89**

Older vintages
CHÂTEAUNEUF-DU-PAPE DA CAPO 2003
Red | 2011 up to 2025   **95**

Rich on the palate, with licorice notes and an astonishing character of candied, raisined grapes, this wine is sweet and deep, rich and ample.

CHÂTEAUNEUF-DU-PAPE DA CAPO 1998
Red | 2011 up to 2025   **96**

Mentholated on the nose, concentrated, with dry raisin flavors, this is a dense and serious wine, rich but elegant, with great intensity.

CHÂTEAUNEUF-DU-PAPE LAURENCE 2004
Red | 2011 up to 2022   **92**

Intense and deep with great richness, this wine marries power and class.

CHÂTEAUNEUF-DU-PAPE LAURENCE 2001
Red | 2011 up to 2020   **92**

Dense, serious, tannic, with beautiful scents of wild herbs, this is an intense and masculine wine, finishing on opulent and rich fruit.

CHÂTEAUNEUF-DU-PAPE RÉSERVÉE 2005
Red | 2011 up to 2020   **90**

Opulent and generous, this is a full and flavorful wine with undeniably great potential.

CHÂTEAUNEUF-DU-PAPE RÉSERVÉE 2004
Red | 2011 up to 2020   **90**
With its notes of tobacco and spices, this honest and seriously structured wine is still a bit linear, but it has great length.

Red: 61.8 acres; grenache noir 85%, mourvèdre 4%, syrah 9%, others 2%. White: 2.5 acres; bourboulenc 10%, clairette 20%, grenache blanc 60%, roussanne 10%.

PERRIN ET FILS

Route de Jonquières
84100 Orange
Phone 00 33 4 90 11 12 00
Fax 00 33 4.90.11.12.19
familleperrin@beaucastel.com
www.perrin-et-fils.com

Perrin et Fils is a family business started by the owners of Château de Beaucastel in Châteauneuf-du-Pape. The Vieille Ferme is a tasty, fruity Côtes du Ventoux blended from a mixture of purchased and estate-sourced wines. Otherwise all of the Perrins' fruit comes from vineyards that the family owns and operates itself. The result is a range of wines that show measurable improvement, both in terms of homogeneous style—clean, vigorous, but never heavy—and faithful expression of their respective terroirs.

Recently tasted
CÔTES DU RHÔNE-VILLAGES CAIRANNE
PEYRE BLANCHE 2007
Red | 2011 up to 2013   **88**

VINSOBRES LES CORNUDS 2007
Red | 2011 up to 2013   **88**

Older vintages
CHÂTEAUNEUF-DU-PAPE LES SINARDS 2006
Red | 2011 up to 2015   **90**
Made from three distinct land parcels—one of Beaucastel's young vines, another to the north of the appellation, and the last situated below the château of Châteauneuf—this wine comes across as unctuous and mellow, very harmonious, and brilliantly aromatic. In brief, excellent.

CÔTES DU RHÔNE PERRIN RÉSERVE 2006
Red | 2011 up to 2013   **86**
This Côtes du Rhône, made exclusively with vines cultivated by the family, is solid and powerful, fleshy and perfumed. Yet there is also a tannic structure that will require a bit of time in the cellar to soften.

CÔTES DU RHÔNE-VILLAGES CAIRANNE
PEYRE BLANCHE 2006
Red | 2011 up to 2013   **86**
A solid and powerful wine also requiring a little time in the cellar to fully express itself.

CÔTES DU VENTOUX LA VIEILLE FERME 2006
Red | 2011 up to 2013   **88**
A delicious and fat red wine, light and fresh.

Gigondas 2006
Red | 2011 up to 2013   **90**
A very solid wine with a refined and tight tannic structure; altogether, this has volume and class.

Gigondas Vieilles Vignes 2006
Red | 2011 up to 2016   **93**
From pre-phylloxera vines, this is a magnificent wine with no hardness. It's very deep, tempting, subtly perfumed, very persistent and racy.

Rasteau 2006
Red | 2011 up to 2013   **87**
An ample and fat wine with good length and a finish that's still a bit acidic. Wait a bit for it.

Vacqueyras 2006
Red | 2011 up to 2013   **88**
Intense notes of olives and bay laurel; ample and soft body; beautiful, deep structure.

Vinsobres Les Cornuds 2006
Red | 2011 up to 2013   **88**
From a vast domaine acquired by the family in the new Drôme appellation, this wine seduces with its svelte and classy length and its intense and elegant balance.

Vinsobres Les Hauts de Julien 2006
Red | 2011 up to 2013   **91**
Beautiful aromas of black olives. This is a deep wine, very typical, with lots of sappy flavor: definitely the best wine of Vinsobres at this time.

Red: 444.8 acres; grenache noir 70%, mourvèdre 15%, syrah 15%. White: 49.4 acres. Annual production: 1,200,000 bottles

DOMAINE RASPAIL-AY

La Filature
84190 Gigondas
Phone 00 33 4 90 65 83 01
Fax 00 33 4 90 65 89 55
raspail.ay@orange.fr

Dominique Ay is one of Gigondas' most emblematic figures. He is, in fact, president of the appellation and his winery is a great example of the wines this appellation can produce: serious wines with powerful tannins that need some time to come around, but that age remarkably well. The older vintages display the wonderful qualities of the Gigondas terroir.

Recently tasted
Gigondas 2007
Red | 2013 up to 2020   **90**

Gigondas 2007
Rosé | 2011 up to 2013   **86**

Older vintages
Gigondas 2006
Red | 2011 up to 2016   **90**
A tight wine, yet refined and complete, with perfectly expressed notes of strawberries, raspberries, and wild herbs. The tannins are firm yet ripe.

Gigondas 2005
Red | 2011 up to 2016   **89**
Strong in color and deep, this is a fleshy and rich wine with ripe and silky tannins, though it has closed down a bit. Cellar it for a few years—it'll be worth the wait!

Gigondas 2000
Red | 2011 up to 2013   **89**
A powerful, massive wine, with dark-berry and leather notes. The bouquet is beginning to mature, offering noble tertiary nuances: beautiful mushrooms. On the palate, the tannins are still firm. It's a powerful wine that took a long while to soften and find its balance, but today, it is beginning to offer itself up: intact, complete, a bit rough, but authentic.

Gigondas 1995
Red | 2011 up to 2013   **92**
No trace of defects. The wine is pure and deep, with a lightly wild edge, dense and authentic. The bouquet feels natural and fresh. This is a wine at the peak of its form, with no perceptible off flavors. It could still keep a while. The finish remains streamlined, with freshness and lots of structure.

Red: 44.5 acres; grenache noir 80%, mourvèdre 5%, syrah 15%. Annual production: 55,000 bottles

CHÂTEAU RAYAS

84230 Châteauneuf-du-Pape
Phone 00 33 4 90 83 73 09
Fax 00 33 4 90 83 51 17
www.châteaurayas.fr

Château Rayas stands out from the other Châteauneuf estates, with its sandy, breezy terroir and shady pine groves. It is the complete antithesis of modern trends in wine aging, fermenting all of its wines in concrete tanks then aging them in barrels so old they appear to have fossilized. But when it comes to the essentials, Rayas is way ahead of its time: low-yield vines; late harvesting at peak ripeness; natural vinification that avoids maximum extraction. These are the principles that have been deftly but unassumingly applied by Emmanuel Reynaud since he took charge in 1997. His wines tend to lack color when young (as do those from Château des Tours, his Vacqueyras property), something that the impatient taster will no doubt find disconcerting. Time, however, adds a majestic grace to their refined bouquet, delicate texture, and fresh length.

CHÂTEAUNEUF-DU-PAPE 2006
Red | 2016 up to 2030   96
This wine, rich, ample, and brilliantly spicy on the palate, has enormous promise.

CHÂTEAUNEUF-DU-PAPE 2006
White | 2011 up to 2020   92
Fruity, fat and long, this has good structure and a superb, fresh balance. Good potential.

CHÂTEAUNEUF-DU-PAPE 2005
Red | 2011 up to 2030   98
This wine expresses a supreme elegance that undeniably places it in the ranks of the most successful crus since the mythic 1990 and 1995, with perhaps a refinement of texture and a precision that is even more accentuated. This is great art!

CHÂTEAUNEUF-DU-PAPE 2005
White | 2011 up to 2015   92
A wine with a wonderful bouquet, smooth and full. Splendid harmony on the palate.

CHÂTEAUNEUF-DU-PAPE 2004
Red | 2011 up to 2025   96
Rayas has achieved yet again its incomparably velvety texture. This is a smooth wine, ethereal, with a bouquet of raspberries and a freshness without equal in Châteauneuf—yet it has the expected largesse and depth. A great accomplishment.

CHÂTEAUNEUF-DU-PAPE 2003
Red | 2011 up to 2025   92
Deeply colored, this wine expresses a racy range of aromas, pairing delicate spice notes with stone fruits and blackberries. Well structured on the palate, it is ample and fat, with great length. Nevertheless, the tannins are slightly drying.

CHÂTEAUNEUF-DU-PAPE 2001
Red | 2011 up to 2025   96
This wine is complete and deeply refined. It is a superb Rayas, unctuous, high-class, with a texture of unparalleled elegance in this appellation.

CHÂTEAUNEUF-DU-PAPE PIGNAN 2005
Red | 2011 up to 2025   92
Delicately spiced, deep and refined, this is blessed with a touch of tannins resembling in their elegance those of a grand wine. A magnificent wine.

Red: 54.4 acres; grenache 100%. White: 7.4 acres. Annual production: 70,000 bottles

DOMAINE LA RÉMÉJEANNE

Cadignac
30200 Sabran
Phone 00 33 4 66 89 44 51
Fax 00 33 4 66 89 64 22
remejeanne@wanadoo.fr
www.laremejeanne.com

Rémy Klein is the foremost ambassador of the terroirs of the right bank of the Rhone River. With a strict work ethic and organic viticultural practices he produces wines that are complex and structured, with fresh fruit and lots of character. Many different wines are offered here, each bearing the name of a plant that grows wild in the surrounding "garrigue" forests. The most powerful wines, Les Arbousiers and Les Églantiers, are well worth cellaring for a few years.

Recently tasted

CÔTES DU RHÔNE CHÈVREFEUILLE 2008
Red | 2011 up to 2013   87

CÔTES DU RHÔNE CÔTÉ LEVANT 2008
Red | 2011 up to 2013   86

CÔTES DU RHÔNE LES ARBOUSIERS 2007
Red | 2011 up to 2014   88

CÔTES DU RHÔNE-VILLAGES LES ÉGLANTIERS 2007
White | 2011 up to 2013   89

Older vintages

CÔTES DU RHÔNE CHÈVREFEUILLE 2007
Red | 2011 up to 2013   87
From young vines (grenache, syrah, and mourvèdre) as well as 30 percent old-vine counoise, carignan, and cinsault, this is a straight and linear wine with notes of red berries, pepper, and sweet spice. Its acidity renders it delectable and pleasant.

CÔTES DU RHÔNE-VILLAGES GENEVRIERS 2007
Red | 2011 up to 2014   89
Intensely fruity, with notes of licorice and black pepper, here's a dense wine, with ripe and well-integrated tannins. Cellar it for a few years.

CÔTES DU RHÔNE-VILLAGES LES ÉGLANTIERS 2006
Red | 2011 up to 2016   91
A vineyard situated at 656 feet in altitude produced a superbly concentrated and long wine with notes of blackberries, black currants, and licorice. The tannins are firm and harmonious.

Annual production: 110,000 bottles

DOMAINE RICHAUD

Route de Rasteau
84290 Cairanne
Phone 00 33 4 90 30 85 25
Fax 00 33 4 90 30 71 12
marcel.richaud@wanadoo.fr

Marcel Richaud has a lively, perfectionist, engaging personality that perfectly embodies his spirit of winegrowing: unpretentiously classy and endlessly soul-searching. Few take so much trouble with their wines, that's for sure. From the basic table wines to a cuvée as ambitious as L'Ebrescade or Les Estrambords, every wine in the range is sure to delight your taste buds: fruity, cheerful, and refined, luscious but never heavy, and always perfectly balanced. Absolute benchmarks for the entire region.

Recently tasted

CÔTES DU RHÔNE TERRE DE GALETS 2008
Red | 2011 up to 2013   87

CÔTES DU RHÔNE TERRES D'AYGUES 2008
Red | 2011 up to 2013   87

CÔTES DU RHÔNE-VILLAGES CAIRANNE 2008
Red | 2011 up to 2013   89

CÔTES DU RHÔNE-VILLAGES CAIRANNE
L'EBRESCADE 2007
Red | 2011 up to 2013   92

Older vintages

CÔTES DU RHÔNE TERRE DE GALETS 2007
Red | 2011 up to 2013   88
This cuvée was known as Garrigues until this year. It is deep and dense on the palate, with dark, wild fruit flavor and a more intense personality than the Terre d'Aygues cuvée. It is a fleshy and spicy Côtes du Rhône with perfectly ripe tannins.

CÔTES DU RHÔNE TERRES D'AYGUES 2007
Red | 2011 up to 2013   88
Ultrarich on the palate, this offers up the sappiness of grenache. Full and seductive, this wine comes from a fairly rich alluvial terroir, but the old vines make all the difference! A true delight.

CÔTES DU RHÔNE-VILLAGES CAIRANNE 2007
Red | 2011 up to 2015   90
Rich in very ripe fruit, this wine remains edgy and fresh on the palate. The terroir is present in the ripe tannins, even if they still feel youthful.

CÔTES DU RHÔNE-VILLAGES CAIRANNE
L'EBRESCADE 2005
Red | 2011 up to 2015   **92**
Composed of equal portions of grenache, syrah, and mourvèdre, this cuvée comes from a parcel with perfect exposition. It offers scents of spicy fruit with notes of licorice, and it's still marked by its aging in demi-muids. Long and serious, it has a silky fruitiness and ripe tannins, finishing with elegance and harmony.

Red: 118.6 acres; carignan 10%, counoise 5%, grenache 55%, mourvèdre 15%, syrah 15%. White: 4.9 acres. Annual production: 150,000 bottles

DOMAINE DE LA ROQUETTE

2, avenue Louis-Pasteur
BP 22
84230 Châteauneuf-du-Pape
Phone 00 33 4 90 33 00 31
Fax 00 33 4 90 33 18 47
vignobles@brunier.fr
www.vignoblesbrunier.fr

The estate belongs to the Brunier family (of Vieux Télégraphe fame). The winery is located near the center of Châteauneuf, while the vineyards are spread across three different areas: in La Roquette itself, planted in sandy terrain over a clay-limestone subsoil that suits the white wines; on the Pied-Long plateau (pebbles); and in Pignan (sandier soils). The red wine is very harmonious—no trace of heaviness and more focused on finesse than Vieux Télégraphe.

Recently tasted
CHÂTEAUNEUF-DU-PAPE 2007
Red | 2011 up to 2020   **86**

CHÂTEAUNEUF-DU-PAPE L'ACCENT 2007
Red | 2012 up to 2017   **88**

CHÂTEAUNEUF-DU-PAPE L'ACCENT 2006
Red | 2012 up to 2017   **88**

Older vintages
CHÂTEAUNEUF-DU-PAPE 2006
Red | 2011 up to 2013   **86**
A fat, fleshy wine, expressing notes of strawberry jam supported by solid tannins.

CHÂTEAUNEUF-DU-PAPE 2005
Red | 2011 up to 2013   **87**
The body is fat, ample, fleshy, and rather long, but the tannins lack the finesse of those in the cuvée L'Accent.

CHÂTEAUNEUF-DU-PAPE CLOS LA ROQUÈTE 2006
White | 2011 up to 2013   **95**
Deliciously subtle, this long, svelte white wine develops on smooth notes of candied citrus and milky caramel on a very persistent palate. The style is taut and fresh. Bravo!

Red: 66.7 acres. White: 4.9 acres. Annual production: 110,000 bottles

DOMAINE ROGER SABON

🦀🦀🦀🦀🦀

Avenue Impériale
84232 Châteauneuf-du-Pape
Phone 00 33 4 90 83 71 72
Fax 00 33 4 90 83 50 51
roger.sabon@wanadoo.fr
www.roger-sabon.fr

The vineyard here is owned by one of the oldest documented landholders in Châteauneuf-du-Pape. Its numerous component parcels are divided between three properties in La Crau, Courthézon, and Les Cabrières. The grenache is by far the dominant grape, though slightly less so in the cuvée Réserve. The property also makes a Marsellan-based table wine, which is tasty, generous, and satisfyingly fruity.

Recently tasted

CHÂTEAUNEUF-DU-PAPE PRESTIGE 2007
Red | 2014 up to 2020　　　　　　　　**91**

CHÂTEAUNEUF-DU-PAPE PRESTIGE 2006
Red | 2012 up to 2020　　　　　　　　**91**

CHÂTEAUNEUF-DU-PAPE RÉSERVE 2007
Red | 2012 up to 2018　　　　　　　　**90**

Older vintages

CHÂTEAUNEUF-DU-PAPE LES OLIVETS 2005
Red | 2011 up to 2015　　　　　　　　**86**
A spicy and fruity Châteauneuf in a rather energetic style.

CHÂTEAUNEUF-DU-PAPE LES OLIVETS 2003
Red | 2011 up to 2015　　　　　　　　**86**
The color has a ruby tint and the bouquet offers hints of stone fruit paired with black olives. It is long on the palate, with sober tannins and coffee notes that show some evolution. It's a classic Châteauneuf, held together by its alcohol and spice, but with character.

CHÂTEAUNEUF-DU-PAPE PRESTIGE 2005
Red | 2011 up to 2020　　　　　　　　**90**
Nicely colored, deep and suave, expressing stone-fruit notes. It is persistent, without any burning alcohol sensation. Good cellar potential.

CHÂTEAUNEUF-DU-PAPE PRESTIGE 2004
Red | 2011 up to 2015　　　　　　　　**88**
A beautiful, classic, and elegant Châteauneuf. The plum and spice bouquet has limited depth, yet the wine is rich in flavor.

CHÂTEAUNEUF-DU-PAPE PRESTIGE 2003
Red | 2011 up to 2020　　　　　　　　**82**
The color is deep, the spices showy in the bouquet. Soft on the palate, it is seriously lacking in vigor.

CHÂTEAUNEUF-DU-PAPE PRESTIGE 2001
Red | 2011 up to 2020　　　　　　　　**87**
The color is deep. The bouquet is somewhat reduced, but then spice and woodland berry scents emerge. The palate is straightforward, dense, and well structured, finishing on jammy notes.

CHÂTEAUNEUF-DU-PAPE RENAISSANCE 2006
White | 2011 up to 2014　　　　　　　**90**
Fat and generously structured, this Châteauneuf nevertheless shows both aromatic subtlety and true textural finesse.

CHÂTEAUNEUF-DU-PAPE RENAISSANCE 2004
White | 2011 up to 2013　　　　　　　**88**
Pale in color, oaked, refined, and delicious, this is not without elegance, and is rather well structured.

CHÂTEAUNEUF-DU-PAPE RÉSERVE 2005
Red | 2011 up to 2015　　　　　　　　**89**
An ample Châteauneuf, velvety and generous, this has scents of bay laurel and thyme. It's mellow and comfortable on the palate, with no heaviness.

CHÂTEAUNEUF-DU-PAPE RÉSERVE 2003
Red | 2011 up to 2020　　　　　　　　**84**
A balanced wine, soft and mellow, with simple fruit and appropriate length.

CHÂTEAUNEUF-DU-PAPE RÉSERVE 2001
Red | 2011 up to 2020　　　　　　　　**87**
Deeply colored, this easily offers dark-berry notes that develop into a rich and delicious sensation on the palate. Generous, in a rather relaxed style.

CHÂTEAUNEUF-DU-PAPE SECRETS 2004
Red | 2011 up to 2020　　　　　　　　**91**
Rich, this intense wine has great aromatic and flavorful length. The tannins are tight, but with no roughness.

Red: 111.2 acres; cinsault 10%, grenache 65%, mourvèdre 10%, syrah 10%. **White:** 4.9 acres. **Annual production:** 73,000 bottles

CHÂTEAU DE SAINT-COSME

84190 Gigondas
Phone 00 33 4 90 65 80 80
Fax 00 33 4 90 65 81 05
louis@château-st-cosme.com

Saint-Cosme is probably the oldest estate in Gigondas, built on a site that attests to wine-growing from Gallo-Roman times. It was acquired by present owner Louis Barruol's forebearers in the late fifteenth century and has remained in the same family ever since, located at the heart of the appellation and richly supplied with old vines, some of them replanted just after the phylloxera epidemic. The vineyard boasts an astounding diversity of soils, product of geological upheavals to the north of the village where two faults merge. Clays, limestone, and sands provide Louis Barruol with a rich palette that he weaves into a well-orchestrated range of deep, original Gigondas wines. He also runs a small merchant business, sourcing wines from promising terroirs throughout the Rhone Valley that complete the Barruol portfolio.

CHÂTEAUNEUF-DU-PAPE 2004
Red | 2011 up to 2013   84
Supple, smooth, and round, here's a very classic Châteauneuf of medium intensity, honest and balanced.

CÔTE RÔTIE 2005
Red | 2011 up to 2013   84
Very fruity, fat, and immediately seductive, this Côte Rôtie plays on its roundness and freshness more than on its depth.

CÔTES DU RHÔNE 2007
Red | 2011 up to 2013   87
The 2007 vintage is ample and deep, with superb richness on the palate. It's very grenache, with scents of bay laurel, thyme, and undergrowth. Supple and delicate tannins. A truly pleasing wine.

CÔTES DU RHÔNE LES DEUX ALBIONS 2006
Red | 2011 up to 2013   88
Supple and silky in the mouth, with notes of cherries, tobacco, and dead leaves. Good structure, ripe tannins.

GIGONDAS 2005
Red | 2011 up to 2013   89
A harmonious and delicately spiced wine, with silky tannins that bear witness to a mastery of enology.

GIGONDAS HOMINIS FIDES 2006
Red | 2011 up to 2016   90
Very powerful in the mouth, with young and taut tannins. Perfumed, with floral and sweet spice notes. Delicately oaky in the finish, with a touch of tobacco.

GIGONDAS LE CLAUX 2006
Red | 2011 up to 2018   92
From very old vines on yellow clay soils. The result: a wine of extraordinary finesse, with scents of candied prunes, rich and racy. The tannins are delicate and perfectly integrated, the wood present and toasty, the finish superbly long.

GIGONDAS LE POSTE 2006
Red | 2011 up to 2014   90
Beautifully oaked, with a lovely bouquet. Delicate scents of wild blackberries and toasted bread. It finishes on youthful tannins and elegant wood.

GIGONDAS VALBELLE 2006
Red | 2011 up to 2016   90
Powerful and deep, with notes of small dark berries and sweet spices. With the addition of 10 percent syrah, it is slightly more tannic than the other cuvées. It will require a few years of cellaring.

SAINT-JOSEPH 2005
Red | 2011 up to 2013   82
Supple, simple, but a classic Saint-Joseph. Easy to drink.

VIN DE TABLE LITTLE JAMES' BASKET PRESS 2006
Red | 2011 up to 2013   88
A tasty, seductive, and eminently likable table wine: it is consistent, brilliantly fruity, and very balanced.

CLOS SAINT-JEAN

18, avenue Général De Gaulle
84231 Châteauneuf-du-Pape
Phone 00 33 4 90 83 58 00
Fax 00 33 4 90 83 58 02

The Clos Saint-Jean is a large family property that remained somewhat anonymous for many years despite having been one of the first to sell bottled wine (before World War I). Production has been transformed in recent years, spurred on by brothers Pascal and Vincent Maurel with guidance from enologist Philippe Cambie. Two cuvées are especially noteworthy: La Combe des Fous and the Deus ex Machina, made from the grenache but with a hefty whack (40 percent) of new-oak-matured mourvèdre. Clos Saint-Jean is a stellar example of modern-style Châteauneuf-du-Pape: expressive, lush, and fruity, if sometimes a bit too emphatic. All of these wines are built to age, but with a generous character and exuberant aromas that also make them ideal for early drinking.

CHÂTEAUNEUF-DU-PAPE 2005
Red | 2011 up to 2017 **91**
The wine has found its balance, gaining in aromatic finesse and even more in velvety texture. It has a warming depth, unctuous texture, and pleasing aromatic persistence.

CHÂTEAUNEUF-DU-PAPE 2003
Red | 2011 up to 2015 **89**
This seduces with its texture and structure. With its lack of heaviness, delicate tannins, flesh, and alcoholic balance, it is a classic wine that will age well.

CHÂTEAUNEUF-DU-PAPE DEUS EX MACHINA 2005
Red | 2011 up to 2018 **89**
An imposing wine with deep color, this expresses rather delicate notes of dark fruit. It is generous and unctuous on the palate, with length and round tannins.

CHÂTEAUNEUF-DU-PAPE DEUS EX MACHINA 2003
Red | 2011 up to 2020 **92**
Beautifully deep ruby in color, this has a bouquet of dark berries. The body is very fat, the tannins powerful, preventing the wine from attaining perfect finesse. Instead, it is a wine of grand, rich volume, with a surprising mellowness and seductive depth.

CHÂTEAUNEUF-DU-PAPE LA COMBE DES FOUS 2005
Red | 2011 up to 2020 **89**
Inky, with a precise bouquet of dark berries. Unctuous, with length dominated by the alcohol, yet with lots of richness. Good volume in a rather modern style.

CHÂTEAUNEUF-DU-PAPE LA COMBE DES FOUS 2003
Red | 2011 up to 2017 **90**
Beautifully deep in color, this has an expressive bouquet of red-berry jam. It is soft and fleshy in the mouth, yet reinforced with tannic solidity and generous alcohol.

Red: 1050.2 acres. White: 37.1 acres. Annual production: 100,000 bottles

CLOS SAINT-MICHEL

84700 Sorgues
Phone 00 33 4 90 83 56 05
Fax 00 33 4 90 83 56 06
mousset@clos-saint-michel.com
www.clos-saint-michel.com

The Clos Saint-Michel is located in Sorgues, south of Châteauneuf-du-Pape, and is owned by Olivier and Franck Mousset. The blend of red grapes (in both cuvées) is now much better balanced than it has been, thanks to more or less equal quantities of syrah, grenache, and mourvèdre.

Recently tasted

CHÂTEAUNEUF-DU-PAPE 2008
White | 2011 up to 2013   86

Older vintages

CHÂTEAUNEUF-DU-PAPE 2004
Red | 2011 up to 2013   89
Deeply colored. Dark berry and bay laurel flavors, very languid. Delicately spiced on the palate. Supple and round.

CHÂTEAUNEUF-DU-PAPE 2003
White | 2011 up to 2013   86
Golden, fat, supple, and fleshy, this pairs white-fruit flavors with honey nuances that are quite pronounced. Seductive right now, it should be drunk soon.

CHÂTEAUNEUF-DU-PAPE 2001
Red | 2011 up to 2013   88
Deeply colored, this is rich with tasty fruit, pairing extract and length. It is powerful yet refined.

CHÂTEAUNEUF-DU-PAPE RÉSERVÉE 2004
Red | 2011 up to 2013   90
A beautiful deep color. Dark fruit, delicate spice, long and smooth on the palate. Pedigreed and unctuous, deep and enveloping.

CHÂTEAUNEUF-DU-PAPE RÉSERVÉE 2003
Red | 2011 up to 2018   90
The color is full without being opaque. The delicate nose pairs notes of dark berries with those of red berries. Unctuous on the palate, with good, well-controlled, and velvety tannins. Smooth and elegant length.

Red: 32.1 acres. White: 3.5 acres. Annual production: 65,000 bottles

DOMAINE LE SANG DES CAILLOUX

Route de Vacqueyras
84260 Sarrians
Phone 00 33 4 90 65 88 64
Fax 00 33 4 90 65 88 75
le-sang-des-cailloux@wanadoo.fr
www.lesangdescailloux.com

Top Vacqueyras winegrower Serge Férigoule was an employee here until, with no other buyers in sight, he seized the opportunity to buy the estate himself. Since then, Férigoule has revolutionized this garrigue vineyard, working the soil and using only organic materials. The vineyard lies on the plateau between Sarrians and Vacqueyras and is overwhelmingly planted with old grenache vines. The wines show fabulous density and concentration thanks to naturally tiny yields year after year. Every successive vintage of the classic cuvée is named after one of Férigoule's daughters, Azalaïs, Floureto, or Doucinello. The Lopy comes from a parcel of very old grenache and syrah vines and is even more assertive than the classic cuvée.

Recently tasted

VACQUEYRAS FLOURETO 2007
Red | 2011 up to 2013   92

VACQUEYRAS LOPY 2007
Red | 2012 up to 2020   91

VACQUEYRAS UN SANG BLANC 2007
White | 2011 up to 2017   90

Older vintages

VACQUEYRAS AZALAÏS 2006
Red | 2011 up to 2016   88
Highly perfumed with a sunny bouquet, this classic cuvée expresses the 2006 vintage well. Round on the palate with silky tannins and notes of seductive, candied fruit, it's a complex wine that will mature well.

VACQUEYRAS DOUCINELLO 2005
Red | 2011 up to 2015   91
Elegant and generous, with a bouquet of very concentrated dark berries. Silky on the palate, the wine is supported by its delicate and round tannins, and finishes on notes both refined and fresh.

VACQUEYRAS LOPY 2006
Red | 2011 up to 2016   91
Intense and marked by its wood at this time. This property's old vines are perfectly expressed in this cuvée. It's warm on the palate, with notes of plums and sweet spices. A beautiful and deep wine.

VACQUEYRAS LOPY 2005
Red | 2011 up to 2015   **92**
The style is more modern, but the extraction is perfect, the fruit concentrated. This wine has real sappiness, with silky tannins. It is very well aged.

VACQUEYRAS UN SANG BLANC 2005
White | 2011 up to 2013   **90**
Delectable and rich on the palate, with floral notes (lilacs), this is a concentrated wine, beautifully textured, fat, and long.

Red: 39.5 acres; cinsault 3%, grenache noir 70%, mourvèdre 7%, syrah 20%. White: 2.5 acres Annual production: 60,000 bottles

DOMAINE DE LA SOLITUDE

Route de Bédarrides
BP 21
84230 Châteauneuf-du-Pape
Phone 00 33 4 90 83 71 45
Fax 00 33 4 90 83 51 34
domaine.solitude@orange.fr
www.domaine-solitude.com

This major Châteauneuf estate owns a hundred-acre single-block vineyard on the road from Châteauneuf to Bédarrides. Other assets are a long tradition of wine-making dating back to the Barberinis, the Tuscan family who founded the Avignon papacy in the Middle Ages; plus magnificent vineyards that include a sizable portion of La Crau. These qualities are now being fully taken advantage of (somewhat belatedly, giving new strength to the latest vintages). The red wine contains a balanced blend of grenache and syrah, supported by just the right amount of mourvèdre; the Réserve Secrète relies exclusively on (mainly barrel-aged) syrah and grenache.

Recently tasted
CHÂTEAUNEUF-DU-PAPE 2007
Red | 2012 up to 2016   **88**

CHÂTEAUNEUF-DU-PAPE BARBERINI 2007
White | 2011 up to 2015   **88**

Older vintages
CHÂTEAUNEUF-DU-PAPE 2006
Red | 2011 up to 2016   **90**
Deeply colored, with a beautiful red-berry sorbet scent: this is very elegant, with refined tannins and beautiful length.

CHÂTEAUNEUF-DU-PAPE 2005
Red | 2011 up to 2016   **89**
Deeply colored, with scents of blackberries and blueberries, this is a big wine, intense and deep, with suave roundness. Seductive and long.

CHÂTEAUNEUF-DU-PAPE 100% GRENACHE 2006
Red | 2011 up to 2022   **94**
Charming scents of delicious strawberries. Savory length. Very refined, all velvet.

CHÂTEAUNEUF-DU-PAPE 100% GRENACHE 2005
Red | 2011 up to 2022   **97**
Delicate notes of black olives. Racy, with great length and a superfine texture. Unctuous and mellow.

CHÂTEAUNEUF-DU-PAPE BARBERINI 2006
White | 2011 up to 2015   **92**
Great personality and an intensity on the palate matched by few in the appellation: the aromas are complex and refined; the palate is silky and beautifully structured, with great persistence.

CHÂTEAUNEUF-DU-PAPE BARBERINI 2006
Red | 2011 up to 2019   **92**
With good color and delicate wood, this is high-class, with notes of blackberries and small red berries. Grand and smooth length.

CHÂTEAUNEUF-DU-PAPE BARBERINI 2005
Red | 2011 up to 2018   **90**
A smooth and mild wine, long and fat, nonetheless showing good freshness and flavorful balance.

CHÂTEAUNEUF-DU-PAPE BARBERINI 2004
White | 2011 up to 2013   **92**
Very beautiful golden green. Good aging, with refined and long body. Quite well done in an ambitious style.

CHÂTEAUNEUF-DU-PAPE RÉSERVE SECRÈTE 2006
Red | 2011 up to 2023   **92**
Wonderfully deep in color, powerful, chocolaty and intense. Beautiful wood, long and deep potential.

CHÂTEAUNEUF-DU-PAPE RÉSERVE SECRÈTE 2005
Red | 2011 up to 2023   **94**
A remarkable bouquet of black olives and herbs. The attack is refined, the length brilliant. A structured, dense, and superbly realized wine.

CHÂTEAUNEUF-DU-PAPE RÉSERVE SECRÈTE 2004
Red | 2011 up to 2018   **96**
Deep and brilliantly colored, with a noble bouquet. Intense on the palate, with strong notes of dark berries, bay laurel, and licorice and a very unctuous texture. Perfect and persistent finish. Superb volume.

Red: 89 acres; cinsault 8%, counoise 1%, grenache noir 65%, mourvèdre 8%, syrah 18%. **White:** 9.8 acres; bourboulenc 5%, clairette 10%, grenache blanc 60%, roussanne 25%. **Annual production:** 100,000 bottles

DOMAINE LA SOUMADE

84110 Rasteau
Phone 00 33 4 90 46 13 63
Fax 00 33 4 90 46 18 36
dom-lasoumade@hotmail.fr

André Roméro, now assisted by his son, is a leading Rasteau producer and one of the region's most charming ambassadors. His wines have long been impressive for their full-throttle style and solid tannins, and we are delighted to say that they are even better since he sought advice from Stéphane Derenoncourt. They now display a silky texture that in no way detracts from their sincerity, energy, and power. The portfolio of wines explores the many facets of the Rasteau terroir, both inside and outside the appellation. In addition to the Vin Doux Naturel, a generous and powerful amber-colored Rasteau, there is for instance an equally robust and interesting cabernet sauvignon Vin de Pays. Of the red wines, the Fleur de Confiance is an enormously endowed wine made from old grenache vines that grow in soils composed of pure blue clays.

Recently tasted
CÔTES DU RHÔNE LES VIOLETTES 2007
Red | 2012 up to 2017   **91**

GIGONDAS 2007
Red | 2012 up to 2016   **92**

RASTEAU CONFIANCE 2007
Red | 2013 up to 2018   **92**

RASTEAU CÔTES DU RHÔNE VILLAGES 2007
Red | 2011 up to 2015   **88**

RASTEAU FLEUR DE CONFIANCE 2007
Red | 2015 up to 2018   **93**

RASTEAU PRESTIGE 2007
Red | 2012 up to 2017   **91**

Older vintages
CÔTES DU RHÔNE LES VIOLETTES 2006
Red | 2011 up to 2013   **90**
This wine has gained in finesse, freshness, and perfumed nuances, with its delicate flower notes and hints of dark berries, without losing any of the delectable generosity that has always been a hallmark of André Roméro's wines. Quite a competitive Côtes du Rhône!

GIGONDAS 2006
Red | 2011 up to 2018   **92**
With no hardness whatsoever, this is a superb Gigondas, elegant, very refined, and deeply profound, with beautiful aromatic intensity.

RASTEAU CONFIANCE 2005
Red | 2011 up to 2018   **91**
Deep in color and very forward in fruit and spice on the nose and palate. Generous length. Intense, with firm yet finely expressed tannins, this wine still shows lots of restraint.

RASTEAU CONFIANCE 2004
Red | 2011 up to 2015   **92**
Languid yet powerful, this cuvée shines. It is full but not overtly forceful, with a refined and rich perfume and superb generosity.

RASTEAU FLEUR DE CONFIANCE 2005
Red | 2011 up to 2020   **94**
The blue clay soils have given this wine tremendous precision and intensity in this vintage. It is very unctuous, rich, and finely spiced, with notes of bay laurel and olive. The length is extraordinary, holding onto its freshness and tannic structure throughout, with no trace of heaviness. This wine, among the best ever made by the Roméro family, has great cellaring potential.

RASTEAU PRESTIGE 2004
Red | 2011 up to 2015   **91**
A superb aromatic range marries delicate spice and persistent blackberry notes. It is long and harmonious, with definite balance, even with its generously alcoholic finish.

RASTEAU VIN DOUX NATUREL 2003
Sweet Amber | 2011 up to 2022   **91**
Spice cake and candied fruit notes. Well structured on the palate, fleshy with residual sugar but no heaviness. A beautiful Vin Doux Naturel (fortified wine), muscled and delicately spiced.

Red: 69.2 acres; cabernet sauvignon 10%, grenache 55%, merlot 5%, mourvèdre 5%, petit verdot 5%, syrah 20%. Annual production: 120,000 bottles

TARDIEU-LAURENT

Les Grandes Bastides
Route de Cucuron
84160 Lourmarin
Phone 00 33 4 90 68 80 25
Fax 00 33 4 90 68 22 65
info@tardieu-laurent.com
www.tardieu-laurent.com

Tardieu-Laurent wines have become a reference point for the wines of the Rhone Valley. Michel Tardieu's négociant business has grown enormously since its beginnings in the mid-1990s, with the help of willing accomplice and specialist in barrel-aged Burgundies, Dominique Laurent. The quantities released under the Tardieu-Laurent label are always very small, but you can nevertheless find bottles of Tardieu's equally excellent second-label wines, Les Grandes Bastides, plus a range of simpler, very prettily crafted offerings marketed under the Becs Fins label (and often widely distributed). All Tardieu-Laurent wines are raised in barrels but with rather less use of new oak than in the early years. Ambitiously made but by no means standardized, they develop a refined structure and definition that, after one to three years in the bottle (and the potential to last much, much longer), makes them extremely expressive of their terroir. Tardieu is above all a connoisseur of Rhone Valley wines (from the north and south alike), and his range of offerings is always the choicest: flawless, from the Guy-Louis Côtes du Rhône (which can compete with any Grand Cru) to the magnificent Hermitage and Châteauneuf Cuvée Spéciale.

Recently tasted

CHÂTEAUNEUF-DU-PAPE 2007
Red | 2013 up to 2022   **95**

CÔTE RÔTIE 2007
Red | 2014 up to 2024   **95**

CÔTES DU RHÔNE GUY-LOUIS 2007
Red | 2011 up to 2017   **92**

GIGONDAS VIEILLES VIGNES 2007
Red | 2014 up to 2027   **95**

HERMITAGE 2007
Red | 2015 up to 2025   **98**

RASTEAU 2007
Red | 2011 up to 2018   **92**

Older vintages

BANDOL 2004
Red | 2011 up to 2025   **92**
Peppery, deep, long, racy, very intense: a great, classic Bandol, clearly made to cellar for a while.

CHÂTEAUNEUF-DU-PAPE 2006
Red | 2011 up to 2018   **90**
This smooth and unctuous Châteauneuf is a fat and ample wine with no tannic aggressivity. It will open beautifully in a few years.

CHÂTEAUNEUF-DU-PAPE 2003
Red | 2011 up to 2020   **89**
A beautiful, very ripe Châteauneuf with very expressive aromas and a silky palate marked by integrated, highly refined tannins. It has a chewy style, fresh and harmonious, but nonetheless retains the depth and intensity of the best of this appellation.

CHÂTEAUNEUF-DU-PAPE 2001
Red | 2011 up to 2020   **89**
The wine is going through a closed-down phase that will reveal its excellent élevage, but will adversely affect the strong fruit flavors or, rather, simplify them. The palate is evenly elegant, structured, with refined and ripe tannins.

CHÂTEAUNEUF-DU-PAPE CROZES-HERMITAGE 2006
Red | 2011 up to 2017   **86**
At this time this wine is dominated by oak. It's fruity, well made, to be tasted again in the future.

CHÂTEAUNEUF-DU-PAPE CUVÉE SPÉCIALE 2006
Red | 2011 up to 2020   **95**
The blackberry and plum aromas are very expressive, even dominant in this wine, giving it personality. Its incredible depth and energy promise a great future.

CHÂTEAUNEUF-DU-PAPE CUVÉE SPÉCIALE 2003
Red | 2011 up to 2025   **92**
The style of the vintage is fully expressed in this wine's bouquet of prunes, wild herbs, cocoa, and licorice. On the palate, this generosity is paired with far-from-dry tannins, perceptible but ripe and perfectly tuned by the high-class aging in cask. The wine has lots of length and so much more. It seems not to be flabby in the least, supported by its tannins and alcohol as well as acidity. It is definitely still holding back.

CHÂTEAUNEUF-DU-PAPE CUVÉE SPÉCIALE 2001
Red | 2011 up to 2025   **97**
A magnificent wine, this has great structure and excellent fruit. It also has the characteristic elements of the terroir, and the tannic elegance common to wines made by Michel Tardieu. It has power, aromatic elegance, and equally great tannic silkiness, as well as undeniable restraint. It is a wine of great class.

CHÂTEAUNEUF-DU-PAPE SPÉCIALE 2007
Red | 2014 up to 2027   **94**
Pure, long, ideally balanced, this is a lovely Châteauneuf, generous and deep, with unctuous and finely spiced length.

CHÂTEAUNEUF-DU-PAPE SPÉCIALE 2005
Red | 2011 up to 2030   **95**
The eternal classic style of Châteauneuf: racy, light, deep without heaviness. Reminiscent of a Rayas or a Bonneau. Purity, superb!

CHÂTEAUNEUF-DU-PAPE TL 2005
Red | 2011 up to 2015   **90**
This superb cuvée expresses tremendous elegance for the appellation, and for a very nice price!

CHÂTEAUNEUF-DU-PAPE VIEILLES VIGNES 2006
Red | 2011 up to 2021   **94**
Big yet smooth attack; delicate spices paired with bay laurel and dark berries; depth and velvet texture. Beautiful promise.

CHÂTEAUNEUF-DU-PAPE VIEILLES VIGNES 2005
Red | 2011 up to 2013   **92**
A wine of great intensity, deeply black, with scents of blackberries and unctuous flesh, knit together by present yet delicate tannins: a modern-style Châteauneuf.

CHÂTEAUNEUF-DU-PAPE VIEILLES VIGNES 2003
Red | 2011 up to 2020   **97**
A wine of very great intensity, both in its generous alcohol content and its tannins, supporting mature fruit with a beautiful, spicy, chocolaty character. It's a superlative wine, very powerful yet with perfectly silky tannins, intense and long. It will need a minimum of fifteen years in the cellar, even if its tannic finesse makes it a pleasure to drink already!

CHÂTEAUNEUF-DU-PAPE VIEILLES VIGNES 2001
Red | 2011 up to 2020   **90**
Assuredly, the wine is passing through a closed-down phase that will minimally affect its extremely rich and deep character; it's nearly a liqueur. It has equally present acidity, which, for the moment, feels in opposition to the sweetness, rather than balancing it. It should come together with a bit of time. Leave it in the cellar, and taste it again in a few years.

Cornas Coteaux 2006
Red | 2011 up to 2015   **91**
Soft and fruity, this lacks the intensity of a great Cornas, but it is subtle and delicately built.

Cornas Grandes Bastides 2006
Red | 2011 up to 2016   **87**
Velvety, fruity, very pure, straight, and svelte: a good, classic Cornas that can be enjoyed relatively young.

Cornas Veilles Vignes 2005
Red | 2011 up to 2030   **98**
Michel Tardieu is, alas, obliged to abandon this cuvée because the vines from which it is made have been sold. What a shame, as this Cornas has been at the top of his portfolio every year, for reasons that can be tasted in the extraordinarily brilliant 2005: deep and unctuous sap, refined and intense length, volume, and ultra-precise fruit perfectly honed by an élevage without equal in Cornas.

Côte Rôtie 2006
Red | 2011 up to 2022   **92**
Powerful, concentrated, not yet revealing all its nuances: an intense wine worth waiting for.

Côtes du Rhône Becs Fins 2006
Red | 2011 up to 2009   **88**
A beautiful Côtes du Rhône, fleshy and ample, expressing superb scents of black cherries and blackberries. It is long and balanced, to be enjoyed for its fruit.

Côtes du Rhône Guy-Louis 2006
Red | 2011 up to 2017   **91**
The velvet texture and the tannins are those of a great wine: unctuous, silky, and expressing very pure fruit. It is most definitely an unusual Côtes du Rhône, with a fresher balance than the 2005.

Côtes du Rhône La Pièce sous le Bras 2006
Red | 2011 up to 2009   **86**
Fat and easy to drink, this is a fruity and seductive Côtes du Rhône with no heaviness.

Côtes du Rhône-Villages Rasteau Grandes Bastides 2006
Red | 2011 up to 2016   **89**
An ample, well-structured wine with scents of black cherries and wood. Deep length.

Gigondas Vieilles Vignes 2006
Red | 2011 up to 2020   **97**
A great and noble wine, without the rusticity or hardness that one, alas, finds too often still in this appellation. It has magnificent fruit and it's ultra-persistent, with superfine tannins, power, and length, as well as velvety finesse. It is certainly the best Gigondas of the vintage, and one of the great bottles of the valley.

Hermitage 2006
White | 2011 up to 2018   **92**
This wine offers an aromatic range in its bouquet that is already turning toward acacia blossom honey. The wine, very rich and fat, is refined by its aging. It finishes with freshness today.

Hermitage 2006
Red | 2011 up to 2022   **92**
Subtle and deep, a lovely Hermitage blending its mineral and fruit elements with pure joy. Good potential.

Hermitage Grandes Bastides 2006
Red | 2011 up to 2017   **88**
A straight, very mineral wine. Long and promising, even if the tannins could be more refined.

Rasteau 2006
Red | 2011 up to 2018   **92**
Softer but also more immediately balanced than the 2005, this is a subtle and flavorful Rasteau. It is delicious and pleasing right now, even though it surely has beautiful potential for cellaring.

Saint-Joseph 2006
Red | 2011 up to 2021   **95**
An intense and generous wine, mineral and fruity, very deep, without austerity. It has a rich and concentrated finish. Beautiful restraint.

Saint-Joseph Grandes Bastides 2006
Red | 2011 up to 2016   **90**
A joyous, old-school Saint-Joseph, playing perfectly among notes of minerals, granite, black olives, and stone fruit. It comes to a finish that's well padded yet very pure.

Vacqueyras 2006
Red | 2011 up to 2016   **90**
In this vintage, the wine is more solid but also more linear than the Rasteau. It's a Vacqueyras to cellar.

Vacqueyras 2005
Red | 2011 up to 2013   **91**
Deep and intense, serious but fresh. This wine offers today the definition of harmony and suavity.

Vacqueyras Grandes Bastides 2006
Red | 2011 up to 2017   **90**
Subtler than the Rasteau, this is a smooth and supple wine with notes of bay laurel and very velvety length.

Annual production: 100,000 bottles

CHÂTEAU DES TOURS

Les Sablons
84260 Sarrians
Phone 00 33 4 90 65 41 75
Fax 00 33 4 90 65 38 46
www.châteaudestours.fr

This small but famous cru produces a style of wine very similar to Château Rayas, vinified and matured by owner Emmanuel Reynaud. With the exception of the often excellent syrah-based cuvée, the linchpin of production is the grenache, even though it only accounts for half of total red plantings. All Reynaud wines need time to firm up in the bottle and those below are no exception: unlike most good, modern-style Côtes du Rhône, these do not play on lushness and exuberant fruit. What you get instead is depth, ultrarefined texture and unmistakable class. The whites have come on nicely, too.

Recently tasted
CÔTES DU RHÔNE 2005
Red | 2011 up to 2014   87

VIN DE PAYS DU VAUCLUSE DOMAINE DES TOURS 2005
White | 2011 up to 2015   88

Older vintages
CÔTES DU RHÔNE 2004
Red | 2011 up to 2013   87
Silky, long and rich in the mouth, this wine unfolds on notes of black cherries. Good balance.

CÔTES DU RHÔNE 2004
White | 2011 up to 2013   86
A cuvée of white grenache, this is dominated by vegetal notes on the nose. On the palate, it is fat and expansive, very rich.

CÔTES DU RHÔNE GRANDE RÉSERVE 2002
Red | 2011 up to 2013   87
A lovely wine with supple and tender balance. Ready to drink.

VACQUEYRAS 2005
Red | 2011 up to 2018   93
Unctuous, long, and very harmonious. The wine develops a superb aromatic range of delicate spices.

VACQUEYRAS 2004
Red | 2011 up to 2016   90
Great depth, long and defined, harmonious, flavorful and intense. Notes of kirsch, mint, and spices.

VACQUEYRAS 2003
Red | 2011 up to 2013   89
An astonishing and exceptional 2003, with notes of raisins and liqueur, this is a sunny grenache, with hints of roasted figs. The heat of the vintage is perceptible, but the wine finishes with a very surprising freshness.

VACQUEYRAS 2002
Red | 2011 up to 2013   88
Fresh, long, and racy. A true success in a difficult vintage. Ready to drink.

VACQUEYRAS 2001
Red | 2011 up to 2013   92
Emblematic of this domaine, this wine is perfectly matured, rich, and truffled, with flavorful flesh and a long and fresh structure. Refined and ready to enjoy.

VIN DE PAYS DU VAUCLUSE 2004
Red | 2011 up to 2009   86
Supple, pleasant, with good fruit expression.

VIN DE PAYS DU VAUCLUSE DOMAINE DES TOURS 2005
Red | 2011 up to 2013   87
Rich and floral with a very pleasant fullness in the mouth. The fresh finish bears the domaine's signature cherry and strawberry notes.

Red: 91.4 acres; cinsault 15%, counoise 5%, grenache 66%, merlot 3%, syrah 8%. White: 7.4 acres; clairette 50%, grenache blanc 50%. Annual production: 165,000 bottles

DOMAINE PIERRE USSEGLIO ET FILS

Route d'Orange
84230 Châteauneuf-du-Pape
Phone 00 33 4 90 83 72 98
Fax 00 33 4 90 83 56 70
domaine-usseglio@wanadoo.fr

The 1990s marked a turning point for this very classical Châteauneuf-du-Pape estate. It started producing intensely sunny and sappy wines, followed by the Cuvée Mon Aïeul, a wine built for long aging; the style nevertheless remains as traditional as ever. The wines evolve toward that smooth, deep character typical of Châteauneuf, sometimes with tannins that are very slightly rough around the edges.

Recently tasted

CHÂTEAUNEUF-DU-PAPE 2008
White | 2011 up to 2013   90

CHÂTEAUNEUF-DU-PAPE MON AÏEUL 2007
Red | 2012 up to 2017   88

Older vintages

CHÂTEAUNEUF-DU-PAPE 2006
Red | 2011 up to 2016   87
Medium-deep in color, this is a supple wine from lovely, fine grenache. Soft and long enough, it has a small note of acidity in the finish that will go away with time.

CHÂTEAUNEUF-DU-PAPE 2005
Red | 2011 up to 2020   88
Round and persistent. Stone fruit, delicate spice, and strawberries. Expansive finish.

CHÂTEAUNEUF-DU-PAPE 2003
Red | 2011 up to 2018   90
Beautiful ruby color. A delicately chocolate bouquet. Fleshy, elegant, supple, refined, and spicy: this is a wine with lovely length, suave and persistently classy.

CHÂTEAUNEUF-DU-PAPE 2001
Red | 2011 up to 2018   91
Deeply colored. The bouquet seems rustic, with notes of curry, but when aerated, stone fruits and black olives emerge. It's fat and intense on the palate, profound, a very classic, powerful Châteauneuf style.

CHÂTEAUNEUF-DU-PAPE 1999
Red | 2011 up to 2015   88
Deeply colored with cashew nuances, yet still somewhat young, this is seriously structured and has scents of toast and wild game. It is fat, unctuous, and rustic but generous.

CHÂTEAUNEUF-DU-PAPE 1998
Red | 2011 up to 2013   88
Beautiful color. The wine needs to be drunk now, but the volume is intense.

CHÂTEAUNEUF-DU-PAPE MON AÏEUL 2006
Red | 2012 up to 2017   88
Deep color. Strawberries and young leather in the bouquet. Unctuous body, rather refined.

CHÂTEAUNEUF-DU-PAPE MON AÏEUL 2005
Red | 2011 up to 2020   90
Deeply colored and very seriously built, with good, deep length, this is somewhat firm at this time, but without any tannic rigidity: it simply needs time in the cellar.

CHÂTEAUNEUF-DU-PAPE MON AÏEUL 2003
Red | 2011 up to 2020   90
The color is vibrant and deep. The wine is very spicy and develops long and full volume. Still rather linear, but with true balance and great depth.

CÔTES DU RHÔNE 2006
Red | 2011 up to 2013   86
Vinified in a classic style, this wine has notes of cherries preserved in alcohol and thyme on the nose. The palate is supple, silky on the attack, with a sensation of alcohol. It finishes on the soft tannins of old wood.

Red: 66.7 acres; cinsault 5%, grenache 80%, mourvèdre 5%, syrah 10%. **White:** 2.5 acres; bourboulenc 10%, clairette 10%, grenache 80%. **Annual production:** 80,000 bottles

DOMAINE RAYMOND USSEGLIO

84230 Châteauneuf-du-Pape
Phone 00 33 4 90 83 71 85
Fax 00 33 4 90 83 50 42
info@domaine-usseglio.fr
www.domaine-usseglio.fr

Francis Usseglio came to Châteauneuf-du-Pape as a sharecropper before buying his own property after the war. Since developed by son Raymond, this estate now boasts more than fifty acres in the appellation, plus a further twelve in the Côtes du Rhône. The estate offers two red wines, both grenache-driven; the prestige cuvée Impériale is made from the vineyard's oldest plantings. The wines are traditionally styled but of excellent quality, and they age to perfection.

Recently tasted
CHÂTEAUNEUF-DU-PAPE IMPÉRIALE 2007
Red | 2012 up to 2016   88

Older vintages
CHÂTEAUNEUF-DU-PAPE 2006
Red | 2011 up to 2016   87
A supple wine, fat and sweet: good, fresh grenache.

CHÂTEAUNEUF-DU-PAPE 2005
Red | 2011 up to 2018   88
This wine is maturing well: it is garnet-colored, with clear notes of strawberries in the bouquet. The body is deep and refined, suave and subtle. The finish has become more elegant.

CHÂTEAUNEUF-DU-PAPE 1999
Red | Drink now   90
Perfect right now: fresh, soft, with supple length and excellent freshness.

CHÂTEAUNEUF-DU-PAPE IMPÉRIALE 2006
Red | 2011 up to 2017   91
Deeply colored, this has beautiful intensity, red-berry notes, refined tannins, persistence, and freshness.

CHÂTEAUNEUF-DU-PAPE IMPÉRIALE 2005
Red | 2011 up to 2017   92
A deeply colored wine, very unctuous and delicious, refined and long, with a magnificent velvety texture.

CHÂTEAUNEUF-DU-PAPE IMPÉRIALE 2004
Red | 2011 up to 2018   89
This prestige cuvée seduces with its unctuous and smooth body and its refined softness, all in an aromatic register of stone fruit.

Red: 46.9 acres; cinsault 2%, counoise 2%, grenache 80%, mourvèdre 10%, syrah 6%. White: 7.4 acres. Annual production: 60,000 bottles

DOMAINE DE LA VIEILLE JULIENNE

CD 72
84100 Orange
Phone 00 33 4 90 34 20 10
Fax 00 33 4 90 34 10 20
contact@vieillejulienne.com
www.vieillejulienne.com

The vineyards here are situated in a single block at the northern end of the Châteauneuf-du-Pape appellation, with an equal amount of acres classified for Vin de Pays, Côtes du Rhône, and Châteauneuf-du-Pape. The estate converted to organic viticulture in 1990 and has been fully biodynamic for five years. Destemmed red grapes account for two red bottlings, one classical, the other based on very low-yield, old grenache vines. The latter, known as the Réservée, plainly ranks as one of the deepest, most intense cuvées currently produced under this appellation.

Recently tasted
CHÂTEAUNEUF-DU-PAPE 2006
Red | 2011 up to 2016   89

CÔTES DU RHÔNE CLAVIN 2006
Red | 2011 up to 2013   87

Older vintages
CHÂTEAUNEUF-DU-PAPE 2005
Red | 2011 up to 2020   90
Spicy, with hints of fig. Deep and remarkably built, this wine has brilliant dimension. It's no doubt a future classic for this domaine.

CHÂTEAUNEUF-DU-PAPE 2004
Red | 2011 up to 2020   92
Long, silky, with spices and licorice. Classically made, nicely round with a firm, tannic structure. An intense, thoroughbred wine that will need years of cellaring to express its great potential.

CHÂTEAUNEUF-DU-PAPE RÉSERVÉE 2005
Red | 2011 up to 2025   96
At its summit, this is a powerful wine with a tight texture yet superb balance and greatly refined flavor. Superb length.

CHÂTEAUNEUF-DU-PAPE RÉSERVÉE 2003
Red | 2011 up to 2020   90
A fat and deep wine with rich and ripe tannins, this is powerful on the palate, a bit drier than the 2001.

CHÂTEAUNEUF-DU-PAPE RÉSERVÉE 2001
Red | 2011 up to 2025   95
Ultra-dense with great extract, this wine is still monolithic, with great depth and a very classy intensity. Here, too, expect great cellar potential.

CHÂTEAUNEUF-DU-PAPE RÉSERVÉE 1999
Red | 2011 up to 2025   92
Fresher than the 1998, with lots of sap, this is a deep and classy wine, persistent with delicate spice notes. It has lots of character, and great potential for cellaring.

CHÂTEAUNEUF-DU-PAPE RÉSERVÉE 1998
Red | 2011 up to 2025   95
Deeply colored and still very young, this has a superbly expressive bouquet of olives, spices, and stone fruits. It has outstanding intensity on the palate and stands out for its length and density. Great potential, great length.

CÔTES DU RHÔNE CLAVIN 2005
Red | 2011 up to 2013   87
Beautiful intensity. Dense, concentrated, rich, but balanced, with notes of licorice and wild herbs. Could be cellared for a couple of years.

Red: 66.7 acres; grenache 60%. **White:** 1.2 acres.
Annual production: 45,000 bottles

LE VIEUX DONJON
🌿 🌿 🌿 🌿 🌿

9, avenue Saint-Joseph
BP 66
84232 Châteauneuf-du-Pape
Phone 00 33 4 90 83 70 03
Fax 00 33 4 90 83 50 38
vieux-donjon@wanadoo.fr

The cellars here are located in the village of Châteauneuf-du-Pape, but the small, thirty-seven-acre vineyard lies more to the north of the appellation. The wines are sourced from meticulously cultivated vines and are entirely gimmick free: simply vinified, with poised balance, exceptionally good aging potential, and a deep, savory style.

Recently tasted
CHÂTEAUNEUF-DU-PAPE 2007
White | 2011 up to 2013   88

Older vintages
CHÂTEAUNEUF-DU-PAPE 2007
Red | 2011 up to 2014   88
A beautiful wine, pale in color, delicately floral and delicious in character. The finish is supple. This wine could be enjoyed now.

CHÂTEAUNEUF-DU-PAPE 2006
Red | 2011 up to 2022   95
Intensely built, this is a remarkably deep and flavorful wine, quite structured yet maintaining a perfectly tender and velvety finish with good freshness and balance. It's a major success for this vintage.

CHÂTEAUNEUF-DU-PAPE 2004
Red | 2012 up to 2019   90
For the first time, the grapes were fully destemmed. The wine is less impressive than some prior vintages from this domaine, but it is beautifully unctuous, with silky tannins. Time will reveal its finesse.

CHÂTEAUNEUF-DU-PAPE 2003
Red | 2011 up to 2013   92
Profoundly deep color. Dense, with chocolate notes yet no heaviness. Very unctuous, deep, and ample on the palate, with eminently racy tannins. Great freshness in the finish. An elegant wine that will cellar well.

Red: 34.6 acres; grenache noir 75%, mourvèdre 10%, syrah 10%, others 5%. **White:** 2.5 acres; clairette 50%, roussanne 50%. **Annual production:** 50,000 bottles

DOMAINE DU VIEUX TÉLÉGRAPHE

꿈꿈꿈꿈꿈

3, route de Châteauneuf-du-Pape
BP 5
84370 Bédarrides
Phone 00 33 4 90 33 00 31
Fax 00 33 4 90 33 18 47
vignobles@brunier.fr
www.vignoblesbrunier.fr

This splendid property in Bédarrides is one of the leading Châteauneuf-du-Pape holdings, owner of a vast, single-block vineyard that is entirely located on the Crau plateau. Winemaking is classical: partial destemming and tank fermentation, followed by aging first in tanks then in oak vats. The Vieux Télégraphe has been one of the most consistently superior Châteauneufs since the early 1990s, especially the extraordinary 1998. The Brunier family owns two other domains: La Roquette in Châteauneuf and Les Pallières in Gigondas.

Recently tasted
CHÂTEAUNEUF-DU-PAPE 2008
White | 2011 up to 2013   86

CHÂTEAUNEUF-DU-PAPE 2007
Red | 2012 up to 2016   88

Older vintages
CHÂTEAUNEUF-DU-PAPE 2006
White | 2011 up to 2013   90
This wine has vibrancy and freshness: it beautifully expresses delicate notes of lightly acidic tangerines. Very charming.

CHÂTEAUNEUF-DU-PAPE 2006
Red | 2011 up to 2020   88
Beautifully deep in color, with a blackberry-jam bouquet, a generous attack, and solid tannins, this is a fleshy wine, rather firm in the finish at this time.

CHÂTEAUNEUF-DU-PAPE 2005
Red | 2011 up to 2025   92
Deeply colored and voluminous, this has a fresh bouquet of red berries. Fat and long, it is still young.

CHÂTEAUNEUF-DU-PAPE 2004
White | 2011 up to 2013   87
Pale, with surprising notes of dried apricots and hazelnuts. Ample on the palate.

CHÂTEAUNEUF-DU-PAPE 2004
Red | 2011 up to 2020   92
Rather rich color. Nose of chocolate. A wine of beautiful substance, fat and deep. Its velvety texture gives it class.

CHÂTEAUNEUF-DU-PAPE 2003
Red | 2011 up to 2020   93
A beautifully colored wine with aromas of stone fruit and olives. The palate is very taut, with length, distinction, and allure. A wine of great character; a svelte thoroughbred. Beautifully done.

Red: 160.6 acres; cinsault 4%, grenache noir 66%, mourvèdre 15%, syrah 15%. White: 12.4 acres; bourboulenc 16%, clairette 34%, grenache blanc 34%, roussanne 16%. Annual production: 280,000 bottles

DOMAINE VIRET

Quartier les escoulenches
26110 Saint-Maurice-sur-Eygues
Phone 00 33 4 75 27 62 77
Fax 00 33 4 75 27 62 31
domaineviret@domaine-viret.com
www.domaine-viret.com

The Viret family proudly describe their wines as produced in accordance with the principles of "cosmoculture." Loosely translated as "cosmic farming," this is a concept based on organic principles, with particular attention (heré as in other great French wineries) to the role of magnetic forces and the interaction between cosmic and telluric influences. This has led, among other things, to the building of a fantastic cathedral-like winery. The wines are terrifically intense and powerfully built on a solid core of tannins. They will reward patient cellaring—preferably in cool conditions since they contain hardly any sulfur.

Recently tasted

CÔTES DU RHÔNE LA COUDÉE D'OR 2008
White | 2011 up to 2013   **89**

CÔTES DU RHÔNE-VILLAGES SAINT-MAURICE EMERGENCE 2007
Red | 2011 up to 2016   **90**

CÔTES DU RHÔNE-VILLAGES SAINT-MAURICE LES COLONNADES 2006
Red | 2011 up to 2016   **88**

CÔTES DU RHÔNE-VILLAGES SAINT-MAURICE RENAISSANCE 2007
Red | 2011 up to 2016   **91**

VIN DE TABLE AMPHORA ROUGE VII 2007
Red | 2011 up to 2013   **91**

Older vintages

CÔTES DU RHÔNE-VILLAGES SAINT-MAURICE EMERGENCE 2005
Red | 2011 up to 2015   **89**
Deeply colored. The aromas recall blackberry brambles, blackberries, and spice. The palate is powerfully built with slightly drying tannins. The élevage demands more time to be assimilated.

CÔTES DU RHÔNE-VILLAGES SAINT-MAURICE LES COLONNADES 2005
Red | 2011 up to 2015   **90**
Old-vine grenache is the primary ingredient for this cuvée. It is an intense wine, with lots of sap and a deep bouquet of dark berries that will become more complex with age.

CÔTES DU RHÔNE-VILLAGES
SAINT-MAURICE MARÉOTIS 2005
Red | 2011 up to 2015   **89**
A blend of grenache and syrah, this parcel selection benefits from ambitious aging in oak. It is impressive in its tannic density.

CÔTES DU RHÔNE-VILLAGES
SAINT-MAURICE RENAISSANCE 2005
Red | 2011 up to 2013   **88**
This is the domaine's primary cuvée. The wine is intense, powerful, and very rich, with fruit that expresses itself with notes of black olives and blackberries.

VIN DE TABLE AMPHORA ROUGE VI 2006
Red | 2011 up to 2013   **86**
Supple and more focused on the fruit than the domaine's other wines, this good table wine is presented in 16.7-ounce bottles. It can be enjoyed right away.

Red: 68 acres. White: 6.2 acres. Annual production: 100,000 bottles

Bettane & Desseauve
Selections for the Southwest

The Southwest

The wines from this wonderfully diverse and picturesque region have always been closely linked to local culinary traditions. Today we are reaping the benefits of this relationship. Though the wines never became international prize-winners they remain wines to be enjoyed with a meal, and that is exactly what most foodies and wine lovers are looking for. The prices are still within reach, too!

Appellation Overview

The Bergerac Wine Region

• **Bergerac and Côtes de Bergerac:** The basic Bergerac appellations for straightforward, honest, and often very inexpensive red, rosé, and white wines.

• **Pécharmant:** A red wine appellation, centered on the village of Pécharmant, making Merlot-driven wines in a style reminiscent of Bordeaux but without the depth. The appellation is in need of a star producer, though, in order to drive quality and awareness.

• **Montravel:** The appellation traditionally reserved for white Bergerac wines. A few ambitious producers ferment their wines in wood, in the manner of modern-style white Bordeaux. Following a change in the rules in 2001, red wine may also be labeled Montravel.

• **Monbazillac, Côtes de Bergerac Moelleux, Haut-Montravel, and Saussignac:** The appellations for the sweet white wines of Bergerac. Performance is very uneven, but some of these wines are real gems and still very affordable—a fine demonstration of the benefits of AOC standards.

The Borders of Aquitaine

• **Côtes de Duras, Buzet, and Côtes du Marmandais:** Vineyards neighboring the Bordeaux region, planted with a similar mix of red and white varietals. The wines offer good value for the money and are well represented by two high-performance cooperative wineries.

The Haut Pays (Fronton, Gaillac, Cahors)

• **Côtes du Frontonnais:** Vineyards near Toulouse, making simple but honest fruit-forward reds.

• **Gaillac:** Not an easy appellation to characterize due to the sheer number of varietals approved for both white and red wine production. The white wines seem the more interesting of the two.

• **Cahors:** A region long renowned for its red wines. Classically made Cahors is a dense wine, predominantly based on the cot grape (also known as malbec), that can be quite rough around the edges but smoothes out nicely with age. The quality of the wines has improved over the past two or three years.

Pyrenees Appellations

• **Madiran:** A red wine appellation, making deeply colored, robust, and tannic wines. A new generation of young winemakers is now producing wines that are more accessible and less rustic than those of their predecessors.

• **Pacherenc du Vic-Bilh:** The appellation for white Madiran wines, dry and sweet alike. The sweet wines lack the depth and class of a Jurançon, but the best of them are certainly worth a look.

• **Côtes de Saint-Mont:** An AOC mainly represented by an exceptional wine cooperative, making simple, well-balanced, and affordable red, rosé, and white wines.

• **Jurançon:** Very classy dry and sweet wines. Both are remarkably crisp and lively and the sweet wines age magnificently.

• **Irouléguy, Tursan:** Two small appellations in the Basque Country (Irouléguy) and the Landes (Tursan), well represented by a handful of ambitious producers.

Southwest Vineyards

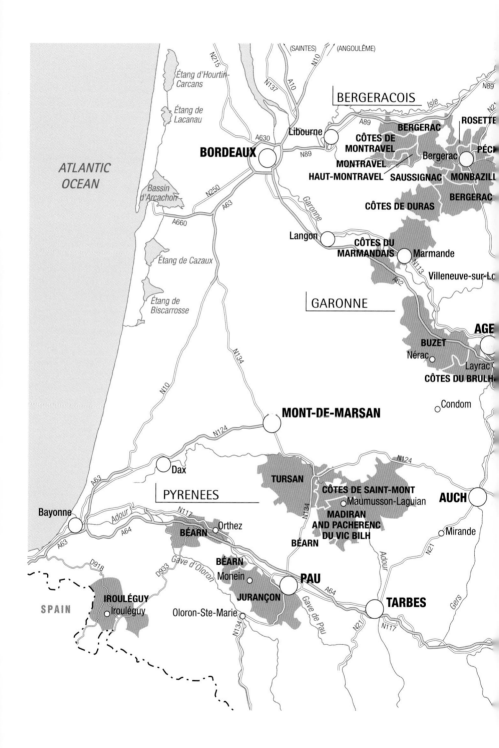

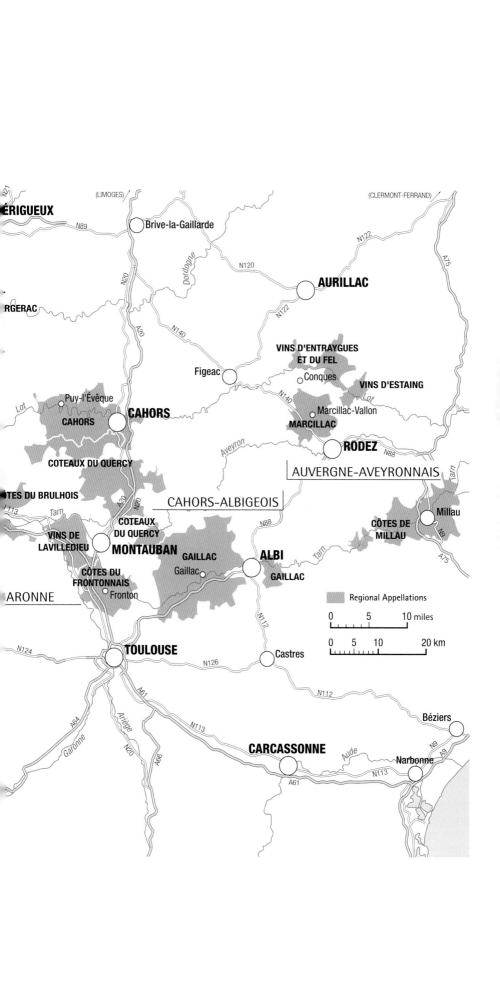

PÉRIGUEUX

(LIMOGES)

(CLERMONT-FERRAND)

N21

N89

Brive-la-Gaillarde

Dordogne

N120

N122

N122

A75

AURILLAC

N140

RGERAC

A20

N140

VINS D'ENTRAYGUES
ET DU FEL

Figeac

Conques

VINS D'ESTAING

Lot

Lot

Puy-l'Évêque

N140

Marcillac-Vallon

CAHORS

CAHORS

MARCILLAC

COTEAUX DU QUERCY

Aveyron

RODEZ

N88

AUVERGNE-AVEYRONNAIS

TES DU BRULHOIS

CAHORS-ALBIGEOIS

Tarn

113

A20

N20

COTEAUX
DU QUERCY

N88

CÔTES DE
MILLAU

Millau

A75

N9

Tarn

VINS DE
LAVILLEDIEU

MONTAUBAN

GAILLAC

ALBI

GAILLAC

Gaillac

GAILLAC

CÔTES DU
FRONTONNAIS

Fronton

ARONNE

N124

TOULOUSE

N126

Castres

N112

Regional Appellations

0   5   10 miles

0   5   10   20 km

A61

N112

Béziers

A64

Ariège

N20

A66

N113

Garonne

CARCASSONNE

Aude

N9

A9

Narbonne

A61

N113

DOMAINE ARRETXEA

Maison Arretxea
64220 Irouléguy
Phone 00 33 5 59 37 33 67
Fax 00 33 5 59 37 33 67
arretxea@free.fr

This exemplary estate in Irouléguy owns some exceptionally steep vineyards that are cultivated in accordance with strict ethical standards. Its red and white wines alike are deliciously complete, with that natural but perfectly controlled expression of powerful terroirs. These are wines made in the best Pays Basque tradition.

IROULEGUY 2007
Rosé I Drink now   86
Made in part with tannat and cabernet franc, by maceration, this deeply colored aperitif rosé will be able to hold its own throughout the meal.

IROULEGUY ARRETXEA ROUGE TRADITION 2007
Red I 2011 up to 2014   86
With dark, appetizing fruit, this wine has a texture and body carried by palpable tannins. They are sure to soften in the future.

IROULEGUY ARRETXEA ROUGE TRADITION 2005
Red I 2011 up to 2013   86
Precise, supple, lively, natural, and easy-going, not too big.

IROULEGUY HAITZA 2007
Red I 2011 up to 2014   89
The delicious fruitiness of this cuvée is held up by extremely light tannins.

IROULEGUY HAITZA 2006
Red I 2011 up to 2013   89
Lightly marked by black currants, spicy and powerful, this is ready to drink now for its fruit.

IROULEGUY HEGOXURI 2007
White I 2011 up to 2015   89
Yellow fruits, peach. Behind the delicate bouquet comes a lightly saline finish.

IROULEGUY HEGOXURI 2005
White I 2011 up to 2020   94
A brilliant green-gold, this is very complex and refined, with a refreshing acidity and a very beautiful purity.

Red: 16.1 acres; cabernet franc 25%, cabernet sauvignon 25%, tannat 50%. White: 4.9 acres; gros manseng 55%, petit courbu 10%, petit manseng 35%. Annual production: 37,500 bottles

CHÂTEAU D'AYDIE

64330 Aydie
Phone 00 33 5 59 04 08 00
Fax 00 33 5 59 04 08 08
contact@famillelaplace.com
www.famillelaplace.com

The Laplace family makes classic Madiran wines with above-average finesse thanks to just the right proportion of cabernet and a vinification process that avoids over-extraction. Many of the other offerings from this estate (red and white alike) are rather less remarkable though all are carefully crafted. The 2006 is sure to please despite its difficult vintage, thanks to a style that perfectly captures the terroir.

Recently tasted
MADIRAN 2006
Red I 2011 up to 2013   85

Older vintages
MADIRAN 2005
Red I 2011 up to 2013   84
A wine with more suppleness than body, this is a bit monotone aromatically but has no obvious flaws. It is, however, not a great expression of the terroir.

MADIRAN CHÂTEAU D'AYDIE PRESTIGE 2005
Red I 2011 up to 2025   88
Deeply colored, a little oaky. Made with very ripe fruit, this wine is beautifully dressed, with its wood notes well integrated into the tender texture. Commercial. Good work, but slightly lacking in energy.

MADIRAN ODÉ D'AYDIE 2005
Red I 2011 up to 2015   90
There is a lot of delicacy and textural elegance in this subtle Madiran. It is classic, long, superbly vinified and aged, but at the opposite end of the style spectrum from the flamboyant Montus.

PACHERENC DU VIC BILH 2007
Sweet White I 2011 up to 2017   90
A great richness of citrus in the primary aromas. Long in the mouth. Remarkably vinified. Astonishing.

VIN DE TABLE MAYDIE TANNAT VINTAGE 2006
Sweet Red I 2011 up to 2018   91
An astonishing attempt to vinify tannat as a Vin Doux Naturel (fortified wine). The result is remarkably muted, long, and complex. On level with the most successful efforts of the Roussillon, and certainly an example to follow.

Red: 111.2 acres; cabernet franc 20%, cabernet sauvignon 20%, tannat 60%. White: 24.7 acres; arrufiac 20%, courbu 10%, gros manseng 30%, manseng 40%. Annual production: 600,000 bottles

DOMAINE BELLAUC

Chemin de Las Bordes
64360 Monein
Phone 00 33 9 75 97 34 56
Fax 00 33 5 59 21 27 17
domaine@bellauc.com
www.bellauc.com

This tiny and very young artisan winery has holdings in the celebrated Clos Cancaillaü. Its wines proved a real revelation in our last tastings: uncompromising, with precise expression of terroir and enormous potential! The Cuvée Marie Blanque was particularly irresistible. A talented "new" producer who deserves to go far.

Recently tasted
JURANÇON 2007
White I 2011 up to 2015   **89**

Older vintages
JURANÇON 2006
White I 2011 up to 2016   **90**
This has a bouquet as subtle as that of the dry wine, but with delicate truffled notes that don't in any way dominate the nuanced candied fruit or citrus. It is pure, elegant, a wine that for once deserves the term "authentic."

JURANÇON BELLAUC 2005
Sweet White I 2011 up to 2025   **93**
A clear gold. Remarkable oak. Long, complex, well aged, not heavy, somewhat jammy, with a great future.

JURANÇON SEC MARIE BLANQUE 2006
White I 2011 up to 2014   **89**
The many subtle nuances of the bouquet are borne from grapes pressed to perfection. Don't serve it too cold. This is a wine that could be listened to, its music so well written, rather akin to notes from a piano.

JURANÇON SEC MARIE BLANQUE 2005
White I 2011 up to 2025   **88**
Pale, with light scents of petrol, this is complex, rich, and acidic, with fruit on the second level. Tannic, dense, complete enough.

White: 4.9 acres; petit manseng 100%. Annual production: 2,000 bottles

DOMAINE BELMONT

Le Gagnoulat
46250 Goujounac
Phone 00 33 5 65 36 68 51
Fax 00 33 5 65 36 60 59
belmont@domainebelmont.com

This domaine is one of Cahors' latest greatest discoveries. Because it just happens to fall outside the appellation area, its owner, Christian Belmont, a celebrated Cahors architect with a passion for vines and wine, can plant whatever grapes he chooses. With shrewd advice from Claude Bourguignon, Belmont picked chardonnay for white wines and cabernet franc and syrah for the reds, carefully selecting only the finest clones (the syrah comes from chez Chave!). Viticulture embraces organic principles and the grapes are picked at the peak of ripeness. Belmont's passionate commitment to his superb terroirs has had immediate results. The white wine is by far the best for miles around while the reds possess a finesse and quality of fruit that should make other Cahors producers a bit thoughtful! Ask to sample the small, experimental pure cabernet franc cuvée and you will see why!

Recently tasted
VIN DE PAYS DU LOT chardonnay 2007
White I 2011 up to 2013   **92**

VIN DE PAYS DU LOT syrah-cabernet franc 2007
Red I 2012 up to 2017   **87**

Older vintages
VIN DE PAYS DU LOT chardonnay 2006
White I 2011 up to 2014   **92**
With an absolutely remarkable purity and frankness in its bouquet, this wine could easily compete for the trophy for the best French Vin de Pays chardonnay. From one vintage to another, this wine gets better thanks to the work in the vineyards.

VIN DE PAYS DU LOT syrah-cabernet franc 2006
Red I 2011 up to 2016   **88**
With its lively color, precise and frank aromas of dark fruit, good tannins, and full body, free of heaviness, this demonstrates a remarkable marriage of grape varieties. The vines are still young, but a Grand Cru is quietly gathering its forces.

VIN DE PAYS DU LOT syrah-cabernet franc 2005
Red I 2011 up to 2017   **88**
An intense color, with a bouquet of small red berries. A complete body with very elegant tannins. Unusual and far superior in its finesse than most Cahors.

DOMAINE BERTHOUMIEU

Dutour
32400 Viella
Phone 00 33 5 62 69 74 05
Fax 00 33 5 62 69 80 64
barre.didier@wanadoo.fr
www.domaine-berthoumieu.com

Didier Barré is one of the most experienced and talented winemakers in all of Southwest France. His wines have that combination of fullness and finesse rarely seen in a Madiran. The Charles de Batz cuvée is a very powerful red sourced from beautifully manicured, premium parcels that produce a wine of terrific purity but without those disturbing animal notes that spoil so many local wines. The recent Pacherencs are stunners, our anxious winemaker having finally come to terms with overripe white grapes!

Recently tasted
MADIRAN CUVÉE CHARLES DE BATZ 2007
Red I 2011 up to 2013   88

MADIRAN HAUTE TRADITION 2007
Red I 2013 up to 2019   90

Older vintages
MADIRAN CUVÉE CHARLES DE BATZ 2006
Red I 2011 up to 2018   89
A bit more tobacco and mocha in the bouquet than in the Haute Tradition. Its time in barrel has tightened its texture and tannins. Well made, elegant, clean and precise, more intellectual than sensual.

MADIRAN HAUTE TRADITION 2006
Red I 2011 up to 2016   88
Beautiful color, with a rather pure and fruity bouquet. Clean. Supple and fleshy, adroitly elegant tannins.

PACHERENC DU VIC BILH SEC 2007
White I 2011 up to 2015   90
An opulent nose. Harvested riper than many other dry wines of this type. Long and complex, this is a remarkable expression of the merit of local grape varieties. A friendly but serious rival to the great Bergeracs.

Red: 56.8 acres; cabernet 25%, fer servadou 5%, tannat 70%. White: 7.4 acres; courbu 10%, gros manseng 25%, petit manseng 65%. Annual production: 180,000 bottles

DOMAINE BORDENAVE

Quartier Ucha
64360 Monein
Phone 00 33 5 59 21 34 83
Fax 00 33 5 59 21 37 32
contact@domaine-bordenave.com
www.domaine-bordenave.com

Gisèle Bordenave has taken her family estate to a high level of quality, thanks as much to the excellence and consistency of her wines as to the beautifully renovated tasting room where guests receive a real lesson in local viticulture. As so often in the Jurançon, the sweet wines do remain preferable to the dry ones. The 2005 vintage is beyond reproach.

Recently tasted
JURANÇON CUVÉE DES DAMES 2007
Sweet White I 2011 up to 2019   90

Older vintages
JURANÇON CUVÉE DES DAMES 2006
Sweet White I 2011 up to 2013   88
A very balanced dessert wine, very fruity but without notes of truffles. With its flavorful and significant sweetness, it will become far more complex over time.

JURANÇON CUVÉE SAVIN 2004
Sweet White I 2011 up to 2024   90
Very golden, a note of mint, a very typical 2004. The sweetness is a bit flabby, lacking style but not richness. Flavors of lemon verbena and lemongrass.

JURANÇON HARMONIE 2006
Sweet White I 2011 up to 2013   87
A dessert wine deserving of its name. Not too rich in sweetness, but already a touch marked by the raisining of the grapes. Gracefully vinified.

JURANÇON LES COPAINS D'ABORD 2006
Sweet White I 2011 up to 2014   86
Golden in color, this is a very fluid wine, smooth and easy to drink, and, in tune with its name, friendly. Very approachable and a pleasure to recommend!

JURANÇON SEC SOUVENIRS D'ENFANCE 2007
White I 2011 up to 2013   87
A pale color, quite lemony, with strong notes of carbon accenting the flirty side of the bouquet. A modern vinification has preserved all the characteristics of these varieties, which comes across with very pleasing tropical notes that will please many.

White: 29.7 acres; gros manseng 55%, petit manseng 45%. Annual production: 55,000 bottles

DOMAINE BRANA

3 bis, avenue du Jaï-Alaï
64220 Saint-Jean-Pied-de-Port
Phone 00 33 5 59 37 00 44
Fax 00 33 5 59 37 14 28
brana.Étienne@wanadoo.fr
www.brana.fr

Jean, a fourth-generation Brana, planted this Irouléguy vineyard in 1985 as a complement to the family's négociant business. The soils are a mixture of sandstone, clay, and limestone, and the winemaking facilities are ultramodern. Cabernet franc, known here as axeria, receives particular attention, being mainly barrel-aged for long periods. The Branas also purchase grapes from outside suppliers; one of their wine-growing partners is Basque-born Jean-Claude Berrouet, winemaker at Pétrus. The Branas operate Berrouet's few acres in Irouléguy, vinifying and marketing these wines under the label Domaine Herri-Mina (which means "homesickness" for the Basque country).

Recently tasted
IROULÉGUY 2007
Red | 2011 up to 2013   89

IROULÉGUY BRANA 2008
White | 2011 up to 2013   92

Older vintages
IROULÉGUY 2006
Red | 2011 up to 2015   90
This has smoky notes of ashes and tobacco. The tannins are well rounded, encouraging a bit of patience for this wine to mature.

IROULÉGUY 2005
Red | 2011 up to 2013   89
Predominantly cabernet franc, with tannat and cabernet sauvignon, this is powerful and dense, a full-bodied wine with depth, good balance, and no astringency.

IROULÉGUY AXERIA 2006
Red | 2011 up to 2013   89
The delicate anise in the bouquet heralds the beautiful volume on the palate. Refined and classic, this is a model cabernet franc.

IROULÉGUY AXERIA 2005
Red | 2011 up to 2013   87
Fruit forward, completely free of astringency and charming in its approachability. Long and full, it is creamy, an unusual yet successful style for a cabernet franc.

IROULÉGUY BRANA 2006
White | 2011 up to 2013   92
A blend of gros and petit manseng with a bit of petit courbu, this is harmonious, with a powerful bouquet. It finishes with a superb sweetness, yet it is perfectly dry.

IROULÉGUY DOMAINE HERRI MINA 2005
White | 2011 up to 2013   88
Based on gros manseng, this offers flavors of pineapple, peach, apricot, spice, and honey. It is a gastronomic white wine, perfect for serving with food. With this cuvée, Jean-Claude Berrouet sought to produce a wine that reflects its terroir, with a minimum of human intervention.

IROULÉGUY DOMAINE HERRI MINA 2005
Red | 2011 up to 2015   88
This is impressively powerful yet still highly drinkable, made from a harvest of only 127 gallons per acre (12 hectoliters per hectare). The mineral notes in the finish build into a superb finale, long, silky, and dense.

IROULÉGUY HARRI GORI 2005
Red | 2011 up to 2013   86
A wine filled with fruit, unctuous and fleshy. With a creamy finish, it is a pleasure-giving wine.

Red: 37.8 acres; cabernet franc 55%, cabernet sauvignon 10%, tannat 35%. White: 19 acres; courbu 40%, gros manseng 45%, petit manseng 15%.
Annual production: 50,000 bottles

DOMAINE BRU-BACHÉ

Rue Barada
64360 Monein
Phone 00 33 5 59 21 36 34
Fax 00 33 5 59 21 32 67
domaine.bru-bache@orange.fr

Claude Loustalot may not be as outgoing as his uncle, the celebrated Georges Bru-Baché, but he is proving a worthy successor: his wines are highly expressive of their fruit and terroir, especially the richer cuvées, Éminence and Quintessence. The dry wines, though, are less consistent. The 2005 edition of the Éminence is flawed by obvious volatile acidity and is best avoided. The other 2005s fared somewhat better.

Jurançon Les Casterasses 2004
Sweet White | 2011 up to 2020   **91**
Golden, toasty, rich and complex, very Jurançon. Refined and energetic in its style, very rich in extract.

Jurançon Quintessence 2005
Sweet White | 2011 up to 2015   **85**
A strong acidity, with a slight bitterness. A tasty wine with precise fruit, a bit less complete than expected.

Jurançon Quintessence 2004
Sweet White | 2011 up to 2019   **90**
Golden, a bit bitter, medicinal. Less pure than could be desired at this stage.

Jurançon Sec Les Casterasses 2005
White | 2011 up to 2013   **84**
Very dry with a strong presence of bitterness. Not disagreeable, but this producer is clearly not at ease with this type of wine.

White: 24.7 acres; gros manseng 20%, petit courbu 5%, petit manseng 75%. **Annual production:** 40,000 bottles

DOMAINE CAUHAPÉ

Quartier Castet
64360 Monein
Phone 00 33 5 59 21 33 02
Fax 00 33 5 59 21 41 82
contact@cauhape.com
www.cauhape.com

This is by far the largest private estate in the Jurançon area, and the brand most widely purchased by leading restaurateurs and luxury wine merchants. Henri Ramonteu has perfected a very restricted offering of richly sweet wines with spectacular aromas and fascinating length, while also producing large-volume dry wines that are no doubt less characteristic but of consistent quality nonetheless. Their exotic aromas are very skillfully developed and their formidable acidity is beautifully kept in check.

Recently tasted
Jurançon Noblesse du temps 2007
Sweet White | 2011 up to 2019   **93**

Jurançon Sec Chant des vignes 2008
White | 2011 up to 2013   **88**

Jurançon Sec La Canopée 2007
White | 2011 up to 2015   **91**

Older vintages
Jurançon Noblesse du temps 2005
Sweet White | 2011 up to 2015   **89**
This has a strong acidity matched by an equal amount of bitterness. It has more body and texture than the Symphonie de Novembre and a beautiful sweetness, but less complexity than other vintages.

Jurançon Sec La Canopée 2006
White | 2011 up to 2014   **87**
Brilliantly gold and green, with a precise and affirmed bouquet of hazelnut. Well aged, this is a firm wine, unusual, balanced, and one of the best of its genre.

Jurançon Sec La Canopée 2005
White | 2011 up to 2015   **92**
Golden green, luminous. Sumptuous, a noble bouquet, grapefruit. A grand musical suite in the mouth.

Jurançon Sec Sève d'Automne 2006
White | 2011 up to 2015   **89**
This has green highlights similar to the Canopée, but far more unusual and harmonious scents of grapefruit and very ripe grapes. With well-integrated wood, it is also denser, more flavorful, and more harmonious. The pinnacle of a dry Jurançon.

White: 103.8 acres; gros manseng 40%, petit manseng 60%. **Annual production:** 260,000 bottles

CAUSSE MARINES

Le Causse
81140 Vieux
Phone 00 33 5 63 33 98 30
Fax 00 33 5 63 33 96 23
causse-marines@infonie.fr
www. causse-marines.com

Patrice Lescarret is an exceptional wine-grower, and it shows in his extraordinary wines—so extraordinary, in fact, that they regularly fall outside the rules of the AOC and are relegated to the category of table wine. All of them testify to an integral approach that aims for consistency and intelligence across the board. Viticulture is of course organic and well on the way to becoming biodynamic; vinification uses only indigenous yeasts; even marketing reflects the same standards. The entire range is highly recommended, from the sparkling Préambulles to the "classical" Gaillacs (famously including the Zacmau and Rasdu, backwards-slang for Mauzac and Duras) and especially the Gaillacs Doux (Grain de Folie Douce, Délire d'Automne, and Folie Pure), not forgetting the stylish, sherry-like vin de voile, called Mystère. Prices can be steep but worth it, considering Lescarret's relentless commitment to quality and his tiny yields.

Recently tasted

VIN DE TABLE DENCON 2007
White sparkling | 2011 up to 2015   88

VIN DE TABLE PRÉAMBULLES 2008
Brut White sparkling | 2011 up to 2013   88

VIN DE TABLE ZACMAU 2007
White | 2011 up to 2014   88

Older vintages

GAILLAC GRAIN DE FOLIE DOUCE 2006
Sweet White | 2011 up to 2014   88
A pleasant aromatic palette (spice cake, honey, apples); a modest sweetness. Well balanced, fresh, and pure.

GAILLAC GRAIN DE FOLIE DOUCE 2005
Sweet White | 2011 up to 2013   89
A complex and refined bouquet. Notes of cooked apples, tea, flowers, and honey. Smooth on the palate, refined, with a beautiful richness. All its components are balanced by a fresh finish. A very beautiful, sweet Gaillac. Very pure.

GAILLAC LE CAUSSE 2004
Red | Drink now   87
A ripe, frank and open bouquet. Beautiful red fruits and sweet spices. The palate is ripe, the tannins tender. An honest wine, with beautiful roundness.

GAILLAC LES GREILLES 2006
White | 2011 up to 2014   86
Good fruit (citrus), round and ripe. On the palate it is rich and expressive, balanced by a lovely aromatic freshness in the finish.

GAILLAC LES GREILLES 2005
White | 2011 up to 2013   88
An expressive and open bouquet, with notes of orange zest. Very fruity. The sensation on the palate is pure and straightforward, with beautiful fruit flavors (always citrus). Good length. Less rich and less long than the Zacmau, this is still a very beautiful introductory wine.

GAILLAC PEYROUZELLES 2006
Red | 2011 up to 2013   88
A concentrated bouquet, strong in mineral notes (smoke, graphite). Unusual but very interesting! The palate is ripe, the tannins pleasurable, the beautiful, peppery juice well concentrated. Of medium length, since it also includes juice from young vines. The price is a steal!

MOÛT DE RAISIN PARTIELLEMENT FERMENTÉ
DÉLIRE D'AUTOMNE 2003
Sweet White | 2011 up to 2013   95
Extraordinary! The sensation in the mouth is that of a concentrated cocoa liqueur. The length is magnificent. This is unclassifiable but superb! Delicious, long and, most of all, fresh and balanced. At last, a sweet white wine that can be enjoyed with a chocolate dessert (milk chocolate!). It finishes on a light rancio note.

MOÛT DE RAISIN PARTIELLEMENT FERMENTÉ
FOLIE PURE 1999
Sweet White | 2011 up to 2013   97
Amber-hued. The bouquet is concentrated. The palate is broad: spices, cinnamon, yellow and white fruit, honey. In the mouth the sensation is pure syrup. But the finish stays fresh, with a note of salted butter caramels. To be drunk *as* dessert rather than *with*.

VIN DE TABLE 7 SOURIS 2007
Red | 2011 up to 2015   86
A lean syrah, but straightforward and honest on the attack, with a good freshness. Tasty.

VIN DE TABLE DENCON 2006
White sparkling | 2011 up to 2013   87
This is ripe and powerful on the nose, with flavorful floral and citrus (orange) notes, and rich and pleasing in the mouth, but it does not have the tension and depth of the Zacmau.

VIN DE TABLE MYSTÈRE 1996

White | 2011 up to 2013   **88**

The bouquet reveals a wine aged sous voile: curry, cheese rind. The sensation in the mouth is rich, with beautiful volume. The finish stays fresh and concentrated. Yet again a beautiful exercise in style. Great purity. The finish ends on beautiful fruit notes.

VIN DE TABLE PRÉAMBULLES 2006

Brut White sparkling | 2011 up to 2013   **86**

Cloudy. Scents of apples. Complex and tasty. Medium long but rich in flavor. An unusual wine, to be drunk before dinner.

VIN DE TABLE PRÉAMBULLES 2005

Brut White sparkling | 2011 up to 2013   **89**

The color is cloudy. This is a rich wine that virtually exhales Mauzac. It's not very varied in its bouquet (dominated by apples and white fruit), but it comes across as natural. There are fermented nuances on the palate. Delicious, an ideal wine before dinner.

VIN DE TABLE RASDU 2006

Red | 2011 up to 2014   **86**

Concentrated, fleshy, with notes of spices and meat, this is a generous and ripe wine with round tannins. Delectable. A finish of spices and red fruit.

VIN DE TABLE RASDU 2004

Red | 2011 up to 2013   **88**

A well-concentrated wine, this has straightforward aromas of meat and red fruits. The palate is suave with a beautiful expression of minerality in the finish. It merits being decanted a half-hour before drinking.

VIN DE TABLE ZACMAU 2005

White | 2011 up to 2015   **87**

A refined bouquet, with notes of apple pastries. It feels rich in the mouth, with a mineral edge that brings tension and a touch of bitterness to the finish. Wait a bit.

VIN DE TABLE ZACMAU 2004

White | 2011 up to 2013   **90**

Very beautiful floral and fruit notes: delicate apples (apple tart), tea. The sensation on the palate is rich, with a delightful fattiness. Long, fat, and complex, this wine is superb. Very great purity. Mineral finish.

Red: 13.6 acres. White: 17.3 acres. Annual production: 50,000 bottles

CHÂTEAU DU CÈDRE

Bru
46700 Vire-sur-Lot
Phone 00 33 5 65 36 53 87
Fax 00 33 5 65 24 64 36
châteauducedre@wanadoo.fr
www.châteauducedre.com

Regional viticulture may be in the doldrums but this estate continues to set an example for the entire appellation by its painstaking viticulture and vinification. Pascal Verhaegue is an expert at picking perfectly ripe malbec grapes and coaxing out that spicy, taut, and subtle cachet typical of his magnificent terroirs. The overextraction seen in the past is now no more than a bad memory. The Cuvée Grand Cru is a bit saturated when young, but it won't be after another three to five years' aging.

Recently tasted

CAHORS 2007

Red | 2011 up to 2015   **86**

CAHORS 2006

Red | 2012 up to 2016   **90**

Older vintages

CAHORS CHÂTEAU DU CÈDRE 2006

Red | 2011 up to 2016   **88**

With strong scents of prunes, this wine shows better wood integration than past examples. It is graced with a generous texture—an excellent beginning!

CAHORS CHÂTEAU DU CÈDRE 2005

Red | 2011 up to 2025   **89**

This has a lot of grace and clarity in the bouquet, with notes of truffles and cedar. The tannins are well managed, with very present wood. A wine perfectly matched to the flesh and texture of duck!

CAHORS GC 2006

Red | 2011 up to 2018   **90**

This wine has a tighter texture than that of the prestige cuvée, with an inevitably strong reduction due to its bottle aging. The tannins are quite present for the moment, but not excessive. A wine to cellar.

CAHORS LE CÈDRE 2004

Red | 2011 up to 2020   **90**

The wood is still obvious, but this is full of life, an opulent wine with licorice tannins, long, complex, and generous. Great future.

Red: 64.2 acres: malbec 90%, merlot 5%, tannat 5%. White: 2.5 acres; viognier 100%. Annual production: 120,000 bottles

CHÂTEAU DE CHAMBERT

Les Hauts Coteaux
46700 Floressas
Phone 00 33 5 65 31 95 75
Fax 00 33 5 65 31 93 56
info@chambert.com
www.chambert.com

With well-placed vineyards planted on the sparse limestone terroirs of the Causse, Chambert was one of the leaders of the appellation in the early 1980s. It fell into a bit of a rut after that time, but with the arrival of Stéphane Derénoncourt and his team, Chambert is once again a benchmark in the region! The holdings are vast (nearly 150 acres) and homogeneous. The prestige bottling Orphée was excellent in 2005, but with the 2006 they have changed the style, aiming at more refined texture and tannins.

Recently tasted
CAHORS CHAMBERT GRAND VIN 2007
Red | 2012 up to 2017   **86**

Older vintages
CAHORS 2006
Red | 2011 up to 2016   **89**
It's not the most deeply colored wine of the appellation, but its spicy aromas, with their note of violet, are among the most refined, just like its texture. A lovely wine, with rare elegance for this region.

CAHORS ORPHÉE 2005
Red | 2011 up to 2017   **88**
One of the most successful wines of the year, from old vines (thirty-five years) planted at the center of the property, and 50 percent aged in new wood. It reveals complex, spicy flavors, firm tannins, good presence, and an assured style. It lacks only a touch of grape maturity.

Red: 148.3 acres. Annual production: 250,000 bottles

DOMAINE COSSE MAISONNEUVE

Les Beraudies
46700 Lacapelle-Cabanac
Phone 00 33 6 87 16 68 08
Fax 00 33 5 65 24 22 37
laquets.maisonneuve@gmail.com

Mathieu Cosse and Catherine Maisonneuve share the workload here, Mathieu making the wines while Catherine grows the grapes in accordance with increasingly biodynamic principles. Their prestige Cuvée Les Laquets is a full-bodied, complex, tannic thoroughbred from an incomparable terroir on the Causse and takes its place among the finest of all Cahors wines. The Sid is sourced from younger vines and is particularly striking for its natural fruit. Last we heard, the couple had just acquired extra acres in exceptional terroirs—much to the delight of all Cahors lovers.

CAHORS LES LAQUETS 2006
Red | 2012 up to 2016   **88**
The nose is quite muted, save the slight notes of reduction that mask the fruitiness of the palate. The core of the wine is, without a doubt, one of the richest made in this difficult vintage, the tannins still tightly wound, but the structure is a stark contrast to most of the other lifeless wines of the vintage.

CAHORS LES LAQUETS 2005
Red | 2011 up to 2020   **92**
Intense in color, with great nobility in its aromas, this shows an intimate fusion of wine and wood. Velvety tannins, complex. An extension of a Grand Cru, one of the best-realized expressions of this appellation.

CAHORS LES LAQUETS 2004
Red | 2011 up to 2016   **90**
Great color, rare intensity of extract, masterfully extracted tannins. The unique distinctiveness of the Causse terroirs, to their great advantage and future.

VIN DE TABLE LA FAGE 2006
Red | 2011 up to 2014   **86**
This wine from lesser parcels merits the appellation it bears by its honesty, fullness, and pure gustatory pleasure, rare in Cahors.

Red: 42 acres; malbec 95%, merlot 3%, tannat 2%.
Annual production: 60,000 bottles

CAVE DE CROUSEILLES

64350 Crouseilles
Phone 00 33 5 59 68 10 93
Fax 00 33 5 59 68 14 33
d.degache@crouseilles.com

This pioneering Madiran wine co-op, sur-rounded by its historic vineyards, has not looked back since it was taken over by the Plaimont co-op. The merger lent wings to the Crouseilles winemaking team, who now turn out some exceptional wines at very friendly prices. The red single-vineyard offerings such as the Château d'Arricau-Bordes, Château de Mascaras, and Château de Crouseilles now show all the body and dimension one would expect. But it was the staggering improvement in the Pacherencs (sweet and dessert wines) that impressed us most: fabulously complex and expressive, with an overall standard of quality that vies with Jurançon for top billing in the pantheon of great wines from Southwest France. The 2005 Mascaras Pacherenc du Vic Bilh and Arricau-Bordes Pacherenc du Vic Bilh are truly exceptional.

Recently tasted
PACHERENC DU VIC BILH GRAINS DE GIVRE 2007
Sweet White | 2011 up to 2013   90

PACHERENC DU VIC BILH L'HIVERNAL 2007
Sweet White | 2011 up to 2013   89

Older vintages
BÉARN LES HAUTAINS 2007
Red | 2011 up to 2013   85
Very clean fruit, with classic reductive scents of stainless-steel tank fermentation. Supple, fleshy, ripe. The result of an excellent vinification, and an impeccable wine for the price.

MADIRAN CHÂTEAU DE CROUSEILLES 2005
Red | 2011 up to 2014   88
Well vinified, sufficiently rich yet balanced, precise yet powerful.

MADIRAN CHÂTEAU DE MASCARAS 2005
Red | 2011 up to 2015   88
Simpler, more classic. A lovely Madiran with good tannins. Excellent.

MADIRAN CHÂTEAU LA MOTTE 2005
Red | 2011 up to 2015   88
More classic, tannic, very streamlined, with fruit at the fore. Well made.

MADIRAN FOLIE DE ROI 2005
Red | 2011 up to 2020   93
Lemony, with very lovely wood. Long and entrancingly graceful.

MADIRAN PLÉNITUDE 2005
Red | 2013 up to 2017   87
Well done. Notes of licorice. Long, classic, very subtle, sensual. A pleasing wood presence. Rather aristocratic. To drink soon.

PACHERENC DU VIC BILH
CHÂTEAU DE MASCARAS 2005
Sweet White | 2011 up to 2020   92
Remarkable. Salty, long, and complex. A lively and powerful wine. Bravo!

PACHERENC DU VIC BILH CHÂTEAU LA MOTTE 2005
Sweet White | 2011 up to 2020   92
Pure, unctuous, angelic, and delicate. Long in the mouth. Ravishing, with marvelous balance.

PACHERENC DU VIC BILH GRAINS DE GIVRE 2006
Sweet White | 2011 up to 2017   88
The grapes for this cuvée are richer with more roasted notes than those for the Harmonie cuvée. It is lightly wooded and well balanced, pure, fat, elegant and sweet without being heavy. Remarkable quality for the price.

PACHERENC DU VIC BILH GRAINS DE ROY 2006
Sweet White | 2011 up to 2013   84
A tender wine, pleasant, but with less complexity and structure than the Harmonie cuvée.

PACHERENC DU VIC BILH GRAINS DE ROY 2005
Sweet White | 2011 up to 2015   88
Slightly bitter, complex, well built, long and stylish.

PACHERENC DU VIC BILH HARMONIE 2006
Sweet White | 2011 up to 2016   86
Pale in color with delicate notes of honey, chamomile, and non-woody vanilla, this is a tender wine that would be very pleasant before dinner. A good introduction to sweet wines.

PACHERENC DU VIC BILH HARMONIE 2005
Sweet White | 2011 up to 2015   90
Ultra-classic, complete, tannic, and impeccable.

PACHERENC DU VIC BILH SEC LES OMBRAGES 2007
White | 2011 up to 2013   85
A perfectly dry wine, less a "primeur" than the Motte. It has a discreet but light bouquet of white fruits. Refreshing without being heavy. Precise and well made.

Red: 1,443.2 acres; cabernet franc 23%, cabernet sauvignon 10%, fer servadou 2%, tannat 65%. White: 261.9 acres; arrufiac 10%, gros manseng 20%, petit courbu 10%, petit manseng 60%. Annual production: 3,000,000 bottles

ELIAN DA ROS

47250 Cocumont
Phone 00 33 5 53 20 75 22
Fax 00 33 5 53 94 79 29
e_daros@club-internet.fr

The hilly countryside around Marmande is home to this forty-acre estate in Cocumont. It encompasses three different types of soil: clay-limestone in the Clos Baquey, clay-gravel in Chante Coucou, and clay-silt mixed with iron slag (known locally as crasses de fer) in the Vignoble d'Elian. The vines are biodynamically grown, using principles learned by owner Elian Da Ros in his years as right-hand man at the Domaine Zind-Humbrecht. Vinification follows suit, with the occasional nasty surprise that comes from avoiding sulfur dioxide. Generally speaking, however, the wines show character and clout and measure up to their appellation.

Recently tasted

CÔTES DU MARMANDAIS LE VIN EST UNE FÊTE 2007
Red | 2011 up to 2013   **85**

Older vintages

CÔTES DU MARMANDAIS CHANTE COUCOU 2006
Red | 2011 up to 2013   **88**
The color is deep and impenetrable, nearly black. The nose is still a bit closed. Harmonious on the palate, with good length punctuated by beautiful, silky tannins on the finish.

CÔTES DU MARMANDAIS CLOS BAQUEY 2005
Red | 2011 up to 2013   **91**
Dark in color, with a rather closed bouquet. Beautiful on the palate, well dressed, silky, with freshness and beautiful length. A lovely wine with good potential.

CÔTES DU MARMANDAIS CLOS BAQUEY 2004
Red | 2011 up to 2013   **92**
Full in the mouth, this has good volume, presence, and harmony as well freshness and minerality punctuated by the beautiful tannins on the finish. A clean and precise wine.

CÔTES DU MARMANDAIS VIGNOBLE D'ELIAN 2004
Red | 2011 up to 2013   **88**
Dense in color, nearly black. The bouquet is a bit reduced. This is a massive wine, voluminous in body, with a beautiful tannic structure and delightful spicy notes.

DOMAINE D'ESCAUSSES

La Salamanderie
81150 Sainte-Croix
Phone 00 33 5.63.56.80.52
Fax 00 33 5.63.56.87.62
jean-marc.balaran@wanadoo.fr
www.domainedescausses.com

Winegrower Jean-Marc Balaran is one of the most respected men of this appellation, and so he should be. All of Balaran's wines are magnificently expressive, except for Les Drilles (a bit too supple): reds with soft, fat tannins, sweet wines with stunning fruit and freshness. Price is eminently reasonable for wines of this quality.

GAILLAC LA CROIX PETITE 2006
Red | 2011 up to 2016   **88**
Fat, round tannins. A civilized and modern wine that holds true to the spirit of the Gaillac terroir.

GAILLAC LA VIGNE BLANCHE 2006
Red | 2011 up to 2014   **87**
A bouquet of red fruit and spices. Full body with well-enrobed tannins. Good length.

GAILLAC LA VIGNE MYTHIQUE 2005
Red | 2011 up to 2013   **90**
A very pure and concentrated bouquet, with scents of asphalt and black fruit, rather severe but ripe and intense. The sensation in the mouth is straightforward and very pure, with a well-integrated élevage. It finishes on mineral and saline notes. A delicious wine with firm but nicely enrobed tannins.

GAILLAC LES VENDANGES DORÉES 2006
Sweet White | 2011 up to 2016   **89**
Superb, rich sweetness. Flavorful, very pure.

GAILLAC LES VENDANGES DORÉES 2005
Sweet White | 2011 up to 2013   **88**
An intense bouquet, with beautiful botrytis and jammy notes of pineapple and very ripe yellow fruit, this is a very seductive wine with no heaviness. The sensation in the mouth is pure, with a beautiful, sweet richness. The finish brings freshness along with beautifully roasted fruit. Delicious.

Annual production: 180,000 bottles

DOMAINE ETXEGARAYA

64430 Saint-Étienne-de-Baïgorry
Phone 00 33 5 59 37 23 76
Fax 00 33 5 59 37 23 76
etxegaraya@wanadoo.fr
www.etxegaraya.com

The red wines from this small artisan winery are an exemplary articulation of Marianne and Joseph Hillau's fastidious management: fleshier than your average Irouléguy red, with less of those mouth-puckering tannins. The top bottling is as always the very dependable Lehengoa—now one of the classics of Southwest France!

Recently tasted
IROULÉGUY 2008
Rosé | 2011 up to 2013   85

IROULÉGUY 2007
Red | 2011 up to 2013   86

Older vintages
IROULÉGUY 2007
Rosé | Drink now   84
Tart cherry in color and very full-bodied, this rosé can be served like a red wine with the meal. Barbecued meats would go quite nicely with it.

IROULÉGUY LEHENGOA 2005
Red | 2011 up to 2015   84
Marianne Hillau maintains a high level of quality at her small, artisanal property. Dominated by tannat, the Lehengoa cuvée is built in the classic style of an Irouléguy: solid with staunch power.

IROULÉGUY LEHENGOA 2004
Red | 2011 up to 2015   86
Tannic, a bit untamed, a touch bitter, this lacked refinement in its extraction. Solid.

Red: 18.5 acres; cabernet franc 30%, cabernet sauvignon 20%, tannat 50%. Annual production: 30,000 bottles

LA CAVE D'IROULEGUY

Route de Saint-Jean-Pied-de-Port
64430 Saint-Étienne-de-Baïgorry
Phone 00 33 5 59 37 41 33
Fax 00 33 5 59 37 47 76
contact@cave-irouleguy.com
www.cave-irouleguy.com

This is a medium-size wine co-op (330 acres) but it plays a pivotal role in the local economy of the tiny Irouléguy appellation. Vineyards are held to strict environmental standards, producing red, white, and rosé wines with all the liveliness and aromatic charm of real "mountain" wines. The red Domaine de Mignaberry and Cuvée Omenaldi and the white Xuri d'Ansa can all be bought with confidence, even by non-Basques!

Recently tasted
IROULÉGUY ANDERE D'ANSA 2008
White | 2011 up to 2013   88

IROULÉGUY DOMAINE DE MIGNABERRY 2006
Red | 2011 up to 2013   87

IROULÉGUY GORRI D'ANSA 2007
Red | 2011 up to 2013   86

IROULÉGUY XURI 2008
White | 2011 up to 2013   89

Older vintages
IROULÉGUY ANDERE D'ANSA 2007
White | 2011 up to 2013   88
Pale gold in color, this mineral white has good length and is carried by its acidity, discreet yet present in service of its elegant fruit.

IROULÉGUY AXERIDOY 2007
Rosé | 2011 up to 2009   85
A delicate rosé with a delicious, long finish rich in lovely red fruit.

IROULÉGUY PREMIA 2006
Red | 2011 up to 2013   84
With its fruit and long, clean finish, this simple, harmonious wine is a good example of Basque reds. You could even cellar it a bit to give the tannins time to soften.

IROULÉGUY XURI 2007
White | 2011 up to 2013   90
Impressive right from the start. Xuri is aged in oak barrels. On the nose, noble aromas of peaches prepare the mouth for the wine's great volume, lightly smoky and quite refined, long and pleasing. What a finish!

Red: 303.9 acres; cabernet franc 30%, cabernet sauvignon 15%, tannat 55%. White: 29.7 acres; gros manseng 72%, petit courbu 6%, petit manseng 22%. Annual production: 650,000 bottles

MICHEL ISSALY

Domaine de la Ramaye
Sainte Cécile d'Avès
81600 Gaillac
Phone 00 33 5 63 57 06 64
Fax 00 33 5 63 57 35 34
contact@michelissaly.com
www.michelissaly.com

Michel Issaly is a committed winegrower who was quite ready to make a drastic reduction in the scale of his estate so as to achieve his goals. Today he makes do with just over seven acres of plantings that he looks after lovingly and intelligently, using a combination of organic and biodynamic methods, though his vineyards are not officially certified as either. His approach as a winemaker is defined by his total hands-off policy from the end of fermentation to the following June. The wines spend the winter on their lees, aging in tanks at low temperatures. The finished product is rich, expressive, and deliciously pure on the palate—nothing like typical Gaillac, and so quite likely to fall afoul of some of the stricter aspects of AOC legislation. Michel Issaly now makes all of his wines under his own name, which replaces the former Domaine de la Ramaye label.

Recently tasted

GAILLAC LE SOUS-BOIS DE RAYSSAC 2006
Sweet White | 2011 up to 2016   **94**

VIN DE PAYS DES CÔTES DU TARN
LE GRAND TERTRE 2007
Red | 2011 up to 2013   **88**

VIN DE TABLE LES CAVAILLÈS BAS 2007
White | 2011 up to 2014   **86**

Older vintages

GAILLAC LA COMBE D'AVÈS 2007
Red | 2011 up to 2015   **86**
Rich, tannic structure, ripe. Fruity finish, pleasing.

GAILLAC LA COMBE D'AVÈS 2005
Red | 2011 up to 2015   **88**
Complex and rich on the nose, appetizing. Dark fruit, menthol, spices. Chewy, with good, fat tannins.

GAILLAC LA COMBE D'AVÈS 2003
Red | 2011 up to 2013   **90**
Very open on the nose. Ripe fruit, typical of the vintage, but fresh, not cooked. Well-integrated notes of oak (twenty-eight months in barrels!). A wine that must be decanted. Magnificent flavor, with a texture both refined and delicate. The tannins are fat and well enrobed; the length is fresh and velvety.

GAILLAC LE SOUS-BOIS DE RAYSSAC 2005
Sweet White | 2011 up to 2013   **90**
The nose smells of very ripe apples. In the mouth it is rich, with a lovely sweetness and, most of all, great purity. The finish is lightly caramelized. Overall, it is a wine with superb freshness and magnificent balance—a treat, a dessert in itself.

VIN DE PAYS DES CÔTES DU TARN
LE GRAND TERTRE 2006
Red | 2011 up to 2016   **90**
Concentrated fruit, red and black. Rich on the palate, with well-enrobed tannins and a dense and fresh finish.

VIN DE TABLE LES CAVAILLÈS BAS 2007
White | 2011 up to 2013   **86**
Very floral, pure, with a touch of minerality. Streamlined and taut, this is a wine that will show best when enjoyed with a meal.

Red: 7.2 acres. White: 7.2 acres. Annual production: 18,000 bottles

LES JARDINS DE BABYLONE

Chemin de Cassienla
64290 Aubertin
Phone 00 33 5 59 04 28 15
Fax 00 33 5 59 04 28 15
silex@wanadoo.fr

This winery was set up a few years ago by the late sauvignon blanc master Didier Dagueneau, who pulled out all the stops to achieve his driving purpose: to make the greatest possible sweet wine. His first job was to replant these steep, very difficult terraces with their highly characteristic soils; but his greatest undertaking was the installation of a very expensive, ultramodern mini winery. It gave him a level of wine-making precision that most winegrowers can only dream of. To judge from his first vintages, Didier Dagueneau's plan was a success, he gambled and won—even if there won't be enough to go around!

JURANÇON LES JARDINS DE BABYLONE 2005
Sweet White | 2011 up to 2020   95
A sumptuous accomplishment. The bouquet has an extravagant complexity and richness, blending candied fruit, spice, and the most pure floral honey notes. It's a sweet wine with remarkable richness and a finish that never ends.

White: 6.2 acres; petit manseng 100%.

CLOS LE JONCAL

Le Joncal
24500 Saint-Julien d'Eymet
Phone 00 33 5.53.61.84.73
Fax 00 33 5.53.61.84.73
rolandtatarddujoncal@gmail.com
www.closlejoncal.com

Ex-fighter-pilot Roland Tatard returned to his eighteen-acre family estate in 1995 and has been converting it to organic farming ever since. The wines are deep and lush but with a distinctly mineral quality. Inspired by Luc de Conti, aka the prince of Bergerac, this estate is a stellar example of the revival of the Dordogne wine industry.

Recently tasted
BERGERAC MYSTÈRE DU JONCAL 2006
Red | 2011 up to 2013   85

BERGERAC MYSTÈRE DU JONCAL 2003
Red | 2011 up to 2013   84

BERGERAC SEC 2004
White | 2011 up to 2013   82

CÔTES DE BERGERAC MIRAGE DU JONCAL 2006
Red | 2011 up to 2013   86

Older vintages
BERGERAC LES HAUTS DE FONTETTE 2005
Red | 2011 up to 2013   87
Straightforward, with firm but ripe tannins. An elegant wine, long, fresh, and tasty.

BERGERAC MYSTÈRE DU JONCAL 2005
Red | 2011 up to 2013   88
Ripe and fully expressive, this is a modern wine with dark fruit and sweet spice aromas. Seductive, in an international style.

BERGERAC SEC 2006
White | 2011 up to 2013   83
Powerful and oaky, this rich wine is dominated by its élevage. For those who love a rich oaked style, it is a good choice!

CÔTES DE BERGERAC MIRAGE DU JONCAL 2005
Red | 2011 up to 2013   89
Ripe, with fleshy tannins, this is a rich and powerful wine with true presence. It comes across with more freshness and balance than the Mystère du Joncal.

Annual production: 30,000 bottles

DOMAINE LABRANCHE-LAFFONT

32400 Maumusson-Laguian
Phone 00 33 5 62 69 74 90
Fax 00 33 5 62 69 76 03
labranchelaffont@aol.com

Christine Dupuy has turned this estate into a very respectable performer despite the challenging growing conditions. The wines are fleshy and consistent with just a hint of rusticity. They include the nectar-like Madiran Vieilles Vignes: a velvety gem of a wine from vines more than a hundred years old. Of the Pacherencs, the 2005 Mascaras and Arricau Bordes bottlings are truly exceptional.

Recently tasted
MADIRAN 2007
Red | 2012 up to 2017   **89**

MADIRAN VIEILLES VIGNES 2006
Red | 2011 up to 2016   **91**

Older vintages
MADIRAN 2005
Red | 2011 up to 2017   **89**
Excellent fruit, rich in extract yet balanced. Remarkable grape maturity. A lot of precision and a clean edge in the finish. Beautiful work.

MADIRAN VIEILLES VIGNES 2005
Red | 2012 up to 2019   **90**
A very powerful wine, structured, sculpted by the almost aggressive tannins extracted from the old-vine fruit. Certainly more complete than the normal cuvée, but the harmony of the regular bottling is preferred.

PACHERENC DU VIC BILH SEC 2007
White | 2011 up to 2015   **86**
Intelligently vinified in a modern style, bringing to the fore fruity notes of grapefruit, with strong acidity. Unusual, pure. Very aromatic for this vintage.

Red: 42 acres; cabernet franc 15%, cabernet sauvignon 10%, tannat 75%. White: 7.4 acres; gros manseng 40%, petit manseng 60%. Annual production: 100,000 bottles

CHÂTEAU LAFFITTE-TESTON

32400 Maumusson
Phone 00 33 5 62 69 74 58
Fax 00 33 5 62 69 76 87
info@laffitte-teston.com
www.laffitte-teston.com

Jean-Marc Laffitte has perfected a highly original style of Madiran wine: reds focused on refined tannins and balance, and Pacherencs made in a dry style but from perfectly ripe fruit. Both hit the spot, though the prize has to go to the whites, especially the famous cuvée Éricka that continues to reign supreme over the local wines. Jean-Marc's daughter Éricka is gradually taking the reins, following her father's lead. All of the latest offerings are particularly well balanced for Madiran wines—an area known for its love of excess!

Recently tasted
MADIRAN VIEILLES VIGNES 2007
Red | 2011 up to 2013   **85**

PACHERENC DU VIC BILH SEC ERICKA 2008
White | 2011 up to 2014   **88**

PACHERENC DU VIC BILH SEC ERICKA 2007
White | 2011 up to 2015   **88**

Older vintages
MADIRAN VIEILLES VIGNES 2006
Red | 2011 up to 2016   **86**
An excellent example of the Laffitte style: this has suppleness and a lovely silkiness of texture that is not easy to achieve with Tannat. An honest wine pulling no unnecessary punches, this will only fully reveal itself at the dinner table.

MADIRAN VIEILLES VIGNES 2005
Red | 2011 up to 2015   **86**
A weaker wine with unbalanced wood, cedar notes. Short.

PACHERENC DU VIC BILH SEC ERICKA 2005
White | 2011 up to 2020   **90**
Marvelously unctuous, long and very pleasant. The epitome of a well-made white wine.

Red: 75.4 acres. White: 21 acres. Annual production: 230,000 bottles

DOMAINE LAFFONT

32400 Maumusson
Phone 00 33 5 62 69 75 23
Fax 00 33 5 62 69 80 27
pierre@domainelaffont.fr

Belgian native Pierre Speyer is crazy about "grand vin." This small, 8.6-acre estate in Maumusson is where he persistently attempts the impossible. He doesn't always pull it off, but when he does the result is a wine to rival the masterpieces of the Domaine Brumont: outrageously generous character, fabulous radiance, and long length on the palate. May Hecate and Erigone forever watch over the creator of the cuvées that bear their name.

Recently tasted
MADIRAN ERIGONE 2007
Red | 2013 up to 2017   86

MADIRAN HÉCATE 2007
Red | 2014 up to 2019   88

Older vintages
MADIRAN 666 2006
Red | 2011 up to 2013   92
Once again, a remarkably crafted wine, in a way more classic, less baroque in its form and tastes than Hécate, superbly balanced tannins, long, well rounded; a highly recommended wine!

MADIRAN ERIGONE 2006
Red | 2011 up to 2016   91
A superb aroma of red fruit, the voluptuous texture of perfectly aged tannat, very successful élevage; once again, a master stroke from this uncommon producer.

MADIRAN ERIGONE 2005
Red | 2011 up to 2025   93
Very deep color, close to the pinnacle of what this wine can be, drawn-out licorice notes, complex, velvety.

MADIRAN HÉCATE 2006
Red | 2011 up to 2018   92
A pinnacle of the appellation. Admirably velvety texture, length, class, voluptuous but with tautness in its voluptuousness. Bravo!

Red: 8.6 acres; cabernet franc 22%, tannat 78%. White: 1.2 acres; petit manseng 100%. Annual production: 30,000 bottles

CHÂTEAU LAGRÉZETTE

Domaine de Lagrézette
46140 Caillac
Phone 00 33 5 65 20 07 42
Fax 00 33 5 65 20 06 93
adpsa@lagrezette.fr
www.château-lagrezette.tm.fr

This blue-chip Cahors estate is largely the work of its patron Alain-Dominique Perrin, who has poured a great deal of his own money into creating and maintaining a model winery, within an appellation that is racked with uncertainty and defections. With the help of Michel Rolland, Perrin has revolutionized the taste and texture of Cahors wines by aiming for riper grapes and more luxurious aging. His early-drinking spring bottling preludes the standard Cahors and the two prestige cuvées, Dame Honneur and Le Pigeonnier (the latter only fully integrates its wood after seven to eight years of bottle aging). Château Lagrézette continues to set an example to other producers, growing its grapes and vinifying its wines in accordance with strict practices worthy of the Bordeaux Grands Crus.

Recently tasted
CAHORS DOMAINE DE LAGRÉZETTE 2006
Red | 2012 up to 2016   87

Older vintages
CAHORS 2006
Red | 2011 up to 2014   87
This is most likely the Dame Honneur cuvée, but in our blind tasting, it was not indicated. Strong red and black fruit aromas, a body more fully fleshed out than the average. Velvety tannins, with wood just a bit insistent.

CAHORS LE PIGEONNIER 2005
Red | 2011 up to 2016   88
An ample bouquet, toasted, modern, with notes of mocha brought by the wood. Some will find this wine a bit insistent, but experience shows that it will mellow after five or six years. The grapes for this vintage were riper than usual, and the tannins have been judiciously extracted.

Red: 192.7 acres; cabernet franc 2%, malbec 84%, merlot 11%, syrah 2%, tannat 1%. White: 17.3 acres; chardonnay 34%, viognier 66%. Annual production: 275,000 bottles

CHÂTEAU LAMARTINE

Lamartine
46700 Soturac
Phone 00 33 5 65 36 54 14
Fax 00 33 5 65 24 65 31
château-lamartine@wanadoo.fr
www.cahorslamartine.com

This pristine property sets the pace for the entire Soturac area. Its vineyards are mainly located on the finest terraces in Cahors, producing wines that are somewhat austere when young but develop a lovely finesse in bottle. The Cuvée Particulière tends to show a more pleasing balance of wood than the luxury Cuvée Expression, which is distinctly denser and more robust.

CAHORS 2005
Red | 2011 up to 2015   **88**
Deep color; the oak brings to mind the style of a great champagne, with focused and manicured notes of violet, enrobed tannins. A serious, distinguished, and virile wine.

CAHORS EXPRESSION 2006
Red | 2011 up to 2016   **88**
One of the more complex wines of 2006 in this appellation, with subtle notes of cedar and graphite and a dense texture. Both distinguished and frank, this is quite a success.

Red: 79.1 acres; malbec 90%, merlot 6%, tannat 4%.
Annual production: 180,000 bottles

CLOS LAPEYRE

La Chapelle-de-Rousse
Chemin du Couday
64110 Jurançon
Phone 00 33 5 59 21 50 80
Fax 00 33 5 59 21 51 83
contact@jurancon-lapeyre.fr
www.jurancon-lapeyre.fr

Jean-Bernard Larrieu is among the cream of Jurançon winegrowers, within an appellation that is blessed by some very good vignerons indeed. He tends his vines immaculately and produces skillfully crafted dry and dessert wines; those occasional irregularities seen in the mid-1990s are nothing but a distant memory now. The best of his offerings develop that emphatic nose of white or black truffles (depending on the vintage) that are typical of the vineyards around the Chapelle de Rousse, an area unlike any other in the Jurançon.

Recently tasted
JURANÇON LAPEYRE 2007
Sweet White | 2013 up to 2019   **89**

JURANÇON SEC VITATGE VIELH 2006
White | 2011 up to 2015   **88**

Older vintages
JURANÇON LA MAGENDIA 2005
Sweet White | 2011 up to 2020   **90**
Pineapple. Rich, generous, clean, precise. Well crafted, as expected. Good work.

JURANÇON LAPEYRE 2005
Sweet White | 2011 up to 2013   **88**
A balanced sweetness, delicately lemony, pure, with a slight hint of truffle. Easy to drink, and very recommendable in the category of not-too-rich dessert wines.

JURANÇON LAPEYRE 2004
Sweet White | 2011 up to 2025   **90**
Full, lemony, long, very pleasant.

JURANÇON SEC LAPEYRE 2006
White | 2011 up to 2014   **88**
Dry, with rather remarkable hazelnut notes that bring to mind certain Vouvrays. Quite fine, straightforward, subtle, with nothing exotic. A wine of the terroir, vinified with enviable precision.

JURANÇON SEC VITATGE VIELH 2005
White | 2011 up to 2017   **89**
Unusual, remarkable in its purity and finesse. Made in a tighter style than the 2006. Not a technological wine, but nothing haphazard either. A style we applaud and defend.

White: 42 acres; gros manseng 45%, petit manseng 50%, others 5%. Annual production: 70,000 bottles

CAMIN LARREDYA

Rousse
64110 Jurançon
Phone 00 33 5 59 21 74 42
Fax 00 33 5 59 21 76 72
jm.grussaute@wanadoo.fr
www.caminlarredya.fr

Here is an excellent source for semi-sweet and sweet wines, with lots of character, that tend to age rather quickly in bottle. The best of the terraced vineyards can even make for exceptionally rich and subtle wines at very reasonable prices.

Recently tasted

JURANÇON A SOLVÉHAT 2007
Sweet White | 2012 up to 2019   **92**

JURANÇON SEC A L'ESGUIT 2008
White | 2011 up to 2013   **86**

Older vintages

JURANÇON A SOLVÉHAT 2005
Sweet White | 2011 up to 2018   **87**
Golden in color, quite concentrated. Long and complex in the mouth with citrus notes, but also with biting acidity, not completely precise. A dessert wine, without a doubt a bit over the top, but tasty.

JURANÇON AU CAPCÉU 2006
Sweet White | 2011 up to 2016   **89**
A wine very rich in sweetness, yet long and pure, clearly the result of precise and careful vinification, with not the least deviation. It finishes with a note of violets that lends it an undeniable allure.

JURANÇON COSTAT DARRER 2005
Sweet White | 2011 up to 2020   **92**
A magnificent expression of manseng, this is very complex, long, and generous, with a note of truffles. A remarkable wine clearly reflecting its terroir!

JURANÇON SEC A L'ESGUIT 2007
White | 2011 up to 2013   **84**
Unusual, this is honeyed with a slight oxidative cast, lending the wine notes of bread or yeast. The finish is straightforward.

JURANÇON SEC A L'ESGUIT 2005
White | 2011 up to 2015   **86**
Balanced in body, with delicate notes of tropical fruits. Flavorful, though a bit thin on the finish.

White: 19.8 acres; gros manseng 25%, petit courbu 5%, petit manseng 70%. **Annual production:** 40,000 bottles

CHÂTEAU LES MIAUDOUX

24240 Saussignac
Phone 00 33 5 53 27 92 31
Fax 00 33 5 53 27 96 60
gerard.cuisset@wanadoo.fr

Nathalie and Gérard Cuisset belong to that group of "musketeers" who shook up the sluggish Bergerac region and showed the world its capacity for greatness. Modeling themselves on Luc de Conti, they adopted growing and winemaking methods that made the reputation of the great neighboring Bordeaux wines: grapes picked at optimum ripeness, aging in good-quality barrels, plus rigorous parcel selection. The aptly named Inspiration has everything it takes to inspire new talent.

BERGERAC SEC L'INSPIRATION 2005
White | 2011 up to 2013   **86**
Highly floral, this wine is both expressive and powerful. With good volume in the mouth, it has an ample finish.

BERGERAC SEC L'INSPIRATION 2004
White | 2011 up to 2009   **87**
This pleasant and fresh wine develops with aromas of acacia flowers.

SAUSSIGNAC 2005
Sweet White | 2011 up to 2015   **90**
This wine has a lovely golden hue and a citrus bouquet. It has good volume on the palate, with soft notes of citrus, and delightful freshness, good acidity, and beautiful length.

CHÂTEAU MONTUS – CHÂTEAU BOUSCASSÉ

🎖🎖🎖🎖

32400 Maumusson-Laguian
Phone 00 33 5 62 69 74 67
Fax 00 33 5 62 69 70 46
brumont.commercial@wanadoo.fr
www.brumontalain.com

Alain Brumont sets the pace for the whole of Southwest France with a selection of reds that have all the other Madiran and Côtes de Gascogne wines beat—and by a wide margin! The tannat grape ripens to perfection in his incomparable Montus and La Tyre terroirs, but it is winemaking and aging that capture its full potential. Brumont's wines are monumental, with an obvious strength and aggression that are totally tamed and kept in check—quite an achievement! The white Pacherencs show the same spirit and complexity, the same luxurious crafting—sure to ignite the imagination of wine lovers. All of these offerings are, as they say, well worth the trip!

Recently tasted
MADIRAN CHÂTEAU BOUSCASSÉ VIEILLES VIGNES 2006
Red | 2012 up to 2018   91

MADIRAN CHÂTEAU MONTUS 2006
Red | 2013 up to 2018   91

MADIRAN LA TYRE 2007
Red | 2015 up to 2022   92

PACHERENC DU VIC BILH MONTUS BRUMAIRE 2007
Sweet White | 2015 up to 2019   92

PACHERENC DU VIC BILH SEC CHÂTEAU MONTUS 2007
White | 2011 up to 2017   89

Older vintages
MADIRAN CHÂTEAU BOUSCASSÉ VIEILLES VIGNES 2005
Red | 2011 up to 2017   90
Great color, discreet nose, spicy, with impressive volume in the mouth delivered via a silky texture. The tannins nonetheless claim their rights. A solid and complete wine, as to be expected.

MADIRAN CHÂTEAU BOUSCASSÉ VIEILLES VIGNES 2003
Red | 2011 up to 2015   92
Beautiful to the eye, with a bouquet of dark fruit and spice. Ample presence on the palate like a 2003, but with slightly more vigorous tannins than the norm. It finishes with a noble bitterness and a touch more length, as it is only at the beginning of its aging. Masterful.

MADIRAN CHÂTEAU BOUSCASSÉ VIEILLES VIGNES 2002
Red | Drink now   87
The nose is spicy and slightly animal; the tannins are more bare and dry than in the 2003 or 2005. It is beginning to become gamey. Ready to drink!

MADIRAN CHÂTEAU BOUSCASSÉ VIEILLES VIGNES 2001
Red | 2011 up to 2013   90
With a bouquet of spice and licorice, this has lots of body and tannins, but the middle of the palate is comfortable, mellow, with impressive length. More character than the 2002.

MADIRAN LA TYRE 2005
Red | 2011 up to 2017   96
A wine with a large and complex bouquet. The texture is marvelous. It is rather high in alcohol, but that is a necessity for such noble texture. Great length. This is one of the most perfect Madirans ever made.

MADIRAN LA TYRE 2001
Red | 2011 up to 2013   88
Not as well made as in recent vintages, this is veering toward animal flavors, but it still shows acidity and acceptable body. Its energetic finish is that of a true Madiran.

Red: 271.8 acres; cabernet franc 5%, cabernet sauvignon 15%, tannat 80%. **White:** 74.1 acres; courbu 50%, manseng 50%. **Annual production:** 800,000 bottles

CHÂTEAU MOULIN CARESSE

1235, route de Couin
24230 Saint-Antoine-de-Breuilh
Phone 00 33 5 53 27 55 58
Fax 00 33 5 53 27 07 39
moulin.caresse@cegetel.net
www.pays-de-bergerac.com/vins/
château-moulin-caresse

This vineyard is partly on clay-limestone slopes and partly on a 240-foot-high plateau of alluvial clay-limestone soils, known locally as boulbènes, looking out over the Dordogne Valley. The wines produced are very refined and original, with an abundance of character: the red wines were largely instrumental in defining the production guidelines of the new Montravel Rouge AOC. All of the wines show much more skillful use of oak plus significantly better balance than five or six years ago.

Recently tasted
BERGERAC MAGIE D'AUTOMNE 2008
Red | 2011 up to 2015 **89**

BERGERAC MERLOT 2008
Red | 2011 up to 2013 **88**

MONTRAVEL 100 POUR CENT 2007
Red | 2011 up to 2016 **89**

MONTRAVEL MAGIE D'AUTOMNE 2008
White | 2011 up to 2013 **89**

Older vintages
HAUT-MONTRAVEL MAGIE D'AUTOMNE 2005
Sweet White | 2011 up to 2013 **87**
A complex and elegant bouquet. The sensation on the palate is fleshy yet balanced, with a beautiful, velvety length.

MONTRAVEL 100 POUR CENT 2005
White | Drink now **86**
This ample and silky wine is marked by its delicate bouquet, round and fatty mouthfeel, and beautiful volume.

MONTRAVEL 100 POUR CENT 2005
Red | 2011 up to 2019 **92**
Nice oak, rich and elegant. Fleshy and generous on the palate, with a beautiful elegance, this is a civilized wine, although a bit expensive!

MONTRAVEL 100 POUR CENT 2004
Red | 2011 up to 2019 **90**
This dark-hued Montravel, with its refined bouquet, develops smoothly on the palate with an elegant finish and delicate tannins.

Red: 54.4 acres; cabernet franc 15%, cabernet sauvignon 14%, malbec 13%, merlot 58%. White: 29.7 acres; muscadelle 17%, sauvignon blanc 31%, sauvignon gris 6%, sémillon 46%. Annual production: 200,000 bottles

DOMAINE NIGRI

Quartier Candeloup
64360 Monein
Phone 00 33 5 59 21 42 01
Fax 00 33 5 59 21 42 59
domaine.nigri@wanadoo.fr

This is another Jurançon winery that is serious about artisan wines. It is run by skilled winemaker Jean-Louis Lacoste, who knows how to ferment wines to perfect dryness and maintains plantings of rare varietals such as camaralet and auzet that make his wines that bit more original.

Recently tasted
JURANÇON SEC 2008
White | 2011 up to 2013 **88**

JURANÇON SEC RÉSERVE 2007
White | 2011 up to 2013 **86**

Older vintages
JURANÇON SEC 2006
White | 2011 up to 2016 **86**
Notes of apricot and lemon, remarkably free of any oxidation. Precise, flavorful, but less complex than those produced in other terroirs.

JURANÇON SEC CUVÉE DOMAINE 2007
White | 2011 up to 2014 **88**
Very pale in color; a finely expressive nose, richer in aromas than the 2006. Fatter, more complete, yet modern in style. Quite sophisticated, with the scent of grape skins at the fore.

JURANÇON SEC CUVÉE DOMAINE 2006
White | 2011 up to 2013 **86**
Pale in color and rather light in texture, this has slightly bitter notes that are in balance with the acidity. It is not very full-bodied or long, but this suits its delicacy.

JURANÇON SEC CUVÉE DOMAINE 2005
White | 2011 up to 2015 **88**
Pale, green, a little wood, ripe, long, unctuous. The fruit arrives later.

JURANÇON SUPÉRIEUR 2005
Sweet White | 2011 up to 2020 **88**
Clear. Honey, acacia flower. A little stale, not too heavy, not much grandeur.

Red: 12.4 acres; cabernet sauvignon 30%, fer servadou 10%, tannat 60%. White: 32.1 acres; camaralet 3%, gros manseng 32%, lauzet 3%, petit manseng 62%. Annual production: 70,000 bottles

DOMAINE PLAGEOLES

Très-Cantous
81140 Cahuzac-sur-Vère
Phone 00 33 5 63 33 90 40
Fax 00 33 5 63 33 95 64
vinsplageoles@orange.fr
www.vins-plageoles.com

Robert Plageoles, now joined by son Bernard, triggered a revival of interest in Gaillac wines by familiarizing consumers across France with the many different faces of the mauzac varietal. What makes his estate so different is a huge range of single-varietal, separate bottlings—an interesting exercise in style but a bit baffling perhaps for seekers of the truth hoping to identify genuine Gaillac character. Be that as it may, all of these wines are good, though the best offerings are plainly the sweet white wines, which achieve exceptional purity and balance.

Recently tasted
GAILLAC ONDENC 2008
White | 2011 up to 2013   **86**

Older vintages
GAILLAC BRAUCOL 2007
Red | 2011 up to 2013   **86**
A lovely wine, very fruity, delicious. More structure than the Mauzac Noir.

GAILLAC BRAUCOL 2006
Red | 2011 up to 2013   **88**
A bouquet of black fruit and undergrowth. Good richness in the mouth. The finish is tasty, with a mineral note, clean and precise. Lots of personality.

GAILLAC DURAS 2007
Red | 2011 up to 2013   **86**
With good, ripe fruit, this is a rich wine with lots of licorice notes.

GAILLAC DURAS 2006
Red | 2011 up to 2013   **87**
Very beautiful color. A wine with good structure, spicy, with the scents of flowers (violets). Beautiful fleshiness in the mouth. More potential than the Mauzac Noir.

GAILLAC LEN DE LEL 2007
Sweet White | 2011 up to 2017   **89**
Beautiful floral elegance. Pure and delicate juice with notes of golden herbs and dried flowers. Balanced with a fresh finish.

GAILLAC MAUZAC NOIR 2007
Red | 2011 up to 2013   **84**
Good fruit. A ripe wine, light and minimally tannic, but fruity.

GAILLAC MAUZAC ROUX 2007
Sweet White | 2011 up to 2015   **88**
The nose smells of pears, brown sugar. Delicious on the tongue, with a pleasant richness. Beautiful balance on the finish. Tasty. A dessert wine that makes you salivate.

GAILLAC MUSCADELLE 2007
Sweet White | 2011 up to 2017   **89**
Beautifully sweet richness in a fruity wine. Good concentration on the palate, pure, straight, and fresh. More concentrated than Le Loin de l'Oeil, but perhaps less original aromatically.

GAILLAC ONDENC 2007
White | 2011 up to 2013   **85**
A beautifully aromatic palette (fennel, anise, flowers). Fat and ripe in the mouth.

GAILLAC ONDENC 2007
Sweet White | 2011 up to 2015   **88**
Elegant, but lacking the purity of the juicy fruit in the Mauzac Roux. But it has good balance and will age well. Fresh finish.

GAILLAC PRUNELARD 2007
Red | 2011 up to 2013   **85**
A deep black color! Dark berries, a touch of minerality. A thick weave of tannins. Rich, fleshy, dense, with a tight finish.

GAILLAC PRUNELARD 2006
Red | 2011 up to 2013   **89**
A bouquet marked by delicate woodland berries. Rich flavors in the mouth, with fat and silky tannins. Beautiful, velvety. Superb fruity finish. Fat texture.

GAILLAC SYRAH 2006
Red | 2011 up to 2013   **87**
A concentrated bouquet. A bit reduced (that's the syrah). It is rich in the mouth, but without the length and volume of other red wines. A strict, straight-up, pure wine. The finish is precise.

GAILLAC VIN D'AUTAN 2007
Sweet White | 2011 up to 2022   **89**
Very rich in extract, this is a wine that has not yet found its balance. The sweet body has notes of yellow fruits, a touch floral. It finishes straight and fresh.

Red: 17.3 acres; braucol 29%, duras 42%, syrah 29%.
White: 39.5 acres; len de l'ehl 5%, mauzac 70%, muscadelle 7%, ondenc 15%. **Annual production:** 80,000 bottles

PRODUCTEURS DE PLAIMONT

Route d'Orthez
32400 Saint-Mont
Phone 00 33 5 62 69 62 87
Fax 00 33 5 62 69 61 68
f.lhautapy@plaimont.fr
www.plaimont.com

The genial André Dubosc steered this great ship from complete obscurity to fame. Now that he has retired, we can only hope his successors will be as talented. He began by organizing co-op members in a way unheard of anywhere else, giving them joint responsibility for quality. He equipped the winery with state-of-the-art technical systems allowing gentle but efficient grape handling, even introducing compulsory hand harvesting for white AOC varietals. Most important, he succeeded in building strong, well-respected brands based on well-made, fruity wines that were right for the times, using his unique flair for marketing to create a highly diversified portfolio. All of the wines set an example for other producers in Southwest France, from the top-end offerings Arte Benedicte, Plénitude, and Faîte to the middle-of-the-range Passé Authentique. Following the acquisition of small local wineries in places such as Crouseilles, the range now includes Madiran and Pacherencs wines that are even more expressive.

Recently tasted
MADIRAN LAPERRE COMBES 2007
Red | 2011 up to 2015   85

PACHERENC DU VIC BILH MAGIE D'OR 2007
Sweet White | 2011 up to 2015   88

Older vintages
MADIRAN ARTE BENEDICTE 2005
Red | 2011 up to 2015   92
A very beautiful bouquet. Magnificently vinified, elegant, long. Excellent value.

PACHERENC DU VIC BILH MAGIE D'OR 2005
Sweet White | 2011 up to 2025   95
Very complex, sumptuous, fabulous.

PACHERENC DU VIC BILH SAINT ALBERT 2005
Sweet White | 2011 up to 2025   96
Pure and complex. Fabulous purity.

LE ROC

31620 Fronton
Phone 00 33 5 61 82 93 90
Fax 00 33 5 61 82 72 38

This property definitely leads the way in quality Fronton wines. Its entries came out on top in all of our blind tastings thanks to their extra fleshiness and fragrance and more velvety texture. All of these wines age well; we recently tasted the Cuvée Réservée 2001 and it was in excellent condition!

FRONTON 2007
Rosé | Drink now   86
Deeply colored with good, expressive red fruit, this is a rich and flavorful rosé. Delicious.

FRONTON DON QUICHOTTE 2006
Red | 2011 up to 2013   84
Salty. A wine with lovely juice, nicely scented on the palate.

FRONTON DON QUICHOTTE 2005
Red | 2011 up to 2013   89
Beautiful and expressive fruitiness, with notes of undergrowth. The palate is rich, with a lightly chalky and salty finish. This cru is pure, fresh, and rather long. Well balanced. A very lovely wine.

FRONTON RÉSERVÉE 2006
Red | 2011 up to 2013   86
Saline notes on the palate. A ripe wine, with well-enrobed tannins.

FRONTON RÉSERVÉE 2005
Red | 2011 up to 2013   86
The fruit is fresh and forward. The palate is rich, with firm tannins. A good medium-level wine.

Red: 50.7 acres; cabernet franc 5%, cabernet sauvignon 10%, négrette 60%, syrah 25%. White: 1.2 acres; chardonnay 40%, muscadelle 20%, sémillon 40%. Annual production: 90,000 bottles

DOMAINE ROTIER

Petit-Nareye
81600 Cadalen
Phone 00 33 5 63 41 75 14
Fax 00 33 5 63 41 54 56
rotier.marre@domaine-rotier.com
www.domaine-rotier.com

This estate is run by Alain Rotier, president of the Gaillac AOC, and was acquired by his parents in 1975. Vineyard practices have eased up over the past two years, now consisting of tilling with the intention of ending the use of weed killers. When it comes to winemaking, Rotier prefers demi-muids (barrels with a capacity of roughly 98 gallons) and seasoned casks, rather than new barrels. He offers three categories of wine: Initiale (négociant wines, sold under the Rotier label); Gravels (named after the estate's gravel soils); and Renaissance (the top-of-the-range offerings). Quality is exceptionally consistent across the range.

GAILLAC INITIALE ROTIER 2006
Red | 2011 up to 2013   88
Dominated by red berries and spices on the nose, with a touch of cocoa. The flavors are rich, with a lovely fatness. The tannins are delicate. It finishes on the cocoa note, with a very velvety feel. Charming. To be drunk young and chilled.

GAILLAC LES GRAVELS 2007
Sweet White | 2011 up to 2013   85
Aromatic, floral. A pleasant sweet wine to drink young.

GAILLAC LES GRAVELS 2006
Red | 2011 up to 2013   85
Beautiful bouquet, spicy, smoky. On the palate, supple, round, and ripe.

GAILLAC LES GRAVELS 2005
Red | 2011 up to 2014   88
Marked by dark berries, tar, earth. But the flavors are suave and pleasing, with a beautiful texture. A ripe wine, long, with good balance; very pure. An expressive style. A good wine for an elegant meal, perhaps with duck breast.

GAILLAC RENAISSANCE 2006
Sweet White | 2011 up to 2014   88
Candied notes (lemon zest, citrus). Beautiful sweetness on the palate. Concentrated, reinvigorated by its fresh finish. Delicious.

GAILLAC RENAISSANCE 2006
Red | 2011 up to 2014   87
Rich, chewy, ripe. Good tannins. Pure and honest.

GAILLAC RENAISSANCE 2005
Sweet White | 2011 up to 2013   91
A bouquet of wax, tropical fruit, and yellow-fruit jam. Highly concentrated, very pure. The richness of the liqueur is superb and well balanced by a good freshness in the finish. (The virtue of noble rot!) A great wine at a very affordable price. And it isn't just sugar!

GAILLAC RENAISSANCE 2005
Red | 2011 up to 2013   89
The nose is still marked by oak, but that will soften with time. It is rich in the mouth, with a well-balanced finish.

GAILLAC RENAISSANCE 2004
Red | 2011 up to 2013   90
Intense on the nose with dark berries, graphite. Good depth. The palate is pleasing, with lovely juice and a smooth finish. Very pure and seductive, with lots of personality and a salty finish. The price is quite reasonable.

Red: 590.6 acres; cabernet sauvignon 13%, duras 34%, fer servadou 23%, gamay 2%, syrah 28%. **White:** 25.7 acres; len de l'ehl 70%, sauvignon blanc 30%. **Annual production:** 180.000 bottles

CHÂTEAU DE ROUSSE

La Chapelle-de-Rousse
64110 Jurançon
Phone 00 33 5 59 21 75 08
Fax 00 33 5 59 21 76 54
châteauderousse@wanadoo.fr

Truffle character and a sensational, unforgettable bouquet make this your classic Jurançon wine. Though largely unheard of outside the village of Gan, it deserves to be included on more restaurant wine lists.

Recently tasted

JURANÇON TRADITION 2007
Sweet White | 2011 up to 2017   **90**

Older vintages

JURANÇON PRESTIGE 2006
Sweet White | 2011 up to 2018   **90**
A complex bouquet with notes of tropical fruit and light caramel in a tasty marriage. Very sweet with fruit jam flavors. Long. An excellent source for this type of wine.

JURANÇON SEC TRADITION 2005
White | 2011 up to 2025   **92**
Deeply golden in color, caramelized, with beautiful acidity. Long, complex, fresh and vibrant. A wine of the terroir made with sincerity.

JURANÇON SÉDUCTION 2006
Sweet White | 2011 up to 2016   **90**
Very strong terroir character, strong acidity, remarkably pure notes of lemon. Good length, with a drier finish than the Prestige cuvée. The grapes were largely raisined. A very beautiful wine.

JURANÇON TRADITION 2006
Sweet White | 2011 up to 2016   **86**
Pale in hue, this has a well-developed bouquet with pleasant lemon notes. The sweetness feels natural and well done, partnering with a light acidity and delicate bitterness. It is lacking a little of the roasted notes that would make it a truly great wine.

JURANÇON TRADITION 2005
Sweet White | 2011 up to 2020   **88**
Golden and evolved, with notes of spice cake, good terroir character and some length. Well vinified.

White: 24.7 acres; gros manseng 31%, petit courbu 19%, petit manseng 50%. Annual production: 45,000 bottles

DOMAINE DE SOUCH

805, chemin de Souch
64110 Laroin
Phone 00 33 5 59 06 27 22
Fax 00 33 5 59 06 51 55
domaine.desouch@neuf.fr

This small winery, with its vineyard enviably located right on the slopes of the village of Jurançon, shot to fame overnight after its charismatic owner, Yvonne Hegoburu, was featured in Nossiter's film *Mondovino*. A lover of pure, genuine wine, Yvonne stands out for her uniquely successful approach to making great dessert wines. Their power and individual expression are simply unmatched by any wine today. The dry wines continue to aspire to that perfect balance that the climate and local grape varieties make so difficult to attain. Wine lovers will rush to buy the sublime Pour René and Marie Kattalin cuvées, the absolute pinnacle of modern-day Jurançon, with an irresistible truffled nose.

Recently tasted

JURANÇON DOMAINE DE SOUCH 2007
Sweet White | 2011 up to 2019   **92**

JURANÇON MARY KATTALIN 2007
Sweet White | 2013 up to 2019   **94**

JURANÇON SEC 2008
White | 2011 up to 2015   **90**

Older vintages

JURANÇON DOMAINE DE SOUCH 2004
Sweet White | 2011 up to 2014   **88**
Very light in color, acidic, minimally raisined, garlic notes. Needs cellaring.

JURANÇON MARY KATTALIN 2005
Sweet White | 2011 up to 2017   **95**
A well-developed bouquet of rare finesse, with subtle notes of caramel and sugar marvelously integrated into the texture. A noble finish, long and pure. A model of its style.

JURANÇON MARY KATTALIN 2004
Sweet White | 2011 up to 2024   **95**
Lemony, very long, very pure with lively acidity. A delicious and pure mountain wine!

JURANÇON SEC 2007
White | 2011 up to 2016   **88**
Light in color, with beautiful lemon notes on the palate. A very pleasant fruit acidity, with significant dry extract. Without a doubt, this is the best dry wine in the recent history of this domaine.

White: 16.1 acres; gros manseng 20%, petit courbu 10%, petit manseng 70%. Annual production: 25,000 bottles

CLOS THOU

Chemin Larredya
64110 Jurançon
Phone 00 33 5 59 06 08 60
Fax 00 33 5 59 06 87 81
clos.thou@wanadoo.fr

With holdings in some of the most celebrated vineyards in this appellation, Thou is renowned as a producer of wines with consistent Jurançon character. The best by far is its sublimely sweet, fantastically truffled Suprême de Thou cuvée, but every bottle listed here shows real character.

Recently tasted

JURANÇON SUPRÊME DE THOU 2007
Sweet White | 2011 up to 2017   **92**

Older vintages

JURANÇON DÉLICE 2006
Sweet White | 2011 up to 2016   **90**
The pure, refined, citric nose is heading in a slightly truffled direction that lends great hope for the future. In the mouth, it is perfectly balanced, long, precise, classic, impeccable!

JURANÇON SEC CUVÉE GUILHOURET 2007
White | 2011 up to 2013   **85**
A lightly honeyed bouquet with notes of ferns. Clean, fatty, entirely acceptable yet far from recognizing the full potential of a sweet wine!

JURANÇON SUPRÊME DE THOU 2006
Sweet White | 2011 up to 2016   **88**
Rich, caramelized, long and unctuous, this is more sweet than delectable, in a style that is a bit less balanced and pure than desired. Nonetheless it is a beautiful wine.

JURANÇON SUPRÊME DE THOU 2004
Sweet White | 2011 up to 2019   **95**
A luminous golden green! Extraordinarily complex bouquet of lemon, pineapple, and mango. Has finesse, purity, and phenomenal acidity.

White: 18.5 acres; camaralet 3%, gros manseng 25%, petit courbu 5%, petit manseng 67%. Annual production: 30,000 bottles

CHÂTEAU TIRECUL LA GRAVIÈRE

24240 Monbazillac
Phone 00 33 5 53 57 44 75
Fax 00 33 5 53 61 36 49
infos@vinibilancini.com
www.vinibilancini.com

Tirecul is a world leader in sweet-wine production, notable for wines of outstandingly generous character and pristine crafting sufficient to rival the great Château d'Yquem itself. Claudie and Bruno Bilancini are experts in the harvesting and vinifying of fully botrytised grapes, capturing that extravagant range of perfumes that are too often oversimplified in poorly vinified wines. They give new meaning to the word "Monbazillac," and quality, of course, comes at a price. They also produce tiny quantities of a very warm but rather overly oaked Pomerol!

Recently tasted

MONBAZILLAC 2005
Sweet White | 2011 up to 2030   **98**

MONBAZILLAC MADAME 2005
Sweet White | 2011 up to 2030   **99**

MONBAZILLAC MADAME 1999
Sweet White | 2011 up to 2017   **95**

Older vintages

MONBAZILLAC 2004
Sweet White | 2011 up to 2019   **90**
Fine, elegant, with a bouquet of great purity. The sensation on the palate is concentrated and unctuous, with a fresh finish. Magnificently balanced.

MONBAZILLAC 2003
Sweet White | 2011 up to 2018   **90**
Straw colored, this has a strong bouquet of floral honey and milky caramel, lightened by notes of chamomile. Full and sumptuously sweet on the palate, with well-integrated oak.

MONBAZILLAC MADAME 2004
Sweet White | 2011 up to 2029   **94**
More concentrated, purer, and a bit fresher than the "simple" cuvée, this is a superb wine, ample and generous. It could unblushingly rival the greatest sweet wines of Bordeaux!

MONBAZILLAC MADAME 2003
Sweet White | 2011 up to 2023   **92**
This has more energy on the nose than the typical Monbazillac, and more perceptible noble rot. With its deeply rich body and a good balance of acidity and sweetness, it is delicate despite the new oak, an imposing and complex dessert wine with a great future.

VIN DE PAYS DU PÉRIGORD MADEMOISELLE 2007
White | 2011 up to 2013   88
Fresh and precise, with a pure and elegant
floral bouquet. Streamlined, fresh, balanced.

VIN DE TABLE MARGUERITE 2007
White | 2011 up to 2015   90
Subtle aromas of fruit and flowers. Ripe and
mature. The sensation on the palate is pure,
distinguished, fresh and tasty. A wine of
superb finesse and pure fruitiness.

White: 14.8 acres

CHÂTEAU TOUR DES GENDRES

Les Gendres
24240 Ribagnac
Phone 00 33 5 53 57 12 43
Fax 00 33 5 53 58 89 49
familledeconti@wanadoo.fr
www.châteautourdesgendres.com

Château Tour de Gendres has been in the
Conti family since 1981. It occupies the site
of an ancient Gallo-Roman villa, on clay-
limestone soils that feature three specialties: very limestone in Gendres, iron rich
("crasse de fer") in Grand Caillou, and
loamy ("boulbène") in Saint-Julien. Luc de
Conti is known as a real stickler for quality
and his wines are there to prove it. But the
real measure of this great winegrower is
his commitment to the cause of the
regional wines and generosity toward so
many of his fellow winegrowers.

Recently tasted
BERGERAC SEC TOUR DES GENDRES
CUVÉE DES CONTI 2007
White | 2011 up to 2013   88

Older vintages
BERGERAC ANTHOLOGIA 2005
Red | 2011 up to 2019   91
Spicy, intense black fruit as well as round
tannins characterize this cuvée, which is
currently shutting down like many 2005s.
You must be patient.

BERGERAC SEC MOULIN DES DAMES 2006
White | 2011 up to 2014   88
More concentrated, richer, and deeper than
the Conti cuvée. A beautiful wine, both elegant and racy.

BERGERAC SEC TOUR DES GENDRES
CUVÉE DES CONTI 2006
White | 2011 up to 2013   86
A fresh wine, very nervy, floral, and ripe.

CÔTES DE BERGERAC MOULIN DES DAMES 2005
Red | 2011 up to 2015   90
Good concentration. A rich wine with good
volume in the mouth. Deep and satisfying.

CÔTES DE BERGERAC TOUR DES GENDRES
LA GLOIRE DE MON PÈRE 2006
Red | 2011 up to 2013   86
A wine with ripe fruit, flavorful, with good
tannins. Very accessible.

Red: 74.1 acres; cabernet 40%, malbec 25%, merlot
35%. White: 56.8 acres; muscadelle 15%, sauvignon
35%, sémillon 50%. Annual production: 250,000
bottles

CLOS TRIGUEDINA

46700 Puy-l'Évêque
Phone 00 33 5 65 21 30 81
Fax 00 33 5 65 21 39 28
contact@jlbaldes.com
www.jlbaldes.com

Clos Triguedina is widely available in restaurants in France and abroad and remains a preferred ambassador for the Cahors appellation. The wines are fleshy and generous, especially the Cuvée Prince Probus, and there are many vintages for sale. But performance is a bit sluggish these days; none of Triguedina's wines shone in the latest blind tastings.

Recently tasted
CAHORS CLOS TRIGUEDINA 2006
Red I 2011 up to 2014   85

CAHORS NEW BLACK WINE 2006
Red I 2011 up to 2016   88

Older vintages
CAHORS PRINCE PROBUS 2006
Red I 2011 up to 2014   86
Firm color, generous and balanced in body. Currently lacking in finesse, but with a truly velvety texture. This wine requires a lot of aeration.

Red: 131 acres. White: 24.7 acres. Annual production: 400,000 bottles

CLOS D'UN JOUR

Le Clos d'un Jour
46700 Duravel
Phone 00 33 5 65 36 56 01
Fax 00 33 5 65 36 56 01
s.azemar@wanadoo.fr
www.leclosdunjour.blogg.org

This tiny property has rocketed to the top of its appellation by following the example of some of the best winegrowers in Southwest France. In fact, owners Véronique and Stéphane Azemar have managed to one-up their peers with Un Jour sur Terre, a stunning red cuvée whose intriguing name refers to the method of élevage or maturation—in earthenware jars, as in Roman times! The aim is to favor a measure of oxygen exchange with the wine, but with none of those oaky aromas that you get with barrels. This sort of commitment to quality is a real shot in the arm for the Cahors appellation!

Recently tasted
CAHORS CLOS D'UN JOUR 2006
Red I 2011 up to 2014   84

CAHORS UN JOUR SUR TERRE 2007
Red I 2011 up to 2017   88

Older vintages
CAHORS UN JOUR 2006
Red I 2011 up to 2014   86
One of the most refined wines of the vintage. Tender and fleshy, finishing on serious tannins, with true terroir character.

CAHORS UN JOUR SUR TERRE 2005
Red I 2011 up to 2017   88
More full-bodied than Un Jour, this has strong notes of chocolate, a rich body, and a tight structure with no dryness. A wine with a strong local character, this won't pass unnoticed!

Red: 16.7 acres; malbec 93%, merlot 7%. Annual production: 20,000 bottles

CLOS UROULAT

Chemin Uroulat
64360 Monein
Phone 00 33 5 59 21 46 19
Fax 00 33 5 59 21 46 90
contact@uroulat.com
www.uroulat.com

Jurançon wines from these more easily cultivated vineyards around Monein are more remarkable for their finesse and harmony than for the uniqueness of their bouquet. The region favors the production of dry or dry-styled wines, which the very likeable Charles Hours certainly makes better than anyone else—despite the stupid ruling that limits residual sugar content to just 4 grams per liter. This explains why his sumptuous 2003, containing 6 grams per liter, is downgraded to a simple Vin de Table. It nevertheless remains the masterpiece of his portfolio and once again stole the show at our blind tastings. We ask only that the label distinguish between his estate-produced wines and those made with purchased grapes, even if the quality is close to identical!

Recently tasted
JURANÇON HAPPY HOURS 2007
Sweet White | 2011 up to 2017   87

JURANÇON UROULAT 2007
Sweet White | 2012 up to 2019   92

Older vintages
JURANÇON SEC CUVÉE MARIE 2006
White | 2011 up to 2014   87
Delicate notes of acacia. Rich, balanced, tasty, a bit short. This suffers in comparison with the sweet wine, which is far more expressive of the soil and the vintage, yet even as it is, it has few equals!

JURANÇON UROULAT 2006
Sweet White | 2011 up to 2018   95
Perfection itself in the balance of fruit and acidity. The flavor is noble, filled with delicious candied and dried-fruit notes, and very long. This wine approaches the ideal of a Jurançon! Perfect today, and surely superb in ten years!

JURANÇON UROULAT 2005
Sweet White | 2011 up to 2020   94
Ample and precise fruit, a balanced body, a highly noble texture and finish. It has yet to show its full potential.

JURANÇON UROULAT 2004
Sweet White | 2011 up to 2019   90
Golden, evolved, sticky, with beautiful freshness and acidity. Of the terroir, with good length.

VIN DE TABLE CUVÉE MARIE 2003
White | 2011 up to 2018   95
We dishonored ourselves by denying this wine the appellation label because it had a few too many grams of sugar! The bouquet is majestic, and the sensation on the palate is explosive and harmonious. This has reached a new level of perfection rare in this type of dry wine. Let us clarify: very dry. So rarely found in Jurançon!

White: 39.5 acres; gros manseng 50%, petit manseng 50%. Annual production: 90,000 bottles

VIGNOBLE DES VERDOTS

24560 Conne-de-Labarde
Phone 00 33 5 53 58 34 31
Fax 00 33 5 53 57 82 00
verdots@wanadoo.fr
www.verdots.com

This is one of Southwest France's most iconic estates, owned by enterprising, talented winemaker David Fourtout, whose achievements have now earned him a place among the top-ranking French wineries. His red wines, with their notes of lush, ripe fruit and thick, dense substance, are built for aging. The white wines are big and obviously (even) more complex than the reds—well on their way to becoming absolute benchmarks for Bergerac, the likes of which it would be nice to see in Bordeaux! The wines are grouped into three categories, distinguished by name and label: Clos des Verdots (the fruit-driven, basic bottlings); Tour des Verdots (oakier, blended wines); and Les Verdots (what David Fourtout considers the grand vin, sourced from the best parcels).

Recently tasted
BERGERAC SEC GRAND VIN LES VERDOTS 2007
White | 2011 up to 2017   90

Older vintages
BERGERAC CLOS DES VERDOTS 2006
Red | 2011 up to 2013   84
A wine filled with fruit, supple, with ripe tannins, to enjoy for its simple fruitiness.

BERGERAC GRAND VIN LES VERDOTS 2006
Red | 2011 up to 2016   89
A big wine, richly matured, with ripe and well-enrobed tannins and delicious fruit aromas. Tasty.

BERGERAC SEC CLOS DES VERDOTS 2007
White | 2011 up to 2013   84
Fruity, ripe, and aromatic, this is a dry and edgy wine with a fresh finish.

BERGERAC SEC GRAND VIN LES VERDOTS 2006
White | 2011 up to 2016   90
Now here's a great white Bergerac, ambitiously and lushly vinified and matured, with ripe extract. It's voluminous in the mouth, yet remains fresh and palate-whetting.

BERGERAC SEC GRAND VIN LES VERDOTS 2005
White | 2011 up to 2013   89
A beautifully complex bouquet. Rich and dense on the palate, supple, with lots of freshness. Great length.

BERGERAC SEC LE VIN SELON DAVID FOURTOUT 2004
White | 2011 up to 2013   91
A complex, rich and generous wine with aromas of tropical fruit and citrus.

BERGERAC SEC LES TOURS DES VERDOTS 2008
White | 2011 up to 2015   88
Well ripened. Time on the lees has added richness. It's flavorful and balanced.

CÔTES DE BERGERAC LE VIN SELON DAVID FOURTOUT 2005
Red | 2012 up to 2020   90
Concentrated, rich, very powerful on the palate. True to the vintage, it will always be massive. By comparison, the 2006 grand vin seems fresher.

CÔTES DE BERGERAC LES TOURS DES VERDOTS 2007
Red | 2011 up to 2013   85
Rather rich, this is a wine to chew, although it comes across a bit heavy on the finish, as if lacking freshness.

MONBAZILLAC LES TOURS DES VERDOTS 2006
Sweet White | 2011 up to 2015   89
The color is a lovely gold, rather light. The nose is lively and nervy with notes of honey, citrus, and fruit jam. On the palate it is balanced between sweetness and acidity. Beautiful length.

Red: 54.4 acres. White: 32.1 acres Annual production: 170,000 bottles

Index